WOMEN IN PUBLIC OFFICE

The Center for the American Woman and Politics is pleased to acknowledge those who provided support for updating and expanding the Center's National Information Bank on Women in Public Office. For financial contributions, thanks go to the American Council of Life Insurance; New Jersey Bell; The Home News; and Time, Inc.. Printing services for the questionnaires mailed to officeholders were provided by Avon Products, Inc. of New York and the Playboy Foundation in Chicago, Illinois, The Center is also indebted to the Ford Foundation for continued financial support, without which it would have been impossible to continue collecting national data on women in public life.

As a unit of the Eagleton Institute of Politics at Rutgers-The State University of New Jersey, the Center for the American Woman and Politics benefits from direct and indirect institutional and financial support.

The Center seeks additional funds to update and expand its National Information Bank on Women in Public Office for future editions of this directory as well as for related information services. All contributions are welcome and are deductible for federal income tax purposes.

*   *   *

The Center for the American Woman and Politics (CAWP) was established as a research, education, and service center in 1971 under a Ford Foundation grant to the Eagleton Institute of Politics at Rutgers—The State University of New Jersey. Collecting and disseminating information about women in office are direct outgrowths of CAWP's twofold goal—to develop a body of useful knowledge about women's participation in American public life and to assist efforts aimed at increasing women's contributions to the political process. The data collected for *WOMEN IN PUBLIC OFFICE* have strengthened immeasurably CAWP's capability to document women's political participation and to serve as a resource center for important information about women's status in government and public life.

WOMEN IN PUBLIC OFFICE

A BIOGRAPHICAL DIRECTORY AND STATISTICAL ANALYSIS

Second Edition

Compiled by
CENTER FOR THE AMERICAN WOMAN AND POLITICS
Eagleton Institute of Politics
Rutgers — The State University of New Jersey

Project Staff
KATHY STANWICK, Project Director
MARILYN JOHNSON, Statistical Research Director

Susan Carroll, Research Associate
Lynn Korenblit, Research Associate
Christine Li, Editorial Associate

Diane Bliss, Editorial Typist
Ann Brill, Manuscript Typist

THE SCARECROW PRESS, INC.
Metuchen, N.J. & London
1978

NOTE

Women in Public Office, Second Edition is a reference tool and source of information for those interested in women's contributions to American political life. The directory is not to be used for commercial purposes, for solicitation, or for preparing other general mailing lists. Persons wishing to discuss potential uses of the directory should contact the publisher.

Library of Congress Cataloging in Publication Data

Rutgers University, New Brunswick, N.J.   Center for
    the American Woman and Politics.
    Women in public office.

    Includes index.
    1. Women in politics--United States--Directories.
2. Women in public life--United States--Directories.
I. Stanwick, Kathy.   II. Title.
HQ1391.U5R88 1978   353.002   78-7463
ISBN 0-8108-1142-1

Published by the Scarecrow Press, Inc.
P.O. Box 656, Metuchen, N.J. 08840
Copyright © 1978, Center for the American Woman and Politics
    Eagleton Institute of Politics
    Rutgers—The State University of New Jersey
Manufactured in the United States of America

CONTENTS

FOREWORD ·   *vii*

INTRODUCTION . . . .   *ix*
   Organization of *Women in Public Office, Second Edition*
   Coverage for *Women in Public Office, Second Edition*
   Collecting Information for *Women in Public Office, Second Edition*
   Future Editions
   Acknowledgements

USER'S GUIDE . . . .   *xiii*
   Biography Arrangement
   Sample Entry
   Abbreviations

NUMBERS OF WOMEN IN OFFICE: 1977 State Summaries . . . .   *xvii*

STATISTICAL REPORT: *Profile of Women Holding Office, 1977* 1A

BIOGRAPHICAL DIRECTORY   1

ADDENDUM: Results of November 1977 State Legislative
   Elections (Kentucky, New Jersey and Virginia).   456

APPENDIX: Variations in Types of Offices   457

PAGE COVERAGE OF INDIVIDUAL STATES   460

NAME INDEX   461

782029

FOREWORD

WOMEN IN PUBLIC OFFICE grew out of the public's demand for important new information. During the past six years the Center for the American Woman and Politics has received a growing number of requests from all parts of the country for basic biographical and statistical data about those women who fought and found their way into public office. Requests have come from journalists, researchers, teachers, political consultants and speechwriters, officeholders and party officials, as well as from a wide variety of public agencies and private organizations. In response to these requests and in recognition of the fact that no accurate, comprehensive national data on women in public office were to be found anywhere, the Center for the American Woman and Politics undertook the development of a national data bank on women in public office. This publication consists of data collected by the Center as part of its general effort to develop useful information about American women's political participation.

The first edition of *WOMEN IN PUBLIC OFFICE* (New York: R. R. Bowker, 1976) began the job of circulating basic biographical and statistical information about thousands of female officeholders in the United States. Now the Center is proud to issue this second edition. It contains more categories of officeholders and more women in nearly all categories; it includes information about the women no longer in office since our last survey in 1975; and it offers the first analysis of national data comparing female and male officeholders.

Once again the names, addresses, and levels of office of female officials in each of the fifty states are accessible for immediate reference in a single volume. Important demographic information about women in various levels of office across the country is again available to researchers, writers, and educators. As the only national biographical directory and statistical profile of women serving in elective and appointive office, this book should be a valuable reference tool and source of practical information, as well as a stimulus to broader concerns about women's political roles, interests and status.

This second edition of the directory identifies over 17,000 women currently serving as public officials in local, state, and federal government. The book stands as a telling reflection of American women's political status in the second half of the 1970s. Its publication once more testifies to the decade's interest in women's achievements and changing status. Its size continues to remind us of the numerically small role women played in public office during 1976 and 1977.

Women comprise an estimated 8 percent of all officials holding the offices covered by this directory. This figure is startlingly low relative to the percentages of women in the U. S. population and in the labor force. Nonetheless, it does reflect a steady increase recently in the proportions of women among public officials—from approximately 5 percent of officeholders in 1975 to an estimated 8 percent in 1977.

If the changing status of women implies a trend in the 1970s toward greater participation of women in public office, the lack of prior documentation prevented us from identifying its shape and pattern in the first edition of this book. This second edition of *WOMEN IN PUBLIC OFFICE* contributes important new facts and helps to establish a solid base of information on which to begin building an understanding of the nature and extent of changes in women's political status over recent years. In future studies the Center expects to chart further details and provide new data for comparison with information in the first and second editions of *WOMEN IN PUBLIC OFFICE*. Eventually we shall be able to undertake comprehensive analyses of trends in women's political participation since the early years of contemporary feminism. In the meantime the invaluable body of data collected for this volume will supply many useful clues for those seeking to discover who's who and who's where among today's women in government and politics.

Ruth B. Mandel
Director,
Center for the American Woman and Politics
Eagleton Institute of Politics

INTRODUCTION

ORGANIZATION OF
WOMEN IN PUBLIC OFFICE, SECOND EDITION

Women in Public Office, Second Edition is a reference book about women holding public office in the United States during 1976 and 1977. The volume contains information about women serving in the following offices:

> Federal Executive Appointive
> U. S. Congress
> Federal Judiciary
> State Executive Offices Elected Statewide
> State Cabinet Offices
> State Legislatures
> State Appellate and Trial Courts of General Jurisdiction
> State Boards and Commissions
> County Governing Bodies
> Township Governing Bodies
> Mayoralties
> Local Councils (including cities, towns, villages and boroughs)

This second edition of *Women in Public Office* provides an updated and expanded body of information about the position of women in the political life of the United States. The book has these features: A) a statistical report which examines national data gathered for this volume and profiles women office-holders in 1977; B) a biographical directory of officeholders from federal to local levels; C) the November 1977 election results for state legislative races in Kentucky, New Jersey and Virginia; D) an appendix which explains variations in nomenclature used by different governing bodies; E) a name index.

Statistical Report:
Profile of Women Holding Office 1977

The report presents demographic, biographic and attitudinal data about women in public office in 1977. It examines emergent trends in the numbers and location of officeholders, based on a comparison between current data and information gathered for the first edition of *Women in Public Office* (New York: R.R. Bowker, 1976.) It also explores selected aspects of personal and family characteristics of officeholders, their organizational affiliations, political background and experience, patterns of officeholding, political ambitions, perceptions of women in politics and positions on current social issues. Included in the analysis is an examination of differences among women holding various kinds of offices and a focus on size of election district, year of election, political party, age of the office-holder, presence of female colleagues and political ambitions insofar as these may be associated with characteristics and attitudes of women officials. In addition, comparisons are made between a sub-sample of women currently in office and a parallel sample of male officeholders, and between another subsample of women and a group of women from the 1975 survey who have since left public office.

Biographical Directory

The biographical directory is organized by states, except for a separate section on women serving in federal offices. In the Federal section, entries are grouped and listed as follows:

> Executive Appointments   Alphabetically by name of officeholder
> U.S. House of Representatives   Alphabetically by name of officeholder[1]
> Judicial   First by Circuit Court and then by District Court; within each, alphabetically by name of officeholder

Within each state, entries are grouped and listed in the following way:

> State Executive and Cabinet   Alphabetically by name of officeholder
> State Senate   Alphabetically by name of officeholder
> State House   Alphabetically by name of officeholder
> County Commissions   Alphabetically by name of county; then alphabetically by name of officeholder
> Townships   Alphabetically by name of township; then alphabetically by name of officeholder
> Mayors   Alphabetically by name of city, village, town or borough
> Local Councils   Alphabetically by name of city, village, town or borough; then alphabetically by name of officeholder
> Judges   (State Appellate and Trial Courts) Alphabetically by name of officeholder
> State Boards and Commissions   Alphabetically by name of board or commission; then alphabetically by name of office-holder

Biographical information is provided where available for all offices except State Boards and Commissions. (A roster of names listing members of State Boards and Commissions is supplied.) Each biographical entry includes the following information where applicable: name, party affiliation, date first elected (or appointed) to current office, district number, current board and committee assignments, present and former political party positions and dates, former public offices held and dates, current organizational memberships, education, current occupation, date of birth, address and

---

[1]   U.S. Senate is not included since no women served in the Senate during 1976 and 1977.

telephone. A sample biographical entry with explanatory key is presented in the User's Guide.

Results of November 1977 State Legislative Races

This section lists results of legislative contests in Kentucky, New Jersey and Virginia in November 1977.

Appendix

The appendix describes common variations in nomenclature for the offices covered by this directory. It also cites sources which offer detailed explanations of the variations in names, forms, functions, responsibilities, and types of authority vested in the various governing bodies. In practice, nomenclature varies considerably from state to state as well as within states at county and local levels. For purposes of simplicity and consistency in this volume, standardized designations have been used. They are identified in the section of this introduction entitled "Biographical Directory."

Name Index

The name index, arranged in alphabetical order, cites page references for all officeholders listed in the directory.

COVERAGE FOR
WOMEN IN PUBLIC OFFICE, SECOND EDITION

The second edition of *WOMEN IN PUBLIC OFFICE* reflects CAWP's continued efforts to collect, analyze and disseminate information about women in politics and government. This directory's first edition in 1976 made publically available the first systematic identification of women officials in all fifty states. In response to users' expressed interests, CAWP expanded the coverage and analysis for this second edition by:

- including federal appointments and members of the judiciary at the federal level

- developing a more extensive questionnaire than the one used in 1975 for mailing to officeholders

- collecting data from selected male officials and women former officeholders

First, federal executive appointments and members of the federal judiciary at the district and circuit levels have been added to the biographical directory.[2] Second, a questionnaire nearly twice the length of the one used in 1975 was designed to elicit information for the statistical profile about the officeholding activities, issue orientations, and political background and experience of women in public office. Third, this edition's data analysis

―――――――――

[2] Names listed in the body of this directory cover only those appointments which were made before August 1977.

includes information from a random sample of males serving in state legislatures, county commissions, mayoralties and municipal councils in the following states: Georgia; Kansas; Minnesota; New Jersey; Oregon; Texas; Vermont; and Wyoming. In addition, questionnaires were sent to a random sample of male state legislators and county commissioners in Arizona; Indiana; Maryland; North Carolina; Pennsylvania; South Dakota; Tennessee; and Washington. Finally, questionnaires were also sent to nearly all women officeholders who returned a questionnaire in 1975 but were no longer holding public office in 1977.

Some omissions are the inevitable consequence of an attempt to collect data for a project of this magnitude. In the first edition of *WOMEN IN PUBLIC OFFICE* (1976), most omissions resulted from a lack of available information about the numbers and variety of forms of local governments in each state. In the current second edition (1978), the chart entitled "Women in Public Office: State Summaries 1977" on page *xvii* represents a fuller enumeration of the numbers of women serving in public office nationwide. Some noticeable increases in numbers of female officeholders since publication of the 1975 state summaries result from refinements in the available data. Figures in the state summary table that represent expanded coverage for this edition are indicated with an asterisk (✻). These include:

> Kentucky: Mayors and local councillors
> Michigan: Township officials
> Minnesota: local councillors
> Ohio: Local councillors
> Pennsylvania: Local councillors

COLLECTING INFORMATION FOR
WOMEN IN PUBLIC OFFICE, SECOND EDITION

Identifying the Officeholders

CAWP has turned to many and varied sources for help in gathering names of officeholders for this book. These include staffs of state libraries, legislative reference bureaus, county associations, township associations, municipal leagues and commissions on the status of women.

At the federal appointments level, names were collected from a variety of sources and were verified as current in July 1977 by Mary E. King, Deputy Director, ACTION. Women's Election Central - an election monitoring project conducted by the National Women's Education Fund, the National Women's Political Caucus, and the Women's Campaign Fund - resulted in updated information about the numbers of women in state legislatures after the 1976 elections. In mid-1977 the National Women's Education Fund in Washington, D.C. shared with CAWP its verified list of women state legislators.

At the county and local levels, lists came from state, county and municipal association manuals (where they existed) or from lists prepared in response to our requests and supplied by association offices.

Obtaining and verifying the names of the women who hold political office is an enormous and difficult undertaking. In no state can just one source provide all the information needed for each level of government. In most cases, a minimum of five sources must be contacted to obtain information for various levels of government in each state. In electoral politics, resignations and elections occur year round, and local directories may be somewhat outdated from their moment of publication. Moreover, directories of state or local officials are not necessarily published annually, which makes it imperative to update older directories with information about recent changes. Typically, new lists are issued if a major election has taken place since publication of the last directory in a given locality.

Identifying an officeholder's gender from a roster of names may be problematic. A small proportion of officeholders has first names which most commonly belong to the opposite sex, or which are impossible to identify as typically belonging to females or males.

Inherent in the nature of information gathering for this type of book is the inevitability that some errors of inclusion or omission remain in the published work. There may be some women listed who no longer hold office, and there may be some women who hold office but did not appear on the lists received for this directory, or who were inadvertently missed in the compilation process. There may also be some men included in the directory. Some women with names traditionally assigned to males may not be included. Insofar as possible, all those names which could not be identified as belonging to either a female or male were included in the initial mailing of questionnaires to provide for maximum coverage of women in office.

Because of the complexity of governmental organization and the wide variation in terms used to designate governing bodies, the decision to classify officeholders in categories of functional equivalency may have resulted occasionally in inappropriate classification. An especially troublesome example is that of Townships, whose boundaries may or may not overlap existing municipalities or towns, and whose powers vary greatly. Our decision was to use a separate category (taken from the U.S. Bureau of Census classification) to designate township forms of governments only in states where they exist with municipalities or towns within their boundaries.

This volume reflects extensive efforts to collect complete and accurate information. Nevertheless, some gaps remain. A complete listing at one or more governmental levels was unavailable for inclusion in this book in the following states:

Illinois: Mayors and local councillors
Missouri: Township officials
Nebraska: Township officials
New York: Township officials, mayors and
    local councillors
Wisconsin: Local councillors

Collecting data about state boards and commissions presents greater difficulties than other offices.

Many states do not compile lists of appointees; other states keep lists for some boards and not others; outdated lists are often the only data available. Lists of boards and commissions included in this volume are those which could be verified as recent and complete or nearly complete.

Contacting the Officeholders

After receiving and checking lists of officeholders, CAWP gathered biographical and statistical information by means of a mailed questionnaire. Officeholders who did not respond to the initial mailing received a second questionnaire, followed by a postcard urging a reply. Each mailing included a postage-paid return envelope. Officeholders were invited to telephone collect for additional information about the project. Officeholders whose schedules did not permit them to fill out the questionnaire were urged to send a resume as a substitute source of biographical information.

Variations from the procedure described above occurred when new or updated lists of officeholders were received too late for questionnaire mailings. The states for which lists arrived too late for sending questionnaires were:

Arizona: Mayors and local councillors
Illinois: Township officials
Michigan: Township officials
Mississippi: Mayors and local councillors

In some states, local elections were held while the data gathering process was underway. Because their names were received too late, newly elected local officeholders in the following states were not sent questionnaires: Colorado, Connecticut, Maine, Maryland, Massachusetts, Minnesota, Missouri and Oklahoma. Name listings in the biographical directory, however, do reflect the changes which occurred as a result of local elections in these states.

Apart from the vagaries of the U.S. mail, a minor difficulty encountered in reaching officeholders resulted from unreliable or incorrect mailing addresses. Often the only address available was that of a governmental administrative building, and there was no way of knowing whether questionnaires were forwarded to officeholders from these addresses. Only a very small proportion was returned as undeliverable.

The mailed questionnaire consisted of two sections - a first section requesting basic biographical information for use in the directory listings; a second section requesting data for statistical analysis. Information to be printed under the officeholder's name in the directory was transferred immediately to a biography card. Then, to protect the privacy of individuals included in the statistical analysis, further questionnaire data were coded for computer analysis without identifying names. The questionnaires are kept in locked files and available only to staff investigators for purposes of verifying information in the biographical listing or for computer processing.

Biographical and statistical processing of questionnaires was possible for all responses received <u>before</u> August 15, 1977. In addition, CAWP's staff has utilized available published sources of biographical information describing a small percentage of officeholders for whom questionnaire data were not available. These sources include biographical entries from the first edition of *WOMEN IN PUBLIC OFFICE* for those women who are still holding office, and biographies compiled from other secondary sources, where they exist. Below the congressional and state levels, there is very little published biographical information about public officials. When it exists, the scope of secondary information on a particular officeholder ranges from fairly complete to minimal. Secondary sources consulted by CAWP staff include:

> State, county, township and municipal
> manuals and directories.
> *Who's Who in American Politics, 1975-76*
> (New York: R.R. Bowker, 1975).

Thirty-six percent of the entries for those offices for which biographical data were sought are based on information submitted by officeholders in response to questionnaires mailed by CAWP between May and July 1977. Another seven percent are biographical entries from the first edition of *WOMEN IN PUBLIC OFFICE*. Less than one percent of the biographies derive from secondary sources. A name and address listing is provided for the remaining officeholders, for whom biographical information was unavailable.

FUTURE EDITIONS

This directory is an important building block in the development of CAWP's national information bank on women officials in the United States. The shape of this project in the future depends on the continuation of resources to support collecting, storing, analyzing, and disseminating national data on women's status in politics and government. Since the proportion of women in office is increasing and interest in these data is growing, this project will continue to be feasible only if CAWP has funds available to computerize the entire system so that data collection processes can be facilitated and the data can be maintained in a form readily updated and retrievable.

CAWP takes responsibility for all errors of fact or omission in this second edition. Any corrections, additional information, comments or suggestions should be brought to the attention of CAWP, Eagleton Institute of Politics, Rutgers University, New Brunswick, New Jersey 08901.

ACKNOWLEDGEMENTS

A number of people performed essential tasks during various phases of the project. Teams of valued assistants stuffed and stamped thousands of envelopes. Claire Couture, John Crowley, Joan Cummings, Mary Emery, Barbara Hill, Mary Kay, Elizabeth Kelly, Stacey Pramer and Joseph Somma coded questionnaires. Adrienne Cohen, Maryjane Davies, Nancy Hamilton and Janet Marforio undertook parts of a massive typing job. Barbara Pope and her staff keypunched the computer cards necessary to analyze data. Bill Dolphin assisted in computer processing of the data, and Debbie Person helped to tie up loose ends during various phases of the project.

In addition to CAWP's regular and project staff, numerous people contributed to the production of *WOMEN IN PUBLIC OFFICE, SECOND EDITION*. They are owed many and sincere thanks for their generous help over the past year. Eagleton Institute staff members offered a variety of supporting services, especially Bernice Charwin and Chris Lenart. Ida Schmertz, Chairperson of CAWP's Advisory Committee, provided encouragment, advice and practical assistance, particularly in fund raising activities. Betsey Wright and other good friends at the National Women's Education Fund in Washington, D.C. contributed their expertise about women holding elective office and continued to send out the word that some people in New Brunswick, New Jersey were developing a national data bank about women in office.

Sincere thanks go out to all the individuals, organizations, and agencies across the country who made vital contributions to this publication by providing information essential for identifying and reaching officeholders. Many individuals in offices throughout the United States took time to prepare special lists of officeholders at CAWP's request. Without their help it would have been impossible to obtain otherwise unavailable information.

Our respect, sincere appreciation and thanks are hereby extended to the thousands of busy political women and men who took time to complete a lengthy questionnaire and to send us encouraging letters and enthusiastic notes.

KATHY STANWICK
Research and Information Associate,
Center for the American Woman and Politics

USER'S GUIDE

Arrangement

The body of the biographical directory is divided into two major sections. The Federal section lists officeholders alphabetically within the following offices: Executive Appointive; U.S. House of Representatives; Federal Judiciary. The second section is organized by States. In each state the following offices are listed: State Executive and Cabinet; State Legislative; State Judiciary; County Commissions; Townships; Mayoralties; Local Councils; State Boards and Commissions. Within each state officeholders are listed alphabetically for State Executive and Cabinet, State Legislative and State Judiciary. Also within each state, listings are arranged alphabetically by the name of county, township, municipality or board for the following offices: County Commissions, Townships, Mayoralties, Local Councils and State Boards and Commissions.

Sample Entry

HELEN L. BECK (D)*
1974-. Dist: 25. Bds: Institutions, Health and Welfare; Revenue; Finance and Appropriations. Party: County Com. 1965-73; Municipal Com. 1965-72. Prev: Councilwoman 1958-63; Bd. of Educ. 1939-41. Org: LWV; WPC; Dem. Women's Club. Educ: Conn. Coll. 1929 BA; Rutgers U 1934 MA. Occ: Teacher, B: 8/21/08 NYC. Add: 586 Mountain Ave., E. Brunswick 08816 (201)626-3333.

An asterisk (*) following party affiliation in the entry indicates that biographical material was compiled from secondary sources when the questionnaire was not returned by the officeholder.

The officeholder's party designation appears in parenthesis following her name. Biographical entries provide the following information:

Date first elected
Dist: District number
Bds: Board and Committee assignments, arranged as the respondent listed them.
Party: Current and past political party positions and dates held
Prev: Previous public offices and dates held; includes offices with unexpired terms
Org: Current organizational membership, national, state and local
Educ: Education
Occ: Current occupation
B: Date of birth
Add: Address and telephone number

A double asterisk (**) following party affiliation in the entry indicates that the entry was taken from the first edition of WOMEN IN PUBLIC OFFICE: A BIOGRAPHICAL DIRECTORY AND STATISTICAL ANALYSIS (N.Y.: R.R. Bowker, 1976).

Abbreviations

The following list contains the abbreviations used in this directory.
used in this directory

AA-Associate Arts Degree
AARP-American Association of Retired Persons
AASW-American Association of Social Workers
AAUP-American Association of University Professors
AAUW-American Association of University Women
ABA-American Bar Association
ABAG-Association of Bay Area Governments

ABWA-American Business Women's Association
ACLU-American Civil Liberties Union
ADA-Americans for Democratic Action
Add-Address
Adv-Advisory
AFC-Association of Feminist Consultants
AFL-American Federation of Labor

AFSCME-American Federation of State, County and Municipal Employees
AFT-American Federation of Teachers
AFTRA-American Federation of T.V. and Radio Actors
AGMA-American Guild Musical Artists
Agric-Agriculture
AIP-American Institute of Planners

AK,Alas-Alaska
AL,Ala-Alabama
ALA-American Library Association
ALERT-Women's Leg. Review (Conn.)
Alt-Alternate
AMA-American Medical Association
Amer-American
ANA-American Nurses Association
APHA-American Public Health
    Association
APSA-American Political Science
    Association
Apt-Apartment, Appointed,
    Appointive
AR,Ark-Arkansas
ASPA-American Society of
    Public Administration
Assoc-Association
Asst-Assistant
Atty-Attorney
Ave-Avenue
AWRT-American Women in Radio
    and Television
AZ,Ariz-Arizona

B-Born
BA-Bachelor of Arts Degree
Bd(s)-Board(s)
Bldg-Building
Blvd-Boulevard
BM-Bachelor of Music
BPW-Business and Professional
    Women's Clubs, National
    Federation of
BS-Bachelor of Science Degree

CA,Calif-California
CEWAER-California Elected
    Women's Association for
    Education and Research
CETA-Comprehensive Employment
    and Training Act
Ch-Chairwoman
CIO-Congress of Industrial
    Organizations
Cir-Circle
CLU-Civil Liberties Union
Cmsn(s)-Commission(s)
Cmsnr-Commissioner
Cnty-County
Co-Ch--Co-Chairwoman
Coll-College
CO,Colo-Colorado
Com-Committee
Comsr-Commissioner
Conf-Conference
Conv-Convention
Coord-Coordinator
CORE-Congress of Racial
    Equality
Ct-Court
CT,Conn-Connecticut

D-Democratic
DAR-Daughters of the American
    Revolution
DC-Washington, D.C.
DE,Del-Delaware
Dem-Democratic
Dep-Deputy
Dept-Department

Dev-Development
DFL-Democratic Farm Labor
    Party
Dir-Director
Dist-District
Div-Division
Dr-Doctor, Drive

Educ-Education
EOC-Equal Opportunity
    Commission
ERA-Equal Rights Amendment
Exec-Executive

Fed-Federal, Federation
FEW-Federally Employed Women
FHA-Federal Housing
    Administration
FL,Fla-Florida

GA,Ga-Georgia
Gov-Governor
Govt-Government

HI,Haw.-Hawaii
Hwy-Highway

IA,Ia-Iowa
ICC-Intergovernmental
    Coordinating Council
ID,Ida-Idaho
ILGWU-International Ladies'
    Garment Workers' Union
IL,Ill-Illinois
Inc-Incorporated
IN,Ind-Indiana
Internat-International
IWY-International Womens'
    Year

JD-Doctor of Jurisprudence
Jr-Junior

KS,Kan-Kansas
KY,Ky-Kentucky

La-Lane
LA,La-Louisiana
Leg-Legislative
LI-Long Island
LLB-Bachelor of Laws
LLD-Doctor of Laws
LPN-Licensed Practical Nurse
LWV-League of Women Voters

MA,Mass-Massachusetts
MD,Md-Maryland
ME,Me-Maine
MED-Master of Education
MFA-Master of Fine Arts
Mgr-Manager
MI,Mich-Michigan
MM-Master of Mathematics
MME-Master of Music Education
MN,Minn-Minnesota
MO,Mo-Missouri
MPA-Master of Public
    Administration
MPH-Master of Public Health
MRE-Master of Religious
    Education

MS,Miss-Mississippi
MSW-Master of Social Work
Mt-Mount
MT,Mont-Montana

NAACP-National Association for
    the Advancement of Colored
    People
NAE-National Association of
    Education
NASW-National Association of
    Social Workers
Nat-National
NC-North Carolina
ND-North Dakota
NDC-New Democratic Coalition
NEA-National Education
    Association (state education
    associations appear often as,
    e.g. CEA-Calif. Educ. Assoc.)
NE,Neb-Nebraska
NFLPN-National Federation of
    Licensed Practical Nurses
NH-New Hampshire
NJ-New Jersey
NM-New Mexico
NOW-National Organization of
    Women
NOWL-National Order of Women
    Legislators
NV,Nev-Nevada
NY-New York
NYC-New York, New York

Occ-Occupation
OEO-Office of Economic
    Opportunity
OES-Order of the Eastern Star
OH-Ohio
OK,Okla-Oklahoma
OR,Ore-Oregon
Org-Organization
OWL-Order of Women Legislators

PA,Pa-Pennsylvania
Party-Party Positions held
PhD-Doctor of Philosophy
PIRG-Public Interest Research
    Group
Pky-Parkway
Pl-Place
PO-Post Office
PP-People's Party
PR-Public Relations, Puerto Rico
Pres-President
Prev-Previous Public Office held
Prof-Professor
PTA-Parent-Teacher Association
PTL-Parent-Teacher League
PTO-Parent-Teacher Organization
PTS-Parent-Teacher Society
PTSA-Parent-Teacher Student
    Association

R-Republican
Rd-Road
Rep-Republican
Repr-Representative
Reg-Regional
RFD-Rural Free Delivery
RI-Rhode Island

RN-Registered Nurse
RR-Rural Route
Rt,Rte-Route

SAC-Screen Actors'Guild
SC-South Carolina
SCAG-Southern California
    Area Governments
SCLC-Southern Christian
    Leadership Conference
SD-South Dakota
Sen-Senator
Soc-Society
St-Saint, Street
Sub Com-Subcommittee
SUNY-State University of
    New York

Ter-Terrace
TN,Tenn-Tennessee
Treas-Treasurer
Twp-Township
TX,Tex-Texas

U-University
UDC-United Daughters of
    the Confederacy
UFT-United Federation of
    Teachers
UFW-United Farm Workers
UGN-United Good Neighbor
UN-United Nations
UNESCO-United Nations
    Educational, Scientific
    and Cultural Organization
UT-Utah

V-Vice
VA-Veterans Administration
VA-Virginia
V-Ch-Vice-Chairwoman
VFW-Veterans of Foreign Wars
V-Pres-Vice-President
VT-Vermont

WA,Wash-Washington
Wash, DC-Washington, D.C.
WEAL-Women's Equity Action
    League
WI,Wisc-Wisconsin
WPC-Women's Political Caucus
WV-West Virginia
WY-Wyoming

ZPG-Zero Population Growth

NUMBERS OF WOMEN IN OFFICE: 1977 STATE SUMMARIES

State	U.S. Congress	State Exec.	State Senate	State House	State Judiciary	County Comsn.	Town-ships	Mayor-alty	Local Councils
Alabama	0	5	0	3	1	6	NA	14	174
Alaska	0	1	1	3	0	10	NA	8	105
Arizona	0	2	6	10	6	4	NA	11	37
Arkansas	0	2	1	2	2	45	NA	23	136
California	2	3	1	5	14	26	NA	46	230
Colorado	1	2	2	12	1	7	NA	17	206
Connecticut	0	10	5	32	1	NA	82	18	57
Delaware	0	3	2	6	0	2	NA	5	37
Florida	0	1	2	16	10	18	NA	19	204
Georgia	0	0	1	10	1	11	NA	15	105
Hawaii	0	2	4	5	0	0	NA	0	3
Idaho	0	1	2	8	0	5	NA	10	61
Illinois	1	3	3	18	7	1	87	8[1]	-
Indiana	0	1	3	6	3	2	100	2	65
Iowa	0	2	4	13	1	15	NA	37	412
Kansas	1	2	1	10	1	10	49	23	184
Kentucky	0	2	1	7	1	6	NA	14*	141*

[1] Incomplete information.

NUMBERS OF WOMEN IN OFFICE (Continued)

State	U.S. Congress	State Exec.	State Senate	State House	State Judiciary	County Comsn.	Town-ships	Mayor-alty	Local Councils
Louisiana	1	3	1	1	0	15	NA	12	74
Maine	0	0	2	25	0	0	NA	19	169
Maryland	3	0	3	18	3	12	NA	11	81
Massachusetts	1	3	4	16	0	4	NA	17	133
Michigan	0	0	0	8	6	84	1548*	23	298
Minnesota	0	1	2	10	1	13	NA	28	332*
Mississippi	0	1	0	2	1	4	NA	10	116
Missouri	0	1	2	14	0	8	-	39	303
Montana	0	1	2	12	0	2	NA	9	68
Nebraska	1	1	2 (uni-cameral)		0	3	-	17	99
Nevada	0	1	2	5	0	5	NA	2	7
New Hampshire	0	1	4	110	0	4	NA	7	41
New Jersey	2	4	1	12	2	16	NA	19	269
New Mexico	0	2	1	4	0	5	NA	9	44
New York	2	7	3[2]	6	7	42	256[3]	30[3]	244[3]
North Carolina	0	2	4	19	2	28	NA	16	171
North Dakota	0	0	3	16	0	0	NA	7	82
Ohio	1	2	1	7	8	7	64	28	449*
Oklahoma	0	0	1	6	3	4	NA	21	148
Oregon	0	1	3[4]	9	4	11	NA	11	189
Pennsylvania	0	0	1	10	12	7	NA	19	452*
Rhode Island	0	3	4	7	2	NA	NA	0	18

---

[2]At the beginning of 1978 Carol Bellamy resigned her N.Y. Senate seat to become N.Y.C. Council President.

[3]These figures were taken from Newsvane 6 (November 1977). Newsvane is published regularly by the Department of State of New York. The number of biographical listings for women holding local office in New York in the body of this book varies from the Newsvane figures due to inaccuracies in original lists received from the state of New York.

[4]At the beginning of 1978 Betty Roberts was appointed to the judiciary in Oregon and resigned her Senate seat.

NUMBERS OF WOMEN IN OFFICE (Continued)

State	U.S. Congress	State Exec.	State Senate	State House	State Judiciary	County Comsn.	Town-ships	Mayor-alty	Local Councils
South Carolina	0	2	0	10	0	9	NA	7	71
South Dakota	0	4	2	6	1	5	NA	10	49
Tennessee	1	2	1	2	1	57	NA	10	50
Texas	1	0	1	10	1	21	NA	29	322
Utah	0	1	1	5	0	0	NA	4	50
Vermont	0	1	2	25	0	3	48	3	13
Virginia	0	1	0	9	0	20	NA	11	114
Washington	0	3	7	16	4	8	NA	17	186
West Virginia	0	3	0	12	0	5	NA	7	115
Wisconsin	0	3	2	10	1	85	NA	9	-
Wyoming	0	1	1	6	0	5	NA	4	43
Washington DC	NA	NA	NA	NA	2	NA	NA	NA	4
TOTAL NUMBER OF WOMEN[5]	18[6]	97	102 — 594 (696[7])		110	660	2234	735 — 6961 (9930)	
TOTAL NUMBER OF OFFICEHOLDERS	535	904	1975 — 5583 (7558)		5940	20973[8]		126772[9]	
PROPORTION OF OFFICEHOLDERS WHO ARE WOMEN	3.4%	10.7%	9.2%		1.8%	3.1%		7.8%	

---

[5]Totals listed are current for August 1977, with one exception (see note 7).

[6]In 1977 18 women served in the U.S. House of Representatives (4.1% women of 435 U.S. Representatives). There were no women serving in the 100 member U.S. Senate. In early 1978 Muriel Humphrey of Minnesota was appointed to fill a Senate vacancy created by the death of Hubert Humphrey.

[7]This figure reflects the results of November 1977 State Legislative races in Kentucky, New Jersey and Virginia.

[8]Figure taken from State and Local Government Special Studies No. 68: Governing Boards of County Governments, 1973 (Washington, D.C.: Government Printing Office).

[9]Numbers are estimates arrived at by adjusting figures given in the U.S. Census of Governments, Vol. 6, Popularly Elected Officials of State and Local Governments (Washington, D.C.: Government Printing Office, 1967) p.7. They reflect the changes in total numbers of governing bodies as shown in the U.S. Census of Governments, Vol. 1, Governmental Organization (Washington, D.C.: Government Printing Office, 1972) p.1. A breakdown of figures for the individual totals of townships, mayors, and city councils was unavailable.

STATISTICAL REPORT:
PROFILE OF WOMEN HOLDING OFFICE, 1977

by Marilyn Johnson and Susan Carroll

with Kathy Stanwick and Lynn Korenblit

This profile of women serving in public office is issued by the Center for the American Woman and Politics (CAWP) as part of its continuing commitment to describe and report on the situation of U. S. women in public life. CAWP's first profile of female officeholders (1975) documented the paucity of women at all levels of public decision making throughout the nation.[1] Although limited progress has been made since 1975, women's talents and skills remain seriously underutilized for the development and implementation of public policies. CAWP offers this new report with the conviction that the nature and extent of women's participation in political life and governmental affairs deserve attention of the general public and of the nation's policymakers.

CAWP's 1975 profile of women in public office has found a place in libraries and classrooms, as well as on the reference shelves of journalists, radio and television reporters, corporate managers and public officials. The profile supplied the first nationwide description of the numbers, location, personal characteristics and political backgrounds of women in office at federal, state, county and local levels. As with all first reports, the profile has stimulated as many questions as it answered. Have the numbers of women relative to men in various offices increased over time? How do the backgrounds and officeholding experiences of women compare with those of men? What special difficulties, if any, do women encounter once they have achieved public office? Do women in office, having received appointment from political leaders or approval from voters, perceive themselves as exempt from sex discrimination? Do women perceive their political roles in ways that differ from the role conceptions of men? Are most local officeholders unambitious for political advancement? Why do women leave public office?

Based on a greatly expanded survey, this second national profile of women holding office addresses many of the important questions stimulated by CAWP's earlier research. This survey includes for the first time small samples of federal appointees and members of the judiciary. We also have questioned, in selected states, male officeholders and women who formerly served in office.

Past comparisons of politically active women and men have tended to rely either on very small samples of officeholders in highly restricted locales or on samples of party leaders in which proportionately fewer women than men were public officeholders.[2] The survey of a multi-state sample of men represents an unusual opportunity to examine the role of gender in political leadership among women and men holding equivalent offices.

The inclusion in this analysis of women who have left public office is a first attempt, to our knowledge, to study former officeholders of either sex. Information about former officeholders can provide insight into a number of aspects of the political life of women: the nature of turnover among officeholders, circumstances which cause women to leave office, the degree of continuity in political careers and the impact of officeholding on subsequent activities.

ORGANIZATION OF THE REPORT

The report presents the analysis of information from several thousand questionnaires completed by women currently holding office across the country, by men in selected states, and by women formerly in office. (The questions asked are appended to the report.) The analysis is divided into seven major parts:

Part I describes the numbers and location of women in office in 1977 and assesses change since 1975. It examines the proportion of officeholders who are women, variations among states and regions, size of population of the districts in which women serve, and proportions of women on governing bodies of varying size.

Part II examines personal characteristics, organizational affiliations and family patterns.

Part III analyzes political experience, officeholding activities, and self-ratings of performance.

Part IV considers self-reports of liberalism or conservatism, orientations to selected political issues, and orientations to issues conventionally defined as "women's" issues.

Part V examines evaluations of the situation of women in politics, including perceptions of sex discrimination, of special qualities and skills possessed by women, and of advantages experienced and difficulties encountered as women.

Part VI is devoted to an analysis of political ambitions and, in addition, to a comparison of the characteristics of women who have left public office with those who have remained.

Part VII, the final section, summarizes briefly the major research findings, discusses possible interpretations and implications, and suggests emergent issues deserving further investigation.

DESCRIPTION OF THE SAMPLES

Early in 1977 CAWP collected books, manuals, directories and lists from which we compiled the names of women officials in various governing bodies. Names included women appointed to the federal executive branch and women serving in the U. S. Congress, cabinet-level offices in the state executive, state legislatures, state appellate and trial courts of general jurisdiction, mayoralties and local councils (including cities, towns, townships, villages and boroughs).[3]

The Main Sample

From May through July 1977 more than 13,000 questionnaires were mailed to all officeholders who could be identified as women serving in the categories of office included in the study. A second questionnaire, followed by a reminder postcard, was sent to those who did not respond to the initial mailing. Resumes were requested from officeholders who did not complete the questionnaire. Table 1 describes the numbers of women currently serving in each office and the percentages for whom statistical information is available.[4]

The Sample of Men

Questionnaires were mailed to a sample of male state legislators and county commissioners in sixteen states and to mayors and local councilmen in eight of the sixteen.[5] States were selected to represent a diversity of region.[6] Fifteen percent of those to whom questionnaires were mailed responded, resulting in a sample of 366 male officials.

The subsample of women in office.
For purposes of comparison with men, a subsample of women currently in office has been constructed from the main sample. This comparison sample consists of respondents who hold similar offices in the same states from which men were sampled. The proportions of males holding each kind of office are nearly identical to those of females in the comparison sample. Sixteen percent of the men and 15% of the women are state legislators; 14% of the men and 13% of women are county commissioners; 6% of men and 7% of women occupy mayoralties; 64% of the men and 65% of the women are members of local councils.

Former Officeholders

In an effort to identify some of the conditions and contingencies influencing women to remain in office or to leave, we have questioned a group of women who recently held elective office and responded to the 1975 survey but who no longer serve in office. Respondents to the 1975 survey who were sent questionnaires in 1977 include former state legislators in all states and former local councilwomen, mayors and county commissioners in twenty-five states. Twenty-nine percent of those to whom questionnaires were sent completed

and returned them, yielding a sample of 188 women.

The subsample of current officeholders.
For purposes of comparison with former officeholders, a subsample of 550 women has been selected from the main sample of current officeholders. The group consists of respondents to both the 1975 and 1977 surveys who are from offices and states in which information on former officeholders was received.[7] The sample of former officeholders and the comparison sample of current officeholders are similar in the proportions holding each type of office: former officeholders consist of 19% state legislators, 6% county commissioners, 8% mayors and 67% local councilwomen; corresponding percentages for the comparison sample of women currently in office are 18%, 8%, 9% and 65%.

The Potential for Response Bias

The proportions of nonrespondents mean that caution must be exercised in reviewing the research findings. There is always the danger that those who did not receive questionnaires or who failed to respond are very different from those who replied. A distinct possibility exists that a disproportionate number of completed questionnaires were returned by women with a special interest in the subject of women and politics. The response rate of male officials, as the lowest of the samples, opens the widest potential for bias. Given the sponsorship of the survey and its subject matter, a larger proportion of the men who responded than of nonrespondents may be sympathetic to the concerns of women and to the participation of women in politics. If such a bias does exist, then our data may understate the gender differences among officeholders in attitudes toward women in politics and in positions on "women's" issues.

Since we are unable to pinpoint and adjust for any bias that may exist, caution demands that the reported percentages and averages be regarded as good approximations and not as exact figures. In interpreting tables and research findings, more attention should be paid to the size, consistency and patterning of differences among categories than to any single number.

PRESENTATION OF RESEARCH FINDINGS

In the report to follow, Part I, on numbers and location of officeholders, relies for the most part on analyses of compiled lists of officeholders rather than on responses to questionnaires. The remainder of the report is based on analyses of questionnaire returns. Although the separate parts deal with widely varying topics, a basic strategy for presentation of the findings has been utilized in each section.

Variations by Office

Presentation of a topic begins with a description, through a table or textual commentary or both, of women in nine major categories of officeholding: appointees to the federal executive, members of the U. S. House of Representatives, members of the state executive, state judges, state senators, state representatives, county commissioners, mayors and heads of township governing bodies, members of municipal and township councils.

Special Analyses

In reporting the backgrounds, officeholding activities and attitudes of women holding office, we often shall ask how the basic descriptions may be modified by other dimensions, especially the size of population of the district in which office is held, the age of the officeholder, the year of entry into current office and political party affiliation. These additional analyses are not feasible for every category of office, either because they are not meaningful or because the numbers in some offices are too few to permit subgroupings.

District population. The effect of holding office in a relatively small or relatively large district is examined only at county and local levels, among county commissioners, mayors and local councillors. A distinction is made between districts with populations under 10,000 and those with populations of 10,000 or more.

Age of officeholder. The effect of age is examined among state legislators (upper and lower houses combined) and local councillors. Within these offices, the division of incumbents into four age categories (under 35 yrs., 35-44 yrs., 45-54 yrs., 55+ yrs.) results in subgroups sufficiently large for relatively stable observations.

Year of entry into current office. Subgroupings of officeholders according to year of election or appointment to current office have been made for state legislators (upper and lower houses combined), county commissioners, mayors and local councillors. The analysis distinguishes between those entering their current office in 1974 or earlier and those entering in 1975 or later. This division roughly segregates those achieving office before and after CAWP's earlier survey, which questioned women holding office as of July 1975. Most of the more recent entrants are in their first term of office.

Party affiliation. The association of political party affiliation with other characteristics of officeholders or officeholding is examined among state legislators (upper and lower houses combined), county commissioners, mayors and local council members.

Other special analyses. At various points in the report, research questions are addressed by the introduction of other special analyses that divide officeholders into subgroups. Each of these is described when introduced.

Comparisons of Men and Women

A major theme in this report is a comparison of women with men in office, using the special samples already described. Because the distributions by office for men and women are so similar, we combine offices in presenting the research findings. In reporting differences or similarities based on comparison of the totals, we note whenever a particular pattern does not hold true for every office in the sample.

Tabular Presentation

Tables are utilized in the report as a means of presenting detailed information in more compact form than can be accomplished easily through textual description. (Although the text serves as commentary to the tables, it also contains much information not presented in tabluar form.) The format for tabular presentation has been made as uniform as possible, and every attempt has been made to construct tables which are understandable to those readers relatively unfamiliar with quantitative reports.[8] Each table carries a descriptive title that presents a general statement about information contained therein. Numbers reported consist exclusively of percentages, medians (used to indicate average tendencies), and totals. When totals are so small (under 25) that computations have high risk of being unreliable, percentages are omitted and replaced with raw numbers in parentheses, and medians are reported in parentheses. To assist those who may be unfamiliar with tabular presentation, Footnote 8 supplies simple instructions for reading the tables in this report.

While this report describes basic and previously unavailable information about women in office, many important questions remain unanswered, and some of the research findings may be interpreted in varying ways.[9] (Footnote 9 discusses some problems of interpretation.) Timely reporting of the basic survey results requires postponing some research questions that could be addressed profitably to the data, as well as some of the more complex analyses. Although further analyses of the data constitute an important part of the ongoing research program at CAWP and will appear in future publications, the answers to some questions await the evidence of future research studies. Therefore, CAWP offers this second profile of women in public office as a contribution to the accumulation of research knowledge about political women in the United States.

PART I.   NUMBERS AND LOCATIONS OF WOMEN IN OFFICE

In 1976 and 1977 political women were on the move. Although the changes which have taken place since CAWP's 1975 survey of women in office are not revolutionary, they are noteworthy. Since 1975, the numbers of women have increased in every type of office except the U.S. House of Representatives and the federal judiciary. Nationwide, women comprise more than 9% of state legislators, nearly 11% of state cabinet and equivalent state executive officials, and nearly 8% of mayors and members of township and municipal councils. In 1977, women held approximately 6 to 10% of all offices covered in this survey, while in 1975 they held 4 to 7% of these offices.[10] (See the State Summaries on page xvii for more detail. The reader is cautioned that some changes in the numbers of women serving in office result from more thorough coverage in this second edition. For an explanation of where coverage was expanded and more complete data were available, see the Introduction to this book.)

An overview of women in office at state, county and local levels reveals that no one state or region is consistently high in the numbers of women in every type of office. The diversity in the numbers of women officials may occur for many reasons having no connection with the propensity of women to seek office or their ability to be elected. The numbers are clearly affected by variations in the size of governing bodies, in the number of such bodies within each state, and in the presence or absence of particular offices and governmental forms such as counties or townships.

Federal Offices

In the Carter administration, women received 14% of the presidential appointments as of January 1978. Jimmy Carter is the first president in the history of this nation to have two female cabinet members: Juanita Kreps, Secretary of Commerce and Patricia Roberts Harris, Secretary of Housing and Urban Development. Prior to 1977, only three other women have served in the federal cabinet.

Progress apparent in the federal executive is not paralleled in the judicial branch. No woman has ever served on the Supreme Court. Of 675 U.S. Circuit and District Court Judges, only 5 are women- a decrease of 3 since 1975.

In the 95th Congress 18 women serve in the U.S. House of Representatives. One female U.S. senator, Muriel Humphrey, was appointed to office after the death of her husband, Senator Hubert Humphrey, in early 1978. The numbers of women in Congress are below the previous highs of 19 representatives in the 94th Congress and 2 senators in the 87th Congress. Several factors have contributed to the relatively stable number of women in Congress: it is difficult for women to obtain their party's nomination in districts with open seats; female candidates face male opponents who campaign with the advantage of incumbency; congressional campaigns require large amounts of money. For these and other reasons, a large influx of women into the U.S. Congress is unlikely. Nonetheless, the increase in women's visibility and participation at lower levels of office places them on political paths which could lead to Congress and other high-level offices.

State Offices

Two women serve as governors of their states: Ella Grasso of Connecticut and Dixie Lee Ray of Washington. Three women are lieutenant governors: Evelyn Gandy of Mississippi, Mary Ann Krupsak of New York and Thelma L. Stovall of Kentucky. In 1975 one governor and one lieutenant governor were women.

The number of women in state cabinet or equivalent positions has also increased. In 1975, 84 women were identified as holding state-wide executive positions of cabinet-level or higher. In 1977, 97 women were serving in these offices, constituting nearly 11% of an estimated 904 positions.

In the state judiciary, 110 women--nearly 2% of the total--serve as judges in appellate courts and trial courts of general jurisdiction. This number represents a modest increase from the 92 women judges in 1975.

State Legislatures

Slightly over 9% of state legislators in early 1978 were women--101 out of 1975 senators, and 601 of 5,583 state representatives. The numbers of women in state legislatures have risen steadily from 305 (or 4%) in 1969, to 610 (8%) in 1975, to the current 702 (9%) in 1978.

The increases in the numbers of women legislators represent relatively small increments in a large number of states rather than dramatic increases in one or two, as can be seen in Table 2. The New England, West North Central and South Atlantic regions most consistently exhibit gains.

Despite the general trend, not all states show increases since 1975. Thirteen states have lower percentages of women among their legislators in 1978 than in 1975: Alaska, Arizona, Colorado, Delaware, Hawaii, Michigan, Mississippi, New York, Ohio, Oregon, Tennessee, Utah and Wyoming. States in the Mountain region consistently show either decreases or no change.

In 1975, 17 legislatures had less than 5% women; in 1978, only 8 have less than 5%: Alabama, Arkansas, Louisiana, Mississippi, New Mexico, New York, Pennsylvania and Tennessee. In 1978, as in 1975, we find the southern states and some of the larger, more populous states with the lowest percentages of women in their state legislatures. The highest percentage of women (28%) is found in the New Hampshire legislature, which is also the largest state legislative body in the country. As it did in 1975, New Hampshire accounts for nearly one-fifth of all women serving in the lower houses.

Legislators vs. Other Officeholders

The general political situation of women within a state cannot be ascertained simply from a knowledge of women's participation in one type of office. This point is illustrated by comparing patterns of

Table 1. NUMBERS AND PERCENTAGES OF WOMEN OFFICEHOLDERS INCLUDED IN STATISTICAL REPORT

	Federal[a]	State Judiciary	State Executive	State Senate	State House	County Commission	Mayoralty[b]	Municipal and Township Council
Total women in office	87	110	97	102	594	660	735	9,195
Number analyzed in statistical profile[c]	35	49	54	62	265	288	292	2,204
Number in profile as % of total in office	40%[d]	44%	56%	61%	45%	44%	40%[e]	24%[e]

[a]Includes executive appointments and U.S. House of Representatives as of November 1977. There were no female U.S. Senators at the time of data gathering.

[b]Includes equivalent on council when no mayor exists.

[c]Includes only those from whom questionnaires were received. Totals used for calculation of percentages in subsequent tables may not equal the totals in this table. They will vary with the number of respondents choosing to answer a particular question and with the number of respondents for whom a particular question is applicable. In addition, where information was available from a secondary source, some officeholders who did not return the questionnaire may be included among the total responses.

[d]This figure represents a proportion of the total number of women serving as of 15 November 1977. As a proportion of those who were initially sent questionnaires, the response rate is 54%.

[e]A sizeable proportion of women officeholders at the local level did not receive questionnaires because their names were on lists received in late July, after the cutoff date for mailing. The response rate, excluding those not sent questionnaires, is 42% for mayors and 33% for municipal and township council members.

Table 2. THE PROPORTION OF WOMEN LEGISLATORS HAS INCREASED IN THE MAJORITY OF STATES SINCE 1975

	% Women among State Legislators[a]			% Women among State Legislators[a]			% Women among State Legislators[a]
	1975	1978		1975	1978		1975	1978
NEW ENGLAND			WEST NORTH CENTRAL			WEST SOUTH CENTRAL		
Maine	13	16	Minnesota	4	6	Arkansas	2	2
Vermont	12	14	Iowa	9	10	Oklahoma	4	5
New Hampshire	24	28	Missouri	6	9	Louisiana	1	1
Massachusetts	6	8	North Dakota	10	13	Texas	4	7
Connecticut	14	20	South Dakota	10	10			
Rhode Island	6	8	Nebraska	2	6	MOUNTAIN		
			Kansas	5	7	Montana	9	9
MIDDLE ATLANTIC						Idaho	10	10
New York	4	3	SOUTH ATLANTIC			Wyoming	8	6
New Jersey	8	11	Delaware	16	13	Nevada	12	12
Pennsylvania	4	4	Maryland	10	11	Utah	8	6
			West Virginia	7	9	Colorado	16	15
EAST NORTH CENTRAL			Virginia	4	6	Arizona	20	18
Wisconsin	8	9	North Carolina	9	14	New Mexico	4	4
Illinois	6	9	South Carolina	4	6			
Indiana	6	6	Georgia	4	5	PACIFIC		
Michigan	6	5	Florida	8	11	Washington	12	15
Ohio	7	6				Oregon	12	11
			EAST SOUTH CENTRAL			California	2	5
			Kentucky	4	6			
			Tennessee	4	2	Alaska	15	7
			Alabama	1	2			
			Mississippi	3	1	Hawaii	13	12

Source: Compiled by National Women's Education Fund, Washington, D.C.

[a]See State Summaries, p. xvii, for absolute numbers of women in state houses and senates as of November 1977.

membership in legislatures with patterns of occupancy in state executive and congressional offices. We find that a relatively large number of women in one type of office does not imply a large number in other offices within a given state. States with average or above-average proportions of women among state legislators are no more likely than other states to have an above-average number of state executives. Thirteen of 24 states with an above-average number of women in the legislature and 13 of 26 below-average states have at least two women in state executive positions. The pattern of congressional representation would appear to run counter to the pattern of state legislative office-holding. Among the 14 states represented by women in the U.S. Congress, 10 are states with below-average percentages of women in their state legislatures.

County and Local Offices

The largest increases in women's elective political participation since 1975 have taken place at the local level of officeholding and, to a lesser extent, at the county level. In 1975, 456 women comprised 2% of officials in county governing bodies. In 1977 there were 660 women, 3% of the total. Thirty-five states show increases since 1975 in the numbers of women on county commissions.

The number of women in mayoralties and on municipal and township governing bodies has shown striking increases since CAWP's first survey. In 1975, we identified 5,931 women as holding office at the local level, an estimated 4% of total officials in the offices surveyed. In 1977, women held 9,930 such positions, an estimated 8% of the total. A

Table 3.   LARGE INCREASES IN THE NUMBERS OF WOMEN HOLDING LOCAL OFFICE HAVE OCCURRED SINCE 1975

	Mayors 1975	Mayors 1977	Local Councillors[a] 1975	Local Councillors[a] 1977		Mayors 1975	Mayors 1977	Local Councillors[a] 1975	Local Councillors[a] 1977
NEW ENGLAND					**EAST SOUTH CENTRAL**				
Maine	0	19	87	169	Kentucky	8[b]	14	6[b]	141
Vermont	0	3	44	61	Tennessee	2	10	48	50
New Hampshire	5	7	34	41	Alabama	7	14	78	174
Massachusetts	3	17	45	133	Mississippi	8	10	74	116
Connecticut	13	18	117	139					
Rhode Island	2	0	19	18	**WEST SOUTH CENTRAL**				
					Arkansas	29	23	131	136
MIDDLE ATLANTIC					Oklahoma	17	21	75	148
New York	26[b]	30[c]	161[b]	500[c]	Louisiana	9	12	56	74
New Jersey	15	19	198	269	Texas	36	29	241	322
Pennsylvania	22	19	206	452					
					MOUNTAIN				
EAST NORTH CENTRAL					Montana	6	9	51	68
Wisconsin	10[b]	9	32[b]	-	Idaho	7	10	38	61
Illinois	19	8[b]	170	87[b]	Wyoming	8	4	26	43
Indiana	0	2	132	165	Nevada	0	2	2	7
Michigan	14	23	514	1846[c]	Utah	3	4	37	50
Ohio	29	28	167	513[c]	Colorado	10	17	160	206
					Arizona	6	11	33	37
WEST NORTH CENTRAL					New Mexico	8	9	25	44
Minnesota	23	28	204	332[c]					
Iowa	29	37	275	412	**PACIFIC**				
Missouri	28	39	267	303	Washington	4	17	149	186
North Dakota	4	7	65	82	Oregon	10	11	165	189
South Dakota	12	10	38	49	California	32	46	188	230
Nebraska	12	17	71	99					
Kansas	21	23	184	233	Alaska	2	8	33	105
SOUTH ATLANTIC					Hawaii	0	0	1	3
Delaware	3	5	19	37					
Maryland	5	11	54	81	Washington, D.C.	0	0	3	4
West Virginia	15	7	105	115					
Virginia	6	11	111	114	Total	566	735	5365	9195
North Carolina	10	16	131	171					
South Carolina	5	7	67	71					
Georgia	10	15	67	105					
Florida	13	19	161	204					

[a]Includes Township officials

[b]Incomplete Information

[c]Represents Expanded Coverage over the First Edition of *WOMEN IN PUBLIC OFFICE*

-Information not available

degree of caution should be exercised in noting that the number of women holding local office has nearly doubled since 1975 because in some states an unknown portion of the increase in officeholders reflects the availability of more complete lists for the 1977 survey. Nonetheless, even with adjustments made for changed coverage, the increase in local officeholding appears to be at least 36% above 1975.

Table 3 presents by state and region the numbers of women holding mayoral and local council offices in 1975 and 1977. When examining changes between 1975 and 1977 in the numbers of women holding local office, only limited types of comparisons can be made. The U.S. Census of Governments does not provide a state-by-state description of the number of officeholders within each state. Without such figures, we cannot calculate the number of women as a percentage of the total number of officeholders in each state. In some states, a large increase in absolute numbers may represent relatively slight change when viewed as a change in the percentage of women among total officeholders. Nonetheless, the changes in absolute numbers of women serving at the local level are impressive. If such changes continue with the momentum of the past two years, women will begin to assume a substantial share of the political decision-making in their local communities.

Population of Officeholders' Districts

District population is an important key to under-standing the profiles of officials serving in local and county government. As described in other parts of this report, officeholders from smaller districts differ from those in larger districts in background and family characteristics, political experience and activities of office, positions on issues, perceptions of women's role in politics, and ambition for higher office.

In 1975, we found a majority of mayors and local council members serving in districts under 5,000 population. We speculated then that this pattern might be more true of women than of men, as a manifestation of women's low participation in more

Table 4. THE MAJORITY OF LOCAL OFFICEHOLDERS SERVE IN DISTRICTS UNDER 5,000

District Population	Women[a] Mayors and Councillors %	Men Mayors and Councillors %
under 1,000	26	25
1,000-4,999	34	37
5,000-9,999	14	11
10,000-24,999	16	20
25,000-49,999	6	4
50,000 +	4	3
Total	(507)	(235)

[a]Comparison sample constructed from main sample of women

powerful offices. With the inclusion of a sample of men in the 1977 survey, we are able to compare the size of population of the districts in which men and women serve. As Table 4 reveals, women are no more likely than men to be serving in small districts. Approximately equal proportions of male officeholders and of the comparison sample of women serve at each level of district population. There-fore, if women serve in predominantly small districts, they do so because most districts are small and not because they differ from men in the size of the district in which they are able to achieve office.

An overview of the numbers and locations of office-holders provides the framework for describing the political life of women. But it is only the frame-work. Despite overall changes in representation, women remain a very small proportion of public decision makers. What are their characteristics? What paths to office have they taken, and what are their plans for the future? How do they view their role in politics? How do they compare with men? Are there symptoms of change in the kinds of women who enter office? We address these and other questions in the remainder of this report. We do so with the awareness that their small numbers alone make women in public office a special group of women.

PART II.   BACKGROUND AND FAMILY ROLES OF WOMEN IN OFFICE

Citizenship, minimum age and residence are the only legal qualifications for most public offices. Yet in a number of ways characteristics such as ethnicity, age, education, occupation, income, organizational ties and family roles limit and define the kinds of citizens who do in fact con-stitute the "pool" from which officials are drawn. Some operate as qualifications for office above and beyond legal requirements. Others point to resources of time and money available for invest-ment in political activity. Still others indicate social placement in roles and networks that favor exposure to the political sphere and the subsequent development or maintenance of political ambitions.

The social backgrounds and family roles of women in office are of interest for what we may learn about two processes: recruitment to office and perfor-mance in office. If we learn more about the kinds

of women who achieve public office, we may better understand the nature of the pool of potential officeholders, and of the potential for increases or decreases in the size of the pool. In addition, women may bring special attitudes and priorities to office because they exist in special social situations. If we have knowledge of the social situation of women in office, we may better evaluate the extent to which the increasing number of women officeholders is likely to affect the conduct of government.

The first section of Part II describes the back-grounds and family lives of women officeholders and how these vary according to selected other dimensions. The second section compares women with men in office. A concluding section presents a brief summary.

Table 5. OFFICEHOLDERS NUMBER FEW MINORITY MEMBERS AMONG THEM[a]

Ethnicity	Judi-ciary %	State Exec. %	State Senate %	State House %	County Comsn. %	Mayor-alty %	Local Council %	Total %
Black, Afro-American	6	3	8	3	3	-[b]	2	2
American Indian, Native American	0[b]	5	0	-	-	-	1	1
Chicano, Mexican American	0	0	0	0	0	-	-	-
Puerto Rican	0	0	0	0	0	0	0	0
Other Hispanic	0	0	0	0	0	0	0	0
Asian	0	3	4	1	1	0	-	-
European (identifies 1 or more European countries as heritage)	88	87	80	80	82	89	85	84
'Caucasian', 'white', 'white American'	0	2	4	4	5	4	3	4
'American', 'Yankee', 'Mid-Westerner'	0	0	2	8	5	5	5	5
Other or mixed self-identification	6	0	2	4	4	2	4	4
Total[c]	(34)	(39)	(51)	(221)	(262)	(250)	(1941)	(2813)

[a]Tabulations at the federal level are omitted because of low numbers responding.

[b]In this and all other Tables, '0' = no cases in category; '-' = cases less than .5% of those responding.

[c]In this and all other Tables, those not answering or responding "don't know" have been excluded from bases for percentaging.

Table 6. WOMEN IN OFFICE ARE PREDOMINANTLY MIDDLE-AGED

Age	Fed. Exec.[a]	U.S. House[a]	Judi-ciary %	State Exec. %	State Senate %	State House %	County Comsn. %	Mayor-alty %	Local Council %
Under 30	(0)	(0)	0	2	5	4	2	3	3
30-39	(13)	(3)	8	18	25	24	21	12	23
40-49	(5)	(7)	31	37	28	32	33	25	30
50-59	(4)	(3)	41	37	28	29	35	40	28
60+ years	(0)	(3)	20	6	14	11	9	20	16
Total	(22)	(16)	(39)	(51)	(60)	(267)	(274)	(285)	(2,129)
Median Age	(38)	(47)	52	48	48	47	48	52	47
Total	(22)	(16)	(39)	(51)	(60)	(267)	(274)	(285)	(2,129)
Districts under 10,000 pop.[b]							49	53	48
Total							(119)	(199)	(1,482)
Districts 10,000+ pop.[b]							46	47	46
Total							(128)	(68)	(517)

[a]In this and subsequent Tables, bases lower than 25 are signalled by reporting raw numbers in place of percentages and by placing medians in parentheses.

[b]In this and other Tables, district population is analyzed only at county and local levels.

Table 7. EDUCATIONAL ATTAINMENT RISES WITH LEVEL OF OFFICEHOLDING

Education	Fed. Exec.	U.S. House	Judi-ciary %	State Exec. %	State Senate %	State House %	County Comsn. %	Mayor-alty %	Local Council %
High school or less	0	(0)	0	2	3	10	25	37	37
Some college	0	(1)	0	16	12	20	27	25	24
College graduate	18	(4)	0	28	33	37	30	21	24
Some graduate work	4	(0)	0	3	14	7	3	5	3
One or more graduate degrees	78	(9)	100	51	38	26	15	12	12
Total	(27)	(14)	(47)	(58)	(64)	(270)	(282)	(284)	(2,177)

CHARACTERISTICS OF WOMEN IN OFFICE

A profile of women in office is necessarily complex, for such women are not a strictly homogeneous population. We have routinely inspected the data for a number of questions about variations: Can one generalize about women holding public office without regard to the type of office held? Do the Democratic and Republican parties attract distinct types of women? Are women in small districts -- where most local officeholders are found -- notably different from women in larger districts? Do younger officeholders or those more recently elected exhibit characteristics that may foretell change in the kinds of women who hold public office? For reasons of space, we report answers to these questions selectively, ordinarily commenting only when the analysis reveals differences among categories of officeholders. In the conclusion to Part II, we consider these questions more fully.

Ethnicity

The women in this survey are overwhelmingly Caucasians of European background. Respondents were asked to reply to the question: "What is the principal ethnic or racial heritage with which you identify yourself (e.g. Irish; Afro-American or Black; Chicano; German; etc.)?" A sizeable proportion (15%) made no identification. If those responding present reliable indicators of the total situation, then there are few black women and almost none of any other minority status in state and local governing bodies (Table 5).[12] At least 93% report European, white, or what they seem to consider mainstream American origins. The percentages of minority women among those elected or appointed in 1975 or later are no higher than the percentages among women entering office in earlier years.

At federal levels, minority women are a larger proportion of female officials than at state and local levels. For example, four of 18 women in the 95th Congress are black, and at the end of 1977, there were 11 black, two Asian and eight Hispanic women among the 77 women given major appointments by the Carter administration.

Age of Women in Office

Political elites are predominantly middle-aged. The officeholders in our study are no exception to this well-established fact, as Table 6 confirms. As in the 1975 survey, median age varies little from office to office, though judges, not included in the earlier survey, are similar to mayors in being somewhat older. Federal appointees, also not included in 1975, appear to be markedly younger than other officeholders. At county and local levels of officeholding, women from districts of under 10,000 population are slightly older than women from large districts.

Education

Women holding office are well educated relative to the general population.[13] Most have attended school beyond high school, though only at state and federal levels are the majority college graduates (Table 7). Among state executives, judges and federal officeholders, the majority have one or more graduate degrees.

As is often true of adults in today's society, education is an ongoing process for many officeholders. The percentages who report having taken courses or attended school within the past year range from 15% of state senators to 37% of judges. Seven percent of all officeholders were working toward a degree, though only 3% attended full full time.

Education and age. Similar to age patterns in the general population, older officeholders have less education. For example, the percentage of state legislators aged 55 and over who have completed college is 57%, while 89% of legislators under 35 years old have a college degree. Similarly, 32% of local council members aged 55 or more, but 43% of those under age 35, have completed college. The proportions with graduate degrees among state legislators increase from 19% of those 55 and older to 39% among those under 35 years.

Education and district size. In the smaller districts, proportionately fewer women are college graduates, regardless of age. Indeed, the educational level of officeholders may be more strongly related to district size than to age, as suggested by the fact that 52% of women aged 55 or over in large districts have completed college, in contrast to only 38% of those under age 35 years in small districts.

Employment Status and Occupation

Public office is a part-time activity for many state legislators and for most county commissioners, mayors and local councillors. Substantial proportions of women in these offices, from 30% of state representatives to 56% of local councilwomen, have additional employment outside the home (Table 8).

The present or past occupations of women in office reflect both their elite status and their gender (Table 9). Women in office typically have occupations of higher prestige than do members of the general population, and prestige rises with level of office.[14] Most common are professional/technical occupations, followed by clerical/secretarial and managerial/administrative. The sex-linked nature of the occupations of women officeholders is illustrated in Table 9 by the proportions in selected occupational categories. Among state legislative, county and local officeholders, just four types of occupations -- secretarial/clerical, nursing/health technical, social work and elementary/secondary school teaching -- account for between 30% and 40% of those reporting. Only among state executives, members of the state judiciary, and federal officeholders is there a relative absence of concentration in these four occupations traditionally pursued by women.

Stability vs. change in occupational profiles. Despite the entry of more and younger women into political office in recent years, the occupational profiles of women officeholders show few signs of change. The occupations of local councillors and mayors differ neither by age nor by year of entry into office. Among county commissioners, a larger proportion of recent entrants (22%) than of those entering in 1974 or earlier (12%) are classified as managerial/administrative. This shift is not

Table 8.   MANY WOMEN IN OFFICE ARE EMPLOYED IN OTHER OCCUPATIONS[a]

Employment Status	Fed. Exec.	Judi- ciary %	State Exec. %	State Senate %	State House %	County Comsn. %	Mayor- alty %	Local Council %
% Employed Outside Office	(0)	3	5	40	30	38	51	56
Full time	(0)	0	0	22	15	22	32	37
Part time	(0)	3	5	18	14	14	18	18
Time not specified	(0)	0	0	0	1	2	1	1
% Not Employed Outside Office	(15)	97	95	60	70	62	49	44
Last employed '76-'77	(8)	8	10	5	11	10	3	4
Last employed '72-'75	(0)	13	26	11	16	14	14	12
No recent employment	(1)	30	18	32	34	27	26	23
Date not specified	(6)	46	41	12	9	11	6	5
Total	(15)	(37)	(39)	(62)	(253)	(279)	(286)	(2,170)

[a]Tabulations at the U.S. House level are omitted because of low numbers responding.

Table 9.   THE OCCUPATIONAL EXPERIENCE OF WOMEN OFFICEHOLDERS LIES IN A RESTRICTED RANGE WITH A HEAVY CONCENTRATION IN TRADITIONALLY FEMALE OCCUPATIONS

Current or Past Occupation	Fed. Exec.	U.S. House	Judi- ciary %	State Exec. %	State Senate %	State House %	County Comsn. %	Mayor- alty %	Local Council %
Census Categories									
Professional, technical	(15)	(9)	100	45	64	48	50	36	37
Managers, administrators	(7)	(0)	0	49	16	23	18	20	18
Sales workers	(0)	(0)	0	0	7	8	6	9	8
Clerical, secretarial	(1)	(0)	0	6	11	17	18	21	26
Crafts	(0)	(1)	0	0	0	0	-	1	1
Operatives	(0)	(0)	0	0	0	1	1	3	3
Laborers	(0)	(0)	0	0	0	0	-	1	-
Farm	(0)	(0)	0	0	2	1	4	2	1
Service	(0)	(0)	0	0	0	2	3	7	6
Selected Occupations									
Health workers	(1)	(0)	0	0	0	3	8	7	5
Social workers	(0)	(1)	0	9	3	4	6	1	1
Elem., secondary teachers	(0)	(1)	4	3	16	13	16	14	17
Physicians, dentists	(0)	(0)	0	3	0	0	-	1	-
College teachers	(3)	(0)	6	0	9	6	3	1	2
Editors, reporters	(0)	(0)	0	0	7	2	2	2	2
Real estate, insurance sales workers	(0)	(0)	0	0	5	5	3	5	4
Public administrators	(2)	(0)	0	6	5	3	2	1	1
Lawyers	(8)	(6)	90	10	11	3	2	2	1
Median Occupational Prestige[a]	(72)	(76)	76	56	51	51	50	48	46
Total	(23)	(10)	(32)	(33)	(56)	(240)	(252)	(262)	(2,036)

[a]Hodge-Siegel-Rossi Scores as adapted to the 1970 U.S. Census Occupational Codes by the National Opinion Research Center.

concentrated among the younger officeholders but is true of all age categories. In the state legislatures, no differences appear between newcomers and those with longer tenure, but there are perceptible differences between younger and older legislators. Forty percent of legislators aged 55 and over, 42% of 45-54 year olds, 33% of 35-44 year olds and only 23% of those less than 35 years of age are in the four traditionally female occupations we have singled out as rough indicators of occupational sex-differentiation. Among those under 35, higher proportions are in law (12% vs. 1%-5% at other ages) and college teaching (14% vs. 3%-9% among other age groups). Women aged 35-44 years also show signs of less traditionalism in occupation. Higher proportions are managerial/administrative (28%) than in other age categories (14%-29%), and they are more likely to be college teachers (9%) than those over age 45 (3%).

Organizational Affiliations

Surveys of the general population consistently have found an association between participation in voluntary organizations and heightened political activity.[15] Even organizations that are manifestly nonpolitical in aims often serve as vehicles for the development of political motivations and the exercise of political activity.[16] Therefore women in office, as politically active individuals, can be expected to have a relatively large number of organizational memberships. Moreover, variations in numbers and types of memberships may supply indirect evidence of differing political involvements among women in office.

Number of memberships. On the average, from three to six current, active memberships are reported by every category of officeholder (Table 10). Judges and state legislators report the highest number of memberships, followed by those in state executive and federal offices. Mayors average the fewest affiliations, with county commissioners and local councilwomen reporting almost as few.

Officeholders in larger districts have substantially more memberships than those in smaller districts (see Table 11). This difference is probably the result of a less elaborate organizational structure in less populous areas. It could also reflect the lower education of officeholders in small districts, for past research has shown level of education to be associated with organizational participation.[17]

Except among mayors, women entering their current offices after 1974 belong to fewer organizations (Table 11). Women under age 35 also average fewer memberships, a pattern true of younger women in the general population (Table 11).[18] Do more recent entrants have fewer memberships because they are younger? Or does tenure in public office represent a form of social participation that, regardless of age, stimulates additional organizational involvements? Detailed analysis of local councilwomen by year of entry within separate categories of age reveals that the more recent officeholders average fewer memberships within each age category under 55 years. Among those 55 and older, newcomers have more memberships.[19]

Therefore, with the exception of the older office-

TABLE 10. WOMEN IN OFFICE ARE MEMBERS OF A WIDE VARIETY OF ORGANIZATIONS

Member of at Least One Organization in the Category	Fed. Exec.	U.S. House	Judiciary %	State Exec. %	State Senate %	State House %	County Comsn. %	Mayoralty %	Local Council %
Political (e.g., Democratic or Republican clubs, LWV)	(14)	(11)	46	64	84	86	65	38	43
Professional, business	(14)	(8)	98	68	64	47	37	30	32
Special service (e.g., Red Cross, Sierra Club)	(5)	(6)	40	34	44	39	35	27	29
Cultural[a]	(2)	(5)	26	14	20	34	24	27	29
Youth-school service (e.g., PTA, Girl Scouts)	(3)	(0)	21	16	16	24	25	22	29
Hobby and sports	(3)	(2)	26	24	16	24	22	21	23
General service (e.g., service club auxiliary, Community Chest)	(3)	(1)	33	30	20	27	26	21	19
Church-related	(0)	(0)	5	10	11	18	13	12	16
Alumni and university service (e.g., AAUW)	(7)	(2)	37	24	33	27	13	10	11
Sororal, fraternal auxiliary	(0)	(1)	19	4	5	10	8	13	10
Labor	(0)	(0)	0	8	8	6	3	5	8
Veterans and auxiliary	(0)	(1)	7	2	3	5	7	9	7
Public officials	(3)	(1)	9	14	17	23	12	8	5
Farm	(0)	(1)	0	2	3	3	3	2	2
Ethnic	(0)	(1)	2	6	6	4	2	3	2
Total	(22)	(13)	(43)	(50)	(64)	(263)	(268)	(265)	(1,947)
Median Total Memberships	(4.0)	(4.2)	6.0	4.3	5.5	5.4	3.6	2.6	3.1

[a]Category includes a number of women's groups whose defined purposes appear to be principally cultural-aesthetic.

Table 11.   OFFICEHOLDERS' MEMBERSHIPS VARY WITH
            DISTRICT SIZE, YEAR OF ENTRY AND AGE

Median Number of Memberships:	State Legis.	County Comsn.	Mayor- alty	Local Council
District Population				
under 10,000		2.9 (115)	2.2 (183)	2.7 (1,298)
10,000+		4.8 (125)	4.1 (65)	4.5 (515)
Year of Entry				
1974 or prior	6.0 (189)	4.0 (105)	2.7 (106)	3.4 (766)
1975 or later	5.0 (123)	3.4 (156)	2.6 (153)	2.9 (1,107)
Age				
under 35 years	4.6 (43)	(2.1) (23)	(2.0) (18)	2.4 (240)
35-44 years	5.1 (77)	4.0 (74)	3.1 (56)	3.3 (539)
45-54 years	5.7 (108)	3.7 (98)	3.0 (96)	3.4 (603)
55 and over	6.1 (71)	4.0 (60)	2.3 (92)	3.0 (489)

holders, tenure in office is associated with an increased number of organizational affiliations.[20] Participation in organizations is often viewed primarily as an important antecedent of political participation, a way of developing skills and building constituencies. Our analysis suggests that one must also pay attention to organizational affiliation as a consequence of political activity, perhaps as part of a process by which constituencies are widened and the groundwork laid for political mobility, perhaps merely as an aspect of what officeholders feel is expected of them as officials.

Types of memberships. Women holding office join a wide variety of organizations. This variety is seen in Table 10, which presents the percentages in each

office belonging to one or more organizations of a particular type.[21] In all categories of office, more officeholders belong to political, professional and special service organizations than to any other type of organization. Groups specializing in cultural pursuits, youth or school service organizations, hobby or sports clubs and general service organizations also attract sizeable proportions of officeholders.

The great majority of women officeholders are members of one or more women's organizations, as Table 12 shows. These organizations are classified into five types: feminist social action groups, whose principal aim is to bring about change in the status of women; general service, reform or social action groups, whose aims may include the status of women but are focused primarily on other issues and activities; professional and business organizations; women's partisan political groups; other women's organizations such as sororities, social clubs or women's auxiliaries.

Patterns of membership in feminist organizations are of particular interest because they parallel patterns of orientations to women's issues and women's role in politics, which will be discussed in Parts IV and V. The varying proportions having membership in feminist groups only in part mirror differences in the propensity to join few or many organizations. County and local officeholders, who average fewer memberships in general, are low in the proportions belonging to feminist groups. Yet judges, who have the highest median number of memberships, are also relatively low in feminist affiliations. More than a quarter of other officeholders report membership in one or more feminist groups, with state legislators showing the highest percentages. Membership in feminist organizations is also proportionately more common among women in larger districts, among Democrats and, despite their fewer organizational ties, among women under age 35.

Family Characteristics

The very high levels of social participation of women in public office are apparent from a review of their occupational and organizational involve-

Table 12.   ALTHOUGH MOST WOMEN BELONG TO AT LEAST ONE WOMEN'S ORGANIZATION, LOW PROPORTIONS
            OF OFFICEHOLDERS HOLD MEMBERSHIP IN FEMINIST GROUPS

Membership in at Least One Organization in the Category	Fed. Exec.	U.S. House	Judi- ciary %	State Exec. %	State Senate %	State House %	County Comsn. %	Mayor- alty %	Local Council %
Women's organizations, any type	(14)	(11)	81	74	92	91	75	68	65
Feminist-social action (e.g., NOW, WEAL, WPC)	(8)	(4)	14	26	31	31	13	4	4
General social service (e.g., LWV, AAUW)	(2)	(6)	44	31	66	50	35	26	23
Professional, business (e.g., BPW, women lawyers)	(4)	(5)	51	34	50	41	19	17	14
Women's political (e.g., women's party clubs)	(5)	(5)	9	28	30	40	30	14	15
Other women's (e.g., women's clubs, sororities, DAR, OES)	(2)	(4)	35	30	33	39	36	44	40
Total	(22)	(14)	(43)	(50)	(64)	(264)	(270)	(266)	(1,963)

Table 13.   MOST WOMEN OFFICEHOLDERS ARE MARRIED

Marital Status	Fed. Exec.	U.S. House	Judi- ciary %	State Exec. %	State Senate %	State House %	County Comsn. %	Mayor- alty %	Local Council %
Married	(19)	(8)	84	68	72	80	81	76	78
Divorced, separated	(1)	(0)	11	11	11	8	5	7	5
Widowed	(1)	(4)	0	10	8	6	10	11	12
Single	(3)	(1)	5	11	9	6	4	6	5
Total	(24)	(13)	(45)	(53)	(64)	(278)	(282)	(290)	(2,173)

ments. This multiplicity of public affiliations typically co-exists with the family roles of wife and mother.

Marital status. The overwhelming majority of women in every type of office are married, as demonstrated in Table 13[22]. Marital profiles differ little from office to office. State senators and members of the state executive appear to be slightly less likely to be married and more likely to be single or divorced. Yet the percentages for these offices are based on small numbers and one must be cautious about drawing inferences from them.

Children. Just as most women in office are married, most are mothers, although not of young children. Except for county commissioners (who also have somewhat larger families), the majority in every office have no children under 18 years (Table 14).

Family income. Family income indicates both social status and the extent to which there may be material resources that can be applied to the support of political activity. On the whole, the family incomes of women in office are above average, although few could be classified as enjoying very high incomes (Table 15). Family incomes rise with level of officeholding.

Family and Political Life

Potentially, the family is both resource and focus of strain in relation to political activity. On the one hand, family members may contribute material resources, volunteer labor and psychological support to their politically active members. On the other hand, the demands of political life -- whether full-time career or "spare-time" activity -- may threaten a drain on family resources, a loss of involvement in family life, and a heightening of family tensions. To explore the connection between family life and the political activity of women, we have analyzed responses to two series of questions: about the perceived supportiveness of the husband and about the perceived effects on family life of a high level of political activity.

Husband's degree of supportiveness. Perhaps because of a popular image of politics as the natural domain of men, relatively little attention has been devoted to the support for political activity that women may receive from their families. Yet a supportive family may be even more important for a politically active woman because public roles for women and for men receive differing degrees of social approval. The woman who fails to receive family support faces the double bind of negative sanctions from her family and uncertain public support.

Women in office do report high levels of support from their husbands, as shown by responses to questions about their husbands' interest in politics, approval of their holding office, participation in their political life and assumption of extra house-hold tasks (Table 16).[23] Very large majorities, three-quarters or more in most offices, report that their husbands "approve and actively encourage" their holding office. Few husbands are perceived as even mildly opposed. In addition, most husbands have at least some interest in politics, and from 36% to 74% report their husbands as "very much interested." On the whole, husbands are not as likely to participate in their wives' political lives or to take on extra tasks at home as they are

Table 14.   LOW PROPORTIONS OF WOMEN OFFICEHOLDERS HAVE YOUNG CHILDREN

Age of Youngest Child	Fed. Exec.	U.S. House	Judi- ciary %	State Exec. %	State Senate %	State House %	County Comsn. %	Mayor- alty %	Local Council %
Under 6 years	(3)	(0)	0	4	2	3	6	3	8
6-11 years	(3)	(1)	7	10	10	14	21	13	17
12-17 years	(0)	(1)	28	16	15	21	25	20	22
18+ years	(4)	(1)	42	31	50	47	40	50	41
Age not reported	(0)	(1)	7	11	3	-	1	-	1
No children	(6)	(1)	16	28	20	15	7	14	11
Total	(21)	(5)	(43)	(49)	(59)	(256)	(282)	(288)	(2,163)

Table 15.   MOST WOMEN OFFICEHOLDERS REPORT FAMILY INCOMES IN THE MIDDLE RANGE[a]

Family Income:	Judi-ciary %	State Exec. %	State Senate %	State House %	County Comsn. %	Mayor-alty %	Local Council %
Married							
Under $15,000	0	3	8	9	11	25	20
$15,000-$29,999	7	3	31	32	42	48	52
$30,000-$49,999	21	41	25	37	28	16	19
$50,000 and over	72	53	36	22	19	11	9
Total	(29)	(29)	(39)	(197)	(207)	(206)	(1,571)
Unmarried							
Under $15,000	(0)	(1)	(4)	55	61	62	65
$15,000-$29,999	(0)	(9)	(9)	28	31	24	26
$30,000-$49,999	(6)	(4)	(1)	10	8	5	7
$50,000 and over	(1)	(0)	(1)	7	0	9	2
Total	(7)	(14)	(15)	(42)	(49)	(65)	(453)

[a]Tabulations at the federal level are omitted because of low numbers responding.

to express approval and interest. Nevertheless, the great majority of husbands either often or occasionally facilitate their wives' officeholding through their own participation in political or household activity.

If the political activity of married women is conditional upon spousal support, we would expect higher levels of support among husbands of women in offices that potentially pose the greater threat of family disruption -- offices requiring greater amounts of time or travel away from home. With the exception of members of the judiciary and of the state executive, proportions perceiving political interest, approval, public and household assistance

from their husbands all rise with level of office. The upward trend in political interest and assumption of household tasks is interrupted among judges, and the percentages of state executives reporting interest, approval and public participation are also out of line with the trend. Although the nature of these offices may limit opportunities for the husband's public participation, reasons for lower levels of support in the other dimensions are unclear.

The direction of differences in support among husbands from smaller and larger districts suggests that the reasons for lower supportiveness among husbands of judges and state executives are not to

Table 16.   PROPORTIONS OF RESPONDENTS REPORTING SUPPORTIVE SPOUSES RISE WITH LEVEL OF OFFICE[a]

	Judi-ciary %	State Exec. %	State Senate %	State House %	County Comsn. %	Mayor-alty %	Local Council %
Husband's Interest in Politics							
Strongly interested	58	39	74	61	50	36	39
Somewhat interested	42	54	26	33	41	49	49
Little interest	0	7	0	6	9	15	12
Total	(31)	(28)	(39)	(209)	(222)	(217)	(1,672)
Approval of Wife's Officeholding							
Actively encourages	94	75	77	75	75	62	60
Approves for the most part	6	21	23	23	22	31	33
Mildly to actively opposes	0	4	0	2	3	7	7
Total	(32)	(28)	(39)	(209)	(221)	(215)	(1,669)
Participation in Wife's Political Activity							
Often	62	36	57	43	38	23	24
Occasionally	34	44	33	36	41	40	37
Never	4	20	10	21	21	37	39
Total	(29)	(25)	(39)	(205)	(221)	(214)	(1,655)
Assumption of Extra Household Tasks							
Often	45	79	71	60	43	33	34
Occasionally	29	18	24	27	43	37	38
Never	26	3	5	13	14	30	28
Total	(31)	(28)	(38)	(204)	(221)	(214)	(1,650)

[a]Tabulations at the Federal level are omitted because of low numbers reporting

Table 17. PERCEPTION OF CONFLICT BETWEEN POLITICS AND FAMILY LIFE RISES WITH LEVEL OF OFFICE[a]

Percent agreeing or agreeing strongly	Judi- ciary %	State Exec. %	State Senate %	State House %	County Comsn. %	Mayor- alty %	Local Council %
Men's political activity harms family life	56	63	59	54	49	51	49
Total	(34)	(38)	(53)	(239)	(255)	(251)	(1,946)
Women's political activity harms family life	60	66	65	54	51	54	50
Total	(34)	(38)	(55)	(239)	(261)	(265)	(1,995)

[a]Federal officeholders are omitted because of low numbers reporting.

be found simply in the demanding nature of their wives' offices. Local officeholding in the smaller districts is less demanding and should pose less inconvenience for other family members. Yet consistent with the pattern of higher supportiveness at higher levels of officeholding, husbands of officials in the larger districts are more often perceived as interested, approving, participating and helping. Apparently, the supportiveness of husbands is not so much contingent on minimal inconvenience as it is dependent upon an environment in which husbands develop a nontraditional view of women's roles (or one in which women can select nontraditional husbands).

Perceived effects on family life. Among a series of items dealing with perceptions of women in politics, officeholders were asked to indicate their degree of agreement or disagreement with two statements about family life: "Men can't be really active in politics without having their family life suffer." "Women can't be really active in politics without having their family life suffer." Despite the high levels of support that officeholders perceive from their spouses, they divide fairly evenly in their judgment that being "really active" in politics has deleterious consequences for family life (Table 17). Little distinction between women and men is made in this evaluation.

Perceptions of conflict between an active political life and the quality of family life are proportionately more common among women in higher-level offices, even though women in higher offices tend more often to perceive their husbands as supportive. This apparent anomaly is clarified by Table 18, which presents perceptions of local council members and other officeholders within each category of marital and parental status. Those in higher offices are more likely to perceive conflict between politics and family life only if they have children under 18 years old or, if they have no minor children, if they are divorced or single. Comparing only categories of marital status, we find not the married but the divorced, regardless of whether they have minor children and regardless of level of office, are consistently higher in perceptions of political activity as detrimental to family life. Children do not appear to present the problems that one might predict. The presence of minor children interacts with incumbency of a more demanding office to produce only a slight negative effect on perceptions. Two dimensions contribute in various ways to evaluations of

Table 18. DIVORCED WOMEN AND WOMEN IN HIGHER OFFICES ARE MOST NEGATIVE ABOUT EFFECTS OF OFFICEHOLDING ON THE FAMILY

% Agreeing that Women's Political Activity is Detrimental to Family	Local Councils %	Other Offices %
No children under 18		
Married	50	49
Total	(673)	(381)
Divorced	68	78
Total	(50)	(40)
Widowed	55	46
Total	(185)	(54)
Single	40	62
Total	(93)	(48)
Children under 18		
Married	50	56
Total	(878)	(326)
Divorced	59	64
Total	(46)	(28)
Widowed	54	(13)
Total	(35)	(17)
Single	(4)	(0)
Total	(5)	(0)

political activity as interfering with family life: a relatively demanding office, and the absence of a husband who provides support for political activity.

The importance of spousal supportiveness is confirmed by a comparison of married women whose husbands approve of their officeholding with those whose husbands disapprove. Forty-four percent of local councilwomen and 48% of women in other offices with approving husbands perceive politics as adversely affecting family life. Among those with disapproving husbands, by contrast, 62% of local councilwomen and 70% of women in other offices perceive such ill effects. The small minority of women whose husbands do not approve are similar to divorced women in their tendency to see conflict between family and an active political life. Thus the nature of the conjugal relationship or disruption by divorce of the relationship is strongly associated with the way in which women perceive the connection between family and politics.

CHARACTERISTICS OF WOMEN COMPARED WITH MEN

Recruitment to office is not a random process. The women who enter public office are typically set apart from others by characteristics such as ethnicity, age, education, income or organizational affiliations. To this point, however, our review of the personal attributes and family roles of women in office has failed to address an important question: Have we described the result of selection processes peculiar to women, or have we described the outcome of general processes operating in the selection of both men and women? Undoubtedly, there is no simple answer to this question. We can begin to answer it by comparing women in public office with men holding similar offices. We turn now to this task, utilizing for analysis our sample of men and a comparison sample of women holding similar offices in the same states.

Age of Women Compared with Men

Past research has found women in office to be older than male officials.[24] The most common interpretation of this difference is that men enter politics at a young age, as an extension of their traditional role as representative of the family to the larger society. Women, by contrast, wait until their children are older to become involved in public activity. A second explanation is that women, less involved in the labor force and lacking the professional credentials that are often used informally to define qualifications for office, require a longer period of apprenticeship through alternative structures of community organizations or political parties. Whatever the causes, the consequences of delayed political activity for women are likely to include lowered ceilings on political careers.

Our data confirm only in part the understanding that women in public office are older than men. As can be seen in Table 19, the median age of women is only marginally higher than that of

Table 19. LARGER PROPORTIONS OF MEN IN OFFICE ARE UNDER FORTY OR OVER SIXTY YEARS OLD

Age	Women %	Men %
Under 30 years	2	6
30-39	23	26
40-49	31	27
50-59	31	23
60 and over	13	18
Total	(708)	(361)
Median Age	48	46

men -- approximately two years. An examination of the percentages of men and women in each age category reveals that women are concentrated in the middle years, while slightly higher proportions of men are under 40 and over 60 years of age. The disproportion of older men in relation to women results from the men's longer tenure of office and not from an older age of entry into office. In

fact, among those now aged 60 or more, a higher percentage of the women (60%) than of the men (52%) were at least sixty years old when elected. Thirty percent of the older men but only 9% of the older women entered their current offices more than ten years prior to the survey.

Age at entry into office. Evidence for a trend among women toward a younger age at entry into office was presented in the report of the 1975 survey.[25] If this trend is apparent only for women and not for men, then the age distribution of women in office is converging toward that of men.[26] Underlying such a process would be changes in the general status and roles of women in society. If, instead, age at entry is similarly declining for men, differences in the ages of men and women in office are likely to continue. A pattern of declining age at entry for both sexes could result from general changes in the age structure of the society or from general changes in processes of political recruitment.

Analysis of our data suggests an absence of change in age differences between men and women, for age at entry into office has declined among both sexes by roughly the same number of years. Table 20 presents median age at entry into office, for both

Table 20. AGE AT ENTRY INTO OFFICE IS DECLINING FOR BOTH SEXES

Median Age:	Year of Entry to Current Office				
	76-77	74-75	72-73	70-71	68-69
Of women	44 (278)	46 (241)	44 (109)	48 (31)	(49) (10)
Of men	39 (102)	40 (99)	40 (60)	44 (31)	(45) (19)

the sample of men and the comparison sample of women, in each two-year period over the past decade. In each period, the newly-elected group of women averages at least four years older than its male counterpart. If age at entry into office is an indicator of the potential for similarity between the sexes in patterns of political careers, then we find little to signify that women are becoming more like men in the life-cycle phasing of their political activity.

Education

To the extent that formal education either adds skills or operates as symbolic qualification for office, women are disadvantaged relative to men. In our study, approximately equal proportions of men and women have completed college, but the men are far more apt to have a graduate degree or to have done some graduate work. Twenty-six percent of the men have one or more graduate degrees, and an additional 16% have done graduate work, in comparison to 16% women with graduate degrees and 4% with some graduate study. Equal proportions of men and women had attended school or taken courses within the past year.

Employment and Occupation

Paralleling sex differences in the general population, women in office are much less likely than men to have outside employment. In the sample of men, 86% are employed in addition to holding office, 79% full time. By contrast, only 51% of the comparison sample of women are currently employed, 32% full time.

The current or past occupations of women and men differ in familiar ways. As shown in Table 21, nearly half the women (47%) but relatively few men

Table 21. MALE OFFICEHOLDERS REPORT OCCUPATIONS OVER MORE DIVERSE RANGE THAN WOMEN

Current or Past Occupation	Women %	Men %
Census Categories		
Professional, technical	43	33
Managers, administrators	16	30
Sales workers	8	8
Clerical, secretarial	24	2
Crafts	1	10
Operatives	2	3
Laborers	-	1
Farm	1	10
Service	5	3
Selected Occupations		
Health workers	6	1
Social workers	2	-
Elem., secondary teachers	15	5
Physicians, dentists	-	2
College teachers	4	1
Editors, reporters	2	-
Real estate, insurance sales workers	4	6
Public administrators	2	3
Lawyers	2	4
Median Occupational Prestige[a]	48	50
Total	(678)	(354)

[a]Hodge-Siegel-Rossi Scores as adapted to the 1970 U.S. Census Occupational Codes by the National Opinion Research Center.

(8%) are in four occupations where women traditionally concentrate -- teaching, nursing, social work and secretarial work. Despite the sex concentration of occupations and the somewhat lower educational levels of women, men do not uniformly have the higher status positions. The average occupational prestige of women is approximately equal to that of men in office.[27] Larger proportions of women have professional occupations; men are far more prevalent in managerial and administrative positions. Women predominate in secretarial and clerical occupations; more men are craftspersons and farmers.

Implications of sex differences in occupations.

The pattern of sex differentiation in occupations of officeholders raises questions about special difficulties women may face in using their occupations as credentials or as avenues to political

positions. High occupational prestige is characteristic of both men and women who achieve public office. Although the women officeholders do contain large proportions with conventionally female occupations, we know of no evidence that the skills learned in such occupations are less relevant to political performance than skills learned in, for example, engineering, retail management, crafts or farming. Yet the occupational skills of women may not be perceived and acknowledged as conferring competence for political office because they involve tasks executed by women and may be either unfamiliar to or automatically devalued by influential males. Moreover, women's occupations may well be characterized by lower probabilities of exposure to politically active individuals and networks. Therefore, there is some reason to suspect that the occupations of women, regardless of their formal prestige or intrinsic skills, are not as likely as those of men to aid recruitment to office and political mobility.

Organizational Affiliations

Analysis of the organizational participation of women and men in office suggests that women may compensate for their relative educational and occupational disadvantages by extensive participation in voluntary associations. Women in office average more memberships than men (Table 22). The median for men is 2.6, while that for women is 3.6. The difference is especially pronounced among state legislators, where women average 6.1 to the men's 3.6 memberships.

Table 22. WOMEN IN OFFICE AVERAGE A HIGHER NUMBER OF MEMBERSHIPS THAN MEN

Member of at Least One Organization in Category	Women %	Men %
Political (e.g., party clubs, LWV)	55	34
Professional, business	35	41
Special service (e.g., Red Cross, Sierra)	30	13
Cultural[a]	27	6
Youth-school service (e.g., PTA, Scouts)	26	17
Hobby and sports	28	15
General service (e.g., service clubs, Community Chest)	20	31
Church-related	18	6
Alumni and university service	15	3
Sororal, fraternal	8	14
Labor	9	12
Veteran and auxiliary	6	14
Public officials	7	2
Farm	2	8
Ethnic	3	3
Total	(678)	(346)
Median Number of Memberships	3.6	2.6

[a]Includes groups whose defined purposes appear to be principally cultural-aesthetic.

This finding has significance for understanding sex differences in political recruitment processes. Since surveys of the general population have consistently found women to have fewer organizational ties than men,[28] the more extensive organizational involvement of women officeholders cannot be interpreted simply as a reflection of their gender -- of some feminine impulse to sociability. Instead, it would appear that women who are very active in organizations are able to develop constituencies and build reputations for expertise that facilitate entry into office and maintenance of official status. Even those who lack the professional degrees and occupational ties characteristic of politically active men can find avenues to heightened political participation through organizational ties.

Family Characteristics

Age differences between men and women in office imply differences in their family situations as well. Although men and women do differ in their family characteristics, a causal connection between women's traditionally greater family responsibilities and their older age at entry into office has not been established. The possibility exists that the family characteristics of women are the result and not the cause of their being older than men when they enter office.

Marital status. Lower proportions of women than of their male colleagues are married; higher percentages are divorced or widowed (Table 23). However, since men who have experienced loss of a spouse through

Table 23. A HIGHER PROPORTION OF MALE THAN FEMALE OFFICEHOLDERS ARE MARRIED

Marital Status	Women %	Men %
Married	79	91
Divorced, separated	6	3
Widowed	11	1
Single	4	5
Total	(741)	(360)

widowhood or divorce are much more apt to remarry than women experiencing similar events, differences in the percentages currently widowed or divorced are not reliable indicators of the relative incidence of disruption of marital ties.

Parental status of women vs. men. Female and male officeholders are equally likely to be parents, and they have approximately the same numbers of children. However, a higher percentage of the men are parents of young children, under 12 years of age.[29] The differences are not large: in the total sample, 34% of the men and 24% of the women have children under 12 years. Differences widen at the state legislative level, however, where 35% of men but only 16% of women have young children, even though legislators do not differ in marital status.[30]

Family income. Whether income distributions are to the advantage of male or female officeholders depends upon their marital status. Among the unmarried, women more often have incomes under $15,000 (60% vs. 38% of the men). Among the married, 41% of the women but only 30% of the men report incomes over $30,000. This difference may in part be explained by a slightly higher percentage of currently employed among women officeholders (51%) than among the wives of male officeholders (46%). It could also stem from the fact that a higher proportion of the women are in late middle age, when family income tends to peak. In addition, women in office may have married men of higher status than their male colleagues.

Family and Political Life

The assumption of public, decision-making roles by women has raised many questions among members of the public -- and in the minds of some scholars -- about the stability of the family lives of political women. Apparently, the image of the politically active woman is so at variance with the traditional relegation of women to housework, to child care and to the protective authority of their husbands that many assume the officeholder must pay a high price in domestic harmony for her political ambitions. Yet in our study the men perceive less support from their wives for political activities, and they are more likely to see political activity as having a negative effect on family life.

Support from husbands vs. wives. A comparison of responses of men and women to questions about the political interest, approval, participation and domestic assistance of their spouse is consistent with the hypothesis that the conjugal relationship may be more critical in the political participation of women than of men.[31] On every item higher proportions of female than of male officeholders report the supportiveness of their spouses (Table 24). The differences in spousal supportiveness exist regardless of the age of officeholders and regardless of whether they have minor children.

Table 24. HUSBANDS ARE PERCEIVED AS MORE SUPPORTIVE THAN WIVES BY OFFICEHOLDERS

Percent of Married Reporting:	Women %	Men %
Spouse very much interested in politics	48	26
Actively encourages officeholding	67	44
Participates in officeholder's political life	30	25
Assumes extra household tasks	42	29
Total	(554)	(322)

Perceptions of effects on family life. Men are also substantially more likely than women to perceive a very active political life as in conflict with the family. Proportionately more men than women perceive a high level of political activity as detrimental to the family life of men as well as of women. Seventy-seven percent of the men, but only 49% of the women, agree with the statement

that _women_ cannot be really active in politics
without having their family life suffer. Seventy
percent of the men and 48% of the women subscribe
to this belief in reference to the political
activity of _men_.

The wide differences between male and female officeholders in their perceptions of the effects of
politics on family life occur regardless of marital
status, the presence of minor children, or age of
the officeholder. The differences also persist
unchanged regardless of the level of spousal support,
even though a lower level of support is associated
with an increased tendency among both men and women
to perceive adverse consequences for the family.

The results of this analysis of the relation between
political activity and family roles suggests the
hypothesis that family approval is a far more
important selective criterion for the political
participation of women than of men. It is likely
that women whose families disapprove of their
political activity fail to seek office in the
first place, resulting in a high degree of family
support among those who enter office. Men, taking
for granted positive sanctions for public activity,
perhaps viewing such activity as an important
adjunct to their occupations or as their primary
career commitment, are less likely to seek family
approval before entry into politics. As a consequence, the group of men who do enter politics
contains a fairly high proportion of nonsupportive
families. As will become apparent in Part VI of
this report, in which ambitions for further office
are analyzed, familial disapproval may play a role
in the greater tendency of men to say they plan to
withdraw from public officeholding. Women, too,
whose spouses disapprove are more likely than those
with approving spouses to plan to leave public
office, but relatively few of the women in office
lack the support of their husbands. If our interpretation of differences in the family situations
of men and women is correct, then increases in
women's political participation may depend heavily
upon changing marital relationships.

CONCLUSION TO PART II

In our examination of the social and family
characteristics of women in office, we have considered differences by office, political party,
time of entry into office, age of officeholder and
size of district population. We have also compared
men with women. A brief summary may serve to
clarify the manner in which these dimensions,
utilized throughout this report, are or are not
linked to the social attributes of officeholders.

Variations by Office

Variations by type of office are sufficient to
signal caution before assuming that a description
of incumbents of a particular office is a description of all public officeholders. In some respects,
the higher the level of office, the more elite the
characteristics of officeholders. Education,
occupational prestige and family income all rise
with level of office. Officeholders also differ
in age and number of organizational affiliations,
though not as a simple function of level of office.
Marital status varies little by office. An impli-

cation of such diverse patterning by type of office
is that understanding the nature of women's officeholding requires an office by office examination of
the background, behavior and orientations of incumbents.

Party Affiliation

Despite the fact that Democratic and Republican
women are shown in other parts of this report to
differ in political and social attitudes, political
party does not differentiate to any notable degree
the social characteristics of women in office.
Democrats and Republicans in office are, on the
average, of the same age, educational level (a
slightly higher proportion of graduate degrees
among Democrats), employment status, occupational
prestige, family income (slightly higher among
Republicans at local levels), marital and parental
status. Their husbands are equally likely to
support their officeholding activities. Among the
characteristics we have considered, only ethnicity
(that most minority women are Democrats is well
known) and types of organizational affiliation
differ by political party.

Common knowledge would not predict the lack of
association between party affiliation and social
characteristics frequently observed to be related
to differing ideologies. Since party affiliation
is often "inherited" as an aspect of family
tradition, perhaps the source of differing social
attitudes of Democratic and Republican women in
office lies not so much in their social location
defined by demographic characteristics as it does
in their social location defined by cultural
traditions of family and personal networks.

Tenure of Office

Patterns associated with entry into office before
or since 1975 have been examined with a view to
defining ways in which recent increases in the
numbers of women in office may imply the recruitment of different kinds of women. More recent
entrants to office are younger, not only because
they have less tenure of office but also because
the age of entry into office has been declining
over time. Despite their younger age, newcomers
differ little in social and family characteristics
from women who preceded them into office. Perhaps
the detection of trends in the kinds of women
recruited to office must await a longer period of
observation.

Age of Officeholders

Because age is commonly a sensitive indicator of
many aspects of an individual's attributes, behavior
and attitudes, we give special attention to the age
of officeholders and to the association of age with
other social characteristics. Younger cohorts of
officeholders exhibit patterns typical of their
stage of the life cycle, as reflected in their
lower family incomes or membership in fewer organizations. They also may exhibit patterns that
reflect social change. Like their age mates in the
larger society, younger women in office manifest
ongoing social trends by being proportionately less
often married, less often mothers, more often
college graduates. If such attributes are relevant

to political behavior, then the younger women in office presage changes in the nature of office-holding by women. Yet the anticipation of change should not be exaggerated. Except among state legislators, younger women are no more likely than their older colleagues to possess graduate degrees, and they show few signs to date of deviating from their predecessors in the degree to which their occupational backgrounds are restricted to the traditional pursuits of women.

District Size

The sharpest discriminator of the social character-istics of women in office is the size of the popu-lation of their districts. Women in the smaller districts (defined for purposes of analysis as 10,000 and under) at county and local levels of officeholding differ from those in larger districts in nearly every dimension examined. They are slightly older, more often widowed. When married, their husbands are less supportive of their political activity. The younger among them are more likely than younger women in large districts to have minor children. Tney are less educated, more often employed in addition to holding office, have fewer organizational memberships and of different types. Officeholders in the smaller districts hardly conform to popular stereotypes of the political woman; yet, since the great majority of local officeholders are in such districts, they are more nearly typical of women in office.

Women vs. Men

By implication, the subject of women in politics holds special interest only because it describes a situation that differs from that of men in politics. More than their small numbers distinguish women from their male colleagues. Though the differences are for the most part undramatic, they cumulatively suggest the ways in which the sex differentiation of social life has operated to reduce women's political involvements. Women in office are proportionately more often middle-aged, while men are either younger or older. Women are not as likely to be married and, when married, less likely to have young children. When married, their family incomes are higher than those of their male counterparts. When unmarried, their incomes are lower. The fact that they belong to more organ-izations than the men may serve as counterpoint to their lower likelihood of having educational and occupational credentials that would facilitate political participation. Finally, and perhaps most critical in understanding the process of political recruitment of women, relatively few married women enter politics without the support and encouragement of their husbands but a relatively large group of men in politics lack the support of their wives.

Part III, which is devoted to an examination of political background and officeholding activities, continues our examination of the role of gender in political recruitment and considers a further question: Having achieved office, are women distinguishable from men in their official activities?

PART III. POLITICAL EXPERIENCE AND NATURE OF OFFICEHOLDING

In Part III, our report turns to political activity -- to the experience that women and men have acquired before entering their current offices, to the nature of the offices they have entered, and to the ways in which they view their official roles. Part III has four sections. In the first two sections, we describe the political experience and officeholding activities of women officials, noting variations among women according to the office they hold and other characteristics. In the third and fourth sections, we examine the ways in which the political backgrounds and officeholding of women are similar to or different from those of men.

POLITICAL BACKGROUNDS OF WOMEN IN OFFICE

Because women have been entering office in increasing numbers, a larger proportion are new-comers than would be true if the number of new entrants were equal to the number of women who leave office. A little more than half to three-quarters or more of the women in every type of office except Congress have entered their current office since 1973 (Table 25). Substantial propor-tions, from approximately one-quarter of state judges to 41% of county commissioners and nearly all appointees to the federal executive entered office after 1975. County commissioners, who have shown a large relative increase in numbers although they still constitute a tiny minority on county governing boards, also have the highest proportion of recent entrants.

Number of Terms in Office

The length of a term of office varies by office and locale, from two years in some governing bodies to six or more years in some state judicial posts. Not all officeholders serve fixed terms of office; many members of the executive branches of govern-ment serve at the pleasure of the chief executive, and some judges are appointed for life. Despite such variations, a majority of women in most offices are serving in their first term (Table 26). Exceptions are the U.S. Congress, where no change in the participation of women has occurred in recent years, and the state legislatures where the per-centage increase between 1975 and 1977 is somewhat lower than that taking place in earlier periods.

Election and Partisanship

Because of the offices surveyed, nearly all the women in our study serve in elective office. Exceptions occur among 9% of judges, 38% of members of the state executive, and all women in the federal executive. Even for elective positions, appointment to vacancies with unexpired terms may occur, and by statute some judicial positions are filled initially by appointment followed by election. Thus approx-

Table 25.   MOST WOMEN HAVE SERVED LESS THAN FOUR YEARS IN THEIR CURRENT OFFICE

Year of First Election to Current Office	Fed. Exec.	U.S. House	Judiciary %	State Exec. %	State Senate %	State House %	County Comsn. %	Mayoralty %	Local Council %
1971 or before	(0)	(2)	27	17	23	17	11	13	11
1972, 1973	(1)	(8)	19	3	18	20	14	13	17
1974, 1975	(0)	(6)	28	49	30	31	34	39	40
1976, 1977	(24)	(2)	26	31	29	32	41	35	32
Total	(25)	(18)	(47)	(59)	(66)	(278)	(281)	(286)	(2,133)

Table 26.   MOST WOMEN OFFICEHOLDERS ARE IN THEIR FIRST TERM OF THEIR PRESENT OFFICE

Number of Terms in Office	Fed. Exec.	U.S. House	Judiciary %	State Exec. %	State Senate %	State House %	County Comsn. %	Mayoralty %	Local Council %
First	(22)	(2)	66	72	45	37	63	52	59
Second	(0)	(7)	23	14	23	30	24	31	28
Third or more	(0)	(9)	11	14	32	33	13	17	13
Total	(22)	(18)	(44)	(46)	(62)	(255)	(284)	(283)	(2,153)

imately one-quarter of judges and state executives, 14% of local councilwomen, 12% of mayors, 7% of county commissioners, 8% of state senators, and 1% of state representatives were first appointed to their current offices.

In some locations, election to office is legally nonpartisan, with no party labels appearing on ballots.[32]   Seventy percent of local councilwomen, 74% of mayors, 32% of county commissioners and 67% of judges report that election to their office is nonpartisan.   Slightly higher proportions of women entering office in 1975 or later have won partisan elections at county and local levels: 71% of county commissioners, 28% of mayors and 31% of local councilwomen in contrast to 64%, 23% and 28% respectively entering these offices before 1975.   Although this difference is very small, it suggests the possibility that women are making inroads in

achieving positions that require nomination and endorsement by political parties.

Party Affiliation and Experience

In every office surveyed, the majority of women officeholders are Democrats (Table 27).   Approximately one-third of those in the lower houses of state legislatures and in county or local offices are Republican; one-quarter or less are Republican in state senates, the state executive, the judiciary and the U.S. Congress.

Party identity and year of entry into office.   In some offices, Republicans constitute a higher percentage of those entering office in 1975 or later than of those entering office before 1975.   This is true of state legislators (38% Republicans among recent entrants vs. 33% among earlier), county

Table 27.   DEMOCRATS OUTNUMBER REPUBLICANS IN EVERY OFFICE

Party Affiliation	Fed. Exec.	U.S. House	Judiciary %	State Exec. %	State Senate %	State House %	County Comsn. %	Mayoralty %	Local Council %
Democrat	(20)	(13)	59	73	71	60	59	50	51
Republican	(1)	(5)	24	16	26	36	30	33	33
Independent	(1)	(0)	12	11	3	4	10	17	15
Other	(0)	(0)	5	0	0	0	1	-	1
Total	(22)	(18)	(42)	(56)	(68)	(281)	(281)	(290)	(2,172)

Table 28.   ONLY AMONG STATE LEGISLATORS AND COUNTY OFFICEHOLDERS HAVE A MAJORITY HELD PARTY OFFICE

% Who Report Service in at Least 1 Party Position	Fed. Exec.	U.S. House	Judi- ciary %	State Exec. %	State Senate %	State House %	County Comsn. %	Mayor- alty %	Local Council %
One or more of any type	(7)	(13)	21	49	70	73	53	28	29
Total	(27)	(17)	(47)	(61)	(67)	(292)	(287)	(291)	(2,211)
Party office									
Local	(2)	(4)	10	13	32	31	17	17	18
County	(1)	(2)	17	17	21	27	29	12	11
State	(1)	(4)	1	17	27	19	8	6	3
National	(3)	(6)	2	7	6	4	1	-	-
Total	(27)	(17)	(47)	(60)	(66)	(292)	(286)	(292)	(2,211)
Convention delegation									
State alternate	(0)	(0)	2	8	8	10	9	3	5
State delegate	(2)	(0)	2	33	53	60	31	11	13
National alternate	(1)	(1)	7	6	5	7	3	3	1
National delegate	(3)	(4)	2	19	32	16	5	1	1
Total	(19)	(7)	(41)	(52)	(60)	(256)	(265)	(262)	(1,961)

commissioners (34% vs. 24%) and mayors (36% vs. 30%). It would appear that Republicans have been recapturing districts lost to them in the early 1970s, although it is also possible that the Republican party has improved its relative position in the recruitment of women candidates.

Party offices.   Among women in office, state legislators and congresswomen appear to be most closely tied to political parties.   These officeholders are more likely than others to have past experience or current incumbency in party office at local, county, state or national levels (Table 28).   The only instances in which other officeholders approach the party experience of state legislators and congresswomen are the proportion of county commissioners with experience of party office at the county level and the proportion of state executives who have been delegates to national conventions.

Other than type of office, few categorical differences distinguish officeholders with and without party experience.   Democrats and Republicans are equally likely to have held party posts.   Despite recent observations by journalists and political scientists of a decline in the importance of parties to political affairs, neither younger officeholders nor recent entrants to office have less experience in political parties than do other officeholders. Women in small districts do indicate less involvement with political parties, a pattern that supplies one more instance of the less extensive social participation of women in small districts.

Former Public Offices

The routes to various political offices are not defined by a specific sequence of prior offices. Substantial proportions of officeholders report no past officeholding and, among those with experience, antecedents to current offices are varied.   Moreover, elective and appointive offices do not represent clearly differentiated political careers, with officeholders taking either the elective or the appointive path.   Instead, appointment and election both are part of the experience of officeholders in every type of office.   The lack of strict sequencing of offices is further illustrated by the fact that offices are sometimes held concomitantly.   For example, 11% of women currently in office report second offices, principally as members of appointive boards and commissions.

Table 29.   FOR MANY WOMEN THEIR CURRENT OFFICE IS THEIR FIRST GOVERNMENTAL POSITION

Former Public Offices	Fed. Exec. %	U.S. House	Judi- ciary %	State Exec. %	State Senate %	State House %	County Comsn. %	Mayor- alty %	Local Council %
None	23	(9)	33	39	31	59	63	40	71
Elective only	19	(5)	21	14	40	13	8	30	5
At least one elective and one appointive	4	(2)	15	21	20	6	7	13	3
Appointive only	54	(2)	31	26	9	22	22	17	21
Total	(26)	(18)	(48)	(57)	(67)	(287)	(280)	(286)	(2,141)

Table 30.   WOMEN WHO REPORT PREVIOUS GOVERNMENT SERVICE NAME A WIDE VARIETY OF POSITIONS

Type of Former Office Named	Fed. Exec. %	U.S. House	Judi-ciary %	State Exec. %	State Senate %	State House %	County Comsn. %	Mayor-alty %	Local Council %
Federal Executive	68	(2)	10	8	1	4	0	-	1
U.S. House	4	(0)	0	1	0	0	0	0	-
State Executive	2	(2)	2	11	0	0	0	0	-
State Senate	4	(1)	3	2	0	0	0	0	0
State House	2	(3)	2	8	22	1	1	1	1
Other state position	10	(8)	15	35	23	24	12	3	7
County Commission	0	(1)	0	-	5	2	3	1	-
Special District, other county position	0	(0)	5	14	9	19	34	8	13
Mayoralty	0	(0)	0	3	1	1	1	1	1
Local Council	2	(3)	2	3	8	6	9	36	2
Other local position	4	(0)	5	15	31	43	39	49	74
Judiciary	4	(3)	56	0	0	-	1	1	1
Total responses = 100%	(49)	(23)	(59)	(102)	(91)	(220)	(188)	(263)	(952)
Total cases	(26)	(18)	(48)	(57)	(67)	(287)	(280)	(286)	(2,141)

Table 31.   REPUBLICANS ARE MORE LIKELY THAN DEMOCRATS TO HAVE HELD PREVIOUS ELECTIVE OFFICE

	State Legislature[a]		County Commission			Mayoralty			Local Council		
	Dem. %	Rep. %	Dem. %	Rep. %	Ind. %	Dem. %	Rep. %	Ind. %	Dem. %	Rep. %	Ind. %
Held any past office	48	46	29	53	45	58	62	60	29	30	28
Held past elective office	25	31	10	27	14	36	51	45	8	8	9
Held past appointive office	32	22	24	41	31	32	27	32	24	26	22
Total	(214)	(118)	(163)	(81)	(29)	(143)	(93)	(47)	(1,064)	(692)	(341)

[a]Independent state legislators have not been included in analysis because of small numbers.

Types of past public office. The extent and nature of past public officeholding varies with the office currently held (Table 29). A majority of local councillors, county commissioners and state representatives held no public offices prior to entering their current offices. Although most officeholders surveyed are now holding elective office, all but congresswomen, state senators and mayors are more likely to have held appointive than elective office in the past.

Table 30 presents a profile of the past offices held by those with officeholding experience. Local boards and commissions constitute a large percentage of past offices held by state legislators, county commissioners and local officeholders. School boards, planning boards, parks and recreation commissions frequently are antecedent to current elective offices. Beyond this tendency to gain experience at the local level, there appears to be some specialization of past experience at the same level of government in which office is currently held: that is, the experience of county commissioners is more likely than that of other officeholders to have been at the county level; past offices of present state officials tend to have been at the state level; federal appointees have more experience at the federal level than at other levels of government.

Variations in past officeholding. Past public officeholding varies with district population, political party, age and year of entry into office. Women in small districts have less experience with either elective or appointive officeholding than women in large districts. Except among local council members, Republican women are more likely to have held former elective office than Democrats or Independents (Table 31). The greater elective experience of Republican women probably reflects the preeminence of Democrats in government. With appointive offices less open to Republicans, those who do aspire to political careers are likely to take the electoral route. Since younger women have lived fewer years in which they could accumulate political experience, their lower levels of former officeholding are only to be expected. Less predictable is that recent entrants to office have more former officeholding experience than earlier entrants (Table 32). Except among local councillors, where no differences by year of entry exist, larger proportions of those entering office in 1975 or later have held elective office and larger proportions have also held appointive office. This greater experience among newcomers occurs in spite of the fact that they have entered office at younger ages.[33]

Table 32.   RECENT ENTRANTS HAVE MORE EXPERIENCE OF OFFICEHOLDING PRIOR TO CURRENT OFFICE

% Holding Past Public Office	State Legislature		County Commission		Mayoralty		Local Council	
	elected '74 and prior	elected '75 and later	elected '74 and prior	elected '75 and later	elected '74 and prior	elected '75 and later	elected '74 and prior	elected '75 and later
	%	%	%	%	%	%	%	%
Held any past office	40	59	29	43	45	71	28	31
Held past elective office	22	35	12	17	26	55	8	8
Held past appointive office	22	38	21	35	26	32	22	26
Total	(204)	(133)	(113)	(161)	(112)	(167)	(868)	(1,192)

Table 33.   MOST LOCAL OFFICEHOLDERS RECEIVE UNDER $1,000 OR NO SALARY FROM THEIR OFFICE[a]

Salary	Judiciary	State Exec.	State Senate	State House	County Comsn.	Mayoralty	Local Council
	%	%	%	%	%	%	%
None	0	0	2	–	–	21	18
Under $1,000	0	2	8	18	11	43	49
$1,000-$4,999	0	6	22	17	39	30	28
$5,000-$9,999	0	2	30	32	25	3	3
$10,000-$14,999	0	0	22	20	11	–	1
$15,000-$19,999	0	2	8	8	4	1	–
$20,000-$24,999	3	13	6	7	3	1	–
$25,000 and above	97	75	0	–	2	1	–
per diem, no annual estimate	0	0	2	2	1	0	1
Total	(35)	(48)	(60)	(251)	(274)	(279)	(2,108)

[a]Federal officeholders are omitted because of low numbers responding.

NATURE OF WOMEN'S OFFICEHOLDING

This section considers the activities and concerns of women officeholders -- the extent to which their offices are full time or part time, their committee assignments and preferences, the activities to which they give major emphasis, and their self-ratings regarding effectiveness.

Salary of Office

Although a few, highly visible offices offer substantial salaries, the bulk of public positions are either unpaid or offer only minimal compensation. As can be seen in Table 33, which presents the annual salary of office (with per diem payments calculated at an annual rate by respondents), approximately two-thirds of local offices pay either nothing or under $1,000 per year. Half of county commissioners and about one-third of state legislators in the survey receive less than $5,000.[34] Only among members of the state executive and judiciary and among federal officeholders do most offices offer salaries that imply full-time positions.

Time Devoted to Office

The salaries of officeholders are incomplete indicators of the amount of time that women spend in official activity, for commitments of time reflect both the nature of offices and the characteristics of officeholders. As Table 34 shows, local and county officeholders spend, on the average, less than full time in their positions. The median number of hours per week spent on official matters by other officeholders ranges from 45 hours among state representatives to more than 60 hours among federal officeholders. (An unknown proportion of state legislators appears to have reported the amount of time spent during legislative sessions rather than a year-round average.)

Table 34.   MEDIAN HOURS OF WORK DEVOTED TO OFFICE FALL SHARPLY FROM FEDERAL TO LOCAL LEVEL[a]

Office	Median Hours per Week	Total
Fed. Executive	(64)	(13)
Judiciary	50	(37)
State Executive	60	(44)
State Senate	50	(57)
State House	45	(238)
County Commission	25	(269)
Mayoralty	20	(273)
Local Council	10	(2,002)

[a]Congress omitted because of low number reporting.

Variations in time devoted to office. District size, age, employment and family status are associated with the amount of time spent in official duties (Tables 35 and 36). As one would predict, women holding office in small districts spend notably less time in activities related to office than women in large districts. Except among state legislators, younger women under age 35 and older women over age 55 spend less time in office. Those with outside employment also give fewer hours per week to office. Unmarried women (who also are more likely to be younger or older) give somewhat fewer hours to office than the married.

Table 35.   DISTRICT SIZE, AGE AND OUTSIDE EMPLOYMENT AFFECT TIME GIVEN TO OFFICE

Median Hours of Work per Week in Office by:	State Legis.	County Comsn.	Mayor-alty	Local Council
Size of district:				
under 10,000[a]		20	16	6
Total		(118)	(165)	(1,388)
over 10,000[a]		40	26	20
Total		(130)	(68)	(523)
Year elected:				
1974 or before	44	25	20	10
Total	(175)	(111)	(110)	(801)
1975 or later	48	25	20	8
Total	(111)	(153)	(157)	(1,146)
Age				
under 35	45	(20)	(15)	7
Total	(45)	(23)	(20)	(255)
35 to 44 years	45	30	20	10
Total	(72)	(72)	(54)	(559)
45 to 54 years	40	30	20	10
Total	(100)	(106)	(94)	(629)
55 years and over	48	20	20	6
Total	(62)	(59)	(99)	(510)
Current other employ.				
other employment	40	20	16	7
Total	(99)	(101)	(136)	(1,126)
no other employ.	48	33	23	10
Total	(192)	(163)	(134)	(855)

[a]District population not analyzed for state legislators.

The unmarried, the employed, the older and younger officeholders may give less time to their offices because they are disproportionately found in less demanding offices and not because they make less of a commitment than their colleagues do. However, we have some reason to assume that differences in the amount of time spent in office reflect not only the nature of different offices but also variations in the commitment of individuals.

Self-rating of commitment relative to colleagues. Women officeholders were asked to rate themselves relative to colleagues on "willingness to work hard" and "time spent on official activities." Most women rate themselves above average on these dimensions (as they do on nearly all items asking for self-ratings). Yet categories of officeholders who make relatively lower self-evaluations of their willingness to work hard or of the time they spend in official activity are precisely those categories in which officeholders report fewer hours per week devoted to office.

Official Issues and Projects

Women in office were asked to name "the three issues or projects of most concern to you in your activities as an officeholder." Table 37 presents, for selected offices, responses classified by functional area of specialization. Offices of state legislator, county commissioner and local councillor have been selected for examination because these offices have sufficient numbers to reveal patterns. In addition, a broad enough range of issues is considered by officials in these offices to permit officeholders to vary in defining the issues of highest importance to them.

When viewed in profile, women's concerns are not confined to a few areas but cover the range of governmental activity. To some degree, the salience of issues depends upon the type of office held. Governmental administration, health, education and welfare are the most prominent activities among state legislators. At the county level, these areas plus public utilities, public works and natural resources receive the most attention from office-

Table 36.   UNMARRIED WOMEN WORK FEWER HOURS IN OFFICE THAN THEIR MARRIED COUNTERPARTS

Median Hours of Work per Week in Office by:	All Other Offices	Local Council
Family status		
Married		
children under 18	32	10
Total	(337)	(888)
no children under 18	40	10
Total	(384)	(655)
Unmarried		
children under 18	25	10
Total	(44)	(82)
no children under 18	25	6
Total	(153)	(347)

Table 37.   ISSUES CONSIDERED PRIMARY BY WOMEN OFFICEHOLDERS COVER FULL RANGE OF GOVERNMENTAL ACTIVITY

Three Most Important Official Issues or Projects:	State Legis. %	County Comsn. %	Local Council %
Government responsiveness, citizen involvement, casework	4	6	8
Governmental administration and reform	15	15	9
Intergovernmental relations	1	1	1
Finance, taxation	15	16	12
Health and mental health	6	4	1
Education	10	3	1
Welfare, status of special groups (other than women)	10	12	7
Status of women	5	1	-
Commerce, occupational licensing, consumer protection	3	1	1
Labor and employment	3	1	1
Law, law enforcement, civil rights	8	7	5
Public safety	0	2	3
Public utilities, transportation, communications	3	3	7
Public works	1	8	12
Energy, natural resources	4	2	1
Planning and development, housing, urban renewal	5	11	17
Culture, beautification, parks, recreation	-	2	9
Environment	5	3	3
Mixed, other	2	2	2
Total responses = 100%	(790)	(719)	(5,328)
Total respondents	(278)	(256)	(1,928)

holders. At the local level, cultural activities, parks and recreation, public works, utilities and governmental administration take prominence over issues of health, education and welfare which are major concerns of officials in higher levels of office. At all levels of officeholding, issues of finance and taxation receive a relatively high degree of attention. In every type of office, very few women name any aspect of women's status as among the three issues or projects of greatest concern.

The types of issues and projects preoccupying officeholders vary little with other characteristics of women in office. In the state legislatures, Republican women are less concerned than Democratic women with health, education and welfare and give more attention to issues of finance and governmental administration. However, no differences by political party are apparent at county and local levels. Age and tenure of office do not distinguish the issues and projects of most concern to women in office.

Satisfaction with Committee Assignments

In addition to being questioned about the issues and projects of most concern to them as officials, women in office were asked to identify their assignments as committee members or as official liaisons to other public agencies. The resulting profiles of responses are similar to those for official issues and projects, and therefore are not presented here. The degree of satisfaction with committee assignments varies with the office held. When asked whether there are assignments preferred in addition to or in place of current assignments, 22% of local councilwomen, 35% of county commissioners and 50% of state legislators named one or more assignments that they would prefer.

If women were to receive the assignments they prefer, would they be concentrated in different areas of governmental activity? Some changes would become apparent. There would be less concentration in areas where women traditionally have served and greater concentration in areas traditionally the domain of men.35 In state legislatures and county commissions, proportionately fewer women would be found on health, education and welfare committees, and more would specialize in governmental administration, finance and taxation. On local councils, relatively fewer women would focus on parks, recreation and public works; proportionately more would be active in finance, taxation, law enforcement and planning. Nevertheless, the changes overall would be slight. Although there may be some tendency to assign women to committees on the basis of feminine stereotypes, a majority of officeholders are satisfied with their assignments.

Self-Ratings of Performance

In evaluating their performance in office, women give themselves high marks. Officeholders were asked to rate themselves relative to other public officeholders with whom they work. On a list of nineteen qualities relevant to official performance, they were asked to decide whether they are considerably above average, slightly above average, about the same as their colleagues, slightly lower than average, or considerably lower than average. On nearly every dimension, the majority describe themselves as above average. Self-ratings of average are uncommon and of below average are rare. Even in qualities about which women exhibit less confidence relative to other qualities, a third or more report themselves superior to their colleagues. Even if such high self-evaluations involve an element of public presentation of self as an aspect of questionnaire response, women in office appear to be highly self-confident.[36]

Self-ratings of women in office are so high that one must identify areas of potential uncertainty by examining those items on which relatively lower proportions of women rate themselves as superior. Table 38 presents for selected offices -- state legislator, county commissioner and local councillor -- the qualities on which relatively high and relatively low percentages of women rate themselves above average.[37] The highest proportions of women consider themselves superior to their colleagues in interest in public service, understanding people's behavior and motivations, interest

Table 38.   WOMEN RATE THEIR PERFORMANCE IN OFFICE
            ABOVE THAT OF THEIR COLLEAGUES

Qualities on Which Higher %'s Rate Self Above Average	State Legis.	County Comsn.	Local Council
	%	%	%
Interest in public service	83	84	74
Understanding others' acts	79	80	76
Intrst. in social problems	78	79	72
Time on official activities	83	78	64
Gen'l knowledge, intelligence	85	79	61
Responsive to constituents	78	76	65
Qualities on Which Lower %'s Rate Self Above Average			
Past training, experience	67	64	45
Persuasive in argument	56	61	56
Ability to make contacts	47	59	46
Influence, prestige with colleagues	52	52	43
Financial, economic judgment	49	56	43
Political know-how	49	47	32
Overall effectiveness	71	70	60
Approximate total[a]	(295)	(267)	(2,004)

[a]Slight variations in the numbers responding to each item have been averaged.

in social problems, time spent on official activities, general knowledge and intelligence, and responsiveness to constituents. The time commitment and the "people-orientation" implied by these items are consistent with traditional views of women's contributions.[38]

Relatively lower proportions of women rate themselves above their colleagues in their political know-how, financial and economic judgment, influence and prestige with colleagues, ability to make important contacts, ability to argue persuasively, and past training and experience. These items refer to technical expertise and political skill, in which women are often assumed to be deficient. Whether women are indeed relatively less adequate in these aspects of officeholding or whether their self-ratings merely reflect adoption of popular stereotypes is an important question but one which cannot be answered with the data available.

Effect of district size. Local councilwomen from large districts are more likely than councillors from small districts to rate their performance above average on every quality. County commissioners from the large districts also have higher proportions rating themselves above average on half the items: understanding people, time devoted to official activity, responsiveness to constituents, financial and economic judgment, value of past training and experience, and political know-how. On the one hand, since women in small districts are consistently found in this report to be disadvantaged in the social and political characteristics associated with political achievement, this pattern is unsurprising. On the other hand, since women were asked to evaluate themselves relative to the officeholders with whom they work, the result is not easily interpreted as a simple reflection of the actual characteristics of women in smaller districts. It is possible that women have evaluated themselves, not relative to their colleagues, but relative to some ideal-typical image of the officeholder. It is also possible that women in smaller districts, where a more conventional sex role ideology is likely to prevail,[39] perceive themselves as unequal to their male colleagues proportionately more often than do women in large districts.

Age and self-ratings. In every quality except general knowledge and intelligence, lower proportions of women officeholders under age 35 than of older officeholders rate themselves above average. This pattern exists among both newcomers and those with longer tenure. Why are younger women less confident of performance? One reason may be that younger women in office lack the "seasoning" in their backgrounds that would give them the confidence that their older colleagues display, for younger women are less likely to have held office prior to their current offices and also have lower levels of participation in voluntary organizations. In addition, youth itself may be a threat to self-esteem. Since officeholders are typically middle-aged, young women have the "deviant" status of both youth and feminine gender. Yet an equally plausible explanation is that younger women in office display the lower self-confidence typical of their age, without any special relevance to the fact that they are officeholders. Some research studies of other groups of women have found lower levels of confidence and self-esteem among women under age 35 years than among older women.[40]

Self-ratings and tenure in office. Local councilwomen and state legislators who entered office in 1975 or later are less likely to rate themselves superior to their colleagues in time devoted to office, value of past training and experience, influence and prestige, political astuteness and overall effectiveness. These differences between newcomers and those with longer tenure exist regardless of the age of the officeholder. Yet county commissioners, who have the highest proportion of recent entrants among officeholders, do not differ from their colleagues with longer tenure. The high self-confidence of the newly elected county commissioners is further illustrated by the fact that, whereas county commissioners with longer tenure of office show less confidence on most items than their counterparts in the state legislatures, newcomers among county commissioners show higher levels of confidence than newcomers to the state legislatures. This exceptional pattern is unexplained by our data. Women comprise a smaller percentage of county commissioners than of other types of officeholder. Perhaps it is not unusual for those in the vanguard of change, as are those now entering county governing bodies, to display extraordinary levels of self-confidence.

POLITICAL BACKGROUND OF WOMEN COMPARED WITH MEN

In comparing the social backgrounds of women and men in office, we have noted the educational and occupational disadvantages of women, speculating that the more intensive organizational participation of women may supply a compensatory route to political spheres of activity. Yet if women who achieve public office do take a different path to political participation, they accumulate much the same experience as men once they enter politics. An examination of the political backgrounds of women and men in office suggests that the women differ only in minor ways from their male colleagues.

Number of Terms in Office

A higher proportion of women than of men are in their first term in office: 44% of the men but 59% of the women in the comparison sample. The proportion of officeholders in their first term is a function not only of trends in numbers but also of turnover in office -- of the tendency to remain in office or to be replaced by others. It appears, however, that the proportionate excess of women over men in their first term is principally a reflection of increasing numbers of women occupying public office. The ratio of women in office in 1975 to women in office in 1977 is nearly identical to the ratio of men to women in their first term.[41] If women had higher turnover in office than men, the latter ratio would be lower than the former. The fact that they are approximately equal means that the disproportion of women in their first term of office may be accounted for simply by increases in the numbers of women in office.[42]

Partisanship of Election

Although the male and female samples of officeholders are from the same states and types of office, a slightly higher proportion of the men serve in partisan elective office. Thirty-six percent of male council members and mayors and 30% of women in local offices report that election to their offices is partisan. (However, there are no differences among county commissioners.) This finding with

respect to local officeholders lends limited support to a complaint heard among political women -- that many party leaders try to keep women out of positions of leadership (see Part V).

Party Affiliation and Experience

The Democratic party traditionally has had more appeal than the Republican party for minorities and those who are not members of established elites. Therefore, some political observers have assumed that women would disproportionately find the Democratic party more attractive and that the party, in turn, would be relatively more open to sponsorship of women's candidacies. There is a higher proportion of Democratic women than of Democratic men in our samples (see Table 39), although the difference occurs only at the local level. Since women at local levels of officeholding also are more likely than men to have achieved office in nonpartisan elections, the sex difference in party preference does not imply necessarily that the Democratic party is a more active sponsor of female candidates.

Table 39.   PROPORTIONATELY MORE WOMEN THAN MEN IN LOCAL OFFICES ARE DEMOCRATS

Party	State Legis.		County Comsn.		Local Offices	
	Women %	Men %	Women %	Men %	Women %	Men %
Democrat	71	69	63	60	49	39
Republican	26	26	30	34	37	47
Independent	3	5	6	6	13	14
Other	0	0	1	0	1	-
Total	(111)	(57)	(94)	(52)	(530)	(240)

Despite their slightly greater tendency to hold office in nonpartisan districts, women are a little more likely than men to have held party office. Forty percent of the women and 34% of the men have held some type of party office. This difference is not confined to party participation at the local level, for higher proportions of women than of men have held party offices above the local level, and higher proportions have been delegates to state and national conventions.

Former Public Offices

Approximately equal proportions of women and men have held some past public office (Table 40). Men are more likely to have held elective office (20% men vs. 13% women), while somewhat higher proportions of women have held appointive offices (23% men vs. 30% women). The relatively greater appointive experience of women may derive from their greater involvement in political parties. Among the previous offices held, mayoralties, local council positions and appointments to state boards and commissions are relatively more common in the backgrounds of men. Appointments to local or county boards and commissions are relatively more prominent in the experience of women. The greater elective

Table 40.   WOMEN ARE AS LIKELY AS MEN TO HAVE
HELD PAST PUBLIC OFFICE

Former Public Offices Held	Women %	Men %
None	61	63
Elective only	9	14
At least one elective and one appointive	4	6
Appointive only	26	17
Total	(709)	(360)

experience of the men is further illustrated by the fact that a higher proportion of men than of women have lost elections: 26% of the men and 19% of the women. This pattern of proportionately more losing candidacies among the men is true of every office.

OFFICEHOLDING ACTIVITIES OF WOMEN AND MEN

Although women and men are essentially similar in the amount of political experience they bring to their current offices, gender appears to influence the conduct of office. Women and men differ notably in the time devoted to officeholding, in the like-lihood of chairing committees or obtaining desired committee assignments, in the emphasis placed on relations with constituents, and in the areas of self-confidence in effectiveness as officials.

Time Spent in Official Activity

In every office, women devote more time to their office than men (Table 41). The greater commitment of time by women is accounted for almost entirely by women with no outside employment. Women with outside employment average no more hours per week in official activity than do men. Among the unemployed, however, women give more hours to their offices than either employed or unemployed men.

Table 41.   WOMEN GIVE MORE TIME THAN MEN TO OFFICE
ONLY IF NOT EMPLOYED IN ADDITION

Median Hours/Week in Official Activity	Women	Men
Total Sample	15 (678)	10 (344)
Employed Outside Office	10 (343)	10 (290)
No Outside Employment	20 (328)	15 (49)

Performance Emphases

Women and men appear to hold somewhat differing conceptions of their official duties. Table 42 presents responses to a series of questions about which responsibilities of office are given major emphasis, and which are given moderate or minor

emphasis. Higher proportions of women than of men give major emphasis to seeking available research and information on pending legislation or issues. Women also are slightly more likely to stress independent decision-making and to emphasize the development of policy and legislation. Yet the major respect in which women's conceptions of their offices differ from those of men is in the importance they place on relations with constituents.

Table 42.   HIGHER PROPORTIONS OF WOMEN THAN OF MEN
DESCRIBE THEMSELVES AS ORIENTED TOWARD
CONSTITUENTS

% Giving Major Emphasis To:	Women %	Men %
Relations with public		
Discovering public's views	63	49
Educating public on issues	73	60
Helping on individual problems	50	41
Internal references		
Representing party program	6	5
Seeking colleagues' views	29	28
Effecting compromises with colleagues	22	21
Making independent decisions	83	76
Functional emphases		
Getting own issues on agenda	23	25
Researching pending issues	56	36
Developing policy	55	46
Sponsoring legislation	34	29
Making government more efficient	71	73
Exercising administrative functions	21	25
Approximate total[a]	(690)	(345)

[a]Slight variations in numbers responding have been averaged.

Higher percentages of women report giving major emphasis to discovering the public's views on pending issues, to educating the public about important issues and to helping constituents with their individual problems. This greater emphasis by women on public representation and constituent responsiveness has been suggested in previous research.[43] It appears again in Part V of this report, where relations with the public figure prominently in the advantages women perceive for themselves as officeholders.

The sources of this relatively greater attention by women than by men to representation of the public are unknown, although the difference has significance for the issue of electoral accounta-bility among officeholders.[44] Service to others figures prominently in the socialization of women. However, sex-role socialization does not explain the relatively greater tendency of women office-holders to express a public service orientation. We suggest that the sex difference in officeholders' orientations to the public derives in part from the greater involvement of political women in community organizations.[45] Even if organizational participation by women does not lead directly to open endorsement of their candidacies and subsequent attitudes of political obligation among women in office, their participation is likely to sensitize women to the needs of constituents, to supply ready avenues of communication, and to facilitate the development of conceptions of representation.

Official Issues and Projects

Women have been thought to be highly specialized in their governmental activities, concentrated in health, education and welfare, the status of special populations, good government, culture and beautification.[46] However, our data show that women exhibit much the same spread as men in the focus of their official activities. As illustrated by Table 43, which presents profiles of the issues and projects of most concern to officeholders, there is only a very small tendency for the concerns of women, relative to those of men, to be specialized in areas traditionally the province of women in public life. A slight degree of differentiation between the activities of women and men becomes

Table 43. WOMEN AND MEN OFFICEHOLDERS RATE SIMILAR ISSUES AS MOST IMPORTANT

Three Most Important Issues or Projects:	Women %	Men %
Government responsiveness, citizen involvement, casework	6	5
Government administration, reform	11	13
Intergovernmental relations	2	1
Finance, taxation	13	17
Health, mental health	3	2
Education	3	2
Welfare, status of special groups	7	3
Status of women	1	-
Commerce, occupational licensing, consumer protection	1	1
Labor and employment	1	2
Law, law enforcement, civil rights	6	7
Public safety	2	3
Public utilities, transportation, communications	6	7
Public works	10	12
Energy, natural resources	1	1
Planning and development, housing, urban renewal	15	14
Culture, beautification, parks, recreation	7	4
Environment	3	4
Mixed, other	2	2
Total responses = 100%	(1,780)	(938)
Total respondents	(638)	(335)

apparent only when several functional areas are considered cumulatively. Women do not differ from men in the attention given governmental administration and reform or intergovernmental relations. By only a very slim margin is finance a larger proportion of the activities of men. Less than ten percentage points distinguish the cumulative interest of women and men in environmental protection, parks and recreation, the cultural arts, health, education and welfare. Twenty-four percent of the issues and projects named by women are in these areas; 15% of those named by men are in these same areas. These patterns of little difference in the official activities of women and men exist whether one examines issues and projects of highest concern, committee assignments, or the committee assignment considered most important by the officeholder.

Why do these findings seemingly contradict past evidence and belief? One possibility is that differences in the specializations of women and men depend upon type of office. Our samples of male and female officeholders are heavily weighted with local officials, while past research has focussed principally on state legislators and members of Congress. Another possibility is that, over time, there is a trend toward less differentiation in the governmental concerns of men and women. Finally, we must raise the question of whether the evidence of past research on the governmental activity of women has been misinterpreted, since past studies have often lacked a controlled comparison sample of men or have observed the few women in Congress, where reliable patterns may be difficult to discern. Perhaps women and men are equally concentrated in areas of government thought to be the specialties of women. If so, then the committee memberships of women reflect in large part the nature of governmental committees rather than the disproportionate assignment of women to limited areas of government.

Committee Assignments

Analysis of the relative frequency with which women and men chair committees and of their relative satisfaction with current committee assignments indicates either that women are being discriminated against or that they are not aggressively pursuing their preferences. Women are less likely than men to chair committees. Fifty-eight percent of the male local councillors, county commissioners and state legislators chair one or more committees; 49% of the women in these offices are committee chairpersons. This disparity is not a reflection of the fact that higher percentages of women are in their first term of office. Whether in their first or a higher term of office, women hold proportionately fewer positions as committee chairpersons.

Women exhibit relatively less satisfaction than men with their committee memberships. In profile, the assignments of women differ from those of men only slightly. Yet women are almost twice as likely as men to express a desire for different assignments. Among local councillors, county commissioners and state legislators, 17% of the men but 31% of the women name one or more assignments that they would prefer to have in addition to or in place of current assignments. The relatively greater desire of women for new assignments exists not only among officeholders in their first term of office but also among those in their second term and in their third or higher term. Although the more politically ambitious officeholders are also more likely to prefer different committees, the relative dissatisfaction of women with their committee memberships is not accounted for by women's greater desire to remain in public office (see Part VI). Regardless of plans to remain in public office, women are less satisfied than men with their assignments.

Self-Ratings of Performance

Although women's position with respect to committee assignments indicates that they face some barriers to leadership and performance within the governing bodies in which they serve, women evaluate their overall effectiveness as highly as men rate theirs (Table 44). On most of the nineteen dimensions on which self-ratings were sought, higher proportions of women than of men evaluate themselves above their colleagues. Women are more likely than men to consider themselves above average in interest in public service, understanding people's behavior and motivations, interest in social problems, time spent in official activities, general knowledge and intelligence, and responsiveness to constituents. In addition to these six qualities, shown in Table 44 as those in which women show the highest levels of self-confidence, larger percentages of women than of men consider themselves superior to their colleagues in willingness to work hard, efficiency and organization, getting along with colleagues, imagination, practicality and independence.

Table 44 identifies six areas in which women have exhibited somewhat lower levels of confidence in their performance. The two aspects of performance in which men clearly rate themselves more highly

than women involve elements of technical expertise: past training and experience, and financial and economic judgment. The remaining four items point to specifically political skills: ability to argue persuasively, ability to make important contacts, influence and prestige with colleagues, and political know-how. Sex differences in these areas are negligible. One is reminded of the fact that although women have educational and occupational disadvantages relative to men, they bring similar amounts of political experience to office. If they are relatively less secure in their political skills than in some other areas of performance, they are no less secure than their male colleagues.

CONCLUSION

Increases in the numbers of women in public office have produced a large proportion of female officeholders in their first term. Yet these newcomers are not neophytes. They have as much experience in political parties and more experience in public offices than the women who preceded them. The political backgrounds and official activities of women in office contradict the lingering stereotype of the well-meaning but ineffectual woman who cannot compete with her better qualified and more politically astute male colleagues (see Part V).

In only a few respects is the political experience of women unequal to that of men, and even in these respects the differences are slight. Women have less elective experience (either of winning or of losing) than men in comparable offices, and they are less likely to have run in partisan elections. Once in office, women are relatively less satisfied with their committee assignments and are slightly less likely to chair committees. They are less confident than men of the quality of their past training or of their financial expertise.

These decrements must be weighed against the aspects of women's experience and activities that are no different from, or even superior to, those of their male colleagues. Women have been more active in their political parties, and they have more experience with appointive office. The issues and projects that concern them as officials are little different from those of the men. They are notably more oriented toward constituents. They are more motivated to avail themselves of research and information about pending issues. Those women who are not employed in addition to holding office give more time to official activities. Finally, women in office are self-confident in their abilities. In most respects, they perceive themselves as outperforming their male colleagues.

The women in public office today are still in the forefront of social change and, because they are, they are an unusual group of officeholders. If they are in fact superior to their male colleagues in some aspects of performance, their superiority derives from the fact that public office is not yet as available to women as it is to men. If they are less adequate than male officeholders in some respects, their inadequacies also reflect inequality of opportunity. In brief, the results of our comparison of the political background and activity of women and men in public office should become obsolete as the numbers of women and of men who are active in public affairs approach equality.

Table 44. WOMEN ARE LESS CONFIDENT THAN MEN OF
FINANCIAL JUDGMENT, TECHNICAL TRAINING

Qualities on Which Higher %'s Rate Self Above Average	Women %	Men %
Interest in public service	79	63
Understanding others' acts	80	62
Interest in social problems	74	54
Time on official activities	71	59
General knowledge, intelligence	68	60
Responsiveness to constituents	69	55
Qualities on Which Lower %'s Rate Self Above Average		
Past training, experience	51	65
Persuasiveness in argument	54	59
Ability to make contacts	50	45
Influence, prestige with colleagues	47	52
Financial, economic judgment	44	54
Political know-how	38	42
Overall effectiveness	62	59
Approximate total[a]	(671)	(339)

[a]Slight variations in the numbers responding to each item have been averaged.

PART IV.   ORIENTATIONS TO PUBLIC ISSUES

Is there a woman's point of view in politics? Surveys of mass public opinion abound and some research has been done with political party leaders, but studies which compare the views of women and men in office are rare.

Public opinion surveys over several decades have found either that women are no different from men or are slightly more conservative in their positions on public issues, even issues of women's rights and political participation.[47]   The major exception to this general pattern occurs with respect to issues of force such as military conflict or punishment of criminals.

Among the studies of political party elites, a major investigation of delegates to the 1972 Democratic and Republican national conventions finds women to be more supportive than men of "women's" issues such as day care, abortion on demand or women's rights.   On other issues, women are described as more extreme -- as either more liberal or more conservative than the ideological position of the groups with which they are politically identified.[48]   However, another study of delegates to the 1972 Democratic Convention concludes that women are more liberal on virtually every issue examined.[49]

Public opinion surveys and delegate studies supply inadequate bases for evaluating the extent to which the political views of men and women in public office differ.   As we have noted repeatedly in this report, women in office are a select group who differ in many ways from women in the general population.   Moreover, the results of delegate studies do not invite inferences about women and men in public office because far fewer female than male delegates hold public office.

Comparisons of the policy preferences and behavior of women and men in public office are only beginning to be made.   Women in Congress are both more cohesive and more liberal than can be accounted for by party affiliation alone.[50]   Women in the state legislatures have been found more likely than men to vote for the federal ERA, regardless of party affiliation.[51]   A recent examination of 50 male-

female pairs from local councils in Connecticut finds men to be slightly more conservative in self-described political philosophy and on some women's issues but at least as supportive as female colleagues of ERA, feminism and the women's movement.[52]

Much more research and re-analysis of existing data on both political elites and the general citizenry are required to define precisely the conditions under which sex differences in political perspectives occur, the policies on which women and men differ, and the consequences of these differences for the conduct of public affairs.   For the present, we report our analysis of officeholders' orientations to public issues as an additional step toward understanding the potential consequences of women's participation in political life.   The first section of Part IV describes the views of women officeholders.   The second section is devoted to a comparison of women with men.

POLITICAL ATTITUDES OF WOMEN IN OFFICE

The data to be reported consist of responses to questions about general ideological orientations, the roles of government and industry in promoting equal rights for women, positions on four issues selected as issues of special relevance to women, and positions on five issues selected as not manifestly sex-linked in their content.   (For the precise wording of questions and response categories, see questions 14f, item 5 of 18, and 19 at the end of this report.)   The issues selected for analysis are not intended to supply a complete description of the political views of women.   Rather, they supply a basis for examining women's views on issues of manifest relevance to women in comparison with views on other public issues.

Government, Industry and Women's Rights

Women in office were asked to indicate which of four alternatives is closest to their own feeling about the role of federal government, state government, and private industry in "assuring equal rights for women."   The alternatives included: "should do more about it than it now does," "is now doing just

Table 45.   OFFICEHOLDERS THINK GOVERNMENT AND PRIVATE INDUSTRY SHOULD DO MORE TO PROMOTE EQUAL RIGHTS FOR WOMEN[a]

Agree more should be done to assure women's rights by[b]:	Judi- ciary %	State Exec. %	State Senate %	State House %	County Comsn. %	Mayor- alty %	Local Council %
Federal government	77	84	87	72	62	60	61
Total	(26)	(31)	(47)	(208)	(228)	(215)	(1,685)
State governments	81	88	88	77	67	64	64
Total	(26)	(32)	(48)	(208)	(216)	(199)	(1,611)
Private industry	92	88	94	85	79	76	76
Total	(26)	(32)	(46)	(198)	(211)	(189)	(1,565)

[a]Federal respondents have been omitted because of small numbers reporting.

[b]For precise wording of question and response categories, see item 5 of Question 18 at the end of this report.

about enough," "should be less involved than it now is," "should not get involved at all." Women in office strongly endorse a more active stance from both government and industry in promoting women's rights (Table 45). More action from private industry is desired by the overwhelming majority, between 76% and 94% of women in every type of office. At least six in ten of local and county officials, and even higher percentages of other officeholders, favor a more active role on the part of federal and state governments.

Positions on Issues

As shown in Table 46, clear majorities of women in every office endorse ratification of ERA, oppose a constitutional ban on abortion and favor extension of social security to homemakers. The only women's issue on which opinion is more evenly divided is governmental provision of child care. On other issues, a majority support legislation to ban mandatory retirement because of age and favor returning a larger share of federal revenues to the municipalities. In most offices, a majority deny that busing to achieve racial balance will prove beneficial to the country. Most local officeholders support increasing the severity of criminal penalties as a way of dealing with the crime problem, although women in other offices are more divided on this issue. Officeholders also are divided on whether the defense budget should be reduced.

Table 46.   AMONG WOMEN'S ISSUES, MOST WOMEN OFFICEHOLDERS FAVOR RATIFICATION OF ERA AND
SOCIAL SECURITY FOR HOMEMAKERS, OPPOSE A CONSTITUTIONAL BAN ON ABORTION[a]

Women's Issues[c]:	Judi- ciary %	State Exec. %	State Senate %	State House %	County Comsn. %	Mayor- alty %	Local Council %
Federal ERA should be ratified							
Agree strongly or moderately	77	93	96	82	69	63	62
Neutral	3	2	0	4	16	17	18
Disagree moderately or strongly	20	5	4	14	15	20	20
The Constitution should ban abortion							
Agree strongly or moderately	19	10	8	14	15	19	23
Neutral	7	2	4	6	8	14	10
Disagree moderately or strongly	74	88	88	80	77	67	67
Homemakers should have social security							
Agree strongly or moderately	55	76	76	71	68	65	59
Neutral	3	0	14	9	12	14	14
Disagree moderately or strongly	42	24	10	20	20	21	27
Government should provide child care							
Agree strongly or moderately	48	70	66	52	46	38	39
Neutral	7	8	4	10	8	13	10
Disagree moderately or strongly	45	23	30	38	46	49	51

Other issues[c]:							
Busing for racial balance is desirable							
Agree strongly or moderately	26	50	55	41	30	17	17
Neutral	15	15	7	9	8	15	8
Disagree moderately or strongly	59	35	38	50	62	68	75
Severe penalties would help crime problem							
Agree strongly or moderately	47	39	24	37	56	72	73
Neutral	3	14	2	5	4	4	3
Disagree moderately or strongly	50	47	74	58	40	24	24
The defense budget should be reduced							
Agree strongly or moderately	38	68	73	60	54	38	43
Neutral	14	8	10	11	9	11	13
Disagree moderately or strongly	48	24	17	29	37	51	44
Mandatory retirement should be banned							
Agree strongly or moderately	45	71	71	61	65	70	62
Neutral	13	11	8	13	12	7	10
Disagree moderately or strongly	42	18	21	26	23	23	28
More federal revenue should go to cities							
Agree strongly or moderately	65	59	66	66	81	93	88
Neutral	4	18	18	16	8	2	6
Disagree moderately or strongly	31	23	16	18	11	5	6
Approximate totals[b]	(30)	(38)	(50)	(233)	(257)	(262)	(1,965)

[a]Federal respondents have been omitted because of small numbers reporting.

[b]Slight variations in the numbers responding to each item have been averaged.

[c]For precise wording of questions and response categories, see Question 19 at end of report.

Table 47.   JUDGES, COUNTY AND LOCAL OFFICIALS HAVE MORE CONSERVATIVE IDEOLOGIES[a]

Self-Described Ideology:	Judi-ciary %	State Exec. %	State Senate %	State House %	County Comsn. %	Mayor-alty %	Local Council %
Very conservative or conservative	32	12	5	17	35	37	38
Middle-of-the-road	35	29	36	38	33	43	35
Liberal or very liberal	33	59	59	45	32	20	27
Total	(34)	(42)	(56)	(240)	(272)	(270)	(2,049)

[a]Federal officeholders are omitted because of low numbers reporting.

Table 48.   POSITIONS ON WOMEN'S ISSUES ARE STRONGLY RELATED TO GENERAL IDEOLOGICAL ORIENTATIONS

Agree more should be done for women's rights by[a]:	State Legislature			County Commission			Mayoralty			Local Council		
	Cons. %	Mod. %	Lib. %	Cons. %	Mod. %	Lib. %	Cons. %	Mod. %	Lib. %	Cons. %	Mod. %	Lib. %
Federal government	33	73	89	49	52	83	42	61	78	48	62	78
State governments	44	77	91	51	58	90	49	67	79	50	65	80
Private industry	57	82	96	74	68	92	66	77	88	65	78	86
Approximate totals[b]	(31)	(85)	(124)	(73)	(65)	(75)	(64)	(85)	(43)	(573)	(551)	(437)
Women's Issues:[a,c]												
Agree ERA should be ratified	41	83	98	38	75	95	45	66	85	47	64	81
Disagree Const. ban on abortion	43	83	92	69	73	89	52	74	84	57	69	78
Agree homemaker social security	40	59	94	54	65	84	56	64	78	49	61	69
Agree government child care	18	43	74	22	45	75	26	38	62	26	37	58
Other Issues:[a,c]												
Agree busing desirable	2	32	69	3	27	65	7	16	37	6	17	34
Disagree severe crime penalties	8	52	84	7	42	77	8	21	52	10	23	46
Agree reduce defense budget	8	53	87	24	51	87	32	30	62	30	40	64
Agree ban mandatory retirement	68	56	68	62	68	68	73	67	69	59	61	68
Agree more fed. rev. for cities	59	56	72	80	86	79	93	93	94	89	88	87
Approximate totals[b]	(39)	(100)	(129)	(90)	(79)	(82)	(90)	(108)	(50)	(711)	(661)	(504)

[a]For precise wording of question and response categories, see Questions 18 (item 5) and 19 at report end.

[b]Slight variations in the numbers responding to each item have been averaged.

[c]% agreeing and % agreeing strongly, % disagreeing and % disagreeing strongly have been combined.

In state offices, the highest percentages positive or negative on an issue are those in favor of ERA and those opposed to a constitutional ban on abortion. Among county commissioners, the issue of federal revenue sharing with municipalities receives the highest percentage of supporters. Among mayors and local councillors, the percentages endorsing ERA or opposing a ban on abortion are exceeded by those supporting federal revenues for the cities, opposing mandatory retirement, and approving more severe punishments of criminals.

Interrelations of women's issues.[53]   Positions on women's issues are interrelated, although the association between particular pairs of issues varies in magnitude. The strongest direct relationships occur between ERA and each of the other issues. Thus, among the four issues examined, an office-holder's position on the ERA is the best single predictor of her views on abortion, on social security for homemakers, and on governmental provision of child care.

Ideological Perspective and Positions on Issues

There are variations by type of office held in the proportions of women who describe themselves as liberal, middle-of-the-road, or conservative in their positions on most contemporary issues (Table 47). Relatively higher proportions are liberal and lower proportions are conservative among members of state legislative and executive branches of government. (Federal officials, though reporting in too few numbers for statistical analysis, also tend to be liberal.)

Respondents' self-descriptions as liberal or conservative are strongly related to positions on most of the issues examined (Table 48). Only two issues -- mandatory retirement and municipal sharing of federal revenues -- show little or no relation to ideological divisions. Liberals are more likely than conservatives to support more action from government and industry in assuring women's rights, to favor ratification of ERA, to oppose a constituional ban on abortion, to agree that social security should be extended to homemakers, to believe that government should provide child care facilities, to support busing to achieve racial balance, to oppose more severe penalties as the best way of dealing with the crime problem, and to agree that the defense budget should be reduced. Among the four women's issues, ERA is most strongly related to ideology.

Among the offices examined in Table 48, the link between ideology and positions on particular issues is strongest among state legislators, next strongest among county commissioners and weakest among local councillors.[54] Self-description as liberal or conservative is a better predictor among state legislators than among local council members of views on particular issues. Apparently local officeholders, who more often than not achieve office in nonpartisan elections, are less constrained to bring their positions on particular issues into line with their general views of themselves as liberals or conservatives.

Issue Orientations among Recent Entrants to Office

Legislators and county commissioners entering office since 1974 are, as a group, less liberal and more conservative than earlier entrants to office. Among state legislators, 20% of newcomers describe themselves as conservative and 39% as liberal, in contrast to 12% conservative and 52% liberal among earlier entrants. Among county commissioners, 39% of recent entrants are conservative and 30% are liberal, compared with 31% conservative and 34% liberal among those with longer tenure.

There is a corresponding difference in proportions who are liberal or conservative on specific issues. Somewhat lower proportions of recently elected state legislators take liberal stands on every issue on which conservatives and liberals differ. Among county commissioners, the decline in liberalism is confined to three of the four women's issues: extension of social security to homemakers, ERA and child care.

ORIENTATIONS OF WOMEN COMPARED WITH MEN

Comparison of women officeholders with men in equivalent offices indicates that there is, indeed, a woman's point of view in political affairs, one that is most apparent with respect to women's issues but is not confined to such issues.

Ideology

Higher proportions of women than of men profess liberal political philosophies, while higher proportions of men than of women describe themselves as conservative. Among the women, 30% are liberal or very liberal, 36% are middle-of-the-road, and 34%

are conservative or very conservative. Corresponding proportions for the men are 22% liberal or very liberal, 33% middle-of-the-road, and 45% conservative.

Role of Government and Industry

Women are substantially more likely than men to support increased activity on the part of government and industry in behalf of women's rights. Sixty-five percent of women but only 42% of men endorse a more active role for the federal government. Sixty-eight percent of women and 44% of men feel that state governments should do more to assure equal rights. Seventy-eight percent of women as compared with 58% of men would like to see private industry do more.

Issue Orientations of Women and Men

In addition to greater liberalism in these general perspectives, women in office are more liberal than men on all women's issues analyzed (Table 49). Women and men differ also on some other issues in ways suggestive of a more humanistic outlook among women. Higher proportions of women feel that more severe punishment is not the best way to deal with the crime problem, that mandatory retirement because of age should be banned, and that busing to achieve racial balance will prove good for the country. These differences occur within varied subgroupings of officeholders.

Ideology and positions on issues. Sex differences in the issue positions of women and men in office are not accounted for by the larger proportion of liberals among the women. Although ideology is strongly related to positive or negative views on all issues examined except mandatory retirement and aid to the cities, women differ from men within each category of ideology (Table 50). Among those issues related to ideology, conservative women are more

Table 49.   WOMEN TEND TO TAKE MORE LIBERAL
POSITIONS ON ISSUES THAN MEN

Women's Issues[a]	Women %	Men %
Agree ratify ERA	67	48
Disagree Constitution ban abortion	71	56
Agree homemaker social security	62	44
Agree government child care	39	32
Other Issues[a]		
Agree busing desirable	22	12
Disagree severe crime penalties	31	16
Agree reduce defense budget	46	44
Agree ban mandatory retirement	61	50
Agree more fed. revenue for cities	82	78
Approximate totals[b]:	(662)	(341)

[a]For precise wording of questions and response categories, see Questions 18 (item 5) and 19 at the end of this report. Percent agree and agree strongly, % disagree and disagree strongly have been combined.

[b]Slight variations in the numbers responding to each item have been averaged.

Table 50.   WOMEN ARE MORE LIBERAL THAN MEN ON WOMEN'S ISSUES REGARDLESS OF IDEOLOGY, PARTY AFFILIATION

Agree more should be done for women's rights by[a]:	Ideology						Party Affiliation					
	Cons.		Mid. of Rd.		Lib.		Rep.		Dem.		Ind.	
	Wmn. %	Men %	Wmn. %	Men %	Wmn. %	Men %	Wmn. %	Men %	Wmn. %	Men %	Wmn. %	Men %
Federal government	54	25	59	43	83	70	56	32	74	51	56	39
State governments	52	26	67	42	83	73	57	34	77	54	58	35
Private industry	72	46	77	60	88	76	72	55	84	63	74	46
Approximate totals[b]:	(172)	(124)	(186)	(88)	(170)	(70)	(194)	(123)	(286)	(138)	(65)	(35)
Women's Issues:[a,c]												
Agree ratify ERA	47	33	68	47	88	71	59	33	76	63	54	34
Disagree Constitution ban abortion	60	49	72	52	84	75	75	55	70	62	66	38
Agree homemaker social security	49	38	61	43	78	58	52	34	69	49	62	59
Agree government child care	22	18	35	38	64	55	24	20	53	43	26	24
Other Issues:[a,c]												
Agree busing desirable	6	5	20	6	44	39	11	7	32	18	11	6
Disagree severe crime penalties	9	3	26	9	62	49	19	9	42	25	18	6
Agree reduce defense budget	28	34	42	41	75	65	34	33	57	57	35	30
Agree ban mandatory retirement	60	52	61	42	62	52	55	51	65	48	58	51
Agree more fed. revenue for cities	84	75	84	81	78	80	86	76	79	81	90	81
Approximate totals[b]:	(215)	(149)	(255)	(100)	(189)	(73)	(230)	(140)	(345)	(157)	(80)	(36)

[a]For precise wording of questions and response categories, see Question 18, item 5, and Question 19 at the end of this report.

[b]Slight variations in the numbers responding to each item have been averaged.

[c]% agreeing and % agreeing strongly, % disagreeing and % disagreeing strongly have been combined.

liberal than conservative men on every issue except busing and the defense budget. Women who describe themselves as moderate are more liberal than their male counterparts except regarding social security for homemakers, child care, and the defense budget. Liberal women are more liberal than liberal men on every issue on which conservatives and liberals differ.

Although gender has an independent effect on issue positions, it does not override the influence of liberal/conservative identifications. This can be seen by comparing the percentages for conservative women with those for liberal men in Table 50. On each issue, higher proportions of liberal men than of conservative women take a liberal position.

Party and positions on issues. Unlike ideology, party is a less important predictor than sex of positions on some issues. As can be seen in Table 50, party affiliation is associated with issue positions, with Democrats more liberal on the issues. Despite the fact that higher proportions of women are Democrats, women are more liberal than men on most issues within each category of party affiliation. On action by government and industry to assure equal rights for women, Republican women are more liberal than Democratic men. Higher proportions of Republican women oppose a constitutional ban on abortion, and approximately equal proportions of Republican women and Democratic men support ERA and extension of social security to homemakers. Among women's issues, party affiliation has more influence than gender only with respect to child care. On other issues, party affiliation is more important than sex with respect to crime, the

defense budget and busing; sex is more important than party on issues of mandatory retirement and aid to the cities.

District population and issue positions. Office-holders from small districts are consistently more conservative on issues than those from large districts. Lower proportions of women in small districts than men in large districts describe themselves as liberal. Nonetheless, women from small districts are at least as supportive of women's issues as men from large districts (Table 51). In addition, women from small districts are more likely than men from large districts to oppose mandatory retirement and endorse aid to the cities.

Education and positions on issues. Although education is associated with issue positions among both men and women, women differ from men regardless of their level of education (Table 51). Higher proportions of the most educated men than of the least educated women describe themselves as liberal. Nevertheless, women who are not college graduates are more likely than men with postgraduate degrees to support action from government and industry to promote women's rights. However, on women's issues and other issues, the influence of education tends to outweigh the influence of gender, with the most educated men more liberal than the least educated women.

On women's issues, differences between men and women are wider among the more educated. Except for views on abortion, the relationship between sex and issue position is stronger among those with college educations or graduate degrees than among those who are not college graduates.[55]

Table 51.   SEX DIFFERENCES IN POSITIONS ON ISSUES OCCUR WITHIN EACH CATEGORY OF EDUCATION, DISTRICT SIZE

	Education						District Population			
	Not Coll. Graduate		College Graduate		Post-Grad. Degree		-10,000		10,000+	
Agree more should be done for women's rights by[a]:	Wmn. %	Men %	Wmn. %	Men %	Wmn. %	Men %	Wmn. %	Men %	Wmn. %	Men %
Federal government	61	43	66	34	75	51	61	37	71	50
State governments	61	43	72	34	80	57	63	36	75	55
Private industry	73	56	83	55	86	66	74	55	85	63
Approximate totals[b]:	(280)	(134)	(176)	(87)	(89)	(82)	(308)	(168)	(217)	(124)
Women's Issues:[a,c]										
Agree ratify ERA	58	44	77	46	79	58	60	39	78	62
Disagree Constitution ban abortion	65	45	78	64	80	72	66	54	78	63
Agree homemaker social security	58	50	66	36	71	42	60	45	64	42
Agree government child care	32	26	44	29	53	45	31	24	49	44
Other Issues:[a,c]										
Agree busing desirable	15	8	25	10	36	26	15	11	32	15
Disagree severe crime penalties	22	6	36	17	54	33	21	12	47	22
Agree reduce defense budget	38	41	54	34	60	59	42	38	54	52
Agree ban mandatory retirement	60	51	62	51	64	48	57	49	66	52
Agree more fed. revenue for cities	83	84	85	70	75	77	85	78	79	78
Approximate totals[b]:	(344)	(159)	(204)	(93)	(104)	(89)	(374)	(194)	(251)	(136)

[a]For precise wording of questions and response categories, see Question 18, item 5, and Question 19 at the end of this report.

[b]Slight variations in the numbers responding to each item have been averaged.

[c]% agreeing and % agreeing strongly, % disagreeing and % disagreeing strongly have been combined.

Table 52.   REGARDLESS OF AGE, WOMEN ARE MORE LIBERAL THAN MEN ON WOMEN'S ISSUES

	Age							
	Under 35		35-44		45-54		55+	
Agree more should be done for women's rights by[a]:	Wmn. %	Men %	Wmn. %	Men %	Wmn. %	Men %	Wmn. %	Men %
Federal government	67	53	67	45	65	37	62	35
State governments	71	55	72	48	66	39	63	34
Private industry	80	64	78	57	80	58	75	54
Approximate totals[b]	(66)	(60)	(157)	(91)	(195)	(85)	(120)	(70)
Women's Issues:[a,c]								
Agree ERA should be ratified	76	60	75	55	65	47	58	34
Disagree Constitution should ban abortion	75	61	75	61	73	63	63	42
Agree homemakers should have social security	78	49	63	41	57	40	62	47
Agree government should provide child care	44	37	41	36	42	31	32	24
Other Issues:[a,c]								
Agree busing for racial balance is desirable	27	22	25	15	19	10	20	6
Disagree severe penalties would help crime problem	43	20	39	21	30	16	21	7
Agree defense budget should be reduced	48	51	52	39	44	46	44	42
Agree mandatory retirement should be banned	56	49	61	55	58	42	67	54
Agree more federal revenue should go to cities	92	81	81	80	81	77	82	78
Approximate totals[b]	(70)	(61)	(179)	(97)	(227)	(92)	(163)	(95)

[a]For precise wording of questions and response categories, see Question 19 at end of report.

[b]Slight variations in the numbers responding to each item have been averaged.

[c]% agreeing and % agreeing strongly, % disagreeing and % disagreeing strongly have been combined.

<u>Age and positions on issues</u>. Younger officeholders are more liberal on issues than older officeholders. Yet within each category of age, women are more liberal than men on women's issues (Table 52). Indeed, in nearly every instance younger men are less liberal on women's issues than each older age category of women. On other issues, sex is at least as important as age in influencing positive or negative positions.

CONCLUSION TO PART IV

Among officeholders, gender is more than a minor component of political outlook; it is often more important than characteristics ordinarily receiving greater attention from political analysts. As a predictor of positions on some women's issues, it is more important than political party and age. It has equal importance with education and size of district population. Although gender does not override the association between self-described ideology and positions on women's issues, it has an independent predictive effect.

The importance of sex in the analysis of political orientations is not confined to issues with substance of direct relevance to women. Among issues analyzed, women are more likely than men to oppose tougher penalties against crime, to support busing to achieve racial balance, and to favor legislation to ban mandatory retirement because of age. They differ from men on these issues regardless of their ideology, party affiliation, age, education or the size of their district populations.

These findings are important in evaluating the potential influence of women in government. Women in office may differ from men in office because of divergent socialization processes and gender-linked roles in the larger society. They also may differ because women who achieve public office represent a selection from the general population of women that is dissimilar to the selection of men for office from the general population of men.[56] If sex differentiation in positions on public issues persists, a continued increase in the numbers of women in public office will mean a growing impact of the special political perspectives of women on legislative and executive decision-making.

PART V.   PERCEPTIONS ABOUT WOMEN IN POLITICS

Even in this decade, ambivalence about the role of women in politics has been widespread both among the electorate and among politically elite men. In a nationwide poll in 1972, a majority of respondents felt that women should become more active in politics, but nearly two-thirds of both women and men agreed that most men are better suited emotionally for politics than most women.[57] In a comparison made between voters in this poll and delegates to the 1972 national conventions, female delegates were found to disagree with stereotypical opinions about women's fitness for politics, while male delegates were reported to have much the same opinions as the electorate.[58]

As more women achieve office, many voters and politically elite men may be rejecting a view of women as less well-suited for public life. To the degree that such an opinion continues to be held, however, the behaviors it implies will limit the political roles of women.

Women cannot achieve public office and perform successfully in office solely through their own motivations and characteristics. Quite apart from their actual abilities, aspirations and attitudes, they are dependent upon approval from electorates, from political party leaders, and from officeholders with the power to select others for appointive offices. Once in office, women face additional barriers if sizeable proportions of constituents and colleagues automatically regard their competence and qualifications as suspect because of their gender. Moreover, a tendency of social life is for individuals to share the perceptions that others have of them. If women, even politically active women, adopt conventional stereotypes about themselves, they may limit their own political goals.

In Part V, we examine four aspects of perceptions among officeholders about women in politics: perceptions of <u>barriers in access</u> to public office and political leadership, perceptions of <u>difficulties</u> in office that women experience as a result of being women, perceptions of <u>advantages</u> that women in office experience, and perceptions of the <u>characteristics of women in office</u>. Our investigation is necessarily limited to analysis of only a few of the many questions that might be asked about these topics. It is intended to suggest the nature of the dilemma faced by political women rather than to describe fully its dimensions. As in previous parts of this report, we consider in the first section the perceptions of women in public office and variations among women. In the second section, we compare the perceptions of women with those of men in office.

WOMEN IN POLITICS AS PERCEIVED BY WOMEN IN OFFICE

Large proportions of women in office perceive women as discriminated against in access to political leadership. In their description of the difficulties they encounter while serving in public office, women most often mention various forms of sex discrimination. However, women in politics also see advantages deriving from their gender. They often attribute these advantages to their visibility as a small minority and to special contributions that women make to the political sphere of activity.

<u>Perceptions of Discrimination</u>[59]

Although large proportions of women in office perceive discrimination against women in politics, they are far more likely to identify male party leaders than voters as a source of discrimination (Table 53).

The higher the level of office occupied by women officials, the more likely are women to perceive unequal opportunity for achieving political leader-

Table 53. WOMEN IN OFFICE ARE MORE LIKELY TO SEE MEN IN PARTY ORGANIZATIONS THAN VOTERS AS DISCRIMINATORY

	Judi-ciary %	State Exec. %	State Senate %	State House %	County Comsn. %	Mayor-alty %	Local Council %
Women have just as much opportunity as men to become political leaders							
Agree strongly	17	15	16	21	28	35	31
Agree	35	29	24	33	31	30	32
Disagree	11	22	20	27	20	23	22
Disagree strongly	37	34	40	19	21	12	15
Total[a]	(35)	(41)	(55)	(247)	(270)	(278)	(2,056)
In general, voters are more reluctant to support women candidates							
Agree strongly	11	10	7	3	9	14	13
Agree	31	50	36	36	43	46	43
Disagree	20	22	37	34	29	21	26
Disagree strongly	38	18	20	27	19	19	18
Total[a]	(35)	(40)	(56)	(244)	(271)	(269)	(2,010)
Many men in party organizations try to keep women out of leadership roles							
Agree strongly	30	24	33	22	30	26	32
Agree	44	50	53	46	41	47	43
Disagree	23	18	9	21	20	19	17
Disagree strongly	3	8	5	10	9	8	8
Total[a]	(30)	(38)	(55)	(239)	(250)	(246)	(1,873)

[a]"Undecideds" have been omitted from percentage bases.

ship. A little more than a third of local office-holders but more than two-fifths of county commissioners and state representatives and half or more of state senators, judges and state executives disagree that women have as much opportunity as men to become political leaders.

In contrast to the tendency for higher proportions of women in higher-level offices to perceive unequal political opportunity, local and county office-holders are more likely than women in higher offices (except the state executive) to perceive voter discrimination. Moreover, higher proportions of local and county officeholders perceive voter resistance than perceive unequal opportunity, while higher proportions of state officeholders perceive unequal opportunity than perceive voter resistance.

Thus a proportion of women officials who feel that women have as much opportunity as men to achieve political leadership nonetheless perceive voters as reluctant to support women candidates. Conversely, a proportion of women who define women as having unequal opportunity do not perceive voters as a source of inequality. Apparently, some office-holders think of "political leadership" apart from the electorate, as referring to positions within their governing bodies or within political parties. Perhaps others think of "opportunity" as unequal only if they regard obstacles as insurmountable, since women elected to public office obviously have overcome whatever barriers are imposed by voters.

Far larger proportions of women in every office perceive discrimination from men in political parties than perceive discrimination by voters. Between 68% and 86% agree or agree strongly that many men in party organizations try to keep women from attaining leadership positions. Again, larger proportions of women perceive party discrimination than perceive unequal opportunity for political leadership.

Difficulties Encountered as Women in Office

By far the most common difficulty mentioned by women in office is discrimination. Respondents were asked to reply to this question: "What special difficulties, if any, have you experienced as a result of being a woman holding public office?" The question was designed to elicit a range of responses that would represent the salient concerns of women holding office. Respondents were free to mention family pressures, difficulties of raising money for campaigns, inadequacies in background and skills, problems of travel away from home, prejudice against women or various other difficulties -- and all of these appear with varying frequency, as shown in Table 54.[60]

While a minority report that they have experienced no special difficulties, proportions ranging between 50% and 78% across various categories of office mention one or more problems. The difficulties encountered overwhelmingly refer to prejudice and discrimination, principally from male colleagues or other political leaders but also from constituents. Women complain that they are not taken seriously, are stereotyped in their characteristics, are regarded as sex objects, are excluded from the "old boys' networks," are not consulted on pending issues, are discriminated against in committee assignments, are asked to do clerical work and domestic chores, are asked to assume an unfair share of the work load, are subjected to opposition to

Table 54.   DISCRIMINATION IS THE MAJOR DIFFICULTY EXPERIENCED BY WOMEN IN OFFICE[a]

Type of Difficulty Named:	Judi-ciary %	State Exec. %	State Senate %	State House %	County Comsn. %	Mayor-alty %	Local Council %
Chauvinism, stereotyping, not taken seriously	46	42	33	41	44	38	46
Exclusion from male networks	4	10	12	12	10	5	7
Discrimination in assignments	4	2	5	7	4	2	3
Opposition to programs and ideas	4	7	2	1	1	4	3
Having to prove competence	15	2	12	11	12	20	13
Constituent prejudice	15	10	3	8	10	12	9
Discomfort of minority status	0	12	12	5	9	3	6
Financial support	8	5	3	4	1	1	-
Family pressures	0	5	7	4	3	3	3
Personality difficulty	4	0	3	2	2	2	2
Deficiency in qualifications	0	2	0	2	2	4	4
Other	0	3	8	3	2	6	4
Total difficulties named = 100%	(26)	(41)	(60)	(220)	(242)	(218)	(1,639)
Total naming one or more difficulty	(15)	(25)	(39)	(142)	(151)	(155)	(1,079)
Percent naming one or more difficulty	50%	69%	78%	70%	63%	64%	58%

[a]Federal respondents have been omitted because of small numbers reporting.

their programs and ideas because a woman has initiated them, are expected to prove their competence while that of men is taken for granted, and are sometimes avoided or ridiculed by male constituents. Many comment simply that they confront the "old story" of male chauvinism. From two-thirds to more than eight in ten of women officeholders' comments refer to such forms of discrimination.

In addition, some comments deal with the discomforts of minority status. Among respondents' difficulties in this category are the manner in which they are addressed (e.g., as councilman, as gentlemen, by first name when colleagues are addressed more formally), problems of travel to conferences as the only woman in a group of men, problems of attending official social events without an escort or of placing one's husband in an awkward position by taking him along.

Comments about conflict between officeholding and some aspect of family life constitute only from 3% to 7% of total responses. Either women who achieve and stay in public office find satisfactory ways of combining officeholding with their family roles, or the family problems they do encounter are less salient than the discrimination they face as officials, or they do not regard tensions between family and political life as a problem special to women who hold office (see Part II).

Similarly small percentages of the difficulties mentioned involve the personalities or qualifications of the women themselves. While some women feel that they have had to learn to be more assertive, more direct in their communication or less emotional, others report having to learn to be more patient and accepting, less aggressive, or more subtle in their communication. A few women report felt inadequacies in background or skills such as lack of formal education, lack of business training or experience, lack of technical expertise in matters involving construction or machinery, or lack of political experience and skills.

The overall tendency to mention some form of discrimination or prejudice as distinguished from other types of difficulties does not vary with the characteristics of officeholders. Proportions of responses mentioning discrimination are strikingly similar among all categories of characteristics examined: type of office, party affiliation, size of district population, tenure in office, number of other women serving on governing body, age, education, marital status, presence of minor children, conservative or liberal ideology, and membership in feminist organizations.

Women do vary in patterned ways in the proportions saying that they have experienced one or more difficulties, in comparison with the proportions saying that they have experienced no difficulties. However, the kinds of women who are more likely to mention difficulties are also the kinds of women who are more likely to mention advantages. Thus both difficulties and advantages are named proportionately more often by women in higher-level offices, women in large districts, women with female colleagues, younger women, liberals, college graduates, and members of feminist organizations. Apparently, awareness both of difficulties and of advantages reflects a more general consciousness of self as distinct from other officeholders because of gender.

Advantages Experienced by Women in Office

Just as the majority of women name one or more difficulties they have encountered as women in office, the majority name one or more advantages (Table 55). Answers are given within a variety of perspectives, and the types of answers range widely.

A substantial proportion of responses concerns some aspect of relations with the public. Many women think of themselves as more approachable, more trusted, more responsive to the needs and problems of constituents and more knowledgeable about such problems. A minority of responses refer

Table 55. SERVICE TO PUBLIC, SPECIAL CHARACTERISTICS AND TREATMENT ARE ADVANTAGES CLAIMED BY WOMEN[a]

Type of Advantage Named:	Judi-ciary %	State Exec. %	State Senate %	State House %	County Comsn. %	Mayor-alty %	Local Council %
Constituent service, public representation	33	23	27	22	24	25	34
More approachable	0	0	0	4	5	6	8
More responsive, able to identify needs	0	6	3	6	7	8	12
Public trust	11	11	16	6	5	5	3
Women a special constituency	22	6	8	6	7	6	11
Special skills and performance	9	12	16	30	28	25	27
Superior knowledge and performance	3	3	1	6	4	6	4
More outspoken, independent, innovative	0	0	1	2	3	2	2
Superior interpersonal skills	6	6	2	8	7	6	6
More time; not having to earn a living	0	0	10	12	7	9	9
Women's view, special expertise of roles	0	3	2	2	7	2	6
Visibility, novelty, special treatment	54	56	48	41	40	40	28
Higher visibility, better publicity	46	39	33	29	22	16	10
Special respect for women who achieve	6	3	2	5	8	11	8
Special courtesy, male chivalry	2	14	13	7	10	13	10
Personal satisfactions	2	3	3	0	5	5	7
Other	2	6	6	7	3	5	4
Total advantages named = 100%	(36)	(35)	(63)	(255)	(287)	(252)	(1,923)
Total naming one or more	(22)	(22)	(39)	(150)	(164)	(147)	(1,143)
Percent naming one or more	71%	60%	83%	72%	70%	62%	63%

[a]Federal respondents have been omitted because of small numbers reporting.

to women as a special constituency, stressing service to women and support by women.

A wide variety of qualities, patterns of performance and special perspectives are named by respondents as aspects of officeholding in which they personally or women generally excel. Comments made with some frequency are that women are more persistent, more committed, more knowledgeable about their communities, more willing to seek information, more practical and more honest. Women also frequently mention giving more time to their offices either because they are more committed or because they have more flexible schedules than men.

In their interpersonal skills, women see themselves as more understanding of others, more patient, more skilled in effecting compromises. Some respondents see women as more outspoken and willing to dissent, more independent in their political judgments, more willing to take a fresh perspective and develop new programs.

The "woman's point of view" as a special contribution of women to politics also receives mention. Some women specify this perspective by commenting that their family experience has sensitized them to the needs of women and children in the community, that women's minority status makes them more sympathetic to the needs of other special groups such as racial minorities or elderly citizens, or that women are a humanizing influence in government.

Although women in office often complain of their "token" or minority status, many women consider

their visibility as a minority of some advantage in the treatment and publicity they receive. Responses mentioning visibility or novelty as an advantage occur more frequently at higher levels of officeholding. Special courtesies received also are often mentioned as advantages although some women qualify their comments by indicating that they consider these advantages pleasant but of minor value.

Perceptions of the Qualities of Women in Politics

The advantages mentioned by women holding office suggest that large proportions of politically active women think that members of their sex make distinctive contributions to politics. Part of the conventional wisdom about women in politics is that women make special contributions but are also politically naive and relatively inferior to men in their experience and qualifications. In an effort to examine the extent to which women holding public office may adopt such a conventional stereotype, if not for themselves, then for political women in general, we asked officeholders to indicate their degree of agreement or disagreement with four statements about the characteristics of women in office. Two of these statements assert special contributions of women: commitment of time and expertise in human relations. Two statements describe women in office as inferior to men: in political astuteness and in qualifications and training. Table 56 presents the four statements and the percentages agreeing or disagreeing with each.

Women in office typically agree with statements of

Table 56.   WOMEN SEE THE CHARACTERISTICS OF WOMEN IN OFFICE AS EQUAL OR SUPERIOR TO THOSE OF MEN IN OFFICE

	Judi-ciary %	State Exec. %	State Senate %	State House %	County Comsn. %	Mayor-alty %	Local Council %
Women in office generally devote more time to the job than do men							
Agree strongly	35	43	52	50	57	60	46
Agree	38	30	29	34	30	26	33
Disagree	15	18	19	12	10	7	16
Disagree strongly	12	9	0	4	3	7	5
Total[a]	(26)	(33)	(52)	(217)	(247)	(255)	(1,838)
Women in office are better at the "human relations" aspect of the job							
Agree strongly	30	37	34	38	46	55	48
Agree	49	26	36	33	38	30	36
Disagree	18	26	26	26	13	10	13
Disagree strongly	3	11	4	3	3	5	3
Total[a]	(33)	(35)	(50)	(223)	(249)	(260)	(1,903)
In general, women in office are not as politically astute as men							
Agree strongly	0	10	6	6	10	13	8
Agree	32	10	25	19	20	22	26
Disagree	19	21	25	33	22	24	27
Disagree strongly	49	59	44	42	48	41	39
Total[a]	(31)	(38)	(51)	(242)	(260)	(258)	(1,926)
Women officeholders' qualifications and training usually not as good as men's							
Agree strongly	3	0	6	3	6	6	7
Agree	9	15	14	13	10	17	17
Disagree	21	8	10	22	22	25	23
Disagree strongly	67	77	70	62	62	52	53
Total[a]	(33)	(39)	(51)	(240)	(263)	(263)	(1,965)

[a]"Undecideds" have been omitted from percentage bases.

women's superior contributions and disagree with statements asserting inadequacies. By overwhelming majorities, women in every type of office agree or agree strongly that women give more time to the job than men and are better at human relations. By similarly overwhelming majorities, women in every type of office disagree or disagree strongly that women are not as politically astute as men or as well qualified.

Higher proportions of county and state than of local officeholders believe that women's qualifications and training are not inferior to those of men. In addition, higher proportions of county and local officeholders than of state officeholders agree that women are better at human relations. These findings suggest that women in higher-level offices may be more resistant to conventional stereotypes about women, regardless of whether these stereotypes affirm superiority or inferiority. Alternatively, the patterns of response may reflect actual differences in the behavior and characteristics of women who achieve offices above the local level.

WOMEN'S VS. MEN'S PERCEPTIONS OF WOMEN IN POLITICS

In a number of ways, the perceptions that women in office have of their difficulties, advantages and characteristics are not shared by men in office. Men in office perceive discrimination against women differently, are less likely to perceive superior competencies of women officials, and are more likely to perceive deficiencies.

Perceptions of Discrimination in Access to Office

The men responding to our survey do not differ greatly from women officials in their perceptions of women as subject to unequal political opportunity, party discrimination or voter discrimination (Table 57). Thirty-three percent of men and 38% of women disagree that women have equal opportunity; 60% of men and 55% of women agree that voters are more reluctant to support women. Somewhat larger differences appear in perceptions of discrimination by men in party organizations. Seventy-one percent of women but only 58% of men agree that many men in political parties oppose the attainment of leadership by women.

Although approximately similar percentages of women and men perceive women as having unequal political opportunity, men are more likely to identify voters, and women are more likely to see party leaders as sources of inequality. Among those perceiving unequal political opportunity, 63% of women but 79% of men perceive voters as reluctant to support women candidates, in contrast to 84% of women and 71% of men perceiving discrimination by party leaders. Among those who feel that women have equal opportunity with men, 51% of both men and women perceive voter resistance but a larger proportion of women (63%) than of men (50%) view parties as discriminatory.

Table 57. RELATIVELY MORE WOMEN THAN MEN AGREE
PARTIES DISCRIMINATE AGAINST WOMEN

	Women %	Men %
Women have as much opportunity as men to become political leaders		
Agree strongly	30	28
Agree	32	39
Disagree	21	23
Disagree strongly	17	10
Total[a]	(695)	(344)
In general, voters are more reluctant to support women candidates		
Agree strongly	12	11
Agree	43	49
Disagree	27	27
Disagree strongly	18	13
Total[a]	(679)	(335)
Many men in party organizations try to keep women out of leadership roles		
Agree strongly	30	20
Agree	41	38
Disagree	20	28
Disagree strongly	9	14
Total[a]	(639)	(328)

[a]"Undecideds" omitted from percentage bases.

Men's Perceptions of Difficulties Faced by Women

Men are less likely than women to name sex discrimination as a problem experienced by women serving
in office (Table 58). Larger proportions of the
difficulties named by men are focused on conflicts
between officeholding and the family life of women
officeholders or on perceived inadequacies of
personality and qualifications among female
officials. Forty-five percent of the responses
given by men but only 9% of those made by women
are in these areas. In addition, nearly twice
the proportion of men's responses (17%) as of
women's (9%) refer to the prejudices of constituents. Thus, while women officials perceive their
difficulties largely in terms of the behavior of
their colleagues or of other political men, men
in office perceive women's difficulties as located
in the personal qualities and characteristics of
women officeholders, or in the public's antipathy
toward them.

Men's Perceptions of Women's Advantages

A lower percentage of men (52%) than of women (65%)
perceive one or more advantages experienced by
women in office (Table 59). These figures are in
contrast to men's somewhat greater tendency to
perceive difficulties (68% of men vs. 60% of women).
The advantages named also differ in nature from
those named by women. A higher proportion of the
men's responses mention women's ability to attract
women's votes and to serve the needs of women, but
a lower proportion are concerned with other aspects
of constituent service and representation. Higher
percentages of the men's responses also name aspects
of special skills and performances. These tend to
be heavily, though not entirely, directed to
traditional virtues thought to be possessed by women:

Table 58. MEN'S PERCEPTIONS DIFFER FROM WOMEN'S
REPORTS OF DIFFICULTIES EXPERIENCED

Type of Difficulty Named:	Women %	Men %
Chauvinism, stereotyping	45	26
Exclusion from male networks	7	1
Discrimination in assignments	3	-
Opposition to programs, ideas	3	1
Having to prove competence	14	4
Constituent prejudice	9	17
Discomfort of minority status	6	3
Financial support	1	-
Family pressures	3	11
Personality difficulty	2	17
Deficiency in qualifications	4	17
Other	3	3
Total difficulties named = 100%	(574)	(288)
Total naming one or more	(372)	(215)
Percent naming one or more	60%	68%

Table 59. RELATIVELY FEWER MEN PERCEIVE
ADVANTAGES FOR WOMEN OFFICEHOLDERS:
SPECIAL CONTRIBUTIONS ARE NAMED

Type of Advantage Named:	Women %	Men %
Constituent service, representation	30	22
More approachable	8	1
More responsive, able to identify needs	9	8
Public trust	5	1
Women a special constituency	8	12
Special skills and performance	27	57
Superior knowledge and performance	4	8
More outspoken, independent, innovative	2	5
Superior interpersonal skills	5	9
More time; not having to earn a living	10	18
Women's view, special expertise of role	6	17
Visibility, novelty, special treatment	33	17
Higher visibility, better publicity	15	12
Special respect for women who achieve	9	-
Special courtesy, male chivalry	9	5
Personal satisfactions	6	3
Other	4	1
Total advantages named = 100%	(653)	(238)
Total naming one or more	(393)	(163)
Percent naming one or more	65%	52%

commitment of time because women do not have to earn
a living, the woman's point of view, skill in human
relations, independence and lack of ties to special
interests, conscientiousness, patience with detail,
and knowledgeability.

Perceptions of Women's Characteristics

Examination of the four characteristics selected as

Table 60.   WOMEN AND MEN DIFFER IN THEIR PERCEPTIONS
OF THE CHARACTERISTICS OF WOMEN IN OFFICE

	Women %	Men %
Women in office generally devote more time to the job than do men		
Agree strongly	49	17
Agree	33	34
Disagree	13	30
Disagree strongly	5	19
Total[a]	(637)	(283)
Women in office are better at "human relations" aspect of job		
Agree strongly	45	13
Agree	38	32
Disagree	14	38
Disagree strongly	3	17
Total[a]	(640)	(307)
In general, women in office are not as politically astute as men		
Agree strongly	9	7
Agree	23	32
Disagree	27	37
Disagree strongly	41	24
Total[a]	(656)	(321)
Women officeholders' qualifications and training usually not as good as men's		
Agree strongly	7	8
Agree	16	24
Disagree	21	38
Disagree strongly	56	30
Total[a]	(673)	(323)

[a]"Undecideds" omitted from percentage bases.

indicators of conventional perceptions of the contributions and deficiencies of women officeholders reveals that men are proportionately less likely than women to perceive virtues and are proportionately more likely to perceive deficiencies (Table 60). Lower proportions of men agree that women devote more time to office (which, in fact, they do if unemployed -- see Part III). Lower proportions of men than women also see women as superior in human relations. In addition, men are more likely than women to agree with statements that women's political skills and qualifications are not as good as those of men.

With few exceptions, these patterns of difference between women and men occur regardless of marital status, age of youngest child, education, district size, tenure in office, party affiliation, ideology and age. There are only two instances in which male and female officeholders share similar perceptions about women in office: no sex differences in perceptions of women's political astuteness exist among those under 35 and among liberals, and no sex

differences exist with regard to perceptions of women's qualifications or training among those under age 35, liberals and moderates. These exceptions reflect the fact that age and ideology are strongly related among men (though only weakly related among women) to agreement or disagreement with the statements that women lack political astuteness and qualifications for office.

A more complete picture of the differing perceptions that women and men have of women in office is obtained when we examine the various ways in which beliefs about the four characteristics of time commitment, skill in human relations, political astuteness, and qualifications are patterned in the responses of individuals. Fifty-two percent of women but only 25% of men both affirm the superiority of women in commitment of time and/or human relations and deny inadequacies in training and political astuteness. An additional 34% of women but only 19% of men perceive a traditional sexual division of competencies, defining women officeholders as superior in time and human relations but as deficient in political skill and/or in qualifications for office.

By contrast, only 7% of women officeholders but 36% of the men combine rejection of one or both statements regarding women's special contributions with agreement that women's political skills and qualifications are inferior. Only 7% of women officeholders but 20% of men in office deny all sex-linked differences in characteristics typical of women in office -- the pattern of response that would prevail if gender were perceived as irrelevant to political behavior.

Thus patterns of responses to the four statements about women in politics illustrate the disparities in perceptions that exist. Women tend to perceive women in office as either superior or as exhibiting a traditional sexual division of competencies. Men tend to perceive women officeholders as displaying a traditional sexual division of competencies, as inadequate relative to men, or as no different from men.

Sex-linked stereotypes may be usually true, usually false, or sometimes true and sometimes false. Our data can neither confirm nor refute the validity of any of these patterns of perception. We suggest, however, that the disparities in perceptions may be indicative of tensions in the relations between men and women who are officially colleagues. As we point out in the introduction to this report, the men responding to our survey may well have more interest in women's political participation than men who did not respond. Should our assumption prove correct, the evaluations of women's political roles made by the female and male officeholders in our survey may differ even more widely between women and men in the total population of officials.

PART VI.   POLITICAL PLANS AND PUBLIC OFFICEHOLDING AMBITIONS

Women officeholders view sex discrimination as a widespread problem for politically active women, and we have suggested that such discrimination is one limitation on political achievement. Some

research concludes that an additional restriction on women's political activity is operative: a lack of political ambition.[61] Previous studies which have compared the officeholding ambitions of male and female political elites have found women to be less ambitious politically than men.[62] Lower levels of ambition among women in comparison with men generally have been attributed to differences in sex-role socialization.

The issue of the relative importance of limited ambition versus discrimination as explanations for the lack of greater achievement by women in the political sphere is clearly of more than academic significance. Each explanation implies a different approach to removing obstacles to women's political participation. If the paucity of women in positions of political leadership is due primarily to lower ambition stemming from sex-role socialization, then greater participation must await changes in the attitudes and motivations of women themselves. If the lack of political achievement is due instead to sex discrimination, then increased political involvement by women will depend upon changes in the attitudes of party leaders, voters and others who exercise control over the futures of political women.

To assist clarification of the issue of women's ambition, Part VI is devoted to an examination of the public officeholding aspirations of women in office, as they reported these in 1977. The first section of Part VI describes the ambitions of women currently serving in office and reports the distinguishing characteristics of ambitious women. The second section examines the ambitions of women in comparison with those of men, pointing to the need for revision of the assertion that politically active women are less ambitious than their male counterparts. The third section considers a group of women who have left office since 1975. The concluding section of Part VI briefly summarizes the findings and discusses their implications for the participation of women in public office.

AMBITION AND WOMEN OFFICEHOLDERS

Three questions from our survey are central in analyzing officeholding ambitions. First, respondents were asked if they planned to seek an additional term in the office currently held. Second, respondents were asked if there were any other elective or appointive offices they eventually would like to hold, given the necessary political support and the right opportunities. Third, those who answered this question affirmatively were asked to list all offices which might be of interest.

Women officeholders are politically ambitious. Most women in every category of office definitely or probably plan to seek another term in their present office, and approximately half or more eventually would like to hold some other public office (Table 61).

Those in higher levels of office show some tendency to be more ambitious for additional terms or for other offices. State legislators are more ambitious than county commissioners. In turn, county commissioners are more ambitious than officeholders at the local level. Exceptions to the general pattern occur among mayors, who are no more ambitious than local councillors, and among judges and members of the state executive, who appear less ambitious than state legislators. Perhaps the older average age of mayors and judges, the lengthy term of office of many judgeships, and the appointive nature of some judicial and executive offices affect expressed plans and aspirations of women in these offices.

Among women officeholders who desire other offices, ambitions are affected by current officeholding achievement. Officeholders who aspire to other offices have been classified, on the basis of the highest office desired, as having high, moderate or low officeholding ambition. (See footnote to Table 62 for a complete list of offices considered to reflect each level of ambition.) Consistently greater proportions of state legislators than of county or local officials aspire to federal, state cabinet or other high offices (Table 62). Eighty-nine percent of state senators and 64% of state house members ultimately aspire to these high offices, in contrast to 40% of county commissioners, 20% of mayors and 18% of local councillors.

Leavers, Stayers and Changers

To facilitate more detailed analysis of ambition, officeholders have been classified into three categories on the basis of responses to questions about seeking additional terms in office and seeking other public offices. Those who eventually would like to hold one or more other offices are termed "changers." Officeholders who do not express an interest in other public offices are classified as "stayers" if they plan to seek an additional term in their current office, and as "leavers" if they plan to resign from public officeholding at the end of their current term. Throughout this analysis, changers will be considered more politically ambitious than stayers, and stayers will be con-

Table 61. MOST WOMEN WANT ANOTHER TERM IN CURRENT OFFICE AND/OR AT LEAST ONE MORE PUBLIC OFFICE[a]

	Judiciary %	State Exec. %	State Senate %	State House %	County Comsn. %	Mayoralty %	Local Council %
Probably, definitely will seek additional term in current office	82	63	84	82	72	54	62
Total	(37)	(43)	(58)	(251)	(281)	(287)	(2,142)
Would like one or more other offices	50	66	82	62	56	48	49
Total	(34)	(38)	(54)	(237)	(269)	(267)	(2,013)

[a]Federal offices have been omitted from analysis because of low numbers of responses.

Table 62.   LARGER PROPORTIONS IN STATE THAN IN COUNTY OR LOCAL OFFICES HAVE AMBITIONS FOR HIGH OFFICE[a]

Officeholding Ambition[b]:	Judi-ciary %	State Exec. %	State Senate %	State House %	County Comsn. %	Mayor-alty %	Local Council %
High	(15)	(16)	89	64	40	20	18
Moderate	(1)	(3)	11	34	50	54	49
Low	(0)	(0)	0	2	10	26	33
Total	(16)	(19)	(38)	(132)	(136)	(112)	(896)

[a]Federal offices have been omitted from analysis because of low numbers of responses.

[b]Offices following were considered to reflect high, moderate or low ultimate officeholding ambition:
   High -- Federal: president, vice-president, supreme court justice, senator or representative, cabinet or subcabinet officer, ambassador, district judge; State: governor, lieutenant governor, supreme court judge, attorney general, treasurer, secretary of state; Local: mayor of city of 1,000,000 or more.
   Moderate -- State: senator or representative, trial judge, appellate judge other than of state supreme court, department head not elsewhere listed; Local: mayor of city of less than 1,000,000 but over 100,000.
   Low -- County: head or member of county governing body, judge, other county official or board member; Local: mayor or township head of district less than 100,000 population, municipal judge, member of municipal or township council, other municipal or township official.

sidered more ambitious than leavers. Only two categories of officeholders -- state legislators and local councillors -- are examined in our analysis of leavers, stayers, and changers. These represent the most ambitious and the least ambitious of the categories of officeholders included in our survey, and they also have the advantage of numbers sufficiently large to permit detailed analysis.

The fact that women in office are politically ambitious is further illustrated by the fact that 69% of state legislators and 54% of local councillors are changers, while 26% of legislators and 32% of council members are stayers. Leavers constitute only 5% of state legislators and 14% of local councillors.[63]

Although the majority of legislators and local councillors are changers, changers vary in the level of their officeholding ambition. Among changers at the local level, 18% desire federal, state cabinet or other offices indicating high ambition; 48% aspire to state legislative or other offices reflecting moderate ambition; 34% desire local or county offices indicating relatively low ambition. Among changers in state legislatures, 56% have high officeholding ambition; 42% have moderate ambition; only 2% list an office at the local or county level as the highest office they desire.[64]

Personal Characteristics and Ambition

The personal characteristics of officeholders may represent resources that can be invested in future political activity or obstacles to additional achievement. Among those influencing political ambition, two stand out as of special importance: age and education.[65]

Age and ambition. An individual's sense of what is achievable is likely to become more constrained as

she grows older. While it may seem reasonable for a local councillor of 35 to aspire to Congress, the same aspiration is likely to seem much less reasonable to the councillor of 65. When the proportions of officeholders aspiring to offices other than those now held are examined, the inhibiting effect of age on political ambition is evident (Table 63). Ninety-three percent of state legislators under age 35 are changers, but only 44% of those aged 55 or more desire to seek other offices. Among local councillors, 65% of those under 35 but only 34% of those aged 55 or more are changers. As shown in Table 63, the proportions of both stayers and

Table 63.   YOUNGER WOMEN HAVE HIGHER AMBITIONS

	Legislator Age[a]				Councillor Age			
	-35 %	35-44 %	45-54 %	55+ %	-35 %	35-44 %	45-54 %	55+ %
Ambition:								
Change	93	83	69	49	65	63	56	34
Stay	7	17	31	51	25	28	32	41
Leave					10	9	12	25
Total	(41)	(65)	(91)	(57)	(241)	(523)	(562)	(434)
Changers' Ambition:								
High	82	48	61	42	20	20	17	7
Mod.	18	52	39	58	51	48	48	46
Low					29	32	35	47
Total	(33)	(48)	(54)	(24)	(145)	(309)	(285)	(135)

[a]The 13 legislators classified as leavers and the 3 legislative changers expressing low ambition are omitted from analysis.

leavers among legislators and councillors rise with increasing age.

Among changers, age is strongly related to the level of office ultimately desired. Of the state legislators under age 35 who express a desire to seek other offices, 82% aspire to federal, state cabinet or other comparable offices reflecting high officeholding ambition. The corresponding figure for state legislative changers 55 or older is 42%. While 20% of changers among local council members under age 35 aspire to high office, only 7% of changers 55 and older have high officeholding ambition.

Education. Education may increase an individual's self-esteem and sense of efficacy which, in turn, may lead her to higher aspirations. It also may provide credentials which are perceived both by the individual officeholder and her colleagues as important qualifications for moving on to more powerful or prestigious offices.

Among both legislators and local council members, those with graduate degrees are far more likely to be changers than those who have not completed college, and the better educated among the changers are far more likely to aim for high office than the less educated changers (Table 64).

Table 64. AMBITIOUS OFFICEHOLDERS ARE BETTER EDUCATED THAN LEAVERS, STAYERS

Ambition:	Legislators			Councillors		
	Non-Coll.	Coll.	Post-Grad.	Non-Coll.	Coll.	Post-Grad.
	%	%	%	%	%	%
Changers	60	73	87	50	58	68
Stayers	40	27	13	36	27	21
Leavers[a]				14	15	11
Total	(75)	(114)	(71)	(1,067)	(501)	(214)
Changers' Ambition:						
High	37	60	70	12	21	33
Moderate	63	40	30	46	52	50
Low[b]				42	27	17
Total	(41)	(70)	(54)	(481)	(268)	(135)

[a]Those classified as leavers among Legislators are not analyzed because of small numbers.

[b]Among Legislator changers, the three expressing low ultimate ambition have not been analyzed.

The effects of education on ambition are similar among younger and older officeholders, with one exception. For local councillors over age 45, education fails to differentiate among leavers, stayers, and changers, although it does influence the level of aspirations among changers. Education may not be as critical a credential for older women at the local level, especially those whose aspirations do not include high office.

Spouse's Supportiveness of Officeholding

We found in Part II of this report that married women officeholders, especially those in higher-level offices, tend to have husbands who actively support their wives' officeholding. Just as a supportive husband is likely to be an important consideration in the decision to enter public office initially, one would predict that the spouse's political interest, approval, participation, and willingness to share household tasks are important aspects of the development and maintenance of women's political ambitions after achieving office.

Our data show ambition to be fairly consistently related to spousal support (Table 65). The supportiveness of husbands along each of the four support dimensions affects whether local councillors and state legislators desire to leave public office, remain in their current offices, or seek other offices. Among legislative changers, the level of officeholding ambition appears unaffected by degree of spousal supportiveness. At the local level, however, larger percentages of changers with supportive husbands have high officeholding ambition.

Political Characteristics and Experience

In addition to personal and family characteristics, several aspects of the political backgrounds of women in office distinguish more ambitious from less ambitious officeholders. These include size of district population, organizational, party and officeholding experience, self-identified ideology, and party affiliation.

District population. Local officeholders from small districts are likely to face disadvantages in seeking higher offices where the size of the constituency is large and the costs and efforts of campaigning are great. An officeholder from a small district, in comparison with one from a large district, has neither as broad an electoral base nor as much access to organizational networks that could provide funds, workers, and other support for political campaigns.

Local councillors from large districts are considerably more likely to be changers (73%) than those from small districts (48%). Small districts contain higher proportions both of leavers and stayers than do large districts. Among changers, 30% from large districts and only 11% from small districts aspire to offices reflecting high ambition. Although officeholders from large districts tend both to be younger and better educated, the strong relationship between district population and ambition exists quite apart from the age or education of officials.

Organizational, party and officeholding experience. Experience in voluntary organizations, party activities, and public office can teach important skills, assist in developing interpersonal networks, enhance an individual's qualifications in the eyes of voters and party leaders, and increase self-confidence. Any or all of these benefits may contribute to the maintenance and enhancement of officeholding ambitions.

Differences in organizational and political experience appear far more important in distinguishing

Table 65. SUPPORTIVENESS OF SPOUSES IS RELATED TO FUTURE OFFICEHOLDING AMBITIONS

	Husband's Political Interest[a]			Approval of Officeholding[a]			Participation in Political Life[a]			Extra Household Tasks[a]		
	High %	Some %	Low %	High %	Mod. %	Opposed %	Often %	Some %	None %	Often %	Some %	None %
Legislators												
Changers	76	72	(3)	74	68	(3)	74	76	60	75	67	(15)
Stayers	24	28	(7)	26	32	(1)	26	24	40	25	33	(8)
Total	(134)	(65)	(10)	(158)	(47)	(4)	(98)	(74)	(35)	(129)	(52)	(23)
Changers' Amb.												
High	57	54	(2)	55	62	(0)	51	60	(11)	60	39	(7)
Moderate	43	46	(1)	45	38	(1)	49	40	(7)	40	61	(6)
Total	(86)	(41)	(3)	(100)	(29)	(1)	(63)	(48)	(18)	(86)	(28)	(13)
Councillors												
Changers	64	52	47	59	52	55	64	58	50	64	56	47
Stayers	25	34	34	31	33	19	26	30	34	27	31	34
Leavers	11	14	19	10	15	26	10	12	16	9	14	19
Total	(565)	(682)	(162)	(849)	(463)	(96)	(348)	(536)	(517)	(498)	(537)	(365)
Changers' Amb.												
High	20	16	9	19	16	10	26	12	16	22	15	11
Moderate	48	49	51	47	51	51	43	52	50	47	47	55
Low	32	35	41	34	33	39	31	36	34	31	38	34
Total	(337)	(327)	(69)	(467)	(216)	(49)	(207)	(293)	(232)	(303)	(272)	(156)

[a]For precise wording of questions and response categories, see Question 20, items l-o, at end of report.

the more ambitious from the less ambitious among local councillors than among state legislators. Among council members, changers constitute 70% of those with five or more organizational memberships, 51% of those reporting one to four memberships, and 38% of councillors reporting no organizational affiliations. Sixty-three percent of those with past public officeholding experience are changers, in contrast to 50% of those without such experience. Sixty-eight percent of local officeholders who have held party office are changers, but there are only 48% changers among those who have never held a party post.

In contrast to this pattern among local councillors, organizational affiliations and political experience make little difference in the ambitions of state legislators. Those with a large number of member-ships are slightly _less_ likely to be changers (69%) than those with few organizational ties (81%). Approximately equal proportions of changers are found among those with past officeholding experience (70%) and those without such experience (73%). Changers are only slightly more numerous among those who have held party office (72%) than among those who have not (64%). Apparently, for those who have achieved an office at the level of state legislator, the nature of past experience has little influence on the desire to go on to other offices.

Self-identified ideology. Liberals include the highest proportions, and conservatives the lowest proportions, of changers (Table 66). Moreover, among changers, liberals are more likely than moderates, and moderates are more likely than con-servatives, to have high officeholding ambitions (Table 66).

Table 66. CHANGERS ARE MORE LIKELY TO IDENTIFY THEMSELVES WITH LIBERAL IDEOLOGY

Ambition:	Legislators			Councillors		
	Cons. %	Mod. %	Lib. %	Cons. %	Mod. %	Lib. %
Changers	63	66	79	47	54	63
Stayers	37	34	21	35	33	26
Leavers				18	13	11
Total	(35)	(93)	(124)	(637)	(596)	(489)
Changers' Ambition:						
High	(8)	45	31	15	13	25
Moderate	(11)	55	69	42	52	48
Low				43	35	27
Total	(19)	(49)	(91)	(278)	(294)	(284)

The association between ideology and ambition is not merely a product of the tendency for liberals to be younger, to be better educated, or to reside in large districts. Analysis of our data reveals that ideology is independently related to ambition.[66] A higher percentage of liberals than of conserva-tives have ambitions for further office regardless of other characteristics.

It is not clear precisely why liberalism and political ambition should be related. The most obvious explanation for the relationship between liberalism and greater officeholding ambition among women officeholders would be that liberalism encompasses a less traditional and more flexible conception of the roles which women should play in society. The problem with this explanation is that liberalism is also associated with greater ambition for the sample of men included in this study. Thus, the true explanation for this relationship is not likely to be sex-specific.

Perhaps both political ambition and ideology are related to a more general psychological predisposition which enables an individual to cope with change, and even to desire it -- whether it be change at the societal level, as is the case with liberalism, or change at the personal level, as is the case with officeholding ambitions. This explanation is given some support by the finding that conservative women are nearly as likely as liberal women to desire additional terms in current offices, where no change in responsibilities, colleagues, or location would be necessary.

Party affiliation. Although party affiliation is related to ideological self-identification, it may exert an independent effect on political ambition. Differences in ambitions of Democrats, Republicans and Independents could reflect real differences in the majority-minority standing of the major parties, as well as the limited opportunities available to those outside the major party structures.

In fact, as Table 67 shows, Democrats are slightly more likely to be changers than Republicans and, at the local level, Independents are less ambitious than either. Among changers in state legislatures, Democrats are considerably more likely than Republicans to desire federal, state cabinet and other offices reflecting high ambitions. However, party makes little difference in the level of officeholding ambitions of changers among local councillors.

When self-identified ideology is considered in connection with party identification, we find liberals the most ambitious among Democrats and Independents, but moderates the most ambitious among Republicans. Thus officeholding ambition may

be in part the product of an interaction among the officeholder's personal ideology, the ideological climate of the dominant wing of the officeholder's party, and the structure of opportunity that the party presents for officeholders, especially for women officeholders, to achieve further public offices.

Ambitious Women as Women in Politics

Knowledge of the characteristics associated with political ambition helps us to identify the kinds of women who, if circumstances permit, will continue to serve in public office. Whether because of these characteristics or because of their ambition, we find that ambitious women differ from less ambitious women in their perceptions of the general situation of women in politics, in their evaluations of themselves as officeholders, and in the positions they take on women's issues.

Perceptions of discrimination. Although one might expect perceived limitation in opportunities to hinder the development and maintenance of ambitions, ambitious women are more likely than less ambitious women to perceive obstacles to women's political leadership. Among both local councillors and state legislators, changers -- especially changers with high officeholding ambitions -- are more likely than stayers or leavers to disagree with the statement: "Women have just as much opportunity as men to become political leaders" (Table 68). Similarly, ambitious women are more likely than less ambitious women to agree that "many men in the party organization try to keep women out of leadership roles."

While ambitious women are considerably more likely than less ambitious women to perceive parties as agents of discrimination against women, changers differ little from stayers or leavers in the proportions agreeing that "in general, voters are more reluctant to support women candidates" (Table 68).

Why are ambitious women more likely than less ambitious women to perceive men in the parties as discriminatory, even though they are no more likely to perceive voters as discriminatory? The answer could stem in part from past experience. Changers are more likely than stayers or leavers to have held one or more party positions and, at the local level, to have held one or more elective or appointive offices. As a consequence, if some men in party organizations do try to keep women out of leadership roles, ambitious women probably have had more opportunity than less ambitious women to experience or to observe this discriminatory activity firsthand.

Perceptions of capabilities. We have found ambitious women to be more likely than less ambitious women to perceive leadership opportunities for women as limited and sex discrimination by males in the party as a barrier to women's attainment of leadership roles. Why, then, do ambitious women, who are more likely to perceive obstacles to women's participation, plan to continue on to other offices while those less likely to perceive barriers plan either to stay in the same office or to leave public office completely?

In part, the answer may lie in differences in

Table 67. DEMOCRATS ARE MORE LIKELY TO DESIRE OTHER AND HIGHER OFFICES

Ambition:	Legislators			Councillors		
	Dem. %	Rep. %	Indep. %	Dem. %	Rep. %	Indep. %
Changers	75	68	(7)	60	51	43
Stayers	25	32	(4)	28	33	41
Leavers				12	16	16
Total	(161)	(92)	(11)	(885)	(607)	(290)
Changers' Ambition						
High	69	39	(1)	20	15	14
Moderate	31	61	(4)	45	52	45
Low				35	33	41
Total	(107)	(54)	(5)	(485)	(287)	(110)

Table 68.   AMBITIOUS WOMEN ARE MORE LIKELY TO PERCEIVE DISCRIMINATION WITHIN PARTIES

	State Legislators		Local Councillors		
	Stayers %	Changers %	Leavers %	Stayers %	Changers %
Disagree that women have just as much opportunity as men to become political leaders	40	52	31	30	45
Agree that many men in party organizations try to keep women out of leadership roles	62	76	65	72	80
Agree that, in general, voters are more reluctant to support women candidates	37	39	54	53	57
Approximate totals[a]	(72)	(183)	(226)	(527)	(920)

	Legis. Changers' Amb.		Local Changers' Ambition		
	Moderate %	High %	Low %	Moderate %	High %
Disagree that women have just as much opportunity as men to become political leaders	44	63	33	49	56
Agree that many men in party organizations try to keep women out of leadership roles	72	82	80	80	81
Agree that, in general, voters are more reluctant to support women candidates	38	42	58	57	50
Approximate totals[a]	(68)	(91)	(288)	(328)	(149)

[a]Slight variations in the numbers responding to each item have been averaged.

perceptions of the general capabilities of women in politics and in officeholders' self-ratings of their own performance in office. Relative to leavers and stayers, changers are more likely to agree that women in office devote more time to the job than do men. Changers also are more likely to consider women to be as politically astute as their male colleagues, and to be as well qualified for office.

For most qualities on which officeholders were asked to rate themselves relative to their colleagues, higher proportions of changers than of stayers or leavers rate themselves above average (Table 69). This pattern is more pronounced among local councillors but exists also among state legislators.

Thus, relative to less ambitious women, ambitious women are more likely to view women officeholders generally as equal to or superior to male officeholders. They also give higher ratings to their personal performance in office. It is perhaps this stronger sense of the capabilities both of women generally and of themselves specifically which helps to explain why ambitious women, in spite of their greater tendency to see opportunities as limited, plan to continue in politics while less ambitious women do not.

Views on women's issues. A question of special interest to many concerned with women in politics is whether women who will be serving in political office in the future are likely to be supportive of feminist positions on women's issues. An incomplete but suggestive answer to this question can be gained by comparing the positions of those who desire further office and those who desire to remain in the same office with those who have no plans to continue serving in public office.

Changers at both the state legislative and local levels are more liberal than either stayers or

Table 69.   CHANGERS MAKE HIGHER SELF-RATINGS THAN STAYERS, LEAVERS

Percent Rating Self Above Average[a]:	Legislators		Councillors		
	Stay %	Change %	Leave %	Stay %	Change %
Interpersonal					
Get along w/coll.	69	72	57	64	55
Influence w/coll.	44	56	32	40	48
Argue persuasively	49	61	42	49	66
Make impt. contacts	40	50	34	39	54
Understand others	69	84	68	70	83
Responsive constit.	82	76	56	60	73
Independence	88	94	70	74	87
Commitment					
Interest pub. serv.	81	84	57	69	82
Interest soc. prob.	69	83	59	71	78
Time spent	82	85	49	56	76
Willing work hard	93	95	70	78	89
Knowledge					
General knowledge	69	92	49	51	73
Training and exper.	70	67	39	36	54
Financial judgment	44	56	34	38	49
Political know-how	40	54	16	22	44
Traits					
Organization	63	74	59	63	79
Imagination	61	75	52	62	78
Practicality	65	72	58	61	73
Overall effectiveness	56	77	43	53	72
Approx. totals[b]	(71)	(181)	(232)	(536)	(939)

[a]For precise wording of questions and response categories, see Question 14, item g at end of report.

[b]Slight variations in the numbers responding to each item have been averaged.

Table 70.   CHANGERS ARE MORE LIBERAL ON WOMEN'S ISSUES THAN EITHER LEAVERS OR STAYERS[a]

	State Legislators		Local Councillors		
	Stayers %	Changers %	Leavers %	Stayers %	Changers %
Agree Federal ERA should be ratified	77	88	52	59	70
Disagree Constitution should ban abortion	74	86	61	66	71
Agree homemakers should have social security	65	75	59	55	61
Agree government should provide child care	44	58	31	37	44
Approximate totals[b]	(69)	(180)	(226)	(518)	(922)

	Legis. Changers' Amb.		Local Changers' Ambition		
	Moderate %	High %	Low %	Moderate %	High %
Agree Federal ERA should be ratified	84	95	61	74	83
Disagree Constitution should ban abortion	86	87	66	74	76
Agree homemakers should have social security	70	82	58	62	68
Agree government should provide child care	44	72	38	43	65
Approximate totals[b]	(68)	(92)	(288)	(408)	(151)

[a]For precise wording of questions and response categories, see Question 19 at end of report.

[b]Slight variations in the numbers responding to each item have been averaged.

leavers in their views on the four women's issues included in this study (Table 70). Stayers, in turn, are more liberal than leavers on all issues except social security benefits for homemakers. With this one exception, greater percentages of changers and stayers than of leavers support the ERA, oppose a constitutional amendment to prohibit abortion, favor social security coverage for home- makers, and support government provision of child- care services.

The greatest support for feminist positions on these issues at both the state legislative and local levels is found among changers who aspire to high office. Changers at the local level who aspire to no offices beyond the local or county levels differ little from stayers in their views on women's issues.

The relationship between greater ambition and more feminist issue positions is only in part a re- flection of the more liberal general ideological orientation of the ambitious. When the views of changers, stayers and leavers on women's issues are compared among conservatives, moderates and liberals separately, differences between the ambitious and the less ambitious are diminished but do not dis- appear. Thus, a relationship between feminist issue positions and ambition persists apart from general ideology.

AMBITIONS OF WOMEN COMPARED WITH MEN

Our data show that when women and men who occupy equivalent offices are compared, women are at least as ambitious for public officeholding as men. As noted in the introduction to this report, there is a close correspondence between the percentage of male respondents in each category of office and the percentage of females in the comparison sample who

are in each category of office. Thus, the women and men compared in our study are very similar with regard to current officeholding status.

Previous studies of political elites have found men to be considerably more ambitious politically than women, in contrast to our finding.[67] Research which has explored differences in the ambitions of women and men has for the most part examined delegates to major party conventions. In investigating political ambition, these studies have not compared women and men who are equivalent with respect to current officeholding status. Because male delegates in these studies are much more likely than female dele- gates to hold public office, it is not surprising that women are found to be less ambitious than men with regard to public officeholding.

In addition, past studies frequently have argued that differences in the ambition of women and men are to be expected because of differences in sex-role socialization. However, if one considers instead an alternative approach -- an examination of the various characteristics related to political ambition and the manner in which women and men in office differ in these characteristics -- there is little reason to suspect that female and male officeholders would differ widely in officeholding ambition.

We have found that several characteristics are related to political ambition: age, education, spousal support, district population, organiz- ational memberships, party experience, previous officeholding experience, self-identified ideology, and party affiliation. While women and men in office differ with regard to many of these charac- teristics, the net effect of these differences in contributing to the development of political ambition should favor neither women nor men. Equal proportions of women and men serve in large districts, and equal proportions have prior experience with public officeholding. One would expect the slightly older age of women in office and their lower education relative to men to result in lower ambition for women. However, higher proportions of women in office have supportive spouses, belong to many organizations, have held party office, are Democrats, and are liberals. One would expect these characteristics to lead to higher ambition for women and thus roughly to cancel the effects of older age and lower education in decreasing women's ambition relative to that of men.

Aspirations for Additional Terms, Other Offices

In the samples of women and men currently serving in public office, we find women to be more likely than men to desire an additional term in current office, to be more likely to desire other public offices in the future, and to be about equally as likely to aspire ultimately to a high-level office. Women are more likely than men to be changers and less likely to be stayers or leavers.

Additional term in office. Women are as ambitious and perhaps more ambitious than men in planning to seek an additional term in current office. As Table 71 shows, there are virtually no differences between women and men in this respect among legislators, county commissioners and mayors. Among local councillors, proportionately more women (62%) than men (48%) desire an additional term. In the two samples as a whole, another term

in current office is planned by 64% of the women and by 55% of the men.

Other public office. Intentions to seek one or more public offices other than the one now held display a pattern similar to plans for an additional term (Table 71). Higher percentages of women than men among local councillors and county commissioners desire other public offices. Approximately equal proportions of women and men in state legislatures and mayoralties would like to hold other offices. In the total male and female samples, 57% of men and 44% of women eventually would like to hold other public offices. Again, women appear no less ambitious than men, and perhaps more ambitious.

Highest office desired. Nearly equal proportions of female and male officeholders are ambitious for high-level offices (Table 72). In the total sample, 16% of the men and 14% of the women aspire to federal, state cabinet or other offices reflecting high ambition.

Changers, stayers, and leavers. Similarity in the proportions of women and men aspiring to high office occurs because of two patterns in the data which tend to offset one another: (1) a higher proportion of women than of men are changers and a lower proportion are leavers (Table 73); (2) among changers, male changers more often aspire to high office than do female changers (Table 73). Thus, only among changers could slightly higher proportions of men be considered more ambitious. In the total samples of male and female officeholders, equal proportions

Table 71.   LARGER PROPORTIONS OF WOMEN THAN OF MEN PLAN ADDITIONAL TERMS OR PLAN TO SEEK OTHER OFFICES

	Legislature		County Comsn.		Mayoralty		Local Council		Total	
	Wmn. %	Men %	Wmn. %	Men %	Wmn. %	Men %	Wmn. %	Men %	Wmn. %	Men %
Probably, definitely will seek additional term in current office:	85	80	58	59	51	(11)	62	48	64	55
Total	(96)	(57)	(92)	(51)	(55)	(22)	(475)	(224)	(718)	(358)
Would like one or more other offices:	68	66	58	36	55	(11)	55	41	57	44
Total	(91)	(55)	(85)	(52)	(53)	(21)	(451)	(221)	(680)	(353)

Table 72.   APPROXIMATELY EQUAL PROPORTIONS OF WOMEN AND MEN ARE AMBITIOUS FOR HIGH OFFICE

Highest Level of Other Public Office Desired:	Legislature		County Comsn.		Mayoralty		Local Council		Total	
	Wmn. %	Men %	Wmn. %	Men %	Wmn. %	Men %	Wmn. %	Men %	Wmn. %	Men %
High	45	42	21	13	8	(4)	8	9	14	16
Moderate	14	14	26	15	24	(3)	24	16	23	16
Low	1	2	6	2	17	(3)	21	12	16	9
Office not specified	8	7	5	6	6	(1)	3	5	4	5
Desire no other public office	32	34	42	64	45	(10)	45	59	43	55
Total	(91)	(55)	(85)	(52)	(53)	(21)	(451)	(224)	(680)	(353)

Table 73.   LARGER PROPORTIONS OF WOMEN THAN MEN
            WANT OTHER OFFICES

Ambition:	Wmn. %	Men %
Changers	63	49
Stayers	26	29
Leavers	11	22
Total	(619)	(315)
Changers' Ambition:		
High	27	39
Moderate	43	39
Low	30	22
Total	(360)	(141)

of women and men have high officeholding ambitions.

Other Variables and Sex Differences in Ambition

While our data show women to be no less ambitious than men, we should ask as a final question whether differences between female and male officeholders in characteristics related to ambition have obscured an underlying tendency for women to be less ambitious. If women and men in office were equal in age, education, spousal support, organizational involvements, political experience, party affiliation and ideology, then would we find men more ambitious politically than women? Our data do not permit a complete answer to this question.[68] However, no one of the characteristics associated with ambition accounts for the finding that women are as ambitious as men. When we compare women and men who are in equivalent categories of age, education, spousal supportiveness, size of district, political experience, party affiliation or ideology, we find in each comparison that higher proportions of women than of men are changers, and lower proportions of women than of men are leavers.

Further research on the political ambitions of women relative to men currently serving in comparable positions is needed. Replication of our finding that women are at least as ambitious as men would suggest that the paucity of women serving in offices at the state and federal levels cannot be attributed to lack of political ambition as readily as it has been in the past. Rather, confirmation of our research findings would call attention to the need for closer examination of the way in which structures of political opportunity restrict the achievement of ambitious women.

WOMEN NO LONGER IN OFFICE

The ambitions of officeholders refer to some unknown combination of plans, aspirations and fantasy. Clearly, a number of contingencies intervene in producing various career outcomes, and these contingencies are located in the personal lives and characteristics of officeholders as well as in the structure of opportunities confronting them.

Which officeholders actually leave public office and which remain is a question that has not been addressed directly be researchers. In an effort to

identify some of the circumstances associated with remaining in office or leaving, we have questioned a group of officeholders who responded to the 1975 survey but who are no longer in office. These former officeholders are compared with a group of current officeholders who held similar offices in 1975. (For a description of the samples, see the introduction to this report.)

Leaving Office

Most of the 188 former officeholders in our sample left office voluntarily: 17% resigned before their term of office expired; 47% completed their term of office but decided not to run for re-election; only a little more than a third (36%) were defeated in a bid for re-election. Among those who did not run for re-election, 12% ran for higher office.

Voluntary leavetaking. Reasons for early resignation or failure to run for re-election vary widely, ranging from those bearing on the office itself to occupational demands or preferences, to relocation of the family or other family concerns. Reasons mentioned by more than 5% of voluntary leavers are listed in Table 74. Very few of the former officeholders indicate that they left out of some sense of not performing well. Only 2% feel that they lacked the technical expertise for doing a really effective job, and only 2% report that they felt they could not win re-election. Advanced age is mentioned by only 1%. It appears that women voluntarily leave office largely in

Table 74.   WOMEN LEAVE OFFICE VOLUNTARILY FOR A
            WIDE VARIETY OF REASONS

Reasons for Leaving Office[a]:	Voluntary Leavers %
Wanted to run for higher office	12
Felt I had accomplished what I had set out to do	18
Felt I had done my share and it was someone else's turn	25
Disillusionment with what the office could accomplish	21
Disillusionment with my colleagues in office	14
Demands of a separate occupation	21
Wanted to take a job I felt would be more rewarding	13
Wanted to go back to school	8
Financial pressures	7
Children needed more of my time	16
Husband needed more of my time	13
Husband was actively opposed to my holding office	8
Other family members needed more of my time	7
Family moved to a new area	13
Total[b]	(119)

[a]Reasons given by less than 5% of respondents are omitted from table.

[b]Total percentages do not add to 100 because each respondent could give more than one reason.

response to other opportunities, other role demands with higher priority, or loss of interest in the activities of office.

Election defeat. Among the 80 women defeated for re-election, only 19% lost primary campaigns. Forty-six percent were defeated in partisan general elections, and the remaining 35% lost nonpartisan elections. Defeats took place in multi-member districts nearly as often (46%) as in single-member districts (54%).[69] In neither type of district was there more than a small percentage of instances in which other women emerged as winners, although replacement by a woman appears to be less likely in the single-member district, where only one winner was a woman in 36 races for which information was reported. In multi-member districts, where a total of 108 seats were at stake, women took only eight.

Women who lost elections were asked to comment on any aspect of the election of special significance to them. All of the resulting comments express perceived reasons for losing. As is the case with expressed reasons for leaving office voluntarily, perceived causes for electoral defeat vary widely. Table 75 lists reasons given by more than 5% of election losers. Most prominent among their perceptions -- of interest because these women had already been elected at least once before suffering defeat -- is that opposition to women in politics contributed to their loss. Apart from discrimination against women, the characteristics of the district, the nature of the opposition and the political behavior of the candidate herself are almost equally likely to be mentioned as causes of election defeat.

Table 75.   OPPOSITION TO WOMEN IN OFFICE IS ONE OF MANY PERCEIVED CAUSES OF ELECTION LOSS

Reasons for Defeat[a]:	Election Losers
	%
Opposition to women in office	20
Did not campaign actively	13
Inadequate financial support	12
Lack of party support	12
Smear campaign tactics	12
Loss of constituent support through stands on controversial issues	10
Office especially targeted by opposition	8
Poor media coverage	8
Poor campaign techniques	7
Total[b]	(61)

[a]Reasons given by less than 5% of respondents are omitted from table.

[b]Total percentages do not add to 100 because each respondent could give more than one reason.

Comparison of Former with Current Officeholders

In an effort to learn more about the circumstances of leaving office than might be apparent in the

reasons reported by officeholders, we have compared systematically voluntary leavetakers and defeated officeholders with women who continue to serve in public office. Our comparison has included all the major variables examined in this report and, although some noteworthy differences have emerged, our general conclusion is that former officeholders do not differ widely from women currently serving in public office. We shall return to this point after a brief description of those characteristics that do seem to distinguish former from current officeholders.

Voluntary leavers. In comparison with current officeholders, voluntary leavers have less education and political experience, somewhat less self-confidence about their personal performance as officials, more of a sense of conflict between family and political life, and greater conservatism with regard to women's roles. In some ways, voluntary leavers resemble current officeholders who plan to resign at the end of their current term of office.

Voluntary leavers have less formal education (42% college graduates) than those who remain in office (53% college graduates). Higher proportions of voluntary leavers (75%) than of current officeholders (52%) serve in districts with under 10,000 population. Only 26% of voluntary leavers had held public office prior to their most recent office, in comparison with 40% of current officeholders. Thirty-four percent of voluntary leavers but 40% of current officeholders have held party office. In evaluating their performance as officials, voluntary leavers are less likely than current officeholders to rate themselves highly on general knowledge and intelligence, past training and experience, financial judgment, time devoted to office, and practicality.

Our data offer some evidence that voluntary leavers have relatively more traditional conceptions of women's roles. Although they are similar to current officeholders in perceptions of spousal support, 73% perceive a high level of political activity on the part of women as detrimental to family life, in comparison with 51% of current officeholders. Only 58% of voluntary leavers favor ratification of the ERA, in contrast to 71% of women currently in office. Only 35% support governmental provision of child care, in contrast to 45% of current officeholders.

Defeated officeholders. The dimensions that distinguish officeholders defeated in elections from current officeholders differ somewhat from those that distinguish voluntary leavers. Defeated officeholders differ from current officeholders in age and education, spousal support and perceptions of conflict between family and politics, party involvements, and perceptions of discrimination against women.

Officeholders defeated in elections are slightly older than current officeholders. While there are no differences in the proportions under 40 or over 60, we find 40% of the defeated and 32% of current officeholders in the 50-59 year age category. Conversely, 22% of the defeated but 31% of the current officeholders are between 40 and 49 years of age. Defeated officeholders also have slightly less education as a group, with 47% college graduates in contrast to 53% college graduates among current officeholders. This pattern of differences suggests the possibility that some portion of defeated officeholders may have found their age and education to be disadvantages in their attempts to remain in office.

Defeated officeholders perceive higher levels of spousal support than current officeholders. For example, 65% of the defeated report that their husbands approved and encouraged their officeholding, in comparison with 51% of current officeholders who report high approval from spouses. However, defeated officeholders, like voluntary leavers, are more likely to perceive conflict between women's political activity and family life. Sixty-three percent of the defeated in comparison to 51% of current officeholders see an active political life as damaging to family life. It is possible that defeated officeholders experienced relatively more tension between family and politics as officeholders. It is also possible that the experience of election defeat has contributed to their perception of conflict.

Defeated officeholders are no more liberal in their positions on women's issues than current officeholders. Yet, as already described, defeated officeholders attribute their election loss to oppostion to women in politics more often than to any other single cause. In addition, higher proportions of the defeated than of current officeholders perceive unequal political opportunity for women generally (59% defeated vs. 43% current), discrimination by party leaders (84% defeated vs. 71% current), and discrimination from voters (66% defeated vs. 50% current). They also are more likely to mention one or more difficulties encountered as a result of being a women in office (77% defeated vs. 63% current) and, at the same time, they are less likely to name any advantage to being a woman in office (45% defeated vs. 63% current). Perhaps women defeated in elections have served in districts presenting more than ordinary resistance to women in politics. It is also possible, however, that perceptions of discrimination tend to be heightened by the experience of losing an election.[70]

Those defeated in elections show markedly stronger involvements with political parties than do current officeholders. Sixty-nine percent of the defeated but only 40% of current officeholders have held party office. In addition, more than twice the proportion of defeated (13%) as of current officeholders (6%) report giving major emphasis to representing the programs of their party in their official activities.

Did a strong party involvement play a part in the defeat of officeholders in our sample? Approximately one-third of defeated officeholders lost nonpartisan elections. Perhaps a strong party involvement is a disadvantage in such elections. In addition, we note that defeated officeholders are slightly more likely to be Democrats (62%) than are current officeholders (53%). Since we found in Part III of this report that recent entrants to office are slightly more likely to be Republican than those with longer tenure of office, the defeated officeholders may reflect recent gains by Republicans. Perhaps those with strong party involvements are more likely than others to lose their bids for re-election when electorates shift

their preferences from one party to the other or when they return to usual patterns of voting after a brief period of crossover.

Political Ambitions of Former Officeholders

For large proportions of former officeholders, leaving public office has neither signaled nor precipitated a loss of interest in serving in public office. In their high ambitions for future public office, those defeated in elections resemble the changers among current officeholders. Seventy-four percent of the defeated desire other public offices, in comparison with 59% of current officeholders. Even among voluntary leavetakers, 41% would like to hold public office in the future, suggesting that a number of "voluntary" leavers are in fact "reluctant" leavers. Among officeholders who desire other offices, the defeated (36%) are as likely as current officeholders (32%) to have high officeholding ambitions, although only 17% of voluntary leavers have ambitions for high office.

In our comparison of former with current officeholders, we have noted the differences observed. We also have commented that these differences are few relative to the large number of variables examined. The absence of consistent and strong differences between current and former officeholders, in combination with the finding that large proportions of former officeholders remain ambitious for future office, suggests that external circumstances may be at least as important as characteristics of officeholders in determining which officeholders leave and which remain.

The political ambitions of officeholders represent only one indication of the likelihood of continuing in office. For a clearer understanding of the phenomenon of leavetaking, we must examine also the characteristics of the districts in which officeholders serve. In addition, we must separate from voluntary leavers the "reluctant leavers," who resign from public office because their families move or because of competing demands from family and/or occupation. Finally, in order to evaluate the extent to which gender affects the likelihood of leaving public office and the circumstances of leaving, we require research that includes the study of _men_ who remain and men who leave public office.

CONCLUSION TO PART VI

Politically ambitious women are different from the less ambitious. They are the younger, the better educated, the more experienced organizationally and politically. They serve in the larger districts. They are more likely than other officeholders to rate their own performance in office highly. The married among them are more likely to have the support and encouragement of their spouses. They are more liberal in their ideological orientation, are more liberal in their positions on women's issues, and are more likely to perceive women's capabilities as equal or superior to those of men. These characteristics suggest a nontraditional conception of the role of women and often a desire to change the status of women in society. If politically ambitious women realize their ambitions, then higher-level offices may be filled increasingly by women interested in altering the societal position of women.

The majority of women in office are committed to public officeholding and ambitious for advancement. The typical female officeholder is as ambitious as her male counterpart. Even women no longer in public office display considerable interest in public officeholding, for large proportions would like to hold office in the future.

On the one hand, we find large proportions of women in office to be ambitious. On the other hand, we find large proportions of women in office perceiving discrimination against women, especially from male party leaders and from colleagues. And the more ambitious a woman is, the more likely is she to perceive discrimination. The juxtaposition of ambition and perception of discrimination suggests that one cannot accept without question the validity of assertions that women are not nominated as party candidates or appointed to higher-level positions in larger numbers because of difficulties in finding qualified women who will accept such positions. True, there are women who lack commitment to public officeholding and who would prefer to leave office. There are others who would prefer to remain in their present positions. But such women are proportionately no more numerous than men, perhaps less numerous.

If there ever was a reality to the assumption of low ambition among women, that reality appears to have become a myth. Yet, the persistence of myth also molds reality. The idea of low political ambition among women itself may serve as an obstacle to women's political achievement. If future research supports our finding that politically active women are as ambitious as similarly situated men, then the myth of women's low ambition should be discarded.

PART VII.   CONCLUSION TO PROFILE, 1977

Our purpose in this profile of women in public office has been to present a wide variety of research findings, keeping commentary to a minimum and allowing the reader to select aspects of our description to use for particular purposes. Nonetheless, a number of broader points emerge from this variety, connecting discreet research findings and also raising questions for future research. In this concluding section, we shall comment briefly on a few of these points.

Avenues of Political Recruitment of Women vs. Men

Although the proportions of elective offices filled by women are increasing, women remain a small minority of officeholders. A number of research findings indicate that women who do achieve public office follow routes into office that differ from those typical for men. These differing paths of recruitment may reflect special difficulties experienced by women who wish to enter political office, difficulties stemming in part from the gender-linked roles of women in the society at large, in part from discrimination against women by political leaders.

Political activity has not been as socially legitimate for women as for men. Perhaps as a consequence, family support appears to be a basic condition for officeholding by women. Few married women in office lack the support and encouragement of their husbands. Not only are men in office less likely to perceive their spouses as supportive but also men are more likely to perceive conflict between politics and family life for politically active women and men alike.

Women have less formal education than men in office, and their occupations are heavily concentrated in areas such as teaching and secretarial work that may not receive ready acceptance as qualifications for public officeholding. However, women may compensate for their lack of credentials in these areas through a more intensive apprenticeship in voluntary organizations and political party activities. Women belong to more organizations than do men, and they are more likely to have held offices in their political parties.

Although women have had relatively extensive party experience, most women in public office feel that many men in party organizations try to exclude women from leadership roles. The fact that women's past public officeholding is more likely to have been appointive, while that of men is more likely to have been elective, may be an indirect indicator of a tendency for party organizations to reward party service by women with minor appointive offices in place of nominations for elective office.

The result of lesser educational and occupational credentials, greater organizational and party involvements, and perceptions that party leaders discriminate may be a period of political apprenticeship prior to holding elective office that is longer for women than for men. If so, a longer apprenticeship may help to explain women's relatively older age at entry into office.

Barriers to Mobility

Once in office, women are at least as committed to public officeholding and as ambitious for other public offices as their male colleagues. Yet, women may be encountering gender-based obstacles to political mobility. Women officeholders are less likely than men with similar tenure in office to hold leadership positions within their governing bodies. They are less likely to chair committees, and they are less likely to be satisfied with their committee assignments. Although men in office perceive women's difficulties as related to family pressures, inadequacies of background, personality faults or constituents' prejudices against women, women officeholders perceive their major difficulties to stem from prejudice and discrimination on the part of their colleagues and of male political leaders. The more politically ambitious an officeholder, the more likely she is to perceive discrimination from these sources.

Political Perspective of Women in Office

Gender is a component of political outlook and performance as well as of political recruitment and mobility. Women in office are ideologically more liberal than men, and they take more feminist positions on women's issues such as ERA, abortion, social security for homemakers, child care, and the role of government and industry in assuring equal rights for women. In addition to differing from men in issue positions, women report different emphases in the performance of their official duties. They are more concerned with constituent relations, with policy development and with being well-informed on pending issues.

If these subjective perspectives are being translated into political actions, then the participation of women in public affairs is changing both the style and content of governmental decision-making. The distinctive impact of women is likely to grow as more women achieve public office and will continue as long as women and men continue to have differing roles in the society.

Variations Among Women in Office

To be precise, one should speak not of a profile of women in office but of many profiles. The patterned variations among officeholders are so numerous that one must question the descriptive adequacy of attempts to portray "political woman" as a single type.

Women officeholders vary by type of office held in most characteristics examined: in ethnic or racial identification, in education, occupation, numbers and types of organizational affiliations, family income, spousal support of officeholding, perceptions of conflict between family and political life, self-rating of official performance, ideology, feminist orientation, perceptions of women's situation in politics, and political ambition. Some of these variations form consistent trends, with the proportions possessing a particular characteristic rising or falling regularly from one level of officeholding to the next. But others show less regular patterning, emphasizing the point that caution must be exercised in efforts to generalize to all women in office from studies of women in a particular type of office.

In addition to type of office held, a number of other characteristics divide women officeholders into fairly distinct groups. Among the more important of these are the size of district population, age, and political ambition.

Since both the characteristics of the population and the nature of political offices differ in small and large districts, district population sharply separates the characteristics, orientations and activities of officeholders. Most notably, women holding office in small districts are less educated, are less involved in organizations, are less politically experienced, devote less time to officeholding, are less ambitious politically, and are more conservative ideologically.

The age of officeholders is also important in delineating their political status and behavior.

Younger officeholders often differ from older officeholders in ways characteristic of women in the general population who are at their stage of the life-cycle. For example, younger officeholders are members of fewer organizations than older officeholders, have less political experience, are more likely to describe themselves as liberal, are more ambitious but have somewhat lower levels of confidence. Younger officeholders also manifest ongoing trends in the larger society, for they are less likely to be married or to be mothers, are better educated, and in some offices are less likely to have traditionally female occupations.

Finally, politically ambitious women differ from less ambitious officeholders in a wide variety of characteristics, reflecting both causes and consequences of ambition. Most prominently, ambitious women are younger, are better educated, receive more encouragement from their husbands, serve in larger districts, are more self-confident of their performance as officials, are more liberal, more feminist, and more conscious of sex discrimination.

Women Who Leave Office

The large differences resulting from a comparison between ambitious and unambitious women are not replicated in the comparison of former with current officeholders. Our initial exploration of the circumstances of leaving public officeholding suggests that women who become former officeholders are not dramatically different in their backgrounds, officeholding activities and political orientations from women who continue to serve. Election defeat may be more a function of district characteristics and events than of individual qualities and motivations. Moreover, substantial proportions of voluntary leavetakers relinquish their offices because of external circumstances such as illness or relocation of the family.

An implication of these findings about former officeholders is that political ambition is likely to be a very inexact predictor of future officeholding. Many women who leave office are politically ambitious (and it is likely that many who remain are relatively unambitious). Women who are defeated in elections remain highly ambitious, despite their election loss. A portion of the women who leave office voluntarily are not interested in politics or the activities of office and lack confidence in their own capabilities or qualifications. Even among voluntary leavetakers, however, at least two in five would like to return to public office.

Needed Research

Our report has consisted principally of a description of women in public office. However, description is not explanation, and questions can be appended to most of the findings presented: "Why?" "How?" "With what consequences?" Much additional research and analysis are required, to eliminate competing explanations and thus to provide appropriate interpretations.

Many important questions cannot be answered through ordinary survey research. For example, there is a need for longitudinal studies that will clarify the extent to which women officeholders possess particular characteristics and attitudes before entering office versus the extent to which these change as a consequence of officeholding. There is also a need for studies in which groups, structural patterns or policies -- rather than individuals -- are the focus of analysis, to clarify the manner in which the characteristics and attitudes of women as individuals become reflected in the functioning of governing bodies.

Below are listed a number of questions for additional research that have arisen from our study. Although the list is long, it contains only a sampling of the many research questions stimulated by the findings of our survey.

Variations among officeholders. What explains the differing characteristics and orientations of women in different kinds of political offices? Do women enter different offices from candidate pools that are identifiably distinct though overlapping? Or do women change in patterned ways as a result of holding different types of offices?

Officeholding and the family. What constitutes family support for the political activity of women? How is this support developed and maintained? What are the consequences of lack of support? In what ways do women's definitions of their maternal and spousal responsibilities affect their career patterns?

Age of officeholders. Why are women older than men when they enter office? What are the implications for subsequent career patterns of differing ages of entry into political office?

Appointive vs. elective office. Why are women more likely than men to have served in appointive office? What are the consequences for political careers of differing sequences of elective and appointive offices?

Party experience. Why, since larger proportions of women than men have held party offices, do such large proportions of women perceive discrimination from men in political parties? Are women permitted to hold party office and minor appointive offices while being overlooked as candidates for elective office?

Political ambition. What explains the finding that women are as politically ambitious or more ambitious than men? Are the women recruited to public officeholding such a select group that their political ambition is predictable? Or has a rough equality of ambition between other groups of women and men gone largely unrecognized, obscured by inadequate research analyses? How are the political ambitions of women affected by various experiences of officeholding? By what processes is ambition expanded, decreased, or maintained unchanged?

Officeholding and constituent relations. Why are women officeholders more oriented to constituent relations than men holding office? Does the pattern result from general sex-role orientations that lead women to be more humanistic in outlook and more concerned with service to others? Does it result from more extensive organizational involvement of women prior to and after entry into public office?

What are the consequences of a greater orientation to the public for other aspects of official performances?

Beliefs about women in politics. What explains the differing perceptions of women and men regarding the nature of women's qualifications for office and the extent and sources of sex discrimination? Are women's qualifications being perceived by men through the filter of ill-considered stereotypes? Are women overestimating their qualifications in relation to the demands of their offices? Do women who are excluded from the informal socialization and sponsorship occurring in male networks tend to misunderstand the informal demands and qualifications of officeholding? What are the consequences of sex differences in evaluations of women as officeholders for the effective functioning of governing bodies in which women and men serve as colleagues?

Ideology. To what extent are the greater liberalism and more feminist orientations of women in public office reflections of the kinds of women who seek public office, and to what extent are they the result of experiences in office? In what ways are the more feminist positions of women officeholders apparent in their activities as officials? Do such attitudes affect, for example, voting patterns, attempts to influence political agendas, the kinds of legislation introduced, administrative policy decisions, hiring and personnel practices, political appointments?

The fact that most research findings in this report raise further reserach questions reflects, in part, limitations on the analysis that could be accommodated within these pages. However, it also attests to the recency of research interest in politically active women,[71] and to the need for accumulation of studies that give serious attention to describing and explaining the role of gender in politics. A note of finality in ending this report would be inappropriate. Instead, our final statement must be: to be continued.

NOTES

[1]"Profile of Women Holding Office," by Marilyn Johnson and Kathy Stanwick, is the 37-page statistical essay in Center for the American Woman and Politics, *Women in Public Office: A Biographical Directory and Statistical Analysis* (1976). Reprints of the essay are available for $3.00 from the Center for the American Woman and Politics, Eagleton Institute of Politics, Rutgers University, New Brunswick, N. J. 08901.

[2]Partial exceptions are Diamond (1977), who examines legislators in four New England states, and Leader (1977), who analyzes the ERA vote among state legislators. Among studies with small and restricted samples are: Gehlen's (1977a, 1977b, 1969) studies of Congresswomen; Merritt's (1977) investigation of municipal council members in Cook County, Illinois; Mezey's (1977) analysis of

local council members in Connecticut; Bers' (1976) analysis of school board members in Cook County, Illinois; King and McAuliffe's (1976) comparison of male and female county supervisors in Pennsylvania; Kirkpatrick's (1974) study of state legislators. Studies of party elites include: Soule and McGrath (1977), Kirkpatrick (1976), Costantini and Craik (1972), Jennings and Thomas (1968).

[3]Although extensive efforts were made to collect complete and accurate information, some gaps remain. A complete, current list of officials at one or more governmental levels was unavailable for the states following: Illinois (mayors and local councillors), Missouri (township officials) Nebraska (township officials), New York (township officials, mayors and local councillors), Wisconsin local councillors). In a few states, lists arrived too late for questionnaire mailings: Arizona (mayors and local councillors), Illinois (township officials), Michigan (township officials), Mississippi (mayors and local councillors). In some states, local elections were held while the data-gathering process was underway. Questionnaires could not be sent to newly-elected local officials in Colorado, Connecticut, Maine, Maryland, Massachusetts, Minnesota, Missouri and Oklahoma. However, the total numbers in the state summaries on p. xvii reflect current lists where available, even though questionnaires were not mailed to officeholders in the instances cited above.

[4]Perhaps as a result of a lengthy questionnaire and the time of mailing, the response rate is not as high as it was in the 1975 study. The questionnaire is nearly twice as long as that used in 1975, which may have increased nonresponse. Because we mailed in late spring and early summer, in contrast to the March through May mailing in 1975, a number of officeholders were on vacation and did not receive their questionnaire in time for inclusion in the survey; others, for whom only office addresses were available, did not receive the questionnaire in time because their governing bodies were not in session.

[5]We utilized systematic sampling procedures, selecting every Nth name after a random start on a list of names for a particular office and state. The sampling interval was varied for each office and state to yield a sample for mailing that would roughly equal the number of female officeholders in each category.

[6]State legislators, county commissioners, mayors and local councilmen were sampled in Georgia, Kansas, Minnesota, New Jersey, Oregon, Texas, Vermont and Wyoming. Legislators and county commissioners alone were surveyed in Arizona, Indiana, Maryland, North Carolina, Pennsylvania, South Dakota, Tennessee and Washington.

[7]This procedure has resulted in samples of current and former officeholders from states and categories as follows: state legislators only -- Colorado, Connecticut, Hawaii, Idaho, Michigan, Nevada, New Hampshire, New York, West Virginia; county commissioners, mayors and local council members only -- California, Maryland, Massachusetts, Minnesota, Missouri, Nebraska, North Carolina, Oregon, Rhode Island, Texas, Washington; all four offices --

Arizona, Indiana, Montana, New Jersey, New Mexico, Pennsylvania, South Dakota, Tennessee, Vermont, Wyoming.

[8]Only a few types of tables will be encountered in this report. A common type utilizes percentages that add to 100% down each column of the table, as in Table 4. At the bottom of each column is given in parentheses the number of officeholders constituting the base for calculation of the percentages. Officeholders not answering the question on which the tabluation is based, or to whom the question does not apply, are not included in the percentage base. Whenever the total numbers are too small to justify percentages (less than 25 in this report), this fact is signaled by the practice of presenting absolute numbers in parentheses in place of percentages, as illustrated by federal officeholders in Table 6.

At the top of each column is listed the office or category of officeholders for which the tabulation has been made. Down the left-hand side of the table are the characteristics of officeholders (e.g., ethnic identify, age, education) that are being tabulated. Thus each row of a table represents the percentages of officeholders in each category who display a particular characteristic or attitude. Comparisons among officeholders can be made by reading the percentages in each row across. In Table 5, for example, 6% of female respondents serving in the state judiciary identify themselves as black, as compared with 3% in the state executive, 8% in state senates, etc.

In a few tables, percentages for subcategories may be given in addition to major divisions. In Table 8, for example, the major division employed vs. not currently employed are subdivided by whether current employment is full or part time, and by when those not currently employed were last employed. In Table 9, the percentages in selected occupations are given in addition to the percentages in each of the major occupational categories of the U. S. Census.

In some tables, percentages in each column do not add to 100% because each officeholder may fit into more than one of the categories being tabulated. For example, Table 10 reports the percentages holding membership in various types of organizations.

Occasionally, the percentages in a table refer to items mentioned rather than total number of officeholders. For example, Table 37 shows the percentages of total issues and projects of particular kinds reported by officeholders as of importance to them.

Medians are utilized in some tables. The median is the middle number in a series of numbers; 50% of cases are at or above the median value and 50% are at or below the same value. Thus if the numbers 25, 32, 42, 54 and 67 represent years of age of five officeholders, the median is 42 years. An example of reporting of medians is in Table 6, which shows median ages of officeholders in each category of office and, for county and local officeholders, for those in large and small districts. The number of officeholders included in the calculation of the median is found in parentheses below the median. Whenever the base for calculation is small (less than 25), this fact is signaled by the practice of placing the median in parentheses. For example, the median age of federal appointees is 38 years. The number of officeholders on which the median is calculated is 22. Since this number is less than 25, the median age of federal appointees is shown in parentheses.

[9]Among the many issues of interpretation of research conducted at a single time period, two arise repeatedly in this analysis.

Problems of interpreting the causal direction of events. Statements of relationship between two or more phenomena will appear throughout this report. For example, we note that employed women devote fewer hours to their offices, on the average, than unemployed women. This simple research finding does not lead directly to an understanding of the process at work. It may be that employed women reduce the strain associated with multiple roles by giving fewer hours to their offices. Or it may be that after entering office, some women find that the office requires little of their time and enables them to seek outside employment. It is also possible that employment and hours devoted to office are not directly related in any causal chain. Some additional situation, such as relatively low socio-economic status of the family, may lead some women both into the labor force and into less important and less demanding public offices, with no direct connection between the two events found to occur together.

Problems of interpreting variations by age or by tenure of office. Because of considerable interest in the question of whether women currently entering public office differ significantly from their predecessors, this report comments on differences in our data between younger and older women, and between those in their first term and more experienced officeholders. These differences can be interpreted in several ways. (The more technically minded reader will find a thorough explanation of problems of interpreting age data in Matilda White Riley, Marilyn Johnson and Ann Foner, Aging and Society, Vol. III: A Sociology of Age Stratification. New York: Russell Sage, 1972, Chapter 2.) For example, if women who have held office for more than one term are different from newcomers, this could occur: (a) because newly elected women today differ from newly elected women in past elections; (b) because women entering office are similar no matter when they are elected but change with experience in office; (c) because women are similar when they are elected, but only certain kinds of women go on to serve a second term; (d) some combination of the above. Only successive repetitions of the research over a period of time can help to eliminate all but one of these competing explanations.

[10]Since the actual number of women officeholders continually varies, and since there is no precise and up-to-date count of the total number of officeholders at the local level, we have supplied ranges representing our best estimates.

[11]This figure was calculated by excluding mayors in Kentucky, New York and Wisconsin and local council members in Illinois, Michigan, Minnesota, New York, Ohio, Pennsylvania and Wisconsin.

[12]The National Roster of Black Elected Officials, published annually by the Joint Center for Political Studies, Washington, D.C., supplies a source of detailed information about black women officials. See also Fitch (1977), Prestage (1977), Conyers and Wallace (1976).

[13]See Table 10, page xxvii in Johnson and Stanwick (1976).

[14]We have used the Hodge-Siegel-Rossi scale of occupational prestige as adapted to the 1970 U. S. Census Occupational Codes by the National Opinion Research Center. The scores are constructed from the results of national surveys that ask respondents to estimate the social standing of occupations. When applied to U. S. Census occupational classifications, scores range from 9 (bootblack) to 82 (physician). (For details of the scoring system see National Data Program for the Social Sciences, Codebook for the Spring 1977 General Social Survey, Appendix G. Chicago: National Opinion Research Center, University of Chicago, July 1977.) In the 1977 General Social Survey conducted by NORC, the median score of occupational prestige for a sample of women and men in the general population was 36 (calculated by the author from distributions supplied in the codebook). In contrast, the median score of women in office is 48. Those who have achieved higher-level offices average more prestigious occupational backgrounds, as shown in Table 9.

[15]For example, see Olsen (1974), Verba and Nie (1972), and Erbe (1964).

[16]Verba and Nie (1972).

[17]See, for example, Olsen (1974), Verba and Nie (1972), Hodge and Treiman (1968), Hausknecht (1962).

[18]Cutler (1976), Johnson (1975).

[19]This exception to the general pattern may occur because a disproportionate number of the very old -- those over age 70 -- are found among those entering office before 1975. The reduction of organizational involvements among those of advanced old age is a common phenomenon.

[20]Just as age does not explain differences by tenure of office in the level of organizational affiliation, tenure of offices does not explain age patterns of membership. Among both newcomers and those with longer tenure, officeholders under age 35 average fewer memberships.

[21]The specific organizations named by respondents have been re-classified into fifteen categories. These categories are adaptations of those used in several studies of the population conducted by the National Opinion Research Center (see, for example, Verba and Nie, 1972). Organizations are classified on the basis of type of membership restriction (e.g., ethnic, occupational, religious) and, where such restrictions are not specified, in terms of the manifest primary purpose of the organization. In making classifications, extensive use was made of organizational descriptions in the Encyclopedia of Associations, 8th edition, vol. 1 edited by Margaret Fisk. Detroit: Gale Research Co., 1973.

[22]Our report of women in public office in 1975 showed the marital status of women in public office to be similar to that of women in the general population (Johnson and Stanwick, 1976, Table 14, page xxx).

[23]See Question 20, parts l, m, n, o at the end of this report.

[24]For example, see Stoper (1977, p. 323), Bers (1976), Conyers and Wallace (1976, pp. 83-84), Dubeck (1976), Kirkpatrick (1974, p. 38), and Jennings and Thomas (1968, p. 476). But see also Diamond (1977, p. 38), who notes that proportionately more men are either under 40 years or over 65 years of age; King and McAuliffe (1976, p. 4), who found women younger than men among county supervisors; Costantini and Craik (1972, p. 222), who found no consistent age differences by sex among party leaders.

[25]Johnson and Stanwick (1976, Table 9, page xxvii).

[26]A prediction of ultimate convergence assumes no counter tendency for women to remain in office longer than men.

[27]See Footnote 14 for a description of the Hodge-Siegel-Rossi score of occupational prestige.

[28]See, for example, Johnson (1975), Olsen (1974), Verba and Nie (1972), Hodge and Treiman (1968), Almond and Verba (1963), Hausknecht (1962).

[29]A similar finding is reported by Diamond (1977), Lee (1977), and Stoper (1977).

[30]Whether there are proportionately fewer mothers of young children than fathers of young children among officeholders because women are reluctant to enter politics while their children are still young is an issue for further research.

[31]Evidence for this hypothesis is examined among state legislators by Stoper (1977). In a survey of school board members conducted by the National School Boards Association (1974), the encouragement of family members was more likely to be mentioned by women than by men as influential in the decision to run for election. Lex (1977) also finds that spousal support is important in the reasons given by female state legislators for their decision to run for election or re-election.

[32]Hawley (1973, pp. 16-18) reports that elections of mayors and council members are nonpartisan in 64% of communities with over 5,000 population.

[33]Recent entrants have more past officeholding experience than earlier entrants, even with age controlled.

[34]The low salaries of state legislators reflect in part the large number of women legislators from New Hampshire.

[35]For descriptions of the governmental activities in which women officeholders are concentrated, see Diamond (1977), Gehlen (1977a, 1977b, 1969), Johnson and Stanwick (1976), Kirkpatrick (1974).

[36]Kirkpatrick (1976, 1974) reports similar findings, among state legislators and among national convention delegates.

[37]For a complete list of items, see Question 14g at the end of this report.

[38]See also Diamond (1977, ch. 4), Bers (1976), National School Boards Association (1974).

[39]Note the lower levels of husband's supportiveness reported by women in small districts, described in Part II of this report.

[40]See, for example, Riley and Foner (1968, pp. 240-302).

[41]We have calculated, for the comparison sample of women, the total numbers in the relevant offices in 1975 (1,345 women) and 1977 (1,688 women), omitting local councilwomen for Minnesota because of changes in coverage. The resulting ratio is .80, compared with a ration of .78 of men to women in their first term of office.

[42]The evidence on this point remains tentative because we have compared total numbers of officeholders with survey respondents. It is possible that nonrespondents differ in the proportions serving in their first term of office.

[43]Diamond (1977, ch. 4), Bers (1976).

[44]See Prewitt (1970).

[45]A noticeable minority of women in office -- approximately one-fifth of local officeholders and more than two-fifths of state legislators -- have held membership in the League of Women Voters, an organization that explicitly stresses the position of officials as representatives of the public.

[46]Diamond (1977), Gehlen (1977a, 1977b), Bers (1976), Kirkpatrick (1974), Werner (1968).

[47]For example, see Nunn et al. (1978, ch. 7), Pomper (1975, ch. 4), Louis Harris (1972), Erskine (1971), Gruberg (1968), Campbell et al. (1964), Duverger (1955), Stouffer (1955, ch. 6), Lazarsfeld et al. (1948).

[48]Kirkpatrick (1976, pp. 447-455). Since Kirkpatrick finds sex differences on women's issues but no sex differences on other issues, her finding of high correlations among social, political, and sexual ideologies is worth further analysis.

[49]Soule and McGrath (1977). Differences from the Kirkpatrick findings may reflect sampling differences. Soule and McGrath drew quota samples for each state delegation based on sex, race and age. Kirkpatrick does not appear to have controlled for race or age in her analysis. Both studies control for candidate preference. See also Sullivan et al. (1974, pp. 33-34) for still another view of women and men at the 1972 Democratic Convention.

[50]Frankovic (1977), Leader (1977).

[51]Leader (1977). Diamond (1977, pp. 49-51) finds women slightly more liberal than men on all policy issues examined in her study of New England state legislators.

[52]Mezey (1976). Mezey's finding that men are as supportive of the ERA, feminism and the women's movement is counter to our finding of greater liberalism among women on women's issues. The difference may be due in part to differences in sampling procedures. Mezey paired men with women on the same councils, while we randomly sampled

men from municipalities in selected states, whether or not they were serving on the same councils as female respondents. Perhaps men with female colleagues are more likely to take a feminist position on issues than men with no female colleagues.

[53]The findings described in this paragraph result from an analysis in which responses to issues are dichotomized, and the association between each pair of issues is examined with the others controlled. Yule's Q is employed as a measure of the strength of a relationship.

[54]Findings are based on an analysis of the relative sizes of Yule's Q as measures of the association between liberalism/conservatism and agreement/disagreement on an issue.

[55]For example, women and men who are not college graduates are separated by 8 percentage points in their views on social security for homemakers and by 14 percentage points in their views on the ERA. In contrast, women and men with post-graduate degrees are separated by 29 percentage points on social security and by 21 percentage points on the ERA.

[56]For example, women achieve office at older ages and have unusually supportive spouses.

[57]Louis Harris (1972, pp. 15-16).

[58]Kirkpatrick (1976, pp. 462-470).

[59]The questions analyzed in this section are adaptations of those asked of delegates to the 1972 national Democratic and Republican conventions by Jeane Kirkpatrick and associates. Kirkpatrick, (1976, pp. 458-462, 567.) Although Kirkpatrick combines the items into a single index of perceived discrimination, we find that the items relate in differing ways to a number of other variables and, therefore, we examine them separately.

[60]A maximum of three difficulties named by a respondent have been included in classifications and tabulations. If more than three were named, the first three mentioned were included.

[61]For example, see Kirkpatrick (1976, 1974).

[62]Diamond (1977), Farah (1976), Kirkpatrick (1976), Fiedler (1975), Costantini and Craik (1972), Jennings and Thomas (1968). One exception to the general pattern of findings in previous research is in Merritt (1977), where women are found to be no less ambitious for higher office than men.

[63]Because the 13 state legislators who are leavers do not provide enough cases for additional analysis, they are excluded from further description.

[64]The 3 legislators expressing low officeholding ambition are omitted from further analysis. Categories of offices classified as indicating moderate and high levels of officeholding ambition are different for state legislators and for local councillors because of the greater tendency for state legislators to aspire to federal offices. The following offices are considered to represent moderate ambition for state legislative changers but high ambition for changers among local councillors: federal subcabinet position, federal department head below the cabinet level, federal district judge, lieutenant governor, state supreme court judge, state attorney general, state treasurer, secretary of state. All other offices remain classified as set forth in the footnote to Table 62.

[65]Some characteristics also related to political ambition -- such as marital status, age of youngest child or residential stability -- are so heavily age-related that their separate effects cannot be disentangled in the type of analysis utilized in this report.

[66]Age, education, and district size also are independently related to ambition.

[67]See studies listed in Footnote 62.

[68]Unfortunately, sample size does not permit simultaneous controls for all variables showing independent relationships with ambition.

[69]Since the two-thirds of local districts that are nonpartisan also tend to be multi-member districts, the percentages of defeated officials from nonpartisan and multi-member districts may be low in relation to the percentages of these types of districts among total election districts.

[70]See Kingdon (1967) for a discussion of effects of winning and losing on candidates' perceptions.

[71]The Center for the American Woman and Politics has issued a bibliography of work published or in progress between 1950 and 1976 on the political participation of women in the U. S. See Stanwick and Li (1977).

REFERENCES

Almond, Gabriel A., and Verba, Sidney. The Civic Culture. Princeton, N.J.: Princeton University Press, 1963.

Bennett, Stephen E., and Klecka, William R. "Social Status and Political Participation: A Multivariate Analysis of Predictive Power." Midwest Journal of Political Science 14 (August 1970): 355-382.

Bers, Trudy Haffron. "Local Political Elites: Men and Women on Boards of Education." Paper presented at the annual meeting of the Southern Political Science Association, 1976.

Campbell, Angus, et al. The American Voter. New York: John Wiley, 1960.

Center for the American Woman and Politics. Women in Public Office: A Biographical Directory and Statistical Analysis. New York: R.R. Bowker, 1976.

Conyers, James E., and Wallace, Walter L. Black Elected Officials. New York: Russell Sage Foundation, 1976.

Costantini, Edmond, and Craik, Kenneth. "Women as Politicians: The Social Background, Personality, and Political Careers of Female Party Leaders." Journal of Social Issues 28 (1972): 217-236.

Curtis, James. "Voluntary Association Joining: A Cross-National Comparative Note." American Sociological Review 36 (October 1971): 872-880.

Cutler, Stephen J. "Age Differences in Voluntary Association Memberships." Social Forces 55 (1976): 43-58.

Diamond, Irene. Sex Roles in the State House. New Haven, Conn.: Yale University Press, 1977.

Dubeck, Paula J. "Women and Access to Political Office: A Comparison of Female and Male State Legislators." Sociological Quarterly 17 (winter 1976): 42-52.

Duverger, Maurice. The Political Role of Women. Paris: UNESCO, 1955.

Erbe, William. "Social Involvement and Political Activity: A Replication and Elaboration." American Sociological Review 29 (April 1964): 198-215.

Erskine, Hazel. "The Polls: Women's Role." Public Opinion Quarterly 35 (summer 1971): 275-290.

Farah, Barbara G. "Climbing the Political Ladder: The Aspirations and Expectations of Partisan Elites." In New Research on Women and Sex Roles at the University of Michigan, edited by Dorothy G. McGuigan. Ann Arbor, Mich.: University of Michigan Center for the Continuing Education of Women, 1976.

Fiedler, Maureen, R.S.M. "The Participation of Women in American Politics." Paper presented at the annual meeting of the American Political Science Association, 1975.

Fitch, Nancy E. Black Women in Politics. Washington, D.C.: Library of Congress, Congressional Research Service, Government Division, 1977.

Frankovic, Kathleen A. "Sex and Voting in the U.S. House of Representatives: 1961-1975." American Politics Quarterly 5 (July 1977): 315-330.

Gehlen, Frieda L. "Legislative Role Performance of Female Legislators." Sex Roles 3 (1977a): 1-18.

_____. "Women Members of Congress: A Distinctive Role." In A Portrait of Marginality, edited by Marianne Githens and Jewel L. Prestage. New York: David McKay, 1977b.

_____. "Women in Congress: Their Power and Influence in a Man's World." Transaction 6 (October 1969): 36-40.

Gruberg, Martin. Women in American Politics: An Assessment and Sourcebook. Oshkosh, Wis.: Academia Press, 1968.

Hausknecht, Murray. The Joiners: A Sociological Description of Voluntary Association Membership in the United States. Totowa, N.J.: Bedminster Press, 1962.

Hawley, Willis D. Non-Partisan Elections and the Case for Party Politics. New York: John Wiley, 1973.

Hodge, R.W., and Treiman, D.J. "Social Participation and Social Status." American Sociological Review 33 (October 1968): 722-740.

Jennings, M. Kent, and Thomas, Norman. "Men and Women in Party Elites: Social Roles and Political Resources." Midwest Journal of Political Science 7 (November 1968): 469-492.

Johnson, Marilyn. "Changing Patterns of Voluntary Affiliation in the Later Years." Paper presented at the annual meeting of the American Sociological Association, 1975.

_____, and Stanwick, Kathy. Profile of Women Holding Office. Reprinted from Women in Public Office: A Biographical Directory and Statistical Analysis, compiled by Center for the American Woman and Politics. New York: R.R. Bowker, 1976.

Joint Center for Political Studies. National Roster of Black Elected Officials. Washington, D.C.: Joint Center for Political Studies, published annually.

Karnig, Albert K., and Oliver, Walter B., "Election of Women to City Councils." Social Science Quarterly 56 (March 1976): 605-614.

King, Elizabeth G., and McAuliffe, Joan. "Women County Supervisors: Are They Different?" Paper presented at the annual meeting of the American Political Science Association, 1976.

Kingdon, John W. "Politicians' Beliefs about Voters." American Political Science Review 61 (March 1967): 137-145.

Kirkpatrick, Jeane J. The New Presidential Elite. New York: Russell Sage Foundation, 1976.

_____. Political Woman. New York: Basic Books, 1974.

Lazarfeld, Paul F., et al. The People's Choice. New York: Columbia University Press, 2nd edition, 1948.

Leader, Shelah Gilbert. "The Policy Impact of Elected Women Officials." In The Impact of the Electoral Process, edited by Louis Maisel and Joseph Cooper. Sage Electoral Studies Yearbook, Volume III. Beverly Hills, Calif.: Sage Publications, 1977.

Lee, Marcia M. "Why Few Women Hold Public Office: Democracy and Sexual Roles." In A Portrait of Marginality, edited by Marianne Githens and Jewel L. Prestage. New York: David McKay, 1977.

Lex, Louise. "A Summary of the 1976 Survey of Women State Legislators." Summary of research findings from "The Feminist Movement: Its Impact on Women in the State Legislatures." Ph.D. dissertation, University of Iowa, 1977.

Louis Harris and Associates, Inc. The 1972 Virginia Slims American Women's Opinion Poll. New York: Louis Harris and Associates, Inc., 1972.

Merritt, Sharyne. "Women in Municipal Government: The Case of Cook County." Report to the Center for the American Woman and Politics, 1977.

Mezey, Susan Gluck. "Local Representatives in Connecticut: Sex Differences in Attitudes Toward Women's Rights Policy." Paper presented at the annual meeting of the American Political Science Association, 1977.

National School Boards Association. Women on School Boards. Evanston, Ill.: National School Boards Association, 1974.

Nunn, Clyde Z., Crockett, Harry J., and Williams, J. Allen, Jr. Tolerance for Nonconformity. San Francisco: Jossey-Bass, 1978.

Olsen, Marvin E. "Interest Association Participation and Political Activity in the U.S. and Sweden." Paper presented at the annual meetings of the American Sociological Association, 1974.

Pomper, Gerald. Voters' Choice: Varieties of American Electoral Behavior. New York: Dodd, Mead, 1975.

Prestage, Jewel L. "Black Women State Legislators: A Profile." In A Portrait of Marginality, edited by Marianne Githens and Jewel L. Prestage. New York: David McKay, 1977.

Prewitt, Kenneth. "Political Ambitions, Volunteerism, and Electoral Accountability." American Political Science Review 64 (March 1970): 5-17.

Riley, Matilda White and Foner, Anne. Aging and Society, Vol. 1: An Inventory of Research Findings. New York: Russell Sage Foundation, 1968.

_____, Johnson, Marilyn, and Foner, Anne. Aging and Society, Vol. III: A Sociology of Age Stratification. New York: Russell Sage Foundation, 1972.

Soule, John W. and McGrath, Wilma E. "A Comparative Study of Male-Female Political Attitudes at Citizen and Elite Levels." In A Portrait of Marginality, edited by Marianne Githens and Jewel L. Prestage. New York: David McKay, 1977.

Stanwick, Kathy and Johnson, Marilyn. "Women Appointed to State Boards and Commissions." Report to the Women and Power Committee of the National Commission for the Observance of International Women's Year. U.S. Department of State, 1976.

_____, and Li, Christine. The Political Participation of Women in the United States: A Selected Bibliography, 1950-1976. Metuchen, N.J.: Scarecrow Press, 1977.

Stoper, Emily. "Wife and Politician: Role Strain among Women in Public Office." In A Portrait of Marginality, edited by Marianne Githens and Jewel L. Prestage. New York: David McKay, 1977.

Stouffer, Samuel A. Communism, Conformity, and Civil Liberties. New York: John Wiley & Sons, 1955.

Sullivan, Denis G., et al. The Politics of Representation: The Democratic Convention 1972. New York: St. Martin's Press, 1974.

Van Hightower, Nikki R. "The Recruitment of Women for Public Office." American Politics Quarterly 5 (July 1977): 301-314.

Verba, Sidney and Nie, Norman. Participation in America: Political Democracy and Social Equality. New York: Harper and Row, 1972.

Werner, Emmy E. "Women in State Legislatures." Western Political Quarterly 21 (1968): 40-50.

QUESTIONNAIRE

The following are questions asked of women currently in office. The same questions were asked of men, although in different order. The questionnaire sent to former women officeholders omitted questions 10, 15 and 18 and added the questions designated for former officeholders at the end of this section.

* * *

PART I - FOR YOUR DIRECTORY LISTING (Please print or type)

1. Your name 2. Governmental office address: office telephone: 3. Home address: 4. Date of birth:____
5. What is your party affiliation? ____Democrat ____Republican ____Independent ____Other (PLEASE SPECIFY)____
6. CURRENT GOVERNMENTAL OFFICE (Do not include political party positions in this section. If you currently hold more than one office, indicate that below, but please answer all questions only with reference to the highest level position you now hold)
a. Name and location of your office or position (e.g., St.Rep., 6th Dist.; Mayor,Dallas)
   (1) Highest level position currently held:____
   (2) Other governmental office(s) now held:____
b. Level of government to which your position applies (e.g., federal,state,county,local)
c. Is your office normally___Elective___Appointive? If elective, were you first appointed to fill an unexpired term? ____Yes____No
d. What was the year of your first election or appointment to this office? 19____
e. Is this your ____1st,____2nd,____3rd,____4th, or ____th term of office?
f. If you hold membership on (or act as official liaison to) any committees, boards, or commissions as an assignment of your office, please list below and indicate whether you are the Chair:
7. FORMER PUBLIC OFFICES Please indicate all former governmental offices (including board and commission memberships) you have held, level of government, dates of service, and whether the office was elective (E) or appointive (A). (Do not include political party positions in this section.) Position____ Level (local,county,state,national)____ Years of service____ Elective or appointive____
8. PARTY POSITIONS
a. Were you ever a delegate or an alternate to a state and/or national political convention? In what year(s)?
b. Please list any other positions within your party, elective or appointive, that you currently hold or have held in the past (e.g., precinct leader, county committeewoman). (Do not include political clubs in this section.) Position____Level(local,county,state, national)____Years of Service____Elective or Appointive____
9. EMPLOYMENT AND OCCUPATION In addition to holding office, are you now employed? ____Yes____No
a. If yes: Are you employed____full time or____ part time? What is your occupation?
b. If no: In what year were you last employed? 19____What was your occupation in the year you were last employed?
10. EDUCATIONAL BACKGROUND List schools you attended, dates of attendance, major field of study (if any), and degrees or certificates received (if any).
11. CURRENT EDUCATIONAL ACTIVITY During 1977, have you taken courses or been enrolled in school or received formal training of any kind? ____No ____Yes. If yes, please describe:
a. the nature of the courses or program_____
b. the dates of attendance_____
c. the kind of degree or certificate, if any, that you are (or were) seeking_____
d. whether attendance is (or was) ____full time or ____part time
12. ORGANIZATIONAL MEMBERSHIPS Please list (1) organizations in which you currently hold active membership and (2) organizations in which you are not currently active but in which you have held active membership within the past ten years. Please give the complete name of the organization (not just the initials) and the year in which you first joined.
CURRENT MEMBERSHIPS
a. Professional,occupational,or labor union
b. Civic,social welfare, or reform groups
c. Political clubs
d. School-related and youth groups
e. Social or recreational groups
f. Other (PLEASE SPECIFY)
WITHIN PAST TEN YEARS
a. Professional,occupational, or labor union
b. Civic,social welfare, or reform groups
c. Political clubs
d. School-related and youth groups
e. Social or recreational groups
f. Other (PLEASE SPECIFY)

PART II - FOR STATISTICAL PURPOSES ONLY

Answers to all questions in PART II will NOT BE INCLUDED UNDER YOUR NAME in the directory. They will be used only for statistical charts and analysis, with no names or other identifying materials attached.
13. CHARACTERISTICS OF YOUR OFFICE
a. What is the annual salary, if any, of your office? $____(If payment is in the form of an amount per session or per meeting, please indicate how much would be earned per year for full attendance.)
b. How many women and how many men currently hold office in your governing body? (Please include yourself): ____women and____men, out of ____total members
c. What is the size of population under the jurisdiction of your governing body or office?

d. If your office is elective, what is the population of the district from which you were elected?_____

e. If your office is elective, are elections to your office: ____Partisan(Party label appears on the ballot with the candidate's name) ____Nonpartisan (no party labels appear on the ballot)

14. ACTIVITIES OF OFFICE

a. Please estimate the number of hours per week that you spend on matters related to your office: ____hours/week

b. If you hold membership on more than one committee, board, or commission as an assignment of your office, please name the one you consider: most important___; most time-consuming____.

c. Are there committee, board, or commission assignments you would like in place of or in addition to your current assignments? ____No____Yes If yes, please list in order of preference:

d. What are the three issues or projects of most concern to you in your activities as an officeholder?

e. Considering all the responsibilities of your office, how much emphasis do you place on each of the following? Please indicate the degree of emphasis by placing a number from 1 to 4 in the blank beside each item   1=Major emphasis 2=Moderate emphasis 3=Minor emphasis 4=Not a responsibility of my office

____Educating the public about important issues
____Making government more efficient
____Developing policy
____Helping constituents with their individual problems
____Seeking the opinions of my colleagues on pending issues
____Initiating and sponsoring legislation or ordinances
____Smoothing conflicts and effecting compromises with colleagues
____Getting my own priority issues on the agenda
____Exercising administrative and oversight functions
____Discovering the public's view on pending issues
____Representing the program of my political party
____Seeking available research and information on pending legislation or issues
____Making independent decisions on the merits of each issue

f. On most contemporary issues, do you generally think of yourself as: ____Very conservative ____Conservative____Middle-of-the-road____Liberal ____Very liberal____Other (PLEASE SPECIFY____.

g. Relative to the other public officeholders you work with, please rate yourself on each of the following qualities as: 1=Considerably higher than average 2=Slightly higher than average 3=About the same as my colleagues 4=Slightly lower than average 5=Considerably lower than average 6=Can't evaluate

____General knowledge and intelligence
____Valuable past training and experience
____Financial and economic judgment
____Getting along with colleagues
____Willingness to work hard
____Efficiency and organization
____Influence and prestige with colleagues
____Imagination
____Understanding people's behavior and motivations
____Interest in public service
____Time spent on official activities
____Political know-how
____Ability to make important contacts
____Responsiveness to constituents

____Practicality
____Independence
____Ability to argue persuasively
____Interest in social problems
____Overall effectiveness

15. PAST CANDIDACIES   Have you ever in the past been a candidate for elective office in which you lost the election? ____No____Yes If yes: For which office(s)? In which year(s)? Was the election a primary?

16. POLITICAL PLANS AND GOALS

a. Do you plan to seek an additional term in the office you now hold (or, if you hold appointive office, would you accept a reappointment)? ____Definitely____Probably____Probably not ____Definitely not____Don't know

b. If you had the necessary political support and the right opportunities, are there other elective or appointive political offices at the local,county, state, or national levels that you would eventually hold? ____No. Would prefer to remain in my current office or would prefer not to hold any public office after leaving the one I now hold. (If no, skip to Question 17.) ____Yes. Please list all offices that might be of interest to you.____

c. If you answered yes to b, all things considered, which one office would you like to hold next in the future?____

d. If the future office you are interested in is an elective office, how much money would you guess would be needed to finance you campaign adequately? $____. ____interested in appointive office next

e. Please indicate how important each of the following considerations is likely to be in your decision whether to seek the office you would like to hold next. Beside each item, place the number that comes closest to your own feeling about the matter. 1=So important that I would not seek office without it 2=Important but not critical 3=Somewhat important 4=Of minor or no importance 5=Does not apply to my situation or the office I seek

____Having sufficient numbers of volunteer campaign workers
____Being assured of sufficient campaign funds
____Getting favorable treatment from the media
____Having the support and endorsement of party leaders
____Having the support or endorsement of key organizations
____Being able to run unopposed in the primary election
____Not having to challenge an incumbent in the primary election
____Not having to run against an incumbent in the general election
____Feeling that I can do a better job in office than other potential candidates
____Having financial independence or security
____Not having children still in school
____Having support and encouragement from my husband
____Having an experienced campaign manager
____Being able to hire professional campaign services for literature,polling,targeting the district, etc.
____Being approached for the office rather than having to initiate a candidacy
____Not having to move or travel away from home

17. COMPARISON OF WOMEN AND MEN IN POLITICS

a. What are the special advantages, if any, which you have experienced as a result of being a woman

in public office?____
b. What special difficulties, if any, have you
experienced as a result of being a woman holding
public office?____
c. Beside each statement, please indicate the number
that comes closest to your own opinion. 1=Strongly
agree 2=Moderately agree 3=Moderately disagree
4=Strongly disagree 5=Unable to decide
____Women have just as much opportunity as men to
    become political leaders.
____Many men in the party organizations try to keep
    women out of leadership roles.
____In general, voters are more reluctant to support
    women candidates.
____Men can't be really active in politics without
    having their family life suffer.
____Women can't be really active in politics without
    having their family life suffer.
____Women in office generally devote more time to the
    job than do men in office.
____Women in office usually are better at the "human
    relations" aspects of the job.
____In general, women in office are not as
    politically astute as men.
____The qualifications and training of women in
    public office are usually not as good as those
    of men in office.
18. ROLES OF GOVERNMENT AND INDUSTRY Below is a list
of some common social or individual problems and
needs. For each problem or need, decide which number
comes closest to your own feeling about whether
(a) federal government (b) state government,
(c) private industry 1=Should do more about it than
it now does 2=Is now doing just about enough
3=Should be less involved than it now is 4=Should not
get involved at all
Preventing inflation
Accumulating funds for retirement security
Assuring full employment
Providing mass transportation systems
Assuring equal rights for women
Controlling air and water pollution
Improving the availability and quality of medical
  care
Abolishing poverty
Providing financial aid to students
Assuring equal rights for minorities
Improving the quality of neighborhoods
Protecting the consumer against poor services or
  products and unreasonable prices
Ending discrimination against older workers
Encouraging industrial and commerical development
Supporting the cultural arts
Regulating the supply and distribution of energy
Encouraging technological innovation
Encouraging research on social problems
19. POSITIONS ON CURRENT ISSUES Please indicate
your degree of agreement or disagreement with each
of the following statements by placing a number from
1 to 6 in the blank provided. 1=Strongly agree
2=Moderately agree 3=Neutral 4=Moderately disagree
5=Strongly disagree 6=Don't know
____The best way to handle the crime problem is to
    make punishments more severe.
____Every state should require students to pass a
    test of minimal competency as a condition for
    graduation from high school.
____There should be a constitutional amendment to
    prohibit abortion under all or almost all
    circumstances.
____The defense budget should be reduced.

____In the long run, busing school children to
    promote racial balance will prove to be a
    good thing for the country.
____Social Security coverage should be extended
    to homemakers.
____There should be a federal law forbidding
mandmandatory retirement because of age.
____A larger share of federal revenues should
    be returned to the states.
____A larger share of federal revenues should
    be returned to the municipalities.
____The federal Equal Rights Amendment should be
    ratified.
____Government should provide child care services
    to all parents who desire them, with fees
    charged according to ability to pay.
20. BACKGROUND AND FAMILY CHARACTERISTICS
a. How long have you resided in the community
where you now live?____years. In the state?
----years. In which Congressional District do
you live? (If you do not know the number of your
district, please write the name of your current
Congressman/woman, House of Representatives.)
_____C.D.
b. On the whole, when you were growing up, would
you say that your father and mother were:
                Father
____Very much interested in politics
____Somewhat interested in politics
____Didn't pay much attention to politics
____Father not living or was not raised by father
                Mother
____Very much interested in politics
____Somewhat interested in politics
____Didn't pay much attention to politics
____Mother not living or was not raised by mother
c. What is your age? ____years
d. What is your current marital status?
____Married ____Divorced or separated ____Widowed
____Single, never married
e. How many children have you had? (Include all
your children, living or not, and all adopted
childred.)____children (if no children, write
"none.")
f. If you have children, how old is the youngest
child? ____years
g. What is your religious preference?
____Roman Catholic ____Jewish ____Protestant
____Other (PLEASE SPECIFY)_____
____No religious preference
h. What is the principal ethnic or racial heritage
with which you identify yourself? (e.g., Irish;
Afro-American or Black; Chicago; etc.)
i. What was your combined family income (before
taxes) last year? ____under $5,000
____$5,000-$9,999 ____$10,000-$14,999
____$15,000-$19,999 ____$20,000-$24,999
____$25,000-$29,999 ____$30,000-$39,999
____$40,000-$49,999 ____over $50,000
If you are not currently married, please omit
questions about your husband and skip to the end
of the questionnaire.
j. Please check below the category which tells
how far your husband went in school:
____Grade school or less
____Some high school
____Some high school plus other noncollege training
____Completed high school
____Completed high school plus noncollege training
____Some college
____Completed college (4 years)

_____Completed college plus additional training
_____Has one or more postgraduate degrees
k. What is your husband's occupation?_____
l. On the whole, would you say that your husband:
_____Is very much interested in politics
_____Is somewhat interested in politics
_____Doesn't pay much attention to politics
m. In general, would you say that your husband:
_____Approves and actively encourages your holding office
_____Is for the most part approving
_____Is mildly opposed to your holding office
_____Actively opposes and resists your holding office
n. Has your husband been an active participant in your political life?
_____Yes, he often has participated by doing such things as campaigning, helping to raise money, helping with speeches, substituting for me at public events, etc.
_____Yes, he has occasionally participated.
_____No, he leaves the political activities and officeholding strictly to me.
o. Has your husband taken on extra household or other tasks in ways that free you for the work of your office?
_____Yes, he has often taken on extra tasks.
_____Yes, he has occasionally taken on extra tasks.
_____No, it's up to me to find time for all my activities.

THANK YOU FOR COMPLETING THE QUESTIONNAIRE. PLEASE ENCLOSE IT IN THE POSTAGE PAID ENVELOPE PROVIDED AND MAIL IT PROMPTLY.

✷   ✷   ✷

The following questions were asked only of former officeholders.

6. LEAVING OFFICE Which of the following describes the circumstances of your leaving office?
_____Resigned before the end of my last term and did not serve the remainder of the term (Please answer Part A)
_____Completed my term of office but decided not to run for re-election (Please answer Part A)
_____Was defeated in my bid for re-election (Please answer Part B)

PART A

(1) If you resigned before the end of your term or decided not to run for re-election, please indicate which, if any, of the factors below entered into your decision. (Check all factors that apply)
_____Health
_____Financial pressures
_____Family moved to a new area
_____Husband needed more of my time
_____Children needed more of my time
_____Other family members needed more of my time
_____Husband was actively opposed to my holding office
_____Wanted to go back to school
_____Wanted to take a job I felt would be more rewarding
_____Demands of a separate occupation
_____Felt I could not win re-election
_____Disillusionment with what the office could accomplish
_____Felt I had done my share and it was someone else's turn

_____Lack of interest in the type of work the office entailed
_____Felt I lacked the technical expertise for doing a really effective job
_____Disillusionment with my colleagues in office
_____Felt I had accomplished what I had set out to do
_____None of these was a factor in my decision
(2) Please comment in the space below regarding any other aspects of your leaving office that you consider significant:

PART B

(1) If you were defeated for re-election, was the election: _____A primary _____A partisan general election _____A nonpartisan election
(2) How many candidates were running for the same seat? _____Myself and a single opponent for one seat. Was your opponent: _____a woman or _____ a man? (indicate number) _____candidates for one seat. Was the winner: _____a woman or_____a man? (indicate number) _____candidates for_____seats. How many women won?_____How many men won?_____
(3) Please comment in the space below regarding any aspects of the elction that you consider of special significance:
7. ASSESSMENT OF EXPERIENCE Would you say that your experience as an officeholder is of value to you in your current life and activities? _____Yes _____No. Please comment on your answer in the space below:

BIOGRAPHICAL DIRECTORY

NOTE

Terms used in the directory to identify the levels of office in
all states have been standardized. See the appendix for state-
by-state variations in names of governing bodies.

Federal

BELLA ABZUG (D)
Chairwoman, National Commission on Observance of International Women's Year. 1977-. Party: Exec Com., Nat. Dem. Com. Prev: U.S. Repr. from N.Y. 1970-76. Org: ACLU; Dem. Study Group; Women's Prison Assoc.; Nat. Urban League; UN Assoc. Educ: Hunter Coll. 1942 BA; Columbia U. 1945 JD. B: 7/24/20. Add:252 7th Ave., NYC. 10001 (212) 975-1510.

BETTE B. ANDERSON
Under Secretary of Treasury. 1977-. Org: Nat. Assoc. of Bank Women; BPW; Chamber of Commerce; Amer. Institute of Banking; Amer. Cancer Society. Add: Department of the Treasury, 15th St., and Pennsylvania, NW, Washington, D.C. 20220 (202) 566-2041.

BARBARA ALLEN BABCOCK (D)
Assistant Attorney General, Department of Justice. 1977-. Org: ABA; Nat'l. Legal Aid and Defender; ACLU. Educ: U. of Pa. 1960 BA; Yale Law School 1963 LLB. B: 7/6/38. Add: 4923 Asaby St., NW, Washington, D.C. 20007. (202) 739-3301.

ELIZABETH BAILEY
Member, Civil Aeronautics Board. Add: 1825 Connecticut Ave., NW, Washington, D.C. 20428 (202) 393-3111.

LUCY WILSON BENSON (D)
Under Secretary for Security Assistance, Science and Technology, Department of State. 1977- Bds: Ch., Arms Export Control Bd.; Special Cmsn. on Administrative Review, U.S. House of Reprs. Prev: Secretary, Human Services of Mass. 1975; Special Econ. Policy Mission to Japan 1972; Special Cmsn. on U.S. Trade Policy 1968; Mass. Council on Educ. 1965-68; Mass. Adv. Cmsn. to the U.S. Civil Rights Cmsn. 1964-71; Bd. of Higher Educ. Policy 1962-65; Town Meeting Repr. 1957-75. Org: Catalyst; Women's Action Alliance; Nat. Academy of Public Administration; Advisor to the NWPC, WEAL and Womens' Campaign Fund. Educ: Smith Coll. 1949 BA; 1955 MA. B: 8/25/27. Add: 2700 Virginia Ave., NW, Washington, D.C. 20037 (202) 632-0410.

MARY F. BERRY
Assistant Secretary for Education, Department of Health, Education and Welfare. Add: 330 Independence Ave., SW, Washington, D.C. 20201 (202) 245-8430.

DR. EULA BINGHAM
Assistant Secretary for Occupational Safety and Health Administration. Add: Department of Labor, Third & Constitution NW, Washington, D.C. 20210. (202) 393-2420.

BARBARA DAVIS BLUM (D)
Deputy Director, Environmental Protection Agency. 1977-. Bds: Nat. Consumer Adv. Council of Federal Reserve Bd.; Ch., Georgia Heritage Trust Cmsn. Party: Dep. Campaign Director for Dem. Presidential Campaign 1976. Prev: Ga. Vital Areas Council 1973-74; Health and Soc. Services Adv. Bd. and Govt. Services Adv. Bd. of Atlanta Reg. Cmsn. 1972-74; Org: Nat. Com. for an Effective Congress; Friends of the River; League of Conservation Voters; Sierra Club. Educ: Florida State U. 1958 BS; 1959 MSW. B: 7/6/39. Add: Environmental Protection Agency, 401 M St. SW, Washington, D.C. 20460 (202) 755-2673.

JOAN BRADEN
Coordinator of Consumer Affairs, Department of State. Add: 2201 C St., NW, Washington, D.C. 20520 (202) 655-4000.

CYNTHIA G. BROWN
Deputy Director for Compliance and Enforcement, Office of Civil Rights, Department of Health, Education and Welfare. 1977-. Org: WEAL. Educ: Oberlin Coll. 1965 BA; Syracuse U. 1966 MPA. B: 3/18/43. Add: 1651 Newton St., NW, Washington, D.C. 20010 (202) 245-7320.

BIANDIANA CARDEMAS
Director, Office of Child Development, Department of Health, Education and Welfare. Add: 330 Independence Ave., SW, Washington, D.C. 20201 (202) 245-6296.

ANNE COX CHAMBERS
U.S. Ambassador to Belgium. Add: Department of State, 2201 C. Street, NW, Washington, D.C. 20520 (202) 655-4000.

ANTONIO CHAYES
Assistant Secretary of Air Force, Manpower & Reserve, Department of Defense. Add: The Pentagon, Washington, D.C. 20301 (202) 545-6700.

CARIN ANN CLAUSS
Solicitor, Department of Labor. Add: Third & Constitution NW, Washington, D.C. 20210 (202) 393-2420.

JOAN CLAYBROOK
Administrator, National Highway Traffic Safety Administration. Add: Department of Transportation 400 Seventh St., SW, Washington, D.C. 20590 (202) 426-1828.

MARGARET COSTANZA
Assistant for Public Liason, The White House. Add: 1600 Pennsylvania Ave., NW, Washington, D.C. 20500 (202) 456-1414.

PATSY DANNER
    Federal Co-Chair. of the Ozarks Regional
Commission. Add: U.S. Department of Commerce,
14th St., NW, Washington, D.C. 20230
(202) 783-9200.

JOAN MARIARENEE DAVENPORT
    Assistant Secretary for Energy and Minerals,
Department of Interior. 1977-. Prev: Dir.,
Office of Environmental Assessment, Federal
Energy Administration 1975-77. Org: Audubon
Soc.; National Wildlife Fed., Friends of the
Nat. Zoo. Educ: Georgetown U 1964 BSFS, 1968
MS. B: 1/2/43. Add: Dept. of Interior, C. St.,
NW, Washington, D.C. 20240 (202) 343-1100.

LYNN DAVIS
    Deputy Assistant Secretary for International
Security Affairs, Department of Defense. Add:
The Pentagon, Washington, D.C. 20310. (202)
545-6700.

PATRICIA M. DERIAN (D)
    Coordinator, Human Rights and Humanitarian
Affairs, Department of State. 1977-. Party:
Dem. Nat. Committeewoman 1968. Org: Southern
Reg. Council;ACLU; National Prison Project;
Center for Community Justice. Educ: U. of Vir.
1952 RN. Add: Department of State, 2201 C Street,
NW, Washington, D.C. 20520 (202) 655-4000.

K. MATHEA FALCO (D)
    Senior Advisor to Secretary of State and
Coordinator for International Narcotics Matters.
1977-. Prev: Law Clerk to Chief Judge of the
Juvenile Ct. 1968-69; Asst. to Dir. of OEO's
Office of Legal Service 1969-71; Chief Counsel
and Staff Dir. to Senate Sub Com. on Juvenile
Delinquency; Drug Abuse Council 1973-74. Org:
Bar of Dist. of Columbia, of U.S. Ct. of Appeals,
of U.S. Supreme Ct.; FDA Controlled Substances
Adv. Com. Educ: Radcliffe Coll. 1965 BA; Yale
Law School 1968 JD. B: 10/15/44. Add: 639 E.
Street SE, Washington, D.C. 20003 (202) 632-8464.

CAROL TUCKER FOREMAN (D)
    Assistant Secretary of Agriculture, Department
of Agriculture. 1977-. Bds: Bd. of Dir's.,
Commodity Credit Corp. Prev: Cmsn. on Status of
Women 1972-73; Adv. Com. on Nat. Growth Policy
1976-77; Adv. Council, U.S. Dept. of Commerce
1976-77; Cmsn. on Population Growth 1971-72;
Dept. of HUD 1966-69; Senate Staff 1965;
Congressional Staff 1965. Org: Betterment Assoc;
WEAL; Woman's Nat. Dem. Club; WPC. Educ:
William Woods Coll. 1958 AA; Washington U. 1960
AB. B: 5/3/38. Add: 3717 Morrison St., NW.
Washington, D.C. 20015 (202) 447-4623.

JANE LAKES FRANK
    Deputy Cabinet Secretary. 1977-. Prev: Sub-
Com. on Constitutional Rights, Com. on the
Judiciary 1975-77; Sub-Com. on Repr. of Citizen
Interests, Com. on the Judiciary 1973-75; Cmsn.
of the Churches on Internat. Affairs 1970; Org.
for Rehabilitation through Training 1969. Educ:
Smith Coll. 1966 BA; Harvard U. 1969 JD. B:
6/28/45. Add: The White House, 1600 Pennsylvania Ave., NW, Washington, D.C. 20500
(202) 456-1414.

ARVONNE S. FRASER (D)
    Coordinator, Office of Women in Development,
Agency for International Development. 1977-.
Party: Reg. Coordinator, Dem. Presidential
Campaign in Iowa, Wisc. and Minn. 1976. Org:
WEAL (former Treasurer and President) B: 9/1/25
Add: Agency for International Development (AID),
Dept. of State, Washington, D.C. 20523
(202) 655-4000.

PATRICIA GRAHAM
    Director, National Institute of Education,
Department of Health Education and Welfare.
Add: 1200 19th NW, Washington, D.C. 20208
(202) 254-5800.

PATRICIA ROBERTS HARRIS
    Secretary of Housing and Urban Development.
1977-. Prev: Ambassador to Luxembourg 1965-67;
Alt. Del., General Assembly of the U.N.; Adv.
Com. on Reform of Federal Criminal Law; Com. on
Causes and Prevention of Violence; Trial Attorney,
Dept. of Justice 1960-61. Org: Wash., D.C. Bar
Assoc. Educ: Howard U. BA; George Washington U.
1960 JD. Add: 451 Seventh St., SW, Washington,
D.C. 20410 (202) 655-4000.

ALEXIS HERMAN
    Director, Women's Bureau. Add: Department
of Labor, Washington, D.C. 20210 (202) 393-2420.

LINDA HELLER KAMM (D)
    General Counsel, Department of Transportation.
1977-. Prev: General Counsel, House Budget Com.
1975-77; Assoc. General Counsel, House Budge Com.
1975-76; Counsel, Select Com. on Com's. 1973-75.
Org: ABA. Educ: Brandeis U. 1961 BA; Boston Coll.
1967 LLB. B: 8/25/39. Add: 3316 Rowland Pl., NW,
Washington, D.C. (202) 426-4702.

ROBERTA KARMEL
    Commissioner, Securities and Exchange Cmsn.
Add: 500 N. Capitol St., Washington, D.C. 20549
(202) 755-1200.

MARY ELIZABETH KING (D)
    Deputy Director, ACTION. 1977-. Bds: Nat.
Alliance for Volunteerism. Party: Nat. Del 1976;
Ch., Health Policy Task Force, Carter Pres.
Campaign 1976; Nat. Dir., Carter Pres. Campaign
1976. Prev: Com. of U.S. Nat. Cmsn. for IWY
1975-76. Org: Women's Action Alliance; Women's
Campaign Fund; Amer. Public Health Assoc.; WPC;
Women's Dem. Club. Educ: Ohio Wesleyan U. 1962
BA: B: 7/30/46. Add: 806 Conn. Ave. NW,
Washington, D.C. 20525 (202) 254-8060.

JUANITA M. KREPS
    Secretary of Commerce. 1977-. Prev: U.S.
Special Com. on Aging; Social Security Adv.
Council; White House Conf. on Aging; Nat. Man-
power Adv. Com. Org: Southern Economic Assoc.
Educ: Berea Coll. 1942 BA; Duke U. 1944 MA; 1948
PhD. B: 1/11/21. Add: Dept. of Commerce,
14th St., Washington, D.C. 20203 (202) 783-9200.

CAROL LAISE
    Director General of Foreign Service; Add:
Department of State, 2201 C St., NW, Washington,
D.C. 20520 (202) 655-4000.

JEAN PRICE LEWIS
Assistant Administrator for International Development, Agency for International Development. Add: Department of State, 2201 C St., NW, Washington, D.C. 20520 (202) 655-4000.

KATHERINE C. LYALL (D)
Deputy Assistant Secretary for Housing and Urban Development. 1977-. Org: Amer. Economic Assoc.; Amer. Statistical Assoc.; Council on Applied Research. Educ: Cornell U. 1963 BA; N.Y.U. 1965 MBA; Cornell U. 1969 PhD. B: 4/26/41. Add: 117 Cross Keys Rd., Baltimore, Md. 21210 (202) 755-5980.

ANNE C. MARTINDELL
Director of Foreign Disaster Assistance. Add: Department of State, 2201 C St., NW, Washington, D.C. 20520 (202) 655-4000.

ARABELLA MARTINEZ
Assistant Secretary for Human Development, Department of Health, Education and Welfare. Add: 330 Independence Ave., SW, Washington, D.C. 20201 (202) 245-6296.

VIRGINIA DILL MC CARTY (D)
U.S. District Attorney for Indiana. 1977-. Party: State Del. 1972, '74, '76; Nat. Alt. 1975; Precinct V-Committeewoman 1969-71; Co-Ch., State Platform Com. 1972-74. Prev: Chief Counsel, Marion Cnty. Prosecutor 1975-76; Governor's Com. on Privacy 1976-77; Ind. Com. on IWY 1977; Deputy Asst. Atty. General 1964-69; V. Pres., Ind. Bd. Law Examiners. Org: Ind. Bar Assoc.; WPC; Economic Club; Greater Indianapolis Progress Com.; Dem. Women; Women for Better Govt. Educ: Ind. U. 1945 AB; 1950 LLB. B: 12/15/24. Add: 5809 Washington Blvd., Indianapolis, Ind. 46204 (317) 269-6333.

MARGARET MC KENNA
Deputy White House Counsel. Add: The White House, 1600 Pennsylvania Ave., NW, Washington, D.C. 20500 (202) 456-1414.

PATSY TAKEMOTO MINK
Assistant Secretary of State for Oceans, International Environmental and Scientific Affairs 1977-. Party: State Del. 1954-76; Nat. Del. 1960, '72; Cnty. Committeewoman. Prev: Congress-woman 1965-77; State Senator 1963-64; Territorial Senator 1958-59; Territorial Rep. 1956-58. Org: BPW; ABA; ADA; ACLU. Educ: U. of Hawaii 1948 BA; U. of Chicago 1951 JD; B: 12/6/27. Add: 2201 C St., NW, Washington, D.C. (202) 632-1554.

MARTHA MITCHELL
Special Projects Director. Add: The White House, 1600 Pennsylvania Ave., NW, Washington, D.C. 20500 (202) 456-1414.

AZIE MORTON
Treasurer of the United States and Director of the Mint. Add: 15 St. & Pennsylvania Ave., NW, Washington, D.C. 20220 (202) 393-6400.

ELEANOR HOLMES NORTON
Chairwoman, Equal Employment Opportunity Commission. 1977-. Prev: Ch., Commission on Human Rights, New York City 1970-77; Exec. Asst. to Mayor of New York City 1971-74. Org: ACLU Educ: Antioch Coll. 1960 BA; Yale 1963 MA; 1964 LLB. B: 6/13/37. Add: Equal Employment Opportunity Commission, 2401 E St., NW, Washington D.C. 20506 (202) 634-7040.

GRACIELA OLIVAREZ
Administrator, Community Service Administration, Department of Housing and Urban Development. Add: 451 Seventh St., SW, Washington, D.C. 20410 (202) 655-4000.

ESTHER PETERSON
Assistant for Consumer Affairs. Add: The White House, 1600 Pennsylvania Ave., NW, Washington, D.C. 20500 (202) 456-1414.

ELSA A. PORTER (D)
Assistant Secretary for Administration, Dept. of Commerce. 1977-. Prev: Chief, Analysis and Development Division, Bureau of Personnel Management Evaluation, U.S. Civil Service Cmsn. 1976; Asst. Administrator for Organization Development, Social and Rehabilitation Service, HEW 1971-73. Org: ASPA; Internat. Personnel Management Assoc.; Federally Employed Women; WEAL; Common Cause; Women's Dem. Club. Educ: Birmingham-Southern Coll. 1949 BA; U. of Ala. 1959 MA; Harvard U. 1971 MPA. B: 12/19/28. Add: 14th St., Washington D.C. 20203 (202) 783-9200.

RUTH T. PROKOP
General Counsel, Department of Housing and Urban Development. 1977-. Prev: Special Asst., HUD Secretary 1966-69; Leg. Counsel, Pres's. Com. on Consumer Interest; Leg. Asst., Pres. Cmsn. on Status of Women; Staff Member of V. Pres. of U.S. 1961-62. Org: D.C. Tax Cmsn; ABA. Educ: George Washington U. 1965 JD. Add: U. S. Dept. of HUD, Washington, D.C. (202) 755-5284.

ROZANNE L. RIDGEWAY
U.S. Ambassador to Finland. Add: Department of State, 2201 C Street, NW, Washington, D.C. 20520 (202) 655-4000.

HAZEL ROLLINS
Assistant Administrator, Conservation and Environment. Federal Energy Administration. Add: 12 St. & Pennsylvania Ave., NW, Washington, D.C. 20461 (202) 961-6216.

DONNA E. SHALALA (D)
Assistant Secretary for Policy Development, Department of Housing and Urban Development. 1977- Bds: Ch., Urban and Regional Policy Group; Ch., Redlining Task Force-Interagency. Prev: Dir. and Treasurer, Municipal Assistance Corp. for the City of N.Y. 1975-77. Org: APSA; ASPA; Nat. Municipal League; Dem. Club. Educ: Western Coll. for Women 1962 BA; Syracuse U. 1970 MA, PhD. B: 2/14/41. Add: 451 7th St., SW, Washington, D.C. 20410 (202) 655-4000.

EILEEN SHANAHAN (D)
Assistant Secretary for Public Affairs, Department of Health, Education and Welfare. 1977-. Org: Washington Press Club; Exec. Women in Govt.; WPC. Educ: George Washington U. 1944 AB. B: 2/29/24. Add: 3608 Van Ness St., NW, Washington, D.C. 20008 (202) 245-1850.

GEORGIANA SHELDON
    Commissioner, Federal Power Commission. Add:
825 North Capitol Street, NE, Washington, D.C.
20426 (202) 386-6102.

DEANNE C. SIEMER (R)
    General Counsel, Department of Defense. 1977-
Bds: Defense Investigative Review Council;
Defense Classification Review Com.; Armed Forces
Policy Council. Educ: George Washington U. 1962
BA; Harvard U. 1968 LLB. B: 12/25/40.
Add: 1634 44th St. NW, Washington, D.C. 20007
(202) 695-3341.

MABEL MURPHY SMYTHE
    U.S. Ambassador to Cameroon. Add: Department
of State, 2201 C St., NW, Washington, D.C. 20520
(202) 655-4000.

IRENE TINKER
    Assistant Director, Policy and Planning,
ACTION. Add: 806 Connecticut Ave., NW, Washington
D.C. 20525 (202) 393-3111.

JILL WINE VOLLNER
    Counsel to the US Army. Add: The Pentagon
Washington, D.C. 20310 (202) 545-6700.

FRAN VOORDE
    Director of Scheduling, The White House.
Add: 1600 Pennsylvania Ave., NW, Washington, D.C.
20500 (202) 456-1414.

BARBARA M. WATSON
    Administrator, Bureau of Security and Counselor
Affairs, Department of State. Add: 2201 C St.,
NW, Washington, D.C. 20520 (202) 655-4000.

PATRICIA WALD (D)
    Assistant Attorney General, Department of
Justice. 1977-. B: 9/16/28. Add: Constitution
& Tenth St., NW, Washington, D.C. 20530
(202) 737-8200.

SARAH WEDDINGTON
    General Counsel, Department of Agriculture.
Add: 14th & Independence SW, Washington, D.C.
20250 (202) 655-4000.

MELISSA F. WELLS
    U.S. Representative on the Economic and Social
Council of the United Nations. Add: United States
Mission to the United Nations, 799 United Nations
Plaza, New York, New York 10017.

MITZI M. WERTHEIM (D)
    Deputy Undersecretary of the Navy. 1977-. Prev
Asst. Dir. of Research, The Peace Corps 1963-66.
Educ: U. of Mich. 1960 BA. B: 10/25/37. Add:
3230 Highland Place, NW, Washington, D.C. 20008
(202) 694-5032.

ANNE WEXLER
    Deputy Undersecretary for Regional Affairs,
Department of Commerce. Add: Fourteenth Street,
Washington, D.C. 20203 (202) 783-9200.

JEAN WILKOWSKI
    Nations Conference, Science and Technology.
Add: Department of State, 2201 C St., NW,
Washington, D.C. 20523 (202) 655-4000.

ELOISE WOODS
    Chairwoman, National Credit Union. Add:
2025 M St., NW, Washington, D.C. 20456
(202) 254-9800.

SUZANNE H. WOOLSEY (I)
    Associate Director for Human and Community
Affairs, Office of Management and Budget. 1977-.
Educ: Stanford U. 1963 BA; Harvard U. 1970 MA,
PhD. B: 12/27/41. Add: 6808 Florida St., Chevy
Chase, Md. 20015 (202) 396-4844.

ESTHER CRANE WUNNICKI
    Member, Joint Federal-State Land Use Planning
Commission for Alaska. Add: Department of the
Interior, C St., NW, Washington, D.C. 20240
(202) 343-1100.

Legislative

House of Representatives

LINDY BOGGS (D) *
    U.S. Representative from Louisiana. 1973-.
Dist: 2. Bds: Appropriations. Party: Precinct
Leader, 1939-42; Ch., Dem. Nat. Conv. 1976. Org:
LWV; Congressional Club; Dem. Women's Club; Nat.
Soc. of Colonial Dames; Council for Music and the
Performing Arts. Educ: Sophie Newcomb Coll.
1935 BA; B: 3/13/16. Add: 1519 Longworth, HOB,
Washington, D.C. 20515 (202) 225-6636.

YVONNE B. BURKE (D)*
    U.S. Representative from California. 1972-.
Dist: 28. Bds: Appropriations; Select Com. on
House Beauty Shop; Select Com. on Assassinations.
Party: V. Ch., Dem. Charter Cmsn. 1973-75; V. Ch.,
Dem. Nat. Conv. 1972. Prev: State Assemblywoman
1966-72; Ch., Urban Development and Housing Cmsn.
1971-72. Org: Nat. Athletic Health Institute;
United Negro Coll. Fund; Women's Dem. Forum; Law
Assoc; Dem. Study Group, UCLA Foundation. Educ:
UCLA 1953 BA; USC 1956 JD. B: 10/5/32. Add:
336 Cannon, HOB, Washington, D.C. 20515
(202) 225-7084.

SHIRLEY ANITA CHISHOLM (D) *
    U.S. Representative from New York. 1968-.
Dist: 12. Bds: Rules Com. Party: Dist. Co-Leader
1962-64; Nat. Committeewoman 1968-72. Prev:
State Assemblywoman 1964-68. Org: ADA; LWV;
NAACP; Nat. Assoc. of Coll. Women; Nat. Council
of Negro Women; WEAL; Young Dem. Educ: Brooklyn
Coll. 1946 BA; Columbia U. 1954 MA. B: 11/30/24.
Add: 123 Cannon, HOB, Washington, D.C. 20515
(202) 225-6231.

CARDISS COLLINS (D)
    U.S. Representative from Illinois. 1973-.
Dist: 7. Bds: Ch., Govt. Operations Subcom. on
Manpower and Housing; District of Columbia Com;
Internat. Relations Com. Party: Nat. Del. 1976;
Committeewoman Ward Regular Dem. Org. 1973-.
Educ: Northwestern U. 1967 BS. B: 9/24/31.
Add: 113 Cannon House Office Bldg., Washington,
D.C. 20515 (202) 225-5006.

MILLICENT FENWICK
U. S. Representative from New Jersey. 1974-.
Dist: 5; Bds: Com. on Banking, Finance and
Urban Affairs; Small Business Com.; Com. on
Standards of Official Conduct. Prev: NJ Com. for
the US Cmsn. on Civil Rights; Somerset Cnty.
Legal Aid and Blue Ribbon Com. to Study Drug
Abuse; Com. on Equal Employment Opportunity. B:
2/25/10. Add: 1427 Longworth HOB; Washington,
D.C., 20515 (202) 225-7300.

MARGARET M. HECKLER (R) *
U.S. Representative from Massachusetts. 1966-.
Dist: 10 Bds: Agriculture Com.; Select Com. on
Ethics; Joint Economic Com.; Veteran's Affairs
Com.; Nat. Cmsn. on IWY. Party: Platform Com.
1972. Prev: Governor's Council 1962-66. Org:
ABA; BPW; Rep. Women's Club. Educ: Albertus
Magnus Coll. 1953 BA; Boston Coll. 1956 LLB.
B: 6/21/31. Add: 343 Cannon, HOB, Washington,
D.C. 20515 (202) 225-4335.

MARJORIE S. HOLT (R)
U.S. Representative from Maryland. 1972-.
Dist: 4. Bds: Cnty. Housing Com. of Human
Relations Cmsn.; Com. on Armed Services; Budget
Com. Party: Nat. Del. 1968. Prev: Clerk Anne
Arundel Cnty. Circuit Ct. 1966-72; Cnty. Election
Supervisor 1963-65. Org: ABA; BPW; LWV; Women's
Club. Educ: U. of Fla. 1949 JD. B: 9/17/20.
Add: 1510 Longworth House Office Bldg., Washington
D.C. 20515 (202) 225-8090.

ELIZABETH HOLTZMAN
U.S. Representative from New York. 1972-.
Dist: 16. Bds: Budget Com.; Judiciary Com. Party
Dem. State Committeewoman and Dist. Leader 1970-72
Nat. Del. 1972. Prev: Asst. to the Mayor of NYC
1969-70. Org: Bar Assoc. of NYC. Educ:
Radcliffe Coll. 1962 BA; Harvard U 1965 JD. B:
8/11/41. Add: 1027 Longworth, HOB, Washington,
D.C. 20515 (202) 225-6616.

BARBARA JORDAN (D)
U.S. Representative from Texas. Dist: 18.
Bds: Com. on the Judiciary; Com. on Govt.
Operations; Steering and Policy Com.; House Dem.
Caucus. Prev: State Senator 1966-72. Org: ABA;
Tex. Bar Assoc.; Tex. Trial Lawyers; NAACP. Educ:
Tex. Southern U. BA; Boston U. 1959 LLB; B:
2/21/36. Add: 1534 Longworth, HOB, Washington,
D.C. 20515 (202) 225-3816.

MARTHA KEYS (D)
U.S. Representative from Kansas. 1974-. Dist:
2. Bds: House Ways and Means Com.; Health and
Public Assistance Com. Party: Nat. Del. 1972.
Org: Congressional Rural Caucus; Dem. Adv. Council
of Elected Officials. Educ: U. of Kansas City
BA. B: 8/10/30. Add: 2339 Chris Cr., Manhattan
66502 (202) 225-6601.

MARILYN LAIRD LLOYD (D) *
U.S. Representative from Tennessee. 1974-.
Dist: 3. Bds: Public Works and Transportation
Com.; Science and Technology Com.; Select Com. on
Aging. Org: Dem. Women's Club; BPW; PTA. B:
1/3/29. Add: 1017 Longworth, HOB, Washington,
D.C. 20515 (202) 225-3271.

HELEN S. MEYNER (D)
U.S. Representative from New Jersey. 1974-.
Dist: 13. Bds: Com. on Internat. Relations;
Com. on the Dist. of Columbia; Select Com. on
Aging; Select Com. on the House Beauty Shop.
Party: State Dem. Policy Council 1962-69. Prev:
NJ Rehabilitation Cmsn. 1962-69. Org: Common
Cause. Educ: Colo. Coll. 1950 BA. B: 3/5/29.
Add: 372 Lincoln St., Phillipsburg 08865
(202) 225-5801.

BARBARA ANN MIKULSKI (D)
U.S. Representative from Maryland. 1976-.
Dist: 3. Bds: Interstate and Foreign Commerce
Com.; Merchant Marine and Fisheries Com.; Ad Hoc
Com. on Energy. Party: Ch.; Dem. Party Cmsn. on
Del. Selection and Party Structure 1973. Prev:
Baltimore City Councilwoman 1971-76. Org: Nat.
Center for Urban Ethnic Affairs; LWV; WPC; Urban
Coalition. Educ: Mt. St. Agnes Coll. 1958 BA;
U. of Md. 1965 MSW. B: 7/20/36. Add: 1004
Longworth, HOB, Washington, D.C. 20515
(202) 225-4016.

MARY ROSE OAKAR (D) *
U.S. Representative from Ohio. 1976-. Dist:
20. Bds: Banking Com.; Finance and Urban Affairs
Com.; Select Com. on Aging. Party: State
Committeewoman 1974; Ward Leader. Prev: Cleveland
City Council 1973-76. Org: Fed. for Community
Planning; Community Information Service; Society
for Crippled Children; Near West Side Civic Arts
Center. Educ: Ursuline Coll. 1962 BA; John
Carrol U. 1966 MA. B: 3/5/40. Add: 427 Cannon,
HOB, Washington, D.C. 20515 (202) 225-5871.

SHIRLEY N. PETTIS (R)
U.S. Representative from California. 1975-.
Dist: 37. Bds: International Relations; Educ-
ation and Labor. Org: CEWAER; Amer. Newspaper
Women's Club; NWPC; Amer. Historical Assoc.;
Capitol Hill Club; DAR. B: 7/12/24. Add:
1421 Longworth, HOB, Washington, D.C. 20515
(202) 225-5861.

PATRICIA SCHROEDER (D) *
U.S. Representative from Colorado. 1972-.
Dist: 1. Bds: Armed Services Com; Post Office
and Civil Service Com. Party: Precinct Com.
1968 - present. Org: ABA; LWV; Planned Parenthood; Young Dems. Educ: U. of Minn. 1961 BA;
Harvard U. 1964 JD. B: 7/30/40. Add: 1131
Longworth, HOB, Washington, D.C. 20515
(202) 255-4431.

VIRGINIA SMITH (R) *
U.S. Representative from Nebraska. 1974-.
Dist: 3. Bds: Appropriations Com.; Select Com.
on the House Beauty Shop. Party: Nat. Del. 1956,
1960, 1972; Cnty. Ch. 1970-74. Prev: Governor's
Cmsn. on the Status of Women 1964-68; Neb. Bd. of
Educ. 1950-60; Ch., Presidential Task Force on
Rural Dev. 1971-72; White House Conference on
Children and Youth, 1960. Org: OES; BPW; DAR;
Amer. Farm Bureau Women; Assoc. of Country Women
of the World; Country Life Assoc. Educ: U. of
Neb. 1934 BA. B: 6/30/11. Add: 1005 Longworth,
HOB, Washington, D.C. 20515 (202) 225-6435.

GLADYS NOON SPELLMAN (D) *
U.S. Representative from Maryland. 1974-.
Dist: 5. Bds: Banking, Finance and Urban Affairs
Com.; Post Office and Civil Service Com. Party:
Nat. Com. 1973-present. Prev: Cnty. Councillor
1971-74; Cnty. Csmnr. 1962-71; Cmsn. on Law
Enforcement and the Administration of Justice;
Cmsn. on Functions of Government; Cmsn. to
Determine State's Role in Financing Public Educ.;
State Comprehensive Health Planning Adv. Council.
Org: Nat. Assoc. of Cntys; Council of Gvts.
B: 3/2/18. Add: 1117 Longworth, HOB, Washington,
D.C. 20515 (202) 225-4131.

Judicial

Circuit Judges

SHIRLEY M. HUFSTEDLER
U.S. Circuit Court Judge. Ninth Judicial
Circuit. Los Angeles, California.

District Judges

JUNE L. GREEN
U.S. District Judge. District of Columbia.

CORNELIA G. KENNEDY
U.S. District Judge. Eastern District of
Michigan.

CONSTANCE BAKER MOTLEY
U.S. District Judge. Southern District of
New York.

MARY ANNE RICHEY
U.S. District Judge. District of Arizona.

Alabama

State Executive and Cabinet

MELBA TILL ALLEN (D) *
State Treasurer. 1974-. Bds: State Bd. of
Adjustment; Teachers Retirement System; Employees
Retirement System; Ala. Educ. Auth.; Highway Auth.
Prev: State Auditor 1967-75. Org: Nat. Assoc. of
State Auditors, Comptrollers and Treasurers; Dem.
Women's Club; Amer. Bus. Women's Assoc.; OES.
B: 3/3/33. Add: Box 3, Rte 1, Grandy 36036
(205) 832-3590.

AGNES BAGGETT (D)
Secretary of State. 1975-. Bds: State Bd. of
Adjustment; Healing Arts Bd.; State Canvassing
Bd. Party: Pres. Elector 1968. Prev: Secretary
of State 1951-54, 1963-66, State Auditor
1954-58; State Treasurer 1958-62, 1967-74. Org:
BPW; Altrusa Club; Dem Club. B: 4/9/05. Add:
3202 Montezuma Rd., Montgomery 36109 (205)832-3570

BETTYE JEAN FRINK (D) **
State Auditor 1963-67, 1974-. Bds: State
Bd. of Educ. Party: Del., State Dem. Conv.
1960. Prev: Secretary of State 1959-63. Org:
BPW; LWV. B: 2/19/33. Add: 1943 Talbot Ter.,
Montgomery 36106.

ANNE LAURIE GUNTER (D)
Director, Department of Consumer Protection.
1972-. Bds: Auburn U. School of Home Economics
Adv. Bd. Party: Nat. Del. 1972, 1976. Prev:
Coord., Ala. Office of Hwy. and Traffic Safety
1971-72. Org: Soroptomist; Women in Commun-
ications, Inc.; Soc. of Consumer Affairs
Professionals; Dem. Women's Club. B: 6/23/19.
Add: 66 S. Haardt Dr., Montgomery 36108
(205) 832-5936.

JUANITA MC DANIEL
President, Public Service Commission. Add:
State Capitol, Montgomery 36104.

State Legislature

State House

MARILYN QUARLES (D) **
1974-. Dist: 56. Bds: Health; Educ.; Local
Government; Highway, Traffic and Safety; Women's
Com. Org: NEA; Society for Women Educ. Educ:
U. of Ala. 1970 BS. Occ: School Teacher. B:
12/31/28. Add: 141 Murphy Valley Rd., Springville
35146 (205) 269-1801.

LOUTHENIA THOMAS
931 Arkadelphia Rd., Birmingham 35209.

MRS. SHELBY DEAN WARD
P.O. Box 689, Opelika 36801.

County Commissions

Colbert. JOYCE KATHERINE POSEY (D) **
1968-. Org: BPW; Nat. Assoc. of County
Commissioners; Chamber of Commerce; Medical
Advisory Bd. B: 5/16/25. Add: Route 1, Box 19,
Cherokee 35616 (205) 269-1801.

Conecuh. NINA GORUM
Evergreen 36401.

Henry. KATE W. PALMER
Abbeville 36310.

Montgomery. NANCY COX
Montgomery 36104.

Russell. DOLLY WILSON
     Phenix City 36867.

Tallapoosa. MELBA BARNES
     Dadeville 36853.

Mayors

Atmore. PATRICIA P. MC KENZIE
     P.O. Drawer G, Atmore 36502.

Bay Minette. DOLLIE M. BRYARS (D)
     1975-. Bds: Pres., Cnty. Mayors' Assoc.;
Planning Cmsn.; Adv. Com., Retired Senior Volun-
teer Program. Prev: City Councilwoman 1968-75;
Mayor Pro Tem 1972-75. Org: Chamber of Commerce;
Cnty. Mental Health; Ala. Mental Health and
Retardation; Ala. Soc. for Crippled Children and
Adults. Occ: Shipping Manager. B: 8/5/26. Add:
W. 3rd St., P.O. Box 42, Bay Minette 36507
(205) 937-5502.

Bon Air. MRS. AMIE B. SHAW
     P.O. Box 117, Bon Air 35032.

Brundidge. LILLIAN M. JOHNSON
     104 N. Main Street, Brundidge 36010.

Centre. LILLIAN WHITT WHITE (D)
     1970-. Bds: Gas Bd.; E. Ala. Planning Cmsn.
Prev: Councilwoman 1962-70. Org: Nurses' Assoc.;
BPW; Chamber of Commerce; Dem. Party; PTA. Educ:
Forrest General Hospital 1935 LPN. Occ: Nurse.
B: 12/31/15. Add: 417 Main St., Centre 35960
(205) 927-3281.

Faunsdale. JANICE GUIN (D)
     1976-. Occ: Grocery Checker. B: 8/9/47.
Add: Box 173, Hwy. 255, Faunsdale 36738
(205) 628-4871.

Gaylesville. KATHRYN BLACK
     P.O. Box 126, Gaylesville 35973.

Hammondville. MRS. VESTA HAWKINS
     Rt. 1, Valley Head 35989.

Madrid. VERNA WATSON
     P.O. Box 10, Madrid 36320.

Mentone. ETHEL MANIFOLD
     P.O. Box 16, Mentone 35984.

Oak Grove. VIRGINIA WOMACK
     P.O. Drawer 807, Sylacauga 35150.

Pennington. BERNIECE MC ILLWAIN
     P.O. Box 40, Pennington 36916.

River Falls. MARY HIXON
     P.O. Box 117, River Falls 36476.

Vina. GLORIA BROWN (D)
     Bds: Gas and Water Bd. Occ: Bookkeeper. B:
2/4/26. Add: Box #7, Vina 35593 (205) 356-4996.

Local Councils

Alabaster. CHARLOTTE BURKE
     P.O. Box 277, Alabaster, 35007.

Alabaster, MAYO B. TAYLOR (D)
     1976-. B: 7/27/30. Add: P.O. Box 66, Siluria
35007 (205) 663-7401.

Albertville. EMILY RUDOLPH (D)
     1976-. Bds: Community Action Com. Educ:
U. of Ala. 1947 BS. Occ: Business Manager-Owner.
B: 3/14/23. Add: 600 Brookside Dr., Albertville
35950 (205) 878-0426.

Alexander City. JEAN W. CUMMINS
     P.O. Box 589, Alexander City 35010.

Andalusia. JOANNE L. BOSWELL (D)
     1976-. Bds: Ch., Policy and Fire; Utilities;
Administrative and Recreation. Org: BPW. Occ:
Business-Co-owner. B: 2/22/40. Add: 419 Church
St., Andalusia 36420 (205) 222-3311.

Anniston. GERTRUDE R. WILLIAMS (D)
     1976-. Bds: Retired Police-Fireman Bd.
Org: Retired Teachers. Educ: U. of Ala. 1938 BS;
Jacksonville State U. 1959 MS. B: 8/24/12.
Add: Rt. 1, Box 525, Anniston 36201 (205)236-1860

Ashland. REBECCA BODDIE
     P.O. Box 38, Ashland 36251.

Babbie. WANDA CLARK
        WILIADEAN LEE
     Rt. 2, Andalusia 36467.

Bayou La Batre. WILLIE LOUISE BRYANT
     P.O. Box 517, Bayou La Batre 36509.

Berry. POLLY LAWRENCE BARNES (D)
     1976-. Bds: Ch., Beautification; Street
Maintenance; Ch., Public Relations. Prev:
Medical Bd. 1975-76. Org: NEA; Medical Bd.
Educ: Samford U. 1966 AB; Livingston U. 1971 MEd.
Occ: Special Ed. teacher. B: 3/28/44. Add:
P.O. Box 36, Berry 35546.

Birmingham. BESSIE S. ESTELL (D)
     1975-. Bds: Ch., Public Bldgs. and Environ-
mental Control; Health, Educ. and Welfare Com.;
Planning and Zoning Com. Prev: Community Affairs
1970-77; Chamber of Commerce 1969-77. Org: NEA;
NAACP; Urban League; LWV; Dem. Club; Health
Systems Agency. Educ: Ala. State U. 1940 BS.
B: 4/20/10. Add: 620 Center Way SW, Birmingham
35211 (205) 254-2294.

Birmingham. NINA MIGLIONICO (D) **
     1963-. Bds: Regional Planning Com. Org:
Pres., Nat. Assoc. of Women Lawyers; Pres., BPW;
Pres., Ala. Joint Legislative Council; Pres.,
Ala. Merit System League. Educ: Howard 1933 BA;
U. Of Ala. Law School 1936 LLB. Occ:Attorney.
Add: 2625 Highland Ave., Bham 35205 (205)254-2295

Birmingham. ANGELINE GROOMS PROCTOR (R) **
     1971-. Bds: Health, Educ. and Welfare; Zoning
Environmental Control; Community School Advisory
Com. Org: Society of Interior Designers; Humane
Society. Educ: Auburn U. 1968 BA. Occ: Interior

Designer. B: 10/20/44. Add: 3451 Cliff Rd.,
Birmingham 35205 (205) 254-2294.

Blountsville. JEAN ARNOLD
    1976-. Org: Adv. Com., Regional Planning.
    B: 7/10/31. Add: PO Box 87, Blountsville 35031.

Bon Air. ROSALIE BENTLEY
          JOYCE GENTRY
          GERALDINE PILKINGTON
          PAMELA C. PILKINGTON
          JESSE WAITES
    P.O. Box 117, Bon Air 35032.

Brantley. MARY MOXLEY WEED (I) **
    1972-. Org: Physical Therapy Assoc. Educ:
    U. of NC 1946 BA. Occ: Physical Therapist. B:
    8/4/23. Add: Cherokee, La. Box 106, Brantley
    36009.

Brookside. FRANCES GOODE BEARDEN (D) **
    1972-. Bds: Park and Recreation Bd. Occ: Legal
    Secretary. B: 1/29/43. Add: Price St.,
    Brookside 35036 (205) 674-9275.

Brownville. SARAH ELIZABETH ASBURY (D) **
    1961-. Bds: City Planning and Dev. Bd. Org:
    DAR; Bd. of Dir., Roosevelt Area Family Health
    Center; Secretary, County Historical Society.
    Educ: U. of Montevallo 1935 BS. Occ: Secretary.
    B: 3/26/14. Add: 2301 Ave. K, Bessemer 35020
    (205) 425-0201.

Brownville. JUANITA WATSON
    2120 Avenue K, Bessemer 35020.

Camp Hill. MRS. JESSIE W. SIMS (D)
    1976-. Bds: Ch., Police Com.; Utility Bd.; Ch.
    Finance Com. Org: Ala. Dem. Conf. Educ: Ala.
    A & M U. 1955 BS. Occ: Teacher. B: 2/25/29.
    Add: P.O. Box 271, Camp Hill 36850 (205)896-2291.

Cardiff. GLENDA BROOKS
          ANN T. WALKER
    P.O. Box 37, Cardiff 35041.

Carrville. EVA H. HARPER
    304 Main Street, E. Tallassee 36023.

Clayhatchee. DELORIS SALTER (D)
    1976-. Occ: Electronics Assembler. B: 1/19/45
    Add: Rt. 3, Box 123, Daleville 36322 (205)598-4321.

Clopton. KATE W. PALMER
    Rte. 1, Clopton 36317.

Coffee Springs. SHIRLEY JEAN BALL (D)
    1976-. Bds: Ch., Annual Independence Day
    Celebration; Secretary and Treasurer of Parks
    and Recreation. Occ: Electronics radar technician
    B: 11/13/39. Add: P.O. Box 141, Coffee Springs
    36318.

Coffee Springs. KATHY HENDERSON
    P.O. Box 3, Coffee Springs 36318.

Coosada. KATHLEEN T. CHEATHAM
    1975-. Org: Civic Club; PTA. B: 2/3/20.
    Add: Coosada 36024.

Coosada. MRS. HOMAR A JONES
         MRS. RAYVONNE W. THORNTON
    P.O. Box 356, Coosada 36020.

Cullman. CHARLOTTE MILLER
    P.O. Box 278, Cullman 35055.

Dadeville. SADIE E. CAMPBELL (D)
    1968-. Bds: Ch., Finance; Ch., Cemetery. Org:
    BPW; OES; Amer. Assoc. of Retired Persons. Occ:
    Cashier. B: 6/13/19. Add: 610 Farrington St.,
    Dadeville 36853.

Daphne. DOLORES C. OATES (I)
    1976-. Bds: Ch., Utilities Com.; Streets Com.;
    Recreation Com. Prev: Library Bd. 1972-76;
    Medical Clinic Bd. 1974-76. Occ: Real Estate
    Saleswoman. B: 8/30/40. Add: 1308 Captain
    O''Neal Dr., Daphne 36526.

Dutton. SYLVIA STOCKMAN
    P.O. Box 42, Dutton 35744.

Eclectic. DOROTHY BAUGHMAN (D)
    1976-. Bds: Ch., Christmas Activities; Ch.,
    Swimming Pool. Occ: Author. B: 7/13/40. Add:
    Box 176, Eclectic 36024 (205) 651-2148.

Elkmont. JOYCE RUSS (D)
    1976-. Bds: Ch., Recreation; Ch., Streets;
    Ch., Park. Occ: Quality Control Worker. B:
    9/29/37. Add: P.O. Box 65, Elkmont 35620.

Eunola. JEANETTE POLLARD
         EMMA PHELPS
    P.O. Box 146, Geneva 36340.

Fairfield. BOBBIE C. NE SMITH
    P.O. Drawer 437, Fairfield 35064.

Falkville. ANNIE ELIZABETH JEFFREYS (D)
    1976-. Bds: Ch., Finance Com.; School Tax Bd.;
    Recreation Bd. B: 1/6/32. Add: Rt. 2, Box 4,
    Culver Rd., Falkville 35622.

Falkville. EMMA LOU ROBINSON
    P.O. Box 407, Falkville 35622.

Falkville. JUDITH WILLARD WINTON (D)
    1976-. Bds: Ch., Recreation Com.; Ch., Sani-
    tation Com.; Finance Com. Educ: Miss. State U.
    1969 BS: Occ: Teacher. B: 6/6/47. Add:
    Rt 2, Box 5, Falkville 35622 (205) 784-5922.

Faunsdale. LOUISE R. FULFORD (R)
    1976-. B: 2/6/06. Add: 1 Powers St.,
    Faunsdale 36738.

Florala. SYBIL R. MICKLER (D) **
    1972-. Bds: Water Bd. Prev: Juvenile Officer
    1973-74; Police Commissioner 1942-73. Org: PTA;
    Amer. Public Works Assoc. B: 5/24/20. Add:
    809 North 6th St., Florala 36442 (205)858-3695.

Forkland. EVELYN BAKER
           GERTRUDE WILLIAMS
           MARY VIRGINIA WILLIAMS
    Town Hall, Forkland 36740.

Frisco City. SUSAN B. PHILLIPS
    P.O. Box 119, Frisco City 36445.

Fruithurst. GERALDINE OWENS
     P.O. Box 175, Fruithurst 36262.

Fultondale. HELEN MORRIS FASSINA (D)
     1976-. Bds: Park and Recreation Bd.; Library
Bd. Prev: Beautification Bd. 1968-; Co-Ch.,
Bicentennial 1976. Org: PTA. B: 1/17/38. Add:
1212 Head Rd., P.O. Box 181, Fultondale 35068
(205) 841-6456.

Gainesville. MRS. GROVER HARRISON
     P.O. Box 153, Gainesville 35464.

Gantt's Quarry. RUBY K. CONASTER
                 THELMA L. MC ALISTER
                 JEAN D. PURVIS
     P.O. Drawer 480, Sylacauga 35750.

Geiger. OVETTA MITCHELL
         BEULAH PINSON
     Rt. 1, Box G39A, Geiger 35459.

Goldville. MARY H. POWELL (D)
     1973-. B: 4/25/10. Add: Daviston Rt. 1,
36256.

Gordon. FRANCES DICKSON (D)
     Occ: Nurse's Aide. B: 12/7/22. Add: Gordon
36343.

Gordon. CHRISTINE SMITH
     P.O. Box 42, Gordon 36343.

Goshen. BELINDA C. EDWARDS
     Town Hall, Goshen 36035.

Grant. EARLENE G. SANDERS
     P.O. Box 70, Grant 35747.

Guntersville. SUE JACKSON SORTER (D)
     1968-. Bds: Ch., Bd. of Dir. Top of Ala.
Council Govt. Occ: Store owner. B: 9/3/29.
Add: 1866 Gunter Ave., Guntersville 35976
(205) 582-4222.

Hammondville. ESSIE DOWNER
               VELMA HAMMOND
               PEARL WINSTON
     Rt. 1, Valley Head 35989.

Harpersville. ROSA LEE
     Town Hall, Harpersville 35078.

Heath. ANNA LOIS NALL
     P.O. Box 1414, Andalusia 36420.

Hollywood. ELIZABETH HAAS
            MARY L. SNODGRASS
     P.O. Box 248, Hollywood 35752.

Homewood. EDNA L. MC CUNE
           PAULINE R. MONTGOMERY
     P.O. Box 58066, Homewood 35209.

Homewood. MARGARET ROBERTSON
     1976-. Bds: Library Bd. Occ: Corp. Manager.
B: 9/8/17. Add: 1503 Valley Ave., Birmingham
35209 (205) 933-8813.

Hoover. ELSIE BRADDOCK
     1631 Montgomery Hwy., Hoover 35216.

Huntsboro. MARY KATE STOVALL (D)
     Bds: Family Practice Ctr. Adv. Bd.; E. Ala.
Exec., Bd. of Dir's.; Mental Health and Retard-
ation. Party: Co-Ch. Cnty. Women's Auxiliary
1977. Org: NEA; Russell Cnty. Concerned Group;
NAACP; Ala. Dem. Conf. Cnty. Voters Assoc.; Jr.
Educators of Tomorrow. Educ: Ala. State U.
1949 BS; 1955 MEd.; Atlanta U. 1969 MLS. Occ:
Funeral Dir. B: 12/13/21. Add: P.O. Box 154,
Huntsboro 36860 (205) 667-7679.

Huntsville. JANE MABRY (I)
     1974-. Bds: Planning Cmsn.; Metropolitan
Planning Org.; Central City Assoc. Prev: Local
Govt. Study Cmsn. 1971-73. Educ: U. of Ala.
1957 BA; Ala. U. 1976 MS. B: 10/5/36. Add:
424 Eustis Ave. SE, Huntsville 35801
(205)539-9612.

Jacksonville. HAZEL D. HICKS (D)
     1976-. Bds: Ch., Finance Com.; Utility Com.;
Street Com; Hospital Bd. Org: Concerned Citizens
of Jacksonville. Educ: U. of Ala. 1945 BS; 1951
MS. Occ: Professor. B: 9/4/24. Add: 1006 7th
Ave., Jacksonville 32265 (205) 435-7611.

Kansas. KELLY SUE WAKEFIELD
     Town Hall, Kansas 35573.

Killen. FLORENCE LE MASTER
     P.O. Box 27, Killen 35645.

Kinston. SARA N. BOWDEN (D)
     1976-. Bds: Planning Com. B: 12/10/29.
Add: Peachtree St., Kinston 36453.

Lafayette. RELLA LANDRUM (D)
     1976-. Bds: Ch., Finance; Streets; Parks.
Org: PTA. Occ: Bookkeeper. B: 12/21/21. Add:
206 2nd Ave., Lafayette 36862 (205) 864-3111.

Leesburg. CHRISTINE MACKEY (D) **
     1972-. B: 5/15/15. Add: Leesburg 35983
(205) 526-8299.

Lincoln. MARY C. HENDERSON (I)
     1972-. Bds: Ch., Finance Com.; Library Bd.;
Industrial Bd. Org: AARP. Educ: Huntingdon Coll
1922 BA. B: 6/30/00. Add: Crawford St.,Lincoln
35096 (205) 763-7721.

Lipscomb. BLANCHE S. PERRY
     512 Ave. H, Lipscomb 35020.

Livingston. PATSY CHANEY (D) **
     1972-. Bds: Planning Cmsn.; Beautification
Com.; Library Bd. Org: AAUW; PTO. Educ:
Randolph Macon Woman's Coll. 1963 BA; Georgetown
U. 1965 MA. B: 12/13/40. Add: Picken St.,
Box MM, Livingston 35470 (205) 652-2513.

Loachapoka. ALICE R. ELLINGTON
             IDA W. ROBBINS
     P.O. Box 122, Loachapoka 36865.

Lockhart. BESSIE HENDERSON
     P.O. Box 216, Lockhart 36455.

Loxley. ELSIE S. D'OLIVER
     P.O. Box 57, Loxley 36551.

Lynn.   BARBARA DUKE (R)
    1976-. B: 4/6/39. Add: P.O. Box 73, Lynn
35575.

Lynn.   PENNY WINSLOW
    P.O. Box 145, Lynn 35575.

Margaret.   MAXINE K. MITCHELL
            ANNIE BELL WHARTON
    P.O. Box 127, Margaret 35112.

Mentone.   LINDA BROWN
    P.O. Box 16, Mentone 35984.

Midfield.   JULIA W. PLANT (D) **
    1972-. Bds: Regional Planning Cmsn. Org:
PTA; Bd. of Dir., Chamber of Commerce. B:
11/23/31. Add: 403 10th Ave., Midfield 35228
(205) 788-2460.

Midland City.   MARCINE MC KNIGHT
    P.O. Box 69, Midland City 36350.

Midway.   MARY JANE TURNER (D)
    1976-. Bds: Ch., City License and Permits;
Streets and Lights Com. Org: NEA; NAACP. Educ:
Ala. A & M U. 1973 BS. Occ: Special Educ. Teacher
B: 1/4/51. Add: P.O. Box 149, Midway 36053.

Midway.   DEBORAH L. T. UPSHAW (D)
    1976-. Occ: Plain Laborer. B: 2/15/28.
Add: P.O. Box 103, Midway 36053.

Montgomery.   CATHERYNE W. CASWELL
    P.O. Box 1111, Montgomery 36102.

Morris.   JOYCE BALLARD
    P.O. Box 163, Morris 35116.

Morris.   MARY C. COUNTS (D)
    1976-. Bds: Zoning Bd. Org: Amers. Against
Union Control of Govt.; Freedoms Foundation;
Beautification Bd. Educ: Huntington Coll. 1933
AB. B: 8/18/13. Add: P.O. Box 128, Morris 35116.

Mountain Brook.   MRS. WILLIAM GIVEN
    P.O. Box 9006, Mountain Brook 35213.

Mount Vernon.   AMERLIA E. JONES
    P.O. Box 139, Mount Vernon 36560.

Mulga.   ALMA J. GREEN (D)
    1976-. Org: OES. Educ: Lawson State Jr. Coll.
1972 AA. Occ: Social Worker. B: 4/19/32. Add:
219 1st St., Mulga 35118 (205) 787-4521.

Myrtlewood.   NORA ETHERIDGE
    P.O. Box 70, Myrtlewood 36763.

Myrtlewood.   EVELYN RAY YELVERTON (D) **
    1968-. Bds: Youth Programs; Recreation Bd.
Prev: Justice of Peace 1969-73. Occ: Custodian
of City School Funds. B: 11/20/23. Add: Box 176,
Myrtlewood 36763 (205) 295-5120.

Napier Field.   MYRA HENDERSON
    Rte. 6, Dothan 36301.

Nectar.   MARJORIE HUDSON GARREN (D)
    1976-. Bds: Water Com.; Ch., Beautification.
Org: Amer. Registry of Medical Asst's.; Women
Dem. Org.; OES; Cnty. Welfare Bd.; Dem. Club.
Occ: Registered Medical Asst. B: 3/12/21. Add:
Rt. 1, Cleveland 35049 (205) 559-7431.

Newbern   NORA M. TRUE (I)
    1970-. Org: DAR. Educ: U. of Ala. 1927 AB.
B: 12/11/05. Add: Box 295, Newbern 36765.

New Brockton.   LOIS BAKER
    P.O. Box 70, New Brockton 36351.

Newton.   MARY CARMICHAEL
    P.O. Box 102, Newton 36352.

North Johns.   ELIZABETH DAGNON
             LUCILLE PARSONS
    P.O. Box 156, North Johns 35006.

Notasulga.   BARBARA G. PAYNE
    P.O. Box 207, Notasulga 36866.

Oak Grove.   AILEEN MINOR
    P.O. Drawer 807, Sylacauga 35150.

Oakman.   VELMA SAVAGE
    P.O. Box 267, Oakman 35579.

Odenville.   ALICE BLAKENSHIP
            GLORIA HENDERSON
    P.O. Box 113, Odenville 35120.

Onycha.   EMMA LOU HOOMES
          WILLIE MAE JOHNS
    Rte. 1, Opp 36467.

Paint Rock.   MRS. KATHERINE ROUSSEAR
    P.O. Box 143, Paint Rock 35764.

Pickensville.   MRS. JAMES WRIGHT
    Rte. 2, Carrollton 35447.

Pine Hill.   ROBERTA TOMLINSON JORDAN
    1976-. Bds: Ch., Parks and Recreation Bd.;
Regional Planning Cmsn. Org: BPW. Occ: Office
Manager. B: 1/20/41. Add: P.O. Box 126, Pine
Hill 36769 (205) 963-4442.

Pollard.   VONCILE STANTON
    Rt. 1, Pollard 36441.

Red Bay.   NELL THOMPSON (I)
    1976-. Prev: City Clerk 1949-57. Occ: Book-
keeper. B: 9/20/24. Add: Box 237, Red Bay 35582

Ridgeville.   ALETHIA RICHARDSON
    Rte. 1, Ridgeville 35954.

Robertsdale.   WINONA C. JONES (D)
    1976-. Bds: City Planning Cmsn.; City Repr.
to Library Bd. Org: BPW; Occ: Hospital Exec.
Housekeeper. B: 10/5/38. Add: P.O. Box 545,
Robertsdale 36567 (205) 947-2144.

Rockford.   MARY F. REYNOLDS (D)
    1976-. Org: OES. Occ: Factory Manager. B:
12/23/40. Add: P.O. Box 233, Rockford 35136.

Rosa. SILVIA FAUST
        Rt. 1, Oneonta 35121.

St. Florian. ELENORA U. ECKL
        Rt. 11, Box 318, Saint Florian 35630.

Sardis City. DIXIE JOHNSON
        Box 541, Boaz 35957.

Sheffield. CLAIR S. PITTS
            PATSY L. SAULS
        P.O. Box Q, Sheffield 35660.

Sipsey. GERALDEAN PHILLIPS
         NICKOLENE VANCE
        P.O. Box 156, Sipsey 35584.

Southside. BARBARA JOYCE ROUTON
        Rt. 1, Box 87, Gadsden 35901.

Sulvan Spring. VICKI H. PARKER
        P.O. Box 746, Mulga 35118.

Sylacauga. SHERRY B. ARNOLD
        1976-. Bds: School Bd. Liaison; Park and
        Recreation. Org: Service League; PTA. B: 6/11/45
        Add: 404 W. Spring St., Sylacauga 35150
        (205) 245-6361.

Sylacauga. MRS. REXIE LIGHTSEY
        P.O. Box 390, Sylacauga 35150.

Taylor. RUTH BARTON
         GERALDINE PARKER
         THERMA RONEY
        P.O. Box 402, Rte. 7, Dothan 36301.

Triana. OLIVIA WITHCHARD
        Rte. 3, Box 142, Madison 35758.

Trussville. JEANETTE H. ALEXANDER
        P.O. Box 137, Trussville 35173.

Uniontown. CARRIE B. MC FADDEN
        P.O. Box 6, Uniontown 36786.

Vance. MRS. MARY MARTIN
        P.O. Box 25, Vance 35490.

Vernon. ROSE MARIE SMITH (D)
        1976-. Bds: Water Works and Sewer Bd.,
        Beautification Council; Ch., Public Relations.
        Prev: Bd. of Trustees 1971-78, Lamar Cnty. School.
        B: 8/18/41. Add: 405 2nd Ave., SW, Box 398,
        Vernon 35592 (205) 695-7718.

Vestavia Hills. FRANCES COGGIN (I)
        1976-. Bds: Finance Com. Occ: Exec. in Food-
        Ice Cream Chain. B: 11/21/20. Add: 1532 Hays
        Circle, Vestavia Hills 35216.

Vredenburgh. JOANNE PUGH
              MARY WILLINGHAM
        Town Hall, Vredenburgh 36481.

Waldo. HATTY M. JONES (D) **
        1972-. Educ: Al. State U. 1960 BS; U. of Ariz.
        1966 MEd. B: 12/29/18. Add: Rte. 3, Box 238-1,
        Talladega 35160.

Waverly. MARY WILLIE GRAVES (D)
        1974-. Org: PTA; AEA. Educ: Auburn U. BS,
        MA. B: 2/8/06. Add: Waverly 36879.

Waverly. BARBARA L. TAYLOR (R)
        1975-. Occ: Bookkeeper. B: 6/24/35. Add:
        P.O. Box 126, Waverly 36879.

Weaver. JANA MITCHAM
        P.O. Box A, Weaver 36277.

Webb. ANNETTE GAMBLE (D)
        1976-. Occ: Volunteer Secretary. B: 5/9/45.
        Add: Rt. 1, Box 195A, Webb 36376.

Webb. WILDA HADEN
        P.O. Box 132, Webb 36376.

Wilsonville. MRS. ROBERT JOBE
              MRS. E. W. SCRUGGS
        P.O. Drawer 70, Wilsonville 35186.

Winfield. JOANNE F. MANN (D)
        1976-. Org: NEA. Educ: U. of Tenn. 1955 BSN;
        U. of Ala. 1976 MA. Occ: Special Educ. Teacher.
        B: 9/9/33. Add: P.O. 580, Winfield 35594.

Woodland. EUNICE TRAYLOR LOVVORN (D)
        1967-. Occ: Supervisor. B: 11/23/19. Add:
        P.O. Box 3, Woodland 36280. (205) 449-2222.

Judges

JANIE L. SHORES
        Associate Justice, Montgomery 36104.

State Boards and Commissions

A complete list of state boards and commissions,
and of their membership, was not available for
inclusion.

Alaska

LEE MC ANERNEY (R)
Commissioner, Department of Community and Regional Affairs. 1974-. Bds: Ch., State Census '80 Com.; Ch., State Geographic Names Bd. Party: State Del. 1972; State Alt. 1976. Prev: Mayor of Seward 1973-74; Councilwoman 1971-73. B: 7/14/20. Add: 326 4th St., Apt. 1003; Juneau 99801 (907) 465-4704.

State Legislature

State Senate

KATHRYN E. POLAND (D)
1970-. Dist: L. Bds: Ch., Resources Com.; Commerce Com.; Jobs and Devt. Com. Party: State Del. 1970-72; Precinct Secretary 1956-60, 1964-70. Org: LWV; Dem. Club; Pioneers of Alaska; NOWL. B: 10/12/19. Add: 1411 Kouskov St., Kodiak 99615 (907) 465-3717.

State House

THELMA BUCKHOLDT **
Dist: 9. Bds: Manpower Planning Council. Party: Del. Nat. Conv. 1972. Educ: Mt. St. Mary's Coll. BA. Occ: Planning Consultant. Add: 2607 Kona La., Anchorage 99503.

LISA RUDD (D)
1976-. Dist: 11. Bds: Ch., House Community and Regional Affairs Com. Prev: Cmsn. for Human Rights 1974-75, 1967-70; Alas. Adv. Com. to U.S. Cmsn. on Civil Rights 1961-65; Charter Cmsn. 1970-71; Employee Relations Bd. 1974-75; Governor's EEO Com. 1974-75. Org: ASPA; NOWL; NOW; LWV. Educ: Bennington Coll. 1956 BA; U. of Alas. 1975 MPA. B: 8/11/33. Add: 2827 Lore Rd., Anchorage 99507 (907) 465-3870.

SARAH J. SMITH (D)
1976-. Dist: 20. Bds: Community and Regional Affairs Com.; Labor and Management Com.; Resources Com. Prev: Field Repr., State Community and Regional Affairs. 1974-76. Educ: U. of Ill. 1967 BS. Occ: Saleswoman. B: 1/23/45. Add: 321 Church St., Fairbanks 99701.

County Commissions

Barrow. **ALICE A. SOLOMON** (D)
1974-. Prev: Health Bd. 1974-77. Occ: Nursing Asst. B: 5/13/18. Add: Box 235, Barrow 99723.

Fairbanks. **KAREN PARR**
P.O. Box 1267, Fairbanks 99707.

Haines. **PATTY LOU JONES**
1975-. Org: Amer. Alliance for Health, Physical Educ. and Recreation; Women's Club. Educ:

Mich. State U. 1954 MS. B: 4/25/32. Add: Menaker Rd., P.O. Box 249, Haines 99827.

Kenai Peninsula. **MARGARET A. BRANSON** (R)
1976-. Bds: Ch., Leg. Overview Com.; Cook Inlet Air Resources Management Dist.; Roads and Trails; Solid Waste Com. Org: Community Club. Educ: U. of Denver 1949 BA. Occ: Shop Owner. B: 5/12/27. Add: Box 740 Bean Crk. Rd., Cooper Landing 99572 (907) 262-4441.

Kenai Peninsula. **JEAN B. DOUGLAS**
P.O. Box 850, Soldotna 99669.

Kenai Peninsula. **JO ANN ELSON** (R) **
1974-. Party: Precinct Com. 1969-70. Prev: Advisory School Com. 1972-73. Org: Ch., Alas. Public Employee Assoc.; Pres., Rep. Woman's Club. B: 1/27/37. Add: Box 2788, Kenai 99611.

Kenai Peninsula. **JUDITH F. HAMRICK**
PAMELA F. OLDOW
P.O. Box 850, Soldotna 99669.

Kodiak Island. **SANDRA KAVANAUGH**
BETTY WALLIN
P.O. Box 1246, Kodiak 99615.

Mayors

Allakaket. **STELLA HAMILTON**
Allakaket 99720.

Anderson. **VERA MARIE LAMB**
P.O. Box 4011, Clear 99704.

Haines. **GAIL JEAN WALLACE** (D) **
1974-. Bds: Finance Com.; Streets and Water Com.; Public Health; Parks and Recreation. Prev: Council 1975-76. Org: Art Council; Emblem Club. Occ: Owner of Garage Service Station. B: 4/9/36. Add: Box W., Haines 99827 (907) 766-2571.

North Pole. **CARLETA LEWIS**
P.O. Box 5109, North Pole 99705.

Platinum. **CLARA MARTIN**
1977-. Bds: Ch., Community School Com.; Ch., District Parent Adv. Com.; Ch., Health Com. Prev: Ch., School Bd. 1975-76. B: 7/27/24. Add: (907) 543-2086.

Port Heiden. **ANNIE CHRISTENSEN**
Port Heiden 99549.

Valdez. **LYNN CHRYSTAL**
P.O. Box 307, Valdez 99686.

Wales. **ARLENE ONGTOWASRUK**
Wales 99783.

Wasilla. ELIZABETH HJELLEN (R)
1976-. Bds: Ch., Adv. Planning; Ch., Adv. Airport; Ch., Library. Party: State Alt. 1974. Prev: Councilwoman 1975-76. B: 11/7/16. Add: Lucille Lk., Wasilla 99687 (907) 376-5227.

Local Councils

Akiachak. MARY ANN LOMACK
Akiachak 99551.

Aliak. SOPHIE SAKAR
Chuathbaluk, Aliak 99557.

Allakaket. CAROLINE BERGMAN
LYDIA BERGMAN
VELMA SIMON
RHEA WILLIAMS
Allakaket 99720.

Anchorage. LIDIA SELKREGG
Pouch 6-650, Anchorage 99502.

Anchorage. ARLISS STURGULEWSKI (R)
1976-. Bds: Urban Observatory; Alas.Municipal League. Prev: Adv. Planning Cmsn. 1968-75; Nat. Assoc. of Cnties 1972-74; Bicentennial Cmsn. 1976; Capitol Site Selection Com. 1975-76. Org: Planning Assoc.; Natl. Assoc. of Parliamentarians; Alas. Ctr. for Environment; Alas. Public Research Group; Arts Council; Visual Arts Ctr; LWV. Educ: U. of Wash. 1949 BA. Occ: Personal Investments. B: 9/27/27. Add: 2957 Sheldon Jackson, Anchorage 99504 (907) 264-4311.

Anderson. MARIE LAMB
P.O. Box 4011, Clear 99704.

Aniak. FLORENCE NELSON
LUCY SIMEON
Chuathbaluk, Aniak 99557.

Barrow. MOLLY PEDERSON (I) **
1974-. Prev: School Bd. 1973-74. B: 12/24/35. Add: Box 184, Barrow 99723 (907) 852-5511.

Bethel. BETTY HICKLING
P.O. 388, Bethel 99559.

Chefornak. MARGE LARSEN
Chefornak 99561.

Craig. ELIZABETH M. DENNIS (R)
1975-. Bds: Ch., Finance Com. Occ: Bookkeeper. B: 6/2/21. Add: 3rd & Beach Rd., P.O. Box 31, Craig 99921.

Craig. ANALEE WOODWARD PAUL (R)
1976-. Bds: Ch., Bd. of Dir's., Library Assoc; Health Corp., Garbage Cmsn. Party: Ch., Precinct Election Bd. 1974-77. Org: SE Alas. Health Systems Agency. Educ: U. of Colo. 1969 BS. B: 10/13/46. Add: Box 54, Craig 99921.

Deering. DELORES BARR
Deering 99736.

Dillingham. BARBARA SUSAN LOWY (R)
1975-. Org: Chamber of Commerce. Educ: Lancaster General Hospital School of Nursing 1962 RN. Occ: Asst. Dir. of Nurses. B: 6/4/41. Add: PHS Hospital, Kanakanak, Dillingham 99516 (907) 842-5211.

Elim. LILY FREMERING
Elim 99739.

Galena. ANN MARTIN
Box 149, Galena 99741.

Goodnews Bay. SUSIE BAVILLA
PAULINE GALILA
Goodnews Bay 99589.

Haines. NIKKI HOPPER
P.O. Box 239, Haines 99827.

Holy Cross. JUDI DEMIENTIEFF
MARY DEMIENTIEFF
BETTY JOHNSON
LILLIAN WALKER
Holy Cross 99602.

Homer. NELDA A. CALHOUN (R)
1972-. Party: State Del. 1954; Precinct Committeewoman 1954-60. Prev: School Bd. 1956-59. Org: Chamber of Commerce; Rep. Club. Occ: Manager. B: 11/4/24. Add: P.O. Box 213, Homer 99603 (907) 235-8121.

Huslia. GERTIE BROWN
ANNIE VENT
Huslia 99746.

Huslia. MABEL VENT (R)
1976-. Bds: Treasurer. Party: Local Bd. Member 1976-79. Occ: Manager. B: 3/16/50. Add: Huslia 99746.

Kaltag. MARYLENE ESMAILKA
MARY ETTA NEGLASKA
Kaltag 99748.

Kenai. BETTY JANE GLICK (R)
1976-. Bds: Harbor Cmsn.; Adv. Planning and Zoning Cmsn.; Kenai Peninsula Borough Planning Cmsn. Prev: Adv. Planning and Zoning Cmsn. 1974-76. Occ: Secretary/Bookkeeper. B: 9/15/35. Add: Corner Highbush and Primrose, Kenai 99611 (907) 283-7644.

Ketchikan. ESTELLE THOMPSON
Kasaan, Ketchikan 99950.

King Cove. MARIE LARSON (I)
1976-. Org: Women's Club. Occ: City Clerk. B: 4/9/47. Add: P.O. Box 23, King Cove 99612 (907) 497-2340.

Kivalina. BECKY NORTON
Kivalina 99750.

Klawock. MARY JACKSON
TRINA PERATROVICH
P.O. Box 113, Klawock 99925.

Kodiak. TONI EASTON
           CAROL LECHNER
      P.O. Box 1397, Kodiak 99615.

Kotlik. ISIDORE HUNT
          MAGGIE WASULI
      Kotlik 99620.

Kupreanof. KARIN LINKER (D)
      1975-. Bds: Ch., Planning Com. Org: Alas.
Conservation Society. Educ: U. of Calif Riverside
1970 BA. B: 8/7/48. Add: P.O. Box 707, Petersburg 99832.

Kupreanof. SHARON B. SPRAGUE (R)
      1975-. Bds: Planning Com. Occ: Dental
Technician. B: 9/12/39. Add: Box 567, Petersburg
99833.

Manokotak. BILLIE BARTMAN
      Manokotak 99628.

McGrath. ANN EGRASS
      1975-. Bds: Governor's Adv. Bd. B: 4/15/31.
Add: Box 106, McGrath 99627.

McGrath. ROSE WINKELMAN
      P.O. Box 57, McGrath 99627.

Mekoryuk. FLORA SALLY JACK (I)
      1975-. Bds: Treasurer. B: 1/19/45. Add:
P.O. Box 13, Mekoryuk 99630.

Nelson Island. THERESA CHARLIE
      Nelson Island, Toksook Bay 99637.

Nenana. MEDA LORD
      P.O. Box 177, Nenana 99760.

Newhalen. LINDA JOHNSON
            EVELYN WASSILLIE
            SHIRLEY WASSILLIE
      P.O. Box 31, Iliamna 99606.

New Stuyahok. SOPHIE WALCOTT
      New Stuyahok 99636.

Nightmute. THERESA GEORGE
      Nightmute 99690.

Nome. BLANCHE WALTERS
        VIRGINIA WHITE
      P.O. Box 281, Nome 99762.

Nondalton. ELIZABETH BALLUTA
             HILDA JACKINSKY
      Nondalton 99640.

Noorvik. MINNIE G. SHELDON
      P.O. Box 146, Noorvik 99763.

North Pole. SHIRLEY TOWNE
      P.O. Box 5109, North Pole 99705.

Nuiqsut. LENA BAKER
      Nuiqsut 99723.

Nulato. MARYANN PATSY
      Nulato 99765.

Ouzinkie. ANGELINE ANDERSON
            VERNA BENNETT
      P.O. Box 35, Ouzinkie 99644.

Petersburg. ANNIE L. TAYLOR (D) **
      1974-. Bds: Legislative. Org: Trustee, ILWU.
Occ: Fletcher. B: Florence, Ore. Add: 300 F St.
Petersburg 99833 (907) 772-3129.

Platinum. ANNIE FOX
      Platinum 99651.

Port Alexander. SUSAN TAYLOR
      City Hall, Port Alexander 99836.

Port Lions. MARGARET NELSON
      P.O. Box 278, Port Lions 99550.

Russian Mission. OKALENA POLTY
      Russian Mission 99657.

St. Mary's. SOPHIE GEORGE
      P.O. Box 163, St. Mary's 99658.

St. Michael. ESTHER ANDREWS
      St. Michael 99659.

St. Paul Island. ADRIAN MELOVIDOV
      P.O. Box 98, St. Paul Island 99660.

Selawik. LAURA NORTON
      Box 49, Selawik 99770.

Seldovia. JUDITH HAMRICK
      P.O. Drawer B, Seldovia 99663.

Seldovia. CHERYL A. REYNOLDS
      1976-. Org: Community Relations Org. Occ:
Medical Clinic Administrator. B: 10/12/46.
Add: Drawer J, Seldovia 99663 (907) 234-7643.

Seward. PAMELA F. OLDAW
      P.O. Box 337, Seward 99664.

Shishmaref. MAGGIE NAYOKPUK
      Org: Youth Council. Occ: City Clerk. B:
8/24/56. Add: Shishmaref 99772 (907) 649-3781.

Skagway. MARIAN ROBERTA EDWARDS (D)
      1975-. Bds: Museum Bd., Library. Party:
State Del. 1966; Precinct Committeewoman 1964-67.
Org: OES. Occ: Ticket Clerk. B: 2/3/43. Add:
6th & Spring, Skagway 99840 (907) 983-2297.

Skagway. IRENE HENRICKSEN
      P.O. Box 415, Skagway 99840.

Skagway. LILLIAN LITZENBERGER
      1973-. Org: Chamber of Commerce. Occ: Asst.
Ticket Agent. B: 4/28/18. Add: Box 321,
Skagway 99840 (907) 983-2293.

Skagway. CHRIS ROHLF
      P.O. Box 415, Skagway 99840.

Stebbins. ANATOLE BAGEVAKTUK
      Stebbins 99671.

Tanana. DOROTHY JORDAN (D)
      1977-. Educ: U. of Alas. BA. B: 8/29/50.
Add: Tanana 99777.

Teller. MAGGIE FOSTER
       DOROTHY ISABELL
     P.O. Box 548, Teller 99778.

Tenakee Springs. ROSALIE BEATON
     P.O. Box 52, Tenakee Springs 99841.

Tenakee Springs. VICKI CONVERSE (D) **
     1971-. Bds: Planning Cmsn.; Public Safety Com.
   Party: Secretary, Treasurer, City Com. 1974-75.
   Org: Dem. Club; Pioneers of Alas. B: 12/3/07.
   Add: New Converse House, Tenakee Springs 99841.

Tenakee Springs. KATHRYN SUZANNE WALTERS (D) **
     1973-. Bds: City Council; Planning Cmsn.
   Secretary. Party: V-Ch., Dem. League 1973-76.
   Occ: Librarian. B: 5/29/38. Add: Box 46,
   Tenakee Springs 99841.

Unalaska. BARBARA HAMM
     P.O. Box 89, Unalaska 99685.

Upper Kalskag. OLGA NESBIT
     Upper Kalskag 99607.

Valdez. SUSY COLLINS
     P.O. Box 307, Valdez 99686.

Wasilla. MARCELLA P. PADIE
           DOROTHY PAGE
           PERLIA J. STRASSBURG
           JOANN TORNBERG
     Star Rt., Box 2727, Wasilla 99687.

Whittier. VIRGINIA BENDER
            SUE LEWIS
            FLORENCE RAWHOUSER
     City Hall, Whittier 99502.

Wrangell. JUDITH BAKER
     P.O. Box 531, Wrangell 99929.

Yakutat. EVELYN ANDERSON
           LENA FARKAS
     P.O. Box 6, Yakutat 99689.

State Boards and Commissions

     Office of the Governor, State Capitol Bldg.,
     Pouch A, Juneau 99811.

Administration of Justice, Commission on the
     NORA GUINN
     MELISSA MIDDLETON
     GAIL ROWLAND

Aging, Advisory Committee on
     CAROL DE YOUNG
     KATHRYN FIALA
     VERA SIDARS
     DORIS SOUTHALL
     BETTY WARREN

Alcoholism, Board on
     JACQUELINE PFLAUM

Arts, Council on the
     CONNIE BOOCHEVER
     DOT DARDARSON
     POLLY LEE

JAN MACKIN
BETTIE MC DONALD
ELVERA VOTH

Catastrophic Illness Committee
     BARBARA A. BOWNS

Child Advocacy, Office of Board of Directors
     EDNA APATIKI
     FANNIE CARROL
     LUCY CROW
     NANCY FERGUSON
     SARA HANNAN
     JAMIE JONES
     MARILOU MADDEN
     TONI RAMBOSEK
     BARBARA WOLSTAD

Chiropractic Examiners, Board of
     LINNEA BURNEISTER

Collection Agency Board
     SHARON ANDREW
     LOIS J. INGALLS
     JUDITH WARWICK

Community Mental Health Services Advisory Council
     ANN EGRESS
     ANN GRAHAM
     SUSAN HOLT
     CORNELIA HOWARD
     LYDIA MALUTIN

Dental Examiners, Board of
     JANA M. VARRATI

Developmental Disability Planning and Advisory
Council
     SAVANAH HARGRAVES
     SADIE NEAKOK
     ROSALYN REEDER
     ANN SYMONS
     CAROL WELSH
     ANNIE WHALEY

Dispensing Opticians, Board of
     EDNA LYON

Drug Abuse, Board on
     LENA ANDREE
     PEGGY COLLETTA

Education, Board of
     JAN HOHMAN
     BEVERLY HORN
     KATHERINE T. HURLEY
     THELMA LANGDON
     YVONNE TREMBLAY

Educational Commission of the States
     KATHERINE T. HURLEY
     DORIS RAY

Employment of the Physically Handicapped, Committee
on
     LAURA M. BERGT
     GEORGINA HERRON
     JOERENE HOUT
     MARION KEYES
     JEAN MAHONEY

Environmental Advisory Board
    KATRINA STONOROV

Equal Employment Opportunity Committee
    GEORGIANNA LINCOLN
    THELMA THRASHER

Fisheries Council
    KAY POLAND

Geographic Board
    PHYLLIS DE MUTH

Growth Policy Council
    DIANA TILLION

Hairdressing and Beauty Culture Examiners, Board of
    MRS. IONE LAMBERT
    JUDITH R. MANESS
    MRS. HESTER PUMPHREY

Historical Commission
    MARTHA L. LARSON
    PATRICIA ROPPEL

Historic Site Advisory Committee
    RENE BLAHUTA
    ELLEN LANGE
    KAREN W. WORKMAN

Human Rights, Commission for
    DOROTHY M. LARSON
    CAROL SMITH
    DIANA SNOWDEN

Juvenile Justice and Delinquency Commission
    FANNIE CARROLL
    NANCY FERGUSON
    NORA GUINN
    SARA HANNAN
    JANIE JONES
    MELISSA MIDDLETON
    TONI RAMBOSEK
    GAIL ROWLAND

Libraries, Advisory Council on
    NANCY EBONA
    JEAN M. EISENHART
    WILDA MARSTON
    CAROL WILSON

Local Boundary Commission
    MRS. JO ANDERSON
    SHEILA GALLAGHER JONES

Manpower Planning Council
    JUANITA CORWIN
    KATHERINE T. HURLEY
    MYRTLE JOHNSON
    KATHERINE LLOYD

Manpower Services Council
    JUANITA CORWIN
    KATHERINE T. HURLEY
    MYRTLE JOHNSON
    KATHERINE LLOYD
    JEWEL MASON JONES

Medical Board
    LOUISE M. BEIGHLE

Nursing, Board of
    NORMA J. FRANK
    JOYCE HAZELBAKER
    KANDACE HENRY
    BETTY IRWIN HODO
    BETTY KESTER
    EILEEN MONTANO
    ERNA RASMUSSEN
    JOAN SNYDER
    MARJORIE VAN KOOTEN

Nursing Home Administrators Board
    SARAH JANE HANNA
    MRS. ROBERLEY POTTER
    THERESA PREVOST
    HELEN SANDERSON

Parole, Board of
    BEVERLY DUNHAM

Physical Therapy Board
    DONNA KLOKKEVOLD
    C. PATRICIA MC CABE

Police Standards Council
    DORIS LOENNIG

Post-Secondary Education, Commission on
    MILLIE BANFIELD
    MRS. WADE JACKINSKY
    SHARRON LOBAUGH
    MARY E. LOMEN
    BLANCHE WALTERS

Professional Teaching Practices Commission
    DAPHNE HOFSCHUTE
    RUTH TORDOFF

Psychologists and Psychological Associate Examiners,
Board of
    DOROTHY WHITMORE

Public Accountancy, Board of
    MARGARET BAKER
    MYRNA MC DOUGAL
    CHARLOTTE STUART

Public Broadcasting Commission
    LOUISE COLLINS
    ANITA MC GRATH
    JUNE M. NELSON
    SUE TAYLOR

Public Offices Commission
    WILDA HUDSON
    LOUISE KELLOGG
    JANE PERKINS

Public Utilities Commission
    CAROLYN GUESS
    SUSAN KNOWLES

Real Estate Commission
    HELEN D. BEIRNE
    CAROL MASER

Regents, Board of. University of Alaska
    MILDRED BANFIELD
    MARGARET HALL

Salary Commission
    HELEN BEIRNE
    KATHLEEN DIEBELS

State-Operated Schools. Board of Directors
    JUDITH GEORGE
    SUSAN MURPHY
    CAROL PHILLIPS

Teachers' Retirement Board
    JEAN JOHNSON
    LEAH PETERSON STRANDBERG

Tourism Advisory Board
    MARTHA EDWARDS
    ALICE A. HARRIGAN
    HAZEL HEATH
    LAURA HERMAN

Transportation Planning Commission
    JOYCE GALLEHER

Violent Crimes Compensation Board
    PATRICIA MOORE

Vocational Education Advisory Council
    MRS. LOUIS CHASE
    MRS. CHARLIES M. MOORE
    MRS. FRANCES ROSE
    BETTY WILLIAMS

Water Resources Board
    PEG TILESTON

Arizona

State Executive and Cabinet

MONA SMITH
    Director, Department of Tourism. Add: 11700
W. Washington, Rm. 501, Phoenix 85007.

CAROLYN WARNER (D)
    Superintendent of Public Instruction. 1974-.
Bds: Council of Chief State School Officers; Ariz.
Bd. of Educ.; Ariz. Bd. of Regents. Prev: School
Bd. Member 1968-74. Org: Council on Econ. Educ.;
LWV; Phoenix Exec. Club; Dem. Women's Club;
Western Correctional Assoc; Gov. Adv. Management
Team; Gov. Cmsn. on Environment. B: 8/5/30.
Add: 5245 N. Bartlett Cir., Phoenix 85016
(602) 271-4361.

State Legislature

State Senate

LELA ALSTON
    4133 West Cheery Lynn Rd., Phoenix 85007.

GERTRUDE CAMPING
    1700 W. Washington, Phoenix 85007.

SUE DYE (D)
    1974-. Dist: 12. Bds: Majority Whip; Finance
Com.; Health Com. Party: State Del. 1975-77;
Precinct Committeewoman 1974-. Org: NEA; AAUW;
NOWL; LWV; WPC; Dem. Club; Tucson Press Club.
Educ: Indiana State Teachers Coll. 1951 BA;
Indiana U. 1968 MA. Occ: Teacher. B: 1/28/28.
Add: 1791 E. Hampton, Tucson 85719 (602)271-5261.

POLLY GETZWILLER (D) *
    Dist: 6. Party: Nat. Del. 1968. Org: BPW;
Dem. Women's Club; Women's Club; Nat. Platform
Assoc. B: 3/8/24. Add: Box 127, Casa Grande
85222.

ANNE LINDEMAN (R) **
    Dist: 17. Occ: RN. Add: 6542 West Earll Dr.,
Phoenix 85033 (602) 271-5897.

MARCIA GAIL WEEKS (D) *
    1974-. Dist: 16. Org: LWV. Educ: U. of Ariz.
1967 BS. B: 1/19/38. Add: 3538 W. Mercerla,
Phoenix 85029.

State House

CARMEN F. CAJERO
    104 W. District, Tucson 85714

DONNA J. CARLSON (R)
    1974-. Dist: 29. Party: State Del. 1968, '72,
'76; Nat. Del. 1976; Precinct Captain 1968-74;
State Committeewoman 1968-71; Cnty. Exec. Guidance Com. 1974-77; State Rep. Leg. Campaign Com.
1977-. Occ: Exec. Secretary. B: 2/19/38.
Add: 447 W. Hillview Cir., Mesa 85201.

SISTER CLARE DUNN (D) **
    Dist: 13. Occ: Teacher. Add: 4751 E. Linden,
Tucson 85712 (602) 271-3278.

JUANITA HARELSON (R)
    1972-. Dist: 27. Party: Precinct Committee-
woman 1958-77. Org: Historical Society; Community Council Bd., Rep. Women's Club. Educ:
Ariz. State U. 1945 BA. B: 7/4/23. Add:
1756 El Camino, Temple 85281 (602) 271-3395.

LILLIAN JORDAN
    2941 W. Keim Dr., Phoenix

DIANE B. MC CARTHY (R) **
    1972-. Dist: 16. Bds: House Health Com.
Party: Precinct Com. 1960-75. Org: OWL; State
Bd. Ariz. Civil Rights; Fed. of Rep. Women; PTA;
Redev. Bd.; Rep. Women; State 4-3. Educ: Ariz.
State U. 1960 BA. B: 1/1/39 Add: 5041 West
Kaler Dr., Glendale 85301 (602) 271-3376.

ELIZABETH ADAMS ROCKWELL (R) **
    Dist: 21. Occ: Public Relations. Add: 308
East Palm La., Phoenix 85004 (602) 271-5766.

POLLY ROSENBAUM (D) *
    Dist: 4. Org: BPW; ZONTA; OES. Educ: U. of
Colo. BA; USC MEd. Add: Box 609, Globe 85501.

JACQUE STEINER
    2915 Sherran Lane, Phoenix 85004.

PAT WRIGHT
    5818 W. Northern, Glendale 85301.

County Commissions

Apache. LOUISE A. DESCHEENY (D)
    1976-. Bds: Federal Relations Com.; Regional
Planning and Coord. Council; Navajo Tribal Govt.
Prev: Voter Registration Drive 1976; Get Out the
Vote Drive 1976. Org: Ariz. Assoc. Cnty's.
Educ: Ariz. Western Coll. 1969 AA. Occ: Contracts
and Grants Officer. B: 1/25/49. Add: Box 411,
Chinle 86503 (602) 871-4941 x 434.

Cochise. JUDITH A. GIGNAC (R)
    1976-. Dist:1. Bds: Southeastern Area Govts.
Org.; Health Systems Agency; Advisory Bd., Department Economic Services. Party: State Del. 1972,
'76; Nat. Alt. 1976. Prev: Ch., Bd. of Adjustment
1974-75; Industrial Development Authority, 1976-;
Ch., Charter Bd. of Freeholders 1975-76. Org:
Ariz. Society Public Admin.; BPW; Ariz. of Assoc.
of Cntys.; Westside Civic Assoc.; Chamber of
Commerce; Rep. Women; Assoc. US Army. B: 3/2/39.
Add: 565 Raymond Dr., Sierra Vista 85635
(602) 432-2209.

Mohave. MABEL B. BAILEY (D)
    1976-. Bds: Council of Govts. Prev: Clerk,
Cnty. Bd. of Supervisors 1961-73; General Clerk
1953-61; Treasurer and Assessor 1952-53. Org:
Women's Dem. Club. B: 3/29/20. Add: 539 Pine
St., P.O. Box 344, Kingman 86402 (602)753-2141.

Pima. KATIE DUSENBERRY (R)
    1976-. Bds: Ch., Budget Review Com.; Libraries
Adv. Com.; Judicial Adv. Com.; Judicial Adv. Com.;
Hospital Joint Staff Com.; Party: State Alt. 1968-
70; Precinct Committeewoman 1960-1977. Prev:
School Bd. 1964-74; Airport Authority Bd. 1975-77.
Org: Chamber of Commerce; Woman's Club; Rep.
Women's Club; School Bds. Assoc.; PTA. Educ:
Iowa State U. 1946 BS. B: 7/30/24. Add: 3312 E.
Lester, Tucson 85716 (602) 792-8126.

Mayors

Buckeye. EVERETTE VANSKIKE
    509 Monroe, Buckeye 85326.

El Mirage. MARGARITA REESE
    Box 277, El Mirage 85335.

Hayden. CARMELITA C. HART
    Box 57, Hayden 85235.

Huachuca City. MARGARET JONES
    212 S. Huachuca Blvd., Huachuca City 85616.

Miami. KATIE WEIMER
    622 Live Oak, Miami 85539.

Page. MARJORIE DOLAND
    Box 1865, Page 86040.

Paradise Valley. BARBARA VON AMMON
    9001 N. Martingale Rd., Paradise Valley 85253.

Phoenix. MARGARET HANCE
    251 W. Washington, Room 900, Phoenix 85003.

Oro Valley. LOIS LAMBERSON
    355 W. Calle Concordia, Tucson 85704.

Tombstone. MARGE COLVIN
    Box 339, Tombstone 85638.

Winkelman. SHIRLEY MAE RILEY
    Box 237, Winkelman 85292.

Local Councils

Benson. LOUISE ROSELL
    Box 537, Benson 85602.

Bisbee. COMILLA BROCKBANK
    Box 4086, Bisbee 85603.

Casa Grande. KATE KENYON
    916 N. Coolidge, Casa Grande 85222.

Chino Valley. VIRGINIA CONNER
                LEONA COUCH
                GERTRUDE QUAIN
    Hwy. 89 North, Chino Valley 86232.

Coolidge. GAIL MURRAY
    Rt. 1, Box 156, Coolidge 85228.

Eloy. HELEN HAWSE
    420 E. Third, Eloy 85231.

Fredonia. DIXIE LEE JUDD
    Box 217, Fredonia 86022.

Gila Bend. GINNY BLUE
            NANCY PERDUE
    City Hall, 202 N. Euclid, Gila Bend 85337.

Gilbert. GENEVA CLAY
    Box 837, Gilbert 85234.

Goodyear. BARBARA LA PRADE
    810 Los Alamos, Goodyear 85338.

Guadalupe. FRANCES AMARO
    8829 S. 59 St., Guadalupe 85283.

Hayden. CAROL J. FLORES
          DELORES RAMIREZ
    City Hall, 520 Ray, Hayden 85235.

Holbrook. LIBBY BUDENHOLZER
    524 E. Florida, Holbrook 86025.

Huachuca City. CAROLE VAUGHN
    209 Elgin, Huachuca City 85616.

Jerome. HELEN JANE TROYER
Box 216, Jerome 86331.

Kearny. GAYLE E. CAMPBELL
BONETA STUMP
375 Alden Rd., Kearney 85237.

Kingman. BETTY GROUNDS
Box 270, Kingman 86401.

Mammoth. DONNA CLARK
Gen. Del. Mammoth 85618.

Marana. E. LORRAINE PRICE
14018 N. Aura Rd., Marana 85238.

Mesa. NELL EVANS
ELMA MILANO
55 N. Center, Mesa 85201.

Parker. ESTHER BEAVER
Box AH, Parker 85344.

Patagonia. PATRICIA FORREST
Box 611, Patagonia 85624.

Payson. ELLEN DUDLEY
Box 220, Payson 85541.

Peoria. JO ANNE SMITH
Box 279, Peoria 85345.

Phoenix. JEANNE F. BARLOW (R)
1966-. Bds: Ch., Park Cmsn.; Ch., Finance
Com.; Building Com. Educ: La Salle Extension U.
CPA. Occ: Accountant. B: 11/6/25. Add: 301 N.
Church St., P.O. Box 391, Phoenix 85003
(503) 535-1955.

Phoenix. JOY CARTER
AMY T. WORTHEN
251 W. Washington, Room 900, Phoenix 85003.

Scottsdale. BILLIE GENTRY
3939 Civic Center Plaza, Scottsdale 85251.

Sierra Vista. MARY WADDELL
MARIE ZACKEY
400 Sherbundy, NW, Sierra Vista 85635.

Springerville. BARBARA HOBBS
Box 671, Springerville 85938.

South Tucson. BEATRICE MORALES
JULIA Y. VELEZ
1810 S. 6th Ave., S. Tucson 85725.

Superior. VIRGINIA L. MITCHELL
106 High School Ave., Superior. 85273.

Tempe. BEVERLY HERMON
2086 E. Golf Dr., Tempe 85282.

Tucson. CHERI CROSS
Box 27210, Tucson 85726.

Wickenburg. MARGERY BURKHART
FREDA DIEDRICH
120 E. Apache, Wickenburg 85358.

Willcox. FRANCES A. THOMSEN
809 N. Mesa, Willcox 85643.

Williams. MYRA J. LILLY
Box 3, Williams 86046.

Youngtown. AGNES BOWER
12030 Clubhouse Square, Youngtown 85363.

Yuma. GOLDIE GISS
501 S. 8th, Yuma 85364.

Judges

DOROTHY CARSON (R)
Maricopa Cnty. Superior Court Judge. 1974-.
Bds: Civil Rules Com. Prev: City Judge 1970-74.
Org: Calif., Utah, Ariz. Bar Assocs.; Ariz.
Judges Assoc.; ABA; BPW; AAUW; Rep. Women's Club.
Educ: Utah State U. 1945 BS; Stanford Law School
1948 JD. B: 11/18/24. Add: 1916 W. Cambridge,
Phoenix 85009 (602) 262-3776.

LILLIAN S. FISHER (D)
Pima Cnty. Superior Court Judge. 1974-. Party:
Precinct Committeewoman. Org: ABA; Amer.
Judicature Soc.; Dem. Club. Educ: Brooklyn Coll.
1942 BS; U. of Ariz. 1963 JD. B: 6/18/21. Add:
Rt. 8, Box 582, Tucson 85701. (602) 792-8241.

SANDRA D. O'CONNOR (I)
Maricopa Cnty. Superior Court Judge. 1976-.
Bds: Ch., Judicial Educ. and Training Com.; Leg.
Com. Party: Nat. Alt. 1972; Cnty. Precinct
Committeewoman 1960-65; Dist. Ch. 1962-65. Prev:
State Senator 1969-76; Nat. Defense Adv. Com. on
Women on the Service 1974-77; Cnty. Bd. of
Adjustments and Appeals 1960-63; Governor's Com.
on Marriage and Family 1965; Ch., Cnty. Juvenile
Detention Home Bd. 1966-68. Org: ABA; Historical
Society; Jr. Achievement Bd. Educ: Stamford
1952 AB; LLB. B: 3/26/30. Add: 3651 E. Denton
Ln., Paradise Vly. 85253 (602) 262-3892.

MARILYN A. RIDDEL (R)
Maricopa Cnty. Superior Court Judge. 1969-.
Org: ABA; Amer. Judicature Society; Assoc. of
Trial Ct. Judges; BPW; DAR; YWCA. Educ:
Louisiana State U. 1953 BA; U. of Toledo 1957
LLB, JD. B: 8/22/32. Add: 4519 E. Cheery Lynn
Rd., Phoenix 85018 (602) 262-3831.

MARY MURPHY SCHROEDER (D)
Judge, Court of Appeals. 1975-. Bds:
Phoenix Judicial Selection Nominating Cmsn.
Party: Precinct Committeewoman 1972-75; Dist.
Committeewoman 1972-75; State Committeewoman
1972-75. Educ: Swarthmore 1962 BA; U. of
Chicago 1965 JD. B: 12/4/40. Add: 5608 N.
Quail Run Rd., Paradise Vly. 85253 (602)271-4828.

ALICE TRUMAN
Pima Cnty. Superior Court Judge. Add: County
Courthouse, Tucson 85701.

State Boards and Commissions

Office of the Governor
State Capitol
Phoenix 85007

Air Pollution Control Hearing Board
MURIEL E. BEROZA

Appellate Court Appointments, Commission on
ELIZABETH I. JONES

Arts and Humanities, Commission on
NORMA AMMONS
ALICE FROEB
PAMELA J. GOLDSMITH
HELEN K. MASON
FRANCES B. MC ALLISTER
DR. BARBARA C. VAN SITTERT

Chiropractic Examiners, State Board of
DR. LELIA SCHLABACH

Civil Rights, Advisory Board on
PATRICIA MC GEE
MILDRED J. STARRETT
LOUISE WILLEY

Community Coordinated Child Care Committee
MARTHA AHEARN
MRS. JOHN ALMQUIST, JR.
PHYLLIS ANTONE
ANNA MARIA COPPOLLA
MRS. CRUZ DAVIS
MRS. BOBBIE HANNAH
DR. FLORENCE KARLSTROM
JANET MARCOTTE
MILDRED PERKINS

Community Colleges, Board of Directors of
WANDA G. HALL
MRS. LEONILO LARRIVA, III
ELIZABETH ANNE PACKARD

Cosmetology, State Board of
DOROTHEA HERSCHLEDER
VALERIA I. LOCKWOOD

Day Care Advisory Board
CECILIA AVALOS
NORMA BIFANO
MARLENE R. EVANS
CAROL CAMIN
SHARON LEACH
HELEN SHEA

Deaf and Blind, Board of Directors of the State
School for the
MARTHA CLIFFORD

Dispensing Opticians, State Board of
PHYLLIS M. PRENTICE

Economic Planning and Development Board
GRACE L. CARROLL

Economic Security Advisory Council
LAURA D. GANOUNG
KATHERINE F. HAWKINS
JOAN F. KOENIG
WILMA ROBERTSON

Education, Postsecondary Commission for
PATRICIA MC GEE

Education, State Board of
ELIZABETH PACKARD
MIRIAM SOREY
AMY WORTHEN

Employment Security Advisory Council
EDNA THODE

Environment, Governor's Commission on
JEANETTE BIDEAUX
MARYBETH CARLILE
PAM K. HALT
EVA C. PATTEN

Ethics, Board of
RUTH ADAMS
AMELIA D. LEWIS

Funeral Directors and Embalmers, Board of
MARIAN LUPU

Handicapped, Committee on the Employment of the
JOY CARTER
PATRICIA HARRELL
BETTY JOHNSTON
BETTY D. LOPEZ
PATRICIA J. WILLIAMS
JULIA ZOZAYA

Health Advisory Council
ANNA M. JOLIVET
ISABEL NELSON
CHERYL PATTERSON
JULIA SOTO

Health Facilities Authority Board
MARGARET STARNER

Health Planning Advisory Council
DELIA STORCH

Hearing Aid Dispensers Examiners
DOLORES A. KORDEK

Indian Affairs, Commission of
SISTER MARY ROSE CHRISTY
NOLINE LAMBERT
PATRICIA MC GEE
FRANCES SNELLER

Intergovernmental Relations, Governor's Advisory
Council on
RUTH FINN
SUE LOFGREN
MARY JANE WIENKE

Joint Underwriting Plan Board of Directors
BETTY LEVITT
EMMA MELIKIAN

Judicial Qualifications, Commission on
    MARTHA ELIAS
    ALICE TRUMAN

Law Enforcement Officer Advisory Council
    ELAINE FRYE

Legal Services Advisory Council
    ELIZABETH F. BECK
    BLANCHE F. BERNSTEIN
    VIVIAN FOOTE

Livestock Sanitary Board
    MARY S. RUGG

Medical Examiners, State Board of
    ESTHER CAPIN

Mental Health Advisory Council
    JEANNE CHISHOLM
    NAOMI KARP

Mental Retardation, Board of
    JEAN PHILLIPS

Mineral Resources Board of Governors
    ANN CHESLEY

Nursing, State Board of
    FLORETTA AWE
    DOROTHY CROTHERS
    LILAH M. HARPER
    NANCY MELVIN
    RUTH ANN ZORNOW

Nursing Care Institutions Administrators, Board of
Examiners
    POLLYANNA DE SPAIN

Opticians, Board of Dispensing
    MRS. HARRY CLARK
    PHYLLIS M. PRENTICE

Parks Board
    JOSEPHINE C. BAILEY

Personnel Commission
    MIMI MORRON

Pharmacy, State Board of
    ALICE M. CONLEY
    BETTY D. LOPEZ

Physical Therapy Examiners, Board of
    CHARLOTTE PEROTTI

Power Authority Commission
    THELMA BARBOUR
    MILDRED MALYJUREK
    ZELMA MOORE

Practical Nurse Committee
    VIOLA BOWERS
    JOSEPHINE KING

Private Technical and Business Schools, State
Board of
    LOIS BRADLEY

Psychologist Examiners, State Board of
    DR. MATHILDA B. CANTER

Recreational Coordinating Commission
    PRISCILLA KUHN
    CAROL SCHATT

Retirement System
    SHIRLEY GOETTSCH

Salaries for Elective State Officials, Commission
on
    BETTY LOU HALDIMAN

Structural Pest Control, State Board of
    MARY MAFFEO

Tourism Advisory Council
    JEANNE DALE

Trial Court Appointments, Commission on
    GERALDINE EMMETT
    DOROTHY S. FANNIN
    JEAN HUNNICUTT

Vocational-Technical Education Advisory Council
    ETHEL T. WILLIAMS

Vocational Education Skill Development Advisory
Committee
    BARBARA WELCH

Women's Commission
    JUNE ANDERSON
    SUSAN ARBUTHNOT
    MARY BASS
    BARBY BARONE
    LIBBY BUDENHOLZER
    CARMEN CAJERO
    ANNA CULLINAN
    MARGE LE DUDLEY
    GLORIA FEIGENBAUM
    POLLY GALLARDO
    JACQUELINE GUTWILLIG
    STELLA HANSEN
    JUDY HARDES
    MARY HARO
    MANUELITA HEMSTREET
    JOYCE HUNTER
    DR. HELEN INGRAM
    MARGO INJASOULIAN
    CECILIA DORY
    JUANA LYON
    HARRIET MATTHEWS
    REBA MERRILL
    ANNE NEISSER
    DR. CATHERINE G. NICHOLS
    SHIRLEY ODEGAARD
    PATRICIA L. OFSTEDAHL
    JEAN PARKER
    SELMA PINE
    JUNE REYNOLDS
    WILMA ROBERTSON
    MARTHA RUSSELL
    GLORIA SANDVIK
    BERTHA C. SHEELEY
    MARRY ELLEN SIMONSON
    DELORES SMITH
    GLORIA STARKS
    VERA BROWN STARR
    DR. WILMA STRICKLIN
    PHYLLIS SUGAR
    ELIZABETH TEA
    BARBARA WEYMANN

PAT WILLIAMS
VALERIE VALENCIA
LEVELLE HILLEBRANDT
DOROTHY BRANDT
CAROL TURNBULL

Arkansas

State Executive and Cabinet

ANNE BARTLEY
Director, Department of Natural and Cultural Heritage. Add: State Capitol, Little Rock 72201.

NANCY J. HALL (D) *
1963-. Prev: State Highway Dept. 1925-30; Asst. Sec. of State 1937-61; Sec. of State 1961-63; Org: Dem. Women's Club; BPW; ZONTA; United Daughters of the Confederacy; Women's Chamber of Commerce. B: 10/5/04. Add: 4206 Wood Lawn, Little Rock 72205.

State Legislature

State Senate

VADA SHEID **
1967-. Dist: 44. Prev: County Treasurer. Occ: Furniture; Farming. B: 8/19/16. Add: 911 Baker St., Mountain Home 72653 (501)425-5165.

State House

SHIRLEY MEACHAM (D) **
1974-. Dist: 74. Bds: Public Transportation; Legislative Affairs. Org: PTA. B: 4/17/27. Add: Box 566, Monroe 72108 (501) 372-6211.

CAROLYN JOAN POLLAN (R) *
1975-. Dist: 15. Party: Nat. Alt. 1972; Committeewoman 1972-present; V-Ch., State Com. 1973- present. Org: PTA; Federation of Rep. Women; Mental Health, Amer. Cancer Soc. Educ: John Brown U. BS. Add: 2201 S 40th St., Smith 72901 (501) 782-9014.

County Commissions

Baxter. BETTY ALMON
Baxter County, Mountain Home 72653.

Baxter. IMOGENE ROANE (D)
1968. Org: Ark. Assoc. of Justices of the Peace; Dem. Club. Occ: Payroll Officer. B: 9/5/19. Add: Rt. 5, Box 304, Mt. Home 72653.

Clark. MARILYN L. FLANAGIN (D)
1977-. Dist: 1. Bds: State Rep. Clark Cnty. Quoram Ct. Educ: Henderson State 1947 BA. B: 5/5/23. Add: 620 Hickory, Arkadelphia 71923.

Conway. DORRIS B. DUEWALL (D)
1968. Bds: Ch., Revenue and Appropriations. Party: State Del. 1976. Org: BPW. Occ: Legal Secretary. B: 3/7/28. Add: 1417 Holloway, Morrilton 72110 (501) 354-0125.

Crawford. ALMEDIA H. RUSSELL (D)
1952-. B: 12/22/15. Add: 422 N. 15, Van Buren 72956.

Crittenden. GLORIA JACKSON
County Courthouse, Marion 72364.

Crittenden. MAGGIE MC CORMACK (D)
1977-. Bds: Juvenile Detention Unit Bd. Occ: Insurance Agent. B: 1/6/31. Add: 602 N 14, W. Memphis 72301.

Crittenden. VERA B. SIMONETTI (R)
1976-. B: 1/18/20. Add: Box 26, Marion 72364.

Dallas. MARIE RANEY
County Courthouse, Fordyce 71742.

Desha. BONNIE ZOOK
County Courthouse, Arkansas City 71630.

Drew. MRS. RALPH DEAL (D)
1970.- Occ: Merchant. B: 9/10/20. Add: Rt. 4, Monticello 71655.

Faulkner. ANN HARREL
County Courthouse, Conway 72032.

Faulkner. BETTY PICKETT (D)
1977-. Dist: 10. Bds: Ch., Revenue and Finance Com. Party: State Alt. 1976. Org: Ark. Assoc. of Quorum Cts.; LWV; School Bd. Educ: Hendrix Coll. 1963 BA. B: 11/2/41. Add: Rt. 6, Box 195, Conway 72032 (501)329-5862.

Green. LUCILLE A. JACKSON (D)
1956-. Bds: Office Space Com.; Budget Com.; CETA Program Comm. Org: ANA; Ark. Assoc. of Quorum Cts.; OES. Educ: Ark. State U. 1971 AA; U. of Ark. 1975 RN. Occ: RN. B: 11/22/26. Add: Rt. 4, Paragould 72450.

Greene. LENA D. MC DANIEL (D)
1976-. Bds: Budget Com. Party: State Alt. 1976. Org: AAUW; Dem. Women's Club; Young Dems. of Ark. Educ: U. of S. Miss. 1967 BA; Ark. State U. 1973 MBA. Occ: Coll. Instructor. B: 6/28/41. Add: 416 W. Poplar, Paragould 72450.

Hempstead. LYNN MONTGOMERY
BOBBYE MURPHY
MRS. EDDIE J. WHITMAN
County Courthouse, Hope 71801.

Hot Spring.   ADRIAN LIVINGSTON
                   FAY WELCH
       County Courthouse, Malvern 72104.

Jackson. LOUISE RUNYAN
       County Courthouse, Newport 72112.

Jefferson. JANIE MOORE TOWNSEND (D)
       1976-. Dist: 6. Bds: Finance Com. Party:
State Del. 1976. Org: Amer. Personnel and
Guidance Assoc.; Org. of U. Women; Citizens Org.;
NAACP; Negro Youth Org.; Vietnam Era Veterans
Civic Council. Educ: AM & N Coll. 1947 BS; N.Y.U.
1956 MA; Henderson State Coll. 1971 MS. Occ:
Assoc. Dean of Students. Add: 1117 S. Willow,
Pine Blf. 71603.

Johnson. SALLY MOON (D)
       1976-. Bds: Ch., Budget Com.; Ch., Personnel
Com.; Ad Hoc Bldg. Purchase Com. Party: State
Del. 1974, '76; Cnty. Committeewoman 1974-76.
Org: Charksville Council on Human Relations;
Chamber of Commerce; Cnty. Dem. Women; Historical
Society. B: 7/30/20. Add: 509 Buchanan St.,
Clarksville 72830. (501) 754-8564.

Lee. JUANITA BALLARD
       Lee County Courthouse, Marianna 72360.

Logan. PATSY S. HUBER
       Logan County Courthouse, Paris 72855.

Madison. VIRGINIA KISOR
              BILLIE STAFFORD
       County Courthouse, Huntsville 72740.

Miller. SYLVIA KRING GREEN (D)
       1977-. Dist: 10. Bds: Recreation Com.;
Incentive Com.; Ch., Constables Gasoline Expense
Com. Org: PTA. B: 10/31/36. Add: Rt. 2, Box
197 C, Fouke 71837 (501) 653-2884.

Monroe. VIVIAN JACKS
       County Courthouse, Clarendon 72029.

Montgomery. WANDA HORN MC RAE (D)
       1977-. Bds: Finance Com. Party: State Del.
1967. Org: PTA. Occ: Secretary. B: 7/11/32.
Add: P.O. Box 175, Norman 71960.

Poinsett. MRS. W.O. BURGESS
              MUREL L. MANGRUM
       County Courthouse, Harrisburg 72432.

Polk. GAIL ESTEP
       County Courthouse, Mena 71953.

Pope. FRANCES M. SAMMONS
       County Courthouse, Russellville 72801.

Pulaski. D. ALINE FRAZIER
              CAROL O. HENRY
              JULIE MAE MC DANIEL
       County Courthouse, Little Rock 72201.

Quachita. MARY J. SUTTON
       County Courthouse, Camden 71701.

Randolph. LUCILLE STOLT
       County Courthouse, Pocahontas 72455.

Saline. PEGGY BALLARD BUTLER (D)
       1974-. Bds: Salary Com. Party: State Alt.
1976. Org: Ark. Library Assoc.; Young Dems.
Educ: U. of Ark. 1961 BSE, 1977 MSE. Occ:
Teacher. B: 11/20/39. Add: 2218 Sharon Rd.,
Benton 72015 (501) 778-3288.

Sevier. BRENDA BELTRANI
              MAUDEEN BRINKLEY
       County Courthouse, DeQueen 71832.

Sevier. JUANITA HOOKER (D)
       1977-. Dist: 4. Bds: Ambulance Com.; Ct.
Clerk Com. B: 9/15/29. Add: Rt. 3, Box 194,
DeQueen 71832 (501) 584-2773.

Sevier. MRS. S.A. TOBIN
       1977-. Bds: Ch., Ceta. Org: Ark. Cnty's.
Officers. Occ: Rancher. B: 11/3/22. Add:
Rt. 2, Box 569, DeQueen 71832.

Washington. MARGARET B. ANDERSON (D)
       1976-. Org: Ark. Press Women; AAUW; ACLU;
LWV; Environmental Defense Fund; Common Cause.
Educ: Oberlin Coll. 1943 BA; Mt. Holyoke Coll.
1945 MA. B: 11/16/21. Add: 1599 Halsell Rd.,
Fayetteville 72701 (501) 521-8400.

Washington. PEGGY TREIBER FRIZZELL (D)
       1976-. Bds: Ch., Solid Waste Com.; Bldg.
Com.; Personnel Classification Com. Org: Ark.
Press Women; LWV. Occ: Reporter, Writer. B:
12/4/49. Add: 808 Lawson #4, Fayetteville 72701.

Mayors

Ben Lomond. JUDY YOUNG
       Town Hall, Ben Lomond 71823.

Caldwell. MRS. JOHN C. LINDSEY, JR.
       Town Hall, Caldwell 72322.

Evening Shade. MAURINE M. KRAMER (D)
       1971-. Bds: V-Ch., N. Central Ark. Devt.
Council. Prev: Cnty. Revenue Inspector 1963-66.
Occ: Reporter. B: 9/12/24. Add: 2 Court St.,
Evening Shade 72532.

Fayetteville. MARION ROGERS ORTON (D)
       1970-. Bds: Criminal Justice Council; Adv.
Council for Ark. Dept. of Local Services. Prev:
Mayor 1975-77; Ch., Pollution Control Com. 1971-
74. Org: LWV; Ozark Guidance Center; Historical
Society; Elderly Nutrition Program. Educ: U. of
Ill. 1950 BA. B: 6/22/28. Add: 1641 Halsell Rd.
Fayetteville 72701 (501) 521-7700.

Fulton. NANCY C. MORRISON (I) **
       1973-. Prev: City Recorder 1967-73. Educ:
Belhaven Coll. 1961 BA. Occ: Teacher. B:
1/30/39. Add: Dr. H. Fulton 71838 (501)896-2466.

Garland. MARTHA GREY FRANKLIN **
       1970-. Prev: School Bd. 1967-73; State
Secretary-Treasurer 1948-56. Org: PTA; Mail
Carrier. B: 1/14/21. Add: City Hall, Garland
71839 (501) 683-2355.

Gateway. ADA WALKER
     Town Hall, Gateway 72733.

Gilbert. ETHEL M. MYERS
     Town Hall, Gilbert 72636.

Hartford. NORMA LOCKHART MICHAEL (D) **
     1974-. B: 4/23/30. Add: Box 69, Hartford
72938 (501) 639-2219.

Knobel. MRS. JOE SELLMEYER
     Town Hall, Knobel 72435.

Mansfield. DELOIS JEAN ALLEN
     City Hall, Mansfield 72944.

Mayflower. MARY M. GANDY (D)
     1975-. B: 2/10/10. Add: Rt. 1, Box 166,
Mayflower 72106 (501) 327-4739.

McRae. SARAH GEORGE
     City Hall, McRae 72102.

Melbourne. JAN LAWRENCE (D) **
     1975-. Org: PTA. B: 4/26/28. Add: Box 452,
Melbourne 72556 (501) 368-7875.

Midland. WILMA JEAN KINGORE (D)
     1974-. Bds: V-Ch., Neighborhood Council, Org:
Neighborhood Council. B: 6/13/37. Add: P.O. Box
205, Midland 72945 (501) 639-2635.

Mountain View. LONA ACKERMAN
     City Hall, Mountain View 72560.

Newark. ROSEMARY S. WILLIAMS (D)
     1975-. Bds: Action Com. Municipal League; N.
Central Area Policy Bd. Org: BPW. Occ:
Beautician. B: 4/4/18, Add: 7th & Oak St.,
P.O. Box 314, Newark 72562 (501) 799-3911.

Pruitt. LUCILLE C. HANNON (I)
     1972-. Prev: Recorder-Clerk 1969-73. Org:
Amer. Security Council Adv. Bd. Occ: Income Tax
Consultant. B: 8/3/09. Add: Star Rt. 1, Box 220,
Pruitt 72671. (501) 446-5344.

St. Charles. MARY J. PADGETT
     Town Hall, St. Charles 72140.

Smithville. MRS. ZAY H. HOWARD
     Town Hall, Smithville 72466.

West Memphis. JOYCE T. FERGUSON (D)
     1974-. Bds: Ark. Dept. of Pollution Control
and Ecology; Governor's Adv. Transportation Cmsn.;
Governor's Cmsn. on Status of Women. Org: Altrusa;
Ark. Congress of Parents and Teachers. B: 7/19/25
Add: 450 S. Roselawn, W. Memphis 72301
(501) 735-2720.

Wheatley. GEORGIA L. WALKER (D) **
     1972-. Org: Educ. Assoc.; BPW; Municipal
League. Educ: U. of Central Ark. BS. Occ:
Teacher. B: 3/1/15. Add: Box 31, Wheatley
72392 (501) 457-3031.

Winchester. MRS. LAWRENCE OSWALD
     Town Hall, Winchester 71677.

Local Councils

Amity. MRS. JOAN BEAN
     City Hall, Amity 71921.

Ashdown. MARY LINDSEY
     City Hall, Ashdown 71822.

Barling. LINDA WOMACK (D) **
     1974-. Org: PTA; Community Dev. Council.
B: 7/2/38. Add: Rte. 1, Box 156, Fort Smith
(501) 452-1303.

Bentonville. HARRYETTA BAILEY
                    VIDA SIMPSON
     City Hall, Bentonville 72712.

Bigelow. DEBBIE PHILLIPS
     Town Hall, Bigelow 72016.

Blytheville. ANNE HEARN
     City Hall, Blytheville 72315.

Brinkley. ELMA REECE WILLIAMS (I)
     1977-. Org: NEA; Nat. Business Educ. Assoc.;
Progressive Women's Club; Future Business
Leaders. Educ: U. of Ark. 1953 BSE; 1977 MA.
Occ: Business Teacher. B: 3/23/31. Add:
1101 Charlyne St., Brinkley 72021 (501) 734-3464.

Bryant. MARGARET A. RAMSEY (D) **
     1972-. Bds: Highway & Street Safety. Org:
BPW; Municipal League. B: 3/18/35. Add:
306 Southeast 1st St., Bryant 72022 (501)847-2311.

Burdette. MARGERY HALE (I)
     1972-. Prev: Alderwoman 1972-75. Org: Farm
Bureau; Amer. Society of Agronomy; Bd. Pres. of
Cnty. Mid-Wife Corp.; Comsr. Water System. Educ:
U. of Ark. 1954 BS. Occ: Farmer. B: 1/13/32.
Add: Box 204, Burdette 72321.

Caddo Valley. MAXINE CRAWLEY (D)
     1977-. Occ: Beautician. B: 9/18/25. Add:
Rt. 2, Box 400 A, Arkadelphia 71923 (501)246-5789

Camden. MILDRED J. MATHIS
     City Hall, Camden 71701.

Cammack Village. MRS. SYBIL SMITH
     City Hall, 2710 N. McKinley, Little Rock
72207.

Casa. LORETTA RAINEY
     Town Hall, Casa 72025.

Centerton. RENA J. COPELAND
     1976-. B: 4/12/22. Add: Rt. 1, Box 66,
Bentonville 72712 (501) 795-2750.

Cherry Valley. GAY HORTON
     City Hall, Cherry Valley 72324.

Conway. JANE WILSON (D)
     1974-. Bds: Ch., Light and Water Com.; Health
and Sanitation Com.; Policy Com. Party: State
Del. 1973-76. Prev: Parks and Recreation Cmsn.
1970-73. Occ: Dress Shop Owner. B: 12/25/38.
Add: 1905 Caldwell, Conway 72032 (501)329-3878.

Corning. DOROTHY JOHNSON (D)
1976-. Bds: Bd. of Dir's., Black Rvr. Area
Dev't., E. Ark. Planning & Devt. Dist. Org: BPW;
Chamber of Commerce. B: 1/22/16. Add: 1301 Harb,
Corning 72422 (501) 857-6746.

Daisy. BERTHA MAE TEDDLER
MRS. JODIE WHITE
Town Hall, Daisy 71939.

Delaplaine. DORIS WHITE
1977-. Bds: Ch., Park Com. B: 7/12/35. Add:
P.O. Box 65, Delaplaine 72425 (501) 249-3463.

Delight. CAROLYN CROSS
City Hall, Delight 71940.

Delight. GRACE ANN RILEY (D)
1970-. Prev: Alderwoman 1974. Org: Ark.
Municipal Assoc.; Ark. Health Systems. Occ:
Checker. B: 8/3/29. Add: Delight 71940.

Denning. JUANITA BURNS
JOANNE ROFKAHR
Rte. 1, Altus 72821.

DeQueen. JO ANN HOLCOMBE
GAIL JOHNSON
City Hall, DeQueen 71832.

Earle. MRS. WATT CAMPBELL
City Hall, Earle 72331.

East Camden. PAT PENNY
City Hall, E. Camden 71701.

Emmet. MRS. ELMORE DOUGAN
City Hall, Emmet 71835.

Eureka Springs. ALLISON WESTPHAL
City Hall, Eureka Springs 72632.

Farmington. WANDA NATIONS
City Hall, Farmington 72730.

Fifty-Six. BARBARA COYLE
Town Hall, Fifty-Six 72533.

Foreman. ELVA M. CAPPS (D)
Org: OES. Occ: Art Teacher. B: 2/19/13.
Add: 4th & Spring, Box 146, Foreman 71836
(501) 542-6564.

Friendship. LEATRICE FURR
Town Hall, Friendship 71942.

Fulton. INA J. LOGAN (D)
B: 6/12/02. Add: Box 66, Fulton 71838.

Garland. LINDA DIANE CUTCHALL (D)
1976-. Bds: Ch., Planning & Zonning Cmsn.
Prev: Recorder Treasurer 1975. Occ: Clerk. B:
3/12/54. Add: Garland 71839 (501) 683-2289.

Gateway. BETTIE R. ASH
ELSIE GALYEN
Town Hall, Gateway 72733.

Gillett. HELEN D. WOLFE (D)
1976-. Bds: City Police Cmsn.; Ch., City
Clean-Up. Educ: U. of Ark. 1952 BS. B: 3/31/35.
Add: Gillett 72055 (501) 548-2411.

Gilmore. MRS. TOMMIE JEAN KLINE
Town Hall, Gilmore 72339.

Green Forest. MARGARET G. BUELL
1976-. Bds: Ch., Parks & Recreation. Occ:
Antique Shop Owner. B: 1/9/14. Add: 1209 E.
Main, Green Forest 72638 (501) 438-5518.

Greenway. MRS. JESSIE MIDKIFF
Town Hall, Greenway 72430.

Greer's Ferry. OLIVE R. GREEN (I)
1975-. Org: Ark. Municipal League. Occ:
Cook. B: 3/24/31. Add: Rt. 1, Box 65, Higden
72067 (501) 825-7172.

Harrison. KAY HOLLINGSWORTH
City Hall, Harrison 72601.

Hatfield. PEGGY BRYANT
Town Hall, Hatfield 71945.

Hector. BEATRICE BELL (I)
1976-. B: 8/7/13. Add: Main, Hector 72843.

Helena. JOANN D. SMITH (I)
1974-. Bds: Ch., Sanitation Com.; Insurance
Com.; Ordinance Com. Org: Chamber of Commerce.
Occ: Insurance Agency Owner. B: 12/12/36.
Add: 205 Oakland Ave., P.O. Box 307, Helena
72342 (501) 338-9094.

Higginston. MURIEL PILKINGTON
Town Hall, Higginston 72068.

Holly Grove. DONNA H. HILL (D)
1968-. Org: Monroe Cnty. Mental Health
Council. Occ: Teacher's Aide. B: 9/9/13.
Add: Holly Grove, 72069 (501) 462-3422.

Humphrey. ALICE JEANNE FLYNN (I) **
1975-. Occ: Bookkeeper. B: 10/9/42. Add:
Box 242, Humphrey 72073 (501) 873-4598.

Huntington. DORIS BONDS
City Hall, Huntington 72940.

Johnson. MILLYE POLLOCK
Town Hall, Johnson 72741.

Jonesboro. NANCY A. HAIGLER
1976-. Bds: Finance Com.; Insurance Com.;
Advertising & Promotion Cmsn. Org: Amer.
Institute of CPA's. Educ: Southwestern State of
Okla. 1955 BSE; Okla U. 1965 MSE. Occ: Account-
ing Professor. B: 3/25/31. Add: 906 Melton,
Jonesboro 72401 (501) 972-3037.

Knobel. OPAL FAIRCHILD
LOLA R. FOLCKEMER
IRENE ROWE
LELA HICKS
Town Hall, Knobel 72435.

Knoxville.   WILMA ELAM
    Town Hall, Knoxville 72845.

Lakeview.   MRS. CALLIE FITZHUGH
             LOIS HARDY
    Town Hall, Lakeview 72642.

Leslie.   VIOLET KIMBRELL
          LORNA LACK
    City Hall, Leslie 72645.

Letona.   DOROTHY DUNHAM NEWMAN (I)
    1976-. Occ: Bookkeeper. B: 12/23/29. Add:
    P.O. Box 63, Letona 72085.

Lincoln,   EILENE MORPHIS
    City Hall, Lincoln 74744.

Lincoln.   INA M. ROBERTS (D)
    1975-. Bds: Ch., Planning & Devt. B: 6/10/05.
    Add: 103 S. West, Lincoln 72744 (501) 824-3321.

Little Rock.   MYRA JONES (D)
    1976-. Bds: Ch., Central Ark. Manpower Adv.
    Council. Org: Ark. Municipal League; LWV; WPC.
    Educ: Oberlin Coll. 1957 BME; Drake U. 1963 MME.
    Occ: Business Owner. B: 3/8/36. Add: 37 Pine-
    hurst Cir., Little Rock 72212 (501) 376-6111.

London.   ANNETTE HICKEY (D)
    1977-. Bds: Ch., Publicity. B: 12/28/19.
    Add: Rt. #3, Box 49, Russellville 72801
    (501) 293-4525.

Lonsdale.   MARY IARVIN
    Town Hall, Lonsdale 72087.

Madison.   HELEN MALONE
           JOYCE PROCTOR
    City Hall, Madison 72359.

Magness.   JETRUE G. BATSON (D)
    1969-. Prev: Justice of the Peace 1960-68.
    Occ: Saleswoman. B: 7/1/30. Add: Box 33,
    Magness 72553 (501) 799-3253.

Magness.   EDITH CANADY
           RUBY HARRIS
    Town Hall, Magness 72553.

Mansfield.   A. MARGARET CHAPMAN
    City Hall, Mansfield 72944.

Marion.   ANNA S. UPTON
    City Hall, Marion 72364.

Marked Tree.   ELIZABETH ELDER
               MARY FRANCES WIKE
    City Hall, Marked Tree 72365.

Mayflower.   SANDRA BROWN
    City Hall, Mayflower 72106.

Mayflower.   BERTHA MATCHET WILLETT (I)
    1976-. Bds: Ch., Street Dept. Prev: City-Cnty
    Health Bd. 1971-74; City-Cnty. Beautification
    1972-74. Org: Women's Club. B: 8/11/05. Add:
    Center at Cross St., Mayflower 72106 (501)327-2445

McCaskill.   MRS. ERNEST MORTON
    Town Hall, McCaskill 71847.

McCrory.   IMOGENE DAVIS
    City Hall, McCrory 72101.

Melbourne.   IDAVONNE ROSA (D)
    1976-. Org: ANA· Ark. Municipal League.
    Educ: U. of Central Ark. 1974 AA-RN; Little
    Rock Vocational Tech. 1966 LPN. Occ: RN.
    B: 8/10/21. Add: Box 214, Melbourne 72556
    (501) 368-4377.

Midland.   JUDITH R. THOMPSON
    Town Hall, Midland 72945.

Monette.   MARGARETE REED (I)
    1977-. Bds: Sanitation; Industry, Streets &
    Street Lighting; Ch., Recreation, Parks &
    Cultural. Occ: Office Manager. B: 2/8/37.
    Add: 117 S. Williams, P.O. Box 149, Monette
    72447.

Montrose.   MRS. JO HOWIE
    Town Hall, Montrose 71658.

Moorefield.   MRS. OLLIE COSSEY
    Town Hall, P.O. Batesville, R3, Moorefield
    72501.

Mountain Home.   PHOEBE ATKINS
    City Hall, Mountain Home 72653.

Mountain Pine.   DOROTHY GILBRETH
    City Hall, Mountain Pine 71956.

Mountain View.   MILDRED BENNETT
    City Hall, Mountain View 72560.

Newport.   DORIS MAE BORDERS
    City Hall, Newport 72112.

Norman.   LINDA GREEN
    City Hall, Norman 71960.

Norphlet.   GLADYS B. LONG (D)
    1966-. Bds: Ch., Health & Sanitation; Ch.,
    Legislative; Ch.; Public Relations. Prev:
    Library Trustee 1968-77. B: 5/2/01. Add: Main
    & Ralston Sts., Norphlet 71759.

Norphlet.   DORIS V. WHITE
    City Hall, Norphlet 71759.

Norristown.   MARY FRANCES FRAZIER (D)
    1977-. Bds: Ch., City Planning Cmsn.; Ch.,
    Beautification Program. Occ: Library Asst. B:
    1/20/20. Add: Rt. 5, Box 312, Russellville
    72801.

Norristown.   MRS. POLLY RILEY
    Town Hall, Russellville 72801.

North Little Rock.   MARY E. HESS (D)
    1976-. Org: Ark. Retired Teachers; BPW;
    Woman's Club; Dem. Woman's Club. Educ:
    Hendrix Coll. 1935 AB. Occ: Teacher. B: 1/6/13.
    Add: 2017 Poplar St., N. Little Rock 72114
    (501) 374-2236.

Ogden. SARA T. GOODWIN
        BETTY RUTH MORTON
        PATRICIA A. WARD
        City Hall, Ogden 71853.

Ogden. LOIS W. SHACKELFORD (D)
        1974-. Org: BPW. Occ: Grocery Store Owner.
        B: 9/12/16. Add: P.O. Box 215, Ogden 71853
        (501) 898-3489.

Oil Trough. BILLIE TUCKER BARBER
        1976-. Occ: Bookkeeper. B: 8/16/33. Add:
        P.O. Box 58, Oil Trough 72564.

Oppelo. MRS. PHILLIP LOH
        Town Hall, Morrilton 72110.

Ozark. WILMA MILLER
        1976-. Bds: Ch., Sewer & Water Com.; Sani-
        tation Com. Org: Historical Assoc.; Chamber of
        Commerce; Ark. Municipal League; Recreation Club.
        B: 7/10/20. Add: Rt. 2, Box 74, Ozark 72949.

Pangburn. MRS. PEGGY TAYLOR
        City Hall, Pangburn 72121.

Patmos. DOROTHY RIDER
        Town Hall, Patmos 71856.

Peach Orchard. WANDA BASS
        City Hall, Peach Orchard 72453.

Perla. CATHERINE MITCHELL
        Box 281, Town Hall, Perla 72104.

Perrytown. DOROTHY S. RAYBURN **
        Educ: Tex. Christian U. 1970 BS. B: 11/5/39.
        Add: 6628, Perrytown 71801 (501) 777-8266.

Plainview. BETH BURNHAM
        City Hall, Plainview 72857.

Pocahontas. MRS. LARK SALLEE (I) **
        1974-. Org: Educ. Assoc.; PEO. Educ: Ark.
        State U. 1972 BS; Ark. State U. 1975 MS. Occ:
        Teacher. B: 9/12/50. Add: 207 Baltz St.,
        Pocahontas 72455.

Powhatan. GOLDIE CHAPPEL
        CAROLYN SUE DOWNHAM
        Town Hall, Powhatan 72458.

Pruitt. GENEVIEVE PAULSEN
        MARY ANN SMITH
        Town Hall, Pruitt 72671.

Redfield. MABEL BERRY
        Town Hall, Redfield 72132.

Reed: BERTHA MC GOWAN
        Town Hall, P.O. Reed Rural Sta., Reed 71670.

Roe. MARY ANN DAVIS
        BETTY J. WALTON
        Town Hall, Roe 72134.

Russellville. LINDA BURRIS DARE (D)
        1977-. Bds: Parks & Recreation Com.; Insur-
        ance. Com. Org: School & Community Health &
        Safety Com.; PTA. Occ: Substitute Teacher. B:
        10/18/45. Add: 1905 W. 2nd Pl., Russellville
        72801. (501) 968-2098.

St. Francis. EVA MAE BRAWNER ROTH (D)
        1977-. B: 8/15/07. Add: Gen. Del., St.
        Francis 72464.

St. Francis. MRS. J.A. THOMPSON
        City Hall, St. Francis 72464.

Sherwood. BECKI PEOPST VASSAR (D)
        1977-. Bds: Police Cmsn. Prev: Police Cmsn.
        1975. Org: Chamber of Commerce; Women's Improve-
        ment Group; PTA; Jr. Service League; Bd. of Dir's
        Home for Retarded Children. Educ: Miss. U. for
        Women 1965 BS. B: 7/12/44. Add: 29 Greenview
        Cir., Sherwood 72116 (501) 835-5319.

Stuttgart. MARY STONE
        City Hall, Stuttgart 72166.

Sulphur Springs. GRACE V. BRACKNEY
        City Hall, Sulphur Springs 72768.

Texarkana. MARGARET STUART DICKEY (I)
        1974-. Bds: Civic Ctr. Cmsn.; Ch., Clean
        Community Cmsn.; Chamber of Commerce. Org:
        Assoc. Jr. Leagues; Clean Community System;
        Chamber of Commerce. Educ: Sweet Briar Coll.
        1941 BA. B: 3/12/21. Add: 1902 Ash St.,
        Texarkana 75501 (501) 774-3161.

Tillar. BLUE BELL WELLS
        City Hall, Tillar 71670.

Trumann. NANCY DUDLEY
        City Hall, Trumann 72472.

Tuckerman. GAYLE BAILEY
        City Hall, Tuckerman 72473.

Tyronza. FREDA KIRK
        City Hall, Tyronza 72386.

Waldo. KATHLEEN GILES
        City Hall, Waldo 71770.

Ward. JENNIE SUE LENGEL
        City Hall, Ward 72176.

Washington. CARRIE LONG
        Town Hall, Washington 71862.

Weldon. MRS. DOROTHY T. LONG
        Town Hall, Weldon 72177.

West Memphis. ROBERTA JACKSON
        City Hall, West Memphis 72301.

Winslow. MARSHA CODLEY
        VELMA DUNCAN
        MOZELL SCOTT
        City Hall, Winslow 72959.

Winslow. CELESTER ASLEE PERKINS SHIPLEY (D)
        1969-. B: 8/30/1898. Add: Church St.,
        Winslow 72959.

Judges

BERNICE L. KIZER (D)
Chancery Judge. 1974-. Prev: State Legislator 1961-74. Org: Ark. Bar Assoc.; Ark. Judicial Assoc.; BPW; Soroptimist; Dem. Women's Club. Educ: U. of Ark. 1954-LLB; 1969 JD. B: 8/14/15. Add: 221 May Ave., Ft. Smith 72901 (501) 470-5071.

ELSIJANE TRIMBLE ROY (D)
Supreme Court Judge. 1975-. Bds: Professional Conduct Com. Liason; State-Federal Judicial Council. Party: Committeewoman, State Dem. Com.; V-Ch., Ark. Dem. State Com. Prev: Circuit Judge 1966-67; Ark. Constitutional Revision Study Cmsn. 1967. Org: ABA; Nat. Assoc. Women Lawyers; Altrusa. Educ: U. of Ark. 1939 JD. B: 4/2/16. Add: Riviera Apts. #1101, 3700 Cantrell Rd., Little Rock 72202 (501) 375-8414.

State Boards and Commissions

Office of the Governor, State Capitol, Little Rock 72201.

Abstractors, Board of Examiners
ZETTA MAE DOWNS

Aeronautics, Commission for Department of
MARGE MC LFAN
VIRGINIA PROCTOR

Alcohol Abuse Advisory Council
ANN LAWRENCE

Arts and Humanities Advisory Council
MRS. HAROLD CABE
MARGARET ANN KENWOOD
MRS. THOMAS KING
MRS. J.M. LLEWELLYN
MRS. WILLIAM NOLAN, SR.
MRS. JAMES OLIVER, JR.
MRS. JAMES SHACKLEFORD
JUDY SNOWDEN
MRS. THOMAS SPARKS

Bicentennial Celebration Committee
MRS. BERNARD BRAZIL
MRS. THOMAS F. DODSON
MRS. GEORGE SMITH

Child Care Facilities Review Board
DR. PHYLLIS GREENHOUSE

Collection Agencies, State Board of
JOAN R. ZUMWALT

Commemorative Commission
MRS. BILL FOSTER

Cooperative Area Manpower Planning System
CONNIE BETNER
FLORIDA GUY
MRS. H.C. RUSHING
JO ANNE VANN

Cosmetology, State Board of
VIRGINIA DONALDSON
RUTH HENDRICKSON
MRS. GENEVA MILLER
VEDA TRAYLOR
MRS. GALE YOUNG

Crime and Law Enforcement, Commission of
MARY BURT NASH

Drug Abuse Authority
MANDY ALFORD
EMOGENE FOX
DR. HOPE LEHMAN

Drug Abuse Authority Advisory Commission
MRS. EMOGENE FOX
JANE A. MARTIN

Education Commission of the States
MRS. ARNETT GILL

Education, State Board of
MRS. JAMES W. CHESNUTT

Education Television Commission
MRS. O.P. HAMMONS
MRS. J.R. SINK

Environmental Preservation Commission
MRS. PEGGY MC COOL

Finance, State Board of
NANCY HALL

Governors Mansion Commission
MRS. MELANIE SPEER
MRS. A. HOWARD STEBBINS

Healing Arts Board
DR. ROBERTA BUSTIN

Health Planning Council
CLARA P. FORSBERG
HAZEL C. HICKS
LOIS KIDD
JANE C. MC GEHEE
VADA C. SHEID
STORMY SMITH

Health, State Board of
BARBARA PERRY JOHNSON

Hearing Aid Dispensers, Board of
MRS. SHARON GRAHAM
MRS. LORENE HENDRICKS

Higher Education, State Board of
MRS. FAYDORE HOWARD

History Commission
MRS. GERALD B. MC LANE
MRS. W.A. WOODWARD, SR.

Hospital Advisory Council
CHRIS BURROW
DONNA A. CHACHERE
SISTER JUDITH MARIE
MARY C. WILLIAMS
SISTER ELAINE WILLETT

Inhalation Therapy Exam Commission
MRS. HELEN BUERGLER

Investigation Licensing Board
KAREN D. GULLEY

Justice Building Commission
MARION S. GILL
MRS. MARVIN SUE PARK

Juvenile Training School Board
MRS. CLEON DOZZELL
MRS. CAL LEDBETTER JR.

Kidney Disease Commission
MRS. WILLIAM P. DORTCH, JR.

Labor Board
MRS. DELOIS SMITH
MRS. LORENE WATKINS

Legislative Organization Commission
MRS. EVELENA BERRY
MRS. J.C. MC FARLIN

Library Building Commission
BONNIE OLENE HENDERSON
DR. BESSIE MOORE

Library Commission
MRS. BLANCHE EVANS
MRS. LLOYD HENRY
VERA JACOBS
MRS. VERA KILPATRICK
MRS. JIM MERRITT
DR. BESSIE MOORE

Mansion Advisory Council
DORATHY ALLEN
BERNICE L. KIZER

Mental Retardation Board
MRS. MARION HICKEY

Merit System Council
DR. VERTIE LEE CARTER
MRS. THOMAS LOCKETT

Mobile Home Commission
ELIZABETH BROOKS
IVA TAYLOR

Museum and Cultural Commission
MRS. HENRY W. GREGORY, JR.

Nursing Home Advisory Council
ROSE RUFFIN
MRS. GEORGE TIPPIN

Nursing, State Board of
ERA ASHCRAFT
NELL BALKMAN
GEORGIA BUCANAN
ROSE CLIFTON
ELSIE FERGUSON
PEARL GOOD
GRACE LACKOWSKY
HELEN LIEBHABER
MARIE NOLL
MAXINE OTEY
DAUPHINE WOMACK

Oil and Gas Commission
C.G. BETSY DAVIS

Prairie Grove Battlefield Commission
MRS. BUNN M. BELL
MRS. J.C. PARKS

Private Schools Advisory Council
MRS. RUTH WEST

Psychology Examiners Board
MRS. JUDY DANFORD

Public Building Authority
MRS. JOHN R. GARDNER

Public Employees Retirement System
NANCY HALL
FAY MATHIS

Public Welfare, State Board of
MRS. NELL GUNTER
ANNIE ZACHARY

Recreation and Travel Commission
ANN DAWSON

School For Blind and the Deaf, Board of Trustees
MRS. ERNESTINE CLAYTON
BETTY JO HAYES

Science and Technology Council
DR. JOYCLYN ELDERS

State University, Board of Trustees
MRS. LOU MIXON

Steam Preservation Commission
MRS. JOSEPH CLARK
MRS. HUBERT FERGUSON
MRS. HOWARD S. STERN

Unemployment Insurance Advisory Council
PEGGY KELLER

University of Arkansas, Board of Trustees
DIANE NOLAN

Vo-Tech Education Council
MARY W. HALL
MRS. JO JACKSON
J. MERLE LEMLEY
MRS. HAROLD WOODFIN

Workshop Made Products Commission
KATHLEEN UNDERWOOD

California

CLAIRE T. DEDRICK (R) **
Secretary for Resources. Org: Dir., League of Conservation Voters; Peninsula Conservation Center; Modern Transit Society Advisory Bd., County Environmental Quality Coordination Council. Educ: Ariz. State U. 1952 BS; Stanford U. 1965 PhD. B: 6/28/30. Add: 1416 9th St., Room 1311, Sacramento 95814.

MARCH FONG EU (D)
Secretary of State. 1974-. Bds: State Cmsn. on Voting Machines & Vote Tabulation Devices. Party: State Del. 1966-77; Nat. Alt. 1968; Dem. State Central Com. 1974-77; Cnty. Dem. Central Com. 1974-77. Prev: State Assemblywoman 1966-74. Org: BPW; WPC; LWV; AAUW. Educ: U. of Calif. 1948 BS; Mills Coll. 1951 MEd.; Stanford U. 1956. EdD. B: 3/29/27. Add: 111 Capitol Mall, Sacramento 95814 (916) 445-6371.

CARLOTTA HERMAN MELLON (D)
Appointments Secretary. 1975-. Educ: Immaculate Heart Coll. 1967 BA; Claremont Graduate School 1969 MA; 1973 PhD. B: 10/18/46. Add: 1235 42nd St., Sacramento 95819 (916)445-0658.

State Legislature

State Senate

ROSE ANN VUICH (D)
925 Saginaw Way, Dinuba 93618.

State House

LEONA HELENE EGELAND (D) *
1974-. Dist: 24. Bds: Health Com.; Joint Com. on Legal Equality; Agriculture; Joint Com. on Special Educ; Cmsn. on the Status of Women. Org: NOW; AAUW; NWPC; Zero Population Growth; Dem. Club. Educ: U. of Ariz. 1960 BA; San Jose State U. 1965 MA. B: 4/29/38. Add: 1924 Barry Rd., Davis 95616.

CAROL HALLETT (R)
2560 Alturas Road, Atascadero 93422.

TERESA HUGHES (D)
2630 South Hobart Bldg. #4, Los Angeles 90018.

MARILYN RYAN (R)
1976-. Dist: 51. Bds: Local Govt., Revenue & Tax Resources; Geo-Thermal Task Force; Legis./ U.C. Policy Seminar. Party: State Del. 1977; LA Cnty. Control Com. 1977. Prev: Mayor, Rancho Palos Verdes 1973-76. Org: NOWL; Calif. Elected Women's Assoc.; Soroptimist; LWV; NWPC. B: 12/10/32. Add: 2727 Colt Rd., Rancho Palos Verdes 90274 (916) 445-2112.

MAXINE WATERS (D)
1976-. Dist: 48. Bds: V-Ch., Human Resources; Local Govt; Elections & Reapportionment. Party: State Del. 1973-76; Nat. Del. 1972, '74; Nat. Alt. 1976; Dem. State Central Com. Prev: Chief Deputy 1973-76. Org: Women's Coalition; NAACP. Educ: Calif. State U. 1973 BA. B: 8/15/38. Add: State Capitol, Sacramento (916) 445-2363.

County Commissions

Alameda. VALERIE ANN RAYMOND (D)
1976-. Bds: ABAG Exec. Com.; Mental Health Adv. Bd. Party: Nat. Del. 1974. Org: LWV; Dem. Club. B: 4/17/40. Add: 2368 Buena Vista, Livermore 94550 (415) 874-7367.

Butte. BERTHA MOSLEY
County Courthouse, Oroville 95965.

Calaveras. NANCY WHITTLE
County Courthouse, San Andreas 95249.

Contra Costa. NANCY C. FAHDEN (R)
1976-. Bds: Bay Conservation & Devt. Cmsn.; Local Agency Formation Cmsn.; Mental Health Adv. Bd. Prev: E. Bay Reg. Parks Shoreline Com. 1974-76; Martinez Waterfront Com. 1974-76. Org: LWV; NWPC. Occ: Property Manager. Add: 1053 Hillside Dr., Martinez 94553.

El Dorado. N. ARLIENE TODD
County Courthouse, Placerville 95667.

Fresno. SHARON LEVY (R)
1975-. Bds: Ch., Fresno Cnty. Criminal Justice Com.; Manpower Cmsn.; Council of Govts. Prev: Planning Cmsn. 1971-75. B: 5/11/34. Add: 6475 N. Sequoia Dr., Fresno 93711 (209) 488-3531.

Humboldt. SARA PARSONS (D)
1976-. Bds: Ch., CETA Manpower Com.; Ch., Senior Retired Housing Com.; Mental Health Adv. Com. Prev: Bd. of Educ. 1961-68; Cnty. Grand Jury 1971-72; Status of Women Com. 1974-76. Org: LWV. B: 4/18/16. Add: 44 Hyland, Bayside 95524 (707) 445-7693.

Inyo. WILMA B. MUTH (R)
Dist: 3. Bds: Air Polution Control Dist; Local Agency Formation Cmsn.; Bd. of Dir's,Cnty. Sanatorium. Prev: City Councilwoman 1960-64; State Hospital Adv. Council 1967-70; Local Transportation Com. 1975-77. Org: LWV; Civil Air Patrol. B: 4/13/25. Add: 2758 Glenbrook Way, Bishop 93514 (714) 878-2411.

Marin. BARBARA BOXER (D)
1976-. Bds: Mental Health Adv. Bd.; City/Cnty. Services.Com.; Management Compensation Com. Prev: Cnty. Schools Personnel Cmsn. 1971-73. Org: CEWAER; WPC; Conservation League; Common Cause; Dem. Women's Club. Educ: Brooklyn Coll. 1962 BA. B: 11/11/40. Add: 286 N. Almendor Dr., Greenbrae 94904.

Merced. ANN KLINGER
County Courthouse, Merced 95340.

Mono. JOAN GREEN
County Courthouse, Bridgeport 93517.

Placer. THERESA COOK (D)
1976-. Dist: 3. Bds: Developmental Disa-bilities Area Bd.; Golden Empire Health Systems Agency; Agency on Aging. Party: State Del. 1972-73; Nat. Alt. 1974; Cnty. Dem. Central Com. 1971-73; Assembly Dist. Dem. Com. 1971-72. Org: Soroptimists; BPW; AAUW; Dem. Women's Club. Educ: Sierra Jr. Coll. 1967 AA; Calif. State U. 1977 BA. B: 3/20/34. Add: 255 Sawyer St., Auburn 95603 (916) 823-4641.

Plumas. DELLA J. BLUST (D)
1976-. Dist: 4. Bds: Cnty. Housing Authority; Legal Agencies Formation Council; Mental Health Adv. Bd. Org: Chamber of Commerce. Educ: U. of Wash. 1962 BA. B: 9/18/40. Add: P.O. Box 1071, Quincy, Meadow Vly. 95971 (916) 287-1560.

Sacramento. SANDRA R. SMOLEY (R)
1972-. Dist: 3. Bds: Cnty. Supervisors Assoc. of Calif; Health Services Com.; Governing Bd.-Health Systems Agency. Educ: U. of La. 1959 BS. B: 7/8/36. Add: 1115 Dunbarton Cir., Sacramento 95825 (916) 440-5471.

San Diego. LUCILLE V. MOORE (D)
1977-. Dist: 2. Bds: Local Agency Formation Cmsn.; Mental Health Adv. Bd.; State CETA Council Prev: Councilwoman 1973-76. Org: San Diego Regional Employment Training Consortium Policy Bd; Human Care Services Adv. Bd.; Civil Service Cmsn; LWV; Calif. Fed. of Women's Clubs. Educ: Grossmont Coll. 1969 AA. Add: 1702 Vann Ct., El Cajon 92020 (714) 236-2260.

San Francisco. DIANNE FEINSTEIN (D) **
1970-. Bds: Ch., Rules Com.; V-Ch., Budget & Governmental Efficiency Com., Assoc. of Area Governments; Conservation & Dev. Cmsn.; Water Quality Problems. Org: BPW; LWV; Urban League; Friends of the Earth; Planning & Conservation League; Multi Culture Institute. Educ: Stanford U. 1955 BA. B: 6/22/33. Add: City Hall, San Francisco 94102 (415) 558-5015.

San Francisco. DOROTHY VON BEROLDINGEN (D)
1966-. Bds: Urban & Consumer Affairs; Finance; Health & Environment. Prev: Civil Service Cmsnr. 1964-66; Economic Opportunity Council 1964-66. Org: ABA; BPW; Dem. Women's Forum. Educ: U. of San Francisco School of Law LLB; San Francisco Law School JD. Occ: Attorney. Add: Room 235 City Hall, San Francisco 94102 (415) 558-5015.

Santa Clara County. GERALDINE F. STEINBERG (D)
1973-. Bds: Bay Area Air Pollution Control Bd.; Airport Land Use Com. Prev: Cnty. Planning Comsr. 1972-74. Org: State Bar Assoc.; Community Services Cooperative Bd.; WPC; LWV; Council Relationships; Ch.; Adolescent Services Adv. Bd. Educ: U. of Ill. 1947 BS; Stanford U. Law School 1963 LLB. B: 5/30/25. Add: 10300 W. Loyola Dr., Los Altos 94022 (408) 299-3540.

Santa Cruz. MARILYN LIDDICOAT
County Courthouse, Santa Cruz 95060.

Shasta. BESSIE SANDERS
County Courthouse, Redding 96001.

Sonoma. HELEN B. RUDEE (I)
1976-. Bds: Ch., Joint Hospital Com.; Health Service Agency. Prev: Bd. of Educ. 1965-76. Org: LWV. Educ: Stanford School of Nursing 1940 RN. B: 2/20/18. Add: 725 McDonald Ave., Santa Rosa 95404 (707) 527-2211.

Sutter. MARY KNAPP
County Courthouse, Yuba City 95991.

Tehama. BARBARA CROWLEY
County Courthouse, Red Bluff 96080.

Trinity. AUDREY BUSH
County Courthouse, Weaverville 96093.

Tuolumne. MILDRED FILIBERTI (D)
1976-. Bds: Criminal Justice Planning; Mental Health Adv. Bd. Prev: Juvenile Justice Comsr.; School Dist. Reorg. Bd.; Human Service Adv. Bd. Org: CEWAER; Taxpayers Assoc.; Farm Bureau. Occ: Business Woman. B: 10/14/20. Add: 38 Oak, Sonora 95370 (209) 532-4574.

Yolo. BETSY A. MARCHAND (D) **
1972-. Bds: Calif. Transportation Advisory Bd. Org: Calif. Wildlife Assoc.; County Supervisors Assoc. of Calif.; Davis Dem. Club; PTA; School Tax Over-Ride Com. Educ: Pomona Coll. 1956 BA; Vanderbilt U. 1957 MA. B: 5/19/34. Add: 926 Craig Pl., Davis 95616 (916) 758-2050.

Yolo. TWYLA THOMPSON
County Courthouse, Woodland 95695.

Mayors

Adelanto. JOAN T. ROBINSON
P.O. Box 58, Adelanto 92301.

Albany. JOYCE A. JACKSON
1508 Albany Terrace, Albany 94706.

Anderson. MARIAN A. JAKEZ
3476 Shasta Drive, Anderson 96007.

Arcadia. FLORETTA K. LAUBER
1225 Oaklawn Road, Arcadia 91006.

Arcata. ALEXANDRA FAIRLESS (D)
1972-. Bds: V. Ch., Local Agency Formation
Cmsn.; V. Ch., Humboldt Transit Authority;
Criminal Justice Cmsn. Prev: Cnty. Assoc. of Govt
1974-76. Org: Historical Site Society; LWV; AAUW;
Air Resources Adv. Com.; CEWAER. Educ: Garland
Jr. Coll. 1959 AA; Humboldt State U. 1975 BA.
Occ: Storeowner. B: 7/4/39. Add: 609 J St.,
Arcata 95521 (707) 822-5951.

Artesia. GRETCHEN A. WHITNEY (R)
1976-. Bds: Ch., Sanitation; Finance; Law
Enforcement. Party: Precinct Leader 1960-65.
Prev: Bd. of Educ. 1954-75. Occ: Salesperson.
B: 1/1/13/ Add: 11627 185th, Artesia 90701
(213) 865-6262.

Banning. E. BRIGITTE PAGE (R)
1976-. Bds: Inland Manpower Assoc. Prev:
Economic Devt. Cmsn. 1975-76. Org: Soroptimist.
Occ: Automobile Dealer. B: 9/16/24. Add: 943
Linda Vista, Banning 92220 (714) 849-4511.

Belvedere. SHERRY C. LEVIT (I)
1976-. Bds: Repr., ABAG; Environmental Management Task Force. Prev: Cnty. Park & Recreation Cmsn. 1973-74. Educ: Stanford U. 1964 BA.
B: 6/3/42. Add: 45 Beach Rd., Belvedere 94920
(415) 435-3838.

Claremont. ALBERTA F. SMITH
886 Ottawa Drive, Claremont 91711.

Compton. DORIS A. DAVIS (D) **
1973-. Bds: Mosquito Abatement; Sanitation
Bd. Prev: City Clerk 1965-73. Org: LWV; NAACP;
Nat. Council of Negro Women; Urban League; PTA.
Educ: U. of Ill. BA; Northwestern MA; U. of
Chicago PhD. Add: 409 West Palmer, Compton
90224 (213) 537-8000.

Corona. FLORA SPIEGEL
P.O. Box 878, Corona 91720.

Coronado. VIRGINIA BRIDGE
31 Sandpiper Strand, Coronado 92118.

Covina. ELAINE W. DONALDSON (R)
1976-. Bds: Ch., San Gariel Vly. Assoc. of
Cities; Calif. League of Cities. Party: State
Del. 1976; State Alt. 1974; Cnty. Alt. 1977.
Prev: Councilwoman 1974-76; School Bd. 1963-74.
Org: SCAG; Nat. Adv. Council-Small Business
Administration; Chamber of Commerce; Family
Counseling Bd.;Inter-Community Hospital Foundation
Rep. Club; Rep. Women's Fed. Occ: Controller,
Industrial Distributorship. B: 4/29/23. Add:
785 Rancho El Fuerte, Covina 91724 (213)331-0111.

Del Mar. NANCY HOOVER (D)
1974-. Bds: Ch., Public Participation Com.;
Cmsn. on Status of Women. Org: San Diego Stock-
brokers; League of Calif. Cities; Common Cause
Sierra Club; NOW; Concern for Offshore Oil;
Coalition for Responsible Planning; Civic Assoc.;
PTA; San Diego City Club. Occ: Stock Broker. B:
10/29/38. Add: 367 Pine Needles Dr., Del Mar
92014 (714) 755-9313.

Dixon. ALICE E. ARY (R) **
1972-. Bds: Design & Review Com. Org: NEA;
CTA; Soroptomists. Educ: San Francisco State
1951 BA; Fresno State 1955 MA. Occ: Teacher.
B: 12/18/27. Add: 850 Sievers Way, Dixon
95620 (916) 678-2326.

Downey. HAZEL N. SCOTTO (D) **
1974-. Bds: Transportation Com.; State &
County Transportation Com.; Com. on Aging; Help-
line Counseling Bd.; County Intergovernmental
Com.; Federal Aid to Urban Communities Com. Org:
LWV; Coll. Advisory Com.; League of Cities;
Clean Air Constituents Bd. B: 6/11/21. Add:
9203 Cord Ave., Downey 90240 (213) 861-0361.

Fairfax. JEAN MAHONEY
169 Cascade Drive, Fairfax 94930.

Fillmore. DELORES I DAY (R)
1970-. Bds: Ch., Criminal Justice Planning
Bd.; V-Ch., Ventura Cnty. Assoc. of Govts. Org:
Criminal Justice Planning Bd.; CEWAER; Coord.
Council;Rep. Club. B: 10/13/20. Add: 725 A St.,
Fillmore 93015 (805) 524-3701.

Gonzales. ELLEN MORGAN
522 Brockman Drive, Gonzales 93926.

Gustine. ELIZABETH BETTANCOURT (R)
1976-. Prev: Councilwoman 1970-76. Org:
Native Daughters of the Golden West. B: 11/21/13
Add: 930 West, Gustine 95322 (209) 854-6471.

Hayward. ILENE WEINREB (D)
1974-. Bds: Ch., Recreation Dist; Human
Services; Ch., Shoreline Planning Agency. Prev:
Councilwoman 1968-74. Org: LWV; Mental Health
Assoc.; Dem. Club. Educ: U. of Chicago MA. B:
11/9/31. Add: 30504 Prestwick Ave., Hayward
94541.

Huntington Beach. HARRIETT MARION WIEDER (R)
1974-. Bds: Ch., Environmental Council;
Environmental Quality Com.; Public Safety. Party
State Central Com. 1976-77. Org: CEWAER; Women's
Crusade; LWV; Rep. Women's Club. Educ: Wayne U.
1950 BA. Occ: Nat. Development Dir. B: 10/7/28.
Add: 16261 Tesbury Cir., Huntington Beach
92649 (714) 536-5553.

Ione. AUDREY O. MILLER (R)
1970-. Bds: Local Agency Formation Cmsn;
Cmsn. on Aging; Central Sierra Planning Council.
B: 10/27/08. Add: 415 Preston Ave., P.O. Box 223
Ione 95640 (209) 274-2421.

Laguna Beach. PHYLLIS J. SWEENEY (D)
1976-. Bds: Parking, Transportation & Circul-
ation Com.; Youth Services Bd.; Burglary Manage-
ment Consortium; Cnty. Criminal Justice Council.
Party: State Del. 1966; Precinct Leader 1964-65;
Alt. Cnty. Committeewoman 1967-69; Cnty. Central
Committeewoman 1969-70. Prev: Councilwoman 1972-
76; V-Mayor 1975-76. Org: LWV; Historical Soc.;
Dem. Club. Educ: U. of Md. 1947 BA. Occ:
Realtor. B: 2/23/25. Add: 2775 Temple Hills
Dr., Laguna Beach 92651 (714) 497-3311.

Livermore. HELEN M. TIRSELL (D)
1976-. Bds: Alameda Cnty. Mayors' Conf.; Bay Area Air Pollution Control Dist.; ABAG. Prev: Planning Cmsn. 1972-74; Cnty. Status of Women Com.; Congress of Vly. Agencies 1976-78. Org: LWV; AAUW; Dem. Club: Educ: U. of Ia. 1957 BA; Drake U. 1961 MA. B: 2/25/35. Add: 727 Catalina Dr., Livermore 94550. (415) 447-3931.

Monte Sereno, HELEN NESBET (D)
1975-. Bds: Regional Criminal Justice Planning Bd.; Intercity Council; Ch., Sanitation Dist. Bd. of Dir's. Prev: Santa Clara Cnty. Transportation Cmsn. 1975-77. Org: Dem. Club; AAUW; LWV. Educ: Radcliffe Coll. 1955 AB; Harvard U. 1956 AMT. Occ: Teacher. B: 7/30/33. Add: 17268 Zena Ave., Monte Sereno 95030 (408) 354-7635.

Monte Sereno. BARBARA F. WINCKLER
17887 Vineland Avenue, Monte Sereno 95030.

Moraga. SUSAN HART MC NULTY (R)
1974-. Bds: Ch., Contra Costa Cnty. Mayor's. Conf.; Cnty. Criminal Justice Agency. Org: LWV; Service League. Educ: U. of Wash. 1961 BS, RN. B: 12/24/39. Add: 917 Caming Ricardo, Moraga 94556 (415) 376-5200.

Morgan Hill. VIRGINIA MAE DAYS
16125 Keith Way, Morgan Hill 95037.

Norco. NELLIE K. WEAVER
4286 Old Hamner Avenue, Norco 91760.

Pacifica. JANICE FULFORD (D) **
1974-. Bds: County Solid Waste Advisory; Peninsula Water Agency. Party: Alternate Delegate, Dem. Nat. Conv. 1972. Org: Common Cause; ACLU; Friends of the Earth. Educ: San Jose State 1939 BA. B: 10/27/15. Add: Box 512, Pacifica 94044 (415) 355-4151.

Petaluma. HELEN PUTNAM (D) **
1965-. Bds: Calif. Assoc. of Local Agencies; V-Pres., League of Calif. Cities; County Local Agency Formation. Prev: Pres., Calif. School Bds. Assoc. 1958-59; Pres., Bd. of Educ. 1947-59. Org: Bd. of Dir's., Calif. Elected Women for Educ. & Research; V-Pres., U. of Calif. Alumni Assoc. Educ: U. of Calif. 1930 BA. Occ: Principal & Teacher. B: 5/4/09. Add: 900 B St., Petaluma 94952 (707) 763-2613.

Pismo Beach. MARIAN M. MELLOW (D)
1976-. Bds: San Luis Obispo Cnty. Local Area Formation Com.; Selection Com.; Planning Cmsn. Org: Women's Club. B: 5/9/27. Add: 675 Lemoore St.,Pismo Bch 93449 (805) 773-4657.

Portola Valley. ELEANOR B. BOUSHEY (D)
1964-. Prev: State Scenic Hwy. Adv. Com. 1968-76. B: 8/27/12. Add: 235 Golden Oak Dr., Portola Vly. 94025 (415) 851-1700.

Redwood City. MARGUERITE LEIPZIG (R) **
1972-. Bds: Economic Opportunity Cmsn.; Mosquito Abatement Dist.; Water Agency. Occ: Theater Sales Director. B: 7/1/25. Add: 3628 Highland Ave., Redwood City 94062 (415) 369-6251.

Rosemead. ROBERTA V. TRUJILLO (D) **
1974-. Bds: Rosemead Study Group. Org: PTA; SCAG; Citizens for Civic Action; Calif. Elected Women's Assoc.; Dem. Club. Occ: Community Organizer. B: 10/22/39. Add: 2339 Kelburn, Rosemead 91770 (213) 280-2234.

San Bruno. MARGARET A. KOZKOWSKI (D)
1971-. Bds: ABAG; Governor's Industrial Siting Task Force; Ch., N. San Mateo Cnty. Council of Cities. Party: State Del. 1976. Prev: Ch., School Bd. 1960-71; Recreation Comsr. 1968-71. Occ: Saleswoman. B: 4/15/27. Add: 2681 Valleywood Dr., San Bruno 94066 (415) 583-3083.

San Jose. JANET GRAY HAYES
1975-. Bds: Ch., Urban Devt. Adv. Com.; Cmsn. on Fair Judicial Practices; Mayor's Ad Hoc Task Force on Housing. Party: Nat. Dem. Campaigning Com. 1976; Calif. Dem. Cmsn. on Nat. Platform Policy 1976. Prev: City Council 1971. Org: League of Calif. Cities; Nat. League of Cities; AAUW; LWV. Educ: Ind. U. BA; U. of Chicago MA. Add: City Hall, 801 N. First St., San Jose 95110 (408) 277-4237.

San Pablo. KATHRYN L. CARMIGNANI (D)
1974-. Bds: Emergency Communications; Bay Area Govt.; Cnty. Transportation Adv. Com. Prev: Planning Cmsn. 1961-70. Org: Soroptimist; LWV; Historical Society; Chamber of Commerce; OEO; CEWAER. B: 3/14/26. Add: 5601 Glenn Ave., San Pablo 94806 (415) 234-6440.

Sante Fe Springs. BETTY WILSON
11314 Clarkman Street, Sante Fe Springs 90670.

Sausalito. SALLY STANFORD
56 Marin Avenue, Sausalito 94965.

South Lake Tahoe. DEL LAINE (D)
1976-. Bds: City Recreation & Parks Cmsn.; City Planning Cmsn. Prev: Ch., Recreations & Parks Cmsn. 1973-76; Ch., Tahoe Regional Planning Agency; Citizens Adv. Com. 1973-76; Ch., Urban Design Com. 1974-76. Org: Soroptimist; Historical Society; Dem. Club. Educ: San Francisco City Coll. 1950 AA; Calif. State U. 1953 BA; Calif. State U. 1960 MS. Occ: Co-owner Photography Studio. B: 3/20/30. Add: Box 7322, S. Lake Tahoe 95731 (916) 541-2900.

Stanton. MARTHA V. WEISHAUPT
10551 Courson Drive, Stanton 90680.

Vacaville. BARBARA JONES (R)
1977-. Bds: Environmental Management Policy Com.; Mayors' Conf.; Armed Forces Com. Org: PTA. Educ: Rollins Coll. 1965 BS. Occ: Teacher. B: 11/8/42. Add: 106 Manzanita Dr., Vacaville 95688 (707) 448-1863.

Vallejo. FLORENCE E. DOUGLAS
508 Maine Street, Vallejo 94590.

Victorville. GLADYS M. BUTTS (R)
1962-. Bds: Alt. Repr., SCAG; Alt. Repr., Regional Council; Cnty. Council of Community Services. Org: Inland Manpower; Women's Club. B: 5/10/09. Add: 17053 B St., Victorville 92392 (714) 245-3411.

Local Councils

Adelanto. KAREN I. MC CLURE
P.O. Box 207, Adelanto 92301.

Alameda. ANNE B. DIAMENT (D)
1977-. Bds: Alt., Cnty. Solid Waste Com.; V-Ch., City Beach Erosion Com. Prev: Housing Authority 1968-75. Org: Meals on Wheels; LWV; Women's Town Hall. B: 2/2/19. Add: 1409 St. Charles St., Alameda 94501 (415) 522-4100.

Alturas. LESLEY J. CHACE (R)
1976-. Bds: City Planning Cmsn. Educ: St. Lukes School of Nursing 1965 RN. Occ: RN. B: 5/6/43. Add: 1400 W. 8th, Alturas 96101.

Anaheim. MIRIAM KAYWOOD (R)
1974-. Bds: SCAG Exec. Com.; Dir., Cnty. Sanitation Dist.; Park & Recreation Cmsn. Prev: Planning Cmsn. 1970-73; Santa Ana Rvr. Com. 1970-72. Org: ASPA; Women's Div., Chamber of Commerce; LWV; Women's Club. Add: 2784 W. Wilberta Ln. Anaheim 92804 (714) 533-5626.

Anderson. KAY L. MC QUADE
1977-. Bds: Fire Protection Dist. Add: 1887 Howard, Anderson 96007 (916) 365-2521.

Antioch. ROSEMARIE SPINELLI AGUILAR (D) **
1974-. Bds: Dunes for Recreation; County Housing & Community Dev. Council; Child Dev. Council. Org: LWV; AAUW; PTA. Educ: Brooklyn Coll. 1966 BA; Stanford U. 1967 MA. B: 6/2/45. Add: 3121 Lindley Ct., Antioch 94509 (415)757-3333

Arvin. JANET L. REED
300 Plumtree Drive, Arvin 93203.

Auburn. BERNICE PATE (D)
1966-. Prev: Mayor 1970-73; Sierra Planning Org. 1971-77; Calif. Indian Com. 1967-69. B: 2/1/07. Add: 135 S. McDaniel Dr., Auburn 95603 (916) 885-5661.

Bellflower. MARY E. LEWIS
9911 Ramona Street #20, Bellflower 90706.

Belmont. PAMELA S. KETCHAM
816 Holly Road, Belmont 94002.

Benicia. MARY MC KAY
224 West I Street, Benicia 94510.

Berkeley. SHIRLEY DEAN (D)
1975-. Bds: Mental Health Adv. Bd.; Berkeley Redevt. Agency; Housing Authority. Party: Nat. Del. 1976. Prev: Planning Cmsn. 1971-75; Bd. of Adjustments 1973-75; Waterfront Adv. Bd. 1973-75. Org: LWV; Urban Care; Berkeley Assoc.; Dem. Club.; Women's Dem. Forum; WPC. Educ: U. of Calif. 1956 AA; BA. B: 11/25/34. Add: 924 Santa Barbara Rd. Berkeley 94507 (415) 524-3223.

Berkeley. ILONA HANCOCK (D)
1971-. Org: Berkeley Citizens Action; ACLU; NOW; WPC. Educ: Ithaca Coll. 1963 BA. Occ: Psychologist. B: 4/10/40. Add: 2225 Ward St., Berkeley 94705 (415) 841-0370.

Berkeley. SUSAN MEADOWS HONE (D)
1971-. Bds: Exec. Com., ABAG; E. Bay Div., League of Calif. Cities; Human Resources Steering Com. Party: Dem. State Central Com. 1967-69. Org: LWV; Dem. Club; CEWAER. Educ: U. of Calif. 1961 BA. B: 5/29/38. Add: 3 Tanglewood Rd., Berkeley 94705 (415) 644-6243.

Beverly Hills. DONNA ELLMAN (D)
1974-. Bds: Joint Com. on Tort Liability. Prev: Pres., Civil Service Com. 1972-74. Org: Cnty. Sanitation. B: 7/28/25. Add: 609 N. Crescent Dr., Beverly Hills 90210 (213)550-4705.

Biggs. EUNICE C. SMITH (R)
1975-. Bds: Cnty. Assoc. of Govt.; Cnty. Animal Control Com. Org: Calif. Credit Union; Grange; Dir., Grange; Insurance Assoc. Occ: Manager, Grange Federal Credit Union. B: 12/25/18. Add: 693 B St., P.O. Box 201 Biggs 95917.

Blue Lake. JEAN LEAVITT
P.O. Box 486. Blue Lake. 95525.

Blue Lake. KATHERINE BISHOP WARD (D)
1974-. Bds: Local Agency Formation Com.; Ch., Solid Waste Adv. Com.; Calif. League of Cities. Org: CEWAER; LWV; Chamber of Commerce; Historical Sites Society; Resource Recovery Task Force; Humboldt Cnty. Citizens Welfare Adv. Com.; Cnty. Appointments. Educ: Humboldt State U. 1973 BA; Humboldt State U. 1977 MA. B: 3/22/47. Add: 411 Wahl St., Box 677, Blue Lake 95525 (707) 668-5965.

Bradbury. MYRNA JONES
2238 Gardi Street, Bradbury 94513.

Brentwood. BARBARA J. GUISE (R) **
1974-. Bds: Criminal Justice Bd.; Crime Prevention Com.; Transportation Bd.; Community Dev. Com.; PACCO Com. Org: PTA; Chamber of Commerce; Soroptimist. Occ: Owner Furniture Store. B: 3/10/28. Add: 189 Sherwood Dr., Brentwood 94513 (415) 634-4480.

Brisbane. JEANNINE JONES HODGE (D)
1974-. Mayor Pro Tem. Bds: Criminal Justice Council; San Mateo Cnty. Visitors & Conv. Bureau; E. Bay Dischargers Authority. Prev: Parks, Beaches & Recreation Com. 1973-74. Org: AFT. Educ: San Francisco State U. 1966 BA. Occ: Teacher. B: 8/9/34. Add: 23 San Benito Rd., Brisbane 94005 (415) 467-1518.

Brisbane. ANJA K. MILLER (D)
1973-. Bds: Regional Planning Com.; Airport Land Use Cmsn.; Ch., Parks & Recreation Citizens Adv. Com. Prev: Environmental Quality Com. 1975-76; Open Space Task Force 1974-75. Org: CEWAER; AAUW; Fed. Women's Club. Educ: Helsinki U. 1957 BA; San Francisco State U. 1972 MA. Add: City Hall, Brisbane 94005 (415) 467-1518.

Buena Park. ANN LOU GASS (R)
1976-. Mayor Pro Tem. Bds: League of Calif.
Cities. Prev: Parks & Recreation 1973-75. Org:
Chamber of Commerce. Occ: Hospital Dir. B:
7/7/26. Add: 7865 LaCarta Circle, Buena Park
90620 (714) 521-9900.

California City. MARIE P. WILEY
21820 101st Street, California City 93501.

Calipatria. JAYNE FRANCES COOK (D) **
1974-. Bds: Manpower Planning Council; Recreation Cmsn.; Bicentennial Com. Org: PTA; Occ:
Clerk. B: 10/17/37. Add: Box 262, Calipatria
92233 (714) 348-5012.

Camarillo. MARY REDUS GAYLE (D)
1974-. Bds: Dir., Sanitary Dist.; Alt. Dir.,
Ventura Cnty. Regional Sanitation Dist. Prev:
Planning Cmsn. 1972-74. Org: Bibliographic
Society; Manuscript Society; Assoc. of Coll. &
Research Librarians. Educ: Clarke Coll. 1951 BA;
Immaculate Heart Coll. 1969 MA. Occ: Curator-
Librarian. B: 9/27/29. Add: 1897 Bronson St.,
Camarillo 93010 (805) 482-8921.

Carlsbad. MARY HELEN CASLER (R)
1975-. Bds: Areawide Water Quality Compre-
hensive Planning Org; Senior Citizens Adv. Com.;
Library Bd. of Trustees. Prev: Ch., Carlsbad
Planning Cmsn. 1973-75; Library Bd. of Trustees
1972-73. Org: LWV; Women's Club. Educ: Michigan
State U. 1941 BA. B: 2/9/20. Add: 3843 Highland
Dr., Carlsbad 92008 (714) 729-1181.

Carmel. HELEN ARNOLD
City Hall, Monte Verde & 7th, Carmel 93921.

Carson. KAY A. CALAS
City Hall, 701 C. Carson St., Carson 90745.

Chico. ELIZABETH F. SMITH (D) **
1973-. Bds: Ch., Intergovernmental Relations
Com.; Calif. Dept. of Transportation Advisory Bd.;
League of Calif. Cities; Housing Task Force;
Butte County Area Government Representatives.
Prev: City Planning Cmsn. 1969-73. Org: LWV; WPC;
Sierra Club; NOW; CEWAER; Dem. Club; Tomorrow;
PTA. Educ: Simmons Coll. 1960 BS; Columbia U.
1961 MA. B: 9/30/38. Add: 5th & Main St.,
Chico 95926 (916) 343-0480.

Chino. EILEEN CARTER
4946 Walnut Avenue, Chino 91710.

Claremont. ELEANOR M. COHEN (R)
1974-. Bds: SCAG; Water Quality Com.; Revenue
& Taxation Com. Prev: Planning Cmsn. 1971-74.
Org: Common Cause; Civic Assoc.; Coord. Council;
LWV; Fed. Rep. Women; WPC; Rep. Women's Task
Force; CEWAER. Educ: U.C.L.A. 1961 BS, RN. B:
7/20/40. Add: 440 Greensboro Ct., Claremont
91711 (714) 624-4531.

Claremont. CLAIR K. MC DONALD (D)
1970-. Mayor Pro Tem. Bds: Bd. of Dir's.,
League of Calif. Cities; Tri-City Mental Health
Governing & Adv. Bd.; League of Cities State
Environmental Com. Prev: Planning Cmsnr. 1967-70.
Org: Placement Civic Assoc.; Danforth Assoc.;
CEWAER. Educ: Pomona Coll. 1947 BA. B: 12/28/26.

Add: 239 W. 11th St., Claremont 91711
(714) 624-4531.

Clayton. CAROLYN F. BOVAT (D)
1974-. Bds: League of Calif. Cities E. Bay
Div. Bd. Org: AAUW. Educ: U. of Calif. 1954
BA. B: 7/22/32. Add: 244 Roundhill Pl.,
Clayton 94567 (415) 689-3622.

Clayton. GLORIA E. PATTEN
P.O. Box 242, Clayton 94517.

Cloverdale. MARIE O. VANDAGRIFF
214 Commercial St., Cloverdale 95425.

Coalinga. FLORENCE M. BUNKER (I)
1973-. Mayor Pro Tem. Bds: W. Side Rural
Health Conf. Org: AAUW. Educ: U. of Calif.
1937 BA. Occ: Store-owner. B: 3/11/16. Add:
1515 Coalinga St., Coalinga 93210 (209) 935-1533.

Colfax. JUNE JARRELL (D) **
1974-. Bds: County Industrial Dev.; Ch.,
County Mayors Select Com. Prev: City Treasurer
1966-73; Org: CEWAER; Women's Dem. Club;
Chamber of Commerce; Soroptimists. Occ: Court
Clerk. B: 2/23/29. Add: 185 Culver St., Colfax
95713 (916) 346-8721.

Colton. CONNIE CISNEROS
1410 Latham Stree, Colton 92324.

Concord. JUNE BULMAN (D)
1976-. Bds: Governing Bd., Health Systems
Agency; Regional Airport Planning Cmsn. Prev:
Planning Cmsn. 1974-76. Org: LWV; AAUW; WPC;
PTA. Educ: Miami U. 1948 BA. B: 6/17/26.
Add: 3866 Logan Ct., Concord 94519 (415)671-3158.

Concoran. ALICE GOODRICH
1503 Letts, Concoran 93212.

Corte Madera. JANA GILPIN HAEHL (R)
1973-. Bds: ABAG; Alt., Local Agency Formation Cmsn.; Growth Control Com. Prev: Mayor
1975-76; Pres., Sanitary Dist. of Marin Cnty.
1975-76. Org: Commonwealth Club; WPC; Marin
Women in Govt.; PTA; Conservation League; Sierra
Club. B: 9/17/38. Add: 499 Corte Madera Ave.,
Corte Madera 94925 (415) 924-1700.

Costa Mesa. NORMA C. HERTZOG (R) **
1974-. Bds: Inter City Com.; Crime Prevention; Community Dev.; City-School Liaison. Prev:
Welfare Com. 1972-74. Org: PTA; Women's Groups;
Educ. Assoc. Occ: Pre-School Owner. B: 9/20/28.
Add: 1605 White Oak Dr., Costa Mesa 92626
(714) 556-5285.

Costa Mesa. MARY T. SMALLWOOD
1981 Kornat Drive, Costa Mesa 92626.

Crescent City. GENEVIEVE WAGNER
224 W. 5th Street, Crescent City 95531.

Cupertino. KATHY E. NELLIS
22322 Regnart Road, Cupertino 95014.

Cypress. ALICE J. MAC LAIN (R)
    1972-. Bds: Local Agency Formation Cmsn.;
Orange Cnty. Vector Control; Cnty. League of
Cities. Party: Cnty. Rep. Central Com. 1974-75.
Prev: Cnty. Sanitation Dist. 1972-77; ICC 1973-76.
Org: Women's Club. Educ: Woodbury Coll. BA.
Occ: Administrative Aide. B: 10/16/38. Add:
4219 Dover Cir., Cypress 90630 (714) 828-2200.

Cypress. SONIA SUNNY SONJU (D)
    1974-. Bds: SCAG; Orange Cnty. Housing
Authority; Dept. of Transportation. Party: State
Del. 1977. Prev: Planning Cmsr. 1969-74. Org:
Amer. Society of Planning Officers; LWV; Veterans
Adv. Council; Jr. Woman's Club; NOW. Educ: U. of
Wisc. 1962 BS; Calif. State U. 1976 MA. B:
1/31/39. Add: 11398 Mayshon Ct., Cypress 90630
(714) 828-2200.

Davis. CECILY J. MOTLEY
    Bds: Planning & Conservation League; Calif.
Coastal Alliance. Prev: Cnty. Planning Cmsn.
1966-76; Delta Adv. Planning Council 1968-74;
Davis Planning Cmsn. 1960-66. Org: LWV; Bicycle
Path Adv. Com. Educ: Radcliffe Coll. 1947;
McGeorge School of Law 1975. Add: 534 Villanova
Dr., Davis 95616 (916) 753-3848.

Del Rey Oaks. JOAN G. MOISES (D)
    1974-. Bds: Youth Project Bd., Solid Waste
Disposal Plan Com.; Ch., Parks & Recreation. Org:
CEWAER; LWV; AAUW; Alliance on Aging. Educ: U.
of Calif. 1948 BS. Occ: Optometric Asst. B:
1/6/26. Add: 1040 Paloma Rd., Del Rey Oaks
93940 (408)394-8511.

Dixon. MAUREEN MONSON SOUTHWELL (D)
    1976-. Mayor Pro Tem. Bds: Ch., Ordinance
Review Com.; Citizens Com. Prev: Library Cmsn.
1970-76. Org: NEA; Dem. Club; AAUW. Educ: U.
of Calif. 1942 BS. Occ: Teacher. B: 9/27/21.
Add: 200 S. 7th St., Dixon 95620 (916)678-2326.

El Cajon. LUCILLE V. MOORE (D) **
    1974-. Bds: County Civic Center Authority;
Heartland Fire Training Facility Authority;
Regional Employment & Training Consortium Policy
Bd.; County Local Agency Formation Cmsn. Advisory
Bd.; League of Calif. Cities, Human Resources
Com. Org: LWV; Calif. Elected Women's Assoc.;
East County Dem.; Woman's Club. B: 12/5/27.
Add: 1702 Vann Ct., El Cajon 92020 (714)442-4441.

El Centro. IRIS DE ZARN
    P.O. Box 763, El Centro 92243.

Emeryville. RENA RICKLES (D)
    1975-. Bds: March of Dimes; Ch., Intergovt.
Relations; Public Health and Safety. Party:
State Del. 1975-77; Nat. Alt. 1976. Org: ABA;
NAACP; WPC. Educ: U.C.L.A. 1966 BA. B: 7/16/44.
Add: 6 Admiral Dr., #489, Emeryville 94608
(415) 652-5144.

Escondido. LORRAINE HANDY BOYCE (R)
    1971-. Bds: Ch., League of Calif. Cities
Human Resources Com.; Ch., Health Systems Agency;
Ch., Air Quality Adv. Policy Com. Prev: Governors
Adv. Com. on Early Childhood Educ. 1974-. Org:
Calif. Nurses Assoc.; Ecology; Sierra Club;
Common Cause; NOW. Educ: Los Angeles Cnty.

Medical School of Nursing 1948 RN. Occ: Health
Educator, RN. B: 12/13/27. Add: 384 Cypress
Crest Ter., Escondido 92025 (714) 741-4638.

Exeter. IRELENE M. ELLISON
    1974-. Bds: League of Calif. Small Cities
Com.; Prev: Blue Ribbon Com. 1973-74. Org: BPW;
Exeter Hospital Guild; Exeter Chamber of Commerce; Historical Society. B: 4/5/30. Add:
224 Portola, Exeter 93221 (209)592-3710.

Fairfax. PRISCILLA CLAUDIUS GRAY (I)
    1973-. Bds: Ch., Animal Control Com.; Tax
Equity Com. Prev: School Bd. Trustee 1968-71;
Fairfax Town Treasurer 1971-73. B: 8/7/26. Add:
126 Ridge Rd., Fairfax 94930 (415)453-1584.

Ferndale. EUNICE E. WATSON
    City Hall, 834 Main St., Ferndale 95536.

Firebaugh. ROSEMONDE LEE BARBOA (D)
    1973-. Bds: Ch., Drug Abuse Com. Org: AAUW.
Occ: High School Counselor. B: 8/30/25. Add:
874 G St., Firebaugh 93622 (209) 659-2043.

Fontana. ANNE W. DUNIHUE (D)
    1976-. Mayor Pro Tem. Bds: San Bernardina
Assoc. Govts.; Cnty. Transportation Cmsn. Prev:
Personnel Bd. 1974-76. Org: BPW; United Steel
Workers Local; Steelworkers Old Timers Foundation;
Chamber of Commerce; CEWAER; Management Curric-
ulum Com. Occ: Payroll Clerk. B: 9/22/24. Add:
9395 Mango Ave., Fontana 92335 (714)822-5200.

Fort Bragg. BETTY SEAGRAVES
    420 E. Bush Street, Fort Bragg 95437.

Fort Bragg. JEAN M. TALLMAN (R)
    1976-. Org: Rep. Women. Educ. U. of Calif.
1951 BA. B: 6/8/29. Add: 309 E. Bush St.,
Fort Bragg 95437.

Fort Jones. MARY BERRY
    P.O. Box 117, Carlock St., Fort Jones 96032.

Fortuna. BETH RUNDELL (R) **
    1969-. Bds: Planning Com.; Bicentennial Com.;
County Transportation Authority. Prev: Planning
Cmsn. 1964-69. Org: BPW. Occ: Realtor. B:
4/6/20. Add: Box 811, Fortuna 95540
(707) 725-3308.

Fresno. LINDA MACK
    2326 Fresno St. (City Hall), Fresno 93721.

Fullerton. FRANCES R. WOOD (D)
    1978-. Bds: Flood Protection Agency; Orange
Cnty. Sanitation Agency. Prev: Exec. Com. of
SCAG 1974-77. Org: LWV; AAUS; Cnty. Dems. Educ:
U. of Calif. 1949 BA. B: 10/5/24. Add: 213 S.
Woods Ave., Fullerton 92623 (714) 525-7171.

Garden Grove. KATHRYN L. BARR
    City Hall, 11391 Acacia Pkwy., Garden Grove
92640.

Gridley. DORIS E. LONG (D)
    1976-. Bds: Safety Cmsn.; Electric. Educ:
Chicago State U. 1944 BA; Berkeley Baptist
Divinity School 1948 MA. Occ: Librarian. B:
6/13/23. Add: 197 Vermont St., Gridley 95948.

Grover City. MAYSEL G. FULLER (R)
    1975-. Mayor Pro Tem. Bds: San Luis Obispo
Area Planning Council; Cnty. Transit System; Cnty.
Regional Transportation Study. Prev: Planning
Com. 1970-74; Coastal Vly. Planning Council 1970-
73. Org: BPW; Rep. Club. Occ: Store Owner. B:
12/2/20. Add: 1275 Grand Ave., Grover City
93433 (805) 489-4040.

Grover City. JUANITA QUALLS
    232 North 3rd Street, Grover City 93433.

Hawaiian Gardens. JULIA E. SYLVA (D)
    1976-. Mayor Pro Tem. Prev: Bicentennial Com.
1974-76. Org: Assoc. of Mexican-American Educators; Common Cause; WPC; Dem. Club; Political
Science Student Assoc.; Calif. Scholarship Fed.
Occ: Bilingual Instructor. B: 11/13/55. Add:
21802 Clarksdale Ave., Hawaiian Gardens 90716
(213) 860-2476.

Hayward. GAIL STEELE
    22586 Arlette Avenue, Hayward 94541.

Hermosa. MARY TYSON
    572 25th St., Hermosa Beach 90254.

Hidden Hills. COLLEEN M. HARTMAN (D) **
    1970-. Org: Drug Educ.; Counseling Center
Advisory Council. Educ: Adelphi U. BS. B:
7/24/24. Add: 5747 Jed Smith Rd., Hidden Hills
91302.

Hollister. PAT PICKERING (D)
    1974-. Bds: V-Ch., Local Agency Formation
Cmsn.; Calif. Council on Criminal Justice. Prev:
Mayor 1975-76. Org: BPW; CEWAER. Occ: Business
Manager. B: 8/2/46. Add: 170 McCray, Hollister
95023 (408) 637-4491.

Huntington Beach. NORMA BRANDEL GIBBS (I)
    1970-. Bds: State Human Relations Cmsn.; Nat.
Human Relations Cmsn. Prev: Mayor 1975-76;
Councilwoman 1974-75; V-Ch., Orange Cnty Sani-
tation Bd. 1974-76; Ch., Metropolitan State
Hospital Bd. 1974-77. Org: AAUW; LWV; Soroptimist
BPW; WPC; NOW; CEWAER. Educ: N. Park Coll 1945
AA; U. of Ill 1955 MEd; Northwestern U. 1958 PhD.
Occ: Professor. B: 7/8/25. Add: 17087 Westport
Dr., Huntington Beach 92649 (714) 536-5553.

Imperial. PATRICIA BURK
    708 So. H. Street, Imperial 92251.

Indio. REGENA ZOKOSKY (R)
    1976-. Bds: Goals & Policies Com.; SCAG; Org:
Mayors & Councilman Conf.; League of Calif. Citrus
Belt.; Retired Senior Volunteer Program; Rep.
Women's Club. B: 2/17/32. Add: 81-980 Tournament
Way, Indio 92201 (714) 347-2351.

Irvine. MARY ANN GAIDO
    5071 Berean, Irvine, 92664.

Irvine. GABRIELLE G. PRYOR (D)
    1971-. Bds: Public Safety Com., League of
Calif. Cities. Prev: Councilwoman 1971-77; Canyon
Cnty. Formation Cmsn. 1976; Youth Services Adv.
Bd. 1974-76; Mental Health Adv. Bd. 1974-76. Org:
Planned Parenthood; Dem. Club; CEWAER. Educ:
Stanford U. 1961 BA. B: 1/17/40. Add: 50 Acacia

Tree Ln., Irvine 92715 (714) 754-3605.

Isleton. SALLY FONSECA PATRICK (D) **
    1974-. Org: PTA. Occ: Teacher's Aide. B:
11/10/39. Add: Box 424, Isleton 95641
(916) 777-6082.

Lafayette. BARBARA LANGLOIS (D) **
    1974-. Bds: Mayor's Conf. Org: LWV; Dem.
Club. Educ: U. of Calif. 1943 BA. B: 12/24/21.
Add: 3996 South Peardale Dr., Lafayette
94549 (415) 284-1968.

Laguna Beach. SALLY RHONE BELLERUE (D)
    1976-. Bds: SCAG-Environmental Quality
Com.; Parks & Recreation. Prev: Planning Cmsn.
1973-76. Org: LWV; AAUW; Planning & Conservation
League; Dialogue on Schools. Educ: U. of Mont.
1959 BA. Occ: Volunteer Coord. Elementary
School. B: 2/13/38. Add: 430 Bosque, Laguna
Beach 92651 (714) 494-1124.

La Habra. ROBIN E. YOUNG (D)
    1972-. Bds: Bd. of Dir's. CEWAER; League of
Cities Devt. Com.; Alt., Joint Sanitation Dist's.
Party: Nat. Del. 1976. Org: CEWAER; LWV. Educ:
Fullerton Coll. AA; Calif. State U. BA; The
London School of Economics & Political Science
MS. B: 4/25/48. Add: 591 Magnolia Way, La
Habra 90631 (213) 694-1011.

La Palma. MARY T. WILLIAMS
    7872 Camden Circle, La Palma 90620.

Larkspur. JOAN L. SESTAK (D) **
    1973-. Bds: Alternate to Local Agency
Formation Cmsn. Prev: Library Bd. 1969-71. Org:
LWV; WPC; Conservation League; Sierra Club;
Audubon Society; PTA. Educ: U. of Ill. 1956 BA.
Occ: Insurance Underwriter. B: 12/8/34. Add:
18 Cedar Ave., Larkspur 94939 (415) 925-2405.

Lawndale. SARANN KRUSE (D)
    1976-. Bds: League of Calif. Cities Assoc. -
Public Safety Com.; Juvenile Diversion Policy Bd;
S. Bay Cities Assoc. Party: State Alt. 1976.
Org: Industrial Hygiene Assoc.; Nat. Safety
Council; Soroptimist; Behavior Health Services;
Dem. Club. Occ: Safety & Health Specialist.
B: 1/14/40. Add: 15323 Prairie Ave., Lawndale
90260 (213) 973-4321.

Lemoore. KAREN L. NICKS (D)
    1976-. Bds: Planning Cmsn. Prev: Planning
Cmsn. 1972-76. B: 9/12/43. Add: 640 Wood Ln.,
Lemoore 93245.

Lincoln. LEAH NEVAREZ (I)
    1974-. Bds: Human Relations Cmsn.; Ch.,
Solid Waste Management Com.; Manpower Planning
Council. B: 11/17/42. Add: 420 E St., Lincoln
95648. (916) 645-3314.

Live Oak. LOIS LOCKE (D)
    1972-. Bds: Welfare Adv. Bd.; Bd. of Dir's.,
Mosquito Abatement; Inner-City Adv. Bd. Org:
BPW. B: 10/10/12. Add: 6 Maple Pk., Live Oak
95953 (916) 695-2351.

Lompoc. CHARLOTTE BENTON (R) **
    1964-. Bds: Area Planning Council; Community
Action Cmsn. Org: Accountants Society; Chamber
of Commerce; Mental Health Assoc.; Health &
Welfare Coordination Council; Drug Abuse Council.
Occ: Accountant. B: 5/16/23. Add: 211 South I
St., Lompoc 93436 (805) 736-3434.

Lompoc. ELINOR LEFKOWITZ (R)
    1975-. Bds: Statewide Community Devt. Com.;
Santa Barbara Cnty. Housing & Land Use Com.;
Economic Devt. Assoc. Educ: Calif. Coll of
Commerce 1953 BS. Occ: Property Management. B:
4/24/16. Add: 1720 Sheffield Dr., Lompoc
93436 (805) 736-1261.

Long Beach. RENEE B. SIMON (D) **
    1972-. Bds: Long Beach Park Com.; Compre-
hensive Health Planning Bd.; Los Angeles County
Federal Aid Urban Highway Policy Com. Prev: Los
Angeles Citizens Advisory Planning Council 1972-
73. Org: AAUW; Common Cause; LWV; Women's Council
Chamber of Commerce. Educ: Adelphi U. 1947 BA;
Stanford U. 1948 MS; U. of Calif. 1966 MLS. Occ:
Librarian. B: 3/25/28. Add: 545 Orlena Ave.,
Long Beach 90814 (213) 436-9041.

Los Alamitos. BARBARA M. AUDLEY (R)
    1975-. Prev: Parks & Recreation Cmsn. 1969-75;
Ch., Parks & Recreation Cmsn. 1972-75; Ch., City
Beautification Com. 1967-68. Org: Amer. Society
for Training & Devt.; APSA; Nat. Parks & Recre-
ation. Educ: Calif. State U. 1974 BS. Occ: Coll.
Administrator. B: 4/26/40. Add: 4722 Howard Ave.,
Los Alamitos 90720 (213) 431-3538.

Los Altos. AUDREY H. FISHER (R)
    1964-. Bds: ABAG; Community Health Abuse
Council; Ch., Santa Clara Vly. Water Cmsn. Party:
Nat. Alt. 1960; State Central Com. 1954-74; Cnty.
Central Com. 1955-65. Prev: Mayor 1967-69; State
Health Planning Council 1967-73; Nat. Adv. Council
on Comprehensive Health Planning Program 1971-74;
Regional Water Quality Control Bd. 1975-76. Org:
Rep. Women's Fed. B: 8/30/04. Add: P.O. Box 415,
120 Hawthorne Ave., Los Altos 94022 (415) 948-1491

Los Altos. RUTH H. KOEHLER (I)
    1974-. Bds: Santa Clara Cnty. Planning Policy
Com.; ABAG; Environmental Management Task Force;
San Francisco Bay Area Air Pollution Control.
Org: LWV; AAUW. Educ: Mt. Holyoke Coll. 1948 BA.
B: 10/30/26. Add: 64 Stuart Ct., Los Altos
94022 (415) 948-1491.

Los Altos Hills. LUCILE THERESA HILLESTAD (R)
    1976-. Mayor Pro Tem. Bds: Planning Policy
Cmsn.; Leisure Services; Santa Clara Water Cmsn.
Prev: Freedom From Hunger Foundation 1974-75;
Pathpay Com. 1975-76; Planning Cmsn. Org: Rep.
Women; CEWAER; WPC. Educ: U. of Wis. 1954-AA.
B: 2/19/33. Add: 12843 Normandy Ln., Los Altos
Hills 94022 (415) 941-7332.

Los Angeles. PAT RUSSELL (D)
    1969-. Bds: Ch., Revenue & Taxation. Org:
CEWAER; Nat. League of Cities; LWV. Educ: U. of
Wash. 1946 BA. B: 12/31/23. Add: 7388 W. 81st
St., Los Angeles 90045 (213) 485-3357.

Los Angeles. PEGGY STEVENSON
    City Hall, 200 N. Spring Street, Los Angeles
90012.

Loyalton. ELIZABETH TERYORI
    City Hall, Loyalton 96118.

Manteca. TRENA T. KELLEY
    1015 Tenaya Ct., Manteca 95336.

Marysville. FRANCES S. OWEN (R) **
    1972-. Bds: Community Dev. Agency. Prev:
Mayor 1974. Org: BPW; Calif. Society of CPAs;
Soroptimist; Rep. Women's Club. Educ: Calif.
State U. 1963 BS. B: 2/3/22. Add: 402 Covilland
Pl., Marysville 95901 (916) 743-2001.

Mendota. BLANCHE BARBOZA (D) **
    1974-. Occ: Operations Officer. B: 4/13/45.
Add: 913 Pucheu, Mendota 93640 (209) 655-4298.

Merced. CAROL GABRIAUDT (R)
    1975-. Mayor Pro Tem. Bds: Community Council;
Ch., Cnty. Community Action Agency. Org:
Soroptimist. Occ: Office Manager. B: 8/13/26.
Add: 1218 W. 23rd St., Merced 95340 (209)
722-4131.

Millbrae. MARY GRIFFIN (D)
    1976-. Bds: Ch., Beautification Com.; Milbrae
Arts Cmsn.; ABAG. Party: State Del. 1977. Prev:
Beautification Com. 1971-76; General Plan Com.
1972. Org: Calif. Teachers Assoc.; Chamber of
Commerce; Historical Society; San Mateo Crippled
Children's Society; Children's Home Society;
Woman's Club. Educ: Yuba Coll. 1952 AA, Chico
State U. 1954 BA. Occ: Teacher. B: 5/24/37.
Add: 67 Aura Vista, Millbrae 94030 (415)692-3500.

Mill Valley. JEAN S. BARNARD (D)
    1970-. Bds: League of Calif. Cities Revenue
& Taxation Com.; Ch., City-Cnty. Tax Equity Com.
Party: Alt., Cnty. Com. 1976. Prev: Parks &
Recreation Comsr. 1965-68; Mayor 1972-74. Org:
AAUW; Common Cause; WPC; Dem. Women; Planning &
Conservation League; Save S.F. Bay Assoc. Educ:
Vassar Coll. 1940 BA. B: 10/30/18. Add:
#1 El Capitan, Mill Valley 94941 (415) 388-4033.

Mill Valley. FLORA PRASZKER
    110 Summit Avenue, Mill Valley 94941.

Modesto. PEGGY MENSINGER (R)
    1973-. Bds: Ch., Stanislaus Area Assoc. of
Govts.; Park Com.; Ch., Air Quality Maintenance
Plan Task Force. Party: Precinct Leader 1958-61.
Prev: Library/Culture Cmsn. 1967-73; Human Rights
Cmsn. 1963-64; Charter Revision Com. Org:
Common Cause; AAUW; Historical Society; Ecology
Action Institute; PTA. Educ: Stanford U. 1944
BA. B: 2/18/23. Add: 1320 Magnolia Ave.
Modesto 95350 (209) 524-4011.

Modesto. SUSAN D. SIEFKIN (R)
    1975-. Bds: Ch., Local Agency Formation Cmsn.;
W. Coast Corridor Study Steering Com.; League of
Calif. Cities Transportation Com. Org: CEWAER;
LWV; AAUW; Rep. Women's Fed. Educ: U. of Calif.
1965 BA; Rutgers U. 1966 MA. B: 6/12/43. Add:
1225 Brady Ave., Modesto 95350 (209) 524-4011.

Monrovia. PATRICIA OSTRYE (D)
1974-. Mayor Pro Tem. Bds: Family Service; Reach Out; SCAG. Party: State Del. 1977; Cnty. Committeewoman 1976-. Org: Calif. Elected Women's Assoc.; Soroptimist; Dem. Women. B: 1/12/24. Add: 363 N. Alta Vista, Monrovia 91016 (213) 359-3231.

Montebello. CATHERINE P. HENSEL (D)
1976-. Bds: Youth Division; Chamber of Commerce; Sister City Affiliation. Party: State Del. 1977. Org: Soroptimist. Occ: Corp. Exec. B: 4/25/15. Add: 521 N. 19th St., Montebello 91754 (213) 722-4100.

Monterey Park. LOUISE DAVIS (D)
1976-. Bds: W. San Gabriel Vly. Juvenile Division; Community Relations; Planning. Prev: Cmsnr., Community Relations 1974-75. Org: Coord. Council; Dem. Club; PTA; Senior Citizens; Citizens Adv. Com. on Transportation. B: 3/20/24. Add: 123 S. Marguerita Ave., Monterey Pk. 91754 (213) 573-1211.

Mountain View. EMILY LYON (R)
1976-. Bds: Transportation Cmsn.; Ch., Council Transportation Com.; Council Apportment Com. Prev: Mtn. View Planning Cmsn. 1971-75; Santa Clara Planning Cmsn. 1976-. Org: CEWAER; LWV; Mtn. View Community Services. Educ: Coll. of Wouster 1962 BA; Stanford U. 1963 MA. B: 8/20/40. Add: 530 Victory Ave., Mtn. View 94043 (415) 964-2224.

Mountain View. JUDITH MOSS (D)
1972-. Bds: League of Calif. Cities-Human Resources Dev. Com.; Ch., Communications Com.; Audit Com. Party: Nat. Del. 1972. Prev: Mayor 1974-75. Org: ASPA; LWV; AAUW; Dem. Club. Educ: Vassar 1944 BA; Columbia U. 1947 MA; Stanford U. 1971 MS. Occ: Management Planning. B: 7/11/24. Add: 541 Del Medio, Mountain View 94040 (415) 967-7211.

Mount Shasta. DOROTHY PALFINI
219 E. Jessie Street, Mt. Shasta 96067.

Napa. PHYLLIS M. MOORE
City Hall, 955 School Street, Napa 94558.

Napa. DOROTHY G. SEARCY (D) **
1974-. Bds: City Planning Com.; County Council on Economic Opportunity; County Com. on Aging; Bay Conservation & Dev. Cmsn. Party: County Dem. Central Com. 1971-74; Prev: City Planning Cmsn. 1973-74. Org: Dem. Women; Dem. Club. Educ: Sonoma State Coll. 1971 BA. B: 6/24/20. Add: 3614 Harkness St., Napa 94558 (707) 226-5511.

Needles. LOUISE T. COREY (R) **
Bds: Trustee, Public Cemetery. Org: BPW; Women's Club. B: 10/31/08. Add: 1914 Flora Vista, Needles 92363 (714) 326-2113.

Needles. SHIRLEY J. LACKEY (D)
1976-. Bds: Budget Com.; Desert Land Planning & Airport Cmsn. Org: BPW; Chamber of Commerce. Occ: Bookkeeper. B: 11/9/33. Add: 597 Cibola St., Needles 92363 (714) 326-2113.

Nevada City. ILSE E. BARNHART (D) **
1974-. Bds: Bicentennial Com. Org: Dem. Club; PTA. Educ: Westhampton Coll. 1943 BA. B: 11/7/22 Add: 431 Zion St., Nevada City 95959 (916) 265-4771.

Newark. SHIRLEY SISK (R) **
1972-. Bds: County Library Cmsn.; Bd., East Bay League of Calif. Cities; County Human Relations Com. Prev: Bicentennial Cmsn . 1974-75; City Park & Recreation Cmsn. 1965-72. Org: Rep. Assembly. Occ: Purchasing Agent. B: 11/29/23. Add: 6202 Bellhaven Pl., Newark 94560 (415) 793-1400.

Newman. PAULA C. DAVIS
1058 S Street, Newman 95360.

Newport Beach. LUCILLE KUEHN (R)
1974-. Bds: Ch., Inter-City Com; Community Devt.; Parking. Party: Leg. Ch. 1977. Prev: Cnty. Grand Jury 1964-65; Cnty. Juvenile Justice 1965-66; Cnty. Criminal Justice 1966-67; Cnty. Mental Health 1966-68. Org: Nat. Assoc. Women Deans; LWV; Rep. Women. Educ: U. of Minn. 1945 BA; U. of Calif. 1968 MA. Occ: U. Administrator. B: 5/26/24. Add: 1831 Seadrift Dr., Corona del Mar 92625 (714) 640-2151.

Newport Beach. TRUDI PEABODY ROGERS (R)
1976-. Bds: City School Liaison Com.; Off Street Parking Com.; Central Newport Parking Com. Org: CEWAER; Rep. Women. Educ: U. of Southern Calif. 1943 BA. B: 5/5/21. Add: 429 Seville Ave., Balboa 92662 (714) 640-2151.

Norwalk. MARGARET I. NELSON
12055 Newmire Avenue, Norwalk 90650.

Novato. GAIL M. WILHELM (D) **
1974-. Bds: Community & Housing Dev. Prev: Planning Cmsn. 1970-74; Environmental Quality Com. 1968-70. Org: AAUW; LWV; Conservation League. Educ: U. of Calif. 1961 BS. B: 2/15/39. Add: 21 Hayes St., Novato 94947 (415) 892-4312.

Oceanside. LUCY R. CHAVEZ
515 No. Tremont, Oceanside 92054.

Ontario. FAYE MYERS DASTRUP (D)
1974-. Bds: Cnty. Planning Com. on Criminal Justice; Revenue & Taxation Com.; Cnty. Assoc. of Govts. Prev: City Clerk 1964-73; Deputy City Clerk 1959-64; Deputy City Treasurer 1960-64. Org: Women's Club. Add: 761 W. Hawthorne St., Ontario 91762 (714) 096-1151.

Orland. FLOSSIE THOMAS (D) **
1974-. Prev: City Treasurer 1954-73. B: 7/4/11. Add: 40 Central Ave., Orland 95963 (916) 865-3475.

Oxnard. JANE M. TOLMACH (D)
1970-. Bds: V-Ch., Transportation & Utilities Com.; Cnty. Assoc. of Govt. Transportation Com. Party: State Del. 1958-74, 1977; Nat. Del. 1960, '68, '76; Nat. Alt. 1956, '64; Women's Ch., Dem. State Central Com. 1966-70; Ch., Cnty. Central Com 1959-62; Cnty. Central Com 1953-70. Prev: Planning Cmsn. 1957-62; Cnty. Grand Jury 1958-59. Org: BPW. Educ: U.C.L.A. 1943 BA; Smith Coll.

1945 MSS. B: 11/12/21. Add: 656 Douglas Ave.,
Oxnard 93030 (805) 486-2601.

Pacific Grove. MADELYN ANN SLOAN (D)
    1976-. Bds: Ch., Housing Guidelines Com.;
Monterey Peninsula Youth Project; Regional
Criminal Justice Planning Bd. Prev: Planning
Cmsn. 1973-76. Org: CEWAER; Children's Home
Society; PTA; LWV. Educ: Whittier Coll. 1960 BA.
B: 1/28/40. Add: 822 Laurel Ave., Pacific Grv.
93950 (408) 375-9861.

Palmdale. LYNDA J. COOK
    38471 11th Street, East, Palmdale 93550.

Palm Desert. ALEXIS NEWBRANDER (R)
    1976-. Prev: Regional Planning Cmsn.; City
Charter Comsr. 1956-63. Org: Rep. Club Fed.
Educ: Ohio State U. 1926 BA. B: 4/8/05. Add:
46-260 Cottage Ln., Palm Desert 92260
(714) 346-0611.

Palm Springs. ELIZABETH BEADLING (R)
    1976-. Bds: Inland Cnty's. Manpower Governing
Bd.; Ch., Community Devt. Com.; Community Action
Plan. Prev: Adv. Bd. Senior Center 1974-76. Org:
LWV; Inland Cnty's. Health Systems Agency; Common
Cause; Soroptomists; Calif. Rep. Assembly; NAACP.
Educ: U. of Pittsburgh 1936 BA; U. of Pittsburgh
1941 MA. B: 2/16/15. Add: 775 Plaza Amigo,
Palm Springs 92262 (714) 323-8201.

Palo Alto. ANNE R. WITHERSPOON (R)
    1975-. Bds: Govt. Services Sub-Com.; Santa
Clara Vly. Water Cmsn.; Council Policy & Proced-
ures Com. Org: Jr. League; Senior Coord. Council;
Palo Alto Area Information & Referral Service;
Nat. Trust for Historic Preservation. Educ:
Stanford U. 1960 BA. Occ: Medical Center Dir.
B: 8/9/36. Add: 1255 Hamilton Ave., Palo Alto
94301 (415) 329-2226.

Palos Verdes Estates. ROSEMARIE KALEMKIARIAN (R)
    1976-. Bds: League of Calif. Cities; Tennis
Com.; Ch., Dog Ordinance Com. Prev: Library Cmsnr.
1963-66. Org: Chamber of Commerce; Rep. Women;
Amer. Field Service. Educ: UCLA 1949 BA. B:
4/14/27. Add: 2841 Via Segovia, Palos Verdes Est.
90274 (213) 377-7177.

Pasadena. JO HECKMAN (R)
    1975-. Prev: Planning Cmsn. 1966-75; Human
Relations Com. 1964-66. Org: Zonta. Occ:
Realtor. B: 8/26/13. Add: 2410 Casa Grande,
Pasadena 91104 (213) 577-4311.

Petaluma. M. PATRICIA HILLIGOSS (R)
    1975-. Bds: Parks, Recreation & Music Cmsn.;
Leisure Services Com.; Human Services Task Force
of ABAG. Party: Precinct Ch. 1967; Ch., Rep.
Headquarters 1970-76; Rep. Cnty. Central Com.
1970-77; Rep. State Central Com 1972-78; Women's
Ch. for Dist. 1972. Prev: Ch., Planning Cmsn.
1973-76; Housing Allocation Bd. 1973-74; Environmental Design Plan Com. 1971; Site Design Com.
1973-74. Org: AAUW; Rep. Women; PTA; Womens Club.
Occ: Auto Dealership Advertiser. B: 3/10/24. Add
15 Brown Ct., Petaluma 94952 (707) 762-7556.

Piedmont. CONNIE SHAPIRO (D) **
    1974-. Bds: County Com.on the Status of
Women. Org: LWV; Bd., Jewish Welfare Fed.
Educ: Ohio State U. 1962 BA. Occ: Teacher.
B: 7/15/40. Add: 205 St. James Dr., Piedmont
94611 (415) 653-7204.

Placentia. VIRGINIA C. FARMER (D)
    1976-. Bds: Orange Cnty. Vector Control
Dist. Prev: Library Bd. of Trustees 1968-76.
Org: Women's Opportunities Center; AAUW. Educ:
Fullerton Coll. 1968 AA; U. of Calif. 1971 MA.
B: 5/4/26. Add: 1037 Coventry Circle,
Placentia 92670 (714) 993-8117.

Pleasant Hills. DIONE MUSTARD (D)
    1976-. Bds: Ch., Joint Agency with Recreation
& Parks Dist.; Cnty. Housing & Community Devt.
Cmsn.; Planning Cmsn. Party: State Del. 1972;
Cnty. Registration Ch. 1960-61; Co-Ch., State
Central Com. 1962-63. Prev: City Clerk 1966-76.
Org: Social Services; PTA; Friends of the Earth;
Dem. Club; Historical Society; Historical
Preservation. Educ: Diablo Vly. Coll. 1960 AA.
Occ: Eligibility Worker. B: 5/19/27. Add:
65 Collins Dr., Pleasant Hills 94523.

Pleasanton. JOYCE M. LE CLAIRE (D)
    1974-. Bds: Ch., Growth Management Plan
Com.; Environmental Management Task Force;
Human Services Cmsn. Party: State Del. 1972,
'74, '76. Org: Dem. Club; WPC. Educ: Lamar U.
1961 BA. Occ: Field Repr. B: 7/27/39. Add:
2427 Raven Rd., Pleasanton 94566 (415)792-3838.

Pomona. GEORGIA M. GROVE
    1785 Yorba Drive, Pomona 91766.

Porterville. BETTY JOE FERGUSON
    282 S. H Street, Porterville 93257.

Portola. HELEN JOHNSON
    400 Nevada Street, Portola 96122.

Rancho Mirage. EDNA H. WARNER (R) **
    1973-. Org: Rep. Women's Club. B: 6/18/11.
Add: 71-412 Biskra Rd., Rancho Mirage 92270
(714) 328-8585.

Rancho Palos Verdes. ANN SHAW (R)
    1977-. Bds: Juvenile Dir.; Trails; South Bay
Cities. Prev: Planning Adv. Com. 1973-75; Ch.,
Planning Cmsn. 1975-77. Org: LWV; Common Cause;
AAUW; Rep. Women's Club; Rep. Women Task Force;
CEWAER. Educ: William & Mary 1957 BA. B:
6/18/35. Add: 30036 Via Borica, Rancho Palos
Verdes 90274 (213) 377-0360.

Redding. BARBARA ALLEN GARD (D)
    1976-. Bds: Shasta Cnty. Area Manpower
Planning Council; Cnty. Transportation Cmsn.;
Cnty. Criminal Justice Ctr. Ad. Prev: Parks &
Recreation Cmsn. 1971-76; Citizen Adv. Com.
1968-70; Senior Citizens Facility Adv. Cmsn.
1974-76; Community Devt. Adv. Cmsn. 1974-76;
Bd. of Citizens Adv. Com. for Community Dev.
Prog. Org: AAUW; PTA. Educ: U. of Kan. 1954
BA. B: 8/22/32. Add: 3750 Brian Ct., Redding
96001 (916) 246-1151.

Redlands. BERTAHA ROSE GRACE (D) **
1974-. Bds: Planning Cmsn.; Park Cmsn. Org:
LWV; Dem. Club. Educ: U. of Calif. 1940 BA. B:
8/29/18. Add: 116 Carrie La., Redlands 92373
(714) 793-2641.

Reedley. GAIL BALL
267 W. Ponderosa Avenue, Reedley 93654.

Rialto. JENA R. HAMILTON (R)
1976-. Bds: Public Transit Bd.; San Bernardino
Assoc. Govts.; Transportation Bd. Prev: Planning
Comsn. 1974-76. Org: Amer. Bankers Assoc.;
Chamber of Commerce. Occ: Loan Officer. B:
4/17/40. Add: 885 E. Mariposa, Rialto 92376
(714) 875-3410.

Ridgecrest. FLORENCE L. GREEN (D)
1974-. Bds: Ch., Park & Recreation; Ch.,
Housing; Ch., Police Com. Party: Precinct Leader
1960-64. Prev: Planning Cmsn. 1971-74. Educ:
Bakersfield Coll. 1971 AA; 1974 BA. Occ: Coll.
Professor. B: 6/19/40. Add: 304 Helena, Ridgecrest 93555 (714) 375-1321.

Riverside. ROSANNA BARIL SCOTT (R)
1971-. Bds: Ch., SCAG; Inland Manpower Assoc.;
Council Com. Prev: Community Action Agency; V.
Pres., SCAG; Coord. Com. Org: LWV. Educ: UCLA
1954 BS. B: 4/24/33. Add: 5716 Abilene Rd.,
Riverside 92506 (714) 787-7969.

Rolling Hills. GORDANA SWANSON
2 Chesterfield Road, Rolling Hills 90274.

Rolling Hills Estates. NELL MIRELS (D) **
1972-. Prev: Planning Cmsn. 1967-72. Org:
LWV; PTA; Soroptimist. Educ: Simmons 1952 BS.
Occ: Teacher. B: 4/4/30. Add: 3 Seahurst Rd.,
Rolling Hills Estates 90274 (213) 377-1577.

Rosemead. ROBERTA V. TRUJILLO (D)
1974-. Prev: Calif. Manpower Services Adv.
Bd. B: 10/22/39. Add: 2339 Kelburn, Rosemead
91770 (213) 288-6671.

Ross. JULIE OSTERLOH
Box 1003, Ross 94957.

Sacramento. CALLIE I. CARNEY (D)
1975-. Bds: Sacramento Regional Area Planning
Cmsn.; Govt. Planning & Advisory Council; Office
of Criminal Justice Planning Cmsn. Party: State
Del. 1976; State Alt. 1975; Precinct Leader 1973-
75; Dist. Repr. Dem. Central Com. 1972-75; State
Dem. Central Com. 1976-77. Prev: V-Pres., Nat.
Consumer Law Cmsn. 1974-77; State Adv. Com. on
Drugs & Alcohol 1970-73; State & Nat. Poor People
Rep. OEO 1970-73. Org: Dem. Black Elected
Officers; Sacramento Urban League; Nat. Council
of Negro Women; NAACP; WPC. Educ: Sacramento City
Coll. 1972 AA. B: 7/12/34. Add: 3288 9th Ave.,
Sacramento 95817 (916) 449-5409.

Sacramento. ANNE RUDIN
1410 Birchwood Lane, Sacramento 95814.

St. Helena. GRETA I. ERICSON (R)
1974-. Bds: Napa Cnty. Comsr. on Metropolitan Transit Com. Prev: Mayor 1974-76. Org:
League of Cities; Soroptimist; Chamber of
Commerce. Occ: Apparel Shop Owner. B: 5/5/22.
Add: 1832 Sulpher Spgs. Ave., St. Helena
94574 (707) 963-2741.

San Clemente. DONNA L. WILKINSON
930 Avenida Salvador, San Clemente 92672.

Sand City. FAYE KNIGHT
PEARL PENDERGRASS
City Hall, Sand City 93955.

San Diego. MAUREEN F. O'CONNOR (D) **
1971-. Bds: Economic Opportunity Cmsn.;
Human Care Services Policy Bd.; Regional Employment Training Consortium Policy Bd. Educ: San
Diego State Coll. 1970 BA. B: 7/14/46. Add:
2106 Hickory St., San Diego 92103 (714)236-6622.

San Gabriel. HELEN ACHILLES
1958-. Prev: Mayor 1966-68. Educ: U. of
Calif. BA. B: 11/29/08. Add: P.O. Box 103,
San Gabriel 91778 (213) 282-4104.

San Gabriel. HELEN A. KENNEDY (D)
1964-. Bds: Parks & Recreation Cmsn.; League
of Calif. Cities; League of Calif. Cities-State
of Calif. Resolutions Com. Prev: Music & Performing Arts Cmsn. 1961-; Adv. Bd. Council Atty.
General 1976-; Adv. Council Dist Atty. 1972-;
Bd. of Dir. Sanitation Dist., Bd. of Dir., League
of Cities 1971-. Org: Women's Crusade for
Efficiency & Economy; CEWAER; Historical Society;
Dem. Tuesday Luncheon; Coordinating Council;
Family Counciling. Occ: Consultant. B: 10/30/17
Add: 1101 Abbot Ave., San Gabriel 91776
(213) 282-4104.

Sanger. ANNA MARIE BEATIE
1117 Rawson, Sanger 93657.

San Jacinto. BERTHA J. HAZELTINE (D)
1974-. Bds: Transit Agency; Ch., Parks &
Recreation Com. Org: Parents-Teachers Club.
Occ: Financial Secretary. B: 4/17/31. Add:
637 Estudillo, San Jacinto 92383 (714) 654-7337.

San Joaquin. OLGA A. HILL (D)
1976-. Bds: Council of Govt. Party: Citizens
Adv. Com. 1974-76. Occ: Retail Saleswoman. B:
10/5/16. Add: 8917 9th St., San Joaquin 93660
(209) 693-4311.

San Joaquin. LELA KNAPP
22239 Oregon, San Joaquin 93660.

San Jose. SUSANNE B. WILSON (D)
1973-. Bds: V-Mayor; Ch., Community Devt.
Block Grant Com.; Ch., City Personnel Com.; Exec.
Bd., ABAG. Org: CEWAER; Dem. Party; Nat. League
of Cities; Calif. League of Cities; LWV; AAUW;
WPC. Educ: San Jose State U. BA. B: 9/30/28.
Add: 1743 Valpico, San Jose 95124 (408)277-5226.

San Juan Bautista. BARBARA A. PAGARAN (R)
1976-. Bds: Planning Cmsn.; Chamber of
Commerce Liaison; Library Project Com. Occ:
Bank Supervisor. B: 12/27/41. Add: 63 Franklin
Circle, San Juan Bautista 95045.

San Leandro. FAITH FRAZIER (D)
1974-. Bds: Cmsn. on the Status of Women;
Assoc. of Community Action Programs. Party:
State Del. 1956. Prev: Library Bd. of Trustees
1961-73. Org: AFT; NEA; WPC; NOW; BPW; LWV.
Educ: U. of Calif. 1948 BA. Occ: Teacher. B:
1/28/26. Add: 961 San Jose St., San Leandro
94577 (415) 577-3351.

San Mateo. JANE BAKER (R)
1973-. Bds: ABAG Exec. Com.; Metropolitan
Transportation Cmsn.; CETA Council. Prev: Mayor
1975-76. Org: CEWAER; LWV; AAUW. Educ: Purdue
U. 1944 BS. B: 6/4/23. Add: 1464 Woodberry,
San Mateo 94403 (415) 574-6765.

San Pablo. MARIE DANIELS (R)
1976-. Prev: Human Relations Cmsn. 1971-74.
Org: Chamber of Commerce; Soroptimist. Educ:
Contra Costa Jr. Coll. 1977 AA. Occ: Dir., Mental
Health Drop-In Ctr. B: 1/15/29. Add: 1754 Emeric
Ave., San Pablo 94806 (415) 236-1616.

Santa Barbara. SHEILA LODGE **
Bds: Water Cmsn.; Cmsn. on Aging; Library Bd.;
Conservation & Release Bd.; Operations & Main-
tenance Bd. Prev: Planning Cmsn. 1973-75;
School Adv. Bd. 1973-75. Org: PTA: LWV; Citizens
Planning Assoc.; Dem. League; Dem. Women. Add:
City Hall, Santa Barbara 93101 (805) 963-0611.

Santa Cruz. CAROLE DE PALMA (D)
1975-. Bds: Transportation Cmsn.; Metro-
politan Transit Dist.; City Museum; Water Cmsn.
Prev: City Parks & Recreation 1973-75; Central
Coast Conservation Cmsn. 1975-77. Org: Peoples
Dem. Club. Educ: San Fernando Vly. State Coll.
1965 BA. Occ: Restaurant Owner. B: 5/6/40.
Add: 903 Windham, Santa Cruz 95060 (408)426-5000.

Santa Cruz. SALLY Y. DI GIROLAMO (D) **
1973-. Bds: Criminal Justice Com.; Mayors'
Select Com.; Redevelopment Com. Org: Bd. of
Realtors. Occ: Realtor. B: 11/13/32. Add:
324 Harbor Dr., Santa Cruz 95060 (408) 426-5000.

Santa Cruz. CHARLOTTE MELVILLE
1010 Western Drive, Santa Cruz 95060.

Santa Fe Springs. BETTY WILSON (D)
1957-. Bds: Sister City Com.; Ch., League of
Calif. Cities, L.A. Cnty. Div.; Calif. Contract
Cities Assoc. Party: State Del. 1976. Org: BPW;
Women's Club; Dem. Club; Soroptimist. B: 6/13/15.
Add: 11314 Clarkman St., Santa Fe Springs 90670
(213) 868-0511.

Santa Monica. CHRISTINE EMERSON REED (R)
1975-. Bds: Historical Landmarks Cmsn.; Com.
on Older Amer's.; Ch., Heritage Square Museum
Society Bd. Party: State Del. 1975, '77; State
Alt. 1969, '71; Cnty. Com. 1976-78. Prev: Recreation & Parks Cmsn. 1973-75; Beach Area Study Com.
1973. Org: AAUW; LWV; Common Cause; Chamber of
Citizens; Neighborhood Assoc.; Rep. Club; Rep.

Women's Task Force; Nature Conservancy. Educ:
U.C.L.A. 1967 BA. B: 2/19/44. Add: 859 23rd
St., Santa Monica 90403 (213) 393-9975.

Santa Monica. DONNA O. SWINK
501 11th Street, Santa Monica 90401.

Santa Paula. ELEANOR CROUCH (R) **
1974-. Bds: Liaison to Planning Cmsn.;
County Transportation Advisory Com.; Director,
South Coast Area Transit; Del., SCAG. Prev:
Planning Cmsn. 1972-74; Recreation Cmsn. 1969-
72. Org: PTA. B: 1/25/22. Add: 625 Teague
Dr., Santa Paula 93060 (805) 525-3344.

Santa Rosa. DONNA M. BORN
1201 St. Helena Avenue, Santa Rosa 95404.

Saratoga. MARGARET L. CORR (R)
1974-. Bds: Criminal Justice Planning Bd.;
Adv. Bd., Santa Clara Cnty. Needs Assessment
Study; Adv. Bd., Water Dist. Flood Control.
Party: Alt., Rep. Central Com. 1977. Prev:
Cnty. Com. on Urban Devt./Open Space 1972-74;
Senior Citizen Housing Task Force 1974-76. Org:
LWV; AAUW; Service Guild; Adv. Bd., Information
Referral. Educ: Drexel U. 1943 BS. B: 12/7/21.
Add: 19224 DeHavilland Dr., Saratoga 94070.

Sausalito. VIOLETTA AUTUMN
521 Sausalito Blvd., Sausalito 94965.

Sausalito. ROBIN R. SWEENY (R)
1968-. Bds: Ch., Finance Com.; Liason,
Historical Com. Prev: V-Mayor 1970-72, 1974-77;
Mayor 1972-74. Org: Historical Society. Educ:
Monmouth Memorial Hospital School of Nursing
1946 RN; San Francisco State Coll. 1953 BA. Occ:
RN. B: 8/19/25. Add: 173 San Carlos Ave.,
Sausalito 94965 (415) 332-0310.

Seaside. MICHELE MARTIN
1863 San Pablo, Seaside 93955.

Selma. EMMA ELIZABETH JENSEN (R)
1973-. Bds: Vice Mayor; Ch., Traffic Cmsn.;
Street Com.; Ch., Community Center Study Com.
Prev: Planning Cmsn. 1970-73. Org: Historical
Soc.; Women's Club. Occ: Realtor. B: 10/24/22.
Add: P.O. Box 800, Selma 93662.

Simi Valley. GINGER GHERARDI (D)
1972-. Bds: Bd. of Dirs., Cnty. Sanitation
Dist.; Ventura Cmty. Assoc. of Govts.; League of
Calif. Cities State Transportation Com. Prev:
Planning Cmsn. Ch., 1969-71; Ventura Cnty. Region
al Sanitation Dist. 1974-76; Transportation
Policy Plan Com. 1972-77. Org: AAUW; La Manitas
Children's Home Society; LWV; CEWAER. Educ:
Pratt Institute 1964 BS; 1965 MS. Occ: Teacher.
B: 4/11/43. Add: 2410 N. Justin Ave., Simi
Vly. 93065 (805) 522-1333.

Sonoma. NANCY PARMELEE (R) **
1966-. Bds: ABAG. Prev:Planning Cmsn. 1962-
66. Org: LWV; Woman's Club; Soroptimist. Educ:
U. of Calif. 1955 BA. Occ: Library Technician.
B: 4/18/32. Add: 737 3rd St. East, Sonoma
95476 (707) 996-3681.

South Lake Tahoe. PAT LOWE
   1197 Fairway Box 733, South Lake Tahoe 95705.

South Pasadena. ALVA LEE C. ARNOLD
   1534 Ramona, South Pasadena 91030.

Stanton. ALICITA LEWIS (R)
   1970-. Bds: Calif. League of Cities Community
Devt. Com.; Orange Cnty. League of Cities Resolution Com. Prev: Mayor 1972-73; V-Mayor 1971-72.
Org: Chamber of Commerce; Stanton Community
Service Center; Council for Employment, Environment, Economy & Developement. Occ: Manager. B:
3/2/20. Add: 7881 Santa Catalina, Stanton
90680 (714) 893-2471.

Sunnyvale. ETTA A. LOGAN
   643 Princeton, Sunnyvale 94086.

Taft. FRANCIS L. GREENE (R)
   1974-. Mayor Pro Tem. Bds: Fire Cmsn.;
Police Cmsn. Org: PTA. B: 10/20/25. Add:
328 Warren St., Taft 93268 (805) 763-3611.

Tehama. PATRICIA ANN LANDINGHAM (D)
   1976-. Occ: Postal Clerk. B: 3/28/42. Add:
280 3rd St., Tehama 96090.

Thousand Oaks. FRANCES K. PRINCE (D)
   1976-. Bds: Ch., Govt. Liason Com.; Transportation Policy & Planning Com.; Ch., Open Space
Com. Prev: Planning Cmnsr. 1972-75. Org: AAUW;
Zonta; Historical Society; Dem. Club; PTA. Educ:
San Diego State U. 1960 BA. B: 10/24/37. Add:
2720 N. Granxia Pl., Thousand Oaks 91360
(805) 497-8611.

Torrance. KATY GEISSERT (R)
   1975-. Bds: Los Angeles Cnty. Sanitation Dist.
S. Bay Juvenile Diversion Policy Bd.; Health
Systems Agency. Prev: Park & Recreation Cmsn.
1971-74. Org: LWV; PTA; CEWAER. Educ: Stanford
U. 1948 BA. B: 11/27/26. Add: 439 Calle De
Castellana, Redondo Bch., 90277 (213) 328-5310.

Trinidad. ELEANOR ROBISON (D)
   1974-. Bds: Cemetery Comsr.; Solid Waste Com.;
Cnty. Economic Devt. Org: Fed. Women's Club;
Civic Club. Educ: SUNY 1942 BS; MS. B: 10/6/14.
Add: Box 569, Trinidad 95570.

Tulare. ILA O. HARMON
   City Hall, 411 E. Kern Ave., Tulare 93274.

Tulelake. ROMONA BUTLER
   606 2nd Street, Tulelake 96134.

Union City. CECILIA BOYLE
   34921 Perry Road, Union City 94587.

Upland. INA PETOKAS (R)
   1974-. Bds: SCAG; SCAG 208 Water Program Com;
Street & Light Com. Org: Rep. Women's Club;
Women's Club. Educ: UCLA 1965 BS; UCLA 1967 MA.
B: 8/12/42. Add: 1104 Shannon St., Upland
91786.

Vacaville. CAROLYN VAN LOO (D)
   1976-. Org: S.A.V.E. Environmental Org.; Dem.
Club. B: 3/17/31. Add: 237 Cascade Dr.,
Vacaville 95688 (707) 448-6262.

Ventura. PATRICIA ELLISON
   HARRIET KOSMO
   P.O. Box 99, Ventura 93001.

Victorville. JEAN CAMPBELL DE BLASIS (R)
   1976-. Bds: Ch., City Involvement Plan;
Regional Wastewater Management Adv. Com.; Health
Systems Agency. Prev: Cnty. Grand Jury 1959-60.
Org: Rep. Women's Club. Educ: Pomona Coll. 1941
BA. Occ: Office Manager. B: 9/23/20. Add:
Kemper Campbell Ranch; Victorville 92392
(714) 245-3411.

Victorville. PEGGY SARTOR
   14657 Rodeo Drive, Victorville 92392.

Vista. GLORIA E. MC CLELLAN
   1426 Alta Vista Drive, Vista 92083.

Walnut Creek. MARGARET W. KOVAR
   1078 Hacienda Drive, Walnut Creek 94596.

Waterford. EDITH KIRK
   P.O. Box 356, Waterford 95386.

Waterford. THELMA WOODBRIDGE
   P.O. Box 97, Waterford 95386.

Watsonville. JEAN MC INTYRE MC NEILL **
   1973-. Bds: Metro Transit Dist.; Transportation Cmsn.; Criminal Justice Citizen's
Advisory Com. Party: County Central Com. 1973-
75; Local Precinct 1963-64. Org: Woman's Fed.
Club; Rep. Women; Ladies Elks; Farm Bureau
Women. Educ: Gateside Hospital RN. B: 6/7/11.
Add: 21 St. Francis Dr., Watsonville 95076
(408) 724-1430.

Weed. MARY YOUNG
   P.O. Box 36, Weed 96094.

Westminster. JOY L. NEUGEBAUER (R) **
   Bds: Assoc. of Governments; Bicentennial Com.;
Human Services Com.; Mosquito Abatement Director.
Org: PTA; Women's Club; Chamber of Commerce;
Social Services Com. Occ: Ace Tool Company. B:
11/14/27. Add: 5682 Edita Ave., Westminster
92683 (714) 898-3311.

Wheatland. MARGARET A. LUYSTER
   P.O. Box 125, Wheatland 95692.

Wheatland. JUANITA M. NEYENS (R)
   1974-. Bds: Bi-Cnty./City Intergovt. Relation
Adv. Com. Prev: Mayor 1976; Yuba Cnty. Bicentennial Cmsn. 1974; Local Agency Formation Com.
1974. Org: Rep. Women's Club; Historical Soc.
Occ: Secretary. B: 5/18/21. Add: 401 Main St.,
Wheatland 95692 (916) 633-2761.

Whittier. DELTA L. MURPHY (R)
   1975-. Bds: SCAG; Alt., League of Calif.
Cities. Prev: Park & Recreation Cmsn. 1968-75;
State Exec. Bd. , Park & Recreation 1973-75.
Org: LWV; Rep. Women. B: 7/25/26. Add:
9404 La Alba Dr., Whittier 90603 (213)
698-2551.

Williams. KAY K. NORDYKE (R)
1975-. Bds: Police Cmsr.; Transportation
Cmsn. Prev: Trustee School Dist. 1967-75;
Citizens Adv. Com. 1966-6/; Cnty. Recreation
Com. 1975-76. Educ: U. of Calif. 1954 AA. B:
4/16/35. Add: 753 Venice Blvd., Williams 95987.

Willows. ALLISON HAAPALA (R)
1974-. Org: Children's Home Society; Chamber
of Commerce; PTA. Educ: U. of Calif 1966 BA.
B: 4/5/43. Add: 1120 Cedar St., Willows 95988
(916) 934-7041.

Winters. VERETA SELLERS
213 Anderson Avenue, Winters 95694.

Woodside. OLIVE G. MAYER (D)
1974-. Bds: Solid Waste Adv. Cmsn.; State
Com. on Hotels, Park & Recreation Dept. Org:
Sierra Club; Common Cause; ACLU. Educ: Swarthmore Coll. 1939 BS. Occ: Mechanical Engineer.
B: 11/7/18. Add: 245 Josselyn Ln., Woodside
94062 (415) 851-7764.

Woodside. JOAN MILLER STIFF (D)
1976-. Bds: San Mateo Cnty. Regional Planning
Com. Prev: Planning Cmsn. 1971-76. Org: LWV;
PTA. Occ: R.N. B: 5/6/31. Add:120 Hillside Dr.,
Woodside 94062 (415) 851-7764.

Woodside. SUZANNE WEEKS
106 La Questa Way, Woodside 94062.

Yountville. LOMITA MILLER
2020 Monroe Street, Yountville 94599.

Yountville. ELEANOR VALENZUELA
6765 Jefferson Street, Yountville 94599,

Judges

ROSE ELIZABETH BIRD
Chief Justice, Supreme Court. Add: 4050 State
Bldg., San Francisco 94102.

FRANCES N. CARR
Sacramento Cnty. Superior Court Judge. Add:
Courthouse, Sacramento 95814.

JOAN DEMPSEY KLEIN (D)
Los Angeles Cnty. Superior Court Judge. 1974-.
Bds: Superior Ct. Efficiency & Economy Com.; State
wide Ct. Reorganization Com. Prev: Municipal Ct.
Judge. Org: Calif. Judges Assoc.; Women Lawyers
Assoc.; BPW. Educ: San Diego State U. BA; UCLA
1955 LLB. B: 8/18/24. Add: 6230 Sylmar Ave.,
Van Nuys 91401 (213) 787-3350 x 513.

BETTY LOU LAMOREAUX (D)
Orange Cnty. Superior Court Judge. 1976-.
Prev: Judge, Municipal Ct. 1975-76. Org: Amer.
Bd. of Trial Advocates; Calif. Judges Assoc.
Educ: Weber Coll. 1944 AA; UCLA 1947 BA; San
Francisco Law School 1957 JD. B: 4/24/24. Add:
700 Civic Ctr. Dr. W., Santa Ana 92702
(714) 834-3226.

MILDRED L. LILLIE
Second District Court of Appeals Judge. Add:
3580 Wilshire Blvd., Los Angeles 90010.

BONNIE LEE MARTIN
Los Angeles County Superior Court Judge.
Add: Courthouse, Los Angeles 90012.

MARGARET J. MORRIS (D)
Fourth District Court of Appeals Judge. 1976-
Prev: Municipal Court Judge 1963-66; Superior
Court Judge 1966-76. Org: Calif. Judges Assoc.;
Nat. Assoc. of Women Lawyers; BPW; Zonta. Educ:
Indiana U. 1945 BA; Northwestern U. 1949 JD.
B: 10/8/22. Add: 1332 Arroyo Crest, Redlands
92373 (714) 383-4445.

ROBERTA RALPH
MARY G. ROGAN
BETTY JO SHELDON
Los Angeles County Superior Court Judge.
Add: Courthouse, Los Angeles 90012.

NANCY BELCHER WATSON (R)
Los Angeles County Superior Court Judge. 1972-
Bds: Personnel & Budget Com.; Probation Com.;
Criminal Cts. Com.; Ch., Family Laws Com. for
Com. on Ct. Improvement; Books & Publications
Com. Prev: Municipal Ct. Judge 1968-73. Org:
Calif. Judges Assoc.; ABA; Amer. Judicature
Society; Altrusa. Educ: Stanford U. 1946 BA;
U. of Calif. at Los Angeles 1958 JD. B: 7/14/26.
Add: Dept. 124-Criminal Cts. Bldg. 210 W. Temple
St., Los Angeles 90012 (213) 974-5763.

ARLEIGH WOODS (D)
Los Angeles County Superior Court Judge. 1976-
Educ: Chapman Coll. BS; Southwestern U. 1952 LLB.
Add: 300 E. Olive Ave., Burbank 91502 (213)
849-3353.

MARILYN PESTARINO ZECHER.
Santa Clara County Superior Court Judge. Add:
191 N. First St., San Jose 95113.

ELISABETH E. ZEIGLER (I)
Los Angeles County Superior Court Judge. 1968
Prev: Municipal Ct. Judge 1949-68. Org: Calif.
Judges Assoc.; ABA; Amer. Judicature Soc.;
Soropomist. Educ: U. of So. Calif. 1938 AB;
1941 JD. B: 4/13/17. Add: Cnty. Courthouse,
111 N. Hill St., Los Angeles 90012 (213)974-5775.

State Boards and Commissions

A complete list of state boards and commissions, and of their membership is available
through a compilation entitled the Central
Appointments Registry. It is available in the
State Library, the Secretary of State's Office,
and each County Clerk's Office.

Colorado

MARY ESTILL BUCHANAN (R)
    Secretary of State 1974-. Bds: State Bd. of
Equalization. Party: State Del. 1970, '72. Prev:
Colo. Cmsn. on Status of Women 1971-74; State Bd.
of Agriculture 1971-74. Org: Colo. Centennial-
Bicentennial Com.; Resource Centers for Women;
Industrial Relations Research Assoc. Bd.; BPW.
Educ: Wellesley Coll. 1956 BA; Harvard 1962 MA.
B: 11/21/34. Add: 124 State Capitol, Denver
80220 (303) 892-2762.

BETTY MILLER
    Executive Director, Department of Local Affairs
Add: State Capitol, Denver 80203.

State Legislature

State Senate

BARBARA S. HOLME (D)
    1975-. Prev: Mayors Adv. Cmsn. on Youth,
Denver 1969-70. Party: Co-Pres. Young Dems. 1973-
74. Org: LWV; Nat. Council of Jewish Women.
Educ: Stanford U. 1967 BA. B: 5/24/46. Add:
1232 Gaylord, Denver 80206.

RUTH S. STOCKTON (R)
    1964-. Dist: 14. Bds: Joint Budget Com.;
V-Ch., Appropriations; Transportation. Party:
State Del. 1938-77; Nat. Del. 1948; Precinct
Committeewoman 1938-42, '50-70; Nat. Committee-
woman 1945-56. Prev: State Repr. 1961-65. Org:
BPW; Chamber of Commerce; Women's Rep. Club. B:
6/6/16. Add: 1765 Glen Dale Dr., Lakewood
(303) 892-2316.

State House

POLLY BACA-BARRAGAN (D) **
    1974-. Dist: 34. Bds: Rules Com.; Business
Affairs & Labor Com.; Finance Com.; State
Compensation Insurance Fund. Party: Nat. Com.;
Precinct Com. Org: LWV; Nat. Chicano Planning
Council; Nat. Minority Legislative Educ. Program;
Dem. Women's Caucus. Educ: Colo. State U. 1962
BA. B: 2/13/41. Add: 8747 Santa Fe Dr., Thornton
80221 (303) 892-3006.

LAURA DE HERRERA (D)
    4137 Kalamath, Denver 80211.

NANCY DICK (D) **
    1974-. Dist: 57. Bds: Judiciary; Health,
Environment, Welfare & Institutions; Transportation & Energy. Party: State Rules Com. 1973-
75; County Treasurer 1972-75. B: 7/22/30. Add:
Box 3466, Aspen 81611 (303) 892-3006.

BETTY ANN DITTEMORE (I)
    1968-. Bds: Colo. Housing Finance Authority.
Party: State Del. 1964-76; Precinct Leader 1960-
64; Cnty. V-Ch. 1964-66; Ch., State Political
Educ. 1964-66. Org: Zonta Internat.; OWL; LWV;
BPW; Pres.,Rep. Women's Club; PTA. Educ: 1939
AA. B: 11/12/19. Add: 2239 E. Floyd Pl.,
Englewood 80110 (303) 892-3006.

ANNE MC GILL GORSUCH (R)
    243 S. Fairfax, Denver 80222.

GWENNE HUME (R)
    330 S. 38th Street, Boulder 80303.

LEE RICHARDSON JONES (R)
    1976-. Dist: 47. Bds: Game, Fish & Parks
Com.; State Affairs Com.; Transportation &
Energy. Party: State Del. 1966-76; Secretary
Rep. Cnty. Com. 1967-69; V-Ch., Rep. Central
Committee 1969-72. Org: Women's Rep. Club. B:
3/23/34. Add: 1052 Rosehill Dr., Boulder
80302 (303) 892-3006.

JEAN MARKS (D)
    1974-. Bds: House Business Affairs & Labor;
House Rules; Leg. Audit. Party: State Del.
1968-72. Org: Cnty. Dem's.; WPC. Educ: Metropolitan Coll. 1972 BA. B: 3/6/34. Add:
11106 Elati St., Northglenn 80234 (303) 892-3006
Ext. 215.

BETTY IRENE NEALE (R)
    1975-. Party: Dist. Captain 1970-present;
Nat. Alt. 1972; State Com. 1965-70. Prev:
Denver City Committeewoman 1965-70. Org: Rep.
Roundtable; Symphony Guild; Civic Ballet Guild;
English Speaking Union; Rep. Women's Club. B:
5/20/30. Add: 759 S. Hudson, Denver 80222.

BETTY ORTEN (D)
    1974-. Dist: 35. Party: State Del. 1968-74;
Nat. Del. 1972; Ch., Registration 1966-68; Ch.,
Get-Out-The-Vote 1964; Cnty. V-Ch., 1968-72;
State V-Ch. 1972-74. Org: WPC. Educ: U. of
Colo. 1949 BA. B: 2/3/27. Add: 7978 Stuart
Pl., Westminster 80030 (303) 892-3006.

VIRGINIA L. SEARS (R)
    1973-. Dist: 50. Party: State Central Com.
1972-76; Precinct Committeewoman 1970-72;
Precinct V-Ch., 1972-73. Org: Amer. Women in
Radio & TV; Rep. Women's Club. B: 6/20/06.
Add: 2345 16th St., Greeley 80631.

ARIE P. TAYLOR (D) **
    Dist: 7. Prev: Deputy Clerk, Denver Dist.
Court; Chief Clerk, Election Com. Org: ACLU;
Amer. Legion; NAACP. Occ: Accounting. B:
3/27/27. Add: 2861 Jasmine St., Denver
80207.

County Commissions

Boulder. MARGARET B. MARKEY (D)
1974-. Bds: Bd. of Health; Alt., Denver
Regional Council of Govts.; Cnty. Consortium of
Cities. Prev: Cnty. Long Range Planning Com.
1973-75; Criminal Justice Adv. Com. 1970-71;
Adv. Task Force, Land Use Com. Org: LWV. B:
5/5/35. Add: Sunshine Canyon, Boulder 80302
(303) 441-3500.

Humboldt. SARA PARSONS
Courthouse, Eureka 95501.

Jefferson. JOANNE K. PATERSON (D)
1974-. Bds: Cnty. Mental Health Ctr. Bd.;
Cnty. Community Ctr. Bd.; State Bd. of Social
Services. Org: Colo. Bar Assoc.; Colo. Mental
Health Assoc.; Cnty. Action Ctr.; Cnty. Dem.
Exec. Com. Educ: Barnard Coll. 1945 BA; Western
Reserve Law School 1949 LLB. Add: 258 S. Deklar
Pl., Golden 80401 (303) 279-6511.

Larimer. NONA THAYER (D)
1976-. Bds: Council of Govts; Cnty. Fair Bd.
Party: Cnty. Exec. Com. 1977-. Prev: Land Use &
Transportation Com. 1974-76; Budget Adv. Com.;
Youth Services Bureau Adv. Bd. 1974-76. Org: LWV
Educ: Stanford U. 1954 BA; Colo. U. MA. B:
2/2/32. Add: 1827 Michael La., Ft. Collins
80521 (303) 221-2100 x 266.

Mesa. B. MAXINE ALBERS (R)
1974-. Dist: 3. Bds: Nat. Assoc. of Cnty's.
Land Use Steering Com.; Ch., Cnty. Welfare Bd.;
Hwy. Planning Com. Party: State Del. 1972, '74;
Cnty. Committeewoman 1970-74. Prev: Deputy Cnty.
Treasurer 1952-54. Org: Altrusa; Colo. Cnty's
Inc.; Nat. Assoc. of Cnty's.; Virginia Neal Blue
Ctr. for Women; Cnty. Rep. Women; LWV; Citizens
Adv. Council. B: 7/1/24. Add: 3054 F Rd., Grand
Jct. 81501 (303) 243-9200.

Summit. ELIZABETH H. ETIE (R)
1977-. Bds: Ch., Resource Conservation & Devt.
Com.; Bd. of Equalization; Bd. of Health. Party:
State Del. 1976. Prev: Town Trustee 1973-76;
Regional Planning Cmsn. 1973-77; Planning &
Zoning 1973-74. Org: Nat. Realtors; Rep. Central
Com. Educ: U. of Conn. 1966 BA. Occ: Assayer.
B: 8/17/44. Add: P.O. Box 134, Frisco 80443
(303) 453-2561.

Weld. JUNE K. STEINNARK (D)
1976-. Bds: V-Ch., Council of Govts.; Central
NE Colo. Finance, Central Purchasing & Personnel.
Party: State Del. 1964-74; Ch., Cnty. Dem. Party
1973-75; V-Ch., Cnty. Dem. Party 1971-73; Colo.
Exec. & Central Com. 1971-75; Precinct Committee-
woman 1964-73. Prev: Coord., Cnty. Health
Services 1976-77; Community Devt. Services 1977;
Colo. Cnty's. Inc. Human Resources 1977-78. Org:
LWV. Educ: Colo. Coll. 1962 BA. B: 6/13/40.
Add: 1922 20th St., Greeley 80631 (303)356-4000.
Ext. 200.

Mayors

Arriba. IDA JOHNSON
P.O. Box 113, Arriba 80804.

Basalt. LINDA CROSSLAND (R)
1977-. Prev: Bd. of Adjustments 1975-76; Bd.
of Trustees 1976-77. B: 12/4/44. Add: Box 318,
118 Hillside Dr., Basalt 81621 (303) 927-3322.

Black Hawk. FRANCES A. OLSON (R)
1974-. Bds: Planning Cmsn.; Historical
Foundation; Lace House Restoration Com. Prev:
Councilwoman 1973; Mayor Pro Tem 1973-74. Occ:
Cosmetologist/Salon Owner. B: 8/6/26. Add:
211 Dubois St., P.O. Box 152, Black Hawk
80422 (303) 582-5221.

Cherry Hills Village. BETH HENRY JENKINS (R)
1976-. Bds: Denver Regional Council of
Govt.; Ch., Central N.E. Colo. Health Systems
Agency. Prev: Councilwoman 1972-76. Org: Rep.
Women. Educ: Northwestern U. 1944 BS. B:
7/8/23. Add: 5000 S. Albion St., Littleton
80021 (303) 789-2541.

Durango. MAXINE PETERSON (D)
1973-. Bds: Western Colo. Health Systems
Agency; Resource, Conservation & Devt.; Community
Corrections Bd. Party: Cnty. Dem. Exec. Com.
1977; State Del. 1974. Prev: Planning Cmsn.
1971-73; Youth Advocate Bd. 1974-76; Comprehensive Health Planning 1974-76. Org: Colo.
Municipal League; LWV; Ecological Soc.; Women's
Club. Educ: Beth-El School of Nursing 1953 RN.
B: 1/1/32. Add: 622 3rd Ave., Durango 81301
(303) 247-5622.

Eads. GERMAINE A. LEGG (R)
1976-. Org: Chamber of Commerce. B: 6/20/36.
Add: 1104 Luther St., Eads 81036 (303) 438-5590.

Fairplay. ADA BELLE EVANS (D)
1974-. Org: NEA; NAACP. Educ: Benedict Coll.
1955 BS; U. of Colo. 1974 MA. B: 6/9/32. Add:
525 Hathaway, Fairplay 80440 (303) 836-2924.

Loveland. JEAN GAINES
410 E. 5th St., P.O. Box 419, Loveland 80537.

Morrison. GAILE W. MOLINARO (R) **
1976-. Bds: Water Commissioner; Streets
Commissioner; Regional Council of Governments;
Resource Recovery Management Cmsn. Prev: City
Council 1972-76. Org: PTA. Educ: Western
Washington State Coll. 1959 BA. B: 3/28/37.
Add: Box 206, Morrison 80465 (303) 697-8749.

Olney Springs. IDA E. SPENCER
401 Warner, P.O. Box 35, Olney Springs 81062.

Ordway. CLAIR BIDDISON
315 Main, Ordway 81063.

Poncha Springs. FLORENCE LINDBLOOM
330 Brown Ave., P.O. Box 56, Poncha Springs
81242.

Romeo. GERTRUDE SALAZAR
Box 398, Romeo 81148.

Sugar City. CHRIS GIESE
P.O. Box 69, Sugar City 81076.

Timnath. DORA G. JEFFERS
Box 37, Timnath 80547.

Ward. RAMONA RAPIER
Columbia St., Ward 80481.

Wiggins. PHYLLIS B. FORSCHA (R)
1976-. Prev: Town Clerk 1974-76. Org: Historical Group. Occ: Bookkeeper. B: 11/20/23. Add:
301 Chapman, Wiggins 80654 (303) 483-7450.

Local Councils

Akron. ERNETA ROARK (D)
1976-. Org: Rep. Women Club. B: 10/9/19.
Add: 762 Adams, Akron 80720.

Alma. MADGE GATELY
ETHEL HARPER
City Hall, Alma 80420.

Antonito. VERTHA N. MONTOYA
308 Main St., P.O. Box 86, Antonito 81120.

Arvada. ROSEMARY DOLLAGHAN DOOLEY
1973-. Bds: Planning Cmsn.; Mayors Anti-Crime
Com.; Policy Com., Nat. League of Cities. Educ:
Denver U. 1959 BA. B: 6/16/29. Add: 6579 Lewis
St., Arvada 80004 (303) 420-6579.

Arvada. VESTA H. MILLER (R)
1973-. Mayor Pro Tem. Bds: Ch., Water Quality
Task Force; Ch., State Policy Adv. Group; Urban
Systems Com. Prev: Planning Cmsn. 1972-74; Ch.,
Goals Task Force 1971-73. Org: Nat. League of
Cities; Colo. Municipal League; Jefferson Cnty.
Govt. Assoc.; Arvada Mental Health Adv. Bd.;
Citizens Alert; Rep. Club. Educ: Kan. State U.
1949 BS. B: 10/23/28. Add: 6191 Flower St.,
Arvada 80004 (303) 421-2550.

Aspen. FRANCES JOHNSTON (D)
1975-. Bds: City Finance Com.; Overall
Economic Devt. Program Com.; Chamber of Commerce.
Party: Cnty. Committeewoman 1976-. Prev: Administrative Asst. 1974-. Org: LWV; Colo. Municipal
League; Cnty. Parks Assoc. Educ: Barnard Coll.
1940 BA. B: 12/1/18. Add: 210 E. Cooper, Apt.
2F, P.O. Box 3734, Aspen 81611 (303) 925-5232.

Ault. BETTY LOEWEN
BARBARA SWANSON
201 First, P.O. Box 98, Ault 80610.

Aurora. ALICE DUDICH
1470 South Havana, Aurora 80012.

Aurora. RUTH M. FOUNTAIN (R)
1971-. Bds: Pres., Colo. Municipal League;
Bd., Nat. League of Cities; Party: State Del.
1968-74; State Alt. 1976; Cnty. Committeewoman
1966-71. Prev: Governor's Council Emergency
Medical Service 1976; Governor's Private Employment Agency Adv. Bd. 1971-79. Org: AAUW; Chamber
of Commerce; Historical Society; Rep. Women's
Club; Colo. Women's Rep. Club; Colo. Women's
Forum. Educ: Colo. State Coll. 1963 BA; 1968
MA. B: 6/25/28. Add: 12721 E. 30th Ave., Aurora
80011 (303) 750-5000.

Basalt. BETTY JANE TERRELL
1973-. Bds: Police Adv. Prev: Sanitation
1971-72. Occ: Medical Secretary. B: 10/3/33.
Add: Box 698, 132 W. Sopris Dr., Basalt
81621 (303) 925-1600.

Bayfield. SHARON TALBOT
304 Mill St., P.O. Box 288, Bayfield 81122.

Bennett. NANCY C. BANG
355 4th, Bennett 80102.

Berthoud. FRANCES NIELSON (R)
1975-. Bds: Ch., Finance; Judicial; Cemetery.
Party: State Alt. 1976; Precinct Committeewoman
1960-70. Org: Historical Society; Women's Club;
DAR. Educ: U. of Colo. 1923 BA. B: 5/30/1900.
Add: 620 8th St., Berthoud 80513 (303)532-2206.

Black Hawk. KATHERINE ECCKER
JUDITH HOXEY
ELLEN OLEAN
201 Gregory, Box 327, Black Hawk 80422.

Blanca. JUDITH GROSSWILER ROYBAL (D)
1976-. Occ: Secretary/Bookkeeper. B: 9/11/44
Add: P.O. Box 21, Blanca 81125 (303) 379-3600.

Bonanza City. ETHEL RANSE
City Hall, Bonanza City 81155.

Boulder. RUTH ARMSTRONG CORRELL (D)
1973-. Bds: Housing Authority; Housing Adv.
Com. Party: State Del. 1972. Prev: Human
Relations Cmsn. 1968-71. Org: LWV; Cnty. Dem.
Women. Educ: Ind. U. 1937 BA. B: 10/23/15.
Add: 320 20th St., Boulder 80302 (303)441-3002.

Boulder. JANET S. ROBERTS (D)
1959-. Bds: Ch., City Council. Party: Ch.,
Cnty. Volunteers 1964-; V-Ch., 2nd Congressional
Dist. Central Com. 1965-66. Prev: City Planning
Bd. 1956-59; Boulder Cnty. Regional Planning
1958-59; Air Pollution Variance Bd. 1967-70.
Org: Colo. Municipal League; Nat. League of
Cities; LWV; NOW; Cnty. Dem. Women. Educ:
Wheaton Coll. 1939 BA. B: 5/21/18. Add:
1829 Bluebell Ave., Boulder 80302 (303)441-3002.

Bow Mar. MARY HAMPTON CARTER (R)
1976-. Bds: Colo. Land Use Cmsn.; Colo. Div.
of Parks & Outdoor Recreation; Jefferson Cnty.
Open Space Adv. Com. Party: Block Captain Rep.
Party 1976-78. Org: PTA. Occ: Free lance
writer. B: 2/12/24. Add: 5201 Bow Mar Dr.,
Littleton 80123 (303) 794-5074.

Breckenridge. VERNA ENYEART
JO ANN FRENCH
103 S. Harris, P.O. Box 168, Breckenridge
80424.

Brighton. DORIS DURDY (R)
1974-. Bds: Denver Reg. Council of Govts.;
Human Resource Com.; Clean Water Com. Party:
State Del. 1976; Precinct Committeewoman 1972-;
V-Pres., House Dist. 31 1976-. Prev: Planning
Comsr. 1973-75. Org: BPW; Chamber of Commerce;
NOW; Rep. Club. Occ: Manager. B: 9/20/25.
Add: 792 S. 6th Ave., Brighton 80601
(303) 659-4050.

Brighton. MARY CATHERINE ZINK (R)
1973-. Bds: Environmental Quality Bd.; Policy Com. Party: State Del. 1976. Org: Nat. League of Cities; Colo. Municipal League; Chamber of Commerce; Parent Council. B: 11/23/35. Add: 160 S. 17th Ave. Dr., Brighton 80601.

Broomfield. THELMA BANSCHBACK
GLORIA VAN BUSKIRK
#6 Garden Office Ctr., Broomfield 80020.

Brush. MARY LOU HELD (I)
1976-. Bds: Utilities Com.; Housing Bd. for Rehabilitation; Cnty. Impact Assistance Team. Occ: Realtor. B: 5/2/43. Add: 124 S. Bruse, Brush 80723.

Central City. SHERYL A. WEITZ
Box 204, Central City 80427.

Coal Creek. SALLY M. BOYD
WILMA MASSEY
Box 36, Coal Creek 81221.

Cokedale. PATRICIA SACCAMANNO
P.O. Box 323, Cokedale 81032.

Colorado Springs. MARY KYER
MARGARET VASQUEZ
107 N. Nevada Ave., Box 1575, Colo. Sprgs. 80901.

Commerce City. MARJORIE CHRISTIANSEN (I)
1966-. Bds: Denver Reg. Council of Govts.; Special Com. on Urban System Allocation; Ch., Planning Cmsn. Party: State Del. 1960-76; Cnty. Precinct Committeewoman 1950-77; Dist. Captain 1963-66. Org: Child Care Center Bd.; OES. Add: 5100 Ivy St., Commerce City 80022 (303)287-0151.

Craig. HELEN BARBARA LOYD (R)
1975-. Bds: Ch., Administration Com.; Parks Com.; Finance Com. Prev: City & Cnty. Library Bd. 1965-75. B: 2/27/23. Add: 500 Sandrock Dr., Craig 81625.

Crested Butte. CANDACE LIGHT
308 Third Street, P.O. Box 39, Crested Butte 81224.

Crestone. CYNTELLA HARLAN
FERN VANDERPOOL
P.O. Box 55, Crestone 81131.

Crowley. HELEN BREWER
Broadway, P.O. Box 31, Crowley 81033.

Dacono. ILLA R. WILSON (D) **
1974-. Bds: Planning Cmsn. Org: Amer. Speech & Hearing Assoc. Educ: Denver U. 1954 BA. Occ: Learning Disabilities Teacher. B: 4/19/30. Add: 716 Glen Moor, Dacono 80514 (303) 833-2388.

De Beque. JUDY LAKE
De Beque 81630.

Denver. CATHY DONOHUE
City & County Bldg., Colfax & Bannock, Denver 80202.

Denver. CATHY REYNOLDS (D)
1975-. Bds: Labor Relations Task Force; Ch., Leg. Liason Task Force; Cmsn. on Community Relations. Party: State Del. 1972-75; State Alt. 1976; Precinct Committeewoman. Org: Colo. Women in Municipal Govt.; LWV; Dem. Women's Caucus. B: 11/28/44. Add: 1606 Locust, Denver 80220 (303) 297-3912.

Dillon. JUDY MORGAN (R)
1971-. Bds: Ch., Park Com. B: 11/8/49. Add: Box 41, Dillon 80435 (303) 468-2596.

Dolores. YVONNE RULE
420 Central Ave., Box 621, Dolores 81323.

Eaton. BETTY RAE BATES (R) **
1974-. Bds: Park & Cemetery Com.; Finance Com.; Bldgs. Com. Org: AAUW; Chamber of Commerce. Educ: U. of Colo. 1944 BS. B: 10/28/23. Add: 610 Cheyenne Ave., Eaton 80615.

Edgewater. BONNIE ALLISON (I)
1975-. Bds: Ch., Planning & Zoning; Recreation; Licensing. Educ: Community Coll. of Denver 1977 AA. B: 11/25/36. Add: 2278 Ingalls, Edgewater 80214 (303) 238-0573.

Edgewater. NORMA MIESNER DALY (R)
1973-. Mayor Pro Tem. Bds: Ch., Public Works; Liquor Licensing; Finance; Council Pres. Party: State Alt. 1976. Org: Jefferson Cnty. Govt. Assoc.; Rep. Club. Educ: Colo. State U. 1950 BS; Denver U. 1958 MA. Occ: Teacher. B: 12/7/29 Add: 2580 Lamar St., Edgewater 80214.

Elizabeth. MICHELLE CALDWELL
Box 147, Elizabeth 80107.

Elizabeth. SANDRA H. CASTO (I)
1976-. Bds: Zoning Variance Bd. Org: Citizens for Responsible Action. Educ: Northern Colo. Teachers Coll. 1961 BA. Occ: Bookkeeper. B: 12/10/38. Add: Box 146, Elizabeth 80107 (303) 646-4166.

Empire. EMILY LU S. CROKE
LINDA WALKER
30 East Park Ave., Box 187, Empire 80438.

Erie. SYLVIA MARIE CLEM (D)
1976-. Bds: Ch., Cemetary; Ch., Library; Ch., Parks. Occ: Realtor. B: 5/6/30. Add: 404 Main P.O. Box 403, Erie 80516 (303) 828-3843.

Estes Park. MARGARET HOUSTON (D)
1976-. Bds: Ch., Code & Sanitation Com.; Water Com. Org: BPW; Women's Club. Occ: Gift Shop Clerk. B: 10/28/15. Add: 170 Moraine Ave., Estes Pk. 80517 (303) 586-5331.

Evans. JUNE SIMPSON
815 39th St., P.O. Box 59, Evans 80620.

Federal Heights. GAIL G. IRVINE
2380 W. 90th Ave., Denver 80221.

Firestone. SYLVIA NICHOLS
150 Buchanan Ave., Box 100, Firestone 80520.

Fleming. KATHERINE PYLE
P.O. Box 466, Fleming 80728.

Fort Collins. NANCY P. GRAY (D)
1973-. Party: State Del. 1968-76; State Alt.
1968-76; State Central Com. 1973-76. B: 2/29/32.
Add: 110 Fishback, Ft. Collins 80521.

Frisco. LINDA MC KINLEY
300 Main St., Box 115, Frisco 80443.

Frisco. KATHERINE WOODS (D)
1976-. Bds: Ch., Parks & Recreation. Occ:
Lounge Owner. B: 9/3/45. Add: Box 751, Frisco
80443 (303) 468-2678.

Garden City. MARY FOLKERS
MINNIE GREENWOOD
MARY KREIGER
720 25th St., Box 1214, Greeley 80631.

Georgetown. MARY BLEESZ
KATHERINE SPENCER
P.O. Box 426, Georgetown 80444.

Gilcrest. VIRGINIA CHACON
P.O. Box 8, Gilcrest 80623.

Glendale. LU ELLA TERRY
950 S. Birch St., Denver 80222.

Glenwood Springs. MARIAN IONA SMITH (D)
1976-. Bds: Ch., Cemetery Bd. Party: State
Del. 1976; Precinct Committeewoman 1974-77.
Prev: Cemetery Bd. 1975-77. Org: ACLU; Environ-
mental Action; Nader's Public Citizens; Jane
Jefferson's Dem. Club. B: 10/8/30. Add: 1332
Grand Ave., Glenwood Spgs., 81601 (303)945-5838.

Golden. ADRIENNE H. GILBERT (I)
1976-. Dist: 1. Bds: Jefferson Cnty. Open
Space; Colo. Municipal League; Cnty. Govts. Assoc.
B: 3/12/47. Add: 122 Pike St., Golden 80401
(303) 279-3331.

Granby. AUDREY REECE
JOYCE SCHMIDBAUER
Zero & Jasper, P.O. Box 17, Granby 80446.

Grand Junction. JANE S. QUIMBY (D)
1973-. Bds: Exec. Bd., Colo. Municipal League;
Ch., Western Slope Energy Impact Assistance Com.
Prev: City Planning Cmsn. 1973-77; Housing Authority 1974-76; Housing Bd. 1973-76. Org: Colo.
Municipal League; AAUW; LWV; Dem. Party; Attention
to Youth. Educ: U. of Colo. 1948 BS. B: 9/15/26.
Add: 484 N. Sherwood Dr., Grand Jct. 81501.
(303) 243-2633.

Grand Lake. LUCILLE WAGONER
610 Lake Ave., Box 6, Grand Lake 80447.

Greeley. IRMA PRINCIC (D)
1973-. Bds: Women in Govt. of Colo. Municipal
League; Policy Com. of Colo. Municipal League;
Weld-Larimer Council of Govts. Party: State Del.
1974, '76; State Alt. 1972; Precinct Leader 1976-
78. Prev: Housing Authority 1971-77. Org: LWV.
Educ: Colo. State Coll. 1966 BA; Northwestern U.
1977 CEU. B: 8/9/44. Add: 2624 W. 20th St.,
Greeley 80631 (303) 353-6123.

Green Mountain Falls. ANNE HARTUNG
CATHERINE MC ALLISTER
KATHERINE E. TURNER
735 Oak, P.O. Box 524, Green Mtn. Falls
80819.

Greenwood Village. MARY PHYLLIS SIMPSON
7965 E. Prentice, Bldg. #42, Englewood
80110.

Grover. EVELYN POSTON
P.O. Box 57, Grover 80729.

Haxtun. FILOMENA E. ANICH
145 S. Colorado, Box 205, Haxtun 80731.

Hillrose. ISABEL GILCHRIST (R)
1975-. Org: NEA. Educ: U. of NC 1958 MA.
Occ: Teacher. B: 7/5/20. Add: Box 45, Hillrose
80733 (303) 847-3719.

Hillrose. LILA P. NEIFERT (R)
1974-. Bds: Health & Sanitation; Insect
Control. Org: NEA; BPW. Educ: U. of N.C. 1959
BA. Occ: Teacher. B: 9/7/13. Add: 407 Charles,
Hillrose 80733 (303) 847-3761.

Holly. HELEN LOUISE STEUBEN (R)
1976-. Bds: Ch., Finance Com.; Ch., Parks
Com.; Library Bd. Occ: Music Teacher. B:
11/27/39. Add: Holly 81047 (303) 537-6622.

Holyoke. DOROTHY M. REIMER (D)
1974-. Bds: Ch., City Recreation; Bd. of
Zoning Adjustment; Holyoke Housing Authority.
Prev: Bd. of Zoning Adjustment 1973-77. Org: OES
Educ: Northeastern Jr. Coll. 1973 AA. Occ:
Swimming Instructor. B: 5/27/22. Add: 321 S.
Phelan Ave., Holyoke 80734 (303) 854-2266.

Hooper. ELEANOR SANDERSON
ALVA SMITH
3rd & Main, P.O. Box 1, Hooper 81136.

Hotchkiss. SHIRLEE LIUZZO
202 Bridge, P.O. Box 368, Hotchkiss 81419.

Hot Sulphur Springs. CAROL SCHROER
P.O. Box 116, Hot Sulphur Springs 80451.

Hugo. BARBARA J. STUWE (R)
1975-. Mayor Pro Tem. Bds: Ch., Solid Waste
Study; Airport Com. Party: Cnty. Precinct
Committeewoman 1972. Prev: Ch., Planning Com.
1972-75. Org: Active Com. to Improve our Neigh-
borhood; Assoc. for Research & Enlightenment.
Occ: Secretary. B: 1/4/38. Add: 309 5th St.,
Hugo 80821 (303) 743-2485.

Jamestown. RENA L. MANS
Main Street, Box 273, Jamestown 80455.

Johnstown. ELIZABETH A. WHITMORE (R)
1976-. Bds: Ch., Cemetery; Ch., Ordinance;
Police & Parks. Party: Cnty. Committeewoman.
Occ: Customer Service. B: 3/24/40. Add: 1145 N.
Park Ave., Johnstown 80534.

Keenesburg. BETTY BEAVER
140 S. Main St., P.O. Box 312, Keenesburg
80643.

Keota.   BETTY BIVENS
     CLARA MC CARVER
     Box 144, Keota 80738.

Kim.   WILMA I. GOODE   (I)
     1974-. Educ: U. of Northern Colo. 1967 BA.
B: 2/1/12. Add: Kim 81049 (303) 643-5250.

Kit Carson.   BARBARA KNUDTSON   (R) **
     1974-. Bds: Park Com.; Fire Dept. Prev:
Treasurer, U.S. 287 Highway Assoc. 1971-. Occ:
Motel Owner. B: 5/23/18. Add: Box 195, Kit
Carson 80825 (303) 962-3291.

Lafayette.   PHYLLIS THIEME
     201 E. Simpson St., Lafayette 80026.

Lake City.   EDITH L. SWANSON
     3rd St., P.O. Box 76, Lake City 81235.

Lakeside.   LUCILLE CHADWICK
     MARIE MC LAUGHLIN
     ALINE SWENSON
     LORENE THOMAS
     4601 Sheridan Blvd., Lakeside 80212.

Lakewood.   CAROLYN B. BACHER   (R)
     1973-. Bds: Ch., Finance & Operations Com.;
Public Safety Com.; Citizens Adv. Council. Occ:
Assembly Worker. B: 2/8/31. Add: 2005 Yarrow
St., Lakewood 80215 (303) 234-8605.

Lakewood.   SHARON CARR
     1973-. Bds: Denver Reg. Council of Govts.;
Col. Municipal League; Nat. League of Cities;
Cnty. Historical Cmsn. Party: State Del. 1972-76.
Prev: Jefferson Cnty. Bicentennial Cmsn. 1974-77;
Del., Charter Cmsn. 1972-73. Org: Chamber of
Commerce; Cnty. Historical Society; Cnty. Rep.
Club; PTA. Educ: Col. U. 1958 BA. B: 11/29/38.
Add: 13476 W. Center Dr., Lakewood 80228
(303) 234-8605.

Lamar.   ESTHER ANDERSON   (R)
     1977-. Bds: City Power Bd.; City Library Bd.
Org: Zonta Internat.; Rep. Club. Educ: Garden
City Jr. Coll. 1932 AA. B: 5/30/11. Add: 201
Willow Vly. Rd., Lamar 81052 (303) 336-5874.

Las Animas.   KITTY ANN LONG   (D)
     1976-. Mayor Pro Tem. Bds: Ch., Administra-
tive Com.; Ch., Police Com.; Parks & Recreation.
Party: State Del. 1969; Del., Cnty. Assembly 1976;
Del., Judicial Assembly 1976; Secretary State
Judicial Dist. 1977. Prev: Mayor 1966-71; Mayor
Interim 1972-73; Councilwoman 1974-75; Colo.
Municipal League Exec. Bd. 1976-77; State Nomin-
ations Com. 1977; Cmsn. Status of Women 1971-72;
Library Bd. 1966-73; Planning & Zoning 1966-73.
Org: BPW; Chamber of Commerce; Economic Devt.
Council. Occ: Fashions Store Owner. B: 11/3/25.
Add: 919 6th St., Las Animas 81054 (303)456-0422.

Las Animas.   LILA MAUPIN
     P.O. Box 468, Las Animas 81054.

Le Veta.   DORA RODRIGUEZ QUINTANA   (D)
     1975-. Bds: Planning Cmsn.; Finance Com.;
Park & Recreation. Party: Cnty. Committeewoman
1962-64. Prev: State School Bd. 1968-69. Occ:
Nutrition Instructor. B: 8/3/20. Add: 109 S.

Locust, Le Veta 81055.

Limon.   GLORIA LIGGETT
     200 F Ave., Box 8, Limon 80828.

Littleton.   SALLY H. PARSONS   (R)
     1973-. Bds: Park Com.; Repr., Colo. Municipal
League. Party: Del., Cnty. Assembly. Org:
LWV; Human Resource Council. Educ: U. of Ill.
1956 BS. Occ: Lobbyist. B: 4/8/34. Add:
6777 Southridge Ln., Littleton 80120
(303) 794-4214.

Lochbuie.   IVA BENNETT
     Rt. 4, Box 99, Brighton 80601.

Longmont.   SANDRA L. PARKER   (R)
     1975-. Bds: Planning & Zoning Cmsn.; Water
Task Force; Mental Health Adv. Bd. Party:
State Del. 1976, '74; State Alt. 1972; Cnty.
Captain 1972-74. Prev: Planning & Zoning Cmsn.
1974-76; Accountability Com.1972-74. Org: LWV;
Rep. Roundtable. Occ: Bookkeeper. B: 7/19/39.
Add: 1648 Gillette Ct., Longmont 80501
(303) 776-6050.

Louisville.   MARY DE LORENZO
     749 Main St., Louisville 80027.

Louisville.   BARBARA GAYLE MC DONALD   (R)
     1976-. Bds: V-Ch., Boulder City. Consortuim
of Cities; Louisville Finance Com. Party: Cnty.
Captain 1977; Cnty. Rep. Central Com. Prev:
Cmsnr., Housing Authority 1970-76; Pres., Non-
Profit Corp. 1974-. Org: Colo. Municipal League;
Chamber of Commerce. Occ: Bank V-Pres. B:
3/30/43. Add: 701 Garfield, Louisville 80027
(303) 666-6565.

Loveland.   CAROLYN COULSON
     MARTHA PATTERSON
     410 E. 5th St., P.O. Box 419, Loveland 80537.

Lyons.   ANN FOLTZ
     432 5th Ave., Box 49, Lyons 80540.

Manassa.   GENEVIEVE SMITH
     401 Main St., Manassa 81141.

Manitou Springs.   ELAINE L. PAUL   (D)
     1973-. Bds: Pike Peak Area Council of Govts;
SE Colo. Health Systems Agency. Prev: Planning
Com. 1971-73; Water Com. 1969-71. Org: Histor-
ical Society; Woman's Club; Craft & Art Club. B:
11/20/26. Add: 25 Sutherland Rd., Manitou
Springs 80829 (303) 685-9577.

Manzanola.   ELSIE H. FOX   (D)
     1976-. Bds: Ch., Ordinance; Streets & Alleys;
Water. Org: NEA. Educ: 1974 BA. Occ: Teacher.
B: 12/11/29. Add: 128 Canal, Box 264, Manzanola
81058.

Marble.   MABEL LYKE
     DOROTHEA SEIDEL
     Marble Star Route, Carbondale 81623.

Mead.   PAMELA MATHIESEN
     P.O. Box 217, Mead 80542.

Milliken. DONNA C. JENNIGES (I)
    1976-. Bds: Communication Com. Occ: Bank
Officer. B: 6/4/34. Add: 315 Laura Ave.,
Milliken 80543 (303) 587-4331.

Milliken. BARBARA NEWCOMB
    1118 Broad St., P.O. Box 97, Milliken 80543.

Monte Vista. RUTH ROMERO
    720 1st Ave., P.O. Box 431, Monte Vista 81144.

Monument. CAROL OWENS (I)
    1974-. Bds: Cemetery Assoc.; Parks & Lake.
Occ: School Bus Driver. B: 2/2/32. Add: Box 207,
Monument 80132 (303) 481-2954.

Morrison. LORA PHILLIPS
    110 Stone St., P.O. Box 95, Morrison 80465.

Morrison. SHARI A. RAYMOND (R)
    1976-. B: 4/20/36. Add: 111 Canyon Vista Ln.,
Morrison 80465 (303) 697-8749.

Mount Crested Butte. BARBARA JAMES
    P.O. Box 669, Crested Butte 81224.

Naturita. NANCY MOORE
    230 Main, P.O. Box 377, Naturita 81422.

New Castle. HELEN COLE
    4th St., P.O. Box 166, New Castle 81647.

Northglenn. MARY ELLEN KETTELKAMP (D) **
    1973-. Bds: Regional Council of Governments;
Council on Aging. Prev: School Dist. Advisory
Accountability Com. 1971-74; Planning Cmsn.
1969-71. Org: Municipal League. Educ: St. Mary's
School of Nursing 1957 RN. Occ: Secretary. B:
8/17/36. Add: 9977 Clark Dr., Northglenn
80221 (303)452-1941.

Nucla. JEAN MADOLE
    320 Main St., P.O. Box 219, Nucla 81424.

Nunn. ILA M. DU BOIS (R) **
    1974-. Bds: Centennial-Bicentennial Com. Org:
Women's Club. B: 12/4/37. Add: Box 11, Nunn
80648.

Olathe. CHARLOTTE M. MC GRATH (I)
    1972-. Educ: Ill. State U. 1950 BSEd. B:
10/18/28. Add: Box 528, Olathe 81425.

Ophir. BETSEY HODGES
    P.O. Box 683, Ophir 81426.

Ordway. ELEANOR SYPHER
    315 Main, Ordway 81063.

Otis. JOYCE ARMSTRONG
    102 S. Washington, P.O. Box 95, Otis 80743.

Palisade. LORRAINE FRANKLIN
    175 E. 3rd, Box 128, Palisade 81526.

Palisade. GLEEANNA M. JOHNSON (R) **
    1974-. Bds: Police & Fire Com.; Planning Com.
Org: PTA. B: 8/24/34. Add: 541 South Main,
Palisade 81526 (303)464-5602.

Palmer Lake. ALICE FULLER
    P.O. Box 208, Palmer Lake 80133.

Palmer Lake. FRANCES M. VANAKEN (R) **
    1972-. Bds: Council of Governments; Criminal
Justice Advisory Com. Occ: Floral Designer.
B: 11/24/27. Add: Box 314, Eisenhower Dr. &
Park Ave., Palmer Lake 80133 (303)481-2886.

Paoli. ELSIE FISHBACK
    Main St., P.O. Box 5736, Paoli 80746.

Pierce. BETTY BAKER
    240 Main St., Box 57, Pierce 80650.

Pitkin. ANNA MUSTAIN
    3rd & Main, Pitkin 81241.

Platteville. CONNIE LE CLAIR
    411 Goodrich, Box 6, Platteville 80651.

Pueblo. PAT KELLY (D)
    1969-. Bds: Ch., Energy Cmsn.; Council of
Govts.; S. Colo. Economic Devt. Com. Party:
State Del. 1971. Prev: Colo. Municipal League
Bd. 1970-74; Nat. League of Cities Com. on Energy
& Environment 1971-76. Org: Colo. Municipal
League; Nat. League of Cities; Dem. Party. Educ:
U. of Colo. 1947 BA. B: 11/11/23. Add: 700 W.
17th St., Pueblo 81003 (303)545-0561.

Ramah. VIOLET MAY MC KAY (I)
    1975-. Occ: Liquor Store Owner. B: 5/11/33.
Add: Commercial St., P.O. Box 141, Ramah 80822.

Rangely. PEGGY J. RECTOR
    209 E. Main St., Box 580, Rangely 81648.

Raymer. PAULINE STEFFEN
    P.O. Box 146, Raymer 80742.

Rico. M. ANNA ENGEL
    DIANA FAHRION
    P.O. Box 56, Rico 81332.

Ridgway. MARY THOMSON
    Box 242, Ridgway 81432.

Rifle. CLARE ASHLOCK
    337 East Ave., Box 1908, Rifle 81650.

Rifle. MOLLIE REIGAN (R) **
    1972-. Bds: Planning Cmsn. Org: Rep. Club.
B: 12/16/15. Add: Box 701, Rifle 81650
(303)625-2121.

Rockvale. MARY HORVATH
    510 Railroad St., P.O. Box 305, Rockvale 81244

Rocky Ford. SYLVIA FRANKMORE
    203 S. Main, Rocky Ford 81067.

Rocky Ford. MARION A. VANDYK (R) **
    Bds: Ch., Fire Com.; Police Com.; Civic
Improvement. Occ: Office Manager. B: 7/11/27.
Add: 809 South 6th St., Rocky Ford 81067
(303)254-7414.

Romeo. BERTINA LOPEZ
    Box 398, Romeo 81148.

Rosedale. VENITA ADAIR
         MARILYN COLLINS
         ROSE KENDRICK
         RUTH KENDRICK
      2621 8th Ave., Greeley 80631.

Rye. LILLIAN HAART
      P.O. Box 316, Rye 81069.

Saguache. IRENE A. GRAY (R)
      1974-. Bds: San Luis Vly. Resource, Conser-
   vation & Devt. Project. Party: State Del. 1970,
   '75; State Alt. 1969, '74; Cnty. Secretary-
   Treasurer 1968-77; Cnty. Committeewoman 1960-61;
   Cnty. V-Ch. 1962-68. Prev: Farmers Home Adminis-
   tration 1970-75; Resource Conservation & Devt.
   Project 1975-. Org: Rep. Club. B: 9/19/12.
   Add: 518 San Juan, Saguache 81149 (303)655-2688.

Saguache. ELIZABETH S. WITTMEYER
      P.O. Box 417, Saguache 81149.

Sanford. JANEEN CANTY
      18 S. Main St., Sanford 81151.

San Luis. HENRIETTA P. GARCIA
         LOUISE J. VIGIL
      356 Main St., P.O. Box 56, San Luis 81152.

Silver Plume. CHERYL BARTON (D)
      1975-. Bds: Planning Cmsn.; Coord. Com. Party:
   State Del. 1976; Precinct Committeewoman 1976-.
   Org: Planning Cmsn. Educ: Rivier Coll. 1966 BA.
   Occ: Teacher. B: 2/21/44. Add: Box 39, 10
   Charles St., Silver Plume 80476 (303)569-3118.

Silver Plume. PAULINE MARSHALL
      Box 457, Silver Plume 80476.

Silverton. WANDA MILLER
         NORMA C. WYMAN
      1360 Greene St., P.O. Box 65, Silverton 81433.

Starkville. MARIE CORICH
         LINDA MARTINEZ
      Rt. 1, Box 416A, Starkville 81082.

Steamboat Springs. HELEN D. RICHARDS
      1973-. Prev: Council Pres. Pro Tem; City
   Charter Cmsn. 1972; Zoning Ordinance Cmsn. 1973;
   Flood Plain Ordinance Com. 1976. Org: Horizons
   for the Handicapped. Educ: Oberlin Coll. 1942
   BA. Occ: Reporter/Photographer/Columnist. B:
   10/6/20. Add: Box 192, Steamboat Spgs. 80477
   (303)879-2060.

Sterling. MARCIA R. LUCE (D)
      1973-. Bds: Police Pension Bd.; Fire Pension
   Bd.; Council of Govts. Party: State Del. 1970-76;
   Committeewoman 1970; State Equal Rights Cmsn.
   1972. Org: NEA; AAUW; ACLU. Educ: Northeastern
   Jr. Coll. 1964 AA; Adams State Coll. 1967 BA;
   1970 MA. Occ: Educator. B: 7/25/44. Add: 320
   W. Main St., Sterling 80751 (303)522-2757.

Stratton. VIRGINIA HUBBARD
      P.O. Box 64, Stratton 80836.

Sugar City. PAULINE EICHMAN (D)
      1972-. Bds: Finance Com.; Street & Alley; Ch.,
   Health. Occ: Cook. B: 4/28/18. Add: 424 Iowa,

Sugar City 81076.

Superior. GLORIA ARMSTRONG
      206 W. Coal Creek Dr., Superior Rte.,
   Louisville 80027.

Telluride. JANE CONLIN
         BARBARA LANE
      135 W. Columbia Ave., P.O. Box 902, Telluride
   81435.

Thorton. MARGARET W. CARPENTER (R)
      1973-. Mayor Pro Tem. Bds: Colo. Municipal
   League - Policy Com.; Colo. Municipal League -
   Police & Fire Pension. Party: Precinct Committee-
   woman 1961-65. Org: Colo. Assoc. of School
   Exec's.; Nat'l. Reading Assoc.; Assoc. of
   Curriculum & Devt. Educ: Ottawa U. 1952 BA;
   Colo. State Coll. 1962 MA; U of Northern Colo.
   1972 EdD. Occ: Education Administrator. B:
   11/24/30. Add: 2560 Eppinger Blvd., Thorton
   80229 (303)289-5801.

Timnath. NORMA JOAN WARREN (I)
      1976-. Bds: Street Com. Occ: Landscape Dept.
   Worker. B: 3/3/42. Add: P.O. 145, Timnath
   80547.

Timnath. JEAN C. WEITZ (D)
      1976-. Bds: Water Com. Party: Precinct Del.
   Org: Colo. Assoc. Hospital Volunteer Dir's.;
   LWV. Educ: U. of Wyo. 1950 BA. Occ: Dir.,
   Hospital Volunteer Services. B: 6/25/25. Add:
   5016 5th Ave., Timnath 80547.

Vilas. WILMA HANNAFIOUS
      Main St., P.O. Box 637, Vilas 81087.

Vona. KATHRYN BURD
      Box 126, Vona 80861.

Walden. BETTY J. FOLLETT
         JOANNE K. SHAW
      P.O. Box 337, Walden 80480.

Walsenburg. BETTY RIDGE
      122 E. 6th, Walsenburg 81089.

Ward. DARA SEBASTIAN
      Columbia St., P.O. Box 149, Ward 80481.

Wellington. JEANNETTE BIRCH THIMMIG (R)
      1973-. Bds: Housing Authority; Planning &
   Zoning Bd. Party: State Del. 1974; State Alt.
   1972; Election Judge 1954-74. Prev: Wellington
   Area Devt. Corp. Educ: Colo. State Coll. 1937
   BS. B: 6/7/12. Add: 4006 Cleveland Ave.,
   P.O. Box 147, Wellington 80549.

Westcliffe. WILLA BUZZI (R)
      1972-. Mayor Pro Tem. B: 10/17/22. Add:
   201 Edwards, Westcliffe 81252 (303)783-2418.

Wheat Ridge. MARY JO CAVARRA (R) **
      1973-. Bds: Municipal League; Civil Service
   Cmsn. Org: Chamber of Commerce; Rep. Woman's
   Club. B: 9/2/37. Add: 3805 Robb St., Wheat
   Ridge 80033 (303)421-8480.

Wheat Ridge. LOUISE F. TURNER
7470 W. 38Ave., Box 610, Wheat Ridge 80033.

Wiggins. EVELYN HOPE
JOSEPHINE ROBERTS
GAYLE WEHRER
P.O. Box 287, Wiggins 80654.

Wray. BERTHA K. UTZ (R) **
1966-. Bds: Election Judge. Occ: Director of
Nurses. B: 6/26/01 Add: 302 Douglas, Wray
80758 (303)332-4486.

Judges

AUREL M. KELLY
Associate Justice, Court of Appeals. Add:
608 S.S.S. Bldg., Denver.

State Boards and Commissions

A complete list of state boards and commissions
and of their membership, was not available for
inclusion.

Connecticut

State Executive and Cabinet

KAY V. BERGIN
Deputy Banking Commissioner. 1975-. Bds:
Governor's Com. on Human Rights & Opportunities;
Teacher's Retirement Bd. Prev: Exec. Dir.
Permanent Cmsn. on Status of Women 1973-75. Org:
AAUW; Housing Services; Conn. Women Educ. & Legal
Fund; NOW. Educ: Central Conn. State Coll. 1943
BS; Wesleyan U. 1957 MLS. B: 11/29/21. Add:
25 Steuben St., Waterbury 06708 (203)566-7611.

SANDRA BILOON
Personnel Commissioner. 1976-. Prev:
Personnel Administrator of Ct. Labor Dept. 1958-
75; Asst. Personnel Administrator 1957-58; U.S.
Dept. of Labor Manpower Administration; U.S. Civil
Service Cmsn. Org: Internat. Personnel Management
Assoc.; Nat. Civil Service League. Educ:
Radcliffe Coll. 1951 BA; Trinity Coll. 1971
B: 10/12/30. Add: 306 S. Main St., W. Hartford
16107.

JEANNETTE DILK (I)
Deputy Commissioner of Children & Youth
Services. 1975-. Bds: Ch., Deinstitution-
alization of Status Offenders; Adoption Review
Bd.; Child Day Care Council. Org: NASW; Amer.
Public Health Assoc.; Amer. Public Welfare Assoc.
Educ: Bowling Green State U. 1950 BA; U. of
Mich. 1959 MSW. B: 5/16/28. Add: 16 Edmund Pl.,
W. Hartford 06119 (203)236-3832.

ELLA T. GRASSO (D) *
Governor. 1974-. Bds: Cmsn. on the Status
of Women. Party: Nat. Del. 1960, '64, '68;
Town Com. 1948-74; State Platform Com. 1952-68;
Nat. Platform Com. 1960-68. Prev: State Rep.
1953-57; Sec. of State 1959-71; U.S. Rep. 1971-
74. Org: State Children's Cystic Fibrosis Assoc;
State Institute for the Blind. Educ: Mt. Holyoke
Coll. 1940 BA; 1942 MA. B: 5/10/19. Add:
13 Olive, Windsor Locks 06096.

MARILYN J. GRAVINK (I)
Deputy Commissioner of Mental Retardation.
1976-. Bds: Council on Devt. Disabilities;
Juvenile Justice & Delinquency Prevention Adv.
Council. Org: Amer. Assoc. on Mental Deficiency.
Educ: Houghton Coll. 1952 BA; Boston U. 1953
MEd. B: 4/4/31. Add: 17 Clemens Ct., Rock Hl.
06067 (203)566-4137.

MARY M. HESLIN (D)
Commissioner of Consumer Protection. 1975-.
Bds: Ch., Metric Coord. Com.; Standardization
Com.; Human Richts & Opportunities Cmsn. Party:
State Del. 1973-76; State Alt. 1970-72; Precinct
Leader 1960-70; Town Committeewoman 1968-75.
Prev: City Councilwoman 1970-75; Deputy Mayor
1972-75; Environmental Com.-Nat. League of Cities
1973-75; Ch., Planning & Zoning Com. 1973-75.
Org: BPW; Civic Assoc.; Dem. Women's Club. Educ:
B: 8/5/29. Add: 235 Kenyon St., Hartford 06105
(203)566-4999.

DOROTHY KANE MC CAFFERY (D) *
Deputy Commissioner of Agriculture. Party:
Ch., Town Dem. Committee 1955-65; Dist. Committee
woman 1958-70; Nat. Del. 1956, 1960. Prev:
Cmsnr., Conn. State Bd. of Labor Relations;
Planning Cmsn. 1955-59; Gov's. Clean Water Task
Force 1965-66. Org: LWV; Dem. Women's Club. B:
8/1/16. Add: Kirby Corner, Washington 06793.

CAROLYNE PERRY
Deputy Commissioner of Social Services. Add:
State Capitol, Hartford 06115.

GLORIA SCHAFFER (D)
Secretary of State. 1970-. Bds: Com. on
Appropriations, Corrections & Human Rights;
Public Health & Safety; Ch., Com. on Public
Welfare & Humane Institutions. Party: Del., Nat.
Conv. 1960-72; Co-Ch., Platform Com.-Dem. Nat.
Conv. 1976. Prev: State Council on Human Service
1974-76; State Senator 1958. Org: Assoc. for
Adv. of School Administration. B: 10/3/30.
Add: State Capitol, Hartford (203)566-4135.

MARIN J. SHEALY (D)
Deputy Insurance Commissioner. 1977-. Bds: Cmsn. on Hospitals & Health Care; Teacher's Retirement Bd. Party: State Del. 1974. Prev: Mayor 1973-77; Gov's. Health Systems Area Review Team 1976; Gov's. Housing Assistance Group 1973-74; Ch., Council of Govts. 1973-75; Exec. Com. Council of Small Towns 1974-77; Ch., Cmsn. on Economic Devt. & Environmental Protection 1976-77. Org: LWV. Educ: Barnard Coll. 1952 BS. Occ: Gift Shop Owner. B: 11/12/28. Add: 14 Green Cir., Woodbury 06798 (203)566-2533.

State Legislature

State Senate

AUDREY PHILLIPS BECK (D)
1975-. Bds: Ch., Joint Finance Com.; V-Ch., Joint Govt. Administration & Public Policy Com. of Legislative; Joint Educ. Com. of Legislative. Party: State Del. 1969-77; Nat. Del. 1975. Prev: Bd. of Finance 1965-71; Town Govt. Study Com. 1967-68; Public Works Task Force 1976-77; Cmsn. on Housing Within An Optimum Environment 1970-71. Org: Amer. Society of Planning Officers; AAUW; BPW; Caucus of Dems.; LWV; NOWL; WPC; Cnty. Dem. Assoc.; Fed. of Dem. Women. Educ: U. of Conn. 1953 BA; U. of Conn. 1955 MA. B: 8/6/31. Add: 100 Dunham Pond Rd., Storrs 06268 (203)566-5722.

BETTY HUDSON (D)
1975-. Dist: 33. Bds: Ch., Human Services Com.; Ch., Human Rights & Opportunities Com.; Appropriations Com. Party: State Del. 1974; Dem. Town Com. 1970. Prev: Selectwoman 1972-75. Org: OWL; Nat. Conf. of State Legislators; LWV; NOW; WPC; Madison Assoc. Dem. Women. B: 3/5/31. Add: 155 Bishop Ln., Madison 06443 (203)566-4803.

NANCY LEE JOHNSON (R)
1976-. Bds: Appropriations Com.; Govt. Administration & Policy Com.; Cmsn. on the Status of Women. Prev: Charter Revision Cmsn. 1976. Org: Corrections Adv. Com.; Rep. Town Com. Educ: Radcliffe Coll. 1957 BA. B: 1/5/35. Add: 141 S. Mountain Dr., New Britain 06052 (203)566-3454.

MARY AGNES MARTIN (D) *
1975-. Dist: 18. Prev: Town Meeting Rep. 1964-68; Selectwoman 1969-71; Town Council 1973-74; State Rep. 1971-73. Org: Fed. of Dem. Women. B: 7/18/25. Add: 34 Pegasus Dr., Groton 06340.

BARBARA D. REIMERS (R)
1976-. Dist: 12. Bds: Educ. Com.; Labor Com.; Human Services Com. Party: Town Committeewoman. Prev: Bd. of Educ. 1957-75. Org: Amer. Arbitration Assoc.; LWV; Rep. Party. Educ: Vassar 1939 BA; Lasalle Extension U. 1968 LLB. B: 3/20/19. Add: 258 Pine Orchard Rd., Branford 06405 (203)566-5406.

State House

DOROTHY D. BARNES (R)
1976-. Dist: 21. Bds: General Law Com.; Govt. Administration & Policy Com.; Cmsn. on the Arts. Prev: Secretary, Planning & Zoning Cmsn. 1973-77. Educ: Smith Coll. 1954 BA. B: 10/11/32. Add:

50 High St., Farmington 06032.

JULIE D. BELAGA (R)
1976-. Dist: 136. Bds: Environment Com.; State & Urban Devl. Com.; Public Health & Safety Com. Party: State Del. 1976; State Alt. 1976. Prev: Town Meeting Repr. 1975-76; Coastal Area Management Adv. Com. 1975-76; Ch., Planning & Zoning Adv. Cmsn. 1972-75. Org: LWV; AAUW; Rep. Women's Club; 4th Congressional Rep. Women. Educ: Syracuse U. 1951 BS. B: 7/12/30. Add: 9 Berndale Dr., Westport 06880 (203)566-3492.

ROSALIND BERMAN
80 Barnett St., New Haven 06515.

TERESALEE BERTINUSON (D)
1974-. Dist: 57. Bds: Educ. Cmsn. of the States; State Capitol Preservation & Restoration Cmsn.; Environment Leg. Com. Party: State Del. 1972, '74, '76; State Alt. 1970; Dem. Town Com. 1958. Prev: Bd. of Educ. 1961-69; Conservation Cmsn. 1972-76. Org: WPC; OWL; Community Scholarship Assoc. Educ: Emmanuel Coll. 1943 BA; U. of Denver 1951 MA. B: 6/22/23. Add: 227 Melrose Rd., Melrose 06049 (203)566-4235.

VIRGINIA M. CONNOLLY (R)
1969-. Dist: 16. Bds: Public Health & Safety. Party: State Del. 1970, '74; Nat. Alt. 1976. Prev: Secretary-Housing Authority 1965-70; Ch., Cmsn. on Aging 1971-. Org: Rep. Town Com.; Rep. Women's Club. Educ: Hartford Hospital School of Nursing 1931 RN; St. Joseph Coll. 1950 BS. B: 6/25/14. Add: 91 Old Farms Rd., W. Simsbury 06092.

JACQUELYN C. DURRELL (I)
1976-. Dist: 134. Bds: Educ. Com.; Environment Com.; Banks Com. Party: State Del. 1969-75; V-Ch., Town Com. 1969-73; Ch., Bd. of Educ. 1974-77. Prev: Ch., Bd. of Educ. 1972-77; Bd. of Recreation 1973-75; Town Com. 1966-77. Educ: U. of Minn. 1948 ABA. B: 8/2/27. Add: 223 Jennie Ln., Fairfield 06430.

M. ADELA EADS (R)
1976-. Dist: 64. Bds: Educ.; Public Health & Safety. Party: State Del. 1970; State Alt. 1974. Prev: State Bd. of Educ. 1972-76. Org: Nursing Assoc. Chamber of Commerce; Elderly Housing Repr. to Town Com. B: 3/2/20. Add: RR 1, Box 190, Kent 06757 (203)800-842-1423.

LINDA N. EMMONS (R)
1976-. Bds: Finance Com.; Environment Com. Party: State Alt. 1976, '74; Rep. Town Com. 1970-77. Org: LWV. Educ: Conn. Coll. 1972 BA; U. of New Haven 1976 CPA. Occ: Accountant. Add: State Capital, Capital Ave., Hartford 06443.

DOROTHY FAULISE (D) *
1974-. Dist: 45. Prev: School Bd. 1970-present. Org: Dem. Women's Club; Grange. B: 5/12/29. Add: RFD 3, Norwich 06360.

DOROTHY C. GOODWIN (D)
1974-. Dist: 54. Bds: Ad Hoc Com. on the Arts; Leg. Repr. on New England Bd. of Higher Educ. Party: State Del.; State Alt.; Nat. Alt. 1974; Dem. Town Com. Prev: Bd. of Tax Review; Town Councilwoman; Org: Nature Conservancy; LWV; Common Cause; AAUP. Educ: Smith 1937 BA. U. of Conn. 1957 PhD. B: 9/2/14. Add: 447 Browns Rd., Storrs 06268 (203)566-4239.

ELOISE GREEN (R) **
1961-. Dist: 69. Bds: Ch., Elections Com.; Finance Com. Add: Box 1, Southbury 06488

ASTRID T. HANZALEK (R)
1970-. Dist: 61. Bds: Ch., Ethics Com.; Judiciary Com.; Program Review & Investigations Com. Party: State Del. 1976, '72, '70; State Alt. 1964-74; Co-Ch., State Platform Com. 1974; Ch., Platform Com. 1976; Asst. Majority Leader 1973-74; Asst. Minority Leader 1977-78. Org: Nat. Conf. of State Legislators; Leg. Ch., State Fed. of Women's Clubs; Community Council; Citizens Adv. Com.; Land Conservation Trust; Energy Task Force; Rep. Policy Com. Educ: U. of Pa. 1949 BS. B: 1/6/28. Add: 155 S. Main St., Suffield 06078 (203)566-5175.

PATRICIA T. HENDEL (D)
1975-. Dist: 40. Bds: Ch., Govt. Administration Policy. Party: State Del. 1974-75; Dist. Leader 1974-77. Prev: Charter Cmsn. 1973-74. Org: Conn. Assoc. for Continuing Educ.; LWV; BPW; Historical Society; WPC; NOW. Educ: Barnard Coll. 1953 BA; Conn. Coll. 1968 MA. Occ: Coll. Administrator. B: 1/16/32. Add: 127 Pky. S., New London 06370 (203)566-4553.

JOAN R. KEMLER (D)
1975-. Dist: 18. Bds: Ch., Program Review Com., Appropriations Com.; Human Services. Party: Secretary, Dist. Com. Prev: State Revenue Task Force Cmsn. 1969-71; State Cmsn. on Human Services 1972-73. Org: LWV; Greater Hartford Community Council; Dem. Women; NOWL. Educ: Conn. Coll. 1947 BA; Trinity Coll. 1972 MA. B: 3/28/26. Add: 65 Worwood Rd., W. Hartford 06117 (203)566-4894.

PHYLLIS KIPP (D) **
1973-. Dist: 41. Bds: Human Rights & Opportunities Com.; Insurance & Real Estate Com.; Educ. Com. Add: 58 Nantucket Dr., Mystic 06355.

ELIZABETH M. LEONARD (R)
520 North Salem Road, Ridgefield 06877.

DOROTHY S. MC CLUSKEY (D)
1974-. Dist: 86. Bds: Environment; Regulated Activities & Energy; Govt. Administration & Policy Prev: Conservation Cmsn. 1966-70; Planning & Zoning Cmsn. 1970-74. Org: Amer. Society of Planning Officials; NOWL; LWV; The Nature Conservancy; Dem. Women's Club; Sierra Club. Educ: Wheaton Coll. 1949 BA; Yale U. 1969 MFS. B: 6/28/28. Add: 822 Forest Rd., Northford 06472.

ALICE V. MEYER (R)
1976-. Dist: 135. Bds: Educ.; Govt. Administration & Policy. Party: State Del. 1975; Town V-Ch. 1974. Prev: Conn. Educ. Council 1973-76; Energy Conservation Cmsn. 1974-; Conn. Humanities

Council 1973-76. Org: OWL; AAUW; LWV; Rep. Women's Club. Educ: Barnard Coll. 1941 BA; Columbia U. 1942 MA. B: 3/15/22. Add: 18 Lantern Hl. Rd., Easton 06612.

DOROTHY R. MILLER (R)
23 Cook Drive, Bolton 06040.

MARGARET E. MORTON (D) **
1973-. Dist: 129. Occ: Funeral Home Director. Add: 25 Currier St., Bridgeport 06607.

GEIL ORCUTT (D)
1974-. Bds: Educ.; Public Health & Safety. Org: LWV; WPC. Educ: U. of Mich. 1937 BS; Chicago Theological Seminary 1939 MA. B: 11/3/16. Add: 44 Highland St., New Haven 06511 (203)556-3958.

CLARICE OSIECKI (R)
1972-. Dist: 108. Bds: Ch., Regulations Review Com.; Environment Com.; Judiciary Com. Party: State Del. 1970-76; Ward Ch. 1970-73. Org: Conn. Legal Secretaries; BPW; OWL. Occ: Legal Secretary. B: 10/16/34. Add: 9 Terra Glen Rd., Danbury 06810.

DOROTHY K. OSLER (I)
1973-. Dist: 150. Party: State Del. 1974, '76. Prev: Repr., Town Meeting 1969-77. Org: OWL; LWV; AAUW. Educ: Miami U. of Oh. 1945 BS. B: 8/19/23. Add: 138 Lockwood Rd., Riverside 06878 (800)842-1423.

ANTONINA B. PARKER (R)
1976-. Dist: 31. Bds: Judiciary Com.; Public Health & Safety Com. Party: State Del. 1965. '69 '73; Party Ch. 1976-77; Rep. Recruitment Ch. 1967 76. Prev: Governor's Council on Voluntary Action 1972-76; Bd. of Finance 1971-73; Town Councilwoman 1967-71; Charter Revision Com. 1965-67; Deputy Registrar of Voters 1965-66. Org: Rep. Women's Club; OWL. B: 2/4/21. Add: 187 Sunset Dr., Glastonbury 06033 (203)566-3492.

CATHERINE M. PARKER (D)
1976-. Dist: 125. Bds: Judiciary Com.; Insurance & Real Estate; Human Services. Party: State Del. 1976. Prev: Alderwoman 1971-76. Org: Fed. Dem. Women. Occ: Secretary. B: 7/27/21. Add: 373 Iranistan Ave., Bridgeport 06604.

JANET POLINSKY (D)
1976-. Bds: Ch., Sub-Committee-Natural Resources Appropriations Cmsn.; Ch., Sub-Committee-Planning & Zoning. Party: State Del. 1976-77; Town Committeewoman 1976. Prev: Ch., Planning & Zoning 1973-76; Town Meeting Repr. 1969-71; Charter Com. 1969-70. Org: LWV. Educ: U. of Conn. 1954 BA. B: 12/6/30. Add: 19 E. Neck Rd., Waterford 06385 (203)566-7636.

NATALIE RAPOPORT (D) *
1973-. Dist: 73. Bds: Com. on Aging; Finance Com.; Election Com.; Educ. Com. Party: State Del. 1968, '70, '72; Nat. Del. 1972. Org: Nat. Womens League; Amer. Cancer Society; Planned Parenthood; Dem. Women's Club; Fed. of Dem. B: 4/22/27. Add: 273 Columbia Blvd., Waterbury 06710.

MORAG L. VANCE
    53 Meadow Road, Trumbull 06611.

ELINOR F. WILBER (R) **
    1973-. Dist: 133. Bds: Public Safety &
Health Com.; State Urban Dev. Com.; Transportation
Com. Add: 10 Lalley Blvd., Fairfield 06430.

JOYCE A.WOJTAS (D)
    7 North St., Windsor Locks 06096.

ELIZABETH A. WOODS (R)
    13 Woodruff Ct., P.O. BOx 996, Litchfield
06579.

MURIEL YACAVONE (D)
    1970-. Dist: 9. Bds: Joint Ethics Com.
Party: State Del. 1972; Nat. Del. 1976. Prev:
Health Bd. 1961-63; Economic Opportunity Cmsn.
1963-65; Community Council on Youth 1964-66; Com.
on Drug Abuse 1968-71; State Drug Adv. Council.
Org: LWV; Caucus of Conn. Dem's.; WPC; Fed. of
Dem. Women. Occ: Clerk-Receptionist Supervisor.
B: 5/26/20. Add: 34 Forest St., E. Hartford
06118 (203)566-2932.

Township

Ashford. JOAN E. BOWLEY (R)
    1975-. Party: Treasurer, Town Com. 1975-77.
Prev: Zoning Bd. of Appeals 1973-75; Town
Treasurer 1972-73. Org: Rep. Com. Occ: Secretary
B: 4/20/35. Add: 57 Westford Rd., Ashford,
Stafford Spgs., 06076 (203)429-2750.

Avon. BEATRICE K. MURDOCK (R)
    1975-. Bds: Housing Sub-Com. Org: Capital
Region Council of Govts.; Bd. of Realtors; Assoc.
for Retarded & Handicapped; Rep. Women's Club.
Educ: Mt. Holyoke Coll. 1954 BA. Occ: Real
Estate Saleswoman. B: 10/14/32. Add: 563 W.
Avon Rd., Avon 06001 (203)677-2634.

Bethany. MIRIAM C. NIEDERMAN (D)
    1975-. Party: Town Committeewoman 1972-78;
State Del. 1972. Org: LWV. Educ: Smith Coll.
1948 BA. B: 6/30/26. Add: 429 Sperry Rd.,
Bethany 06525.

Bethlehem. DORIS HORN NICHOLLS
    Main St., Rt. 1, Box 106, Bethlehem 06751.

Bloomfield. MARY Z. HILL
            JANET D. DANIELS
    Town Hall, 800 Bloomfield Ave., Bloomfield
06002.

Cheshire. JUDITH R. FISHMAN (R) **
    1973-. Bds: Youth Services Task Force; Bicen-
tennial; Historic Dist. Study; Cable TV Advisory
Group. Party: Congressional Liaison 1975-; Town
Com. 1960-75. Prev: Charter Revision Cmsn. 1969-
70 & 1972-73. Org: Teacher's Organization;
Women's Rep. Club. Educ: Southern Conn. State
Coll. 1953 BS; Southern Conn. State Coll. 1970 MS.
Occ: Teacher. B: 5/15/31. Add: 15 Williamsburg
Dr., Cheshire 96410.

Cheshire. SELINA H. MC ARDLE
    Town Hall, 84 S. Main St., Cheshire 06410.

Cornwall. PATSY P. VAN DOREN
    Town Hall, Pine St., Cornwall 06753.

Cromwell. LUCY T. BERGER
    5 West St., Cromwell 06416.

Darien. CAROLYN O. BROTHERTON (D)
    1973-. Bds: Bd. of Dir's., Drug Liberation
Program. Party: State Del. 1974, '76; Town Com.
1977. Prev: Repr. Town Meeting 1965-69. Org:
LWV; Dem. Town Com. Educ: Barnard Coll. 1950
BA; U. of Ill. 1954 MA. Occ: History Teacher.
B: 8/22/29. Add: 73 Five Mile Rvr. Rd., Darien
06820 (203)655-8927.

Durham. BETTY C. WAKEMAN
    Town Hall, Town House Rd., P.O. Box 246,
Durham 06422.

East Granby. MARITA D. MC DONOUGH
               CAROLYN B. PHILLIPS
    Town Hall, Center St., E. Granby 06026.

East Hampton. MARY ANN BARTON (R)
    1975-. Bds: Park & Recreation Cmsn.; Public
Health Nursing Assoc. Party: State Alt. 1976.
Org: NASW; Community Health Services; LWV;
Women's Rep. Club; School Health Adv. Com.;
Youth Services Adv. Bd. Educ: U. of Hartford
BA; U. of Conn. MSW. Occ: Social Worker. B:
6/26/30. Add: Day Pt. Rd., E. Hampton 06424
(203)267-4468.

East Hartford. ESTHER B. CLARKE (R)
    1973-. Bds: Emergency Medical Service Com.;
Ordinance Com.; Internal Audit. Party: State
Del. 1974, '76; Committeewoman 1973-77; Town Com.
Secretary 1974-75. Prev: Conn. Adv. Com. 1974-77
Org: Rep. Women's Fed. Occ: Office Mgr./Book-
keeper. B: 1/29/37. Add: 42 Beacon Hl. Rd.,
E. Hartford 06108 (203)289-2781.

East Haven. FRANCES GRIEGO
    250 Main St., E. Haven 06512.

East Haven. PEARL A. MATTIE (R) **
    1969-. Bds: Administrative. Party: Com.
1969-75. Org: Nurse's Assoc. Educ: Bridgeport
Hospital School of Nursing 1948 RN. Occ: Head
Nurse. B: 3/14/26. Add: 18 Summit Ave., East
Haven 06512 (203)469-5311.

East Haven. MARILYN M. VITALE (D)
    1975-. Bds: Ch., Educ., Library, School Bldg.;
Public Health & Safety; Public Service-Park &
Recreation. Party: State Del. 1976; Town
Treasurer 1974. Org: LWV; Woman's Dem. Club.
Occ: Bookkeeper. B: 9/8/35. Add: 48 Forest St.,
E. Haven 06512 (203)469-5311.

Ellington. JANET S. BATT
    55 Main St., P.O. Box 236, Ellington 06029.

Enfield. JAYNE C. AYOTTE
    820 Enfield St., Enfield 06082.

Essex. EVELYN R. LIBBY (R)
    1973-. Bds: Zoning Cmsn.; Zoning Bd. of
Appeals; Renovation Com. Party: State Del.; Ch.
& Sec. of Rep. Town Com. Prev: Registrar of
Voters. Occ: Bookkeeper. B: 10/19/16.

Add: 4 Kings La., Essex. 06426 (203)767-8201.

Farmington. ABIGAIL C. MAHANNAH
Town Hall, 1 Monteith Dr., Farmington 06032.

Glastonbury. MARCIA W. ERLEY
JANET R. MAHER
2108 Main St., Glastonbury 06033.

Hamden. VIRGINIA P. FERGUSON (R)
1974-. Bds: Ch., Human Services Com.; Finance
& Administrative Com.; Educ. Com. Party: Rep.
Town Com. 1966-74. Educ: Larson Jr. Coll. 1938
AS. Occ: Partner in Theater Company. B: 1/29/19.
Add: 178 Haverford St., Hamden 06517 (203)
288-5641.

Hampton. JANE W. GILLARD
Town Office Bldg., Old Rt. 6, P.O. Box 143,
Hampton 06247.

Harwinton. JANET W. BURRITT
Town Office, Hutchings Rd., Harwinton 06790.

Hebron. CYNTHIA G. WILSON
Town Office Bldg., Rt. 85, P.O. Box 156,
Hebron 06248.

Kent. DOROTHY OSBORNE
Town Hall, RFD Box M5, S. Main, Kent 06757.

Ledyard. JANET SITTY (D)
1973-. Bds: Finance; Public Works; Library
Cmsn.; Water & Sewer Cmsn. Party: State Del.
1974; Town Committeewoman 1976-present. Prev:
Zoning Cmsn. 1969-71; Planning Cmsn. 1972-73.
Org: LWV; Dem. Town Com.; Caucus of Conn. Dems.;
PTO; Historical Soc. Educ: Central Conn. Coll.
1964 BS; U. of Conn. 1970 MA. B: 2/19/42. Add:
21 Oakridge Dr., Gales Ferry 06335.

Madison. ADELAIDE P. AMORE (D)
1974-. Bds: Planning & Zoning Cmsn.; Library
Bd. Party: State Del. 1976. Prev: Bd. of Educ.
1971-74. Org: AAUP; LWV; Dem. Women's Club; PTO.
Educ: Southern Conn. State Coll. 1959 BS; 1963 MA.
Occ: Asst. Prof. of English. B: 4/4/38. Add:
406 Warpas Rd., Madison 06443.

Manchester. VIVIAN FIRATO FERGUSON (R)
1971-. Bds: Health Systems Agency. Party:
State Del. 1972, '74, '76; State Alt. 1970; V-Pres
Congressional Women 1975-77. Org: Rep. Women's
Club; Women's Nat. Rep. Club. Occ: Radio Personality. B: 5/4/25. Add: 78 Forest St., Manchester
06040 (203)649-5281.

Manchester. PHYLLIS V. JACKSTON
IRENE R. PISCH
MILDRED M. SCHALLER
Town Hall, 41 Center St., Manchester 06040.

Mansfield. SHEILA B. AMDUR (D)
1973-. Bds: Ch., Personnel Com. Party: Town
Committeewoman 1972-74. Prev: Housing Com. 1971-
73. Org: NASW; Conn. Health Assoc.; LWV; Conn.
Human Resources Assoc.; Regional Com. Council;
Dem. Women's Club; PTO. Educ: U. of Pittsburgh
1963 BA; U. of Conn. 1967 MSW. Occ: Social Worker
B: 1/2/42. Add: 28 Beech Mt. Cir., RFD #3,
Willimantic 06226.

Mansfield. BARBARA M. JORDAN
954 Storrs Rd., Storrs 06268.

Monroe. ELIZABETH M.N. BOVARD
Town Hall, 11 Fan Hill Rd., Monroe 06468.

Monroe. VIVIAN N. CAPOCCITTI (D) **
1973-. Bds: Monroe Builds Communications;
Planning & Zoning; Bd. of Educ.; Finance Bd.
Party: Town Com. 1969-76; Campaign Ch. 1975.
Org: LWV; Dem. Club; PTA. B: 5/31/31. Add:
88 Swendsen Dr., Monroe 06468 (203)261-3651.

Monroe. KAYE F. FARKAS
Town Hall, 11 Fan Hill Rd., Monroe 06468.

Monroe. EDITH M. SERKE (R)
1975-. Party: State Alt. 1974. Prev:
Planning & Zoning Cmsn. 1965-68; Charter Revision
Cmsn. 1973-74; Regional Agency 1970-73. Org:
LWV; Rep. Women's Club. Educ: U. of Bridgeport
1951 AA; 1974 BA. Occ: Assoc. Dir. of SW Conn.
Agency on Aging. B: 12/6/30. Add: 17 Sunrise
Terr., Monroe 06491 (203)261-3651.

Naugatuck. ANITA C. BOWLEY
Town Hall, 229 Church St., Naugatuck 06770.

Naugatuck. MARJORIE ANN CARLSON (D)
Bds: Park Bd.; Ch., Elderly Cmsn.; Day Care.
Party: Dem. Town Com. Org: Family Service; PTA.
B: 8/23/27. Add: 23 Myrtle Ave., Naugatuck
06770.

Naugatuck. BARBARA ANN ROSSI
Town Hall, 229 Church St., Naugatuck 06770.

New Canaan. JENNIFER W. DELAGE (R) **
1973-. Bds: Drug Liberation Program. Prev:
Council Member 1970-73. Org: Rep. Women's Club;
Audubon Society. Educ: U. of Conn. 1950 BA. B:
3/31/29. Add: 34 Adams La., New Canaan 06840
(203)966-1687.

New Canaan. ELIZABETH P. ERB (D) **
1970-. Bds: Municipal Services & Functions
Com.; Parks & Conservation Com. Org: Audubon
Society; LWV. B: 12/21/18. Add: 237 Greenley
Rd., Box 537, New Canaan 06840.

New Canaan. ERNA J. GREEN (D)
1975-. Bds: Educ. Com.; Municipal Services
Com.; Parks & Conservation Com. Party: State
Del. 1976. Org: LWV; NAACP. Educ: U. of Miami
1958 BBA; U. of Bridgeport 1971 MA. B: 5/14/36.
Add: 210 Main St., New Canaan 06840 (203)966-5211

New Canaan. PRISCILLA S. RUTHERFORD (D)
1973-. Bds: Municipal Services; Finance;
Ordinance. Party: State Del. 1974-77; V-Ch.,
Town Com. 1964-73. Org: LWV; Visiting Nurse
Assoc.; Dem. Women's Club. Educ: Jackson Coll.
1948 BA; Tufts U. 1949 MA. B: 3/22/27. Add:
62 Ludlowe Rd., New Canaan 06840 (203)966-5211.

Newington. SONIA A. SHIPMAN
131 Cedar St., Newington 06111.

New Milford. GERTRUDE K. BARYSH
AGNES L. KNOWLES
HHP Annex, Town Hall, Box 360, New Milford

North Branford. PHYLLIS NEWBERRY
Administration Bldg., Rt. 80, N. Branford
06471.

Orange. L. NATALIE SANDOMIRSKY
Town Hall, 617 Orange Ctr. Rd., Orange 06477.

Oxford. MARGARET R. COSTELLO (I)
1975-. Party: Town Com. V-Ch. 1974-76. Org:
Women's Rep. Club; PTA. B: 12/13/26. Add:
14 Hawkstone Ter., Oxford 06483 (203)888-2543.

Plainfield. MARY ESPINOLA (R) **
1972-. Bds: Eastern Conn. Rural Health Assoc.;
Dog Track Task Force. Party: Town Com. 1959-67;
Del., State Conv. 1972. Prev: Community Coll.
Trustee 1971-; School Bd. 1961-73; Governor's
House Task Force 1971-72. Org: Nat. Secretary
Assoc. Occ: Office Manager. B: 6/21/21. Add:
Pond St., Plainfield 06374 (203)774-8553.

Ridgefield. LILLIAN E. MOORHEAD (D)
1973-. Party: State Del. 1974. Org: NAACP;
LWV; Dem. Club; WPC; PTA. Occ: Office Manager.
B: 4/16/32. Add: 92 Ashbee Ln., Ridgefield
06877 (203)438-7301.

Rocky Hill. MIRIAM L. LIFSHITZ
MARIE C. MORGANTI
Town Hall, 699 Old Main St., Rock Hill 06067.

Simsbury. ILVA L. BERGMAN
Box 495, 760 Hopmeadow St., Simsbury 06070.

Simsbury. MARGARET M. DONOHUE (D) **
1972-. Bds: Library Bd.; Health & Welfare
Com. Party: Dem. Town Com. 1974. Org: LWV; PTA;
Visiting Nursing Assoc.; Trustee, Library. Educ:
Northeastern U. 1947 BA. B: 12/7/25. Add: 17
Firetown Rd., Simsbury 06070 (203)658-4455.

South Windsor. CECILE M. DECKER (D)
1975-. Bds: Ch., Public Health & Safety;
Planning & Zoning; Economic Development. Party:
State Del. 1974, '76; District V-Ch., 1974-76.
Prev: Bd. of Education 1968-75. Org: Bd. of
Realtors. Educ: Douglass Coll.1952 BA. Occ:
Realtor. B: 6/23/34. Add: 91 Berle Rd., S.
Windsor 06074 (203)644-2511.

Stratford. ROSEMARY W. HERMANN
CARMELLA M. VITALE
Town Hall, Rm. 101, 2725 Main St., Stratford
06497.

Tolland. CAROLE M. GORDON (D)
1975-. Bds: Ch., Police Protection Com.; Ch.,
Public Safety; Planning & Zoning Com. Prev:
Registrar of Voters 1974-75. Org: WPC. Occ:
Bookkeeper. B: 12/4/42. Add: 474 Mile Hi. Rd.,
Tolland 06084 (203)872-4320.

Trumbull. JOYCE FABIANO
MAXINE MURRAY
MRS. MORAG VANCE
JANE ZEHNDER
5866 Main St., Trumbull 06611.

Vernon. MARIE A. HERBST (D)
1975-. Bds: Ch., Open Space; Ch., Merit Bd.;
Budget Com. Party: State Del. 1967-77; State
Alt. 1967-77; Voter Registration Ch. 1967. Prev:
Bd. of Educ. 1967-73. Org: NEA; Dem. Town Com.
Educ: SUNY 1950 BA; Columbia Teachers Coll. 1952
MA. Occ: Teacher. B: 5/26/28. Add: 245 Brandy
Hill Rd., Vernon 06066 (203)872-8591.

Vernon. MARIAN J. NARKAWICZ
GAIL E. SLICER
Memorial Bldg., 14 Park Pl., P.O. Box 246,
Vernon 06066.

Wallingford. GLADYS BELCHER
IRIS PAPALE
LAURA VERNE
Municipal Bldg., 350 Center St., P.O. Box 427,
Wallingford 06492.

Waterford. PATRICIA M. SMITH
Hall of Records, 200 Boston Post Rd., Waterford 06385.

Watertown. EVELYN O. GRABOSKI
THERESA P. MITCHELL
KATHRYN SHELHART
BRENDA ZURAITIS
Town Hall, 37 Deforest St., Watertown 06795.

West Hartford. MARY S. GLYNN
RUTH P. KRONICK
BETTY H. PAVLAK
CATHERINE C. REYNOLDS
Town Hall, 28 S. Main St., West Hartford
06107.

Weston. SUSAN J. HUTCHINSON (R)
1975-. Bds: Land Acquisition Com.; Ch.,
Community Service Adv. Council. Party: State
Del. 1976; State Alt. 1974; Treasurer, Rep. Town
Com. Prev: Planning & Zoning Comsr. 1973-75.
Org: Conn. Conf, of Municipalities; LWV; Women's
Club; Young Women's Club; Women's Rep. Club; PTO.
Educ: Nasson Coll. 1963 BA; N.Y.U. 1968 MBA. B:
9/18/42. Add: 18 Cartbridge Rd., Weston 06883
(203)226-3341.

Weston. BARBARA WAGNER
56 Norfield Rd., Box 1007, Weston 06880.

Wethersfield. MARIAN H. CHRISTENSEN
JUDITH P. WHITEHEAD
505 Silas Deane Hwy., Wethersfield 06109.

Winchester. SUSAN L. MC CANN
Town Hall, 338 Main St., Winsted 06098.

Wolcott. ALICE G. MOSS
PATRICIA C. YURGAITIS
10 Kenea Ave., Wolcott 06716.

Woodbridge. AUDREY L. FETTER
Town Hall, 11 Meetinghouse Ln., Woodbridge
06525.

Mayors

Deep River. LORRAINE C. WALLACE (R)
     1971-. Bds: Police Chief; Tree Warden; Dir.
of Social Services. Party: State Del. 1966-72;
Presidential Elector 1976; V-Ch., Rep. Town Com.
1961-65; Ch., Rep. Town Com. 1965-71. Prev:
Public Health Nursing Bd. 1962-68; Planning Cmsn.
1964-66. Org: Soroptimist; Rep. Women's Club;
Historical Soc.; Amer. Cancer Soc. Occ: Practical
Nurse. B: 1/10/14. Add: Westbrook Rd., Deep
River 06417 (203)526-2309.

Groton. BETTY JEAN CHAPMAN (R)
     1975-. Prev: Councilwoman 1973-75. Org:
Public Health Nurses Inc.; Child & Family Agency.
Educ: Silvermine Art Coll. BA. B: 8/19/29. Add:
164 Shore Ave., Groton City 06340 (203)445-8591.

Madison. VERA DALLAS
     Town Hall, P.O. Box 605, Madison 06443.

Mansfield. AUDREY HAVICAN BARBARET (D)
     1972-. Bds: Ch., Reg. Municipal Officials
Assoc. Party: Town Committeewoman 1966-67. Prev:
Conservation Cmsn. 1964-68. Org: Day Care Center
Bd.; Historical Soc.; LWV; Dem. Women's Club.
B: 10/27/29. Add: 45 Farrell Rd., Storrs 06268.

Norwalk. JENNIE F. CAVE
     City Hall, N. Main St., S. Norwalk 06854.

Old Saybrook. BARBARA JOYCE MAYNARD (R) **
     1973-. Bds: Resource Recovery Authority;
Waste Disposal; Registrar 1958-73; Deputy
Registrar 1956-58. Org: Women's Club; Women's
Rep. Club. B: 2/8/27. Add: 174 Ingham Hill,
Old Saybrook.

Portland. MARIE T. LARSON
     Town Hall, 265 Main St., Portland 06480.

Salisbury. CHARLOTTE H. REID (D) **
     1973-. Bds: Bd. of Resources; Recovery
Authority. Party: Town Com. 1963-. Prev: Ch.,
School Bd. 1957-73. Educ: Barnard 1939 BA; U. of
Hartford 1963 MA. B: 6/8/18. Add: Elm St.,
Lakeville 06039 (203)435-9512.

Seymour. ANNA LO PRESTI (D)
     1973-. Bds: Bd. of Public Works; Cmsn. on
Aging; Safety. Party: State Del. 1974. Prev:
Library Bd.; Bd. of Health. Org: Woman's Club;
Dem. Women; PTA. Educ: Teachers Coll. 1941 BA;
MA. B: 12/22/07. Add: 852 S. Main, Seymour
06483 (203)888-2511.

South Windsor. SANDRA J. BENDER (D)
     1975-. Bds: Capital Reg. Council of Govts.;
Fire Dept. Bd. Party: State Del. 1976; Town
Committeewoman 1972-77. Prev: Public Health &
Safety Com. 1971-75; Solid Waste Disposal Dist.
1971-73; Capital Improvement Com. 1971-72;
Community Action Dev. Plan 1969-71. Org: LWV;
Dem. Women's Club; Community Service Council.
Occ: Commercial Banking Officer. B: 10/30/42.
Add: 96 Greenfield Dr., S. Windsor 06074.

Union. ANNA MAE PALLANCK (R)
     1974-. Party: State Del. 1952, '74; V-Ch.,
Town Com. 1975-77; Town Committeewoman 1967-77.
Prev: State Repr. 1952-57; Planning & Zoning
Cmsn. 1954. Org: Historical Society; Women's
Rep. Club. B: 12/5/22. Add: 755 Buckley Hwy.,
Union 06076 (203)684-3812.

West Hartford. ANNE P. STREETER (R)
     1975-. Bds: Regional Council of Govts.;
Hartford Process; Conn. Conf. of Municipalities.
Prev: Councilwoman 1973-77. B: 7/21/26. Add:
26 Claybar Dr., W. Hartford 06117 (203)236-3231.

Westport. JACQUELINE P. HENEAGE (D)
     1973-. Bds: Ch., Sewer Authority; Ch.,
Traffic Authority; Ch., Bd. of Electors. Party:
State Del. 1975; Nat. Alt. 1976. Prev: Zoning
Bd. of Appeals 1971-73. Org: Conn. Conf. of
Municipalities; Metropolitan Regional Council;
Internat. City Managers; LWV; Dem. Women; WPC;
Women's Club. Educ: U. of N.H. 1948 BS. B:
9/19/25. Add: 81 S. Compo Rd., Westport 06880
(203)227-0891.

Wethersfield. A. CYNTHIA KOSMAS MATTHEWS (D) **
     1973-. Bds: Senior Citizens Advisory;
Contracts & Land Acquisition; Ecological Com.;
Ambulance Com.; Emergency Medical Services
Council. Party: Voter Registration Ch. 1974-75.
Org: LWV; Dem. Women's Club. Educ: Barnard 1946
BA. B: 2/1/24. Add: 66 Collier Rd., Wethers-
field 06109 (203)529-8611.

Wilton. ROSE MARIE VERRILLI
     Town Hall, 238 Danbury Rd., Wilton 06897.

Winchester. YOLANDA M. BARRETT (D)
     1974-. Bds: Ch., Bd. of Finance; Regional
Planning Com. of Govts. Party: State Del. 1972,
'76; V-Ch., Town Com. 1971-. Prev: Bd. of Tax
Review 1971-72; Selectwoman 1972-73; Town
Bicentennial 1970-71. Org: Dem. Town Com. Occ:
Real Estate Broker. B: 1/1/31. Add: 65 Woodruff
Ave., Winsted 06098 (203)379-0684.

Woodstock. SHIRLEY E. RAPOSE
     Town Office Bldg., P.O. Box 123, Rt. 169,
Woodstock 06281.

Local Councils

Ansonia. EDITH BEHRLE
          MONICA P. LONARDO
          JEAN MC EVOY
     City Hall, 253 Main St., Ansonia 06401.

Bridgeport. RITA E. MILLER
     City Hall, Rm. 124, 45 Lyon Ter., Bridgeport
06604.

Bridgeport. IRMA N. PALKO (D)
     1975-. Bds: Community Devt.; Finance; Educ.
Org: League Dem. Women Voters; PTO. Educ: St.
Vincent's Hospital School of Nursing 1953 RN. B:
3/13/33. Add: 26 Davis Ave., Bridgeport 06605.

Bridgeport. YOLANDA M. RICCIO
     City Hall, Rm. 124, 45 Lyon Ter., Bridgeport
06604.

Bristol. PATTI D. EWEN (D)
1975-. Bds: Park Bd.; Com. on the Handicapped;
Day Care Cmsn. Party: State Alt. 1970; Town
Committeewoman 1972-77. Prev: Charter Revision
Com. 1971-72. Org: Dem. Woman's Club. Educ:
U. of Me. 1958 BA; Boston U. 1961 MSW. Occ:
School Social Worker. B: 10/21/35. Add: 41
Broadview St., Bristol 06010 (203)583-1811.

Bristol. LILLIAN E. FIOROT
111 North Main St., Bristol 06010.

Danbury. ELIZABETH CRUDGINTON
ANNE ERIQUEZ
ROSEMARY LAVELLE
City Hall, 155 Deer Hill Ave., Danbury 06810.

Danbury. SHEILA MILLMAN (D) **
1973-. Bds: Police Pension Com. Org: PTO;
LWV; Dem. Women's Club. Educ: Upsala 1973 BA.
Occ: Manager, Retail Store. B: 9/16/43. Add:
15 Redline Rd., Danbury 06810 (203)744-1760.

Danbury. ELLA MARIE ROUNTREE (D)
1973-. Party: State Del. Prev: Library Bd.
1970-73. Org: NEA; NAACP; Dem. Women's Club;
Black Dem. Club. Educ: Ft. Vly. State Coll. 1957
BS; Western Conn. State 1973 MA. Occ: Teacher.
B: 2/27/36. Add: 20 Harding Pl., Danbury 06810.

Derby. IDA GAROFALO
City Hall, 35 Fifth St., Derby 06418.

Groton. ANNE F. GREGORY
NADINE MAC KINNON
LOUISEANNETTE WRIGHT
Town Hall, 45 Fort Hill Rd., Groton 06340.

Hartford. JACQUELINE ANDERSON (R)
1975-. Bds: Planning & Devt.; Educ. & Human
Resources; Affirmative Action Com. Party: State
Del. 1975; State Alt. 1976; Town Committeewoman
1971. Org: APHA; Alliance of Black Soc. Workers;
Community Council; Conn. Hospital Assoc. Occ:
Dir. of Health Care. B: 7/13/35. Add: 101 Tower
Ave., Hartford 06120 (203)566-6710.

Hartford. BARBARA BAILEY KENNELLY (D)
1975-. Bds: Ch., Zoning Comsn.; Ch., Public
Safety & Zoning Com.; Capitol Reg. Council of
Govts. Party: State Del. 1973, '75, '77; Dem.
Town Com. 1971-75. Prev: Conn. Comsn. on Human
Services 1972-73; V-Ch., Comsn. on Aging 1971-75.
Educ: Trinity Coll. 1958 BA, MA. B: 7/10/36.
Add: 132 Cumberland St., Hartford 06106
(203)566-6710.

Hartford. MARGARET V. TEDONE
OLGA W. THOMPSON
550 Main St., Hartford 06103.

Jewett City. PAULA SCHENA
46 Slater Ave., Jewett City 06351.

Litchfield. ELIZABETH A. WOOD
Town Office Bldg., West St., Litchfield 06759,

Meriden. ELIZABETH A. GREENBACKER (D)
1975-. Bds: Ch., Finance & Claims Com.;
Economic Devt. Com. Party: State Del. 1974;
Town Committeewoman 1973-74. Org: BPW. Educ:
U. of Conn. BA. Occ: Accountant. B: 4/2/49.
Add: 806 Murdock Ave., Meriden 06450.

Middletown. CHRISTIE E. MC LEOD (R)
1975-. Bds: Bd. of Health; Planning & Zoning
Com.; Welfare Com. Party: Town Committeewoman
1975. Prev: State Bd. of Medical Examiners 1975-
Org: Conn. State Medical Society; AMA; AAUW;
Soroptimist. Educ: U. of Vt. 1931 BS; Coll. of
Medicine, U. of Vt. 1934 MD. B: 8/7/09. Add:
466 Maple Shade Rd., Middletown 06457.

Middletown. BARBARA MELLMAN WEISS (R)
Party: State Del. 1975; Town Committeewoman.
Org: Community Health Ctr. Educ: U. of Bridge-
port 1970 AS. B: 2/7/49. Add: 42 Oakcliff Rd.,
Middletown 06457.

Milford. LORRAINE M. CROCCO
City Hall, River St., Milford 06460.

Milford. PATRICIA H. SLAVIN (D) **
1973-. Bds: Ordinance Com.; Rules Com.;
Liaison Bd. of Educ.; Liaison Library Bldg. Com.;
Shredder Investigation Com.; Police Facility
Bldg. Com.; Devon Assoc. Steering Com. for CDA
Funds. Party: Town Com. 1966-. Prev: Bd. of
Health 1964-70. Org: WPC; Fed. of Dem. Women;
PTA. B: 2/17/37. Add: 62 Collingsdale Dr.,
Milford 06460 (203)878-1731.

New Haven. JUDITH M. BALDWIN (D)
1975-. Bds: Ch., Educ. Com.; Water Study Com.
Com. on Special Projects. Party: State Alt.
1976; Ward Committeewoman 1968-77. Org: Community Corp.; Neighborhood Assoc.; Long Range Planning Com. Educ: U. of Mass. 1962 BA. B: 3/5/39.
Add: 151 Livingston St., New Haven 06511.

New Haven. ROSALIND BERMAN
LOUISE DELAURO
Hall of Records, 200 Orange St., New Haven
06510.

New Haven. ANNE-MARIE FOLTZ (D)
1973-. Bds: V-Ch., Plan Cmsn.; Environmental
Adv. Council. Party: State Del. 1974. Org:
Amer. Public Health Assoc.; Common Cause; Caucus
of Conn. Dem's.; PTA. Educ: Cornell U. 1957 BA;
Yale U. 1971 MPH. Occ: Public Health Researcher.
B: 5/6/36. Add: 43 Lincoln St., New Haven
06510 (203)562-0151.

New Haven. CATHERINE ROBINSON
EUGENIA WADLEY
Hall of Records, 200 Orange St., New Haven
06510.

New London. MARGARET MARY CURTIN (D)
1975-. Bds: Ch., Public Safety; Public
Welfare; Administration. Party: State Del. 1968-
74; State Alt. 1964, '66; Nat. Del. 1972; Nat.
Alt. 1968; State Pres., Young Dem. 1969-71;
Young Dem. Nat. Committeewoman 1966-69; Secretary
Town Com. 1970-; Credentials Com. 1972. Prev:
Mayor's Com. on Crime & Juvenile Delinquency;
1969-71; Asst. to Governor 1975; Asst. to

Secretary of State 1971-74. Org: AFSCME; AFL-CIO; Dem. Fed. Women. Occ: Restaurant Owner. B: 9/28/34. Add: 144 Blydenburg Ave., New London 06320 (203)443-2861.

New London. EUGENIE B. KILLY
Municipal Bldg., 181 State St., New London 06320.

New London. RUBY TURNER MORRIS (D)
1962-. Bds: Ch., Public Works Com.; Regional Transit Dist. Party: State Del. 1976; Dem. Town Com. 1952-77. Prev: Mayor 1976. Org: LWV; Dem. Party. Educ: Vassar Coll. 1929 BA; Stanford U. 1930 MA; 1937 PhD. B: 4/28/08. Add: 56 Hawthorn Dr. N #6, New London 06378 (203)443-2861.

Newton. POLLY BRODY
ETHEL E. CONNOR
ANN KRASNICKAS
Edmond Town Hall, 45 Main St., Newton 06470.

Newton. MELISSA MEYER PILCHARD (D)
1975-. Dist: 1. Bds: Ch., Educ. Sub Com. Party: State Del. 1976; Committeewoman 1975-. Org: LWV; Jr. Women's Club. Educ: U. of Md. 1958 BA. Occ: Hostess. B: 4/3/36. Add: RR 1, Poorhouse Rd., Newton 06470.

Norwalk. NANCY H. LASKOS
MARIE L. MASCIA
City Hall, N. Main, Norwalk 06854.

Norwich. SUSAN E. ROBINSON
City Hall, Room 214, Norwich 06360.

Stamford. LINDA D. CLARK
AUDREY M. COSENTINI
Old Town Hall, 179 Atlantic St., P.O. Box 891, Stamford 06904.

Stamford. SANDRA GOLDSTEIN (D)
1975-. Bds: Personnel Com.; Fiscal Com.; Sewer Com. Party: State Del. 1976. Org: Conn. Citizen's Action Group; Nat. Council of Jewish Women; LWV; Dem. Women's Club; PTA. Educ: Brooklyn Coll. 1962 BA. Occ: Designer. B: 10/11/41. Add: 81 Rollingwood Dr., Stamford 06905 (203)358-4024.

Stamford. MARIE J. HAWE
LYNN M. LOWDEN
BARBARA A. MC INERNEY
CHRISTINE M. NIZOLEK
MILDRED J. PERILLO
Old Town Hall, 179 Atlantic St., P.O. Box 891, Stamford 06904.

Stamford. MILDRED S. RITCHIE (R)
1975-. Bds: Personnel Com.; Fiscal Com.; Public Works Com. Party: State Del. 1975; Nat. Del. 1976; V-Ch., Rep. Town Com. 1975-77. Org: Rep. Women's Club. Occ: Administrative Asst. B: 3/31/24. Add: 221 Hubbard Ave., Stamford 06905 (203)327-1234.

Stamford. JEANNE-LOIS MARSCHALL SANTY (R)
1975-. Dist: 18. Bds: Personnel Com.; Health & Protection Com.; Park & Recreation Com. Party: State Del. 1976; State Central Committeewoman 1977-79; Rep. Town Committeewoman 1973-75; V-Ch., Rep. Town Com. 1974-75. Prev: Justice of The Peace 1972-. Org: Amer. Assoc. Occupational Health Nurses. Educ: Stamford Hospital School of Nursing 1952 RN. Occ: RN. B: 6/26/31. Add: 133 Thornridge Dr., Stamford 06903 (203)358-4024.

Waterbury. ALVERA BALANDA (D)
1968-. Bds: Ch., Business Building Code Com.; Delinquent Tax Com.; Housing Code Com. Party: State Del. 1949; Dist. Leader 1949-77. Prev: Public Assistance Cmsn. 1968-70. Org: Bd. of Realtors. Occ: Realtor. B: 11/2/09. Add: 72 Chipman St., Waterbury 06702 (203)574-3944.

Waterbury. MARY J. SLEKIS
City Hall, 235 Grand St., Waterbury 06702.

West Haven. DORIS M. PERRY
ALICE M. RICHARDS
City Hall, 355 Main St., West Haven 06516.

Judges

ELLEN BREE BURNS (I)
Superior Court Judge. 1976-. Bds: State Law Library Adv. Bd. Prev: Common Pleas Ct. Judge 1975-76; Circuit Ct. Judge 1973-75; Dir., Leg. Legal Services 1947-73. Org: New Haven Cnty. Bar Assoc. Educ: Albertus Magnus Coll. 1944 BA; Yale Law School 1947 LLB. B: 12/13/23. Add: 355 River Rd., Hamden 06518.

MARY FITZGERALD ASPELL
Superior Court Judge. Add: Courthouse, W. Hartford.

State Boards and Commissions

Office of the Governor, State Capitol Bldg., Hartford 06115.

Aging, Advisory Council on
MARY GUSTAFSON
MOTHER M. BERNADETTE DE LOURDES
JEANNE M. OSBORNE
RUTH O. TRUEX

Alcohol Advisory Council
MARY AMBLER
KIMBERLY CHENEY
JOANNE S. FAULKNER

Alcohol and Drug Dependence, Advisory Council on
LORETTA BOYD
SHIRLEY WILLIAMS

American and Francophone Cultural Commission
RACHEL BROWN
SISTER BARBARA JOHNSON
ARLETTE LIPPINCOTT

Arts, Commission on the
    MARCIA P. ALCORN
    DENISE M. CURT
    CARMELINA C. KANZLER
    SUSAN R. KELLY
    SHIRLEY W. LAND
    CLARICE C. SEGAL
    TRUDI L. SHIPPENBERG
    JANE N. SMITH
    MARY HUNTER WOLF

Camp Safety Advisory Council
    MRS. KIRBY JUDD

Certification of Teachers, Advisory Board on
    JEANETTE HOTCHKISS
    FRANCES KINSELLAR
    MARIA RIVERA
    MARY SUGGS

Child Day Care Council
    MARGARET KRAH
    DIANE MC ALPIN
    ALICE PIEPER
    MRS. OLINDO SANTOPIETRO

Children and Youth Services, Advisory Council on
    MARY F. ASPEL
    RONNA FEIGENBAUM

Children's Services, Commission on
    MARGARET S. WILSON

Community Affairs, Advisory Council on
    LEAHMAE HIPPMAN
    PEGGY B. SMITH

Comprehensive Health Planning
    ELIZABETH W. CATHLES
    SISTER DOLORES FITZGERALD
    LILLIAN RICHARDSON
    HELEN T. WATSON

Concern for Connecticut Jobs, Committee of
    SANDRA KALOM

Consumers Advisory Council
    ELSIE FETTERMAN
    LINA F. WAGNER
    SHIRLEY PROWN
    PAULING PUTRIMENT

Deaf and Hearing Impaired, Commission on the
    JOSEPHINE BUELL
    BARBARA JOHNSON
    KIT NORTHUP
    GLORIA WHITE

Developmental Disabilities Services and Facilities
Construction Act Advisory Council
    MILDRED ADAMS
    JEAN CORNWELL
    SARAH M. FERGUSON
    MARILYN GRAVINK
    EDITH HARRIS
    CLAIRE LANGTON
    AMY LETTICK
    ELIZABETH PINNER
    ELEANOR STEERE
    ELIZABETH VASKO
    BERNICE VENNERT

Division of Community Services, Department of
Mental Health Advisory Board
    PHOEBE BENNET
    FLORENCE M. CHASE

Drug Advisory Council
    JOAN H. BARTON
    BARBARA MUCHELOT

Drug Council
    MARY M. HESLIN

Eastern Connecticut Rural and Industrial Areas
Preservation Commission.
    BETTY COCHRAN
    LUCY CROSBIE
    LOUISE PEMPEK

Education and Services for the Blind, Board of
    EILEEN AKERS
    SHIRLEY D. LEBOWITZ

Education, Board of
    M. ADELA EADS
    JUNE K. GOODMAN
    ROSE LUBCHANSKY
    CATHERINE V.A. SMITH

Education Council
    KATHLEEN COSGRIFF
    ALICE V. MEYER
    EMMA M. TERRILL

Emergency Medical Service, Advisory Committee on
    MARJORIE C. BENNETT
    MARIE K. CARTER
    ESTHER B. CLARKE
    HELEN GOLDBERG
    MARIA GONZALEZ
    SANDRA PRIMROSE

Employment of the Handicapped, Committee on
    MARGUERITE L. PALLOTTI
    WILMA OLDER
    AMALIA M. TORO

Employment Security, Advisory Council on
    JUNE FORELLA
    RUTH G. HAMILTON

Energy Advisory Board
    JACQUELINE SHAFFER
    MARY B. SULLIVAN

Equine Advisory Council
    JOANNE J. BYRNES
    CANDIDA M. CONWAY
    MARIAN KINGSBURY
    MARIE LISETTE RIMER

Fair Employment Practices, Law and the Public
Accommodations Statute Hearing Examiners
    ANNE DRANGINIS
    PATRICIA A. LILLY
    DIEDRE MAGNELLO

Fitness, Committee on
    MARY U. GRANDE

Higher Education, Commission for
  CAROLYN CHILDS
  ANNE M. HOGAN
  LOUISE KRONHOLM
  BERNICE C. NIEJADIK

Historical Commission
  MARGARET BROWN
  NANCY SPADA

Hospitals and Health Care, Commission on
  ELIZABETH W. CATHLES
  SISTER DOLORES FITZGERALD
  HELEN T. WATSON

Human Rights and Opportunities, Commission on
  ANGELA BONILLA
  FANNIE HIMMELSTEIN
  MARY JANE STINSON

Human Rights and Opportunities, Executive Committee
on
  KAY V. BERGIN
  SANDRA BILOON
  MARY M. HESLIN

Human Services, Council on
  MARY R. HENNESSEY
  BETTY JANE STEPHENS
  ANNE MC KINNE WOLF
  ADELE WRIGHT

Hypertrichologists, Board of Examiners
  ETHYLE W. BEKECH
  FLORENCE E. HAMBLET
  HILDA HARRISON

Indian Affairs Council
  ELAINE S. FERRIS
  HELEN LE GAULT

Investment Advisory Council
  SUSAN LEPPER

Job Innovation and Development, Commission on
  ALICE AYERS

Justice Commission
  KATHRYN FEIDELSON
  SARAH ROMANY

Kidney Disease Advisory Commission
  JANICE HYDE
  JENNEY KITSEN

Landscape Architects, Board of
  HELEN A. TILLAPAUGH

Liquor Control Commission
  ANNA-MAE SWITASKI

Manpower Planning Council
  LILLIAN PITSCHMANN

Manpower Services Council
  SANDRA BILLON
  BEVERLY M. BROWN

Medical Examining Board
  CHRISTIE E. MC LEON

Mental Health, Board of
  MRS. J. KENNETH BRADLEY
  RUTH KIMBALL
  ELEANOR S. KOHN
  SHIRLEY WILLIAMS

Mental Retardation, Council on
  MARGARET V. TEDONE

Natural Area Preserves Advisory Committee
  ELEANOR D. WOLF

Nuclear Power Evaluation Council
  BARBARA FONTAYNE BASS

Nursing, Board of Examiners
  BETTE JANE MURPHY
  ANELINE PETRUNY
  ELAINE C. RAYMOND
  OLIVE SANTAVENERE
  LILLIAN B. WARNER

Nursing Home Administrators, Board of Licensure
  MARIE GONZALEZ
  JANE LOGAN
  ANN L. LUSZCZAK
  SISTER DANIEL MARIE

Occupational Safety and Health, Committee on
  KAREN T. SITARZ

Optometry, Board of Examiners
  ANN J. CAPECELATRO
  RENE G. DESAULNIERS

Organized Crime Prevention and Control, Advisory
Committee on
  MARY R. HENNESSEY

Parole, Board of
  GERTRUDE KOSKOFF
  ARLENE E. LEVINE
  MARGARET K. SMITH

Pharmacy, Commission of
  DOROTHY B. ROMANELLI

Physical Therapists, Board of Examiners
  WILHELMINA J. WERKHOVEN

Power Facility Evaluation Council
  ANNE R. CONOVER

Psychologists, Board of Examiners
  ETHELYN H. KLATSKIN
  JUDITH K. STEIBER

Public Health Council
  CHARLOTTE R. BROWN

Public Utilities Control Authority
  MIRIAM B. BUTTERWORTH

Public Utilities Control Authority Reorganization
Task Force
  RITA D. KAUNITZ
  GLORIA POND

Regional Community Colleges, Board of Trustees for
the
    PATRICIA CROWLEY
    CATHERINE H. JENKINS
    ELIZABETH JOYNER
    DOROTHY C. MC NULTY

Safety Commission
    MARY ELLEN KILLEEN

School Construction Economy Service Advisory
Committee
    MRS. E. H. TRUEX, JR.

Social Services, Citizens' Advisory Committee on
    MARY CLARK
    SARA ELLISON
    JEANNE FARRELL
    IMELDA MORNEAULT
    ELLA NEWKIRK
    ANNE WINGATE

Solid Waste Management Advisory Council
    MARGARET R. BRYAN
    HELEN Z. PEARL

Special Education, Advisory Council for
    SISTER JUDITH CAREY
    MARY H. GELFMAN
    CHARLOTTE C. KENNEDY
    LOUISE M. OKIE
    JOANN SPEAR
    RUTH TRUEX
    MARY H. WOLF

Special Revenue, Commission on
    BEATRICE G. KOWALSKI
    GLORIA M. MORRIS

Speech Pathologists and Audiologists, Advisory
Council on
    MARIAN P. HENNIGES
    MARIE LOVE JOHNSON
    VIRGINIA MACKBACH
    RUTH SANOFSKY

Standardization Committee
    MARY M. HESLIN

State Academic Awards, Board for
    DORIS CASSIDAY
    GRACE W. LINDEN

State Capitol Preservation and Restoration
Commission
    ABIGAIL KENDE

State Colleges, Board of Trustees for the
    PATRICIA A. GEEN
    LUVA M. HOAR
    NANCY W. KAPLAN
    BERNICE C. NIEJADLIK
    MARGARET SHAPIRO

State Library Board
    ELINOR M. HASHIM
    FLORENCE S. LORD
    MRS. ARTHUR L. RANSOHOFF

State Planning Council
    MARY R. HENNESSEY

State Scholarship Commission
    JOYCE BUNTING

Status of Women, Permanent Commission on the
    SHIRLEY R. BYSIEWICA
    RUTH CHURCH
    MARY ERLANGER
    DOROTHY KIMBALL
    BARBARA LIFTON
    KATHLEEN O'LEARY MC GUIRE
    MINERVA H. NEIDITZ
    HELEN Z. PEARL
    ELIZABETH RAWLES
    ELIZABETH SPALDING
    SUZANNE S. TAYLOR
    MRS. CHASE GOING WOODHOUSE

Structure of State Government, Committee on the
    RUTH L. SIMS

Teachers' Retirement Board
    NORINE F. KENNEDY

Tuberculosis Control, Hospital Care and
Rehabilitation Council on
    DELAPHINE E. HATCH

Utility Financing, Special Task Force on
    MARGARET DONOHUE

Vocational and Career Education, Advisory Council
on
    HILDA COOK
    OLIVE SHEEHAN
    BARBARA SOUTHWORTH

Water Company Lands, Council on
    MURIEL LIGHTFOOT
    SALLY RICHARDS

Delaware

LYDIA R. BOYER (R)
Secretary, Dept. of Administrative Services.
1977-. Bds: Capital Projects Review Com.; Central
Data Processing Com.; Records Management Review
Com. Party: State Del. 1966, '68, '70; Nat. Alt.
1964, '68; Committeewoman 1960;76; V-Ch., City
Committee 1962-66; Ch., City Committee 1966-69.
Prev: Governor's Adv. Council on Youth Services
1969-75; Health & Social Services Council 1970-
75; on Corrections 1975-77. Org: Civic Assoc.
Educ: Conn. Coll. 1953 AB. B: 9/1/32. Add:
5701 Kennett Pk., Centreville 19807 (302)678-4706.

PATRICIA C. SCHRAMM (I)
Secretary of Health and Social Services. 1977-
Bds: Ch., State Bd. of Health. Prev: Dir., of
Social Planning 1970-73; Dir., Planning & Devt.
1973-77. Educ: Bryn Mawr Coll. 1959 BA; U. of
Chicago 1963 MA; Bryn Mawr Coll. 1970 PhD. B:
3/25/37. Add: Blackshire Rd., Wilmington, Del.
19805 (302)421-6705.

State Legislature

State Senate

NANCY W. COOK (D) **
Dist: 16. Bds: Administrative Services;
Highways, Transportation & Insurance; Health &
Social Services. Party: County Com. Org: Dem.
Clubs. B: 5/11/36. Add: State Senate, Kenton
19955 (302)653-8725.

WINIFRED SPENCE (R) **
1976-. Dist: Prev: State Repr. 1973-76. Org:
Women's Club. Add: Odessa 19780 (302)834-5075.

State House

MARIAN P. ANDERSON
41 Anglin Dr., Robscott Manor, Newark 19713.

HENRIETTA JOHNSON (D) **
1971-. Dist: 3. Bds: Health & Social Services
Aging; Public Safety. Org: Bd. of Dir., South-
east Wilmington Non Profit Housing Corp.;
Community Council Bd. B: 7/24/14. Add: 1213
Lobdell St., Wilmington 19801 (302)654-1004.

KAREN JENNINGS MILLER (D)
Dist: 31. Bds: Ch., Natural Resource Com.
Party: State Alt. 1974, '76. Org: AAUP. Educ:
Eastern Ill. U. BA; U. of Del. MA. Occ: Asst.
Professor. B: 4/12/39. Add: 836 Miller Dr.,
Dover 19901 (302)678-4132.

RUTH ANN MINNER (D) **
1974-. Dist: 33. Bds: Highway & Transportation; Public Safety; Agriculture. Party:
Dist. & County Com. 1969-74; Finance Com. 1973-
74; State Com. 1973-75. Org: PTA; Dem. Clubs.
B: 1/17/35. Add: RD 3, Box 694, Milford
19963 (302)678-4178.

GWYNNE P. SMITH (R)
1974-. Dist: 10. Bds: Environmental Control;
Energy; Agriculture. Party: Election Dist.
Committeewoman 1972-77; Rep. State Com. 1973-76.
Prev: Coastal Zone Industrial Control Bd. 1971-
76. Org: LWV; AAUW; Common Cause; Del. Nature
Educ. Society. Educ: U. of Del. 1971 BA. B:
Add: 1419 Fresno Rd., Green Acres, Wilmington
19803 (302)678-4124.

SANDRA D. WORTHEN (D)
1972-. Dist: 27. Bds: Ch., Banking & Insurance Com.; Educ. Com. Party: State Del. 1972;
V-Ch., Rep. Dist. 1972-73. Prev: State Repr.
1972-75. Org: LWV. Educ: Amer. U. 1958 BA;
1960 MA. B: 3/12/37. Add: 16 Fairfield Dr.,
Newark 19711 (302)678-4174.

County Commissions

Kent. FRANCES MESSINA
R.D. 5, Box 162, Dover 19901.

New Castle. LOIS M. PARKE (R)
1972-. Dist: 3. Bds: Del., Tri-Cnty. Assoc.;
Ch., Council Finance Com.; Del. Assoc. of Public
Administrators. Party: Committeewoman 1968-72.
Prev: Nat. Adv. Council on Manpower Project 1974-
77; State Del., Manpower Services Council 1974-77;
State Del., Manpower Planning Council 1974-77.
Org: Nat. Assoc. of Cnty's.; Nat. Tax Institute;
Civic League. Educ: Mt. Holyoke Coll. 1957 BA.
B: 12/7/35. Add: 2 Stone Barn Ln., Wilmington
19807 (302)571-7520.

Mayors

Cheswold. DOROTHY L. DEMPSEY (D)
1977-. Prev: Councilwoman 1976-77. Org:
League of Local Govt's. B: 1/12/55. Add: Box 32
Cheswold 19936 (302)734-4932.

Fenwick Island. OLIVE MORRIS (D)
1976-. Bds: Bd. of Adjustment. Prev: Town
Councilwoman 1975-76. Org: Chamber of Commerce.
B: 1/26/15. Add: Rt. 1, Box 262, Fenwick Is.
Selbyville 19975 (302)539-3011.

Henlopen Acres. MILDRED W. POTTS
96 Tidewaters, Henlopen Acres 19971.

Rehoboth Beach. MIRIAM E. HOWARD (R)
    1975-. Prev: City Comsr. 1973-75; City
Treasurer 1970-75. Org: Home Owners Assoc.;
Historical Society. B: 7/21/10. Add: 49 Sussex
St., Rehoboth Bch. 19921 (302)227-6181.

Slaughter Beach. CLARA RUSSELL
    414 Kings Hwy., Slaughter Beach 1996

Local Councils

Bellefonte. ANN FRAMPTON (R)
    1977-. Bds: Ch., Bd. of Adjustment. Party:
State Del. 1974-77; Cnty. Committeewoman 1964-.
Prev: City Comsr. 1964-77. Org: PTA. B: 12/23/34
Add: 1204 Rosedale Ave., Wilmington 19809.

Bowers Beach. ELIZABETH BANKS
              BETTY CUBBAGE
    RD #1, Bowers Beach 19946.

Bowers Beach. LORRAINE E. MADDEN (D)
    1975-. Occ: Auditor. B: 1/31/48. Add: RD #1,
Box 177, Frederica 19946.

Bowers Beach. LORRAINE MOYER
    RD #1, Bowers Beach 19946.

Bridgeville. MILDRED S. BROWN
    209 Market St., Bridgeville 19933.

Camden. SANDRA L. SCOTT
    27 S. Main St., Camden 19934.

Cheswold. ESTHER G. EMORY
    City Hall, Cheswold 19936.

Delaware City. CORDELIA W. BENNETT (D)
    1975-. Bds: Ch., Bd. of Health. Org: PTA.
Occ: Pharmacy Clerk. B: 8/18/37. Add: 105
Warfel Dr., Delaware City 19706 (302)834-4573.

Ellendale. CATHERINE LARE
    City Hall, Ellendale 19941.

Fenwick Island. MARY PAT KYLE
    1975-. Bds: Ch., Ordinance Com.; Ch., Beach
Safety Com. Educ: U. of Maryland 1949 BA. Occ:
Interviewer. B: 1/7/28. Add: 407 Windsor St.,
Silver Spring 20910.

Frankford. BARBARA A. TRUITT
    City Hall, Frankford 19945.

Georgetown. OLIVE D. ADAMS
    22 Chestnut St., Georgetown 19947.

Harrington. ANNA HAMPTON
    103 Fleming St., Harrington 19952.

Hartley. BERNICE BIDDLE
    P.O. Box 84, Hartley 19953.

Houston. VIRGINIA TWILLEY
    City Hall, Houston 19954.

Laurel. ELIZABETH E. ANDERSON
    400 E. 6th St., Laurel 19956.

Leipsic. HELEN MITCHELL
         BARBARA SPANGLER
         MARGARET S. STOREY
    RD #4, Box 356, Dover 19901.

Little Creek. KATHLEEN MARGARET MARY BUNDEK (R)
    1975-. Bds: Ch., Bicentennial Com.; Ch.,
Recreation Project of 1975. B: 4/22/51. Add:
Main St., Little Crk. 19961 (302)674-3528.

Little Creek. BETTY LAMB
    Main St., Little Creek 19961.

Little Creek. DOROTHY K. WRIGHT (D)
    B: 11/18/11. Add: Little Crk. 19961
(302)734-2387.

Magnolia. JANET M. KANOY (D)
    1967-. Occ: Receptionist. B: 11/17/37.
Add: 28 E. Walnut St., Magnolia 19962
(302)335-5891.

Milford. VIRGINIA H. GLENN (I)
    1976-. Bds: Ch., Planning Cmsn. on Liaison;
Ch., Annexation; Street & Sewer. Prev: Planning
Cmsn. 1975-76. Org: Kent Cnty. Bd. of Trustees;
Historical Society. Occ: Realtor. B: 8/28/25.
Add: 419 Kings Hwy., Milford 19963.

Millsboro. THELMA MOORE
            MARIAN V. SMITH
    P.O. Box 137, Millsboro 19966.

Newark. BETTY LEE TRUMAN HUTCHINSON (D)
    1977-. Dist: 3. Bds: Ch., Ad Hoc Com. to
Establish a Conservation Cmsn. Party: Dist. Ch.,
Carter Campaign 1976; Committeewoman 1972, '68.
Prev: Comsr., Housing Authority 1973-77; Mayor's
Revenue Study Com. 1975-76; Tax-Exempt Property
Com. 1972-74; Central Business Dist. Com. 1975-76
Org: LWV; Common Cause. Educ: U. of Pittsburgh
1948 AB. B: 11/18/25. Add: 311 Apple Rd.,
Newark 19711 (302)366-7070.

Newport. PHYLLIS M. CALOMINO
    7 Lynam St., Newport 19804.

Ocean View. MARION DENNY
             LYDIA QUILLEN
    City Hall, Central Ave., Ocean View 19970.

Odessa. RACHEL MANDES
    Mechanix St., Odessa. 19730.

Selbyville. CYNTHIA LEWIS
    Selbyville 19975.

Smyrna. RUTH COLLINS
    1975-. Bds: Recreation Com.; Budget Com.
Org: Historical Society. Occ: Banker. B:
3/1/09. Add: 125 S. Main St., Apt. 1, Smyrna
19977 (302)653-9231.

Townsend. AGNES MANNERING
           WILLANNA VAN HORN
    Main St., Townsend 19734.

Wyoming. CATHERINE HITE
    20 S. Railroad Ave., Wyoming 19934.

Wyoming. NANCY G. TIEMAN
   121 Southern Blvd., Wyoming 19934.

State Boards and Commissions

   Office of the Governor, State Capitol Bldg.,
   Dover 19901.

Aging, Council on the
   MARTHA EVANS
   MILDRED E. SAVAGE

American Revolution Bicentennial Commission
   MURIEL COOPER
   M. CATHERINE DOWNING

Archives and Cultural Affairs, Council on
   ALICE B. DE GRAFF
   EVADNE J. KEMPER
   MRS. ROBERT HUNTER ORR
   MARY T. TRUITT
   MRS. HOUSTON WILSON

Banking, Council on
   NANCY WENDE

Bingo Control Commission
   ALICE C. WOODWARD
   CAROL S. WRIGHT

Blind, Council on the
   AILIE COYNER
   LILLIAN PORTER
   BEATRICE P. SIMONDS

Coastal Zone Industrial Control Board
   GWYNN SMITH

Consumer Affairs Board
   MURIEL E. GILMAN
   ANNA B. KING

Consumer Affairs, Council on
   RUTH ANN BAKER
   LILLIAN E. BURRIS
   JANET C. REED
   CECILE ROCHELEAU

Correction, The Advisory Council on
   LYDIA BOYER
   JOAN CONNOLLY
   HARRIET F. DURHAM
   NANCY W. WOODWARD
   MARGARET E. YOUNG

Cosmetology, State Board of
   HELEN I. FOSKEY
   MARY LOU MURPHY
   AGNES D. PERILLO
   LORRAINE PETERSON
   GRACE ANN YOUNG

Discrimination Review Board
   MARIE C. BIFFERATO

Dover Housing Authority
   PERRY POLLAK
   CLARA WASHINGTON

Drug Control, Council on
   ELISABETH S. CAREY
   VIRGINIA DE SANTIS
   JOANNE MULVENA
   KATHLEEN WILBUR

Education, State Board of
   ELISE GROSSMAN

Employment Services, Council on
   FRIEDA CONNER

Environmental Control, Council on
   LORRAINE FLEMING

Exceptional Children, Advisory Committee on Needs
of
   NANCY ELLEN DAVITT
   LENA HARRIS
   BEE NICKERSON

Funeral Service Practitioners, State Board of
   E. REEVES MARVEL

Health Facilities Authority
   SHIRLEY TARRANT
   JOAN WRIGHT

Highways, Council on
   KATHRYN T. DERRICKSON

Home and Hospital, Council on
   SALLY BROWN
   BETTY JANE HAGERTY
   IDA MAE THOMAS

Housing Authority, Newark
   JOYCE M. CONKEY
   BARBARA GREENFIELD
   BETTY L. HUTCHINSON

Housing, Council on
   ELIZABETH CALHOUN
   HARRIET K. WOLFSON

Human Relations Commission, State
   JANE L. DILLEY
   SISTER CECILE ESTEVES
   REBECCA B. GATES
   LYNNE GRUWELL
   LYNNE KAUFMAN
   PAULA LEHRER
   MYRTLE SHOCKLEY
   MABEL SIMMS
   JOANNE D. SLIGHTS
   MRS. LAWRENCE V. TAYLOR
   DELORES R. WILLIAMS

Interstate Cooperation, Commission on
   MARGARET R. MANNING

Libraries, Council on
   HELEN K. BARNETT
   MARY JEAN KRAYBILL
   HELEN D. ROSS
   LOIS THOMAS
   SARA LOU WILKINSON
   ELSYE WOYKE

Medical Practice, Board of
    ELIZABETH M. LANDIS

Mental Health, Council on
    SHEILA MC MAHON

Mental Retardation, Council on
    BETTY LOU COOPER
    JEAN CROSS
    MARY A. CUYJET
    MAE HIGHTOWER
    HELEN M. HOLLEGER

Nursing, Board of
    ELIZABETH D. CLOUD, R.N.
    THERESE CURRAN, R.N.
    SISTER M. JOSEPH LEO DE FRANK, R.N.
    BERNICE HOWE, R.N.
    BARBARA J. PETERSON, R.N.B.S.M.S.
    ELOISE E. SPARKMAN, L.P.N.
    PEGGY TOWNSEND, L.P.N.

Nursing Home Administrators, State Board of
Examiners for
    CHERRITTA LAWS MATTHEWS
    MARY K. SINIGAGLIO

Parks, Council on
    DIMITY P. CANN
    LEAH ROEDEL

Parole, Board of
    DR. SARAH R. JASTAK
    MARGARET G. SCRIVENS

Personnel Commission, State
    MARTHA V. CALHOUN

Psychologists, Board of Examiners of
    HARRIET AINBINER
    SARAH R. JASTAK

Public Health, Council on
    CHARLOTTE HAMMOND
    CAROLINE H. KEENE
    SARA G. REED
    MARY A. WIESEL

Public Service Commission
    LEE M. CASSIDY
    BERTHA JOHNSON

Real Estate Commission
    ROSE L. ROSE

Regional Transit, Authority for
    MARCIE BIERLEIN
    LOIS MATUSHEFSKE

Speech Pathology and Audiology, State Board of
Examiners for
    HELEN Q. HOLDEN
    SARAH ERICKSON

Standardbred Development Fund, Board of Trustees of
the
    FRANCES E. PITTS

State Buildings, Council on
    LOLA O'DAY

State Planning, Council on
    MARLENE JAMES

Tax Appeals Board
    NETTIE C. REILLY

Technical and Community College
    BARBARA AHERN
    LOUISE MARIE LAMBERTA
    JOAN M. LINDELL
    ANNABEL E. MOORE

Transportation Authority, Statewide Specialized
    BESSIE A. BUNGRY
    CHARLOTTE HUNT

Unemployment Insurance Advisory Council
    LONNIE DILLON

Unemployment Insurance Appeals Board
    EMILIE E. TUGEND

University of Delaware Trustees
    SALLY H. HIGGINS
    MADALINE W. JAMES
    LUNA I. MISHOE

Violent Crimes Compensation Board
    LEAH W. BETTS

Florida

PAULA F. HAWKINS (R) *

Public Service Commissioner. 1972-. Party: Precinct Committeewoman 1964-Present; Nat. Del. 1968, '72; V-Ch., Rep. Nat. Com. 1972. Prev: Cmsn. on the Status of Women 1968-Present. Org: Women's Club; Chamber of Commerce. Add: 700 S. Adams, Tallahassee 32304.

State Legislature

State Senate

ELIZABETH B. CASTOR (D)

1976-. Dist: 23. Bds: Senate Economic, Community & Consumer Affairs Com.; Senate Educ. Com.; Senate Govt. Operations Com. Party: State Dem. Constitutional Revision Com. 1977. Prev: Bd. of Cnty. Msnr.'s. 1972-76; Ch., Bd. of Cnty. Cmsnr's. 1975-76; Cnty. Hospital & Welfare Bd. 1972-76; Ch., Cnty. Hospital & Welfare Bd. 1973-74; Environmental Protection Cmsn. 1972-76; Tampa Bay Regional Planning Council Exec. Bd. 1972-76. Org: Council on Foreign Relations; LWV; Dem. Party; PTA. Educ: Glassboro State Coll. 1963 BA; U. of Miami 1968 MA. B: 5/11/41. Add: 3020 Samara Dr., Tampa 33618 (813)272-6830.

LORI WILSON (I)

1972-. Bds: V-Ch., Judiciary-Civil Com.; Govt. Operations Com.; Exec. Business Com. Prev:Cnty. Cmsn. 1969-72; Human Relations Cmsn. 1972-76; Bicentennial Cmsn. 1972-76; Welfare Bd. 1968-69. Org: BPW; LWV; Learned Scholars Institute; Fed. Women's Club; NOWL; Historical Society; Chamber of Commerce. B: 2/15/37. Add: Pumpkin Ctr. 333 S. Atlantic Ave., Cocoa Bch. 32931 (305)783-5674.

State House

ELAINE BLOOM (D)

1974-. Dist: 100. Bds: Ch., House Fed.-State Appropriations; Ch., Joint Com. on Economic Policy; House Educ. Com. Party: State Del. 1975; Nat. Del. 1976. Org: AWRT; BPW; Women in Govt.; Juvenile Delinquency Task Force; Com. on Foreign Relations. WPC; Post-Secondary Educ. Cmsn.; Right to Read Council; LWV. Educ: Barnard Coll. 1957 BA. B: 9/16/37. Add: 20435 NE 20th St., Miami 33179 (305)371-8611.

BEVERLY B. BURNSED (D)

1976-. Dist: 50. Bds: Health & Rehabilatative Service Com.; Appropriations Com. Org: Junior Women's Club; Young Dems.; Cnty. Dem. Women. Educ: Florida State U. 1962 BA. B: 10/23/41. Add: 511 Woodward St., Lakeland 33803 (813)687-4666.

FRAN CARLTON (D)

1976-. Dist: 41. Bds: Educ. Com.; Corrections, Probation & Parole Com.; Tourism & Economic Devt. Party: Dem. Exec. Com. 1976-. Prev: Ch., Governor's Task Force on Physical Fitness 1975-76. Educ: U. of Fla. 1956 AA; Stetson U. 1958 BS. Occ: TV Show Host. B: 1/19/36. Add: 1250 Henry Balch Dr., Orlando 32810 (305)422-6699.

GWENDOLYN S. CHERRY (D) *

1972-. Dist: 106. Party: Ch., Minority Affairs Dem. Nat. Conv. 1972. Prev: State Rep., Dist. 96, 1970-72. Org: Nat. Assoc. of Women Lawyers; AAUW; ABA; OWL; WPC; Nat. Assoc. of Black Women; NAACP; Bar Assoc.; Southern Regional Council. Educ: Fla. A & M 1946 BS; NYU 1950 MA; Fla. A & M 1965 JD. B: 8/27/23. Add: 636 NW 2nd, Miami 33136.

LINDA COX

5432 NW 18th Street, Lauderhill 33313.

HELEN GORDON DAVIS (D)

1974-. Dist: 70. Bds: V-Ch., Corrections Probation-Parole Com.; Judiciary; Commerce. Prev: Governor's Com. on Judicial Reform 1976-; Governor's Com. on Ct. Reform 1971-72; Cnty. Planning Cmsn. 1972-74; Mayor's Citizen's Adv. Cmsn. 1966-69; Arts Council 1972-74; Quality Educ. Cmsn. 1967-68; Juvenile Delinquency Cmsn. 1965-67; Community Relations Cmsn. 1965-68; Cnty. Local Govt. Study Cmsn. 1963-64. Org: OWL; Common Cause; ACLU; ADA; Dem. Women's Club; WPC. Educ: Brooklyn Coll. 1942 BA. Add: 45 Adalia Ave., Tampa 33606 (813)224-0770.

BETTY EASLEY (R)

1972-. Dist: 56. Bds: Appropriations Com.; Finance & Taxation Com.; Transportation Com. Party: Nat. Del. 1976; Cnty. Committeewoman 1967-; Secretary-Treasurer Cnty. Com. 1970-74; Cnty. V-Ch. 1974-76. Prev: V-Ch., Human Relations Cmsn. 1972-74; Mental Health Bd. 1977-. Org: Zonta Internat.; BPW; Fed. Rep. Women. B: 8/5/29. Add: 801 Camellia Dr., Largo 33540 (813)443-7268.

MARILYN BAILEY EVANS (R)

1976-. Bds: Natural Resources; Health & Rehabilitation Service. Party: State Del. 1974; Nat. Del. 1972; State Committeewoman 1974-78; Cnty. Committeewoman 1972-78. Prev: Mental Health Bd. 1970-76. Org: AAUW; LWV; Rep. Women; Fed. of Rep. Women; Nat. Fed. of Rep. Women. Educ: Duke U. BA. Occ: Realtor. Add: 321 Lynn Ave., Melbourne 32955 (305)254-2121.

ROBERTA FOX (D)

5840 SW 57th Ave., #231, Miami 33143.

PAT FRANK (D)
    1976-. Dist: 67. Prev: Ch., Cnty. School Bd.
1972-76; Cnty. Tax Adjustment Bd. 1972-76; Elec-
tion Bd. 1967; Drug Adv. Council 1974-76; Health
& Rehabilitative Services Adv. Council 1975-76.
Org: Tampa Bay Com. on Foreign Relations; LWV;
PTA. Educ: U. of Fla. 1951 BSBA. B: 11/12/29.
Add: 574 W. Davis Blvd., Tampa 33606
(813)272-6614.

ELAINE Y. GORDON (D)
    1972-. Bds: Ch., Com. on Health & Rehabili-
tative Services; Appropriations Com.; Com. on
Rules & Calendar. Prev: Cmsn. on Status of Women
1970-72; Cnty. Manager's Task Force on Public
Service Employment 1970-72. Org: BPW; NOW; Dem.
Women's Club; LWV; WPC; Human Resources Com.;
Feminist Credit Union; State Health Coord. Council
Occ: Pres., Sales Marketing. B: 9/8/31. Add:
2500 N.E. 135th St., Apt. B705, N. Miami 33181
(305)895-1066.

MARY R. GRIZZLE (R) *
    1963-. Bds: Business Regulation Com.; Environ-
mental Pollution Control & Appropriations Com.
Party: Precinct Committeewoman. Prev: Town
Council; Ch., Fla. Cmsn. on the Status of Women.
Org: PTA; Altrusa; Woman's Club; Nat. Soc. of Arts
& Letters. B: 8/19/21. Add: Rm. 505, Coachman
Bldg., 503 Cleveland St., Clearwater 33515.

MARY ELLEN HAWKINS (R) *
    1974-. Dist: 89. Party: Ch., Cnty. Rep. Com.
1970-72; V-Ch., Dist. Rep. Com. 1970-72. Prev:
Congressional Aide 1945-59. Org: Internat. Platform Assoc. Occ: Freelance Writer. B: 4/18/23.
Add: Collier Cnty. Courthouse Complex, Naples
33940.

TONI JENNINGS (R)
    1030 Wilfred Drive, Orlando 32803.

GWEN MARGOLIS (D)
    1974-. Dist: 102. Bds: Finance & Tax; Tourism
& Economic Devt.; Standard & Conduct. Prev: Bd.
of Adjustment 1970-74; Human Relations Bd. 1972-74.
Org: Planning Assoc.; Women Council of Realtors;
Chamber of Commerce; WPC; BPW; Dem. Women's Club;
Concerned Dem's.; Common Cause; PTA. Occ: Realtor
B: 10/4/34. Add: 13105 Biscayne Bay Dr., N. Miami
33161 (305)949-4541.

DOROTHY EATON SAMPLE (R)
    1976-. Bds: Educ. Com.; Collective Bargaining
Com.; Veteran's Affairs Com. Party: Precinct Com.
Prev: Dist. State Wlefare Bd.; Children's Cmsn.;
Cnty. Pre School License Bd.; Cnty. Educ. Study
Com.; Cnty. Charter Adv. Com. Org: Council of
Neighborhood Assoc.; Tampa Bay Regional Planning
Council; Rep. Club. Educ: Duke U. 1933 BA. Add:
200 Sunset Dr., S., St. Petersburg 33707
(813)823-1722.

County Commissions

Bradford. HAZEL U. PAULK
    County Courthouse, Starke 32091.

Broward. ANN L. KOLB (D) **
    1974-. Bds: Freight Traffic Assoc.; Water
Management Com.; State Housing Bd.; County Child
Care Advisory Com.; Vocational Home Economics
Com. Party: County Exec. Com.; Platform Ch.
1970-78; Precinct Com. 1968-. Org: Common
Cause; Home Economics Advisory Com; Dem. Women's
Club. Educ: St. Louis U. BS. B: 8/10/32. Add:
650 West Tropical Way, Plantation 33317
(305)765-5133.

Dade. CLARA OESTERLE (D) **
    1974-. Bds: Public Health Trustee; Assoc.
of County Com.; Liaison State Legislature. Org:
BPW; LWV; Chamber of Commerce; Dem. Women's Club;
PTA. B: 3/22/25. Add: 18500 Caribbean Blvd.,
Miami 33157 (305)377-5309.

Dade. BEVERLY B. PHILLIPS (D)
    1972-. Bds: Public Health Trust; Baker Mental
Health Clinic Com. Org: LWV; Dir., Council for
the Continuing Educ. of Women. Educ: Northwestern U. 1950 BS. Occ: YWCA Exec. Dir. B: 6/19/28
Add: 9840 SW 12 Ter., Miami 33174 (305)579-5117

Dade. RUTH SCHACK (D)
    1976-. Vice Mayor. Bds: Zoning Bd.; Metro-
politan Planning Org.; Mental Health Bd. Party:
State Del. 1965-68; Nat. Del. 1967-70; Nat. Alt.
1977. Org: LWV; NOW; WPC; PTA; Institute for
Women; Youth Planning Council; Rape Task Force.
Educ: Barry Coll. 1970 BA; U. of Northern Colo.
1975 MA. B: 8/24/31. Add: 1174 NE 110 St.,
Miami 33161 (305)579-5128.

Duval. NANCIE S. CRABB (D)
    1975-. Bds: Ch., Urban Affairs Com.; Finance
Com.; Rules Com. Org: LWV; Dem. Women. Educ:
Fla. Jr. Coll. 1974 AA. B: 4/10/37. Add: 830
La Vista, Jackson 32207 (904)633-3680.

Duval. SALLYE BROOKS MATHIS
    1967-. Bds: Ch., Public Health & Welfare Com.;
Public Services Com. Org: Economic Opportunity;
LWV; Urban League; NAACP; Citizens Com. for
Better Educ.; Opportunities Industrialization Ctr;
Council for Community Involvement; Mental Health
Bd.; Alcoholic Adv. Com.; Black Coalition. Educ:
Tuskegee Coll. BS; Florida A & M U. MA. Add:
1160 Durkee Dr., Jacksonville.

Duval. SYLVIA M. WEBB
    Party: Committeewoman 1977. Org: Northside
Business Men; Women for Responsible Leg. Add:
2066 Hugh Edwards Dr., Jacksonville 32210
(904)633-3131.

Glades. MARGARET VAN DE VELDE
    County Courthouse, Moore Haven 33471.

Hillsborough. FRANCES M. DAVIN **
    Bds: Ch., Community Action Agency; V-Ch.,
Hospital & Welfare Bd.; Regional Planning Council;
Rapid Transit; Expressway Authority; Health
Planning Council; Joint Conf. Com. Org: LWV;
Urban League. Add: County Administration Bldg.,
Tampa 33602.

Indian River. ALMA LEE LOY (D)
1968-. Prev: Fla. Status of Women Cmsn. 1964-69; Assoc. of Hwy. Safety Leaders 1969-77. Org: Civic Arts Cmsn.; Dem. Women's Club. Educ: Rochester Institute of Technology 1950 AAS; U. of Miami 1952 BBA. Occ: Businesswoman. B: 6/10/29. Add: 2036 35th Ave., Vero Beach 32960 (305)567-7242.

Lee. BETTY BOWEN EVANS (R) **
1974-. Bds: Regional Planning Council. Org: WPC; Chamber of Commerce; Rep. Clubs; Rep. Women's Clubs. B: 2/23/29. Add: Route 6 Box 209 N, North Fort Myers 33903 (813)335-2226.

Martin. MAGGY HURCHALLA (D)
1974-. Prev: V-Ch., City Com. 1976-77; Ch., Regional Planning Council 1976-77; Gov's. Com. on Roads 1975-76; Ch., Cnty. Water Bd. 1973-74; Cnty. Charter Bd. 1972-73. Org: Audubon Society; Conservation Alliance; AAUW; Dem. Club; Environmental Ctr. Bd. Educ: Swarthmore Coll. 1962 BA. B: 12/1/40. Add: 5775 S.E. Nassau Ter., Stuart 33494 (305)283-6760.

Nassau. HAZEL E. JONES (D) **
1973-. B: 12/20/17. Add: Route 1, Box 319, Clinch Dr., Fernandina Beach 32034 (904)261-6127.

Okaloosa. DEE PARKTON
County Courthouse, Crestview 32536.

Palm Beach. PEGGY B. EVATT
County Courthouse, West Palm Beach 33401.

Pinellas. JEANNE MALCHON
County Courthouse, Clearwater 33518.

Polk. BRENDA TAYLOR
County Courthouse, Bartow 33830.

Sarasota. BEVERLY CLAY (R) **
1974-. Bds: Public Safety Advisory; Council on Aging. Prev: County Charter Review Bd. 1972-74. Org: Community Action Council; Pres., Woman's Rep. Club; Young Rep. B: 8/11/27. Add: 1000 Longboat Key Club Dr., Sarasota 33577 (813)958-7721.

Mayors

Alachua. MARTHA S. ALDAY
P.O. Box 8, Alachua 32615.

Bunnell. MARGARET JANE DEEN
P.O. Box 756, Bunnell 32010.

Dade City. AGNES H. LAMB
P.O. Box 1355, Dade City 33525.

Dunedin. JUDY GOULD (R)
1976-. Bds: Planning Council; Council of Mayors; Metropolitan Planning Council. Prev: City Comsr. 1972-76. Org: LWV; Civic Assoc.; Historical Society; Women's Rep. Club; Educ: Goucher Coll. 1955 BA. B: 6/6/33. Add: 2346 Demaret Dr., Dunedin 33528 (813)733-4151.

Glen Ridge. ANITA G. YOUNT
1300 Glen Road, Glen Ridge 33406.

Jasper. BETTYE J. SEARS
P.O. Box 1148, Jasper 32052.

Lake Butler. MARGIE F. CASON
125 E. Main St., Lake Butler 32054.

Lazy Lake. PHYLLIS MOORE (R) **
1968-. Party: V-Ch., State Com. 1970-74; State Com. 1966-74; County Com. 1960-74; Precinct Com. 1960-70. Org: Fla. Conservative Union; Women's Rep. Club. Educ: U. of Mo. 1950 BA; St. Elizabeth School of Nursing 1944 RN. B: 5/12/23. Add: 2200 Lazy La., Lazy Lake 33305.

Lynn Haven. MONTEL M. JOHNSON (D)
1976-. Bds: Cnty. & Municipal Govt. League. Prev: City Comsr. 1970-76. Org: LWV; Historical Society; Chamber of Commerce. B: 10/29/22. Add: 116 Carolina Ave., Lynn Hvn., 32444 (904)265-2121.

Mangonia Park. GLADYS M. MALOY (D)
1971-. Educ: U. of Ky. 1956 BA. Occ: Computer Consultant. B: 1/12/35. Add: 4900 Jeffery Ave., Mangonia Pk. 33407 (305)848-1235.

McIntosh. MARSHA STRANGE
City Hall, McIntosh 32664.

Melbourne Village. GRACE D. WALKER
535 Hammock Rd., Melbourne Village 32901.

North Port. MARGARET M. GENTLE
311 N. Port Bld., North Port 33595.

Opa-Locka. CANDY GIARDINO
P.O. Box 86, Opa-Locka 33054.

Painters Hill. MARGARET G. FRASER
P.O. Box 234, Flagler Beach 32036.

Redington Shores. NORA T. CLONEY
17798 Gulf Blvd., Redington Shores 33708.

Riviera Beach. BOBBIE E. BROOKS
P.O. Dwr. 10682, Riviera Beach 10682.

St. Petersburg. CORINNE FREEMAN
P.O. Box 2842, St. Petersburg 33731.

Sweetwater. BLANCHE CARLOW
500 S.W. 109th Ave., Sweetwater 33174.

Local Councils

Altamonte Springs. SANDRA GLENN
225 Newburyport Ave., Altamonte Springs 32701

Altha. FATE SEWELL
P.O. Box 6, Altha 32421.

Bay Harbour Islands. VIVIAN LEVINSON
P.O. Box 546667, Bay Harbour Islands 33154.

Bay Lake. SHARON ANN STREIT
P.O. Box 22066, Lake Buena Vista 32830.

Belleair. CHERYL R. WEIBLE
901 Ponce De Leon Blvd.,Belleair 33516.

Belleair Beach. LUCINDA J. BENEKE (R)
1975-. Org: Bar Assoc.; Women's Rep. Club.
Educ: Fla. State U. 1969 BA; U. of Fla. 1973 JD.
Occ: Atty. B: 9/18/49. Add: 2513 Gulf Blvd.,
Belleair Bch. 33535 (813)595-4646.

Belleair Beach. JOAN LEVY
444 Causeway Blvd., Indian Rocks Beach 33535.

Belleair Beach. MARIE OLIVEN (R) **
1971-. Bds: Finance Officer; Public Relations.
B: 3/17/05. Add: 2450 Mineola Dr. North,
Belleair Bluffs 33540 (813)584-2151.

Belleair Shore. MARTHA NANCE HISGEN (R)
1974-. Bds: Town Clerk. Org: Senior Citizens
Inc. Educ: Fla. State Coll. for Women 1931 BA.
B: 9/21/09. Add: 880 Gulf Blvd., Belleair Shr.
33535 (813)595-4926.

Belleair Shore. CAROL KELLER
880 Gulf Blvd., Indian Rocks Bch. 33535.

Belle Isle. KATHRYN JONES
P.O. Box 13135, Belle Isle 32809.

Biscayne Park. BETTY LADAS (D)
1975-. Bds: Finance Comsr. Org: Municipal
Finance Officers Assoc.; League of Cities; Civic
Club. Occ: Dist. Sales Manager. B: 8/21/29.
Add: 713 NE 119 St., Biscayne Pk 33161
(305)895-7490.

Boca Raton. DOROTHY H. WILKEN (D)
1974-. Prev: Charter Revision Bd. 1972-73;
Ch., Ameration Com. 1974-76. Org: Common Cause;
Dem. Women; Dem. Club. Educ: George Washington
U. 1957 BA. Occ: Art Studio Manager. B: 1/2/36.
Add: 101 Pinehurst Ln., Boca Raton 33431
(305)395-1110.

Bowling Green. VELMA C. ALBRITTON
P.O. Box 608, Bowling Green 33834.

Boynton Beach. EMILY MC CLOUD JACKSON (R)
1974-. Party: Cnty. Rep. Exec. Com. 1962-72.
Prev: Councilwoman 1970-72; V-Mayor 1972-73;
Mayor 1973-74; Planning & Zoning Bd. 1974-75.
Org: Community Improvement Forum; Fed. Rep. Women;
Women for Constitutional Govt. B: 8/7/07. Add:
728 NE 9th Ave., Boynton Beach 33435
(305)732-8111.

Bradenton. LENABELLE COATER (D)
1974-. Bds: Ch., Metropolitan Planning Org.;
Environmental Com., League of Cities; Downtown
Devt. Authority. Prev: Ch., "Solicitation" Bd.
1969-71. Org: Woman's Dem. Club. Add: 209 24th
St. W., Bradenton 33505 (813)748-0800.

Briny Breezes. RITA L. TAYLOR
5000 N. Ocean Blvd., Boynton Beach 33435.

Bronson. HARRIET G. HITCHINGS (D)
1973-. Prev: School Bd. 1953-57. Org: OES;
Amer. Assoc. of Retired Persons. B: 4/2/12.
Add: P.O. Box 57, Bronson 32621 (904)486-2354.

Callaway. SHARON LYNNE SNYDER (D)
1976-. B: 7/13/38. Add: 111 S. Charlene,
Callaway 32401 (904)769-4837.

Cape Canaveral. ANN H. THURM (R)
1972-. Bds: Water Resources Policy; Sewer
Dept. Comsr.; League of Cities. Party: Cnty.
Committeewoman 1970-72. Prev: Ch., City
Recreation Bd. 1964-69; Cnty. Recreation Bd.
1964-68; City Beautification Bd. 1969-72. Org:
Women's Club; DAR. B: 7/4/29. Add: 256 Coral
Dr., Cape Canaveral 32920 (305)783-1100.

Cedar Key. JANIE ROBINSON
City Hall, Cedar Key 32625.

Center Hill. KATHERINE E. SMITH
Prev: Library Bd. 1970-73. Org: PTO. B:
12/28/44. Add: P.O. Box 98, Center Hill 33514
(904)793-4431.

Chipley. CAROL HUDSON
1975-. Org: NEA; Retarded Citizens; Women's
Club; PTA. Educ: Auburn U. 1961 BS; Troy U.
1972 MS. Occ: Teacher. B: 1/16/28. Add:
112 Wells Ave., Chipley 32428.

Clearwater. KARLEEN F. DE BLAKER
KAREN J. MARTIN
P.O. Box 4748, Clearwater 33518.

Cloud Lake. GWEN HUELSKAMP
1 Lang Road, West Palm Beach 33406.

Cocoa. MYRTICE S. THARPE
P.O. Box 1750, Cocoa 32922.

Cocoa Beach. AGATHA I. DOERER
P.O. Box 280, Cocoa Beach 32931.

Cocoa Beach. NANCY GILBERT HUEY (R)
1975-. Bds: Cnty. Solid Waste Adv. Com., Co-
Ch. Planning Adv. Com. Prev: Planning Bd. 1974-
75. Org: Women's Club. Occ: Business Owner.
B: 2/7/29. Add: 448 Carmine Dr., Cocoa Bch.
32931 (305)783-4911.

Coconut Creek. MARILYN BALKANY (D)
1977-. Bds: Recreation Dept. Org: LWV;
Common Cause; Public Citizen. B: 10/21/22.
Add: 2704 Nassau Bend H-1, Coconut Crk. 33066
(305)972-4820.

Crescent City. GERALDINE B. ELLIS
115 N. Summit St., Crescent City 32012.

Dania. JEAN COOK
100 West Beach Blvd., Dania 33004.

Daytona Beach Shores. RUTH KLEIBER
P.O. Box 7196, Daytona Beach Shores 32016.

Deerfield Beach. SYLVIA POITIER
P.O. Dwr. AH, Deerfield Beach 33441.

Dunnellon. KAREN L. THURMAN
P.O. Box 430, Dunnellon 32630.

Eagle Lake. SHARON A. EDMONDSON (D)
1977-. B: 9/6/44. Add: 106 S. Shore Dr.,
Eagle Lk. 33839 (813)293-9090.

Eatonville. EARLENE WATKINS
P.O. Box 2163, Eatonville 32751.

Ebro. LAURA DURRENBURGER
VIRGINIA STRICKLAND
City Hall, Ebro 32437.

Edgewater. RYTA F. WEBBER
P.O. Box 100, Edgewater 32032.

Edgewood. MARCIA JOHNSON
ANIBAL RODRIQUEZ
P.O. Box 13548, Edgewood 32809.

El Portal. MYRA W. LOWRY
500 N.E. 87th St., El Portal 33138.

El Portal. CAROL D. WEIL (D)
1976-. Bds: Ch., Dept. of Parks & Recreation;
Public Service Com.; Law & Finance Com. Party:
Cnty. Committeewoman 1972-76. Org: Civic Club;
LWV. B: 11/3/38. Add: 275 NE 88th St., El
Portal 33138 (305)751-2406.

Eustis. ANN E. HURLEY (D)
1975-. Bds: League of Cities. Org: Meals on
Wheels Adv. Bd. B: 10/16/07. Add: 320 W.
Seminole Dr., Eustis 32726 (904)357-6991.

Everglades City. MINNIE GARDNER ILES (D)
1975-. Bds: Ch., Recreation; Utilities;
Safety. Org: OES. Educ: Smith Coll. 1947 BA;
Stanford U. 1949 MA. B: 2/13/26. Add: 308 S.
Storter Ave., Everglades City 33929
(813)695-3781.

Fernandina Beach. GRACE BUTLER
P.O. Box 668, Fernandina Beach

Flagler Beach. JOAN ERVIN (R)
1977-. Bds: Ch., Recreation Com.; Ch., Life
Guard Com.; Fire Com. Org: Amer. Truckers Assoc.;
Firemen's Assoc. Occ: School Bus Driver. B:
5/31/37. Add: 214 Connecticut Ave., Flagler
Beach 32036 (904)439-2332.

Fort Lauderdale. VIRGINIA S. YOUNG
P.O. Dwr. 14250, Fort Lauderdale 33302.

Fruitland Park. CAROLYN SUE HAMRIC (D)
1976-. Bds: Ch., Armed Forces Day. Educ:
Lk. Sumter Community Coll. 1977 AA. Occ: Exec.
Secretary. B: 12/11/57. Add: 601 Plumosa Ave.,
Fruitland Pk. 32731 (904)787-7977.

Gainesville. ROBERTA LANE LISLE (D)
1976-. Bds: Ch., Human Resources & Services;
Personnel Com.; Regional Utilities Bd. Prev:
Bd. of Adjustment 1975-76. Org: Housing Assoc.;
PTO. Educ: U. of Fla. 1961 B of Design. B:
5/9/39. Add: 1920 NW 8th Ave., Gainesville
32603 (904)373-3647.

Glen Ridge. MARIE HENDERSON
1300 Glen Road, Glen Ridge 33406.

Graceville. MRS. ALYCE BOYD
P.O. Box 636, Graceville 32440.

Greenacres City. NANCY H. GUPTON (D)
1976-. Bds: Charter Revision Com.; Ch.,
Com. Establishing Civil Service Program. Org:
Nat. Assoc. of Bank Women. Occ: Asst. V-Pres.
Bank. B: 11/21/40. Add: 224 Perry Ave.,
Greenacres 33463 (305)965-0388.

Green Cove Springs. ALLIE T. IVEY
229 Walnut Street, Green Cove Springs 32043.

Greenville. LILLIAN DAY
P.O. Box 2, Greenville 32331.

Gulfport. YVONNE JOHNSON (D) **
1972-. Org: PTA, Parlimentarian. B: 5/31/28.
Add: 5012 17th Ave. South, Gulfport 33707
(813)342-8011.

Gulfport. JUDY TONKIN
2401 53rd St. S., Gulfport 33707.

Gulf Stream. JOAN S. LA PORTE
246 Sea Rd., Gulf Stream 33444.

Hacienda Village. VERNA GILLESPIE
ANNA B. GREEN
ALICE HART
3841 State Rd. 84, Hacienda Village 33312.

Haines City. BARBARA R. COSTELLO (D)
1974-. Vice Mayor. Bds: Ch., Finance; Downtown Redevt. Org: BPW. Occ: Exec. Secretary &
Office Manager. B: 6/15/39. Add: 1414 Harriett
Ave., Haines City 33844 (813)422-6969.

Hastings. MRS. LLEWELLYN S. THRIFT (D)
1977-. Org: Nat. Police & Fire Fighters
Assoc.; Nat. Safety Council; Amer. Assoc. of
Retired Persons. B: 6/24/12. Add: 201 1st St.,
Hastings 32045 (904)692-1420.

Haverhill. LUCY J. RENAULT
4585 Charlotte St., West Palm Beach 33409.

Hialeah Gardens. MOLLY GASHUN (D)
1975-. Bds: Police Cmsn. Party: State Del.
1971, '73, '75; State Alt. 1967, '69. Prev:
V-Mayor 1975-76. Org: Senior Citizens; Dem.
Club. B: 7/3/12. Add: 140 Royal Palm Rd.,
Hialeah Gdns. 33016 (305)821-4441.

Highland Beach. RUTH E. MUMFORD (R)
1972-. Educ: N. Central Coll. 1960 BA. B:
8/1/08. Add: 3224 S. Ocean Blvd., Highland
Beach 33421 (305)278-4548.

Hillcrest Heights. JUNE FELT
Babson Park 33827.

Holly Hill. HELEN B. HADLEY (D)
1974-. Mayor Pro Tem. Org: BPW; Chamber of
Commerce; Dem. Club; NEA; OES. Educ: Edinboro
State Coll. 1931 BS; U. of Pittsburgh 1948 MEd.
B: 2/6/07. Add: 1200 Riverside Dr., Holly Hl.
32017 (904)252-7631.

Holly Hill. RUTH NELSON STARR (D)
1975-. Bds: Ch., Civil Service Bd. of Appeals.
Party: Cnty. Committeewoman 1970-77; Precinct
Leader 1965-70. Prev: Community Devt. Project
1973-75; City Charter Review Bd. 1974-75. Org:
Disabled Amer. Veterans; Chamber of Commerce;
Dem. Women Club; Dem. Club. Educ: Daytona Beach
Jr. Coll. 1970 R.E. Occ: Real Estate Assoc. B:
8/21/32. Add: 346 Clifton Ave., Holly Hill
32017 (904)255-2865.

Hollywood. CATHLEEN A. ANDERSON (D)
1975-. Bds: Cnty. Historical Cmsn. Party:
Cnty. Committeewoman. Org: Amer. Institute of
Banking; Civic Assoc.; Chamber of Commerce; Dem.
Club; Women's Club; Concerned Dem's. Occ: Bank
Officer. B: 12/7/34. Add: 1900 Tyler St., Holly-
wood 33020 (305)925-8200.

Holmes Beach. CHARLOTTE LONG
5901 Marina Drive, Holmes Beach 33510.

Homestead. YVONNE H. BRASSFIELD-LEE
790 Homestead Blvd., Homestead 33030.

Homestead. RUTH L. CAMPBELL (D)
1963-. Bds: League of Cities; Municipal
Utilities Assoc. Party: Cnty. Dem. Committeewoman
1961-65. Prev: State Bd. of Cosmetology 1969-73.
Org: Nat. Hairdressers & Cosmetologist Assoc.;
Chamber of Commerce; Women's Club; WPC; Women in
Govt. Service. Occ: Supervisor, Cosmetology
School. B: 6/27/20. Add: 24 N.E. 12th St.,
Homestead 33030 (305)247-1801.

Howey-In-The-Hills. ALICE C. BISHOP (R)
1976-. Prev: Planning Bd. 1955-66. Org: Com.
on Status of Women. Educ: Glassboro State Coll.
1949 BS. B: 11/6/03. Add: 403 S. Palm Ave.,
Howey-In-The-Hills 32737 (904)324-2900.

Howey-In-The-Hills. JUNE V. EBBERTS
P.O. Box 67, Howey-In-The-Hills 32737.

Hypoluxo. EMMA NIEMI
7450 S. U.S. Hwy. 1, Hypoluxo 33462.

Hypoluxo. JUNE ROOS (D)
1976-. B: 7/12/23. Add: 140 Periwinkle Dr.,
Hypoluxo 33462 (305)582-0155.

Indialantic. KATHERINE KOVAC
P.O. Box 3108, Indialantic 32903.

Indian Harbour Beach. BETTY S. WOEHLE
40 Cheyenne Ct., Indian Harbour Beach 32937.

Indian River Shores. SUZANNE M. BODEN (R)
1977-. Org: Nat. Assoc. Women Lawyers. Educ:
U. of Chicago 1944 BA. Occ: Atty. B: 2/23/23.
Add: 261 John's Island Dr., Vero Beach 32960
(305)231-1771.

Indian Rocks Beach. BOBBIE WOODMAN MAC DONALD (R)
1976-. Party: Precinct Committeewoman 1971-75.
Org: League of Cities; Home Owners Assoc.;
Concerned Tax Payers; Young Rep's.; Amer. Conservative Union. Educ: U. of Ala. 1959 BS. B:
3/24/36. Add: 1606 Beach Tr., Indian Rocks Bch.
33535.

Indian Rocks Beach. EDWINA A. WHITNEL
P.O. Box 98, Indian Rocks Beach 33535.

Indian Shores. JEWELL M. ADAMS (D)
1977-. Bds: Bldgs. & Grounds; Legal;
Sanitation. Org: Home Owners Assoc.; Chamber
of Commerce. Occ: Motel Owner. B: 8/15/28.
Add: 19236 Gulf Blvd., Indian Shores 33535
(813)595-4020.

Indian Shores. SUE BREEDING
P.O. Box 235, Indian Shores 33535.

Indian Shores. MRS. JILL VERCHER
P.O. Box 235, Indian Shores 33535.

Inglis. WAUNETA PRICE
P.O. Dwr. 429, Inglis 32749.

Interlachen. LORRAINE G. ALLEN (R) **
1973-. Educ: U. of Fla. Occ: Tax Consultant.
B: 5/24/21. Add: Box 181, Interlachen 32048
(904)684-2151.

Interlachen. RUTH ANN WILSON
P.O. Box 85, Interlachen 32048.

Jennings. KATHRYN ADAMS
P.O. Box 208, Jennings 32053.

Juno Beach. CAROL E. GIBBONS
841 Ocean Dr., Juno Beach 33408.

Jupiter. BERTHA M. BLOOM
P.O. Box 728, Jupiter 33458.

Jupiter. BARBARA JEANNE MONTAGUE (R)
1976-. Bds: Ch., Leisure Time Com.; Ch.,
Beautification Com. Party: Cnty. Committeewoman
1976-80. Prev: Planning & Zoning Cmsn. 1975-76.
Org: LWV; PTO. B: 6/24/37. Add: 605 Douglas
Dr., Jupiter 33458 (305)746-5134.

Keystone Heights. MARY T. BROKAS (D)
1977-. Bds: Ch., Safety; Streets. Occ:
Secretary. B: 6/22/24. Add: P.O. Box 444,
Keystone Hts. 32656 (904)473-4989.

Keystone Heights. FRANCES BUFFINGTON (D)
1977-. Bds: Ch., Finance & Law Com.; Airport.
Educ: St. Johns Rvr. Jr. Coll. 1968 AA; U. of
Fla. 1970 BAE. Occ: Teacher. B: 5/9/36. Add:
Rt. 2, Box 389, Keystone Hts., 32656
(904)473-4807.

Keystone Heights. BARBARA C. OWENS (D)
1976-. Bds: Ch., Streets & Hwy's.; Safety.
Org: Parent Faculty Assoc. Occ: Secretary.
B: 12/07/32. Add: P.O. Box 997, Keystone Hts.
32656 (904)473-4807.

La Crosse. SHIRLEY HILDERBRAN
P.O. Drw. D, La Crosse 32658.

Lake Buena Vista. IMOGENE W. LAND
ELIZABETH J. WISE
P.O. Box 22035, Lake Buena Vista 32830.

Lakeland. WINIFRED C. BROWN (D)
1974-. Bds: Pres., League of Municipalities;
Ch., Ad Hoc Hotel Com.; Ch., Airport Adv. Prev:
Ch., City Beautification Bd.; Ch., Zoning Bd. of
Adjustment & Appeals 1970-73; Mayor 1976. Org:
Chamber of Commerce; Women's Club; Coord. Council
of Women's Clubs; Jr. Achievement; Drug Abuse
Council. Occ: Dress Shop Owner. B: 10/31/15.
Add: 331 Easton Dr., Lakeland 33803 (813)
682-1141.

Lake Mary. LILLIAN GRIFFIN
DELORES LASH
P.O. Box 725, Lake Mary 32746.

Lake Placid. ARLENE TUCK (D)
1975-. Bds: Adv. Bd., Manpower Consortium.
Org: OES. Occ: Legal Secretary. B: 4/6/46.
Add: Rt. 4, 102 Belleview, Lk. Placid 33852
(813)465-4242.

Lake Worth. GRACE S. HUGHES
PATRICIA A. LIN
7 N. Dixie Hwy., Lake Worth 33460.

Largo. MARY GRAY BLACK
LORRAINE B. QUINN
P.O. Box 296, Largo 33540.

Lauderhill. MARIAN CORY (I)
1976-. Party: Precinct Committeewoman 1972-.
Prev: Ch., Charter Review Bd. 1975-76. Org:
Civic Fed. Occ: Exec. V-Pres., Leg. & Govt.
Consultants. B: 7/10/40. Add: 2872 NW 55th Ave.,
Apt. 2A, Lauderhill 33313 (305)584-9521.

Lauderhill. SUSAN G. HATCHER (D)
1973-. Bds: League of Cities Com. on State
Legislation; League of Cities. Prev: Council
V-Pres. 1976-77; Council Pres. 1975-76; Treasurer
1973-74. Org: Civic Fed., Woman's Club. Occ:
Public Relations & Marketing Consultant. B:
8/15/46. Add: 4301 N.W. 23 St., Lauderhill
33313 (305)584-9521.

Lighthouse Point. BETTY A. KIMBROUGH
P.O. Box 5100, Lighthouse Point 33064.

Longwood. JUNE LORMANN
175 W. Warren Ave., Longwood 32750.

Madeira Beach. PATRICIA J. SHONTZ (I)
Bds: Ch., Advertising & Public Relations. Prev:
City Cmsnr. 1972-77. Org: Soroptimist; Civic
Assoc.; Women's Chamber Com.; Women's Rep. Club;
Nat. Fed. Rep. Women. Occ: Corp. Co-Owner. B:
3/29/33. Add: 15334 Harbor Dr., Madeira Bch.
(813)391-9951.

Malabar. ANDREA DE CARO
PRISCILLA HOWARD
P.O. Box 245, Malabar 32950.

Mary Esther. EILEEN PORTER
P.O. Box 397, Mary Esther 32569.

Melbourne Beach. MARGARET F. SCOTT (D)
1977-. Prev: Planning & Zoning Bd. 1972-75;
Bd. of Adjustment 1975-77. Org: LWV. Educ:
Allegheny Coll. 1964 BS. B: 5/10/42. Add: 209
1st Ave., Melbourne Bch. 32951 (305)724-5860.

Melbourne Village. JUNE GOLDER
GLADYS HANSEN
535 Hammock Rd., Melbourne Village 32901.

Miami. ROSE GORDON (D)
1971-. Bds: Ch., City Retirement Plan;
League of Cities; Adv. Com. on Intergovt Affairs.
Party: State Del. 1976. Org: Bd. of Realtors;
Chamber of Commerce; BPW; Urban League; Community
Action Agency; Dem. Women; OES; Fla. Women in
Gov. Serv. in 1975. Occ: Realtor. B: 2/4/18.
Add: 1890 S. Bayshore Dr., Miami 33133
(305)579-6017.

Miami Springs. CAROLYN GRASSO
201 Westward Dr., Miami Springs 33166.

Milton. BETTY ROGERS WILLEY (D)
1972-. Bds: Ch., Youth Council; Ch., Growth
& Devt. Com.; Finance Com. Party: V-Ch., Cnty.
Exec. Com. 1976-77; Ch., Cnty. Exec. Com. 1977-
80; Precinct Committee Repr. 1975. Prev: Cnty.
Draft Bd.; Governor's Review Com. for Retarded-
Program Grants 1977. Org: Bd. of Realtors;
Historical Society; Retarded Assoc.; Chamber of
Commerce; Dem. Women's Club; Youth Council.
Occ: Real Estate Saleswoman. B: 8/2/24. Add:
600 Lakeshore Dr., Milton 32570 (904)623-3661.

Minneola. CLARA CLARK
P.O. Box 678, Minneola 32755.

Miramar. VICTORIA COCEANO (D)
1977-. Party: State Del. 1975; Cnty.
Committeewoman 1963-77; Cnty. Ch. Screening Com.
1968-73; Cnty. V-Ch., Dem. Party 1973-74, 1977-
78; Cnty. Ch., Dem. Party 1974-75. Prev: Safety
Council 1970-74. Org: Bd. of Realtors; Dem.
Club; Women's Club. Occ: Realtor. B: 8/15/23.
Add: 7680 Granada Blvd., Miramar 33023
(305)989-6200.

Miramar. MARY FORZANO
P.O. Box 3838, Miramar 33023.

Mount Dora. ADRIANNE N. LOWE
P.O. Box 176, Mount Dora 32757.

Mulberry. SYLVIA J. EASON (D)
1975-. Bds: Ch., Salary Admin. Review. Prev:
Planning Cmsn. 1974-75. Occ: Maintenance
Scheduler. B: 9/2/35. Add: 105 10th Dr. N.W.,
Mulberry 33860 (813)425-1125.

Naples. VIRGINIA B. CORKRAN (I)
1974-. Bds: Ch., Ad Hoc Water Com.; Ch., Bch.
Com. Org: LWV; Sierra Club. Educ: Conn. Coll.
1945 BA. Occ: Realtor. B: 2/13/24. Add:
3300 Gulf Shore Blvd., Naples 33940.

Neptune Beach. SUE BROWN CHARPENTIER (D)
1973-. Bds: Ch., Beautification, Clean-Up &
Sanitation; Laws & Rules; Ch., Streets, Bulk-
heads & Sidewalks. Org: PTO. Educ: Crawford
W. Long School of Nursing 1961 RN. Occ: R.N.
B: 11/21/39. Add: 1947 Seagull Cove, Neptune
Beach 32233 (904)249-2372.

Newberry. MAGGIE K. HOLDER
P.O. Box 368, Newberry 32669.

New Port Richey. JULIE J. OBENREDER (D)
1976-. Org: BPW; Historical Society; Dem.
Club; Women's Dem. Club; Com. on Council on
Aging. Occ: Author/Teacher. B: 1/7/13. Add:
117 E. Tennessee Ave., New Port Richey 33552
(813)849-2261.

New Smyrna Beach. LILLIAN BENT
P.O. Box 490, New Smyrna Beach 32069.

North Bay Village. DOROTHY COHEN
7903 E. Drive, North Bay Village 33141.

Oakland Park. FLORENCE B. LOSS
3650 N.E. 12th Ave., Oakland Park 33334.

Ocean Breeze Park. DOROTHY GREEBEN
RUTH HOKE
BETTY MAC NAB
P.O. Box 846, Jensen Beach 33457.

Ocean Ridge. VERA J. KLEIN
6450 N. Ocean Blvd., Ocean Ridge 33435.

Oldsmar. DOTTY H. LEE
P.O. Box 100, Oldsmar 33557.

Opa-Locka. BEULAH ROBBINS
P.O. Box 86, Opa-Locka 33054.

Orange City. VIRGINIA L. TRENTHAM
Town Hall, Orange City 32763.

Orange Park. CATIE NICHOLS (R)
1976-. Bds: Zoning Bd. Liason; Environmental
Quality Bd. Liason. Prev: Environmental Quality
Bd. 1971-76. Org: LWV. Educ: Weber Coll. 1942
ABS. B: 2/14/22. Add: 504 Fatio Ln., Orange Pk.
32073 (904)264-9565.

Orchid. JEANNETTE M. LIER
ANNE DENBY MICHAEL
Rt. 2, Box 66, Vero Beach 32960.

Otter Creek. EDNA JEAN WATSON (D)
1974-. Occ: Storekeeper. B: 12/14/47. Add:
P.O. Box 34, Otter Creek 32683.

Otter Creek. PHILENE WILLIAMS
City Hall, Otter Creek 32683.

Pahokee. WYONIA LEE CUMMINGS **
1972-. Bds: Ch., Bicentennial Cmsn. Party:
County Exec. Com. 1969-70. Org: NEA; Rep. Club.
Educ: Morris Harvey 1956 BS. B: 12/21/28. Add:
291 Banyan Ave., Pahokee 33476 (305)924-5659.

Painters Hill. ALMA M. HARRIS
LEOLA R. JONES
P.O. Box 234, Flagler Beach 32036.

Palm Bay. PEG HEWITT (D)
1974-. Bds: Transportation System Policy
Group; Regional Planning Council; City Employee
Retirement Bd. Org: Chamber of Commerce; LWV.
B: 10/22/20. Add: 428 Harvin Ln., Palm Bay 32905.

Palm Beach. YVELYNE DE MARCELLUS MARIX **
1970-. Educ: U. of Calif. 1945 BS. Occ: Owner
Travel Bureau. B: 7/13/25. Add: Box 2029, Palm
Beach 33480.

Palm Beach Shores. MARIE F. ERNST
247 Edwards Ln., Palm Beach Shores 33404.

Palm Shores. ALICIA ELLIOTT (R)
1976-. Org: Chamber of Commerce. Occ:
Motel Manager-Owner. B: 12/5/25. Add: Rt. 1,
Box 396, Palm Shores 32935.

Palm Springs. JEANETTE GUERTY
226 Cypress Ln., Palm Springs 33461.

Parker. ALPHORETTA K. HOLBROOK (D) **
1973-. Educ: U. of West Fla. 1975 BA. Occ:
Substitute Teacher. B: 1/27/30. Add: 5221
Kendrick St., Parker 32401 (904)785-7272.

Parkland. BRENDA C. SELNER
8585 Holmberg Road, Parkland 33067.

Paxton. OLENE STAGGERS
P.O. Box 1186, Paxton 32538.

Pennsuco. BARBARA HAMMACK
SARAH WALKER
14420 N.W. 60th Ave., Miami Lakes 33014.

Pinellas Park. PATRICIA L. BAILEY
5141 78th Ave., Pinellas Park 33565.

Plant City. BETTY JUNE BARKER (D) **
1968-. Org: Dem. Club.; Woman's Club. Educ:
Asbury Coll. 1955 BA. B: 12/22/28. Add: 708
East Tomlin St., Plant City 33566 (813)752-3125.

Pomona Park. NANCY BRADLEY
P.O. Box 518, Pomona Park 32081.

Pompano Beach. EMMA LOU OLSON (I)
1976-. Bds: Bd. of Dir's. League of Cities;
Bd. of Rules & Appeals. Prev: Ch., Zoning Bd.
1971-74; Ch., Annexation Bd. 1974-76; Cnty.
Citizen's Adv. Planning Council 1975-76; Fla.
Selective Service System 1971-76. Org: Bd. of
Realtors; Chamber of Commerce; Nat. Assoc. of
Parliamentarians; Women's Club; Historical
Society; Rep. Club. Women's Exec. Club. Occ:
Realtor. B: 6/18/24. Add: 420 NE 19th Ave.,
Pompano Bch. 33060 (305)942-1100.

Pompano Beach. BETTY L. WISTEDT
P.O. Dwr. 1300, Pompano Beach 33060.

Port Richey. DORIS BURES
1000 U.S. Hwy. 19, N., Port Richey 33568.

Port Richey. HOLLY M. ODER (D)
1973-. Bds: Technical Adv. Com.; League of
Cities. Prev: Deputy City Clerk 1973. Org:
Women's Club; PTA. Educ:Pasco Hernando
Community Coll. 1975 AA. B: 12/30/45. Add:
55 Wildwood St., Port Richey 33568
(813)849-7544.

Port St. Lucie. LOLITA B. KERNOHAN
Morningside Blvd., Port St. Lucie 33452.

Raiford. JOYCE C. NORMAN
P.O. Box 96, Raiford 32083.

Redington Beach. HELEN F. VOLKMER
105 164th Ave., Redington Beach 33708.

Rockledge. SUZANNE F. SCHMITT (R)
1976-. Bds: Ch., Finance Com; Administrative
Com.; Recreation Com. Prev: Citizen's Adv. Com.
1976; Zoning Ordinance Revision Com. 1976. Org:
Chamber of Commerce; Women's Club; Home & School
Assoc. Occ: Newspaper Distributor. B: 3/22/41.
Add: 637 Orange Ct., Rockledge 32955
(305)636-5711.

St. Leo. MARIE CULLITON
SISTER JEROME LEAVY
P.O. Drawer F, St. Leo 33574.

St. Lucie Village. WYNEL A. GRANITZ (D)
1977-. Bds: Ch., Ordinance & Zoning Cmsn.
Org: Mental Health. Educ: Indian River Community
Coll. 1974 AA; Nova U. 1977 BS; Fla. Atlantic U.
1976 MA. Occ: Teacher. B: 12/20/38. Add: Rt. 1,
Box 108, Ft. Pierce 33450 (305)464-0332.

St. Lucie Village. BESSIE HAYES
P.O. Box 3743, Ft. Pierce 33450.

St. Marks. ALLIE MAE ROBERTS
P.O. Box 296, St. Marks 32355.

St. Petersburg. BETTY JANE FINLEY (D)
1977-. Bds: Budget Review; Historical Preservation. Org: Human Rights. Educ: Ga. Wesleyan
1947 BA. Occ: Teacher. B: 1/21/25. Add: 125
9th Ave. N.E., St. Petersburg 33701.

St. Petersburg. SARA C. WALLACE
P.O. Box 2842, St. Petersburg 33731.

St. Petersburg Beach. HELEN L. ERCIUS (R)
1975-. Bds: Regional Planning Council; Waste
Water Treatment Com. Org: Community Club;
Woman's Club. Educ: U. of Tenn. 1940 BS. B:
8/20/19. Add: 109 12th Ave., St. Petersburg Bch.
33706 (813)363-5511.

Sanibel. ZELDA P. BUTLER (R)
1974-. Bds: Energy Action Com.; League of
Cities; Finance Com. Org: LWV. B: 2/9/26. Add:
Loggerhead Cay #503, Sanibel 33957 (813)472-4135.

Satellite Beach. JANIE B. BRIDGERS
510 Cinnamon Dr., Satellite Beach 32937.

Sea Ranch Lakes. VIRGINIA MITCHELL
1 Gatehouse Rd., Sea Ranch Lakes 33308.

Shalimar. KATHLEEN BOWMAN
LUCILLE HANKS
P.O. Box 815, Okaloosa City 32579.

Sopchoppy. ANN HODGE
P.O. Box 72, Sopchoppy 32358.

South Bay. MRS. VERNITA COX
P.O. Box 130, South Bay 33493.

South Miami. BETTY A. LANTZ
CATHY MC CANN
6130 Sunset Dr., South Miami 33143.

Sunrise. PATRICIA BROWN
1277 N.W. 61st Ave., Sunrise 33313.

Surfside. MARION KING PORTMAN (D)
1974-. Bds: Dir., League of Cities; V-Pres.,
Women in Govt. Prev: Mayor 1974-76. Educ:
Harris Teachers Coll. 1945 BA; U. of Miami 1970
MA. Occ: Teacher. B: 2/11/23. Add: 9272 Bay
Dr., Surfside 33154 (305)861-4863.

Suwanee River. LELIA ALLEN
Rt. 1, Box 161B, Trenton 32693.

Tamarac. HELEN C. MASSARO (D)
1972-. Bds: Bd. of Consumer Affairs; Handicapped Transportation Bd. Org: Dem. Club. Occ:
Pres., Structural Steel Corp. B: 10/29/09.
Add: 5601 NW 50th Ave., Tamarac 33319
(305)722-5900.

Tampa. CATHERINE BARJA
City Hall, Tampa 33602.

Tampa. SANDRA WARSHAW FREEDMAN (D)
1974-. Bds: Parks Bd.; Recreation Bd.; Conv.
Bd. Org: Civic Assoc. Educ: U. of Miami 1965
BA. B: 9/21/43. Add: 546 Riviera Dr., Tampa
33606 (813)223-8131.

Tampa. JAN KAMINIS PLATT (D)
1974-. Bds: Ch., Council of Govts.; Drug
Abuse Coord. Council; Housing Authority Study
Com. Prev: Governors Task Force on Coastal Zone
Management 1976-77; Financial Disclosure Campaign
1975-76; Constitution Revision Cmsn. 1977-78.
Educ: Fla. State U. 1958 BA. B: 9/27/35. Add:
4606 Beach Pk. Dr., Tampa 33609 (813)223-8131.

Tavares. PATRICIA FARNER
P.O. Box 1246, Tavares 32778.

Temple Terrace. NANCY R. SEVER (D)
1974-. Bds: Ch., Budget Com.; Audit Com.
Party: Precinct Committeewoman 1977. Prev:
Hillsborough Cnty. Citizens Adv. Com. 1973-75;
Sewer Project Com. 1967-68. Org: LWV; WEAL;
Common Cause; NOW; Public Citizen. Occ: Book-
keeper. B: 4/2/32. Add: 705 Grand Ct., Temple
Ter., 33617 (813)988-5111.

Trenton. FAYE LAYFIELD
P.O. Box 251, Trenton 32693.

Wausau. DOROTHY D. MC DONALD (D)
1973-. Occ: Teacher's Aide. B: 7/14/32.
Add: P.O. Box 53, Wausau 32463.

Weeki Wachee. RUTH BRINZO
97 Highway 19 S., Weeki Wachee 33512.

West Miami. VALERIE C. HICKEY (D)
1974-. Bds: League of Cities. Org: Amer.
Bankers Assoc.; Women in Govt. Service; Citizens
Adv. Com. for Educ. Occ: Asst. Cashier/Manager
Bank. B: 10/7/25. Add: 5930 SW 10th St., Miami
33144 (305)266-1000.

West Palm Beach. CAROL A. ROBERTS
HELEN WILKES
P.O. Box 3366, West Palm Beach 33402.

Wilton Manors. SANDRA KAY JEDLICKA (R)
     1976-. Bds: League of Cities. Party: Precinct
Committeewoman 1969-; V-Ch., Cnty. Com. 1974-76;
Cnty. Membership Ch. 1972-76. Prev: Cnty. Traffic-
ways Com. 1976-78. Org: Internat. Assoc. of
Assessing Officers; Professional Appraisers Assoc;
BPW; Humane Society; Women's Rep. Club. Occ:
Secretary. B: 8/25/39. Add: 8 Middlesex Dr.,
Wilton Manors 33305 (305)566-2467.

Windermere. CAROLYN B. GREER (R) **
     1974-. Bds: West Orange Scholarship Found-
ation. Org: Jr. League. Educ: Fla. State U.
1959 BS. B: 6/30/37. Add: 1119 Oakdale St.,
Windermere 32786 (305)876-2563.

Yankeetown. MRS. JIMMIE WALL
     P.O. Box 280, Yankeetown 32698.

Judges

VIRGINIA Q. BEVERLY (D)
     Circuit Court Judge. 1977-. Org: ABA; Fla.
& Ga. Bar Assocs. Educ: St. Joseph's 1948 BS;
U. of N.C. 1953 LLB. B: 10/20/26. Add: 10157
Lake Lamar Ct., Jacksonville 32216 (904)633-6560.

RHEA PINCUS GROSSMAN (D)
     Circuit Court Judge. 1972-. Bds: State Conf.
of Circuit Judges Bd.; Ch., Rules Com. Prev:
Judge, State Industrial Relations Cmsn. 1970.
Org: ABA; BPW. Educ: U. of Miami 1962 AB; 1965
JD. B: 7/25/41. Add: 4245 N. Bay Rd., Miami
Bch 33140 (305)579-5402.

ELLEN J. MORPHONIOS (D)
     Circuit Court Judge. 1970-. Dist: 11. Prev:
Fla. Bd. Bar Examiners 1968-70. Org: ABA; Amer.
Judicature Soc.; Circuit Judges Conf.; Nat. Assoc.
Women's Lawyers; BPW; NOW. Educ: U. of Miami
1957 JD. B: 9/30/29. Add: 8640 SW 84th Ave.,
Miami 33143 (305)547-7125.

Boards and Commissions

     Office of the Governor, State Capitol Bldg.,
Tallahassee 32304.

Aging, Advisory Council to the Division of
     MARGUERIT BARRINEAU
     JUANITY MAXEY
     HELEN WALKER
     MRS. PARALEE J. WEBB
     MRS. I.E. WILLIAMS

Air and Water Pollution Board
     SUSAN UHL WILSON

Bicentennial Commission
     JOHNNIE RUTH CLARKE
     MRS. RAYMOND MASON
     MRS. ROBERT SHEVIN

Business Regulation, Board of
     MILDRED WIGFALL RAVENELL

Condominium Advisory Board
     MIRIAM S. BLICKMAN
     MRS. JOHN E. HAZARD

Corrections, Task Force On
     SUSAN HARRELL BLACK

Cosmetology, State Board of
     GRACE BLISS
     DOLA HALL
     VIOLET M. LLANEZA
     ALICE B. MELTON

Criminal Justice Standards, Governor's Commission
on
     VIRGINIA YOUNG

Development Commission
     ELISE BROWN

Diabetes Advisory Council
     MILDRED KAUFMAN
     JUDY JORDAN
     PATRICIA SCHULTZ

Economic Development Advisory Council
     MRS. ELISE ASHLER
     GLATYS HARSON

Environmental Regulation Commission
     SUSAN UHL WILSON

Ethics Commission
     CHARLOTTE HUBBARD

Health Coordinating Council
     LUCILLE FRISTOE
     ROSE GORDON
     DOROTHY M. MILTON
     BARBARA ROVINSON
     JEANNE SLOAN
     JAN TUVESON

Health Planning Council
     GLADYS TAYLOR

Historic Preservation Board
     MRS. C.V. BOARD

Housing Authority
     LOUISE TYLER
     NADINE N. WILLIAMS

Housing Goals Council
     ARNETTA BROWN
     MARY SINGLETON

Human Rights Advocacy Committee
     MARY GLOVER
     SISTER CAROL KEEHAN

Independent Post-Secondary Vocational, Technical,
Trade and Business Schools, State Board of
     BETTY W. MC NABB

Judicial Qualifications Commission
     MRS. P.B. PHILLIPS

Jury Commission
     GLADYS M. SMITH

Juvenile Delinquency Task Force for the Governor's
Commission on Criminal Justice Standards and Goals
    MARGARET BALD
    BESS BALL
    ELAINE BLOOM
    LINDA CARTER
    DORIS DUDNEY
    NANCY DELLEY
    DOROTHY PATE
    MRS. FRED ROGERS
    JEANNIE SIFRIT
    BENITA TILLMAN
    GAIL TUCK
    ANN WESTALL

Landscape Architects, Board of
    HELEN HENDRY

Law Revision Commission
    JANET RENO

Marriage and the Family Unit, Task Force on
    ROBERTA FULTON FOX

Medical Examiners, State Board of
    DR. DORIS N. CARSON

Medical Liability Insurance Study Commission
    MRS. I.B. HARRISON

Mental Health, Advisory Council on
    MRS. WAYNE BEVIS

Naturopathic Examiners, State Board of
    DR. LORNA MURRAY

Nursing Home Administrators, Examining Board of
    AGNES CIOLFI

Offender Rehabilitation, Advisory Council to the
Department of
    PEGGY BERG
    SUSAN BLACK
    SUSAN D. CARON
    SISTER ROSEMARY FINNEGAN
    BESSIE H. JACKSON
    ALMA MC KINNEY
    JUNE ROCKER
    VIOLET SALTZMAN
    VIRGINIA M. SHARP
    MRS. ARNOLD SPANJERS, JR.
    JUDY STEPHENS
    HENRIETTA B. SWILLEY
    RENEE TELSON
    SYLVIA WELLS

Physical Fitness, Governor's Task Force on
    DR. RUTH ALEXANDER
    FRAN CARLTON
    SARA JERNIGAN
    JUDY WALKER

Prison Industry Commission
    CLARICE BIGGINS

Psychology Examiners, State Board of
    DR. JACQUELIN GOLDMAN

Public Employees Relations Commission
    ROSEMARY FILIPOWICS

Real Estate Commission
    MAGGIE S. SALLETTER

Regents, Board of
    BETTY ANNE STATON

Resource Recovery and Management Advisory Council
    CHARLENE NEMO

Retirement Commission
    NANCY T. FORD
    EDNA TAIT

State Fair Authority
    MARIE NICHELS

Status of Women, Governor's Commission on
    PEGGY BARNETT
    SUSAN BLACK
    BEVERLY DOZIER
    DOROTHY GLISSON
    EVELYN HOLLAND
    DR. EMMA KITTLES
    MARY KUMPE
    ANNIE LOVE
    DELORES MITCHELL
    ANNE PAJCIC
    JANIS PIOTROWSKI
    RUTH RICHMOND
    CAROLYN VAUGHN
    NANCY WITTENBERG

Teacher Education Center, State Council for
    BEVERLYN BAINES
    PATRICIA LUTTERBIE
    JOY MERCER

Georgia

State Legislature

State Senate

VIRGINIA SHAPARD (D)

1974-. Dist: 28. Bds: Educ. Com.; Human Resources Com.; Consumer Affairs Com. Party: State Del. 1975-77; State Dem. Com. 1975-77; Dem. Com. 1975-77. Prev: Regional Library Bd. 1969-74. Org: Nat. Conf. of State Legislators; LWV; BPW; Utility Club; Farm Bureau. Educ: Randolph-Macon Women's Coll. 1957 BA. B: 2/19/36. Add: P.O. Drawer K, Griffin 30224 (404)656-6885.

State House

HENRIETTA MATHIS CANTY (D)

1975-. Dist: 38. Bds: State Community Affairs; U. System; Retirement. Educ: Johnson C. Smith U. 1949 BA; U. of Pa. 1961 MA. Occ: Personnel Services Owner. B: 10/23/28. Add: 487 Lynn Valley Rd. SW, Atlanta 30311 (404)656-1111.

PEGGY CHILDS (D)

1974-. Dist: 51. Bds: Judiciary; State Institutions & Properties; Retirement. Party: Party Reorg. Com. 1972-73. Org: Child Devt. Ctr.; PTA; Special Educ. Com. Educ: U. of Ga. 1958 BA; 1960 MEd. B: 11/17/37. Add: 520 Westchester Dr., Decatur 30030 (404)378-0593.

BETTY JEAN CLARK (D) *

1973-. Dist: 55. Org: Concerned Citizens of DeKalb. B: 3/13/44. Add: 2139 Flat Shoals Rd., SE, Apt. 3, Atlanta 30316.

DOROTHY FELTON (R)

1974-. Dist: 22. Bds: Governor's Tax Study Cmsn.; Prison Educ. Com.-Sub. Com. of State Institutes & Property. Prev: Cnty. Personnel Bd. 1972-74. Org: LWV; PTA; Woman's Club. Educ: U. of Ark. 1950 BA. B: 3/1/29. Add: 465 Tanacrest Dr., NW, Atlanta 30328 (404)252-4172.

MARY JANE GALER (D)

1976-. Bds: Temperance Com.; Industrial Relations Com.; Defense & Veteran's Affairs. Prev: Cmsn. on Status of Women 1975-. Org: Library Assoc.; AAUP; AAUW; NOW; LWV; Common Cause; Soroptomist; Metropolitan Urban League. Educ: U. of Pittsburgh 1945 BA; Carnegie Institute of Technology 1947 BS. B: 6/30/24. Add: 7236 Lullwater Rd., Columbus 31904 (404)324-2931.

MILDRED GLOVER (D) **

Dist: 32. Occ: Professor. Add: 672 Beckwith St. Southwest, Apt. 7, Atlanta 30314.

GRACE TOWNS HAMILTON (D)

1965-. Dist: 31. Bds: Cnty. Cmsn. Study Com.; Special Rules Com. Party: Cnty. Dem. Exec. Com.; Nat. Dem. Com's. Cmsn. on the Presidential Nomination & Party Structure. Prev: Atlanta Charter Cmsn. 1971-73. Org: NOWL; Nat. Historic Preservation Bd.; Day Nursery Assoc. Bd. Educ: Atlanta U. 1927 BA; Ohio State U. 1929 MA. B: 2/10/07. Add: 582 University Pl., NW, Atlanta 30314.

ELEANOR L. RICHARDSON (D)

1974-. Bds: Health & Ecology; Ch., State Planning & Community Affairs Appropriations. Prev: Ch., Citizens Adv. Com. 1971-73; Ch., Community Relations Com. 1969-73; Economic Appropriations 1969-71. Org: BPW; NOWL; LWV; ACLU; Cnty. Dem. Women; State Dem. Women. B: 3/17/13. Add: 755 Park Lane, Decatur 30033.

EARLEEN SIZEMORE (D)

1974-. Bds: Ch., Agriculture; Ch., Education; Ch., Ways & Means. Party: State Del. 1975. Org: Nat. Assoc. of Educators. Educ: Ga. Southern Coll. 1959 BS; Ga. Coll. 1965 MEd; U. of Ga. 1970 Ed. Sp. Occ: Fed. Program Coord. B: 7/29/38. Add: Rt. 3, Sylvester 31791 (912)776-3098.

CATHEY WEISS STEINBERG (D)

1976-. Dist: 46. Bds: Human Relations & Aging Com.; Retirement Com. Org: LWV; Dem. Party; Dem. Women's Club. Educ: Carnegie Mellon U. 1964 BA; U. of Pittsburgh 1965 MEd. B: 10/6/42. Add: 1732 Dunwoody Pl., Atlanta 30324.

County Commissions

Clarke. **JEWEL JOHN** (D)

1974-. Bds: Ch., Joint Services Study Com.; Ch., Planning Com.; N.E. Ga. Area Planning & Devt. Cmsn. Org: LWV; Women Voters; Recording for the Blind; Mental Health Assoc.; Dem. Women. B: 10/24/21. Add: 199 Spruce Vly. Rd., Athens 30605 (404)546-8330.

Clayton. **ANNIE RUTH FORD** (D)

1977-. Bds: Energy Com.; Assoc. of Cnty. Cmsnrs. Prev: Ch., Cnty. Tax Equalization Bd. 1976. Org: Woman's Club. Occ: Bank Cashier. B: 10/22/25. Add: 9605 Poston Rd., Jonesboro 30236 (404)478-9911.

Dekalb. **LIANE LEVETAN** (D) **

1974-. Bds: More Effective Local Government; School Bd.; Com. on Children & Youth. Org: Dem. Women; PTA. B: 3/19/36. Add: 2250 Chrysler Ter. Northeast, Atlanta 30345 (404)371-2881.

Glynn. LORRAINE DUSENBURY (R)
1972-. Bds: Ch., Coastal Area Planning &
Devt. Cmsn.; Governor's Adv. Council on Coastal
Zone Management; Area Council on Mental Health
& Retardation. Party: State Del. 1973-77. Org:
Civic Assoc.; LWV; Educ: Centenary Coll. for
Women 1939 AA. B: 6/29/20. Add: 22 Capt. Wylly
Rd., Jekyll Is. 31520 (912)265-7600.

Henry. JANICE S. HORTON (D)
1976-. Bds: Ch., Budget Com.; Ch., Community
Services Com. Party: State Del. 1976. Org: BPW;
Chamber of Commerce; Cancer Society; Dem. Club.
Educ: Tift Coll. 1967 BA. Occ: Realtor. B:
1/23/45. Add: 430 Burke Cir., McDonough 30253
(404)957-9131.

Liberty. HAZEL BAGLEY CARTER **
1959-. Prev: Council Member 1949-59. Occ:
Owner, Funeral Home. B: 4/14/14. Add: 308
South Oglethorpe Blvd., Hinesville 31313
(912)876-3523.

Oconee. SUE P. ROACH
Route 3, Box 356, Watkinsville

Richmond. BARBARA MULHERIN SCOTT (I)
1976-. Bds: Ch., Recreation; Hospital
Authority Liaison; Library Bd. Party: State Del.
1977; Exec. Rep. Com. Prev: Cnty. Tax Cmsn.
Org: Nat. Bd. of Realtors; Women's Council; Rep.
Women's Club. Educ: U. of Ga. 1960 BS. Occ:
Realtor. B: 4/17/38. Add: 2418 Williams St.,
Augusta 30904 (404)738-5415.

Schley. IMOGENE D. MC LENDON (D)
1977-. Bds: Library Bd. Party: V-Ch., Cnty.
Com. 1976. Prev: Family & Children's Dept. Bd.
1960-77. B: 5/3/22. Add: Rt. 2, Ellaville
31806 (912)937-2609.

Toombs. MARY BAKER RICE (R)
1977-. Bds: Health Bd.; Child Abuse Bd.;
Athletic Bd. Party: State Alt. 1960; Rep. Nat.
Committeewoman 1960-64. Org: DAR; Woman's Club;
Rep. Women. Educ: Ga. Coll. 1932 BS. B:
6/26/12. Add: 101 6th St., Vidalia 30474
(912)537-3785.

Ware. SARAH DOWLING THRIFT (D)
1977-. Bds: Community Action Agency. Org:
PTA. B: 4/3/47. Add: Rt. 3, Box 375, Waycross
31501 (912)283-7265.

Mayors

Buchanan. EVELYN SHEPARD WADE (D)
1970-. Bds: Water Authority; Ch., Landfill
Corp.; Regional Health Council. Org: Retired
Teachers Assoc.; Health Council; Women's Club;
Municipal Assoc.; Dem. Party. Educ: U. of Ga.
1952 BSE. B: 1/9/07. Add: Buchanan 30113
(404)646-3081.

Decatur. ANN A. CRICHTON (D)
1971-. Bds: Bd. of Educ. Org: Municipal Assoc.
Bd.; State Bd. of Industry & Trade; Ch., Community
Devt. Com.; Mental Health Assoc.; UNICEF; Ga.
Conservancy; Dem. Women; Historical Society. Educ:
Agnes Scott Coll. 1961 BA. B: 2/27/39. Add:

306 Westchester Dr., Decatur 30030
(404)377-9911.

Edison. ANN DISMUKES
City Hall, P.O. Box 327, Edison 31746.

Hiram. MARCIA HARRIS **
1972-. Bds: Water Authority; Industrial
Authority; Airport Authority. Occ: Secretary.
B: 4/3/36. Add: Box 55, Harris Dr., Hiram
30141 (404)943-3726.

Lake Park. INA T. LANE
City Hall, P.O. Box 115, Lake Park 31636.

Manchester. MARGIE S. COOK
City Hall, P.O. Box 166, Manchester 31816.

Marshallville. RACHEL S. BICKLEY
City Hall, P.O. Box 83, Marshallville 31057.

Maysville. MARY L. ARNOLD
City Hall, P.O. Box 86, Maysville 30558.

Norcross. LILLIAN WEBB (R) **
1974-. Bds: Police; Electric Authority.
Party: Dist. Ch. 1972-76; Local Precinct Ch.
1952-74; Del., Nat. Conv. 1972; County Ch.
1964-68. Prev: Council Member 1970-74. Org:
Chamber of Commerce; Municipal Assoc.; Rep.
Clubs. B: 11/13/28. Add: 300 Academy St.,
Norcross 30071 (404)448-2122.

Springfield. DORIS Y. FLYTHE (I)
1974-. Bds: Coastal Area Planning & Devt.
Cmsn.; Gov's. Adv. Bd. for Area Planning & Devt.;
Gov's. Adv. Bd. for the Status of Women. Prev:
Councilwoman 1971-74. Educ: Anderson Jr. Coll.
1948 AA. B: 5/11/28. Add: P.O. Box 93,
Springfield 31329 (912)754-6666.

Tallapoosa. ALTA DRYDEN
City Hall, P.O. Box 155, Tallapoosa 30176.

Villa Rica. JOYCE O. CONNALLY (D)
1975-. Org: PTA. B: 7/5/19. Add: 614
Magnolia St., Box 635, Villa Rica 30180
(404)459-3957.

White. GLENDA B. DUPREE (D)
1974-. B: 12/26/43. Add: P.O. Box 5, White
30184.

Woodland. MARILY DOSTER GOOLSBY (D)
1976-. Org: NEA; Assoc. of Educators. Educ:
Tift Coll. 1965 BS; Columbus Coll. 1976 MEd.
Occ: Teacher. B: 11/5/26. Add: Hwy. 41,
Woodland 31836 (404)674-2200.

Young Harris. IRENE H. BERRY (D)
1974-. Prev: Councilwoman. Add: Young
Harris 30582 (404)379-3223.

Local Councils

Alamo. FRANCES GRIFFIN
City Hall, Alamo 30411.

Albany. MARY YOUNG
City Hall, P.O. Box 447, Albany 31702.

Atlanta.   ESTHER LEFEVER
    1976-.   Bds: Public Safety; Transportation;
Energy Task Force.   Org: LWV.   Educ: Eastern
Mennonite Coll. 1953 AA.   Occ: Exec. Dir.,
Community Devt. Ctr.   B: 3/17/31.   Add: 442 Oak-
dale Rd., N.E., Atlanta 30307 (404)658-6360.

Auburn.   LUCILLE BRADLEY
           NANCY B. FAULKNER
    City Hall, Drawer 134, Auburn 30203.

Augusta.   CARRIE J. MAYS
    City Hall, 530 Greene St., Augusta 30903.

Avondale Estates.   JEAN C. LESLIE   (D)
    1974-.   Mayor Pro Tem.   Bds: Ch., Restoration
Com.; Merchant Com.   Educ: Auburn U. 1938 BS.   B:
7/29/16.   Add: 19 Wiltshire Dr., Avondale Est.
30002.

Baldwin.   MRS. VANCE GALLOWAY
    City Hall, Baldwin 30511.

Ball Ground.   LOUVENIA BARRETT
    City Hall, Ball Ground 30107.

Berlin.   GRACE D. CROFT   (D)
    1977-.   B: 10/18/09.   Add: P.O. Box 73, Ashley
St., Berlin 31722.

Berlin.   BEVERLY JEAN JORDAN
    P.O. Box 156, Berlin 31727.

Berlin.   LONNIE KENT
    1977-.   Org: Woman's Club; PTA.   B: 10/16/44.
Add: P.O. Box 127, Cranford St., Berlin 31722
(912)324-2444.

Bloomingdale.   JACQUELYN W. LOWMAN   (D)
    1974-.   Bds: Ch., Recreation; Ch., Garbage/
Sanitation.   Party: Volunteer Local City Worker
for National & State Elections 1976-77.   Org:
Municipal Assoc.; OES.   Educ: Ga. Southern Coll.
1968 BS; 1976 MA.   Occ: Learning Disabilities
Teacher.   Add: 4 N. Cherry St., Bloomingdale
31302   (912)748-0970.

Bluffton.   DELORIS KEDDINS
    City Hall, Bluffton 31724.

Boston.   ROSA G. BARNES   (D)
    1976-.   Bds: Ch., Water, Streets & Lanes;
Sanitation; Finance.   Org: Nat. Retired Teachers
Assoc.; NAACP; Senior Citizen Club; Human Resource
Office.   Educ: Albany State Coll. BSEd; Florida
A & M U. MEd.   B: 10/12/12.   Add: P.O. Box 731,
Boston 31676.

Bowdon.   MARJORIE F. MIDDLEBROOKS   (D)
    1976-.   Bds: Ch., Recreation & Health; Ch.,
Gas; Finance.   Org: Nat. Assoc. Exec. Secretaries;
PTA.   Occ: Administrative Asst.   B: 5/28/36.
Add: 202 N. Carroll St., Bowdon 30108
(404)258-3725.

Byron.   BETTYE W. GATES
    City Hall, P.O. Box 376, Byron 31008.

Cadwell.   JACKIE FLOREE COLTER   (D)
    1974-.   Educ: Ga. Southern Coll. 1968 BA.
Occ: Secretary/Bookkeeper.   B: 11/29/45.
Add: Box 43, Cadwell 31009 (912)689-4175.

Carrollton.   MIRIAM MERRELL
    Court House Annex, 311 Newnan St.,
Carrollton 30117.

Cave Spring.   MYRTLE A. JOHNSON   (R) **
    1973-.   Party: Del., County Conv.   B: 6/6/09.
Add: Box 176, Cave Spring 30124 (404)777-3382.

Cedartown.   SYBLE BRANNAN
    P O. Box 65, Cedartown 30125.

Chatsworth.   FRANCE ADAMS
    P.O. Box 516, Chatsworth 30703.

Chatsworth.   MARGARET E. ADAMS   (D)
    1973-.   Bds: Ch., Recreation Com.; Street Com;
Ch., Ordinance Com.   Party: Pres., Young Dem.
1966-67.   Prev: Recreation Cmsn. 1970-73.   Org:
NEA; Mental Retardation Assoc.; Dem. Party.
Educ: Lincoln Memorial U. 1957 BS.   Occ:
Physical Educ. Instructor.   B: 3/31/34.   Add:
525 S. 4th Ave., Chatsworth 30705 (404)695-2834.

Claxton.   FRANCES HODGES   (R)
    1977-.   Bds: Ch., Police Dept.; Fire Dept.;
Ch., Civil Defense.   Org: BPW; PTA.   Educ: Ga.
Southern Coll. 1956 BS; 1974 MEd.   Occ: Media-
Specialist.   B: 4/29/33.   Add: 401 Smith St.,
Claxton 30417.

Clayton.   JOSEPHINE KINMAN BREWER   (D)
    1973-.   Bds: Ch., Roads & Streets Cmsn.; Ch.,
Sanitation, Safety, Health Cmsn.; Ch., Community
Ctr.   Org: ANA; Ga. Municipal Assoc.   Educ:
Emory U. 1939 RN; George Peabody Coll. 1941 BS.
B: 1/23/10.   Add: P.O. Box 155, Clayton 30525
(404)782-4513.

Clayton.   NAN SHORT
    City Hall, P.O. Box 702, Clayton 30525.

Climax.   CYNTHIA L. TRULOCK   (R)
    1977-.   Educ: Jacksonville State U. 1968 BS;
U. of Ga. 1970 MEd.   B: 5/13/46.   Add: P.O. Box
146, Climax 31734.

Cochran.   ANTOINETTE JOHNSON
    P.O. Box 8, Cochran 31014.

Cohutta.   DOROTHY S. SEATON   (D)
    1975-.   Org: Woman's Club; Historical Soc.
Educ: U. of Chattanooga 1968 BSEd.   B: 6/5/15.
Add: 5006 Cleveland Rd., Cohutta 30710.

Commerce.   MARLENE DORRIS JOHNSON   (R)
    1975-.   Bds: Ch., Sanitation Dept.; Business
Licensing & Regulations; Waste Water Treatment &
Water Dept.   Party: V-Ch., Cnty.   Prev:
Cnty. Beautification 1975-76.   Educ: U. of Miami
1960 BS; Clemson U. 1963 MS.   Occ: Aquatic
Microbiologist.   B: 12/28/32.   Add: 542 Shankle
Hts., Commerce 30529 (404)335-3164.

Covington.   ALLENE C. BURTON
    2111 Conyers St., Covington 30209.

Cusseta. HAZEL G. SPARKS
     City Hall, P.O. Box 216, Cusseta 31805.

Darien. FREDA S. STEBBINS
     P.O. Box 452, Darien 31305.

Doerun. MRS. ZACKIE HAMMOCK
     City Hall, P.O. Box 37, Doerun 31744.

Douglasville. SUSAN CHERRY
     P.O. Box 218, Douglasville 30134.

Dublin. LENA OPIE
     City Hall, Box 690, Dublin 31021.

Elberton. MRS. SARA KANTALA
     P.O. Box 746, Elberton 30635.

Ellaville. ENDINE HART
     City Hall, P.O. Box 13, Ellaville 31806.

Fitzgerald. LINDA FAYE TAYLOR (D)
     1976-. Bds: Ch., Fire Dept.; License Com.;
Ch., Public Relations. Org: Assoc. of L.P.N.'s.
Educ: Ben Hill Cnty. School of Practical Nursing
1960 LPN. Occ: L.P.N. B: 5/29/41. Add: 601 N.
Main St., Fitzgerald (912)423-3337.

Folkston. MARY ALICE ODOM
     103 N. First St., Folkston 31537.

Forest Park. AGNES B. BATEMAN
     City Hall, P.O. Box 69, Forest Park 30050.

Gray. JOYCE ANNE FOLDS (D) **
     1974-. Bds: Criminal Justice Advisory Com.
Prev: City Clerk 1966-70. Occ: Owner, Flower
Shop. B: 3/17/43. Add: Pinewood Estates, Gray
31032 (912)986-6924.

Grayson. LINDA JENKINS
     Box 208, Grayson 30221.

Hamilton. ELIZABETH F. BLANTON (D) **
     1968-. Org: Assoc. of Educational Secretaries.
Occ: Administrative Assistant. B: 7/12/16. Add:
115 Mill St., Box 243, Hamilton 31811.

Hawkinsville. LINA JONES ARNOLD (I)
     1975-. Bds: Cnty. Library Bd.; Airport Com.
Educ: Wesleyan Coll. 1946 AB. B: 2/3/24. Add:
324 Kibbee St., Hawkinsville 31036
(912)892-3575.

Helen. JANEY STAMEY
     P.O. Box 146, Helen 30545.

Helena. TRUETTE HOWARD
     P.O. Box 222, Helena 31037.

Hiram. JANE S. BROWN
     City Hall, Hiram 30141.

Holly Springs. ADA LITTLE
     City Hall, P.O. Box 603, Holly Springs 30142.

Homerville. LYNEATH M. TYE (D)
     1975-. Bds: Cnty. Recreation Treasurer.
Prev: Cnty. Recreation 1975-77. Org: Library
Com.; Recreational Com. Educ: Stephen Coll.
1959 AA; U. of Ga. 1961 BS. Occ: Shop Owner.
B: 1/3/40. Add: Magnolia St., Homerville
31634 (912)487-2120.

Hoschton. BONNIE WALKER
     City Hall, P.O. Box 61, Hoschton 30548.

Irwinton. DEBORAH ANDERSON
     P.O. Box 169, Irwinton 31042.

Jesup. MARTHA J. BURNS (D)
     1974-. Bds: Ch., Community Action Authority;
Program Planning; Ch., Cnty. Day Care; Ch., Cnty.
Drug Adv. Prev: City Cmsnr. 1975-77. Org: BPW;
Chamber of Commerce; Municipal Assoc. Occ:
Secretary/Bookkeeper. B: 6/2/32. Add: 261 W.
Orange St., Jesup 31545 (912)427-2487.

Jonesboro. VIRGINIA S. OAKES (I) **
     1966-. Bds: Municipal Assoc. Org: PTA. B:
5/10/37. Add: 138 Burnside St., Jonesboro
30236 (404)478-7407.

Kingsland. MYRTLE FUNDERBURK
     City Hall, P.O. Box 397, Kingsland 31548.

Lithonia. ELIZABETH MITCHELL
     MAGGIE C. WOODS
     6980 Main St., Lithonia 30058.

Locust Grove. SARALOUISE B. ROBERTSON (R)
     1973-. Party: Cnty. Secretary. Org:Women's
Club. Occ: Secretary-Treasurer. B: 8/27/15.
Add: Hwy. 42, P.O. Box 401 Locust Grv. 30248.

Loganville. CAROLYN MOON
     City Hall, P.O. Box 128, Loganville 30249

Ludowici. MYRTICE WARREN
     City Hall, P.O. Box 203, Ludowici 31316.

Lula. RONNIE LOGGINS
     City Hall, Lula 30554.

Lumpkin. ALICE R. KEMP
     City Hall, Lumpkin 31815.

Lyons. MARILYN V. DURDEN
     417-19 N. State St., Lyons 30436.

Macon. DELORES BROOKS
     City Hall, P.O. Box 247, Macon 31202.

Macon. DR. MARY R. WILDER (D)
     1975-. Bds: Area & Planning Cmsn.; Daycare
Bd.; Housing Com. Party: Nat. Del. 1976. Educ:
Mercer U. 1954 BA; Peabody Coll. 1963 MA; F.S.U.
1970 PhD. Occ: Professor. B: 10/13/32. Add:
938 Park Pl., Macon 31201 (912)745-6811.

McDonough. JANICE S. HORTON (D)
     430 Burke Circle, McDonough 30253.
     (see Henry Cnty.)

McDonough. LYNDA REEVES RYAN (I)
1976-. Bds: Ch., Street & Light Com.; Water
Com.; Police Com. Educ: Ga. Southern Coll. 1972.
Occ: Teacher. B: 11/25/50. Add: 8 Henry St.,
McDonough 30253 (404)957-5112.

Menlo. KATHRYN MAC VANE
City Hall, P.O. Box 155, Menlo 30731.

Milan. SUSAN HAMILTON
Box 87, Milan 31060.

Molena. BETTY MC CRARY
City Hall, Molena 30258.

Montezuma. GLADYS HAIR
P.O. Box 388, Montezuma 31063.

Nashville. CHRIS BARFIELD
City Hall, P.O. Box 495, Nashville 31639.

Odum. BARBARA HORTON
City Hall, P.O. Box 1808, Odum 31555.

Pearson. NORMA JEAN SMITH
City Hall, P.O. Box 295, Pearson 31642.

Perry. BARBARA CALHOUN
City Hall, P.O. Drawer A, Perry 31069.

Pine Mountain. MRS. O.D. MARSHALL
City Hall, Pine Mountain 31822.

Reynolds. CHARLOTTE E. WHATLEY (D)
1977-. Bds: Environmental Com. of Ga.
Municipal Assoc. Org: Pres., Woman's Club. B:
12/30/39. Add: P.O. Box 187, Reynolds 31076.

Roberta. MARY R.P. SMITH
P.O. Box 278, Roberta 31078.

St. Marys. BETSY THOMAS
418 Osborne St., St. Marys 31558.

Savannah Beach. KAREN LOSEY
City Hall, P.O. Box 128, Savannah Beach 31328.

Screven. MRS. J.L. SHARPE (D)
1973-. Bds: Ch., Cemetery Cmsn.; V-Ch., Exec.
Com. Occ: Medical Secretary. Add: P.O. Box 33,
Screven 31560 (912)579-6614.

Shady Dale. MARY PRESTON
City Hall, Shady Dale 31085.

Smithville. ELNORA HOGG
City Hall, P.O. Box 2, Smithville 31787.

Statham. BELMALENE GENTLEY
JOAN OWEN
City Hall, P.O. Box 26, Statham 30666.

Sugar Hill. HILDA HAYES (D)
1976-. Bds: Planning & Zoning Bd.; Gwinnett
Cnty. Municipal Assoc.; Library. Org: PTA. Occ:
Shipping & Receiving Clerk. B: 8/14/43. Add:
4946 Oak Grove Dr., Sugar Hl. 30518.

Talbotton. ALICE MORRISON
P.O. Box 215, Talbotton 31827.

Tallulah Falls. BARBARA M. DYER (I)
1976-. Org: Municipal Finance Officers
Assoc. Educ: Western Mich. U. 1969 BBA. Occ:
Bookkeeper. B: 6/10/41. Add: Box 57, Tallulah
Falls 30573 (404)965-6752.

Temple. PEGGY DUNAWAY
City Hall, P.O. Box 160, Temple 30179.

Tennille. AUGUSTA LAWSON
City Hall, P.O. Box 145, Tennille 30189.

Thomson. ADELLE D. ADAMS (D)
1972-. Org: Area Mental Health & Mental
Retardation Assoc. Occ: Insurance Saleswoman.
B: 12/22/20. Add: 302 Glenn Stovall Dr.,
Thomson 30824.

Trion. MRS. ROBBIE CAMP
City Hall, Trion 30753.

Valdosta. ELIZABETH REIMET BECHTEL (R) **
1972-. Bds: Electrical Bd.; Drug Abuse;
Sex Educ.; Minority. Org: AAUW; Amer. Cancer
Society; Nat. Wildlife. Educ: Temple U. 1946
BS; Ind. U. of Pa. 1963 MEd; Columbia
Presbyterian School of Nursing 1949 RN. Occ:
Assistant Professor. B: 8/22/26. Add: 208 East
Brookwood Pl., Valdosta 31601 (912)242-2600.

Valdosta. RUTH KIMBALL COUNCIL (D)
1974-. Party: Precinct Leader 1974-77. Org:
NAE; Mental Health Adv. Bd.; Amer. Cancer Soc.;
AAUW; Citizen Adv. Council. Educ: Clark Coll.
1957 BS; Valdosta State Coll. 1974 MEd. Occ:
Curriculum Dir. B: 7/9/34. Add: 822 Bunche Dr.,
Valdosta 31601 (912)242-2600.

Vidalia. JO CULLENS
City Hall, P.O. Box 280, Vidalia 30474.

Vienna. SAYRA AMBROSE (D) **
1973-. Org: Woman's Club. B: 6/24/18. Add:
Box 352, Vienna 31092 (912)268-4505.

Wadley. JOSEPHINE COWART
City Hall, 117 N. Main St., Wadley 30477.

Warner Robins. JOY I. LAND (D)
1974-. Bds: Ch., Finance Com.; Ch., Recreation Com. Party: State Del. 1974; Dem. Cnty.
Exec. Bd. 1974-76. Prev: Cancer Bd. 1969-73.
B: 9/21/30. Add: 109 Freeman Dr., Warner Robins
31093 (912)923-2631 x 221.

Warner Robins. HENRIETTA MC INTYRE (D)
1974-. Bds: Finance Com.; Beautification Com;
Public Safety Com. Party: State Del. 1975-76;
State Alt.; Cnty. Exec. Com. 1975-76. Prev:
Citizen Adv. Com. 1968-77. Occ: Saleswoman. B:
11/17/24. Add: 125 Vernon Dr., Warner Robins
31093 (912)923-2631.

Watkinsville. ELAINE R. VERNER
City Hall, P.O. Box 27, Watkinsville 30667.

Waverly Hall. MILDRED WHEELER
City Hall, P.O. Box 347, Waverly Hall 31831.

Waycross. SHERRY J. SCOTT (D)
1976-. Mayor Pro Tem. Bds: Bd. of Educ.;
Community Action Agency Exec. Com. Org: Ga.
Municipal Assoc.; Intergovt. Relations Com. B:
12/26/36. Add: 1104 Euclid Ave., Waycross 31501
(912)285-4430.

Waynesboro. HARRIETT DOLIN
P.O. Box 230, Waynesboro 30830.

Winterville. FRANCES STEWART
City Hall, P.O. Box #06, Winterville 30683.

Woodland. AUDREY HALL
P.O. Box 96, Woodland 31836.

Judges

PHYLLIS KRAVITCH
Superior Court Judge. Add: Eastern Judicial
Circuit, Savannah 31402.

State Boards and Commissions

Office of the Governor, State Capitol Bldg.,
Atlanta 30311.

Accountancy, State Board of
ELIZABETH A. STERLING

Arts and Humanities, Council for the
CAROLINE ARMSTRONG
ANNE C. BARTON
SHIRLEY C. FRANKLIN
DOROTHY MC CLURE
KATHERINE MIXSON
CAROL MULDAWER
BETTY F. SANDERS
ROSEMARY STIEFEL
HELEN L. STRICKLAND
ISABELLE WATKINS
LOIS C. WOOTEN

Bicentennial Celebration, Commission for the
National
JEAN HENDRIX
MRS. SUE JACKSON
LIANE LEVETAN
MRS. ARTHUR H. WAITE

Compensation, State Commission on
BARBARA MUNTEAN

Consumer Advisory Board
BETTY C. GODWIN
DR. SUE PHELPS
BERNICE TURNER

Correctional Industries Administration
GAYLE N. MANLEY

Corrections, State Board of
SELINA BURCH

Cosmetology, State Board of
CLARISSA HULSEY
MARY BRYANT MILAM
RUTH REDDY
EDNA WEST

Crime Commission, State
CLARICE BAGWELL
MRS. E.C. FRAZER
BETTYE HUTCHINGS
BETTYE KEHRER

Dentistry, Board of
MARILYN E. STONE

Education, State Board of
CAROLYN HUSEMAN
SARALYN B. OBERDORFER

Educational Improvement Council
VIRGINIA SHAPARD

Education, Governor's Task Force on
ELLEN COODY
RUTH DOWNS
DOROTHEA JACKSON
FRANCES LA FARGE
MARY LONG
MARIE B. MARTIN
PEGGY NEAL
JO ANN STALLINGS
KATHERINE STALVEY
VIRGINIA STRINGER
ANNE STROUD
DORIS THOMAS
FLORENCE WARREN
DR. JUSTINE WASHINGTON
GERALDINE WRIGHT

Election Board, State
SHIRLEY ALTMAN

Energy Resources
OMI WALDEN

Ethics Commission
LILLIAN LEWIS

Fine Arts Committee, Executive Center
MRS. CLAYTON H. FARNHAM
MRS. ROY FRANGIAMORE
MRS. JAMES B. GILBERT
MRS. WILLIAM W. GRIFFIN
MRS. EUGENE A. MEDORI, JR.

Heritage Trust Commission
MRS. JAMES J.W. BIGGERS, JR.
LINDA BILLINGSLEY
BARBARA D. BLUM
EUNICE L. MIXON
LENA M. SHEATS
ANN J. SINGER
LORAINE P. WILLIAMS

Higher Education Assistance Corporation
MRS. STANLEY FRIEDMAN
MRS. R.M. HAIR

Hospital Advisory Council
SHIRLEY K. ALTMAN
TONI SAWYER
GLADYS SHAW
WILMA W. SHELNUTT
MARIAN M. STYRON

Human Resources, Board of
SISTER MARY CORNILE

Industry and Trade, Board of
    ANN A. CRICHTON

Judicial Qualifications Commission
    AMILEE GRAVES

Librarians, State Board for the Certification of
    MRS. ROY BOWEN
    DR. VIRGINIA L. JONES
    ELIZABETH MOORE

Marriage and Family Counselor Licensing Board
    FRANCES S. NAGATA
    NAOMI T. WARD

Maternal and Infant Health, Council on
    SABRINA H. ATKINS
    ROBERTA M. BROWN
    JOYCE F. DILLON
    OLA M. FORD
    MRS. BOBBIE RILEY
    NANCE WHITE

Medical Examiners, Composite State Board of
    DR. M. VIRGINIA TUGGLE

Natural Resources, Board of
    MARY IZARD

Nursing, Board of
    VERDELLE B. BELLAMY, R.N.
    PATRICIA N. CONNELL, R.N.
    ROSELLA DERISO, R.N.
    SISTER MARY ANTONETTE MARTINKO
    LORETTA ROBERTS, R.N.
    CHARLOTTE SACHS, R.N.
    DR. DOROTHY THOMPSON WHITE, R.N.

Nursing Home Administrators, State Board of
    CATHERINE SUMMERLIN

Occupational Therapy, State Board of
    BEVERLY U. CURRIE
    SUSAN T. MARCH
    NANCY MOULIN
    BETTY B. NEVES

Pharmacy, State Board of
    BARBARA LEVINE

Physical Therapy, State Board of
    PAT SWAIN COSTEN
    FRANCES A. CURTISS
    GLORY SANDERS

Practical Nurses of Georgia, Board of Examiners
    GLADYS A. BLACKWELL
    GRACE B. KNIGHT
    KATHLEEN MULL
    IULA STIGGERS
    ROSELLE TOBIAS

Professional Examining Boards
    SHIRLEY COWART

Professional Standards Commission
    GWENDOLYN CLEGHORN
    CARY D. HOLT
    BETTY HOUSTON
    EARLINE LOUDERMILK
    SHELLY MC GILL

GWENDOLYN MUNDY
MARGARET THRASHER
LE ANNA C. WALTON
ANN WOODWARD

Real Estate Commission
    PATSY G. COOPER

Speech Pathology and Audiology, State Board of
Examiners for
    MARCIA M. ARNOLD
    DR. WINFRED HARRIS
    JANE B. SEATON

Stone Mountain Memorial Association
    SUSAN ANTHONY

Vocational Education, State Advisory Council on
    DR. DORIS H. ADAMS
    ELLEN COODY
    LYNDA WEISSMAN

Women, Commission on the Status of
    CONNIE SCHLAK, CH.
    MAMIE K. TAYLOR, V-CH.

Hawaii

State Executive and Cabinet

EILEEN R. ANDERSON (D)
Director of Finance. 1974-. Bds: Employees Retirement System, Bd. of Trustees; Hi Health Fund. Org: State Treasurers; Nat. Assoc. State Budget Officers; Hi. Govt. Employees Assoc.; Dem. Party. Educ: U. of Hi. 1950 BA. B: 10/18/28. Add: 1212 Punahou St. #3205, Honolulu 96826 (808)548-2325.

BILLIE BEAMER
Chair, Hawaiian Homes Commission & Department. 1975-. Bds: Hawaiian Home Lands Cmsn. Educ: U. of Hi 1953 BEd.; MEd. B: 6/17/27. Add: Apt. 1408, 700 Richards St., Honolulu 96813 (808)521-2256.

State Legislature

State Senate

MARY GEORGE (R)
1974-. Dist: 3. Party: Nat. Del. 1976; Hi. Conf. of Elected Reps. 1969-. Prev: City Council-woman 1969-74; Ethics Cmsn. 1968-; Nat. Air Quality Bd. 1974-75. Org: LWV; Citizens Against Noise. Educ: U. of Wash. 1937 BA. B: 5/27/16. Add: 782-G N. Kalaheo Ave., Kailua 96734 (808)548-4107.

JEAN SADAKO KING (D) **
1974-. Dist: 6. Bds: Ch., Ecology, Environment & Recreation Com.; V-Ch., Energy & Natural Resources Com.; Ways & Means Com.; Higher Educ. Com.; Coastal Zone Management Policy Coordinating Com.; Governor's Advisory Solid Waste, Energy & Resources Task Force. Prev: State Representative 1972-74. Educ: U. of Hi. 1948 BA; NYU MA; U. of Hi. MFA. Add: State Capitol Room 224, Honolulu 96813 (808)548-7887.

PATRICIA SAIKI (R)
1974-. Bds: Judiciary; Health; Economic Devt. Party: State Del. 1968-75; Nat. Alt. 1968; State V-Ch. 1966-68; State Secretary 1964-66; Cnty. Committeewoman 1962-64. Prev: State Repr. 1968-74; Del., Constitutional Conv. 1968. Org: Govt. Employees Assoc. Educ: U. of Hi. 1952 BS. B: 5/28/30. Add: 784 Elepaio St., Honolulu 96816 (808)548-3867.

PATSY K. YOUNG (D)
1971-. Bds: Ch., Housing; Ch., Hi. Homes Lands. Party: State Del. 1964-76; Precinct Secretary. Prev: Del. Constitutional Conv. 1968; Adv. Council-Dept. of Educ. Org: Zonta; Women's Scholarship Org.; Dem. Party. B: 10/29/29. Add: 94-450 Awamoi St., Waipahu 96797.

State House

FAITH PATRICIA EVANS (R) *
1974-. Dist: 24. Org: PTA; Community Council; Nat. Fed. of Rep. Women. Educ: St. Francis School of Nursing 1958 RN. B: 5/11/37. Add: 687 Ululani, Kailua 96734.

DONNA R. IKEDA (R) *
1975-. Dist: 7. Org: PTA; Communities Council. Educ: U. of Hi. 1962 BA. B: 8/31/39. Add: 918 Wainiha, Honolulu 96825.

KINAU BOYD KAMALII (R) **
1975-. Dist: 11. Bds: Environmental Protection; Public Assistance & Human Resources; Finance; Culture & Arts; Tourism Com. Party: Nat. Com. 1971-75. Org: Amer. Business Women's Assoc.; AFSCME; Audubon Society; PTA. B: 10/24/30. Add: 500 U. Ave., Honolulu 96814.

LISA NAITO (D)
1974-. Bds: Ch., House Com. on Corrections & Rehabilitation; House Com. on Judiciary; House Com. on Economic Devt. Party: State Del. 1972, '74, '76; Nat. Alt. 1972; Precinct Pres. 1972-. Prev: Cmsn. on Status of Women 1972-74. Org: NOWL; BPW; WPC; Suicide Crisis Center; Volunteer Information Service; Dem. Precinct Club. B: 12/11/34. Add: 3696-A Crater Rd., Honolulu 96816 (808)548-6228.

KATHLEEN G. STANLEY (D)
1974-. Dist: 14. Party: State Del. 1972-76; Precinct Ch. 1974-76. Org: NASW; Hi. Govt. Employees Assoc.; LWV; Hi. Assoc. for the Educ. of Young Children; Sex Abuse Treatment Ctr. Educ: Huskingum Coll. 1965 BA; Syracuse U. 1967 MS. B: 9/24/43. Add: 666 Prospect St., #301 Honolulu 96813 (808)548-7559.

County Commissions

Hawaii. **MERLE K. LAI** (D)
1975-. Bds: Finance Com.; Public Services Com.; Planning Com. Party: Precinct V-Pres. 1970-71. Prev: Administrative Aide to Mayor 1972-74; Cnty. Officer of Information & Complaints 1972-74. Org: State Assoc. of Cnty's.; Public Employment Management Assoc.; Dem. Party. Educ: U. of Hi. BA. B: 11/4/44. Add: 2150 Kalanianaole Ave., Hilo 96720.

Kauai. **JO ANN A. YUKIMURA** (D)
1976-. Bds: Ch., Planning Com. of Council; Finance Com. Prev: Mayor's Bikeways Adv. Com. 1975-77; Mayors Beautification Com. 1975-77; State Coastal Zone Citizens Forum 1976-77. Org: LWV; Environmental Action; Citizens Against Noise. Educ: Stanford U. 1971 BA; U. of Wash.

1974 JD. B: 11/1/49. Add: 4728 Kapena St., Lihue 96766 (808)245-4771.

Local Councils

Honolulu. MARILYN BORNHORST (D) **
Party: Dist. Secretary 1968-70; Precinct Pres. 1968-70; Del., State Conv. 1968; Del., County Conv. 1968. Educ: UCLA 1949 BA. B: 5/7/27. Add: 1525 Oneele Pl., Honolulu 96822 (808)523-4000.

State Boards and Commissions

A complete list of state boards and commissions and of their membership, was not available for inclusion.

Idaho

State Executive and Cabinet

MARJORIE RUTH MOON (D)
State Treasurer. 1962-. Party: State Del. 1976, '74; State Alt. 1972; Nat. Del. 1976, 1972; Precinct Committeewoman 1958-60; Editor, State Dem. Newspaper 1956-60. Prev: Ch., Id. Cmsn. on Women's Programs 1971-74; City Planning Bd. 1956-58. Org: Nat. Assoc. of State Treasurers; Dem. Club. Educ: U. of Washington 1948 AB. B: 6/16/26. Add: P.O. Box 207, 2227 Heights Dr., Boise 83701 (208)384-3200.

State Legislature

State Senate

NORMA DOBLER (D)
1976-. Bds: Devt. Disability Council; State Employment & Training Adv. Council; Educ. Com. Prev: State Repr. 1972-76; School Trustee 1963-69. Org: LWV; PTA; AAUW; Common Cause; Conservation League; Chamber of Commerce; NOWL. Educ: U. of Id. 1939 BS. B: 5/2/17. Add: 1401 Alpowa St., Moscow 83843.

EDITH MILLER KLEIN (R)
1948-. Dist: 15. Bds: Law Enforcement Planning Cmsn. Party: State Del.; State Alt.; Nat. Alt. 1960; Precinct Committeewoman. Prev: Governor's Comprehensive Health Planning Cmsn. 1969-76; Governor's Cmsn. on Women's Programs

1965-; Nat. Council on Regional Medical Programs 1973-76. Org: Dist. & State Bar Assoc.; Amer. Judicature Society; Federal Bar Assoc.; Altrusa; Mental Health Assoc.; AAUW; LWV; BPW; Cnty. Rep. Women's Club; State Conf. on Social Work; DAR; Chamber of Commerce; Art Assoc. Educ: U. of Id. 1935 BS; George Washington U. 1946 JD; 1945 LLM. Occ: Atty. B: 8/4/15. Add: 1732 Warm Springs Ave., P.O. Box 475, Boise 83701 (208)343-3676.

State House

PEGGY BUNTING (R)
1972-. Bds: State Affairs; V-Ch., Local Govt. Party: State Del. 1968-76; Precinct Committeewoman 1967-72. Prev: Governor's House Restoration Com. 1965-67. Org: NOWL; Jr. League; Historical Society; Cnty. Rep. Women; Nat. Fed. of Rep. Women. B: 7/5/20. Add: 944 Lewis, Boise 83702 (208)342-3147.

KATHLEEN W. GURNSEY (R)
1974-. Dist: 17. Org: Nat. Leg. Ladies; WPC; Cnty. Rep. Women. Educ: Boise State U. 1976 BA. B: 6/23/27. Add: 1111 W. Highland View Dr., Boise 83702.

ELAINE KEARNES (R) **
1972-. Dist: 30. Bds: State Affairs Com.; Health & Welfare Com. Org: Bd. of Dir., State Mental Health Clinic; Ch., County Cancer Society. Add: 3040 Gustafson Cir., Io. Falls 83401.

DOROTHY H. MC CANN (D) **
1972-. Dist: 4. Bds: State Affairs; Judiciary & Rules; Health & Welfare; Bicentennial Cmsn. Party: State Com. 1970-75; Precinct Com. 1968-72; Secretary, Central Com. 1966-72. B: 2/17/23. Add: 101 Pine St., Box 618, Wallace 83873 (208)384-2000.

PATRICIA L. MC DERMOTT
Box 3, Pocatello 83201.

DOROTHY L. REYNOLDS (R)
1974-. Dist: 11. Bds: Law Enforcement Planning Cmsn. Party: Nat. Del. 1976. Prev: Health & Welfare Adv. Bd. 1975-78; Bureau of Flood & Management 1975-78. Org: NEA; AAUW; Id. Dems.; Cnty. Dems. Educ: Coll. of Id., 1969 BA; MA. Occ: Teacher. B: 10/6/28. Add: 1920 Howard, Caldwell 83605.

VIRGINIA D. SMITH
State Capitol, Boise 83720.

WENDY UNGRICHT
State Capitol, Boise 83720.

County Commissions

Ada. LINDA LUND DAVIS
County Court House, Boise 83720.

Bear Lake. KAY RIGBY
County Court House, Paris 83261.

Latah. DONNA M. BRAY (D)
　　1974-. Bds: Council of Govts.; Dist. Mental
Health Bd. Party: Cnty. Ch.; Cnty. V-Ch. Prev:
State Arts Cmsn. 1970-79. B: 3/1/28. Add:
1314 Deakin, Moscow 83843.

Nez Perce. VERA N. WHITE
　　County Court House, Lewiston 83501.

Twin Falls. ANN S. COVER (R)
　　1975-. Dist: 3. Bds: Cnty. Joint Planning
Council; Harbor House; Waterways. Prev: City
Councilwoman 1972-74. Org: Rep. Club. Educ:
Oberlin Coll. 1947 BA. B: 6/4/25. Add: 1135
Alder Dr., Twin Falls 83301. (208)734-3400.

Mayors

Athol. JOREEN BOHN (I)
　　1976-. Prev: Councilwoman 1965-75; Cnty.
Planning Comsr. 1972-77. B: 4/5/33. Add:
P.O. Box 121, Athol 83801 (208)683-2219.

Culdesac. ELLEN LOUISE BETTINSON
　　Main St., P.O. Box 128, Culdesac 83524.

Fernan Lake. ROSALEA E. MOORE (R)
　　1970-. Prev: Councilwoman 1967-70. Educ:
U. of Id. 1934 BS. B: 12/9/15. Add: P.O. Box
609, Coeur d'Alene 83814 (208)664-6592.

Kootenai. RUTH LANG
　　P.O. Box 177, Kootenai 83840.

Lapwai. LETHA NADINE WALTERS (D)
　　1961-. Bds: Ch., Council; Ch., Street Cmsn.
Prev: Judge 1961-63, 1970-75; Mayor 1974-76;
Councilwoman 1977. Org: Grange. B: 2/4/09.
Add: Lapwai 83540.

Oxford. VA LERE HEGERHORST (R)
　　1977-. Party: State Del. 1971; Precinct
Leader. Occ: Fabric Store Owner. B: 7/17/30.
Add: Oxford Rt., Clifton 83228 (208)747-3402.

Parma. PATRICIA N. ROMANKO (R) **
　　1974-. Bds: Waste Treatment Management Com.;
Dev. Council. Party: Precinct Com. 1970-76.
Prev: Council Member. Org: Bicentennial Com.;
Rep. Women's Club. Occ: Substitute Teacher. B:
5/6/30. Add: 1004 7th St., Parma 83660
(208)722-5138.

Pocatello. DONNA H. BOE (I)
　　1974-. Bds: Parks & Recreation Bd.; Regional
Law Enforcement Planning Cmsn.; Leg. Com.,
Assoc. of Id. Cities. Prev: Safety Council 1967-
70. Org: LWV; Common Cause. Educ: U. of NM
1957 BA. B: 8/7/34. Add: 226 S. 16th, Pocatello
83201 (208)232-4311.

Stateline. MARJORIE PARSONS
　　Rt. 2, Box 133, Post Falls 83854.

Warm River. LILLIAN LEWIES
　　Warm River 83420.

Local Councils

Ammon. CAROL A. DILLE (R)
　　1975-. Bds: City Planning & Zoning Cmsn.;
City Traffic Safety Cmsn.; Cnty. Traffic Safety
Cmsn. Org: Rep. Women. Occ: Interior Designer.
B: 11/28/41. Add: 3095 Central Ave., Idaho Falls
83401 (208)523-4211.

Atomic City. LINDA BROWN
　　Main & 7th Ave., Atomic City 83215.

Bancroft. MARJORIE C. CHRISTENSEN (I)
　　1972-. Bds: Parks & Recreation; Ordinances
& Records. Org: NEA; Business Educ. Assoc.
Educ: 1937 BS. Occ: Teacher. B: 7/9/16. Add:
105 S. Beason, Bancroft 83217 (208)648-7648.

Boise. JOY BUERSMEYER (I)
　　1975-. Bds: Ch., Planning Assoc.; Housing
Authority; Community Devt. Prev: Leg. Exec.
Reorg. Cmsn. 1973-74; City Library Bd. 1974-76;
Mental Health Study Com. 1976-77. Org: Conser-
vation League; LWV. Educ: New Haven State
Teachers Coll. 1953 AA. Occ: Exec. Dir., Mental
Health Assoc. B: 9/27/32. Add: 4924 Allamar,
Boise 83704 (208)384-4422.

Boise. MARGE EWING (I)
　　Bds: Council of Govts.; Metropolitan Trans.
Study; Housing Authority. Org: PTA; AAUW.
Educ: Washington State Coll. 1944 BS. B:
7/26/21. Add: 2318 N. 36, Boise 83703
(208)342-4621.

Caldwell. MARILYN BAUMAN (I)
　　1975-. Bds: Beautification Council; Parks &
Recreation Council. Prev: Ch., Beautification
Cmsn. 1974-75; Planning & Zoning 1976-77; Cnty.
Emergency Medical Care 1973-74; Welfare Adv. Bd.
1974-76. Org: AMA; Assoc. of Id. Cities; LWV;
Conservation League; UNICEF. B: 3/8/36. Add:
910 E. Ash, Caldwell 83605.

Caldwell. ALTA WILLIAMS
　　704 Blaine, Caldwell 83605.

Challis. MILDRED C. FISHER
　　RUBY SWIGERT
　　211 Main St., P.O. Box 587, Challis 83226.

Clark Fork. MAXINE KESTING
　　3rd & Main, P.O. Box 7, Clark Ford 83811.

Clayton. UNIS LEVZINGER
　　P.O. Box 3, Clayton 83227.

Coeur d'Alene. DIXIE REID
　　1976-. Bds: Park & Recreation Com.; Finance
Com.; Personel Com. Prev: Ch., Park & Recreation
Cmsn. 1971-76. Org: Assoc. of Id.Cities. B:
12/27/42. Add: 1144 Lambert Ln., Coeur d'Alene
83814 (208)667-9533.

Craigmont. MURIEL REID
　　109 E. Main, P.O. Box 234, Craigmont 83523.

Donnelly. DOROTHY M. GESTRIN (R)
　　1976-. Occ: Store Owner. B: 4/12/28. Add:
Box 667, Donnelly 83615 (208)325-8540.

Donnelly. R. ILENE OATNEY (D)
 1971 Bds: Parks Comsr. B: 10/11/26. Add: P.O. Box 92, Donnelly 83615.

Downey. ALICE H. OLSON
 Center & Main St., P.O. Box 204, Downey 83234.

Elk River. JEAN DAHLKY
 P.O. Box 153, Elk River 83827.

Fruitland. EDITH M. MELL
 200 Whitley Dr., P.O. Box 324, Fruitland 83619.

Garden City. MARGARET MOCKWITZ
 ANITA WALL
 201 W. 33rd, Garden City 83704.

Glenns Ferry. DORA MAE SELLERS (D) **
 1972-. Occ: Self Employed. B: 8/2/24. Add: 104 East 4th Ave., Glenns Ferry 83623 (208)366-7421.

Gooding. GEORGIA ECHEITA
 420 Idaho St., Gooding 83330.

Grand View. DONNA ANDERSON
 P.O. Box 46, Grand View 83624.

Hagerman. BARBARA JASPER
 218 Main, P.O. Box 158, Hagerman 83332.

Hansen. SANDRA RAE GOLAY
 1974-. Org: Amer. Dental Hygiene Assoc. Educ: Id. State U. 1964 AS. Occ: Dental Hygienist. B: 4/24/43. Add: 202 N. 1st St. W., Hansen 83334 (208)423-5158.

Homedale. BETTY UDA
 1st W. & Wyoming, P.O. Box 757, Homedale 83628.

Idaho City. BARBARA DIXON
 City Hall, Idaho City 83631.

Inkom. MARCELL WANNER
 1973-. Prev: Judge of Election. Occ: School Lunch Program Worker. B: 12/29/22. Add: Box 82, Inkom 83245 (208)775-3372.

Irwin. CONNIE JACKSON
 Irwin 83428.

Kellogg. JUNE H. OLSEN (R) **
 1971-. Bds: Library; Planning & Dev. Council. Prev: Sewer Dist. 1973-75. Org: BPW. Occ: Bookkeeper. B: 6/16/17. Add: Box 955, 523 West Mission Ave., Kellogg 83837 (208)786-9131.

Ketchum. MARTHA POITEVIN (D)
 1973-. Bds: Planning Comsr.; Parks Comsr. Educ: U. of Calif. 1970 BA. Occ: Newspaper Editor. B: 5/24/48. Add: Box 473, Ketchum 83340.

Kootenai. HELEN ALSPACH
 P.O. Box 177, Kootenai 83840.

Lapwai. LA DONNA JUDD
 P.O. Box 336, Lapwai 83540.

Leadore. LA VINNA STROUD (D)
 1973-. Occ: School Bd. Clerk. B: 11/10/32. Add: Box 162, Leadore 83464.

Lewiston. DELITHA J. KILGORE (D)
 1973-. Bds: Energy Task Force; State Policy Adv. Com. on Water Quality Planning; League of Cities, Women in Municipal Govt. Com. Org: AAUW. Educ:U. of Colo. 1962 BS. B: 12/8/40. Add: 3225 8th St. E, Lewiston 83501 (208)746-3671.

Lewisville. MELBA WILLIAMS
 Lewisville 83431.

Melba. DEE FRAZELLE
 P.O. Box 132, Melba 83641.

Melba. AUDREY JEAN MARTINDALE (R)
 1976-. Bds: Cities Disaster Services; Planning & Zoning; Sanitary Land Fill Com. B: 9/21/37. Add: Box 111, Melba 83641 (208)495-2722.

Melba. CHARLOTTE M. NELSON
 1975-. Bds: Ch., Park Cmsn. Org: Businessmen's Assoc. Occ: Postmaster. B: 3/6/13. Add: 406 Randolph, Melba 83641 (208)495-2722.

Menan. RUTH RYAN
 P.O. Box 127, Menan 83434.

Moscow. DEANNA DRISKILL HAGER (D)
 1973-. Bds: Ch., Traffic Safety Cmsn.; Administrative Com. Party: State Del. 1972, '74; Precinct Committeewoman 1972-75. Org: Assoc. of Id. Cities; Nat. League of Cities; LWV. Occ: Assoc. Dir., Community Devt. Center. B: 7/29/42. Add: 860 E. 7th, Moscow 83843 (208)882-5553.

Mountain Home. LUCILE H. PEARCE (R)
 1973-. Bds: Planning & Zoning; Traffic & Safety; Library Bd. Prev: School Bd. 1970-72. Occ: Library Manager. B: 2/17/19. Add: 500 N. 4th Street E., Mt. Home 83647 (208)587-3031.

Mullan. MILDRED E. GRANT (D)
 Party: Precinct Committeewoman 1971-76. Prev: City Clerk 1968-69. B: 8/24/35. Add: 237 Copper, Mullan 83846 (208)744-1515.

Nampa. MARGUERITE S. BROWN (I)
 1975-. Bds: City Planning & Zoning Cmsn.; Nampa Housing Authority. Party: State Del. 1973, '74; Precinct Committeewoman 1972-74; Young Rep. Nat. Committeewoman 1948-50. Prev: Nampa Public Library Trustee 1961-66, '68-73; Id. Cmsn. on Women's Programs 1972-74. Org: Assoc. of Id. Cities. Educ: NW Narazene Coll. 1946 AB. B: 7/19/23. Add: 119 Davis Ave., Nampa 83651 (208)466-9221.

Notus. ELIZABETH COULTER
 Elgin Ave. (Hwy. 20) P.O. Box 257, Notus 83656.

Osburn. BEULAH THOMAS
 1975-. Bds: Police Comsr. Educ: U. of Id. 1941 BSEd. Occ: Coin-Op Laundry Owner. B: 7/16/18. Add: 114 N. 6th, Osburn 83849 (208)752-0001.

Osburn. ANNA J. WILSON (D)
   1976-. Bds: Sewer Cmsn. Party: State Del.
1949-52, 1946-48; Precinct Committeewoman 1946-
52, 1973-77; Org: Amer. Society of Radiologic
Technologists; BPW; OES; Dem. Central Com.;
Mental Health Adv. Bd. Occ: Radiological Technician. B: 6/13/26. Add: 204 W. Chestnut,
Box 111, Osburn 83849 (208)752-0001.

Oxford. LUCILLE FRANSON
   Clifton, Oxford 83228.

Payette. DOROTHA B. WOLFE (I)
   1970-. Ch., Finance; Ch., Recreation. Org:
Civic League. Occ: Secretary. B: 7/1/13. Add:
2061 Center, Payette 83661.

Pinehurst. BETTY DUDLEY (D)
   1975-. Occ: Scheduling Clerk. B: 6/16/30.
Add: 306 Lewiston St., Pinehurst 83850
(208)682-3721.

Post Falls. HILDE KELLOGG
   208 E. Hwy. 10, P.O. Box 789, Post Falls
83854.

Rexburg. DARLENE BLACKBURN
   12 N. Center, P.O. Box 245, Rexburg 83440.

Ririe. NONA L. DUTSON (I)
   1972-. Org: NEA. Educ: Ricks Coll. 1948 AA;
Brigham Young U. 1962 BS. Occ: Teacher. B:
11/28/25. Add: Box 387, Ririe 83443.

St. Maries. PRISCILLA K. DERRY (D)
   1975-. Bds: Planning Cmsn.; Panhandle Area
Council; Ch., Bldg., Planning & Zoning Com. B:
3/22/41. Add: 501 Scott Ave., St. Maries
83861 (208)245-2837.

Sandpoint. EMMA HOOK
   2nd Ave., Sandpoint 83864.

Spirit Lake. EDNA M. GUILD
   Maine St., P.O. Box 308, Spirit Lake 83869.

Stanley. FRAN ELLIS
   P.O. Box 53, Stanley 83278.

Stateline. HATTIE HOWARD
   Rt. 2, Box 133, Post Falls 83854.

Stites. GENEVA COOPER
   Main St., P.O. Box 127, Stites 83552.

Sun Valley. JO ANN ALGIERS LEVY (D)
   1976-. Bds: Planning & Zoning; Hospital Bd.
Party: Precinct Leader 1971-72. Prev: City
Councilwoman of Ketchum 1970-72. Org: Assoc. of
Id. Cities. Educ: U. of Hi. 1963 BEd., MEd.
Occ: Disc Jockey. B: 5/28/40. Add: Box 714,
Sun Vly. 83353 (208)622-4438.

Terreton. ELLEN A. SEEDALL (D)
   1970-. B: 7/16/41. Add: Terreton 83450
(208)663-4397.

Weippe. EVA MAE WOLFE (D) **
   1972-. Bds: Bldg. Comsn.; Library Bd.; Cmsn.
on Women's Rights; City Beautification; Planning.
Party: Local Precinct Com. 1955-; Secretary,

County Central Com. 1972. Prev: Historical
Bd. 1972-74. Org: Young Dem. Occ: Correspondent. B: 5/16/16. Add: Box 181, Weippe
83553 (208)435-4243.

State Boards and Commissions

   Office of the Governor, State Capitol Bldg.,
Boise 83702.

Aging, Advisory Council on
   NELLIE BRONCHO
   MARIA GALVAN
   RUTH SHOVE
   FERN TRULL

Arts & Humanities, Committee on
   MARJORIE BICKMORE
   DONNA BRAY
   KELLIE COSHO
   SYLVIA LE MOYNE
   MAUREEN MC FADDEN
   DOROTHY STANSBURY
   MARY WALKER

Building Authority
   MARION WALKER

Cancer Coordinating Committee
   DONA BARALOU
   MARY LOU ENGLAND
   JULIA FORD
   PHOEBE LINDSEY
   EVELYN TREMAINE

Canvassers, Board of
   MARJORIE RUTH MOON

Correction, Board of
   MARGERY MOSER

Cosmetology, Board of
   ROYCIE CARMACK
   VIRGINIA COCKRANE
   REVA CLEGG
   LINDA COS
   HELEN DANIELS
   SUSANNE EVERTS
   UNA FRITCHIE
   NOLA KAY PRICE
   SUSAN SMITH
   SHARON WICK

Dairy Products Commission
   RUTH E. MILLER

Developmental Disabilities, Planning Council for
   MILDRED BROWN
   HELEN BUSHNELL
   SEN. NORMA DOBLER
   SHIRLEY FRITCHOFF
   MARGARET GIGRAY
   IDA HOLDEN
   SHARON HUBLER
   JULIE YODER

Education, Board of
   JANET S. HAY

Education Commission of the States
LOUISE JONES
HOPE KADING

Employment Advisory Council
IDA T. HOLDEN

Employment and Training Advisory Council
MONA HUBENTHAL
TAMMY SELLARS
CELESTE TAYLOR

Factory Built Housing Board
NANCY MANDL

Geologists, Registration for Professionals
NORMA RADFORD

Health and Welfare, Board of
PAMELA BOWEN
DONNA PARSONS
MARY WITTMAN

Health Coordinating Council, Statewide
NORMA BUCHANAN
KIMIKO CAMARA
MARGE EWING
SISTER HELEN FRANCES
SUE GRAY
DOLLY HARTMAN
LOUISE REHWALT
MAXINE RIGGERS
EULA SIMS
GRACE SMITH
YVONNE SWANSTROM

Health Education, Advisory Board for
SISTER WILLIAM MARY MURPHY

Higher Education, Western Interstate Commission on
BEVERLY BISTLINE
MARTHA JONES

Historical Records Advisory Board
HELEN MILLER
VIRGINIA RICKETTS

Historic Sites Review Board
MARY LESSER

Housing Agency
FERN TRULL

Human Rights, Commission on
CONSUELO DE PEARCE
IDAHO PURCE
LIZ SULLIVAN
MAE TAYLOR

Indian Advisory Council
DIXIE ABRAHAM
ANGELA BUTTERFIELD

Judicial Council
HELEN MC KINNEY
PAT WOODWORTH

Juvenile Justice Advisory Council
NORMA BUCHANAN
DRUCILLA GOULD
EMILY HANSEN
IDA HAWKINS
BARBARA J. STERLING

Legal Services Council, Advisory Council for
KAYE BURMAN

Legislative Compensation Commission
LOUISE SHADDUCK
ANN WHEELER

LEPC
SENATOR EDITH M. KLEIN
DOROTHY REYNOLDS

Library Board
MARY JANE KINNEY

Library Service and Construction Act Advisory Council
ANNABELLE ALEXANDER
MARGUERITE BROWN
MAXINE EDMO
MARY JANE HILL
DIANNA HULL
RUTH MC BIRNEY

Licensed Practical Nurse Advisory Council
MAXINE HOMER
CAROL SIMONS

Magistrates Commission
DONNA BOE
DONNA BRAY
LINDA DAVIS
VERA WHILE

Nursing, Board of
ILLA HILLARD
SISTER MARY AGNES REICHLIN
ROSEMARY SHABER
MILDRED WADE

Nursing Home Administrators Board, Examiners of
LAURA G. LARSON

Off-Road Vehicle Commission
MISS LOUISE SHADDUCK

Parks and Recreation Board
JOYCE E. WILSON

Personnel Commission
EMILY MC DERMOTT

Physically Handicapped, Committee on Employment of
MRS. PATRICIA CARR
MRS. LOIS T. DAVIS
MRS. MARY MAURO
MRS. EDNA SIGGELKOW

Professional Standards Commission
SUE HOVEY
BETTY MOORE
LEILA MORFITT
KATHRYN EAST
ELLEN HOWARD

Psychologist Examiners, Board of
   SHANNA MC GEE

Public Assistance, County Councils of
   MARILYN BAUMAN
   GERTRUDE M. EATON
   SUE ELLEN GRAY
   PHYLLIS HAND
   FRANCES HILL
   NORMA A. JONES
   RAMON KEYNA
   MRS. RUTH LINDSEY
   MARGERY MOSER
   MARY PATTE
   LYNN PEARSON
   MARY LOU REED
   MRS. HELEN SANDERS
   MRS. NAOMI SCHANT
   ANNA WANDER

Social Workers Licensure
   LOLLY BARTON
   BETTY PHILLIPS

Uniform Building Code Board
   MRS. CHUCK BARNES
   NANCY MANDL

Veterans Affairs Commission
   CLAIRE WETHERALL

Vocational Education, Advisory Council for
   BETTY BANKS
   MARCELINE KEVIS
   RUTH SMITH
   ALICE WALTERS

Vocational Rehabilitation Service Advisory Board
   JANET ANDERSON
   MAE BROWER
   IDA HOLDEN
   CAROL MOENS
   ALICE WALTERS

Women's Programs, Commission on
   JANELL BURKE
   PAT EHRLICH
   DOROTHY ELLIS
   AFTON FALTER
   ELNA GRAHN
   E. KAY HAMILTON
   PAULINE HINMAN
   SANDRA JENSEN
   EDITH M. KLEIN
   SARA KUGLER
   HELEN MC KINNEY
   PHYLLIS MILLER
   BERNICE MOFFETT
   MARJORIE RUTH MOON
   KAREN MORGAN
   ROSALIE NADEAU
   MARCIA PORTER
   LOUISE REID-CRAIGMONT
   MARGARET ROBBIN
   CHRISTY STRANGE
   MARGARITA SUGIYAMA
   GLADYS SWANK
   MARGE TITUS
   ZWAN VAN BEEK

BETTY PENSON WARD
GRACE WICKS
EVA WOLFE

Illinois

State Executive and Cabinet

JOAN K. ANDERSON
   Director, Department of Registration and
   Education. Add: State Capitol, Springfield
   62706.

MICHELE C. KANE
   Director, Department of Finance. 1977-. Bds:
   State Employer's Retirement System; Data Information Systems Cmsn. Org: ASPA. Educ: SUNY 1972
   BA; Syracuse U. 1973 MPA. B: 11/17/50. Add:
   814 W. Edwards St., Springfield 62706
   (217)782-9490.

JOSEPHINE K. OBLINGER (R)
   Director, Department of Aging. 1977-. Bds:
   Ill. Council on Aging. Party: State Del. 1962-
   65; Nat. Alt. 1972; Cnty. Ch. 1962-67. Prev:
   Sangamon Cnty. Bd. 1955-62; Cnty. Clerk 1962-70;
   Dept. of Registration & Educ. 1970; Governor's
   Office of Voluntary Action, Exec. Dir. 1970-73.
   Org: AFL-CIO; Assoc. for Administration of
   Volunteer Services; Ill. Bar Assoc.; Community
   Action; Alcohol & Drug Council; Retired Senior
   Volunteer Program; Rep. Women's Club; Ill. Fed.
   of Rep. Women; Planning Consortium for Services
   to Children in Ill; Amer. Judicature Society;
   Altrusa; NAACP; Ill. Assoc. Community Action
   Agencies. Educ: U. of Ill. 1933 BS; U. of
   Detroit 1943 JD. B: 2/17/13. Add: Box 130 RR 1,
   Sherman 62684 (217)782-4917.

State Legislature

State Senate

EARLEAN COLLINS (D)
   120 S. Grove Ave., Oak Park 60453.

VIVIAN VEACH HICKEY (D)
   1974-. Dist: 34. Bds: Ch., Com. Higher Educ.;
   Appropriations Com.; Cmsn. on the Status of
   Women. Prev: Ill. Bd. of Higher Educ. 1973-74.
   Org: AAUW; LWV; Dem. Women's Club. Educ: Rock-
   ford Coll. 1937 BA; U. of NC 1938 MA. B:3/25/16.
   Add: 1234 National Ave., Rockford 61103
   (217)782-7154.

DAWN CLARK NETSCH (D) **

1972-. Dist: 13. Bds: Public Health; Welfare
& Correction; Tax Com.; Status of Women; Revenue
& Finance. Org: AAUW; Bd. of Dir., ACLU; Bar
Assoc.; LWV; Advisory Bd., Nat. Program for Educ.
Leadership; Municipal League. Educ: Northwestern
U. 1948 BA; Northwestern School of Law 1952 JD.
Occ: Professor. B: 9/16/26. Add: 20 East Cedar,
Chicago 60614.

State House

JANE M. BARNES (R)

9825 S. Tripp Ave., Oak Lawn 60453.

PEG MC DONELL BRESLIN (D)

RFD 2, Ottawa 61350.

SUSAN CATANIA (R) **

Dist: 22. Bds: Com. on Child Care; Judiciary
Com.; Agriculture & Natural Resources Com.;
Urban School Dists. Cmsn.; Com. on Employment of
Women & Minorities in State Government. Party:
Precinct. Org: ACLU Women's Rights Cmsn.; Amer.
Chemical Society; Bd. of Directors, Flexible
Careers; League of Black Women; LWV; NOW; WPC;
State Women's Rights Cmsn.; Rep. Women's Club.
B: 12/10/41. Add: 2801 South Mich., Chicago.

EUGENIA S. CHAPMAN (D)

1964-. Dist: 3. Bds: Ch., House Human
Resources Com. Party: State Del. 1972-76; Nat.
Del. 1972. Prev: Bd. of Educ. 1961-64. Educ:
Chicago State U. 1944 BEd. B: 1/10/23. Add:
16 S. Princeton Ct., Arlington Hts., 60005
(217)782-8110.

GOUDYLOCH DYER (R)

1969-. Dist: 41. Bds: Higher Educ.; Cmsn. on
Children; Cmsn. on Status of Women. Party:
Precinct Committeewoman 1961-71. Prev: Cnty.
Cmsnr. 1961-68. Org: BPW; LWV; AAUW; PTA;
Women's Rep. Club. Educ: Agnes Scott Coll. 1938
BA. B: 5/28/19. Add: 441 E. 3rd St., Hinsdale
60521 (217)782-8022.

ADELINE J. GEO-KARIS (R) **

1972-. Dist: 31. Bds: Labor & Commerce Com.;
Public Utilities Com.; Human Resources Com.;
Dangerous Drugs Advisory Com.; Rape Study Com.;
Bd. of Aeronautics; Energy Resources Cmsn. Prev:
Assistant State's Attorney; Justice of the Peace.
Org: Amer. Business Women's Assoc.; Bar Assocs.;
BPW; LWV. Educ: DePaul U. LLB. Occ: Attorney.
Add: Box 33, Zion 60099 (312)623-8811.

BETTY J. HOXSEY (R)

RFD 3, Ottawa 61350.

MARY LOU KENT (R) **

1973-. Bds: Transportation Com.; Appropri-
ations; Economic & Fiscal Cmsn.; Ch., Tourism
Advisory. Party: County Central Com. Org: Rep.
Women's Club, Exec. Com. Spokeswoman. B: 10/3/21.
Add: 22 Spring Lake, Quincy 62301 (217)782-8096.

VIRGINIA B. MAC DONALD (R) **

Dist: 3. Bds: Delegate, State Constitutional
Conv.; Water Pollution & Water Resources Cmsn.
Party: Secretary, House Caucus; County Ch.; Town-
ship Com. Org: Rep. Clubs. Add: 515 South

Belmont Ave., Arlington Heights.

LYNN MORLEY MARTIN (R)

1976-. Dist: 34. Bds: Appropriations;
Cities & Villages; Exec. Party: State Del.
1972; Minority Leader, Cnty. Bd. 1973-76; Exec.
Com.; Rep. Party. Prev: Cnty. Cmsnr. 1973-76.
Org: Chamber of Commerce; AAUW; Jr. League; LWV;
Cnty. Repub. Women. Educ: U. of Ill. 1960 BA.
B: 12/26/39. Add: 1419 National Ave., Rockford
61103 (815)962-7703.

PEGGY SMITH MARTIN (D)

1972-. Dist: 26. Bds: Human Resources Com.;
Judiciary Com.; Public Utilities Com. Party:
Nat. Del. 1972; Precinct Captain 1951-53. Org:
Urban League; NAACP; Political Rights Defense
Fund; Nat. Blacks in the Criminal Justice System;
Black Political Caucus; Concerned Women-War on
Crime; Volunteers for Housing. Educ: Governors
State U. 1976 BS. B: 5/22/31. Add: 6810 S.
Loomis Blvd., Chicago 60636 (217)782-8088.

PENNY PULLEN (R)

1976-. Bds: Human Resources; Cnty's. & Twps.;
Public Utilities. Party: State Del. 1972-76;
Precinct Captain 1973-. Org: Historical Society;
DAR; Regular Rep. Org.; Rep. Women. Educ: U. of
Ill. 1969 BS. B: 3/2/47. Add: 2604 W. Sibley,
Park Ridge 60068 (312)823-2023.

BETTY LOU REED (R)

1974-. Dist: 32. Bds: Cnty. & Twp. Com.;
Environment, Engergy & Natural Resources;
Aeronautics Cmsn. Party: Cnty. Rep. Committee-
woman 1964-76; Rep. Party Platform Com. 1975;
State Central Committeewoman 1970-72; Cnty. Rep.
Ch. 1964-72; Ch., Nat. Rep. Women's Conf. 1969;
Del., Nat. Rep. Women's Conf. 1962-64, '68.
Prev: State of Ill. Dept. Local Govt. Affairs
1972-73; Cnty. Supervisor 1969-72; Comsr., Cnty.
Forest Preserve 1969-72; Pres., Cnty. Twp.
Officials Assoc. 1971-72; Mid-West Region Adv.
Council - Small Business Admin. 1971-72; Com. on
Youth 1972-74; Urban Cnty's. Council 1971-72.
Org: Women's Rep. Club; Exec. Dir., Rep. Women
Power; Senior Citizen Adv. Bd. B: 3/23/27.
Add: 927 Holly Ct., Deerfield 60015
(217)782-8037.

HELEN F. SATTERTHWAITE (D)

1974-. Dist: 52. Bds: House Elementary &
Secondary Educ. Com.; House Appropriations Com.;
Cmsn. on Mental Health & Devt. Disabilities.
Party: State Del. 1974, '76; Election Judge
1963-68. Prev: Co-Ch., Task Force on Mental
Retardation 1973; Joint Review Com. on Funding
of Champaign Cnty. Mental Health Programs 1973.
Org: OWL; Women's Internat. League for Peace &
Freedom; LWV; NOW; United Nations Assoc.; Dem.
Study Group; WPC; Assoc. for Mentally Retarded.
Educ: Duquesne U. 1949 BS. B: 7/8/28. Add:
101 E. Florida Ave., Urbana 61801 (217)356-8557

CELESTE M. STIEHL (R) **

Bds: Appropriations; Educ.; Insurance; Public
Utilities Coms.; Internat. Trade & Port Promotion
Advisory Cmsn.; Legislative Advisory Com. to
Southwest Ill. Metropolitan Area Planning Cmsn.;
Bi-State Dev. Visitation Com.; Energy Resources
Cmsn. Party: County Women; Exec. Com., Women

Power. Org: LWV; Ill. Positive Action Task Force; Exec. Com., Rep. Women's Club; Bd. of Directors, County Health & Welfare Council; County Rep. Women; PTA; Zonta; OWL. B: 9/7/25. Add: 25 Lake Inez Dr., Belleville 62220.

MARY LOU SUMNER (R)
3000 Pines, Dunlap 61525.

ANNE W. WILLER (D)
1974-. Bds: Human Resources; Judiciary; Cmsn. on Children. Prev: Constitutional Conv. 1969-70. Org: BPW; NOWL; LWV; Independent Dem's.; Com. on Ill. Govt.; Common Cause; PTA. B: 12/14/23. Add: 107 Howard, Hillside 60162 (217)782-5108.

WYVETTER YOUNGE (D)
1617 N. 46th, East St. Louis 62204.

County Commissions

Randolph. RUTH E. ROBINSON GILSTER **
1973-. Bds: Archives Bd.; Economic Council. Prev: Planning Cmsn. 1974-. Occ: Farmer. Add: Randolph County Court House, Chester 62233 (618)826-3642.

Township

Bureau. LOIS M. LAWLER
Bureau 61315.

Bureau. HARRIET MUELLER
R 2, Sheffield 61361.

Bureau. BERNIECE WEST
Wyanet 61379.

Carroll. EUNICE FELKER
R 1, Box 27, Savanna 61074.

Cass. ESTHER MORRISON
Box 37, Arenzville 62611.

Cass. DOROTHY J. SCHUETTER
1111 State St., Pearlstown 62618.

Champaign. LEOTA BUCKLEY
Rosamond 62083.

Champaign. MARIE KAIN
Kincaid 62540.

Champaign. PAULINE M. MEIER
R 4, Champaign 61820.

Champaign. MARJORIE E. SODERMAN
3203 Valley Brook, Champaign 61820.

Christian. HELEN IRWIN
Edinburg 62531.

Clinton. MARIE VON BOKEL
1151 Franklin, Carlyle 62231.

Coles. BETTYE BENNETT
Box 192, Oakland 61943.

Cook. KIKI BHOTE
493 Woodlawn, Glencoe 60022.

Cook. NANCY FOLLETT
105 South Oak Park Ave., Oak Park 60302.

Cook. FLORENCE HEEREN
834 Lill St., Barrington 60010.

Cook. GRACE S. LEE
1769 Highland Ave., Northbrook 60062.

Cook. ANN PAINTER
5800 S. Brainard, LaGrange 60525.

DeKalb. SANDRA K. FROST
Hinckley 60520.

DeKalb. HELEN G. HARRIS
417 S. 6th St., DeKalb 60115.

DeWitt. MARGARET M. TOEPKE
504 W. Water, Farmer City 61842.

Douglas. MRS. WM. P. HANCOCK
Villa Grove 61956.

DuPage. DORIS KARPIEL
23 W. 630 Forest Dr., Roselle 60172.

DuPage. BARBARA WHEAT
4512 Sterling Rd., Downers Grove 60515.

Edgar. CARRIE DE ATLEY
Box 24, Hume 61932.

Edgar. MABEL SCOTT
R 1, Chrisman 61924.

Fayette. LUCILE FISHER
Brownstown 62418.

Fayette. DOROTHY PORLETT
Roberts 60962.

Fayette. LORRAINE SAGER
R 1, Herrick 62431.

Franklin. YVONNE CLEMENS
Ipava 61441.

Franklin. DOROTHY REED
R 3, Benton 62812.

Franklin. MARY RUTH WRIGHT
RR, Smithfield 61477.

Greene. GLENNA S. KILLEBREW
Hillview 62050.

Greene. RUBY POSTLEWAIT
Kane 62054.

Hamilton. DELORIS TAYLOR
R 2, McLeansboro 62859.

Hamilton. BETTY WHITLOW
R 4, McLeansboro 62859.

Hancock. LOIS E. KENDALL
Plymouth 62367.

Henry. SANDRA L. KAISER
Altona 61414.

Jefferson. MARY BURNS
R 5, Centralia 62801.

Jefferson. LILLIAN CLARK
R 2, Woodlawn 62898.

Jefferson. NORMA CONNER
Ina 62846.

Jersey. ETHEL SCHAAKE
R 1, Bow 62022.

Jo Daviess. CAROL J. HALL
Elizabeth Rd., Galena 61036.

Jo Daviess. CHARLOTTE M. MILLS
Box 464, Hanover 61041.

Jo Daviess. TWYLA REUSCH
R 2, Elizabeth 61028.

Kane. MARILYN J. UNRUH
557 Barrington Ave., Dundee 60118.

La Salle. MARILYN TRUCKENBROD
R 3, Mendota 61342.

Lawrence. ETHEL M. KERCHNER
Quiet Acres, R 2, Box 253, Amboy 61310.

Livingston. JANET COUP
R 1, Pontiac 61764.

Logan. JO ANN KRETZINGER
Chestnut 62518.

Macoupin. VIRGINIA HUNTER
223 S. Springfield, Virden 62690.

Macoupin. MABEL D. MARCH
Hettick 62649.

Madison. PEARL PETERS
18 Jacob Ct., St. Jacob 62281.

Madison. FRANCES M. ROBERTS
100-A E. Broadway, Alton 62002.

Mason. CAROL VANCE
Forest City 61532.

McHenry. ANITA SHERWOOD
6004 Smith Rd., Crystal Lake 60014.

McLean. FREDA L. HORINE
Arrowsmith 61722.

McLean. MAXINE E. SCHULTZ
216 Eddy Bldg., Bloomington 61701.

Mercer. MARY CLOSE
R 1, Reynolds 61279.

Mercer. NORMA DAHL
New Boston 61272.

Montgomery. MARGARET L. FRICKE
RR 1, Nokomis 62075.

Moultrie. NEVA FOSTER
Box 458, Bethany 61914.

Ogle. NANCY GROEN
Leaf River 61047.

Ogle. VENUS L. VAUGHN
711 Franklin St., Oregon 61061.

Peoria. DOROTHY M. LADD
1617 N. Benedict, Chillicothe 61523.

Pike. HELEN BETHEL
Pearl 62363.

Rhode Island. LILLIAN D. CARLSON
24720 1 Ave. N., Hillsdale 61257.

Richland. JEANNE DEHLINGER
R 6, Olney 62450.

Sang. RUTH HINDS
2108 N. Grand Ave., Springfield 62702.

Schuyler. LEONA H. CALVERT
601 N. Bess, Marissa 62257.

Stephenson. SHEILA HOOPER
328 W. Douglas, Freeport 61032.

Vermilion. MARION F. DYSERT
R 2, Fithian 61844.

Vermilion. WILBA B. MORRIS
Hoopeston 60942.

Washington. ELEANORA CARSON
Oakdale 62268.

Washington. NANCY GRATHWOHL
Richview 62877.

Washington. GALE KOELLING
Box 226, Irvington 62848.

Wayne. MARILYN HOLT
R 2, Cisne 62823.

Whiteside. IRENE HUNT
R 1, Erie 61250.

Whiteside. HAZEL JAMES
Morrison 61270.

Will. VIRGINIA N. RICHARDS
203 Meadowood Dr., Joliet 60435.

Will. LIESE L. RICKETTS
Nacke Rd., Crete 60417.

Winnebago. ANNA PORTER
5647 Elevator Rd., Roscoe 61073.

Mayors

A complete current listing of women serving as Mayors was not available at the time the book was being compiled. A current listing can be obtained from the Illinois Municipal League, P.O. Box 3387, Springfield, Il. 62708.

Bolingbrook. ELEANOR WIPFLER
    131 E. Boughton Rd., Bolingbrook 60439.

Crystal Lake. ARLENE B. FETZNER (R) **
    1974-. Bds: Ch., Bd. of Local Improvements; Ch., Liquor Cmsn.; Ch., Bd. of Election Cmsn. Prev: Council Member 1971-74. Org: BPW; LWV; United Fund; Rep. Women's Club. B: 8/10/31. Add: 1335 Ivy La., Crystal Lake 60014 (815)459-2020.

Darien. JOYCE S. STAHL (R) **
    1973-. Bds: Municipal League; Community Dev. Cmsn. Prev: City Clerk 1971-73. Org: Woman's Club. B: 8/2/41. Add: 7337 Bunker Rd., Darien 60559 (312)852-5000.

DeKalb. JUDY KING (D)
    1977-. Bds: Ch., Bd. of Local Improvements; Cnty. Planning Cmsn.; Statewide Health Co-Ord. Council. Prev: DeKalb Cnty. Bd. 1972-77; Ch., Local Govt. Affairs Adv. Council 1973-77; Ch., Comprehensive Health Planning 1973-77. Org: LWV; Urban Counties Council; Ill. Municipal League; Dem. Women's Club; U. Women's Club. Educ: St. Xavier Coll. 1963 BA. B: 1/3/42. Add: 731 Hillcrest, DeKalb 60115 (815)756-4881.

Glencoe. FLORENCE H. BOONE
    675 Willage Court, Glencoe 60022.

Glen Ellyn. CONSTANCE C. ZIMMERMAN (R) **
    1973-. Bds: Community Dev. Cmsn.; Liquor Commissioner; Pres., Bd. of Local Improvement; Planning Cmsn.; Law Enforcement Cmsn. Org: LWV; Municipal League. Educ: Fla. State U. 1954 BA. B: 6/30/31. Add: 640 Forest Ave., Glen Ellyn 60137 (312)469-5000.

Hoffman Estates. VIRGINIA M. HAYTER (R) **
    1973-. Bds: County Manpower; County Office of Economic Opportunity; Fire Dept. Pension Bd.; Labor Relations Com. Party: Precinct Captain 1969-. Prev: Village Trustee 1969-73; Elementary School Bd. 1965-69. Org: LWV; Ill. Municipal League; PTA; Rep. Women's Organization; Rotary Club; Woman's Club. B: 11/23/33. Add: 384 Carleton, Hoffman Estates 60172 (312)882-9100.

Oregon. CRISSIE E. MARTIN
    115 N. 3rd Street, Oregon 61061.

Local Councils

A current listing of women serving on local councils was not available at the time this book was being compiled. A current listing can be obtained from the Illinois Municipal League, P.O. Box 3387, Springfield, Il. 62708.

Judges

MARY HEFTEL HOOTON
    Circuit Court Judge. Add: 70 E. Walton Pl., Chicago 60615.

HELEN C. KINNEY (R)
    Circuit Court Judge. 1976-. Dist: 18. Prev: Assoc. Judge 1972-76; Del., 6th Ill. Constitutional Conv. 1969-70; Asst. States Atty. 1962-69. Org: ABA; Women's Bar. Educ: DePaul U. 1944 AB; 1959 JD. B: 10/21/20. Add: 201 Reber St., Wheaton 60187.

MARILYN ROZMAREK KOMOSA
    Circuit Court Judge. 1976-. Bds: Coord. Com. Ill. Judicial Conf. Prev: Magistrate 1964; Assoc. Judge 1971. Org: Ill. Bar Assoc.; Women's Bar Assoc.; Advocates Society. Educ: Northwestern U. 1952 BS; Loyola School of Law 1956 JD. Add: 2900 N. Milwaukee, Chicago 60618.

HELEN J. MC GILLICUDDY
    Appellate Court Judge. Add: Civic Center, 30th Floor, Chicago 60602.

MONICA DOYLE REYNOLDS
    Circuit Court Judge. Add: 6161 N. Lemont Ave. Chicago 60646.

EDITH S. SAMPSON
    Circuit Court Judge. Add: 1236 Madison Pk., Chicago 60615.

DOROTHY W. SPOMER
    Circuit Court Judge. Add: Alexander County Courthouse, Cairo 62914.

State Boards and Commissions

A complete list of state boards and commissions, and of their membership, was not available for inclusion.

Indiana

State Executive and Cabinet

MARY AIKINS CURRIE (D) **
     State Auditor 1970-. Bds: Finance; Revenue;
Depositories; Tax & Financing. Party: State Com.
1962-72; V-Ch., State Dist. 1962-72; County Ch.
1968-72; County V-Ch. 1960-68; Town V-Ch. 1950-70;
Local Precinct 1950-70. Prev: Council Member
1958-62. Org: BPW; WPC; Dem. Women's Club. B:
12/27/10. Add: 201 South Buckeye St., Osgood
47037 (317)633-5700.

State Legislature

State Senate

JULIA M. CARSON (D)
     1976-. Dist: 34. Bds: Ch., Com. on Metro-
politan Affairs; Com. on Public Health; Com. on
Elections. Party: State Del. 1970-76; Nat. Del.
1972; Precinct Committeewoman 1968- ; Dem. Nat.
Committeewoman 1976- . Prev: State Repr. 1972-
76. Org: Fed. of Professional Women; Urban
League; Nat. Council of Negro Women; State Dem.
Women; WPC. Occ: Manager, Cummins Engine Co. B:
7/8/38. Add: 2534 N. Park, Indianapolis 46205
(317)269-3424.

JOAN GUBBINS (R) **
     1969-. Dist: 30. Bds: Educ.; Government
Affairs; Labor & Penal Institutions; Public
Health, Welfare & Pensions. Party: Del., State
Conv. 1966, 1968, 1970, 1974; Precinct Com. 1966-
70. Org: Nat. Fed. of Rep. Women; State Legislators Club; Citizen's Forum. B: 7/2/29. Add:
1000 East 81 St., Indianapolis 46200
(317)269-3500.

KATIE HALL (D)
     1976-. Bds: Ch., Educ.; V-Ch., Metropolitan
Affairs; Govt. Affairs. Party: State Alt. 1974.
Prev: State Repr. 1974-76; City Housing Bd. 1973-.
Org: AFT; Nat. Council for Social Studies; Nat.
Council Negro Women; AAUW; NAACP; Ind. Black
Political Assembly; Conf. State Legislators; NEA.
Educ: Miss. Vly. State U. 1960 BS; Ind. U. 1969
MS. Occ: Teacher. B: 4/3/38. Add: 1937 Madison
St., Gary 46407 (317)269-3400.

State House

DORIS DORBECKER (I)
     1968-. Bds: Cnty. Library Bd. Party: State
Del. 1962-70; V-Precinct Committeewoman 1952-67;
Ward Ch. 1967-72. B: 6/21/19. Add: 409 Mello-
wood Dr., Indianapolis 46217 (317)888-8851.

JANET L. HIBNER (R)
     1976-. Dist: 40. Bds: Governor's Traffic
Safety Adv. Com.; Elections Com.; Roads & Trans-
portation Com. Party: State Del. 1974; Cnty.
Secretary 1972-74; V-Ch. GOP 1974-76. Org:

Women's Rep. Club. Educ: Ind. U. 1957 BA. B:
7/26/35. Add: 3190 Toddsbury Ln., Richmond
47374.

LILLIAN M. PARENT (R)
     1977-. Dist: 47. Party: State Del. 1974.
Prev: Cnty. Treasurer 1969-76. Org: Women's
Rep. Club; BPW; OES. Occ: Asst. Cashier. B:
10/21/22. Add: P.O. Box 172, Danville 46122.

MARILYN F. SCHULTZ (D)
     1972-. Bds: Ways & Means; Elections. Org:
WPC; AAUP. Educ: U. of Tex. 1964 BA; 1968 MA.
Occ: Retail Merchant. B: 1/7/44. Add: 800 N.
Washington, Bloomington 47401 (812)339-2200.

ESTHER WILSON (D)
     2727 Poplar Street, Portage 46368.

MARNA JO WORMAN (I)
     1976-. Dist: 14. Bds: Insurance & Corpora-
tion Com.; Cities & Towns Com.; Education Com.
Party: Vice-Committeewoman 1976- . Prev: Dep.
Assessor 1970-72. Org: BPW; OES; Rep. Women's
Club; Rep. Quest; PTA. B: 11/18/32. Add:
9735 Gerig Rd., Box 303A, Grabill 46741.

County Commissions

Gibson. MARY MC CONNELL
     Gibson Cnty. Courthouse, Princeton 47570.

Morgan. THELMA T. GRAY (D) **
     1968-. Bds: Planning Com.; Agriculture Agent
Bd. Party: Precinct Com. 1950-64. Prev: County
Recorder 1961-68. Org: Women's Rep. Club. B:
8/19/29. Add: 269 East Green St., Martinsville
46151 (317)342-5563.

Townships

Abington. LOUELLA M. GRIMME
     RR #1, Centerville 47330.

Beaver. CLETHA KESTLE
     RR #2, Winamac 46996.

Blue River. RUTH M. CHURCHILL (R)
     1974-. Party: Twp. Committeewoman 1970. Org:
Women's Rep. Club. Occ: Clerk. B: 11/13/34.
Add: R #1, Box 9, Depauw 47115 (812)347-2669.

Boon. DORIS I. MUNDY
     504 W. Walnut Street, Boonville 47601.

Boston. MARJORIE L. DENISON
     204 S. Salem, Boston 47324.

Brandywine. HARRIET H. STROTMAN
     Box 157, Fairland 46126.

California. DOROTHY A. WHITE (D) **
1969-. Party: Precinct Com. 1972-74. Org:
Dem. Women. Occ: Bookkeeper. B: 2/3/30. Add:
Route 3, Box 657, Knox 46534 (219)772-3249.

Center. HELEN J. SALEK
122 South Avenue, LaPorte 46350.

Center. HAZEL SCHALL
153 Parkview Heights, Knox 46534.

Center. MYRTLE I. SPARKS (R) **
1970-. Org: Zonta; BPW; Women's Rep. Club.
B: 7/28/16. Add: 859 Myrtle Ave., Frankfort
46041. (219)654-5714.

Cicero. ANNA DOVERSBERGER
RR #4, Atlanta 46031.

Clark. LUCILLE VAN WINKLE
Bristow 47515.

Clay. ISABELLE H. SCHROER (D) **
1975-. Org: Bicentennial Com.; Women's Dem.
Club. B: 7/12/25. Add: RR 2, Columbus 47201
(812)372-1082.

Clinton. JEANETTE AUST
P.O. Box 235, Millersburg 46543.

Clinton. RUTH BALLOCK (D) **
1974-. Party: Treasurer, County Central Com.
1955-75. Prev: County Recorder 1967-74; Water
Utility Bookkeeper 1955-66. Org: BPW; Dem.
Woman's Club. B: 10/27/08. Add: 431 Elm St.,
Clinton 47842 (317)832-6258.

Coal Creek. EDITH E. FULTZ (R)
1974-. B: 7/15/13. Add: R #1, Wingate
47994 (317)275-2729.

Decatur. HELEN L. DAVIS (D)
1975-. Bds: Adv. Bd., Trustee Assoc. Party:
Cnty. Election Clerk 1959-74; Cnty. Voter Registor
1959-74. Org: Farmer's Union; Dem. Club. Occ:
Business Partner. B: 3/21/25. Add: 4336 S. Foltz
Rd., Indianopolis 46241 (317)248-8458.

Erie. DOROTHY L. BUTT (D) **
1971-. Bds: County Welfare Bd. Org: PTA.
Occ: Clerk. B: 6/5/31. Add: RR 2, Box 208,
Peru 46970 (317)473-9402.

Eugene. ESTHER GRAGG
RR #1, Cayuga 47928.

Fairmount. RUTH L. BAKER
1970-. Org: Chamber of Commerce; Rep. Women's
Club. B: 12/4/19. Add: 112 N. Main, Fairmount
46928 (317)948-5335.

Forest. PEGGY CALDWELL
RR #1, Forest 46039.

Franklin. MILDRED BENNETT
2406 W. 10th, Marion 46952.

Franklin. VIRGINIA HUBLAR
RR #1, Elizabeth 47117.

Franklin. MARY LONG
Darlington 47940.

Gill. ALICE M. SMILEY (D)
1970-. Party: State Del. 1968; State Alt.
1972; Precinct Committeewoman 1968-70; Precinct
V-Committeewoman 1970-77. Org: Improvement
Assoc.; Dem. Women's Club. B: 2/23/17. Add:
P.O. Box 104, Merom 47861 (812)356-4629.

Green. RUTH E. GABY (D) **
1974-. Occ: Farmer. B: 12/28/14. Add:
RR 1, Argos 46501 (219)892-5936.

Greensfork. FRANCES E. MACY (R)
1972-. B: 2/23/19. Add: RR 2, Lynn 47355
(317)874-8913.

Haddon. DAISY R. NICOL
RR #3, Carlisle 47838.

Harris. JOYCE JOZWIAK (R)
1975-. Org: NEA. Educ: Bethel Coll. 1964
BSEd; Ind. U. 1974 MAEd. Occ: Teacher. B:
8/9/31. Add: 14245 Brick Rd., Granger 46530
(219)272-8142.

Harrison. BONNIE BAKER
RR #1, Logansport 46947.

Harrison. MARY LOUISE HAYMAKER
RR #4, Martinsville 46151.

Harrison. NANCY K. NICEWANDER (D)
1975-. Org: Dem. Women; Ind. Trustees Assoc.;
Assessor/Trustee Assoc. Occ: Secretary. B:
4/10/39. Add: R 9, Box 171A, Muncie 47302
(317)284-2804.

Harrison. DORIS PORTER
RR #2, Russiaville 46979.

Harrison. CLARIBEL THOMAS (I)
1966-. Party: V-Ch., Precinct Committee 1966-
77. B: 10/27/12. Add: RR #2, Box 58, Harrison,
Ohio 45030 (512)638-8456.

Highland. DELORIS HICKS
RR #1, Perrysville 47974.

Indian Creek. CAROLYN WITHAM
RR #2, Star City 46985.

Iroquis. ESTIL DAVIS
Brook, 47922.

Jackson. BEULAH BICKNELL
Hymera 47855.

Jackson. JUANITA MARIE CROSBY (D) **
1967-. Prev: Deputy Assessor 1959-67. Org:
Dem. Women's Club. Occ: Insurance Sales. B:
11/5/28. Add: RR 2, Roachdale 46172
(317)596-7884.

Jackson. VIRGINIA GOLDING
RR #4, Box 239, Knox 46534.

Jackson. BETTY HUFF
8440S 400 W, Lafayette 47902.

Jackson. LUCILLE KOONTZ (R) **
  1970-. Bds: Hospital Bd.; Township Assessor.
Party: V-Precinct Com. 1960-70. Org: Rep.
Women's Club; Trustee Assoc. B: 7/11/08. Add:
Box 104, Sidney 46566 (219)839-2495.

Jackson. HELEN PARKER
  RR #1, Morgantown 46160.

Jefferson. SUE ARMSTRONG
  RR #1, Delphi 46923.

Jefferson. EDITH L. EVERSOLE (R)
  Org: Twp. Trustees Assoc.; OES; BPW. Occ:
Bookkeeper. B: 12/5/13. Add: 359 W. High St.,
Hagerstown 47346 (317)489-4824.

Jefferson. CATHERINE FISHBACK (D)
  1975-. Party: State Del. 1974; Treasurer,
Cnty. Dem. Central Com. 1965-77. Org: Welfare
Bd.; Women's Dem. Club; State Trustees Assoc. B:
1/29/12. Add: RR 3, Tipton 46072 (317)947-5557.

Jefferson. ELLEN SUE TEAGUE
  Box 165, Otwell 47564.

Johnson. ALICE BRIDGE (D)
  1974-. Org: Women's Dem. Club. B: 9/22/18.
Add: Rt. 1, Box 43, Deputy 47230 (812)794-2605.

Johnson. DEBBIE RAWLINGS
  RR #1, Forest 46039.

Jordan. VIRGINIA NOLIN (R) **
  1966-. B: 4/21/15. Add: Route 3, Williamsport 47993 (317)893-4190.

Keener. DOROTHY BOISSY (R) **
  1970-. Bds: County Ambulance Service. Party:
Precinct Com. Prev: Township Clerk 1963-71. B:
3/12/38. Add: RR 1, Box 366, De Motte 46310
(219)987-2342.

Kent. PATRICIA WRIGHT (D) **
  1970-. Party: Treasurer, County Central Com.
1970. B: 11/24/26. Add: Box 57, State Line
47982 (317)793-3593.

Knox. MARY PREMER
  RR #1, Dunkirk 47336.

Lake. MARSHA WATKINS
  Lake Village 46349.

Laughery. CATHRYN DICKEY
  705 S. Park, Batesville 47006.

Liberty. KATHLEEN HALL (R)
  1967-. Bds: Twp. Assessor. Occ: Cattle
Raiser. B: 7/27/17. Add: RR 2, Box 452, Clayton
46118 (317)539-6499.

Liberty. BERDINA HEAD (R)
  1974-. Bds: Ind. Assoc. of Trustees. Org:
Nat. Women's Realtors. Occ: Realtor. B: 2/2/41.
Add: Box 181, RR #2, Sharpsville 46068
(317)963-5643.

Liberty. FAITH B. LAIRD
  RR #1, Waldron 46182.

Licking. MARY CHANEY
  RR #1, Hartford City 47348.

Lincoln. KAY SELLERS
  RR #2, Box 120, Walkerton 46574.

Madison. SHIRLEY BRATTAIN (D)
  1975-. Org: 4-H Council; OES. B: 2/21/34.
Add: RR 4, Greencastle 46135 (317)653-4913.

Middle. MARGARET SPOON (D) **
  1970-. Party: V-Com. 1952-72. Prev: Deputy
Assessor 1955-66. Org: Dem. Women's Club. Occ:
Store Clerk. B: 6/14/21. Add: Box 309,
Pittsboro 46167 (317)892-4571.

Millgrove. JUDY PENICK (R)
  1975-. B: 4/12/39. Add: R #1, Orland
46776 (219)829-5381.

Monroe. ELSIE M. BARRETT
  Spurgeon 47584.

Morgan. WANDA WILSON
  RR #1, Poland 47868.

Mound. JUDITH JENNINGS
  RR #2, Dovington 47932.

Nevins. HAZEL HERB
  Box 66, Fontanet 47851.

New Garden. HELEN S. MEYER (I)
  1972-. B: 6/5/07. Add: 5807 US 27 N.,
Richmond 47374 (317)847-2412.

North. ELMA E. KONYA (D)
  1975-. Prev: Deputy Assessor 1967-74. B:
7/31/21. Add: RR 3, Bremen 46506 (219)784-3491.

Northwest. ALICE MOFFATT (D)
  1974-. Bds: Ch., Twp. Adv. Bd.; Hindostan
Community Ctr. Bd. Occ: Hospital Housekeeping
Aide. B: 3/10/14. Add: Rt. 2, Box 93, W. Baden
Springs 47469 (812)936-4403.

Ohio. EDNA L. SCHUBLE (D) **
  1970-. Bds: Advisory Bd. Org: Dem. Women.
B: 9/26/23. Add: RR 1, Chandler 47610
(812)925-6339.

Paoli. RUTH E. BABCOCK (R)
  1971-. Org: Nat. Fed. Rep. Women. B: 12/9/17.
Add: RR 2, Paoli 47454 (812)723-3153.

Penn. GRACE J. BROWN
  Box 176, Bloomingdale 47832.

Perry. CAROLYN FINKENBINDER
  9639 E. 100S, Lafayette 47902.

Pike. MARIAN JEAN ELLIS (R) **
  1974-. Bds: Welfare Bd. B: 4/28/32. Add:
Route 1, Bennington 47011 (812)667-4250.

Prairie. DORIS A. MILLS (R) **
  1971-. Bds: County Bd. of Educ.; State Assoc.
of Trustees. Org: Township Farm Bureau; County
Bd., Farm Bureau. B: 10/10/20. Add: R1 17519,
S St., RD 39, Hanna 46340 (219)797-3275.

Prairie. JUNE THOMAS (R)
    1975-. Bds: Civic Ctr. Bd. Occ: Drapemaker.
B: 6/9/39. Add: RR 4, Box 144, Warsaw 46580
(219)858-2356.

Preble. ALICE MARIE EHLERDING (D) **
    1974-. Educ: Ind. U. 1974 BA. Occ: Accountant
Secretary. B: 11/3/51. Add: Route 1, Decatur
46733 (219)547-4255.

Railroad. JUDITH K. ECKERT (D) **
    1974-. Org: PTO; Trustees Assoc. Educ: Ind.
U. School of Nursing 1961 BS. B: 9/6/39. Add:
RR 1, San Pierre 46374 (219)828-4201.

Richland. MARGARET HINTON
    Newtown 47969.

Richland. JOAN M. LEWIS
    425 Cedar Drive, Ellettsville 47429.

Richland. EVELYN WEIR
    RR #2, Rushville 46173.

Robinson. EMMA NEUMANN
    RR #2, Wadesville 47638.

Russell. REGINA SHANNON (D) **
    1974-. Party: Local Precinct Com. 1974. Prev:
Deputy Clerk 1951-55; Deputy Recorder 1947-51.
Org: Dem. Women's Club. B: 8/28/26. Add: RR 1,
Roachdale 46172 (317)739-2244.

Springfield. DELLA L. RHINESMITH (I)
    1971-. Org: Council on Aging; Trustee Assoc.
Occ: Nursing Home Aide. B: 6/9/34. Add: Box 12,
Mongo 46771 (219)367-2348.

Sugar Creek. MARDENNA SEIFERT
    New Palestine 46163.

Sugar Ridge. DORIS L. BARNHART (R)
    1974-. Org: OES. B: 8/11/27. Add: RR 2,
Center Pt.,47840.

Tippecanoe. DONNA L. ROMEIN (R) **
    1970-. Bds: Welfare Bd. Party: Precinct Com.
1966-75. Org: Women's Rep. Club. Occ: Bus
Driver. B: 11/6/33. Add: Route 2, Box 125,
Delphi 46923 (317)564-3403.

Tobin. ERNESTINE HARRIS
    Rome 47574.

Troy. THELMA HARDEN
    722 Jefferson, Covington 47932.

Union. HELEN SPENCER (D) **
    1970-. Bds: Advisory Bd. B: 9/5/31. Add:
Magnet 47555 (812)843-2571.

Vermillion. THELMA GRADY
    Newport 47966.

Wabash. VIRGINIA L. BECKER (D) **
    1974-. B: 10/6/24. Add: 726 Lindberg Rd.,
West Lafayette 47906 (317)463-3016.

Washington. BEVERLY SUE BEE
    RR #2, Box 106, Gaston 47342.

Washington. DELIGHT PIERCE (D)
    Occ: Nursing Home Housekeeper. B: 12/24/16.
Add: Rt. 3, Hartford 47348 (317)348-2084.

Washington. FERN RIPPERDAN (R) **
    1970-. Party: Precinct Com. 1969-75. Org:
Trustee Assoc.; Rep. Women. B: 7/14/18. Add:
Box 99, Central 47110 (812)732-4712.

Waterloo. TOBY ANN MAZE (D)
    1974-. Bds: Fayette Cnty. Welfare Bd. Org:
State Assoc. of Twp. Trustees. B: 7/31/38.
Add: RR 1, Box 127-A, Brownsville 47325
(317)825-2014.

Wayne. LILLIAN J. DOLEZAL (D) **
    1964-. Bds: County Fair Bd.; Recreation Bd.
Occ: Owner, Clothing Store. Add: Route 1,
North Judson 46366 (219)896-2022.

Wayne. RUTH MC CARTY
    RR #1, Gosport 47433.

West. BETTY J. WADE (D)
    1975-. Bds: Emergency Medical Service;
Welfare. B: 1/31/29. Add: Rt. 3 Plymouth
46563 (219)936-9489.

Westchester. EMILY E. BUSHORE (R)
    1969-. Bds: Ambulance Cmsn. Party: State
Del. 1965; State Precinct Committeewoman 1962-64.
Org: Cnty. Women's Rep. Club. B: 3/4/17. Add:
420 S. 15th St., Chesterton 46304 (219)926-1405.

York. DONELDA AUSTIN
    Angola 46703.

Mayors

Frankfort. MARY JANE MC MAHON (R)
    1975-. Bds: Pres., Common Council; Ch. Bd. of
Public Works & Safety; Pres., Police Pension.
Party: State Del. 1976; State Alt. 1972; Precinct
Leader 1956-77. Prev: Cnty. Bd. of Tax Review
1964-65; Clerk-Treasurer 1966-75. Org: Ind.
Cities & Towns; Zonta; BPW; Chamber of Commerce;
Rep. Women's Club; Rep. Mayors Assoc.; Nat. Rep.
Mayors Assoc.; Big Brother & Big Sisters. B:
8/24/25. Add: 957 N. Clay St., Frankfort 46041
(317)654-7332.

Mishawaka. MARGARET H. PRICKETT
    City Hall, Mishawaka 46544.

Local Councils

Attica. JANIS SICHTS
    City Hall, Attica 47918.

Bedford. JANET LEE
    City Hall, Bedford 47421.

Bluffton. LINDA ANN STULTZ (R)
    1976-. Bds: Liason to City Police; Area
Planning & Zoning Cmsn.; Review Com. for Zoning
Bd. Occ: Loan Officer. B: 3/6/39. Add: 404 W.
Market St., Bluffton 46714 (219)824-2510.

Carmel. MINNIE M. DOANE (R)
    1976-. Bds: Planning Cmsn.; Sub Div. Residential Com.; Ch., Finance. Org: BPW; Chamber of Commerce; Senior Citizen Service, Inc.; Cnty. Rep. Women's Club. B: 5/5/10. Add: 621 1st Ave., NE, Carmel 46032.

Carmel. JANE A. REIMAN (R)
    1976-. Bds: Chaplain to Council. Party: Precinct Committeewoman 1972-75; V-Precinct Committeewoman 1970-72. Org: Historical Society; Rep. Woman's Club. B: 2/9/33. Add: 4433 Somerset W. So., Carmel 46032 (317)846-7092.

Columbia City. CLAIR KNAPP
    City Hall, Columbia City 46725.

Columbus. CAROLYN ADLER LICKERMAN (D)
    1976-. Dist: 5. Bds: Capital Improvement's Budget Com.; City Hall Bldg. Com.; Community Devt. Adv. Com. Prev: Redevt. Cmsn. 1968-75; Human Rights Cmsn. 1966-70; School Bd. Nominating Com. 1971-73. Org: Chamber of Commerce; LWV; Dem. Ladies League. Educ: Ind. U. 1976 BS. Occ: Asst. Portfolio Manager. B: 12/21/29. Add: 3354 Woodland Pkwy., Columbus 47201 (812)372-0111.

Connersville. RUTH L. KING KENNEDY (D) **
    1971-. Party: Precinct Com. 1961- ; Sec.-Treas., Central Com.; Del., State Conv. 1962-70; V-Ch., Precinct Com. 1959-61. Org: Dem. Women's Club; Realtors Assoc. Occ: Realtor. B: 8/4/18. Add: 708 West 3rd St., Connersville 47331.

Connersville. FRANCES MC LAUGHLIN (D)
    1972-. Bds: Pres. of Council. Org: AAUW; AFT; Women's Dem. Club. Educ: Purdue U. 1942 BS; Miami U. 1967 MA. Occ: Teacher. B: 8/14/19. Add: 625 Tulip La., Connersville 47331 (317)825-4211.

Crawfordsville. LOIS P. PHILON (D)
    1975-. Bds: Cmsn. on the Environment; Ordinances & Petitions Com.; City Planning Cmsn. Party: State Del. 1974, '76; Precinct Committeewoman 1974-78. Prev: City Plan Cmsn. 1974-76; City Bd. of Zoning Appeals 1974-76; Judicial Study Cmsn. 1973-76; Devt. Cmsn. 1975-77; Manpower Devt. Adv. Council 1976-77. Org: ANA; Amer. Judicature Society; Council on Aging; Ind. Juvenile Justice Task Force; Mental Health Assoc.; WPC; LWV; PTA. Educ: Methodist-Kohler School of Nursing 1957 RN. Occ: Journal Clerk. B: 11/17/35. Add: 1311 Durham Dr., Crawfordsville 47933 (317)269-3531.

Crown Point. JOYCE GRAVES
    City Hall, Crown Point 46307.

Decatur. ELOISE HOFFMAN
    City Hall, Decatur 46733.

Decatur. NANCY R. MC MURRAY (R)
    1976-. Bds: Plan Cmsn.; Ch., Finance Com.; N. Ind. Health Systems Agency. Party: Ch., Precinct Com. 1976. Org: Women's Club. Educ: Lees McRae Jr. Coll. 1955 AA. B: 1/27/35. Add:412 Limberlost Trl., Decatur 46733 (219)724-7171.

Dunkirk. MABEL LE FEVRE
    City Hall, Dunkirk 47336.

Dunkirk. HELEN WHITESELL (D)
    1970-. Bds: Water Bd. Org: Blackford Jay Labor Council. Occ: Clerk. B: 5/16/20. Add: 336 Walnut St., Dunkirk 47336 (317)768-6713.

East Chicago. HATTIE LEONARD
                ROSE PARKER
    City Hall, East Chicago 46312.

East Gary. ANN ARVESTA HOUSE (D)
    Party: Precinct Committeewoman 1966-76; V-Precinct Committeewoman 1976- . Org: Bd. of Realtors; Women's Council of Realtors; Community Club; Chamber of Commerce; Dems. for Good Govt. Occ: Realtor. B: 2/23/28. Add: 2308 W. 37th Ave Hobart 46342.

Evansville. BETTY LOU JARBOE (D)
    1976-. Bds: Historic Preservation Com.; Administration, Safety & Dev. Com. Party: Precinct Committeewoman 1970. Org: Women's Dem. Club; PTA. B: 9/30/34. Add: 3919 Clement St., Evansville 47712.

Evansville. BETTY K. SMITH
    City Hall, Evansville 47708.

Fort Wayne. VIVIAN G. SCHMIDT (D)
    1971-. Bds: City Plan Cmsn.; Fire Merit Study Com.; Ch., Regulations Com. Party: State Del. 1976, '74, '72; Nat. Del. 1976; Precinct Committee 1976-77. Prev: Dir., Mayors Cmsn. on the State of Women 1973-74; Plan Cmsn. 1972-75; Metropolitan Human Relations Com. 1973-74; Transportation Planning Bd. 1973-75; Ch., Finance Com. 1975-76. Org: LWV; Fort Wayne Women's Bureau; Common Cause; IWY; Allen Cnty. Dem. Women's Club; WPC. Educ: Cornell U. 1956 BS; Cornell U. 1959 MS. B: 10/14/35. Add: 2621 E. Maple Grove Ave., Fort Wayne 46806 (219)423-7183.

Frankfort. ANNABELL GREENO
    City Hall, Frankfort 46041.

Franklin. DOROTHY RAINEY
            DEBRA SWINEHAMER
    City Hall, Franklin 46131.

Greencastle. CLAIR WILLIAMS
    City Hall, Greencastle 46135.

Greenfield. BEVERLY GARD
    City Hall, Greenfield 46140.

Hartford City. NANCY BARRY
    City Hall, Hartford City 47348.

Huntington. BONNIE SUSAN OSTROW (R)
    1975-. Dist: 2. Bds: Ch., Ordinance Com. Party: Rep. Cnty. V-Ch. 1976- ; Precinct Committeewoman 1976- ; Precinct V-Committeewoman 1975-76. Org: Cnty. Rep. Women's Club. Occ: Sales Secretary. B: 10/8/40. Add: 1915 Dean St., Huntington 46750.

Indianapolis. JOYCE BRINKMAN
    City Hall, Indianapolis 46204.

Indianapolis. BEULAH COUGHENOUR (R)
1975-. Dist: 24. Bds: Public Works Com.;
Transportation Com.; Community Affairs Com. Org:
Amer. Society of Medical Technology; Twp. Rep.
Club; Rep. Women's Club; Adv. Bd. of Young Americans for Freedom. Educ: Taylor U. 1951 BA. B:
4/26/30. Add: 3804 Meridee Dr., Indianapolis
46227 (317)787-1725.

Indianapolis. PAULA HART
LULA JOURNEY
City Hall, Indianapolis 46204.

Lafayette. JOHANNA C. DOWNIE (D) **
1971-. Bds: Railroad Relocation Com.; Commun-
ity Dev. Com.; Educ.; Finance; Sewer & Water;
Redev.; Annexation & Zoning. Party: Precinct
Com. 1969-75; Precinct V-Com. 1967-69. Org:
Human Dev. Coalition; WPC; Dem. Women's Club.
Educ: SUNY Potsdam 1938 BA. B: 2/6/17. Add:
505 Lingle Ter., Lafayette 47901 (317)742-8404.

Lawrence. JOAN GERRISH
City Hall, Lawrence 46226.

Lawrenceburg. JEAN MARIE FRANZE (D)
1976-. Bds: Parks & Playground Com.; Fire
Dept.; Sanitation & Grievances. Org: OES; Dem.
Women; PTA. Occ: Clerk. B: 10/17/27. Add: 113
1st St., Lawrenceburg 47025.

Ligonier. MARCIA HICKS
City Hall, Ligonier 46767.

Logansport. MARY A. COTNER (D)
1976-. Bds: Ch., Street Com.; Utility Com.
Party: State Del. 1970-76; Precinct V-Committeewoman 1962-64. Prev: Ch., Cass Cnty. Election
Bd.1974-76; Ch., Animal Control Bd. 1971- ; Cnty.
Youth Service Bureau 1977- . Org: Youth Service
Bureau; Juvenile Justice. Occ: Teacher Aide. B:
9/16/23. Add: 8 E. Mildred St., Logansport
46947.

Logansport. ELLEN GLENDENING
MRS. JACK REEDER
City Hall, Logansport 46947.

Marion. HELEN JEAN THOMPSON (D) **
1968-. Org: Amer. Business Assoc.; AFL-CIO;
Dem. Women's Club. B: 2/14/26. Add: 3644 South
Gallatin, Marion 46952 (317)662-6681.

Michigan City. EVELYN DELIA BAKER (D)
1975-. Bds: Ch., Plan Cmsn.; Zoning Bd.;
Finance Com. Party: State Del. 1972; Precinct
Leader 1965-73, 1975-77. Org: BPW; Nat. Cosme-
tologists Inc.; Dem. Civic Club; Humane Society;
Women's Dem. Club. Occ: Dir., Mich. City Beauty
Coll. B: 4/1/28. Add: 3146 Cleveland Ave.,
Michigan City 46360.

Michigan City. BERYLE BURGWALD
City Hall, Michigan City 46360.

Mishawaka. JEAN BODINE (D)
Party: State Del. 1976; State Alt.; Nat. Coord.
1976. Org: BPW; Women's Dem. Club. Add: 2515
Greenlawn Blvd., Mishawaka 46544.

Mishawaka. RUTH M. MEEHAN (D)
1976-. Bds: City Planning Cmsn.; Ch.,
Public Safety; Ways & Means. Party: State
Del. 1975; Precinct Committeewoman 1965-77. Org:
Dem. Women's Club. Occ: Deputy-Cnty. Recorder.
B: 10/3/27. Add: 1014 Alabama, Mishawaka 46544.

Monticello. RUTH COTTRELL.
City Hall, Monticello 47960.

Nappanee. ROSE MARIE METZLER (I)
1975-. Bds: Planning Cmsn. Org: Rep. Club.
Educ: Indianapolis Methodist School of Nursing
1947 RN. B: 1/16/26. Add: 556 W. Van Buren St.
Nappanee 46550.

Nappanee. BETTY M. SINCLAIR (D)
1976-. Bds: Bd. of Works & Safety; Plan
Cmsn.; Bd. of Zoning Appeals. Party: State Alt.
1976; V-Precinct Committeewoman 1974-77. B:
6/2/21. Add: 356 N. Hartman, Nappanee 46550.

Oakland City. JANICE REED
City Hall, Oakland City 47660.

Portland. LOLA V. JOY (R)
1972-. Bds: City Plan Cmsn.; Park Bd. Party:
Service Repr. 1977- . Org: Citizens Anti-Crime
Com.; Rep. Women's Org. Occ: Group Insurance
Administrator. B: 10/18/30. Add: 709 E. Race
St., Portland 47371.

Rensselaer. JO KATHRYN BUNDY HANIFORD (R)
1975-. Bds: Park Bd.; Cemetery Bd. Prev:
School Bd. 1967-71; Cnty. Tax Bd. 1968-76. Org:
Rep. Women; DAR. Educ: DePauw U. 1944 BM. B:
3/6/22. Add: Box 45, RR 3, Rensselaer 47978
(219)866-5212.

Rochester. CAROLINE STEPHEN (D)
1975-. Bds: Street Com.; Fire Com. Party:
State Alt. 1976. Org: Cnty. Dem. Women's Club.
Occ: Bookkeeper. B: 2/16/46. Add: 504 E. 9th
St., Rochester 46975 (219)223-2510.

Rushville. ROSEMARY BROWN (R)
1970-. Dist: 2. Bds: Cnty. Civil Defense
Com. Org: Cnty. Mental Health. Occ: Asst. Bank
Cashier. B: 7/8/33. Add: 843 Roosevelt St.,
Rushville 46173 (317)982-4151.

Salem. MARY BARNARD (D)
1975-. Bds: Planning & Zoning Com. Party:
State Del.; Precinct Committeewoman. Org: BPW.
Occ: Clerk. B: 11/24/12. Add: 305 E. Market
St., P.O. Box 293, Salem 47167.

Salem. ZELLA CAULBE
City Hall, Salem 47167.

Seymour. MYRA HILL (R)
1975-. Bds: Ch., Traffic Control & Parking
Com.; Planning & Zoning Cmsn.; Streetlight &
Fireplug Com. Org: Rep. Women. Occ: Drapery
Maker. B: 4/22/35. Add: 608 N. Walnut, Seymour
47274.

Shelbyville. MARILYN J. HENDRICK (R)
     1976-. Bds: Senior Citizens Adv. Bd.; City
Sewer Com.; Ch., City Water & Electric Com.
Party: State Del. 1974, '76; Ch., Precinct 1972.
Org: Historical Society; Rep. Club; Women's Rep.
Club. Educ: Ind. U. 1975 BA. B: 6/1/22. Add:
44 S. High Gardens, Shelbyville 46176
(317)398-6624.

South Bend. MARY ADAMS
     City Hall, S. Bend 46601.

Southport. SHIRLEY A. KING
            GRADA A. SAYERS
     City Hall, Southport 46227.

Sullivan. YVONNE LONGFIELD
     City Hall, Sullivan 47882.

Valparaiso. MARTHA A. SATTERLEE (R)
     1975-. Bds: Police Com.; Fire Com.; Ch.,
Ordinance Com. Org: Ind. Assoc. of Cities &
Towns; Regional Plan Cmsn.; Rep. Women's Club.
Educ: Valparaiso U. 1962 BSHE. B: 3/16/40. Add:
601 Franklin St., Valparaiso 46383.

Wabash. MRS. OMBRA KEFFABER
     City Hall, Wabash 46992.

Washington. FLORENCE C. CAVANAUGH (D)
     1973-. Bds: Council Pres.; Office Of Economic
Devt.; Senior Citizens Site Com.; Downtown Modernization Com. Org: Bicentennial Steering Com.;
Humane Society; PTA. Occ: Business Asst. B:
8/14/30. Add: 411 NE St., Washington 47501
(812)254-3410.

West Lafayette. MARJORIE J. GORDON (D)
     1975-. Dist: 5. Bds: Environmental Cmsn.;
Health Dept. Council; Public Utilities Council.
Prev: Area Plan Cmsn. 1976-77. Org: LWV; Women's
Club. Educ: Ind. U. 1949 BA; 1951 MA; 1953 PhD.
B: 9/24/22. Add: 2800 Henderson Ave., W.
Lafayette 47906 (317)463-3750.

West Lafayette. KATIE HUNTER
     City Hall, W. Lafayette 47906.

Judges

BETTY BARTEAU (D)
     Superior Court Judge. 1974-. Bds: Domestic
Relations Counseling, Ch. Party: V. Committee-
person 1966-68; Cnty. Ch. of Young Dem. 1967-68.
Prev: Cnty. Atty. 1966-68; Deputy Prosecutor
1965-68; Local Judge 1967-69. Org: Assoc. of
Family Conciliation Cts.; Ind. State Bar; Indianapolis Bar Assoc.; BPW; Cnty. Dem. Club. Educ:
Ind. U. Law School 1965 LLB. B: 10/19/35. Add:
4363 N. Central Ave., Indianapolis 46205
(317)633-3850.

PHYLLIS SENEGAL
     Superior Court Judge. Add: Courthouse, Gary
46401.

V. SUE SHIELDS
     Superior Court Judge. Add: Courthouse,
Noblesville 46060.

State Boards and Commissions

     Office of the Governor, State Capitol Bldg.,
     Indianapolis 46204.

Addiction Services Advisory Commission
     DELORES BAKER
     HAZEL MINNEFIELD
     MARGARET SNYDER

Aging and Aged, Commission of the
     ALICE BIRD
     MRS. KERMIT BURROUS
     EDNA TROTH WALKER

American Revolution Bicentennial Commission
     MRS. JAMES B. DEAN
     MRS. RITA EYKAMP
     MRS. HERBERT R. HILL
     MRS. ROBERT KIESWETTER
     ELIZABETH KURTZ

Arts Commission
     RUTH ADAMS
     SUSAN BURNS
     JEANNE COOPER
     BOBBIE CARVER
     JANET I. HARRIS
     DOREEN LE MASTERS
     CAROLYN MAC AVOY
     SHIRLEY MACK
     EMELITA TOLENTINO
     MARIAN VENABLE

Arts and Humanities, Commission for the
     MRS. HENRY F. DE BOEST
     JANET I. HARRIS
     MARY ANN KIESLER
     PAT RAHE

Arts and Humanities in Education, Commission for
     MRS. HENRY DE BOEST
     JANET I. HARRIS
     MARY ANN KIESLER
     PAT RAHE

Beauty Culturist Examiners, Board of
     LUCILLE MESSICK
     HELEN JEAN MOHR
     PATSY NIX
     IRENE SEBREE
     ODESSA WALKER

Bedding Advisory Board
     JACKIE RAVENSCROFT
     MIRIAM WHITECOTTON

Child Mental Health Advisory Committee
     DARLA CHRISTIE

Civil Defense Advisory Council
     MRS. MOISELLE M. MAUS

Civil Rights Commission
     MARY E. WYATT

Correction, Board of
     THERESE MARIE RAZZINI

Correctional Code Commission
SHARON FRUECHTENICHT
VIRGINIA H. HAYS

Criminal Justice Planning Commission
MARGARET MOORE POST

Criminal Justice Planning Commission Advisory Board
MATTIE CONEY

Criminal Law Study Commission
HARRIETTE B. CONN

Deaf Advisory Committee
BETTY COBB

Depositories, Board for
MARY AIKINS CURRIE

Disability Determination Advisory Committee
DORIS PARKER
ANNE VARBLE

Education, Board of
BETTY CROWE
CHRISTINA HARRIS
BETTYE LOU JERREL
JANET WICKERSHAM

Egg Board
MRS. DON IDDINGS

Emergency Medical Services Commission
MRS. JEWELL SPEARS

Employees Appeals Commission
BARBARA CURRAN

Employment of the Handicapped, Task Force for the
PATRICIAL NOEL

Employment Security Division Advisory Council
JOANNE THROCKMORTON

Environmental Management Board
CAROLE RUST

Epilepsy Advisory Committee
BETTY HARRELL

Fair Board
LOLA YODER

Finance, Board of
MARY AIKINS CURRIE

General Education, Commission on
SHIRLEY BRYAN
JEANETTE MOELLER

Governor's Mansion Commission
MRS. J. IRWIN MILLER
MRS. RICHARD O. RISTINE
MRS. MATTHEW WELSH

Health, Board of
EVA H. ROSSER

Health Facilities Council
MAMIE BEAMON
NANCY E. DAYHOFF

MRS. CECIL M. HARDEN
MARION N. STEFFY

Hemophilia Advisory Committee
KATIE MILBURN

Higher Education, Commission for
MRS. WILLIAM G. BRAY

Highway Extension and Research Program for Indiana Counties Advisory Board
JOY L. BROWN

Hospital Regulating and Licensing Council
SISTER MARY BROOKS
IRENE KARDASEN

Library and Historical Board
SUZANNE WARE

Library and Historical Building Expansion Commission
HELEN ACHOR SHOEMAKER

Little Calumet River Basin Commission
MRS. ROBERT Q. ASHCRAFT
MRS. CLAYTON ROOT, JR.

Medical Assistance (Medicaid), Advisory Committee for
CHARLOTTE AKINS
MILDRED LAWSON
PEARL MYERS
MARIE PEACOCK

Medical Distribution Loan Fund, Board of Trustees
BETTY LARAMORE

Mental Health, Advisory Council for
BARBARA BACKER
NORMA BOWEN
DARLA CHRISTIE
DOROTHY KAZMIERZAK
MARY WESSELMAN

Mental Health Laws, Committee for the Study of
HARIETTE BAILEY CONN

Mental Retardation and Other Developmental Disabilities Advisory Committee
KATHIE CURTIS
MURIEL LEE
JEANNETTE P. REILLEY
GENEVIEVE RILEY

New Harmony Memorial Commission
HELEN ELLIOTT
SHERI B. DUNNINGTON
MRS. WILLIAM H. KECK
MRS. B. A. TANNER

Nurses' Registration and Nursing Education, Board of
HELEN J. BERRY
MARGUERITE F. CLARK
MARTHA LEE GODARE
PEARL MYERS
SHIRLEY ANN ROSS
MARY B. RUNNELS
DOROTHY P. SMITH

Parole Board
    RUTH M. PAPPERT

Personnel Board
    MILDRED RICHEY

Pharmacy, Board of
    BARBARA NELSON

Physical Therapist Examining Committee
    FRANCES EKSTAM
    MARGARET KREISLE

Public Accountants Administrative Committee
    BLANCHE WEAN

Public Transportation Advisory Committee
    REBECCA BEASLEY

Public Welfare Committee
    MARION M. HILGER
    ARVELLA M. STANTON

Recreational Development Commission
    MRS. DONALD STOCKER

Registration and Education, Board of Health Facility
Administrators
    ELSIE DREYER
    SISTER CATHERINE KRIETER
    LAURA L. PETERSON

Rehabilitation Service Board
    SUE HETHERINGTON
    CHRIS PARASCHOS
    CAROLYN TUCKER

Scholarship Commission
    SISTER M. VIVIAN BRAND
    MRS. ARDATH BURKHART
    LYNNE L. MERRITT

School for the Blind Advisory Committee
    MRS. ROBERT REED
    MRS. LEROY SHINE
    MRS. FRANK A. WHITE

School for the Deaf Advisory Committee
    MRS. LESTER MENKE

Services for the Blind Advisory Committee
    KATHLEEN BYRN
    MRS. VERNON KOESTER

Sickle Cell Anemia Advisory Committee
    NANCY MC COY

Silvercrest Disability and Chronic Disease Facility
Advisory Committee
    MRS. CHARLES H. TINSLEY

Soldiers' and Sailors' Children's Home Advisory
Committee
    MRS. ORIN NOWLIN
    MRS. WILLIAM E. STECKLER

Soldiers' Home Advisory Committee
    MRS. ROBERT DAVIDSON
    ANN HAYWORTH

Speech Pathology and Audiology, Board of
Examiners on
    MRS. JESSIE WHITE

Tax Commissioners' Advisory Council
    LUCILLE DAVIDSON
    MARY CATHERINE HERR

Teacher Training and Licensing Commission
    ALEENE PFAFFINGER
    LUCILLE TURNER

Teachers' Retirement Fund, Board of Trustees
    NELL BETHEL

Traffic Safety Advisory Committee
    DONNA AGNESS
    MRS. HORTENSE MYERS
    BARBARA VAN CLEVE

Vocational and Technical Education, Advisory
Council on
    ELIZABETH BRIDGEWATERS
    PAULA W. CARTER
    ARLINE C. ERLICK
    EVE PURVIS
    SARAH JEAN THARP

Vocational Rehabilitation Division Advisory
Committee
    CORRINE WALKER

Voluntary Action Program
    BARBARA AHLERING
    JACQUELINE KERR
    LINDA KOLB
    SUSAN KUHN
    CONNIE STATON

Wage Adjustment Board
    EVE PURVIS

War Memorials Commission
    ELEANOR J. GARBER

Youth Council
    MRS. C. B. BARTHOLD
    BARBARA BURNAM
    LUCILLE DE VOE
    MAXINE GARRETT
    JANET GORRELL MC CARTHY
    JUDY ROGERS
    SUSAN WARNER

Iowa

State Executive and Cabinet

MARY F. HOLSTAD (I)
State Commerce Commissioner. 1975-. Org: Des Moines Financial Analysis; Nat. Assoc. Regional Utility Com.; Chamber of Commerce; Nat. Secretaries Assoc.; Altrusa. B: 12/8/19. Add: 622 S.E. Huches, Des Moines 50315 (515)281-5896.

COLLEEN P. SHEARER
Director of Job Service. Add: 1000 E. Grand, Des Moines 50319.

State Legislature

State Senate

MINNETTE DODERER (D)
1968-. Party: State Del. 1952-76; Nat. Del. 1968, '74; Cnty. V-Ch. 1956-59; Precinct Co-Ch. 1952-56. Prev: State Repr. 1964-69. Org: BPW; WPC; LWV; WEAL; NOW; New Frontier Dem. Club. Educ: U. of Ia. 1948 BA. B: 5/16/23. Add: 2008 Dunlap Ct., Iowa City 52240 (515)281-3721.

ELIZABETH MILLER (R) ☆☆
Dist: 20. Bds: Transportation; Natural Resources; State Government. Prev: State Representative. Org: BPW; OWL; Parliamentarians; Rep. Women's Club; Retarded Children's Assoc.; Women's Club; Farm Bureau. B: 8/24/05. Add: RR 3, Marshalltown 50158.

JOAN ORR (D)
1970-. Dist: 36. Prev: Parks Bd. 1971-72; Community Action Program Bd. 1968-70; Cmsn. on the Aging 1975-76; Educ. Cmsn. of the States 1976-77. Org: LWV; Ia. Civil Liberties Union; United Nations Assoc.; Common Cause; Ia. Tax Reform Action Coalition; Cnty. Assoc. for Retarded Citizens; Farm Bureau. Educ: Oberlin Coll. 1946 BMEd. B: 2/10/23. Add: 10 Merrill Park Cir., Grinnell 50112.

ELIZABETH SHAW (R)
Dist: 40. Prev: State Repr. 1967-71. Org: Ia. Bar Assoc.; Bd. Ia. Law Enforcement Academy; Cnty. Rep. Women. Educ: Drake U. 1945 BA; U. of Ia. 1949 JD. Occ: Lawyer. B: 10/2/23. Add: 29 Hillcrest Ave., Davenport 52803

State House

DIANE BRANDT (D)
1974-. Dist: 35. Party: State Del.; State Alt. Prev: Planning & Zoning Cmsn. 1972-74. Org: LWV; WPC; NAACP. Educ: Ia. State U. 1961 BS. B: 8/28/38. Add: 2507 Willow Ln., Cedar Fls. 50613 (515)281-3221.

BETTY JEAN CLARK (R)
1976-. Dist: 11. Bds: Human Resources; Judiciary & Law Enforcement; Transportation. Party: State Del. 1976. Org: Internat. Platform Assoc.; BPW; Chamber of Commerce; LWV; WPC; Fed. of Rep. Women. B: 4/18/20. Add: Rt. 2, Box 12, Rockwell 50469 (515)281-3221.

SONJA EGENES (R) ☆☆
Dist: 43. Bds: Commerce; Natural Resources; Ways & Means. Org: Fed. of Rep. Women's UN Assoc. Educ: Ia. State U. 1951 BS. B: 10/19/30. Add: 905 Lafayette, Story City 50248 (515)279-9891.

JULIA B. GENTLEMAN (R)
1974-. Dist: 65. Party: State Del. 1964-70; State Alt. 1972-76; Precinct Committeewoman 1964-72; Cnty. Exec. Com. 1970-72. Org: Ia. Civil Liberties Union; LWV; Jr. League; Amer. Patients Assoc.; WPC. Educ: Northwestern U. 1953 BS. B: 8/24/31. Add: 2814 Forest Dr., Des Moines 50312 (515)281-3221.

MATTIE HARPER (D) ☆☆
Dist: 90. Bds: Agriculture; Appropriations; Transportation; Ethics. Org: BPW; Dem. Women's Club; Legislative Ladies League. Educ: Miss. State U. BA. B: 12/15/23. Add: Box 22, West Grove 52538.

BETTY A. HOFFMAN (R)
2005 Circle Dr., Muscatine 52761.

JOAN LIPSKY (R)
1966-. Bds: Asst. Minority Leader; Council on Child Abuse; Genetic Counseling Adv. Council. Party: State Del. 1968-76; Nat. Del. 1976; State Platform Com. 1970, '76; Nat. Platform Com. 1976. Prev: Task Force on Human Relations 1972-75; Midwest Conf. of State Govt. 1970-75; Employment Security Adv. 1968-74; Medical Adv. Council 1970-74. Org: LWV; AAUW; Altrusa. Educ: Northwestern U. 1940 BS. B: 4/9/19. Add: 655 Cottage Grv., Cedar Rapids 52403 (515)281-3625.

JOYCE LONERGAN (D)
1974-. Dist: 44. Bds: V-Ch., Commerce; Rules; Human Resources. Party: State Del. 1972, '76; Secretary, Cnty. Central Com. 1968-72. Org: NOWL; Leg. Ladies League; Amer. Business Women's Assoc.; WPC; Cnty. Dem's.; Historical Society. B: 3/5/34. Add: 1215 Mamie Eisenhower Ave., Boone 50036 (515)281-3221.

OPAL L. MILLER (D)
1974-. Dist: 47. Bds: V-Ch., Educ.; Agriculture; Social Services Budget. Party: State Del. 1970-76; Asst. Dem. Cnty. Ch. 1970-73. Prev: Cnty. Deputy Recorder 1950-57, 1962-67; Secretary & Aid to State Repr. 1972-74.

Org: Leg. Ladies League; WPC; BPW; Fed. Women;
OES; Historical Society; Assoc. of Dem. Women
State Legislators. Occ: Farm Owner. B: 10/6/15.
Add: RR #2, Rockwell City 50579 (515)281-3221.

MARY O'HALLORAN (D) **
   1972-. Dist: 36. Bds: House Energy Com.;
House Natural Resources Com.; House Appropriations
Com.; Governor's Task Force on Sex Role Stereo-
typing in Educ. Party: County Central Com. 1972-
75; Del., Nat. Mini Conv. 1974; Precinct Ch. 1971-
72. Org: LWV; WPC. Educ: Clarke Coll. 1966 BA.
B: 5/1/43. Add: 1939 Coll St., Cedar Falls
50613 (515)281-3221.

NANCY J. SHIMANEK (R)
   1976-. Dist: 22. Party: State Del. 1976, '74.
Org: ABA; BPW; Ia. Fed. of Rep. Women; WPC. Educ:
Clarke Coll. 1970 BA; U. of Ia. 1973 JD. Occ:
Attorney. B: 12/1/47. Add: 107 Monterey Trail,
Monticello 52310 (515)281-3221.

LINDA A. SVOBODA (D) **
   1974-. Dist: 72. Org: WPC. Educ: Marquette
U. BA. Add: RR, Amana 52203 (515)281-3221.

PATRICIA L. THOMPSON (R)
   1976-. Dist: 66. Party: State Del. 1976.
Org: Chamber of Commerce; WPC; Community Educ.
Dist Adv. Com.; Women's Club. Educ: U. of Nebr.
1947 AA. Occ: Bank Employee. B: 9/17/27. Add:
1512 Mountain Ave., W. Des Moines 50265
(515)281-3221.

County Commissions

Benton. HOPE ROGERS (D)
   Vinton 52349 (319)4722365.

Black Hawk. LYNN CUTLER (D) *
   1974-. Bds: Nat. Assoc. of Cntys.; Adv. Cmsn.
on Intergovernmental Relations; Pres., Ia. Assoc.
of Reg. Councils; Ch., Con.of Women, Nat. Assoc.
of Cntys. Party: State Del.; Platform Com. 1972;
Ia. Cnty. Officials for Carter-Mondale 1976;
Coord., 51.3% Com. in Ia. 1976. Org: WPC; Junior
League. Prev: Ia. Adv. Com. to U.S. Cmsn. on
Civil Rights; Cnty. Ch. 1975-76. Add: 705
Prospect Blvd., Waterloo 50701 (319)291-2416.

Black Hawk. SONIA A. JOHANNSEN (R)
   Waterloo 50703 (319)291-2416

Cedar. JEAN PENNINGROTH (R)
   Tipton 52772 (319)886-6346

Jasper. JEANNE BRIDENSTINE (D)
   Newton 50208 (515)792-7016.

Johnson. LORADA CILEK (D)
   Iowa City 52240 (319)338-5442.

Lee. DARLENE MORRISON (D)
   Ft. Madison 52627 (319)372-6557.

Linn. JEAN OXLEY (D)
   Cedar Rapids 52401 (319)398-3421.

Mitchell. BETTY MC CARTHY (D)
   Osage 50461 (515)732-4989.

Muscatine. JOAN AXEL (R)
      JANIS TORRENCE (R)
   Muscatine 52761 (319)263-5821.

Polk. FRANCES L. WHITEHURST (D)
   Cnty. Administration Bldg., Des Moines
50309 (515)284-6083.

Union. AGNES MC CANN (D)
   Creston 50801 (515)782-7918.

Wayne. FAY CRAIG (D)
   Corydon 50060 (515)872-2242.

Woodbury. RITA H. KLINE (D)
   Cnty. Administration Bldg., Sioux City
51101 (712)279-6525.

Mayors

Ames. MRS. LEE FELLINGER
   City Hall, Ames 50010.

Bagley. SANDRA S. GUBER (R)
   1976-. Bds: Ch., Fire Dist. Bd.; Cnty. Conf.
Bd. B: 9/2/34. Add: 200 1st Ave., Bagley
50026 (515)427-5600.

Beacon. N. RUTH MC CARTIE (I)
   1973-. Org: OES. B: 6/30/24. Add: 200
Grant St., Beacon 52534 (515)673-8993.

Benton. HELEN M. BLUNCK (R) **
   1962-. Bds: County Solid Waste Land Com.
Party: Precinct Com. 1960-74. Org: Young Rep.
Occ: Nurse's Aid. B: 7/24/13. Add: City Hall,
Benton 50835 (515)785-2259.

Bloomfield. HAZEL NARDINI
   City Hall, Bloomfield 52537.

Blue Grass. LAURETTA M. SCHUTTE
   City Hall, Blue Grass 52726.

Center. EILEEN M. NEENAN (D)
   1973-. Bds: Exec. Com., Non-Metro Coord. Com.;
Cnty. Conf. Bd.; Compensation Bd. Party: State
Del. Cnty. Committeewoman; Precinct Leader. Org:
Agency on Aging; Dem. Women's Club; Historical
Society. Educ: Coll. of St. Teresa Mercy,
Radiologic Technology RI. Occ: Coord., Adult
Educ. Program. B: 4/18/24. Add: 1121 Central
Ave., Center Pt. 52213 (319)849-1508.

Correctionville. GLORIA ANN HINK (R)
   1975-. Bds: Woodbury Cnty. Conf. Bd. Org:
Cnty. Mayor's Assoc.; Cnty. Communications Cmsn.
Educ: Ia. State Teachers Coll. 1960 BA. Occ:
Substitute Teacher. B: 11/1/40. Add: 418 6th
St., Correctionville 51016 (712)372-4791.

Delmar. FLORENCE MC CUTCHEON
   City Hall, Delmar 52137.

Edgewood. IMOGENE DEBES
   1976-. Prev: Councilwoman 1974-76. Occ:
Letter Carrier. Add: P.O. Box 393, Edgewood
52042 (319)928-7001.

Elgin. MARY S. CAPPER (I)
1976-. Org: Fed. Women's Club. B: 1/10/44.
Add: Mill Ave., Elgin 52141.

Ellston. JEANINE WALTERS
City Hall, Ellston 50074.

Floris. ALICE HUNTER
City Hall, Floris 52560.

Fontanelle. BETTY V. BURCHAM (D)
1973-. Bds: Ch., Fire & Rescue Cmsn. Org:
OES. Occ: Beautician. B: 9/20/22. Add:
Fontanelle 50846 (515)745-3961.

Galt. MRS. FRANCYS BRIGGER
City Hall, Galt 50101.

Iowa City. MARY CAMERON NEUHAUSER (D)
1975-. Bds: Johnson Cnty. Regional Planning
Cmsn.; Exec. Com. of Johnson Cnty. Reg. Planning
Cmsn.; Comprehensive Plan Coord. Cmsn. Prev:
Riverfront Cmsn. 1973-75. Org: LWV; WPC. Educ:
Radcliffe Coll. 1956 BA. B: 8/27/34. Add: 914
Highwood, Iowa City 52240 (319)354-1800.

Kalona City. ELDA G. WAY (R)
1976-. Prev: Councilwoman 1972-76. Occ: Bank
Officer. B: 8/6/16. Add: 603 H Ave., Kalona
52247 (319)656-2310.

Lake City. MARILYN MC CRARY (R)
1975-. Bds: V-Ch., Dist. Council of Govts.;
V-Ch., State Council of Govts. Bd. of Dir's.,
Ia. League of Municipalities. Party: State Del.
1964-70; V-Ch., Cnty. 1954-60; City V-Ch. 1950-51.
Educ: Gulfport Coll. 1944 AA; U. of Ia. 1946 BA;
Drake U. 1950 JD. B: 1/28/25. Add: 819 W.
Madison, Lake City 51449 (712)464-3111.

Larrabee. MARGARET YOUNG
City Hall, Larrabee 51029.

Laurel. BEVERLY L. BOLLHOEFER (D)
1973-. Bds: Exec. Bd. of Region Planning. B:
12/10/21. Add: Box 62, Laurel 50141 (515)476-
3436.

Lehigh. HAZEL MICKELSON (D) **
1973-. Bds: Library Bd. Org: Women's Club.
Occ: Secretary. B: 11/16/09. Add: Lehigh 50557
(515)359-2627.

Leland. JEAN ORTHEL
City Hall, Leland 50453.

Littleport. LORAINE THEIN
City Hall, Littleport 51523.

Marathon. MARGARET WALDSTEIN
City Hall, Marathon 50565.

Missouri Valley. DOROTHY M. PALMER (R)
1976-. Prev: Justice of the Peace 1958-64.
B: 1/3/24. Add: 567 N. 1st, Missouri Vly.
51555 (712)642-4424.

Monticello. JANET M. FRASER (D)
1975-. Bds: Cnty. Crime Cmsn.; Cnty. Solid
Waste Landfill Com.; V-Ch., E. Central Ia. Assoc.
of Regional Planning Com. Party: State Del.
1968, '72; Nat. Del. 1974; Precinct Committeewoman 1965; Cnty. Ch. 1969-71; State Dist. Ch.
1972-75. Prev: City Councilwoman 1972-75. Org:
Cnty. Retarded Child; WPC; LWV; Cnty. Dem's.
B: 6/4/23. Add: 5 Spring Farm Ln., Monticello
52310 (319)465-4230.

Moorland. MARY MC CARVILLE
City Hall, Moorland 50566.

Mount Vernon. DORIS L. PRINGLE (R)
1975-. Prev: Cnty. Conf. Bd. 1976-78. Org:
OES. B: 2/10/03. Add: 615 "A" Ave., S.,
Mt. Vernon 52314 (319)895-8742.

New Hartford. MARY J. BRINKMAN
City Hall, New Hartford 50660.

North Buena Vista. SELMA BOYCE
City Hall, North Buena Vista 52066.

Pulaski. DEBORAH BAUGHMAN
City Hall, Pulaski 52584.

Sabula. BONNIE LEE CALENTINE **
1975-. Org: BPW; Typographical Union. Occ:
Owner, Restaurant, Motel. B: 12/13/38. Add:
412 Elk St., Sabula 52070 (319)687-2420.

Stanwood. KATHARINE K. WINSOR (R) **
1974-. Bds: Crime Cmsn.; East Central Intergovernmental Assoc. Educ: Culver 1943 BA. B:
10/2/22. Add: Stanwood 52337 (319)945-3340.

Thayer. BETTY FIZER
City Hall, Thayer 50254.

Treynor. ELSIE M. BRYANT (R)
1976-. Party: Cnty. Com. Woman 1968-77. Org:
NEA; Cnty. Rep. Party; Cnty. Historical Society.
Educ: U. of Neb. BS. Occ: Teacher. B: 6/10/08.
Add: Box 297, Treynor 51575 (712)487-3787.

Volga. MRS. SHIRLEY GRANT
City Hall, Volga 52077.

Yetter. GLADYCE FAHAN
City Hall, Yetter 51433.

Local Councils

Ackworth. BEVERLY GINDER (I)
1975-. Occ: Printer. B: 3/13/40. Add:
Box 3, Ackworth 50001.

Adel. BETTE SCOTT
City Hall, Adel 50003.

Afton. HALLIE MOORE
City Hall, Afton 50830.

Ainsworth. NORMA WHITE
City Hall, Ainsworth 52201.

Albion. MARY LOU TAPPE
City Hall, Albion 50005.

Al Burnett. ARDITH SMITH
City Hall, Al Burnett 52202.

Alleman. JOY WANDER
City Hall, Alleman 50007.

Allerton. LUELLA CARPENTER
City Hall, Allerton 50008.

Allison. CHRISTENA HAMPEL (R)
1973-. Bds: Cemetery Com.; Sanitation; Bldg.
Org: Rep. Women's Club; Occ: Insurance Saleswoman.
B: 12/14/10. Add: 308 9th St., Allison 50602
(319)267-2245.

Ames. BARBARA A. KOERBER **
1971-. Party: Procedures Revision Com. 1975;
Ch., Com. 1974; Platform 1972. Org: LWV; WPC. B:
12/6/29. Add: 1206 Orchard Dr., Ames 50010
(515)232-6210.

Anamosa. MALINDA ENGELBART
City Hall, Anamosa 52205.

Anita. RUBY LITTLETON (D)
1976-. Occ: Receptionist. B: 11/29/29. Add:
610 Chestnut, Anita 50020.

Arion. JOANNE GORDEN (R)
1973-. Occ: Waitress/Bartender. B: 9/2/44.
Add: P.O. Box 434, Arion 51520.

Arion. MARGARET ROAD
City Hall, Arion 51520.

Asbury. DELORES A. KLOSER (R)
1972-. Prev: Council Ch. 1974-76. B: 7/5/31.
Add: 4903 Asbury, Dubuque 52001.

Asbury. MARTHA THOMAS
City Hall, Asbury 52001.

Athelstan. LEONA WILLIAMS
City Hall, Athelstan 50832.

Atkins. BLANCHE ELEANOR PADLEY (R)
1976-. Bds: Ch., Park Com. Party: State Del.
1976; Cnty. Central Com. 1974-77. Org: Cnty. Rep.
Women. Educ: Coe Coll. 1937 BA; U. of Ia. 1965
MA. B: 4/6/16. Add: 322 "A" Ave., Atkins 52206
(319)446-7810.

Atlantic. SHARON BROWN (R)
1976-. Bds: Liaison to Chamber of Commerce;
Land Preservation Policy Com.; Public Safety Cmsn.
Org: FACT (For Atlantic Community Tomorrow)
Foundation. Educ: Iowa State U. 1961 BS. Occ:
Office Assistant. B: 5/24/38. Add: Atlantic
50022 (712)243-3616.

Ayrshire. JEAN ROUSE HILL (I)
1974-. Mayor Pro Tem. Org: Teacher's Council.
Educ: Buena Vista Coll. 1968 BA. Occ: Teacher.
B: 3/8/25. Add: Box 1, Ayrshire 50515
(712)426-2371.

Badger. JUDY JENSEN (I)
1977-. Org: PTA. B: 10/21/42. Add:
210 Maher St., Badger 50516.

Baldwin. GERALDINE BODENHOFER
City Hall, Baldwin 52207.

Bankston. MARCELLA MULLER
City Hall, Bankston 52045.

Bassett. GLORIA BUCKNELL
City Hall, Bassett 50645.

Beacon. JUDITH C. ROORDA (D)
1975-. Bds: Mahaska Cnty. Solid Waste Management Cmsn. Org: Ia. Div. Independent Truckers
Assoc.; OES. B: 1/22/44. Add: 208 Grant St.,
Beacon 52534.

Beacon. SHIRLY SMITH
City Hall, Beacon 52534.

Beaconsfield. FAIGE HAGEN
City Hall, Beaconsfield 50030.

Bedford. KAY JOHNSON
City Hall, Bedford 50833.

Bennett. BETTY L. SMITH (R)
1970-. B: 11/5/24. Add: 135 W. 3rd St.,
Bennett 52721.

Benton. KATHLEEN BUTLER
Benton 50835.

Benton. ELEANORA G. CAVENDER (D)
Org: Head Start. B: 4/14/05. Add: Benton
50835.

Benton. KARYN KAY GRAHAM (R)
1974-. B: 5/16/47. Add: Benton 50835.

Benton. DOROTHA HALEY
VIOLA NICKLES
City Hall, Benton 50835.

Berkley. MILDRED GIBSON
City Hall, Berkley 50220.

Berkley. STELLA L. KEPPLE (D)
1975-. Occ: Babysitter. B: 12/5/19. Add:
Rt. 1, Perry 50220 (515)275-4257.

Bevington. PAULINE BUSSANMAS
City Hall, Bevington 50033.

Birmingham. MRS. LARRY PENCIL
City Hall, Birmingham 52535.

Blairsburg. BETTY L. KAREKEL (R)
1972-. Mayor Pro Tem. B: 6/7/32. Add:
Blairsburg 50034 (515)325-6292.

Blairsburg. BETTY ANN SPONSEL (D)
1975-. Bds: Solid Waste Cmsn.; Ch., Park
Cmsn. Party: State Del. 1976; Local Committeewoman 1970-76; Precinct Leader 1970-74. B:
1/3/46. Add: Box 76, Blairsburg 50034
(515)325-6363.

Blockton. DELORIS HENSON
City Hall, Blockton 50836.

Bouton. PATRICIA MC CAIN
City Hall, Bouton. 50039.

Brunsville. BEA RAMHORST
City Hall, Brunsville 51008.

Buckeye. MILDRED B. RADOHL (D)
1974-. Party: State Del. 1970-76; Precinct Committeewoman 1970-77; Cnty. Treasurer - Central Com. 1972-77. Org: Dem. Women's Club. Occ: Cafe Worker. B: 8/4/15. Add: Box 14, Buckeye 50043.

Calamus. MARJORIE MALAVOLTI
City Hall, Calamus 52729.

Callender. EMMA HANSON
FLORENCE JONDLE
City Hall, Callender 50523.

Cambridge. SHIRLEY MOORE (R) **
1972-. Bds: Ch., Finance Com.; Cemetery Com.; Social Concerns. Party: Historian 1962-68; Com. 1962-66. Prev: Library Bd. 1960-72. Org: Rep. Women's Club. Occ: Accountant. B: 4/26/25. Add: Box 496, Cambridge 50046 (515)383-4541.

Carbon. EVA MAAS
City Hall, Carbon 50839.

Carroll. VALERIE WINDSCHITL
City Hall, Carroll 51401.

Carter Lake. JEANNINE POLDBERG
City Hall, Carter Lake 68110.

Carter Lake. WANDA ROSENBAUGH (R)
1973-. Bds: Rescue Squad Com. Party: Cnty. Del. 1976-77. Prev: Planning Cmsn. 1970-73. Org: Improvement Club. Occ: Bookkeeper. B: 11/11/18. Add: 1617 13th St., Carter Lake 68110 (712)347-6320.

Casey. PATRICIA JENSEN
JO ANN MORRIS
City Hall, Casey 50048.

Center Junction. SANDRA RICKLEF (D)
1975-. Bds: Community Betterment Program Bd. B: 9/6/41. Add: Box 344, Center Junction 52212 (319)487-2821.

Centerville. ZEORA FISHER (R)
1974-. Bds: Community Devt.; Chamber of Commerce. Org: OES. Educ: Chillicothe 1934 BA. Occ: Credit Union Officer. B: 6/7/03. Add: 511 Haynes, Centerville 52544 (515)856-3224.

Centralia. HELEN K. WUERTZER (D)
1959-. Prev: City Clerk 1968-73. Occ: Tavern Owner. B: 10/20/28. Add: Rt. 1, Box 163, Centralia, P.O. Peosta 52068 (319)556-5971.

Chariton. LANORA DE VORE
City Hall, Chariton 50049.

Charter Oak. NANCY L. ROSBURG (I)
1974-. Bds: Zoning Com.; Recreation Com. Occ: Legal Secretary. B: 9/19/46. Add: 553 1st St. S,

Charter Oak 51439 (712)678-3580.

Cherokee. ELIZABETH BRASSER
City Hall, Cherokee 51012.

Churdan. JOANN K. DENNEY (D)
1973-. Occ: Insurance Secretary. B: 9/21/42. Add: Box 64, Churdan 50050.

Clare. MARIE PROCHASKA
City Hall, Clare 50524.

Clarinda. ANNA R. SMITH (R)
1973-. Bds: Community Betterment Com.; Employee Relations Com.; Cnty. Water Assoc. Party: State Del. 1972; Precinct Co-Ch. 1976. Org: AAUW; Community Betterment Com.; Cnty. Rep. Women. Educ: Northwest Mo. State U. 1957 BSEd.; U. of Kan. 1963 MMEd. Occ: Exec. Dir. of Clarinda Town of Tomorrow. B: 3/3/36. Add: 601 S. 16th, Clarinda 51632.

Clarion. ALICE KAY
City Hall, Clarion 50525.

Clayton. ANNA BALK
City Hall, Clayton 52149.

Clermont. EILEENE OLSON
City Hall, Clermont 52135.

Clio. ALTA ELOISE ALLEN (R)
1969-. Party: Precinct Committeewoman 1964-77. B: 10/21/05. Add: Clio 50052.

Clio. BETTY A. STILES (R)
1975-. Occ: Secretary. B: 3/21/27. Add: RR, Clio 50052.

Clive. EDNA MURIEL KAUFFMAN (D)
1974-. Bds: Center Ia. Regional Assoc. of Local Govts.; Parks Com.; Ch., Personnel Com. Org: OES. Occ: Manager. B: 10/8/30. Add: 1480 NW 96th, Clive 50322 (515)279-9793.

Coburg. MAYE ALM
City Hall, Coburg 51566.

Coggon. LOIS HEFFERNEN
City Hall, Coggon 52218.

Colesburg. JANICE MARILYN SCHERBRING (R)
1976-. Occ: Waitress. B: 10/15/37. Add: Box 135, Colesburg 52035.

Colfax. DONNA JONES
City Hall, Colfax 50054.

Collins. PEGGY L. EVANS (R)
1975-. Bds: Ch., Finance Com.; Parks & Bldgs. Org: OES. Occ: Bookkeeper. B: 12/19/51. Add: Box 101, Collins 50055.

Conway. HAZEL MILLER
City Hall, Conway 50834.

Coon Rapids. LUCILLE LAMP (R)
Bds: Park & Recreation. Occ: Cafe Owner/ Waitress. B: 10/19/20. Add: 311 7th Ave., Coon Rapids 50058.

Coralville. JULIA LYON
City Hall, Coralville 52241.

Correctionville. GAYLE D. JACOBS (D)
1975-. Bds: Cnty. Com. Action Agency; City
Park Supervisor. Org: Women's Fed Club. Occ:
Motel Owner. B: 5/21/45. Add: Box 52, Correctionville 51016 (712)372-4791.

Council Bluffs. DOROTHY L. STROHBEHN (R)
1971-. Bds: Operation Pride; Transportation;
Crime. Party: State Del. 1976; Precinct Committee
Woman 1964-72. Prev: Ia. Crime Com. 1968-73. Org:
Altrusa; Rep. Women. Educ: Ia. State U. 1951 BS.
B: 1/5/30. Add: 35 Royal Rd., Council Bluffs
51501 (712)328-4601.

Creston. JUNE JOANN LOUDON
1973-. Org: BPW. Occ: Realtor. B: 1/11/32.
Add: 1207 W. Mills, Creston 50801 (515)782-5217.

Creston. IRENE SMITH
City Hall, Creston 50801.

Cumming. SHERYL WEBB
City Hall, Cumming 50061.

Cylinder. CHRISTINE FREEMAN (I)
Bds: Recreation Dir. B: 5/20/50. Add: Box 37,
Cylinder 50528 (213)424-3967.

Davenport. BURDETTE DOHSE
City Hall, Davenport 52800.

Davis City. FLOSSIE SCHOONOVER
City Hall, Davis City 50065.

Dayton. LINDA JOREAN HANSEN (I)
1975-. Bds: Ch., Finance. Educ: Ia. State U.
1975 BS. B: 3/10/46. Add: 101 W. Skillet,
Dayton 50530.

Decorah. JOYCE EPPERLY
City Hall, Decorah 52101.

Deep River. GAYNELLE HOPWOOD (I)
1975-. Bds: Ch., Street Improvements; Water
Dept. Occ: Clerk. B: 11/14/41. Add: Box 132,
Deep River 52222 (515)595-3161.

Defiance. VERA MUNCHRATH
City Hall, Defiance 51527.

Delaware. CAROL TUTTON
City Hall, Delaware 52036.

Delmar. EDNA GISEL.
City Hall, Delmar 52137.

Delta. JUNE WYLLIE (R)
1975-. Bds: Sanitation; Ch., City Health Cmsn;
City Safety Comsr. Org: Fed. Women's Club;
Senior Citizen Housing. Occ: Cafe Manager/Owner.
B: 2/20/34. Add: P.O. Box 91, Delta 52550.

Denison. JANE MC KIM FLOOD (D)
1975-. Bds: Council of Govts.; Park Cmsn.;
Youth Foundation Bd. Educ: Georgetown Visitation
Jr. Coll. 1955 AA; Maryville Coll. 1957 BA. B:
8/31/35. Add: 1316 2nd Ave. N, Denison 51442
(712)263-3143.

Derby. PEARL TEATER
City Hall, Derby 50068.

Desoto. MARILYN DUPUY
City Hall, Desoto 50069.

Dexter. IRIS NOPOULOS
City Hall, Dexter 50070.

Dickens. BARBARA TEILBUR
City Hall, Dickens 51333.

Dixon. DOROTHY GIBSON
City Hall, Dixon 52745.

Donahue. MARGERY SCHROEDER
City Hall, Donahue 52746.

Donnan. MARGARET GAGE
ELINOR PORTER
CYNTHIA WEST
City Hall, Donnan 52139.

Donnellson. LORRAINE B. THOMAS (I)
1975-. B: 11/13/42. Add: RR 1, Donnellson
52625 (319)835-5798.

Donnellson. PEARL WOODS
City Hall, Donnellson 52625.

Doon. BARBARA B. ROSS (D) **
1973-. Bds: Park Cmsn.; Sanitation Cmsn.
B: 7/31/35. Add: Box 251, Doon 51235
(712)726-9390.

Drakesville. NELLIE F. HILL (R)
1972-. Mayor Pro Tem. B: 9/24/1897. Add:
Drakesville 52552.

Duncombe. MARY BETH BOCK
MAXINE PETERSON
City Hall, Duncombe 50532.

Dunkerton. NATALIE BAUGHER
City Hall, Dunkerton 50626.

Dunlap. RUTH L. LACEY (D) **
1974-. B: 3/25/34. Add: 1006 Jeroleman,
Dunlap 51529.

Durango. HELEN LEIK
MARGARET ROSE SCHEMMEL
City Hall, Durango 52039.

Dysart. AGNES DOCEKAL
City Hall, Dysart 52224.

Earlham. CLAIRE WAUGH
City Hall, Earlham 50072.

East Peru. VIRGINIA ROBBINS
City Hall, East Peru 50222.

Elberton. KAY BATES
City Hall, Elberton 52225.

Eldon. JACQUELINE JONES
City Hall, Eldon 52554.

Elliott. DOROTHY BRADEN (D)
    1975-. Org: Fed. Women's Club. Educ: Drake
U. BS. B: 12/18/09. Add: Elliott 51532.

Emmetsburg. NANCY O'CONNER
    City Hall, Emmetsburg 50536.

Essex. PHYLLIS DOBBS
    City Hall, Essex 51638.

Fairfax. KATHY A. HANKE (D)
    1975-. B: 7/18/48. Add: 206 Prairie St.,
Fairfax 52228.

Farmersburg. DELORES MATHEWS
    City Hall, Farmersburg 52047.

Farmersburg. LINDA SEDLMAYR (R)
    1973-. Mayor Pro Tem. Org: NEA. Educ: Upr.
la. Coll. 1967 BS. Occ: Teacher. B: 12/02/39.
Add: Farmersburg 52047 (319)536-2390.

Farragut. LINDA L. BONNES (D)
    1976-. Bds: Park Comsr. Educ: Clarinda
Community Coll. 1961 AA. Occ: Office Manager.
B: 10/22/41. Add: 203 Lincoln, Farragut 51639.

Fayette. ELLEN LANE
    City Hall, Fayette 52142.

Ferguson. PEARL OLSEN
    City Hall, Ferguson 50078.

Floris. CELMA A. BIRDSALL (D)
    1977-. Mayor Pro Tem. Org: Nat. League of
Postmasters; Nat. Assoc. of Postmasters. Occ:
Postmaster. B: 7/24/08. Add: P.O. Box 562,
Floris 52560 (515)459-2218.

Floris. KAY BROWN
         VIOLA FIEDLER
         BETTY ROSENSTANGLE
    City Hall, Floris 52560.

Floyd. VALARIA DYRE
    City Hall, Floyd 50435.

Fonda. JANETTE GARLOCK
    City Hall, Fonda 50540.

Fort Atkinson. MARY ROSE MOSER
    City Hall, Ft. Atkinson 52144.

Franklin. JEAN MAAG
           LORRAINE THOMAS
    City Hall, Franklin 52625.

Galva. MARTHA SCHULKE (D)
    1973-. Bds: Ch., Park Cmsn. Org: Civic Club.
B: 9/18/07. Add: 205 Woodbury, Galva 51020.
(712)282-4228.

Garden Grove. DARLEAN ERB (D) **
    1971-. Occ: Housekeeper. B: 5/27/14. Add:
Main St., Box 4, Garden Grove 50103 (515)443-3653

Garden Grove. LORNA NOECKER
    City Hall, Garden Grove 50103.

Garnavillo. CHERYL B. SIEBRECHT
    City Hall, Garnavillo 52049.

Garner. CAROL E. OMANS
    City Hall, Garner 50438.

Garrison. CINDY PATTEE
    City Hall, Garrison 52229.

Geneva. PATRICIA BONEWITZ
         DOROTHY SILVER
    City Hall, Geneva 50633.

Gilbert. MARGARET CLOUSER
    City Hall, Gilbert 50105.

Gilman. ESTHER WERTZ
    City Hall, Gilman 50106.

Gilmore City. LOIS WISEMAN
    City Hall, Gilmore City 50541.

Glidden. ARLENE DAVIS
    City Hall, Glidden 51443.

Graf. JEAN MAYNE (I)
    1975-. Occ: Sales Clerk. B: 6/9/48. Add:
103 Graf Ct., Durango 52039.

Graf. BLANCHE SCHMITT
    City Hall, Graf 52039.

Grandview. LOIS BONNICHSEN (D)
    1974-. Occ: Grocery Store Owner. B: 6/11/32.
Add: Grandview 52752 (319)729-2151.

Gravity. MARG LAND
    City Hall, Gravity 50848.

Green Island. MARGARET MOHR
    City Hall, Green Island 52051.

Greenville. JOANNE ARTHUR
    City Hall, Greenville 51343.

Gruver. EVELYN KIRCHNER
         GLADYS MUSTARD
    City Hall, Gruver 51344.

Hamilton. MARLENE ALLEN
           ELLA JOHNSON
           ALICE WALLACE
    City Hall, Hamilton 50116.

Hardy. DONNA RATHKE
    City Hall, Hardy 50545.

Harlan. NANCY A. ROSS (D)
    1975-. Bds: Ch., Utilities Com.; Sanitation
Com.; Sidewalk Com. Prev: Library Bd. 1971-77;
Cnty. Bd. of Social Services 1972-77. Educ:
Grinnell Coll. 1956 BA. B: 7/13/34. Add: 2002
Willow St., Harlan 51537 (712)755-5137.

Harper. JOANNE MILLER
    City Hall, Harper 52231.

Harpers Ferry. EMMA BENSON
    City Hall, Harpers Ferry 52146.

Hartwick. JOAN MC CONNELL
    City Hall, Hartwick 52232.

Havelock. MARGARET BLAHA
City Hall, Havelock 50546.

Hazleton. LORAINE CHASE
ARLENE WHITE
City Hall, Hazleton 50641.

Hillsboro. ROBERTA BOITSCHA (D)
1975-. Bds: Park; Sanitation. Party: Precinct
Leader 1969-77. Org: Women's Club; Dem. Club;
Ch., Bicentennial. B: 7/8/17. Add: Hillsboro
52630 (319)253-3645.

Hornick. LUCILLE SIEGER
City Hall, Hornick 51026.

Houghton. JUDY MOELLER
City Hall, Houghton 52621.

Humeston. REVA GOULD
City Hall, Humeston 50123.

Hurtsville. WILMA EYE
GLORIA MANNING
LORANN SUMMERS
City Hall, Hurtsville 52060.

Imogene. LETTY DAVIS
WILMA MAHER
BETTY MC GARGILL
City Hall, Imogene 51645.

Indianola. JOAN D. HOLT (D)
1975-. Org: LWV; Dem. Club. Occ: Manager.
Add: 1104 W. Salem, Indianola 50125
(515)961-5361.

Inwood. MARY ANN MUENZENMAY
City Hall, Inwood 51240.

Ionia. GLADYS DIESBURG
RUTH WEIGLEIN
City Hall, Ionia 50646.

Iowa City. CAROL W. DE PROSSE (D)
1973-. Bds: Regional Planning Cmsn.; Compre-
hensive Planning Coord. Com.; Transportation Com.;
Nat. League of Cities. Org: ACLU; Southern
Poverty Law Ctr. B: 3/19/42. Add: 1113 E.
College St., Iowa City 52240 (319)354-1800.

Jamaica. CONNIA MEINECKE
City Hall, Jamaica 50128.

Janesville. MILDRED M. MITCHELL (D)
1967-. Bds: Ch., General; Ch., Library;
Sanitation. Party: State Del. 1964, '68; Precinct
Ch. 1956-72. Org: Dem. Women's Club. B: 8/20/22.
Add: 126 Main, Janesville 50647 (319)987-2905.

Jefferson. DOROTHY VAN HORN (R)
1973-. Bds: Recreation Cmsn.; Cnty. Solid
Waste Agency. Party: State Del. 1974-76. Org:
League of Ia. Municipalities Bd.; Cnty. Day Care
Ctr.; Soroptimist; Community Betterment. Educ:
U. of Ia. 1946 BA. B: 12/24/23. Add: Maple Hl.
Pl., Jefferson 50129 (515)386-3111.

Joice. RUTH ELWOOD
City Hall, Joice 50446.

Kanawha. LOIS SCHROEDER (R)
1973-. Bds: Ch., Street Cmsn. Org: Woman's
Club. Educ: Io. State Coll. 1942 BS. B:
10/28/20. Add: 210 East 6th St., Kanawha 50447
(515)762-3632.

Kellerton. SANDRA S. CAMPBELL (D) **
1973-. Org: OES. Occ: Beautician. B:
4/23/38. Add: Box 206, Kellerton 50133
(515)783-2510.

Keokuk. BROOK DUNN (I)
1975-. Bds: Tri-State Bridge Com.; Downtown
Devt. Corp. Org: Ia. League of Municipalities.
B: 1/2/45. Add: 629 Fulton, Keokuk 52632
(319)524-2050.

Keomah. MARY JOHNS
City Hall, Keomah 52577.

Kirkman. CAROL FISCUS
SANDRA RONFELDT
City Hall, Kirkman 51447.

Klemme. ELSA K. DIRKS (I) **
1973-. Bds: Public Safety; Utilities; Finance,
Bills & Trust Agencies; Public Relations &
Community Dev. Occ: School Bus Driver. B:
3/28/44. Add: RR, Klemme 50449 (515)587-2600.

Knoxville. PAMELA SMITH TODD (R)
1974-. Bds: Repr., Central Ia. Regional
Assoc. Local Govts.; Community Betterment Com.
Educ: William Penn Coll. 1974 BA. Occ: Sub-
stitute Teacher. B: 4/16/40. Add: 114 S. 7th,
Knoxville 50138 (515)842-3647.

Lamoni. WILMA I. RUNKLE
City Hall, Lamoni 50140.

Larrabee. JUDY LOUCKS
PAMILA WESPHAL
City Hall, Larrabee 51029.

LeGrand. MARY LOUISE LOERWALD (D)
1976-. Bds: Water & Sewer; Park. Party:
State Del.; Cnty. Committeewoman 1970-75. Prev:
Planning & Zoning 1973-76. Occ: Secretary. B:
9/6/40. Add: 201 N. Webster, LeGrand 50142.

Leland. BARBARA A. SMITH (I)
1975-. Org: Nat. Assoc. of Flight Instructors.
Educ: U. of Colo. 1972 BFA; Mary Immaculate
Hospital School of Nursing 1955 RN. Occ: Chief
Pilot-Flight Instructor. B: 7/13/30. Add: RR 1,
Box 95, Leland 50453.

Lemars. BONNIA DULL
City Hall, Lemars 51031.

Leroy. EDNA CLARK
JOAN MUNDELL
ZULA PATTERSON
City Hall, Leroy 50123.

Letts. JUDY OHARA
City Hall, Letts 52754.

Libertyville. SHERRY ANGSTEAD
DORIS ECKLUND
City Hall, Libertyville 52567.

Lime Springs. ELLEN NELSON
    City Hall, Lime Springs 52155.

Lincoln. KIM SIENKNECHT
    City Hall, Lincoln 50652.

Lineville. DORIS KILTABIDLE
            RUTH OWENS
    City Hall, Lineville 50147.

Little Sioux. VIOLET BREELING
               NINA BURNS
    City Hall, Little Sioux 51523.

Little Sioux. ANNA MARIE FLINT (R) **
    1973-. Bds: Park Cmsn.; Street Cmsn.; Better-
ment Com. Org: PTA; RNA. Occ: Secretary. B:
7/18/32. Add: 400 1st St., Little Sioux 51545
(712)649-2187.

Lohrville. HELEN MC LAIN
    City Hall, Lohrville 51453.

Lone Tree. LETHA M. GRAY
    1972-. Mayor Pro Tem. Org: Chamber of
Commerce. Occ: Bookkeeper. B: 7/2/15. Add:
Lone Tree 52755.

Lost Nation. BETTY M. FLEMMING (I)
    1966-. Bds: Ch., Sewer; Auditing; Cnty.
Planning. Prev: Councilwoman 1966-72. Occ: Auto
Mechanic. B: 6/6/26. Add: 801 Winter, Lost
Nation 52254.

Lovilia. SUSAN MARIE BEARY (D)
    1976-. Bds: Ch., Community Betterment Com.
Party: State Del. 1976. Org: Community Club; Dem.
Women's Club; WPC. Occ: Home Health Aide. B:
8/26/50. Add: Box 91, Lovilia 50150
(515)946-3411.

Lovilia. ELEANORA SOFRANKO (D)
    1972-. Bds: Ch., Planning & Devt.; Ch., Fair
Housing Officer; Equal Rights Officer. Org:
Community Club. B: 9/21/14. Add: 606 W. 18th,
Lovilia 50150 (515)946-3411.

Lowden. LANA RUGGEBERG
    City Hall, Lowden 52255.

Luana. MYRNA GORDON (R)
    1976-. Bds: Ch., Better Devt. Com. Party:
State Del. 1976; Precinct Leader 1976; Cnty. Com.
1976; Cnty. Ch. 1976. Org: Cnty. Rep. Women.
Occ: Beautician. B: 5/12/37. Add: Box 56, Luana
52156 (319)539-2960.

Luana. JOYCE LANGE
    City Hall, Luana 52156.

Lucas. BELVAH BAKER (R) **
    1973-. Org: Telephone Pioneers; Treasurer,
John L. Lewis Labor; Women's Club. B: 7/4/09.
Add: 305 Division, Lucas 50151 (515)766-2722.

Lucas. OPAL JAMES
    City Hall, Lucas 50151.

Luverne. EUNICE BLAKE
    City Hall, Luverne 50560.

Lynnville. MARY YODER
    City Hall, Lynnville 50153.

Macedonia. ALICE ALLENSWORTH (R)
    1969-. Bds: Ch., Street Dept.; Water Dept.
Occ: Meat Cutter. B: 11/13/24. Add: Macedonia
51549.

Macksburg. ESTEL WELCH
    City Hall, Macksburg 50155.

Malcolm. SHERYL SMITH
    City Hall, Malcolm 50157.

Manly. MRS. DON OSTLUND
    City Hall, Manly 50456.

Manning. THELMA MOHR
    City Hall, Manning 51455.

Marble Rock. FLORENCE I. SHOOK (D) **
    1973-. Bds: Public Grounds; Park; Library.
B: 11/27/34. Add: Box 14, Marble Rock 50653.

Marengo. VIRGINIA BENSCOTER
          DORIS FRY
    City Hall, Marengo 52301.

Marion. JANICE KOPEL
    City Hall, Marion 52302.

Marion. MARY LOU PAZOUR (D)
    1975-. Bds: Park Bd.; Metropolitan Community
Adv. Bd. Org: NEA; Amer. Security Council; Nat.
Trust for Historic Preservation. Educ: Coe Coll.
1958 BA. Occ: Elementary Physical Educ.
Instructor. B: 12/14/36. Add: 1609 3rd Ave.,
Marion 52302 (319)377-1581.

Marshalltown. JEAN COOPER
    City Hall, Marshalltown 50158.

Marshalltown. ROSEMARY E. JOHNSON (I)
    1973-. Bds: Ch., Traffic Com.; Utilities Com;
Airport Com. B: 1/3/19. Add: 1507 E. Nevada St.
Marshalltown 50158 (515)752-2512.

Marysville. ANNETTA ROBERTS
    City Hall, Marysville 50116.

Masonville. MARY KING
    City Hall, Masonville 50654.

Massena. LINDA J. EILTS (I)
    1976-. Bds: Ch., Sanitation & Equipment;
Buildings & Ordinances; Ch., Streets & Alleys.
Occ: Postal Clerk. B: 8/9/47. Add: Rt. 1,
Box 68, Massena 50853 (712)779-2295.

Matlock. LILA BOERHAUE
    City Hall, Matlock 51244.

McClelland. MAXINE SCHULTZ
             DARLENE SHARRETT
    City Hall, McClelland 51548.

McIntire. NORMA ARMSTRONG
           VIOLET LOCKIE
    City Hall, McIntire 50455.

Mechanicsville. LA VERNA M. KOCH (D)
    1975-. Bds: Finance. Occ: Paint & Lumber
Clerk. B: 12/21/27. Add: 206 N. Linn St.,
Mechanicsville 52306.

Melbourne. WILMA V. COPENHAVER (D)
    1975-. Bds: Streets; Sanitation; Ch., Finance.
Occ: Factory Worker. B: 7/29/24. Add: 301 2nd
St., Melbourne 50162.

Melrose. COLLEEN SEARS
    City Hall, Melrose 52569.

Melvin. MARILYN DAMMAN (R)
    1973-. Org: Rep. Women; Fed. Club. Occ: Bank
Cashier. B: 9/12/36. Add: Melvin 51350.

Merrill. SHARON THILL
    City Hall, Merrill 51038.

Millersburg. MICHEL BESLEY
    City Hall, Millersburg 52308.

Millville. GERMAINE WEYANT
    City Hall, Millville 52052.

Milton. JANE HARGROVE
    City Hall, Milton 52570.

Minburn. VIRGINIA M. NELSON
    City Hall, Minburn 50167.

Mitchell. FRANCINE VULK
    City Hall, Mitchell 50461.

Moneta. ROSIE SABOE
    City Hall, Moneta 51352.

Monmouth. JANE MILLER
    City Hall, Monmouth 52309.

Mont Rose. DIANE HAGMEIER
    City Hall, Mont Rose 52639.

Moorland. GARLAND BALL
             MAXINE FERRIA
    City Hall, Moorland 50566.

Moorland. DOLORES LEEPER (D)
    1976-. Bds: Fire Dept. Bd. B: 5/14/35. Add:
Moorland 50566   (515)549-3457.

Morrison. ANNA BEENKEN (D) **
    1974-. B: 6/8/32. Add: Box 46, Morrison
50657   (319)345-2694.

Moulton. TRACY CORDER
    City Hall, Moulton 52572.

Mount Auburn. LEONA WILSON (D)
    1975-. B: 8/31/13. Add: Box 87, Mt. Auburn
52313.

Mount Pleasant. JOANN SANKEY
    City Hall, Mt. Pleasant 52641.

Mount Vernon. JOANN NEFF
    City Hall, Mount Vernon 52314.

Murray. MARGARET J. COX (I)
    Occ: Inspector; Shipping Clerk. B: 8/17/20.
Add: Murray 50174.

Neola. HELEN FREY
        BARBARA LANGIN
    City Hall, Neola 51559.

New Hampton. ELAINE M. GUNDACKER (I)
    1975-. Bds: Finance Com.; Ch., Ordinance
Com.; Sanitation Com. Prev: City Clerk 1966-73.
Occ: Technical Asst. to Local Govt. B: 6/11/33.
Add: P.O. Box 144, New Hampton 50659
(615)394-2109.

New Market. RHODA MC COMB
    City Hall, New Market 51646.

Newton. MARJORIE DENNISTON
    1973-. Bds: Conf. Bd. Org: LWV; WPC. Educ:
Coll. of Emporia 1947 BS. B: 7/5/26. Add:
1506 N. 7th Ave. W., Newton 50208.

New Virginia. CHERYL A. BOLES (R)
    1975-. Bds: Ch., Street Lighting Com.; Park
Com. Org: OES. B: 7/18/48. Add: Box 102, New
Virginia 50210.

New Virginia. BETTY ROBERTS
    City Hall, New Virginia 50210.

Nodaway. GLORIA BALDWIN
    City Hall, Nodaway 50857.

North Buena Vista. CELESTINE LUDOVISSY
    City Hall, N. Buena Vista 52066.

North English. JEAN E. COFFMAN (R)
    1975-. Bds: Finance Com. Party: State Del.
1973; Precinct Committeewoman 1973-77. Org:
Ch., Ia. Assoc. of Insurance Agents; Commercial
Club; Cnty. Rep. Women; OES. Occ: Insurance
Agency Manager. B: 6/9/20. Add: 108 E. Oak St.,
N. English 52316 (319)664-3616.

North Liberty. MARY ELLEN COMLY (R)
    1976-. Org: ALA; Common Cause; Opera Guild;
Friends of Art. Educ: Monmouth Coll. 1941 BS;
Cottey Coll. 1939 AA; U. of Ia. 1972 MLS. B:
10/30/20. Add: Quail Crk. 2-E, RR1, N. Liberty
52317   (319)626-2853.

Numa. ANNA MAC PARTIN
        LINDA RICK
    City Hall, Numa 52575.

Oakland Acres. KATHERINE REDIGER
                SANDRA SANGER
    City Hall, Oakland Acres 50112.

Oakville. DOROTHY MITCHELL
    City Hall, Oakville 52646.

Okoboji. HELEN GIBSON
    City Hall, Okoboji 51355.

Olin. GOLDIE E. BENISCHEK (D)
    1975-. Bds: Ch., Street Cmsn.; Library Bd.
B: 8/9/18. Add: Maple St., Olin 52320.

Olin. NORMA LUCKSTEAD
City Hall, Olin 52320.

Onawa. DARLENE FARBER
City Hall, Onawa 51040.

Oneida. INA ANTRIM
City Hall, Oneida 52057.

Osage. ROBERTA F. LOVE (R)
1975-. Bds: Ch., Parking Com.; Sewer & Water;
Wages. B: 2/10/19. Add: 719 S. 5th, Osage 50461.

Owasa. ALICE HERROLD
City Hall, Owasa 50126.

Oxford. VIOLET REIHMAN
BETTY ROHRET
City Hall, Oxford 52322.

Oxford Junction. SHARYN JENSEN
City Hall, Oxford Junction 52323.

Palo. DONNA HILL
MILDRED ZELLER
City Hall, Palo 52324.

Panama. DONNA MAHLBERG
City Hall, Panama 51562.

Panora. EVELYN EMBREY
City Hall, Panora 50216.

Panorama Park. LELA E. CARY (D)
1968-. Bds: Road Cmsn.; Ch., Finance Com.;
Public Health Com. B: 12/20/07. Add: 904 Park
Ave., Panorama Pk. 52722.

Panorama Park. ALTA GRAPENGETER
DOROTHY HICKS
City Hall, Panorama Park 52722.

Parnell. VIOLA BURKHOLDER
JUDY CARNEY
JENNY MC DONALD
JEAN O'BREIN
City Hall, Parnell 52325.

Patterson. ANNA G. FAUX (D) **
Occ: Operator, Mobil Home Park. B: 7/27/26.
Add: Box 25, Patterson 50218.

Paullina. MARLO EBEL
BERTHA SJAARDA
City Hall, Paullina 51046.

Peosta. MARY E. DARDIS (I)
Prev: Fed. Postmaster 1963-77. Occ: Postmaster
B: 3/1/20. Add: Post Office, Peosta 52068
(319)556-6212.

Peosta. DONNA WEYDERT
City Hall, Peosta 52068.

Perry. VIRGINIA JOY POFFENBERGER (R)
1973-. Bds: Civic Ctr. Bd. Party: State Del.
1968-74; Cnty. Co-Ch. 1964-67; Precinct Leader
1968-72. Org: Student Bar Assoc.; Mental Health
Ctr. Bd.; Day Ctr. Bd. Educ: Ia. State U. 1957 BS
B: 11/12/34. Add: 1816 Willis Ave., Perry 50220.

Pilot Mound. ANN H. STARK (D)
1969-. Bds: Dog Control. Org: Soroptimist.
Occ: Trust Officer. B: 8/7/21. Add: Box 116,
Pilot Mound 50223 (515)353-4224.

Plain View. MARTHA DIETSCH
LEONA HOLDORF
HANNAH KOESTER
City Hall, Plain View 52773.

Pleasant Hill. PAULINE THURMAN
City Hall, Pleasant Hill 50317.

Plymouth. JEANETTE M. NICHOLSON (I)
1975-. Mayor Pro Tem. Bds: Roads Bd. B:
9/5/35. Add: 600 Main, Box 295, Plymouth 50464
(515)696-5613.

Pocahontas. M. ANTONETTE HALLMAN (D)
1975-. Bds: Park Cmsn. Occ: Bookkeeper. B:
5/28/15. Add: 400 1st Ave SW, Pocahontas 50574.

Portsmouth. JUDY FUNK
City Hall, Portsmouth 51565.

Primghar. SHIRLEY J. OMER (D)
1972-. Bds: Cnty. Communications Cmsn. Org:
Ia. Press Assoc.; Community Betterment Council;
Historical Society. Occ: Newspaper Editor. B:
9/22/27. Add: 620 12th St., Primghar 51245
(712)757-4055.

Promise City. AMY ROBERTSON
City Hall, Promise City 52583.

Quimby. EVA M. NELSON (D)
Occ: Upholsterer. B: 7/29/18. Add: Quimby
51049.

Ralston. VERNA STOUGARD
City Hall, Ralston 51459.

Randall. MYRTLE CHRISTENSON (D)
1973-. Educ: Drake U. 1942 BS. B: 1/20/15.
Add: Randall 50231.

Randall. A. ELIZABETH SMITH (R)
1971-. Org: Women's Club. Occ: Accounting
Clerk. B: 8/6/14. Add: Box 124, Randall 50231.

Rathbun. ELIZABETH CHEBUHAR
ROSE STARCEVICH
City Hall, Rathbun 52545.

Raymond. MARIE SACHS
City Hall, Raymond 50667.

Readlyn. LORRAINE JOHNSON
BETTY KOSCHMEDED
City Hall, Readlyn 50668.

Redfield. BONNIE D. KOTE (D) **
1975-. Bds: Parks & Recreation; Finance &
Health. Occ: Bookkeeper. B: 9/16/35. Add:
City Hall, Redfield 50233 (515)833-2566.

Renwick. REBECCA ANN NAGEL (I)
1976-. Bds: Ch., Improvement; Public Health
Com.; Purchasing Com. Org: WPC; OES. Occ: Bank
Teller. B: 4/1/42. Add: 217 Montgomery, Renwick
50577 (515)824-3511.

Ridgeway. HATTIE M. RINGOEN (R)
    1969-. Org: Bd. of La Crosse Lutheran Hospital;
Heritage Club-Lutheran Hospital; Sons of Norway;
Chamber of Commerce; Ridgeway Rental Housing Apts.
Occ: Postal Clerk. Add: Ridgeway 52165
(319)737-2220.

Ringsted. LILLIAN DAVIDSON (D)
    1969-. Bds: Ch., Task Force for Land Use;
Streets and Sewers. Occ:Cafe Owner. B: 8/25/22.
Add: Box 66 Maple St., Ringsted 50578
(712)866-2501.

Robins. SHIRLEY L. HOPPE (D)
    1975-. Bds: Ch., Recreation Cmsn.; Ch., Bd.
of Control. B: 1/16/47. Add: 25 Timber Lane
RR 1, Marion 52302 (319)377-1687.

Robins. BARBARA PFEIFFER
    City Hall, Robins 52328.

Rockford. THELMA KOCK (R)
    1974-. Bds: Ch., Library. Org: Women's Club.
B: 12/4/28. Add: 404 2nd Ave., NE, Box 215,
Rockford 50468.

Rock Rapids. DORIS CALKINS (R)
    1975-. Org: BPW; Rep. Women's Club. Educ:
Westmar 1958 BA. Add: 1008 S. Tama, Rock Rapids
51246.

Rock Rapids. DOROTHY MC CORMACK (R)
    1969-. Bds: Human Devt. Com.; Home & Community
Environment; Summer Recreation Com. B: 1/15/27.
Add: 510 S. Bradley, Rock Rapids 51246
(712)472-2511.

Rodney. VERA HECK
    City Hall, Rodney 51051.

Rowan. GLADYS WOODLEY
    City Hall, Rowan 50470.

Rowley. VIVIAN DAVIS
    City Hall, Rowley 52329.

Runnells. IOLA B. WEAVER (D) **
    1950-. Prev: Mayor. B: 4/1/20. Add: 401
Garfield, Runnells 50237 (515)966-2042.

Russell. VIRGINIA ORWIG
    City Hall, Russell 50238.

Ruthven. NANCY ANN BAEDKE
    1974-. Occ: Waitress/Cook. B: 10/12/40. Add:
Box 216, Ruthven 51358.

Rutland. ARLENE TILLE
    1975-. Bds: Ch., Recreational Facilities;
Water Comsr. Party: Senior Treasurer 1976.
Org: Jr. Citizens. Occ: Restaurant Owner. B:
2/3/36. Add: Box 96, 105 Grand Ave., Rutland
50582 (515)332-1412.

Sac City. DOROTHY WEDDELL (R)
    1976-. B: 2/19/22. Add: Box 17, Rt. 2,
Sac City 50583.

St. Ansgar. LAUREL A. KIMBER (R)
    1976-. Bds: Ch., Community Protection;
Policy & Administration; Street Improvements.
Party: State Del. 1974-76; Election Bd. Official
1976. Org: Chamber of Commerce. Occ: Gas
Station/Restaurant Owner. B: 8/22/47. Add:
513 W. 4th St., St. Ansgar 50472.

St. Anthony. LOIS DRUMMER
                RUTH MACKIN
    City Hall, St. Anthony 50239.

St. Charles. CONNIE KEPHART
    City Hall, St. Charles 50240.

St. Donatus. HELEN KALMES (D) **
    1970-. Party: Ch. 1972-74. Occ: Bookkeeper.
B: 8/11/39. Add: St. Donatus 52071.

St. Marys. FRANCES BUSSANMAS
    City Hall, St. Marys 50241.

Sanborn. JEANETTE RAYMOND
    City Hall, Sanborn 51248.

Sandyville. OLEVIA PHILLIPS
    City Hall, Sandyville 50001.

Scarville. SANDRA ARNIVIK
                BLANCHE NESSA
    City Hall, Scarville 50473.

Scranton. KIM J. BATES (I)
    1976-. B: 11/2/51. Add: Scranton 51462.

Searsboro. IONE RAYL
    City Hall, Searsboro 50242.

Shannon City. JANE VAN TYLE
    City Hall, Shannon City 50861.

Shelby. LOIS HETRICK
    City Hall, Shelby 51570.

Shenandoah. KAYE NORTON
    City Hall, Shenandoah 51601.

Silver City. EDNA BOLTE
    City Hall, Silver City 51571.

Sioux City. MARGARET M PRAHL
    1973-. Bds: Planning & Zoning Cmsn.; Housing
Advisory Cmsn.; Mayor's Youth Com. Prev: City
Planning & Zoning Cmsn. 1970-73. Org: LWV; Jr.
League; Sioux City Center for Women. Educ: U. of
Neb. 1960 BA. B: 11/12/38. Add: 3638 Linden-
wood, Sioux City 51104 (712)279-6102.

Stanwood. SALLY I. TAYLOR (D)
    1976-. Prev: Park Bd. 1966-72. Occ: News-
paper Editor. B: 3/14/34. Add: 205 S. Ash,
Stanwood 52337 (319)945-3340.

Storm Lake. MARY L. LENHART
    City Hall, Storm Lake 50588.

Superior. MARDELLE HASBROOK
    City Hall, Superior 51363.

Sutherland. MARCELLE SCHULTZ
      City Hall, Sutherland 51058.

Swaledale. KATHLEEN BOHL
      City Hall, Swaledale 50477.

Swea City. FAYE BOLAND (D)
      1976-. B: 10/28/47. Add: RR 2, Box C-2,
Swea City 50590.

Tabor. GLADYS GERBER (D)**
      1974-. Bds: Street Commissioner. Prev:
Justice of the Peace. B: 5/18/01. Add: Tabor
51653 (712)629-3865.

Tama. BESS INGLES
      City Hall, Tama 52339.

Terril. BEVERLY DALLMAN
      City Hall, Terril 51364.

Thayer. NONA ALEXANDER
      DOROTHY CLAYPOOL
      City Hall, Thayer 50254.

Thayer. REKA QUEE **
      1965-. B: 1/11/07. Add: Thayer 50254
(515)338-2327.

Thurman. ELAINE LEEKA (D) **
      1974-. Party: Ch., County 1972-76; V-Ch.,
County 1960-72. Org: WPC; Women's Clubs. Educ:
U. of Neb. 1931 BA; State U. of Ia. 1936 MA. B:
6/20/08. Add: Box 166, Thurman 51654
(712)628-3491.

Tiffin. JANIS STRATTON
      City Hall, Tiffin 52340.

Tipton. DORIS A. HARGRAVE (R)
      1976-. Bds: Ch., Ambulance Com.; Ch., Finance
& Insurance Com.; Ch., Ordinance Com. Party:
State Del. 1964; Precinct Committeewoman 1950-77;
Cnty. Treasurer 1974-76. Org: Nat. Retail Farm
Equipment Assoc. Occ: Bookkeeper/Corp. Secretary.
B: 12/29/13. Add: 310 W. 9th St., Tipton 52772
(319)886-6187.

Titonka. ROBERTA MOVICK
      Titonka 50480.

Toledo. CAROLEE DOYLE (R)
      1971-. Bds: Joint Recreation Bd. Org: Tama
Cnty. Bd. of Realtors. Occ: Real Estate &
Insurance Saleswoman. B: 12/26/37. Add: 801 E.
State, Toledo 52342 (515)484-2160.

Treynor. BEVERLY C. ANDERSEN (R)
      1976-. Occ: Bookkeeper. B: 12/26/34. Add:
Box 348, Treynor 51575 (712)487-3353.

Tripoli. HAZEL M. KIRCHHOFF (D) **
      1974-. Bds: City Housing; Sanitation; Library
Bd.; Recreation. Party: Election Bd. 1970-75;
Central Com. Org: City Housing. Occ: Owner,
Antique Shop; Inventory Specialist. B: 8/29/34.
Add: Box 213, Tripoli 50676 (319)882-4801.

Truesdale. JEWEL EDWARDS
      BARBARA VANLANDINGHAM
      City Hall, Truesdale 50592.

Truro. DIANA CISLER
      City Hall, Truro 50257.

Truro. HELEN A. ELBEN (R)
      1976-. Mayor Pro Tem. Org: OES. Occ:
Secretary. B: 1/5/24. Add: Box 162, Truro
50257 (515)765-4586.

Udell. CHALLICE HEDGECOCK
      City Hall, Udell 52593.

Urbana. NANCY M.NEWTON (D)
      1975-. Bds: Ch., Community Betterment
Council; Ch., Parks & Recreation. Occ: Plastics
Operator. B: 5/27/44. Add: Box 384, Urbana
52345.

Ute. EILEEN HINRICHSON
      City Hall, Ute 51060.

Vail. COLLETTE M. HUNTLEY (I)
      1976-. Bds: Zoning Com.; Swimming Pool Bd.
Org: NEA. Educ: Ia. State U. 1969 BS. Occ:
Teacher. B: 2/16/47. Add: Box 62, Vail 51465.

Van Horne. LOLA BOSSLER
      City Hall, Van Horne 52346.

Van Wert. MARY LOU SCHULDT
      City Hall, Van Wert 50262.

Victor. RUTH GWIN
      City Hall, Victor 52347.

Vining. ADELE RIHA (D)
      1970-. B: 4/28/07. Add: Vining 52348
(515)489-2264.

Vinton. JANE LA GRANGE (D)
      1973-. Bds: Regional Planning Com.; Ambulance
Bd. Org: Ia. League of Municipalities; Common
Cause; Hawkeye Area Community Action Program Adv.
Bd.; WPC; AAUW. Educ: U. of Ia. 1952 BA. Occ:
Piano Teacher; Newspaper Correspondent. B:
1/28/31. Add: 1314 C Ave., Vinton 52349.

Vinton. DORIS A. PIPPERT (R)
      1973-. Org: WPC. Occ: Saleswoman. B:
4/15/29. Add: 701 E. 3rd St., Vinton 52349.

Walnut. MARY JUNE DORSCHER
      City Hall, Walnut 51577.

Wapello. CAROLYN HICKLIN
      City Hall, Wapello 52653.

Waterloo. MARY J. LICHTY
      City Hall, Waterloo 50705.

Waucoma. ANNA JANE TOMASEK (D)
      1975-. Bds: Ch., Streets. Org: Cnty. Dem.
Club. B: 8/22/21. Add: Waucoma 52171.

Waverly. JEANETTE M. NORQUIST (R)
      1976-. Bds: Selection Com. for City Adminis-
tration; General Govt. Com.; Public Safety Com.
Prev: Planning & Zoning Cmsn. 1974-76. Org: LWV;
Rep. Women's Club. Educ: Col. Women's Coll. 1949
AA. Occ: Music Instructor. B: 6/13/30. Add:
113 8th Pky. SE, Waverly 50677 (319)352-4252.

Waverly. EVELYN L. RATHE (R)
1975-. Bds: Public Safety Com.; Ch., Ambulance
Study Com.; Public Works Com. Org: LWV. Educ:
Columbia U. 1954 BS. B: 7/27/32. Add: 1324
Hillcrest Dr., Waverly 50677 (319)352-4252.

Wellman. MARLYN ALLEN
City Hall, Wellman 52356.

Welton. FRANCES SCHMIDT
City Hall, Welton 52774.

Westfield. MARGARET FAUST
City Hall, Westfield 51062.

Westgate. AGNES POTRATZ
City Hall, Westgate 50681.

West Liberty. MILDRED GREGG (I)
1974-. Bds: Community Betterment Council;
Ch., Finance & Ordinance Com. Org: Ia. Realtors
Assoc. Occ: Realtor. B: 1/24/39. Add: E. 4th
St., W. Liberty 52776 (319)627-4020.

Westside. VIVIAN MARTENS
City Hall, Westside 51467.

Willey. WANDA TIGGES
City Hall, Willey 51401.

Winterset. C. JEAN BRISTOW
City Hall, Winterset 50273.

Woodbine. ROSALIE BROWN (R) **
1973-. Bds: Finance; Ch., Weed Com.; Gas &
Street Com. Org: Rep. Ch's. Club; Rep. Women's
Club. B: 11/22/26. Add: Box 8, Woodbine 51579
(712)647-2050.

Yale. GRACIA E. FOX (D)
1976-. Bds: Ch., Construction of Sewer
Systems. Occ: School Bus Driver. B: 8/21/21.
Add: West St., Yale 50277.

Judges

LYNNE E. BRADY
District Associate Judge. Add: 1st Ave.,
Gridge, Cedar Rapids 52401.

State Boards and Commissions

Office of the Governor, State Capitol Bldg.,
Des Moines 50319.

Accounting Board
RUTH E. KUNEY
RUTH ROBERTS

Accounting Practitioner Advisory Committee
VERNA E. FRANK

Aging Commission
HARRIETTE J. BAUM
DOROTHY DONCARLOS
LOUISE M. ROSENFELD
COLLEEN SHAW

Air Quality Commission
HELEN J. GLEESON

Alcoholism and Drug Abuse, Task Force on
RUTH ANDERSON
TONI FONTANINI
CAROLE HARDER

Alcoholism Citizens, Advisory Council on
JUANITA BLACK
MARTHA G. KNUTSEN

Alcoholism, Commission on
RUTH ANDERSON
ROSEMARY SHAW SACKETT

Architectural Examiners, Board of
MARGARET APOSTLE
NANCY G. MC HUGH

Arts Council
ALICE R. BOWERS
ANN JORGENSEN
MARY ELLEN KIMBALL
PHYLLIS LEPKE
RHODA M. MC CARTNEY
MARIE MILLARD
MARIBETH JESSIE SCHECTMAN
LINDA HANSEN SOLHEIM

Banking Board
JULIA ANDERSON

Barber Examiners, Board of
CAROL A. BROWN
PATRICIA E. CORNICK

Beer and Liquor Control Council
JOAN BALLANTYNE

Blind, Commission for the
NEL BONNELL
SALLY FRUDDEN

Campaign Finance Disclosure Commission
JOLENE STEVENS

Capitol Planning Commission
POLLY MOORE

Certification Board
BEVERLY B. EVERETT

Child Abuse Information Council
MARGARET HURST
JEAN A. PURDY

Child Labor Committee
PENNY BINGER

Children, Council for
BETTY A. BERNHAGEN
EVELYN DAVIS
ANNE L. FORSTON
HELEN MC DONALD
KATHLEEN A. SANDUSKY
ELIZABETH S. TURNER

Chiropractic Examiners, Board of
MARY XAVIER COENS
GRETCHEN N. SCHREFFLER

City Development Board
SHARON NAIL

City Finance Committee
BETTY JO HARKER

Civil Rights Commission
GRETCHEN M. BATAILLE
HARRIETTE BRUCE
EVELYN R. VILLINES
GRETCHEN WALSH

Commerce Commission
MARY F. HOLSTAD

Conservation Commission
CAROLYN T. LUMBARD
MARIAN PIKE

Conservation of Outdoor Resources, Committee on
DOROTHY BARINGER
DOROTHY BUCKINGHAM
HELEN CRABB
BARBARA DAWSON
RUBY L. KRUSE
MURIEL MINGLIN
ELIZABETH SAMMONS

Corrections Relief, Advisory Commission on
JANET A. JOHNSON

Cosmetology Examiners, Board of
DORIS ELLWOOD
BARBARA A. FAILOR
HELEN MEFFERD
CAROLE TRACY
NANCY E. WELTER

Crime Commission
MARY H. BERDELL
DOROTHY BUCKINGHAM

Deaf Advisory Committee
BECKY MORGAN
EUNICE TICE
NORMA JEAN WEILAND

Dental Examiners, Board of
JUDITH E. GLASGOW
CONNIE PRICE
JEAN A. TESTER
MARCIA L. WIEDMEYER

Development Commission
DONNA KEPPY
MARDELLE NOBLE

Developmental Disabilities Council
EUGENIE M. DEAN
HELEN HENDERSON
FRAN KURTZ
LOU LYON
WANDA SCHNEBLY
CONNIE TOLAND
MARGARET G. WESTERHOF

Drug Abuse Authority Advisory Council
KAY E. DULL
CAROLE HARDER
JERI JENNER

Early Childhood Development, Task Force on
KATHLEEN E. COLLISON
EVELYN DAVIS
JEANNE DIXON
THELMA JOHNSON
HELEN MC DONALD
ALICE MC KEE
SUSAN MORGAN
JEAN PARKER
LEONA RINGGENBERG
BERNICE SANACHE

Economic Advisory Council
MARGARET B. ANDERSEN

Education Commission of the States
MINNETTE F. DODERER
SONJA EGENES
ELIZABETH SHAW

Educational Radio and TV Facility Board
LOIS M. CHARLTON

Emergency Medical Service Council
JANICE FRYETT
MARY A. STATLER

Employment of the Handicapped, Commission on the
ANGELINE L. ANDERSON
LAVONNE EARWOOD
GAIL GREENWALD
LINDA HANSSEN
HELEN SETTLE
VERA E. SMITH
KRISTIN WRIGHT

Energy Policy Council
HARRIETTE LINDBERG
LILLIAN M. MC ELROY
VIRGINIA E. PHIPPS

Engineering Examiners, Board of
DAWN E. CHAPMAN

Family Practice Education Advisory Board
CLAUDINE MANSFIELD
MADGE PHILLIPS

Funeral Directors and Embalmer Examiners, Board of
DONNA P. GABRIEL

Local Government Task Force
BARBARA A. KOERBER
SHARON W. NAIL

Health Board
MARY D. KENNEDY

Health Coordinating Council
KAREN ROSEANN BLUE
ARDELLE J. CONNER
MARILEE FREDERICKS
VERA V. FRENCH
MARY W. GREENLEAF
HELEN B. HENERSON

LYNNE M. ILLES
LINDA KAMP

Hearing Aid Dealers Examining Board
MARGARET BAEHR
MILDRED F. COUGHLON

Higher Education Facilities Commission
JOANN C. COLE

Historical Board
THELMA E. HEFLIN
PRISCILLA L. WANATEE

Historical Records Advisory Board
JOYCE GIAQUINTA
PATTI ODELL
GLENDA RILEY
HELEN M. VIRDEN

Hospital and Health Facilities Advisory Council
NELMA L. BEDSOE
LINDA GARTEN
JUNE GOLDMAN
MARY CLARENCE MC DONALD
JEAN MC MURRAY
BERNICE WOLF

Housing Finance Authority
FREDINE M. BRANSON
CONSTANCE C. FOSTER

Interstate Cooperation Commission
COLLEEN P. SHEARER

Ipers Advisory Investment Board
BETTY S. MAXHEIMER

Job Service Appeal Board
NORMA I. LOCK

Judicial Nominating Commissions
ANITA M. ANDRIES
SARA CALDWELL
JUDITH CARLSON
VIRGINIA DEARDORFF
KATHY P. HELGESON
CATHERINE H. HOGUE
CAROLYN HOUK
CORINNE M. HUBBELL
GEORGIA HUTCHISON
CATHERINE IRONS
JEWELL JURY
CHARLOTTE KELLY
DOROTHY KELLY
BETTY KLECHNER
VAL MOELLER
ODETTA MOORE
BETTY SANDERS
BETTY SCHWARTZKOPF
JEAN SWISHER
MARSHA THUDIUM
ELIZABETH VAN DEN HEUVEL
ALICE JANE WALTER
ADA WATERS
NELL WEBER
JANET WINSLOW
BARBARA WOODSTRA

Judicial Qualifications Commission
JANE BEARD
DORIS ANN PEICK

Juvenile Justice Advisory Council
CAROL W. AUGUSTINE
BONNIE BROWN EVANS
JOSEPHINE GITTLER
LILY RITCHIE HILL
JANET LEE LAYMAN
LAURA M. LEHMANN
DIANE J. MAXSON
MAGGI LYNN MOSS
MARILYN MURPHY
KATHLEEN M. NEYLAN
MARIE RUNNING MOCASSIN PEARSON
CATHERINE G. WILLIAMS

Landscape Architectural Examiners, Board of
NANCY SIEBERLING

Legal Services Advisory Council
MARY ELLEN KERR
ILA R. PLASENCIA
MARY SHARP

Library Commission
MARIE WALLINGA

Life Support of Dependent Adults Task Force
HELEN B. HENDERSON
DELORES LOWE
LEONA I. PETERSON
EVELYNE R. VILLINES

Manpower Planning Council
PATRICIA D. BRENNER
JACQUELINE DAY

Manpower Services Council
ALICE MC KEE
COLLEEN P. SHEARER
PATRICIA A. STEIGER

Medical Assistance Advisory Council
MARY ELLEN EVANS
RUTH HANNAGAN
VIRGINIA R. PETERSEN

Medical Examiners, Board of
ROSALIE B. NELIGH, M.D.
SHEILA SIDLES

Mental Hygiene Committee
LOUISE GOLDMAN
ELOISE LEE
ELIZABETH MC TIGUE

Merit Employment Commission
THELMA HEITSMAN
ALICE A. MC KEE

Mississippi Parkway Planning Commission
MARY MAJORS
PHYLLIS M. PERRY

Natural Resources Council
JOYCE REPP
LINDA A. TIGGES

Nursing Board
PEARL FORBES
DONNA R. HEALD
NELLIE OSTERLUND
BARBARA ANN STEEN
RUTH M. TURNIS

Nursing Home Administrators, Board of
PHYLLIS J. PETERS
LOIS M. SHERMAN
DORCAS W. SPEER

Occupational Safety Health Review Commission
ALICE VAN WERT

Optometry Examiners
BERTHA J. KIRKWOOD
MARTHA H. PECK
KATHERINE R. STROUD

Parole Board
JANET A. JOHNSON

Pharmacy Examiners, Board of
VENNETTA M. FIEDLER
SUSAN C. LUTZ

Physical Fitness and Sports Council
CEIL HERBOLD
BETTY A. HOFF
JANE ROSS
GWENDOLYN D. WIEGMANN

Physical Therapy Examiners, Board of
JANET K. DUNN
SISTER BERNADINE PIEPER
GRACE RASMUSSEN
HELEN REICHART

Physicians Assistance Programs Advisory Committee
ELIZABETH BURROWS
VIRGINIA LAWRENCE

Podiatry Examiners, Board of
LOIS ECKHARDT
SHIRLEY A. THOMPSON

Preserves Advisory Board
DOROTHY M. BARINGER

Psychology Examiners, Board of
ELSIE GRANT
JOAN JACOB
JOAN MC KEAN
IRENE WIEMERS

Public Instruction Board
JOLLYANN DAVIDSON
VIRGINIA HARPER
SUSAN M. WILSON

Real Estate Commission
KATHRYN L. GRAF
GRACIE M. RUDEN
JULIE ZELENKA

Regents, Board of
MARGARET COLLISON
MARYLOUISE PETERSEN

School Budget Review Committee
ENID DAVIS

Social Service Council
LOIS EMANUEL
MADALENE R. TOWNSEND

Soil Conservation Commission
LOUISE MOON

Solid Waste Disposal Commission
ANN FRENZEN
ROSEMARY SHEARER

Spanish Speaking Peoples Commission
IRENE MUNOZ
ILA R. PLASENCIA

Speech Pathology and Audiology Examiners, Board of
DIANE M. BROWN
FRANCES P. LANGDON

Status of Women, Commission on the
MARGARET S. ANDERSON
FRANCES CALHOON
ROXANNE CONLIN
MARY DRENNAN
MARILYN J. DUNN
MILDRED I. FREEL
PATRICIAL GEADELMANN
KATHLEEN M. GREEN
CAROLYN HANNAN
ROSA L. HOWELL
PHYLLIS HOWLETT
JUANITA LOPEZ
MARY JEAN MONTGOMERY
ANITA M. NORTHUP
JOAN POE
JANE ANN ROBBINS
EDITH SACKETT
MADELEINE MARIE SCHMIDT
B. FRANCES VAN WINKLE
KRISTELLE L. VORHAUS
SANDY WILLIAMS

Teaching Practices Commission
JOANN BURGESS
BARBARA K. SMELTZER

Transportation Commission
BARBARA J. DUNN

Transportation Regulation Board
SHERRI Y. ALSTON

Two Thousand Planning Committee
MARY BAUMHOVER
BEVERLY EVERETT
CAROLYN FARRELL
JANE LAGRANGE
BURTINE MOTLEY
SUE MULLINS
BETTY SCHUTTER

United Nations Day Committee
DOROTHY SCHRAMM

Venereal Disease Task Force
    JANE CARSON
    MINNETTE DODERER
    ETHEL HAMDORF
    THELMA JOHNSON
    ELIZABETH E. KERR
    ELAINE OLSON
    ENID WORTMAN

Veterinary Medical Examiners, Board of
    CATHY SUE KELLY

Vocational Education Advisory Council
    FRANCES MELVOLD
    PHYLLIS MOERSHEL
    DOROTHY K. PECAUT
    FAY WINTERS

Voting Machine Examiners
    LOIS SCHNOOR

Watchmaking Examiners, Board of
    MARIAN R. HAAF

Kansas

State Executive and Cabinet

JOAN FINNEY (D)
    State Treasurer. 1974-. Bds: Ch., Pooled
Money Investment Bd. Prev: Cnty. Elections Cmsr.
1970-72; Administrative Aide to Mayor 1973-74;
Senator's Asst. 1953-69. Org: Big Brother-Big
Sister; WPC; Dem. Century Club; Dem. Action Com.;
Fed. of Rep. Women; Fed. of Dem. Women; Latin-
Amer. Dem. Club; Kan. Women for Hwy. Safety;
Women Aware; Cnty. Dem. Club; Nat. Assoc. of State
Treasurers; BPW. B: 2/12/25. Add: 4600 W. 19th,
Topeka 66604 (913)296-3172.

ELWILL M. SHANAHAN (R) **
    Secretary of State 1966-. Bds: Bd. of
Canvassers; Election Bd.; Administration Rules &
Regulations. Org: Amer. Business Women's Assoc.;
Nat. Assoc. of Secretary of State; Rep. Women's
Club. Add: Capitol Bldg., Topeka 66612.

State Legislature

State Senate

JAN MEYERS (R) **
    1972-. Dist: 8. Bds: Ch., Mid Amer. Regional
Council; Bd. of Dir., Water Resources Assoc.;
Health, Welfare & Recreation; Council on Crime
& Delinquency. Prev: Pres., City Council.
Org: Nat. League of Cities; League of Kan.
Municipalities; LWV. Educ: U. of Neb. BA. Add:
8408 West 90th, Overland Park 66212 (913)648-7516

State House

GENEVA JUNE ANDERSON (D) **
    1974-. Dist: 101. Bds: Agriculture & Live-
stock; Transportation; Commercial & Financial
Institutions. Party: Local Precinct Com. 1963-
65, 1974-76. Org: Amer. Institute of Banking;
BPW; Nat. Assoc. of IRS Employees; Dem. Women's
Club. Occ: Bank Teller. B: 11/24/18. Add:
618 Highland, Mulvane 67110 (913)354-7651.

SHARON HESS (R) **
    1974-. Dist: 87. Bds: Public Health &
Welfare; Transportation. Party: Precinct Com.
1970-74. Org: Advisory Bd., County Mental
Health Society. Educ: U. of Kan. BGS. B:
3/5/48. Add: 816 South Estelle, Wichita
67211 (913)354-7651.

GLEE CARREL JONES (R)
    1970-. Bds:Elections; Public Health &
Welfare; Governor's Common Children & Youth.
Prev: Council Children & Youth; Adv. Health
Council. Org: Farm Bureau; BPW; Cnty. Rep.
Women. B: 12/10/20. Add: RR 3, Hiawatha 66434.

RUTH LUZZATI (D)
    1972-. Dist: 84. Bds: Ways & Means; Educ.;
Leg. Post Audit. Party: State Del. 1972; Precinct
Committeewoman 1964-65, 1972-76. Org: LWV; WPC;
Cnty. Dem. Club; ACLU. B: 10/19/22. Add: 5203
Plaza Ln., Wichita 67208 (913)296-7510.

ARDENA MATLACK (D)
    1974-. Dist: 93. Party: State Del. 1975-76;
Precinct Committeewoman 1960-66. Org: BPW; Fed.
Women's Study Club; Dem. Club; Women's Dem. Club;
Neighborhood Club. Educ: Wichita State U. 1969
BA. B: 12/20/30. Add: 615 Elaine, Clearwater
67026 (913)296-7577.

ANITA G. NILES (D)
    1974-. Bds: Health & Welfare; Elections;
Energy & Natural Resources. B: 8/3/19. Add:
RR #2, Lebo 66856.

BELVA J. OTT (R)
    1977-. Dist: 92. Bds: Com. on Educ.; Com.
on Elections. Party: State Alt. 1976-77;
Precinct Committeewoman 1974-77; Ward Ch. 1975-
77. Prev: Citizen Participation Org. 1975-77.
Org: Cnty. Rep. Women; Fed. of Rep. Women; Cnty.
Rep. Party; PTA; LWV; WPC. Occ: Medical
Secretary. B: 6/5/40. Add: 211 N. Sedgwick,
Wichita 67203.

KATHRYN SUGHRUE (D)
    Bds: Secretary, Arts Council. Party: V-Pres.,
Ford Cnty. Dem. Central Com.; Secretary Cnty.
Dem. Women's Club. Educ: Kan. State U. BS;
Colo. State U. MS. Add: 810 Central, Dodge City
67801.

MARJORIE J. THOMPSON
416 E 12, Winfield 67156.

RUTH WILKIN (D)
1972-. Dist: 56. Bds: Bd., Assessment & Taxation Com.; Public Health & Welfare Com. Org:
NOWL; Nat. Conf. of State Legislators; LWV; AAUW;
WPC; Common Cause; Council on Crime & Delinquency;
Dem. Action Club. Educ: U. of Kan. 1940 AB. B:
9/9/18. Add: 1610 Willow, Topeka 66606.

County Commissions

Allen. PHYLLIS MARIE DE TAR (R)
1972-. Bds: Exec. Bd., Cnty. Comsr's. Assoc.;
Governor's Task Force on Transportation. Party:
State Del. 1968. Org: Cnty. Cmsnr's. Assoc.;
Rep. Women's Club. B: 4/7/29. Add: Rt. 2, Iola
66749 (316)365-2921.

Barton. JANICE I. CRISSMAN (R)
1976-. Bds: Economic Devt. Cmsn. Org: LWV;
Rep. Women. Occ: Bookkeeper. B: 7/30/32. Add:
3106 24th, Great Bend 67530 (316)793-5261.

Cowley. MARILYN J. JOHNSON (R)
1975-. Bds: Chair. of Bd., Cnty. Juvenile Ctr.
Party: Cnty. Precinct Leader 1965-77. Org: Rep.
Club. Occ: Farmer. B: 9/4/27. Add: Rt. 5,
Winfield 67156 (316)221-4066.

Douglas. BEVERLY BRADLEY
Rt. #2, Lawrence 66044.

Geary. JOSEPHINE C. YOUNKIN (D)
1974-. Dist: 1. Bds: City-Cnty. Health Bd.;
NE Dist. Cnty. Cmsnr's. & Engineers; Facilities
Officers. Party: Precinct Com. 1925-62; Cnty.
Committeewoman 1962-76. Prev: Cnty. Treasurer
1963-68; State Repr. 1969-74; Cnty. Cmsnr. 1975-
Org: BPW; Area Agencies for Aged; Council on
Aging; Dem. Women's Club. B: 7/27/03. Add:
128 W. Pine St., Junction City 66441
(913)238-4300.

Haskell. GAIL AUGEROT HALE (D)
1975-. Party: Cnty. Ch. 1975-77. Org: Cnty.
Dems. B: 10/6/28. Add: 406 Ponca, Satanta
67870 (316)675-2234.

Hodgeman. MARIE V. BURKE
Kinsley 67547.

Lyon. GAIL GASCHE
Emporia 66801.

Reno. MILDRED J. BAUGHMAN (D) **
1966-. Bds: Economic Dev. B: 11/18/29. Add:
128 West 18th, Hutchinson 67501 (316)662-4411.

Shawnee. MARY L. BOGART (D)
1974-. Bds: Chair. of Bd.; Solid Waste Adv.
Bd.; Cnty. Bd. of Health; N.E. Kan. Health Systems
Agency. Org: Nat. Assoc. of Cnty's.; Young Dem's.
Educ: Washburn U. 1971 BEd. B: 8/31/49. Add:
5731 N.E. Whiteside Dr., Topeka 66617
(913)295-4040.

Stafford. HAZEL JORDAN
St. John 67576.

Townships

Aurora. BERTHA C. DALLEN (D)
1975-. Occ: Cook. B: 2/14/19. Add: Aurora
67417 (913)464-3416.

Banner. MYRTLE LARSON
Smith Center 66967.

Belleville. JOAN GREER
Chautauqua

Bonaville. EVERETTE JOHNSON
Gypsum 67448.

Cedar. LINDA M. RICE (D)
1975-. Org: Young Women's Club. B: 11/8/48.
Add: Athol 66932 (913)476-2610.

Center. VERNICE HAUG
Vermillion 66544.

Cherokee. RUBY SCOTT
RFD #1, Wier 66781.

Cheyenne. LAURAINE SHAY
Healy 67850.

Coolidge. HELEN HESSE (D) **
1970-. Bds: City Treasurer. Party: Local
Com. Occ: Bookkeeper. B: 3/23/15. Add: Box 15,
Coolidge 67836 (316)372-8602.

Dodge. LORENE ZIMMER
RFD #2, Dodge City 67801.

Drum Creek. FERN SCHENK
RFD #2, Independence 67301.

Elk. ARLENE F. COUTURE
1974-. Occ: Bus Driver. B: 6/10/32. Add:
Clyde 66938.

Englewood. ELLEN HARRINGTON
Englewood 67840.

Evergreen. GAIL MILLER
McDonald 67745.

Greene. MAE DAVIS
South Haven 67140.

Guilford. LOLA SHIVELY
Benedict 66714.

Hallet. OLLIE HILL
Jetmore

Hayes. GAIL HAUSERMAN
Clay Center 67432.

Hazelton. CLAIR RUCKER
Hazelton 67061.

Highland. LILLIE MAE SMITH
RT. #1, Walton 67151.

High Prairie. MARILYN L. LINDSAY (R)
1976-. Bds: Fire Dept. Org: Regional Planning Cmsn.; PTA. B: 4/27/35. Add: Rt. 1, Box
183, Leavenworth 66048.

Iola. DORIS E. GORDEN (R) **
    1969-. Party: County Com. 1964-68. Org:
Retarded Citizens. B: 9/27/22. Add: RR 1, Iola
66749 (316)365-5388.

Iowa. WINIFRED WOODRUFF
    White Cloud 66094.

Jefferson. SHARON K. STEVENS (R)
    1974-. Org: Cnty. Health Planning Counci; PTO.
Occ: Secretary. B: 2/21/47. Add: RR 1,
Winchester 66097.

Keysville. LORRAINE COUCHMAN
    Garfield 67529.

Kirwin. MRYTLE BENNETT
    Kirwin 67644.

Lacey. FREIDA JENSEN
    Gem 67734.

Logan. EILEEN BAUMAN (D)
    1976-. Occ: Bookkeeper. B: 5/18/20. Add:
Rt. 1, Box 92, Goodland 67735.

Logan. VONA LEA DEMPEWOLF (R) **
    1972-. Bds: Solid Waste Disposal Com. Occ:
Bus Driver. B: 9/26/30. Add: Route 2, Hoxie
67740.

Marion. IVA JEAN ISSAC
    Uniontown 66779.

Montana. MARY LEWIS
    Oswego 67356.

Parker. JUANITA WRIGHT
    Independence 67301.

Pawnee. MILDRED PETERSON
    Bellaire 66934.

Paw Paw. ELIZABETH DELLINGER (R) **
    1956-. Bds: Solid Waste; Health. Party: Com.
1956-75. Org: Farm Bureau Women. B: 3/30/11.
Add: RFD 2, Howard 67349 (316)374-2618.

Paxton. LULA DIRKS
    Leoti 67861.

Pleasant. BARBARA K. STRUCKHOFF (D)
    1973-. Org: PTA. B: 12/29/43. Add: RR 1,
Athol 66932 (913)695-2241.

Richland. ROBERTA WEST
    Mankato 66956.

Rock Creek. DONNA LEE BARKER
    RFD #2, Douglass.

Sedan. ROSE HUTTON
    Sedan 67361.

Silver Lake. CHARLENE ABBOTT
    401 Pottawatomie, Silver Lake 66539.

Summit. LUCILLE CLEMONS (I)
    1968-. Bds: Cemetery Bd. Prev: Committee-
woman 1968-76. Occ: Bookkeeper. B: 8/18/16.
Add: RR 2, Jamestown 66948 (913)439-6520.

Sycamore. JUDY HOY REMSBERG (R) **
    1974-. Party: Precinct Com. Org: PEA.
Educ: Kan. State U. 1961 BS. B: 8/10/39. Add:
RR 1, Cassoday 66842.

Verdigris. DOROTHY DUCKWORTH
    Toronto 66777.

Walton. FRANCES WHINERY
    RR #3, Parson 67357.

Wheatland. CELESTINE PFANNENSTIEL
    Munjor Route, Hays 67601.

Mayors

Andover. GOLDIE BUCHANAN
    City Hall, 1601 N. Main, Andover 67002.

Anthony. PATRICIA WILLIAMS (R)
    1973-. Bds: Planning Cmsn. Org: OES. Educ:
U. of Kan. 1957 BA, BS. Occ: Bank Worker. B:
10/17/32. Add: 702 N. Bluff, Anthony 67003.

Arkansas City. JEANNE FEARNOW (R)
    1977-. Bds: Hospital Bd.; Library Bd.;
Strother Field Bd. Org: Soroptimist; Day Care
Bd. Educ: Mercy Hospital RN. Occ: Nurse.
B: 11/1/17. Add: 1326 N. "C", Arkansas City
67005 (316)442-0735.

Bird City. DORA SEYMOUR
    City Hall, 111 E. 4th, Bird City 67731.

Carlton. IRENE MEYER
    City Hall, Main St., Carlton 67429.

Coolidge. MARJORIE BARRETT (D)
    1975-. Bds: Cnty. Zoning Bd.; Library Bd.
Prev: Councilwoman 1963-67. Occ: Postal Clerk.
B: 11/2/22. Add: P.O. Box 67, Coolidge 67836
(316)372-8201.

Cullison. CRISS BOOI
    City Hall, Cullison 67124.

Kechi. SANDRA K. COOK (D)
    1975-. Bds: Ch., Water Dept. Prev: Cnty.
Councilwoman 1974-78. B: 10/3/42. Add: 4604 E.
61st N., Wichita 67220 (316)744-2431.

Lawrence. MARJORIE HAYES ARGERSINGER (D)
    1975-. Bds: Citizens Com. for Crime Pre-
vention; Publications Com., League of Kan.
Municipalities; Transportation Com. Nat. League
of Cities. Party: Precinct Committeewoman.
Prev: Citizens Adv. Com. 1975-76. Org: LWV; U.
Women's Club. Educ: U. of Kan. 1950 BA; 1968
MA. B: 6/7/22. Add: 325 Park Hl. Ter.,
Lawrence 66044 (913)841-7700.

Lenexa. JOHNNA LINGLE (R) **
    1973-. Bds: County Council of Mayors; Bd. of
Water Resources. Org: Assoc. of Commerce &
Industry; Rep. Women's Club. Occ: Exec. Manager.
B: 9/2/41. Add: 12217 West 93, Lenexa 66215.
(913)492-8800.

Lincoln Center. DEE GOURLEY
    219 E. South, Lincoln Center 67455.

Oketo. JUDY E. REMMERS
City Hall, Main St., Oketo 66518.

Ottawa. VIOLA L. REUSCH
1972-. Bds: Governor's Task Force on State Transportation. Occ: Store Owner. B: 9/19/15. Add: 1203 S. Elm; Ottawa 66067 (913)242-2910.

Pittsburg. RUTH M. LEMON (D) **
1973-. Party: Local Com. 1950-54. Org: LWV; Red Cross. B: 9/1/22. Add: 110 East Carlton, Pittsburg 66762 (316)231-4100.

Princeton. SHARON HIGGINS
City Hall, Princeton 66078.

Reserve. KATHLEEN SANDERS
City Hall, Reserve 66529.

St. Paul, GERTRUDE GALLO
City Hall, St. Paul 66771.

Scranton. BETTY LEE
City Hall, Scranton 66537.

Sterling. MARY ANN SHEPHERD (R)
1976-. Bds: Medical Facilities; Kan. Municipalities Leg. Action Com. Party: Committeewoman. Prev: Town Comsr. 1975-78. Org: Cnty. Rep. Women. B: 5/24/21. Add: 116 W. Jefferson, Sterling 67579.

Sylvia. BEVERLY MILLER
City Hall, P.O. Box 247, Sylvia 67581.

Syracuse. MAGDALENE HASLETT
N. Lester St., Syracuse 67878.

Turon. LOIS DIGEL (D)
1974-. B: 11/25/18. Add: Box 221, Turon 67583 (316)497-6443.

Virgil. MARY ELLEN LONG (R)
1971-. Bds: Cnty. Economic Devt. Cmsn.; League of Kan. Municipalities; Kan. Mayor's Assoc. Org: Kan. Inspectors Assoc.; Mental Health Assoc. Educ: Phillips U. 1943 BSEd. B: 12/3/20. Add: P.O. Box 164, 203 S. Main, Virgil 66870.

Westphalia. HOLLIE MC GHEE
City Hall, Westphalia 66093.

Local Councils

Abilene. LILLIE MAE HELM
2101 N. Buckeye, Abilene 67410.

Alta Vista. DELORIS ASHBURN
City Hall, Main St., Alta Vista 66834.

Altoona. BETTY HARSHMAN
FAYE STANELY
City Hall, P.O. Box 263, Altoona 66710.

Anthony. PATRICIA WILLIAMS
702 N. Bluff, Anthony 67003.

Arcadia. VIDA CULLMAN
YVONNE MAUS
City Hall, Arcadia 66711.

Arlington. WILLA SPENCE
City Hall, Main St., Arlington 67514.

Assarie. BONNIE HAMILTON
MAURENE SCRIVEN
City Hall, Box 205, Assarie 67416.

Atchison. GAYLE G. CARLSON
1709 Santa Fe Ter., Atchison 66002.

Atchison. EDNA SUTLIEF (D)
1973-. Bds: Community Devt. Loan & Grant Com. Prev: Human Relations Cmsn. 1969-77. Org: BPW; Area on Aging. B: 5/7/21. Add: 1206 Pacific, Atchison 66002 (913)367-5081.

Atchison. MARY JANE THUM (D)
1975-. Bds: Mo.-Kan. Regional Council; Regional Dir., Women in Municipal Govt.; Nat. League of Cities. Prev: Library Bd. 1968-74. Org: AAUW. Educ: UCLA 1942 BA. Occ: Secretary. B: 6/19/21. Add: 401 N. 12th St., Atchison 66002 (913)367-5081.

Attica. ERNESTINE HEATH
City Hall, 101 N. Main, Attica 67009.

Augusta. PRISCILLA ALL (D) **
1973-. Bds: County Health Dept. Org: PEO. B: 2/1/43. Add: 1911 Meadow, Augusta 67010 (316)775-7448.

Basehor. ANNA MARY LANDAUER (R)
1975-. Bds: Ch., Finance & Administration; Street & Equipment. Prev: Planning Cmsn. 1972-75. B: 5/5/18. Add: 15422 State Ave., Basehor 66007 (913)728-2058.

Basehor. MARGARET STERNER
City Hall, 2718 N. 155th, Basehor 66007.

Bassett. SHARON K. BUSS
P.O. Box 101, Iola 66749.

Bassett. RUTH ROUSH
R.R. #3, Iola 66749.

Bazine. MARJORIE NIEDENS (D)
1975-. Bds: Ch., Com. to Improve Safety Street Signs. Org: BPW; Chamber of Commerce. Occ: Art Studio Owner. B: 11/20/19. Add: Bazine 67516 (913)398-2695.

Bentley. ETHEL SIMPSON (D)
1974-. Prev: Assoc. Fire Chief 1975-76. Occ: Antique Shop Owner. B: 11/20/18. Add: 102 S. Davidson St., Bentley 67016 (316)796-1251.

Beverly. ROWENA SCHROEDER
City Hall, Main St., Beverly 67423.

Bonner Springs. MARY ANN ALLEN
518 Allcutt, Bonner Springs 66012.

Brookville. SHIRLEY A. COLE (D) **
1971-. Occ: Secretary. B: 9/7/42. Add: Box 11, Brookville (319)225-3175.

Buffalo. BETTY CRUMRINE
City Hall, P.O. Box 122, Buffalo 66717.

Byers. RUTH NAOMI HUGHES (R)
1976-. Org: Historical Society. Occ: Avon
Repr. B: 12/24/10. Add: Byers 67021.

Carlton. CLARA BAMFIELD (D)
1972-. Party: Dem. Committeewoman 1976. Occ:
Cook. B: 1/12/17. Add: Box 14, Carlton 67429.

Carlton. M. BARBARA COATES (R) **
1971-. Org: PTA. Occ: Bookkeeper. B:
2/15/43. Add: Box 35, Carlton 67429 (913)
949-2847.

Colby. FAWNA J. HAREMZA (R)
1976-. Prev: Citizens Adv. Bd. for Community
Devt. 1974-76. Org: BPW. Occ: Secretary/Bank
Teller. B: 10/25/34. Add: 890 S. Grant Ave.,
Colby 67701 (913)462-3973.

Colony. CLAIR WILEY
City Hall, 339 Cherry, Colony 66015.

Concordia. BETTY JANE HUMES (R)
1973-. Bds: City Cmsn. on Aging. Prev:
Mayor 1975-77. B: 9/29/26. Add: 1219 Washington,
Concordia 66901.

Coolidge. RUTH SCHWERDFGER
City Hall, Main St., Coolidge 67836.

Corning. ALLIE NIEHUES
City Hall, Corning 66417.

Cottonwood Falls, MARY BELL
City Hall, Cottonwood Fls. 66845.

Cottonwood Falls. RUEA THURSTON (R)
1975-. Bds: Ch., Street-Alley Com.; Solid
Waste; Swimming Pool. Prev: Mayor 1951. Org:
NEA. Educ: Coll. of Emporia 1942 BA. Occ:
Business Teacher. B: 8/2/21. Add: 201 Cedar St.,
Cottonwood Fls. 66845 (316)273-6666.

Council Grove. DORIS HIGHT
629 S. Neosho, Council Grove 66846.

Council Grove. CHARLENE MC RAE (D) **
1973-. Bds: Fire; Ordinance; Utilities.
Party: County Precinct Com. 1974. Occ: Secretary.
B: 12/9/36. Add: 325 Chick St., Council Grove
66846 (316)767-5417.

Council Grove. SIDRA WILKERSON (D) **
1973-. Bds: Appropriation; Ordinances Com.;
Streets; Parks & Lakes. Educ: Emporia State
Teacher's Coll. 1964 BA. Occ: Owner, Restaurant.
B: 3/21/41. Add: 913 Donnon, Council Grove
66846 (316)767-5417.

Countryside. LAURA ROSS
5924 W. 61st Ter., Countryside 66202.

Cullison. ALMA JENKINS
City Hall, Cullison 67124.

Deerfield. DORIS ZUBECK
City Hall, Deerfield 67838.

Dodge City. NANCY JO TRAUER
City Hall, 709 1st Ave., Dodge City 67801.

Douglass. JANET POLK
120 S. Poplar, Douglass 67039.

Dwight. ANNA MAE ROBIDUE
City Hall, P.O. Box 233, Dwight 66849.

Elkhart. VERNA REAZIN
22 Sunset Dr., Elkhart 67950.

Ellis. EVELYN L. SCHUMACHER (I)
1975-. Bds: Ch., Cemetery; Ch., Finance.
Party: Precinct Committeewoman 1973- ; Cnty.
V-Ch., 1975-77. Org: BPW; Nat. Assoc. of Bank
Women; Adv. Council Good Samaritans; Senior
Citizen Council; Community Day Care Bd. Occ:
Banker. B: 10/22/32. Add: 103 Cedar Cir. Dr.,
Ellis 67637 (913)726-4562.

Ellis. AGNES WASSINGER (D)
1975-. Party: State Del. 1972; Precinct
Committeewoman 1964- . Occ: Bookkeeper. B:
4/27/27. Add: 1800 Spruce St., Ellis 67637.

Ellsworth. ALYCE PFLUGHOEFT
302 Missouri, Ellsworth 67439.

Ellsworth. VANDELIA VAN METER (I)
1975-. Bds: Park Bd., Recreation Cmsn. Org:
NEA. Educ: Kan. Wesleyan U. 1957 BA; Emporia
State U. 1970 MLS. Occ: Media Specialist. B:
7/17/34. Add: 403 Court, Ellsworth 67439
(913)472-3941.

Elwood. BARBARA COX
City Hall, Elwood 66024.

Emmett. IRENE I. HLADKY (D)
1976-. Bds: Street. B: 10/19/21. Add:
Emmett 66422.

Englewood. ALTHEA JACQUES
City Hall, Main St., Englewood 67840.

Ensign. RUTH SCHRINER
City Hall, P.O. 40, Ensign 67841.

Erie. WINONA BATES
404 N. Grant, Erie 66733.

Eskridge. ILA BUSH
City Hall, Eskridge 66423.

Fairview. REVA M. SPEER (I)
1975-. Bds: City Treasurer. Party: Precinct
Committeewoman 1966-70. Prev: Atchison Cnty.
Treasurer 1963-67. Org: Women's Rep. Club; OES.
B: 5/23/14. Add: Fairview 66425 (913)467-3701.

Fairway Shawnee Mission. MARY BALLINGER
Bds: Ch., Recreation; Pool & Park; Police.
Org: LWV. B: 2/10/27. Add: 6100 Fontana,
Fairway Shawnee Msn. 66205.

Fall River. ALICE GIPE
City Hall, Fall Rvr. 67047.

Fontana. JUANITA FEIGHNER
City Hall, Fontana 66026.

Fort Scott. BRENDA DENTON
402 S. Main, Fort Scott 66701.

Freeport. VIRGINIA PAYNE
    City Hall, Freeport 67049.

Galena. LOIS WARD
    920 N. Henning, Galena 66739.

Garden Plain. BARBARA J. SMITH
    City Hall, Garden Plain 67050.

Goff. SHARON SHUMAKER
    City Hall, Goff 66428.

Gove City. HELEN ENGEL
            DELORIS PACKARD
    City Hall, Main St., Gove City 67736.

Great Bend. GAIL LUPTON
    1408 Roosevelt, Great Bend 67530.

Great Bend. ANN PRINGLE (R)
    1976-. Bds: Golden Belt Regional Planning
Cmsn. Org: LWV. Educ: U. of Nebr. 1944 BS. B:
9/9/27. Add: 2501 Jefferson, Great Bend 67530.

Hanover. MARIE DOEBELE
    City Hall, P.O. Box 416, Hanover 66945.

Hardtner. VIVIAN SCHARR
    City Hall, Hardtner 67057.

Harper. ZELLA HELSBY (D)
    1976-. Bds: Ch., Personnel; Park; Health.
Party: Cnty. Committeewoman. Org: Chamber of
Commerce. Occ: Printer. B: 4/13/14. Add:
704 Oak, Harper 67058 (316)896-7586.

Harris. JUDY AHRING
         CLARA BEARD
         AUDRA GRIMES
         PAM MONROE
    City Hall, W. 2nd St., Harris 66034.

Haven. VIRGINIA FINNIN
    302 N. Reno, Haven 67543.

Haysville. ROSIE ALSPACH (R)
    1976-. Bds: Finance Com.; Pioneer Days Com.
Occ: Coin Laundry Owner. B: 11/25/29. Add:
233 Baughman, Haysville 67060.

Haysville. MARGUARITE DESMARTEAU
    503 German, Haysville 67060.

Hesston. CONNIE R. OETINGER (R)
    1975-. Bds: Com. on Administration, Streets &
Public Safety. Org: Nat. League of Nursing.
Educ: Presbyterian Hospital School of Nursing
1957 RN; Wichita State U. 1976 BS. Occ: RN B:
4/24/32. Add: 116 Willow Ln., Hesston 67062.

Hoisington. GLENDA JAHNKE
    255 W. 1st, Hoisington 67544.

Howard. IRMA CRISP
    City Hall, 110 N. Pine, Howard 67349.

Inman. MARTHA WIENS (I)
    1975-. Bds: Law Enforcement. Prev: Recreation
Cmsn. 1975-77. Occ: Office Manager. B: 6/8/18.
Add: 209 S. Locust, Inman 67546.

Hope. JEAN L. LARDENOIS
    City Hall, Main St., Hope 67451.

Jetmore. AUDREY LONNBERG
    City Hall, Main St., Jetmore 67854.

Jetmore. SHIRLEY NEVINS (D)
    1975-. Party: Precinct Committeewoman 1972- ;
Cnty. V-Ch. 1973-76; Cnty. Ch. 1976- ; State
Committeewoman 1976- . Prev: Crippled Children
Cmsn.; Cnty. Probate Judge. Org: WPC. Occ:
Abstracter. B: 9/13/28. Add: 516 W. Hwy.,
Jetmore 67854.

Kiowa. VIVIAN DIEL
    204 N. 9th, Kiowa 67070.

Kirwin. HAZEL ACHISON
         ESSIE WESTBROOK
    City Hall, Kirwin 67644.

Labette. ROWENA E. HIGGINS
    City Hall, Labette 67350.

Lakin. MINNIE E. HEFNER
    211 W. Western St., Lakin 67860.

Lakin. SALLYANN MC CUE (R)
    1974-. Bds: Regional Planning Cmsn.; Ch.,
City Park Cmsn. Party: V-Ch., Cnty. Rep. Party
1976; Ch., Women's Rep. Party 1976- . Org: S.W.
Regional Planning Com.; Rep. Women's Club. Occ:
Secretary/Clerk. B: 2/10/47. Add: Box 676,
Lakin 67860 (316)355-6252.

Lancaster. RITA THURN (R)
    1974-. Bds: Recreation & Parks; Ch., City
Hall. Org: RN Club. Educ: St. Joseph's
Hospital School of Nursing 1955 RN. Occ: RN.
B: 2/20/34. Add: Box 37, Lancaster 66041.

Langdon. EVA CLOUGH
          EDITH SWAN
    City Hall, Langdon 67549.

Lansing. ELIZABETH GREGORY
    City Hall, 108 S. Main, Lansing 66043.

Latham. LORIENE BROWER (R)
    1977-. Bds: Council Ch. Org: OES. Occ:
Clerk/Bookkeeper. B: 3/19/28. Add: 312 Blain,
Latham 67072 (316)965-2233.

Latham. DOROTHY WOLF
    City Hall, Latham 67072.

Leawood. JEAN WALTUCH WISE (R)
    1976-. Bds: Ch., Budget & Finance Com.; Insur
ance Com.; Newsletter Com. Prev: City Recreation
Cmsn. 1973- . Org: LWV; Women's Club. Educ:
Washington U. 1964 BA. B: 6/30/42. Add: 2610 W.
105th St., Leawood 66206 (913)642-5555.

Lecompton. MARGIE FISHER
    City Hall, Elmore St., Lecompton 66050.

Leon. LOUISE SEWARD
    101 Ola, Leon 67074.

Leonardville. PEGGY DETTMER (D)
    1975-. Occ: Grocery Checker. B: 12/12/29.
Add: 203 S. Kansas, Leonardville 66449.

LeRoy. IRENE HOBART
    City Hall, LeRoy 66857.

Lincoln Center. HARRIET M. WAHL
    315 S. 2nd, Lincoln Center 67455.

Linwood. ARLENE E. PRITCHARD (D)
    1962-. Occ: Substitute Rural Mail Carrier.
B: 1/21/32. Add: 124 Park St., Linwood 66052
(913)723-3333.

Lucas. BETTY DUWE (R)
    1975-. Bds: City Parks Com. Party: Precinct
Committeewoman 1968-77. Prev: Bd. of Dirs.,
Library 1975-77. Org: Chamber of Commerce; Cnty.
Women's Rep. Club; OES. Educ: Kan. State U. 1951
BS. Occ: Storeowner. B: 10/4/29. Add: Box 147,
Lucas 67648.

Lyndon. MYRTLE WHALEY
    314 W. 6th, Lyndon 66451.

Lyons. VIRGINIA LOUISE COX (D)
    1972-. Bds: Ch., Cemetery; Housing Authority;
Ch., Health; Parks. Party: Local Committeewoman
1968. Occ: Beauty Salon Owner. B: 7/26/25.
Add: 205 N. Euclid, Lyons 67554.

McFarland. CAROL GASPERICH
    McFarland 66501.

Medicine Lodge. MRS. IREE BOYTER
    926 Elm, Medicine Lodge 67104.

Melvern. CLEORA BURNS
    City Hall, Melvern 66510.

Melvern. DOREEN ROBERTS
    1975-. B: 2/19/25. Add: Mayes, Melvern
66510.

Menlo. HAZEL NEAL (D)
    1971-. Party: Precinct Committeewoman 1975-77.
Prev: Postal Clerk. Org: NEA; Women's Service
Group. Educ: Kan. State Coll. 1959 BS. B:
3/14/04. Add: Menlo 67746.

Merriam. IRENE B. FRENCH (R)
    1973-. Bds: Leg. Com., Kan. League of Munici-
palities; Ch., General Govt. Com. Party: State
Del. 1974-77; Nat. Del. 1972; State V-Ch. 1977- ;
State Secretary 1975-77; Cnty. V-Ch. 1969-76;
Cnty. Committeewoman 1965- . Prev: Planning Cmsn.
1971-73. Org: Chamber of Commerce; Women's Rep.
Club. Occ: Medical Secretary. B: 9/2/27. Add:
10235 W. 70th, Merriam 66203 (913)722-3330.

Mildred. LUCILLE C. BROWN (R) **
    1969-. Party: County Com. 1968- ; Local Com.
1966- ; Central Com., Treasurer. Prev: City
Treasurer 1967-69. Org: PTA; Fed. of Rep. Women.
Occ: Postmaster. B: 5/31/21. Add: 10 West Main
St., Mildred 66055 (913)439-5424.

Mildred. WILMA BYNUM
        DOROTHY WALTON
    City Hall, Mildred 66055.

Minneapolis. LETHA SCHEIBELER
    410 N. Concord St., Minneapolis 67467.

Mission. KATHY LAMPHEAR
    6107 W. 58th, Mission 66202.

Mission Hills. JEAN C. SMITH
    6532 Sagemore Rd., Mission Hills 66208.

Morganville. PATRICIA GILBERT
    City Hall, Morganville 67468.

Morrill. MILDRED LIVENGOOD
        KATHERINE REYNOLDS
    City Hall, P.O. Box 146, Roxana St., Morrill
66515.

Mound City. MARIE KRULL (D)
    1975-. Occ: Corp. Pres. B: 6/20/22. Add:
612 Fletcher, Mound City 66056 (913)795-2202.

Mulberry. WINFRED BEAN
    9th St., Mulberry 66756.

Ness City. PAULA MC CREIGHT
    City Hall, 109 S. Iowa, Ness City 67560.

New Albany. RUBY IRENE RICHARDS ANDERSON (D) **
    1969-. Bds: Street & Alley. B: 8/25/15.
Add: RR 3, Fredonia 66736.

Nickerson. LINDA FLEMING
    P.O. Box 542, Nickerson 67561.

Oak Hill. ANNA LARGENT
        LEONA WALKER
    City Hall, Oak Hill 67472.

Olathe. JANE SHEPPARD
    312 E. Mulberry, Olathe 66061.

Olsburg. MRS. JESSE YANTISS
    City Hall, Olsburg 66520.

Otis. MARY ANN POOL
    City Hall, Otis 67565.

Overland Park. JANET D. LEICK (D)
    1975-. Bds: Transportation Com.; V-Ch.,
Community Devt. Com.; Steering Com. on the Fine
Arts Liason. Party: Precinct Committeewoman
1974-77; Cnty. Dem. Party Exec. Bd. 1975-77.
Prev: Cnty. Youth Services Cmsn. 1973-75. Org:
Kan. League of Municipalities; Nat. League of
Cities; LWV; WPC; Mental Health Assoc.; Dem.
Club; Cnty. Dem. Women; PTA. Educ: Coll. of
Wooster 1962 BA; Kan. State U. 1963 MS. B:
1/19/40. Add: 6500 W. 65th Terr., Overland Park
66202 (913)381-5252.

Oxford. ZOE E. NICEUM (R)
    1975-. Bds: Ch., Park; Ch., Health; Swimming
Pool. Org: Women's Club. Occ: Upholsterer. B:
7/16/16. Add: 302 N. Iowa, Oxford 67119.
(316)455-2222.

Paola. BETTY M. NICHOLS (I)
    1974-. Org: Kan. Chiropractor Assoc. Educ:
Palmer Coll. 1948 DC. Occ: Chiropractor. B:
8/7/23. Add: 208 Brookside Dr., Paola 66071.

Penalosa. BONNIE HART
City Hall, Penalosa 67121.

Pittsburg. SHERRY STRECKER (I)
1973-. Bds: Pres., Bd. of Comsrs. Prev: City
Clerk 1964-73. Org: City Clerks Assoc. of Kan.;
Amer. Business Women's Assoc.; Altrusa Club; OES.
Occ: Manager, Insurance Co. B: 6/29/32. Add:
406 Fieldcrest Dr.; Pittsburg 66762 (316)
231-4100.

Pleasanton. MILDRED L. JUSTUS (R) **
1970-. Org: Nurse's Assoc. Educ: Mercy
Hospital School of Nursing 1940 RN. B: 4/4/18.
Add: Box 166, Pleasanton 66075 (913)352-8455.

Powhattan. ALICE CRANE (R)
1973-. Party: Precinct Leader. B: 12/30/1900.
Add: Box 52, Powhattan 66527.

Powhattan. VIRGINIA MC LAUGHLIN
City Hall, Commercial St., Powhattan 66527.

Preton. LANITA CARPENTER
City Hall, Main St., Preton 67569.

Quenemo. JO ANN ALLEN
JANICE TRENDEL
City Hall, 109 E. Maple, Quenemo 66528.

Randall. PHYLLIS WILSON
City Hall, 111 Main, Randall 66963.

Rantoul. WANDA BRIGGS
GLENDA MEDLEN
City Hall, Rantoul 66079.

Roseland. MARY POMATTO
City Hall, Roseland 66773.

Russell. NANCY KATHERINE LAND (D)
1974-. Bds: Pres., City Council. Prev: City
Planning Cmsn. 1973-74. Org: NEA; AAUW. Educ:
U. of Kan. 1964 BS. Occ: Teacher. B: 1/20/41.
Add: Box 484, Russell 67665 (913)483-3322.

Russell Springs. JOYE ROGGE
City Hall, Russell Springs 67755.

St. Paul. GERALDINE M. HILL
City Hall, St. Paul 66771.

Scott City. ROSELLA MARIE HEDGES (I)
1975-. Bds: Ch., Parks; Ch., Dog Control;
Police Cmsn. Org: NEA. Educ: Garden City Community Coll. 1957 AS; Kan. State U. 1962 BS. Occ:
Librarian. B: 8/17/35. Add: 805 Era, Scott City
67871.

Sedan. MARGO BOULANGER
City Hall, 111 W. Chautauqua, Sedan 67361.

Shawnee. DEANNA J. GASTL
6117 Ballantine, Shawnee 66203.

Shawnee. CHARLOTTE A. HARGIS (R)
1972-. Party: Cnty. Exec. Com.; Precinct
Committeewoman 1962-70, 1972-74. Occ: File
Supervisor. B: 9/28/24. Add: 11320 W. 49 Ter.,
Shawnee 66203 (913)631-2500.

Simpson. SANDRA PAUL
City Hall, Simpson 67478.

South Haven. GRACE MIRT (D)
1975-. Party: Cnty. Committeewoman 1971-75.
B: 10/4/13. Add; Box 422, S. Haven.

Sublette. SHIRLEY SHOTTON
City Hall, 103 S. Cody, Sublette 67877.

Treece. ROSE ASHWORTH
IMOGENE HURD
City Hall, Park Ave., Treece 66778.

Tribune. ERMA M. JOHN (R)
1972-. Bds: Ch., Shade Tree Cmsn.; Medical
Bd.; Ch., Park & Recreation. Party: Cnty.
Committeewoman 1965-70; Rep. Com. Treasurer 1965-
68. Org: Cnty. Extension Council. Occ: Bookkeeper. B: 8/27/27. Add: 303 3rd, Tribune
67879.

Troy. MARGARET SUTHERLAND
124 N. Centre St., Troy 66087.

Tyro. MICHELLE DENNY
City Hall, Main St., Tyro 67364.

Udall. BARBARA WILLIAMS
City Hall, S. Main, Udall 67146.

Ulysses. BEVERLY L. HAEFELE (R)
1975-. Prev: City Park Bd. 1971; City Tree
Bd. 1973. B: 5/3/28. Add: 602 E. Wheat,
Ulysses 67880.

Valley Center. NORMA L. DANIELS
130 Miles, Valley Center 67147.

Valley Falls. PATTY BROWN
916 Linn, Valley Falls 66088.

Virgil. GRACE C. KERR (D)
1974-. B: 11/18/1896. Add: 202 Main St.,
Virgil 66870.

Virgil. NORMA M. KULANDER (R)
1971-. B: 4/2/1898. Add: Virgil 66870.

Virgil. JULIE MC KENZIE
ERMA SHERMAN
City Hall, P.O. Box 84, Virgil 66870.

Waldron. FLOSSIE BETTES
City Hall, Waldron 67150.

Washington. VERA FAYE ROSENKRANZ (R)
1975-. Bds: Ch., Park; Ch., Library; Ch.,
Ambulance. Prev: School Bd.; N. Central Kan.
Library Assoc. 1974-75. Org: Rep. Women's Club;
OES. Educ: U. of Kan. 1929 BA. Occ: Teacher.
B: 11/25/07. Add: 110 W. College, Washington
66968.

Wellington. ELEANOR CAMPBELL LEE (R) **
1972-. Bds: Ch., Park Bd. Org: Chamber of
Commerce; PEO. B: 6/6/28. Add: 819 South
Washington, Wellington 67152 (316)326-3631.

Westmoreland. BARBARA DIANE EBERT (R) **
    1973-. Org: Amer. Dental Hygiene Assoc. Educ:
U. of Mo. 1972 BS. Occ: Dental Hygienist. B:
9/28/50. Add: Box 38, Westmoreland 66549.

Westwood. NANCY M. JEFFRIES (D)
    1972-. Educ: State U. of Ia. 1957 BSN. B:
10/23/34. Add: 4831 Booth, Westwood 66205
(913)362-1550.

Westwood Hills. NANCY BUTLER (R)
    1977-. Bds: Ch., Communications; Ways & Means.
Org: MENSA. Occ: Secretary. B: 6/13/41. Add:
2111 W. 48th Ter., Westwood Hls. 66205.

Westwood Hills. BARBARA GRIGGS
    4929 Glendale Rd., Westwood Hills 66205.

Wheaton. CONNIE DEPEW
    City Hall, Wheaton 66551.

White Cloud. FLORA TAYLOR
    City Hall, White Cloud 66094.

Williamsburg. SANDRA LINK
    City Hall, 123 W. Williams, Williamsburg
66095.

Wichita. CONNIE A. PETERS (D)
    1973-. Party: Precinct Committeewoman 1975-76.
Prev: City Com. 1973-77; Governor's Bd., Kan.
League of Municipalities 1973-76; U.S. Com. on
Civil Rights 1973-77. Org: Dem. Women's Club.
Occ: Saleswoman. B: 8/11/40. Add: 541 N.
Pershing, Wichita 67208 (316)268-4331.

Winchester. VERA SIEBEN (D)
    Party: Committeewoman 1967-77; Cnty. V-Ch.,
1971-77; Precinct Leader 1967-77. Org: Farm
Bureau; Senior Citizens. Occ: Surgical Technician
B: 8/17/06. Add: Winchester 66097.

Winchester. GLENDA THOMPSON
    City Hall, Winchester 66097.

Yates Center. CATHRINE JANE CHATTERTON (R) **
    1973-. Party: County Com. 1955- . Org: Rep.
Women's Club. B: 8/16/28. Add: 611 South Main,
Box 333, Yates Center 66783 (316)625-2252.

Judges

KAY MAC FARLAND (R)
    Shawnee Cnty. District Court Judge. Add:
Courthouse, Topeka 66603.

State Boards and Commissions

Arts Advisory Council
    LUCINDA FOSTER
    JANICE LEE
    JANE STEFFES

Arts Commission
    CAMILLA CAVE
    MARTHA DODGE NICHOLS
    CHRISTINE PECK

Community Junior College Advisory Council
    M. PRUDENCE HUTTON
    PHYLLIS KRAFT

Consumer Credit, Council of Advisors
    NONA BERGHAUS

Dealer Review Board
    EVELYN V. FATELEY

Dental Board
    CYNTHIA G. BARRETT

Developmental Disabilities Services, State Planning
and Advisory Council on
    BEVERLY S. BENNETT
    DOROTHY OKESOR
    GLORIA RUSSELL
    BETTY SMITH
    JOAN WESSELOWSKI
    SUSANNE D. WOODS

Economic Development Commission
    JEAN GRAGG

Education Commission of the States
    M. PRUDENCE HUTTON

Education, State Board of
    DOROTHY G. GROESBECK
    MARILYN HARWOOD
    RUTHANN OELSNER
    EVELYN WHITCOMB

Educational Television and Radio Authority
    DOROTHY BALLARD
    MARY PHARES

Emergency Medical Services Advisory Council
    CAROLYNN DARBY
    JANIE STEIN

Energy and Natural Resources, Governor's Commission
on
    JEANETTE R. HOLMES
    JOYCE LIVINGSTON

Fire Protection Personnel Standards and Education
    MARION SCHROLL

Governmental Ethics Commission
    KATHLEEN SEBELIUS

Nursing, Board of
    CECILIA G. WAGONER
    SISTER MARY ANN KLEIN
    GLORIA L. KILIAN

Pharmacy, Board of
    MARIE WYCKOFF

Physical Therapy, State Examining Committee for
    L. JANE WEISBENDER

Public Television Commission
    MRS. RAYMOND SCHMIDT

Supreme Court Nominating Commission
    ELEANOR L. MC COY

Wheat Commission
    ANNA JANE BAIRD

Kentucky

State Executive and Cabinet

FRANCES JONES MILLS
    Treasurer. Add: State Capitol, Frankfort
40601.

THELMA L. STOVALL (D) *
    Lt. Governor 1975-. Prev: Sec. of State 1956-
60; 1964-68; 1972-75; State Treasurer 1968-72;
State Repr. 1950-56. Org: BPW; OES. B: 4/1/19.
Add: 104 Valley Rd., Louisville 40204
(502)564-3490.

State Legislature

State Senate

GEORGIA M. POWERS (D)
    1967-. Dist: 33. Bds: Rules Com.; Labor &
Industry; Cities. Party: Nat. Del. 1968. Prev:
Leg. Ch. 1964-68. Org: NAACP; Urban League. B:
10/29/23. Add: 733 Cecil Ave., Louisville
(502)774-3476.

DAISY WIGGINTON THALER (D) **
    1973-. Dist: 34. Bds: Business & Pro-
fessions; Public Utilities. Party: V-Ch., Local
1974-76. Org: PTA; Women's Club; Dem. Women's
Club; Secretary, Assoc. for Childhood Educ. Educ:
Western U. BS; U. of Louisville MEd. Occ:Manager.
B: 8/27/34. Add: 5804 Lovers La., Louisville
40299 (502)969-3029.

State House

GERTA BENDL (D) *
    1975-. Dist: 34. Bds: Dept. of Educ.,
Citizens Adv. Com.; Water Management Com.; Nat.
League of Cities, Environmental Com. Prev: Alder-
woman 1971-75. Org: BPW. Add: 2403 Newburg Rd.,
Louisville 40205.

GLENNA A. BEVINS (D) *
    Dist: 77. Org: Nat. Assoc. of Prof. Educators;
Amer. Businesswoman's Assoc. Educ: Eastern Ky. U.
BA; U. of Ky. MA. Occ: Teacher. B: 1/8/23. Add:
1709 Normandy Rd., Louisville 40504.

ALLENE A. CRADDOCK (D) *
    Dist: 25. Org: BPW; Chamber of Commerce;
Dem. Women's Club; Cnty. Real Estate Board.
Occ: Bank Dir. & Realtor. Add: 710 Woodland
Rd., Elizabethtown 42701.

MAE KIDD (D) **
    1968-. Dist: 41. Org: Urban League; Dem.
Clubs. Add: 2308 Chestnut West, Louisville
40211.

CHARLOTTE MC GILL (D) **
    1972-. Dist: 42. Party: County Exec. Com.;
State Central Com. Org: NAACP; Neighborhood
Service Center. Educ: Howard BA; Ind. U. MA.
Occ: Self Employed. Add: 3016 River Park Dr.,
Louisville 40211.

DOLLY MC NUTT (D)
    1976-. Dist: 3. Bds: Cities Com.; Public
Utilities. Prev: City Comsr. 1968-70; Mayor
1972-76. Org: BPW; Women's Club; Historical
Society; Dem. Women's Club. B: 6/22/17. Add:
105 Country Club Ln., Paducah 42001
(502)442-1783.

DOTTIE PRIDDY (D) **
    1970-. Dist: 45. Org: BPW; Women's Club.
Educ: U. of Louisville BS. Occ: Bookkeeping
Agency. B: 1/9/35. Add: 3702 South Park Rd.,
Louisville 40219.

MARY ANN TOBIN (D) *
    1975-. Dist: 18. Educ: U. of Ky. BS. Occ:
Horse Stable Owner & Farmer. B: 7/23/41. Add:
Irvington 40146.

County Commissions

Ballard. MARTHA HOWLE
    County Courthouse, Wickliffe 42087.

Boyle. RITA L. DECKER (D)
    1974-. Bds: Ch. Decorating Courthouse; V-Pres.
Ky. Magistrates Assoc. Occ: Telephone Supervisor
B: 6/10/23. Add: Waterworks Rd., Danville
40422 (606)236-2020.

Elliott. DONNA SUE KEGLEY
    County Courthouse, Sandy Hook 41171.

Fulton. BONNIE MIKEL
    County Courthouse, Hickman 42050.

Perry. ELIZABETH DUNCAN
    County Courthouse, Hazard 41701.

Wayne. KATHERINE LAIR (D) **
    1973-. Org: Dem. Women's Club; OES. B:
12/6/16. Add: 125 Cherry St., Monticello
42633 (606)348-6041.

Mayors

Allensville. GENEVIEVE H. PACE
    Town Hall, Allensville 42204.

Concord. DAISY REDDELL SPRIGGS (R)
1963-. Prev: Police Judge 1963- ; Mayor 1963-.
B: 8/13/02. Add: Box 112 Concord 41131.

Edmonton. MARY NELL VAN ZANT (R)
1973-. Bds: Barren River Area Devt. Dist;
V-Ch., Ambulance Service; Governor's Cmsn. on
Economic Devt. Prev: Dir., Airport Bd. 1968-73.
Org: BPW; Woman's Club. Occ: Cashier. B:
5/24/22. Add: P.O. Box 352, Edmonton 42129
(502)432-4242.

Germantown. MARY JO MORAN
Town Hall, Germantown 41044.

Gilbertsville. DOROTHA GLENN
Rte. 1, Gilbertsville 42044.

Indian Hills. JEANNE BEAM RICHERT (R)
1973-. Party: Precinct Captain 1973; Cnty.
Campaign Manager 1977. Prev: City Clerk 1967-73.
Org: Crusade Against Crime. Educ: U. of La.
1943 BA. B: 5/26/23. Add: 25 Southwine Rd.,
Louisville 40207.

Lationia Lakes. MARGARET BOSSE
6155 Club House Dr., Lationia Lakes 41015.

Livingston. MRS. BERTIE B. RICE
Town Hall, Livingston 40445.

Plantation. SUE BAKER
City Hall, Box 22252, Plantation 40222.

Pleasureville. DORISLYNN N. LEACH
Town Hall, Pleasureville 40057.

Sharpsburg. PATSY PREWITT RATLIFF (D)
1974-. Bds: Cnty. Planning Bd.; Regional Adv.
Council. B: 8/4/24. Add: Main St., Sharpsburg
40374 (606)247-2141.

Shepherdsville. MARGIE EDDINGTON
1005 W. Second, P.O. Box 398, Shepherdsville
40165.

Vicco. BETTY JANE CUMMINGS
City Hall, P.O. Box 163, Vicco 41773.

Wilder. GLORIA TERRELL
400 Licking Pike, Wilder 41071.

Windy Hills. BETTY WALSH (D)
1967-. Party: State Precinct 1972. Org:
Women's Chamber of Commerce; Women's Assoc. of
Allied Beverage Industries; Dem. Women's Club;
Jr. Achievement. B: 10/7/19. Add: 708 Marrifield
Rd., Windy Hls. 40207 (502)895-0230.

Woodlawn. HELEN PURVIS
City Hall, 27 Woodlawn Ter., Woodlawn 41071.

Local Councils

Anchorage. ANN MC CLOSKEY
City Hall, Box 266, Anchorage 40223.

Bancroft. LINDA CRUMP
7412 Greenlaw, Louisville 40222.

Bedford. FRIEDA C. TINGLE (D)
1971-. Occ: Clerk. B: 9/9/04. Add:
Bedford 40006.

Beechwood Village. EVELYN E. FLEMING (D)
1975-. Bds: Ky. Municipal League; Senior
Citizens Council. Org: NASW; Mental Health
Assoc. Educ: Syracuse U. 1933 BA; Columbia U.
1944 MS. B: 10/14/12. Add: 4511 Blenheim Rd.,
Louisville 40207 (502)895-1787.

Benham. MRS. ALPHA SHIRER
LOUISE STURGILL
City Hall, Box 38, Benham 40807.

Briarwood. MARY GRAFF
P.O. Box 22111, Louisville 40222.

Brownsboro Farm. HENRIETTA OWEN
8455 Brownsboro Rd., Louisville 40222.

Brownsboro Village. MARCIA L. COTTERMAN
3701 Old Brownsboro Rd., 2nd Presbyterian
Ch., Louisville 40207.

Calhoun. WINFRED WILLIAMS
2nd & Branch, Calhoun 42327.

California. ROSE ELLEN SMITH (D)
1972-. Dist: 23. B: 1/29/48. Add: Madison
St., P.O. Box 44, California 41007.

Carrollton. NANCY J. GROBMEYER (D)
1974-. Bds: Recreation Bd.; Finance Com.
Org: Ky. Music Teachers Assoc.; Chamber of
Commerce; Women's Club; Historical; DAR. Educ:
Christian Coll. 1947 AA. Occ: Music Instructor.
B: 11/25/27. Add: 304 9th St., Carrollton
41008.

Cherrywood Village. LOIS COHEN
City Hall, Louisville 40206.

Clay. NORMA HOLOOMAN
MONA RUSSELL
W. R.R. St., City Hall, Clay 42404.

Clay City. BERTHA BLANKENSHIP
City Hall, Clay City 40312.

Clinton. MARGARET CAMPBELL
LUCILLE OWINGS
City Hall, P.O. Box 103, Clinton

Cold Spring. CATHERINE E. MOELLMAN
40 James Ct., City Hall, Cold Spring 41076.

Crab Orchard. BETTY LOU ADAMS
City Hall, P.O. Box 87, Crab Orchard 40419.

Crittenden. MARY FOLZ
Town Hall, Crittenden 41030.

Dayton. MARY ANNE DUCHIN (D)
1975-. Bds: Ch., Parks & Real Estate Com.;
Youth Cmsn.; Finance Com. Prev: Secretary, Park
Bd. 1975. Educ: Eastern Ky. U. 1969 BA. Occ:
Teacher. B: 8/5/46. Add: 1319 Dayton Ave.,
Dayton 41074 (606)491-1600.

Devondale. PAT ASHBROOK
  7204 Boxwood Rd., Louisville 40222.

Douglass Hills. HELEN K. BURDETTE
  300 Ronnoch Ct., Louisville 40243.

Earlington. FERN STOKES
             HELEN TROVER
  City Hall, W. Main St., Earlington 42410.

Edgewood. JUNE CORNELUIS HEDGER (R)
  1976-. Bds: Ch., Park & Recreation. Party:
Precinct Leader 1976-77. Org: Nurses Assoc. of
Oh.; Civic Club; Cnty. Rep. Women's Club; State
Rep. Party; PTA. Educ: Our Lady of Mercy Hospital
1949 LPN. Occ: Nurse. B: 6/26/24. Add: 3042
Bellflower Ct., Edgewood 41017 (606)331-5910.

Edgewood. MAUREEN TOWNSEND
  City Hall, 436 Dudley Rd., Edgewood 41017.

Elizabethtown. PATRICIA VENCILL DURBIN (D)
  1973-. Bds: Ch., Recreation Com. Org: NEA;
Chamber of Commerce. Educ: Eastern Ky. U. 1959
BS; 1961 MA. Occ: Teacher. B: 11/28/37. Add:
303 Morningside Dr., Elizabethtown 42701
(502)765-6121.

Elkhorn City. TELMA CANTRELL
  City Hall, Box 57, Elkhorn City 41522.

Erlanger. CAROLYN LOWER LAINHART (D)
  1971-. Bds: Ch., Public Affairs Com.; Repr.,
Chamber of Co-merce; Ky. Municipal League Effective Govt. Policy Com. Prev: City Councilwoman
1971-77. Org: BPW. Occ: Airport Security Coord.
B: 3/27/43. Add: 623 Hollam Ave., Erlanger 41018.

Evarts. MINNIE GRIGGS (D)
  1974-. Org: NEA. Educ: La Grange Coll. 1929
BA; Union Coll. 1968 MA. Occ: Remedial Reading
Teacher. B: 9/17/08. Add: Box 356, Evarts 40828.

Evarts. BARBARA SUE MOORE (I)
  1975-. Occ: Office Clerk. B: 2/15/40. Add:
Box 303, Evarts 40828.

Fairmeade. MRS. DALE S. WELLS
  121 Fairmeade Rd., City Hall, Fairmeade 40407.

Fincastle. MARY MICHAEL
            BARBARA TINSLEY
            MARTHA WALLINGFORD
  City Hall, P.O. Box 22052, Louisville 40222.

Flat Woods. JEAN BROWN
             BECKI LUCAS
             GOLDIE SAYES
  City Hall, 2411 Argillite Rd., Flat Woods
41139.

Flemingsburg. MARJORIE DAVIS
  City Hall, P.O. Box 126, Flemingsburg 41041.

Forest Hills. JOAN DAUGHERTY (R)
  1975-. Bds: Ch., Planning & Zoning. Party:
Cnty. Precinct Worker 1954-72. Prev: City Clerk
1973-75; Plan & Zoning Com. 1973-75. Org: Historical Society; Amer. Business Women's Assoc. Educ:
U. of Louisville 1967 BSC; 1970 MBA. Occ:
General Accounts Supervisor. B: 9/17/31. Add:

2112 Canterbrook Dr., Jeffersontown 40299
(502)491-6802.

Forest Hills. CHARLANN W. HORAN (R)
  1973-. Bds: Police Com. Party: Precinct
Co-Captain 1971-77. Org: Jefferson Cnty.
Teachers Assoc. Educ: Western Ky. State U.
1970 BA. Occ: Home Economics Teacher. B:
9/9/45. Add: 2302 Janlyn Rd., Forest Hills
40299 (502)267-1432.

Fort Mitchell. GLORIANNE F. CARLIN (D)
  1973-. Bds: Ch., Recreation Cmsn.; Cnty.
Municipal League; Liaison State Municipal League.
Org: Printing House Craftsman Women's Group.
B: 1/2/28. Add: 28 Pleasant Ridge Ave., Ft.
Mitchell 41017 (606)331-1212.

Frankfort. PATRICIA L. LAYTON (D)
  1975-. Org: Dem. Women's Club. Educ: Watts
Hospital School of Medical Technology 1959 ASMT.
Occ: Ice Cream Store Owner/Manager. B: 9/7/38.
Add: 603 Leawood Dr., Frankfort 40601
(502)227-2201.

Fulton. MRS. ROBERT MORGAN
  101 Nelson Tripp Pl., Fulton 42041.

Germantown. ANNA B. MC NAMARA
  Town Hall, Germantown 41044.

Glenview Hills. RELLA KORT (D)
  1975-. Occ: Realtor. Educ: U. of Miami 1952
BBA. B: 1/12/31. Add: 2906 Glenhill Ct.,
Louisville 40222.

Glenview Manor. MRS. P.H. COCHRAN
  2305 Glenview Ave., Glenview Manor 40222.

Goosecreek. NANCIANN D. BRENEMAN (R)
  1965-. Party: Committeewoman 1967. Occ:
Nurses Aide. B: 1/6/32. Add: 3114 Limerick Ln.,
Louisville 40222.

Hartford. JUDY MOORE
  City Hall, 114 Washington, Hartford 42347.

Hazard. ELIZABETH SNYDER DUNCAN (R)
  1970-. Prev: Planning & Zoning Cmsn. 1970-74.
Org: BPW; Women's Club; School Adv. Com. Occ:
Bookkeeper. B: 7/10/26. Add: 716 Oakhurst Ave.,
Hazard 41701 (606)436-3311.

Highland Heights. MARGARET TRUNICK
  City Hall, 112 Renshaw Rd., Highland Hts.
41076.

Hodgenville. LOUISE REED
  205 E. Water St., Hodgenville 42748.

Hopkinsville. MARY EVE DAVIS
  101 N. Main St., City Hall, Hopkinsville
42240.

Independence. DOLORES KLEIN RICHARDSON (D)
  1974-. Bds: Ch., Budget Com.; Ch., Sign Com.
Prev: City Clerk-Treasurer 1971-74. Occ:
Receptionist-Secretary. Add: 93 Roselawn Dr.,
Independence 41051 (606)356-5302.

Independence. MRS. P. DYAN VAUGHN (D)
1975-. Bds: Recreation Cmsn. Org: PTA;
Women's Club. B: 6/18/43. Add: 4214 Arbor Ct.,
Independence 41051.

Independence. THERESA WISHMAN (I)
1975-. Bds: Recreation. Occ: Beautician. B:
1/2/39. Add: 5027 Madison Pk., Independence
41051 (606)356-5302.

Keeneland. BETTY GUENTHNER
City Hall, 2000 Dugoon, Keeneland 40299.

Kenton Valley. DELORES HAYDEN
ALICE LOWRY
3124 Madison Ave., Covington 41015.

Kingsley. NECTAR KAZANJIAN
SHIRLEY MORRELL
2352 Tyler Ln., Louisville 40205.

Kuttawa. ROSAMOND SMITH
City Hall, P.O. Box 398, Kuttawa 42055.

Lebanon. NORA MOTLEY
113 S. Proctor Knott Ave., Lebanon 40033.

Lexington. ELEANOR H. LEONARD (D)
1975-. Bds: Ch., Planning & Evaluation Com.;
Public Works Com. Leg.-Judicial Com. Org: PTA.
Educ: Colo. Coll. 1959 BA. Occ: Business Manager.
B: 12/12/36. Add: 1806 Charleston Dr., Lexington
40505 (606)255-5631.

Lexington. MARY M. MANGIONE
136 Walnut St., Lexington 40507.

Lexington. PAM MILLER (D)
1973-. Dist: 4. Bds: Ch., Housing & Community
Devt. Com.; Employees Pension Bd.; Ch. Leg. Com.
Party: State Del. 1972; Nat. Alt. 1976; Co-Ch.,
Congressional Dist. 1976. Org: WPC; LWV; Common
Cause; Dem. Women's Club.; PTA. Educ: Smith Coll.
1960 BA. B: 9/7/38. Add: 140 Cherokee Pk.,
Lexington 40507 (606)255-5631.

Lockport. SANDRA JO FROST
BEATRICE HACKETT
LEOTA LYONS
MILDRED SPURR
Town Hall, Lockport 40036.

Louisville. MARY MARGARET MULVIHILL (D)
1975-. Bds: Senior House Bd. Party: State
Del.1976-77; Leg. Dist. Ch. 1977-80. Org: Special
Educ.; Com. on Aging; Dem. Club. Educ: U. of
Louisville 1969 BS. B: 12/15/42. Add: 1018
Greenleaf, Louisville 40213.

Ludlow. ETHEL EUBANKS
231 Elm St., Ludlow 41016.

Lynch. CYNTHIA ALLEN
DOROTHY MORROW
City Hall, P.O. Box 667, Lynch 40855.

Lynnview. JACQUELINE LEGER
City Hall, P.O. Box 13144, Cp. Taylor Br.
40213.

Manor Creek. KAY LUBAY
3403 Hastings Cir., Manor Creek 40222.

Manor Creek. F. JO ANNE MC CRARY
1975-. Educ: Siena Hts. Coll. 1957 BS. B:
3/9/36. Add: 3408 Ascot Cir., Louisville 40222

Maryhill Estate. MRS. J.L. MEAGHER
4111 Crestview Rd., Maryhill Est. 40207.

Meadowbrook Farm. CLAIRE BROUILETTE
NARCISSA VAN PELT
2101 Terriwood Ct., Louisville 40223.

Meadowview Estate. ELIZABETH G. ABELL (D)
1970-. Party: Campaign Treasurer Repr. 1975,
'77. Prev: City Clerk. 1968-74. Org: Amer.
Business Women's Assoc. Occ: Secretary. B:
9/9/17. Add: 3765 Taylorsville Rd., Louisville
40220 (502)458-1417.

Middlesboro. BETTY JEAN HAYES (D)
1976-. Bds: Ch., Finance Com.; Building Com.
Org: Nat. Assoc. for Bank Women; Bank Adminis-
tration Institute; Ken. Bankers Assoc.; Red Cross;
Dem. Women's Club; Chamber of Commerce. Occ:
Banking Executive. B: 3/3/27. Add: 814 Chester
Ave., Middlesboro 40965 (606)248-5950.

Midway. BETTY BRIGHT (D)
1973-. Bds: Ch., Cemetery; Ch., License.
Prev: Planning 1976. Add: Midway 40347.

Millersburg. EDITH BEEDING
City Hall, Box 265, Millersburg 40338.

Monterey. LELA M. BALLARD (D)
1976-. B: 4/13/07. Add: Monterey 40349.

Monterey. MRS. JOHN SPICER
Town Hall, Monterey 40349.

Moorland. MARY CAHILL
SANDRA J. DOYLE
9408 Farnham Dr., Louisville 40223.

Moorland. JO ANN METTS (D)
1973-. Bds: Dir., Public Safety. Org: OES.
Occ: Secretary. B: 7/9/33. Add: 9403 Earlham
Dr., Louisville 40223.

Mount Sterling. DOROTHY LAVOIL
City Hall, 40 Broadway, Mt. Sterling 40353.

Newport. IRENE DEATON
4th & York St., City Hall, Newport 41071.

Norbourne Estate. BERNADETTE SMITH
4021 St. Ives Court, Louisville 40207.

Norwood. MARIE EMBRY
7501 N. Park Pl., Louisville 40222.

Oakland. NANCY ALEXANDER
City Hall, Oakland 42159.

Oakland. ZULA STEENBERGEN (D)
1975-. B: 9/4/16. Add: Box 47, Oakland
42159.

Owensboro. CLAUDIA MYLES
    City Hall, P.O. Box 847, Owensboro 42301.

Park Hills. VIRGINIA SCHMITZ
    1106 Amsterdam, Park Hills 41011.

Parkway Village. MARIE EMBRY
    828 Perennial Dr., Louisville 40207.

Pembroke. BETTE L. JACKSON (D)
    1976-. Bds: Ch., Sanitation Com. Org:Women's
Nat. Farm & Garden Assoc. B: 9/25/25. Add: RR 1
Main St., Pembroke 42266 (502)475-4343.

Pineville. ANN BROUGHTON
    City Hall, Box 688, Pineville 40977.

Plantation. MARGARET FOSTER
             NANCY FULLER
    City Hall, Box 22252, Plantation 40222.

Princeton. LILLIE BELL CHILDRESS
            VIRGINIA MC CASLIN
    206 N. Jefferson, Princeton 42445.

Prospect. ALICE SENIOR
    7601 Hunting Creek Dr., Prospect 40059.

Providence. JUDITH GREEN
    City Hall, P.O. Box 128, Providence 42459.

Radcliff. MARTHA P. BAKER
    City Hall, 411 W. Lincoln, Radcliff 40160.

Ridgeview Heights. SUE HADDIX
    416 Ridgeview Dr., Ridgeview Hts. 41051.

Riverwood. MRS. P. STEWART
    2106 Starmont Rd., Louisville 40207.

Robinswood. BARBARA BRICK
    City Hall, 419 Blankenbaker, Robinswood 40207.

Russellville. PEGGY RUDDER
    City Hall, Park Square, Russellville 42276.

Sacramento. MAGDALENE BARNETT (D)
    1975-. Bds: Water Bd. Party: Precinct Worker
1975-77. Org: PTA. Occ: Grocery Clerk. B:
11/24/08. Add: W 3rd St., Sacramento 42372.

St. Regis Park. EVELYN NORFLEET
    4413 Mt. Vernon Rd., Louisville 40220.

Salyersville. MARY LOU BROWN
    1975-. Org: Ky. Civil Liberties Union. B:
2/26/25. Add: Box 331, Salyersville 41465
(606)349-3984.

Salyersville. BETSEY CONNELLY
    City Hall, P.O. Drawer A, Salyersville 41465.

Sandy Hook. ESTA LOU BOWLING
            EDNA PENNINGTON
    City Hall, Box 274, Sandy Hook 41171.

Sebree. FERN DENTON
    City Hall, Spring St., Sebree 42455.

Sharpsburg. IDA M. CAMPBELL
             ROBERTA SHROUT
    Town Hall, Sharpsburg 40374.

Sheperdsville. BETTY MARAMAN
    1005 W. 2nd, P.O. Box 398, Sheperdsville
40165.

Smith Grove. MARGARET BEVARLEY
    City Hall, Box 114, Smith's Grove 42171.

Union. BEVERLY HOLIDAY (I)
    1976-. Bds: Cnty. Planning & Zoning Cmsn.
Org: WPC. Occ: Administrative Asst. B: 6/6/47.
Add: P.O. Box 148, Mt. Zion Rd., Union 41091.

Versailles. BRENDA YEARY
    City Hall, 196 S. Main, Versailles 40383.

Vicco. JO ANN STANLEY
    City Hall, P.O. Box 163, Vicco 41773.

Villa Hills. LOIS BRUNS (D)
    1971-. Bds: Ch., Budget; Bldg. Prev: Council-
woman 1971-77. Org: Nat. Assoc. of Realtors;
Civic Club. Occ: Realtor Assoc. B: 12/14/30.
Add: 2505 Buttermilk, Villa Hills 41046
(606)341-1280.

Warsaw. BETTY GRAY
    City Hall, Main Cross, Warsaw 41095.

Washington. CHRISTINE GANTLEY
             JANE HENDERSON
    City Hall, Box 34, Washington 41096.

Whipp's Millgate. FRANCES MILLER
    City Hall, P.O. Box 832, Whipp's Millgate
40223.

Whitesville. WANDA BROOKS
    City Hall, P.O. Box 51, Whitesville 42378.

Wilder. LORENA ZIEGLER
    400 Licking Pike, Wilder 41071.

Woodlawn Park. SHERRY HYDE
    1975-. Org: PTA. Occ: Secretary. B:
9/21/44. Add: 6916 Ambridge Cir., Louisville
40207.

Woodlawn Park. JEANNINE HAINES LIVESAY (R)
    1975-. Bds: Ch., Ordinances. Org: Younger
Women's Club. Educ: U. of Ky. 1963 BA. Occ:
Boutique Owner. B: 3/26/41. Add: 111 Ahland Rd.
Louisville 40207 (502)425-5758.

Woodland. KAY MELLOY
    City Hall, P.O. Box 7891, Woodlawn Pk. 40207.

Worthington. HAZEL I. SMITH (D)
    1975-. Bds: Ch., Sewer Com.; Police Com.;
Fire Dept. Com.; Prev: Bd. of Educ. 1953-56.
Org: Younger Women's Club; PTA; Wild Life Assoc.
Occ: Interviewer, Public Opinion Research. B:
4/11/15. Add: 1016 Prospect Ave., Worthington
41183.

Worthville. SUE TOLES
    City Hall, Box 134, Worthville 41098.

State Boards and Commissions

A complete list of state boards and commissions and of their membership, was not available for inclusion.

Louisiana

State Executive and Cabinet

SHIRLEY MC NAMARA
Secretary, Department of Revenue and Taxation. Add: State Capitol, P.O. Box 44004, Baton Rouge 70804.

MARY EVELYN PARKER
State Treasurer. 1968-. Party: Nat. Dem. Committeewoman 1948-52. Prev: Ch., State Bd. of Public Welfare 1950-51; State Cmnsr. of Public Welfare 1956-63; Ch., White House Conf. on Children & Youth 1960; State Cmnsr. of Administration 1964-68. Educ: Northwestern State Coll. BA. B:11/8/20. Add: P.O. Box 44154, Baton Rouge 70804 (504)389-5686.

SANDRA S. THOMPSON (D)
Secretary, Department of Culture, Recreation & Tourism. 1976-. Bds: Parks & Recreation Com.; Tourist Devt. Com.; Museum Bd.; Arts Council; Archaeological & Antiquities Com.; Library Bd.; Historic Preservation Review Bd. Prev: Exec. Asst., Sec. of State 1971-72; Exec. Dir., Atchafalaya Basin Div. 1972-76; Coord., La Trails Council 1974-76; Dir., Gov's. Beautification Program 1975-76. Org:Ecology Ctr.; Friends of Archives; WPC. B: 10/4/46. Add: 6048 Hibiscus Dr., Baton Rouge 70808 (504)389-2567.

State Legislature

State Senate

VIRGINIA KILPATRICK SHEHEE (D)
1976-. Dist: 38. Bds: Regional Bicentennial Cmsn.; Governor's Beautification Cmsn.; Citizens Adv. Bd. to Governor's Council on Environmental Quality. Party: Caucus 1972. Org: NOWL Educ: Centenary Coll. 1943 BA. Occ: Pres., Life Insurance Company. B: 7/12/23. Add: 2500 Crestwood Dr., Shreveport 71108 (504)389-5061.

State House

DIANE ELIZABETH BAJOIE (D) *
1976-. Dist: 91. Party: Nat. Del. 1972. Org: Southern U. Alumni Assoc.; Southern Political Science Assoc.; Save our Community; Community Development Corp. Educ: Southern U. BA. B: 2/8/48. Add: 2303 Milan St., New Orleans 70115 (504)899-2193.

County Commissions

Beauregard. MARY ANN E. LE RAY
DeRidder 70634.

Caddo. DORIS MC WILLIAMS (R)
1975-. Bds: N. La. Health Systems Agency; Citizens Blood Supply Com. Party: Parish Exec. Com. 1976-80. Org: LWV; Rep. Women; AAUW. Educ: Butler U. 1946 BA. B: 10/1/24. Add: 10021 Smitherman Dr., Shreveport 71115 (318)226-6911.

Calcasieu. MARGARET LOWENTHAL
Lake Charles 70601.

Calcasieu. WILDRED ROBERTS (D)
1975-. Bds: Ch., Mosquito Control Com.; Road & Bridge Com.; Agenda Com.; Claims Com. Org: PTA. B: 12/22/28. Add: Rte. 5, Box 1250, Lake Charles 70601 (318)433-3661.

Calcasieu. BONNIE H. SMITH (D)
1976-. Bds: Ch., Bids & Claims Com.; Intergover-mental Planning Com.; Finance Com. Org: Credit Women Internat.; Internal. Consumer Credit Assoc.; Credit Executives, Inc.; BPW; Nat. Assoc. of Public Accountants; La. Women in Politics; ABWA; OES. Educ: Northwestern U. 1962 BS. Occ: Accounting Firm Owner. B: 10/28/31. Add: 211 Wayside Dr., Westlake 70669 (318)439-3656.

East Baton Rouge. JEWEL J. NEWMAN
Baton Rouge 70807.

Natchitoches. MRS. JAMES D. MARTIN
Goldonna 71031.

Rapides. GAYLE JOSEPH CRAIG (D)
1975-. Bds: Rapides Area Planning Cmsn.; Ch., Recreation Com.; Recreation Dist. Party: State Del. 1972; Cnty. Committeewoman 1964. Org: Social Service Org.; AAUW; Dem. Women. Educ: La. State U. 1962 BA. Occ: Teacher. B: 2/11/41. Add: 209 Pleasant Dr., Alexandria 71301 (318)445-3617.

Rapides. JILL ELDRED GLASSCOCK (D)
1975-. Bds: Intergov't. Affairs & Zoning; Finance; Roads & Bridges. B: 9/17/38. Add: 113 Hudson St., Pineville 71360 (318)445-3617.

St. Bernard. CELESTINE MELERINE
Violet, 70092.

St. Mary. MATILDA ALOISIO (D) **
　1971-. Bds: Ch., Ordinance Com.; Legislative
Com. Prev: Councilwoman 1958-66. Org: Chamber of
Commerce. Occ: School Bus Driver. B: 12/18/21.
Add: 404 William St., Patterson 70392
(318)385-2520 Ext. 220.

Tangipahoa. GERTRUDE B. WITTIE (D) **
　1958-. Bds: V-Pres. Fire Bd.; Courthouse Com.;
Road Com.; Memorial Com. Org: BPW. B: 12/30/12.
Add: Hammond 70401 (506)345-7249.

West Baton Rouge. MYRTIS ALEXANDER (D)
　1975-. Bds: Ch., Drainage & Equipment; Fire
Protection & Solid Waste; Finance & Personnel.
Occ: Sugar Chemist. B: 6/15/21. Add: P.O. Box
116, Brusly (504)383-4755.

West Carroll. JEANETTE COPES
　Pioneer 71266.

West Carroll. LEE LOIS JONES
　Pioneer 71266.

Mayors

Dixie Inn. MADIE L. MATHENY (D)
　1972-. Bds: Ch., Monthly Council Meetings;
Ch., Special Meetings of Bd. of Aldermen. Org:
Retail Clerks Union; Al-Anon; PTA; Park Com. B:
12/18/24. Add: 50 Shell St., Minden 71055
(318)377-6855.

Elton. MILDRED LA FLEUR
　City Hall, Elton 70532.

Folsom. VERA FAYE FORBES (D)
　1971-. Org: St. Tammany Municipal Assoc.; OES.
Occ: Bookkeeper. B: 2/6/33. Add: P.O. Box 74,
Folsom 70437 (504)796-5607.

Gibsland. NOMIE M. NAMIE
　City Hall, Gibsland 71028.

Haughton. ELIZABETH OWEN SHERWIN (R)
　1976-. Prev: Alderwoman 1972-76. B: 9/11/18.
Add: 505 W. McKinley Ave., Haughton 71037
(318)949-0600.

Many. VIRGINIA GADDIR GODFREY (D)
　1965-. Org: BPW; DAR; Colonial Dames. Educ:
Southern Methodist Coll. 1932 BA. Occ: Manager.
B: 9/19/10. Add: 875 N. Nabours, Many 71449
(318)256-3651.

Maurice. CORBETTE A. LE BLANC
　Town Hall, Maurice 70555.

Port Barre. DORRIS GODET
　City Hall, Port Barre 70577.

St. Francisville. MARIE H. WENGER
　City Hall, St. Francisville 70775.

Tullos. ETHEL H. DOYLE
　Town Hall, Tullos 71479.

Wilson. JEWEL E. RAVENCRAFT
　Town Hall, Wilson 70789.

Local Councils

Athens. MRS. WILLIE B.S. ARM
　　MRS. CLYDE SHERRILL
　　MRS. G.W. SIMS
　City Hall, Athens 71003.

Baker. SHERRY ANN FISHER (D)
　1976-. Bds: City Ct. Adv. Bd.; Planning &
Zoning Bd.; Capitol Reg. Planning Cmsn. Org:
La. Municipal Assoc.; Amer. Bank Consumer Bd.
Educ: Tex. Woman's U. 1963 BS. Occ: Teacher.
B: 12/22/42. Add: 231 Ray Weiland Dr., Baker
70714 (504)778-0300.

Basile. HILDA FONTENOT
　City Hall, Basile 70515.

Bastrop. MRS. JERALD L. JORDAN (D)
　1973-. Bds: Ch., Public Safety; Finance;
Recreation. Org: N. La. Fair Bd.; Industrial
Dev. Bd. Occ: Special Assignments Newspaper
Reporter. B: 2/14/31. Add: 719 Highland Ave.,
Bastrop 71220 (318)281-4644.

Bastrop. JULIA MAE SCOTT SMITH (D)
　1973-. Bds: Ch., Public Works. Prev:
Recreation Bd. 1953-57. Org: NEA; NAACP; Council
on Aging; La. Education Assoc. Occ: Teacher.
B: 9/3/13. Add: 531 Haynes Ave., Bastrop 71220.

Baton Rouge. PEARL GEORGE
　　JEWEL J. NEWMAN
　City Hall, Baton Rouge 70821.

Benton. MRS. FRANKIE CAMPBELL
　City Hall, Benton 71006.

Benton. RUTHA L. RICHARDSON (D)
　1976-. Occ: Teacher. B: 7/10/35. Add:
P.O. Box 404, Benton 71006.

Bielville. ANNE BAXTER
　Town Hall, Bielville 71008.

Bogalusa. MAXIE C. CAMPBELL
　City Hall, Bogalusa 70427.

Boyce. EVELYN R. STEWART (D) **
　1974-. Bds: Street Com.; Utility Com. Org:
LTA; CTA; Ch., Farmers Market. Educ: Northwest
State U. BA. Occ: Teacher. B: 11/4/25. Add:
Box 65, Boyce 71409 (318)793-2360.

Campti. MRS. LARRY GILL
　City Hall, Campti 71411.

Cankton. WILHELMINA SAVOIE
　Town Hall, Cankton 70584.

Clayton. BARBARA JEAN RUTLAND (D)
　Mayor Pro Tem. Org: NEA; La. Municipal Assoc;
Park & Recreation Assoc. Educ: Grambling State U.
1961 BS; Ind. U. 1969 MA. Occ: School Counselor.
B: 6/10/38. Add: P.O. Box 176, Clayton 71326
(318)757-8540.

Collinston. VERA I. BUTLER (D) **
　1973-. Org: DAR; Women's Insurance Club. B:
1/5/07. Add: Box 44, Collinston 71229
(318)874-2558.

Cullen. NELLIE B. LA CASE
City Hall, Cullen 71021.

Delta. SARAH MERCIER
City Hall, Delta 71233.

Denham Springs. MONITA P. JACKSON (D) **
1974-. Educ: LSU 1938 BA. B: 8/14/14. Add:
Box 105, Denham Springs 70726 (504)665-2249.

Deridder. COREAN GIBBS
City Hall, Deridder 70634.

Deridder. HELEN W. JOHNSON (D) **
1974-. B: 11/10/26. Add: 1413 Blankenship
Dr., Deridder 70634.

Dodson. SADIE HOLLINGSWORTH (D) **
1974-. Mayor Pro Tem. Org: Retired Teachers
Group. Educ: Grambling State U. 1950 BS. B:
3/25/05. Add: Rt. 2, Box 6, Dodson 71422
(504)628-3775.

Downsville. POLLY WALLACE MC GEHEE (D) **
1972-. Educ: La. Polytechnic Inst. 1946 BS.
B: 12/4/25. Add: Box 38, Downsville 71234.

Elizabeth. DOROTHY E. HUSSONG (D) **
1973-. Org: PTA. Occ: Supervisor, Paper
Company. B: 6/12/24. Add: P.O. Box 146,
Elizabeth 70638 (318)634-5100.

Eros. IRMA SHARP
City Hall, Eros 71238.

Estherwood. FRANCES K. TRUMPS (D)
1974-. Org: PTA. B: 11/17/36. Add: 521
Jackson St., P.O. Box 32, Estherwood 70534
(318)783-7428.

Eunice. VERNITA POWELL
City Hall, Eunice 70535.

Farmerville. TINY W. TALLEY (D) **
1968-. Bds: Ch., Finance. Org: Amer. Accounting Assoc.; BPW. Educ: La. Technical U. 1973 BS.
B: 10/21/17. Add: 1114 Pine Dr., Farmerville
71241 (318)368-6041.

Georgetown. DOLLY E. TULLY
Town Hall, Georgetown 71432.

Golden Meadow. ENA LEONARD
City Hall, Golden Meadow 70357.

Gonzales. MARY B. WILLIS (D)
1976-. Mayor Pro Tem. Bds: Ch., Public
Relations; Ch., Insurance Com. Org: BPW. Occ:
Kindergarten Teacher. B: 6/15/31. Add: P.O. Box
421, Gonzales 70737 (504)644-2841.

Grambling. ROSETTA HILL DAYS (D)
1973-. Bds: Bd. of Dir's. Lincoln Cnty. Indus-
trialization Ctr. Prev: Mental Health Assoc.
Org: Amer. Personnel & Guidance Assoc.; Assoc. for
Counselor Educ. & Supervision; Amer. Coll. Person-
nell Assoc.; Educ. Assoc.; ACLU; League of Voters;
LWV. Educ: Grambling State U. 1957 BS; U. of
Mich. 1964 MS. Occ: Asst. Professor. B: 12/23/36
Add: 608 E. Grand, Grambling 71245 (318)247-6696

Grayson. MRS. DELL KENWORTHY
City Hall, Grayson 71435.

Greensburg. ELOIS SMITH MC NABB (D)
1972-. Bds: Capitol Reg. Planning. Occ:
Accountant. B: 8/10/26. Add: P.O. Box 184,
Greensburg 70441.

Hornbeck. BERNICE O. CABRA
City Hall, Hornbeck 71439.

Hornbeck. BETTY PAULINE HOWARD (D) **
1974-. Bds: City Clerk. Occ: Secretary.
B: 4/10/43. Add: Rt 1, Box 174N, Hornbeck
71439 (318)565-4659.

Ida. MRS. CLIFFORD CHILDRESS
Town Hall, Ida 71044.

Jackson. JULIA W. ADAMS
SYBIL MARCANTEL
City Hall, Jackson 70748.

Jonesville. MRS. T. L. MORRIS (D) **
1974-. Occ: Self-employed. B: 2/25/28.
Add: 503 E. Park St., Jonesville 71343
(318)339-7859.

Killian. BARBARA WILD (D) **
1973-. B: 12/4/40. Add: Rt. A-2, Box 55,
Springfield 70462 (504)695-3557.

Krotz Springs. VYRONA M. WILTZ (D) **
Bds: Finance; Recreation; Council on Aging;
Industrial Com. Educ: U. of Southwest La. 1974
BA. Occ: Self-employed. B: 5/21/51. Add:
Box 216, Krotz Springs 70750 (318)566-3703.

Madisonvilla. MRS. PAT PELLOAT
City Hall, Madisonvilla 70447.

Mamou. MAXIME FONTENOT
City Hall, Mamou 70554.

Marksville. SHIRLEY W. SCIONEAUX
City Hall, Marksville 71351.

Maurice. BARBARA PICARD
Town Hall, Maurice 70555.

Mermentau. CAMILLE A. LA POINT
Town Hall, Mermentau 70556.

Montgomery. EVERETTE NELMS
City Hall, Montgomery 71454.

Montpelier. MARY RYAN WILLIAMS (D)
1974-. Org: Senior Citizens. B: 1/25/08.
Add: Rt. 1, Box M-4, Montpelier 70422
(504)777-4400.

Natchez. ELEANOR GOLDBERG
Town Hall, Natchez 71456.

Newellton. CLARA THOMAS BASS (D)
1976-. Org: Nat. Teacher Assoc.; La. Assoc.
for Public Continuing; La. Recreation & Park
Assoc.; Voter's League; PTA; Recreational Club.
Educ: Grambling State Coll. 1969 BS. Occ:
Elementary School Teacher. B: 12/4/46. Add:

204 McDonald St., P.O. Box 236, Newellton 71357
(318)467-5050.

Oakdale. CHARLENE SOLOMAN
    City Hall, Oakdale 71463.

Oak Ridge. HAZLE MOTT
    Town Hall, Oak Ridge 71264.

Oberlin. PATRICIA A. FONTENOT (D) **
    1973-. Bds: Planning Cmsn. Occ: Teacher's
Aid. B: 9/5/41. Add: City Hall, Oberlin 70655
(318)639-4344.

Oil City. WILLA MC CORD
    Town Hall, Oil City 71061.

Olla. ELAINE NELSON GOUGH (D) **
    1968-. Occ: Florist. B: 8/30/22. Add:
P.O. Box 207, Olla 71465.

Parks. CAMILLE LASSEGNE
    Town Hall, Parks 70582.

Parks. VIVA PERIOU (D)
    1960-. Org: Social Welfare Assoc. Educ:
U.S.L. 1964 BS. Occ: Social Worker. B: 8/31/22.
Add: Parks 70582 (318)845-4654.

Pearl River. ANITA L. BROWN (D)
    1975-. Bds: Ch., Humane Society; Parish
Planning. Org: Civic Club; PTA; Humane Society.
Occ: Insurance Agent. B: 7/6/38. Add: P.O. Box
243 Pine St., Pearl River 70452 (504)863-5800.

Plain Dealing. EVERETTE PITTMAN
    Town Hall, Plain Dealing 71064.

Pleasant Hill. JUANITA W. FALLIN
    Town Hall, Pleasant Hill 71065.

Powhatan. MRS. O. V. HALL
    Town Hall, Powhatan 71066.

Rayne. MARJORIE BERNARD
    City Hall, Rayne 70478.

Reeves. NETTIE HEINTZ (D) **
    1974-. B: 1/20/20. Add: Edith St., Reeves
70658.

Ruston. HILDA ANNE TAYLOR (D)
    1975-. Bds: Ch., Public Works; Ch., Community
Devt.; Finance Com. Org: La. Teachers Assoc.;
Nat. Council Teachers of English; BPW. Educ: La.
Technical U. 1976 BA; MA. Occ: English Teacher.
B: 9/22/39. Add: Rt. 1, Box 477, Ruston 71270.

Sarepta. VERA PARKER STILES (D)
    1976-. Bds: Ch., Finance & Administration.
Org: BPW; Bureau of Status of Women; School-
Community Council. Occ: Office Clerk/Bookkeeper.
B: 8/20/24. Add: N. Main, Sarepta 71071
(318)847-4333.

Sicily Island. KATIE N. CONEY
    Town Hall, Sicily Island 71368.

Simsboro. OPAL CHOATE (D)
    1974-. Occ: Accountant. B: 10/19/25. Add:
Box 188, Simsboro 71275 (318)247-6350.

Slaughter. MARIAN RUTH GREMILLION (D)
    1976-. Org: Ladies Civic Club. B: 6/21/32.
Add: Box 222, Slaughter 70777 (504)654-4278.

South Mansfield. DOLLIE M. GODEJOHN
    Town Hall, S. Mansfield 71052.

Sulphur. IVY J. DAVID
    City Hall, Sulphur 70663.

Ville Platte. HELEN RAY L. DARDEAU (D) **
    1974-. Educ: U. of Southwestern La. 1955
BA. B: 9/21/36. Add: P.O. 327 - 1503 Lincoln
Rd., Ville Platte 70586.

Waterproof. MARIE BACHUS
    City Hall, Waterproof 71375.

Waterproof. YVONNE T. BURNS (D) **
    1974-. Party: Exec. Com. 1970- . Org: NEA;
TEA; PTSA. Educ: Grambling 1956 BA; Southern U.
1969 M.Ed. Occ: Teacher. B: 7/24/29. Add:
Box 151, Waterproof 71375 (318)749-5292.

State Boards and Commissions

    A complete list of state boards and commissions
and of their membership, was not available for
inclusion.

Maine

State Senate

MINNETTE H. CUMMINGS (R)
1973-. Bds: Ch., Public Utilities Com.; Legal
Affairs Com.; Party: State Del. 1970-76; Nat. Del.
1972. Prev: School Board 1955-68. Org: Adv. Com.
on Alcholism & Drug Abuse Prevention; Adv. Cmsn.
Civil Emergency Defense. Educ: Bennington 1940
BA. B: 1/26/20. Add: Rowell Rd., Hampden 04444.
(207)289-3601.

OLYMPIA J. SNOWE (R)
114 Nottingham Rd., Auburn 04210.

State House

ANGELA Z. ALOUPIS (R)
15 Astor Place, Bangor 04401.

ANNE JAMESON BACHRACH (D) ☆☆
1974-. Dist: 91. Bds: Human Resources; Audit.
Party: Town Com. 1965-75. Prev: Councilwoman
1970-75. Org: LWV; WPC. B: 7/19/19. Add: 17
Meadowbrook Rd., Brunswick 04011 (207)725-2134.

SHARON B. BENOIT (D)
1976-. Bds: Natural Resources Com.; Perform-
ance Audit Com. Party: State Del. 1970, '76. Org:
NEA; Political Action Conf. for Educators; NAACP.
Educ: Westbrook Coll. 1963 AA; U. of Me. 1973
BSEd. Occ: Educator. B: 11/28/44. Add: 75
Parrott St., S. Portland 04106 (207)289-2866.

GEORGETTE B. BERUBE (D) ☆☆
Dist: 6. Bds: Governor's Message; Local &
County Government; Ch., Performance Audit; Natural
Resources. Add: 195 Webster, Lewiston 04240
(207)782-2272.

ANNE BOUDREAU (D) ☆☆
Dist: 21. Bds: Business Legislation; Ch.,
Election Laws. Add: 81 Lincoln, Portland 04103
(207)622-5804; (207)774-3518.

KAREN LEE BROWN (R)
1976-. Dist: 63. Bds: Energy Com.; Natural
Resources Com. Party: State Del. 1976; State Alt.
1972; Nat. Alt. 1976; Oxford Cnty. GOP 1976. Org:
Historical Society. Educ: U. of Mass. 1976 BS.
B: 4/14/53. Add: Box 32, Bethel 04217
(207)389-2866.

LORRAINE CHONKO (D) ☆☆
Dist: 88. Bds: Labor. Add: New Lewiston
Road, Topsham 04067 (207)725-8993.

NANCY RANDALL CLARK (D)
1972-. Dist: 27. Bds: Ch., Com. on Business
Leg.; Com. on Veterans & Retirement. Party:
State Del. 1972-76; Local V-Ch., 1972-76; Cnty.
Committeewoman 1972-78; Dem. Party Platform
Secretary 1972-76; V-Pres., Selection Cmsn. 1973-
74. Prev: Governor's Adv. Council on the Status
of Women 1973-75; Educ. Subsidy Cmsn. 1974-75.
Org: NEA; OES; NOWL; WPC; Historical Society.
Educ: Husson Coll. 1962 BS; U. of Me. 1968 MEd.
Occ: Teacher. B: 5/6/38. Add: RFD#2, Box 156,
Lambert Rd., Freeport 04032 (207)622-2866.

LENA C. DURGIN (R) ☆☆
Dist: 107. Bds: Election Laws, Energy. Add:
6 Cook St., Kittery 03904 (207)439-1323.

BARBARA A. GILL (R)
70 Springwood Rd., South Portland 04106.

KATHLEEN WATSON GOODWIN (D) ☆☆
1968-. Dist: 90. Bds: Com. on Aging. Party:
Secretary, State Com., 1968-75; City Com. 1963-
75; Del. Nat. Conv. 1972; County Com. 1964-66.
Org: Bd. of Governors, Nat. Society of State
Legislators. B: 11/13/40. Add: 409 High St.,
Bath 04530. (207)289-3591.

SHERRY F. HUBER (R)
1976-. Dist: 22. Bds: Joint Com. on Natural
Resources; Joint Com. on Energy. Party: State
Alt. 1976; Fund Raising Ch. 1975-76. Prev:
Conservation Cmsn. 1974-77. Org: Audubon Society;
Natural Resources Council; LWV. Educ: Smith
Coll. 1959 BA. B: 9/27/37. Add: 430 Blackstrap
Rd., Falmouth 04105 (207)289-2866.

MARJORIE C. HUTCHINGS (R)
1975-. Bds: Transportation; Human Resourses.
Party: State Del. 1970-76; Nat. Del. 1976; State
Committeewoman 1960-75; Del., State Com. 1976-78.
Org: Bd. of Realtors; WPC; Improvement Assoc.
Occ: Real Estate Assoc. B: 11/25/22. Add:
RFD 1, Lincolnville 04849.

MARY E. KANE (R)
131 Cony St., Augusta 04330.

JUDY C. KANY (D)
1974-. Dist: 52. Bds: Cmsn. on Me's. Future.
Party: State Del.; Nat. Del. 1976. Org: ACLU;
LWV; Common Cause; AAUW. Educ: U. of Mich. 1959
BBA; U. of Me. 1975 MPA. B: 5/27/38. Add:
18 West St., Waterville 04901 (207)289-2866.

JOYCE E. LEWIS (R) ☆☆
Dist: 4. Bds: Educ. Add: RR 3, Auburn
04210 (207)782-1628.

ANTOINETTE C. MARTIN (D) **
    Dist: 91. Bds: Local and County Government.
Add: 24 Hawthorne St., Brunswick 04011
(207)725-5358.

NANCY N. MASTERTON (R)
    1976-. Dist: 34. Bds: Joint Standing Com. on
State Govt. Party: State Del. 1976. Prev: Adv.
Com. on Coastal Devt. & Conservation 1976- ;
House Apportionment Com. 1973- ; Senate Approtion-
ment Cmsn. 1971; Task Force on Govt. Reorganization 1976-79; Cape Elizabeth Planning Bd. 1973-
76. Org: Me. Assoc. of Planners; Portland Com.
on Foreign Relations; LWV; Natural Resources
Council. Educ: Boston U. 1952 BA. B: 11/28/30.
Add: 36 Delano Park, Cape Elizabeth 04107
(207)289-2866.

ELIZABETH MITCHELL (D) **
    1974-. Dist: 50. Bds: Educ. Cmsn. of States.
Party: Town Ch., 1974- . Org: LWV. Educ: Furman
U. 1962 BA; U. of NC 1967 MAT. B: 6/22/40. Add:
RFD #1, Vassalboro 04330 (207)289-1110.

MARY NAJARIAN (D) **
    1972-. Dist: 21. Bds: Legislative Council.
Party: County Com. 1972- ; City Com. 1972- . Org:
LWV; NOW; WPC; Dem. Women's Club. Educ: West
Virginia U. 1954 BS. B: 8/13/32. Add: 173
Pleasant Ave., Portland 04103 (207)289-3281.

MERLE NELSON (D)
    1976-. Dist: 21. Bds: Health & Institutions
Com.; Me. Com. on the Problems of the Mentally
Retarded. Party: City Dem. Com. 1976-78. Org:
Portland Symphony Women; Jr. League; LWV; WPC;
NOW; Citizens Adv. Bd.; Parents Council. Educ:
Lesley Coll. 1959 BS; Harvard Graduate School of
Educ. 1961 Ed.M. B: 5/8/35. Add: 71 Carroll,
Portland 04102.

BONNIE D. POST (D) **
    1974-. Dist: 56. Party: State Com. 1974- ;
County Com. 1972- ; Town Com. 1972- . Org: Conservation Cmsn. Educ: Mary Hitchcock School of
Nursing 1965 RN. B: 1/27/44. Add: Owl's Head
04841 (207)289-2866.

CHARLOTTE ZAHN SEWALL (R)
    1974-. Dist: 60. Bds: Joint Standing Com. on
Judiciary. Party: State Del. 1972-76; Cnty.
Committeewoman 1972-76; Ch., Town GOP 1972-77.
Org: Cnty. Rep. Women's Club; Nat. Fed. of Rep.
Women. B: 11/28/47. Add: Glidden St., Newcastle
04553.

GAIL H. TARR (R) **
    Dist: 24. Bds: Labor; Public Utilities. Occ:
Secretary. Add: RFD 1, North High St., Bridgton
04009 (207)622-5804; 647-2025.

BARBARA M. TRAFTON (D)
    RFD 3, Box 140, Auburn 04210.

Mayors

Alfred. DOROTHY HILL (R)
    1975-. Bds: Bd. of Dir., York Cnty. Community
Action Program. Org: Historical Soc. B: 11/30/32
Add: Bennett Rd., Alfred 04002 (207)324-3521.

Arundel. MARGARET PEARSON
    Kennebunkport 04066.

Beddington. MARY LANE
    Star Rte., Cherryfield 04622.

Caribou. ELIZABETH B. HAMILTON (R)
    1977-. Bds: Health Systems Agency Bd.; Ch.,
Municipal Bldg. Com. Prev: City Councilwoman
1972-76. Org: Chamber of Commerce; AAUW. Educ:
Wellesley Coll. 1954 BA. Occ: Craft Retailer.
B: 3/28/33. Add: 339 Main St., Caribou 04736
(207)493-3324.

Centerville. MARJORIE GAUDETTE
    Town Hall, Columbia Falls 04623.

Columbia Falls. SUSIE OLIVER (D)
    1976-. Bds: Overseer of Poor; Road Cmsnr.
Prev: Tax Assessor 1966. Occ: Bookkeeper. B:
2/1/30. Add: Columbia Falls 04623
(207)483-4067.

Cutler. CYNTHIA ROWDEN
    Cutler

Dresden. MRS. JOHN FOSTER
    Town Hall, Dresden 04342.

Eastbrook. LOUISE ASHE
    RFD 1, Franklin 04634.

Frenchville. VALERE TARDIS
    Town Hall, Frenchville 04745.

Lewiston. LILLIAN L. CARON
    City Hall, Lewiston 04240.

North Haven. PATRICIA S. CURTIS
    Town Hall, North Haven 04853.

Poland. MARY BENNETT
    RFD #2, Oxford 04270.

Prospect. MARION B. LA FORGE (I)
    1958-. Bds: Overseer of Poor. Party: Ch.,
Town Com. 1960-68. B: 8/25/03. Add: Prospect
RFD, Stockton Springs 04981 (207)567-3481.

Stonington. MARGARET H. GRINDLE (R)
    1972-. Prev: Treasurer, Recreation Com. 1976.
Occ: Manager, School Lunch Program. B: 11/12/25.
Add: Town Office, Stonington 04681
(207)367-2351.

Vienna. MARIE KOHTALA
    Town Hall, Vienna 04360.

Warren. MARIANNE LOWDEN
    Town Hall, Warren 04864.

Washington. DOROTHY A. SAINIO
    Washington

Woolwich. SYLVIA CARLETON
    Wiscasset 04578.

Local Councils

Abbot. ALLISON RICHARDS
    Town Hall, Abbot 04406.

Alna. GAIL ANTONIOLI
    RFD, Wiscasset 04578.

Auburn. CAMILLE CARRIER
    City Hall, Auburn 04210.

Aurora. JOAN A. LARSON (R)
    1973-. Bds: Cnty. Regional Planning Cmsn.;
Planning Bd. Party: Cnty. Rep. Com. 1975-77.
Prev: Bd. of Trustees, Airline Community School
1972-75. Occ: Clerk. B: 11/9/46. Add: Town
Hall, Aurora 04408.

Bangor. PATRICIA A. FINNIGAN (D)
    1975-. Bds: Penobscot Valley Reg. Planning
Cmsn.; Area Transportation Com.; Ch., Community
Dev. Com. Party: State Alt. 1974, '76; Dem. City
Com.; State Platform Com. 1976. Prev: Co-Ch.,
Citizens Adv. Com. 1972-73. Org: LWV; WPC. Educ:
U. of Me. 1974 BA. B: 10/31/52. Add: 129 Palm
St., Bangor 04401 (207)947-8321.

Bangor. BARBARA G. MC KERNAN
    73 Harlow St., Bangor

Bar Harbor. PATRICIA S. CURTIS
    Main Street, Bar Harbor

Baring Platation. KATHLEEN DOTEN
    Town Hall, Baring Plantation 04610.

Barnard Plantation. SUSAN DEAN
    RFD 1, Brownville 04414.

Bath. DOROTHY E. KELLEY
    City Hall, Bath 04530.

Beals. EILEEN L. BEAL (D)
    1968-. Bds: Govt. Grants for Town Projects.
Party: Warden Voting Booths 1968-77; Ballott
Clerk 1974-77. Prev: Postal Clerk. Org: Histor-
ical Society; Bicentennial Com. B: 12/31/18.
Add: Perio Pt., Beals 04611 (207)497-2286.

Beddington. MARY M. LANE (I)
    1975-. B: 1/9/22. Add: Star Route P/O,
Cherryfield 04622 (207)638-2311.

Belgrade. KATHERINE DAMEN
    Town Hall, Belgrade 04917.

Boothbay Harbor. LEONIE GREENWOOD-ADAMS
    Oak Street, Boothbay Harbor

Brewer. ANN MARIE DYER (D) **
    1973-. Bds: Regional Planning Cmsn. Educ:
U. of Maine 1970 BA; Eastern Maine General School
of Nursing 1957 RN. Occ: Nurse. B: 1/28/36.
Add: 364 N. Maine, Brewer 04412.

Brooklin. LORNA J. BRYANT
    Town Hall, Brooklin 04616.

Brownville. ROBERTA SMITH
    Town Hall, Brownville 04414.

Brownville Junction. CAROLYNE JONES
    Brownville Jct.

Brunswick. CHARLOTTE Y. GUPTILL
    61 Federal St., Brunswick

Brunswick. HELEN GREENE SCHLAACK (R) **
    1973-. Bds: Notary Public. Org: Medical
Group Managers Assoc. Educ: Radcliffe 1942 BS.
Occ: Business Manager, Medical Group. B:
4/13/18. Add: 9 Curtis St., Brunswick 04011.

Bucksport. DOROTHY L. SEEKINS
    Main Street, Bucksport

Byron. MELITA LA BRECQUE (D)
    1975-. Bds: Town Tax Assessor. Org: Me.
Teachers Assoc.; NEA. Educ: St. Lawrence U.
1972 BS. Occ: Teacher. B: 7/28/50. Add:
Rt. 17, Byron 04275.

Calais. LUCY P. THOMPSON (R)
    1975-. Bds: Ch. Property Com.; Schools &
Welfare Com. Educ: Bates Coll. 1939 BS. Occ:
Manager, Meals on Wheels Program. B: 6/14/17.
Add: 18 Lafayette St., Calais 04619
(207)454-2521.

Camden. SHIRLEE CARLSON
    92 Washington St., Camden

Cape Elizabeth. STELLA B. PATTEN
    Town Hall, Cape Elizabeth 04107.

Caribou. LEOLA GUERRETTE (D)
    1972-. Bds: Ch., Solid Waste Com.; Bicen-
tennial Com.; Cemetery Com. Party: State Del.
1970,'74; Local Secretary/Treasurer 1970-75;
Cnty. Secretary 1970-75. Prev: Deputy Mayor
1976-77. Org: BPW; Legal Secretaries Assoc.
Occ: Legal Secretary. B: 5/15/39. Add: RFD #4,
Box 44, Caribou 04736 (207)498-2581.

Carmel. MARY PERRY
    Town Hall, Carmel 04417.

Carrahassett Valley. MARTHA J. AYOTTE
    Carrahassett Valley.

Cary Plantation. LAURA MC GARY
    North Amity 04465.

Carroll Plantation. SHIRLEY BURRILL
                ANITA TOBY
    Springfield.

Caslo. EVORA JORDAN (D)
    1975-. Bds: Budget Com.; Planning Bd.; Study
Com. Party: State Del. 1968-76; Local Dem. Ch.
1975-77; Local Dem. Secretary/Treasurer 1970-75.
Prev: Educ. Finance Cmsn. 1976-77; Budget Com.
1970-75. Org: NEA; Dem. Club; Cnty. Dem's.
Educ: U. of Me. 1966 MA. Occ: Teacher. B:
11/17/31. Add: Box 134, Rt. 121, Caslo 04015
(207)627-4515.

Charleston. NANCY NOYES
    P.O. Box 102, Charleston.

Cherryfield. BARBARA R. KNEELAND
    Academy Building, Cherryfield.

China. GLORIA ELLIS
    South China 04926.

Columbia. NANCY GREENE
    Town Hall, Columbia Falls 04623.

Columbia Falls. DAWN MAYNARD
    Columbia Falls.

Columbia Falls. SALLY D. THOMPSON (D)
    1970-. Org: PTC. Educ: Wash. State Teachers
    Coll. 1965 BS. B: 4/21/43. Add: Columbia Falls
    04623 (207)483-4067.

Cranberry Isles. MARGARET BUNDY
    Cranberry Isles.

Cranberry Isles. KAREN BUNKER
    Islesford.

Cranberry Isles. POLLY STOREY
    Cranberry.

Cumberland. MARY LOUISE SMITH
    Box 206, Cumberland.

Cutler. ARLENE DENNISON
    Cutler.

Cutler. RUTH MC NEELAND
    Town Hall, Cutler 04626.

Dallas Plantation. MARY-LYN FIELD
                     HERMIA STEWARD
    Rangeley.

Damariscotta. MARILYN HARVIE (D)
    1975-. Prev: Planning Bd. 1973-75. Occ:
    Bookkeeper. B: 8/4/42. Add: Egypt Rd.,
    Damariscotta 04543 (207)563-5168.

Deblois. LENA O. TORREY
    1938-. Prev: Town Treas.; Town Clerk. B:
    5/13/1895. Add: Deblois 04622.

Deblois. VIRGINIA A. TORREY
    1957-. Bds: Town Clerk 1957-present. B:
    2/8/22. Add: Deblois 04622 (207)638-2271.

Denmark. LESLEE K. POLLINA (I)
    1977-. Prev: Town Clerk 1974-77. B: 9/4/50.
    Add: RR 1, Denmark 04022 (207)452-2163.

Dexter. ARLENE M. PAGE (D)
    1974-. Org: Dexter Devt. Occ: Store Owner.
    B: 7/22/14. Add: 21 Lion Hl., Dexter 04930
    (207)924-7427.

Dover-Foxcroft. KATHRYN D. MERRILL (R)
    1975-. Bds: Tax Assessing Cmsn.; Ch., Health
    & Welfare Cmsn. Party: State Del. 1977. Occ:
    Clerk. B: 12/11/23. Add: Box 52, Dover-Foxcroft
    04426.

Durham. BARBARA ELIZABETH CHESLEY (D)
    1974-. Bds: Bd. of Dir's., Me. Municipal Assoc.
    Prev: Planning Bd. 1970-74. Org: Me. Assoc. of
    Assessing Officers; Welfare Dir. Assoc. B:

9/13/24. Add: RR #1, Pownal 04069
    (207)353-2561.

Easton. JACKALENE BRADLEY
    Easton.

East Plantation. MARIE BREWER
    Blaine 04734.

Ellsworth. RUTH FOSTER
    City Hall, Ellsworth.

Fairfield. DOROTHY C. POULIN
    Town Hall, Fairfield 04937.

Falmouth. JEAN H. MAYHEW
    54 Johnson Road, Falmouth.

Falmouth. MARY W. PAYSON
    Town Hall, Falmouth 04105.

Fort Fairfield. TRESSA HETHERINGTON
    Town Hall, Fort Fairfield 04742.

Fort Kent. ROSE NADEAU
    Town Hall, Fort Kent 04743.

Franklin. VERONICA PALMER
    Franklin.

Freeport. NORMA CARTER
             VAUGHNDELLA CURTIS
    Lambert Rd., Ext., Freeport.

Glenburn. AGNES R. BRAYSON (D)
    1976-. Prev: School Bd. 1942-47. Org:
    Senior Citizens Club. B: 2/28/12. Add: RFD 1,
    Box 223 A, Bangor 04401.

Gorham. EVELYN KING
    163 Main St., Gorham.

Gouldsboro. RITA W. CHELLI
    Box 69, Prospect Harbor

Grand Falls Plantation. THELMA HARRIMAN
    Town Hall, Burlington 04417.

Grand Falls Plantation. CYNTHIA J. HOBBS (R)
    1977-. Prev: Bd. of Health 1974-77; School
    Com. 1974-77. B: 10/3/47. Add: Rt. 188, Grand
    Fls. Pltn.

Greene. MARGARET RICHMOND
    Town Hall, Greene 04236.

Greenville. MARTHA R. BURTON
    Box 46, Greenville.

Greenwood. MARGERY R. SWAN (R)
    1976-. Prev: Treas. 1968-76. Org: Me.
    Municipal Assoc.; Assoc. of Assessing Officers.
    B: 12/2/34. Add: E. Bethel Rd., Locke Mills
    04255 (207)875-2773.

Hammond Plantation. IRIS MC IVER
    RFD 1, Houlton 04730.

Hampden. SANDRA PRESCOTT
    MRC Box 11, Bangor 04401.

Harrington. GWENDOLYN GRANT
Harrington.

Harrington. LEAH M. PARKER (D)
1976-. Bds: Conservation. Prev: Rd. Cmsnr.
1975-77; Town Clerk 1968-77. Occ: Vista Volunteer
B: 2/27/15. Add: Old Addison Rd., Harrington
04643 (207)483-2221.

Haynesville. BARBARA ALDRICH
Town Office, Haynesville.

Hersey. JEANETTE GALLAGHER
Patten.

Houlton. SARA DOUGLAS
Town Hall, Houlton 04730.

Industry. SONYA CIRKS
Rt. #1, Farmington 04938.

Jonesport. GLORIA FEENEY
Town Office, Jonesport.

Lisbon. LINDA WOODARD
Perry Road, Lisbon.

Livermore Falls. PATRICIA A. ROWE (D)
1976-. Bds: Cnty. CETA. Party: State Del.
1968; State Alt. 1976; Town Treasurer 1976. Prev:
Sewer Com. 1975-76; Recreation Com. 1974-76.
Educ: Regis Coll. 1959 BA; Ind. U. 1961 MSEd.
B: 3/3/38. Add: Heritage Rd., Livermore Fls.
04254 (207)897-3321.

Lubec. ANN UNOBSKY THEEMAN
Town Hall, Lubec 04652.

Machias. SHIRLEY LOOK
Town Hall, Machias 04654.

Macwahoc Plantation. JUNE BERG
Town Hall, Kingman 04451.

Magalloway Plantation. FAY VAUGHN
Town Hall, Errol, NH 03579.

Mattawamkeag. PATRICIA GRAHAM
Mattawamkeag.

Millbridge. ESTHER M. BEAL
Town Hall, Milbridge 04658.

Millinocket. NATHALIE V. MC GIBBON (D) **
1971-. Bds: Bd. of Dir. Housing Corporation;
Nursing Cmsn. Org: Dem. Club. B: 6/18/32. Add:
101 Massachusetts Ave., Millinocket 04462
(207)723-8277.

Millinocket. LAURETTA RUSH (D)
1966-. Bds: CETA; Me. Leg. Com.; Criminal
Justice Com. Party: State Del. 1936-77; Nat. Del.
1936-70; Cnty. Ch. 1940-46; Cnty. Committeewoman
1936-77; Town Secretary 1936-54; Cnty. Secretary
1936-54. Prev: Me. Leg. Com. 1965-72; CETA 1976;
Criminal Justice Com. 1976-77. Org: Ct. Clerks
Assoc.; Friends of Retarded; Dem. Town Club; Dem.
Cnty. Club. B: 10/19/12. Add: 153 Maine Ave.,
Millinocket 04462 (207)723-9701.

Milo. JANET S. VALENTE
Prespect Street, Milo.

Monhegan Plantation. RUTH PADDOCK STANLEY (D)
1973-. Bds: Monhegan Water Co.; Planning
Com. Org: City & Town Clerk's Assoc. Educ:
Bennington Coll. 1971 BA. B: 1/6/49. Add:
Monhegan Island 04852 (207)372-9663.

Monson. DOROTHY A. HOLMBOM (D)
1975-. Prev: Planning Bd. 1973-75; School Bd.
1965-69; CETA Cnty. Bd. 1975-77. Org: Me.
Family Planning Assoc.; Women's Club.; Historical
Society. Occ: Retail Store Clerk. B: 8/3/26.
Add: RFD 2, Guilford, 04443 (207)997-3641.

Monticello. PHYLLIS WADE
Town Hall, Monticello 04760.

Montville. LOIS DAVIS
Thorndike.

Moro Plantation. CARRIE T. PALMER
RFD 1, Smyrna Mills 04780.

Mount Desert. PEARL S. BORDEAUX
Town Office, Northeast Harbor.

Naples. NANCY L. BUSHELL (D) **
1974-. Bds: Legislative Policy Making Com.
B: 11/24/36. Add: Box 2, Lake House Rd., Naples
04055 (207)693-6364.

Nashville Plantation. SHIRLEY A. CHARETTE (R)
1962-. Prev: Town Clerk 1961-75; School Bd.
1962-70. Occ: Busdriver. B: 2/25/40. Add:
Rte. 1, Box 107A, Ashland 04732 (207)435-6537.

Nashville Plantation. ERNESTINE DONOVAN
RFD 1, Ashland 04732.

Norridgewock. NYOKA BISHOP
Town Office, Norridgewock.

Norway. WINONA PALMER
Town Hall, Norway 04268.

Orland. BETTY S. CHAVAREE
Castine Road, Orland.

Orland. MRS. EARL SOPER
Star Rt., Orland.

Orono. PATRICIA ANN CLARK (D)
1972-. Bds: Ch., Municipal Sewer Com.; Bus
Com.; Finance Com. Prev: Urban Renewal Cmsn.
1970-72. Org: LWV. Educ: U. of Me. 1975 BA.
Occ: Bank, Bd. of Dir's. B: 3/24/29. Add: 15
Mayo St., Orono 04473 (207)866-4781.

Orono. MADELEINE R. FREEMAN (D)
1971-. Bds: Exec. Com., Me. Municipal Assoc.;
Penobscot Cnty. Manpower Planning Council; Ch.,
Ordinance Com. Org: LWV; Health Assoc. B:
2/10/26. Add: 13 Glenwood St., Orono 04473.

Orrington. HELEN M. TUPPER
RFD #2, Orrington.

Otis. BRENDA TATE
    Ellsworth.

Oxbow Plantation. JEAN RHINEHALT
    Town Hall, Oxbow Plantation 04764.

Passamaquoddy Indian Reservation. MARY ALTVATER
    Pleasant Point 04563.

Passamaquoddy Indian Reservation. PHILOMENE DANA
                                    DELIA MITCHELL
    Indian Township 04668.

Passamaquoddy Indian Reservation. JEANNETTE NEPTUNE
    Pleasant Point 04563.

Patten. SUSANNE A. CHASE (I)
    1974-. Bds: Overseer of Poor. Prev: Budget
Com. 1973-75; Overseer of Poor 1974-75. Org:
Housing Authority. B: 11/1/38. Add: Box 159,
Patten 04765.

Penobscot Reservation. EVA BISULCA
                        GAIL DAIGLE
                        VIOLET FRANCIS
                        BERNICE LOLAR
                        VIVIAN MASSEY
                        BEATRICE PHILLIPS
                        EVELYN SAPIEL
                        ERNESTINE TOMER
    Indian Island, Old Town 04468.

Phippsburg. DONNA GAIL ROBERTS (R)
    1974-. Org: PTA. B: 1/29/34. Add: Star Rte.
Box 60, Phippsburg 04562 (207)389-2653.

Presque Isle. BRENDA B. BROWN
               JEAN B. HARDING
    City Hall, Presque Isle 04769.

Reed Plantation. BEATRICE BROWN
    Wytopitlock 04497.

Richmond. GALINA PANKO
    Sampson Street, Richmond.

Ripley. SYLVIA BUBAR
    RFD #1, Harmony 04942.

Rockport. MARJORIE C. JONES
    Town Hall, Rockport 04856.

Roque Bluffs. SUSAN ZURHORST
    Rt. #1, Machias.

Sabattus. ANNETTE B. STURTEVANT
    Town Hall, Sabattus 04280.

St. George. MARJORIE J. COOK (D)
    1968-. Bds: Assessor. Party: Me. Dem. Com.
1966-70; Cnty. Dem.; Local Dem. Com. Prev: Keep
Maine Scienic Com.; Me. Leg. Task Force Fisheries;
Me. Library Task Force. Educ: U. of Me. 1978 BS.
Occ: VISTA Volunteer. B: 12/28/21. Add: Wallston
Rd., Tenants Harbor 04860.

Scarborough. REBECCA I. WARREN
    102 Fogg Rd., Scarborough.

Shapleigh. RUTH HAM
    P.O. Box 66, Shapleigh.

Shirley. MARY NYE
    Shirley Mills.

Solon. MIRIAM A. CORO (D)
    1974-. Prev: Tax Collector 1961-73. B:
11/27/21. Add: 59 S. Main St., Solon 04979
(207)643-2541.

Somerville. VIRGINIA A. BRANN
    Box 32, Windsor 04363.

South Berwick. DORIS BLANCHARD
                NORMA R. TUTELIAN
    180 Main St., South Berwick.

South Thomaston. NANCY POMROY (D)
    1976-. Bds: Planning Bd. Party: State Del.
1972-76; Ch., Town Com. 1972-78; Sec., Cnty. Com.
1972-76; Member, Platform Com. 1976. Prev:
School Bd. 1974-75. Occ: Taxidermist. B:
10/12/39. Add: So. Thomaston 04858
(207)596-6584.

Southwest Harbor. SANDRA LEWIS
    Town Office, Southwest Harbor.

Springfield. RUTH LEWIS
    Springfield.

Surry. ALFREDA J. DAIGLE (I)
    1976-. Occ: Mail Driver. B: 4/9/35. Add:
Morgan Bay Rd., Surry 04684 (207)667-2082.

Swanville. CATHERINE MIKLOVICH
    Rt.#2, Belfast.

Thomaston. NELLIE HICKMAN
    258 Main St., Tomaston.

Tremont. ROSE E. GALLANT
    Seal Cove 04674.

Tremont. ELEANOR MAYO
    Bass Harbor.

Tremont. ESTHER M. TRASK
    Bernard.

Veazie. DOROTHY D. HENDERSON
         MARY E. SILVER
    MRB, Box 337, Bangor.

Vinalhaven. OLGA CARLETON
    Town Office, Vinalhaven.

Waldo. KATHERINE C. LITTLEFIELD
    RFD 3, Waldo 04915.

Waldoboro. BETTY LOU LEE
    Town Hall, Waldoboro 04572.

Warren. JUDITH BARTER
    Rt. #1, Thomaston 04861.

Waterville. LOUISE SMITH
    City Hall, Waterville 04901.

Wayne. ELINOR H. AULT
    Wayne.

Wellington. KAREEN ANDRUS
     Wellington.

Wells. HELEN B. COLBY (R)
     Bds: Ch., Bicycle Safety Com.; York Cnty.
Health Services. Org: Cnty. Law Enforcement; Cnty.
Extension Women; Women of Me. Extension Assoc.;
Citizens for Better Courts. B: 10/6/22. Add:
R.D. #2, Box 455, Wells 04090.

Westbrook. JANET L. CARGILL
     35 Longfellow Dr., Westbrook.

Westmanland Plantation. BARBARA MILLER
     RFD 1, Stockholm 04783.

Westport. DANA CROCKER
     RFD #2, Wiscassett.

Winslow. LOIS J. SHAW
     Joe Ave., Winslow.

Winthrop. DONNA S. IRVINE
     Central St., Winthrop.

State Boards and Commissions

     Office of the Governor, State Capitol Bldg.,
     Augusta 04330.

Aging, Committee on
     MARION S. BARABY
     CONSTANCE H. CARLSON
     KATHLEEN GOODWIN
     SARAH E. MORSE
     LEORA PRENTISS

Alcohol and Drug Abuse Prevention and Treatment,
Council on
     SISTER MARY ANASTASIA
     MINNETTE H. CUMMINGS
     ALBERTA R. NICOLA
     OLYMPIA J. SNOWE

Archives Advisory Board
     DORRIS ISAACSON

Arts and Humanities, Commission on
     RACHEL ARMSTRONG
     BETSEY COE
     ANNE R. ERWIN
     ADA GRAHAM
     ANNE HAZLEWOOD-BRADY
     NANCY LEE
     MARGARET T. MAST
     JANE MOODY

Capitol Planning Commission
     LILLIAN UTTERBACK

Children and Youth, Committee on
     CYNTHIA BALDWIN
     FLEURETTE R. BANNON
     ALICE BEAN
     LINDA DUNNING
     LINDA FAIRBANKS
     KATHERINE B. FINNEGAN
     FRANCES SEAMAN
     SUZANNE E. K. SMITH
     BEVERLY TEAGUE

MARY A. WHEELER

Corrections Advisory Commission
     PAULA H. ELKINS
     KATHRYN C. SMITH

Cosmetology Board
     MARILYN BEDIGAN
     FRANCES COTTA DAVIS
     LEONIE B. KNOWLES
     LINDA J. MOODY

County Records Board
     OLIVE B. MOORE

Critical Areas Advisory Board
     LINDA CLARK
     L. CORINNE MANN
     PATRICIA STIMETS

Education, Board of
     SYLVIA V. LUND
     JULIA L. NAULT
     LUCILLE SHEPPARD

Education Finance, Commission on
     ELIZABETH MITCHELL

Employment of the Handicapped, Committee on
     RONA BACKSTROM
     LILLIAN CARON
     ELAINE GAGNE
     PEGGY HARNOIS

Environmental Protection, Board of
     EVELYN JEPHSON

Hearing Aid Dealers and Fitters, Board of
     CORA L. BROWN
     ANNE P. GIROUX

Historic Preservation Commission
     HELEN CAMP
     GLORIA DUCLOS
     ANN V. MICHAUD

Human Rights Commission
     JEANNINE CLARK
     TERRY ANN LUNT-AUCOIN
     MEREDITH RING

Land Use Regulation Commission
     MARY MC EVOY

Library Commission
     BETSEY COE
     ELSA COHEN
     JANE ANN COOPER
     CAROLYN CORNETT
     LENORE HILTON
     HELEN OLIVER

Licensure of Administrators of Medical Care
Facilities other than Hospitals, Board of
     ETHEL STOVER

Maine Institution for the Blind, Board of Directors
     MARJORIE AWALT
     FLORENCE HARRIETT CHARRON
     SUZANNE D. KANNEGIESER
     RUTH B. LEAVITT

Maine's Future, Commission on
    MARION FULLER BROWN
    LILLIAN CARON
    ESTHER HAWLEY
    SYLVIA LUND
    JENNIE MAGARO
    MARY MERRILL
    ABIGAIL C. NORLING
    SISTER LUCY POULIN
    MARY RINES THOMPSON
    ROBERTA WELL

Medical Laboratory Commission
    LORRAINE M. DUSTIN
    JANICE O. NICHOLS

Milk Commission
    JULIA S. HAHNEL
    MARIA HURLEY
    THELMA LIPMAN

Municipal Records Board
    JUDITH HUNTER
    WILMA MOSES

Nursing, Board of
    FAY E. INGERSOL
    MARION M. KLAPPMEIR
    NAOMI MC IVOR
    BARBARA ROACH
    JUDITH T. STONE
    SISTER MARY CONSUELA WHITE

Optometry, Board of
    BETTY HANSEN

Personnel Board
    LAURA NAWFEL
    CHRYSTAL POMROY
    PATRICIA E. RYAN

Post-Secondary Education Commission
    PHYLLIS D. ABBOTT

Probation and Parole Board
    FRANCES M. JACKSON

Problems of Mentally Retarded, Committee on
    GAYLE E. CORNELL
    FRANCES N. FINK
    RUTH L. PENNELL
    SHEILA D. ROGERS
    CHARLOTTE H. WHITE

Public Broadcasting, Committee on
    PATRICIA M. COLLINS
    MARYLINE WHITE

Real Estate Brokers and Salesmen, Board of
    ELAINE B. LITTLEFIELD

Registration of Voters, Board of
    NELLIE ARSENAULT
    DOROTHY M. BOWLEY
    THERESA M. BRENNAN
    F. EVELYN CATES
    FLORENCE COUTURIER
    ALINE FONTAINE
    RITA FORTIER
    JEAN A. GWAYDOSKY
    EMMA JORDAN

    OLIVINE LIBHART
    MARILLA MAC ISAAC
    DORIS MICHAEL
    LILLIAN MICHAUD
    LORRAINE MORREY
    LILLIAN MURPHY
    MARION B. NOBLE
    JUNE NOYES
    VIRGINIA O'REILLY
    DOROTHY POULIN
    LOUISE E. ST. ONGE
    ESTHER G. SMITH
    PHYLLIS STAFFORD
    BARBARA TEMPLE
    ELEANOR M. VAN BLARCOM
    MARILYN WORREY

Revise the Statutes Relating to Juveniles,
Commission to
    JEANNE A. ROSSE

Revision of the Criminal Laws, Commission to
Prepare a
    CAROLINE GLASSMAN
    EDITH L. HARV

Scenic Committee
    MARJORIE J. COOK

Social Worker Registration, Board of
    EILEEN CROCKER FRANCIS

State Museum Commission
    NATALIE BUTLER
    ANN M. DICKINSON
    RUTH REED MRAZ
    NANCY L. SNOW
    DORIS PIKE WHITE

Veterans Small Business Loan Authority
    PAULYNE D. BULL
    BERNADETTE A. MORIN

Maryland

State Legislature

State Senate

ROSALIE SILBER ABRAMS (D)
1970-. Bds: Ch., Humane Practices Cmsn. of Md.; Governor's Cmsn. on ERA; Special Senate Com. on Rape & Related Offenses. Party: Coord., Md. Com. for Carter 1976; Exec. Com., State Central Com. 1976. Prev: State Del. 1966-70. Org: Exec. Council, Community Involvement Com.; OWL; Safety First Club of Md.; Amer. Physical Therapy Assoc.; Md. Cmsn. on Women; Bd. of Dir's., Md. Food Com.; Govt. Relations Com., Jewish Council. Educ: Sinai Hospital School of Nursing 1938 RN; Johns Hopkins U. 1963 BS; 1969 MA. Occ: Realtor. B: 6/2/16. Add: 6205 Wirt Ave., Baltimore 21215 (301)486-6374.

MARGARET C. SCHWEINHAUT (D)
1961-. Dist: 18. Bds: Ch., Exec. Nominations Com.; Judicial Proceedings Com.; Legislative Policy Com. Prev: State Rep. 1954-60. Org: BPW; LWV; Nat. Council on Aging. Add: 3601 Saul Rd., Kensington 20795 (301)946-3111.

VERDA WELCOME (D) **
1963-. Dist: 40. Bds: Legislative Council; Governor's Com. on Human Relations; Md. Cmsn. on Status of Women; Security Guard Cmsn.; Health & Welfare Council; Day Care Licensing Advisory & Study Com. Party: Del., 1964 Dem. Nat. Conv. Bd. of Governor's, District Org. Prev: Md. House of Delegates 1959-63. Org: ACLU; ADA; AAUW; Citizens Planning & Housing Assoc.; Internat. League of Peace & Freedom; LWV; NAACP; Southern Regional Educ. Bd.; Urban League; Women's Dem. Club. Educ: N.Y.U. 1943 MA. Add: 2101 Liberty Heights Ave., Baltimore 21217 (301)267-5794.

State House

PATRICIA L. AIKEN (D)
1974-. Dist: 33. Party: Precinct Leader 1965-77. Prev: Soil Conservation Supervisor 1972-77. Org: NOWL; Leg. Study Group; WPC; LWV; Common Cause; Mental Health Assoc.; Women's Dem. Club. B: 5/27/22. Add: 501 Epping Forest Rd., Annapolis 21401 (301)269-2345.

KAY G. BIENEN (D)
1974-. Dist: 21. Bds: Ch., Sub Com. on Flood Control; Governor's Cmsn. on Funding Educ. of Handicapped Children; Energy Com. Party: Nat. Del. 1972; Chief Cnty. Election Judge 1968-74. Prev: Prince George's Cnty. Goals Adv. Com. 1971-72; Cnty. Child Abuse Task Force 1974-75. Org: OWL; Leg. Study Group; Mental Health Assoc.; Civic Assoc.; LWV; Dem. Club; PTA. Educ: Skidmore Coll. 1959 BA. B: 1/1/19. Add: 12411 Radnor Ln., Laurel 20811 (301)269-2741.

BERT BOOTH (R)
1974-. Dist: 11. Org: OWL; LWV; NOW; Citizen's Planning & Housing Assoc.; Md. Conf. of Social Concern; GOPhers. B: 8/24/25. Add: 11231 Greenspring Ave., Lutherville 21093 (301)269-2546.

MARILYN GOLDWATER (D)
1974-. Dist: 16. Party: Precinct Ch. 1965-68. Org: ANA; Nurses Coalition for Action in Politics; LWV; Concerned Citizens for Juvenile Justice; Women's Nat. Dem. Club. Educ: Mt. Sinai Hospital School of Nursing 1958 RN. B: 1/29/27. Add: 5508 Durbin Rd., Bethesda 20014.

HATTIE N. HARRISON (D)
1973-. Party: Ch., Dist. State Central Com. 1971-73; Leg. Sub Com. Prev: Dunbar Neighborhood Facilities Ctr. 1973- ; Senior Community Aide 1968-73. Org: Citizens for Fair Housing; Eastside Dem. Org.; Md. Assoc. for Mental Health; Neighborhood Management System Parent Group; NOWL; Nat. Black Caucus; LWV; NAACP; NOW; Nat. Laboratory for the Advancement of Educ. Educ: Antioch Coll. 1976 BA. B: 2/11/28. Add: 2721 Mura St., Baltimore 21213.

SHEILA K. HIXSON (D)
1976-. Dist: 20. Bds: Environmental Matters Com. Party: State Central Com. 1974-76; Cnty. Central Com. 1974-76; State Officer 1964-66; Dist. Secretary 1963-67. Org: BPW; Nat. Dem. Club; Women's Dem. Club. Educ: Northern State Teachers Coll. 1953 BS. Occ: Consultant. B: 2/9/33. Add: 1008 Broadway Cir., Silver Spring 20904 (301)269-2354.

ANN R. HULL (D)
1966-. Dist: 22. Bds: Md. Cmsn. on Intergovt. Cooperation. Org: Assoc. of Amer. Geographers; NOWL; LWV; Md. Community Coord. Child Care. Educ: U. of Wash. 1945 BA; Syracuse U. 1948 MA. B: 2/24/25. Add: 1629 Drexel St., Takoma Park 20012 (301)269-2741.

NANCY K. KOPP (D)
1974-. Bds: Appropriations Com.; Ch., Joint Com. on Program Review in Educ. & Social Services; Com. on Leg. Improvement & Modernization. Party: Precinct Ch., 1970-71. Prev: Montgomery Cnty. Cmsn. on Women 1970-71. Org: APSA; Women's Caucus for Political Science; Suburban Md. Fair Housing; LWV; Alliance for Dem. Reform; Historical Society; Citizens Assoc.; Womens Suburban Dem. Club. Educ: Wellesley Coll. 1965 BA; U. of Chicago 1968 MA. B: 12/7/43. Add: 6301 Dahlonega Rd., Bethesda 20016 (301)269-2651.

HELEN L. KOSS (D)
1970-. Dist: 19. Org: OWL; LWV; AAUW; Nat.
Women's Dem. Club. Educ: Bennington Coll. 1942
BA. B: 6/3/22. Add: 3416 Highview Ct., Wheaton
20902 (301)269-2651.

LENA K. LEE (D) *
1967-. Dist: 38. Org: ABA; NOWL; BPW; NAACP;
Urban League; Women's Club; Amer. Judicature Soc.
Educ: Morgan State Coll. 1939 BS; NYU 1947 MA; U.
of Md. 1952 LLB; 1971 JD. Add: 1818 Madison Ave.
Baltimore 21217 (301)267-5072.

LUCILLE MAURER (D)
1969-. Dist: 19. Bds: Ways & Means; Ch., Md.
Com. on Intergovt. Coop.; Council Postsecondary
Accreditation: Party: Cnty. Liason 1974. Prev:
Md. Constitutional Conf. 1967-68; Montgomery Cnty.
Bd. of Educ. 1960-68. Org: BPW; AAUW; LWV; Child
Day Care Assoc.; Common Cause; Mental Health
Assoc.; WPC; NOW; WEAL; Women's Suburban Dem's;
Dem. Club; Alliance for Dem. Reform; Historical
Society; OWL. Educ: U. of NH 1942 BA; Yale U.
1945 MA. B: 11/21/22. Add: 1023 Forest Glen Rd.,
Silver Spg. 20901 (301)269-2651.

PAULINE H. MENES (D)
1966-. Dist: 21. Bds: Ch., Maryland Women's
Legislative Caucus; Ch., Special Joint Com. on
Corrections; Cmsn. on Aging. Prev: Campaign Com.
Secretary 1962. Org: BPW; NOWL; Mental Health
Assoc.; Coll. Pk. Woods Civic Assoc.; St. John's
Council on Crime; LWV; Women's Nat. Dem. Club;
Coll. Pk. Youth Service Bd. Member; The Smith-
sonian Assoc. Educ: Hunter Coll. 1945 BA. B:
7/16/24. Add: 3517 Marlbrough Way, College Park
20740.

CATHERINE I. RILEY (D)
1974-. Dist: 6. Bds: House Environmental
Matters Com.; Joint Com. on Program Open Space;
V-Ch., Joint Special Com. on Energy. Party: Dem.
Co-Ch. 1970. Org: NOWL; Com. to Study Implement-
ation of ERA; Md. Service Corps Adv. Council;
Council on Alcoholism; Council of Community
Service; Young Dem's; Dem. Club; Citizens Inter-
ested in Political Expression; N. Md. Society for
Retarded Children. Educ: Towson State U. 1969 BA.
Occ: Legal Asst. B: 3/21/47. Add: 20 Office St.,
Bel Air 21014 (301)838-7010.

IDA G. RUBEN (D) *
1975-. Dist: 20. Bds: Montgomery Ad Hoc Com.
to Study the Status of Women. Party: Precinct Ch.
1964-74. Prev: White House Conferences on Youth,
Aging & Handicapped. Org: Dem. Club; WPC; Legal
Aid Society; PTA; Dem. Women's Club. Add: 11
Schindler Ct., Silver Spring 20903 (301)439-2332

MADELINE RUTKOWSKI (D) *
1975-. Dist: 37. Add: 314 Washburn, Baltimore
21225.

LORRAINE M. SHEEHAN (D)
1974-. Dist: 26. Bds: House Judiciary Com.;
Joint Com. on Rape & Related Offenses; Cnty.
Affairs Com. of the Prince George's Del. Party:
Precinct Coord. for Congressional Campaign 1972;
Campaign Coord. 1976. Prev: Citizen Adv. Bd.
1972-75; Task Force on Community Educ. 1972-73.
Org: Citizen Assoc.; LWV. B: 5/2/37. Add:

3600 Dianna Rd., Suitland 20023 (301)
420-7050.

ELIZABETH S. SMITH (R) *
1975-. Dist: 33. Bds: Com. to Promote
Employment of Handicapped; Legislative Com.
Party: Nat. Alt. 1972; Precinct Leader 1972-74.
Org: Chamber of Commerce; ZONTA; OWL; Rep. Club.
Occ: Radio Station Exec. B: 3/18/34. Add:
Rte. 2, Box 96-C, Davidsonville 21035
(301)267-1344.

JUDITH COGGESHALL TOTH (D)
1974-. Dist: 15-B. Bds: Environmental
Matters; Leg. Adv., Governor's Com. on the
Annotated Code. Party: Precinct Ch. 1967-74.
Org: Civic Fed.; Metropolitan Wash. Cong. of
Citizens; ACLU; New Dem. Coalition; Alliance for
Dem. Reform. Educ: Northwestern U. 1959 BA. B:
10/21/37. Add: 6611 80th Pl., Cabin John
20034 (301)269-2519.

County Commissions

Anne Arundel. VIRGINIA P. CLAGETT (D)
1974-. Dist: 7. Bds: Coastal Zone Management
Cmsn.; Bd. of Dirs. , Anne Arundel General
Hospital; W. Chesapeake Basin Study Phase II.
Org: Md. Assn. of Cntys.; Civic Assoc.; Chesapeake
Environmental Protection Assoc.; Cnty. Dem. Club;
LWV. Educ: Smith Coll. 1965 BA. Occ: Farm
Manager. B: 7/18/43. Add: Holly Hill, Friend-
ship 20758 (301)224-1401.

Anne Arundel. ANN STOCKETT
Dist: 6. Bds: General Devt. Plan Com.;
Regional Planning Council; Bd. of Dir's., Md.
Assoc. of Cnty's.; Cmsn. to Study Implementation
of ERA. Prev: Bd. of Zoning Appeals 1972-74;
Salary Standards Cmsn. 1973; V-Ch., Charter
Revision Cmsn. 1971-72. Org: COPE; Civic Assoc.;
New Dem. Coaltion; Dem. Club. Educ: Hood Coll.
1961 BA. B: 4/11/39. Add: 100 Claude St.,
Annapolis 21401.

Caroline. RACHEL COLLISON
County Courthouse, Denton 21629.

Cecil. MARY A. MALONEY (D)
1970-. Bds: Ch., Wilmington Area Metropolitan
Coord. Council; Eastern Shore Criminal Justice
Cmsn.; Resource Conservation & Devt. of Eastern
Shore. Prev: Cnty. Tax Study Cmsn. 1962-64.
Org: Md. Assoc. of Cnty's.; Women's Club; Women
for Federal Restoration; Md. Historic Trust;
Women Dem. Club. Occ: Outdoor Advertiser. B:
11/17/24. Add: RD #7, Frenchtown Rd., Elkton
21921 (301)398-4100.

Charles. ELEANOR F. CARRICO
County Courthouse, LaPlata 20646.

Howard. RUTH U. KEETON (D) **
1974-. Bds: Ch., Regional Planning Council;
Area Housing Council; Regional Manpower Council;
Regional Transportation Steering Com. Prev:
County Housing Agency 1972-74; Councilwoman 1970-
73. Org: LWV; NAACP; Dem. Clubs. Educ: North-
western U. 1940 BA. B: 3/19/19. Add: 10989
Swansfield Rd., Columbia 21044 (301)465-5000.

Montgomery. ESTHER P. GELMAN (D) **
1974-. Bds: County Del., County Senate.
Party: Precinct Ch. Prev: County Planning Bd. &
State Agency 1970-75; Md. Nat. Capitol, Park &
Planning Cmsn. 1970-75. Org: Anti-Defamation
League; County Civic Assoc.; Dem. Club; PTA.
Educ: U. of Colorado 1952 BA. B: 6/14/31. Add:
8719 Postoak Rd., Potomac 20854 (301)279-1234.

Montgomery. JANE ANN MOORE (D)
1974-. Bds: Health Systems Planning Bd.;
Council of Govt. V-Pres.; Ch., Health Com. Org:
Amer. Sociological Assoc.; African Studies Assoc.;
Common Cause; LWV; Suburban Fair Housing; Help,
Inc.; NAACP. Educ: Oh. Wesleyan U. 1952 BA; Yale
Divinity School 1956 BD; Boston U. 1961 MA; 1966
PhD. Occ: Teacher. B: 3/11/31. Add: 11400
Cloverhill Dr., Silver Spring 20902 (301)
279-1231.

Montgomery. ELIZABETH L. SCULL (D) **
1970-. Bds: Bd. of Social Services; Human
Resources Com. Prev: State Bd. of Educ., Advisory
Com., 1969-70; Housing Authority; Human Relations
Cmsn. 1963-65. Occ: Secretary-Treasurer, Property
Management Firm. B: 6/15/23. Add: 9315 Greyrock
Rd., Silver Spring 20910 (301)279-1231.

Prince George. SARAH ADA KOONCE (D)
1974-. Bds: Energy Cmsn.; Ch., Special Deten-
tions Com.; Ch., Youth Services Com. Prev: State
Repr. 1963-65; Cnty. Assignment Comsr. 1965-74.
Org: NOWL; Civic Assoc.; Dem. Club. B: 10/23/22.
Add: 5409 Chesterfield Dr., Camp Springs 20031
(301)449-6103.

Prince George's. DARLENE Z. WHITE
County Courthouse, Upr. Marlboro 20870.

Somerset. HELEN SUE WARD (I)
1974-. Bds: Hospital Bd.; Cmsn. on Aging.
Org: BPW. Educ: St. Mary's Memorial Hospital
1948 RN. B: 12/9/27. Add: P.O. Box 647,
Crisfield 21817 (301)651-0320.

Mayors

Barnesville. ELIZABETH H. TOLBERT
Bds: Bicentennial Com. Party: V-Ch., Precinct
1960-64. Org: Citizen Assoc.; Historical Society;
Bicentennial Com.; Municipal League. Educ:
Garfield Nursing School 1947 RN. B: 12/5/15.
Add: 18120 Barnesville Rd., Barnesville 20703
(301)972-8460.

Bel Air. JUNE WEEKS
39 Hickory Avenue, Bel Air 21014.

Bladensburg. SUSANNA K. CRISTOFANE
P.O. Box 39, Baldensburg 20710.

Bowie. AUDREY EBBA SCOTT (R)
1976-. Bds: Nat. League of Cities; Council of
Govts.; Md. Municipal League. Party: Precinct Ch.
1970-77. Prev: City Councilwoman 1975-76; Pres.
Bowie Health Center 1971-75. Org: Women in
Municipal Govt.; Women's Club; Citizen's Assoc.;
Rep. Club; Women's Rep. Club; Rep. Breakfast Club.
Educ: Tufts U. 1957 BA. B: 11/25/35. Add: 12109
Long Ridge Lane, Bowie 20715 (301)262-6200.

Brookview. DORIS COLLINS
Rt. 1, Rhodesdale 21659.

Chevy Chase. ANNE K. BUSHART (D)
1974-. Prev: Council Secretary 1974-76.
Educ: Baldwin-Wallace Coll. 1939 BS. Occ:
Chief of Recreational Therapy. B: 4/19/16.
Add: 7406 Ridgewood Ave., Chevy Chase 20015
(301)654-7144.

Delmar. FLORENCE MC GEE
14 E. State St., Delmar 19940.

Friendsville. KAROL RUSH
P.O. Box 6, Friendsville 21531.

Highland Beach. EUNICE M. MATTHEWS (D)
1973-. Org: Nat. Medical Assoc.; Nat. Council
of Negro Women; Neighborhood Club. Educ: Howard
U. 1944 BA; NYU MA. B: 1/11/06. Add: 4628
Blagden Ter. NW, Washington, D.C. 20011
(301)267-6777.

Kensington. JAYNE H. PLANK (R)
1974-. Party: Precinct Ch. 1968-74; Regional
Ch. 1972-74; Asst. Precinct Ch. 1974- . Prev:
Councilwoman 1967-74. Org: Md. Municipal League;
Women's Community Club; Women's Rep. Club; Rep.
Mayor's Assoc.; Rep. Women's Federal Forum.
Educ: George Washington U. 1954 BA. Add: 10005
Frederick Ave., Kensington 20795 (301)949-2424.

Mount Rainier. LAVINIA NALLS (R)
3409 Rhode Island Ave., Mount Rainier 20822.

University Park. RUTH TAYLOR LUTWACK (R)
1974-. Bds: Liason, Prince George Cnty.
Council. Org: Women's Club. Occ: Yarn Shop
Asst. B: 3/30/16. Add: 4308 East-West Hwy.,
University Pk. 20782 (301)927-4262.

Local Councils

Baltimore. VICTORINE Q. ADAMS
100 N. Holliday St., Baltimore 21202.

Baltimore. MARY PAT CLARKE (D)
1975-. Dist: 2. Bds: Central Md. Health
Systems Agency; Mental Health Adv. Com. Prev:
Pres., Greater Homewood Community Corp. 1971-73.
Org: BPW; Health & Welfare Council; Md. Conf. of
Social Concern, Public Relations Com.; Neighbor-
hood Assoc.; New Dem. Club; LWV; PTA. Educ:
Immaculate Coll. 1963 BA; U. of Pa. 1966 MA. B:
6/22/41. Add: 3911 Cloverhill Rd., Baltimore
21218 (301)396-4811.

Baltimore. ROCHELLE SPECTOR
100 N. Holliday St., Baltimore 21202.

Barnesville. IDA LU PRICE (D)
1975-. Org: Nat. Assoc. of Postmasters of
the US; Nat. League of Postmasters; Soroptimist;
Citizens Assoc.; PTA; Bicentennial Com. Occ:
Postmaster. B: 11/4/26. Add: 18200 Barnesville
Rd., Barnesville 20703.

Betterton. KAY BECKER
P.O. Box 154, Betterton 21610.

Boonesboro. SHIRLEY E. METZ
11 St. Paul St., Boonsboro 21713.

Brookview. PATRICIA ROGERS
Rt. 1, Rhodesdale 21659.

Capitol Heights. MARTHA A. TAYLOR (I) **
1974-. Bds: Model Neighborhood Action Bd.
Org: NAACP. B: 9/24/33. Add: 107 Sultan Ave.,
Capitol Heights 20027 (301)336-0626.

Chestertown. JANE B. NEAL
P.O. Box 38, Chestertown 21620.

Cheverly. JOY A. MARCY
6401 Forest Road, Cheverly 20785.

Cheverly. DOROTHY MC CLAIN (D)
1974-. Bds: Ch., Zoning & Open Space Com.;
Prince Georges Combine Communities in Action ;
Adv. Bd. Community Block Grant. Prev: Election
Bd. 1966-72. Org: NAACP; Concerned Citizens of
Cheverly; Democratic Alliance Club; Women's Club.
Occ: Administrative Assistant. Add: 1710 62 Ave.,
Cheverly 20785 (202)576-7187.

Cheverly. DOROTHY H. RYAN (D) **
1974-. Org: Women's Club. B: 10/5/24. Add:
2302 Cheverly Ave., Cheverly 20785 (301)773-8360

Chevy Chase. JULIE W. DAVIS (D) **
1972-. Bds: Environmental Quality Com.; Wash.
Metropolitan Council of Governments; Citizens
Advisory Com. on Health & Environmental Protect-
ion. Party: Ch., Dem. Precinct 1971- . Org:
Alliance for Dem. Reform; Civic Assoc.; Dem. Club;
Environment Coalition; PTA; Women's Dem. Club.
Educ: Duke Univ. 1961 BA. Occ: Information
Analyst. Add: 14 W. Irving St., Chevy Chase
20015 (301)654-6363.

Chevy Chase. PAULINE S. MC GUIRE
P.O. Box 9807, Chevy Chase 20015.

Church Creek. ELIZABETH D. GULLETTE
Church Creek 21622.

College Park. ROSE FIEGHENNE
4500 Knox Road, College Park 20740.

Colmar Manor. MARY FERGUSON
RUTH MERKEL
3701 Lawrence St., Colmar Manor 20722.

Cottage City. AUDREY L. BATEMAN
3700 40th Ave., Cottage City 20722.

Delmar. MARY ANNE SMITH
14 E. State St., Delmar 19940.

Denton. CAROL D. STOCKLEY
P.O. Box 246, Denton 21629.

District Heights. MIRIAM S. HOOK
2000 Marbury Dr., District Heights 20028.

Eagle Harbor. MARY BENNET
HARRIET HUNTER
City Hall, Eagle Harbor 20608.

Edmonston. MABEL M. BASS
MARGARET A. SULLIVAN
5005 52nd Ave., Edmonston 20781.

Fairmount Heights. MAMIE QUARLES
717 60th Pl., Fairmount Heights 20027.

Federalsburg. KAY D. COOPER
103 S. Main, Federalsburg 21632.

Forest Heights. EDITH HART
5508 Arapahoe Dr., Forest Heights 20021.

Frederick. ELIZABETH PYLES BURKET (D)
1973-. Bds: Ch., Transportation Cmsn.;
Historic Dist. Com.; Parks, Streets, Sanitation
Com. Org: Zonta; BPW; Cnty. Civic Fed.; Improvement Foundation. Educ: U. of Md. 1932 BA; 1933
MA. B: 10/8/10. Add: 5 James St., Frederick
21701 (301)662-5161 x 54.

Frostburgh. MARGARET C. JONES
City Hall, Frostburgh 21532.

Galena. MARGARET A. CERENZIA
Galena 21635.

Garrett Park. MABEL M. PETERSON (D)
1975-. Prev: Pres., Garrett Pk. Citizens
Assoc. 1970-75. Org: Md. Municipal League.
Occ: Exec. Asst., Hospital. B: 6/27/20. Add:
4405 Cambria Ave., Garrett Pk 20766.

Glen Rock. NANCY C. LONG
6106 Harvard Ave., Glen Echo 20768.

Goldsboro. DEBORAH A. CONKLIN
MARY E. JACKSON
P.O. Box 32, Goldsboro 21636.

Henderson. ANNABEL CLARK
PEARL JONES
Box 175-B, Henderson 21640.

Hyattsville. MARY MARGARET HALEY
4307 Jefferson St., Hyattsville 20781.

Hyattsville. MILDRED D. HARKNESS (D) **
1972-. Party: Precinct Fund Raiser 1960-75.
Prev: Urban Renewal 1962-70; Youth Com.; Cultural
Cmsn.; Community Action Com. Org: Dem. Club;
PTA; Women's Dem. Club. B: 10/23/24. Add: 5022
38th Ave., Hyattsville 20782 (301)927-0194.

Hyattsville. POLLY ROGERS
4307 Jefferson St., Hyattsville 20781.

Kensington. DOROTHY M. GOODING
KITTY L. RAUFASTE
3710 Mitchell St., Kensington 20795.

Landover Hills. ANNA LEX
4219 70th Ave., Landover Hills 20784.

Laytonsville. JACQUELINE ELLINGTON
P.O. Box 938, Laytonsville 20760.

Luke. GLADYS E. GIFT (R) **
1968-. B: 7/2/10. Add: 133 Mullan Ave.,
Luke 21540 (301)359-3922.

Mardela Springs. EDITH PHILLIPS JOHNSON (R)
    1975-. Bds: Md. Municipal League. Prev: Cnty.
Health Planning Com. 1976- . Org: ANA. Educ:
U. of Md. 1966 BSN. Occ: RN. B: 6/29/31. Add:
Main St., Box 125, Mardela Spgs. 21837 (301)
742-1025.

Midland. ELAINE M. MILLER (R)
    1974-. Bds: Ch., Bicentennial Com. B:
10/17/29. Add: Cemetery Rd., Midland 21542.

Midland. LORRAINE THRASHER
    P.O. Box 43, Midland 21542.

Morningside. BONNIE KAMENICKY
    6601 Woodland, Morningside 20023.

Mountain Lake Park. ETHEL D. BOLTZ (I)
    1974-. Org: NEA. Educ: Fairmont State Normal
Coll. 1946 AB. B: 6/28/07. Add: Oak Hall Dr.
124, Oakland 21550.

Mount Ranier. CHARLOTTE B. MC DONALD
    3409 Rhode Island Ave., Mount Ranier 20822.

New Carrollton. VERA C. WEINBACH (R)
    1976-. Org: Civic Assoc. Educ: U. of Evans-
ville 1960 BS. Occ: Mgr., Educ. Corp. B:
10/14/24. Add: 8340 Verona Dr., New Carrollton
20784 (301)459-6100.

North Beach. MAXINE KERN CRAWFORD
            PATRICIA J. HAYNES
    City Hall, North Beach 20831.

North Brentwood. EDITH L. DAVIS
    P.O. Box 196, North Brentwood 20722.

North Chevy Chase. JAYN ZOPF
    8903 Montgomery Ave., N. Chevy Chase 20015.

Oakland. FRANCES C. RILEY (R)
    1972-. Bds: Ch., Md. Municiapl League; Ch.,
Tri-Cnty. Council for W. Md., Cmsn. on Aging.
Org: Civic Club of Oakland; LWV; Rep. Women's
Club. B: 1/14/10. Add: 321 N. 3rd St., Oakland
21550.

Ocean City. THELMA CONNER
    P.O. Box 158, Ocean City 21842.

Pocomoke. PAIGE V. WEBB
    P.O. Box 29, Pocomoke City 21850.

Poolesville. MARY LU MOYER
    P.O. Box 158, Poolesville 20837.

Port Deposit. ERMA M. KEETLEY
    P.O. Box 95, Port Deposit 21904.

Rising Sun. JO ANN E. HALL (D)
    1976-. Bds: Ch., Maintenance. Prev: Zoning &
Planning Appeals Bd. 1970-76. Org: Md. Municiapl
League. Educ: Md. Coll for Women 1949 BS. B:
11/11/26. Add: N. Walnut St., Rising Sun 21911
(301)658-5353.

Rock Hill. ROSALIE KUECHLER
    P.O. Box 8, Rock Hall 21661.

Rockville. PHYLLIS B. FORDHAM
    1976-. Bds: Health & Environmental Protection
Policy Com.; Human Resources Com.; Council of
Govts. Org: Historical Preservation. Educ: U.
of Md. 1977 BA. B: 1/24/36. Add: 699 Coll. Pky.
Rockville 20850 (301)424-8000.

St. Michaels. HELEN K. PLUMMER (D)
    Bds: Ch., Public Relations. Prev: Pres. of
Council. Org: Municipal League; OES; Historical
Society. Occ: Legal Secretary. B: 1/13/11.
Add: 410 St. Mary's Square, St. Michaels 21663
(301)745-9535.

Seat Pleasant. ROSALIE JONES
            GEORGIANN P. SCOTT
    54 Addison Rd., Seat Pleasant 20027.

Sharpsburg. ANNA L. JAMISON (I)
    1973-. Bds: Planning & Zoning. Occ: Clerk
Typist. B: 12/1/24. Add: 211 W. Main St.,
Sharpsburg 21782.

Somerset. MARY H. CURZAN (D)
    1975-. Org: APSA. Educ: Mich.State U. 1961
BA; Yale U. 1965 PhD. Occ: Editor. B: 10/28/39.
Add: 5519 Uppingham St., Chevy Chase 20015
(301)656-9256.

Sykesville. MAGRUDA H. CARLYLE (D)
    1971-. Bds: Council Pres.; Recreation &
Parks; Ch., Town House Maintenance & Upkeep.
Prev: City Budget 1971-73; Town House Upkeep
1974-76; Police Com. 1974-76. Org: Md. Classi-
fied Employees Assoc. B: 3/28/17. Add: 7316
Brown St., Sykesville 21784 (301)795-0757.

Sykesville. THERESA MORRIS
    7547 Main St., Sykesville 21784.

Takoma Park. MARY ANN MEDINA (D)
    1974-. Bds: Montgomery Cnty. Community Devt.
Block Grant Citizens Adv. Com.; Council of Govt.
Transportation Planning Bd.; Bd. of Dir's.
Project Turnaround. Educ: George Washington U.
1959 BA. B: 10/19/37. Add: 7425 Buffalo Ave.,
Takoma Pk 20012 (301)270-1700.

Taneytown. PHYLLIS SINGEL
    16 E. Baltimore St., Taneytown 21787.

Templeville. BERNICE COLEMAN
    City Hall, Templeville 21670.

Union Bridge. VIVIAN S. NUSBAUM (D)
    1975-. Bds: Council Pres.; Ch., Community
Ctr. Bd. Org: OES. Occ: Clothing Company Worker
B: 7/5/24. Add: 102 E. Locust St., Union Bridge
21791.

University Park. ELLA MAE LEMON
    Box 187, Hyattsville 20781.

Upper Marlboro. HELEN M. WILSON
    P.O. Box 280, Upper Marlboro 20870.

Washington Grove. ANN K. BRIGGS
            JANE PUGHE
    City Hall, Washington Grove 20880.

Williamsport. PATRICIA K. CUSHWA
    Town Hall, Williamsport 21795.

Judges

MARY ARABIAN
    Circuit Court Judge. Add: Baltimore City
Courthouse, Baltimore.

RITA C. DAVIDSON
    Associate Judge. Add: Court of Appeals Bldg.,
Annapolis 21401.

SHIRLEY B. JONES
    Associate Judge. 1961-. Prev: Orphans' Ct.
1959-61; Asst. Atty. General 1958-59; Asst. City
Solicitor 1952-58; Att., Md. Dept of Employment
Security 1946-52. Org: Md. Bar Assoc.; ABA;
Historical Society. Educ: U. of Baltimore AA;
1946 JD. B: 6/27/25. Add: Baltimore Courthouse,
Baltimore City.

State Boards and Commissions

    Office of the Governor, State Capitol Bldg.
    Annapolis 21404.

Aging, Commission
    VIOLA M. GARDNER
    BETTY K. HAMBURGER
    PAULINE H. MENES

Agriculture, Board of Review
    MARGARET G. PROUTY

Alcoholism Control, Advisory Council on
    GLADYS L. AUGUSTUS
    BEVERLY D. DOPKIN
    JANE I. HAYMAKER
    WENDY MATTERS
    DIXIE J. MILLER
    DELORES STREET

Apprenticeship Information Center Advisory Committee
    MARIAN GOETZE
    LORRAINE HOFFMAN
    SUE HOPPE
    JEAN JACKSON
    NANCY MARTIN

Architectural Registration Board
    CONSTANCE R. CAPLAN

Arts Council
    BEATRYCE L. PROSTERMAN
    SHIFRA M. RUBIN

Atomic Energy, Advisory Commission on
    JEAN STIFLER, M.D.

Audiologists
    BETH J. URBAN

Baltimore City Hospital-Nursing Home Study
Commission
    MATILDA SCHAFERBEIN
    MRS. GEORGE VAN BUSKIRK
    CHARLOTTE WHEATLEY

Blind Industries and Services
    GEORGIA MYERS
    DORIS SAMUELS

Capital City, Commission on the
    MRS. J.M.P. WRIGHT

Children's Program Awards Committee
    JEANETTE JOHNSON

Circuit Court Unification, Task Force to Study
    MADELINE SCHUSTER

Civil Defense and Disaster Preparedness Advisory
Council
    MRS. WILLIAM F. WENDLER

Commission to Study the Feasibility of an All-
Purpose Performing Arts Facility in the City of
Annapolis
    ELIZABETH S. SMITH
    BETH M. WHALEY
    MARTHA WRIGHT

Community Colleges, State Board for
    JOSEPHINE BARR
    MRS. HOWARD CRIST

Correction, Parole and Probation, Advisory Board
for
    MARGARET M. DUDLEY
    SUSAN B. HARRIS
    EILEEN MARION

Cosmetologists, State Board of
    CHRISTINA J. ANDERSON
    MARY ELLEN BROOKE
    MRS. HOWARD MC INTYRE
    ELLEN P. MC LANE

Criminal Law, Commission on
    MARY ARABIAN
    ELLEN LUFF

Credit Union Insurance Corporation
    DOROTHY GEORGE

Crime, Task Force on
    PAULINE H. MENES

Developmental Disabilities Council
    MARY ACKERLEY
    CAROL E. BAKER
    NANCY BATHON
    RENNE DIXON
    MARGUERITE HASTINGS
    MRS. ERNIE HONIG
    MURIEL ROSE
    MARGARET ULLE

Domestic Relations Laws, Commission to Study
    BEVERLY ANNE GRONER
    HATTIE N. HARRISON
    DOROTHY CURTIS MELBY

Drug Abuse, Advisory Council on
    PATRICIA RUTH SHER

Economic and Community Development Advisory
Commission
    MARGIE H. MULLER

Education, State Board of
    MARY ELIZABETH ELLIS
    JOANNE T. GOLDSMITH

Election Laws, State Administrative Board of
    ANN SCHISSLER

Emergency Resources Priorities Board
    MRS. RUSSELL POPE

Employees Retirement Review Board
    GLADYS SPRINKLE

Employment Agency Advisory Board
    VERA LE CATO

Environmental Trust
    MRS. NORMAN BAETJER
    MRS. T. HUGHLETT HENRY, JR.
    MRS. HOLGER B. JANSSON

Equal Rights Amendment, Governor's Commission to
Study Implementation of the
    ROSALIE S. ABRAMS
    BE BE BAILEY
    KATHLEEN O'FERRALL FRIEDMAN
    LUCY ANN GARVEY
    BEVERLY ANNE GRONER
    SHIRLEY MC CLENDON
    HELEN PARKER
    CONSTANCE PUTZEL
    CATHERINE I. RILEY
    ANN STOCKETT

Ethics, Board of
    NATALIE R. ZIMMERMAN

Fair Campaign Financing Commission
    MARY CATHERINE BELL
    ETHEL RICH

Financial Disclosure Advisory Board
    DELIA B. SPENCER

Foresters, State Board of Registration for
    NANCY ERWIN

Governor's Consulting Committee for the National
Register of Historic Places in Maryland
    RHODA DORSEY

Handicapped Children, Commission on Funding the
Education of
    KAY G. BIENEN
    ANN C. STOCKETT
    VERDA WELCOME

Health Services Cost Review Commission
    NATALIE BOUQUET

Hereditary Disorders, Commission on
    SHIRLEY R. CLINTON
    MARIAN SCARBOROUGH

High Blood Pressure Commission
    CARMALYN SIMIRAGLIA

Higher Education Loan Corporation
    MRS. W. KENNETH ROOT

Higher Education, State Board
    LUCY KEKER
    MARY L. NOCK

Historical Records Advisory Board
    MARY A. BOCCACCIO
    MRS. ARTHUR STARIN
    MRS. GERRY WOOLDRIDGE

Historical Trust
    MRS. RALPH DONNELLY
    MRS. COLEMAN du PONT
    MRS. EDWIN GRAMKOW
    EILEEN MC GUCKIAN
    MRS. GLENFORD M. MUSSENDEN

Hospital Licensing, Advisory Board on
    VIRGINIA LAYFIELD

Hospitals and Juvenile Institutions, Educational
Coordinating Council for
    MRS. CHARLES B. ANDERSON, JR.
    LEAH S. FREEDLANDER

Humane Practices Commission
    ROSALIE SILBER ABRAMS
    LORRAINE M. SHEEHAN

Human Relations Commission
    MRS. LANE K. BERK
    LINDA GOLDEN
    MURIEL WEIDENFELD

Human Resources
    EDITH G. BLOUNT
    FLORENCE CAVEY

Juvenile Services, Advisory Board of
    FRIEDA L. COLEMAN
    ORA JOHNSON
    VERA M. MC CULLOUGH
    SHERRY PERRIN
    ALMA RANDALL
    BONNIE SNEED
    MYRNA S. TEPPER

Kidney Disease, Commission on
    EDYTH SCHOENRICH

Landlord-Tenant Laws Study Commission
    BONITA DANCEY
    RUTH FRANQUET
    LUCILLE GORHAM

Landscape Architects, Examiners of
    JANET PHILLIPPE

Law Enforcement and the Administration of Justice,
Commission on
    ROSETTA CHASE

Libraries, Advisory Council on
    ANNIE T. REID
    MRS. WILLIAM F. ROBIE
    MRS. EDWARD SATTERTHWAITE
    GRACE SLOCUM

Manpower Planning Office, Advisory Council
    ELAINE NEWMAN

Mental Hygiene, Advisory Council on
    MRS. ERNEST A. LYTE

Nurses, State Board of Examiners of
    JEAN S. FRIZELL
    MARY L. MILLER
    GLADYS PEEVY
    DORIS H. REESE
    SHIRLEY LOU SMACK

Nursing Home Administrators, Board of Examiners of
    SISTER MARY SCHOLASTICA HANDREN
    MARJORIE MAGUIRE
    MARTHA TARUTIS

Ocean City Convention Hall Commission
    ELIZABETH D. SANFORD

Parks Advisory Commission
    ANNE DE JONG

Physical Fitness, Commission on
    RITA KNOX
    ELEANOR M. TICKNER
    JOANNE T. WEINBERG

Physical Therapy Examiners
    JANE SATTERFIELD

Post-Mortem Examiners Commission
    JEAN ROSE STIFLER, M.D.

Practical Plumbing, Commissioners of
    HELEN BURWELL

Psychologists Board
    EVELYN F. HILL

Public Accountancy, State Board of
    YOLANDA D. BROOKS

Public Broadcasting Commission
    REBECCA E. CARROLL
    MARY ROBINSON

Real Estate Commission
    MILDRED B.JONES

Residential Needs of the Retarded, Commission to
Study the
    KAY G. BIENEN
    LUCILLE MAURER

Scholarship Board
    MRS. JOHN E. HESS
    ELIZA MC DANIEL
    SUSAN WRIGHT

School Construction Program, Commission to Study
Revision of the
    JOANNE T. GOLDSMITH
    KITTY SHOAP

Schools for the Deaf, Board of Visitors
    MARGY FEIGELSON
    MARGARET S. KENT
    MRS. JOHN N. MAGUIRE
    MRS. CHARLES MC C. MATHIAS, JR.
    WILMA J. MAUSE

Social Services, Board of
    ROXANNE BERNERT
    SHIRLEY MC NEILL
    JANET ROSEN
    HARRIET TRADER

Spanish-Speaking People, Commission on the Concerns
    ANN A. BEUSCH
    RONA LOIEDERMAN
    BLANCA M. WESTGATE

Speech Pathologists
    MARY STUART FARQUHAR

State Employees Deferred Compensation Plan
    DORIS P. SCOTT

Student Affairs for the University of Maryland,
Advisory Commission on
    MELISSA CABLE
    ALEXANDRIA COSGROVE
    MARY ENO
    BETH HAVLIK
    PATRICE LEWIS
    MARIANNE SCHMITT
    JILL SHEINBERG
    RENEE SILVER

Transportation Commission
    DOROTHY H. STREAKER

Universities and Colleges, Board of Trustees of the
    JOYCE R. PHILLIP
    J. MILLARD TAWES

University of Maryland, Board of Regents
    MARY H. BROADWATER

Veterinary Medical Examiners, State Board of
    CAROL JOHNSON

Vocational-Technical Education, State Advisory
Council on
    NORMA H. DAY
    DELORES HUNT
    PHYLLIS E. REED

War Memorial Commission
    RUTH S. LEVY

Women, Commission for
    ROSALIE S. ABRAMS
    SHOSHANA S. CARDIN
    KATHLEEN M. CARTER
    DAISY B. FIELDS
    LUCILLE GORHAM
    JILL M. GREENBERG
    HATTIE N. HARRISON
    WINIFRED G. HELMES
    ANNE D. HOPKINS
    EDNA D. JOHNSON
    BERTINA A. NICK

JO-ANN ORLINSKY
BETTY PIKE
LEE JOYCE RICHMOND
LINDSAY SCHLOTTMAN
JEAN E. SPENCER
EMILY M. TAYLOR
ESTHER S. VINES
DIANE H. WEAVER
JEANETTE R. WOLMAN

Workmen's Compensation Laws, Commission to Review
Laws Governing the
    ADA EVANS

Science Advisory Council
    RUTH M. DAVIS

Security Guards and Special Police, Commission to
Study the Operation of
    BEATRICE F. MARTIN
    VERDA WELCOME

Massachusetts

State Executive and Cabinet

DOLORES L. MITCHELL (D)
    Cabinet Coordinator. 1975-. Party: State
Del. 1964-68; State Committeewoman 1964-72; Town
Committeewoman 1976. Org: ACLU; Mass. Research
Ctr. Bd.; Americans for Dem. Action; LWV; Finance
Com.; NAACP; Mass. Childrens Lobby; Metropolitan
Council for Educ. Opportunities. Educ: Oh. State
U. 1951 BA. B: 7/23/29. Add: 37 Russell Ave.,
Watertown 02172 (617)727-7185.

EVELYN F. MURPHY (D)
    Secretary of Environmental Affairs. 1975-.
Bds: New England River Basins Cmsn.; Martha's
Vineyard Cmsn. Educ: Duke U. 1961 BA; Columbia
U. 1963 MA; Duke U. 1965 PhD. B: 5/14/40. Add:
20 Dawes Rd., Lexington 02173 (617)727-7700.

CHRISTINE B. SULLIVAN (D)
    Secretary of Consumer Affairs. 1976-. Bds:
Ch., Energy Facilities Siting Council. Party:
State Dem. Committeewoman 1976-80. Prev: New
England Regional Cmsn. 1976; Dir., Energy Facilit-
ies Sitting Council. Org: Health Planning Council.
Educ: Vassar Coll. 1965 BA; Harvard U. 1976 MPA.
B: 5/24/44. Add: Ashburton Pl., Boston 02108.

State Legislature

State Senate

CAROL C. AMICK (D)
    1977-. Bds: Governor's Hanscom Field Task
Force; Com. on Urban Affairs; Com. on Trans-
portation; Com. on Natural Resources. Party:
Town Committeewoman 1971-present. Prev: Charter
Cmsn. of Bedford 1972-73; Library Trustee of
Bedford 1976-present; Com. on Criminal Justice
1975-76; State Repr. 1974-June 1977. Org: Mass.
Legislators Assoc.; Women in Communications;
Mass. Caucus of Women Legislators; Human Relations
Council; LWV; Cmsn. on Status of Women; Citizens
Participation in Political Action. Educ: Iowa
State U. 1968 BS. Add: 277 Great Road, Bedford
01730 (617)727-2571.

ANNA BUCKLEY (D) **
    1973-. Bds: Election Laws & Legislations;
V-Ch. Local Affairs. Party: Secretary, State
Com. Prev: City Councillor, 1972-73. Org:
AFL-CIO; County Dem. League. B: 3/21/24. Add:
16 Rutland Square, Brockton 02401 (617)727-8100.

MARY L. FONSECA (D) **
    1953-. Bds: Asst. Majority Leader; Ch., Educ.
Prev: Fall River School Com., 1945-53. Org: BPW;
Dem. Women's Club. B: 3/30/15. Add: 400 David
St., Fall River 02720 (617)672-4100; 727-5095.

SHARON MARGARET POLLARD (D)
    1976-. Dist: 3. Bds: Commerce & Labor Com.;
Energy Com.; Human Services & Elderly Affairs.
Party: State Del. 1977. Org: Bd. of Trade;
Mass. Legislator's Assoc.; DAR; Women's Civic
Club; Nat. Trust for Historic Preservation;
Citizens for Participation in Politics; LWV.
Educ: Dunbarton Coll. 1972 BA. B: 9/21/50. Add:
12 Pleasant St., Methuen 01844 (617)727-2740.

State House

DORIS BUNTE (D) **
    Dist: 9. Org: Nat. Tenants Assoc.; NAACP;
Citizen's Housing & Planning Assoc.; Mental
Health Center. B: 7/2/33. Add: 120 Humboldt
Ave., Boston 02121 (617)727-2351.

ELEANOR CAMPOBASSO (D) **
    1965-. Dist: 10. Bds: Public Service.
Prev: Town Meeting 1954-70. Org: Municipal
Employees Assoc.; Traffic Policewomen's Assoc.
B: 8/10/23. Add: 15 University Rd., Arlington
02174 (617)727-7676.

GENEVRA COUNIHAN (D) **
    1974-. Dist: 40. Bds: Public Service Com.;
Urban Affairs Com. Educ: U. of Okla. 1944 BA;
Yale U. 1947 JD. B: 12/15/25. Add: 349
Nashawtoc Rd., Concord 01742 (617)727-8206.

MARY FANTASIA (D) **
    1971-. Dist: 8. Party: Nat. Com.; State
Com.; Presidential Elector 1960; 1964. Org:
Legislator's Assoc.; United Fund. B: 10/1/19.
Add: 181 Hudson St., Somerville 02143
(617)721-2560.

ANN C. GANNETT (R) **
1968-. Dist: 53. Bds: Equal Educ. Opportunity; Study of Vocation & Technical Schools; Privacy; Recodify Animal Laws. Org: Common Cause; Ripon; Social Work Agency. B: 11/7/16. Add: 85 Old Connecticut Path, Wayland 02133 (617)727-2584.

MARY H. GOODE (D) **
1975-. Dist: 10. Occ: Assoc. Director. B: 7/2/27. Add: 20 Hawthorne St., Boston 02100 (617)721-5374.

SAUNDRA M. GRAHAM (D)
1977-. Dist: 4. Bds: Urban Affairs Com. Party: Nat. Del. 1972; Ward Dem. Com. 1975- . Prev: V-Mayor, Cambridge 1976- ; City Councilwoman 1972- . Org: Mass. Black Caucus; WPC; Nat. Black Caucus. Educ: U. of Mass. BA; Harvard U. MA. B: 9/5/41. Add: 189 Western Ave., Cambridge 02139 (617)727-7035.

BARBARA E. GRAY (R)
1973-. Dist: 56. Bds: Ways & Means. Party: V-Ch., Local Com. 1975-77. Prev: Planning Bd. 1961-73. Org: LWV; Women's Club. Hot Line. Educ: Conn. Coll. 1948 BA. B: 11/11/26. Add: State House, Boston.

IRIS K. HOLLAND (R)
1972-. Dist: 2. Bds: Joint Leg. Com. on Health Care; Leg. Research Council; Cmsn. on Elder Affairs. Party: Town Com. 1972- . Org: Nat. Assoc. of Legislators; Zonta; Caucus of Women Legislators; Dir., Mental Health Assoc. Educ: Rider Coll. 1940 BS. B: 9/30/20. Add: 38 Hazelwood Ave., Longmeadow 01106 (413)567-1529.

MARIE E. HOWE (D)
1965-. Dist: 7. Bds: V-Ch., Com. on Commerce & Labor; Rules Com. Party: State Del. 1968; Ward & City Com. 1965- . Educ: New England School of Law 1969 JD. Add: 19 Pembroke St., Somerville 02133 (617)727-7676.

ELIZABETH N. METAYER (D) **
1974-. Bds: Transportation Com.; Health Care Com. Party: Town Com. Prev: Ch., Technical Advisory Com., 1965-67. Org: LWV; Secretary Civic Assoc. B: 8/21/11. Add: 33 Arthur St., Braintree 02184 (617)727-5374.

MARY JEANNETTE MURRAY (R)
30 Margin Street, Cohasset 02025.

ELAINE NOBLE (D)
1974-. Dist: 6. Bds: Com. on Educ.; Com. on Rules; Com. on Ethics. Org: NWPC; AAUW; Mass. Civil Liberties Union. Educ: Boston U. 1966 BA; Emerson Coll. 1970 MS; Harvard U. 1974 MEd. Add: 403 Marlborough St., Boston 02115 (617)536-4911.

LOIS PINES (D) **
1973-. Dist: 19. Org: Alderwoman 1972-73; Bar Assoc. Educ: Barnard 1960 BA; Cincinnati School of Law 1963 JD. Occ: Lawyer. B: 8/16/40. Add: 40 Helene Rd., Newton 02168 (617)965-1633; 727-4646.

CAROLINE J. STOUFFER (D)
1976-. Dist: 1. Bds: Nat. Resources & Agric. Party: Nat. Del. 1972; Town Committeewoman 1972-80. Prev: Governor's Cmsn. on Status of Women 1973-74. Org: AGMA; LWV; WPC; ACLU. Educ: Middlebury Coll. 1954 BA. B: 4/5/33. Add: 7 Howard Rd., Hingham 02043 (617)727-2023.

KAREN J. SWANSON (R)
1974-. Dist: 14. Bds: Health Care Com.; Public Service Com. Party: State Del. 1976; Ward Dem. City Com. 1975. Org: BPW. Educ: U. of Mass. 1976 BA. B: 1/15/54. Add: 237 Menlo St., Brockton 02401.

County Commissions

Dukes. SHIRLEY K. FRISCH (R)
1970-. Bds: Martha's Vineyard Cmsn.; Cnty. Extension Service. Party: Town Committeewoman 1974-77. Prev: Finance Com. 1955-75. Org: Zonta; LWV. Educ: Beth Israel Hospital School of Nursing 1940 RN. B: 7/15/19. Add: State Rd., Vineyard Haven 02568 (617)627-5535.

Essex. KATHERINE M. DONOVAN
Superior Courthouse, 32 Federal St., Salem 01970.

Nantucket. ESTHER U. GIBBS
Superior Courthouse, Cnty. Bldg., Broad St., Nantucket 02554.

Worcester. LILLIAN M. KELLY
Superior Courthouse, 2 Main, Worcester 01608.

Mayors

Acton. JULIA D. STEVENS (D)
1974-. Prev: Housing Authority 1970-74. Org: ANA; LWV. Educ: Mass. General Hospital School of Nursing 1954 RN. Occ: RN/Piano Instructor. B: 9/26/33. Add: 3 Long Ridge Rd., Acton 01720.

Amherst. DIANA H. ROMER (D)
1975-. Bds: Town Meeting. Prev: Finance Com. 1971-75; Town Meeting 1961- . Educ: Smith Coll. 1953 BA. B: 10/8/31. Add: 155 Woodside Ave., Amherst 01002 (413)253-9707.

Andover. SUSAN TREANOR POORE (R)
1976-. Bds: Mass. League of Cities & Towns; Solid Waste Com. Org: Selectman's Assoc.; LWV. Educ: Bradford Jr. Coll. 1961 AS; Lesley Coll. 1963 BSEd. B: 7/13/41. Add: Hobby Horse Farm, 85 Osgood St., Andover 01810 (617)475-5560.

Boxborough. JEANNE S. KANGAS (R) **
1973-. Bds: Bd. of Health; Sanitary Landfill Subcom.; Tax Reform Com.; Governor's Com. on the Status of Women. Party: State Platform Com. 1974- ; Ch., Town Com. 1966-70. Prev: Finance Com. 1968-73. Org: ACLU; Interstate Com. on Status of Women; NOW; WPC; Selectmens Assoc.; Mental Health Assoc.; Tax Reform Com. Educ: Simmons Coll. 1960 BA. Occ: Legislative & Public Information Officer. B: 8/25/40. Add: 959 Hill Rd., Boxborough 01719 (617)263-4595.

Danvers. MARJORIE WATTERS MURRAY
16 Martin St., Danvers 01923.

Dedham. MARILYN MORRIS (D)
1973-. Bds: Joint Regional Transportation
Com.; Ch., Emergency Medical Services Com.; Sign
by Law Com. Prev: Town Meeting 1972-73; Ch., Bd.
of Selectmen 1976-77; Ch., Growth Policy Com.
1975-76; V-Ch., Youth Cmsn. 1972-73. Org: Mass.
Selectmen Assoc.; Mass. League of Cities & Towns;
Family Service; LWV. B: 3/11/29. Add: 42
Norwell Rd., Dedham 02026 (617)326-5770.

Groton. LORETTO C. MOEN (I)
1975-. Bds: Lowell Reg. Transit Authority;
Women Elected Municipal Officials. Org: Middle-
sex Cnty. Selectmen's Assoc.; Women's Club;
Historical Society. B: 5/3/17. Add: 99 Chicopee
Row, Groton 01450 (617)448-2069.

Hanson. PATRICIA L. STEARNS (R) **
1975-. Bds: Ch., Advisory Bd.; Drainage Com.;
Conservation Cmsn.; Highway Commissioner. Party:
Ch., Town Com. 1966-68; Secretary, Town Com. 1962-
66. Prev: Library Trustee 1963-70; Council 1970-
75. Educ: Boston U. 1939 BS. B: 2/24/18. Add:
971 Whitman St., Hanson 02341 (617)293-2131.

Merrimac. NANCY C. MAC GREGOR (R) **
1975-. Bds: Regional Transportation Advisory
Bd. Party: Town Com. 1965-75. Prev: Council
1973-75. Org: Counsel for the Elderly. Educ:
Bates Coll. 1947 BA; Boston U. 1975 MS. Occ:
Rehabilitation Counselor. B: 3/5/25. Add:
Locust St., Merrimac 01860 (617)346-8900.

Mount Washington. BETTE C. WRIGHT (R) **
1975-. Prev: Council 1973-75. B: 10/23/17.
Add: East St., Mount Washington 12517
(413)528-0579.

Needham. LORETTA REYNOLDS *
1975-. Prev: Town Meeting Member 1971-76;
Business Adv. Com. 1971-76; Ch., Town Report Com.
1970-74; Housing Com. 1970-72; Govt. Review Com.
1973-75; Drug Abuse & Alcohol Com. 1973-75. Add:
149 Harris Ave., Needham 02192.

North Reading. ESTER V. ZEIMETZ (I)
1975-. Bds: Middlesex Cnty. Adv. Bd. Prev:
CETA 1972-77; Ch., Planning Council 1975-77;
State Manpower Services Council 1975-77; Economic
Devt. Com. 1973-75; Ch., School Com. 1966-73;
Conservation Com. 1960-62. Org: LWV; Mass.
Selectmen's Assoc. Educ: Simmons Coll. 1944 BS;
MS; Andover Newton Theological School 1969 MRE.
B: 10/8/23. Add: 5 Grandview Rd., N. Reading
01864 (617)664-2671.

Plainfield. FRANCES ALLETSON
Main St., Plainfield 01070.

Provincetown. MARY JO AVELLAR (D)
1976-. Bds: Growth Policy Com. Prev: By-Law
Revision Com. 1973-76. Org: Dem. Town Com. Educ:
U. of Mass. 1968 BS. Occ: Waitress. B: 2/3/46.
Add: 114 Commercial St., Provincetown 02657
(617)487-3900.

Richmond. RUTH H. BASS (I) **
1975-. Bds: Bd. of Health. Prev: Council
1971-75. Org: Civic Assoc.; Health Assoc.;
PTA. Educ: Bates Coll. 1955 BA; Columbia U.
1956 MS. Occ: Free-Lance Writer. B: 7/18/34.
Add: View Drive, Rt. 49, Pittsfield 01201
(413)698-3353.

Salem. JEAN A. LEVESQUE
City Hall, Salem 01970.

Shutesbury. JEAN FOOTIT (I)
1975-. Bds: Energy Com. Org: New England
Women's Ctr. for Women in Transition; Community
Union. Educ: U. of Mass. 1966 BA; U. of Conn.
1971 MSW. Occ: Social Worker. B: 1/31/45.
Add: Locks Pond Rd., Shutesbury 01072.

Southwick. VIVIAN V. BROWN (R)
1975-. Bds: Police Comsr.; License Comsr.;
Personnel Bd. Party: Ch., Rep. Com. 1974-75.
Prev: School Com. 1967-75; Westfield Area Mental
Health & Retardation Bd. 1974-75. Org: BPW;
Cnty. Selectmen's Assoc.; Rep. Town Com.; OES;
Western Mass. Public Health Assoc. Educ: East-
man School Dental Hygiene 1944 DH. Occ: Dental
Hygienist. B: 6/2/23. Add: 27 Feeding Hls Rd.,
Southwick 01077 (413)569-5995.

Topsfield. MARY L. WENDEL (I)
1976-. Prev: Long Range School Planning 1969-
73; Area Transportation Authority 1976-77. Org:
LWV. Educ: St. Lawrence U. 1959 BA. B: 9/12/37.
Add: 86 Parsonage Ln., Topsfield 01983
(617)887-8571.

Warwick. MARGARET ADAMS STRIEBEL (D)
1975-. Party: Ch., Dem. Com. 1976-77. Prev:
Conservation Cmsn. 1972-73. Occ: Housing &
Community Devt. Consultant. B: 8/5/47. Add:
Orange Rd., Warwick 01364.

Wayland. MARCIA P. CROWLEY (I)
1975-. Prev: Finance Com. 1971-75. Org:
ASPA; Amer. Society of Training & Devt.; Governor's Cmsn. on the Status of Women. Educ: Colby
Sawyer Coll. 1942 BA. Occ: Dir., Career Planning
B: 6/14/23. Add: 6 Wayland Hls. Rd., Wayland
01778 (617)358-7701.

Wenham. MARJORIE A. DAVIS (R)
1972-. Bds: Metropolitan Area Planning Cmsn.;
Cnty. Adv. Bd. Party: Committeewoman 1964.
Prev: Recreation Study Com. 1970-71; Ch., Bicen-
tennial Com. 1973-76. Org: Community Services
Assoc. Educ: Wellesley Coll. 1939 BA. Occ:
Exec. Dir., Girl Scout Council. B: 7/1/17.
Add: 143 Grapevine Rd., Wenham 01984 (617)
468-4468.

Winchester. BARBARA S. HANKINS
1975-. Bds: Cash Management Com.; Middlesex
Cnty. Adv. Bd. Prev: Ch., Finance Com. 1972-75;
Ch., Town Govt. Study Com. 1968-72. Org: LWV;
Historical Society; Mass. Selectmen's Assoc.
Educ: Cornell U. 1954 BS; Boston U. 1959 MBA.
Occ: Accountant. B: 5/28/33. Add: 37 Cabot St.,
Winchester 01890 (617)729-1100.

Acton. JOAN GARDNER (I)
1974-. Bds: V-Ch., Mass. Selectman's Assoc.;
Ch. Mass. League of Cities & Towns. Prev:
Finance Com. 1972-74; Library Trustee 1968-72.
Org: Mass. Selectman's Assoc.; Mass. League of
Cities & Towns; LWV; Historical Society. Educ:
Simmons Coll. 1959 BS. B: 11/13/37. Add: 53
Woodbury Ln., Acton 01770 (617)263-2617.

Agawam. ANITA M. DAVILLI
229 N. St., Feeding Hills

Amherst. NANCY B. EDDY (D)
1971-. Bds: Town Meeting. Prev: Town Meeting
1966- ; Planning Bd. 1968-71; Exec. Bd., Mass.
League of Cities & Towns 1975- . Org: Mass.
League of Cities & Towns; LWV; NAACP. Educ: Mt.
Holyoke Coll. 1959 BA. Occ: Staff Assoc.,
Industrial Engineering. B: 12/27/37. Add:
127 Mill Ln., Amherst 01002 (413)253-9707.

Arlington. ANN MAHON POWERS *
1975-. Prev: Town Clerk 1959-68; Town Meeting
Member. Add: 274 Mountain Ave., Arlington
02174 (617)646-0756.

Arlington. MARGARET H. SPENGLER (D)
1973-. Bds: Leg. Com. - Mass. Selectmen's
Assoc.; Women's Municipal Com.; Ch., Vandalism
& Youth Problems Com. Prev: Finance Com. 1969-
73; Mass. Bd. of Higher Educ. 1965-67; Mass.
State Coll. Bldg. Authority 1965-71. Org: LWV.
Educ: Misericordia Coll. 1940 BS. B: 11/21/17.
Add: 189 Jason, Arlington 02174 (617)643-6720.

Ashby. JANET L. UMPHRESS (R)
1976-. Bds: Middlesex Cnty. Adv. Bd. Org:
Mass. Selectmen's Assoc.; League of Cities &
Towns; LWV. Educ: Oh. State U. 1957 BSEd. B:
4/15/31. Add: New Ipswich Rd., Ashby 01431.

Athol. EVELYN KING
134 Drury Ave., Athol 01331.

Attleboro. JUDITH HOFFMAN ROBBINS (R)
1973-. Bds: Ch., Ordinance Com.; Streets Com.;
Transportation Com. Party: Rep. City Com. 1976-
77. Prev: Charter Cmsn. 1971-73; Planning Bd.
1967-73. Org: Mass. League of Cities & Towns;
LWV; AAUW. Educ: Stanford U. 1958 BA. B:
2/24/37. Add: 20 Ashton Rd., Attleboro 02703
(617)222-2548.

Barnstable. MARY K. MONTAGNA
990 Iyanough Rd., Hyannis 02601.

Bedford. GRACE THOMAS ERDMAN (D)
1975-. Bds: Personnel Bd. Prev: Personnel Bd.
1973-75. Org: Mass. Selectmen's Assoc.; Common
Cause; Mass. Fair Share; AAUW; LWV; Historical
Society. Educ: Oh. State U. 1947 BS. B: 9/25/25
Add: 23 Wildwood Dr., Bedford 01730 (617)
225-1111.

Bedford. LOUISE COLE MAGLIONE (I)
1974-. Bds: Conservation Cmsn.; Planning Bd.;
Youth Study Com. Prev: Conservation Com. 1972-
73. Occ: Educator. Add: 8 Glenora Dr., Bedford
01730 (617)275-1111.

Belchertown. SHIRLEY A. DOREY
1976-. Bds: Council on Aging; Recreation
Com.; Historical Com. Prev: Land Evaluation
Study Com. 1975-76; Personnel By-Law Study
Com. 1975-76; Parks & Recreation Com. 1974-76;
Municipal Bldg. & Site Study Com. 1972-74. Org:
Mass. Selectmen's Assoc.; Mass. League of Cities
& Towns; Arts and Humanities Council. Educ:
Boston U. 1950 BS. B: 4/26/28. Add: 41 Spring-
field Rd., Belchertown 01007 (413)323-7251.

Beverly. FRANCES F. ALEXANDER (D)
1976-. Bds: Ch., Legal Affairs. Prev:
Beverly School Com. 1970-76. Org: Civic Assoc.
Occ: Dir., Nursery School. B: 6/16/19. Add:
80 Lothrop St., Beverly 01915 (617)922-0015.

Blandform. JOAN PITONIAK *
1975-. Prev: Finance Com. 1972-76. Educ:
Our Lady of the Elms Coll. BA; Syracuse U. MEd.
Add: Shepard Rd., Blanford 01008.

Boston. LOUISE DAY HICKS (D)
1970-. Bds: Ch., Ways & Means Com.; Ch.,
Health & Hospital; Ch., Confirmations. Party:
State Del. 1976; State Committeewoman 1976; Ch.,
Ward Com. 1976. Prev: US Repr. 1971-72. Org:
Mass. Bar Assoc.; Mass. Assoc. Women Lawyers;
Mass. Women on Wheels; Civic Assoc.; Residents
Group. Educ: Boston U. BS; LLD. Occ: Atty.
B: 10/16/23. Add: 1780 Columbia Rd., S. Boston
02127 (617)725-4376.

Brookline. ELEANOR MYERSON (D)
1970-. Prev: Finance Com. 1957-63; Com. on
Town Org. & Structure 1963-69; Town Meeting 1956-
70. Org: Mass. Selectmen's Assoc.; Women's
Elected Municipal Officials; ADA; Common Cause;
LWV; Mental Health Assoc.; Dem. Town Com. Educ:
Smith Coll. 1943 BA. B: 5/9/22. Add: 175
Rawson Rd., Brookline 02146 (617)232-9000.

Cambridge. BARBARA ACKERMANN *
1975-. Prev: School Com. 1962-68. Educ:
Smith Coll. BA. Add: 41 Gibson St., Cambridge
02138 (617)876-2629.

Cambridge. SAUNDRA GRAHAM
189 Weston Ave., Cambridge 02139.

Carlisle. NANCY P. PENHUNE (D) **
1972-. Bds: County Advisory Bd.; Regional
Refuse Bd. Org: LWV. B: 12/29/37. Add: 1019
North Rd., Carlisle 01741 (617)369-6136.

Carver. VIRGINIA FORD
Box 96, N. Carver 02355.

Chester. MARIE L. MORRISSEY (D) **
1972-. Prev: Finance Com. 1969-72. Org:
Dem. Women's Club; OES. Occ: Secretary. B:
11/16/28. Add: Emery St., Chester 01011
(413)354-7760.

Chesterfield. JANET LA FOND *
1975-. Prev: Finance Com. 1973-75; Recreation
Com. 1967-72. Add: Main Rd., W. Chesterfield
01012.

Chicopee. VERONICA C. LA FLUER
243 Carew St., Chicopee 01013.

Chicopee. MARY ANNE MINOR
147 Morean Dr., Chicopee 01013.

Chicopee. LUCILLE G. OUIMETTE
21 Academy St., Chicopee 01013.

Chilmark. ELIZABETH BRYANT
South Rd., Chilmark 02535.

Cohasset. MARY JEANETTE MURRAY
30 Margin St., Cohasset 02025.

Concord. MARGUERITE M. PURCELL (D)
1977-. Prev: Celebrations Com. 1975-76. Org:
Mass. Selectmen's Assoc.; LWV. Educ: Pembroke
Coll. 1949 BA. B: 1/15/27. Add: 330 Musketaquid
Rd., Concord 01742 (617)369-2100.

Deerfield. ELIZABETH KIRKWOOD
King Phillip Ave., S. Deerfield 01373.

Dighton. MYRNA D. ADAMS (I)
1975-. Bds: League of Cities & Towns Joint
Legislative Conference; Adv. Council on Water
Quality. Prev: Clerk, Water Dist. 1973-77; Sec.,
Fire Dept. Needs Study Com. 1973-74. Org: Mass.
Selectmen's Assoc. B: 4/1/40. Add: 455 Center
St., Segreganset 02773 (617)669-6431.

Dover. ANN R. WISE *
1975-. Prev: Local Growth Policy Com. 1976;
Long Range Planning Com. 1975-76; Warrant Com.
1971-74. Educ: Chatham Coll. BS. Add: 54 Glen
St., Dover 02030.

Eastham. LAURA UNDERHILL *
1975-. Prev: Coastal Zone Management Com.
Educ: Cornell U. BA; Brown U. MA. Add: Box 681,
Eastham 02642 (617)255-1162.

Egremont. NANCY LEHMBECK
Baldwin 01258.

Everett. LINDA A. HIBBS (I)
1975-. Bds: Annuities & Pensions; Printing.
Org: League of Cities & Towns. Educ: Boston State
Coll. 1974 BSEd. Occ: Clerk. B: 9/14/51. Add:
119 Irving St., Everett 02149 (617)223-0915.

Everett. ROSE M. LECOURS (D)
1972-. Bds: Protection of Persons & Property;
Senior Citizens; Public Safety. Occ: Taxi Driver.
B: 8/24/09. Add: 12 Miller St., Everett 02149
(617)389-2100.

Fall River. MARILYN J. RODERICK *
1975-. Prev: Administrative Asst. to Mayor
1972. Educ: Southeastern Mass. U. BS; Boston U.
MEd. Add: 378 Oak Grove Ave., Fall River 02720.

Fitchburg. ELLEN M. DIGERONIMO
31 Ash Street, Fitchburg 01420.

Fitchburg. MARY M. MAYNE (D)
1976-. Bds: Ch., Claims Com.; Public Safety
Com.; Leg. Affairs Com. Org: City Dem. Com. Occ:
Sales Clerk. B: 5/13/42. Add: 12 Boxwood Cir.,
Fitchburg 01420 (617)345-4394.

Foxborough. HARRIET J. BLOOMBERG
40 South Street, Foxborough 02035.

Foxborough. CAROLE A. BURNS
11 Wayne Dr., Foxborough 02035.

Gay Head. HELEN MANNING *
1975-. Prev: Martha's Vineyard Land & Water
Com.; Finance Com. 1972-74. Add: Box 144, State
Rd., Gay Head 02535.

Gill. GENEVIEVE KREJMAS
Main Rd., Box 201, Gill 01376.

Hampden. JEANETTE S. GREEN
3 Colonial Vlg., Hampden 01036.

Hanover. JANET O'BRIEN
128 Washington St., Hanover 02339.

Holden. MARY JANE MACKENNE
4 Pioneer Rd., Holden 01520.

Holyoke. MARY M. O'NEILL (D)
1974-. Bds: Ch., Public Service Com.;
License Com.; Ch., Transportation Com.; Party:
Ward Ch. 1973- . Prev: Assoc. Cnty. Cmsnr. 1974-.
Org: New England Women in Media; Valley Press
Club; Holyoke Dem. Club; Chamber of Commerce.
Occ: Journalist. B: 11/18/43. Add: 182 Oak St.,
Holyoke 01040 (413)534-5838.

Hopkinton. SALLYANN W. MACINTOSH
22 Main St., Hopkinton 01748.

Ipswich. ADELE C. ROBERTSON
176 Argilla Rd., Ipswich 01938.

Lanesborough. JEANNETTE E. SULLIVAN (I) **
1974-. Bds: Civil Defense Dir. Prev:Deputy
Sheriff. Org: Interstate Police Assoc.; Select-
men's Assoc. Educ: Smith Coll. 1945 BA. Occ:
Junior Clerk-Typist. B: 5/27/31. Add: 633 South
Main St., Lanesborough 01237.

Lee. MARIA D. BETTEGA
66 Railroad St., Lee 01238.

Leverett. NANCY J. RASKEVITZ *
1975-. Prev: Leverett School Bldg. Renovation
Com. 1972-73. Educ: Mass. General Hospital
School of Nursing, Cooley Dickinson Hospital
School of Nursing RN. Add: 200 Long Plain Road,
RFD 3, Amherst 01002.

Lexington. MARGERY M. BATTIN (I)
1974-. Bds: Ch., Drug Adv. Com.; Auditing
Com.; Library Trustee. Prev: Town Meeting 1969-
74; Ch., Structure Town Govt. Com. 1966-69. Org:
Dir., Mass. Assoc. Mental Health; Human Services
Coalition; Adv. Council Dept. Public Management
& Administration. Educ: Wellesley Coll. 1948
BA. Occ: Consultant. B: 3/25/27. Add: 15 Paul
Revere Rd., Lexington 02173.

Lexington. MARY W. MILEY (D)
1976-. Bds: Ch., School Site Conversion;
Youth Adv. Cmsn. Party:Dem. Town Com. 1976.
Prev: Town Meeting 1973; Precinct Officer 1975-
76; Town Meeting Exec. Bd. 1975-76; Suburban
Responsibility Com. 1976-77. Educ: Regis Coll.

1943 BS. B: 8/5/22. Add: 29 Robinson Rd.,
Lexington 02175 (617)862-0138.

Lincoln. ANN SUTHERLAND
Grasshopper Ln., Lincoln 01773.

Ludlow. JENNIE TYBURSKI
164 Root St., Ludlow 01056.

Lunenburg. ANN P. HALL
195 Rolling Acres Rd., Lunenburg 01462.

Lynn. PATRICIA A. MC INTIRE (D)
1973-. Bds: Ch., Public Safety Com.; Ordinance
Com.; Public Property. Prev: Ch., Planning Bd.
1970-74. Org: Lynn Industrial Devt. Corp. Occ:
Purchasing Asst. B: 2/5/40. Add: 10 Great Woods
Rd., Lynn 01904 (617)598-4000.

Marblehead. MARILYN A. REIS
9 Basselt St., Marblehead 01945.

Marlborough. JOSEPHINE P. PLAS
83 Kings View Rd., Marlborough 01752.

Marlborough. CYNTHIA D. VAIL (I)
1975-. Bds: Legal & Legislative; Transportation; City Property. Prev: Planning Bd. 1972-
75. Org: Mass. Fed. of Planning Bds.; LWV; Local
Charter. B: 11/4/39. Add: 47 Roundtop Rd.,
Marlborough 01752 (617)481-0971.

Medfield. SANDRA MUNSEY
8 Clark Rd., Medfield 02052.

Medford. MARILYN CATINO PORRECA (D)
1975-. Bds: Fed-State Liaison Com.; Senior
Citizens Com. Party: State Del. 1956, '58, '62,
'64, '77; Dem. City Com. 1953-77. Prev: Welling-
ton Dev. Com. Org: Women Elected Municipal
Officials; Dem. Women's Club; PTA. Educ: Boston
U. 1953 BS. B: 4/21/32. Add: 10 Maverick St.,
Medford 02155 (617)396-5500.

Melrose. JOAN T. MOORE (D)
1975-. Bds: Ch., Health, Educ. & Welfare Com.;
Protection & License Com.; Appropriations. Org:
LWV; Eastern Middlesex Mental Health. Educ: U. of
Mass. 1975 BA. B: 12/28/22. Add: 237 Upham St.,
Melrose 02176 (617)665-0604.

Middleborough. THERESA S. KILPATRICK (D)
1973-. Org: Mass. Selectmen's Assoc.; Mass.
League of Cities & Towns; Historical Assoc.;
Women's Club; N.E. Public Power Assoc. Occ:
Information Specialist. B: 11/17/30. Add: 131
Miller St., Middleborough 02346 (617)947-0780.

Milford. MARIE J. PARENTE (D) **
1973-. Bds: Blackstone Valley Consortium.
Party: Precinct Com. 1972-75. Org: Concerned
Citizens. Occ: Secretary. B: 5/22/28. Add: 24
Union St., Milford 01757 (617)473-0023.

Millbury. MABEL G. STOCKWELL
5 Grove St., Millbury 01527.

Nantucket. ESTHER U. GIBBS (I)
1972-. Bds: Bd. of Appeals. B: 7/19/11. Add:
67 N. Centre St., Nantucket 02554 (617)228-1122.

Natick. ERICA ESTHER BALL (D)
1975-. Bds: V-Ch., S. Middlesex Opportunity Council; V-Ch., Middlesex Cnty. Adv. Bd.;
Leg. Liaison to Mass. League of Cities & Towns.
Org: LWV; Good Govt. Educ: Brandeis U. 1958
BA. B: 3/30/37. Add: 11 Russell Cir., Natick
01760 (617)653-7191.

New Bedford. ROSALIND POLL BROOKER (R)
1969-. Party: State Del. 1974; Nat. Alt.
1972; Rep. State Committeewoman 1972-77. Prev:
Industrial Accident Cmsn. 1973-75. Org: Mass.
Bar Assoc.; Mass. Assoc. for Women Lawyers;
Assoc. for Retarded Citizens; BPW. Educ: Boston
U. 1949 AAB; 1952 LLB. Occ: Atty. Add: 419
Union St., New Bedford 02740.

New Braintree. BETTY DAVIS
Hardwick Rd., New Braintree 01531.

New Braintree. BERNICE KLEM
Moore Rd., New Braintree 01531.

New Salem. CLAIRE KLEMENT
Jennie Horr Rd., New Salem 01355.

Newton. CAROL ANN SHEA (R)
1975-. Bds: Land Use Com.; Planning Com.;
Public Health & Safety Com. Party: Ward Com.
1973-77. Org: Community Assoc.; LWV. Educ:
U. of Penna. 1966 BA. B: 4/5/44. Add: 215
Auburndale Ave., Newton 02166.

Newton Centre. JOAN H. SAKLAD (D)
1974-. Bds: Finance Com.; City Planning
Com.; Consumer Affairs Com. Prev: Crime Cmsn.
1974-76. Org: LWV; Activity Ctr. for Cerebral
Palsy. Educ: Adelphi Coll. 1954 BA. Occ:
Business Manager. B: 10/21/32. Add: 45 Miller
Rd., Newton Ctr. 02159.

Newton Centre. SUSAN DOREMAN SCHUR (D)
1973-. Bds: Ch., Consumer Affairs & Licenses
Com.; Public Works; Neighborhood Area Council.
Party: State Del. 1972; Dem. City Com. 1970- ;
Secretary, Dem. City Com. 1972-74. Prev: Con-
sultant to Human Resources Administrator 1967;
Field Repr., Office of Economic Opportunity;
Program Officer, Agency for Internat. Devt.
1962-64; Housing & Home Finance Agency 1961-62.
Org: LWV; Common Cause; Waban Improvement Society;
PTA. Educ: Goucher Coll. 1961 BA. B: 2/27/40.
Add: 130 Nehoiden Rd., Newton 02168 (617)
244-1470.

Newton Centre. ETHEL W. SHEEHAN (D)
1976-. Bds: Land Use; Legislation & Rules;
Street Traffic. Party: State Del. 1972; Ch.,
Ward Com. 1972-76. Org: LWV. B: 1/2/23.
Add: 6 Crescent Ave., Newton Centre 02159.

Norfolk. DIANE C. POWERS
15 Diamond St., Norfolk 02056.

Northampton. MARY T. MC COLGAN *
1975-. Prev: Council on Aging 1970-76.
Educ: Mercy Hospital School of Nursing, RN.
Add: 218 South, Northampton 01060.

Northampton. FRANCES H. MC NULTY (D)
    1973-. Bds: Fire Com.; Military Affairs Com.
Party: State Del. 1977; Ward Com. 1973- ; Ward
Com. Treasurer 1976-77. Prev: V-Pres., Citizens
Adv. Com. 1969-72. Org: Mass. League of Cities
& Towns; Women Elected Municipal Officials.;
LWV; Historical Society; Florence Civic & Business
Assoc.; WPC. Educ: Becker Jr. Coll. 1960 AS; Amer.
Internat. Coll. 1964 BA. Occ: Citizen Advocacy
Coord. B: 10/25/40. Add: 9 Greeley Ave.,
Florence 01060 (413)586-1683.

Northampton. MARION E. MENDELSON (D)
    1975-. Bds: Ordinance Com.; Finance Com.;
Military Affairs Com. Org: LWV. Educ: Barnard
Coll. 1943 BA. B: 5/4/23. Add: 15 Barrett Pl.,
Northampton 01060.

North Attleboro. SUSAN B. NELSON (R)
    1976-. Bds: Local Growth Policy Com.; Ch.,
Cnty. Adv.; Leg. Liason Mass. League of Cities &
Towns. Prev: Finance Com. 1971-74; Bd. of Health
1975-76. Org: LWV. Educ: Wheaton Coll. 1964 BA.
B: 1/3/42. Add: 19 Stonehill Rd., N. Attleboro
02760 (617)695-0981.

Northbridge. ANGELA M. ZANCHETTI
    52 East St., Whitinsville 01588.

Northfield. CAROLYN B. PARENTEAU
    8 Main St., Northfield 01360.

Oakham. HAZEL M. YOUNG
    Turnpike Rd., Oakham 01068.

Peru. MARGARET KELLY
    E. Windsor Rd., Peru 01235.

Petersham. HOPE W. STREETER (R)
    1976-. Bds: Franklin Cnty. Regional Planning
Bd.; Rural Consortium. B: 4/29/19. Add: Hardwick Rd., Petersham 01366 (617)724-3275.

Phillipston. OPAL E. CLARK
    State Rd., Phillipston 01331.

Rehoboth. SUE ELLEN SNAPE (R)
    1975-. Bds: SE Regional Planning & Devt. Dist;
Bd. of Health. Party: Town Committeewoman 1975-77.
Prev: Town Bicentennial Cmsn. 1974-75. Educ: U.
of Del. 1973 BA. B: 10/13/41. Add: 78 County
St., Rehoboth 02769 (617)252-3758.

Revere. ELVIRA CURCIO
    146 Patriot Pky., Revere 02151.

Revere. RITA SINGER
    14 Bellingham Ave., Revere 02151.

Rochester. JULIA S. ENROTH (D)
    1976-. Bds: Conservation Cmsn.; Growth Policy
Com.; Regional Planning Cmsn. Prev: Finance Com.
1969-75; Master Plan Com. 1972-76. Org: LWV.
Educ: U. of N.C. 1960 BA. B: 8/5/38. Add: New
Bedford Rd., Rochester 02770.

Rockland. CATHERINE YOUNG
    68 Payson Ave., Rockland 02370.

Salem. FRANCES J. GRACE (D)
    1975-. Bds: Ch., Natural Resources;
Community Devt., Licenses & Permits; Municipal
Services. Party: State Del. 1977; Del., Dem.
State Issues Conv. 1977. Org: Teamsters Union;
BPW; Historic Salem; LWV; Mass. Elected Women
Officials; PTA. Occ: School Bus Driver. B:
3/5/42. Add: 3 Hillside Ave., Salem 01970
(617)744-0224.

Salem. JEAN-MARIE ROCHNA
    15 Cherry St., Salem 01970.

Sandisfield. ROBERTA MYERS
    P.O. Box, Otis 01253.

Scituate. ALICE C. PROCTOR
    1973-. Bds: State Scenic Rivers Steering
Com.; Council on Aging; Land Use Com. Prev:
Charter Cmsn. 1971-72. Org: Beautification
Cmsn.; Historical Assoc. Educ: Mt. Holyoke
Coll. 1935 BA. Add: 34 Curtis St., Scituate
02066 (617)545-9082.

Scituate. ROSE ZOOB
    41 Surfside Rd., N. Scituate 02060.

Seekonk. ELIZABETH B. BARKER
    166 Hope St., Seekonk 02771.

Sharon. COLLEEN M. TUCK (D)
    1976-. Bds: Capital Outlay Com. Prev:
Nominating Com. for the Warrant Com. 1973-74.
Org: LWV; Common Cause; Women Elected Municipal
Officials. Educ: Simmons Coll. 1962 BS. B:
4/16/40. Add: 27 Maskwonicut St., Sharon
02067 (612)784-6909.

Springfield. BARBARA J. GARVEY (D)
    1973-. Bds: Ch., Community Devt.; Parks &
Recreation; Finance. Party: State Del. 1964-
68; Dem. State Com. 1964- . Org: Mass. Council
of Social Studies; Mass. Assoc. for Legal Educ.;
APSA. Educ: Our Lady of the Elms 1951 BA; U. of
Mass. 1971 MA. Occ: Teacher. B: 9/25/30. Add:
127 Gillette Ave., Springfield 01118
(413)736-2711.

Stoughton. GENEVIEVE R. GLENNON (I) **
    1974-. Bds: Ambulance Study Com.; Advisory
Bd. - Multi-Service Health Center. Org: Amer.
Nurses Assoc.; LWV; Mass. Mental Health Nurses
Assoc.; Selectmen's Assoc. for Exceptional
Citizens. Educ: Boston U. 1959 BSN; State Coll.
of Bridgewater 1968 MEd. B: 8/16/08. Add:
80 Pearl St., Stoughton 02072 (617)344-7133.

Stoughton. MAMIE C. GRAY (I)
    1974-. Bds: Traffic Study Com. Prev: Town
Meeting Repr. 1969-71. Org: Nat. Teacher Assoc.;
Concerned Citizens for Conservation; Grange;
Exceptional Children; LWV. Educ: Winthrop Coll.
1943 BA. Occ: Math Teacher. B: 1/22/22. Add:
34 Rockland St., Stoughton 02072 (617)344-9231.

Sturbridge. JEANNETTE C. BAILLARGEON (I)
    1976-. Bds: Leg. Liaison, Mass. Selectmen
Assoc.; Leg. Liaison, Mass. League of Cities &
Towns. Educ: Notre Dame School of Nursing 1948
RN. B: 3/24/27. Add: RFD 1, Box 159, Brookfield
01506 (617)347-3000.

Sunderland. CATHERINE N. HUBBARD *
    1975-. Prev: Bd. of Appeals 1969-71. Educ:
Mass. State Coll. BS; Boston U. MEd. Add:
Amherst Rd., Sunderland 01375.

Taunton. REGINA F. CALVEY
    71 Power St., Taunton 02780.

Templeton. GLADYS I. SALAME
    Barry Rd., Templeton 01468.

Tisbury. CORA S. MEDEIROS
    Fairfield Ave., Vineyard Haven 02568.

Townsend. JANE L. JACKSON (D)
    1976-. Bds: Leg. Liason; Public Safety Cmnsr.;
Union Negotiator. B: 4/25/47. Add: 14 Blood Rd.,
Townsend 01469 (617)597-6612.

Walpole. JO ANN SPRAGUE
    236 Plympton St., Walpole 02032.

Waltham. KATHLEEN BRENNAN MC MENIMEN (D)
    1976-. Bds: Ch., Public Works Com.; Finance
Com.; Community Devt. Com. Party: State Del.
1977; Nat. Alt. 1976; Ward Secretary 1976-77.
Prev: Bd. of Dir's., John F. Kennedy Multiservice
Center 1970-72. Educ: Boston Coll. 1966 BS;
Boston Coll. 1974 MEd. B: 6/15/44. Add: 147
Trapelo Rd., Waltham 02154 (617)893-4040.

Ware. GERTRUDE T. HAMELIN *
    1975-. Party: Rep. Town Com. 1950-76. Prev:
Home Rule Com.; Conservation Com.; Bd. of
Registrars; Town Steering Com.; Local Growth
Policy Com.; School Com. 1959-61. Add: 20 Spring
St., Ware 01082.

Wareham. JANE BEATON
    Bourne's Pt., Wareham 02371.

Wareham. CLAIRE J. MC WILLIAMS
    1970-. Bds: Ch., Cemetery Cmsn.; Permanent
Town Bldg. Needs Com.; Bicentennial Cmsn. Prev:
Pres., Plymouth Cnty. Selectmen's Assoc. 1974-75;
Secretary, Mass. Selectmen's Assoc. 1975-76; Cnty.
Adv. Bd. 1976-77; Assessor 1970-73. Org: BPW;
Historical Society. B: 1/21/28. Add: 138 Hatha-
way St., Wareham 02571 (617)295-0800.

Warren. LEONA A. WROBEL (D)
    1976-. B: 12/12/37. Add: 15 Liberty, Warren
01083.

Wayland. CATHERINE SEILER
    87 Lincoln Rd., Wayland 01778.

Wellesley. JEAN W. KELLY (R)
    1977-. Bds: Bd. of Fire Engineers. Party:
Rep. Town Com. 1975-77. Prev: School Board 1969-
75. Org: LWV; Rep. Women; Women Elected Mass.
Officials; AAUW. Educ: Brown 1975 BA. B:
10/10/24. Add: 9 Bay State Rd., Wellesley 02181
(617)235-0262.

West Bridgewater. DORIS HAIGHT
    2 Crescent St., W. Bridgewater 02379.

Westfield. ELLA M. FLAHIVE (D)
    1971-. Bds: Ch., Council Computer Liaison
Com.; Off-Street Parking Com.; Personnel.
Party: State Del. 1977. Prev: Jr. High Bldg.
Com. 1957-59. Org: Nat. Retired Teachers;
Ecology; Dem. Club. Educ: Framingham State
Coll. 1930 BSEd; U. of Mass. 1933 MSEd. B:
6/11/08. Add: 10 Highland Cir., Westfield
01085 (413)562-3518.

Westminster. MARY E. VEDOE
    33 Lanes Rd., Westminster 01473.

Weston. JOAN B. VERNON
    15 Conant Rd., Weston 02193.

Westport. PHYLLIS G. BERNIER
    11 Reed Rd., Westport 02790.

Westwood. JANET E. JEGHELIAN (D)
    1972-. Bds: Ch., Growth Policy Com.; Ch.,
Traffic Study Com. Party: Dem. Town Com. 1964-
77. Prev: Adv. Bd. of Health 1968-72. Org:
Amer. Physical Therapy Assoc.; Mass. Selectmans
Assoc.; LWV; Bd. of Dirs. Norfolk-Bristol Home
Health Service; Dem. Town Com. Educ: Boston U.
1956 BS; NYU 1959 MA. Occ: Radio Broadcaster.
B: 4/28/34. Add: 161 Pleasant Vly. Way, West-
wood, 02090 (617)326-6450.

Williamsburg. JEANNE E. HEMENWAY
    Hemenway Rd., Williamsburg 01096.

Windsor. IRENE A. WELLS (I)
    1976-. Bds: Bd. of Health; Licensing Author-
ity; Veterans Benefits. Prev: Library Trustee
1976-77. Org: Mass. Selectmen's Assoc. B:
1/29/38. Add: North St., Windsor 01270
(413)684-3878.

Woburn. MARION C. BOBBIE FINNERTY *
    1975-. Prev: School Com. 1968-73; Northeast
Reg. Vocational School Com. 1964-67. Educ:
Lowell State Coll. BSE. Add: 8 Mishawum Rd.,
Woburn 01801.

Woburn. MARY PAES
    9 Mount Ida, Woburn 01801.

Worthington. JULIA J. SHARRON (D)
    1976-. Bds: Hampshire Cnty. Budget Hearings;
Council on Aging; Ch., Park Com. Prev: Bd. of
Registrars 1970-76. Org: PTO. B: 9/22/40.
Add: Buffington Hill Rd., Worthington 01098
(413)238-5361.

Wrentham. KAREN KOHUT
    67 Park St., Wrentham 02093.

State Boards and Commissions

    A list of state boards and commissions, and of
their members, was not available for inclusion.

Michigan

State Legislature

State House

CONNIE BINSFELD (R) **
1974-. Dist: 104. Bds: Towns & Counties;
Mental Health; State Affairs; Transportation.
Party: Del., State Conv. 1970-75. Prev: County
Commissioner 1970-74. Org: WPC; Rep. Women's
Club. Educ: Siena Heights Coll. 1945 BS. B:
4/18/24. Add: RR 2, Maple City 49664 (517)
373-1789.

MARY C. BROWN (D)
1976-. Dist: 46. Bds: Urban Affairs; Towns
& Cntys.; Civil Rights. Party: State Del. 1974-
77; Cnty. Ch. 1975-76. Org: LWV. Educ: Syracuse
U. 1957 BA;1960 MS. B: 8/18/35. Add: 1624 Grand
Kalamazoo 49007 (517)373-1785.

BARBARA-ROSE COLLINS (D) **
1974-. Dist: 21. Bds: Constitutional Revision
& Women's Rights; Urban Affairs; Public Health;
Housing Policy; Human Rights. Prev: School Bd.
1970-73. Org: Afro-Amer. Museum Trustee. B:
4/13/39. Add: 2256 Leland, Detroit 48207
(517)373-2616.

DAISY ELLIOTT (D) **
Dist: 8. Bds: Ch., Labor; V-Ch., Constitu-
tional Revision & Women's Rights; Coll. & U.;
Educ.; Administrative Rules. Prev: Mich. State
Constitutional Conv. 1961-62. Org: Dem. Black
Caucus; LWV; NAACP; OWL; United Black Coalition.
Add: 8701 Lasalle Blvd., Detroit (517)373-2617.

ROSETTA FERGUSON (D) **
1964-. Dist: 20. Bds: Ch., Social Service;
V-Ch., Civil Rights; Public Safety; Roads &
Bridges. Party: State Central Com.; County Dem.-
Rep. Human Relations Council on Civil Rights. Org:
NAACP; Trade Union Leadership Council; People's
Community Civic League, Inc.; PTA. Occ: Staff
Manager, Real Estate Firm. B: 7/1/20. Add: 2676
Arndt St., Detroit 48207 (517)373-1178.

LUCILLE H. MC COLLOUGH (D)
1954-. Bds: Ch., Educ. Com.; Public Health;
Senior Citizens & Retirement. Party: Precinct
Del. 1950-55. Prev: City Councilwoman 1950-54.
Org: Aviation Property Owners; Fed. of Civic
Assoc.; Dem. Club; NOWL; LWV; BPW; Historical
Society. B: 12/30/05. Add: 7517 Kentucky,
Dearborn 48126 (517)373-0847.

RUTH B. MC NAMEE (R)
1974-. Dist: 63. Bds: Towns & Cnty's; V-Ch.,
Consumer; Constitutional Review. Party: State
Del. Prev: Mayor 1970-71; City Comsr. 1965-74;
Cnty. Supervisor 1968; Youth Assistance Com. 1966-
70; Community Action Com. on Drug Abuse 1970-74;
Planning Bd. 1964. Org: AAUW; LWV; Altrusa.
Educ: Bucknell U. BA. B: 6/2/22. Add: 1271
Lakeside Rd., Birmingham 48009 (517)373-0824.

JOYCE SYMONS (D) **
1964-. Dist: 30. Bds: Ch., Mental Health;
Public Health; State Affairs; Towns & Counties.
Org: OWL; Dem. Club; Women's Club. B: 9/10/27.
Add: 9648 Buckingham, Allen Park 48101 (517)
373-0843.

County Commissions

Allegan. FLORA V.MOORE
510 W. River St., Otsego 49078.

Baraga. JUNE FOREST
Box 194, Baraga 49908.

Barry. CAROLYN G. COLEMAN (R)
1972-. Bds: Cmsn. on Aging; Mental Health
Bd. Prev: Child Guidance Clinic Bd. 1959-65.
Educ: Christian Coll. 1947 AA; U. of Mich. 1949
BA. B: 12/21/27. Add: 109 W. State Rd., Hasting
49058.

Barry. RAE M. HOARE (D)
1975-. Bds: Ch., Dept. of Public Works; Ch.,
Human Resources; Substance Abuse. Party:
Election Precinct Ch. 1958-75. Prev: Dep. Clerk
1973-74; Ch., Bd. of Review 1973-75. Org: Cnty.
Dem's. Add: 10944 Houvener Rd., R #3, Delton
49046.

Benzie. ULEDENE MERRILL (R)
1976-. Bds: Planning Cmsn.; Ch., Leg. Com.;
Social Service Com. Party: State Alt. 1976.
Org: Neighbor Extension Group; Cnty. Farm Bureau.
B: 2/28/34. Add: 6258 Grace Rd., Benzonia
49616 (616)882-4939.

Berrien. NANCY F. CLARK (R)
1969-. Bds: State Manpower Council; Tri-
Cnty. Human Resources Com. Org: Health Services
Agency; Human Resources Com.; Juvenile Adv.
Council; State Manpower Bd. Educ: U. of Mich
1943 BA. B: 9/21/21. Add: 178 Meadow Ter.,
Benton Hbr., 49022 (616)983-7111.

Branch. RUBY LOEHR
130 E. Chicago St., Coldwater 49036.

Calhoun. MARIAN E. BURCH
36 Greenwood, Battle Creek 49017.

Calhoun. BESS JORDAN (D)
1972-. Bds: Bd. of Public Works; Drain Bd.;
Planning Council. Party: Nat. Del. 1976;

Precinct Del. 1960-77; V-Ch. Cnty. 1960-76. Org:
Dem. Women's Org. B: 8/31/30. Add: 21103-2
Mile Rd., Battle Creek 49017 (616)781-9811.

Cass. GENEVIEVE V. TOOTHAKER (R)
1977-. Dist: 1. Bds: Operations Com.;
Services Com.; Safety & Law. Party: Treasurer
1955-77; Cnty. Rep. 1977. Org: Cnty. Rep. Women.
Educ: 7/22/10. Add: Cass Cnty. Court House,
Cassopolis 49047.

Chippewa. MARGARET L. KAUNISTO (R)
1977-. Bds: Ch., Health & Social Services;
Ch., Emergency Services; Sheriff Dept. Prev:
Community Service Bd. 1972-80. Org: Parks &
Recreation Com. Occ: Insurance Saleswoman. B:
11/19/30. Add: 1127 E. Spruce St., Sault Ste.
Marie 49783.

Clinton. VIRGINIA ZEEB
2840 Herbison Rd., RR #1, Bath 48808.

Crawford. MARY E. HARLAND (R)
1976-. Bds: Ch., Animal Control; Finance;
Personnel. Prev: Regional Planning 1968-70; Cnty.
Planning Com. 1970-74; Planning & Zoning Bd. 1968-
77. Org: Amer. Business Womens Assoc.; PTA. Occ:
Manager. B: 12/13/24. Add: Rt. 2, Box 2500,
Grayling 49738 (517)348-8949.

Delta. ELNORA STRAHAN VADER (D)
1974-. Dist: 3. Bds: Ch., Six-Cnty. Consort-
uim for Employment & Training; Cnty. Mental
Health Cmsn.; Delta-Menominee Dist. Bd. of Health.
Party: State Del. 1965-77; Nat. Del. 1960, '72,
'76; Cnty. V-Ch. 1970- ; Precinct Del. 1972- ;
Dist. V-Ch. 1970-76; State Central Com. 1962- .
Org: NEA; Nat. Council for the Social Studies; LWV.
BPW; Common Cause; Public Citizen; ACLU; Cnty.
Dem. Womens Club. Educ: W. Mich. U. 1939 BA;
Ut. State U. 1968 MS. Occ: Teacher. B: 3/13/15.
Add: 1115 10th Ave. S, Escanaba 49829 (906)
786-2237.

Emmet. PAULINE MENGEBIER (R)
1975-. Bds: Community Mental Health Services
Bd.; Ch., Mich. Assoc. of Cnty's Social Services
Com. Party: Precinct Del. 1975-76. Prev: Health
Planning Council 1973-74. Org: Common Cause;
Planned Parenthood; Arts Council; Historical
Society. Educ: McGill U. 1954 BS. B: 10/2/33.
Add: 2855 Maxwell Rd., Petoskey 49770.

Emmet. ANABELLE C. SMITH (R)
1973-. Bds: NW Mich. Regional Planning & Devt.
Cmsn.; Ch., Health Systems Agency; Conservation &
Roads Com. Party: Pres., Cnty. Rep. Women 1975-
76. Org: Historical Society; Cnty. Rep. Women;
Women's Resource Center. Educ: Capital City
School of Nursing 1954 RN. B: 9/17/32. Add: 513
Bay St., Petoskey 49770.

Genesee. CHARLOTTE L. WILLIAMS (D)
1968-. Dist: 4. Bds: Ch., Nat. Assoc. of
Cnty's; Ch., Cnty. Bd. of Health; V-Ch., Bd. of
Cnty. Institutions. Party: Dem. Adv. Council of
Elected Officals. Prev: State Assoc. of Bds. of
Health; OEO Adv. Com.; Nat. Assoc. of Regional
Councils. Org: NAACP; Urban League; Mich League
for Human Services; Dem. Party. Educ: Flint
School of Practical Nursing 1961 LPN. B: 5/28/28.

Add: 2030 Barks St., Flint 48502 (313)
766-8926.

Gladwin. JACQUELINE RUSSEL
RR #4, Gladwin 48624.

Gratiot. GERALDINE L. PALMER (R)
1977-. Bds: Mid-Mich. Dist. Health Dept. Bd.;
Mental Health Bd.; Ch., Cnty. Bd. of Cmsnr's. -
Health Com. Party: State Alt. 1974, '76;
Precinct Del. 1974-78; Cnty. Exec. Com. 1976-78.
Org: BPW; Cnty. Rep. Women; OES. Occ: Business
Owner. B: 3/21/22. Add: 535 Corinth St., St.
Louis 48880 (517)681-3123.

Gratiot. DORATHA E. STOLZ
315 Euclid, Alma 48801.

Hillsdale. VELMA I. LEMKE (R)
1976-. Bds: Ch., Civil Claims Com.; Ch.,
Youth Home; Equalization Com. B: 4/13/37. Add:
121 W. Main St., (Cambria) Rt. 2, Hillsdale
49242 (517)437-3391.

Houghton. AGNES MARIE SEPPANEN (D)
1974-. Dist: 4. Bds: Ch., Equalization;
Ch., Planning & Zoning; Ch., Parks & Recreation.
Party: State Del.; Precinct Del. 1962-77;
Treasurer of Cnty. Com.; Pres., Women's Dem.
1966-68. Prev: Cnty. Register of Deeds 1962-68;
Secretary of State 1970-75. Org: Extension
Club. B: 4/9/15. Add: 511 Ethel Ave., Hancock
49930 (906)482-8307.

Ingham. SHERRY FINKBEINER
602 Evergreen, E. Lansing 48823.

Ingham. M. ANN LEONARD
1626 Shubel, Lansing 48910.

Ingham. JACQUELINE MC KEON
4269 Greenwood, Okemos 48864.

Ingham. DEBBIE STABENOW
2525 Deerfield, Lansing 48910.

Isabella. KATHLEEN LOUISE LING (D)
1976-. Dist: 7. Bds: Bd. of Health; Central
Mich. Mental Health Services. Party: State
Del. 1972. Prev: Planning Cmsn. 1976; Mental
Health Services Bd. 1976- . Org: Mich. Assoc.
of Cnty's.; Nat. Assoc. of Cnty's.; LWV; PTA.
Educ: Wayne State U. 1967 BS. B: 6/7/45. Add:
1000 E. Preston, Mt. Pleasant 48858 (517)
772-0911.

Jackson. MARY KEITH BALLANTINE (R) **
1970-. Bds: Public Works; Manpower Consortium. Party: Precinct Com. Org: AAUW. Educ:
U. of Ky. 1948 BA; Ind. U. 1950 MA. B: 8/30/26.
Add: 1809 Herkimer, Jackson 49203 (517)
787-3800.

Jackson. EVELYN CRAWFORD
1132 Napoleon Rd., Jackson 49201.

Jackson. GERTRUDE TITUS (D) **
1965-. Bds: Intergovernmental Personnel Com.;
Assoc. of Counties; Mental Health Bd. Org: BPW;
Zonta. Occ: Clerk, Bookkeeper. B: 1/29/23.
Add: 935 S. Gorham, Jackson 49203.

Juce. MARY JO HETRICK
    Turnbull St., Newberry 49868.

Kalamazoo. MARGARET E. MILLER (D)
    1975-. Dist: 12. Bds: Human Resources Com.;
Administrative Com.; Human Services Cmsn. Party:
Precinct Del. 1973-75. Org: NAACP; Dem. Party.
Educ: NC Central U. 1955 BA; U. of NC 1960 MSLS.
Occ: Librarian. B: 11/19/34. Add: 1605 N.
Church St., Kalamazoo 49007 (616)383-8700.

Kent. AGGIE KEMPKER (D)
    1977-. Dist: 11. Bds: Leg. Com.; Juvenile
Detention Study Com.; Community Action Program
Repr. Party: Precinct Del. Prev: Citizens
Community Devt. Com. 1974-77. Org: Amer. Business
Women Assoc.; Community Action Program. Educ:
Grand Vly. State Coll. 1975 BS. B: 11/2/22. Add:
619 Milwaukee Ave. NW, Grand Rapids 49504
(616)454-6796.

Kent. CAROL S. LANDHEER
    2041 Paris Ave., S.E., Grand Rapids 49507.

Keweenaw. ROSALIE KARVONEN
    Allouez 49805.

Keweenaw. DONNA D. LASSILA
    Mohawk 49950.

Lake. LEE ANN RUSSELL (R)
    1975-. Bds: Tri-Cnty. Health Dept.; Civil
Defense Asst. Org: Women's Club. Occ: Abstractor
B: 1/27/46. Add: P.O. Box 128, Baldwin 49304
(616)745-4641.

Lapeer. VIRGINIA JACQULINE JUBELT (D)
    1976-. Dist: 2. Bds: Ch., Leg.; Public Works
& Planning; Human Resources. Party: State Del.
1970-76; Cnty. Committeewoman 1974-76. Prev:
Twp. Clerk 1970-74. Org: Mich. Assessors Assoc.;
Mich. Dem's; BPW. Educ: Wayne State U. 1946 BS;
U. of Mich. 1973 CA. Occ: Accountant. B: 7/11/21
Add: 2614 Mitchell Lk. Rd., Lum 48452 (313)
664-4911.

Lenawee. JANE C. DAVIS (R)
    1977-. Dist: 1. Bds: Bldgs. & Grounds; Tax
Equalization; Human Services. Party: State Del.
1965. Prev: Tax Bd. of Review 1968-69; Community
Mental Health Bd. 1972-77. Org: Cnty. Bd. of
Realtors; Nat. Assoc. of Realtors; Common Cause
Ctr. for Dem. Action; AAUW. Educ: Bucknell U.
1942 BA; U. of Mich. 1976 GRI. Occ: Realtor. B:
9/27/21. Add: 8670 Cherry Pt., Manitou Bch.
49253 (517)263-8831.

Lenawee. NANCY NICHOLS (D)
    1974-. Bds: Ways & Means; Ch., Human Services;
Judicial. Party: State Del. 1974; State Alt.
1976; Local Exec. Bd. 1974-77. Org: Amer. Public
Health Assoc.; Dem. Party; OES; Mich. Assoc. of
Bds. of Health. B: 12/1/39. Add: 216 N. Oneida,
Tecumseh 49286 (517)263-8831.

Livingston. LYNNE MARIE JAMIESON
    1974-. Bds: Ch., Law Enforcement & Public
Safety; Ch., Court House Preservation; Building
& Grounds; Criminal Justice Planning Council.
Org: Mich. Assoc. of Cntys.; Nat. Assoc. of Cntys.
B: 3/22/40. Add: 205 Mason Rd., Howell 48843

(517)546-3520.

Livingston. LOIS J. WILES
    4500 Fausett Rd., Howell 48843.

Macomb. MARY LOUISE DANER (D) **
    1974-. Bds: Full Bd. Party: County Exec.
Bd. 1972-75; Del. State Central Com. 1972-74;
Local Precinct Del. 1972-74. Org: Young Dems.
Educ: U. Miami 1970 BA. B: 7/16/48. Add:
89 Riverside Dr., Mt. Clemens 48043 (313)
465-1211.

Macomb. CAROLINE SKUPNY
    28605 Gratiot, Roseville 48066.

Manistee. BETTY H. NOTEWARE (R)
    1976-. Bds: Mental Health Bd.; Health Dept.
Bd.; Social Services Bd. Party: State Alt.
1954; Cnty. V-Ch. 1954; State Central Com.
1976; Cnty. Exec. Com. 1977-79. Prev: Bd. of
Educ. 1955-66. Org: Fed. Women's Club; Cnty.
Rep. Women's Club. Educ: State U. of Ia. 1941
BA. B: 2/24/14. Add: 3506 Lakeshore Rd.,
Manistee 49660 (616)723-9047.

Marquette. RUBY CHEATHAM
    610 Talon, K.I. Sawyer AFB 49843.

Marquette. SALLY MAY (D)
    1972-. Bds: Ch., Cnty. Lands & Bldgs. Com.;
Alger-Marquette Community Action Bd.; Area
Agency on Aging. Party: Cnty. Exec. Com. 1973- ;
Org: Mich. Assoc. of Cnty's.; Nat. Assoc. of
Cnty's; Humane Society; Upr. Peninsula Environ-
mental Coalition; NOW; WPC; PTA; Nonmotorized
Trails Council. Educ: UCLA 1960 BS. B: 5/1/38.
Add: 425 Lakewood Ln., Marquette 49855 (906)
228-8500.

Midland. PATTIE L. ARMSTRONG (D)
    1977-. Bds: Operations & Purchasing; Planning
Dev.; Taxation Com. B: 9/29/28. Add: 1183 W.
Chippewa Riv. Rd., Midland 48640 (517)835-6881.

Midland. ANNE E. SCHILLING (R)
    1975-. Bds: V-Ch., Human Resources Com.;
Law Enforcement Com.; Ambulance Bd. Party:
State Del. 1974; Cnty. Rep. Exec. Com. 1975.
Prev: Cnty. Social Service Bd. 1974. Org:
Women's Rep. Club. Educ: Oh. State U. 1947 BS.
B: 6/1/25. Add: 6100 Siebert St., Midland
48640 (517)835-6881.

Missaukee. JESSIE HELSEL
    Lake City 49651.

Monroe. DOROTHY BAILEY
    15277 S. Dixie Hwy., Monroe 48161.

Monroe. DOROTHY B. NAVARRE (D)
    1976-. Dist: 2. Bds: Mental Health Bd.;
Mich. Assoc. of Cnty. Leg. Com.; Inter-Cnty.
Hwy. Cmsn. Party: State Del. 1956-62; State Alt.
1953, '54. Org: Nat. Dental Hygiene Assoc.;
Dem. Party; Cnty. Dem. Women. Occ: Dental
Hygienist. B: 11/16/27. Add: 1485 Bates Ln.,
Monroe 48161.

Montcalm. ELAINE M. BAXTER (R) **
    1972-. Bds: Regional Planning. Occ: Secretary. B: 11/28/45. Add: 716 Rosewood, Greenville 48838 (517)831-5272.

Montcalm. KATHLEEN LOIS BURLISON (D)
    1974-. Dist: 8. Bds: Ch., Law Enforcement Com.; Finance Com.; Equalization Com. Prev: Cnty. State Social Services Bd. 1974-76; Ambulance Com. 1974-76. Org: Mich. Assoc. of Cnty's; Mid-Mich. Health Dept.; Planning Com.; OES. Educ: Blodgett School of Nursing 1944 RN, AS. B: 2/5/24. Add: 9454 N. Greenville, Lakeview 48850 (517) 831-5226.

Newaygo. MARY KENDALL (R)
    1976-. Bds: Ch., Health Com.; Ch., Cmsn. on Aging; Personnel Com. Party: State Del. 1974-76; State Alt. 1977; Nat. Del. 1976; Ch., Cnty. 1974-77; Cnty. Secretary 1973-74; Ch., Headquarters 1972. Prev: Charter Cmsn. 1968-69. Org: AAUW; Life Counseling Service; Chamber of Commerce; Rep. Party. Educ: U. of Calif. 1944 BA. B: 12/20/22. Add: 216 S. Woods, Fremont 49412.

Oakland. BETTY J. FORTINO (D)
    1974-. Dist: 5. Bds: Parks & Recreation Cmsn.; Family Focus; Ch., Tourist & Conv. Cmsn. Party: Precinct Del. 1975-77; Congressional Dist. V-Pres. 1975. Prev: Cnty. Cmsnr. 1975-77. Org: Nat. Action Group; Council on Aging; Community Services; Dem. Club; PTA; Pro Life. B: 12/16/35. Add: 747 Joyceil, Pontiac 48054.

Oakland. PATRICIA KELLY
    605 Gardendale, Ferndale 48220.

Oakland. LILLIAN V. MOFFITT (R) **
    1972-. Dist: 15. Bds: V-Ch., Personnel Practices; Public Services Com. Party: County Com. 1968-73; Local Precinct Captain 1964-68; Del., State Conv. Org: AAUW; LWV; PTO; Rep. Women's Club. Educ: De Paul U. 1948 BS. B: 8/3/25. Add: 6828 Cathedral Dr., Birmingham 48010 (313)858-0100.

Oakland. MARGUERITE SIMSON (D)
    1965-. Bds: Emergency Medical Service/Disaster Control; Cnty. Library Bd. Prev: City Cmsnr. 1973-76; Cnty. Supervisor 1965-69; Cnty. Cmsnr. 1971-73. B: 8/12/12. Add: 140 W. Brooklyn, Pontiac 48055 (313)858-0100.

Ogemaw. CLARICE L. SPERRY (D)
    1976-. Dist: 2. Bds: Ch., Welfare, Resolutions & Veteran Affairs; Parks & Recreation; Ambulance. Party: State Del.; State Alt.; Cnty. V-Ch. 1975-77; Cnty. Ch. 1970-74. Org: State Dem. Women's Caucus. Occ: Ct. Transcriber. B: 3/2/33. Add: 105 N. Burgess, W. Branch 48661.

Ottawa. EUNICE K. BARESHAM (R)
    1972-. Bds: Ch., Finance; Ch., Equalization; Ch., Improvement. Party: State Del. 1952-76; Nat. Del. 1976; Rep. Cnty. Ch. 1974-76; Rep. State Central Com. 1977-78. Prev: Cnty. Jury Cmsn. Org: BPW; Mich. Assoc. of Cnty's.; Nat. Assoc. of Cnty's. B: 5/23/25. Add: 530 Grandview, Spring Lake 49456 (616)846-8295.

Ottawa. MARILYN WYNGARDEN SHERWOOD (I)
    1974-. Dist: 3. Bds: Ch., Cnty. Devt. Com.; Planning Cmsn.; Social Services Com. Party: State Del. 1976; Exec. Com. Rep. Party 1974-77. Org: NOWL; ZPG; ACLU; LWV; Environmental Action Council; Counterpart. Educ: U. of Mich. 1960 BSEd. B: 1/1/38. Add: 15983 Harbor Pt. Dr., Spring Lake 49456 (616)846-8310.

Saginaw. MARIE DAVIS
    732 Athens, Saginaw 48601.

St. Clair. PATRICIA LEWIS
    1112 Minnie, Port Huron 48060.

St. Joseph. GRACE E. MC CALLY (R)
    1977-. Dist: 4. Bds: Sheriff Com.; Planning Bd.; Parks & Recreation Bd. Prev: City Planning Bd. 1962-66; City Cmsnr. 1966-71; Mayor 1971-73. Org: BPW; Woman's Club. Occ: Interior Decorator. B: 10/16/19. Add: 1506 8th St., Three Rivers 49093 (616)467-6361.

St. Joseph. JOANNE SADEWASSER (R)
    1977-. Bds: Ch., Exec. Com. B: 7/3/27. Add: 3205 Clark St., Centerville 49032 (616) 467-6205.

St.Joseph. LA VENIA STEVENS
    301 N. Nottawa, Sturgis 49091.

Tuscola. DONNA RAYL
    RR #2, Clark Rd., Akron 48701.

Tuscola. MARGARET A. WENTA (D)
    1974-. Bds: Ch., Tri-Cnty. Transportation Com.; Health Bd., Manpower. Party: Strategy Com. 1975-76. Org: AFSCME; Mich. Assoc. of Cnty's.; Dem. Club. Occ: Bus Driver. B: 12/7/25. Add: 9570 Foster, Fostoria 48435.

Van Buren. SHIRLEY K. JACKSON (R)
    1976-. Dist: 9. Bds: Ch., Auditing & Purchasing; Finance; Administrative Affairs. Party: State Del. 1956-58; Cnty. Rep. Exec. Com. 1975-77; Precinct Del. 1970-77. Prev: Cnty. Jury Bd. 1973-76; City Housing Cmsn. 1968-77; Deputy Twp. Clerk 1963-77. Org: Bicentennial Exec. Com.; Cnty. Rep. Women. B: 6/18/31. Add: 121 Lakeview Ter., PawPaw 49079 (616)657-5581.

Van Buren. RUTH WOLFF LYTLE
    Keeler 49057.

Van Buren. LINDA MARIE SPARKS (D)
    Dist: 6. Bds: Mental Health Bd.; Public Works Com.; Administrative Affairs Com. Party: Del., Cnty. Conv. 1974-77. Occ: Medical Transcriptionalist. B: 5/28/48. Add: 307 Union St., Bangor 49013 (616)427-8411.

Washtenaw. KATHLEEN M. FOJTIK (D) **
    1972-. Bds: Mental Health Bd.; Council of Governors; Agency on Aging; Comprehensive Health Planning. Party: Exec. Com. 1972-75; Women's Caucus 1972-75; Ch. of Issues 1970-71. Org: ACLU; Common Cause; NOW; Occupational Therapy Assoc.; Youth Exchange Assoc. Educ: Mich. State U. 1967 BA; Eastern Mich. U. 1973 BS. B: 11/22/44. Add: 925 E. Ann St., Ann Arbor 48104 (313)994-2402.

Washtenaw. MARGARET A. KUEBLER (D) **
      1972-. Bds: Human Services Com.; Social
Services; Manpower Sub-Com.; OEO Bd. Party:
County Com. 1972- ; Precinct Captain 1970-75;
Precinct Del. 1970-75; Ch. 1972-74. Prev: Parks
& Recreation Com. 1973- . Org: NAACP. B: 7/31/36.
Add: 809 Dwight, Ypsilanti 48197 (313)994-2402.

Washtenaw. CATHERINE MC CLARY
      1125 Michigan Ave., Ann Arbor 48104.

Washtenaw. MERI LOU MURRAY (D)
      1972-. Bds: Parks & Recreation Cmsn.; Urban
Area Transportation Policy Com. Party: State
Del. 1966-76; Ward Ch. 1964-73. Prev: Zoning Bd.
of Appeals 1970-73; Leg. Com. 1975-76; Ch., Bd.
of Cmsnr's. 1975-77. Org: Cnty. Dem's.; Mich.
Dem. Party. Educ: U. of Mich. 1953 BA. Add:
2871 Sorrento, Ann Arbor 48104 (313)994-2400.

Washtenaw. MARGARET O'CONNER
      4300 Saline Rd., Ann Arbor 48104.

Wayne. MARY E. DUMAS (R)
      1970-. Bds: Criminal Justice Coord. Council;
Emergency Medical Services; Crime & Public Safety
Com. Party: State Del. 1964-77; State Alt. 1963;
V-Ch., Congressional Dist. Rep.; Precinct Del.
1964-74. Prev: Dist. Ct. Probation Officer 1969-
71; SE Mich. Council of Govt. 1968-71. Org:
BPW; Chamber of Commerce; United Community Service;
LWV; Rep. Club; Livonia GOP Women. Educ: U. of
Wis. 1947 BA. B: 2/12/22. Add: 17659 Loveland,
Livonia 48152 (313)224-0946.

Wayne. JACKIE CURRIE
      726 City-County Bldg., Detroit 48226.

Wayne. ROSE MARY ROBINSON
      4221 Avery, Detroit 48208.

Wayne. JARRETTE SIMMONS (D) **
      1974-. Prev: Road Cmsn. Org: Dem. Club.
Add: 726 City-County Bldg., 2 Woodward Ave.,
Detroit 48226 (313)224-0908.

Wayne. LORETTA YOUNG
      14304 Schoolcraft, Detroit 48227.

Wayne. MAXCINE YOUNG
      7720 LaSalle Blvd., Detroit 48206.

Wexford. PHYLLIS B. YEARND (R)
      1974-. Bds: Mich. Assoc. Bds. of Public
Health; NW Mich. Substance Abuse Adv. Council;
V-Ch., Mental Health Bd. Party: State Del. 1974;
State Alt. 1976; Precinct Del. 1964-77; Cnty.
Exec. Com. 1964-77. Prev: Cnty. Cmsnr. 1974-76.
Org: BPW. Occ: Funeral Home Owner. B: 8/19/28.
Add: 118 N. Shelby, Cadillac 49601 (616)775-3474.

Townships

Acme. VICTORINE L. KNOPF
      Box 8, Acme 49610.

Acme. BONITA LARKIN
      R. #1, 3313 Michael Dr., Williamsburg 49690.

Adams. BETH A. CASWELL
      114 Vreeland St., North Adams 49262.

Adams. ELIZABETH M. DUBEY
      R #1, Sterling 48659.

Adams. ELSIE M. ESKOLA
      84 Third St., South Range 49963.

Adams. ELEANOR M. MAKI
      17 Fourth St., South Range 49963.

Adams. LOUISE WILLIAMS
      66 Dawn Dr., Hillsdale 49242.

Addison. MARY ANN THOMPSON
      7 E. Elmwood, Leonard 48038.

Aetna. JOYCE MUMAH
      MARGARET WHIPPLE
      R. #2, Morley 49336.

Alabaster. HOPE RESCOE
      140 Center, Tawas City 48763.

Alabaster. FANNIE WALSTEAD
      1693 S. US 23, Tawas City 48763.

Alabaster. ALICE MAKINEN
      1864 Huron Rd., Tawas City 48763.

Alaiedon. GAIL B. THORBURN
      3159 Willoughby Rd., Mason 48854.

Alamo. RITA A. GEARHART
      7888 West D Ave., Kalamazoo 49009.

Alamo. EMMA G. KISINGER
      8081 West D Ave., Kalamazoo 49009.

Albert. FLORENCE MOLINE
      P.O. Box 484, Lewiston 49756.

Albion. DOROTHY JOHNSON
      9644 25 1/2 Mile Rd., Homer 49245.

Alcona. GENEVIEVE GAUTHIER
      JEAN LANGENBURG
      Box 37, Black River 48721.

Algansee. DOLORES COLLINS
      720 Kelly Rd., Reading 49274.

Algoma. DORIS M. GRAY
      11332 Grange Ave., Sparta 49345.

Algoma. LELA R. PECK
      11731 Pine Island Dr., Sparta 49345.

Allen. DOROTHY LETENDRE
      641 W. Chicago, Allen 49227.

Allen. GLADYS E. PEIRCE
      353 Edon Rd., Allen 49227.

Allis. ESTHER DUMSCH
      M-33, #2, Onaway 49765.

Allis. HAZEL PAULY
      R. #2, Onaway 49765.

Allouez. ELLEN MOTTONEN
17 Parnell St., Ahmeek 49901.

Allouez. JUDITH OILA
1030 Ahmeek St., Mohawk 49950.

Almena. DIANE M. TRIQUET
R. #3, Almena Dr., Paw Paw 49079.

Almena. DORIS E. YOUNG
R. #3, 30th St., Paw Paw 49079.

Almer. DORIS REAVEY
R. #1, Box 36, Akron 48701.

Almira. JANET BURCH
Box 75, Lake Ann 49650.

Almira. SHIRLEY E. JOHNSON
R. #1, Empire 49630.

Almira. LUCILLE THOMAS
Box 17, Lake Ann 49650.

Almont. GLORIA HOWE
5430 Cochrane Rd., Almont 48003.

Almont. MARJORIE MUIR
6371 Dryden Rd., Dryden 48428.

Aloha. JOYCE BARR
R. #4, Box 213, Cheboygan 49721.

Aloah. ETHEL PALLISTER
R. #4, Cheboygan 49721.

Alpena. GENIE DIAMOND
1101 Hinckley, Alpena 49707.

Alpena. CHRISTINE M. DUBEY
3000 US 23 N., Alpena 49707.

Alpine. FLORENCE BRECHTING
841 Alpine Church Rd., Comstock Park 49321.

Alpine. MARY HENDERSHOT
841 Alpine Church Rd., Comstock Park 49321.

Amber. SUSAN C. GENSON
R. #2, Scottville 49454.

Amboy. CLAIRE LEININGER
868 E. Territorial Rd., Waldron 49288.

Ann Arbor. VIRGINIA A. AMO
3177 Warren Rd., Ann Arbor 48105.

Antioch. MARGARET HANSEN
DORIS SHERBURNE
HELEN STYSKAL
R. #1, Mesick 49668.

Antrim. CLARA M. PASCO
10378 Godfrey Rd., Bancroft 48414.

Antrim. DONNA J. TIDERINGTON
12295 Bancroft Rd., Morrice 48857.

Antwerp. RUTH COULSON
R. #2, Box 39B, Lawton 49065.

Arbela. RUTH S. O'REILLY
9538 Barkley, Millington 48746.

Arbela. MARY C. WARREN
9451 N. Belsay Rd., Millington 48746.

Arcada. THEORA BERRY
1741 N. Jerome Rd., Ithaca 48847.

Arcadia. JOY HOPWOOD
17341 6th St., Arcadia 49613.

Arcadia. ELLEN MATTER
2614 Mitchell Lake Rd., Lum 48452.

Arcadia. OLIVE MORTENSON
St. Pierre Rd., Arcadia 49613.

Arcadia. SHIRLEY A. SWAIN
1800 Mitchell Lake Rd., Lum 48452.

Arenac. EVELYN OSIER
1808 US 23, R. #1, Omer 48749.

Arenac. ELAINE PULA
2234 Sterling Rd., Rt. #1, Omer 48749.

Argentine. JO ANNE M. COX
12349 Lillie Rd., Byron 48418.

Argyle. HAZEL FOOTE
Frieburg Rd., Snover 48472.

Armada. FAYLENE BEAUDETT
23121 E. Main St., Armada 48005.

Armada. DOROTHYANNE F. TALLMAN
78409 Romeo, Plank, Romeo 48065.

Arthur. EDITH M. NEWMAN
10852 Jefferson, Clare 48617.

Arvon. LEONA E. JANDA
RR Box 185, Skanee 49962.

Arvon. ARLINE VAN BUREN
Skanee 49962.

Ashland. IONE ROBINSON
11496 McClelland, R. #1, Grant 49327.

Assyria. NIANNE A. JARRARD
Guy Rd., R #3, Nashville 49073.

Athens. KATHALEEN TOMLINSON
307 E. Burr Oaks St., Athens 49011.

Atlas. CAROLYN LAWNICZAK
7295 McCandlish Rd., Grand Blac 48439.

Atlas. CORALYN SYMANZIK
8146 Baldwin Rd., Goodrich 48438.

Atlas. NANCY TENNISWOOD
9412 Brendonwood Rd., Goodrich 48438.

Attica. NORENE IRISH
2310 S. Lake Pleasant Rd., Attica 48412.

Au Gres. JOSEPHINE M. COREY
1677 Manor Rd., Au Gres 48703.

Au Gres. MARION J. MIX
1479 E. Huron Rd., Omer 48749.

Augusta. CAROL KOVALAK
10262 Willow Rd., Willis 48191.

Augusta. JOANNE L. LADD
10165 Talladay Rd., Willis 48191.

Aurelius. JUDY CLARK
5726 W. Curtice Rd., Mason 48854.

Au Sable. RHEA MATTHEWS
720 Farnsworth, Oscoda 48750.

Au Sable. RUTH SCHWALM
Robinson Lake Rd., St. Helen 48656.

Au Sable. CARMELLA SHIEL
7902 N. St. Helen Rd., St. Helen 48656.

Au Sable. MORNELVA SNITCHLER
322 Harbor, Oscoda 48750.

Au Sable. MARY SPENCER
303 5th, Oscoda 48750.

Austin. HELEN M. BURDEN
R. #1, Pierce Rd., Stanwood 49346.

Austin. CLAIRE GRIGKA
R. #2, Ubly 48475.

Austin. MARGUERITE HOISINGTON
R. #1, Buchanan Rd., Stanwood 49346.

Avery. GAYLE FERGUSON
R. #3, Box 329, Atlanta 49709.

Avon. GLADYS I. CORBIN
MILDRED P. KNUDSEN
THELMA G. SPENCER
407 Pine St., P.O. Box 250, Rochester 48063.

Backus. ANN COLLINS
3280 S. Maple Valley Rd., St. Helen 48656.

Backus. MARGE LONDRY
3830 S. Maple Valley Rd., St. Helen 48656.

Backus. BARBARA J. MAYER
4054F S. Maple Valley Rd., St. Helen 48656.

Bagley. SHIRLEY JENKINS
P.O. Box 191, Gaylor 49735.

Bainbridge. BEVERLY KOROCH
6100 E. Empire, Benton Harbor 49022.

Baldwin. JOYCE KLENOW
488 Miller Rd., Tawas City 48763.

Baldwin. FRIEDA REMPERT
658 Bischoff Rd., Tawas City 48763.

Baltimore. ANNA CAIRNS
5170 S. Charlton Park Rd., Hastings 49058.

Baltimore. PATRICIA NEWTON
550 E. Cloverdale Rd., Hastings 49058.

Baltimore. KAY SEXTON
4414 E. Dowling Rd., Dowling 49050.

Bangor. RUTH CHARBONNEAU
Bay City 48706.

Bangor. EILEEN NUTTING
R. #2, Bangor 49013.

Bangor. SHARON SHAW
3101 E. Birch Dr., Bay City 48706.

Bangor. VIRGINIA R. WEISS
3921 Wheeler Rd., Bay City 48706.

Banks. MARION SITZEMA
R. #1, Charlevoix 49720.

Baraga. NORINE OSTERMAN
EDITH E. PATOVISTI
Box 246, Baraga 49908.

Bark River. BEVERLY FOURNIER
R. #1, Box 37, Bark River 49807.

Barry. LOIS BROMLEY
R. #2, Delton 49046.

Barry. JUDITH WOOER
10410 Cedar Creek Rd., R. #2, Delton 49046.

Barton. MAXINE R. BATTLE
R. #1, Box 72, Paris 49338.

Batavia. RUTH RIGG
189 W. Colon Rd., Coldwater 49036.

Bates. CLARA KAPUSTA
R. #1, Box 294, Iron River 49935.

Bath. JUNE F. BURNETT
5060 Drumheller Rd., Bath 48808.

Battle Creek. RUTH I. GLADY
957 Hillbrook Dr., Battle Creek 49015.

Bay. MARGARET E. SMITH
2775 Wildwood Harbor Rd., Boyne City 49712.

Bay De Noc. JOANNE SMITH
R. #2, Rapid River 49878.

Bay Mills. MAYBELLE BADDER
R. #1, Box 221, Brimley 49715.

Bay Mills. NANCY A.M. HASCALL
R. #1, Box 178A, Brimley 49715.

Bay Mills. JANET SPRECKER
R. #1, Brimley 49715.

Bear Creek. MARY H. WINTER
4415 Country Club Rd., R. #2, Petoskey 49770.

Bearinger. PATRICIA BOSLEY
Box 157, Huron Beach, Ocqueoc 49763.

Bear Lake. CHARLOTTE HEJL
6716 S. Shore Rd., Bear Lake 49614.

Bear Lake.   INEZ REYNOLDS
      P.O. Box 191, 7899 Lake St., Bear Lake   49614.

Bear Lake.   BERNICE SY
      Box 193, W. Bear Lake Rd., Kalkaska   49646.

Beaugrand.   ELLEN MARTIN
             GERTRUDE M. ROCHELEAU
      R. #3, Cheboygan   49721.

Beaver.   PAMELA CAMPBELL
      950 W. Beaver Rd., Auburn   48611.

Beaver.   KATHERYN C. KIRK
      R. #1, 11 Mile Rd., Bitely   49309.

Beaver.   ROSILEA THOMPSON
      R. #3, 8177 8 Mile Rd., Hesperia   49421.

Beaver Creek.   VIRGINIA MILLIKIN
      R. #1, Box 814 - M Woodland, Roscommon   48653.

Beaver Creek.   ANNA MAE NEILSON
      R. #1, Box 813, Roscommon   48653.

Beaver Creek.   JOAN PATTERSON
      R. #1, Box 794-A, Roscommon   48653.

Beaverton.   MARGARET KILLIAN
      5361 S. Roehrs Rd., Beaverton   48612.

Beaverton.   EUNICE PAYNE
      P.O. Box 67, Beaverton   48612.

Bedford.   PEARL M. ALBERT
      7364 Colonial Dr., Lambertville   48144.

Bedford.   ELIZABETH ANN ARMSTRONG
      107 Markham Ave., Battle Creek   49017.

Bedford.   JO CAROLYN TRACK
      1207 Oakmont Dr., Temperance   48182.

Belknap.   IVA SCHALK
      8150 S. Rogers Rd., Hawks   49743.

Bellevue.   PANSY L. GARDNER
      201 N. Main St., Bellevue   49021.

Belvidere.   DIANN J. CARLSON
      R. #2, Lakeview   48850.

Bengal.   MARILYN K. IRRER
      R. #4, St. Johns   48879.

Bennington.   JACQUELINE C. KELLEY
      4837 Mohican Trail, Owosso   48867.

Benona.   DORIS REAMES
      1400 S. 36th Ave., Shelby   49455.

Benona.   ELEANOR SMITH
      6005 W. Buchanan Rd., Shelby   49455.

Bentley.   LOUISE KREVINGHAUS
      R. #1, 4530 Estey Rd., Rhodes   48652.

Benton.   MARGARET A. CRISHAL
      1565 US 33, Benton Harbor   49022.

Benton.   NORA JEFFERSON
      212 Collins, Benton Harbor   49022.

Benton.   BETTY LETSON
      R. #6, 375 E. Vermontville Hwy., Charlotte
      48813.

Benton.   CATHERYN J. SIRK
      1952 E. Empire Ave., Benton Harbor   49022.

Benton.   HULDA STERZICK
      5131 Billwood Hwy., Potterville   48876.

Benton.   JO ANN WIXSON
      R. #2, 3471 Orchard Beach, Cheboygan   49721.

Benzonia.   NANCY P. KAGE.
      438 S. Michigan, Beulah   49617.

Benzonia.   CONNIE J. ROSE
      1720 Harris Rd., Beulah   49617.

Bergland.   AGNES BONIN
            SHARON NEWHOUSE
      Bergland   49910.

Berlin.   HELEN CHRISTIAN
      14108 Hough Rd., Allenton   48002.

Berlin.   REMI WYLIN
      14560 Gilbert Rd., Allenton   48002.

Berline.   SHIRLANN WELLNER
      5651 Trombley, Newport   48166.

Berrien.   ESTER I. SOMMERS
      R. #1, Box 258, Berrien Center   49102.

Bertrand.   TRELLA L. ROUGH
      2065 Mayflower Rd., Niles   49120.

Bessemer.   CATHERINE FESNICK
      R. #1, Box 196, Bessemer   49911.

Bessemer.   JEAN F. CHAICH
      R. #1, Box 316, Bessemer   49911.

Bessemer.   VERONICA P. MINKIN
      R. #1, Box 26, Bessemer   49911.

Bethany.   MARY SULLIVAN
      R. #1, St. Louis   48880.

Bethel.   JANET L. RZEPKA
      438 S. Snow Prairie, Bronson   49028.

Big Creek.   GERMAINE E. DENNIS
      P.O. Box 447, Mio   48647.

Big Creek.   CHRISTINE MC GREGOR
      P.O. Box 488, Mio   48647.

Big Prairie.   MILDRED CORLEW
      R. #2, Box 276, Newaygo   49337.

Big Prairie.   SANDRA CRAWFORD
      R. #2, Box 313-D3, Newaygo   49337.

Big Prairie.   ELAINE HOLT
      R. #3, Box 112-E, White Cloud   49349.

Big Rapids. JOANNE G. EMMONS
        MAXINE MC CLELLAND
    R. #2, Big Rapids 49307.

Billings. FRANCES FLETCHER
    1130 Pinconning Rd., Beaverton 48612.

Billings. MARY OFFENBECKER
    4301 Martin Rd., Beaverton 48612.

Bingham. MARY DRAPER
    R. #3, Box 535, Traverse City 49684.

Bingham. LYOLA DUNKEL
    1504 E. Walker Rd., St. Johns 48879.

Bingham. INEZ KOPIETZ
    R. #3-B398, Traverse City 49684.

Birch Run. MARCIA STRONG
    8445 E. Burt, Birch Run 48415.

Bismarck. BEATRICE BRIETZKE
    4556 W. 638 Hwy., Hawks 49743.

Bismarck. MABEL KREFT
    Hawks 49743.

Blaine. CHARLOTTE C. PUTNEY
    6352 Putney Rd., Arcadia 49613.

Blaine. MARY JANE TONDU
    Frankfort 49635.

Blair. VIRGINIA E. DUROCHER
    R. #5, Box 480, Traverse City 49684.

Blair. MATILDA J. FASHBAUGH
    719 Brakel Rte. Dr., Traverse City 49684.

Blair. CLARA A. SCHNEIDER
    R. #2, Hilltop Rd., Grawn 49637.

Bliss. CATHERINE KILPATRICK
    S.R., Levering 49755.

Bliss. ALICE MARSHALL
    R. #1, Levering 49755.

Bliss. DONNA SEARLES
    S.R., Levering 49755.

Blissfield. MARY JANE HULL
    9402 Rouget Rd., Blissfield 49228.

Blissfield. JUNE MC KOWN
    412 Giles Ave., Blissfield 49228.

Bloomfield. NADINE LIABENOW
    R. #2, 7350 N. Lueus Rd., Manton 49663.

Bloomfield. DELORIS V. LITTLE
    3185 Franklin Rd., Bloomfield Hills 48013.

Bloomfield. PAULINE PROCTOR
    R. #2, Manton 49663.

Bloomfield. EMMA WOODKE
    R. #2, Port Hope 48468.

Bloomingdale. RUTH H. CORRELL
    P.O. Box 265, Bloomingdale 49026.

Blue Lake. EMELIE ALBRECHT
    R. #2, Mancelona 49659.

Blue Lake. EUNICE L. KARSEN
    11333 Nichols Rd., Holton 49425.

Blue Lake. MINNIE KENEL
    R. #1, Kalkaska 49646.

Blue Lake. EUGENIA VOLLER
    R. #2, Mancelona 49659.

Bohemia. SARAH DANNEELS
    R. #1, Mass 49948.

Bohemia. LEVONA J. NICHOLS
    R. #1, Rousseau, Mass 49948.

Bois Blanc. ANNA ANDERSON
    Box 955, Pointe Aux Pins 49775.

Bois Blanc. MARIAN I. HOFFMAN
    Box N, Pointe Aux Pins 49775.

Bois Blanc. FLORENCE L. VARGO
    Box L, Pointe Aux Pins 49775.

Boon. RUTH BEARSE
    R. #1, Boon 49613.

Boon. SANDRA MC BEATH
    109 Davis, Harrietta 49638.

Bordman. KAREN K. BUXTON
    Box 9B, So. Boardman 49680.

Boston. PATRICIA WYMAN
    6943 Weeks Rd., Saranac 48881.

Bourret. MILDRED LEWIS
    4461 Sycamore, R. #1, Alger 48610.

Bourret. JENABELLE TONEY
    5078 Evergreen Tr., R. #1, Alger 48610.

Bowne. SANDRA KOWALCZYK
    8793 Alden Nash S.E., Alto 49302.

Boyne. JANE I. DE NISE
    Box 1110, Deer Lake Rd., Boyne City 49712.

Boyne. LOUISE MAGEE
    R. #1, Box 39, Boyne Falls 49713.

Brady. LOUISE BARNABY
    R. #3, Vicksburg 49097.

Brady. PATRICIA ANN GOODRICH
    14570 Brady Rd., Chesaning 48616.

Brady. JEAN SHUTES
    R. #3, Vicksburg 49097.

Brampton. FLORA LARSON
    R. #1, Gladstone 49837

Branch. SHIRLEY BRAYTON
R. #1, Fountain 49410.

Brandon. LEONA I. ANDERSON
EDNA M. BURTON
LYNN C. NELSON
LESLIE L. WRIGHT
395 Mill St., Ortonville 48462.

Breen. JUDY CARLSON
Foster City 49834.

Breitung. ROBERTA GRIBBEN
1333 Quinnesec Ave., Quinnesec 49876.

Brevort. REVA SCHIMMELPENNY
Moran 49760.

Bridgehampton. ETHEL SEE
Ruth Rd., Deckerville 49427.

Bridgehampton. DIANE WISIENSKI
Basler Rd., Carsonville 48419.

Brighton. MURIEL BEURMANN
8650 Hyne Rd., Brighton 48116.

Brighton. KAREN C. SMENDZIUK
2964 Pleasant Valley Rd., Brighton 48116.

Brighton. MARGARET E. WENZEL
10872 Spencer Rd., Brighton 48116.

Briley. PATRICIA J. BOLSER
P.O. Box 212, Atlanta 49709.

Brockway. LOUISE KAMMER
12021 Wilkes Rd., Yale 48097.

Bronson. FLORENTINE KEESLAR
R. #2, 584 Bawden Rd., Bronson 49028.

Brookfield. YVONNE WILLIAMSON
7792 Brookfield Rd., Charlotte 48813.

Brooks. MARJORY BOISSONEAU
1376 88th St., Newaygo 49337.

Brooks. SHIRLEY I. GARNDER
R. #1, Grant 49327.

Brooks. MARTHA KALKOFEN
Emerald Lake, Newaygo 49337.

Brooks. JOYCE E. OLWIN
715 76th St., Newaygo 49337.

Brown. RUTH C. HICKOK
8319 Kerry Rd., Manistee 49660.

Brown. MARCELLA ZUPIN
5154 Tompke Rd., Manistee 49660.

Browntown. ROSE M. LEGG
21100 Dean, Romulus 48174.

Browntown. PHOEBE A. STROMP
15850 Bulley Dr., Rockwood 48173.

Bruce. DONNA BATHO
PSR, Sault Ste. Marie 49783.

Bruce. MARY LOU WITZKE
433 Wonderlane, Romeo 48065.

Buchanan. DONNA NEWSOM
1006 Chippewa, Buchanan 49107.

Buchanan. RUTH ROSE
R. #1, Box 400B, Buchanan 49107.

Buckeye. ADRIENNE COURNEY
2199 Weber Rd., Gladwin 48624.

Buena Vista. COLLEEN BENDER
1860 N. Portsmouth, Saginaw 48601.

Bunkerhill. BARBARA RISNER
5234 Freiermuth Rd., Stockbridge 49285.

Burdell. FRANCES ERICKSON
11272 W. Ina Rd., Tustin 49688.

Burleigh. LEONA CHIPPS
R. #1, 2210 S. Putnam Rd., Whittemore 48770.

Burleigh. SHARON OTT
6916 Siefert, Whittemore 48770.

Burlington. LUCILE LOVE
R. #1, Burlington 49029.

Burlington. JANICE MILLER
9972 Main St., Box 207, Clifford 48727.

Burlington. RUBY M. WIESCHOLEK
R. #1, Burlington 49029.

Burr Oak. BEVERLY GRESHAW
R. #1, Burr Oak 49030.

Burr Oak. MARY ANN SMITH
R. #5, 870 Kelley Rd., Sturgis 49091.

Burt. SHIRLEY A. REIMANN
R. #1, Box 142, Cheboygan 49721.

Burtchville. CECILY HILL
4652 Burtch Rd., North Street 48049.

Bushnell. BARBARA DRAPER
1853 Boyer Rd., R. #1, Fenwick 48834.

Bushnell. PHEBE M. WILSON
8129 S. Sheridan Rd., R. #1, Sheridan 48884.

Butler. HILDA CURTIS
944 Curtis Rd., Quincy 49028.

Butler. JOYCE VAN KAMPEN
1180 Crandell Rd., Litchfield 49252.

Butman. PAULA BAILEY
6149 Rou Rd., Gladwin 48624.

Butman. JEAN L. EASTMAN
4411 Ash Rd., Gladwin 48624

Butterfield. MARY CARPENTER
IDA LONG
LULAH VANDENBASS
Merritt 49667.

Caldwell. IDA MAY SNYDER
    NANCY WILSON
    R. #2, Manton 49663.

Caledonia. WINIFRED BALDWIN
    5872 Bennett Rd., Box 62, Hubbard Lake 49747.

Caledonia. RUTH V. DAHL
    1306 E. Spruce Rd., Spruce 48762.

Caledonia. NANCY M. GIAR
    6655 76th St., Caledonia 49316.

Caledonia. MARJORIE RENWICK
    3365 E. Hibbard Rd., Corunna 48817.

Caledonia. SHIRLEY TOLAN
    5325 108th St., Caledonia 49316.

California. PEARL MINER
    R. #3, Fremont 46737.

California. MARY PRIDGEON
    R. #1, Montgomery 49255.

Calumet. GRACIA BRACCO
    2232 Middle St., Calumet 49913.

Cambria. EMMA F. BEECHER
    372 S. Hillsdale Rd., R. #3, Hillsdale 49242.

Cambria. IVA MAY BUTTS
    125 E. Reading Rd., R. #3, Hillsdale 49242.

Cambria. DONITA M. FRITZE
    305 Steamburg Rd., R. #3, Hillsdale 49242.

Cambridge. VIRGINIA DAVIS
    201 Pine St., Brooklyn 49230.

Camden. EVELYN ORTH
    320 N. Main St., Camden 49232.

Camden. ETHEL ROGERS
    210 S. Main St., Camden 49232.

Cannon. BERNADETTE TERPSTRA
    8005 Ramsdell Rd., Rockford 49341.

Canton. ANNE BRADLEY
    6438 Canton Center, Canton 48187.

Canton. C. LYNNE GOLDSMITH
    43951 Bannockburn, Canton 48187.

Carlton. THELMA SWEERS
    1949 Carlton Ctr. Rd., Freeport 49325.

Carmel. RUTH M. GRIER
    R. #5, Charlotte 48813.

Carmel. ISABELLE M. SMITH
    R. #6, Charlotte 48813.

Carp Lake. BERNADINE L. SIBERT
    R. #1, Levering 49755.

Casco. GRACE JOHNSTON
    R. #4, South Haven 49090.

Casco. HELEN M. WAUGH
    10426 Meisner Rd., Richmond 48062.

Case. ELIZABETH J. FREEL
    BERTHA SKINNER
    MARY J. SMITH
    Millersburg 49759.

Caseville. ELAINE M. CLEAVER
    Caseville 48725.

Casenovia. LUCILE M. PENDELL
    17641 Pine St., Bailey 49303.

Castleton. GENEVA BRUMM
    313 Center Ct., Nashville 49073.

Castleton. GERALDINE M. LONG
    9404 Thornapple Lake Rd., Nashville 49073.

Cedar. JOYCE APSY
    R. #3, Reed City 49677.

Cedar. BERNADETTE M. FORREST
    R. #3, Box 427A, Reed City 49677.

Cedar Creek. EDITH DAVIS
    5994 Ryerson Rd., Twin Lake 49457.

Cedar Creek. MARY E. HALL
    5815 Ryerson Rd., Twin Lake 49457.

Cedar Creek. HELEN HILTON
    R. #2, Manton 49663.

Cedar Creek. MARY E. OBENAUF
    4022 Obenauf Rd., Twin Lake 49457.

Cedarville. ALICE ANDERSON
    Cedar River 49813.

Center. DONNA BATCHELDER
    R. #1, Pellston 49769.

Centerville. INEZ KIRT
    R. #1, Box 104, Cedar 49621.

Centerville. MAXINE SCHOPIERAY
    R. #1, Cedar 49621.

Central Lake. WILDA BURNETT
    P.O. Box 152, Central Lake 49622.

Central Lake. DORIS SHOOKS
    R. #1, Box 140, Central Lake 49622.

Champion. WAINO E. LIUPAKKA
    R. #1, Box 34, Champion 49814.

Chandler. MEREDITH BARNES
    R. #1, Boyne Falls 49713.

Chandler. HILDA NIESCHULZ
    Limerick Rd., Caseville 48725.

Chandler. PHYLLIS PENFOLD
    R. #1, Box 133A, Boyne Falls 49713.

Chandler. MARY PETERS
    R. #1, Box 146, Boyne Falls 49713.

Charleston. DOROTHY J. HARMAN
12151 Fort Custer Dr., Galesburg 49053.

Charlevoix. ROSE BERGMANN
R. #3, Division Ave., Charlevoix 49720.

Charlevoix. JO ANN ELZINGA
R. #3, Box 96, Charlevoix 49720.

Chapin. DELLA SHOLTZ
19884 Ridge Rd., Henderson 48841.

Charlton. LILA MAE KESKINE
Star Rt., Box 192, Johannesburg 49751.

Charlton. MAXINE KOSCIELNIAK
Star Rt., Box 211, Johannesburg 49751.

Chassell. PENNY SOUMIS
103 4th, Box 126, Chassell 49916.

Cherry Grove. ISABELL GILLE
3733 W. M-55, Cadillac 49601.

Cherry Valley. ELSIE AVERY
R. #1, Queens Hwy. & 40 St., Chase 49623.

Cherry Valley. WYOMA CANNON
R. #1, Idlewild 49642.

Chesaning. ARLOWA S. HIMM
420 W. Brady St., Chesaning 48616.

Cheshire. SHIRLEY GREIFFENDORF
R. #1, Box 60, Bloomingdale 49026.

Chester. VIRGINIA M. CREAGER
4635 Harding, Conklin 49403.

Chester. LAURA KORONKA
R. #1, Gaylord 49735.

Chester. MAXENE SCHWARTZ
21451 Kenowa, N.W., Sparta 49345.

Chester. MARY T. ZIMBICKI
R. #1, Box 374, Gaylord 49735.

Chesterfield. GLORIS GOIKE
45871 Edgewater, Mt. Clemens 48045.

Chesterfield. CATHERINE MOHR
28606 Cotton Rd., Mt. Clemens 48045.

Chestonia. MILDRED MORRIS
Alba 49611.

Chestonia. MARY STARK
R. #1, Box 264, Mancelona 49659.

Chikaming. LENA ABRAHAMSEN
R. #2, Box 247, Three Oaks 49128.

Chikaming. VIRGINIA M. SPERRY
P.O. Box 156, Sawyer 49125.

China. LEONA MARKEL
JULIE SCHUNK
4560 Indian Trail Rd., Marine City 48039.

Chippewa. THERESA CONROY
4199 S. Shepherd Rd., Mt. Pleasant 48858.

Chippewa. CATHERINE HYNES
8223 E. Remus Rd., Mt. Pleasant 48858.

Chippewa. DORIS LAMOREAUX
Star Rte. #81, Box 14, Eckerman 49728.

Chippewa. ELEANOR J. MARTINDALE
Star Rte. #81, Box 11, Eckerman 49728.

Chippewa. WYNNE NELLIS
R. #1, Rodney 49342.

Chippewa. LOUISE SOULLIERS
Star Rte. #81, Eckerman 49728.

Chocolay. HELEN KOPENSKI
426 Lakewood Lane, Marquette 49855.

Churchill. VERNICE BEDTELYON
1564 Bedtelyon Rd., W. Branch 48661.

Churchill. LUANA LAURIA
5900 Gerald H. Miller Rd., W. Branch 48661.

Churchill. HENRIETTA VOGAN
1139 Gerald H. Miller Rd., W. Branch 48661.

Clam Lake. AMELIA R. BENSON
10345 E. 46 Mile Rd., Cadillac 49601.

Clarence. LINDA GILL
18321 28 Mile Rd., Albion 49224.

Clarendon. GLORIA J. COMBS
23701 T. Dr. S., Homer 49245.

Claredon. CHRISTINE E. MILLER
20584 Q Dr. S., Tekonsha 49092.

Clark. JUDITH A. IZZARD
R.F.D. Swede Rd., Cedarville 49719.

Clay. PATRICIA A. COX
5803 Jankow Rd., Algonac 48001.

Clay. JACQUELINE G. DOWNING
P.O. Box 429, Algonac 48001.

Claybanks. ARLENE M. DAVEY
R. #1, Montague 49437.

Claybanks. LILLIAN R. KIRK
R. #1, Box 172, New Era 49446.

Clayton. SHIRLEY BURTCH
LOIS HARTWICK
CAROL E. KIMSEL
ELAINE MOGG
R. #1, Sterling 48659.

Clayton. NORMA J. WRACAN
12090 Bristol, Lennon 48449.

Clearwater. ESTHER AMIDON
R. #2, Box 346, Rapid City 49676.

Clearwater. VERA DOLEZAL
R. #1, Box 461, Rapid City 49676.

Clearwater. VIRGINIA L. LEE
P.O. Box 43, Rapid City 49676.

Clement. PEARL DOUGLASS
R. #1, 4739 Eastshore Dr., Alger 48610.

Cleon. MARILYN TOEPFER
R. #1, Box 110, Copemish 49625.

Cleveland. BESSIE MUSIL
R. #1, Maple City 49664.

Climax. LUELLA EYRE
14759 OP Ave., Climax 49034.

Climax. SANDRA SIBSON
13515 ON Ave., Climax 49034.

Clinton. MARLA GREEN
ALICE PFAFF
ELNORA STUTEMAN
Comins 48619.

Clinton. MARY HULL
126 Brown St., Clinton 49236.

Clinton. JANET L. WELCH
115 W. Franklin St., Clinton 49236.

Clyde. ANNAMAE C. DAVIS
4893 118th Ave., R. #3, Fennville 49408.

Clyde. MARIE D. NIELSON
R. #4, Box 365, Fennville 49408.

Coe. INA MAE PHILO
108 W. Hall, Shepherd 48883.

Cohoctah. MARGARET E. HOLMES
6685 Byron Rd., Howell 48843.

Coldsprings. CLARA R. DONAHUE
R. #3, Box 358, Kalkaska 49646.

Coldsprings. LUCILLE C. MOTT
R. #1, Box 34, Kalkaska 49646.

Coldwater. LORAINE CONLEY
9320 W. Coleman Rd., Lake 48632.

Coldwater. IRMA GIFFORD
149 E. Garfield Rd., Coldwater 49036.

Colfax. PATRICIA E. FLANERY
Walkerville 49459.

Colfax. MARION JEFTS
R. #2, Big Rapids 49307.

Colfax. ELSIE KRIMM
HAZEL ORDWAY
BETTY L. SCOTT
MILDRED E. SMITH
Thompsonville 49683.

Colfax. JANET TIDEY
R. #1, Manton 49663.

Colfax. NANCY WRIGHT
R. #1, Cadillac 49601.

Coloma. NONA STEWART
4919 Paw Paw Lake Rd., Coloma 49038.

Colon. CATHERINE D. FRISBIE
1234 Decker Rd., Colon 49040.

Colon. NANCY A. PERCIVAL
628 Maple St., Colon 49040.

Columbus. BETTY D. STONE
McMillan 49853.

Columbus. ELIZABETH SCHMIDT
2140 Mayer Rd., St. Clair 48079.

Columbus. MARY LOU WESTRICK
2670 Palms Rd., Richmond 48062.

Comins. LOTIS MILLER
1515 Rogers Rd., Fairview 48621.

Comins. ELIZABETH NEFF
Box 147, Miller Rd., Fairview 48621.

Comins. DONNA YODER
2333 M 33, Comins 48619.

Comstock. ELEANOR WESTRATE
Box 14, Comstock 49041.

Concord. GEORGIA GARDNER
5521 Parsons Rd., Concord 49237.

Concord. JEAN D. WILDT
204 S. Union St., Concord 49237.

Convis. ABIGAIL J. ALBRIGHT
13659 N. Dr., Battle Creek 49017.

Convis. LENORA L. HEWITT
12408 Old Bellevue Rd., Battle Creek 49017.

Conway. SONJA KLEIN
8095 Gregory Rd., Fowlerville 48836.

Cooper. CAROLE M. CULVER
DONNA J. MATYAS
1590 West D Ave., Kalamazoo 49007.

Corwith. MARIAN E. OLIVER
410 W. Main St., Vanderbilt 49795.

Covert. VIOLA LOGAN
R. #2, Box 42, Covert 49043.

Covert. CAROLYN STUCKUM
R. #2, Box 88, Covert 49043.

Covert. LURLEAN TISCHLER
R. #3, Box 167, So. Haven 49090.

Covington. MARTHA AALTO
Box 40, R. #1, Covington 49919.

Crockery. GENEVIEVE CZINDER
13009 Cleveland Rd., Nunica 49448.

Cross Village. MARGARET GASCO
Division Rd., Cross Village 49723.

Cross Village. MARIE KRUPA
Oak Dr., Cross Village 49723.

Croton. EMILY M. BROMLEY
R. #3, Box 104B, Newaygo 49337.

Crystal. PHYLLIS GREINER
R. #2, Hart 49420.

Crystal. ARLENE TURNER
Box 111, Crystal 48818.

Crystal Falls. KALEVA PUOTINEN
R. #1, Box 229, Crystal Falls 49920.

Crystal Lake. JOSEPHINE PETERSON
1169 Frankfort Hwy., Frankfort 49635.

Crystal Lake. IRENE SPAFFORD
Box 506, Frankfort 49635.

Cummings. PATRICIA K. RIEGLE
679 E. Sage Lake Rd., Rose City 48654.

Cummings. RITA SNYDER
2195 N. M-33, Rose City 48654.

Custer. ORLA ALLISON
MARY E. JONES
KATHLEEN LEONARD
LILLIAN E. MAYER
R. #1, Custer 49405.

Custer. ANNA SIMPSON
R. #1, Box 181, Mancelona 49659.

Dallas. JOSEPHINE C. GEORGE
11215 W. 2nd St., Box 216, Fowler 48835.

Dalton. RUTH A. BUELL
2477 N. Pillon Rd., Twin Lake 49457.

Davison. MARY L. MC ARA
8295 Lippincott, Davison 48423.

Day. BEVERLY SMITH
Box 126, Mc Bride 48852.

Dayton. ELOISE KUNNEN
3571 S. Green Ave., Fremont 49412.

Dayton. KAREN ROBERSON
3397 Shay Lake Rd., Mayville 48744.

Dayton. CLAUDIA SCOTT
5932 S. English Rd., Silverwood 48760.

Decatur. MAY KAPLAN
308 W. St. Marys St., Dacatur 49045.

Decatur. JERILEE KLINKERS
115 W. S. Marys St., Decatur 49045.

Deep River. JULIA DERENIAK
2560 Husak Rd., Standish 48658.

Deep River. MARSHA L. MC COY
829 M-70, Sterling 48659.

Deep River. JEANNETTE WOJTOWICZ
4115 Ellison Rd., Standish 48658.

Deerfield. MARJORIE DAMON
147 W. River St., Deerfield 49238.

Deerfield. THERESE Y. DEEDS
10515 N. Latson Rd., Howell 48843.

Deerfield. JOAN MC MACKEN
5035 Center Rd., Linden 48451.

Deerfield. JANET L. ROWLAND
R. #2, Morley 49336.

Deerfield. RITA TAYLOR
231 Indian Trail, Columbiaville 48421.

Delaware. MARY GOETZE
8183 Goetze Rd., Minden City 48456.

Delhi. ELIZABETH S. AUGENSTEIN
2708 Ramparte Path, Holt 48842.

Delhi. BILLIE L. DOWELL
1544 Aurelius Rd., Holt 48842.

Delta. BARBARA BARRETT
1825 N. Willow Hwy., Lansing 48917.

Denver. JEANNE H. EPPLE
H. BEULAH KREINER
R. #5, Mt. Pleasant 48858.

Denver. ARLENE ROBERSON
8333 One Mile Rd., Hesperia 49421.

Denver. SHARON ROBERTSON
7394 One Mile Rd., Hesperia 49421.

Denver. MARIAN STRAUCH
R. #4, Clare 48617.

De Tour. META GEYER
HAZEL SCHOPP
De Tour Village 49725.

De Witt. EILEEN M. CORR
682 Northcrest, Lansing 48906.

De Witt. ALTA CATHERINE REED
780 E. Wieland Rd., Lansing 48906.

De Witt. DONNA B. SYVERSON
780 E. Wieland Rd., Lansing 48906.

De Witt. ENID L. WHITE
780 E. Wieland Rd., Lansing 48906.

Dexter. ARLENE HOWE
7197 Lakeshore, Chelsea 48118.

Dexter. LORINDA JEDELE
13175 N. Territorial, Dexter 48130.

Douglass. VIVIAN HEY
Miles Rd., R. #1, Stanton 48888.

Douglass. LELA PETERS
Grow Rd., R. #1, Stanton 48888.

Dover. JOYCE E. BAILOR
N. State Rd., Luther 49656.

Dover. LUCILLE E. BOUGHNER
R. #1, Box 216, 8748 Sparr Rd., Gaylord 49735.

Dover. EDITH FIKE
2576 Sword Hwy., Adrian 49221.

Dover. EDITH NOVAK
9297 E. 7 Mile Rd., Luther 49656.

Dover. ELIZABETH ROETHIG
9092 E. 7 Mile Rd., Luther 49656.

Dover. KAREN D. SEWELL
R. #1, Box 150D, 4018 Marquardt Rd., Gaylord
49735.

Doyle. VERNA GOUDREAU
Gillver Lake, Gulliver 49840.

Doyle. EVELYN MAC GREGOR
Box 116, Gulliver 49840.

Drummond. JUDITH A. BRITTON
Drummond 49726.

Dryden. MARJORIE AVERY
4042 S. Mill St., Dryden 48428.

Dryden. ALICE L. CLARK
3630 Rochester Rd., Dryden 48428.

Duncan. VIRGINIA HANSEN
Box 132, Kenton 49943.

Duncan. ARLENE SHELLEY
Box 66, Sidnaw 49961.

Dundee. JANET GOETZ
483 Franklin St., Dundee 48131.

Dundee. CLARIBEL ROD
426 Main St., Dundee 48131.

Duplain. KELLEY CARTER
213 E. Main St., Elsie 48831.

Duplain. DORIS MOORE
9870 Gratiot Rd., Elsie 48831.

Eagle. ALICE SULLIVAN
10945 Grand River Hwy., Grand Ledge 48837.

Eagle Harbor. GERTRUDE LAMERAND
SANDRA WHELAN
Eagle Harbor 49951.

East Bay. DONNA J. FINNILA
3351 4 Mile Rd., Traverse City 49684.

East Bay. FLORENCE M. HERALD
1579 4 Mile Rd., Traverse City 49684.

East China. CAROL J. SAUNDERS
4071 S. River Rd., St. Clair 48079.

Easton. MYRTLE ARNOLD
1734 Johnson Rd., Saranac 48881.

Easton. MEREDITH SANDBORN
1286 W. Main, Ionia 48846.

Eaton. BERTHA SEDERLUND
1940 E. Clinton Tr., Charlotte 48813.

Eaton. IRENE P. SMITH
5870 Island Hwy., Charlotte 48813.

Eaton Rapids. CLAIRE A. BRUNTON
6447 Island Hwy., Eaton Rapids 48827.

Eaton Rapids. MYRTLE MAY
9413 Island Hwy., Eaton Rapids 48827.

Echo. SHIRLEY BEAL
R. #3, E. Jordan 49727.

Echo. KATHLEEN L. WILLSON
R. #3, Box 142, E. Jordan 49727.

Eckford. ZELLA ROCKEY
8900 19 Mile Rd., Marshall 49608.

Eckford. JANICE SUNDAY
20748 F Dr. S., Marshall 49068.

Eden. FRANCES BREDEWEG
CLARIBEL E. BRUNNER
ELSIE KESSEL
R. #1, Irons 49644.

Eden. EDITH R. RATHBUN
R. #1, Box 747, Scottville 49454.

Edenville. BETTY BERGMAN
2871 Curtis Rd., R. #2, Coleman 48618.

Edenville. PHYLLIS M. BOMAN
6276 W. River Rd., Sanford 48657.

Elba. ILA C. LINDSAY
383 Harsen Rd., Lapeer 48446.

Elba. BONNIE PURVIS
1470 Lake Nepessing Rd., Lapeer 48446.

Elbridge. DOROTHY I. CUTTER
R. #3, Hart 49420.

Elbridge. NANCY M. TATE
R. #1, Hart 49420.

Elk. DOROTHY KASARSKIS
AUDREY MC CLELLAN
EVELYN MYERS
R. #1, Irons 49644.

Elkland. FAY MC COMB
4292 Maple St., Cass City 49726.

Elkland. CAROLYN M. WARE
4653 Hospital Dr., Cass City 48726.

Elk Rapids. DERONDA ARNOLD
Box 461, R. #2, Williamsburg 49690.

Elk Rapids. HELEN LARSON
Elk Rapids 49629.

Elk Rapids. CAROLINE G. SCHULER
707 Evergreen Bay, Elk Rapids 49629.

Ellington. PEARL A. PUTNUM
3897 Hurds Corner Rd., Caro 48723.

Ellington. HAZEL I. TOMLINSON
1698 S. Colwood Rd., Caro 48723.

Ellis. BERNICE CADDICK
MARY D. EVERARD
R. #1, Wolverine 49799.

Ellis. ESTHER MC CLARY
P.O. Box 9, Afton 49705.

Ellsworth. ANNA SHAFER
206 Elm St., Luther 49656.

Elmira. CATHLENE BRANDENBURG
R. #5, Box 5108 Alba Rd., Gaylord 59735.

Elmira. VIVA KELSO
P.O. Box 27, Elmira 49730.

Elm River. LORNA BRUSO
Twin Lakes Rte., Toivola 49965.

Elm River. JEANNE GOURNEAU
Twin Lakes Rte., Toivola 49965.

Elm River. JOYCE LEPPANEN
Winona Rte., Toivola 49965.

Elmwood. ARLENE R. LAUTNER
12596 W. Bay Shore Dr., Traverse City 49684.

Elmwood. JOANNE SATTELBERG
2777 E. Dickerson Rd., Unionville 48767.

Elmwood. NANCY C. SCOTT
10076 Grand View Ct., Traverse City 49684.

Ely. MARY KIRKER
R. #1, Box 622A, Ishpeming 49849.

Ely. ELISE PETRO
R. #1, Box 625, Ishpeming 49849.

Emerson. JUDITH EICHORN
3345 N. Baldwin, Alma 48801.

Emerson. MARIAN SCHLEDER
2386 E. Polk, Ithaca 48847.

Emmett. DIANE BURROWS
15174 Ackerson Dr., Battle Creek 49017.

Emmett. ELEANOR BUTLER
3291 Quain Rd., Emmett 48022.

Emmett. MARGUERITE GARDNER
620 Cliff St., Battle Creek 49017.

Empire. FRANCES W. BRANDL
R. #2, Box 39, Maple City 49664.

Empire. DOROTHY J. MANNING
10168 Front St., Empire 49630.

Empire. MARIAN E. MINGUS
Box 202, 11679 LaCore Ave., Empire 49630.

Ensign. VIRGINIA PAJNICH
R. #3, Rapid River 49878.

Erie. MARGARET M. DUSSEAU
2060 Manhattan St. Box 187, Erie 48133.

Erwin. JOANNE KAISER
R. #2, Box 363, Ironwood 49938.

Erwin. EVELYN NELSON
R. #2, Box 235, Ironwood 49938.

Erwin. LILLIE POHJOLA
R. #2, Box 305, Ironwood 49938.

Escanaba. LUELLA SMITH
R. #1, Box 443, Gladstone 49837.

Essex. MARCIA NEMCIK
R. #1, St. Johns 48879.

Eureka. ESTELLE COOPER
791 Baldwin Lake Dr., Greenville 48838.

Eureka. M. PATRICIA KREMERS
9350 W. Shows Lake Rd., Greenville 48838.

Eureka. VIRGINIA WEBER
9393 S. Berridge Rd., Greenville 48838.

Evangeline. ELIZABETH E. HOUSER
2664 Wildwood Harbor Rd., Boyne City 49712.

Evangeline. BETTY M. PINNEY
3365 Glenwood Beach Rd., Boyne City 49712.

Evart. BETTY ELDER
EMMA PARSONS
R. #1, Evart 49631.

Eveline. LINDA HILDERBRANT
Box 1660, Boyne City 49712.

Eveline. ZOLA KEMP
R #2, E. Jordan 49727.

Everett. DIANE C. THOMPSON
R. #1, Box 405, White Cloud 49349.

Evergreen. MARGARET KELLNER
4850 S. Staines Rd., Sheridan 48884.

Ewing. IRENE AALTO
ELMA BAKKA
TOINI NIEMELA
R. #1, Rock 49880.

Excelsior. BARBARA COTTON
ELLEN HALL
R. #2, Kalkaska 49646.

Excelsior. CAROLYN WEBBER
R. #3, Kalkaska 49646.

Exeter. MARGARET M.BRUCK
10120 S. Stoney Creek, Carleston 48117.

Fairbanks. MAYME GIERKE
R. #1, Fayette 49830.

Fairbanks. ISABEL THILL
R. #1, Fayette 49830.

Fairfield. BEVERLY A. COWELL
4138 Packard Rd., Sand Creek 49279.

Fairfield. EVA MUNSON
8488 W. Riley Rd., Elsie 48831.

Fairfield. ILENE PURVES
R. #2, 7071 Allen Rd., Elsie 48831.

Fairfield. NORMA J. RIES
8924 Sand Creek Hwy., San Creek 49279.

Fairplains. CAROL NITENGALE
8838 Miller Rd., Greenville 48838.

Fairplains. MARY ELLEN WILSON
8200 Holland Rd., Sheridan 48884.

Faithorn. BETHEL CARLSON
R. #1, Vulcan 49892.

Fawn River. VENICE CARLS
NANCY INMAN
R. #1, Sturgis 49091.

Fenton. DOROTHYANN PHILLIPS
12060 Mantawauka, Fenton 48430.

Ferris. MARY L. CARD
R. #1, Riverdale 48877.

Ferris. COLLEEN WALDRON
R. #2, Edmore 48829.

Fife. JULIA DOWNEY
Maple St., Fife Lake 49633.

Fillmore. VERNA BOEVE
A4521 52nd St., Holland 49423.

Flint. BEVERLY HUNT
1490 S. Dye Rd., Flint 48504.

Flint. MARYANNE KONRAD
G-3422 Hull Ave., Flint 48504.

Flowersfield. DORIS CURTIS
R. #3, Bliss Rd., Marcellus 49067.

Flowerfield. GENEVIEVE WRIGHT
R. #3, Chamberlain Rd., Marcellus 49067.

Flushing. DORENE M. JONES
6111 N. McKinley Rd., Flushing 48433.

Forest. MARY JANE BRECKENRIDGE
11468 N. State Rd., Otisville 48463.

Forest. CATHERINE C. LAING
131 E. Main St., Otisville 48463.

Forest. VIOLET MARTINSON
JERI MC GEE
R. #1, Lake City 49651.

Forest. ELSIE SHIVLIE
R. #2, Lake City 49651.

Forest. LOIS VEIHL
Tower, 49792.

Fork. JOANNE E. BRAND
R. #1, Box 215, Barryton 49305.

Forsyth. SHARON G. CONNORS
Box B, Gwinn 49841.

Forsyth. EVELYN J. HEIKKILA
Box 536, Gwinn 49841.

Frankenlust. MARIE PIOTROWSKI
1826 Delta Rd., Bay City 48706.

Franklin. MARTHA ANDERSON
R. #1, Box 138, Hancock 49930.

Franklin. VELMA DAVIS
11909 Meredith Grade, Gladwin 48624.

Franklin. EVA ECKLIN
7029 E. Long Lake Rd., Harrison 48625.

Franklin. LOIS MATTHEWS
9524 E. Long Lake Rd., Harrison 48625.

Franklin. EMMA RISKE
9303 Meredith Grade, Harrison 48625.

Fraser. ANNA HOLYSKO
R. #2, Box 100, Pinconning 48650.

Fraser. MARIE SCHOTT
R. #2, Box 265, Linwood 48634.

Frederick. MILDRED O. HARMER
R. #1, Frederick 49733.

Frederick. VIOLA MIDDLETON
R. #1, Frederick 49733.

Freedman. MILDRED BLAIN
9051 Monroe, Lake 48632.

Freedman. DELBERTA HOWARD
6526 W. Mannsiding, Lake 48632.

Freedom. RENA L. GIRBACH
8750 Pleasant Lk. Rd., Ann Arbor 48103.

Fredonia. RUTH L. ALBAUGH
193 Perrett Rd., Marshall 49068.

Fredonia. JACQUELINE WARSOP
16274 J. Dr. S., Marshall 49068.

Fremont. LILLIAN DUCKER
131 E. Main St., Mayville 48744.

Fremont. LESLIE KAATZ
895 Saginaw Rd., Mayville 48744.

Frenchtown. ARLENE M. GERWECK
3600 Chinook Ind. Tris., Monroe 48161.

Friendship. ALICE L. CETAS
R. #1, Box 96, Harbor Springs 49740.

Friendship. ALICE B. JERICHOW
R. #1, Lightfoot Rd., Harbor Springs 49740.

Friendship. MARGARET KOHLMAN
R. #1, Harbor Springs 49740.

Frost. NANCY DUTCHER
8982 Clare Ave., Harrison 48625.

Frost. LANORA SCHUTZ
7163 Clare Ave., Harrison 48625.

Fruitland. EMAJEAN LOBENHERZ
5842 Duck Lake Rd., Whitehall 49461.

Fruitport. FLORENCE FLICKINGER
3461 Black Creek Rd., Muskegon 49444.

Fruitport. JANET THOMAS
2645 White St., Muskegon 49444.

Fulton. LORETTA FIRST
5100 Taft Rd., Ferrington 48871.

Gaines. BETTY J. DOLEHANTY
9210 Nichols Rd., Gaines 48436.

Galien. DOROTHY MURDOCK
R. #1, Galien 49113.

Garden. CONNIE WILSON
Box 93, Garden 49835.

Garfield. SANDRA DAY
R. #1, 1155 N. Carter, Linewood 48634.

Garfield. ANNA FEIGER
4969 N. Long Lake Rd., Traverse City 49684.

Garfield. SHARON GRABILL
1385 W. Spring Dr., Newaygo 49337.

Garfield. MARILYN MELVIN
1361 W. 68th, Newaygo 49337.

Garfield. DOROTHY NEEPER
8340 Gibson Rd., Lake 48632.

Garfield. BETTE M. ROWLEY
9930 W. Rock Rd., Lake 48632.

Garfield. DELORES WOJDA
R. #1, Linwood 48634.

Genesee. BETTY J. CARD
4231 Independence Rd., Flint 48506.

Genesee. BETTY J. FAWCETT
4475 Richfield Rd., Flint 48506.

Geneva. GRACE M. LEWIS
3280 N. Lewis Rd., Coleman 48618.

Geneva. SALLY P. WARD
3234 N. Walter, Coleman 48618.

Genoa. LUCILLE A. GLYNN
2980 Dorr Rd., Brighton 48116.

Genoa. DOROTHY MUSCH
3500 Pineridge Ln., Brighton 48116.

Genoa. WENDY W. PETERSON
2980 Dorr Rd., Brighton 48116.

Germfask. SANDRA CHENARD
Box 31, Germfask 49836.

Germfask. MAXINE EDWARDS
Box 55, Germfask 49836.

Germfask. MARY LYTLE
R. #1, Germfask 49836.

Gerrish. MILLIE ROBSON
R. #2, Box 451, Roscommon 48653.

Gerrish. KATHRYN STIEFELMAYER
R. #2, Box 451, Roscommon 48653.

Gilead. BURNIECE MC CLELLAND
R. #1, Bronson 49028.

Gilead. BEVERLY WEAVER
R. #4, Bronson 49028.

Gilmore. MABEL LOVEGROVE
Elberta. 49628.

Gilmore. BONNIE NESS
735 Lincoln, Elberta 49628.

Golden. VADA BEGGS
Box 34, Mears 49436.

Goodar. JANET E. ARNTZ
5365 Goodar, S. Branch 48761.

Goodar. BERENICE PETERS
4507 Alcona, S. Branch 48761.

Goodland. LEA J. LOCKWOOD
2144 N. Summers Rd., Imlay City 48444.

Goodwell. SHIRLEY HARRIS
MARY KAISER
R. #2, White Cloud 49349.

Gore. MARY ANN JAHN
Port Hope 48468.

Gourley. COLLEEN STRAHL
R. #1, Wilson 49896.

Grand Island. ORVA GOLLINGER
Powells Pt., Munising 49862.

Grand Island. BARBARA STARK
Westwood, Munising 49862.

Grant. EDNA ANSCHUETZ
R. #1, 4051 M-55, Tavas City 48763.

Grant. LUCILE BLACKMORE
1199 Sand Lake Rd., National City 48748.

Grant. MARILYN BURCH
7274 Wildcat Rd., Jeddo 48032.

Grant. BERNADINE FEND
R. #1, Free Soil 49411.

Grant. KATHLEEN M. HART
R. #2, Box 248, Cheboygan 49721.

Grant. REBECCA A. JACOBS
R. #4, Box 72A, Big Rapids 49307.

Grant. HELEN MERKEY
R. #2, Free Soil 49411.

Grant. MARGA J. PALMER
Lac La Belle, Mohawk 49950.

Grant. BETTY PETERSON
R. #4, Box 100, 160th Ave, Big Rapids 49307.

Grant. LUCILLE RANDALL
10782 S. Grant Ave., R. #3, Clare 48617.

Grant. CLARE SEAVER
R. #2, Montague 49437.

Grant. RUTH VIAU
R. #4, Box 342, Cheboygan 49721.

Grant. EDITH WALTON
12410 Willow Ave., Grant 49327.

Grant. MARY WENTWORTH
2847 Surrey Rd., R. #3, Clare 48617.

Grass Lake. MARJORIE A. CLARK
1652 Norvell Rd., Grass Lake 49240.

Grass Lake. JANICE G. LABADIE
235 Wimple St., Grass Lake 49240.

Grayling. EVELYN GARDINER
R. #2, Box 2872, Grayling 49738.

Grayling. ELIZABETH H. WIELAND
R. #3, Box 3030, Grayling 49738.

Green. DOROTHY C. JURY
R. #1, Lechine 49753.

Green. CLARE REDNER
19901 Northland Rd., R. #1, Big Rapids 49307.

Greenbush. RUTH DOBBS
4439 S. US 23, Greenbush 48738.

Greenbush. ONALEE MANEVAL
R. #3, 7714 Welling Rd., St. Johns 48879.

Greenbush. RUTH PERSCHON
3392 S. US 23, Greenbush 48738.

Greenbush. LYNN PROCUNIER
5048 E. Main St., Greenbush 48738.

Greendale. ELGA DEGASE
1178 S. Geneva Rd., R. #1, Shepherd 48883.

Greendale. DOROTHY LITTLE
4435 W. Isabella Rd., R. #1, Shepherd 48883.

Greendale. PAULINE VASOLD
4473 W. Isabella Rd., R. #1, Shepherd 48883.

Green Lake. JUDITH LINDENAU
4501 Lakeview Dr., Interlochen 49643.

Greenland. CAROL J. KIN
Greenland 49929.

Greenland. MARY C. MIILU
R. #1, Mass 49948.

Greenleaf. CLARE BROWN
R. #2, Ubley 48475.

Greenleaf. ALETHA FOX
R. #1, Cass City 48726.

Greenleaf. VERA NICOL
R. #1, Cass City 48726.

Green Oak. BEVERLY JOHNSON
9766 Silverside Dr., South Lyon 48178.

Green Oak. JO ANN MURPHY
6210 Marcy, Brighton 48116.

Green Oak. SHIRLEY A. WICKMAN
10789 Silver Lake Rd., South Lyon 48178.

Green Oak. SALLY A. YORK
10789 Silver Lake Rd., South Lyon 48178.

Greenwood. HENRYETTA HOPPE
R. #2, 9505 Garfield Rd., Hesperia 49421.

Greenwood. MARY HULETT
R. #2, Kingsley 49649.

Greenwood. SHIRLEY A. MAYFIELD
2786 N. Harding Ave., Harrison 48625.

Greenwood. ALLEGRA PRIELIPP
5781 N. Old State Ave., Harrison 48625.

Greenwood. CLAIR SCOTT
ANITA WHITE
R. #1, Manton 49663.

Greenwood. LORRAINE ZELDENRUST
9230 200th Ave., Holton 49425.

Grout. LYDIA A. PERRY
R. #3, 1350 S. Bard Rd., Gladwin 48624.

Groveland. ELAINE K. PHILLIPS
3918 Bald Eagle Lake Rd., Holly 48442.

Gun Plain. MARGARET HYDER
371 6th St., Plainwell 49080.

Gustin. CONSTANCE STUTZMAN
204 Fisk, Lincoln 48742.

Hadley. SYLVIA E. BONDS
4115 Diehl Rd., Metamora 48455.

Hagar. WINIFRED ANDERSON
4990 Fikes Rd., Coloma 49038.

Haight. ELIZABETH ANDRUS
MARGARET HAMMOND
Bruce Crossing 49912.

Hamburg. ELLEN S. MC AFEE
4115 E. M 36, Pinckney 48169.

Hamilton. DOROTHY LIEBER
6418 Eugene St., Harrison 48625.

Hamilton. PHYLLIS SENSABAUGH
6981 Buchanan, Ithaca 48847.

Hamilton. PATRICIA SHAW
6383 Nelson, Ashley 48806.

Hamilton. IRENE WEBER
R. #2, Box 54, Decatur 49045.

Hamilton. ELDA ZELT
1603 N. Hoover Ave., Gladwin 48624.

Hamlin. LITA J. GILLETT
R. #1, Eaton Rapids 48827.

Hamlin. EDNA RYON
P.O. Box 100, Ludington 49431.

Hamlin. NANCY LEE SCHOTT
P.O. Box 100, Ludington 49431.

Hampton. ELLA JANE MARTINI
1277 W. Cecelia Dr., Essexville 48732.

Hampton. MARGARET VAN SUMEREN
760 S. Schearmann, Bay City 48706.

Handy. KATE RUDNICKI
314 W. Grand River, Fowlerville 48836.

Hanover. JACQUELINE CADE
MARGARET CADE
Buckley 49620.

Haring. YVONNE M. DE BOER
618 16th St., Cadillac 29601.

Haring. JULIE MODDERS
5081 45 1/2 Mile Rd., 49601.

Harrison. DOROTHY R. GARVEY
38169 Chartier, Mt. Clemens 48045.

Harrisville. MARIE PLEW
4656 Dean Rd., Harrisville 48740.

Hartford. HELEN E. MAYHAK
R. #1, Hartford 49057.

Hartwick. FAY SHANAFELT
R. #2, Evart 49631.

Hastings. VIRGINIA SHERRY
3041 S. Charlton Pk. Rd., Hastings 49058.

Hastings. JUANITA A. SLOCUM
3853 S. Broadway Rd., Hastings 49058.

Hatton. ROSEMARY CARTER
2318 S. Cornwell Ave., Clare 48617.

Hatton. JUDITH DE VALL
1987 Arthur Rd., Harrison 48625.

Hatton. ANN KLEINHARDT
2041 S. Clare Ave., Clare 48617.

Hatton. SHIRLEY RILETT
5914 Eberhart Rd., Clare 48617.

Hawes. VIOLET SCHRAM
1711 Trask Lake Rd., Lincoln 48742.

Hay. MARY ANN SHERWOOD
1726 E. Highwood Rd., Beaverton 48612.

Hayes. ANGELA NOWAK
5460 Gronda Rd., Harrison 48625.

Hayes. MARY ELNOR SEELEY
5383 N. Clare Ave., Harrison 48625.

Hayes. VERONICA SKOP
R. #1, Box 99, Elmira 49730.

Hayes. MARJORIE A. TOLMAN
R. #4, Box 604, Gaylord 49735.

Haynes. MARGARET GREEN
P.O. Box 338, Bay Shore 49711.

Haynes. SANDRA SOMERVILLE
Box E, Bay Shore 49711.

Haynes. MAXINE STERNER
2212 N. Poor Farm Rd., Harrisville 48740.

Hazelton. AUDREY A. ROACH
9454 Butturnut St., New Lothrop 48460.

Hebron. MARGARET ARMANTROUT
R. #1, Levering 49755.

Hebron. ARLEEN DOUGLAS
NANCY DOUGLAS
MRS. DANIEL WHEELOCK
R. #3, Cheboygan 49721.

Hematite. BEVERLY DALLAFIOR
Box 213, Amasa 49903.

Hematite. ILMI LLOYD
R. #1, Crystal Falls 49920.

Henderson. ALICE A. GALVANEK
9160 S. 21 Mile Rd., Cadillac 49601.

Henderson. RUTH E. PERKINS
9030 S. 21 Mile Rd., Cadillac 49601.

Hendricks. ESTHER BEAUDAIN
Star Rte., Naubinway 49762.

Hendricks. LORRAINE BROGG
Star Rte., Naubinway 49762.

Hendricks. BERNICE HOOD
Star Rte., Naubinway 49762.

Henrietta. DOROTHY CHEVRIE
10100 N. Meridian Rd., Pleasant Lake 49272.

Henrietta. RUTH LAYTON
11520 N. Meridan Rd., Pleasant Lake 49272.

Hersey. VENA ZIMMERMAN
311 3rd St., Hersey 49639.

Higgins. MARJORIE E. BIDDLE
　　　LEOLA M. MURPHY
Box 236, Roscommon 48653.

Highland. JOYCE IZZI
　　　LILLIAN ANN WALKER
205 N. John St., Highland 48031.

Hill. ESTHER M. FISCHER
2515 Shady Shores Rd., Lupton 48635.

Hill. ALICE WILLIAMS
2620 Shady Shores Rd., Lupton 48635.

Hillsdale. CATHERINE E. LEWIS
340 S. Broad, R. #4, Hillsdale 49242.

Holland. ELIZABETH CHERNIK
　　　MARGARET FORBES
R. #1, Falmouth 49632.

Holland. LA VERNE JOHNSON
606 Oak Valley Dr., Holland 49423.

Holly. BERNICE ALEXANDER
3500 Grange Hall Rd., Holly 48442.

Holton. LINDA WILKS
7463 Brickyard Rd., Holton 49425.

Holton. JOYCE ZERLAUT
8375 Holton Rd., Holton 49425.

Home. BERENICE JENSEN
222 South Second St., Edmore 48829.

Homer. BARBARA RADOSA
R. #2, Midland 48640.

Homestead. MAUDE MEAD
Honor 49640.

Homestead. JUNE MINER
Box 52, Honor 49640.

Homestead. JEAN ROSA
R. #1, Goose Rd., Beulah 49617.

Hope. SHIRLEY R. CASE
1061 W. Brogan Rd., Hastings 49058.

Hope. DOROTHY STILLWAGON
823 Hull Rd., Hope 48628.

Hopkins. JANE HITZLER
515 Selby St., Hopkins 49328.

Houghton. ANTONIA J. STIGLICH
Phoenix Rte., Mohawk 49950.

Howard. KATHERINE MARTIN
1040 Almaugus Dr., Niles 49120.

Howell. CHRISTINE M. BUNTING
5739 Byron Rd., Howell 48843.

Howell. DIANNE HARDY
2091 Oak Grove Rd., Howell 48843.

Hudson. VIVIAN BRIGHTON
R. #1, Hudson 49247.

Hudson. PATRICIA DERUSHA
Star Rte., Box 27, Naubinway 49762.

Hudson. CELIA R. SEVENSKI
R. #1, Box 17, Elmira 49730.

Hudson. JOAN M. WASYLEWSKI
R. #1, Box 17A, Elmira 49730.

Hudson. DORIS WEBB
R. #1, Vanderbilt 49795.

Hudson. MARGIE WEBER
Garnet 49734.

Hulbert. MAXINE PANGBORN
Box 38, Hulbert 49748.

Humboldt. JANE ANDERSON
R. #1, Champion 49814.

Humboldt. JACQUELINE KOSKI
R. #1, Champion 49814.

Huron. LEONA MUTER
Huron City Rd., Port Hope 48468.

Huron. SANDRA RHODES
36983 Evans, New Boston 48164.

Ida. IONE PARKER
12011 Ida West Rd., Ida 48140.

Imlay. CHARLOTTE SIEGERS
Box 185, 7245 Imlay City Rd., Imlay City
48444.

Independence. ELIZABETH J. HALLMAN
90 N. Main St., Clarkston 48016.

Indianfields. MARION RUSHLO
R. #3, Caro 48723.

Ingallston. AGNES KLEINKE
S.R. 235, Menominee 49858.

Ingham. BEVERLY RISNER
Box 137, Dansville 48819.

Inland. BARBARA J. DOW
　　　MARY ANN JUSTIN
　　　GLADYS WILSON
R. #1, Interlochen 49463.

Interior. ARLENE OLSON
Box 110, R. #1, Trout Creek 49967.

Interior. LOIS J. PERTTULA
Box 83, R. #1, Trout Creek 49967.

Inwood. MARGARET CANTRALL
P.O. Box G, Thompson 49889.

Inwood. KATHLEEN ROCHEFORT
P.O. Box G, Thompson 49889.

Ionia. DEBORAH E. BENSINGER
2548 Clyde Rd., Ionia 48846.

Ionia. ALYCE A. DURAK
4307 E. Riverside Dr., Lyons 48851.

Iosco. LINDA L. ROBERTS
5080 Bradley, Gregory 48137.

Iosco. NANCIE M. STAHL
9797 Lamoreaux Rd., Fowlerville 48836.

Ira. OLGA MELDRUM
8737 Dixie Hwy., Fair Haven 48023.

Iron River. DOROTHY VERVILLE
R. #2, Box 292, Iron River 49935.

Ironwood. RUTH I. HENDRICKSON
P.O. Box 211, Mt. Zion Rd., Ironwood 49938.

Ironwood. SAIMA M. WALKONEN
R. #1, Box 103, Ironwood 49938.

Irving. SANDY SCHONDELMAYER
6900 Soloman, Middleville 49333.

Isabella. DONNA J. PROUT
4144 N. Mission, Rosebush 48878.

Ishpeming. GLADYS RAJALA
US 41 W., Ishpeming 49849.

James. ELEANOR C. HART
5540 Swan Creek Rd., Saginaw 48603.

Jamestown. MYRTLE NEWHOUSE
1687 32nd Ave., Hudsonville 49426.

Jefferson. MARJORIE GEILCZUK
R. #2, Dailey Rd., Edwardsburg 49112.

Jefferson. MARIAN GIER
341 S. Lamb Rd., Osseo 49266.

Jefferson. GLADYS MOLTER
R. #2, Box 172, Cassapolis 49031.

Jefferson. EVELYN POULSON
585 E. Reading Rd., Osseo 49266.

Johnstown. JUNE DOSTER
1815 Lacey Rd., Dowling 49050.

Jonesfield. JUNE C. PLAYFORD
19995 Gratiot Rd., Merrill 48637.

Jordan. SANDRA NEMECEK
LEONA R. STANEK
R. #1, E. Jordan 49727.

Joyfield. IMOGENE GRAY
R. #1, 4319 Rice Rd., Benzonia 49616.

Kalamazoo. PATRICIA HIATT
912 Dwillard Dr., Kalamazoo 49004.

Kalamo. PAULINE OSMAN
7140 Carlisle Hwy., Vermontville 49096.

Kalamo. PEARL G. JOHNSON
7640 Carlisle Hwy., Vermontville 49096.

Kalkaska. JANE KING
P.O. Box 625, Kalkaska 49646.

Kalkaska. LINDA SIETING
R. #3, Box 223, Kalkaska 49646.

Kasson. VIOLET STACHNIK
P.O. Box 2, Maple City 49664.

Kawkawlin. KATHLEEN BRAGIEL
2184 S. Fraser Rd., Kawkawlin 48631.

Kearny. HELEN A. DERENZY
R. #1, Box 319, Bellaire 49615.

Kearny. ROBERTA KOUTNIK
P.O. Box 121, Bellaire 49615.

Keeler. LILLIAN MONTEN
R. #2, Hartford 49057.

Keene. JEAN BURTON
R. #2, 8425 Potters Rd., Saranac 48881.

Keene. MAXINE GASPER
2500 N. Marble Rd., Belding 48809.

Kenockee. MARY BRENNAN
3875 Cogley Rd., Emmett 48022.

Kimball. CONSTANCE HYDE
6320 Griswold Rd., Smiths Creek 48074.

Kinderhook. MARY A. FREEMAN
363 Dragon Lake Rd., Coldwater 49036.

Kingston. VICTORIA WOLAK
2083 S. Kingston Rd., Kingston 48741.

Klacking. DORIS M. DE ROSO
2371 Sage Lake Rd., W. Branch 48661.

Klacking. KATHRYN FRITZ
M-33, R. #3, W. Branch 48661.

Klacking. DEBRA A. THOMAS
Houghton Creek Rd., R. #1, Klacking 48661.

Koehler. ROSE DAVISON
Box 66A, Afton 49705.

Koylton. AILENE R. MC LAUGHLIN
R. #1, Marlette 48453.

Krakow. SHIRLEY M. BELUSAR
Box 123 Bolton Rd., Posen 49776.

Krakow. MARY T. HIGGINS
Box 131-B Bolton Rd., Posen 49776.

Lafayette. GAYLE STELLOW
R. #2, Breckenridge 48615.

La Grange. LUCILLE E. KING
401 E. Jefferson, Cassopolis 49031.

Laird. MARTHA MAKI
R. #1, Box 134, Pelkie 49958.

Laird. MARGARET WESTENBERG
P.O. Box 64, Nisula 49952.

Lake. GLENNA MANEKE
R. #1, Lake City 49651.

Lake. ELSIE RECK
8559 Gast Rd., Bridgman 49106.

Lake. DEBI TAGLIARENI
R. #1, Big Star Lake Rd., Baldwin 49304.

Lake. LOIS WEINEL
R. #79, Box 306, Houghton Lake 48629.

Lakefield. SUSAN MACAULAY
R.R., Mc Millan 49853.

Lakefield. PEGGY A. MUNGER
20420 Lakefield Rd., Merrill 48637.

Lakefield. MARY SULLIVAN
19081 Lakefield Rd., Merrill 48637.

Laketon. KYRAN J. KANE
80 Green Creek Rd., Muskegon 49445.

L'Anse. LOIS M. TEMBRUELL
106 S. 4th St., L'Anse 49946.

Lansing. MARTHA C. BISSINGER
1307 Shaffer Court, Lansing 48917.

Lapeer. ILA M. BURRIS
2065 S. Lapeer Rd., Lapeer 48446.

Larkin. RUTH A. ROBEL
R. #8, 4986 Letts Rd., Midland 48640.

Larkin. DIANNE L. DAVIS
R. #1, Hubbard Rd., Midland 48640.

Leavitt. LEOLA FORNER
P.O. Box 242, Walkerville 49459.

Lebanon. GAYLE FITZPATRICK
R. #1, Fowler 48835.

Lee. THELMA BARNHART
23182 21 Mile Rd., Olivet 49076.

Lee. EDITH KROTZER
800 N. 11 Mile Rd., Sanford 48657.

Lee. VIRGINIA KRUGER
1254 S. Eight Mile Rd., Midland 48640.

Lee. VERA LAING
18424 19 Mile Rd., Marshall 49068.

Leelanau. DOROTHY CRAKER
P.O. Box 224, Northport 49670.

Lenox. FRANCES R. GOLDENBOGEN
58869 Pine St., New Haven 48048.

Leoni. JO ANN MIDDLEBROOK
913 Fifth St., Michigan Center 49254.

Leonidas. SELMA COMSTOCK
R. #1, Box 87, Mendon 49072.

Leonidas. GERTRUDE SAXMAN
1089 E. M-60, Leonidas 49066.

Leonidas. PATRICIA A. SAXMAN
N. Maple, Leonidas 49066.

Leroy. JOAN K. ACKER
1757 Elm Rd., Webberville 48892.

Leroy. PATRICIA DECKER
7991 3 1/2 Mile Rd., E. Leroy 49051.

Leroy. MARGARET D. EDSTROM
400 Houghton, Leroy 49655.

Leroy. DORRANCE RISCH
5000 Dennis Rd., Webberville 48892.

Leroy. LUANA M. SAWYER
4689 Holt Rd., Webberville 48892.

Leroy. INGRID THACKER
R. #2, Leroy 49655.

Leslie. ERMA BIGG
4965 E. Main St., Leslie 49251.

Leslie. MARIAN PARKER
5074 State Rd., Leslie 49251.

Lexington. SHIRLEY LANDBERG
Wixson Rd., Croswell 48422.

Liberty. PATRICIA A. LEUTZ
11465 Culver Rd., Cement City 49233.

Liberty. ROBERTA S. SCHWARTZ
9735 Gillette Rd., Clark Lake 49234.

Lilley. LYDIA BRIGGS
P.O. Box 13, Bitely 49309.

Lilley. DAISY THOMAS
R. #2, Bitely 49309.

Lima. LEILA C. BAUER
13000 Scio Church Rd., Chelsea 48118.

Lima. JEAN L. TILT
1031 N. Steinbach Rd., Dexter 48130.

Lincoln. EVA G. BEEBE
R. #2, Pleasant Valley Rd., Shepherd 48883.

Lincoln. LYNN BROWN
R. #2, E. Fremont Rd., Shepherd 48883.

Lincoln. JEAN DROUSE
4260 Melita Rd., Standish 48658.

Lincoln. LESLIE EICHENBERG
R. #3, Reed City 49677.

Lincoln. DOROTHY KOELSCH
4012 Melita Rd., Standish 48658.

Lincoln. HELEN A. KOWALK
3210 Finley Lk. Rd., Harrison 48625.

Lincoln. DIANE SCRAMLIN
2195 1/2 Price Rd., Midland 48640.

Lincoln. SALLY SMITH
336 Parkway Dr., Lake George 48633.

Lincoln. BERNICE TRETHEWAY
CHRISTINE WELCH
P.O. Drawer L, Stevensville 49127.

Lincoln. VIRGINIA WUNCH
R. #4, Quincy St., White Cloud 49349.

Litchfield. PATRICIA BLONDE
764 Jonesville Rd., Allen 49227.

Little Traverse. JANE TAYLOR
Pleasantview Rd., Harbor Springs 49740.

Livingston. ISADORE KOZLOWSKI
R. #1, 2966 Wilkinson Rd., Gaylord 49735.

Locke. DOROTHY FINGER
3959 Rowley Rd., Williamston 48895.

Locke. BEATRICE WAITE
4405 Rowley Rd., Williamston 48895.

Lodi. GRACE M. DIUBLE
4441 S. Parker Rd., Ann Arbor 48103.

Logan. MARY ELLEN GALLINGER
4497 E. M-55, Prescott 48756.

Logan. JEANNE THOMPSON
R. #1, P.O. Box 139, Branch 49402.

Long Lake. VIRGINIA FEWINS
R. #2, Box 400, Traverse City 49684.

Long Rapids. BONNIE KING
4003 M-65 North, Lechine 49753.

Loud. ROSEMARY BEAUREGARD
R. #3, Box 181, Atlanta 49709.

Loud. ELSIE BIXEL
County Line Rd., Comins 48619.

Lowells. MARGIE HARWOOD
R. #3, Box 3512, Grayling 49738.

Lowells. HELEN M. SPENCER
R. #3, Box 3558, Grayling 49738.

Lyndon. DORIS M. FUHRMANN
R. #2, Roepke Rd., Grass Lake 49240.

Lyndon. BARBARA RODERICK
9508 Beeman Rd., Grass Lake 49240.

Lynn. VIRGINIA MEIKLE
14520 Speaker Rd., Yale 48097.

Lynn. ELENA ROOT
15685 Dudley Rd., Brown City 48416.

Lyon. MARY CANFIELD
EVELYN HERALD
57100 Pontiac Trail, New Hudson 48165.

Lyon. JOAN V. HILLEARY
P.O. Box 81, Higgins Lake 48627.

Lyon. GWENDOLYN S. KNAPP
57100 Pontiac Trail, New Hudson 48165.

Lyon. JOYCE REDMON
P.O. Box 14, Higgins Lake 48627.

Lyons. CLARE J. PUNG
2641 Hubbardston Rd., Pewamo 48873.

Lyons. BERNETTIA E. SMITH
10875 Kimball Rd., Pewamo 48873.

Mackinaw. LA VONYA S. FUSS
925 S. Huron, Mackinaw 49701.

Mackinaw. ROSE M. SCOTT
US 27, Mackinaw City 49701.

Macon. SANDRA BORTEL
11890 N. Ridge Hwy., Tecumseh 49286.

Macon. BEATRICE GILMORE
10148 Welch Rd, Britton 49229.

Madison. LARRAINNE SEAMAN
2240 Cadmus Rd., Adrian 49221.

Mancelona. MARGARET M. BOGERT
304 Lincoln St., Mancelona 49659.

Manchester. DOROTHY R. BURCH
648 W. Main, Manchester 48158.

Manchester. WILMA E. LENTZ
9415 Grossman Rd., Manchester 48158.

Manistee. NORMA ANDERSON
165 W. Kott Rd., Manistee 49660.

Manistee. ALMA GIBSON
1130 E. Parkdale Ave., Manistee 49660.

Manistee. HELEN OLSEN
126 W. Kott Rd., Manistee 49660.

Manistique. ESTHER ERICKSON
R. #1, Box 523, Manistique 49854.

Manistique. HELEN SCHNURER
R. #1, Box 477, Manistique 49854.

Mansfield. ANN CLEMENT
GERTRUDE COLONY
EVA STREAM
ROSE ZAVADA
Star Rte., Crystal Falls 49920.

Maple Forest. EDNA BABBITT
R. #1, Frederic 49733.

Maple Forest. SUSAN M. KEENE
R. #1, Frederic 49733.

Maple Forest. MARTHA J. PETERSEN
R. #1, Frederic 49733.

Maple Grove. MARY JARRARD
9950 S. Clark Rd., Nashville 49073.

Maple Grove. MARY L. LENZ
R. #1, Joy Rd., Kaleva 49645.

Maple Grove. JOYCE STARRING
8510 Cloverdale Rd., Nashville 49073.

Maple Ridge. NANCY M. JOKELA
R. #1, Rock 49880.

Maple Ridge. LILLIAN KINGSBURY
5868 Dietz Rd., Alpena 49707.

Maple Ridge. PATRICIA LUND
R. #1, Rock 49880.

Maple River. DORIS BUDNIK
R. #1, Brutus 49716.

Maple River. SALLY SCHREIER
Tower Rd., Pellston 49769.

Maple Valley. CLARE BARTLE
6610 Bailey Rd., Brown City 48416.

Maple Valley. VIRGINIA PARKER
13452 Briggs Rd., Trufant 49347.

Marathon. LETA SECORD
4643 Middle St., Columbiaville 48421.

Marathon. MARGARET TRAVER
4170 LeValley, Columbiaville 48421.

Marcellus. EDITH L. DAVIS
Box 218, Marcellus 49067.

Marilla. MILLIE REPO
R. #1, Copemish 49625.

Marion. MARTHA FORDYCE
306 Carland, Marion 49665.

Marion. DOROTHY HOLDEN
4255 Mason Rd., Howell 48843.

Marion. DORIS HONAMAN
9065 S. Merrill Rd., Brant 48614.

Marion. DORIS JOHNSON
R. #2, Black Rd., Charlevoix 49720.

Marion. DOROTHY POHL
3575 Jewell Rd., Howell 48843.

Marion. BERNICE WAUN
2368 Black River St., Deckerville 48427.

Markey. ALICE HARDAWAY
R. #2, Box 355, Houghton Lake 48629.

Markey. LOUISE SULLENGER
R. #2, Box 52A, Roscommon 48653.

Marquette. CAROL HUEMPFNER
2393 Badger, Marquette 49855.

Marquette. CAROLE A. SIMILA
2343 Werner St., Marquette 49855.

Marquette. MARJEEN WISE
Pickford 49774.

Marshall. JUNE HINDENACH
15495 A. Dr. N., Marshall 49068.

Martiny. VIRGINIA GEASLER
R. #1, Rodney 49342.

Mason. SILVA BRACK
1160 N. Lehman Rd., Twining 49766.

Mason. EDNA P. CLICK
R. #1, Box 87, Edwardsburg 49112.

Mason. ALICE LIEBER
1707 N. Fire Rd., Twining 49766.

Masonville. LILLIAN M. BJURMAN
R. #1, Box 1587, Rapid River 49878.

Masonville. RUTH A. SUNDBERG
R. #2, Box 148, Rapid River 49878.

Matchwood. AGNES HOKENS
R. #1, Ewen 49925.

Mathias. PAULINE M. WEBBER
Box 78, Trenary 49891.

Matteson. MARY DEAN
R. #3, Bronson 49028.

Matteson. RUTH M. HURLEY
R. #1, Sherwood 49089.

Mayfield. MABEL M. BOTT
7622 Bott Rd., Buckley 49620.

Mayfield. BARBARA L. POTTER
2442 Haines Rd., Lapeer 48446.

McKinley. SALLY JUDSON
R. #1, Levering 49755.

McKinley. IDA MC CABE
Pellston 49769.

McMillan. IDA MALNAR
R. #1, Ewen 49925.

Meade. DORIS REID
R. #2, Box 76A, Freesoil 49411.

Meade. HELEN SCHMITT
2186 Crown Rd., Filion 48432.

Meade. ELIZABETH SMALLEY
R. #2, Box 114, Freesoil 49411.

Mecosta. RUTH HESS
R. #2, 8 Mile Rd., Stanwood 49346.

Mecosta. JEAN ULRICH
R. #3, 10085 Northland Dr., Big Rapids 49307.

Medina. ELAINE NOFZINGER
R. #1, Morenci 49256.

Melrose. MARY W. ERB
Walloon Lake, 49796.

Mendon. ORTHA DAUGHERTY
838 Silver St., Mendon 49072.

Menominee. DOROTHY BUYARSKI
RA 663, Menominee 49858.

Mentor. EDNA CRANE
Box 444, Mio 48647.

Mentor. RUTH ANN KINNEY
Box 96, Mio 48647.

Mentor. PHYLLIS MATTSON
R. #1, Wolverine 49799.

Mentor. LOIS WEHRMEISTER
R. #2, Box 59, Mio 48647.

Meridian. CARLENE WEBSTER
2247 Kenmore Dr., Okemos 48864.

Meridian. VIRGINIA L. WHITE
5100 Marsh Rd., Okemos 48864.

Merrill. JOSEPHINE CARTER
R. #1, Bitely 49309.

Merrill. CHARLOTTE PAIGE TUCKER
R. #1, Box 66, Bitely 49309.

Merritt. MARCIA COLBERG
163 E. Munger Rd., Munger 48747.

Metamora. ELAINE M. BECHILL
1384 Kile Rd., Metamora 48455.

Metamora. MARY HELEN KUREK
1640 Hendrie Rd., Metamora 48455.

Metz. MARY KASZUBOWSKI
R. #2, Box 22, Posen 49776.

Meyer. JANE ST. JULIANA
Fourth St., Hermansville 49847.

Meyer. MARY ELLEN PLUNGER
R. #1, Hermansville 49847.

Michigamme. ALICE CITTADINO
Star Rte., Box 227, Michigamme 49861.

Michigamme. JEAN D. HOWE
P.O. Box 27, Michigamme 49861.

Middle Branch. PATRICIA MITCHELL
R. #1, Marion 49665.

Middlebury. H. ELIZABETH PUTNAM
7940 W. Hibbard Rd., Ovid 48866.

Middlebury. DELORES J. SIMPSON
6235 W. Simpson Rd., Ovid 48866.

Midland. JOYCE L. HAGLE
2094 E. Stewart Rd., Midland 48640.

Midland. DELORIS H. MC KELLAR
3117 E. Gordonville Rd., Midland 48640.

Mikado. HELMA A. LEE
4916 Alvin Rd., Mikado 48745.

Mikado. BERTHA M. SILVERTHORN
3616 M-41, Mikado 48745.

Milan. LOIS J. HEATH
11666 Wabash, Milan 48160.

Milan. SUE C. MURRAY
17495 Hickory, Milan 48160.

Milford. ORMA C. MC CRANER
C. ELAINE SKARRITT
1100 Atlantic, Milford 48042.

Millbrook. DOROTHY COULSON
MARIE CUMMINGS
R. #2, Blachard 49310.

Millen. DE LORIS MANIGLIA
66 Sanborn Rd., Barton City 48705.

Millen. MARJORIE REEVES
1338 W. M-72, Barton City 48705.

Millington. WANDA SERGENT
4912 Barnes Rd., Millington 48746.

Mills. MAXINE M. BRINK
5561 N. Sturgeon Rd., Midland 48640.

Mills. CATHERINE LEHNER
DONNA L. WILKINS
2441 Greenwood, Prescott 48756.

Milton. MARIAN E. BUSSA
R. #1, Box 176, Rapid City 49676.

Milton. MARGARET J. FALES
R. #1, Box 415, Kewadin 49648.

Milton. JOYCE F. PIERSON
218 Ironwood Dr., Niles 49120.

Milton. DORIS WESLEY
191 Fir Rd., Niles 49120.

Minden. DEANNA JO LAUTNER
7795 Rangeline Rd., Minden City 48456.

Minden. JUNE SPAETZEL
1717 Main St., Minden City 48456.

Mitchell. CATHRYN PALMER
R. #1, Curran 48728.

Moffatt. KATHLEEN MC ALISTER
6784 S. Forest Lake, Alger 48610.

Moltke. CAROLINE D. LA LONDE
1649 N. Ward Dr. Rd., Rogers City 49779.

Monroe. LETA EAMES
Box 23, Brohman 49312.

Monroe. MARGUERITE FERGUSON
R. #2, White Cloud 49349.

Monroe. CYNTHIA LITTICH
R. #4, White Cloud 49349.

Monroe. SUE JOHNS
4925 Dunbarr Rd., Monroe 48161.

Monterey. VALERIE ARNDT
R. #5, Allegan 49010.

Monterey. LUCILLE COON
R. #1, Hopkins 49328.

Montmorency. SYLVIA I. CONNON
R. #2, Box 85, Hillman 49746.

Montmorency. SHIRLEY KLOTZ
R. #2, Box 216, Hillman 49746.

Montmorency. PATSY SHOOKS
R. #2, Box 112, Hillman 49746.

Montrose. PEARL THORSBY
139 S. Saginaw St., Montrose 48457.

Moore. CLARE DORMAN
2900 Ubly Rd., Snover 48472.

Moorland. DONNA TYERS
2023 Mason Rd., Ravenna 49451.

Moorland. DOROTHY J. VANDERLAAN
11961 White Rd., Ravenna 49451.

Moran. JANIS A. CHEESEMAN
R. #2, Box 127, St. Ignace 49781.

Moran. LOUISE HAGEN
Brevort, R. #2, Moran 49760.

Morton. NANCY SHEEHAN
485 W. Main, Mecosta 49332.

Moscow. VERA RICHARDS
Moscow 49257.

Mottville. MARY JANE ALMASI
R. #2, Box 325, White Pigeon 49099.

Mount Forest. BERNICE ADAMS
5179 Garfield Rd., Pinconning 48650.

Mount Morris. VIOLET L. GROSCH
G-3026 W. Coldwater Rd., Mt. Morris 48458.

Mount Morris. HELEN MURPHY
G-3026 W. Coldwater Rd., Mt. Morris 48458.

Mueller. VIOLET FREELAND
Box 184, Gulliver 49840.

Mueller. MARION PETERS
P.O. Box G, Thompson 49889.

Mueller. SANDRA PRICE
Box 170, Gulliver 49840.

Mullett. ELEANOR M. SPENCER
1466 Patterson, Tapinabee 49791.

Munising. ELEANOR STORM
R. #1, Box 37, Shingleton 49884.

Munro. JACQUELINE COATTA
R. #1, Levering 49755.

Munro. LINDA GINOP
R. #1, Hellman Rd., Box 187, Levering 49755.

Muskegon. CHARLOTTE L. RUSCH
287 N. Sheridan Dr., Muskegon 49442.

Mussey. CLAIRE D. KRIESCH
324 N. Hunter, Capac 48014.

Mussey. LA VERNE W. NEWMAN
4824 Martin Rd., Capac 48014.

Nadeau. JULIA GRONMARK
DOROTHY SPEHAR
R. #1, Carney 49812.

Nahma. SUZANNE POMEROY
R. #3, Rapid River 49878.

Negaunee. DOROTHY COLLINS
230 Wilderness Rd., Negaunee 49866.

Nester. CAROLYN CORLEW
12790 Nolan Rd., R. #4, Gladwin 48624.

Nester. MARY ANN ROZA
6745 Muma Rd., R. #4, Gladwin 48624.

Nester. VIOLA STOKUS
7706 Muma Rd., R. #4, Gladwin 48624.

New Buffalo. JEANNINE J. DALTON
P.O. Box 12, New Buffalo 49117.

New Buffalo. JOANN P. FLECK
R. #1, Box 597, New Buffalo 49117.

Newberg. FLORENCE NORTON
R. #5, Box 80, Three Rivers 49093.

Newfield. LAURA P. RICE
7256 E. Hayes Rd., Hesperia 49421.

New Haven. MILDRED BARNES
102 S. Bliss Rd., R. #1, Sumner 48889.

Newkirk. EDNA MAE FULLERTON
Robbins Rd. RFD, Luther 49656.

Newkirk. MARY E. KESSEL
P.O. Box 16, Luther 49656.

Newton. LILA H. BAKER
JEAN D. BUNCE
RACHEL A. MC NEIL
ANNE TREMBLEY
KATHLEEN M. VOGL
Gould City 49838.

Noble. GAIL METZGER
R. #1, Bronson 49028.

Norman. RITA CROW
16156 Caberfae Hwy., Wellston 49689.

Norman. CORA KNIGHT
16848 West Sixth St., Wellston 49689.

Norman. FRANCES SCHUESSLER
483 Tipp Dam Rd., Wellston 49689.

North Allis. MARJORIE BENAWAY
            VIVIAN M. ELLENBERGER
     M-211 Rd., R. #1, Onaway 49765.

Northfield. BEVERLY J. BATER
     9317 Main St., Whitmore Lake 48189.

Northfield. ROSE C. LAVENDER
     9158 Jay St., Whitmore Lake 48189.

Northfield. JUDITH F. STEELE
     58 Margaret St., Whitmore Lake 48189.

Northville. CLARICE SASS
     16300 Sheldon Rd., Northville 48167.

Norvell. ANNA A. DALTON
     11321 Wamplers Lake Rd., Brooklyn 49230.

Norvell. GENEVIEVE SANDERS
     12886 Austin Rd., Brooklyn 49230.

Norvell. BARBARA J. TROLZ
     115 Sweeney Lake Rd., Norvell 49263.

Norway. THERESA HAMMILL
     R. #1, Vulcan 49892.

Norway. BEATRICE ZYCHOWSKI
     R. #1, Vulcan 49892.

Norwich. YVONNE MC KEOWN
     R. #2, Lake City 49651.

Norwich. ILENE OLSON
     R. #3, Box 323, Big Rapids 49307.

Norwich. LOIS WHIPPLE
     4840 E. Morrestown Rd., Moorestown 49651.

Norwood. RUTH ANN CAMPBELL
          BERTHA E. PARSONS
     R. #1, Charlevoix 49720.

Nottawa. BARBARA J. WEBER
     424 E. Main, Centreville 49032.

Novesta. JEAN CLARKE
     Cass City 48726.

Novesta. GAIL PARROTT
     3446 Philips Rd., Cass City 48726.

Novesta. ARLEON RETHFORD
     Gilford Rd., Deford 48729.

Nunda. PATRICIA A. BURROWS
     R. #1, Wolverine 49799.

Nunda. MARGUERITE SWARTZ
     P.O. Box 126, Wolverine 49799.

Oakland. MARILYN M. MALINOWSKI
          CAROLYN L. PHELPS
     4393 Collins Rd., Rochester 48063.

Ocqueoc. RUTH MILBOCKER
     M-68 Hwy., Millersburg 49759.

Odessa. NANCY HICKEY
     R. #3, Box 457, 8963 Eaton Hwy., Lake Odessa

Odessa. LINDA SWIFT
     1122 Lakeview Dr., Lake Odessa 48849.

Ogemaw. HAZEL BUTLER
     R. #2, 4362 W. M-76, W. Branch 48661.

Ogemaw. VIRGINIA LINSENMAN
     R. #2, 4428 W. Brewer Rd., W. Branch 48661.

Olive. RUTH BARTELS
     0-7140 120th Ave., Holland 49423.

Olive. EDITH JACOBSEN
     8283 120th Ave., W. Olive 49460.

Oliver. BETTY J. DUNHAM
     R. #2, Sigma Rd., Kalkaska 49646.

Oliver. DOROTHY HENDRICKS
     R. #2, Cool Rd., Kalkaska 49646.

Oneida. IDA GREY
     5640 Grand River Dr., Grand Ledge 48837.

Oneida. JOHANNA PARSHALL
     12699 Kenyon Rd., Grand Ledge 48837.

Onondaga. DOROTHY M. CLARKE
     4815 S. Waverly Rd., Onondaga 49264.

Onondaga. ELIZABETH A. WATSON
     6251 Rossman Rd., Onondaga 49264.

Ontonagon. CAROLE J. MONVILLE
     414 Walnut St., Ontonagon 49953.

Ontwa. HELEN J. PARSONS
     R. #3, Box 379, Edwardsburg 49112.

Orange. ELEANOR FERRIS
     4872 Kelsey, Ionia 48846.

Orange. MARILYN MUNRO
     R.R., South Boardman 49680.

Orangeville. DARLENE M. HARPER
     11031 Wildwood Rd., R. #1, Shelbyville 49344.

Oregon. LYNN K. PORRITT
     2643 Reynolds Circle, Columbiaville 48421.

Oregon. KENNA R. SCHLEGEL
     5083 Mt. Morris Rd., Columbiaville 48421.

Oregon. ROSEMARY L. SIMPSON
     3490 Northwood Dr., Columbiaville 48421.

Orient. GLADYS BOWNS
     R. #1, Box 167, Sears 49679.

Orient. AGNES LLOYD
     R. #1, Box 436, Sears 49679.

Orion. MARJORIE L. HODGES
        JO ANN VAN TASSEL
     571 S. Lapeer Rd., Lake Orion 48035.

Orleans. GERTRUDE HEPPE
     514 Meade Rd., Orleans 48865.

Osceola. VIRGINIA ANDERSON
Box 122, Hubbell 49934.

Osceola. SHARON L. BEERS
R. #2, Evart 49631.

Osceola. EVELYN M. CORNELL
6625 Brophy, Howell 48843.

Osceola. R. ELAINE FORGET
Box 205, Hubbell 49934.

Osceola. ELIZABETH MEYER
R. #3, Evart Rd., Evart 49631.

Osceola. ALINE K. SMITH
R. #1, 5491 E. Forest Hill Rd., Evart 49631.

Oscoda. MAXINE BISSONETTE
110 S. State St., Oscoda 48750.

Oshtemo. LOIS BROWN
4162 S. 1st St., P.O. Box, Oshtemo 49077.

Oshtemo. JEAN VANDER LYKE
7874 W. Main, Kalamazoo 49009.

Ossineke. BERTHA GERKE
9913 Wolf Creed Rd., R. #1, Hubbard Lake 49747

Otsego. SHIRLEY DOXEY
35 20th St., Otsego 49078.

Otsego Lake. VERGELINE MILLER
R. #3, Box 577, Gaylord 49735.

Otsego Lake. CECELIA SCHOTTE
P.O. Box 45, Waters 49797.

Otto. MARY EDGERTON
Wilke Rd., Rothbury 49452.

Ovid. NANCY AKER
2023 Lake Dr., Coldwater 49036.

Ovid. CAROL A. BASHORE
3485 S. Meridian Rd., Ovid 48866.

Ovid. KATHERINE KELLEY
R. #2, 1774 S. Shepardsville Rd., Ovid 48866.

Oxford. CLARA J. SANDERSON
DIANA C. TURNBULL
18 W. Burdick, Oxford 48051.

Palmyra. LINDA L. EHLERT
8997 Rouget Rd., Palmyra 49268.

Paradise. VESTA A. SEDLACEK
Box 311, Kingsley 49649.

Paris. THERESA STOMACK
Minden City 48456.

Park. CORALYN HAAN
988 Sycamore Dr., Holland 49423.

Park. CAROL E. SNOW
R. #2, Three Rivers 49093.

Parma. GERALDINE G. KOHLER
3737 Brown Rd., Parma 49269.

Parma. MARGARET N. LANDON
16420 Devereaux Rd., Albion 49224.

Paw Paw. JUDITH E. HAEFNER
P.O. Box 20, Paw Paw 49079.

Pavillion. NANCY K. MLECZEWSKI
8660 E. Q Ave., Scotts 49088.

Peacock. EDNA M. BUZZO
R. #2, Box 242, Baldwin 49304.

Peacock. BARBARA A. CAMPBELL
R. #2, Wolf Lake, Baldwin 49304.

Peacock. RUTH O. MOORE
R. #1, Box 125, Irons 49644.

Peacock. GLORIA ROOT
R. #2, Wolf Lake, Baldwin 49304.

Peaine. ROSE CONNAGHAN
Beaver Island, St. James 49782.

Peaine. GLADYS SCHAUDIGEL
Beaver Island, P.O. Box 85, St. James 49782.

Peaine. BONNIE WAGNER
St. James 49782.

Peninsula. MARY K. BELDING
17630 Smoky Hollow Rd., Traverse City 49684.

Peninsula. MERRY S. WORDEN
6271 E. Shore Rd., Traverse City 49684.

Pennfield. JULIA SWEET NEWMAN
P.O. Box 99, Battle Creek 49016.

Pennfield. WANDA M. WALTON
10700 Gorseline Rd., Battle Creek 49017.

Pere Marquette. CONSTANCE C. ANDERSEN
R. #1, S. Lakeshore Rd., Ludington 49431.

Pere Marquette. ETHEL M. LISTER
3140 S. Pere Marquette Rd., Ludington 49431.

Perry. MARTHA BREHM
4880 W. Britton Rd., Perry 48872.

Perry. PATSY FORCE
14738. S. Morrice Rd., Morrice 48857.

Perry. BENNITA SWEETER
5087 W. Church, Perry 48872.

Perry. JOYCE WILLARD
2246 E. Union, Shelby 49455.

Pierson. VERA PAULEN
Waterwheel Rd., Pierson 49339.

Pine. DORIS J. SWEM
2393 N. Greenville Rd., Stanton 48888.

Pine Grove. VERA HEINTZMAN
7866 16th, Gobles 49055.

Pine Grove. MARY H. RENDEL
R. #1, Gobles 49055.

Pioneer. ZELDA CHAFFEE
NONDIS HUTCHINSON
LUELLA MUSSELMAN
HELEN SLOAT
R. #2, Lake City 49651.

Pipestone. PATRICIA KIRK
5783 Old Pipestone, Eau Claire 49111.

Pittsford. EVELYN MONROE
1113 Union Rd., R. #2, Pittsford 49271.

Plainfield. BARBARA MALCHO
R. #2, Box 1365, Hale 48739.

Plainfield. ELIZABETH TIMMER
Box 495, Hale 48739.

Platte. LINDA L. DAVIS
R. #1, Box 349, Honor 49640.

Platte. VERA PARKER
Fowler Rd., Honor 49460.

Pleasanton. JUDY GIRVEN
MARJORIE REED
R. #2, Bear Lake 49614.

Pleasant Plains. GAIL MARSHALL
845 Beech St., P.O. Box, Baldwin 49304.

Pleasant View. LELIA BETWAY
R. #1, Box 174, Alanson 49706.

Pleasant View. JANE WURST
R. #1, Box 184, Alanson 49706.

Plymouth. HELEN I. RICHARDSON
42350 Ann Arbor Rd., Plymouth 48170.

Pokagon. EDNA DARESH
R. #4, M-62 W., Dowagiac 49047.

Pokagon. BARBARA ROCKWELL
R. #1, M-51 S., Dowagiac 49047.

Pontiac. DOROTHY A. BABB
VERONICA C. NEW
2060 Opdyke Rd., Pontiac 48057.

Portage. CHARLOTTE BUSBY
R. #1, Box 171, Houghton 49931.

Portage. M. JEANNE EDWARDS
P.O. Box 38, Curtis 49820.

Portage. CAROL HAAPAPURO
R. #1, Houghton 49931.

Portage. SALLY OLLILA
R. #1, Box 149, Houghton 49931.

Port Austin. PAULINE ADAMSON
267 State St., Port Austin 48467.

Port Austin. ELIZABETH BROCK
36 Washington, Box 320, Port Austin 48467.

Porte Aux Barques. HELEN P. GILBRIDE
1951 Cliff Rd., Port Austin 48467.

Porter. BIANCA HEBRON
R. #1, Jones 49061.

Porter. CAROLE A. PACKER
R. #1, Box 488, Lawton 49065.

Port Huron. BEULAH F. HOWARD
3110 Strawberry Lane, Port Huron 48060.

Portland. JEAN M. DAWDY
8559 Oak Dr., Portland 48875.

Portland. FLORA B. KRAUSZ
5250 Lyons Rd., Lyons 48851.

Port Sheldon. JUDITH ELENBAAS
ESTHER VAN SLOOTEN
16201 Port Sheldon Rd., W. Olive 49460.

Portsmouth. ELIZABETH A. NEERING
70 Tierney Rd., Bay City 48706.

Posen. ALICE M. HOPPE
W. Long Lake Rd., R. #3, Alpena 49707.

Prairie Ronde. ZELLA STREW
15401 S. 6th & XY Ave., Schoolcraft 49087.

Prairieville. ELEANOR HOUVENER
10580 Houvener Rd., Delton 49046.

Prairieville. ELINOR WELTY
R. #1, Box 137, Delton 49046.

Presque Isle. PEGGY A. CRILLEY
P.O. Box 91, Presque Isle 49777.

Presque Isle. SHIRLEY ANN SNAY
11541 Bell Bay Rd., Alpena 49707.

Presque Isle. NANCY V. WENDLAND
P.O. Box 26, Presque Isle 49777.

Pulaski. FLORINE KELLERMEYER
11725 Hanover Rd., Hanover 49241.

Pulaski. JOYCE WELTER
11245 Hanover Rd., Hanover 49241.

Pulawski. EILEEN DARGA
Box 191, Posen 49776.

Pulawski. MARIE WYREMBELSKI
Box 200, Posen 49776.

Putnam. MARGARET DE SMEDT
11280 Patterson Lake Dr., Pinckney 48169.

Putnam. KATHLEEN A. URBANY
134 Pearl St., Pinckney 48169.

Quincy. GLORIA KARPPINEN
R. #1, Box 414, Hancock 49930.

Quincy. ELAINE J. RAASIO
302 McKinley St., Hancock 49930.

Quincy. VIVIAN SATTLER
72 W. Chicago St., Quincy 49082.

Raber. KATHRYN MACIAG
Stalwart 48789.

Raisin. MARJORIE COMFORT
5423 Sutton Rd., Britton 49229.

Raisin. SHIRLEY ROBACK
3700 Westgate Place, Tecumseh 49286.

Raisinville. MARIE JANSSENS
7837 N. Custer Rd., Monroe 48161.

Ransom. LINDY KIRKINGBURG
1017 S. Bird Lk Rd., R. #1, Osseo 49266.

Rapid River. JOAN BRAND
Westwood Trail, R. #1, Alden 49612.

Rapid River. DOLORES DEXTER
2609 Westwood Rd., R. #2, Mancelona 49659.

Rapid River. ANNIE LUCILLE FERGUSON
Priest Rd., R. #2, Mancelona 49659.

Ravenna. SHARON RUST
12930 Harrisberg, Ravenna 49451.

Ray. CAROL A. VITALE
22000 27 Mile Rd., New Haven 48048.

Readmond. FLORA BELLE KRUZEL
JENNIE LASLEY
Cross Village 49723.

Readmond. KATHLEEN A. SELLICK
Lakeshore Dr., Harbor Springs 49740.

Redding. MINNIE CASTLE
634 E. Davis, R. #1, Harrison 48625.

Redding. LEONA L. KENNEDY
499 So. Main, Rt. #1, Harrison 48625.

Redding. ANNA L. KRICHMAR
6435 W. Lily Lake Rd., Harrison 48625.

Redford. RUTH SULLIVAN
15145 Beech Daly, Detroit 48239.

Reeder. KAY ROBERTS
R. #1, Lake City 49651.

Reno. WINONA REDMOND
6821 Carpenter, Whittemore 48770.

Republic. RUTH MYKKANEN
Box 127, Republic 49879.

Reynolds. MARGARET E. HILL
107 Grant St., Howard City 49329.

Rich. ELLA MAE LYON
2041 Sarles Rd., Silverwood 48760.

Richfield. MARY M. MASTERS
10251 Richfield Rd., Davison 48423.

Richfield. DOROTHY L. MC NEIL
8831 South St., St. Helen 48656.

Richfield. CAROL D. SULLIVAN
2101 North St., Helen Rd., St. Helen 48656.

Richland. SUSAN A. BRANTLEY
Box 151, Vestaburg 48891.

Richland. BETTY J. BROWN
8655 East DE Ave., Richland 49083.

Richland. DORIS BRUMELS
R. #2, McBain 49657.

Richland. ELIZABETH L. DROLET
8719 East DE Ave., Richland 49083.

Richland. CLARE PREUSS
13555 Geddes, Hemlock 48626.

Richland. CLARE V. SMITH
R. #1, McBain 49657.

Richmond. CLAUDIA M. O'CONNOR
26245 Prinz Rd., Armada 48005.

Riley. STEPHANIE FREY
13439 Burgess Rd., Allenton 48002.

Riley. LINDA HAZELTON
401 Braidwood, Memphis 48041.

Riley. ANDREE LAMBERT
12245 Hough Rd., Memphis 48041.

Riverton. AUDREY VAN NORTWICK
R. #1, Ludington 49431.

Riverton. PHYLLIS J. SCHWARTZ
1050 Washington Rd., Pentwater 49449.

Rives. MARIAN J. HERL
1947 Perrine Rd., Rives Junction 49277.

Rives. BARBARA S. HAMMOND
4000 Broughwell Rd., Rives Junction 49277.

Robinson. MAXINE TEN BRINK
9634 Lake Mich. Dr., W. Olive 49460.

Rockland. MARGARET ERICKSON
CATHERINE FREDRIKSON
Rockland 49960.

Rock River. KATHY J. MAKI
Eben Jct. 49825.

Rock River. MARY A. PILIPPO
Chatham 49816.

Rock River. EDITH L. SMITH
Box 11, Eben Jct. 49825.

Rolland. GERTRUDE BEACH
Box 136, Blanchard 49310.

Rolland. MARY C. WICHERT
    R. #2, Blanchard 49310.

Ronald. MARGIE POWELL
    R. #2, Ionia 48846.

Ronald. EVELYN RANSOM
    Rt. #1, Ionia 48846.

Roscommon. BETTY L. SAXTON
    R. #79, Box 347J, Houghton Lake 48629.

Roscommon. CHARLOTTE WHITE
    P.O. Box 283, Houghton Lake 48629.

Rose. BARBARA ALDERTON
    VIOLET COSAND
    P.O. Box 32, Lupton 48635.

Rose. JOYCE V. SLAUGHTER
    MARGARET I. THORSBY
    204 Franklin St., Holly 48442.

Rose Lake. FLORENCE JOHNSON
    R. #1, LeRoy 49655.

Rose Lake. KATHRINE M. SWANSON
    R. #1, Hogback Lake, LeRoy 49655.

Ross. MARY E. BOWMAN
    7690 N. 41st St., Augusta 49012.

Ross. BETTE SHROYER
    304 N. Wester, Augusta 49012.

Roxand. BEULAH LAWRENCE
    R. #1, Mulliken 48861.

Royal Oak. VIVIAN BELL
    SYLVANIA GUINN
    HELLEN ROSE MADDOX
    21075 Wyoming Ave., Ferndale 48220.

Rubicon. PEGGY L. EMERICK
    3195 N. Lakeshore Dr., Port Hope 48468.

Rush. BETTY CRIM
    205 E. Main St., Henderson 48841.

Rush. AMY SMITH
    1720 W. Henderson Rd., Henderson 48841.

Rust. ISMA BANKS
    R. #1, Box 45, Hillman 49746.

Rust. MARILYN J. KELLEY
    R. #1, Box 181, Hillman 49746.

Rust. VIOLET KLEIN
    R. #1, Box 102, Hillman 49746.

Rutland. MARY LOU PRATT
    2982 Irving Rd., Hastings 49058.

Sage. RUTH L. GERTZ
    R. #5, Gladwin 48624.

Sage. PHYLLIS RAYMOND
    R. #6, 1446 Chapel Dom Rd., Gladwin 48624.

Saginaw. ESTHER M. FUHRHOP
    NANCY SPENCER
    4980 Shattuck Rd., Saginaw 48603.

Sagola. SOPHIE HARVATH
    Star Rte. #1, Iron Mountain 49801.

Sagola. LUCILLE SAYERS
    Channing 49815.

St. Charles. VIVIAN VOGELAAR
    8702 Fergus, St. Charles 48655.

St. Ignace. DONNA B. HARJU
    Box 59, R. #1, St. Ignace 49781.

St. Ignace. SANDRA K. LITZNER
    Box 144, R. #1, St. Ignace 49781.

St. Ignace. BESSIE A. MATSON
    R. #1, St. Ignace 49781.

St. James. VIVIAN H. VISSCHER
    VERA M. WOJAN
    Beaver Island, St. James 49782.

St. Joseph. SALLY MUTZ
    146 W. Napier, Benton Harbor 49022.

Salem. DORIS COATS
    4278 30th St., Burnips 49314.

Salem. NANCY M. GEIGER
    5379 Five Mile Rd., South Lyon 48178.

Salem. DOROTHY SHUCK
    4279 30th, Burnips 49314.

Saline. MARILYN M. GORDON
    4725 Willow Rd., Saline 48176.

Sanborn. MARILYN CREVIER
    Ossincke 49766.

Sands. HILMA MUNSON
    P.O. Box 237, Marquette 49855.

Sands. NATALIE HENDERSON
    Star Rte., Box 477, Gwinn 49841.

Sandstone. PRISCILLA J. STERRETT
    3805 N. Parma Rd., Parma 49269.

Sandstone. THERESA TAYLOR
    321 Grove St., Parma 49269.

Sanilac. MARY SCHLICHTING
    Box 43, Port Sanilac 48469.

Sauble. VERNA J. BARTOLETTI
    Box 109-D, Irons 49644.

Sauble. AMANDA A. EVANS
    R. #1, Five Mile Rd., Irons 49644.

Sauble. VIRGINIA M. KESTER
    R. #1, Five Mile Rd., Irons. 49644.

Schoolcraft. EVIE M. BURR
    R. #3, Box 23, Vicksburg 49097.

Schoolcraft. JULIA A. CHAMBERLAIN
    14535 S. 16th St., Schoolcraft 49087.

Schoolcraft. GRAYCE SLONAKER
    834 Front St., Lake Linden 49945.

Schoolcraft. IDA SMITH
    520 Front St., Lake Linden 49945.

Scio. GAY F. KONSHUH
        EVELYN P. NAVARRE
    827 N. Zeeb Rd., Ann Arbor 48103.

Sciota. BERNICE A. GRAHAM
    8475 Doyle Rd., Laingsburg 48848.

Scipio. JUDY HOLLENBAUGH
    1037 Rainey Rd., Jonesville 49250.

Scipio. MARY L. MC MILLAN
    1163 Rainey, Litchfield 49252.

Sebewa. HAZEL M. FENDER
    11336 Cassel Rd., R. #1, Portland 48875.

Sebewaing. LOIS BOHN
    Liken Rd., Sebewaing 48759.

Secord. JOSEPHINE BOMAN
    2853 Lakeshore, Gladwin 48624.

Secord. ANNA MAY HORNER
    3370 Lakeshore, Gladwin 48624.

Secord. DORIS MC KAY
    2985 Three Rivers, Gladwin 48624.

Secord. ELAINE ST. LOUIS
    3767 Lakeshore, Gladwin 48624.

Seneca. CATHERINE FORD
    R. #2, Brower Rd., Morenci 49256.

Seney. JENNIE NELSON
    P.O. Box G, Thompson 49889.

Seville. BONNIE M. CARROLL
    R. #1, Elwell 48832.

Shelby. EILEEN BUCKMATER
    65 Rankin, Shelby 49455.

Shelby. MARY S. HOLMES
    8430 Pamela, Utica 48087.

Shelby. LOIS MC ALPINE
    11260 Pierson, Washington 48094.

Shelby. MARY ELLEN PARROTT
    53436 Northrup, Utica 48087.

Shelby. JOY L. PLUMMER
    2275 S. 88th Ave., Shelby 49455.

Shelby. ELLEN PRINCE
    4600 S. Redwood, New Era 49446.

Sheridan. HELEN BUDZYNSKI
    R. #1, Fountain 49410.

Sheridan. ORMA GINGRICH
    R. #2, Remus 49340.

Sheridan. JOYCE LANDENBERGER
    17520 28 Mile Rd., Albion 49224.

Sheridan. NORMA JEAN MORSE
    R. #1, Fountain 49410.

Sherman. FRANCES C. ADAMS
        RUTH G. CALKINS
        DORIS E. EGGLE
        BEVERLY MICKEVICH
        MARY RICARD
        PRINCESS STOCKING
    Fountain 49410.

Sherwood. ELLA M. YOUNGS
    506 N. Main, Sherwood 49089

Sidney. CECILE M. THOMAS
    751 Lakeside Dr., Stanton 48888.

Silver Creek. NELLIE J. PRICE
        RUTH SARABYN
    R. #5, Dowegiac 49047.

Sims. MARIE A. WARR
    5557 AuGres Ave., AuGres 48703.

Sims. CAROLE J. ZANNER
    Point Lookout, AuGres 48703.

Skandia. GLORIA MAKI
    R. #1, Carlshend 49811.

Slagle. KATHRYN L. KLINGBEIL
    R. #1, Harrietta 49638.

Sodus. VIRGINIA PAILS
    4598 Tabor Rd., Sodus 49126.

Somerset. LOUISE M. ALLEY
    867 Alley Rd., Jerome 49249.

Somerset. LOUISE K. MECKLEY
    1069 S. Jackson Rd., Cement City 49233.

Soo. ALICE EAGLE
    R. #1, Box 130, Sault Ste. Marie 49783.

South Arm. HELEN CHERRY
    R. #1, E. Jordan 49727.

South Arm. ANNA M. OLSTROM
    R. #2, E. Jordan 49727.

South Branch. VIRGINIA DRILL
    9500 S. 11 Mile Rd., Cadillac 49601.

South Branch. MURIEL MICHAEL
    R. #4, Box 45-E, Roscommon 48653.

South Branch. MARY M. MOLLON
    R. #4, Box 45-E, Roscommon 48653.

South Branch. HELEN G. STIMAC
    R. #1, Wellston 49689.

Southfield. ELEANOR A. MC GEE
18321 Saxon Dr., Birmingham 48009.

Southfield. ELLEN M. REED
30125 Marimoor, Birmingham 48009.

South Haven. EMILIA MILLER
R. #3, South Haven 49090.

South Haven. RUTH C. TORP.
R. #3, 72nd St., South Haven 49090.

Spalding. BONNIE L. BARKER
LUELLA MURRAY
Spalding 49886.

Speaker. MARY RECTOR
10556 Fisher Rd., Yale 48097.

Spring Arbor. ESTELLA BEARDSLEE
153 Harmony, Spring Arbor 49283.

Springfield. DOROTHY M. CLARK
R. #1, Box 99, Shippy Rd., Fife Lake 49633.

Springfield. JOYCE M. INGERSOLL
Puffer Rd., Fife Lake 49633.

Springfield. PATRICIA L. KRAMER
650 Broadway, Davisburg 48019.

Springvale. LELIA TERPENING
R. #2, Petoskey 49770.

Springville. SHERYL SPARRKS
R. #2, Mesick 49668.

Spurr. EDITH KOSKI
Star Rte. Box 5, Michigamme 49861.

Spurr. MARY SKYTTA
Box 40, Michigamme 49861.

Spurr. MARTHA WILTJANEN
Star Rte. #4, Michigamme 49861.

Stambaugh. CAROLINE MEHLBERG
R. #3, Box 74, Iron River 49935.

Stambaugh. BERNICE ROSETTI
R. #3, Box 55, Iron River 49935.

Standish. JEANNETTE LEMMER
R. #1, Box 67, Standish 48658.

Standish. JEAN STODOLAK
R. #1, Box 240, Standish 48658.

Stannard. ALICE LINNA
Box 31, Bruce Crossing 49912.

Stanton. BETTY RUOHONEN
R. #1, Box 255, Houghton 49931.

Stephenson. LORAINE L. VANDENHOUTEN
R. #2, Box 162, Stephenson 49887.

Stockbridge. JOYCE DICKINSON
217 Williams Ave., Stockbridge 49285.

Stockbridge. JO ANN OWEN
315 Water St., Stockbridge 49285.

Stronach. HELEN GENTZ
5513 Caberfae Hwy., Manistee 49660.

Sturgis. CHRISTINE FELLER
R. #4, Sturgis 49091.

Sugar Island. JANET T. COWAN
Sugar Island, Star Rte., Saulth Ste. Marie 49783.

Summerfield. MINNIE KRICHMAR BINGLEY
1971 Muskegon Rd., Harrison 48625.

Summerfield. HAZEL BURTRAW
11043 N. Harding Ave., Harrison 48625.

Summerfield. JUDITH A. DUSA
1092 Rose Rd., Petersburg 49270.

Summerfield. JENNIE R. HOLCOMB
17671 Railroad, Petersburg 49270.

Summerfield. RUTH P. JONES
6183 N. Old State Ave., Harrison 48625.

Summit. SHIRLEY M. ANTHONY
R. #1, Ludington 49431.

Summit. DOROTHY E. COLESTOCK
2320 Francis St., Jackson 49203.

Sunfield. ALMA GRINAGE
11721 Clinton Trail, Sunfield 48890.

Superior. MARY LINK
Brimley 49715.

Superior. DIANA M. PARKES
8924 Nottingham Dr., Ypsilanti 48197.

Superior. RUTH L. URTON
9740 Cherry Hill Rd., Ypsilanti 48197.

Superior. JUANITA WILSON
P.O. Box 155, Brimley 49715.

Surrey. JOANNE GEYER
3909 Ludington Rd., Farwell 48622.

Suttons Bay. SALLY KONOLD
R. #2, Stoney Pt. Rd., Suttons Bay 49682.

Suttons Bay. ROSEMARIE MOE
R. #2, Box 466, Suttons Bay 49682.

Sweetwater. SUE E. GLEASON
R. #1, Box 24, 40th St., Branch 49402.

Sweetwater. JOYCE MAVIS
R. #1, Branch 49402.

Sweetwater. MARY RADER
R. #1, Box 32, 48th St., Branch 49402.

Sylvan. CLARA HUNTOON
R. #2, Evart 49631.

Tawas. MARIAN ULMAN
404 Lorenz Rd., Tawas City 48763.

Tawas. IRENE HUGHES
251 Meadow Rd., Tawas City 48763.

Taymouth. GERALDINE J. CASIDAY
12601 Nichols Rd., Burt 48417.

Tecumseh. HELEN M. SHARPE
9255 Tonneberger Dr., Tecumseh 49286.

Tekonsha. ESTHER DEMAREST
134 Allen, P.O. Box, Tekonsha 49092.

Tekonsha. MARY MAIN
119 S. Murry, Tekonsha 49092.

Texas. JOYCE NEUBAUER
1316 Crooked Lake Dr., Kalamazoo 49009.

Thetford. MARGARET L. LAND
12466 N. Center Rd., Clio 48420.

Thetford. SHARON K. NORRIS
2485 E. Farrand Rd., Clio 48420.

Thomas. SHIRLEY P. MILLER
561 N. Miller, Saginaw 48603.

Thompson. ILENE PIERCE
P.O. Box 127, Thompson 49889.

Thornapple. DONNA KENYON
407 Johnson St., Middleville 49333.

Three Oaks. MARJORIE E. DRIER
6 Orange St., Three Oaks 49128.

Tilden. ELLA M. ALDERTON
Box 26, National Mine 49865.

Tilden. AILI BENVENUE
Box C, National Mine 49865.

Tobacco. IRENE M. BOYER
2594 Glidden Rd., Beaverton 48612.

Tobacco. CONNIE M. FREEMAN
4997 S. M-18, Beaverton 48612.

Tompkins. DOROTHY DACK
10843 Wilcox Rd., Onondaga 49264.

Tompkins. HELEN TENNANT
11670 Onondaga Rd., Onondaga 49264.

Torch Lake. MILLICENT J. KIVELA
R. #1, Lake Linden 49945.

Torch Lake. ESTELLE PERREAULT
Mildred St., Hubbell 49934.

Torch Lake. MARGARET RHEAULT
R. #1, Lake Linden 49945.

Trowbridge. ELEANOR L. NIELSEN
2753 108th Ave., R. #1, Allegan 49010.

Troy. IDA MAY CONKLIN
ERICA QUICK
MAXINE WOLGAMOTT
R. #1, Bitely 49309.

Turin. RUTH PERKINS
Rock 49880.

Turner. MARIAN PETERSON
477 E. Turner Rd., Turner 49765.

Tuscarora. PHYLLIS L. SCHULTZ
3147 Gratiot, Indian River 49749.

Tuscarora. MELBA TEETERS
1920 Straits Hwy., Indian River 49749.

Tuscola. CAROLYN BALDWIN
9012 Church, Tuscola 48769.

Tyrone. BETTY PRESSLER
8189 Faussett Rd., Fenton 48430.

Unadilla. ELLEN JACOBS
17852 M-36, Gregory 48137.

Union. DOROTHY A. BALOWSKI
Union City 49094.

Union. JUNE M. CARPENTER
221 N. Broadway, Union City 49094.

Union. ALMA V. HAAG
R. #1, Fife Lake Rd., Fife Lake 49633.

Union. PAULINE HUFFMAN
11612 Cedar Creek Rd., Fife Lake 49633.

Union. MARGARET JACKSON
2046 Florence St., Box 146, Mt. Pleasant
48858.

Union. VERA C. LAW
5683 Knight Rd., Kingsley 49649.

Union. ROSEMARY W. REID
4936 E. Mackenzie Lane, Mt.Pleasant 48858.

Union. HELEN UTTERBACK
3397 S. Lincoln Rd., Mt.Pleasant 48858.

Van Buren. DOREEN CRAVEN
11514 Fisher, Belleville 48111.

Van Buren. PATRICIA CULLIN
13375 Lenmoore, Belleville 48111.

Van Buren. DOROTHY YORK
47215 Ayres, Belleville 48111.

Vassar. ANN M. GLEESON
5171 Oak Rd., Vassar 48768.

Vassar. BETTY J. KOCHALKA
6205 S. State Rd., Vassar 48768.

Venice. MARCIA L. HARRIS
11237 Lennon Rd., Lennon 48449.

Venice. JUDITH A. KINGSBURY
1387 Byron Rd., Lennon 48449.

Vermontville. BABETTE HOEFLER
174 East First, Vermontville 49096.

Vermontville. JANE THRUN
7111 Vermontville Hwy., Vermontville 49096.

Vernon. OLIVE IRWIN
8159 Whiteville Rd., Clare 48617.

Vernon. GERALDINE M. JONES
7600 E. Newburg Rd., Durand 48429.

Verona. DELIA APLEY
Hellems Rd., Bad Axe 48413.

Verona. LENA MC CREA
1484 N. Van Dyke Rd., Bad Axe 48413.

Vevay. SARAH L. LO VETTE
3142 W. Kipp Rd., Mason 48854.

Vevay. BLANCHE A. WHEELER
3254 W. Tomlinson Rd., Mason 48854.

Victor. JANET MALKIN
R. #1, Laingsburg 48848.

Victory. MYRTLE C. DENNIS
R. #3, Dennis Rd., Ludington 49431.

Victory. FRIEDA JOHNSON
R. #3, Victory Dr., Ludington 49431.

Vienna. HAZEL DU PONT
Brown Rd., Box 222, Johannesburg 49751.

Vienna. FLORENCE FERGUSON
R. #2, Box 191, Atlanta 49709.

Vienna. LOIS MC LEAN
11034 Varna, Clio 48420.

Vienna. MARY SCHLICHER
R. #2, Box 185, Atlanta 49709.

Vienna. MILDRED THOMPSON
Star Rte., Box 250, Johannesburg 49751.

Volinia. EDITH L. CHURCHILL
R. #1, Cassopolis 49031.

Volinia. ESTHER M. MEAD
Marcellus 49067.

Wakefield. SHIRLEY A. NEWMAN
Box 435, R. #1, Wakefield 49968.

Wakefield. ALICE C. SALO
Box 455, R. #1, Wakefield 49968.

Wakeshma. DONNA M. BROOKING
13329 44th St., Fulton 49052.

Wales. LULA M. BENNETT
8003 Sparling Rd., Goodells 48027.

Wales. DIANE SHARPE
8488 County Park Dr., Goodells 48027.

Walker. ROSEMARY WILSON
Afton 49705.

Walton. ALICE M. WILLIAMS
4469 S. Bradley, Charlotte 48813.

Warren. ETHEL R. OBERDORF
R. #2, 4462 Magruder, Coleman 48618.

Washington. SHARON KINDEL
R. #1, Ashley 48806.

Washington. SARAH M. RITTER
155 S. Rawles, Romeo 48065.

Washington. MARILYN WHITFORD
R. #1, Ashley 48806.

Waterford. NAOMI F. GRIFFIN
5204 Lake Rd., Pontiac 48054.

Waterloo. CAROLYN FOX
10131 Mt. Hope Rd., Munith 49259.

Waterloo. CLARE WAHL
5250 Clear Lake Rd., Grass Lake 49240.

Watertown. FLOSSIE HOWAY
9324 S. Edwards Rd., Fostoria 48435.

Watertown. MILDRED F. MC DONOUGH
8588 Corrison Rd., Grand Ledge 48837.

Watertown. BETTY JEAN VALENTINE
8689 S. Edwards Rd., Fostoria 48435.

Watervliet. ELEANOR A. KRELL
Blatchford Rd., R. #1, Box 946, Watervliet
49098.

Watervliet. BARBARA J. TYLER
38 Beechwood Circle, Watervliet 49098.

Watson. PATRICIA A. MAHER
2035 20th St., Allegan 49010.

Waucedah. MARY BUYTAERT
P.O. Box 26, Loretto 49852.

Waucedah. MINERVA M. PHILLIPS
P.O. Box 52, Loretto 49852.

Wawatam. FLORENCE A. TRACY
502 W. Central Ave., Mackinaw City 49701.

Wayland. PEARL M. FOX
Box 15, Bradley 49311.

Wayland. MARY L. MARCOTT
R. #1, Wayland 49348.

Wayne. DORIS A. GREEN
R. #3, Dowagiec 49047.

Weare. GERMAINE MALBURG
LOIS MALBURG
R. #2, Hart 49420.

Webber. VERA E. CHILDRESS
R. #1, Box 388, Baldwin 49304.

Webber. MARGIE LEE DAVIS
R. #1, Box 142, Baldwin 49304.

Webber. ADA MAE DAY
R. #1, Box 2186, Baldwin 49304.

Webber. ALICE RINDGE
R. #1, Box 185, Baldwin 49304.

Webster. WANA M. BALDUS
6755 Webster Ch. Rd., Dexter 48130.

Webster. MARGARET MYNNING
5020 N. Territorial, Dexter 48130.

Weldon. LOIS B. HUGHES
R. #1, Lindy Rd., Thompsonville 49683.

Weldon. CONNIE STEVENS
Box 7, Thompsonville 49683.

Wells. PHYLLIS M. BENNICK
R. #3, Hurds Corner Rd., Caro 48723.

Wells. MARION HUFF
R. #3, 376 Murray Rd., Caro 48723.

Wells. DORA JOHNSON
MARILYN MANNINEN
Cornell 49818.

West Bloomfield. BETTY SUE DUPREE
7230 Stonebrook, Birmingham 48010.

West Bloomfield. LILLIAN S. WARNER
3425 W. Long Lake, Orchard Lake 48033.

West Branch. VIRGINIA BARAVETTO
BEATRICE BECKER
P.O. Box 31, Ralph 49877.

West Branch. EVANGELINE BERGLUND
R. #1, Box 16, Skandia 49885.

West Branch. DONNA COOTWARE
P.O. Box 30, Ralph 49877.

West Branch. SHERRY DIXON
P.O. Box 7, Ralph 49877.

West Branch. AUDREY DOSS
P.O. Box 13, Ralph 49877.

West Branch. ROSE FILLIS
P.O. Box 14, Ralph 49877.

West Branch. EVELYN M. OLLILA
Box 28, Skandia 49885.

West Branch. MARY ANN WAGNER
R. #1, Lake City 49651.

West Branch. BETTY L. WANGLER
R. #3, 445 S. Cambell Rd., W. Branch 48861.

West Branch. BESSIE WETZEL
R. #2, Lake City 49651.

West Traverse. VELDA J. LAUER
R. #2, Harbor Springs 49740.

West Traverse. JORETTA A. BETHKE
R. #2, Harbor Springs 49740.

Wexford. MARION KELLOGG
R. #1, Buckley 49620.

Wheatfield. AGNES BEACH
940 Linn Rd., Williamston 48895.

Wheatfield.. LAURA CARSON SHEFFIELD
2340 Dennis Rd., Williamston 48895.

Wheatland. DEANNA C. MILLER
1435 Hoxie Rd., Addison 49220.

Wheatland. MARY RICHARDS
2195 Nine Mile Rd., Remus 49340.

Wheeler. SHIRLEY DONLEY
130 Elm St., Breckenridge 48615.

Wheeler. MABLE POINDEXTER
7205 McClelland Rd., Breckenridge 48615.

Whiteford. BETTY CREQUE
10165 M-151, Riga 49276.

White Oak. PAULINE NOTTINGHAM
4665 E. Cooper Rd., Stockbridge 49285.

White Oak. CAROL OESTERLE
4675 E. Iosco Rd., Webberville 48892.

Whitewater. MARGARET BECKWITH
R. #1, Box 37B, Williamsburg 49690.

Whitewater. ELLEN L. OSTLUND
R. #2, Williamsburg 49690.

Whitney. FLORENCE BISCHOFF
1921 N. Huron Rd., R. #2, Tawas City 48763.

Whitney. BESS ELLISON
300 N. Delano Rd., R. #1, AuGres 48703.

Wilber. BETTY CROSS
2013 N. Wilber Rd., East Tawas 48730.

Wilber. OPAL MALLON
179 Curtis, East Tawas 48730.

Wilcox. JANICE B. EATON
R. #2, Box 249, White Cloud 49349.

Williams. JEAN KACZMAREK
4437 S. Nine Mile Rd., Auburn 48611.

Williams. MARY PUTT
5841 Garfield Rd., Auburn 48611.

Williamstown. GLENDORA G. BIXBY
1840 Rowley Rd., Williamston 48895.

Williamstown. DOROTHY M. ROBINSON
1703 Barry Rd., Williamston 48895.

Wilmot. LUCILLE GEARHARD
13866 S. Straits Hwy., Wolverine 49799.

Wilson. JOAN C. OLIVER
Box 1229, Boyne City 49712.

Windsor. DOROTHY HULL
8309 Vermontville Hwy., Dimondale 48821.

Windsor. JOYCE NELSON
8406 Windsor Hwy., Dimondale 48821.

Winfield. MYRTLE KOHL
R. #2, Howard City 49329.

Winfield. LIDA ROSSMAN
R. #1, Lakeview 48850.

Winsor. CLARE J. DAST
7071 Clabuesch St., Pigeon 48755.

Winterfield. LUCILLE PRIELIPP
R. #2, Marion 49665.

Wise. YVONNE N. MORLEY
8675 Wise Rd., R. #4, Clare 48617.

Wisner. MILDRED HILL
R. #1, Fairgrove 48733.

Wisner. ELLEN WHALEY
8295 W. Dickerson Rd., Akron 48701.

Woodhull. DOREEN DUZENBURY
10455 S. Fenner Rd., Perry 48872.

Woodhull. EDNA FULLER
12458 Warner Rd., Laingsburg 48848.

Woodhull. WANDA LYON
12850 Warner Rd., Perry 48872.

Woodland. CAROL HEWITT
5336 N. Clark Rd., Woodland 48897.

Woodland. LUCY JORDAN
6841 N. Woodland Rd., Woodland 48897.

Woodstock. SARAH HARBAUGH
136 Woodstock St., Cement City 49233.

Worth. BONNIE LAYMAN
6471 Burns Line, Lexington 48450.

Worth. DONNA MATTHEWS
7185 Wildcat, Croswell 48422.

Wright. SHARON L. DAVIS
Waldron 49288.

Yates. MURIEL CASTALLANTE
199 Wilson Dr., Box 112, Idlewild 49642.

Yates. EDNA MC KINNEY
334 Wilson, R. #1, Box 149, Idlewild 49642.

York. ELEANOR W. BENJAMIN
12310 Platt Rd., Milan 48160.

York. CHRISTINA L. CLARKE
4112 Briarhill Dr., Milan 48160.

York. BEULAH DICKASON
8595 Crane Rd., Milan 48160.

York. SANDRA RICHARDSON
1315 Milan Oakville Rd., Milan 48160.

Ypsilanti. RUTH ANN GOODRIDGE
ANNA J. STEPP
7200 S. Huron River Dr., Ypsilanti 48197.

Zilwaukee. PATRICIA KAECKMEISTER
5271 N. Towerline, Saginaw 48601.

Zilwaukee. IRMA MC GUIRE
880 Kochville Rd., Saginaw 48604.

Mayors

Algonac. KAREN COLE
City Hall, Algonac 48001.

Barton Hills Village. ELIZABETH LANGFORD (R)
1973-. Party: Del., Cnty. Conv. 1968-74.
Educ: U. of Mich. 1941 BA. B: 5/21/21. Add:
859 Oakdale Rd., Barton Hills., Ann Arbor
48105 (313)662-0635.

Burlington. BARBARA REESE
City Hall, Burlington 49029.

Calumet. RITA FINCH (I)
1976-. Org: BPW. Occ: Barber. B: 9/28/21.
Add: 101 8th St., Calumet 49913 (906)337-1713.

Coleman. CHRISTINE O'LAUGHLIN
City Hall, Coleman 48618.

Copemish. ALICE R. DIXON (R)
1976-. Prev: Bd. of Educ. 1968. Occ:
Manager. B: 7/26/32. Add: Corner Beech & 4th
Ave., Copemish 49625.

Corunna. BERNICE HAGADON (D)
1975-. Prev: City Clerk 1954-69; Councilwomen 1971-73. Occ: Newspaper Correspondent.
B: 1/22/17. Add: 615 Walnut St., Corunna
48817 (517)743-3650.

Ecorse. DORA GAINES
City Hall, Detroit 48229.

Evart. MARTHA ANN PATTEE (D)
1977-. Bds: Planning Cmsn.; Labor Relations.
Prev: City Councilwoman 1973-77. B: 1/4/28.
Add: 807 N. Pine, Evart 49631 (616)734-2181.

Gladstone. PATRICIA A. FINLAN (I)
1977-. Bds: Delta Cnty. Chamber of Commerce;
Industrial Devt. Corp.; Bd. of Review. Prev:
City Cmsnr. 1975-77; Election Bd. 1974-75. Org:
LWV; Parent-Teacher Club. Educ: U. of Mich.
1970 BS. B: 6/16/48. Add: 1018 Michigan Ave.,
Gladstone 49837 (906)428-9470.

Lennon. MAVOURNEEN KRANZ
City Hall, Lennon 48449.

Mackinac Island. MARGARET DOUD
City Hall, Mackinac Is., 49757.

Madison Heights. VIRGINIA M. SOLBERG
City Hall, Royal Oak 48071.

Marquette. HOLLY S. GREER (D)
     1975-. Bds: Council on Aging; Bd. of Dir's.,
Mich. Municipal League. Party: Precinct Del.
1971-72. Prev: City Comsr. 1972; Community
Action 1970. Org: BPW; AAUW; NOW; Citizens to
Save Superior Shoreline. Educ: Smith Coll. 1953
BA; Northern Mich U. 1971 MA. Occ: Dir., Women's
Center for Continuing Educ. B: 6/10/31. Add:
423 W. College, Marquette 49855 (906)228-8200.

Millersburg. FLORENCE HUGHS
     City Hall, Millersburg 49759.

Mount Pleasant. SIBYL MARIE ELLIS (I)
     1976-. Prev: Housing Cmsn. 1975-76. B:
9/30/34. Add: 1119 Kent, Mt. Pleasant 48858
(517)773-7971.

Negaunee. ELAINE H. JUIDICI (D)
     1974-. Party: State Del. 1968-76; Precinct
Del. 1968-76; V-Ch., Dem. Party 1970-77. Prev:
Superior Systems Library Bd. 1974-77. Org: BPW;
NEA; Cnty. Dem. Party. Educ: N. Mich. U. 1962
BA; 1964 MA. Occ: Teacher. B: 3/31/29. Add:
132 Iroquois Dr., Negaunee 49866.

Petoskey. BARBARA WATERS
     City Hall, Petoskey 49770.

Portage. BETTY LEE C. ONGLEY (R) **
     1973-. Bds: Metropolitan Council; Substance
Abuse Bd.; Area Transportation Study Policy Com.
Prev: Councilwoman 1968-73; Park & Recreation Bd.
1965-68. Org: AAUW; LWV; NOW. Educ: Western
Mich. U. 1947 BS; MA. Occ: School Guidance
Coordinator. B: 1/25/26. Add: 8615 Tozer La.,
Portage 49081 (616)327-3081 Ext. 247.

St. Ignace. SARAH H. TAMLYN
     City Hall, St. Ignace 49781.

South Range. AGNES KOIVUNEN (D) **
     1973-. Prev: Councilwoman 1968-73. Org: PTA.
B: 1/31/24. Add: 41 2nd St., South Range 49963
(906)482-3514.

Sylvan Lake. BETTY B. WILSON (I) **
     1971-. Bds: Parks & Recreation; Community
Center Com.; Planning Cmsn.; Bicentennial Com.
Org: PTA; Women's Club. Occ: Driver Safety
School. B: 3/18/24. Add: 1466 Oakwood Ave.,
Sylvan Lake 48053 (313)682-1440.

Watertown. MRS. DOROTHY KOZIOL
     City Hall, Watertown 55388.

Local Councils

Addison. LOU ANNE STAMBOUGH
     City Hall, Addison 49220.

Adrian. JUNE M. MERRILL (D)
     1975-. Bds: Liason, Cnty. Bd. of Cmsnr's.
Party: State Del. 1977; State Alt. 1974-76;
Precinct Leader 1974-78; Cnty. Committeewoman
1974-78. Org: BPW; LWV; Dem. Women's Caucus; Nat.
Assoc. of Parlimentarians. Occ: Bank Teller. B:
6/23/27. Add: 530 Frazier Dr., Adrian 49221.

Ahmeek. ANNIABLE SPAGNOTTI
     City Hall, Ahmeek 49901.

Ahmeek. EDNA TULPPO (R)
     1966-. Bds: Water & Sewage; Fire Hall. Prev:
Cnty. Bd. of Review 1970-72. B: 6/3/17. Add:
5 Vivian St., Ahmeek 49901 (916)337-3152.

Alanson. IRIS LESH
     City Hall, Alanson 49706.

Albion. FRANCES B. COSTIANES **
     1972-. Bds: Hospital Bd.; Ambulance Bd.;
Recreation Bd.; Library Bd.; School Com.; Parking. Occ: Camp Dir. & Newspaper Pressroom. B:
8/19/28. Add: 810 Prospect, Albion 49224
(517)629-2846.

Algonac. JUNE E. CROCKER
     City Hall, Algonac 48001.

Allegan. JEANETTE RUMERY
     City Hall, Allegan 49010.

Allegan. NORMA J. STONE (I) **
     1969-. Bds: Planning Cmsn.; County OEO; Bldg.
Com.; Ambulance Com. Party: County Com. 1973-74.
Org: BPW; PTO. Occ: Real Estate Sales. B:
8/6/34. Add: 719 Linn St., R. 6, Allegan 49010
(616)673-4594.

Allen. CHARLOTTE BENGE
     City Hall, Allen 49927.

Alma. MARCIA E. O'BRIAN (R)
     1971-. Bds: Ch., Community Educ., Parks &
Recreation; Mid-Mich. Community Action Council.
Party: State Alt. 1973. Org: Women's Club;
Gratiot Cnty. Rep. Party; Dictician Assoc. Educ:
Oh. Wesleyan U. 1946 BA. Occ: Dietician B:
9/18/24. Add: 808 W. Center St., Alma 48801.

Ann Arbor. CAROL JONES
     City Hall, 100 N. 5th Ave., Ann Arbor 48108.

Ann Arbor. ELIZABETH KOEGH
     City Hall, 100 N. 5th Ave., Ann Arbor 48108.

Ashley. IRENE KECK (R)
     1972-. Org: NEA; Cnty. Rep. Women. Educ:
Central Mich. U. 1965 BS. Occ: Teacher. B:
6/29/20. Add: 306 S. Ann, Ashley 48806
(517)847-4701.

Athens. JANET N. VUNOVICH
     1975-. B: 9/9/16. Add: P.O. Box 62, Athens
49011 (1-616)729-5515.

Augusta. HELEN GODDE
     City Hall, Augusta 49012.

Augusta. SANDRA S. NOTEBOOM (I)
     1968-. Bds: Ch., Purchasing & Salary; Police;
Water. Prev: Police Cmsr. 1972-77. Educ:
Kalamazoo Vly. Community Coll. 1974 AA. Occ:
Cnty. Deputy Sheriff. B: 7/3/38. Add: 404 W.
Michigan Ave., Augusta 49021 (616)731-5517.

Bad Axe. CAROLYN TALASKI
     City Hall, Bad Axe 48413.

Battle Creek. BETSY UNRUE
City Hall, E. Michigan Ave., Battle Creek
49014.

Belding. VIRTUE D. MEHNEY
1975-. Prev: Inspector of Elections 1968-75.
Org: Municipal League; Chamber of Commerce; OES.
B: 12/30/20. Add: 222 W. Liberty St., Belding
48809 (616)794-1900.

Bellevue. MARILYN FRANKENSTEIN
City Hall, Bellevue 49021.

Benton Harbor. MILDRED WELLS
City Hall, Benton Harbor 49022.

Benzonia. JOAN CRAIN
City Hall, Benzonia 49616.

Beulah. MILDRED HARWOOD
City Hall, Beulah 49617.

Beverly Hills. MARILYNN A. QUICK
City Hall, Beverly Hills

Big Rapids. RUTH M. LUCAS
City Hall, Big Rapids 49307.

Bingham Farms. MIRIAM L. BARRIS
1973-. Bds: Ch., Housing. Org: Nat. Council
of Jewish Women. Educ: Wayne U. 1942 BA. B:
4/25/20. Add: 23616 Shagwood, Birmingham 48010.

Birmingham. DOROTHY J. CONRAD (R) **
1973-. Bds: Watershed Council; Bicentennial
Com.; Regional Planning Agency. Org: LWV; PTA;
Rep. Women's Club. Add: 2252 Yorkshire, Birmingham 48008 (313)644-1800.

Birmingham. ANN DROPIEWSKI
City Hall, Birmingham 48025.

Birmingham. PATRICIA K. WATT
City Hall, Birmingham 48025.

Blissfield. THELMA SEETHALER (R)
1976-. B: 3/22/11. Add: 302 Giles Ave.,
Blissfield 49228.

Boyne City. THELMA BEHLING
City Hall, Boyne City 49712.

Boyne Falls. IRENE HAUSLER
City Hall, Boyne Falls 49731.

Bridgman. MARILYN WILTSHIRE STANARD (I)
1976-. Bds: Park & Recreation Cmsnr. Educ:
Western Mich. 1964 BA. Occ: Piano Instructor.
Add: Rt. #1, Box 34D, Bridgman 49106.

Brighton. IRMA S. TRUANCE (I)
1975-. Party: State Del. 1972; Local Treasurer
1968-69, 1972-74. Org: LWV. Occ: Bookkeeper. B:
1/28/09. Add: 118 E. Grand Rvr., Brighton 48116.

Britton. NELLIE DENNY
City Hall, Britton 49229.

Brooklyn. DONNA J. HOWARD (R) **
1974-. Bds: Community Library; Bicentennial
Com.; Christmas Decoration; Mich. Week Com. Org:
AAUW; PTA. Educ: Eastern Mich. U. BS. Occ:
Teacher. B: 12/14/30. Add: Box 536, 102 King
St., Brooklyn 49230 (517)592-8844.

Brooklyn. LINDA WEATHERWAX
City Hall, Brooklyn 49230.

Brown City. RUTH CARMAN
City Hall, Brown City 48416.

Buchanan. MILDRED E. ANDERSON
1971-. Mayor Pro Tem. Bds: Treasurer, S.E.
Berrien Cnty. Landfill Authority. Org: LWV.
Educ: Mich. State U. 1933 BA. Occ: Librarian.
B: 1/10/12. Add: 301 N. Detroit St., Buchanan
49107 (616)695-3844.

Buckley. VERNITA HARTZELL
EILEEN KING
JULIE WAGNER
City Hall, Buckley 49620.

Burlington. VERA LUX
City Hall, Burlington 49029.

Burr Oak. MARY AULT
FLORENCE FRYE
City Hall, Burr Oak 49030.

Burton. MARILYN M. ESTEP (D) **
1973-. Bds: Planning Cmsn. B: 6/11/30.
Add: G-4355 Lapeer Rd., Burton 48509
(313)743-3876.

Caledonia. CHRISTINE DOELE (I)
1976-. Bds: Ch., Public Information. Org:
NEA. Educ: U. of Mich. 1968 BA. Occ: English
Teacher. B: 10/8/46. Add: 216 Pleasant,
Caledonia 49316.

Calumet. MARIE BIANCHI
MARY LEWIS
City Hall, Calumet 49913.

Capac. MARIANNE KELLER
City Hall, Capac 48014.

Cassopolis. STELLA CASSEY
City Hall, Cassopolis 49031.

Center Line. MARY ANN ZIELINSKI
City Hall, Center Line 48015.

Charlevoix. SUE ERBER
JEANNINE WALLACE
City Hall, Charlevoix 49720.

Charlotte. BARBARA DENISON
City Hall, Charlotte 48813.

Clawson. MARY F. AIRRIESS
1973-. Bds: SE Mich. Council of Govts.
Prev: Parks & Recreation 1967-69; Planning Cmsn.
1969-73. Org: BPW; Women's Club; Historical
Society; Cnty. Bd. of Realtors; LWV; Women's
Conf. of Concerns. Occ: Realtor. B: 2/26/26.
Add: 1301 Shenadoah Dr., Clawson 48017.

Clifford. OTHELIA ESSARY
JANET MC ALPINE
City Hall, Clifford 48727.

Climax. KATHLEEN DIANE HARPER (R)
1974-. Bds: Ch., Public Safety Com.; Finance
Com. Educ: Bronson Methodist Hospital School of
Nursing 1966 RN. B: 3/26/44. Add: 106 Ebinger,
Climax 49034.

Clio. ALICE BOYSE **
1971-. Bds: Finance; Library Bd. Org: Educ.
Assoc. Educ: U. of Mich. 1931 BA. Occ: Teacher.
B: 7/21/10. Add: 120 Butler St., Clio 48420
(313)686-9311.

Coldwater. ALICE PUORRO
City Hall, Coldwater 49036.

Coloma. WAVIA NOACK (R) **
1973-. Bds: City Coms. Occ: Secretary. B:
5/8/10. Add: P.O. Box 401, Coloma 49038
(616)468-6125.

Columbiaville. HAZEL SIMMS
1973-. Bds: Ch., Property Com.; Ordinance;
Ch., Finance. B: 6/12/07. Add: 4374 Golden Glow
Dr., Columbiaville 48421.

Concord. DOROTHY SPRY
City Hall, Concord 49237.

Constantine. MARCIA L. GEISLER (R)
1975-. Educ: Albion Coll. 1966 BA. Occ:
Nursery School Teacher. B: 4/29/44. Add: 420
Centreville St., Constantine 49042 (616)435-5315.

Copemish. ALICE DIXON
City Hall, Copemish 49625.

Crystal Falls. PATRICIA M. JEWELL (R)
1974-. Bds: Downtown Devt. Com. Party: State
Del.; State Alt.; Cnty. V-Ch. Occ: Bookkeeper.
B: 3/4/26. Add: 125 High St., Crystal Falls
49920.

Daggett. VIVIAN LEA AYERS (I)
1976-. Bds: Bldgs. & Parks Com.; Recreation
Com.; Sanitation Com. Org: Amer. Occupational
Therapy Assoc.; Mich. School Bd. Assoc.; Mich.
Municipal League. Educ: Western Mich. U. 1966 BS.
B: 11/26/44. Add: Daggett Medical Bldg., Daggett
49821 (906)753-4734.

Dansville. VICKY LAWSON
City Hall, Dansville 48819.

Dearborn Heights. MARIE G. SCOTT (D)
1975-. Bds: City Pension. Party: State Del.
1977. Prev: City Beautiful Com. 1964-75. Org:
LWV; Nat. League of Cities; Municipal League of
Cities; Civic Assoc.; Dem. Club. Occ: Airline
Agent. B: 12/5/32. Add: 5327 Syracuse, Dearborn
Hts. 48125 (313)277-6832.

Decatur. ELEANOR SMITH
City Hall, Decatur 49045.

Detroit. ERMA L. HENDERSON (D) **
1972-. Bds: Nat. Council on Crime & Delin-
quency; Jail Advisory Com.; Land Use Task Force;
Community Coll., Bd. of Trustees; Cable TV
Study Com. Party: Dist. Member. Org: ACLU; Bd.
of Black Broadcasters; BPW; LWV; NAACP; Nat.
Black Caucus; Nat. Council Negro Women; Social
Worker Assoc.; United Com. on Negro History;
Urban Alliance; W.O.M.A.N.; Women's Conference
of Concerns. Educ: U. Mich. BA; Wayne State
U. MA. Add: 1340 City-County Bldg., Detroit
48226 (313)224-4505.

Detroit. MARYANN MAHAFFEY (D) **
1973-. Bds: Advisory Cmsn. on Nutrition;
Rape Task Force. Party: State Central Spokes-
woman; Dist. Exec. Com.; Precinct Del. Prev:
Advisory Com. on the Status of Women; Bd. of
Educ; Ch., Task Force on Hunger & Malnutrition;
Cmsn. on Children & Youth; Health Care Com.;
Social Work Council. Org: ACLU; AFL-CIO; AFT;
AAUP; Dem. Women's Caucus; LWV; NAACP; Nat.
Assoc. of Social Workers; Nat. Council of Negro
Women; Nat. Women's Political Educ. Fund; NOW;
Urban Alliance. Educ: Cornell Coll. 1946 BA;
USC 1951 MSW. Occ: Professor. B: 1/18/25.
Add: 19468 Avon, Detroit 48219 (313)224-4545.

Dewitt. BARBARA JEAN TOWNS (R)
1976-. Bds: Ch., Parks & Recreation; Ch.,
Grant Coord.; Finance. Party: State Del. 1964-65.
Org: Dewitt Merchants Assoc.; Mich. Park & Recre-
ation. Educ: Lansing Community Coll. 1977 ABA.
Occ: Store Owner. B: 11/22/32. Add: 909 W.
Geneva Dr., Dewitt 48820 (517)669-5559.

Dexter. DONNA LAMBERT
City Hall, Dexter 48130.

Diamondale. JOANNE HUMMEL
City Hall, Diamondale 48821.

Dundee. SHIRLEY FRIESS
City Hall, Dundee 48131.

Eagle. MARY FELDPAUSCH
MARLEEN HIGBEE
City Hall, Eagle 48822.

East Detroit. HERRIET LANE
City Hall, E. Detroit 48021.

East Jordan. VIRGINIA GIACOMELLI (R)
1973-. Prev: Councilwoman 1973-75; Mayor
1976. Occ: Advertising Consultant. B:
11/10/21. Add: 213 N. Lake, E. Jordan 49727.

Eastlake. PATRICIA A. SCHMIDT (D)
1975-. Bds: Zoning Bd. B: 10/9/34. Add:
584 Wall St., Eastlake 49626.

East Lansing. MARY P. SHARP (R)
1965-. Mayor Pro Tem. Bds: Capital Area
Community Services Bd.; Tri-Cnty. Aging Consortium Bd.; Tri-Cnty. Water Com. Prev: Fair Employment Practices Comsr. 1961-63; Adv. Com. on
Services to Children 1960-64; Human Relations
Com. 1963-65. Educ: U. of Mich. 1939 BA; JD.
B: 1/10/17. Add: 950 Audobon Rd., E. Lansing
48823 (517)337-1731.

Edwardsburg. LOIS KELLER (R) **
1973-. Bds: Bicentennial; Council on Aging;
Area Park Bd. Org: Council on Community Adult
Educ.; Library Assoc. Educ: Mich. State U. 1970
MLS. Occ: Librarian. B: 5/1/07. Add: P.O. Box
311, Edwardsburg 49112.

Edwardsburg. DOROTHY ELNORA SMITH (R) **
1973-. Bds: Police Bd. Org: BPW. Occ: Owner-
Operator Dry Cleaning Store. B: 2/7/17. Add:
110 Cass St., P.O. Box 31, Edwardsburg 49112
(616)663-8484.

Elberta. LOUISE RENA KIRBACH (D)
1972-. Org: OES. B: 4/24/21. Add: 174
Furnace Ave., Elberta 49628.

Elberta. EVELYN ROMMELL
City Hall, Elberta 49628.

Elks Rapids. MARY A. HOCKSTAD (I)
1973-. Bds: Council Pres. Pro Tem.; Finance
Com.; Parks & Recreation; Ch., Charter. Org:
Mich. Newspaper Assoc.; Nat. News Assoc.; Chamber
of Commerce; OES. Educ: U. of Mich. 1956 BA.
Occ: Editor-Publisher - Local Newspaper. B:
7/28/34. Add: 305 S. Bayshore, Elk Rapids 49629
(616)264-9274.

Essexville. SHIRLEY SHOWALTER
City Hall, Essexville 48732.

Farmington Hills. ANNA JANETTE DOLAN (R)
1975-. Bds: Housing Cmsn.; Beautification
Cmsn. Org: Beautification Cmsn. Educ: U. of
Akron 1949 BA. B: 1/15/27. Add: 30324 Wicklow
Rd., Farmington Hls. 48018 (313)474-6115.

Farmington Hills. JOAN D. DUDLEY
City Hall, Farmington Hls.

Farmington Hills. JOANNE SMITH
City Hall, Farmington Hls.

Farwell. BERDETTE HILLIARD
City Hall, Farwell 48622.

Fenton. LUCILLE M. BRABON
1975-. Org: Chamber of Commerce. Occ: Assoc.
News Editor. B: 7/30/33. Add: 613 Park St.,
Fenton 48430.

Ferndale. DOROTHY M. WEBB (R)
1975-. Bds: Plan Cmsn.; Parks & Recreation
Adv. Bd.; Ordinance Cmsn. Party: State Del. 1974;
State Alt. 1976; Exec. Com. 1974-78; Precinct
Del. 1974-78; Cnty. Conv. Del. 1974-76; Com. on
Permanent Organization & Order of Business 1976.
Org: Women in Municipal Govt.; Nat. League of
Cities; BPW; Rep. Club; DAR. B: 1/25/19. Add:
1546 Albany St., Ferndale 48220 (313)547-6000.

Ferndale. HELEN MARIE WEBER (D) **
1973-. Bds: Recreation Advisory Bd.; Employee
Pension Bd.; Housing Bd. of Appeals. Party:
Precinct Del. 1972-74; Resolution Com. 1973. Prev:
Library Bd. 1972-73. Org: ACLU; Another Mother
for Peace; Common Cause; NOW; Dem. Club. Educ:
Marygrove Coll. 1964 BA; 1969 MEd. Occ: Administrative Assistant. B: 10/9/41. Add: 464 W. Marshall, Ferndale 48220 (313)547-6000.

Fife Lake. MARGARETTE NEWELL
City Hall, Fife Lake 49633.

Flat Rock. BARBARA FEDON
City Hall, Flat Rock 48134.

Flat Rock. DOROTHY MAY REED (D)
1975-. B: 4/1/20. Add: 27046 James St.,
Flat Rock 48134 (313)782-2455.

Flint. SANDRA APPLEGATE
1973-. Bds: Ch., Employees Retirement Fund;
Economic Devt. Cmsn.; Planning Cmsn. Prev:
Cnty. Prosecutor's Consumer Council 1973-76;
Human Relations Com. 1971-73; Cnty. Coord. Child
Care 1970-73. Org: Nat. League of Cities; Mich.
Municipal League; NOW; Cancer Society; Institute
of Arts; Drug Abuse Cmsn. Educ: Mich. State U.
1955 BS. B: 4/4/33. Add: 2607 Circle Dr., Flint
48507 (313)766-7418.

Fountain. JANET LE BRUN
City Hall, Fountain 49410.

Fowlerville. MARJORIE CARLON
City Hall, Fowlerville 48836.

Frankfort. ALICE W. HOLLENBECK (I)
1975-. Bds: Ch., Ways & Means Com.; Claims &
Accounts; Police & Fire. Prev: Trustee, School
Dist. 1958-67. Org: LWV. Educ: Pomona Coll.
1942 BA; Western Reserve U. 1945 MA. Occ: Dir.,
Social Agency. B: 8/19/21. Add: 591 Day Ave.,
Frankfort 49635 (616)352-4123.

Franklin. VIRGINIA DE BENHAM RODGERS
1972-. Bds: Ch., Bicentennial; Cnty. Cultural
Council. Prev: Councilwoman 1972-76. Org:
Historic Society; Rep. Women's Club; PTA; Parent
Adv. Council. Occ: Public Relations. B: 7/5/27.
Add: 26980 Wellington Dr., Franklin 48025
(313)626-9666.

Free Soil. CLARA M. TRIPP (I)
1976-. Org: Senior Citizens. B: 4/26/08.
Add: 2759 E. Michigan, Free Soil 49411.

Fremont. ANN HARTSEMA
City Hall, Fremont 49412.

Fruitport. JANET M. JAMES
City Hall, Fruitport 49415.

Garden City. GERALDINE F. KIESSEL (I)
1975-. Bds: Del. S.E. Mich. Council of Govts.
Prev: Charter Comsr. 1973-75. Org: School Admin-
istrators Political Action Committee; BPW. Educ:
Eastern Mich. U. 1968 BS; 1973 MA. Occ: Educ.
Administrator. B: 2/2/33. Add: 29014 Alvin Ct.,
Garden City 48135 (313)421-1262.

Grand Beach. LOUISE M. KRIJCI
City Hall, Grand Beach

Grand Haven. MARJORIE ANN BOON (R)
1973-. Bds: Planning Cmsn.; Ch., Audit Com.;
Ch., Senior Citizens Housing Com. Prev: Ch.,
Planning Cmsn. 1970-73. Org: LWV. Educ: Hope
Coll. 1952 BA. Occ: Teacher. B: 6/28/30. Add:
315 Terrill, Grand Haven 49417 (616)842-3210.

Grand Rapids. NORENE J. BROOKS (I)
1976-. Bds: Recreation Bd.; Regional Planning
Cmsn.; Environs Transportation Study Policy Com.
Party: State Del. 1954-60; Precinct Del.; Party
V-Ch. 1958-60. Org: AAUW; W. Mich. Environmental Action
Council. Educ: Mich. State U. 1949 BA. B:
5/22/26. Add: 3104 Dorais Dr. NE, Grand Rapids
49503 (616)456-3857.

Grass Lake. JO ANN SAVOY (PP)
1974-. Bds: Ch., Street Com.; Ch., Water Com.;
Ch., Sewage Com. B: 12/29/41. Add: 1471 Wolf
Lk. Rd., Grass Lk. 49240 (517)522-5230.

Grass Lake. THELMA SNODGRASS
City Hall, Grass Lake 49240.

Grayling. HELEN M. JOHNSON (I)
1976-. Org: Amer. Business Women's Assoc.;
Women's Club. Occ: Bookkeeper. B: 12/21/24.
Add: 503 Elm St., Grayling 49738 (517)348-2131/
6811.

Greenville. ANNE D. POWERS
1975-. Bds: Bldg. Bd. of Appeals. Org:
Chamber of Commerce. Occ: Retailer. B: 3/4/42.
Add: 509 Van Deinse Ave., Greenville 48838.

Gross Pointe Farms. NANCY J. WAUGAMAN
City Hall, Grosse Pointe Farms

Gross Pointe Park. CAMILLE S. PETERSON
City Hall, Grosse Pointe Park

Grosse Pointe Woods. JOAN M. MULLAN (I) **
1973-. Bds: Beautification Cmsn.; Bicentennial
Cmsn.; Taxation Com.; Planning Com.; Public
Relations Com. Party: Del., County Conv. 1965-67.
Org: PTA. Educ: Polyclinic Hospital School of
Nursing 1956 RN. B: 5/17/36. Add: 1087 Sunningdale, Grosse Pointe Woods 48236.

Hamtramck. ESTELLE JAWORSKI (I)
1971-. Bds: Planning Cmsn.; Beautification
Com. Occ: Secretary. B: 7/4/14. Add: 11549
Fleming, Hamtramck 48212 (313)TR4-2400.

Hamtramck. HELEN JUSTEWICZ
City Hall, Detroit 48212.

Harper Woods. WILMA A. PAGE
City Hall, Detroit 48212.

Harrietta. NORMA ROWE
EVELYN SPOLAR
City Hall, Harrietta 49638.

Harrison. ELIZABETH B. FOOTE
City Hall, Harrison 48625.

Harrisville. PATRICIA SYSAK (I)
1976-. Bds: Streets; Ch., Airport; Sewer. B:
1/23/25. Add: 308 W. Main St., Harrisville
48740 (517)724-6666.

Hart. MARILYNN ENEMANN
City Hall, Hart 49420.

Hartford. LOIS BUDREAU
LOUISE ENGLE
City Hall, Hartford 49057.

Highland Park. ETHEL TERRELL (D)
1968-. Bds: Council Pres.; City Retirement
Bd.; Police Cmsn. Party: State Del. 1964; Nat.
Del. 1954-77; State Central Com. 1964-66. Prev:
Sec. of State 1964-67. Org: NAACP; Nat. Council
of Negro Women; OES; Dem. Club. Occ: Dir., Day
Care School. B: 2/28/26. Add: 12209 Woodward
Ave., Highland Pk. 48203 (313)867-7171.

Hillsdale. MARGERY SCHUSTER
City Hall, Hillsdale 49242.

Holland. BEATRICE WESTRATE
City Hall, Holland 49423.

Homer. ELAINE RALSTON
City Hall, Homer 49245.

Honor. KAREN MILLER
City Hall, Honor 49640.

Honor. MARGA OLIGNEY (R)
1974-. Occ: Accountant. B: 1/25/25. Add:
2018 South St., Honor 49640 (616)325-2922.

Houghton. GERTRUDE R. SMITH (R)
Org: Civic League. Occ: Antique Shop Owner.
B: 11/3/26. Add: 706 W. South St., Houghton
49931.

Howard City. CONNIE STEVENS
City Hall, Howard City 49329.

Hudson. LEE ANN MINTON (I)
1976-. Bds: Ch., Police Com. Org: NEA.
Educ: U. of Mich. 1958 BA; Eastern Mich. U. MA.
Occ: Teacher. B: 4/13/37. Add: 326 Wood St.,
Hudson 49247 (517)448-3271.

Kalamazoo. PATRICIA M. CAYEMBERG (R)
1973-. Bds: South Central Mich. Reg. Planning
Council Treasurer; Water Quality Cmsn.; Crime
Cmsn. Exec. Bd. Party: State Del. 1975; State
Alt. 1975; Precinct Del. 1975-76. Org: Mich.
Assoc. of Regions; Mich. Women in Govt.; Rep.
Women's Club; LWV. Educ: Western Mich. U. 1976
BA. Add: 709 Egleston Ave., Kalamazoo 49001.

Kalamazoo. CAROLINE R. HAM (D)
1975-. Bds: Planning Cmsn.; Cnty. Human
Services Cmsn.; Community Relations Com. Org:
LWV. Educ: Kalamazoo Coll. 1948 BA. B: 2/2/27.
Add: 2105 Waite Ave., Kalamazoo 49008
(616)342-2123.

Kaleva. EILEEN MANNISTO
City Hall, Kaleva 49645.

Kingston. JANE ANNE LALKO (D)
1968-. Mayor Pro Tem. Bds: Ch., Recreation;
Ch., Insurance; Finance. Prev: Recreation Cmsn.
1972-76; Library Cmsn. 1970-79. Org: Library
Bd. Occ: Special Educ. Teacher Aide. B:
10/26/30. Add: 3244 River St., Kingston 48741
(517)683-2680.

Klingston.   MARLENE POWELL
     City Hall, Kingston   48741.

Kingston.   PATRICIA SOPER
     City Hall, Kingston   48741.

Laingsburg.   D. JEAN AUSTIN   (I)
     1973-.   Bds: Police Com.; Fire Com.; Library
Bd.   Org: NEA; Conservation Club.   Educ: Mich.
State U. 1957 BA; Mich. State U. 1961 MA.   Occ:
Teacher.   B: 1/1/33.   Add: 302 W. Grand River,
Laingsburg   48848   (517)651-6101.

Laingsburg.   DOROTHY WITCHELL
     City Hall, Laingsburg   48848.

Lake Ann.   MARGARET MENKE
     City Hall, Lake Ann   49650.

Lake Orion.   MILDRED EDWARD
          KATHERINE E. JACOBS
     City Hall, Lake Orion   48035.

Lakeview.   BARBARA DISHER
     City Hall, Lakeview   48850.

Lakewood Club.   MARJORIE JOHNSON
     City Hall, Lakewood Club

Lakewood Club.   PATRICIA E. JOHNSON   (D)
     1976-.   Bds: Ch., Planning Cmsn.; Finance Com.;
Pres. Pro Tem.   Prev: Treasurer 1969-76; Bicentennial Ch. 1976.   Org: Civic Builders; Big Sister
Occ: Wax Injector.   B: 1/27/43.   Add: 96 W. Ashland, Rt. 2, Twin Lk.,   49457.

L'Anse.   DONNA E. BLOOD   (D)
     1976-.   Bds: Ch., Police Com.; Ch., Recreation
Com.; Labor Com.   Org: OES.   Occ: Gym Teacher.   B:
5/7/31.   Add: 521 N. Main, L'Anse   49946   (906)
524-6116.

Lansing.   LUCILE E. BELEN   (D)
     1955-.   Bds: Ch., Capitol Area Council of Govts;
Lansing Conv. Bureau; Tri-Cnty. Aging Consortium
Party: State Del. 1940, '55; Nat. Alt. 1948;
Precinct Del.; State Com.   Prev: Cnty. Supervisor
1957-68; Ingham Cnty. Bd. of Health 1958-68.
Org: Chamber of Commerce; Zonta Club; Eleanor
Roosevelt League of Women; Dem. Party.   Occ:
Flower Shop Owner.   B: 12/28/12.   Add: 610 W.
Ottowa, Apt. 1203, Lansing   48933   (517)487-1378.

Lathrup Village.   BEVERLY CLEMO
     City Hall, Southfield   48075.

Lennon.   TERESA GLOWACKI
     City Hall, Lennon   48449.

Leslie.   BELVA F. SYLER   (D)
     Prev: Councilwoman 1974- .   B: 5/24/34.   Add:
429 W. Bellevue St., Leslie   49251.

Lincoln.   MARY BUCHANAN
     City Hall, Lincoln   48742.

Ludington.   MARILYN AMES   (R)
     1976-.   Bds: Ch., Pollution; Salary & Labor
Relations; Fire & Police.   Occ: Real Estate Saleswoman.   B: 10/27/31.   Add: 301 N. William, Ludington   49431   (616)845-6237.

Luna Pier.   DOROTHY BAUMGARTNER
          THELMA WARNER
     City Hall, Luna Pier   48157.

Lyons.   VERA DADD   (I)
     1958-.   B: 1/16/1899.   Add: 511 Isham,
Lyons   48851.

Manistique.   MARY MOFFAT
     City Hall, Manistique   49854.

Manton.   DORIS DEIKE
          ELEANOR SOSENKO
     City Hall, Manton   49663.

Marine City.   OTTOLYN E. COHRS   **
     1972-.   Bds: Community Center.   Prev: City
Clerk 1964-70.   Occ: Accounting Clerk.   B:
10/15/29.   Add: 834 Robertson St., Marine City
48039   (313)765-8830.

Marion.   NORMA TURNER
     City Hall, Marion   49665.

Mattawan.   CAROL J. DALY   (I)
     1976-.   Occ: Archivist.   B: 6/14/46.   Add:
198 2nd Ave., Mattawan   49071   (616)668-2128.

Melvindale.   PATRICIA A. HALL   (D)
     1976-.   Bds: Coord., City Beautification Com.
Org: Beautification Council; Mich. Municipal
League; Dems. for Progress; Dem. Club.   B:
7/3/42.   Add: 18550 Henry, Melvindale   48122
(313)381-8750.

Mendon.   CASSANDRA CRABTREE
     1971-.   Bds: Ch., Civic Affairs; Recreation;
Water Dept.   Prev: Councilwoman 1972-74.   Educ:
Glen Oaks Community Coll. 1977 AS.   Occ: Postal
Clerk.   B: 3/17/45.   Add: 315 Jackson St.,
Mendon   49072.

Menominee.   NINA JOAN TOMEK   (D)   **
     1972-.   Bds: Public Works; Planning; Commun-
ity Action Bd.; Schools; Bldgs. & Grounds.   Org:
PTA.   Occ: Assistant Personnel Dir.   B: 11/15/36.
Add: 1801 18th Ave., Menominee   49858   (906)
863-9474.

Metamora.   MARIETTA LEE
          DELORIS PAYNE
     City Hall, Metamora   48455.

Middleville.   VALERIE OWEN
     City Hall, Middleville   49333.

Midland.   WILMA M. DIESEN
     City Hall, Midland   48640.

Minden City.   VIRGINIA KROETSCH
     City Hall, Minden City   48456.

Mineral Hills.   MARIAN PETERSON
     City Hall, Mineral Hills

Montague.   JEWEL WINTERS
     City Hall, Montague   49437.

Mount Clemens. ADA D. EISENFELD (I) **
1971-. Bds: Retirement Bd.; Bicentennial Com.
Org: LWV. Educ: U. of Mich. 1948 BS. B: 1/23/27.
Add: 38 Breitmeyer Pl., Mt. Clemens 48043.

Mount Clemens. BETTY POWERS (D)
1975-. Org: Liberal Dem. Caucus; Interfaith
for Social Justice. Occ: Office Manager. B:
4/19/36. Add: 745 Cumberland, Mt. Clemens 48043.

Mount Pleasant. CAROL L. SCHERER (D) **
1972-. Bds: Municipal League; Ch., Resource
Recovery Com.; Ch., Park Study Com.; Labor Relations Com. Party: County V-Ch. 1970- ; Precinct
Del. 1970- . Org: LWV; PTA. Educ: Ohio State U.
1965 BS. B: 9/28/43. Add: 302 E. High St., Mt.
Pleasant 48858 (517)773-7971.

Mount Pleasant. DORIS ANN SHERWOOD (I)
1976-. Bds: Regional Planning Council; Liaison,
Chamber of Commerce. Prev: Planning Cmsn. 1971-76.
Org: NEA; LWV. Educ: Stetson U. 1958 BA; Central
Mich. U. 1962 MA. Occ: Music Teacher. B:
12/25/36. Add: 1109 Watson Rd., Mt. Pleasant
48858 (517)773-7971.

Munising. CHARLOTTE J. WEST (R) **
1974-. Party: County Ch. 1974. Org: Library
Bd.; Schools Advisory Bd. B: 9/13/27. Add: 208
E. Varnum, Munising 49862.

Muskegon. MARGUERITE HOLCOMB (R)
1975-. Bds: Planning Cmsn.; Citizens Dist.
Council on Housing; Historic Dist. Cmsn. Org:
BPW; Zonta; Women's Div., Chamber of Commerce;
Urban League; Cnty. Women's Rep. Club; Independent
Rep. Action Com. Occ: Corp. Pres. B: 4/9/17.
Add: 1891 Lakeshore Dr., Muskegon 49441 (616)
759-0991.

Muskegon. RUTH S. STEVENS (R)
1975-. Bds: Ch., Personnel Com.; Sewer &
Special Assessment Appeal Bd.; Landfill Com. Org:
Women's Div., Chamber of Commerce; Women's
Political Action Com. Educ: Grand Vly. State Coll.
1971 BA. B: 3/21/40. Add: 3922 Norton Hls. Rd.,
Muskegon 49441.

Muskegon Heights. RILLASTINE WILKINS
City Hall, Muskegon Hts. 49444.

Nashville. LOIS ELLISTON
115 E. Francis St., Nashville 49073.

Newberry. LUCY BRADLEY
City Hall, Newberry 49868.

New Buffalo. CAROL BOND
City Hall, New Buffalo 49117.

New Haven. IRMA WILSON
City Hall, New Haven 48048.

New Lothrop. JANE RALEIGH
City Hall, New Lothrop 48460.

North Muskegon. MARY ANN CROWELL FREEMAN
1976-. Bds: City Street Com. Party: Rep.
Town Com. 1969-72. Org: AAUW; LWV. Educ:
Wellesley Coll. 1951 BA. Occ: Hospital Community
Relations & Dev. Dir. B: 3/17/31. Add: 456 E.

Circle Dr., N. Muskegon 49445.

North Muskegon. MARGARET SEROCZYNSKI
City Hall, N. Muskegon 49445.

Northport. MARTHA ROBERTS
City Hall, Northport 49670.

Norton Shores. CHRISTEL G. WILLIAMS
City Hall, Norton Shores

Novi. MARTHA HOYER
City Hall, Novi 48050.

Novi. PATRICIA A. KAREVICH (I)
1975-. Bds: Regional Fire Study Com.;
Community Devt. Com. Prev: Election Cmsn. 1972-
74; Citizens Adv. Com. 1974-75; Parks & Recreation
B: 12/16/42. Add: 25904 Clark, Novi 48050
(313)349-4300.

Novi. ROMAINE ROETHEL (D)
1973-. Bds: SE Mich. Council of Govts.;
Council on Regional Devt.; Municipal League Urban
Affairs Com. Org: BPW; Common Cause; LWV; Cnty.
Dem. Club. Occ: Bookkeeper/Legal Secretary. B:
4/19/25. Add: 22461 Brook Forest, Novi 48050
(313)349-3445.

Oakley. JEAN M. POLLICK (D)
1976-. Bds: Finance Com. Occ: School
Custodian. B: 2/21/35. Add: 203 E. 4th St.,
Oakley 48649.

Oak Park. CHARLOTTE M. ROTHSTEIN (D)
1973-. Mayor Pro Tem. Bds: Recreation Adv.
Bd.; Arts & Cultural Cmsn.; Beautification Adv.
Cmsn. Org: Mich. Parks & Recreation Assoc.;
Municipal League. Occ: Media Center Dir. B:
11/14/24. Add: 24601 Westhampton, Oak Park
48237 (313)547-1331 Ext. 201.

Olivet. KATHY FULLENWIDER
City Hall, Olivet 49076.

Omer. MAXINE MARTIN (D)
1976-. B: 8/9/29. Add: 100 Broad, Omer
48749 (517)653-2531.

Orchard Lake Village. BETTY MACDUFF
City Hall, Orchard Lk. Vlg.

Ortonville. PEGGY A. PIDDINGTON (R)
1975-. Bds: Ch., Rent & Leasing Com.; Insurance Coverage Com. Party: Precinct Del. 1973-75.
B: 8/16/46. Add: 149 Mill St., Ortonville
48462 (313)625-3560.

Otter Lake. BETTY SCHNEIDER
City Hall, Otter Lake 48464.

Ovid. JANET BIRNEY
City Hall, Ovid 48866.

Owasso. VIRGINIA TEICH (R)
1973-. Bds: Mich. Municipal League-Trustee;
Planning Cmsn. Party: State Del. 1975-76; State
Alt. 1973-74; Precinct Del. 1973-77; State Dist.
Repr. 1975-77; Rep. State Central Com. 1975-77.
Org: Municipal League; Sheaivassee Cnty. Real
Estate Assoc.; Rep. Party; Arts Council; DAR;

Geneological Society. Educ: John Wesley Coll. 1975 BA. Occ: Real Estate. B: 12/21/23. Add: 1253 Ada St., Owasso 48867 (517)723-5221.

Parchment. VIRGINIA C. ALDRICH (I)
1974-. Bds: Recreation; Park. Educ:Kalamazoo Coll. 1935 BA. Occ: Library Aide. B: 5/7/13. Add: 360 Glendale Dr., Parchment 49004 (616) F19-3785.

Parma. CAROL BARE
DOROTHY TOOK
City Hall, Parma 49269.

Paw Paw. ANN M. GRIFFITH (R)
1975-. Bds: Senior Citizens. Party: State Del.; State Alt.; Cnty. Committeewoman 1976. Org: BPW; Bicentennial Com.; PTO. Occ: Deputy Cnty. Clerk. B: 11/1/34. Add: R. #2, Maple Lk., Paw Paw 49079 (616)657-5470.

Pentwater. MARIE S. DU MONT (D)
1974-. Bds: Ch., Parks & Recreation; Finance Com.; Zoning Bd. of Appeals. Org: Women's Club. B: 9/3/03. Add: 114 Park St., Pentwater 49449.

Pentwater. DELORES MODENA
City Hall, Pentwater 49449.

Perry. NATALEE BILLSBROUGH
City Hall, Perry 48872.

Pierson. NORMA J. BEAN (R)
1975-. Occ: Teacher's Aide. B: 8/31/42. Add: 158 Grand St., Pierson 49339.

Pierson. MILDRED RUNYON (D)
1973-. B: 1/17/19. Add: 153 Elm St., Pierson 49339.

Pinconning. EILEEN FORD
1973-. Bds: Planning Cmsn.; Police Cmsn.; Ch., Bills and Accounts. Occ: Secretary & Book-keeper. B: 9/28/20. Add: 600 Mercer, Pinconning 48650 (517)879-2199.

Plainwell. DORALDYNE SACHS (I) **
1974-. Bds: Park & Recreation Bd.; Public Works Com.; Tree Cmsn.; Bicentennial Com. Org: Environmental Action Council; Municipal League; Civic Assoc. Educ: Western Mich. U. 1966 BS. B: 7/20/35. Add: 131 N. Sunset, Plainwell 49080 (616)685-6821.

Plymouth. MARY B. CHILDS (R)
1975-. Bds: Parking Com. Prev: Planning Cmsnr. 1968-75; Bd. of Appeals 1973-75. Org: Municipal League; Community Ctr.; Historical Society; Woman's Club; LWV. Educ: Miami U. 1944 BSEd. Occ: Substitute Teacher. B: 5/25/23. Add: 1439 Ross, Plymouth 48170 (313)453-1234.

Plymouth. BEVERLY DIPPEL MC ANINCH (D)
1975-. Prev: City Comsr. 1971-73; Mayor 1973-75. Org: Detroit Economic Club; LWV. Educ: U. of Mich. 1949 BA; Wayne State U. 1957 MBA. Occ: Coll. Instructor. B: 9/12/26. Add: 539 S. Sheldon Rd., Plymouth 48170 (313)453-1234.

Pontiac. ELIZABETH STOGDILL
City Hall, Pontiac

Port Huron. AUDREY PACK
City Hall, Port Huron 48060.

Potterville. FRANCES DIANE KUSSMAUL (I)
1975-. Bds: Budget Com.; Community Educ. Council. Occ: Account Exec. B: 10/5/42. Add: 428 E. Cherry, Potterville 48876 (517)645-7673.

Quincy. LILAH M. BAKER (R)
1976-. Bds: Finance & Budget; Streets; Ordinance. Party: State Del. 1972. Org: BPW; Rep. Women; Women's Club. B: 8/15/10. Add: 11 E. Chicago, Quincy 49082 (517)639-4065.

Reed City. PATRICIA IVKOVICH
City Hall, Reed City 49677.

Reese. MARY JO RUMMEL
City Hall, Reese 48757.

Richmond. ADALINE GOHLKE
City Hall, Richmond 48062.

Rochester. FRANCES A. WEAVER (I)
1975-. Bds: Library Bd. Party: State Del. 1968, 1972; Precinct Del. 1968-74. Org: ACLU; Another Mother for Peace; Common Cause. Educ: Western Mich. U. 1947 BS, BA; Colo.State U. 1955 MA. B: 10/15/24. Add: 719 Ludlow, Rochester 48063 (313)651-0308.

Romulus. JOAN A. LEE
BEVERLY MC NALLY
City Hall, Romulus 48174.

Roscommon. NORMA EMERY
City Hall, Roscommon 48653.

Roseville. MARY MATUJA (D)
1975-. Bds: School Liason. Org: Dem. Club; PTO. B: 1/4/39. Add: 19273 Shadowoods Dr., Roseville 48066 (313)778-2800.

Roseville. CAROLINE SKUPNY
MARGARET SPYBROOK
City Hall, Roseville 48066.

Roseville. NANCY A. SWITALSKI (D)
1977-. Bds: Co-Ch., Com. for Mich. Week. Educ: Marymount Coll. 1948 BA. B: 12/13/25. Add: 16950 Martin Rd., Roseville 48066 (313) 778-2800.

Royal Oak. BARBARA A. HALLMAN
1973-. Ch., Bicentennial Cmsn.; Ch., Apple Day; Ch., Beautification Council. Prev: Parks & Recreation Adv. Bd. 1969-71. Org: Art Educ. Assoc.; Potter's Assoc.; Craftsman Council; NEA; Mich. Educ. Assoc.; PTA; LWV. Educ: Western Mich. U. 1956 BS; Wayne State U. 1957 MEd. Occ: Art Educator. Add: 512 Lexington Blvd., Royal Oak 48073 (313)546-1000.

Royal Oak. ALICE L. SCHOENHOLTZ
City Hall, Royal Oak 48073.

Saginaw. PAMELA LECKIE (R) **
1972-. Bds: Equal Educ. Opportunity Com.; School Liaison. Party: Precinct Leader; County Del. Org: PRA; Rep. Club. Educ: U. of Mich. 1952 BA. Occ: Juvenile Probation Officer. B:

3/3/30. Add: 225 Garden La., Saginaw 48602.
(517)799-2821.

Saginaw. SISTER ARDETH PLATTE (I)
1973-. Bds: Mortgage Appeals Bd.; Saginaw
Arts. Org: Mental Health Society; Retarded
Children's Assoc.; LWV. Educ: Aquinas Coll. 1959
BA; 1963 MA. Occ: Dir. of Alternative Educ. B:
4/10/36. Add: 1419 Veterans Memorial Pky.,
Saginaw 48601 (517)753-5411.

St. Ignace. JEAN KALBFLEISCH (R)
1971-. Bds: Library Bd., Ch., Procurement of
Doctors for Area. Org: BPW; Chamber of Commerce;
OES. Educ: U. of Mich. 1950 MA; Northern Mich.
Coll. of Educ. 1948 BS. Occ: Teacher. B: 6/9/26.
Add: 10 E. Stockbridge St., St. Ignace 49781
(906)643-8545.

St. Louis. MARY C. MEAD (R)
1974-. Mayor Pro Tem. Org: Mich. Kidney
Foundation. Educ: Saginaw Gen. Hospital School
of Nursing 1949 RN. Occ: Registered Nurse. B:
8/17/27. Add: 115 York Rd., St. Louis 48880.

Saline. MARY LOU HESS (R)
1973-. Mayor Pro Tem. Occ: Receiving Clerk.
B: 2/9/39. Add: 600 Canterbury, Saline 48176
(313)429-4907.

Sanford. DONNA DRAVES
City Hall, Sanford 48657.

Saranac. JOYCE KLEIN
City Hall, Saranac 48881.

Saugatuck. VIOLA FOX
City Hall, Saugatuck 49453.

Scottville. BETTY GUNNINGHAM
City Hall, Scottville 49454.

Southfield. LILLIAN JAFFEE
City Hall, Southfield 48075.

Southfield. JEAN MC DONNELL (I)
1958-. Bds: Site Plan Review Com.; Human
Resources Com.; Community Resources Com. Prev:
Zoning Planning Cmsn. 1956-59; Oakland Cnty. Bd.
of Supervisors 1968-70. Org: BPW; Community
Resources Com.; Historical Society. Add: 19860
W. 12 Mile Rd., Southfield 48076 (313)354-9380.

Southgate. DOROTHY RUPP (I) **
1973-. Bds: Cultural Cmsn.; City Beautiful;
Bicentennial Com. B: 12/17/34. Add: 14427
Trenton Rd., Southgate 48195 (313)283-1300.

South Rockwood. VIOLA LUXMOORE
City Hall, S. Rockwood 48179.

Sparta. DORIS M. JOHNSON (R)
1951-. Bds: Ch., Bd. of Appeals; Finance Com.;
Fire Com. B: 11/11/21. Add: 24 Division, Sparta
49345.

Springport. DONNA M. LEIGHTVER (I)
1975-. Bds: Water Com.; Drains & Sewer;
Police. Org: OES. Occ: Type Setter. B: 6/30/16.
Add: 130 Willow St., Springport 49284.

Standish. AUDREY LE VENT
LOIS RANSIER
City Hall, Standish 48658.

Stephenson. CARMEN ANDERSON
City Hall, Stephenson 49887.

Sunfield. DEBBIE SHEPARD
City Hall, Sunfield 48890.

Swartz. KAY M. HART
City Hall, Swartz 48473.

Taylor. MARY WASHBURN (D) **
1973-. Party: Dist. Exec. Bd. 1973- ;
Precinct Com. 1971- . Prev: Planning Cmsn.
1973-75. Org: BPW; Community Service; Dem.
Clubs. Educ: Wayne State U. 1973 BA. B:
4/6/15. Add: 24939 Chernick, Taylor 48180
(313)287-6550; 287-6262.

Tecumseh. MARY A. BOWERS (R)
1974-. Prev: City Councilwoman. Org: Nat.
Assoc. of Bank Women; Historical Society. Occ:
Bank V-Pres. B: 6/14/26. Add: 603 Red Mill Dr.,
Tecumseh 49286 (517)423-8373.

Tekonsha. DONNA BROWN
BETTY STEFAN
City Hall, Tekonsha 49092.

Three Oaks. HANNAH NOBLE
City Hall, Three Oaks 49128.

Three Rivers. PEARL MITCHELL (D)
1975-. Bds: S. Central Mich. Planning & Devt.
Council; State Crime Cmsn.; State Municipal
League. Party: State Del. 1965-73; Nat. Alt.
1972; Dist. Secretary 1968-73; State Conventions
Secretary 1970-72; V-Pres., Dem. Black Caucus
1970-73. Prev: Human Relations Com. 1969-73.
Org: Mich. State Employees Assoc.; NAACP; Black
Social Workers of Amer. Occ: Employment Inter-
viewer. B: 2/4/26. Add: 900 5th St., Three
Rivers 49093 (616)273-7815/1075.

Traverse City. DIANE GILBO (I)
1972-. Mayor Pro Tem. Bds: Grand Traverse
Cnty. Assoc.; Joint City-Cnty. Bldg. Com. Org:
Amer. Society of Clinical Pathologists; Assoc.
for Retarded Citizens; PTA; AAUW. Educ: Coll.
of St. Teresa 1956 BS. Occ: Medical Technologist.
B: 5/8/34. Add: 2014 E. 8th, Traverse City
49684.

Troy. JEANNE STINE.
City Hall, Troy 48084.

Turner. MAXINE CANTO
City Hall, Turner 48765.

Ubly. LANA MAURER
City Hall, Ubly 48475.

Union City. ROWENA SCHRAGG (D)
1972-. Bds: Ch., Park Bd. Org: Women's
Fellowship; PTSA. B: 9/11/38. Add: 204 John
St., Union City 49094 (517)741-7773.

Union City. DOROTHY SMITH
City Hall, Union City 49094.

Unionville. DOROTHY SCHMUCK
City Hall, Unionville 48767.

Utica. HELEN SCHWARK
City Hall, Utica 48087.

Vandalia. JOSEPHINE EBERHARDT
City Hall, Vandalia 49095.

Vanderbilt. CLARE WIMMER
City Hall, Vanderbilt 49795.

Vicksburg. ANNA BROWN
City Hall, Vicksburg 49097.

Vicksburg. SUSAN A. NOBLE (I)
1976-. Bds: Ch., Budget; Recreation Council;
Street & Bridge Com. Org: Ladies Library. Educ:
Western Mich. U. 1949 BS. B: 11/1/27. Add: 124
E. Maple, Vicksburg 49097 (616)649-0642.

Walker. JOYCE D. STARK (R)
1975-. Bds: V-Ch., Bd. of Zoning Appeals;
Economic Devt. Administration; Awards Com. Org:
Grandville Educ. Assoc.; LWV; PTA. Educ: Grand
Vly. State Coll. 1972 BS; Western Mich. U. 1975
MA. Occ: Teacher. B: 5/7/32. Add: 5 Cummings,
N.W., Walker 49504.

Walkerville. KATHRYN TRENARY
City Hall, Walkerville 49459.

Walled Lake. HEATHER HILL
City Hall, Walled Lake 48088.

Warren. CARMELLA SABAUGH (D)
1975-. Bds: Retirement Bd.; Beautification
Cmsn. B: 8/3/38. Add: 27520 Sutherland, Warren
48093.

Watervliet. SANDRA JEAN PRITCHETT (I)
1976-. Bds: Ch., Park Com.; Sanitation Com.;
Bldg. & Equipment. Occ: Librarian. B: 12/8/49.
Add: 124 Sutherland, Watervliet 49098 (616)
463-6769.

Wayland. MARIE J. HALL (I)
1976-. Bds: Ambulance Bd. Org: ANA. Occ:
RN. B: 5/12/35. Add: 119 W. Pine, Wayland
49348.

Wayne. MILDRED JANE BATTERSON (I)
1973-. Bds: Recreation Adv. Bd. Prev: Repr.,
State Parks & Recreation 1972-77; Recreation Adv.
Bd. 1970-73; Summer Festival Com. 1970-73. Educ:
Eastern Mich. U. 1958 BS. Occ: Sales Repr. B:
1/8/38. Add: 35252 Winston, Wayne 48184.

Westland. JUSTINE BARNS (D) **
1966-. Bds: Hospital Authority; Free Clinics;
Bicentennial Com. Party: State Com. 1974- ;
County Com. 1964- ; Precinct Del. 1958- ; V-Pres.
Precinct 1962-64; Secretary Precinct 1960-62.
Prev: County Charter Cmsn. 1968; Planning Cmsn.
1963-67; Local Charter Cmsn. 1964-66. Org:
Municipal League; PTA. B: 2/2/25. Add: 34139
Tawas Tr., Westland 48185 (313)PA1-6000.

Westland. H. GAIL MC KNIGHT (D)
1976-. Prev: Zoning Bd. of Appeals 1975-77;
Bicentennial Cmsn. 1975-76. Org: ABA; Amers.
for Dem. Action; Dem. Club. Educ: U. of Detroit
1967 BA; Wayne State U. 1976 JD. Occ: Atty./
Wayne Cnty. Prosecuter. B: 7/31/45. Add: 8249
Ravine, Westland 48185 (313)721-6000.

Whitehall. ELSA M. ANDERSON
EDNA K. BLOMDAHL
City Hall, Whitehall 49461.

Williamston. DRUSCILLA ROEHM **
1973-. Bds: Regional Planning Cmsn. Prev:
Planning Cmsn. 1971-73. Educ: U. of Mich. 1960
BBA. B: 11/3/38. Add: 302 Jackson St., Williamston 48895 (517)655-2774.

Wixom. LILLIAN SPENCER
City Hall, Wixom 48096.

Wolverine Lake. SYLVIA S. BAIZE
PAT HOWARTH
City Hall, Wolverine Lake

Woodland. MARY MAKLEY
City Hall, Woodland 48897.

Ypsilanti. MATTIE L. DORSEY
City Hall, Ypsilanti 48197.

Ypsilanti. NATHALIE E. EDMUNDS (R) **
1970-. Bds: Watershed Council; Transportation
Study; Liquor Study; Community Schools; Historic
Dist. Cmsn. Party: Precinct Leader. Org: Art
Council; Historical Society; Rep. Club. Educ:
U. of Mich. 1949 BA. B: 5/3/27. Add: 1303
Westmoreland, Ypsilanti 48197.

Ypsilanti. SUSAN GAIL LINDSAY (D) **
1973-. Bds: Recreation Coordinating Com.
Party: State Com.; County Com. 1973-75; Precinct
Leader 1972-75; Precinct Secretary 1971-72. Org:
AFL-CIO; Fed. of Teachers; NAACP; Dem. Club.
Educ: Wayne State U. 1970 BS. Occ: Teacher. B:
4/2/47. Add: 505 Emmet, Ypsilanti 48197 (313)
483-1100.

Judges

SUSAN D. BORMAN
Judge, Recorders Court. Add: 1441 St.
Antoine, Detroit 48226.

PATRICIA J. BOYLE (D)
Judge, Recorders Court. 1976-. Prev: Asst.
US Atty. 1964-69; Asst. Prosecuting Atty. 1969-
75. Org: Women Lawyers of Mich.; State Bar of
Mich.; Nat. Adv. Bd.-Rape Crisis; NOW; Dist.
Dem. Party; Mich. Dem. Party. Educ: Wayne State
U. 1963 BA; Wayne Law 1963 JD. B: 3/31/37.
Add: 15925 Warwick, Detroit 48219 (313)
224-5531.

MARY STALLINGS COLEMAN (R)
Supreme Court Justice. 1973-. Bds: Liaison,
Probate & Juvenile Court Judges Assoc.; Judicial
Reporting. Prev: Probate & Juvenile Court
Judge 1961-73. Org: ABA; BPW; AAUW; Nat. Women
Lawyers; Amer. Judicature Society; Jr. League;

Altrusa. Educ: U. of Md. 1935 BA; George Wash. U. 1939 JD. Add: 355 E. Hamilton Land, Battle Creek 49015 (517)373-0128.

GERALDINE BLEDSOE FORD
Judge, Recorder's Court. Add: 1441 St. Antoine St., Detroit 48226.

ALICE L. GILBERT
Judge, Circuit Court. Add: Courthouse Tower, 1200 N. Telegraph Rd., Pontiac 48053.

DOROTHY C. RILEY
Judge, Court of Appeals. Add: 900 1st Federal Bldg., 1001 Woodward Ave., Detroit 48226.

State Boards and Commissions

Aging, Commission on Services
MARGHERITTA S. ALLARDICE
ADELA M. CAMARENO
HELEN I. COOVER
GWENDOLYN R. EDWARDS
ELEANOR HARGROVE
MICHALENE LEWANDOWSKI

Agriculture Commission
REBECCA TOMPKINS

Agricultural Labor, Commission on
MIRTA C. CARRION
ESTHER M. HUIZENGA
RUTH M. RIGG

Agricultural Marketing and Bargaining Board
CLARE MC MANUS

Air Pollution Control Commission
MARTHA REYNOLDS

American Revolution Bicentennial Commission, A Special Committee
MARGO R. CARLIN
CAROL L. EVANS
MILDRED A. PASTOR
DOROTHY L. WALKMEYER
DELORES WHARTON

Art in State Buildings, Special Commission
MARY ANN KEELER
HELEN MILLIKEN

Arts, Council on
PEGGY BRANSDORFER
LOIS COHODAS
CAROLYN T. HOAGLAND
THELMA GRAY JAMES
JUDITH RIECKER MANOS
BETTY PARSONS
SUSAN A. PRICE
JUDITH RAPANOS

Awards Commission for Distinguished Public Employees
JUDITH HECHT

Barrier Free Design Board
NAN E. SMITH

Bay County Metropolitan Transportation Authority
ARLENE BUSH
SUSANNAH HARRISON

Beef Industry Commission
JOANN HIGBY

Building Commission
LUCILE E. BELEN

Canvassers, Board of State
NANCY CHASE
JESSIE M. DILLARD
ESTHER WAITE

Carnival-Amusement Safety Board
JOAN CLEVER

Child Care Study Committee
LAVON BLIESENER
ILENE TOMBER

Chiropractic Examiners, Board of
MARIE M. RAGUCKAS

Civil Defense Advisory Council
ALICE E. TUNISON

Civil Rights Commission
CATHERINE BLACKWELL
CAROLE L. CHIAMP
HILDA R. GAGE

Collection Practices Advisory Board
CAROL S. JOSEPHSON
KATHERINE M. WILLIS

Community Planners, Registration for Professional
ANN O. FLETCHER

Consumer Affairs, Citizens Committee
POLLY GIBSON
HARRIET ROTTER
SUE K. WILLISON

Corrections Commission
FLORENCE CRANE

Cosmetology, Board of
LUELLA M. MC KAY
MARGUERITE PRESTON

Criminal Justice, Commission on
FLORENCE CRANE
RUTH RASMUSSEN
ROSEMARY SARRI
ILENE TOMBER

Crippled Children Commission
LAURA L. WILLIAMS
VIRGINIA WILSON

Developmental Disabilities Services and Facilities Construction Advisory Council
RUTH H. KARSLAKE
MARION R. MC DONNELL
EVELYN PROVITT
ANN ZUZICH

Education Commission of the States
    ELIZABETH B. KUMMER
    DANA P. WHITMER

Education Council
    MARY K. KOSA

Electrical Administrative Board
    DEANNA D. HANIESKI
    LEE ANNE KENT

Employment Security Advisory Council
    M. JANE KAY

Environmental Education Interim Committee
    MRS. WILLIE C. EVANS
    ODESSA KOMÈR

Environmental Review Board
    MARY ANNE WILLIAMS

Ethics, Board
    MARGARET FOERCH

Fair Authority
    LILLIAN DAVEY
    MERLE M. JOHNSON

Financial Institutions, Commission on Regulation of
    JOSEPHINE STARKWEATHER

Handicapped, Commission on the Employment of the
    ROSALYN CLARK
    ARDYCE J. GERMAIN
    MIRIAM F. KING
    DOROTHY L. MOSER
    PEGGY S. TENNEY
    BERNICE WHITE

Health and Safety Compliance and Appeals Board
    VICKI KENNEDY

Health Coordinating Council
    NINA O. BUELL
    ESTHER CANJA
    VIRGINIA S. CLELAND
    ROBERTA F. COTTMAN
    LILLIAN R. DAVEY
    MARY R. DE FOE
    ELIZABETH GOULAIS
    ANNAMARIE G. HAYES
    LOIS LAMONT
    MARGARET MORROW
    JARRETTE SIMMONS
    MYRA L. SUNDBECK
    LEA M. TOBAR
    HOPE Y. TRAPP

Health Facilities Commission
    HELEN B. KELLY

Health Maintenance Organization Commission
    ELLA BRAGG
    MARY LOVE CLAVON

Hearing Aid Dealers, Board
    PAT S. TARITAS

Higher Education Assistance Authority
    JEAN R. MORAN
    PATRICIA J. SHONTZ

Historical Commission
    ELIZABETH ADAMS

Indian Affairs, Commission on
    DORIS ADAMS
    JOAN BEMIS
    VIOLA G. PETERSON
    ELAINE M. TUFFELMIRE
    MURIEL YOUNGBLOOD

Interstate Cooperation Committee
    LILLIAN MOFFIT

Juvenile Justice Advisory Committee
    MARY E. DUMAS
    BETH GOEBEL
    VIRGINIA LEE
    ROSEMARY SARRI
    KAREN M. SCHROCK
    CARYLE SEIM
    MARY A. TEAGUE
    ILENE TOMBER

Juvenile Justice Services Commission
    PATRICIA W. BARNES-MC CONNELL
    Y. GLADYS BARSAMIAN
    LINDA FELDT
    MARIA MERGENTIME

Law Examiners, Board of
    KAY D. SCHLOFF

Legal Services Corporation Advisory Council
    DOLORES C. BLACKBURN
    EVELYN SIMS
    ODESSA SMITH

Libraries, Board of
    JANE R. CAMERON
    DIANE E. HOLBEL
    MARGARET STEFFENS

Marriage Counselors, Board of
    REBECCA A. VAUGHAN

Massage, Board of
    MARY LOU BARTH
    VERNA M. HICKS

Medical Practice Board
    CAROL H. PEARSON

Mental Health Advisory Council
    ELOISE C. WHITTEN

Natural Resources, Commission
    JOAN L. WOLFE

Neighborhood Education Authority
    HELEN B. HARRIS

Nursing, Board of
    ROSEMARY BELL
    SANDRA J. BRIDGES
    EDITH J. FROST
    MARTHA J. HARPER
    BARBARA J. HORN
    FRANCES E. JACKSON
    LORRAINE RUCINSKI
    HAZEL SMITH

VIRGINIA ANN SMITH
BARBARA C. THAYER

Nutrition, Advisory Commission on
ALICIA V. COPPOLA
ANITA MARIE HERALD
LAURA B. HESS
LYNNE MARIE JAMIESON
MARYANN MAHAFFEY
EDNA MAE MC INTOSH
VIRGINIA SOLBERG
KATHLEEN WEBB
LYNN E. WYMAN

Occupational Health Standards Commission
LUCILE M. PORTWOOD

Officers Compensation Commission
BARBARA DARIN
DOLORES ANN KINZEL

Osteopathic Medicine Advisory Board
MYRTLE F. BLACK

Osteopathic Registration and Examination
BETSY DURBIN

Pharmacy, Board of
LINDA GROSSMAN
PEGGY A. MEZIER

Physical Fitness and Health, Council on
PATTY LYN ATKINSON
JEAN HOOK
PHYLLIS TERWILLIGER
JANET A. WESSEL

Physicians' Assistants, Committee on
D. ANNETTE ADAMS
KAREN D. KOTCH
SALLY MOLDWIN

Public Health Advisory Council
ROSEMARY BELL
ESTHER O. RUPRIGHT
SONDRA C. SHAW

Public Health Statue Review Commission
A. JOSEPHINE BROWN
DOLORES LYONS
SONDRA SHAW
ELLA MARY SIMS

Public School Employees Retirement Board
DONNA J. FAHLEN
MABEL MATTHEWS

Radiation Advisory Committee
DARLENE F. BENNETT

Recreation Advisory Committee
MARGARET HOSSACK
DELORA YORI

Recreational Land Acquisition Trust Fund, Board of
Trustees
PATRICIA HUXTABLE

Resource Recovery Commission
PAMELA FRUCCI

Small Business Advisory Council
MILDRED H. DUNNELL
MERIAM B. LEEKE

Social Services Advisory Board
MARTHA W. GRIFFITHS
SELMA E. GOODE
SARA HARDY
ERMA L. HENDERSON

Social Workers, Board of Examiners
SHARON DALTON
ROSE MARY SIMON
MARGERY VANDER PLOEG
ELOISE C. WHITTEN

Spanish Speaking Affairs, Commission on
ANITA M. ALFARO
THERESA LEDESMA
MARGARITA ORTIZ
MARIA D. RAMIREZ
DEBORAH W. SANCHEZ
MARIA Y. SCHULMEYER

State Employees Retirement Board
BERNEICE LOHMAN
PATRICIA PICKETT

Substance Abuse Services, Advisory Commission on
MARIANNE E. BRICKLEY
MARGARET CLAY
ANN M. POWELL

Tenure Commission
MARIAN GIBSON

Travel Commission
NINA O. BUELL

Upper Peninsula State Fair Board
RUTH BUTLER

Volunteers in Michigan, Commission on
RACHEL J. ANDRESEN
ROSE BELL
CAROLINE A. DAVIS
DORETTA M. DISE
MARIAN G. KLEIN
ROBERTA M. PICKETT
DOROTHY RAPPA

Wage Deviation Board
EILEEN K. NUTTING

Water Resources Commission
HELEN S. WILLIS

Wilderness and Natural Areas Advisory Board
GENEVIEVE GILETTE

Women's Commission
N. LORRAINE BEEBE
PATRICIA BURNETT
MARGARET R. COOKE
ROSA DAHYA
CLARE C. DANIELS
BERNADINE N. DENNING
NORMA J. LASKEY
BARBARA T. MAC QUEEN
MARIE MYLAN

SHIRLEY OCZUS
LORNA JEAN OTTO
IRENE PROPHATER
ANN MARIE SHAFER
CONNIE TARRAN
MARTHA WYETH

Workmen's Compensation Appeal Board
MOLLY A. BEITNER

Youth Advisory Commission
KATHLEEN A. MAISNER
MARIA T. MERGENTIME
ELIZABETH PHILLIPS

Minnesota

State Executive and Cabinet

JOAN ANDERSON GROWE (D)
Secretary of State. 1974-. Bds: Exec. Council; Investment Bd.; Ch., Canvassing Bd. Prev: State Repr. 1973-75. Org: Nat. Assoc. of Secretaries of State; Zonta; BPW; LWV; NOW; Common Cause; DFL; WPC; Minn. Shares for Hunger. Educ: St. Cloud State Coll. 1956 BS. B: 9/28/35. Add: 15 S. 1st St., Minneapolis 55401 (612)296-2079.

State Legislature

State Senate

NANCY OSBORN BRATAAS (R) **
1975-. Dist: 33. Bds: Educ.; Labor & Commerce; Nursing Homes. Party: Dir. of Nat. Phone Campaign; Com. for the Reelection of the Pres.; State V-Ch.; GOP Ch. 1957-59, 1960-61; Pres., County GOP Workshop 1957-58. Org: AAUW, LWV; ZONTA. Occ: Pres., Nancy Brataas Assoc. B: 1/19/28. Add: 839 10 1/2 St. SW, Minneapolis 55901 (612)296-4848.

EMILY ANNE STAPLES (D)
1976-. Dist: 43. Bds: Council on the Economic Status of Women. Party: State Del. 1964; State Alt. 1972; Dem. Precinct Ch. 1974-75; Rep. Precinct Ch. 1964-66; Dist. Co-Ch. 1966-68. Prev: Ch., Women's Adv. Com. to Minn. Dept. of Human Rights. 1965-70; Ch., Cnty. Bicentennial Cmsn. 1973-76. Org: NOW; WEAL; AAUW; LWV; BPW; WPC; Jr. League; DFL Feminist Caucus; Com. on Foreign Relations. Educ: U. of Minn. 1950 BA. B: 5/3/29. Add: 1640 Xanthus Ln., Wayzata 55391 (612)296-4137.

State House

LINDA BERGLIN (D)
1972-. Bds: Ch., Council on the Economic Status of Women. Party: State Del. 1972; Precinct Convener 1974-77. Prev: Ch., Model Cities Resident Bd. 1971-72. Org: Neighborhood Assoc.; Action Council; Community Org.; DFL; WPC. Educ: Minneapolis Coll. of Art & Design 1967 BFA. B: 10/19/44. Add: 2309 Clinton Ave. S., Minneapolis 55404 (612)296-4261.

MARGARET MARY BYRNE (D)
1974-. Bds: Educ.; Labor; Criminal Justice. Party: State Del. 1974; Caucus Del. 1974. Educ: U. of Minn. BA. B: 12/17/49. Add: 524 Van Buren, St. Paul 55103 (612)296-4245.

JANET CLARK (D) **
Dist: 60A. Add: 3025 Cedar Ave. S, Minneapolis 55407 (612)724-8318.

MARY M. FORSYTHE (R)
1972-. Dist: 39A. Bds: Nat. Conf. of State Legislatures; V-Ch., Human Resources Task Force; Minn. Cmsn. on Economic Status of Women; Leg. Review Cmsn. Party: State Del. 1974-77; State Alt.; Nat. Alt. 1976; Precinct Ch. 1968-74; State Rep. Workshop Bd.; Cnty. Rep. Com. Org: Nat. Conf. of State Legislators. Educ: St. Olaf Coll. 1942 BM. B: 5/23/20. Add: 4605 Edina Blvd., Edina 55424 (612)296-4363.

SHIRLEY ANN HOKANSON (D) **
1974-. Dist: 37A. Party: Ch., Exec. Com. 1970-73; Central Com. 1970-72; Local Exec. Com. 1966-70. Org: LWV; Minn. Social Service Assoc.; Sons of Norway; DFL; Chamber of Commerce; PTA. Educ: U. of Minn. 1958 BA. B: 2/8/36. Add: 7345 Russell Ave., S, Richfield 55423 (612) 296-4239.

PHYLLIS KAHN (D)
1972-. Dist: 57A. Bds: Agriculture Com.; Appropriations Com.; Environment Com. Party: Precinct Del. 1972-78. Prev: Women's Adv. Com. to Human Rights Dept. 1970-72. Org: Amer. Assoc. for Advancement of Science; Fed. of Amer. Scientists; NOW; WEAL; WPC; Feminist Caucus. Educ: Cornell U. 1957 BA; Yale U. 1962 PhD. B: 3/23/37. Add: 100 Malcolm Ave. S.E., Minneapolis 55414 (612)296-4257.

ARLENE I. LEHTO (D)
1977-. Dist: 8A. Bds: Natural Resources & Environment Com.; Criminal Justice Com.; General Leg. & Veterans Affairs Com. Party: State Del. 1974; Precinct Ch. 1974-77; Prev: Regional Devt. Cmsn. 1970-72; State Esthetic Environment Task Force 1975-76. Org: BPW; Chamber of Commerce; OES; Save Lake Superior Assoc.; LWV; Community Club; DFL; DFL Feminist Caucus; WPC. Occ: Print Shop Manager. B: 9/14/39. Add: 901 E. 7th St., Duluth 55805.

MARY MURPHY (D)
6794 Arrowhead Rd., Duluth 55811.

LINDA J. SCHEID (D)
1976-. Bds: Com. on Taxes; Local & Urban
Affairs Com.; Health & Welfare Com. Prev:
Capital Long Range Improvement Com. 1975-77.
Org: AFSCME; LWV. Educ: Coe Coll. 1964 BA. B:
6/16/42. Add: 5316 81st Ave. N., Brooklyn Pk.
55443 (612)296-3751.

ANN J. WYNIA (D)
1976-. Dist: 62A. Party: State Del. 1974;
Congressional Dist. Central Com. 1974-76. Org:
Minn. Political Science Assoc.; Minn. Environ-
mental Citizen Control Assoc.; WPC. Educ: U. of
Tex. 1965 BA; U. of Wis. 1968 MA. Occ: Coll.
Intructor. B: 7/29/43. Add: 1550 Branston, St.
Paul 55108 (612)296-3824.

County Commissions

Chisago. SARAH MOLD
Center City 55012.

Douglas. EDITH M. KELLY (D)
1975-. Bds: Ch., W. Central Minn. Communities
Action; Cnty. Social Welfare Bd.; Devt. Achieve-
ment Ctr. Party: State Del. 1966; Cnty. Ch.
1958-62; Precinct Leader. Prev: Cnty. Social
Welfare Bd. 1960-68. Org: BPW; WPC; Assoc. of
Retarded Citizens. Occ: Bookkeeper. B: 2/4/29.
Add: 304 12th Ave. E., Alexandria 56308.

Fillmore. JEAN L. OLSON
Preston 55965.

Hennepin. NANCY K. OLKON (D)
1976-. Bds: Community Action Agency; Cnty.
Criminal Justice Coord. Council. Party: State
Del. 1972; Nat. Alt. 1972; Precinct Ch. 1969-74;
House Dist. Ch. 1972-74; Congressional Dist. Dir.
1974-76. Org: Minn. State Bar Assoc. Educ: U.
of Minn. 1971 BA; William Mitchell Coll.of Law
1968 JD. B: 8/26/41. Add: 3515 Zenith S.,
Minneapolis 55416 (612)348-3080.

Itasca. SHIRLEY JOKINEN
Grand Rapids 55744.

Lac Qui Parle. MARY E. TOLLEFSON
1976-. Dist: 3. Prev: Community Fund Bd.
Org: General Fed. Women's Club; PTA. Educ:
Winthrop Coll. 1945 BA. B: 11/16/23. Add: 118
E. 8th St., Madison 56256.

Lake. LENORE M. JOHNSON **
1975-. Dist: 5. Bds: Planning & Zoning; Recreation. Occ: Bookkeeper. B: 4/29/38. Add:
Rt. 1, Box 152A, Two Harbors 55616.

Lake of the Woods. HOPE GULLINGSRUD
Baudette 56623.

Olmsted. ROSEMARY AHMANN (D)
1972-. Dist: 1. Bds: Public Safety;Ch., Nat.
Assoc. of Cnty's. Party: Cnty. Nominating Com.
Prev: Halfway House 1974-75; Probation Rehabili-
tation & Training Officers 1974-76; Community
Corrections 1973-75. Org: LWV; Common Cause.
Educ: Milwaukee Cnty. School of Nursing 1956 RN;
Rochester Community Coll. 1972 AA. B: 4/26/35.
Add: 521 14th Ave. SW, Rochester 55901 (507)

285-8115.

Olmsted. CAROL KAMPER (R)
1976-. Bds: Public Works; Zumbro Vly.
Mental Health; Welfare Bd. Prev: Alderwoman
1971-76; Cnty. Health Bd. 1974-76. Org: Nat.
League of Cities; Nat. Assoc. of Cntys.; AAUW;
Rep. Party; PTA. Educ: Hope Coll. 1962 BA;
Rutgers U. 1963 MA. B: 12/21/40. Add: 2204
Valkyrie Dr. NW, Rochester 55901 (607)285-8115.

Ramsey. DIANE AHRENS (D)
1974-. Bds: Gov. Study Cmsn.; Hospital
Cmsn.; Legislative Com.; Environment & Engineer-
ing Com. Org: Nat. Assoc. of Cnty. Officials;
Social Service Assoc.; LWV; Urban League; NAACP;
ACLU; WPC; Common Cause; Environmental Concerned
Citizens. Educ: U. of Maryland 1952 BS; Yale
U. 1954 MRE. B: 5/30/31. Add: 842 Osceola,
St. Paul 55105 (612)298-4145.

St. Louis. DEIDRE DODGE (D)
1974-. Bds: Ch., Finance Com.; V.-Ch., Cnty.
Bd.; Welfare Bd. Org: BPW; Minn. Social
Service Assoc.; LWV; WPC. Educ: Vermillion Jr.
Coll. 1965 AA; U. of Minn. 1970 BA. B: 3/1/45.
Add: 322 N. 21st Ave. E., Duluth 55812 (218)
723-3507.

Wilkin. KATHLEEN M. VERTIN (I)
1974-. Bds: Ch., Bd. of Cnty. Cmsnrs.;
Opportunity Council; Extension Com. Org: WPC;
Common Cause; Comprehensive Health Planning
Council; Medical Complex Negotiating Com.;
Medical Facilities Com.; Home Governing Bd.
Occ: Secretary/Treasurer. B: 1/16/13. Add:
321 8th St. N., Breckenridge 56520 (218)
643-4981.

Mayors

Badger. LOIS M. JOHNSON (D)
1971-. Party: Badger Dem. Ch. 1967-74.
Prev: Councilwoman 1969-70. Occ: Proprietor.
B: 4/10/34. Add: Box 194, Badger 56714 (218)
528-3258.

Bethel. RUTH M. NETTEBERG (D)
1977-. Bds: Chief of Police. Party: Dist.
Del. 1970. Org: Minn. Fed. of Teachers. Educ:
St. Cloud State Coll. 1970 BS. Occ: Teacher.
B: 6/21/25. Add: 154 237 Ave. NW, Bethel 55055
(612)434-5669.

Buhl. MRS. RICHARD WILMAN
City Hall, Buhl 55713.

Carlton. A. JANICE GRANNES (R)
1977-. Bds: Planning Cmsn. Party: Precinct
V-Ch. 1972-74; City V-Ch. 1974-76; City Sec.
1972-74. Prev: Park & Recreation Com. 1973-76.
Org: Businessmen's Group; Cnty. Rep's. Educ:
Concordia Coll. 1961 BS. Occ: Corporation
Secretary-Treasurer. B: 4/27/37. Add: 217
Ashland, Carlton 55718 (218)384-4215.

Champlin. JOSEPHINE D. NUNN (D)
1971-. Bds: Metropolitan Sports Facilities
Cmsn.; League of Minn. Cities Bd.; Assoc. of
Metropolitan Municipalities. Prev: Councilwoman
1970-71. Org: Minn. Mayor's Assoc.; Common
Cause; Minn. Civil Liberties Union; Women's Club.
B: 8/7/19. Add: 401 Elm Creek Rd., Champlin
55316 (612)421-8064.

Cloquet. ARLENE H. WOLNER
320 2nd Street, Cloquet 55720.

Crosslake. ORENA M. FOGELBERG (R)
1974-. Bds: Police Cmsnr.; Municipal Telephone
System. B: 6/14/04. Add: Box 115, Crosslake
56442 (218)692-2688.

Foreston. PHYLLIS CHRISTIANSON (D)
1975-. Party: Central Dem. Com. 1975-77.
Prev: Councilwoman 1974-75. B: 6/2/27. Add:
Foreston 56330 (612)294-5462.

Ghent. MARION WIGNES
City Hall, Ghent 56239.

Hampton. COLLEEN MARSCHALL
City Hall, Hampton 55031.

Island View. ANGELINE BRASCUGLI (D) **
1976-. Bds: Planning Cmsn.; Com. on Zoning;
Nat. Park Com.; Minn. Future Com. Prev: Council
1972-76. Org: Welfare Bd. Educ: Boston U. 1927
BS. B: 9/27/06. Add: Rte. 8, Box 435A, International Falls 56649 (218)286-5225.

Kinney. MARY ANDERSEN (D)
1975-. Party: State Alt. 1976; Central Com.
1976-77. Prev: Justice of the Peace 1960-75.
Occ: Nurse. B: 6/8/15. Add: Kinney 55788.

Lake Bronson. ALICE DANIELSON
City Hall, Lake Bronson 56734.

Maple Plain. MARCENE SHAFFER (D)
1976-. Party: State Del. 1975-77; Precinct
Leader 1974-76; Political Educ. Dir. 1974-75;
Senate Dist. Finance Dir. 1976-77. Org: NEA;
Congressional Club. Educ: St. Cloud State U. BS.
Occ: Teacher. Add: 1769 Howard Ave., Maple Plain
55359 (612)479-1123.

Menahga. IONE E. ELLINGSON **
1974-. Prev: Justice of the Peace 1966-74.
B: 12/8/33. Add: Box 274, Menahga 56464 (218)
564-4557.

Minnetrista. ELIZABETH K. REED (R)
1975-. Bds: Parks & Recreation Cmsn. Prev:
Councilwoman 1973-75; Planning Cmsn. 1971-73.
Org: Minn. Field Trial Assoc. Educ: Radcliffe
Coll. 1944 AB; U. of Minn. 1949 MA. Occ: Under-
writer. B: 2/23/22. Add: Birdsong - 7300 Cnty.
Rd. 26, Maple Plain 55359 (612)472-3484.

New Richland. MARGARET A. ENGESSER (I)
1971-. Bds: Regional Cmsn.; Park Assoc. Org:
Devt. Assoc. Educ: St. Lukes Hospital School of
Nursing 1946 RN. Occ: Newspaper Ad Saleswoman/
Reporter/Photographer. B: 1/9/22. Add: 100 N.
Birch, New Richland 56072 (507)465-3514.

Ortonville. SARAH S. EGERT (R)
1975-. Bds: Regional Manpower Cmsn. Party:
Cnty. Del. 1975-77. Org: US Daughters of 1812;
DAR; Daughters of Amer. Colonists; Huguenot
Society. Educ: Hamline U. 1958 BS. B: 10/12/35.
Add: 551 4th St. NW, Ortonville 56278 (612)
839-2909.

Otter Lake. ALFA J. SPOONER (R)
1976-. Bds: Sewer Planning. Prev: Vlg.
Council 1973-76. Occ: Real Estate. B: 9/9/20.
Add: 5860 Benson Ave., Otter Lk. 48464 (313)
793-6223.

Osseo. VICTORIA JOYNER (R) **
1953-. Bds: County Nursing Dist. Bd. Org:
BPW; League of Municipalities; PTA. Occ: Self-
employed. B: 9/29/04. Add: 233 6th St. NW,
Osseo 55369 (507)425-2104.

Pequot Lakes. HENRIETTE GREER (D)
1974-. Party: State Del. 1948-64; Cnty. Ch.
1948-59. Prev: Cnty. Welfare Bd. 1960-67. Org:
Fed. Women's Club. B: 2/6/03. Add: Pequot Blvd.
Box 297, Pequot Lakes 56472 (218)568-8966.

Roseville. JUNE DEMOS (R)
1975-. Bds: V-Pres., Assoc. of Metropolitan
Municipalities. Party: State Del. 1970-76; Leg.
Dist. Ch. 1975-77; V-Ch., Congressional Dist.
1968-70; V-Ch., Leg. Dist. 1966-68; Precinct Ch.
1962-66. Prev: Councilwoman 1973-75; Planning
Cmsnr. 1968-73. Org: BPW. B: 5/30/24. Add:
1850 Ryan Ave. W., Roseville 55113 (612)
484-3371.

St. Clair. RAMONA M. FITZLOFF (I)
1976-. Org: School Adv. Bd. Occ: Office
Manager. B: 4/20/25. Add: P.O. Box 189, St.
Clair 56080 (507)245-3433.

Shelly. ALOINA SWENSON (I)
1977-. Prev: School Bd. Treasurer 1961-65.
Occ: State Bank Cashier. B: 3/29/26. Add:
Box 37, Shelly 56581.

Sherburn. NEDRA A. WESEMAN (R)
1977-. Prev: Councilwoman 1969-76. Org:
LWV; Community Service Club. B: 12/8/17. Add:
315 N. Lake, Sherburn 56171 (507)764-4491.

Shevline. THELMA NORGAARD
City Hall, Shevline 56676.

Solway. CHRISTINE SOLT
City Hall, Solway 55678.

Willernie. LOIS V. MILLNER (D)
1974-. Bds: Planning Com.; Joint Consultation
Bd. Party: Cnty. Ch.; Precinct Leader 1970.
Org: Common Cause; Ralph Nader; LWV. Occ:
Vocational Instructor. B: 12/3/24. Add:
Montclair Pl., Willernie 55090 (612)429-2977.

Wilton. JANE HILLIGAN (R) **
1974-. Bds: Water Commissioner. B: 5/29/23.
Add: Wilton 56687 (218)751-5207.

Local Councils

Ada. EVELYN L. SITTKO (R) **
    1974-. Bds: City Library; Municipal Hospital.
Org: Women's Study Club. Educ: Moorhead State
Teachers 1934 BE. B: 5/5/11. Add: 201 2nd Ave.
E, Ada 56510.

Adams. KAREN SWANSON
    City Hall, Adams 55909.

Alexandria. DOROTHY E. KOBS (R)
    1974-. Bds: Planning Cmsn.; Budget Com.
Party: Precinct Leader 1973-74. Prev: Projects
Com. 1972-74; Leg. Com. 1974-75. Org: BPW; LWV.
Occ: Administrative Secretary. B: 10/27/15.
Add: 118 10th Ave. W., Alexandria 56308 (612)
762-1511.

Alexandria. MARGARET LEUTHNER (I) **
    1975-. Bds: Library Bd.; Liquor Cmsn. Educ:
St. Catherine 1945 BA; U. of Minn. 1951 BS. Occ:
Religious Educ. Coordinator. B: 2/4/23. Add:
315 Hawthorne St., Alexandria 56308 (612)
763-6678.

Alpha. EMMA CRAWLEY
    City Hall, Alpha 56111.

Andover. MARY C. VANDER LAAN (D) **
    1974-. Bds: Personnel Com. B:4/18/44. Add:
2120 154th La., NW, Andover 55303 (612)755-5100.

Anoka. RUTH FRANKLIN (R)
    1975-. Bds: Cnty. Joint Law Enforcement
Council; Assoc. of Metropolitan Municipalities.
Party: State Del. 1968-74; City Ch. 1971-74; V-Ch.
Rep. Women 1969-71. Occ: Accountant. B: 4/19/30.
Add: 430 Rice St., Anoka 55303 (612)421-6630.

Appleton. SHARON L. HANSON
    1976-. Bds: Western Plains Regional Library
Bd. Org: Govt. Officials Training Bd. Occ:
Fabric Shop Owner. B: 7/19/42. Add: 231 E.
Snelling, Appleton 56208 (612)289-2389.

Apple Valley. M. ROBINETTE FITZSIMMONS (R)
    1976-. Bds: City Parks & Recreation Com.
Party: State Alt. 1976; Precinct Del. 1976-78;
Cnty. Precinct Del. 1976-78. Prev: Architectural
Com. 1976-77. Org: LWV. Educ: Coll. of William
& Mary 1964 BA. B: 4/10/42. Add: 13360 Findlay
Ave., Apple Vly. 55124 (612)432-7105.

Apple Valley. BARBARA LUND SAVANICK (D)
    1976-. Bds: Planning Cmsn.; Metropolitan
Council Transportation Adv. Bd. Party: State Cen.
Com. 1974-75; Precinct Ch. 1974-75, 1977- . Org:
LWV; Dem. Club. Educ: Portland State U. 1960 BA.
B: 11/22/37. Add: 154 Juniper La., Apple Valley
55124 (612)432-7105.

Ault. RUTH MC KINNEY
    Brimson 55602.

Austin. DONNA JEAN ROBBINS (R)
    Bds: Ch., Public Safety; Finance, Federal
Funding; Ordinance & Health. Party: State Del.;
State Alt.; Precinct Ch. Prev: Charter Cmsn.;
Human Relations Cmsn. Org: LWV. B: 1/20/34.
Add: 310 21st St. SW, Austin 55912 (507)437-7671.

Balkan. LAURI SALO
    Chisholm, R. 1, Box 161 E 55719.

Ball Bluff. LAURI HILLSTROM
    FLORENCE SAARI
    Jacobson 55752.

Baudette. AUDREY M. GRUND (R)
    1977-. Bds: Planning Cmsn.; Economic Devt.
Org.; Cemetery Bd. Occ: Bookkeeper. B:
11/10/26. Add: Box 191, Baudette 56623.

Baxter. MRS. RICHARD MC PHERSON
    1970-. Bds: Lake Area Council of Govts.;
Brainerd Rural Fire Repr.; Ch., Recreation Cmsn.
Prev: City Treasurer 1970-76; City Councilwoman
1976-80. Org: Crow Wing Cnty. Health Bd. Occ:
Secretary. B: 6/30/28. Add: Rt. 11, Box 172,
Brainerd 56401 (218)829-3862.

Beardsley. HAZEL GIBSON
    City Hall, Beardsley 56211.

Beaver. NANCY TIMONEN
    Strugeon Lake 55783.

Beaver Bay. LA JEAN ROY FIRMINHAC (D)
    1976-. Party: State Del. 1974-76; State
Alt. 1972; Assoc. Cnty. Ch. 1976-77; Cnty. Bd.
of Dir's. 1974-77. Org: NEA. Educ: Duluth U.
1964 BS. Occ: Teacher. B: 5/15/30. Add:
Box 364, Beaver Bay 55601.

Beaver Bay. MARTHA ROWE
    City Hall, Beaver Bay 55601.

Beaver Creek. MARIAN VANCE
    City Hall, Beaver Creek 56116.

Becker. LOIS A. FOUNTAIN (I)
    1974-. Bds: Planning Com. Org: Assoc. for
Retarded Citizens. Occ: Cook. B: 10/4/14.
Add: Becker 55308 (612)261-4302.

Bejou. ALICE KUCHYNKA
    City Hall, Bejou 56516.

Belle Plaine. CONNIE DENZER
    706 S. Meridian, Belle Plaine 56011.

Belle Plaine. FRANCES SCHUMAN (D)
    1975-. Bds: Ch., Parks & Public Property;
Ambulance Com. Prev: Justice of the Peace 1956-
69. Occ: Molder. B: 12/20/17. Add: 311 S.
Willow, Belle Plaine 56011 (612)873-6281.

Belview. JUDY GRANNES
    Box 63, Belview 56214.

Bemidji. MRS. CAMERON MC MAHON
    2407 Birchmont Drive, Bemidji 56601.

Bena. LUELLA SEELYE
    City Hall, Bena 56626.

Bethel. BEATRICE HUTCHINS
    City Hall, Bethel 55005.

Birchwood. MARY M. HAUSER (R)
    1973-. Bds: Ch., Personnel; Ch., Building;
Park Devt. Party: Precinct Ch. 1976-77; Cnty.
Platform Com. 1973-75; Ch., Platform Com. 1973-75;
Ch., Credentials Com. 1973. Prev: Planning Cmsn.
1971-73. Org: LWV; Community Services Com.;
Women's Club. B: 10/23/32. Add: 616 Hall Ave.,
White Bear Lk., 55110.

Biwabik. EDNA REBROVICH
    Box 246, Biwabik 55708.

Biwabik. HELEN SEDGEMAN
    Gilbert, R. 1, Box 47 55741.

Blackduck. MRS. LEE KOHL
    City Hall, Blackduck 56630.

Blaine. MARGARET M.LANGFELD (D)
    1976-. Dist: 3. Bds: Liaison to Cnty. Bd.
of Comsr's.; Liquor Store Operation Review Com.;
Comprehensive Planning Com. Prev: City Charter
Cmsn. 1975-77. Org: LWV; A.C.T. for Battered
Women; DFL Club. B: 9/30/42. Add: 832 120th
Lane N.E., Blaine 55434 (612)784-6700.

Bowstring. ISABELLE PERRY
    Deer River, Inger Rt. 56636.

Boy River. SHARON CLEVELAND
    City Hall, Boy River 56632.

Brainerd. MARY KOEP (R)
    1970-. Bds: Ch., Lk. Region Council of Govt.;
Minn. Assoc. of Regional Councils; Nat. Assoc. of
Regional Councils. Party: State Alt. Org: Minn.
Planning Assoc.; Zonta. B: 10/15/32. Add: 123
Laurel, Brainerd 56401.

Brainerd. MILDRED MICHAELIS
    1004 S.E. 15th Street, Brainerd 56401.

Breckenridge. PATRICIA ANN MULLENIX (D)
    1976-. Bds: Ch., Wage, Grievance & Recommend-
ation Com.; Ch., Finance Com.; Parks & Recreation.
Org: Clay-Wilkin Opportunity Council. Occ:
Quality Control Specialist. B: 10/7/35. Add:
223 N. 14th St., Breckenridge 56520.

Browns Valley. BEVERLY RAW
    City Hall, Browns Valley 56219.

Brownsville. FERN HEILLER
    City Hall, Brownsville 55919.

Bruno. EDITH MOLGAARD (D)
    1977-. Org: Community Club. Occ: Cook. B:
8/13/39. Add: P.O. Box 116, Bruno 5712 (612)
838-4473.

Bruno. MAUREEN SEIBERT
    City Hall, Bruno 55712.

Bull Moose. EDYTHE BARTLETT
    Backus 56435.

Burnsville. CONSTANCE MORRISON (R)
    1976-. Party: State Del. 1972-74; Precinct
Ch. Occ: Public Information Coord. B: 12/11/35.
Add: 909 W. 155th St., Burnsville 55337 (612)
890-4100.

Burtrum. DORIS FINK
    City Hall, Burtrum 56318.

Butterfield. MARGARET SALEM
    City Hall, Butterfield 56120.

Canton. HELEN DOTZENROD
    JUNE SHANKS
    City Hall, Canton 55922.

Carver. SUZANN NELSON
    City Hall, Carver 55315.

Chatfield. MARGARET A. PERKINS (R) **
    1969-. Party: State Del. 1975; Ch., Precinct
1970-74; County Del. 1960. Org: Rep. Club;
Women's Club. B: 11/25/37. Add: 322 Winona St.
Chatfield 55923 (507)867-3810.

Chisholm. MARJORIE LEVCHAK PETERSON
    Bds: Cmsnr., Water Dept. Prev: Recreation
Bd. 1975-77. Org: Chamber of Commerce; DFL.
B: 8/16/24. Add: 405 7th St. SW, Chisholm
55719 (218)254-3353.

Circle Pines. PATRICIA JEAN OMAN (D)
    1975-. Occ: Bookkeeper. B: 12/30/39. Add:
242 N. Star Ln., Circle Pines 55014 (612)
784-5898.

Clearwater. KITTY HELGET
    City Hall, Clearwater 55320.

Clearwater. NAN KAMPA
    City Hall, Clearwater 55320.

Clinton. SHIRLEY FINBERG
    City Hall, Clinton 56225.

Clitherall. JOELLEN SEIDEL
    City Hall, Clitherall 56524.

Clover. ARVILLA BAKEWELL
    Park Rapids, Itasca St. Rt. 56470.

Cologne. BONNIE LEIKAM
    City Hall, Cologne 55322.

Cook. ELEANOR HOWARD
    City Hall, Cook 55723.

Coon Rapids. SUSAN GREEN
    10913 Woody Lane, N.W., Coon Rapids 55433.

Cornish. LOUISE SWANSON
    Jacobson 55752.

Crookston. LYNN E. THOEN (R)
    1969-. Bds: Ch., Finance Com.; Ch., License
Com.; Airport. Party: Precinct Ch. Prev: Airport Zoning Cmsn. Org: PTA. Educ: U. of ND
1958 BSEd. B: 4/13/36. Add: 815 Woodland Ave.,
Crookston 56716 (218)281-5717.

Crosby. FRANCES VIDMAR
    20 4th St., N.W., Crosby 56441.

Crosslake. ELIZABETH ANDOLSHEK (R)
    1975-. Bds: Ch., Telephone Cmsn. Party:
State Alt. 1976-77. Occ: Hearing & Vision Technologist. B: 9/20/20. Add: P.O. Box 35,

Crosslake 56442 (218)692-2688/2777.

Culver. CAROLINE BONG
Culver 55727.

Currie. JOANNE CARTER
City Hall, Currie 56123.

Dassel. HELEN RAMEY
City Hall, Dassel 55325.

Decoria. FAYETTE WILDER
Mankato, R. 4, Box 259 56001.

Deephaven. JANE DAYTON HALL (R)
1975-. Bds: Ch., Park & Recreational. Party:
State Alt.; Precinct Ch.; Rep. Workshop Bd. Prev:
Planning Cmsn. 1969-75. Occ: Broadcasting Commun-
ications Exec. B: 6/9/25. Add: 3650 Northome
Ave., Deephaven 55391.

Deer River. SHARON OTT
City Hall, Deer River 56636.

Denham. VIVIAN LARSON
Rt. 1, Sturgeon Lake 55783.

Denham. RUTH SWANSON
City Hall, Denham 55728.

Denmark. BEVERLY ANNE MC CUMBER
Hastings, 6959 Peller Ave. S. 55033.

Dennison. PHYLLIS BESTUL
MRS. PAT HUSCHLE
City Hall, Dennison 55018.

Dexter. IRENE ELIT
City Hall, Dexter 55926.

Duluth. MAUREEN E. BYE (D)
1973-. Acting Mayor. Bds: Economic Policy
Adv. Com.; Bd. of League of Minn. Cities. Party:
Precinct Del. 1970-76. Prev: Gov. Comsn. on
Crime Prevention & Control 1971-74; Org: League
of Minn. Cities; Nat. League of Cities. Educ:
Coll. of St. Scholastion 1966 BA. B: 2/6/43.
Add: 609 W. 2nd St., Duluth 55806 (218)723-3340.

Duluth. ELNORA J. JOHNSON (D) **
1970-. Bds: Regional Dev. Cmsn.; Parks &
Recreation Com.; Interstate Policy Cmsn. Party:
Precinct Ch. 1970-74. B: 5/16/30. Add: 5717
Olney St., Duluth 55807 (218)727-4522.

Dunnell. JOANNE JANSSEN (D) **
1972-. Bds: Civil Defense. Occ: Teacher's
Aid. B: 11/6/18. Add: Dunnell 56127 (507)
695-2364.

Eagle Bend. JEANETTE J. HANSEN (D) **
1975-. Bds: Water & Sewage; Streets; Redevelopment Com. Org: Educ. Assoc. Occ: Teacher. B:
10/23/19. Add: Box 277, Eagle Bend 56446 (218)
738-3362.

East Bethel. CAROL EGAN
1104 219th Ave., N.E., Cedar 55011.

Eden Prairie. JOAN MEYERS
6930 Boyd Avenue, Eden Prairie 55343.

Eden Prairie. SIDNEY PAULEY
17450 W. 78th St., Eden Prairie 55343.

Edina. JUNE A. SCHMIDT (I)
1973-. Bds: Human Services Bd.; Adv. Health
Bd.; Red Cross Bd. Prev: Environmental Quality
Com. 1971-73; Govt. Com. 1972-73; Housing Needs
Com. 1972-73. Org: Woman's Club. Educ: U. of
Minn. 1949 BS. B: 6/29/28. Add: 7005 Bristol
Blvd., Edina 55435 (612)927-8861.

Effie. JEAN M. CUTLER
1976-. Educ: U. of Minn. 1968 BS. Occ:
Consultant Dietitian. B: 11/21/46. Add: Box 65,
Effie 56639.

Elgin. NEVA PRESCHER
City Hall, Elgin 55932.

Elko. MARILYN R. BLOHM (I)
1976-. Prev: Treasurer 1971-76; Planning
Cmsn. 1974-76. Org: Women's Club. B: 9/21/44.
Add: Box 7, Elko 55020 (612)461-2098.

Ely. HELEN BACHAR
343 E. Chapman St., Ely 55731.

Ely. MARGARET M. LIKAR (R)
1974-. Bds: Budget Com.; Finance Com. Party:
State Alt. 1976-77. Org: Minn. Nurses Assoc.;
ANA; Reps. of Minn. Educ: Coll. of St. Catherine
1953 RN. Occ: RN. B: 3/22/32. Add: 141 W.
Sheridan St., Ely 55731 (218)365-3224.

Embarrass. BARBARA KALLIO
Embarrass, R. 1, Box 49A 55732.

Emmons. EDITH SHAW.
LORNA TROE
City Hall, Emmons 56029.

Eveleth. ANNE F. GERENCHER (D)
1954-. Bds: Golf Cmsn.; Fire Study Cmsn.
Org: MEA. Educ: Eveleth Jr. Coll. 1939 AS; St.
Cloud State Teachers Coll. 1941 BS. B: 7/7/19.
Add: 710 Summit, Eveleth 55734.

Excelsior. LUCILLE CROW
540 Wheeler Drive, Excelsior 55331.

Excelsior. JANICE HORNICK
174 3rd Street, Excelsior 55331.

Fairbanks. HAZEL JOHNSON
Brimson 55602.

Fergus Falls. BARBARA EBERSVILLER (R)
1974-. Bds: Ch., Park, Planning & Devt.;
Leg. Review; Employee Relations. Party: State
Del. 1968-74; Area Ch. 1971-75. Prev: Park Bd.
1972-74. Org: Rep. Women's Club. Educ: U. of
Minn. 1947 BS. Occ: Interviewer. B: 2/21/26.
Add: 501 W. Birch, Fergus Falls 56537.

Fort Ripley. MRS. LYLE PEARSON
City Hall, Fort Ripley 56449.

Frazee. JOYCE WOTHE
City Hall, Frazee 56544.

Frederick. C. ELIZABETH BURKET
N. Market St., Frederick 21701.

Freeborn. LOIS EVENSON
City Hall, Freeborn 56032.

French. CLAIRE LANDSKOV
Side Lake 55781.

Fridley. CARROLL A. KUKOWSKI (D) **
1974-. Bds: Community Educ.; Suburban Rate
Authority. Org: BPW; DFL; PTA. B: 7/15/41.
Add: 1338 Hillcrest Dr., NE, Fridley 55432
(612)571-3450.

Funkley. EVELYN BALSIGER
City Hall, Blackduck 56630.

Garrison. MAXINE GRIFFEN
Garrison, Star Rt. 56401.

Gem Lake. EILEEN BIGELOW (R)
1963-. Party: State Alt. 1962-64. Educ:
Vassar Coll. 1926 BA. B: 2/15/05. Add: 1270
Goose Lake Road, White Bear Lake 55110.

Genola. IRENE LUBBERTS
Pierz 56364.

Ghent. BERNADETTE ENGELS (I)
1976-. Occ: Income Tax Practitioner. B:
11/7/32. Add: Ghent 56239 (507)428-3477.

Gilbert. MARGE BOZICH (I)
1973-. Bds: Ch., Police Consolidation Com. B:
6/2/24. Add: 205 S. Broadway, Gilbert 55741
(218)741-9443.

Glencoe. MILDRED S. BENEKE (R)
1974-. Bds: Library Bd. Liason; Nutrition
for Elderly, Liaison; Senior Citizens Bd. Liaison.
Party: State Del. 1969-77; State Alt. 1973; Rep.
Cnty. Ch. 1969-73; Ward Ch. 1967-69; Rep. State
Central Com. 1969-75; Rep. State Platform Com.
1970- . Org: BPW; Project Interaction, Inc.; WPC;
GOP Feminist Caucus; Common Cause; Diversion
Program. B: 5/1/20. Add: Glencoe Woods, Glencoe
55336 (612)864-4751.

Golden Valley. MARY ANDERSON
3030 Scott Avenue, N., Golden Valley 55427.

Golden Valley. GLORIA JOHNSON
4200 Golden Valley Road, Golden Valley 55427.

Golden Valley. ROSEMARY THORSEN (I) **
1975-. B: 12/5/28. Add: 2625 Vale Crest Rd.,
Golden Valley 55422 (612)545-3781.

Gonvick. JULIA KNUTSON
City Hall, Gonvick 56644.

Goodridge. MARLENE HANSON
City Hall, Goodridge 56725.

Good Thunder. MARILYN ROBINSON
City Hall, Good Thunder 46037.

Grafton. JOAN A. ANDERSON
Buffalo Lake 55314.

Grand Marais. LINDA BYSTROM
City Hall, Grand Marais 55604.

Grand Rapids. CAROLYN KASTNER
726 5th Ave. N.W., Grand Rapids 55744.

Granite Falls. EVELYN ERNSTON
343 5th Avenue, Granite Falls 56241.

Grattan. ANNA WINKLEMAN
Northome 56661.

Grey Eagle. MARILLA MUELLNER
City Hall, Grey Eagle 56336.

Grove Park. MARION LEE
Mentor 56736.

Hamburg. DELORES A. THOELE (D)
1976-. Occ: Secretary. B: 1/12/34. Add:
421 Lousia St., Hamburg 55339.

Hammond. LORETTA LUCILLE HOFFMAN (D)
1977-. Org: Credit Women Internat.; Recreational Assoc. Occ: Accounts Payable Clerk. B:
9/21/23. Add: Hammond 55938.

Hanley Falls. DELORES ANDERSON (D)
1976-. Bds: Health Bd.; Liquor Bd. Educ:
St. Cloud State Coll. 1962 BS. Occ: Teacher.
B: 2/21/39. Add: Box 64, Hanley Fls. 56245
(507)768-3570.

Hastings. MARY FISCHER
1936 Ashland, Hastings 55033.

Hatfield. IRENE E. PESCHON
City Hall, Hatfield 56135.

Hayward. MARILYN E. MATSON (R)
1974-. Party: Precinct Leader 1970-77. Org:
Freeborn Cnty. Rep's.; PTA. Occ: School Bus
Driver. B: 10/18/34. Add: Box 362, Hayward
56043.

Henriette. MRS. JOHN POVONDRA
City Hall, Henriette 55036.

Hermantown. SAUNDRA D. MONSON (I)
1976-. Bds: Utilities Cmsn.; Recreation
Council; Finance Com. Org: Jr. League; Right-
to-Read. Educ: U. of Minn. 1963 BA; U. of Minn.
1966 BS. B: 8/27/41. Add: 6721 Arrowhead Rd.,
Hermantown 55811 (218)729-6331.

Hill City. MARGY GILLSON
Box 127, Hill City 55748.

Hill River. LAURIE FINSETH
McIntosh 56556.

Houston. BERNICE ONSGARD
430 S. Sheridan Street, Houston 55943.

Hutchinson. KAY PETERSON
16 Grove Street So., Hutchinson 55350.

International Falls. MARY JANE FURMAN
Box 296, Rte. 7, International Falls 56649.

Inver Grove Heights. ELEANOR NELSON
9115 Inver Grove Trail, Inver Grove Heights 55075.

Inver Grove Heights. JO TEARE (R)
1971-. Bds: Planning Cmsn.; Consulting Planner. Party: State Del. 1968-71; City Ch. 1968-72. Org: LWV; Rep. Party. Occ: Administrative Asst. B: 11/30/26. Add: 6444 Babcock Trl., Inver Grove Hts. 55075.

Irving. PHILLIS HANSON
Hawick 56246.

Island View. DIANNE CASARETO
International Falls 56649.

Jackson. BETTY ABRAHAM (D) **
1975-. Bds: Finance Com.; Planning Cmsn. Party: Conv. Del. 1974- ; County Secretary/Treasurer 1964-65; Precinct Com. 1964-65. Org: LWV. B: 1/2/33. Add: 1013 W. Highway, Jackson 56143 (507)847-4410.

Jordan. ROSEMARY LUCIUS
213 4th St. W, Jordan 55352.

Kasota. JERI JANSEN
City Hall, Kasota 56050.

Kasota. DIANE A. VOGT
1976-. Bds: Planning Com.; Health Dept.; Bldg. Com. Prev: Vlg. Treasurer 1975-76. B: 6/23/53. Add: 631 Rice St., Kasota 56050 (507) 931-2829.

Kego. NORA SHEPARD
Longville 56655.

Kelliher. MARION COLLINS
Kelliher 56650.

Kenyon. HELEN AASE
1973-. Org: ANA; Amer. Vocational Assoc.; NEA; Historical Society. Educ: U. of Minn. 1955 BS; Mankato State Coll. 1968 MS. Occ: Nursing Instructor. B: 10/11/21. Add: RR 3 Trondheim Rd., Kenyon 55946.

Kertsonville. FRANCES FROEHLER
Crookston, R. 3 56716.

Kettle River. EVELYN E. MARSYLA (D)
1977-. Org: AFL-CIO. Occ: Senior Janitor. B: 3/29/24. Add: 103 Main St., Kettle Rvr. 55757.

Kiester. LYNN MONGE (I)
1975-. Bds: State Senator's Com. on Local Govt. Org: ALCW. B: 5/28/43. Add: Box 218, Kiester 56051.

Kilkenny. REGINA R. KEWATT
City Hall, Kilkenny 56052.

Kinbrae. MARCELLA HAUGH
City Hall, Kinbrae 56148.

Kinghurst. MRS. BURNELL FERGUSON
HELEN WALLER
Northome 56661.

Kugler. IRENE JANKOWSKI
Tower, St. Rt. Box 52 55790.

Lake Elmo. DOROTHY LYONS
10072 10th St. N., Lake Elmo 55042.

Lake Hattie. JOYCE STILLWELL
Laporte 56461.

Lakeland. MAXINE BACHTLE
Rt. 1, Lakeland 55043.

Lakeland. MARJORIE HUMPHRIES (I)
1974-. Bds: State Park Com.; Metropolitan Transit Adv. Cmsn. Org: AAUW; LWV; Sierra Club; Council of State Parks. Educ: U. of Minn. 1937 BSEd. B: 10/16/15. Add: 1531 N. Rivercrest Rd., Lakeland 55043.

Lake St. Croix. GLORIA SWELANDER
P.O. Box 268, Afton 55001.

Lake Shore. MARY ELLEN JOHNSTON (R)
1974-. Bds: Planning Cmsn.; Bd. of Adjustment. Prev: Planning Com. 1972-74; Bd. of Adjustment 1972-74. Org: Women's Club. Educ: 1948 BS. Occ: Volunteer Tutor. B: 7/23/26. Add: Rt. 6, Box 337, Brainerd 56401.

Lakeville. MARIANNE CURRY (R)
1976-. Bds: Public Works Com.; Youth Adv. Com.; Natural Resources Com. Party: Cnty. Precinct Alt. 1972-74. Prev: Cnty. Budget Ch. 1974-76. Org: League of Minn. Cities; Minn. Planning Assoc.; LWV; Chamber of Commerce; PTA. Educ: U. of Minn. 1960 BA. B: 7/11/38. Add: 19039 Junelle Path, Lakeville 55044 (612) 469-4931.

Lancaster. JOANIE BARBO
City Hall, Lancaster 56735.

Landfall Village. SHIRLEY GRAMS
302 Dellwood Sq. No., St. Paul 55119.

Landfall Village. RUTH WOOLGAR
20 Ivy Lane, St. Paul 55119.

Lanesboro. IRENE STROM (I)
1976-. B: 5/6/27. Add: Lanesboro 55949 (507)467-3365.

La Prairie. DIANNE L. JOHNSON
1812 Spruce Street, Grand Rapids 55744.

La Prairie. FAYE MOSTOLLER
710 Walter Avenue, Grand Rapids 55744.

Lauderdale. JANE IRVIN BANZHAF LINDBERG (R)
1975-. Bds: N. Suburban Senior Citizens Council; Coord., Senior Citizens Group & Activities. Org: Lauderdale Civic Club; Internat. Institute of Minn. B: 5/23/23. Add: 1892 Carl St., Lauderdale 55113 (612)631-0300.

Lavell. DOROTHY SCHMIDT
Hibbing, St. Rt. 4 55746.

Lengby. JEANETTE FENSKE
City Hall, Lengby 56651.

Leonard. EDITH ERICKSON
City Hall, Leonard 56652.

Leonidas. CAROL HOGLUND
144 No. 2nd Street, Eveleth 55734.

Leonidas. KATHY MOSTAD
149 No. 2nd Street, Eveleth 55734.

Le Roy. ESTHER ENGELSEN
City Hall, Le Roy 55951.

Lexington. MILDRED HUSE
Box 98, Circle Pines 55014.

Lexington. MAYME PINKERTON
9064 Dunlap, Lexington 55112.

Liberty. EULAH L. CUSTER
SHIRLEY A. PAGE
Wirt 56688.

Little Falls. VIOLA M. ZETTEL
1027 NE 3rd Avenue, Little Falls 56345.

Littlefork. JUDY AREL (D) **
1974-. Bds: Recreation Cmsn. Occ: Secretary.
B: 8/29/43. Add: P.O. Box 136, Littleford 56653
(218)285-5430.

Long Lake. DIANE J. GALLAGHER (I)
1977-. Bds: Park Bd. Prev: Park Bd. 1975-76.
Educ: St. Luke's School of Nursing 1963 RN. Occ:
RN. B: 12/6/41. Add: 68 S. Brown Rd., Long
Lake 55356.

Lynd. DIANNE POPE
City Hall, Lynd 56157.

Mabel. MYRNA O. NELSON (I)
1974-. Bds: Zoning Com.; Liquor Store Improvement Com.; Nursing Home Com. Prev: Zoning 1975-
78; Ambulance 1976-77; Special Drug Com. 1976-77.
Occ: Secretary. B: 1/7/39. Add: 205 N. Elm,
Mabel 55954.

Madelia. CLAIRE SEIBERT
City Hall, Madelia 56062.

Mahnomen. LOIS L. BRANDON (D)
1977-. Bds: Library Bd. Occ: Storeowner. B:
10/18/34. Add: Box 394, Mahnomen 56557.

Mahtomedi. MARILYN KING
735 Warner Road, Mahtomedi 55115.

Mankato. ARLINE BROWN (D)
1968-. Bds: Housing & Redevt. Authority.
Party: Del., Cnty. Conv. 1976. Org: Midwest
Economic Assoc.; Nat. Assoc. Housing & Redevt.
Officers; Common Cause; LWV. Educ: Tarkio Coll.
1931 BA; Ia. State U. 1943 MS. B: 10/1/11. Add:
1216 Highland Ave., Mankato 56001.

Mantrap. JUDY OLSON
Park Rapids, R. 3 56479.

Marine-On-St. Croix. MARGARET F. ARNASON
Marine-On-St. Croix 55047.

Marshall. EVA M. CARLSON (R) **
1974-. Bds: Legislative Com.; Hospital
Com. Prev: Planning Cmsn. 1972-74. Org:
Chamber of Commerce. Occ: Office Work. B:
5/8/14. Add: P.O. Box 615, Marshall 65258.

McGrath. AUDREY GANZ
City Hall, McGrath 56350.

McIntosh. RUBY D. CHRISTOPHERSON (D)
1974-. Occ: Cafe Owner. B: 5/31/31. Add:
285 Cleveland, McIntosh 56556.

Meadowlands. KATHLEEN A. MOREHOUSE
1976-. Occ: Stenographer. B: 12/29/44.
Add: Box 114, Meadowlands 55765.

Medicine Lake. SANDRA ANN GEIER
1974-. Org: PTA; Women's Club. Occ: Secretary. Add: 244 Peninsula Rd., Minneapolis
55441 (612)544-1037.

Medina. NANCY LAURENT
895 Hamel Road, Hamel 55340.

Mendota. RITA E. DREW (D) **
1974-. Occ: Clerk. B: 9/3/34. Add: 1676
4th St., Mendota 55150.

Middle River. ISABELLE HANSON
City Hall, Middle River 56737.

Milaca. PATRICIA BECKER (D)
1973-. Party: Precinct Leader 1974-76. Org:
Minn. Community Educ. Assoc. Educ: St. Cloud
State U. 1964 BS. Occ: Community Educ. Dir. B:
10/29/42. Add: 340 10th St., Milaca 56353
(612)983-3141.

Minneapolis. ALICE WHALEN RAINVILLE (D)
1975-. Bds: Ch., Capital Long Range Improvements Com.; Transportation Adv. Bd.; Ch. Consumers
Services Com. Party: State Del. 1972; Precinct
Ch. 1970-74; Credentials Ch. 1970-71; Assoc. Ch.
1971-73; Dist. Ch. 1973-75. Org: DFL. B:
10/15/28. Add: 4727 Girard Ave. N., Minneapolis
55438 (612)348-2204.

Minnesota Lake. DONNA M. ARMSTRONG (D)
1977-. Prev: Cnty. Adv. Bd.-Human Services
1976-77; Cnty. Welfare Bd. 1970-76; Comprehensive Social Service Planning Task Force 1976-
77. Org: Woman's Club; Minn. Social Service
Assoc.; Cnty. Dem. Party. Occ: Insurance Agent.
B: 6/6/29. Add: Box 246, Minnesota Lake 56068
(507)462-3525.

Moorhead. RUTH M. WENSEL (I)
1952-. Bds: Nutrition Program Senior Citizens;
Planning Com.; Public Safety Com. Add: 419 S.
8th St., Moorhead 56560.

Moose Lake. VIRGINIA WALCH
Pennington 56663.

Morris. JUDY JOHNSON (D)
1976-. Bds: Community Educ. Adv. Council;
Co-Ch., Housing Task Force; Library Bd. Prev:
Charter Cmsn. 1974. Org: LWV. Educ: State U.
of Iowa 1957 BA. Occ: Optometrist Asst. B:
7/8/35. Add: 408 W. 5th, Morris 56267

Morristown. IVY HOFFMAN
City Hall, Morristown 55052.

Mounds View. JUDY ROWLEY
City Hall, 2401 Hwy. #10, St. Paul 55112.

Mount Iron. MARGARET KRALL
City Hall, Mt. Iron 55768.

Nassau. RUTH ANN ZAHN (D)
1970-. Occ: Bartender. B: 8/17/13. Add:
Nassau 56272.

Nerstrand. BONNIE KAY SWARTS (D)
1976-. B: 7/2/47. Add: 101 Main St., Nerstrand
55053 (507)334-3648.

Newfolden. MURIEL MERCIL (D)
1976-. Bds: Tri-Cnty. Health Adv. Bd. Occ:
Supervisor, Youth Work Program. B: 2/1/29. Add:
Box 62, Newfolden 56738 (218)874-8745.

New Hope. DOROTHY I. HOKR (R)
1976-. Party: State Candidate Search Com.
1972-74; Precinct V-Ch. 1970-72. Prev: Human
Rights Cmsn. 1969-70. Org: LWV; Rep. Women's
Club. B: 6/22/23. Add: 8308 40th Ave. N., New
Hope 55427 (612)533-1521.

New Market. SANDY SIMON
City Hall, New Market 55054.

New Richland. CAROL BATTENFELD (I)
1977-. Occ: Bookkeeper. B: 10/13/43. Add:
352 S. Balsam Ave., New Richland 56072.

New Ulm. VIRGINIA L. BURNETT (I)
1976-. Bds: Park & Recreation Dept. Cmsn.;
New Ulm Business/City Council Liaison Com. Prev:
Human Rights Cmsn. 1973-76; Criminal Justice
Adv. Council 1974. Org: LWV. Educ: U. of Kan.
School of Nursing 1946 RN. Occ: Administrative
Asst. B: 6/16/24. Add: 717 S. Franklin, New
Ulm 56073 (507)354-6245.

New Ulm. KATHLEEN R. KASTEN (D)
1976-. Party: Cnty. Del. 1976. Org: AAUW.
Educ: Mankato State U. 1960 BS. B: 1/18/39.
Add: 206 Bianchi Dr., New Ulm 56073 354-2252.

Nore. MRS. FRANCES NELSON
Northome 56661.

Normanna. DORIS SOLEM
1298 French River Rd., Duluth 55804.

Northfield. MARIE JENSEN (D)
1976-. Bds: Ch., Community Services Council
Com.; Community Devt. Council Com.; Task Force
on Reorganization Devt. Party: Precinct Leader
1976-77. Prev: Park Bd. 1976- ; Community Devt.
Com. 1975-76. Org: Nat. Parks & Conservation
Assoc.; NARAL; LWV; Common Cause; ZPG. Educ:
Carleton Coll. 1947 BA; U. of Mich. 1948 MA.
Occ: Music Instructor. B: 7/19/26. Add: 7 Hill-
side Ct., Northfield 55057.

North Mankato. LIN WILKER (I)
1976-. Bds: Planning Cmsn. Prev: Planning
Cmsn. 1975; Region Devt. Sub-Cmsn. 1976-77. Org:
LWV. Educ: U. of Northern Ia. 1962 BA. B:

6/18/40. Add: 833 Nicollet Ave., N. Mankato
56001 (507)625-4141.

North Oaks. MARY ANN YAKEL
56 E. Pleasant Lake Road, St. Paul 55110.

North Redwood. DOROTHY JENSEN
City Hall, No. Redwood 56275.

Oakdale. MYRA LUBECK (R)
1975-. Bds: Park Liaison; School Adv.;
Assoc. of Metropolitan Municipalities. Party:
State Del. 1973-75; State Alt. 1970-73; Cnty.
V-Ch., 1971-72; Precinct Leader 1967-74; Leg.
Ch. 1972-74; Senate Ch. 1974-75. Prev: Ch.,
Park Cmsn. 1973-74. Org: State Coord. for
Women in Municipal Govt. B: 3/1/39. Add:
1636 Hilo Ave. N., Oakdale 55119 (612)
739-6338.

Oakdale. BEVERLY M. PETERSON
1976-. Bds: Planning Cmsn. Occ: Secretary.
B: 7/1/30. Add: 2350 Hadley Ave. N., Oakdale
55119.

Ogilvie. EVELYN OSTERHUIS (R)
1976-. Org: Women's Club. Occ: Interviewer.
B: 6/27/27. Add: Box 124, Ogilvie 56358.

Olivia. MARGARET MEHLHOUSE (D)
1976-. Bds: Planning Cmsn. Prev: Planning
Cmsn. 1975. Org: AAUW; OES. Educ: Mankato
State Coll. 1950 BS. Occ: Librarian. B:
5/18/28. Add: 300 E. Oak, Olivia 56277.

Orono. MARY C. BUTLER (D)
1971-. Bds: Park Cmsn.; Assoc. of Metropolitan Municipalities. Prev: Governors Manpower Cmsn. 1973-75; Metropolitan Council Adv.
Com. 1971-73; Planning Cmsn. 1970-71. Occ:
Exec. Secretary. B: 10/17/37. Add: 3145 Casco
Circle, Wayzata 55391 (612)473-7357.

Oronoco. JEAN TEMPLETON
City Hall, Oronoco 55960.

Osseo. IDA DOCHNIAK
324 4th Ave. N.E., Osseo 55369.

Owatonna. ROBERTA M. ANDERSON (R)
1974-. Bds: Ch., License Com.; Personnel
Com.; Road & Bridges Com. Party: State Del.;
State Alt.; Ward Precinct Ch. 1970-72. Org:
Minn. League of Cities; Chamber of Commerce;
LWV; Arts Council; Women's Club. B: 3/16/23.
Add: 353 Thomas Ave., Owatonna 55060.

Park Rapids. ALICE JUNE HOLK (I) **
1973-. Bds: Police Com.; Park; Health. Occ:
Bailiff. B: 6/4/29. Add: N. Central Ave.,
Park Rapids 56420 (218)732-4567.

Payne. SHIRLEY FIROVICH
Meadowlands 55765.

Paynesville. JOANNE BRAUN
P.O. Rt. 3, Paynesville 56362.

Pierz. DOROTHY ANN THIELN
City Hall, Pierz 56364.

Pike Bay. LYNNE ZOTHMAN
Cass Lake 56633.

Pine Lake. DORIS BROWN
Whipholt, Box 104 56485.

Pine River. PAULINE K. GRIEP (D)
1976-. Bds: Sewer Cmsn.; Ch., Water Streets
Park Com. Party: State Del. 1970, '64, '60; Cnty.
Secretary 1959-62; Cnty. Ch. 1962-72. Org: NEA;
School Nurses of Minn.; Future Nurses of Amer.
Educ: St. Mary Hospital 1944 RN. Occ: School
Nurse. B: 10/29/22. Add: Box 4, Pine River
56474. (218)587-2440.

Pleasant Grove. CLAIRE FOGARTY
Rochester, R. 3 55901.

Pleasant Lake. ERMALINE LAHR
Rt. 4, St. Cloud 56301.

Poppleton. LAVERNE ISAACSON
Lancaster 56735.

Port Hope. PAULINE SPANGLER
Bemidji, R. 5 56601.

Preston. DORIS MILDRED STRAHL (R) **
1975-. Bds: Park Bd. B: 2/2/21. Add: Box 5,
Preston 55965 (507)765-9997.

Preston Lake. LEA DOBBERSTEIN
Buffalo Lake, R. 2, Box 78 55314.

Proctor. MARY ANN HANSON
9 4th Street, Proctor 55810.

Ranier. DORLYN DESENS
City Hall, Ranier 56668.

Red Wing. MARY JANE TAYLOR (D)
1975-. Bds: Ch., Ordinance Com.; Public
Utilities Com.; Ch., Adv. Com. Red Wing Area Vo-
Tech. Prev: Library Bd. 1974-77. Org: LWV.
Educ: Mich. State U. 1951 BS. B: 7/12/29. Add:
106 E. Ave., Red Wing 55066 (612)388-6734.

Regal. VI BLOOMQUIST
JEANETTE WINTERS
City Hall, Regal 56366.

Richville. DARLENE GRANT
GOLDIE GROVER
City Hall, Richville 56576.

Riverton. PAMELA DOBSON
City Hall, Ironton 56455.

Robbinsdale. MERRY M. OLSON (D)
1976-. Bds: Human Relations Cmsn.; Flood
Control Cmsn. Org: LWV. Occ: Manager. B:
5/21/42. Add: 3400 Beard Ave. N., Robbinsdale
55422 (612)537-4534.

Rochester. MRS. DONALD HALLING
406 23rd St. S.W., Rochester 55901.

Ronneby. DONNA ALBRIGHT
MARDELL STAR
City Hall, Ronneby 56370.

Rose Creek. MRS. ARDIS MAY
City Hall, Rose Creek 55970.

Rosemount. MARI VAN KLEEK (I)
1974-. Prev: Planning Cmsn. 1971-73. Org:
Chamber of Commerce. B: 2/14/34. Add: 12769
Bolivia Ave. W., Rosemount 55068 (612)
423-4411.

Rushford. MARION JOHNSON
City Hall, Rushford 55971.

St. Anthony. SALLY ANN HAIK
2901 Silver Lake Court, N.E., Minneapolis
55418.

St. Anthony. DONNA LOIS STAUFFER (D)
1973-. Bds: Ch., Task Force on Chemical
Dependancy; Metropolitan Agencies Com. of Assoc.
of Metropolitan Municipalities; Joint Task Force,
State League of Cities. Party: State Alt. 1968,
'76. Prev: Human Relations Adv. Com. 1972-73;
Metropolitan Significance Adv. Com. 1974-75.
Org: Amer. Occupational Therapy Assoc.; Dem.
Club; PTSA. Educ: U. of Minn. 1954 BS. B:
5/12/32. Add: 3000 Croft Dr., Minneapolis
55418.

St. Bonifacius. SHIRLEY BREN (D)
1977-. Bds: Police Cmsn. Prev: Town Clerk
1968-72. Occ: Waitress. B: 12/4/37. Add:
8656 Kennedy Memorial Dr., St. Bonifacius
55375 (612)446-1061.

St. Cloud. SYBIL HOLLERN
501 4th Ave., So., St. Cloud 56301.

St. Cloud. ALICE M. WICK (D)
1972-. Bds: Park & Recreation Bd. Org: LWV;
AAUW. Educ: State U. of Ia. 1938 BS; St. Cloud
State U. 1963 MS. B: 1/7/17. Add: 1720 N. 6th
Ave., St. Cloud 56301 (612)251-5541.

St. James. MARGARET WARLING
1014 3rd Avenue So., St. James 56081.

St. Louis Park. ROSE-MARY GRIAK (R) **
1971-. Bds: Educ. Com.; Community Relations
Com.; Municipalities Bd.; Watershed. Org: LWV.
Educ: U. of Minn. 1950 BS. Occ: Teacher's Aid.
B: 5/20/27. Add: 8921 Stanlen Rd., St. Louis
Park 55426 (612)920-3000.

St. Paul. RASALIE BUTLER
City Hall, St. Paul 55102.

St. Paul. RUBY HUNT
1972-. Bds: Ch., Council Public Works Com.;
City Council Finance Com.; Utilities Com. Prev:
City Council Pres. 1973-75. Org: LWV; PTA; Ch.,
Charter Cmsn.; Urban Coalition; Minn. League of
Cities. Add: 1148 Edgcumbe Rd., St. Paul 55105.

St. Peter. BONNIE DOWLING (D) **
1974-. Bds: Ways & Means; Sanitation &
Sewer; Educ. Council; Bd. of Zoning Adjustment.
Occ: Store Owner-Manager. B: 7/29/25. Add:
816 Lower Johnson Circle, St. Peter 56082
(507)931-4840.

St. Rosa. DELLA KLASEN
Rt. 2, Melrose 56352.

Sauk Centre. GRACE K. PETTIT
626 Pine Street, Sauk Centre 56378.

Sauk Rapids. MILDRED BENNER (R)
1976-. Bds: Ways & Means Com.; Water. Org:
Historical Society; Minn. Citizens Concerned for
Life; Minn. Com. to Restore the Constitution;
Industrial Devt. Corp.; PTSA. B: 11/9/18. Add:
1117 S. Broadway, Sauk Rapids 56379.

Seavey. ARLENE HATFIELD
Isle 56342.

Sebeka. CLAIRE POLMAN
City Hall, Sebeka 56477.

Shakopee. DOLORES M. LEBENS
1973-. Bds: School Bd.; Community Educ. Bd.
Org: League of Women. Occ: Interior Designer.
B: 1/3/19. Add: 538 W. 4, Shakopee 55379
(612)445-3650.

Shoreview. MARY ELIZABETH NEWBOLD (D)
1976-. Party: Precinct Del. 1971-73. Prev:
Human Rights Cmsn. 1973-75. Educ: Simmons Coll.
1962 BS. Add: 3531 Owasso St., Shoreview 55112
(612)484-3353.

Shorewood. JANICE M. HAUGEN (R)
1975-. Bds: Planning Cmsn.; Ch., City Public
Relations; League of Minn. Cities. Party: State
Del. 1974-//; Minn. Precinct Chairman 1970-77;
Asst. to Cnty. Chairwoman 1960-64. Org: Assoc.
of Metropolitan Municipalities; League of Minn.
Cities; LWV; Rep. Party; Community Services.
Educ: Stephens 1948 AA. B: 4/18/28. Add: 4780
Lakeway Terrace; Shorewood 55331 (612)474-3236.

Slayton. MARJORIE D. JEROME (D)
1976-. Bds: Water & Sewer Cmsn.; Airport
Cmsn.; City Dump Cmsn. Prev: Dir., Civil Defense
1968-73. Org: Assoc. of Civil Defense; Amer.
Security; Slayton Adv. Council. B: 8/5/29. Add:
2502 20th St., Slayton 56172 (507)836-6756.

Solway. JANET JOHNSON
Duluth, 4158 Rose Rd. 55811.

South St. Paul. KAREN W. FROWNFELTER (D)
1975-. Bds: Ch., Parks & Recreation Council
Com.; Planning & Metropolitan Affairs Council
Com.; Personnel Council Com. Party: State Del.
1974; State Alt. 1968; DFL State Central Com.
1972-76; DFL Dist. Central Com. 1972- . Org: S.
St. Paul Dem. Farmer/Labor Club. B: 10/11/36.
Add: 100 16th Ave. S., S. St. Paul 55075.

South St. Paul. VIRGINIA E. LANEGRAN (D)
1976-. Party: State Del. 1954, '70, '72, '76;
Nat. Committeewoman, Young Dem's. 1957-59; State
Secretary, Young Dem's. 1952-54. Prev: Charter
Cmsn. 1971-76. Org: Assoc. of Amer. Historians;
Amer. Studies Assoc.; Org. of Amer. Historians;
Women Historians of the Midwest; AAUP. Educ:
Macalester Coll. 1953 BA; U. of Minn. 1968 MA.
Occ: Coll. Professor. B: 6/20/30. Add: 257 4th
Ave. S., S. St. Paul 55075.

Spalding. JOYCE MILBERG
McGregor, R. 2 55760.

Spicer. MRS. DORRANCE DAVICK
City Hall, Spicer 56288.

Spring Park. ELLIE E. HELLER
1974-. Org: Minneapolis Assoc. of Retarded
Citizens; Assoc. of Residences for Retarded in
Minn.; Minn. Foster Parent Assoc.; PTA; Parents
Adv. Council; Women's Club. Occ: Professional
Foster Parent. B: 11/27/23. Add: 3801 Sunset
Dr., Spring Pk. 55384 (612)471-8304.

Stillwater. ANN MARIE BODLOVICK (I) **
1974-. Bds: Planning & Equalization. Occ:
Secretary-Treasurer. B: 8/25/29. Add: 1511 W.
Olive St., Stillwater 55082 (612)439-6120.

Stillwater. CATHY BUCK
Stillwater, 13630 116th St. N. 55082.

Sugar Bush. BARBARA PRESTON
R. 2, Hines 56647.

Sunfish. MARY HAMMES
331 Salem Church Road, St. Paul 55118.

Syron. VIRGINIA RAATZ
Syron 55920.

Tenney. OPAL HARDIE
City Hall, Tenney 56582.

Thief River Falls. ELEANOR J. BOTHMAN (R)
1976-. Bds: Airport Com.; Park & Recreation;
Tax & Assessment. Occ: Travel Consultant. B:
9/24/17. Add: 919 N. Arnold Ave., Thief Rvr.
Fls. 56701.

Thomson. BERTHA ANTON
35 Dalles Avenue, Carlton 55718.

Tonka Bay. JO ANN CARROLL
235 Lakeview Avenue, Tonka Bay 55331.

Tonka Bay. SUSAN R. REID (D)
1977-. Bds: Ch., Vlg. Employee Salary Com.;
Animal Warden. Party: State Del. 1974. Educ:
U. of Minn. 1969 BA. B: 8/1/47. Add: 25 Fair-
hope Ave., Tonka Bay 55331 (612)474-7994.

Tonka Bay. RUTH M. SHERMAN
90 Birch Bluff Rd., Tonka Bay 55331.

Tracy. CLAIRE HANNASCH
587 Harvey, Tracy 56175.

Tracy. JEANNE STANTON (D)
1974-. Bds: Planning Cmsn. Occ: Inventory
Clerk. B: 6/6/31. Add: 325 6th St., Tracy
56175.

Trail. PAMALA SAMSON
City Hall, Trail 56684.

Trosky. STELLA BRANCHAUD (R)
1977-. Org: NEA. Educ: Northern State Coll.
BS. Occ: Teacher. B: 7/1/25. Add: Trosky
56177.

Turtle River. STELLA CARTER
Rt. 5, Bemidji 56601.

Twin Lakes. SHIRLEY GRAY
HELEN RILEY
City Hall, Twin Lakes 56089.

Tyler. RUTH E. RILEY (I)
1972-. Educ: RN. B: 4/10/43. Add: 105 E.
Oak, Tyler 56178.

Underwood. RUBY HENDERSON
City Hall, Underwood 56586.

Upsala. BARB POLMAN
City Hall, Upsala 56384.

Van Buren. BERNICE JOHNSON
Floodwood 55786.

Verndale. EVELYN R. ERCKENBRACK (I)
1975-. Prev: City Civil Defense Dev. 1964-73.
Occ: Custodian. Add: Box 53, Verndale 56481
(218)445-5879.

Victoria. JEAN KLEIN STROHM (R)
1976-. Bds: Planning Cmsn. Party: State Alt.
1964-70; Cnty. Campaign Ch. 1974; Ch., Ways &
Means 1970-72; Precinct Ch. 1972-76; Cnty. Del.
1972-76. Prev: Regional Dir. 1973-76. Org:
Women in Leadership; Minn. GOP. Occ: Realtor.
B: 1/4/30. Add: 6728 Iris, Excelsior 55331
(612)443-2363.

Viking. MRS. HAROLD KAGG
City Hall, Viking 56760.

Wabana. EMMA C. LONG
Grand Rapids, R. 2, Box 589 55744.

Waconia. TERESE MILLER
240 E. Main Street, Waconia 55387.

Waltham. SHARON EHMKE
City Hall, Waltham 55982.

Waseca. MRS. ROMELLE DEEF (R)
1972-. Bds: Le Sueur Group Home Bd.; Liquor
Com.; Joint Powers Bd. Prev: Bd. of Appeals &
Adjustments 1971-72; Planning Bd. 1972. Org:
Historical Society. B: 4/17/29. Add: 201 6th St.
S.E., Waseca 56093.

Watkins. EILEEN SPODEN (D) **
1973-. Bds: Police Commissioner; Health Com.
Party: Precinct Leader 1970-75; 1967-69. Occ:
Bookkeeper. B: 6/13/22. Add: Watkins 55389
(612)764-2110.

Wawina. LILLIAN HEIKKINEN
Box 87, R. 1, Floodwood 55736.

Wawina. BETTY KARKIAINEN
Box 102, Wawina 55794.

Wayzata. MARY W. VAUGHAN (R)
1975-. Party: State Del. 1956; Vlg. Committeewoman 1956-60. Org: PTA. Educ: Smith Coll. 1949
BA. B: 7/31/28. Add: 2875 Gale Rd., Wayzata
55391.

Westbrook. DONNA J. GOEHRING (R)
1976-. Bds: Building. Org: Library Bd.;
Right to Read. Educ: U. of S.D. 1963 BSEd;
1971 MA. Occ: Teacher. B: 6/16/41. Add:
456 Cedar, Westbrook 56183.

White Bear Lake. ROSEMARIE JOHNSON
3756 Auger Avenue, White Bear Lake 55110.

White Bear Lake. MADONNA F. RASK (D)
1975-. B: 2/27/40. Add: 1469 N. Birch Lk.
Blvd., White Bear Lk. 55110 (612)429-3552.

Willmar. IRMA LOUISE PETERSON (R)
1969-. Bds: Ch., Finance Com.; Public Works
Com.; Regional Devt. Cmsn. Party: State Del.
1965-66; Cnty. Ch.; Cnty. Committeewoman 1960-75.
Prev: Charter Cmsn. 1976-78; Human Rights Cmsn.
1974-78. Org: Medical Auxiliary; League of
Cities; Social Concerns Com; Rep. Club; General
Fed. of Women's Clubs. B: 6/9/13. Add: 314 E.
Trout, Willmar 56201.

Willmar. KAREN WESTBY (R) **
1973-. Bds: Public Works; Legislative; Surety;
Finance. Org: LWV. Educ: Macalester Coll. 1960
BS. B: 12/24/38. Add: 506 Knollwood Dr.,
Willmar 56201 (612)235-5524.

Windom. MARION E. UHLHORN (R)
1976-. Bds: City Planning Cmsn.; Personnel.
Occ: Factory Supervisor. B: 10/10/25. Add:
1069 Redding Ave., Windom (507)831-2363.

Winnebago. BETTY ENGELBY
City Hall, Winnebago 56098.

Winona. JANETTE P. ALLEN (R)
1975-. Bds: Coll. Relations; Senior Citizens
Task Force; Traffic Com. Party: State Del.
1962- ; Precinct Ch. 1958-64; Cnty. Co-Ch. 1968-
74; Dist. V-Ch. 1974-76; State Central Com.
1974- . Org: Volunteers in Ct. Service; Chamber
of Commerce; Rep. Women; LWV; WPC. Educ: Winona
State U. 1950 BA; 1975 MA. Occ: Realtor. B:
7/2/28. Add: 203 E. Broadway, Winona 55987
(507)452-8550.

Winona. SUSAN K. EDEL (D)
1975-. Bds: Ch., Coll. Relations Com.; Ch.,
Traffic Com.; Ch., Senior Citizens Center Task
Force. Party: State Del. 1974, '72; State Alt.
1976; Associate Cnty. Ch. 1972-76; State Central
Com. 1972- . Org: Birthright; WPC. Educ: Coll.
of St. Teresa 1969 BA. B: 3/21/47. Add: 1257
West 5, Winona 55987 (507)452-8550.

Winsted. JOANN SNEER
382 Southshore Drive, Winsted 55395.

Winthrop. DARLENE A. MAJESKI (D)
1977-. B: 2/4/34. Add: 307 S. Carver,
Winthrop 55396 (507)647-2146.

Winton. MARGARET ELIZABETH WHITING (I)
1977-. Org: Boundary Waters Conservation
Alliance. B: 1/6/48. Add: 218 Main St., P.O.
Box 168, Winton 55796.

Wirt. GLENDA HETCHLER
Wirt 56688.

Wolf Lake. HILMA KANGAS (I)
1975-. Party: State Alt. 1960. Prev: Tri-Cnty. Community Council 1972-75. Occ: Financial Worker. B: 3/23/21. Add: Box 46 Wolf Lake 56593 (218)538-6686.

Woodbury. LAVON OLANDER (R)
1977-. Bds: Administration; Parks. Org: Community Club. Occ: Nursery School Dir. Add: 7140 Coachwood Cr., Woodbury 55119 (612) 739-5972.

Woodstock. FRANCES CULLEN
City Hall, Woodstock 56186.

Wuori. BETTY H. JOHNSON
St. Rt., Virginia 55792.

Zimmerman. ANNA MAE ILIFF (R)
1975-. Bds: Health & Welfare. Org: Zimmerman Civic Club. Occ: Model Home Attendant. B: 7/20/13. Add: Box 114, Zimmerman 55398.

Judges

SUSANNE C. SEDGWICK
District Court Judge. 1974-. Prev: Municipal Ct. Judge 1970; Asst. Cnty. Atty. 1968-70; Staff Atty., Legal Aid Society of Minn. Org: Bd. of Dir's., Community Health & Welfare Council; State Bar Assoc.; Dist. Ct. Judges Assoc. Educ: U. of Minn. BA; William Mitchell Coll of Law JD. Add: Courthouse, Minneapolis.

ROSALIE WAHL
Justice, Supreme Court. Add: State Capitol, St. Paul 55155 (612)296-2581.

State Boards and Commissions

Accountancy, Board of
JANET JASPER

Appointments Commission, Governor's
VIRGINIA RICHARDSON

Architects, Engineers, Land Surveyors and Landscape Architects, Board of
MARY ANN MURPHY
EDYTHE NADDY

Community College Board
ELNA PONTO

Cosmetology, Board of
CYNTHIA ALLEN

Crime Control Planning Board
ROSEMARY AHMANN
RUTH CAIN
CAROL LEMCKE
CHERYL MORRISON
LISE SCHMIDT

Dentistry, Board of
CAROL SCHUPPEL
JANET SPODIS

Designer Selection Board
LILLIAN MERKEL

Environmental Quality Board, Citizens
SISTER TRESSA PIPER

Ethical Practices Board
MARY JO RICHARDSON

Handicapped, Governor's Council on the
SANDRA GORDON

Health Advisory Committee
PATRICIA BRAUN
BRIDGET COLEMAN

Higher Education Coordinating Board
GERALDINE CARTER
MAXINE GAINES
VERNA WOOD

Medical Examiners, Board of
DOROTHY BERNSTEIN

Merit Systems Council
VONDELL HOLBERT

Nursing, Board of
GHULAM HANIFF
MARY HEINEN
SHIRLEY ROSE

Nursing Home Administrators
EVA LARSON

Optometry, Board of
EILEEN BEACH

Peace Officers Standards and Training Board
CAROLYN BAILEY
ANN DARBY
DIEDRE DODGE

Pharmacy, Board of
KITTY ALCOTT

Psychology, Board of
PATRICIA LILLIGREN

Public Employment Relations Board
LORRAINE CLARK

Public Service Commission
JUANITA SATTERLEE

Soil and Water Conservation Board
MARGLYN DENEEN

State University Board
JEAN FARRAND
ALICE KELLER

Teaching, Board of
MARGERY HARRIS
JO MALMSTEN
MARIE MC NEFF
KATHRYN RAYBURN
NOREEN WELCH

Telephone Systems Advisory Committee, 911 Emergency
PRISCILLA WHITE

Watchmaking, Board of Examiners in
TRUDY MAIER

Workers' Compensation Study Commission
WENDY BORSHEIM
TOBEY LAPAKKO
NADEEN JAMES

Zoological Board, State
CONNIE DE LAND
SANDRA STOKESBARY

Mississippi

State Executive and Cabinet

EDYTHE EVELYN GANDY (D)
Lieutenant Governor. 1975-. Bds: State Bldg. Cmsn.; Cmsn. of Budget & Accounting; Agriculture & Industrial Bd. Prev: State Treasurer 1960-64, 1968-72; Public Welfare Cmsnr. 1964-67; Insurance Cmsnr. 1972-76. Org: ABA; BPW; Miss. Women's Cabinet of Public Affairs; Miss. Official Women's Club. Educ: U. of Southern Miss. BA; U. of Miss. Law School JD. B: 9/4/20. Add: 727 Arlington St., Jackson 39202.

State Legislature

State House

BETTY JANE LONG (D) **
1956-. Dist: 24. Bds: Rules Com.; Appropriations Com.; Constitution Com.; Judiciary Com. Org: AAUW; Farm Assoc.; BPW. B: 5/8/28. Add: 2219 49th Ave., Meridian 39301.

HELEN MC DADE **
1968-. Dist: 24. Org: Amer. Judicature Legal Society; Nat. Assoc. of Women Lawyers; State Bar Assoc.; DAR. B: 5/15/18. Add: Box 112, DeKalb 39328.

County Commissions

Marshall. BERNICE E. TOTTEN (D) **
1974-. Org: NAACP; PTA. B: 9/1/21. Add: Rt. 3, Box 98, Holly Springs 38635 (601)337-2285.

Quitman. CONNIE L. SIMPSON (I)
1975-. B: 5/18/36. Add: Rt. 2, Box 50, Sledge 38670 (601)326-2661.

Scott. MRS. WALDO PRYOR
464 Broad St., Forest 39074.

Washington. JAN ACKER (D)
1976-. Bds: Miss. State Educ. Com. Org: Miss. Nursing Assoc.; DAR. Educ: Warner Brown School of Nursing RN. B: 7/17/35. Add: 498 Idlewild Dr., Greenville 38701 (601)332-1595.

Mayors

Blue Springs. SHIRLEY D. NEWTON
Bryer Patch Farm, Blue Springs 38828.

Brooksville. MRS. LOTTIE F. SMITH
P.O. Box 304, Brooksville 39739.

Doddsville. MRS. MONTEZ COLEMAN
Doddsville 38736.

Gunnison. VIOLET LEGGETT
Gunnison 38746.

Hickory Flat. REBECCA GRESHAM
Box 171, Hickory Flat 38633.

Mayersville. UNITA WRIGHT
Mayersville 39113.

Ruleville. VIRGINIA TOLBERT
City Hall, Ruleville 38771.

Shubuta. FLORENCE BUSBY
Box 416, Shubuta 39360.

Wesson. RENE W. CURTIS
Box 127, Wesson 39191.

West. MRS. A.J. STEVENS, III
Box 55, West 39192.

Local Councils

Arcola. MARY CURRO
Box 38, Arcola 38722.

Bassfield. MATILDA BOOTH
P.O. Box 124, Bassfield 39421.

Beaumont. MINNIE B. FREEMAN
P.O. Box 155, Beaumont 39423.

Beauregard. ANNA S. HARTGRAVES
Rte. 11, Wesson 39191.

Boyle. LORRAINE T. ACORD
MARCIE MULLINS
P.O. Box 367, Boyle 38730.

Brandon. VIRGINIA H. KING
P.O. Box 526, Brandon 39042.

Brooksville. IRENE DURHAM
TRUDY GENO
DOROTHY F. WILKINS
Box 256, Brooksville 39739.

Bruce. STACEY GABBERT
Box 667, Bruce 38915.

Byhalia. SARA P. WILLIAMS
Box 412, Byhalia 38611.

Cary. MARGIE GERRARD
Cary 39054.

Coldwater. BETTY WILKERSON CRUMP
Box 94, Coldwater 38618.

Crawford. HELEN FAYE O'NEAL
Box 65, Crawford 39743.

Crowder. JUDY BYARS
P.O. Box 97, Crowder 38622.

Derma. MARY E. CANNON
ANN BAILEY LANGSTON
Box 95, Derma 38839.

D'lo. MARGARET SMITH
D'lo. 39062.

Ethel. CHARLENE BLAINE
Box 91, Ethel 39067.

Falcon. LILLIE MAE SHAW
Box 55, Falcon 38628.

Fayette. DOROTHY A. HUMPHREY
Box 146, Fayette 39069.

Florence. DORIS BRADSHAW
Rte. 6, Box 165, Florence 39073.

Flowood. IVY R. GRAHAM
Box 252, Mangum Dr., Rte 4, Flowood 39208.

French Camp. HELEN BRANNING
MELBA CURTIS
French Camp 39745.

Friars Point. JOYCE D. FILI
Box 185, Friars Point 38631.

Gattman. TOMMIE JEAN BAILEY
EDNA WEST
Gattman 38844.

Greenville. SARA JOHNSON
Box 5572, Greenville 38701.

Heidelberg. AUDREY MC CLELLAN
Heidelberg 39439.

Horn Lake. ANNA CALVI
LOUISE THOMAS
Box 167, Horn Lake 38637.

Houston. NETTIE MAE ALEXANDER
104 Depot St., Houston 38851.

Indianola. CHARLOTTE BUCHANAN
111 Clover Dr., Indianola 38751.

Jonestown. LAURA CHRISTIAN
MYRTLE B. SHANKS
P.O. Box 110, Jonestown 38639.

Lake. PRISCILLA COOKSEY
MRS. MATTIE R. EVANS
P.O. Box 39, Lake 39092.

Lambert. MARIE KOGER
P.O. Box 161, Lambert 38643.

Leakesville. EMMA JANE WILKERSON
Box 143, Leakesville 39451.

Leland. KATHLEEN JACOBS MULCAHY
108 Peninsula Dr., Leland 38756.

Long Beach. BETTY ANN JONES
NINA MANLY
Box 378, Long Beach 39560.

Louise. LINDA RENFROE
Box 246, Louise 39097.

Louisville. FRANCES BALL
AVA MERLE CUNNINGHAM
P.O. Box 147, Louisville 39339.

Lucedale. HILDA M. HAINES
Box 264, Lucedale 39452.

Lula. MRS. W.L. BARBEE
MRS. D.B. CANNON
MRS. J.W. HANKS
BETTY C. HOPKINS
ALENE S. SPEIGHT
Box 326, Lula 39644.

Maben. ETHELYN HESTER
Box 187, Maben 39750.

McComb. JEWEL CONERLY
Box 997, McComb 39648.

Magnolia. ROSE M. MURPHY
230 Gene St., Magnolia 39652.

Marion. LOUISE GREEN
Rte. 8, Box 33, Meridian 39301.

Mayersville. MILDRED FLEMMING
LORRAINE MABUS
GERALDINE MARSHALL
Mayersville 39113.

Memphis. DIXIE AUSTIN
JOSEPHINE AUSTIN
Walls 38680.

Monticello. EUTHA DAVIS
Monticello 39654.

Morton. IMOGENE WARD
Box 301, Morton 39117.

Moss Point. PATTI C. GUNN
EVERETTE E. WELLS
163 Denny St., Moss Point 39563.

Mount Olive. MRS. IVAL MURPHY
Box 61, Mount Olive 39119.

New Albany. MARY R. PHYFER
Box 329, New Albany 38652.

New Augusta. DELORES MC GOWEN
Box 105, New Augusta 39462.

Newport. EVELYN S. DOLLAHITE
        IRENE SHANNON
    Lake Cormorant 38641.

North Carrollton. SARA W. GRANTHAM
    Box 31, North Carrollton 38947.

Okolona. NORMA WELFORD
    Maine Street, Okolona 38860.

Pachuta. PATRICIA C. ATWOOD
        LINDA PERRY
    Box 96, Pachuta 39347.

Pascagoula. RUBY K. BAGGETT
        PEGGY HOOVER
    Box 908, Pascagoula 39567.

Pass Christian. KITTY FLOYD
        MARIE M. ROGERS
    P.O. Drawer 368, Pass Christian 39571.

Pelahatchie. LILA TANNER
    Box 711, Pelahatchie 39145.

Pickens. ETTA B. GREER
    Box 331, Pickens 39146.

Pittsboro. MRS. JOHN ELLARD
    Box 187, Pittsboro 38951.

Polkville. MABLE MOORE
        LORA PHILLIPS
    Rte. 4, Morton 39117.

Pope. FRANCES MANN
    Box 86, Pope 38658.

Potts Camp. DOROTHY FULLER
    Box 57, Potts Camp 38659.

Prentiss. CHERRY T. DEDDENS
    Box 40, Prentiss 39474.

Purvis. NELL VAN
    Rte. 1, Box 1, Purvis 39475.

Raymond. MARIE C. MAXWELL
    Box 346, Raymond 30154.

Rolling Fork. MRS. HOMER ATCHLEY
    200 West Ave., Rolling Fork 39159.

Roxie. PEGGY ARNOLD.
    Box 213, Roxie 39661.

Schlater. MRS. W.P. BROWN, JR.
    Schlater 38952.

Senatobia. MAUDINE F. HANKS
    210 Camille St., Senatobia 38668.

Shannon. SUE C. COLLINS
    Rte. 2, Shannon 38868.

Shelby. MRS. W.G. PHILLIPS
    Box 108, Shelby 38774.

Silver Creek. KAY CHANCE
    Box 96, Silver Creek 39663.

Sledge. MARILYN C. STARR
    Box 276, Sledge 38670.

Smithville. MRS. JAMES E. COWLEY
    Box 125, Smithville 38870.

Starkville. MARY LEE BEAL
    2103 McArthur Dr., Starkville 39759.

State Line. DOROTHY BARKLEY
    State Line 39362.

Sturgis. MARGARET MOOR
    Box 14, Sturgis 39769.

Sylvarena. BLANCHE JAMES
        MAXINE SIMS
    Rte. 2, Raleigh 39153.

Tchula. MRS. JESSIE BANKS
    Box 321, Tchula 39169.

Thaxton. JUNE HALE
    Thaxton 38871.

Tillatoba. MRS. GUY RAY WEIR
    Box 102, Tillatoba 38961.

Tremont. KATHERINE ZEPP
    Tremont 38876.

Tutwiler. MARTHA BOX
    Box 176, Tutwiler 38963.

Verona. LINDA BOST
    Box 263, Verona 38879.

Walthall. AUDREY BAILEY
        MRS. JAMES F. EIDSON
        NOLA LOVETTE
        RUBY TENHET
    302 Walthall, Walthall 39771.

Webb. MRS. GEORGE BERRY
    Box 112, Webb 38966.

Wiggins. PENNY ALEXANDER
    720 W. College, Wiggins 39577.

Winstonville. LENA WEATHERSPOON
    Winstonville 38781.

Woodland. RUBYE CROWSON
    Box 96, Woodland 39776.

Judges

BETTY JANE LONG
    Judge, Chancery Court. Add: Hinds County
    Courthouse, Jackson.

State Boards and Commissions

A complete list of state boards and commissions,
and of their membership, was not available for
inclusion.

Missouri

CAROLYN M. ASHFORD (D)

Director, Department of Natural Resources. 1977-. Bds: Ch., Inter-Agency Council of Outdoor Recreation; State Historic Preservation Officer; Upr. Miss. Rvr. Basin Com. Educ: U. of Mo. 1968 BA; 1969 MA. B: 7/1/46. Add: 823 Dean Dr., Jefferson City 65101 (314)751-4422.

State Legislature

State Senate

MARY GANT (D) **

Dist: 9. Bds: Banks, Banking & Financial Institutions; Higher Educ.; Ch., Industrial Dev. & Aviation; Public Health, Welfare & Environment. Add: 5804 East 14th St., Kansas City 64126 (314)751-3785.

HARRIETT WOODS (D)

1976-. Dist: 13. Bds: Leg. Com. Party: State Del. 1976; Precinct Leader. Prev: Transportation Com. 1974-76; Highway Com. 1974-76; City Council 1967-74. Org: LWV; NAACP; WPC; Women's Crusade Against Crime; Dem. Club. Educ: U. of Mich. 1949 BA. Occ: Film Maker. B: 6/2/27. Add: 7147 Princeton, University City 63130 (314)751-4010.

State House

KAREN MC CARTHY BENSON (D)

1976-. Bds: Educ. Com.; Consumer Protection Com.; Atomic Energy & Industrial Devt. Party: Nat. Alt. 1972; Precinct Leader 1970-72. Org: LWV; Environmental Defense Fund; Com. for Cnty. Progress; Citizen's Assoc.; WPC. Educ: U. of Kan. 1969 BS; U. of Mo. 1976 MA. B: 3/18/47. Add: 1111 Valentine Rd., Kansas City 64111 (314)741-2723.

MARION G. CAIRNS (R)

1976-. Bds: Educ.; Consumer Protection; State Parks, Recreation & Natural Resources. Party: State Del. 1964-76; Bd., Rep. Club 1968-76; Pres. Women's Club 1968-70; Precinct Leader 1958-76. Org: Rep. Club; Rep. Women's Club. Educ: Monmouth Coll. 1950 BA. B: 6/8/28. Add: 17 E. Swon Ave., Webster Groves 63119 (314)751-4187.

DE VERNE CALLOWAY (D)

1962-. Dist: 81. Bds: Ch., Educ.; Elections; State Institutions & Properties. Party: State Del. 1968-76; Nat. Del. 1976, '74. Educ: LeMoyne Owen 1938 BA. B: 6/17/16. Add: 4309 Enright, St. Louis 63108. (314)751-3282.

DOTTY DOLL (D)

1974-. Dist: 29. Bds: Appropriations; Consumer Protection; V-Ch., Urban Affairs. Org: NOWL; Neighborhood Coalition; ACLU; U. Assoc.; Common Cause; WPC; Mo. Dem. Com.; Citizens Assoc; Historic Kansas City Foundation. Educ: Chicago Teachers Coll. 1958 BEd. B: 7/20/36. Add: 5400 Rockhill Rd., Kansas City 64110 (314) 751-4908.

DELLA M. HADLEY (D)

Dist: 31. Bds: Educ. Com.; Govt. Review Com.; V-Ch., Motor Vehicle & Traffic Regulations. Prev: V-Pres., City School Bd. 1970-74. Org: ACLU; LWV. Educ: Purdue U. 1952 BS. B: 1/27/29. Add: 7345 Belleview, Kansas City 64114 (314) 751-4931.

ORCHID IRENE JORDAN (D) **

1970-. Dist: 25. Bds: Ch., Bills Perfected & Passed; Retirement & Pensions; Social Services & Medicaid. Party: Nat. Com. 1973- ; State Com. Org: NAACP; Urban League. B: 8/15/10. Add: 2745 Garfield, Kansas City 64127 (816)751-4138.

JEWEL KENNEDY (R)

1966-. Bds: Fees, Salaries & Pensions; Municipal Corporations; Fed-State Relations. Party: State Del. 1968; Nat. Del. 1968; Cnty. Committeewoman 1964-66; V-Ch., Congressional Dist. 1964-66. Org: Chamber of Commerce; WPC; Rep. Club. B: 2/7/10. Add: 6111 Harris, Raytown 64133 (314)751-4828.

GLADYS MARRIOTT (D) **

1966-. Dist: 37. Bds: Ch., Retirement & Pensions; Legislative Research Appropriations. Party: Dem. Caucus Ch. Org: OWL; PTA; Women's Chamber of Commerce; Women's Club. B: 1/3/22. Add: 9001 Leeds Rd., Kansas City 64129.

JUDITH O'CONNOR (D) **

Dist: 70. Bds: Public Health & Safety; Workmen's Compensation. Add: 4252 Brampton, Bridgeton 63042 (314)751-2726; 739-1482.

CAROLE ROPER PARK (D)

1976-. Dist: 35. Bds: Public Health & Safety Cmsn.; Social Services & Medicaid; State & Fed. Relations & Veteran's Affairs. Party: Campaign Manager. Org: AFT; Business & Civic Club; Dem. Club; WPC. Educ: U. of Mo. 1964 BA. B: 9/18/39. Add: 11415 E. Gill, Sugar Creek 64054 (314)751-2984.

SUE SHEAR (D)

1972-. Bds: Ch., State Institutions & Properties; Civil & Criminal Justice; Educ. Party: State Del. 1960, '76; Nat. Del. 1976. Prev: Cmsn. on Status of Women 1966-72. Org: LWV; White House Conf. on Educ.; Rep. Dem. Club.

B: 3/17/18. Add: 200 S. Brentwood, Clayton 63105
(314)751-4163.

KAYE STEINMETZ (D)
    1976-. Dist: 57. Bds: Consumer Protection;
Educ.; Social Services & Medicaid. Party: State
Del. 1976; State Alt. 1974; Precinct Captain
1974-77. Prev: Planning & Zoning 1974-76; Ch.,
Senior Citizens Adv. Com. 1972-77; Community
Betterment 1972-77. Org: Mo. Chamber Exec's.;
Soroptimist; BPW; Planning & Zoning; Senior
Citizens Adv. Bd.; Mo. Aid for Amer. Indians;
Cnty. League of Chambers; Dem. Club; Historic
Society. Educ: Columbia Coll. 1958 AA. B:
3/5/38. Add: 13 Longhenrich Dr., Florissant
63031 (314)751-4481.

IRENE E. TREPPLER (R)
    1972-. Bds: Governmental Organizations; Local
Govt. & Related Matters; Consumer Protection.
Party: State Del. 1968-76; Nat. Alt. 1976;
Precinct Captain 1960-72. Org: Rep. Club; Rep.
Women's Club; NOWL. B: 10/13/26. Add: 4681
Fuchs Rd., St. Louis 63128 (314)751-2887.

WINNIE P. WEBER (D)
    3626 Lakeshore, House Springs 63051.

County Commissions

Boone. CAROLYN LOUISE LATHROP (D)
    1975-. Bds: V-Ch., Mid. Mo. Area Adv. Man-
power Bd.; Retirement Center Bd.; Extension
Council. Org: Mo. Assoc. of Counties; Mo. Assoc.
Cnty. Judges; Zonta Internat.; Cnty. Dem. Women.
B: 10/3/38. Add: Rt. 3, Columbia 65201 (314)
874-7510.

Greene. SHIRLEY MADDY
    1700 Sycamore Ln., Springfield 65801.

Jackson. MAMIE F. CURRIE HUGHES (D) **
    1972-. Bds: Regional Council; Alternates;
Truman Medical Center. Org: Freedom, Inc.;
Minority Women's Coalition on Human Rights; NAACP;
Nat. Council of Negro Women. Educ: Fisk U. 1949
BA. B: 5/3/29. Add: 1763 Woodland, Kansas City
64108. (816)881-3163.

Jackson. KAY CRONKITE WALDO (D)
    1975-. Dist: 3. Bds: Ch., Health & Justice
Com.; Land Use Com.; Ch., Housing Policy. Org:
ASPA; Women's Chamber of Commerce; WPC; Com. for
Cnty. Progress; Citizen's Assoc. Educ: U. of Kan.
1960 BS; U. of Mo. 1969 MA. Occ: Human Relations
Consultant. B: 3/30/38. Add: 811 W. 69 Ter.,
Kansas City 64113 (816)881-3750.

Jefferson. KATIE BENTON
    Rt. 3, Hillsboro 63050.

Oregon. DOROTHY ELLIS (D) **
    1970-. Bds: Extension Bd.; Child Welfare Bd.;
Regional Planning Cmsn. Party: County Com. 1955-
75; State Com. 1957-58. B: 6/13/20. Add: Rte. 1,
Thayer 65791 (417)778-7475.

St. Louis. VIRNAMAY BEHRENS
    7601 Manchester Rd., Maplewood 63143.

St. Louis. BETTY FLYNN VAN UUM
    7900 Forsyth, Clayton 63101.

Mayors

Allendale. MARIAN DANIELS
    City Hall, Allendale 64420.

Annapolis. EDNA COX
    202 W. 2nd St., Annapolis 63620.

Aurora. YVONNE SWEARINGEN
    City Hall Bldg., Aurora 65605.

Bertrand. JOAN M. HARRIS
    City Hall, Bertrand 63823.

Bethel. MRS. JOHNNIE L. JONES
    City Hall, Bethel 63434.

Blackwater. JANE SPRIGG (D)
    1976-. Occ: Bookkeeper. B: 12/16/36. Add:
Blackwater 65322 (816)846-4411.

Blodgett. RUTH DODSON
    City Hall, Blodgett 63824.

Bonne Terre. FAITH C. BUNCH
    8 N. Division St., Bonne Terre 63628.

Carrollton. ELISABETH ANN DANIELS
    201 W. Benton St., Carrollton 64633.

Centerview. MARJORIE TODD
    City Hall, Centerview 64019.

Chillicothe. MARY E. SMITH
    City Hall, Chillicothe 64601.

Commerce. ANN HUCK (D)
    Org: Community Club. Add: Box 45, Commerce
63742 (314)264-4470.

Crocker. NORMA LEA MIKALEVICH
    P.O. Box 116, Crocker 65452.

Edina. PAULINE S. CAMPBELL (R) **
    1974-. Bds: Health Planning Bd.; Planning
Cmsn. Prev: Councilwoman 1969-74. Org: OES;
Rep. Women; Senior Citizen Housing Bd. B:
8/11/12. Add: Box 188, Edina 63537 (816)
397-3251.

Gower. JIMMIE LOU COURTNEY (D)
    1973-. Bds: Regional Planning Cmsn. Prev:
Alderwoman 1972-73. Occ: Secretary. B: 3/5/25.
Add: 101 Field St., Gower 64454.

Green Ridge. BARBARA STARK
    City Hall, Green Ridge 65332.

Hallsville. JANE SOUTH
    City Hall, Hallsville 65255.

Hannibal. LILLIAM M. HERMAN
    4th & Broadway, Hannibal 63401.

Hunnewell. VERA M. YANCEY (R)
1974-. Party: State Alt. 1960; Nat. Alt. 1960; V-Ch., Local Com. 1946-77; State Ch., Publicity 1962-64. Prev: Postmaster 1932-44; Nat. Postal Clerk 1944-51. Org: Nat. Ind. Bankers Assoc.; Nat. Press Women; Fed. Women's Club; Historical Society; Civic Club; Senior Citizens Housing; Rep. Women's Club. Educ: U. of Mo. 1962 BA. Occ: Bank Pres. B: 1/31/03. Add: P.O. Box 111, Center St., Hunnewell 63443 (314)983-2484.

Kimberling City. MARY ELIZABETH EDGINGTON (R)
1977-. Prev: Councilwoman 1974-76; Planning & Zoning Com. 1974-76; Budget Com. 1974-76. Org: BPW. B: 1/18/23. Add: 6 Stone Edge Rd., Kimberling City 65686 (417)739-4903.

Ladue. EDITH J. SPINK
9345 Clayton Rd., St. Louis 63124.

Lanagan. JEAN WILSON
Box 16, Lanagan 64847.

Leasburg. GLADYS L. NICHOLSON (I) **
1975-. Prev: Trustee 1971-75. Org: Community Club. Occ: Gas Station Attendant. B: 3/26/20. Add: P.O. Box 66, Leasburg 65535 (314)245-6223.

Matthews. A.W. WAGLEY (I) **
1972-. Educ: School of Practical Nursing, Mo. 1969 RN. Occ: Nurse. B: 8/16/16. Add: Matthews 63867 (314)471-4383.

Morrisville. MARY ANDERSON
City Hall, Morrisville 65710.

Mountain View. JOAN SMITH
City Hall, Mountain View 65548.

Nelson. RUTH YOUNGER
City Hall, Nelson 65347.

Nixa. EDNA B. WASSON (D)
Prev: US Postmaster 1933-72. Org: Local Adv. Council; Amer. Assoc. of Retired Persons; OES. Educ: Southwest Baptist Coll. 1932 AA. B: 3/23/12. Add: 8H Wilderness Rd., Nixa 65714 (417) 725-3785.

Novinger. JAUNITA SUMMERS
City Hall, Novinger 63559.

Odessa. ESTEL SMITH
125 S. 2nd St., Odessa 64076.

Old Monroe. SHARON ANN BRINKMAN
1976-. Org: VFW; PTA. Occ: Bank Teller. B: 1/17/47. Add: 2 St. & Wende, Old Monroe 63369 (314)665-5113.

Rogersville. PEARL LEE SWEARENGIN
City Hall, Rogersville 65742.

St. George. MARY JO FITZPATRICK
9041 Southview Lane, St. Louis 63123.

Stella. VERNA HINTON
P.O. Box 166, Stella 64867.

Trimble. CAROLYN ROGERS
City Hall, Trimble 64492.

Walker. BERNIECE MARTIN
City Hall, Walker 64790.

Wayland. MARY D. STEVENS
P.O. Box 282, Wayland 63472.

Weatherby. MILDRED M. HELMS (D)
1975-. Party: Committeewoman 1975-79. Occ: Machine Operator. B: 10/15/20. Add: Box 193, Weatherby 64497 (816)449-5641.

Wentzville. NANCY REYNOLDS SCOTTI (D)
1974-. Bds: Planning & Zoning; Park; Ch., Finance. Party: State Del. 1974-76; Cnty. Committeewoman. Org: NEA; Bd. of Dirs, Cnty.; Community Club; Historical Society; State Dem. Club; Cnty. Dem. Club; Water Pollution Nat. Bd.; Industrial Dev. Bd. Educ: Fontbonne 1957 BA; U. of Mo. 1970 MEd. Occ: Educ. Specialist. B: 7/21/33. Add: 612 Scotti Ct., Wentzville 63385 (314)327-5101.

Local Councils

Aldrich. JO ANN MARRISON
City Hall, Aldrich 65601.

Anniston. SHIRLEY CHAMBERS
City Hall, Anniston 63820.

Appleton. DIANA E. BURTON
4th St., Appleton 64724.

Arcadia. RUTH MANNING
West Orchard St., Arcadia 63621.

Atlanta. ALVA MAGRUDER
City Hall, Atlanta 63530.

Ava. BETTY HOUSE (R)
Bds: Zoning Bd.; Ch. Light Dept. Party: State Del. 1976; Cnty. Committeewoman 1972-76; Cnty. V-Ch. 1976. Org: Adv. Council. Occ: Storeowner. B: 5/18/20. Add: 1503 S. Jefferson, Ava 65608 (417)683-5849.

Baker. SUSAN BAKER
City Hall, Essex 63846.

Battlefield. BARBARA SILVEY
5474 S. Daniel, Battlefield 65807.

Bella Villa. JOAN SCHREMP
3989 Bayless Rd., Lemay 63125.

Bellefontaine Neighbors. PHONSE HURLEY (D)
1975-. Bds: Parks & Recreation Cmsn.; Repr., St. Louis Cnty. Municipal League; Exec. Bd. of Dir's., St. Louis Cnty. Municipal League. Org: Cancer Crusade; Citizens for Educ. Freedom; Dem. Club; Parents Assoc. B: 12/31/39. Add: 1160 Poelker Ct., Bellefontaine Neighbors 63137 (314)867-0077.

Bellerive. MRS. HUGH O'NEILL
Box 5717, St. Louis 63121.

Bel-Nor. MELBA S. RUDOLPH
8416 Natural Bridge, Bel-Nor 63121.

Belton. CALLA SAULTZ
506 Main, P.O. Box 230, Belton 64012.

Berkeley. IRIS STUART
6140 N. Hanley Rd., Berkeley 63134.

Bethel. JOSEPHINE PARKER
City Hall, Bethel 63434.

Bevier. LYNN COX
City Hall, Bevier 63532.

Bigelow. BETTY BOMAR
City Hall, Bigelow 64425.

Blackwater. JOANN FENICAL
City Hall, Blackwater 65322.

Blue Springs. EULA B. MAHAN
903 Main St., Blue Springs 64015.

Boonville. MABEL SIMMONS
6th & Spring Sts., Boonville 65233.

Breckenridge. MAXINE FULTON
City Hall, Breckenridge 64625.

Brentwood. BERNICE A. MC ANANY
2348 Brentwood Blvd., Brentwood 63144.

Brownington. GLADYS J. MOORE (D)
1974-. Party: Local Committeewoman 1946-50.
Prev: Dem. Twp. Committeewoman 1946-50. B:
6/25/11. Add: Rt. 2, Deepwater 64740 (417)
644-2946.

Buckner. HELEN SANDERS
11 W. Washington, Buckner 64016.

Buffalo. WANDA WILSON
City Hall, Buffalo 65622.

Bunceton. RUBY SMITH
City Hall, Bunceton 65237.

Caledonia. JANE FARIS
City Hall, Caledonia 63631.

Callao. HORTENSE HOLMAN (D)
1975-. B: 3/23/16. Add: Callao 63534.

Calverton Park. BETTY TURNER
52 Young Dr., Ferguson 63135.

Canton. NANCY WILSON
124 N. Fifth St., Box 231, Canton 63435.

Carterville. NEVA JONES
VIRGINIA MILLER
100 E. Main, Carterville 64835.

Caruthersville. VIRGINIA JOSEPHINE VAN CLEVE (D)
1973-. B: 10/6/06. Add: 600 Eastwood,
Caruthersville 63830.

Centerview. LYNERA CHURCH
City Hall, Centerview 64019.

Centerview. MITTIE MARTIN (D)
1975-. Occ: Counselor. B: 2/6/23. Add: Rt. 1,
Box 255, Centerview 64019 (816)656-3589.

Champ. ROSEMARY BANGERT
Rt. 1, Box 260, Hazelwood 63042.

Charlack. SHIRLEY M. MAY (I)
1967-. Bds: Pres., Bd. of Aldermen. Occ:
Cashier/Bookkeeper. B: 7/7/29. Add: 2515
Pomona Pl., Charlack 63114 (314)427-4715.

Charleston. JACKIE WHITESIDE
200 N. Main St., Charleston 63834.

Chillicothe. WILLA JANE SMITH
City Hall, Chillicothe 64601.

Clarksburg. JEWEL MANESS
P.O. Box 144, Clarksburg 65025.

Clarkson Valley. BEVERLY B. MACKIE
15925 Kettington Rd., Chesterfield 63017.

Clarksville. HELEN BARRON
113 Howard St., Clarkesville 63336.

Claycomo. JENNIE M. BRANDT
1975-. Chair Pro Tem. Prev: City Clerk
1959-75. Org: Amer. Business Women's Assoc.
B: 9/9/08. Add: 159 Longfellow, Claycomo
64119 (816)452-5539.

Clayton. ELIZABETH THURMOND ROBB (D)
1975-. Bds: Ch., Ways & Means; Public
Works; Public Safety. Prev: Parks & Recreation
Com. Occ: Realtor. B: 12/23/43. Add: 6312
Alamo, Clayton 63105 (314)727-8100.

Clifton Hill. MAY D. WEBSTER
City Hall, Clifton Hill 65244.

Clinton. HELEN MACHNICKE
215 S. Washington, Clinton 64735.

Columbia. FRAN BEACH (I)
1973-. Bds: Mo. Council of Govts. Org: LWV;
AAUW; Amer. Judicature Society; PTA. Educ:
Cornell U. 1961 BA; Columbia Teachers Coll.
1964 MA; U. of Mich. 1970 MS. Occ: Science
Teacher. B: 6/23/39. Add: 108 Parkhill,
Columbia 65201.

Cool Valley. EILEEN KAPELLER
100 Signal Hill Dr., Cool Valley 63121.

Cooter. PAULICE ALEXANDER
City Hall, Cooter 63839.

Country Club Village. BARBARA IRWIN
R.R., St. Joseph 64501.

Country Life Acres. IONE GUCCIONE
7 Country Life Acres, St. Louis 63131.

Crane. DORRIS JOHNSON
Box 17, 120 N. Commerce, Crane 65633.

Crestwood. PATRICIA KILLOREN
#1 Detjen Dr., Crestwood 63126.

Creve Coeur. PEGGY VICKROY
11631 Olive Blvd., Creve Coeur 63141.

Crocker. GLORIA ROBBINS
        City Hall, Crocker 65452.

Curryville. KATHERINE S. MOTLEY
            LUCILLE STEVENS
        City Hall, Curryville 63339.

Dearborn. LYNN CASSITY (D)
        1976-. Educ: Mo. W. State Coll. 1975 BS. B:
8/16/52. Add: Box 223, 107 May St., Dearborn
64439.

Dellwood. KATHLEEN BASILE
        1415 Chambers Rd., Ferguson 63135.

Dennis Acres. BEULAH JACKSON
        City Hall, Joplin 64801.

DeSoto. IRIS BERNHARDT
        413 South Second St., DeSoto 63020.

Dewitt. LILLY SIMS
        FREIDA WINFREE
        City Hall, Dewitt 64639.

Diggins. MRS. PALMA BRONNER
        City Hall, Diggins 65636.

Dimmswick. GEORGIA CROW
        Box 27, Dimmswick 63053.

Doolittle. CATHERINE E. HILL
        MARY JANE SMITH
        R.R. #2, Rolla 65401.

Duenweg. MARY F. WEAVER (D)
        1975-. Occ: Clerk. B: 3/27/15. Add: 706
Patterson, Duenweg 64841.

Easton. NADINE KAISER
        City Hall, Easton 64443.

Edgerton. CONNIE CONSTANT
        IRENE ROBERTS
        VIRGINIA YORK
        City Hall, Edgerton 64444.

Edmundson. MARIANNE KALTENBACH
        4440 Holman Lane, St. Louis 63134.

Eldorado Springs. VIRGINIA R. STRAIN (D)
        1970-. Bds: Ch., Municipal Band. Prev: Park
1964-66. B:11/10/13. Add: 122 Hightower St.,
Eldorado Springs 64744.

Elmo. MARIDEE PRUITT
        City Hall, Elmo 64445.

Elsberry. JO ANN CORDSIEMON (D)
        1975-. Add: 703 Bailey, Elsberry 63343
(314)898-2669.

Esther. PHYLLIS YOUNG
        7th & Jefferson, Esther 63601.

Eureka. JOAN P. ROMERO (D)
        1976-. Bds: Road Com. Org: Community Better-
ment. Educ: Providence Coll. of Nursing 1963 RN.
Occ: Insurance. B: 6/4/42. Add: 90 Edward Dr.,
Eureka 63025 (314)938-5233.

Exeter. BEE SINKLIER
        City Hall, Exeter 65647.

Fayette. HELEN AKINS (D) **
        1974-. Bds: Steeet Cmsn. Occ: Business
Owner. B: 10/10/41. Add: 507 Watts Ave.,
Fayette 65248.

Fenton. FRANCES J. PICKLES
        JEAN GERBER
        625 No. Highway 141, Fenton 63026.

Flat River. MARILYN JEANNE CALVIRD (R)
        1976-. Org: Mo. Assoc. of Juvenile Officers.
Occ: Deputy Juvenile Officer. B: 10/11/35.
Add: 213 Munger, Flat Riv. 63601 (314)431-3577.

Florissant. JO CURRAN (I)
        1973-. Org: BPW; LWV; Bd. of Dirs. County
Municipal League; Chamber of Commerce; Soropti-
mists. B: 3/25/40. Add: 9 Cantabrian Ct.,
Florissant 63033 (314)921-7754.

Foley. LUCILLE STONEBRAKER
        P.O. Box 81, Foley 63347.

Foley. SOPHIE STONEBRAKER
        1975-. Occ: Beautician. B: 8/12/26. Add:
Addison St., Foley 65347 (314)662-2272.

Fredericktown. WANDA A. PRIEST (D)
        1976-. Bds: Ch., Planning & Zoning; Bd. of
Health. Org: Municipal League. Occ: Beautician.
B: 8/10/27. Add: 307 E. Mine La Motte, Frederick-
town 63645 (314)783-3683.

Fredericktown. LEOTA REAGAN
        124 West Main St., Fredericktown 63645.

Frontenac. JOAN M. BAYER
        MARJORIE R. HARWOOD
        10555 Clayton Rd., St. Louis 63131.

Fulton. WILMA M. JONES
        4th & Market Sts., Fulton 63251.

Garden City. CAROLYN CLARK
        City Hall, Garden City 64747.

Gerald. BEVERLY MERK
        City Hall, Gerald 63037.

Gladstone. WILMA OGDEN
        7010 N. Holmes, Gladstone 64118.

Glendale. REBECCA DUGGAN
        424 N. Sappington Rd., Glendale 63122.

Golden City. MARTHA HUBER
        City Hall, Golden City 64748.

Graham. EUGENIA HARVEY LINVILLE (R)
        1973-. Bds: Street Cmsnr. Org: Amer. Assoc.
Retired Teachers; Housing Corp. Bd.; Historical
Society; Women's Social Progressive. Educ:
Park Coll. 1932 BA. B: 9/2/10. Add: 115 Lynn,
Graham 64455.

Grain Valley. SARA P. ROGERS (R)
    1975-. Bds: Fire Dept. Cmsnr.; Secretary,
Planning Zoning Bd. Prev: Mayor 1963-66. Occ:
Office Worker. B: 8/28/31. Add: 616 Gregg,
Grain Vly. 64029 (816)229-6275.

Grandview. PATRICIA L. BISHOP
    1200 Main St., Grandview 64030.

Grantwood Village. JOANNA GEORGE (I)
    1976-. Org: Chamber of Commerce; Red Cross.
Occ: Physician's Asst. B: 1/10/40. Add: 12
Zinzer Ct., Grantwood Village 63123 (314)
842-2268.

Greendale. JANET R. FRANTZEN
    7407 Leadale Dr., Normandy 63133.

Green Ridge. BARBARA HARMS
    City Hall, Green Ridge 65332.

Guilford. DEBBIE PEDERSON
    City Hall, Guilford 64457.

Hamilton. PHARES LINVILLE
    201 S. Davis, Hamilton 64644.

Hanley Hills. CAROL A. WILHELM (D)
    1976-. B: 1/6/39. Add: 7812 Alert, St. Louis
63133 (314)725-0909.

Harrisonville. PEGGY J. CLUM
                JEAN OVERBEY
    300 E. Pearl, Box 367, Harrisonville 64701.

Hayti Heights. MARTHA DEAN
    P.O. Box 426, Hayti Hgts. 63851.

Hazelwood. MOLLIE C. RICKEY
    7900 N. Lindbergh, Hazelwood 63042.

Hazelwood. CECELIE RYAN
    Rt. 1, Box 260, Hazelwood 63042.

Henrietta. GENEVA GARDNER
    City Hall, Henrietta 64036.

Henrietta. BEATRICE HEGER (D)
    Bds: V-Ch., Bd. of Dir's., Fellowship Senior
Citizens; V-Ch., Cnty. Council on Aging. B:
8/23/09. Add: P.O. Box 483, Henrietta 64036
(816)494-5445.

Higbee. DEALIA BOLLES
    City Hall, Higbee 65257.

Higginsville. KATE POWELL
    P.O. Box 110, Higginsville 64037.

Hillsdale. MARGARET AMANDA ARCHAMBAULT (I)
    1954-. Bds: Ch., Derelict Housing Com.; Ch.,
Health; Ch., Ways & Means. Educ: Southeast
Teachers Coll. 1950 BS. Occ: Bus Driver. Add:
2117 Erick Ave., St. Louis 63121.

Hillsdale. DOROTHY MOORE
             MARGARET MORGAN
             RAYE ROBERTSON
    6428 Curtis Ave., St. Louis 63121.

Holden. DORIS NICOLI
    101 W. 3rd St., Holden 64040.

Holt. RYNTHIA C. FRANKE
       NANCY HOPKINS
       DOLLIE NICHOLSON
    City Hall, Holt.

Holts Summit. CAROL MAXEY
    Box 66, Holts Summit 65043.

Homestown. AMIE EDMOND
            MRS. MOZETTA HENRY
    P.O. Box 142, Wardell 63879.

Huntsville. SHARON HARLAN
             MARY RUTH SUMMERS
             MARY ELLEN ZWONITZER
    205 S. Main St., Huntsville 65259.

Illmo. MARGARET HILL SHIPMAN (R) **
    1973-. Bds: Finance Ch.; Library Bd. Org:
OES. Educ: Southeast Mo. State U. 1930 BA. B:
3/20/08. Add: Box 142, Illmo 63754 (314)
264-2189.

Independence. MITZI ANN OVERMAN (D)
    1974-. Bds: V-Ch., Municipal League; Mid-
Amer. Regional Council Com. on Utilities; Mid-
Amer. Regional Council Com. on Housing. Prev:
Ch., Bicentennial Com. 1973-74. Org: Amer.
Public Power Assoc.; Chamber of Commerce; AAUW;
Jr. Service League; Congress of Dem. Clubs.
Educ: U. of Mo. 1950 BS. B: 9/29/29. Add:
12001 Newbury Ln., Independence 64052 (816)
836-8300.

Jackson. DAISY LONG
    225 S. High St., Jackson 63755.

Jefferson City. CAROLYN MC DOWELL
    240 E. High, Jefferson City 65101.

Jonesburg. DARYLENE HAUSKINS
    City Hall, Jonesburg 63351.

Joplin. KAY WELLS
    303 E. 3rd St., P.O. Box 1355, Joplin 64801.

Kansas City. JOANNE M. COLLINS (R)
    1974-. Dist: 3. Bds: Mid-Amer. Regional
Council. Party: State Del. 1968, '70; Nat. Alt.
1972, '76; Sec., Cnty. Com. 1971-75; State
Committeewoman 1971-73. Prev: Cnty. Transition
Com. 1971-72. Org: Nat. Alliance of Postal &
Federal Employees; Metropolitan Concern; Citizens
for Prison Reform; LWV; Nat. Fed. of Rep. Women;
Citizen's Assoc. B: 8/29/35. Add: 4030
Bellefontaine Ave., Kansas City 64130 (816)
274-1321.

Keytesville. JANET WEAVER
    408 W. Bridge, Keytesville 65261.

Kingsville. SHEILA MC FARLAND
    City Hall, Kingsville 64061.

Kinloch. JOHNIE MAE BRYANT
    5625 Martin Luther King Bldg., Kinloch 63140.

Kirksville. ELIZABETH LAUGHLIN (I)
1974-. Bds: Planning & Zoning Cmsn.; Humane
Society Bd.; City Cemetery Bd. Prev: Planning
& Zoning Com. 1965-77; Major Toroughfare Tech.
Planning Com. 1965-70. Org: AAUW; Humane Society;
Environmental Defense Council. Educ: Northeast
Mo. State Coll. 1963 AA; Northeast Mo. State Coll.
1963 BS; 1965 MA. B: 5/6/21. Add: 2916 S. 1st,
R#1, Box 37, Kirksville 63501 (816)665-7792.

Lake Lotawana. NINA AULT
Rt. #4, Lake Lotawana 64063.

Lake Ozark. MARGE C. CAMPBELL (R) **
1971-. Occ: Shop Owner. B: 12/15/14. Add:
Twin Oaks La., Box 59, Lake Ozark 65049.

Lake Tapawingo. MARY STEPHENS
LOUISE SUTTLES
R. 2, Box 135, Blue Springs 64015.

Lake Tapawingo. FRANCIS ELOISE VAUGHN (D)
1976-. Bds: Ch., Street & Light Cmsn.; Ch.,
Waste Management Cmsn.; Ch., Cmsn. on Aged. Org:
Nat. Treasury Employees Union; Mo. Municipal
League; Red Cross; UDC; Women's Club. Occ: Tax
Examiner, Internal Revenue Service. B: 7/20/23.
Add: 52-D Lk. Tapawingo, Rt. 2, Box 237, Lk.
Tapawingo 64015 (816)229-3722.

Lee's Summit. SUSAN HENDRICKS
220 S. Main St., Lee's Summit 64063.

Levasy. BETTY CARROL
LA RUE WELCH
City Hall, Levasy 64066.

Liberty. DOROTHY D. ALLEN (I)
1974-. Mayor Pro Tem. Bds: Alt., Bd. Member,
Mid-Amer. Regional Council; Leg. Com., Mo.
Municipal League. B: 8/9/35. Add: 1632 Magnolia,
Liberty 64068 (816)781-7100.

Liberty. GLENNA TODD
16 South Missouri St., Liberty 64068.

Licking. ANN FOX
VERA KIRKMAN
City Hall, Licking 65542.

Louisianna. JEANNE HALLOWS
121 No. 7th St., Louisianna. 63353.

Marceline. KAREN J. STAUFFER (D)
1975-. Bds: Recreation Bd. Org: Amer. Business
Women's Assoc.; Regional Manpower Adv. Com.;
Recreation Bd. B: 11/2/45. Add: 128 W. Ritchie,
Marceline 64658 (816)376-3528.

Marquand. LOUISE HANKS (D) **
Org: Chamber of Commerce; PTA. B: 4/11/25.
Add: Fleming St., Marquand 63655 (314)783-2090.

Marquand. MARY LEACH
City Hall, Marquand 63655.

Mayview. JUDITH PRAGMAN (I) **
1974-. Bds: Street Dept.; Park Com.; CETA
Summer Work for Youth. Org: PTA. B: 10/4/47.
Add: 400 E. Marshall, Mayview 64071 (816)237-4353.

McFall. JOYCE AINSWORTH
City Hall, McFall 64657.

Merwin. JUANITA DYER (R)
1975-. Prev: Twp. Assessor 1972-74. Occ:
Factory. B: 8/16/34. Add: Box 75, Amsterdam
64723.

Merwin. MRS. JOE KELSO
Rt. 1, Amsterdam 64723.

Milan. VERDA FRANKLIN (D)
1975-. Bds: Airport Bd., Utilities. Org:
Dem. Women's Club; OES. Occ: Physician Asst.
B: 7/3/16. Add: 320 E. 4th, Milan 63556
(816)265-4411.

Mokane. MRS. WALTER ROEWE
City Hall, Mokane 65059.

Mooresville. FAE FAIR
City Hall, Mooresville 64664.

Mosby. MRS. EYELA HENRY
Main St., Mosby 64073.

Mountain View. MILDRED BARMUN
City Hall, Mountain View 65548.

Mount Vernon. LORENE FIEKER
ANNABELLE JUSTUS
P.O. Box 70, Mt. Vernon 65712.

Neelyville. EMMA PAYNE
City Hall, Neelyville 63954.

New Franklin. MICHELLE PATRICK
City Hall, New Franklin 65274.

New Madrid. VIRGINIA LAVALLE CARLSON (I)
1976-. Prev: Cnty. Child Welfare Bd. 1970-74.
Org: Chamber of Commerce; Community Betterment.
B: 12/26/34. Add: 900 Davis, New Madrid 13869.

Noel. HAZELL R. ALBINS (I)
1975-. B: 1/12/13. Add: Box 404, Noel
64854.

Normandy. MARTHA HOFFSTETTER
3620 Oakmount Ave., Normandy 63121.

Normandy. ANN WILLIS
2803 Maywood, Normandy 63121.

North Lilbourn. NELLIA MILLER
City Hall, Lilbourn 63862.

Northmoor. DOROTHY THARP
2300 N.W. Vivion Rd., Kansas City 64151.

Northwoods. LUCILLE B. POTTER (R) **
1972-. Bds: Personnel; Police Advisory.
B: 12/28/09. Add: 6719 Mathew St., Northwoods
63121.

Northwye Village. BECKY COLLET
Rt. 5, Box 10, Rolla 64501.

Northwye Village. BLANCHE PAISTE (D)
     1973-. Party: Cnty. Committeewoman 1976-78.
Org: Dem. Women's Club. Occ: Tax Consultant. B:
11/17/22. Add: Rt. 5 Box 36, Rolla 65401 (314)
364-1685.

Norwood. LEVETA SHORES
     City Hall, Norwood 65717.

Norwood Court. ELIZABETH LAMMERT
     5534 Norway Dr., Normandy 63121.

Oak Grove. RACHEL HOLLAND
     Sullivan 63080.

Oakland. BARBARA BRICKNER
     1007 Oakland Ave., Kirkwood 63122.

Oaks. DOROTHY VEST
     520 Northeast Dr., Kansas City 64118.

Oakview. JO JARRETT
     P.O. Box 19766, Kansas City 64118.

Oakwood. MARTHA ALLEN
               SHIRLEY GARNER
     Kansas City 64118.

Oakwood Manor. CLAREEN BAEHR (R)
     1976-. Bds: Ch., Water & Trash Collection.
Prev: Sewer Collection System 1976-77. Org:
Meals on Wheels. Educ: Allen School of Nursing
1949 RN. B: 4/26/26. Add: 5718 N. Tracy, Kansas
City 64118.

O'Fallon. PHYLLIS JUNE SCHABER (I)
     1975-. Bds: Parks & Recreation; Budget &
Insurance; Planning, Zoning Bd. Org: PTA;
Athletic Assoc. Occ: Kindergarten Teacher. B:
9/7/39. Add: 505 St. Patrick Dr., O'Fallon
63366.

Old Monroe. MARY C. BURKEMPER
     City Hall, Old Monroe 63369.

Olivette. JANET MONSEY
     9473 Olive Blvd., Olivette 63132.

Olympian Village. LOIS W. NEAL (D)
     1974-. Bds: Planning Cmsn.; Health Cmsnr.
Prev: City Clerk 1971-74; Bldg. Cmsnr. 1973-74.
B: 7/18/26. Add: Rt. 4, Box 369, Desoto 63020
(314)586-4359.

Oran. ROSALIA FRIGA
     City Hall, Oran 63771.

Otterville. CECI HITE
     City Hall, Otterville 65348.

Pacific. EILEEN HARRIS
     221 S. 1st St., Pacific 63069.

Pagedale. DARLINE CRAWLEY
             LEATRICE J. DOWD
     1404 Ferguson Ave., Pagedale 63133.

Parkdale. CAROL BONE
             IVA BROWN
     Rt. 2, Box 217, High Ridge 63049.

Parma. AGNES HARDESTY
     City Hall, Parma 63870.

Parnell. SUSAN MARIE MAXWELL (D)
     1976-. Org: Amer. Legion Auxiliary. Occ:
Grocery Clerk. B: 11/20/49. Add: Box 141,
Parnell 64475.

Pasadena Hills. BELVA JANE WEAVER (I)
     1972-. Bds: Municipal Clerks Assoc. Educ:
U. of Mo. 1951 BSEd. Occ: Flg. Clerk. B:
4/18/29. Add: 7248 S. Winchester Dr., Pasadena
Hls. 63121 (314)382-4453.

Pasadena Park. JUNE MUELLER
     P.O. Box 5696, Normandy 63121.

Peerless. LORENA HENDERSON
     100 Hwy. 141, Peerless 63088.

Perry. IDA REYNOLDS
     City Hall, Perry 63462.

Pevely. PAT KALTENBRONN (I)
     1976-. Bds: Public Works Com.; Police Com.
Occ: Teacher's Aide. B: 6/13/43. Add: 1072
Oak Trl., Pevely 63070 (314)479-4454.

Pickering. SHIRLEY MC KEE
     City Hall, Pickering 64476.

Pierce City. PAULINE M. TALARSKI
     City Hall, Pierce City 65723.

Pine Lawn. ANGELA M. COREY
     6250 Forest Ave., Pine Lawn 63121.

Pineville. PATRICIA ATPELESY
     City Hall, Pineville 64856.

Pineville. MARY ANN BRADLEY (D) **
     1973-. Org: Mental Health Com.; Nurse Assoc.
Educ: Okla. U. 1949 RN. B: 11/17/28. Add:
Box 306, Pineville 64856 (417)223-4351.

Pleasant Valley. AVA B. BOUCHER (R) **
     1964-. Bds: Budget Com. Occ: Bookkeeper.
B: 4/20/25. Add: Rt. 2, Box 569, Liberty
64068 (816)781-3996.

Pleasant Valley. CAROL HOBBS
                   CAROL THOMPSON
     R.R. #2, Box 276, Liberty 64068.

Poplar Bluff. JANE SCHERRER
     301 S. Broadway, Poplar Bluff 63901

Portage Des Sioux. JULIA E. FINN (I)
     1974-. Org: AAUW; Nat. Wildlife Fed.
Educ: Wash. U. 1947 BA; 1963 MAEd. Occ: Guid-
ance Counselor. B: 8/10/26. Add: 1850 Main
St., Portage Des Sioux 63373.

Powersville. TWYLA BATES (R)
     1976-. Occ: Interior Decorator. B: 8/26/23.
Add: Powersville 64672.

Powersville. CORA GATREL
     City Hall, Powersville 64672.

Powersville. MARY E. VARNER (R) **
    1974-. Org: Teachers Assoc. Educ: Northeast
Mo. State U. BS. Occ: Teacher. B: 5/29/18. Add:
Box 144, Powersville 64672.

Purdin. MAXINE KOLLASCH
    City Hall, Purdin 64674.

Quitman. MRS. MERRILL HELLER
    City Hall, Quitman 64478.

Raytown. SHIRLEY MUNSTERMAN
        MARY PISCIOTTA
    10000 E. 59th St., Raytown 64133.

Rayville. DOROTHY WILHITE
    City Hall, Rayville 64084.

Redings Mill. RUBY C. FINK
    Rte. 4, Box 73A, Joplin 64801.

Renick. ALLIENE MANGUS
    City Hall, Renick 65278.

Richmond. CAROL THOMAS
    303 S. Thornton, Richmond 64085.

Riverview. PATRICIA TURNBULL
    9699 Lilac Drive, St. Louis 63137.

Rocheport. MARIE GARDNER
        FRANCES TURNER
    City Hall, Rocheport 65279.

Rockaway Beach. BARBARA TAYLOR
    Box 315, Rockaway Beach 65740.

Rock Port. JOYCE T. STONER (R)
    1969-. Party: Cnty. Committeewoman 1960-68.
Educ: Ia. State U. 1953 BS. B: 2/12/31. Add:
517 E. Ridge Ct., Rock Port 64482.

Rogersville. BETTY N. HANIE (D)
    1973-. Party: State Del. 1976; Cnty. Committee-
woman. Add: 100 Helesy Ave., Rogersville 65742.

Rolla. MRS. LOU MC FARLAND
        SHARON TRYON
    204 E. 8th St., Rolla 65401.

Rush Hill. CAROL RICHARDSON (D)
    1976-. Org: PTA. B: 12/30/40. Add: Box 86,
Rush Hill 65280.

St. Charles. GRACE NICHOLS
    101 S. Main St., St. Charles 63301.

St. Cloud Village. LEOLA M. REITZ (I)
    1963-. B: 12/22/06. Add: Rt. 2, Box 2,
Bourbon 65441 (314)732-4651.

St. George. AUDREY GREGORY
    9041 Southview Lane, St. Louis 63123.

St. Joseph. JOYCE WINSTON (D)
    1974-. Bds: Ch., City Council Com.; Mo. Local
Govt. Employees Retirement. Party: State Del.
1976. Org: Assoc. Volunteer Bureau; LWV; Historical Society; PTSA. Educ: Mo. Western State Coll.
1972 BS. B: 12/7/37. Add: 5018 Mockingbird Ln.,
St. Joseph 64506 (816)232-5408.

St. Louis. NELLENE JOYCE
        DAISY MC FOWLAND
    City Hall, 12th & Markets Sts., St. Louis
63103.

St. Louis. GERALDINE OSBORN (D) **
    1973-. Party: State Dist. Com. 1969-73;
Ward Com. 1968-73. Org: Business Women's
Assoc.; LWV; Dem. Club; PTA. B: 6/13/34. Add:
3966 Juniata, St. Louis 63116 (314)865-2327.

St. Louis. VIRGINIA PATTON
        MARY ROSS
    City Hall, 12th & Market Sts., St. Louis
63103.

St. Louis. MARY G. STOLAR (D)
    1973-. Bds: Ch., Welfare Com.; Housing &
Urban Devt. Hearing; Parks Com. Party: State
Del. 1972. Org: ACLU; Neighborhood Community
Environmental Groups; Dem. Club. Educ: Wash.
U. 1962 AB; 1970 MSW. B: 1/24/40. Add: 59
Kingsbury Pl., St. Louis 63112 (314)453-3287.

St. Louis. JO ANNE WAYNE
    City Hall, 12th & Market Sts., St. Louis
63103.

St. Martins. RUTH BRAUMER
    R.R. 1, Jefferson City 65101.

St. Peters. NORMA SIMS
    P.O. Box 9, St. Peters 63376.

Savannah. JANICE VIESTENZ
    402 Court St., Savannah 64485.

Seymour. JANICE BLANKENSHIP
        MARY DOGGETT
    Washington St., Box 247, Seymour 65746.

Silver Creek Village. JO RAUDENBUSH (R)
    1975-. Org: Council for the Arts; Rep.
Women; PTA. B: 3/26/25. Add: 4507 Hickory Ln.,
Joplin 64801. (417)623-6162.

Smithville. ELIZABETH BLACKWELL
    P.O. Box B, Smithville 64089.

South Gifford. DONNA GRAY
        BARBARA WARREN
    R. 4, La Plata 63549.

Sparta. KATHY GAMEL
    City Hall, Sparta 65753.

Stella. PEARL COLLIER (D)
    1973-. B: 7/6/03. Add: Stella 64867
(417)628-3404.

Stewartsville. JOAN SCHLEICHER
    City Hall, Stewartsville 64490.

Strasburg. VICKIE BROWN
    City Hall, Strasburg 65090.

Sugar Creek. EDNA VAN VLACK
    Drexel 64742.

Sumner. VEDA JOHNSON
    City Hall, Sumner 64681.

Sunset Hills. RUTH WOOLDRIDGE
     Rt. 1, 10875 Sunset Hills, St. Louis 63127.

Sycamore Hills. BEATRICE I. CATES (D)
     Bds: Ch., Finance Cmsn. Org: Dem. Club. B:
10/10/05. Add: 2463 Northland Ave., Sycamore
Hls., 63114 (314)427-0811.

Tina. CONNIA PETERSON
     City Hall, Tina 64682.

Town & Country. JANE T. MUDD (R)
     1975-. Bds: Ch., Planning & Zoning. Educ:
Vassar Coll. 1963 BA; Middlebury Coll. 1964 MA.
B: 9/24/41. Add: 7 Country Ave., Town & Country
63131 (314)432-4696.

Tracy. MARILYN INOJOS
     P.O. Box 6, Tracy 64091.

Trenton. DOROTHY MILLER
     113 E. 10th St., Trenton 64683.

Trimble. DOROTHY DUBOIS
     City Hall, Trimble 64492.

Twin Oaks. MARILYN M. BAUER
     5 Ann Ave., Valley Park 63088.

Unionville. FRANCES J. KLINGINSMITH (D)
     1976-. Bds: Streets, Alleys & Health; Planning
& Zoning Cmsn. Org: BPW. Occ: Bookkeeper. B:
4/16/27. Add: 522 S. 20th St., Unionville 63565
(816)947-2141.

University City. ELSIE BECK GLICKERT
     1969-. Bds: Cmsn. on Human Relations. Prev:
Park Bd. 1963-69. Occ: Secretary. B: 2/1/25.
Add: 6712 Etzel, University City 63130 (314)
863-0100.

Urich. E. ELAINE URTON (I)
     1975-. Bds: Park Bd. B: 12/16/42. Add:
105 N. Locust, Urich 64788 (816)638-4415.

Vanduser. MURIEL BURTON
     City Hall, Vanduser 63784.

Velda Village Hills. MYRTLE L. O'GORMAN
     3501 Avondale Ave., Normandy 63121.

Verona. JANE JOHNSON (R) **
     1972-. Bds: Bicentennial. Party: Local Com.
1954-58. Occ: Owner, Printing Business. B:
1/13/19. Add: Box 97, Verona 65769.

Verona. BOBBIE PRUENTE
     City Hall, Verona 65769.

Vinita Park. VIRGINIA A. BIRA
     8374 Midland Blvd., St. Louis 63114.

Vinita Terrace. ELEANOR A. FINNERAN
                 LAURA FREEMAN
                 RUTH TATE
     7956 Page, St. Louis 63114.

Walker. HAZEL WOOD
     City Hall, Walker 64790.

Warrensburg. DELORES HUDSON (D)
     1976-. Mayor Pro Tem. Bds: V-Ch., Regional
Planning Cmsn.; Health Services Agency; Traffic
Cmsn. Prev: Beautification Cmsn. 1975-76. Org:
AAUW; Mo. Municipal League; Community Council.
Educ: Kan. State Teachers Coll. 1959 BSEd; 1962
MS. Occ: Teacher. B: 12/6/36. Add: 6 Locust
La., Warrensburg 64093 (816)747-9131.

Warrenton. DORENE E. REESE (R)
     1976-. Bds: Liaison, Dispatchers Bd.;
Regional Manpower Adv. Bd. B: 9/14/27. Add:
208 Thurman, Warrenton 63383 (314)456-8293.

Washington. L. JUNE KLEBERGER (R)
     1975-. Bds: Bd. of Health. Party: State
Del. 1976; City Committeewoman 1975-77. Org:
Mo. Society of Professional Engineers; Cnty.
Rep. Central Com. Occ: Consulting Engr. Firm
Promoter. B: 6/5/32. Add: 111 Old Pottery Rd.,
Washington 63090 (314)239-4724.

Waverly. NAIDA FENNER
     City Hall, Waverly 64096.

Weatherby. ERMA HUTSON
     City Hall, Weatherby 64497.

Weaubleau. VIRGINIA MURNAN (I)
     1972-. Prev: Cnty. Library Bd. 1970-78.
Educ: Central Mo. State U. 1930 BS. Add:
Weaubleau 65774.

Webb City. KATHRYN PATTEN
     P.O. Box 30, 35-37 Main St., Webb City
64870.

Webster Groves. DOROTHY ANNE CARROLL DRINKHOUSE(R)
     1972-. Bds: Health Cmsn. Org: LWV. Educ:
DePauw U. 1952 BA. B: 10/18/30. Add: 222 S.
Maple, Webster Groves 63119 (314)961-4100.

Wellston. VELDIA BROWN
     6205 Dr. Martin Luther King Dr., Wellston
63133.

Wenchester. MRS. LORE CROWE
     109 Lindy, Manchester 63011.

Wentzville. GLORIA JEAN EHLL (I)
     1975-. Bds: Park Bd., Selection Com. for
City Administration. Prev: Insurance Com. 1975-
77. Educ: U. of Mo. 1970 BS. B: 5/26/49.
Add: 524 Cheryl Ann Dr., Wentzville 63385
(314)327-5101.

Wilbur Park. YVONNE BALDRIDGE
     9018 Rosemary, Afton 63123.

Winfield. MABLE HARDING
     City Hall, Winfield 63389.

Wright City. PEGGY FLEIHMAN
     P.O. Box 436, Wright City 63390.

Wyatt. ETHEL D. SMALL
     City Hall, Wyatt 63882.

State Boards and Commissions

Governor's Office, State Capitol Bldg.,
Kansas City 64126.

Aging, Advisory Council on
VIRGINIA BEARD
QUINNE BENTON
MARGARET CAREY
MAMIE F. HUGHES
CHRISTINE JONES
JEANE JONES
SISTER M. MAGDALENE
CAROL W. PATTERSON
JOYCE RAYE PATTERSON
MRS. PAT WALKER

Alcoholism and Drug Abuse, Advisory Council on
KATIE BLANCHARD
MARY BOEGER
GERALDINE FOX
VIRGINIA GRADY
ARAMINTA SMITH
MARTHA STEPHENSON

Appellate Judicial Commission
ROSE MARIE NEHER

Bi-State Development Agency
JACQUELINE PHILLIPS

Blind Advisory Committee, Bureau for the
CHARLYN ALLEN
MARIE BUSCH
ELVA HAYES
SHERI STINEBAKER
ELLEN THOMAS

Clean Water Commission
BETTY WILSON

Compensation Commission
MRS. G. DUNCAN BAUMAN

Comprehensive Health Planning, Advisory Council on
SISTER JOSEPHINE ATCHISON
ANITA BANKS
MRS. WILLIAM BOWIE
JOAN CRAWFORD
MARCELLA DE ALMEIDA
A.C. MARCELLA ESTERLY
MRS. JOHN NUNNINK
JUNE RHODES
CLAIRE RODRIGUEZ
MRS. FRED STEWARD
NADINE THURMAN
NORMA TOLO
LOLA UPSHAW
PAT WEIER

Cosmetology Board
RUTH ALLEN
WANDA BOLTON
BETTY SUE CROW
CARLENE ORR

Criminal Justice, Council on
LINDA SELF

Day Care Advisory Committee
VIRGINIA FISHER

MARGE GRANT
MARTY K. HIDE
JODY NEWMAN
PEGGY PEARL
ROSALIND PHILLIPS
MARY SHOCKLEY
SHIRLEY STUBBS
MARIANNE THOMAS
KARIN VAIL
FERN WEBSTER

Embalmers and Funeral Directors, Board of
CONNIE PICKERING
VORA WILSON
JULIE WINDLE

Emergency Medical Services
ADELLA BARE

Energy Council
CAROLYN LEUTHOLD
MRS. WILLIAM G. PHILLIPS
MRS. RHEAT SMITH

Environmental Improvement Authority
JANET EPPERSON

Governmental and Community Service Programs
CAROLYN FRICK
DOROTHY MOORE
CAROL PRICE
SHIRLEY ANN RENDLEN
VIRGINIA SWEARINGEN

Governor's Mansion Preservation Advisory
Commission
MRS. JOHN M. DALTON
MRS. LLOYD C. STARK

Handicapped, Coordinating Commission for the
HELEN ADREA
GRACE ROTH
MILLIE WIEJACZKA

Health, Board of
MARTHA HAMLINE
MARTHA RABE

Health Coordinating Council
MRS. LARRY BUTCHER
MARCELLA DE ALMEIDA
BETTY DICKEY
MRS. HARLAN FERGUSON
PRUDENCE FINK
SALLIE HAILEY
DOROTHY HARRISON
KATHLEEN ISRAEL
MRS. BARRY JACKSON
DONNA LINDAMON
VIVIENNE PONCE
JUNE RHODES
SISTER MARY ROCKLAGE
ANN ROSE
ESTELLA SMITH

Higher Education, Coordinating Board of
LELA BELL
VIRGINIA YOUNG

Historic Preservation, Advisory Council on
BARBARA IDE

Humanities, Committee for the
VERA F. BURK
CLAUDINE COX

Human Rights, Commission on
JEAN COLLINS
CARRIE L. DUNSON
JOAN KRAUSKOPF

Judicial Circuit Commission
MRS. PHILIP L. CHAMBERLAIN

Lewis and Clark Trail Commission
MRS. MARK THOMPSON

Manpower Planning, Office of
BETTY ADAMS

Mental Health Commission
BARBARA STARKS

Mental Retardation and Community Health, Advisory
Council on
MRS. DONALD WILCOX

Mental Retardation and Other Developmental
Disabilities, Advisory Council on
MARY PEREZ
SARIJANE FREIMAN
B. JANE GARRETT
MILDRED MARKS
GLADWOYN NORMAN
JOYCE WEBER

Mississippi River Parkway Commission
BETTY MILLS

Missouri School for the Blind Advisory Board
MARTHA HAMILTON

Nursing Board
SISTER MARY JEREMY BUCKMAN
MARY RUTH CUDDY
ZELLA HARRINGTON
JANET PORT
AUDREY ROBERTS
NORMA WILSON

Nursing Home Administrators, Board of
MRS. MAUDE GUNN
JANE PRESNELL

Nursing Home Advisory Council
SISTER AUGUSTINE CATON

Pharmacy Board
CAROLYN DICKSON

Public Defenders Commission
RUTH BENDER

Soil and Water District Commission
BETTY BROEMMELSIEK

State Tax Structure Study Commission
SUE ANN COCHRAN

Status of Women, Commission on the
BETTY ADAMS
VERA FUNK

MARJORIE GARANSSON
VIRGINIA HENDRICK
LEONA HUDAK
MARGERY LEHENBAUER
ALBERTA MEYER
KAREN PASSAGE
GERRY PRICE
SAPHRONIA RENFRO
WILMA SUTTON
DATHERIN WEYHRICH

Thomas Hart Benton Homestead Memorial Commission
MRS. JESSIE BENTON LYMAN

Transportation Commission
BINA S. DAVIS

Vocational Education, Advisory Council on
MRS. CHARLES BAILEY
MARY C. KASTEN
BETTY WATT

Youth Services Advisory Board
ELIZABETH JORDAN

Montana

State Executive and Cabinet

GEORGIA RUTH RICE (D)
    Superintendent of Public Instruction. 1977-.
Bds: Land Bd.; Library Bd.; Bd. of Public Educ.
Org: Amer. Fed. of Teachers; LWV; Amer. Assoc.
Health, Physical Educ. & Recreation; NEA; Nat.
Safety Council. Educ: Eastern Mont. Coll. 1957
BSEd. B: 6/4/36. Add: P.O. Box 947, Helena
59601 (406)449-3654.

State Legislature

State Senate

PAT REGAN (D)
    204 Mountain View, Billings 59101.

MARGARET S. WARDEN (D)
    1974-. Bds: Ch., Fish & Game Com.; V-Ch.,
Environmental Quality Council; Ch., Ad Hoc
Archives Preservation Com. Party: State Del.
1975. Prev: White House Conf. on Libraries 1975-;
Com. on Libraries 1975- ; Adv. Council for
Vocational Ed. 1976; State Library Com. 1973-75.
Org: ALA; Society Amer. Archivists; LWV; Rati-
fication Council ERA; State Dem's.; Cnty. Dem's.
B: 7/18/17. Add: 208 3rd Ave. N., Great Falls
59401.

State House

ESTHER G. BENGTSON (D) **
    Dist: 59. Educ: Eastern Mont. Coll. BS. Occ:
Teacher. B: 10/30/27. Add: Shepherd 59079.

DOROTHY BRADLEY (D)
    1970-. Party: State Del. 1976, '72; Nat. Del.
1976, '72. Org: ACLU; Common Cause; WPC; Dem.
Women's Club. Educ: Colo. Coll. 1969 BA. B:
2/24/47. Add: 427 N. Tracy, Bozeman 59715
(406)449-3064.

EDITH E. COX (R)
    1976-. Dist: 74. Bds: Natural Resource Com.;
Health Com.; Capitol Ground & Improvement Interim
Com. Party: State Del. 1976; Nat. Del. 1976;
Campaign Ch., 1974-75; V-Ch., Cnty. Central Com.
1974-77. Org: Nat. Music Teachers Assoc.; Rep.
Women's Club. Occ: Piano Teacher. B: 7/15/21.
Add: 316 N. 5, Livingston 59047 (406)222-1016.

AUBYN A. CURTISS (R)
    P.O. Box 102, Fortine 59918.

ANN MARY DUSSAULT (D) **
    1974-. Dist: 95. Bds: Educ.; Public Health,
Welfare & Safety; Advisory Council Office of
Public Instruction; Select Com. on Censure; Child
Abuse, Dept. of Social & Rehabilitation Services.
Org: Assoc. for Music Therapy; LWV; Dem. Club;
Dem. Women's Club. Educ: Mich. State U. 1971
BA. Occ: Coordinator, Child Dev. Center. B:
5/23/46. Add: Rt. 2, Mullan Rd., Missoula
59801.

JO ELLEN ESTENSON (D)
    608 North Rodney, Helena 59601.

EDNA A. GUNDERSON (D)
    612 Ninth Street, Havre 59501.

ORA J. HALVORSON (D)
    Dist:16. Bds: State Coal Oversight Com.;
Appropriations; Local Govt. Party: State Del.
1972-76; State Alt. 1970; Precinct Committee-
woman 1966- . Org: Fed. of Women's Clubs; DAR;
Dem. Party; NOW; Nat. Women Legislators; WPC.
Educ: Flathead Vly. Community Coll. 1969 AA;
Goddard Coll. 1973 BA. B: 12/31/13. Add:
244 Woodland Ave., Kalispell 59601.

POLLY HOLMES (D)
    1972-. Dist: 67. Bds: V-Ch., Public Health
& Safety; House Judiciary. Party: State Del.
1972, '74; Precinct Committeewoman 1968-72.
Org: Common Cause; Faculty Women's Club. Educ:
State U. of Ia. 1945 BS. B: 5/10/23. Add:
1620 Ave. F, Billings 59102 (406)449-5600.

V. JEAN MC LANE (R)
    Box 186, Laurel 59044.

HELEN O'CONNELL (D) **
    Dist: 34. Prev: City Council Alderwoman.
B: 7/15/17. Add: 703 4th Ave., SW., Great
Falls 59404.

AUDREY ROTH (R)
    Box 489, Big Sandy 59520.

County Commissions

Petroleum. MRS. ROBERT WEINGART
    Winnett 59087.

Silver Bow. BEVERLY HAYES (D)
    1977-. Bds: Ch., Community Service; Public
Works; Judicial. Org: Women's Protective; Dem.
Women; Historical Preservation. Occ: Cafe Owner.
B: 5/25/30. Add: 801 W. Galena, Butte 59701
(406)722-6655.

Mayors

Belt. SHIRLEY MURPHY
    City Hall, Belt 59412.

Boulder. OLIVE HAGADONE
    City Hall, Boulder 59632.

Broadview. BETTY BREWINGTON (R) **
Prev: Alderwoman 1968-75. Occ: Postal Clerk.
B: 8/3/23. Add: Box 96, Broadview 59015 (406)
667-4463.

Clyde Park. FERN LOGAN
City Hall, Clyde Park 59018.

Eureka. BARBARA J. MORGAN (R) **
1975-. Bds: Health Bd.; Planning Cmsn. Prev:
Alderwoman 1973-75. B: 3/6/29. Add: Box 331,
Eureka 59917. (406)296-2821.

Fairfield. GAYLE E. WOOD (I)
1977-. Bds: Cnty. Planning Bd.; Cnty. Mental
Health Bd. Org: Women's Club. B: 11/17/40.
Add: P.O. Box 22, Fairfield 59436 (406)467-2510.

Helena. KATHLEEN RAMEY
1977-. Prev: Central Neighborhood Council
1968-71; Model City Bd. of Dir's. 1968-71. Org:
NEA; Zonta; Amer. Business Women. Educ: Creighton
U. 1945 BA; 1947 MA. Occ: Russian-English Teacher.
B: 5/25/17. Add: 1511 1/2 Railroad Ave., Helena
59601 (406)442-2817.

Jordan. MARY ANN ENGDAHL
City Hall, Jordan 59337.

Kalispell. NORMA E. HAPP
City Hall, Kalispell 59901.

Local Councils

Bearcreek. PEARL DE VILLE (D)
1977-. Org: Nat. Retired Teachers Assoc.;
Woman's Club. Educ: Eastern Mont. Coll. 1935
BSEd. B: 9/23/15. Add: Bearcreek 59007.

Bearcreek. FIINA H. FORD.
City Hall, Bearcreek 59007.

Bearcreek. PEARL A. JONES (R)
B: 2/12/07. Add: Box 269, Bearcreek 59007.

Belt. MARJ DICKMAN
City Hall, Belt 59412.

Big Timber. LOIS D. BJORNDAL (R)
1974-. Bds: Ch., City-Cnty. Planning Bd.; Ch.,
Finance; Ch., Fire & Water. Org: Women's Club;
Chamber of Commerce; Rep. Women's Club. Occ:
Secretary & Bookkeeper. B:11/18/45. Add: 512 E.
4th, Big Timber 59011 (406)932-2489.

Big Timber. MARGARET LAVOID
City Hall, Big Timber 59011.

Billings. JANE A. LLOYD (I)
1977-. Bds: City-Cnty. Planning Bd. Prev:
Citizens Transportation 1975-77; Citizens Planning
Com. 1975-77. Org: LWV; PTA. Educ: Niagara U.
1956 BS. B: 1/19/35. Add: 2117 Iris Lane,
Billings 59107 (406)248-7511.

Billings. LUCILLE MILLS
City Hall, Billings 59101.

Billings. MARIE THOMPSON (D)
1973-. Bds: Personnel Com. Prev: Cmsn.
Community Affairs 1975-77; Animal Control 1975-
77; Personnel Com. 1975-77; Recreation Bd. 1975-
77; Park Bd. 1973-75. Org: Jr. League; Dem.
Women; Dem. Party. Educ: Dickinson State Coll.
1960 BS; U. of Colo. 1962 MA. B: 11/18/38.
Add: 123 Lewis, Billings 59101 (406)248-7511.

Cascade. CLARA MAE FRASER
Bds: Ch., Cemetery Com. Prev: Cemetery Bd.
1965-77. B: 11/19/31. Add: 324 2nd St. N.,
Cascade 59421 (406)468-2836.

Chester. BONNIE JOHNSON
DEANNA KEITH
City Hall, Chester 59522.

Clyde Park. MURIEL HANSEN
ETHEL RICHARDSON
City Hall, Clyde Park 59018.

Denton. DORIS E. MOSSEY
B: 3/4/13. Add: 819 Lehman Ave., Denton
59430 (406)567-2228.

Denton. MAUDE ROWE
City Hall, Denton 59430.

Dillon. BILLIE ANN MC GOVERN
City Hall, Dillon 59725.

Dodson. LILA KODALEN
City Hall, Dodson 59524.

Dutton. LAURA J. NOWLIN
City Hall, Dutton 59433.

Ekalaka. BEVERLY COONS **
1975-. Bds: Park; Swimming Pool. Org: Geological Society. Educ: Eastern Mont. Coll. 1974
BS. Occ: Teacher. B: 12/31/29. Add: Box 343,
Ekalaka. 59324.

Ekalaka. BETH DEAN
LORNA GROSS
City Hall, Ekalaka 59324.

Ennis. LAURA DYER **
1975-. Occ: Office Manager. B: 4/15/35.
Add: Box 454, Ennis 59729 (406)682-4287.

Eureka. EVA JEAN EKHOLT
City Hall, Eureka 59917.

Fairfield. PAULINE DAHL
City Hall, Fairfield 59436.

Fromberg. DORIS COLLINS
City Hall, Fromberg 59029.

Glendive. MARY LOU BRENNER
INEZ SVINGEN
City Hall, Glendive 59330.

Hamilton. JUANITA H. HORK (R) **
1968-. Bds: Council on Aging; Human Society
Bd.; Library Bd. Party: State Com. 1966-74;
V-Ch., County Central Com. 1967-74; Precinct
Com. 1964-74. Org: AAUW; League of Cities.

Educ: U. of Mont. 1964 BA. B: 8/12/20. Add:
521 S. 8th, Hamilton 59840 (406)363-2101.

Hardin. ELIZABETH BRENNAN
     City Hall, Hardin 59034.

Harlem. JOAN COLUMBUS
     City Hall, Harlem 59526.

Harlowton. CONNIE J. THOMPSON (I)
     1976-. Bds: Police Com.; Recreation Com.;
Sanitation. Occ: Saleswoman. B: 2/12/46. Add:
415 3rd St., S.E., Harlowton 59036 (406)
632-4697.

Havre. BARBARA ABELL CONLEY (D) **
     1971-. Bds: Ordinance Com.; Water Com.; Sewer
& Plumbing; Bd. of Adjustments. Party: Precinct
Com. 1970- ; County Central Com. Prev: Deputy
Registrar 1968-70. Org: PTA. Occ: Office
Manager. B: 11/8/32. Add: 518 2nd St., Havre
59501 (406)265-6719.

Havre. SALLY THOMPSON
     City Hall, Havre 59501.

Ismay. BERDETTE ASKIN
     City Hall, Ismay 59336.

Kalispell. JEAN R. BLEKEN
          LAUREN GRANMO
     City Hall, Kalispell 59901.

Laurel. SUSAN CARTER
     City Hall, Laurel 59044.

Lima. BONNIE MERRELL
     City Hall, Lima 59739.

Malta. SHIRLEY A. LEGG (I)
     1977-. Prev: Ch., Local Govt. Study Cmsn.
1974-77. Org: FEW; Chamber of Commerce. Occ:
Mgr., Credit Union. B: 9/29/30. Add: 612 6th
Ave. E., Malta 59538 (406)654-1251.

Manhattan. LOIS WHITE
     City Hall, Manhattan 59741.

Melstone. MARY G. WALKER (R)
     1977-. B: 1/11/28. Add: Box 6, Melstone
59054 (406)358-3841.

Miles City. LEOTA L. HENRICHS (D) **
     1973-. Bds: Police & Fire; Lands; Public
Transportation; Community Dev. Org: School
Community Council. B: 10/2/34. Add: 718 N.
6th, Miles City 59301 (406)232-3462.

Missoula. JEANNE RANSAVAGE
     City Hall, Missoula 59801.

Moore. ELIZABETH H. DAVIS (I)
     1972-. Bds: Road Com.; Ch., Library Com.
Occ: Hot Lunch Program Supervisor. B: 12/29/15.
Add: Box 58, Moore 59464 (406)374-2274.

Nashua. BARBARA BONER (D) **
     1973-. Org: Dem. Club; Nurses Assoc.; PTA.
Educ: St. Joseph School of Nursing 1943 RN. Occ:
Head Nurse. B: 11/14/19. Add: Box 52, Nashua
59248 (406)746-3461.

Plains. WILMA WEST
     City Hall, Plains 59859.

Plevna. LILLIAN ANDERSON
     City Hall, Plevna. 59344.

Poplar. JEAN DANIELSON
     City Hall, Poplar 59255.

Richey. MARILYN BUECHLER
     City Hall, Richey 59259.

Roundup. JEANETTE E. DEVINE (D)
     1977-. Bds: Ch., Garbage Com.; Flood.
Party: State Del. 1976; Sec., Dem. Cnty. Com.
1976. Prev: Study Cmsn. on Local Govt. 1974-76.
Org: Dem. Women's Club. Occ: Asst. Mgr.,
Lumberyard. B: 11/16/32. Add: 945 1st St., W.,
Roundup 59072.

Roundup. THELMA KEY
     City Hall, Roundup 59072.

Saco. ALMA MC CUIN
     City Hall, Saco 59261.

St. Ignatius. ESTHER S. BICK (R) **
     1971-. Org: PTA. Occ: Clerk, Bookkeeper;
Meat Cutter. B: 11/21/35. Add: Box 168, St.
Ignatius 59865 (406)745-2656.

Sunburst. BONNIE DYRDAHL
     City Hall, Sunburst 59482.

Superior. MARY GUNDERSON
     City Hall, Superior 59872.

Terry. DOROTHY SCHEID
     City Hall, Terry 59349.

Townsend. MARY ALICE UPTON
     City Hall, Townsend 59644.

Twin Bridges. MARIE MC ALEAR (R)
     1975-. Bds: Ch., Judiciary & Public Order
Standing Com.; Leg. Com., Mont. League of Cities
& Towns; City & Cnty. Planning Bd. Party:
State Del. 1976-77; Precinct Committeewoman 1976-;
Cnty. Committeewoman 1977- . Prev: Cnty. Census
Dir. 1970; Local Govt. Study Cmsn. 1975-77.
Org: AAUW; Resource Conservation & Devt.; Mont.
League of Cities & Towns; Com. for Mont. Chil-
dren's Ctr.; Mont. Women's Resource; Cnty.
Rep's.; WPC. Educ: U. of Mont. 1965 BA;
Western Mont. Coll. 1973 MS. Occ: Bookkeeper.
B: 5/29/43. Add: Box 364, Twin Bridges 59754.

Virginia City. COLLEEN CRANE
               VAEDA SCHEITLIN
     City Hall, Virginia City 59755.

Walkerville. MAURINE M. DENNEHY (D)
     1975-. Occ: Taxi Dispatcher. B: 4/15/21.
Add: 506 W. Daly St., Walkerville 59701.

West Yellowstone. CHERYL LYONS
     City Hall, West Yellowstone 59758.

Whitehall. LYNDA ZIESING
     City Hall, Whitehall 59759.

White Sulphur Springs. NETTEMAE BINNIE
    City Hall, White Sulphur Springs 59645.

Winnett. EVA LENGEMANN
          HELEN QUIGG
    City Hall, Winnett 59087.

State Boards and Commissions

A complete list of state boards and commissions,
and of their membership, was not available for
inclusion.

Nebraska

State Executive and Cabinet

M. ANNE CAMPBELL (R)
    Commissioner of Education. 1975-. Bds: Cmsn.
on Drugs; Cmsn. on Alcoholism; Dev. Disabilities
Cmsn. Party: State Del. 1958-62, '68. Prev:
Cnty. Superintendent of Schools 1955-63; Cmsn. on
the Status of Women 1962-72. Org: Amer. Assoc.
of School Administrators; AAUW; BPW; LWV; Nat.
Adv. Council for Women's Educ. Programs. Educ:
U. of N. Colo. 1938 BA; Wayne State Coll. 1959
MS; U. of Neb. 1969 EdD. B: 11/13/17. Add: 7500
South St. #8, Lincoln 68506 (402)471-2465.

State Legislature

State Senate

BERNICE LABEDZ
    4417 S. 40th Street, Omaha 68107.

SHIRLEY MAC MARSH (R)
    1974-. Dist: 29. Bds: Appropriations Com.;
Intergovt. Cooperation Com.; V-Ch., Com. on Com's.
Party: Cnty. Del., Rep. Cnty. Conv. 1976. Org:
BPW; AAUW; NOWL; Neb. Welfare Assoc.; Neb. Fed. of
Rep. Women; Neb. Adv. Com. to the U.S. Cmsn. on
Civil Rights. Educ: U. of Neb. BA. B: 6/22/25.
Add: 2701 S. 34th St., Lincoln 68506 (402)
471-2734.

County Commissions

Buffalo. DORALENE E. WEED (R)
    1977-. Bds: Ch., Welfare Com.; Law Enforcement
Com. Party: State Alt. 1968-76; Secretary, Cnty.
Rep. Women 1970-74; Precinct Leader 1968-72.

Org: Cnty. Rep. Women. Occ: Saleswoman. B:
6/25/31. Add: 2805 Ave. F, Kearney 68847
(308)237-5981.

Cherry. MABEL D. JONES (R)
    1975-. Bds: Ch., Welfare; Multi-Social;
V-Ch., Mental Health Governing Bd. Prev: Cnty.
4-H Council Ch. 1960-66; Pres., Cnty. Rural
Schools 1973-75; Sec., Cnty. Re-Org. Bd. 1970-
74; Sec., Cnty. Dist. 1972-75. Org: Neb. Stockgrowers; Neb. Cowbelles; Drug Council; NE Neb.
Opportunity Ctr. Adv. Bd.; Educ. Com. of Stockgrowers. Occ: Rancher. B: 3/31/14. Add:
Whitman 69366 (402)376-2420.

Dixon. DOROTHY MATTES
    Allen 68710.

Mayors

Auburn. AUDRE BLANKENSHIP (R) **
    1974-. Bds: Civic Affairs. Prev: Council-
woman 1972-74. Org: Children & Youth Bd. Occ:
Medical Insurance Claims. B: 1/17/16. Add:
1211 17th St., Auburn 68305 (402)274-3420.

Belvidere. VIOLA BRUNING
    City Hall, Belvidere 68315.

Craig. VIVIAN E. CARLSON
    City Hall, Craig 68019.

Crawford. BETTY M. NORGARD (R) **
    1976-. Bds: Nursing Homes. Prev: Council
1972-76. Org: Nat. Assoc. of Parliamentarians;
Chamber of Commerce; Rep. Women's Club. B:
11/9/30. Add: 920 4th St., Crawford 69339
(308)665-1336.

Curtis. JOYCE PETERSON
    City Hall, Curtis 69025.

Gandy. ARWILLA KRAMER
    City Hall, Gandy 69137.

Gilead. LORAINE GIBSON
    City Hall, Gilead 68362.

Gordon. JANE D. MORGAN (D)
    1975-. Bds: Planning Cmsn. Prev: Council-
woman 1974-75. Occ: Office Manager. B:4/23/41.
Add: 325 Elm, Gordon 69343 (308)282-0837.

Lincoln. HELEN G. BOOSALIS (D) **
    1965-. Bds: Implementation Com.; Officials
Com.; Health Planning Council. Prev: Councilwoman 1959-75. Org: Assoc. of Health Planners.
B: 8/28/19. Add: 3019 Jackson Dr., Lincoln
68502. (402)475-5611.

Merriman. VIVIAN M. THAYER (R)
    1976-. Occ: Store Clerk. B: 6/19/38. Add:
Box 164, Merriman 69218 (308)684-3356.

Nebraska City. EDITH FENSTERMACHER
    City Hall, Nebraska City 68410.

North Loup. BONNIE B. SEVERANCE (R)
    1976. Bds: Ch., Health Bd. Prev: Vlg. Bd.
1974-78. Org: Community Improvement. Occ:
Cafeteria Manager/Dietician. B: 5/2/31. Add:
Box 68, N. Loup 68859 (308)496-4891.

Sidney. LEE-ELLEN MATZKE
    City Hall, Sidney 69162.

Silver Creek. JANET J. BROCKMAN (R)
    1974-. Bds: Ch., Bd. of Trustees. Org:
Civic Club. Occ: Banker. B: 12/13/32. Add:
Silver Creek 68663 (308)773-2477.

Snyder. GALE MAHNKE
    City Hall, Snyder 68664.

Steele City. SUSAN V. TAYLOR (D) **
    1974-. Bds: Agency on Aging. Org: DAR; OES.
Educ: 1925 BA; U. of Neb. 1949 BS. B: 6/18/03.
Add: City Hall, Steele City 68440 (402)442-2681.

Terrytown. BARBARA CARPENTER
    City Hall, Terrytown 69341.

Local Councils

Ainsworth. LOIS CAMPBELL
    City Hall, Ainsworth 69210.

Alexandria. ERMA BENNETT
    Village Hall, Alexandria 68303.

Arthur. JANET MAGNUSON
    City Hall, Arthur 69121.

Atkinson. JOYCE WHITE
    City Hall, Atkinson 68713.

Aurora. BERNADINE A. WANEK (D)
    1975-. Bds: Com. of Improvement & Dev.; Ch.,
Police Com.; Licenses & Permits. Educ: St. Agnes
School of Nursing 1951 RN. Occ: RN. B: 4/12/30.
Add: 1411 12th St., Aurora 68818 (402)694-3571.

Bartlett. KAREN DAY
    Town Hall, Bartlett 68622.

Bassett. LYNDA PARSON RADANT (R)
    1976-. Bds: Ch., Parks & Recreation Bd. Org:
Community Improvement Assoc.; Child Care Ctr.;
Cultural Arts Council. Educ: U. of Nebr. 1972
BS. Occ: Home Economist. B: 7/7/49. Add: 401
Clark St., Bassett 68714.

Bayard. VERN HUCK
    City Hall, Bayard 69334.

Bellevue. INEZ M. BOYD (R)
    1972-. Org: Jr. Women's Club; Bd. of Dir's.,
League of Municipalities. Educ: Kan. State U.
1957 BS. B: 1/2/36. Add: 1416 Fairfax Rd.,
Bellevue 68005.

Belvidere. LINDA HUDSON
    City Hall, Belvidere 68315.

Benedict. JOAN BITTINGER
    City Hall, Benedict 68316.

Bennington. LEOLA BONGE
    City Hall, Bennington 68007.

Berwyn. LYNN FOSTER
    City Hall, Berwyn 68819.

Bladen. BONNIE SCHILLING
    City Hall, Bladen 68928.

Blue Hill. LUCILLE M. KINNEY (D)
    1974-. Org: OES. B: 5/17/22. Add: Box 327,
Blue Hill 68930 (402)742-6441.

Brady. LUCILLE FERN WHIPPLE (D)
    1975-. Prev: Ch., Community Improvement
1967-72. Org: Extension Club. Occ: Upholstery
Shop Owner. B: 5/31/37. Add: Box 97, Brady
69123.

Brewster. BLANCHE NORRIS
    City Hall, Brewster 68821.

Broadwater. MARTHA EUSE
    City Hall, Broadwater 69125.

Brownville. ETHEL MINER
    City Hall, Brownville 68321.

Campbell. MADIE BURG
    SANDRA POE
    City Hall, Campbell 68932.

Ceresco. BONNIE J. FINLEY (D)
    1976-. Bds: Ch., Parks & Recreation. Occ:
Credit Mgr. B: 11/19/36. Add: Box 205,
Ceresco 68017 (402)665-2391.

Chadron. MARY V. HORSE
    City Hall, Chadron 69337.

Comstock. MARILYN KALLHOFF (D)
    1976-. Bds: Park & Sewer. Occ: Barmaid.
B: 8/29/35. Add: Comstock 68828.

Cornlea. KATHERINE KORTH
    City Hall, Cornlea 68630.

Crab Orchard. SHIRLEY ROTHELL
    City Hall, Crab Orchard 68332.

Crete. LILLIAN L. DUDLEY (D)
    1974-. Bds: Personnel & Finance; Ch., Bldg.
& Grounds. Prev: Library Bd. 1970-74. Org:
NEA. Educ: Doane Coll. 1955 BA; U. of Nebr.
1971 MM. Occ: Music Teacher. B: 4/21/34.
Add: RFD 1, Crete 68333 (402)826-4311.

Dakota City. SHIRLEY F. HUGHES
    City Hall, Dakota City 68731.

Dakota City. SHIRLEY YVONNE SIDES (R)
    1976-. Org: Postal Union. Occ: Rural Mail
Carrier. B: 4/25/35. Add: 1709 Myrtle, Dakota
City 68731.

Du Bois. GRACE HAIGHT
    City Hall, Du Bois 68345.

Dwight. PAULINE C. KADAVY (D)
    1974-. Party: Election Bd. Counting Judge
1976 . Occ: Teacher. B: 1/27/27. Add:

Box 123, Dwight 68635.

Elba. SHARON L. CONLEY
City Hall, Elba 68835.

Elm Creek. BARBARA I. SWARTZ (I)
1976-. Occ: Motor Home Court Operator. B:
1/4/11. Add: Arendt Ave. & Beecroft St., Elm
Creek 68836 (308)856-4256.

Elmwood. KATHY COWAN
City Hall, Elmwood 68349.

Elsie. ELIZABETH BROWN
SANDY MC COWN
City Hall, Elsie 69134.

Emmet. THERESA SCHAAF
FAYE WHEELER
City Hall, Emmet 68734.

Eustis. NANCY JOHNSON
City Hall, Eustis 69028.

Eustis. ELSIE W. KOCH (R)
1972-. Bds: Council of Govts . B: 3/31/13.
Add: Eustis 69028.

Fairbury. SHIRLEY HOWELL
City Hall, Fairbury 68352.

Farnam. BEVERLY EDSON
City Hall, Farnam 69029.

Geneva. MARY ANN NAJMON (I)
1973-. Party: State Del. 1972; Cnty. V-Commit-
teewoman 1968-72. Org: ANA; Women's Club. Educ:
St. Catherine's Hospital 1957 RN. Occ: Dir.,
Nursing Service. B: 12/12/36. Add: 909 B.,
Geneva 68361.

Geneva. PAULETTE WISE
City Hall, Geneva 68361.

Gering. MATTIE LOU JONES
City Hall, Gering 69341.

Gothenburg. IRENE E. AYRES (R)
1977-. Org: Women's Club. Occ: Bookkeeper.
B: 6/30/19. Add: 2122 Ave. F, Gothenburg 69138
(308)537-3677.

Grand Island. LOU ANN SNYDER (R)
1974-. Prev: Health Bd. 1972-74. Org: LWV;
Dir., Goodwill Industries; Dir., Retired Sr.
Volunteer Program; PTA. B: 8/16/37. Add: 2515
Cochin, Grand Island 68801.

Greenwood. SANDRA L. HAMMERS (R)
1974-. Bds: Planning Com.; Park & Recreation.
B: 5/14/43. Add: Rt. 1, Greenwood 68366 (402)
789-2300.

Greenwood. ROBERTA HANSEN
City Hall, Greenwood 68366.

Gresham. VIOLET SWANSON
City Hall, Gresham 68367.

Harbine. MAXINE E. SCHWISOW (D) **
1974-. Bds: Historical; Election Bd. Party:
Local Precinct Com. 1962-64. Occ: Secretary &
Bookkeeper. B: 10/13/28. Add: Rt. 1, Jansen
68377 (402)754-4061.

Harrison. VIRGINIA C. COFFEE (R)
1973-. Bds: Ch., Park Bd. Prev: Ch., Sioux
Cnty. Bicentennial 1973-76; Governor's Ft.
Robinson Centennial Cmsn. 1973-75; State
Historical Society Foundation 1975- . Org:
Historical Society; Ladies Community Club.
Educ: Chadron State Coll. 1942 BA. Occ: Book-
keeper/Secretary. B: 12/8/20. Add: Box 336,
Harrison 69346 (308)668-2445.

Hebron. ELEANOR B. RIZEK (R)
1977-. Bds: Ch., Recreation; Finance;
Ordinance. Educ: Kan. State U. 1954 BA. B:
8/23/30. Add: 710 Olive Ave., Hebron 68370.

Holdrege. PATRICIA A. NELSON (R)
1976-. Bds: Ordinance Com.; Public Bldgs.
Com. Org: Service League. Educ: Lincoln Gen.
Hospital School of Nursing 1961 RN. Occ: RN.
B: 11/9/40. Add: 1024 Hancock, Holdrege 68949
(308)995-8681.

Homer. THELMA BAUGOUS
City Hall, Homer 68030.

Hooper. SUSAN KAY DEDIC (R) **
1974-. Bds: Streets & Sidewalk; Parks &
Bldgs. Prev: Library Bd. 1972-74. Org:
Bicentennial Com. Educ: U. of Neb. 1968 BS.
B: 10/14/46. Add: Box 44, Hooper 68031 (402)
654-3343.

Imperial. LAURINE MEININGER
City Hall, Imperial 69033.

Inglewood. RHODA PEARSON
City Hall, Inglewood 68025.

Lincoln. SUE OGDEN BAILEY (D) **
1973-. Bds: Downtown Advisory Com.; Crime
Cmsn.; Jail Study Com. Org: ACLU; LWV; PTA.
Educ: U. of Miami 1944 BA. B: 12/27/23. Add:
1800 S. 22nd St., Lincoln 68502 (402)473-6515.

Litchfield. THELMA LANG
City Hall, Litchfield 68852.

Lorton. LELA GAEDEN
City Hall, Lorton 68382.

Lushton. SARAH FRIESEN
City Hall, Lushton 68383.

Malcolm. LA VERA M. BENISCHEK (I)
1974-. Occ: Transcriber. B: 11/16/25. Add:
455 S. Lincoln, Malcolm 68402.

Marquette. EMILY MERSCH
City Hall, Marquette 68854.

Martin. CLAIR WALKER
Franklin 68939.

Maxwell. SANDRA S. KELLY (D)
    1976-. Occ: Bookkeeper. B: 12/19/46. Add:
Box 183, Maxwell 69150.

Nemaha. GLENDA PALMER
    City Hall, Nemaha 68414.

Oconto. ROBIN HENDRICKSEN
    City Hall, Oconto 68860.

Orchard. LYNN THELANDER
    City Hall, Orchard 68764.

Orleans. FLORENCE BLEES (D)
    Prev: Vlg. Treasurer. Org: Chamber of
Commerce; Civic Club. Occ: Cashier. B: 10/2/20.
Add: Box 375, Orleans 68966.

Oxford. JANICE ALLEN
    City Hall, Oxford 68967.

Ragan. MARIE SLOAN
    City Hall, Ragan 68969.

Republican City. LINDA LEWTON
    City Hall, Republican City 68971.

Roca. HARRIET GLOVER (D)
    1976-. Org: AFSCME. Occ: Gardener. B:
5/21/42. Add: Roca 68430 (402)423-3402.

Rogers. CLAIRE CONNERLEY
    City Hall, Rogers 68659.

Rulo. LUCILLE PRATER
    City Hall, Rulo 68431.

Scotia. DONNA FOXWORTHY (R)
    1976-. Org: Women's Club. B: 8/22/32. Add:
Scotia 68875 (308)245-4101.

Scottsbluff. MARJORIE L. MANDUJANO (D)
    1976-. Party: Precinct 1975-. Org: Nebr.
School Counselors; NEA. Educ: U. of Wyo. 1966 BA;
U. of N. Colo. 1975 MA. Occ: School Counselor.
B: 7/25/44. Add: 2413 Ave. D, Scottsbluff 69361.

Seneca. FLORENCE FINNEY
         SANDY HANSEN
         RETA MICHAEL
    City Hall, Seneca 69161.

Shubert. DONNA A. HALL (D) **
    1974-. Bds: Bicentennial Com.; Village Park
Bd. B: 12/19/47. Add: Box 51, Shubert 68437.

Silver Creek. FRANCES SOHL
    City Hall, Silver Creek 68663.

South Sioux City. VERN LARSON
    City Hall, South Sioux City 68776.

Springfield. VIRGINIA BUSKIRK
    City Hall, Springfield 68059.

Stratton. BEV EARNEST
    City Hall, Stratton 69043.

Sutton. MARLO MONSON
    City Hall, Sutton 68979.

Talmage. JUDY EICHENBERGER
    City Hall, Talmage 68448.

Tecumseh. ELLYN L. HOLDEN (R)
    1976-. Bds: Library Bd. Org: NFLPN. Educ:
Lincoln Technical Coll. 1970 LPN. Occ: LPN.
B: 2/7/21. Add: 261 N. 13, Tecumseh 68450
(402)335-3570.

Thayer. BEVERLY BRISTOL
    City Hall, Waco 68460.

Trenton. DOROTHY I. POWERS
    City Hall, Trenton 69044.

Valley. DOLORES M. LEWIS (D)
    1977-. Bds: Police Cmsnr. B: 11/21/35.
Add: 110 S. Pine, Valley 68064 (402)359-2251.

Walthill. CONNIE YOUNG
    City Hall, Walthill 68067.

Wauneta. DORTHY DUDEK
    City Hall, Wauneta 69045.

Wayne. CAROLYN FILTER
    City Hall, Wayne 68787.

Winslow. KAREN F. MEIERHENRY
    City Hall, Winslow 68072.

Wymore. BETTY BENDA
    City Hall, Wymore 68466.

Wynot. ELAINE UTESCH
    City Hall, Wynot 68792.

York. PATRICIA J. BLUM
    City Hall, York 68467.

Yutan. SHARON OGDEN
    City Hall, Yutan 68073.

State Boards and Commissions

        Office of the Governor, State Capitol Bldg.,
        Lincoln 68509.

Advisory Council
    BELLE KEITGES

Aging Advisory Panel, Commission on
    MABEL BAIRD
    CAROLYN CATHROE
    ESTHER HAMON
    IDA HEIL
    ALICE PORTER
    NETTIE RASS
    HELEN STORMS

Aging, Commission on
    RUTH BLANKENSHIP
    JOCIELL BULL
    LUCILLE DORWART
    IRMA ELROD
    CLAUDELLE GERLACH
    SISTER MARTHA HUND

JANET PETERSON
MARY STOTTS
DOROTHY SWITZER

Agricultural Products Industrial Utilization Committee
HOLLY HODGE

Alcoholism Advisory Council
DARLENE CORDING
BARBARA K. DETLEFSEN
MARY DIXON

Ambulance Advisors Board
MELBA SCOTT

American Revolution Bicentennial Commission
KATHY BLACKSTONE
MRS. WILLIAM H. HASEBROOCK
MRS. ALBERT A. KJAR
MRS. STANLEY A. MATZKE, SR.

Arts Council
MARIAN ANDERSEN
DIANE BRIDGE
DOROTHY CREIGH
BRETA DOW
BARBARA DOYLE
JANE GILMORE
JOAN NELSON

Certifications Advisory Committee
SARA EDWARDS
SISTER GENEVIEVE SCHILLO
SHIRLEY SLOUP
MRS. MARVIN C. STEWART

CHP Advisory Council
MADELINE AUFDENGARTEN
HELEN BOOSALIS
BEVERLY DOSE
MRS. ROBERT SHOEMAKER

College Approval Advisory Committee
MARTHA FRICKE
SHIRLEY KREUTZ
SISTER MARY PATRICUS MALONEY

Cosmetology, Board of Examiners
WILMA R. FEIT
ALTA SCHAFER
ANNA TIBBS

County Welfare Directors Program Committee
GARNET BROOM
DORIS CROCKER
LA VERN DICKINSON
FRANCES EVANS
GLADYS FITZGERALD
CLARA GRAMLICH
MILDRED JORGENSEN
ERMA RIPLEY
LA VERNE WEERS

Crippled Children's Committee
ELEANORE ENERSEN
EILEEN M. NOVOTNY
MRS. WILLIS H. TAYLOR, JR.

Developmental Disabilities Planning and Advisory Council
ANNE CAMPBELL
DEANNA COALSON
JANE HOFFART
HARRIET MAJOR
JANE MC MARTH
MARY MITCHELL
SANDY PEEKS

Drugs, Commission on
MADELINE CODER
MARY A. NEJEZCHLEB
PENNI PIRSCH
VIOLET RICHTER
KATHLEEN ROBACKER
MIRIAM WALDBAUM

Education and Vocation Education, Board of
DOROTHY CREIGH
MARILYN FOWLER
MARGARET LOCKWOOD

Election Commissioner
PATRICIA J. KREIFELS

Employment of the Handicapped, Committee for
NANCY ERICKSON
SUZI FISCHER
MAMIE M. LEACH
BETH MACY
KAY NEIL
MARY SANTIN
LOIS O. SCHWAB
FRANCES WARNSCHOLZ

Environmental Control Council
BETTY ABBOTT
MARGARET SUTHERLAND

Equal Opportunity Commission
BARBARA J. COFFEY
FRANCES DUNSON
DOROTHY HOLSTEIN

ETV Commission
M. ANNE CAMPBELL
MADELINE CODER

Hall of Fame Commission
MRS. PAUL ARMSTRONG
PAULINE STUCKEY
NELLIE YOST

Health, Board of
SHARON HOLYOKE
MRS. EMMETT SMITH

Historical Society
NELLIE SNYDER YOST

Home Economics Association of Organized Agriculture
ROSE FRAHM
KATHY SULLIVAN
JEANENE WEHRBEIN

Hospital and Medical Facilities, Advisory Council on
JEANETTE BECKNER

Indian Commission
MARY ELLEN HENRY
DOLORES KILLS
REBECCA PRENTICE
PAULINE TYNDALL

ITV Curriculum Advisory Committee
MARY ELLEN GOODENBERGER
JAN JOHANSEN
MARLYS MORTENSEN SAY

Judicial Nominating Commission
MRS. GAYWELLE GOODRICH

Law Enforcement and Criminal Justice, Commission on
MRS. DON ABERNETHY
MOLLY S. HIGGINS
MRS. CLIFFORD JORGENSEN

Library Commission
BARBARA SWANSON
MRS. FORREST SWOBODA

Manpower Planning, Advisory Council for
MYRNA WOODSIDE

Manpower Services Council
ANNE CAMPBELL

Massage, Board of Examiners
AGNES SWITZER

Mental Health Advisory Committee
DONNA CARSTENSON
WANDA MINDT
JENNY PEDERSON

Mental Retardation, Advisory Committe to the Office of
DOROTHY BEAVERS

Merit System Council
HELEN M. LASSEK

Nursing, Board of
EVELYN BAKER
LORETTA BURTIS
ROSANNA DYKEMAN
MARY ANN HOEFLER
PHYLLIS KENDLE
LINDSAY LEIBEE
MILDRED MEIER
SUE MORRISSEY
SHIRLEY ROBINS
SHEILA RYAN
RUTH WHITE

Nursing Home Administrators, Examiners for
MARY HANNA

Nursing Home Advisory Council
MRS. ROLAND CHRISTENSEN
ELAINE M. CONNELLY
CLARA FOX
JOAN HEINZMAN
SISTER ESTHER MARIE MILLER
MAXINE MORRISON

Parole, Board of
DORIS D. COLLINS
CATHERINE DAHLQUIST

Postsecondary Education, Coordinating Council for
ANNE CAMPBELL
MARY CAREY

Professional Practices Commission
NLYA ALEXANDER
LORENE KERNAN
HELEN KRAUSE
THELMA L. LANG
THERESA RAMIG
ANNE RANKS
GRACE W. SCHUMANN

Psychologists, Board of Examiners
MARGARET M. KRUSEN
DAWN E. PURINTON
CAROLINE SEDLACEK

Public Buildings Safety Advisory Committee
NANCY ERICKSON

Public Employees Retirement System
MARGARET SULLIVAN

Public Institutions for Visually Impaired, Advisory Committee to the Department of
MARSHA BANGERT
SHARON E. CARR
MRS. FRED FRANK
DOROTHY NIETO
DOROTHY PATRICK

Public Roads Classifications and Standards, Board of
MRS. PAT PETTERSEN

Public Water Supply, Advisory Council on
CATHERINE CODER
FRANCES MC CALL

Public Welfare Advisory Committee on Assistance and Services
DOROTHY BRUNT
SHARON CROSBY
SALLY DITMAR
MRS. CLIFFORD H. JORGENSON
GRACE LEE
LOTUS NICHOLAS
SALLE SAWYER
CHARLOTTE SHROPSHIRE
EVA WARE
RAMONA WOLFE
JOAN WOOTEN

Public Welfare, Institutions and Corrections Advisory Committee
SALLY BATES
MRS. ROBERT MATZ

Racing Commission
VIRGINIA M. COFFEY

Regional Child Care and Development Advisory Committee
THELMA ANDERSON
PAT APPALA
JODIE BAMESBERGER
MRS. ARLIS BURNEY
DOROTHY CALAHAN
GEORGELLA CALDWELL
BETTY COOKE

JOAN CROMER
MRS. LUCRETIAL DAILY
PAT DENNISON
KAREN DILLIN
ELOISE DILLON
SISTER JOAN DUNNING
BARB FLECK
JAN FLOHR
JANE FORD
MRS. LARRY FRIEDLAN
CAROL FRY
JERDA GAREY
KAREN GENRY
LINDA GONZALES
MRS. JONQUIL HABERER
MRS. DERALD HAMM
PAT HARDING
PAT HENDRICKS
THERESA HINMAN
DONNA HOWARD
ANGELA KEIERLEBER
CHARLOTTE KERN
MARY ANN KIRBY
JEAN LAING
CAROL LANE
MARY LIKES
MARILYN LOWERY
DOROTHY MAGNUSSON
BILLYE JO MAY
MATILDA S. MC INTIRE
MRS. LARRY MORGAN
LOIS MORRIS
SISTER ANNE MARIE MULLEN
MRS. JERRI MYFFLER
CAROL OLSON
LAVEDA PARKS
RITA PEREZ
DOROTHY PLUMMER
MARLENE RHOADES
EUNICE RIENSCHE
CHERRILL RIVERA
MYRTIS ROSS
MARY JO RYAN
KATHY SCHINKER
IRMA SCHROEDER
SUZIE SHARP
LILA SHERRERD
NANCY SMITH
GLORIA SNOW
WILMA STUTHEIT
ANNA Q. SUN
KAREN SWIHART
JULIE VAN METER
SALLY WENGERT
MARJORY WITULSKI
JOANIE ZIEGELBEIN

Renal Disease Advisory Committee
CAROL ANGLE

Right to Read Advisory Council
MAXINE ALLARD
YOLANDA CHAVES
BETTY JACOBSON
KATHY KAUFMAN
JOAN MONTGOMERY
MARY PETERSON
DOROTHY PORTER
NORMA STULL

Rural Rehabilitation Advisory Committee
MADELINE CODER
RUTH THOMPSON

School District Reorganization, Committee for
MARGARET ROBINSON

Special Education Advisory Council
SALLY MAJORS
MARGARET MC INTEER
MRS. WAYNE MEENTS
MRS. FRANK MIRIOVSKY
MRS. MARVIN NELSON
MRS. JACK STARK

Special Education Appeal Board
POLLY FEIS
MARJORIE HARTNETT
MARY KRIDER
DOROTHY LEY
MARJORIE SEDERBERG
MRS. JACK STARK

State Accreditation Committee
PAULINE BOTTORFF
MILDRED BROWNELL
MRS. K. BUCKLE
KATHY FARRIS
MRS. ROBERT MATZ

State Personnel Board
HELEN M. LASSEK

Status of Women, Commission on the
DOROTHY ANDREWS
PAULINE BENSON
PRINCIE BROWN
VIRGINIA COFFEY
GLADYS DALTON
MARYALICE DENNIS
SEANNE EMERTON
HOPE EDDY
FAYE D. GOMEZ
MARTHA GREER
MARY V. HORAN
JOAN KOCINA
BARBARA KRANTZ
RUTH KRUSE
KATHLYN KING LUNDGREN
RUTH MARESH
ROBERTA MC GOWEN
SHIRLEY L. MECKEL
THERESA MACIASMEDINA
MAXINE MOUL
MARTHA MUELLER
CATHERINE NORE
SUZANNE PANKONIN
MRS. JACK PLASTERS
NORMA STRUNK
JOAN I. TOMLINSON
MARIE VOGT
JULIE C. WOLSTROM
CLODY WRIGHT

Student Advisory Committee
ROBERTA GOODROAD
MALANIE GROSS
JANICE KLUCK
DONNA WANT

Technical Community Colleges, Board of
LORETTA DRAPER

Technical Community Colleges, Coordinating
Commission for
ANNE CAMPBELL
LORETTA DRAPER
RITA SHELDON

Title IV ESEA State Advisory Council
PATRICIA BECKENHAUER
POLLY J. FEIS
JANE GESKE
MARY ELLEN GOODENBERGER
DOROTHY LEY
SHIRLEY A. PETERSON
MARILYN SAMPSON

Title VI-B EHA Advisory Committee
SALLY MAJORS
MARGARET MC INTEER
MRS. WAYNE MEENTS
MRS. FRANK MIRIOVSKY
MRS. MARVIN NIELSON
MRS. JACK STARK

Trustees, Board of Nebraska State Colleges
ANNE CAMPBELL
TERESA GRAVES
ELDONNA HAZEN

Veterans' Advisory Commission
NELL KRAUSE

Vocational Education, Advisory Council for
JACQUELINE CRAWFORD
LORETTA DRAPER
CYNTHIA SUE DREVO
SISTER GENEVIEVE SCHILLO
DONNA SUHR
VIRGINIA A. VIEREGG
CODY WRIGHT

Nevada

State Executive and Cabinet

PEGGY GLOVER (D) **
Dir. of General Services. B: 4/25/23. Add:
230 S. Iris St., Carson City 89701 (702)
885-4094.

State Legislature

State Senate

MARGIE ELLEN FOOTE (D)
1975-. Dist: 2. Bds: Leg. Cmsn.; Interim.
Study Com.-State Dept. Educ. Party: State Del.
1956-64; Nat. Alt. 1964; Cnty. V-Ch. Prev:
State Assemblywoman 1967-75; Employment Security
Council 1965-66. Org: OES. Occ: Children's
Apparel Store Owner. B: 12/23/29. Add: 5585
Wedekind Rd., Sparks 89431.

MARY GOJACK (D)
1972-. Bds: Western Fed. Regional Council.
Prev: State Assemblywoman 1972-74. Org: AAUW;
NOWL; BPW; Common Cause; ACLU; Dem. State &
Cnty. Central Cmsn.; Nevadans for ERA; ASPA.
Educ: U. of Nev. 1968 BA. Occ: Bank Marketing.
B: 2/19/36. Add: 3855 Skyline Blvd., Reno
89509 (702)825-9652.

State House

EILEEN B. BROOKMAN (D)
1967-. Dist: 9. Bds: Senior Citizen Resource
Ctr. Adv. Bd.; Indian Affairs Cmsn.; Human
Relations Cmsn.; Nat. Com. for the Support of
Public Schools; Leg. Cmsn. Party: Cnty. Dem.
Central Com. Org: NAACP; National Conf. of
Christians & Jews; BPW. B: 10/25/21. Add:
1900 Cochran St., Las Vegas 89105.

NANCY A. GOMES (D)
1976-. Bds: Health & Welfare Com.; Educ.
Com.; Labor Com. Party: State Del. 1970-74;
State Treasurer 1972-74. Prev: Cnty. School
Trustee 1972-76; Deputy Dir. OEO 1968-70. Educ:
U. of Nev. 1948 BA. B: 6/19/26. Add: 1650
Reyburn Dr., Reno 89503 (702)885-5627.

KAREN WOOD HAYES (D)
1974-. Bds: Ch., Interim Com. on Transportation. Party: State Del. 1976. Org: OWL; S.
Nev. Drug Abuse; Citizens for Responsible Govt.;
Women's Dem. Club; PTA. Educ: Brigham Young U.
1959 BS. B: 10/16/35. Add: 6010 Euclid,
Las Vegas 89120.

SUE WAGNER (R)
1974-. Dist: 25. Party: State Del. 1974-76;
Cnty. Com. 1974-78; State Central Com. 1974-78;
Cnty. Exec. Com. 1974-78. Prev: Mayor's
Citizen Advisory Com. 1973-76. Org: BPW; AAUW;
Rep. Club; Women's Club. Educ: U. of Ariz.
1962 BA; Northwestern U. 1964 MA. B: 1/6/40.
Add: 845 Tamarack Dr., Reno 89509.

PEGGY WESTALL (D)
211 Galleron Way, Sparks 89431.

County Commissions

Carson City. THELMA DAVIS CALHOUN (R)
1974-. Bds: Nev. Cnty. Comsr's. Assoc.;
Nev. League of Cities; Devt. Review Bd. Prev:
Exec. Bd. of State Council on the Arts 1967-77;
State Land Use Cmsn. 1975-77; State Silver

Centennial Cmsn. 1959-60. Org: Rep. Women. Educ: Artist. B: 8/19/13. Add: 301 N. Anderson St., Carson City 89701 (702)882-5114.

Clark. THALIA M. DONDERO (D)
1975-. Bds: Areawide Policy Adv. Com.; Ch., Cnty. Criminal Justice Review Com.; CETA Exec. Bd. Party: State Del. 1973-76; Precinct Captain 1968-72. Prev: State Parks Cmsn. 1968-73. Org: Jr. League; Soroptomist; Dem. Club; PTA. B: 1/23/21. Add: 808 Bonita, Las Vegas 89101 (702)386-4011.

Douglas. YVONNE BERNARD (R)
1977-. Bds: Planning Cmsn.; Bd. of Equaliz-ation; Ch., Data Processing Com. Org: ANA; Cnty. Rep. Women's Club; Parent Faculty Group. Educ: St. Joseph Coll. 1958 RN. B: 1/20/38. Add: 118 10th St., Box 222, Minden 89423 (702)782-2763.

Storey. LORA M. DEL CARLO
Virginia City 89440.

Mayors

Caliente. DORIS MC GHIE
591 Main St., Caliente 89008.

Carlin. WANDA BORDEN (D)
1975-. Org: Nev. State Women. Occ: Beautician B: 8/4/29. Add: 125 Cortez Cir., Carlin 89822 (702)754-6354.

Local Councils

Carson City. THELMA DAVIS CALHOUN
See Carson City Cnty.

Ely. ADELE RATTAZZI
1174 Lyons Ave., Box 907, Ely 89301.

Gabbs. AILEEN M. WAKEFIELD
110 Main St., Gabbs 89409.

Henderson. LORNA JOLLEY KESTERSON (D)
1975-. Bds: Memorial Bd.; Regional Planning Council. Party: Precinct Leader. Occ: Managing Editor. B: 12/30/25. Add: 110 Fir St., Henderson 89015 (702)565-8921.

North Las Vegas. CYNTHIA BAUMANN
2608 Magnet St., N. Las Vegas 89030.

Reno. PAT HARDY LEWIS (R)
1973-. Bds: Reno-Sparks Joint Sewer Com.; Washoe Council of Govts.; V-Ch., Joint Airport Zoning Bd. Educ: U. of Nev. 1947 BA. B: 3/13/27. Add: 1290 W. Plumb Ln., Reno 89509.

Wells. CATHERINE I. IGOA
Shell Crest Motel, Wells 89835.

State Boards and Commissions

Office of the Governor, State Capitol Bldg., Carson City 89701.

Accountants' Grievance Committee
MARY O. KNAPP

Alcohol and Drug Abuse Advisory Board
MARTHA COON
MARRIETT SHELDON

American Revolution Bicentennial Commission
PAULEEN FOUTZ
HELEN HERR
SISTER MARGARET MC CARRAN
VICKI NASH

Archeological Council
SHEILAGH BROOKS
FLORENCE LEE CAHLAN
CELESTA LOWE
EDNA B. PATTERSON
MARY RUSCO
MARY ELLEN SADOVICH
MARGARET SCHNEIDER

Arts, Council on the
THELMA CALHOUN
DORIS EXBER
CHARLENE GOLDMAN
ELAINE S. LOPEZ
GLORIA MC DONALD
LILLIAN NALL
DOROTHY L. NEZ
GERI PALMERI
JOAN SNYDER
ARLENE SOUTHARD
MARIAN WELLS

Arts, Executive Board of the Council on the
CHARLENE GOLDMAN

Child Care Services Policy Board
ADELE BELLAS
JANET BUBNIS
MARY BURNETT
ROXIE CLAIBORNE
JEAN DUNN
JAN SPETH
LINDA THOMAS

Children and Youth, Advisory Council on
REBA E. DOLAN
EVELYN J. HARPER
LIESE HOLBERT
KATHLEEN LOU KELLEY
E. LAVONNE LEWIS
FRANCES F. MARTIN
LINDA EBERT OLSON
CARLEY L. SULLIVAN
JANIE TOBMAN

Colorado River Advisory Commission
EVELYN J. WEIKEL

Comprehensive Health Planning Advisory Council
ANNETTE EZELL
AUTUMN KEYES
SYLVIA RODRIGUEZ
JULIA VIANI
RITA ZAJAC

Conservation Commission
RILDA ERICKSEN

Cosmetology, Board of
    DOROTHY FEENEY
    BLANDA GANN
    DORA WILLIAMS
    MARILYN M. WILLIAMS

Credit Union Advisory Council
    MARGUERITE M. TOURREUIL

Crimes, Delinquency and Corrections, Commission on
    SISTER RICCARDA MOSELEY
    NANCY WILLIAMS

Dairy Commission
    PHYLLIS BERKSON
    MURIEL STEVENS

Education, Board of
    ROSEMARY K. CLARKE
    CYNTHIA W. CUNNINGHAM
    JOAN KENNY
    SHIRLEE A. WEDOW

Education Communications Commission
    HELEN CANNON

Eldorado Valley Advisory Group
    MARILYN R. HAMILTON
    JAN MAC EACHERN
    MRS. HENRY WEINSTEIN

Emergency Telephone Number Study Committee
    THALIA DONDERO

Employee-Management Relations Advisory Committee
    LEONA HENRY

Employment of the Handicapped, Committee on
    CATHY OLSON

Employment Security Council
    MRS. KAZUKO NOJIMA
    ELAINE WAR

Energy Resources Advisory Board
    PATTI BELDEN
    PAT HARDY LEWIS
    JEAN MAGOWAN
    MRS. JAY NELSON
    ADELE RATTAZZI

Environmental Commission
    ELLEN SHIRLEY

Environmental Education, Advisory Committee for
    RUTH J. ARMSTRONG
    MARY BARNETT
    BARBARA BURFORD

Equalization, Board of
    STEPHANIE A. SIRI

Fish and Game Advisory Board
    CARRIE DANN

4-H Camp Advisory Council
    BARBARA BYLINGTON
    BARBARA CURTI
    JUDY GARBARINO
    JUNE HANSON

    MRS. DE VOY MUNK
    SHIRLEY PARKER
    ANITA SMITH

Gaming Commission
    IRENE F. MORROS

Gaming Policy Committee
    JEAN STOESS

Health, Board of
    MRS. RICHARD FULSTONE
    JO GLEESON

Health Facilities Advisory Council
    MRS. MERTON DOMONOSKE
    MARJORIE ELMORE
    EDYTHE KATZ
    AUDREY L. MC CRACKEN
    JACQUELINE STORMSON

Hearing Aid Specialists, Board of
    HELEN CIBULKA

Higher Education, Western Interstate Commission for
    PATRICIA A. GEUDER

Historical Society Board of Trustees
    EDNA B. PATTERSON
    MARY ELLEN SADOVICH

Indian Commission
    JANET ALLEN
    WINONA L. HOLMES

Industrial Development Division Advisory Board
    SELMA BARTLETT

Land Use Planning Advisory Council
    THELMA CALHOUN
    MAGGI COLEMAN
    JANET H. EYRE
    MARYANNA HAMER
    DORIS MC GHIE

Landscape Architects, Board of
    MARJORIE B. IVARY

Libraries, Council on
    VERLIA G. DAVIS
    HAZEL M. POTTER

Local Government Employee-Management Relations Board
    SALLY S. DAVIS
    DOROTHY EISENBERG

Marriage and Family Counselor Examiners, Board of
    JUDI HAVAS KOSINSKI

Mental Hygiene and Mental Retardation Advisory Board
    ELEANOR GOTTSCHALK
    IDA HUBER
    SISTER MARIE BRIGID MC DONALD

Mobile Home and Travel Trailer Advisory Commission
    PAULINE T. DEWEY

Multiple Use Advisory Committee on Federal Lands
 ANNE L. ANDERSON

Nevada Girls Training Center Advisory Board
 ROSEMARY CONNOR
 LESLIE REGINATA
 HELEN CONAWAY
 DOROTHY RAGGIO
 MARJORIE RUBINSON

Nevada Youth Training Center Advisory Board
 MYRNA J. SPALDING

Nursing, Board of
 ALENE R. DICKINSON
 ALICIA M. GIANNOTTI
 JULIA IBARRA
 JANET I. KIMAK
 JULIA C. MAHER
 PATRICIA A. PEER
 RUTH ANN PURHONEN
 HILDA VARNEY

Occupational Safety and Health Review Board
 RUTH TINSLEY

Older Americans, Advisory Committee on
 SYBLE ASKENETTE
 EILEEN B. BROOKMAN
 FRANCES DE LOUCHE
 CATHERINE LOUGHLIN
 ALICE SMITH
 MARY WILD

Oriental Medicine, Board of
 BARBARA GREENSPUN

Parole Commissioners, Board of
 IDA MAE CROCKETT

Park Advisory Commission
 ANNE L. ANDERSON
 RUTH E. GONZALES
 MARIE RIPPS

Peace Officers Standards and Training Committee
 NANCY WILLIAMS

Physical Therapy Examiners, Board of
 PATRICIA CONN
 HELGA LOTT
 NANCY C. THORPE

Postsecondary Institutional Authorization,
Commission on
 CYNTHIA W. CUNNINGHAM
 MRS. BERNIE LENZ
 NANCY R. CUMMINGS
 PENNY MOEZZI
 PAT ZIMMERMAN

Public Works Board
 HAZEL J. GAY

Real Estate Advisory Commission
 ELIZABETH M. KROLAK
 OLIVIA D. SILVAGNI

Regents, Board of. University of Nevada
 LILY FONG
 MOLLY KNUDTSEN
 BRENDA D. MASON

Renal Disease Advisory Council
 MARY LOU KEEVER

Rural Housing Authority
 GERTRUDE GOTTSCHALK

Savings Association Appeal Board
 ELEANOR LUBA PERKINS

State Communications Board
 PEGGY GLOVER

State Museum Board of Trustees
 FLORENCE L. CAHLAN
 MOLLY F. KNUDTSEN
 CAROL MC NAMEE
 MIMI RODDEN

Tax Commission
 RUBY DALTON
 E. EVELYN GEROW

Textbook Commission
 KATHLEEN BROWN
 SUSIE T. MEDINA

Veterans' Advisory Commission
 CATHERINE E. PERROTTI
 SUSAN D. PRICE
 DOROTHY E. M. WERNER

Vocational-Technical Education, Advisory Council
for
 HOPE ROBERTS
 RUBY DUNCAN

Welfare Board
 DONNA ANDREAS
 BARBARA H. HENRY
 JO ANN KELLEY
 ALICE SMITH

Youth Services Agency Advisory Board
 JACQUELINE ZUNINI

New Hampshire

DUDLEY W. DUDLEY (D)
Executive Council Member. 1976-. Party: State Del. 1972-76; Nat. Del. 1972; Exec. Com. Dem. State Com. 1972-78; Co-Ch., Platform Com. 1972. Prev: State Repr. 1972-76. Educ: U. of N.H. 1959 BS. B: 8/4/36. Add: 25 Woodman Rd., Durham 03823.

State Legislature

State Senate

EILEEN FOLEY (D)
1965-. Dist: 24. Bds: Cmsn. Studying Problems of Elderly; Ch., Cmsn. Studying Bicycle Laws; Cmsn. Studying Liquor Laws. Party: State Del. 1960-77; Nat. Alt. 1968; V-Ch., State Dem. Com.; V-Ch., Cnty. Com.; Ch., City Com. Prev: Mayor 1968-71; Bd. of Educ. 1960-68; Bd. of Registrars 1952-56. Org: BPW; Rehabilitation Ctr.; Mentally Retarded Bd.; City Com. Dem's. Educ: Syracuse U. 1940 BA; U. of N.H. 1950 MEd. Occ: Field Worker for U.S. Senator. B: 2/27/18. Add: 39 Sunset Rd., Portsmouth 03801 (603)21-2600.

EDITH B. GARDNER (R) **
1961-. Dist: 4. Bds: Finance Com. Prev: State Representative 1943-55. Org: OWL. Occ: RN. B: 1/1/1899. Add: Rte. 5, Laconia 03246.

MARY LOUISE HANCOCK (D)
33 Washington St., Concord 03301.

PHYLLIS M. KEENEY (R)
1976-. Dist: 14. Bds: Ch., Environment Com.; V-Ch., Cities Leg. Com.; Judiciary Com. Party: State Del. 1964-76; Cnty. Rep. Party Secretary 1974-76; Town Rep. Party Exec. Com. 1964-72. Prev: State Repr. 1967-72; Cnty. Exec. Com. 1970-72; Selectwoman 1974-77. Org: Women's Club; BPW; Historical Society; LWV; OWL. Educ: Pa. State U. 1946 BA; Columbia U. 1952 MS. Occ: Librarian. B: 12/10/25. Add: 152 Wason Rd., Hudson 03051.

State House

LEA H. AESCHILMAN (D)
1977-. Dist: 18. Bds: State Institutions Com. Party: State Del. 1976. Prev: Library Trustee 1969-75. Org: LWV. Educ: Smith Coll. 1964 BA. B: 5/15/43. Add: 24 Kensington Rd., Portsmouth 03801.

GRETA M. AINLEY (R)
1957-. Bds: Appropriations. Party: State Del; Nat. Del. 1950, '54, '60, '64; Nat. Alt. 1968. Prev: Ballot Cmsn. 1960-79; Health & Welfare 1959-75. Org: LWV; City Rep. Club; State Rep. Club;

Women's Club; Historical Club. B: 8/14/1900. Add: 1165 Union St., Manchester 13104 1-800-472-1809.

MELISSA APPEL (R)
1975-. Org: Rep. Women's Club. Educ: Occidental Coll. 1957 BA; U. of N.H. 1975 MPA. B: 12/5/36. Add: 433 Central Rd., Rye 03870 (603)271-3315.

PATTI BLANCHETTE (D)
1974-. Bds: Health & Welfare Com. Party: State Del. 1976; State Committeewoman 1976. Educ: U. of N.H. 1974 BA. Occ: Social Worker. B: 3/6/52. Add: 33 Elm St., Newmarket 03857.

BARBARA B. BOWLER (R)
1973-. Dist: 3. Prev: Conservation Cmsn. 1972-75; Law Enforcement & Study Cmsn. 1968- B: 5/26/32. Add: Silver Lake Rd., Box 85, Lochmere 03252.

RITA M. BRACK (D)
1975-. Dist: 28. Bds: State Educ. Com.; Curriculum Com. Party: State Del. 1970-76; State Conv. Ch. 1971, '74. Org: AAUP; Dem. Club; Women's Dem. Club; Governor's Com. on Public Educ. Educ: Boston State Coll. 1939 BSEd.; Rivier Coll. 1965 MEd. Occ: Dir., Counseling & Placement. B: 5/15/18. Add: 60 Hubbard St., Manchester 03104.

SHARON E. BRODY (D)
25 Tenby Drive, Nashua 03060.

MARILYN R. CAMPBELL (R)
1973-. Bds: Environment & Agriculture. Party: State Del. 1972-76. Org: BPW; Farm Bureau; NOWL. Educ: U. of N.H. 1954 BS. Occ: Farmer. B: 7/31/32. Add: 79 Brady Ave., Salem 03079.

ETHEL CANNEY (R)
1973-. Dist: 2. Party: State Del. Org: Women's Club; Pres., State Rep. Women's Club. B: 2/3/03. Add: 232 Meadowborn Rd., Rochester 03867.

MAURA CARROLL (D)
14 Grove Street, Concord 03301.

MINNIE F. CARSWELL (R) **
1973-. Hillsborough 13. Org: Women's Club. Add: Longa Rd., Merrimack 03054.

MARY P. CHAMBERS (D)
1972-. Bds: Deputy Minority Leader; Ch., Dem. Policy Com. Party: State Del. 1972-76; Dem. State Com. 1974; Dem. Cnty. V-Ch. 1976. Org: LWV; Dem. Town Com. Educ: W. Va. Wesleyan Coll. 1952 BA; George Peabody Coll. 1955 MA.

Occ: Dir., Adult Basic Educ. B: 8/31/31. Add: Box 284, Etna 03750 (603)271-2136.

DOROTHY F. COLSON (R) **
1974-. Hillsborough 12. Bds: Health & Welfare Com. Prev: School Bd. 1966-72. Org: Nat. Assoc. of Social Workers; Advisory Com. Needs Workshop; Advisor Visiting Nurse Service. Educ: Mt. Holyoke Coll. 1942 BA; Boston School of Social Work 1948 MS. Occ: Social Work Consultant. Add: 8 Merrill La., Hollis 03049 (617)271-2548.

MARION L. COPENHAVER (D) **
1973-. Grafton 13. Bds: Advisory Council to Mental Health Center. Org: LWV. Add: 42 Rayton Rd., Hanover 03755.

MARGARET S. COTE (D) **
1969-. Hillsborough 19. Bds: Exec. Dept. & Administration. Party: County Exec. Com. 1971-75. Prev: Bd. of Educ. 1963-75. Org: AFT; Dem. Women's Club. Educ: NHU 1922 BA; Boston U. 1952 MA. B: 3/13/1898. Add: 273 Main St., Nashua 03060.

MARY ELIZABETH COTTON (D)
1973-. Bds: Rockingham Cnty. Del.; Cnty. Bicentennial Com.; Com. on State Institutions. Party: State Del. 1972-76; Nat. Committeewoman Young Dem's. 1974-75; State Bd. of Dem. Women 1974-76. Prev: Ward Clerk 1975-76. Org: NOWL; Nat. League of Nursing; Dem. Women. Educ: Mercy Central School of Nursing 1964 RN. Occ: Nurse. B: 11/7/45. Add: 1155 Islington Apt. 5, Portsmouth 03801 (603)271-1110.

ELIZABETH ANN LUPIEN CRORY (D)
1976-. Bds: Com. on Commerce & Consumer Affairs; Grafton Cnty. Del. Party: State Del. 1974, '76; Dem. Exec. Com. 1968-77; Cnty. Dem. Com. 1974-77. Prev: Del., N.H. Constitutional Conv. 1974-84; Adv. Com. on Bldg. Height 1976-77; School Bldg. Com. 1976-77. Org: OWL; N.H. Social Welfare Council. Educ: U. of Mass. 1954 BA; Dartmouth Coll. 1975 MALS. Occ: Property Manager. B: 9/12/32. Add: 40 Rip Rd., Hanover 03755.

BONNIE LEWIS DANFORTH (R)
1975-. Dist: 7. Bds: State Institutions Com. Party: State Del. 1974-77. Prev: Del., Constitutional Conv. 1974-84. Educ: High Pt. Coll. 1944 BS. B: 3/31/24. Add: Scribner Rd., Fremont 03044.

CATHERINE-ANN DAY (D) **
1975-. Hillsborough 26. Prev: Del., Constitutional Conv. Org: WPC. Educ: Mt. St. Mary BA; Middlebury MA. Occ: Teacher. Add: 284 Hawthorne St., Manchester 03104.

GRACE L. DE CESARE (D) **
1974-. Rockingham 5. Party: Del., President's Conv. 1972. Prev: Del., Constitutional Conv. 1974. Org: Dem. Women's Club. Add: Sandy Beach Rd., Salem 03079.

ARLINE L. DION (D)
47 Cartier St., Manchester 03104.

L. PENNY DION (D)
6 Booth Street, Nashua 03060.

HELENE R. DONNELLY (D) **
1965-. Strafford 17. Bds: Bicentennial Com. Org: OWL; Dem. Club. B: 8/12/04. Add: 2 Broadway, Apt. 5, Dover 03820 (603) 742-5404.

DOROTHY J. DREWNIAK (D) **
1975-. Hillsborough 30. Party: Ward Clerk; Ward Ch.; Secretary, City Com. Org: Dem. Women's Club. B: 8/1/39. Add: 765 Page St., Manchester 03103.

NATALIE SMITH FLANAGAN (R)
1974-. Bds: Pres., N.H. Fed. of Rep. Women; State Rep. Steering Com. Party: Ch., Town GOP 1968-72; Cnty. GOP 1973- . Org: Family Service; Internat. Women; Rep. Women. B: 8/6/13. Add: Maple Ave., Atkinson 03811 (603)271-3319.

M. SUSAN FOUND (R)
1977-. Dist: 2. Bds: Commerce & Consumer Affairs. Party: State Del. 1976; Cnty. Clerk Del. 1977-78. Org: Carroll Cnty. Human Services Coord. Council. Occ: Bookkeeper. B: 3/24/54. Add: Kearsarge St., N. Conway 03860.

MARTHA MC DANOLDS FRIZZELL (R)
1950-. Dist: 7. Party: State Del. 1976, '50; Cnty. Ch. Prev: New England Bd. of Educ. Org: Rep. Party; Grange. Educ: U. of NH 1924 BS. B: 11/18/02. Add: Claremont Rd., RFD Box 245, Charlestown 03603.

BEVERLY A. GAGE (R) **
1975-. Rockingham 5. B: 2/1/34. Add: 45 Pelham Rd., Salem 03079.

GABRIELLE VIRGINIA GAGNON (D) **
1974-. Hillsborough 21. Bds: Health & Welfare Com.; Dem. City Com. Party: Local Com. 1974- . Prev: Del, Constitutional Conv. 1974- . Org: OWL; V-Pres. N.H. State Assoc. Emblem Club; V-Pres. Retail Clerks Assoc., AFO-CIO; Pres., Dem. Women's Club; Senior Citizens, Senior Power. B: 3/15/13. Add: 22 Maurice St., Nashua 03060.

NANCY R. GAGNON (R)
Bedford Rd., Merrimack 03054.

BARBARA THORPE GANLEY (D)
1974-. Bds: Resources; Recreation; Devt. Party: State Del. 1972-76; Secretary, Cnty. Dem's 1974-76; V-Ch., Cnty. Dem's 1976; State Platform Com. 1976. Org: Save our Shores; Seacoast Anti-Pollution League; Society for Protection of NH Forests; Dem. Women; Day Care Ctr. Educ: U. of NH 1966 BA. B: 5/20/33. Add: 10 Elliot St., Exeter 03833 (603)271-2136.

ELIZABETH E. GOFF
205 Main St., 113, Salem 03079.

ANNE B. GORDON (R)
1957-. Dist: 8. Bds: Regulated Revenues Com.; Cheshire Cnty. Exec. Com.; Cnty. Ct. House Bldg. Com. Party: Secretary, State Com. 1973-75; Cnty. V-Ch. 1971-73; Local Co-Ch. 1951-77. Prev: School Bd. 1955-70; Town & School Auditor 1952-54; Bicentennial Council 13 States 1970-77; State Leg. Council 1957-59. Org: OES; Grange; N.H. Fed. Rep. Women's Club; Cnty. Rep. Women's

Club. B: 4/27/08. Add: RFD Box 282, Jaffrey 03452.

ELIZABETH A. GREENE (R)
    1961-. Bds: Ch., State Solid Waste Com. Prev: State Air Pollution Com. 1965-69. Educ: U. of N.H. 1927 BA. B: 5/21/06. Add: 399 South Rd., Rye 03870.

RUTH L. GRIFFIN (R) **
    1971-. Rockingham 19. Bds: Rules. Party: State Policy Com., 1975; Nat. Conv. 1972. Org: DAR; OWL. Educ: Wentworth Hospital 1946 RN. B: 7/9/25. Add: 479 Richards Ave., Portsmouth 03801 (603)271-3661.

MARGARET M. HARTFORD (R)
    P.O. Box 282, New Castle 03854.

JOANNE C. HEAD (R)
    1976-. Dist: 10. Bds: Labor Com. Org: LWV; Common Cause. Educ: Antioch Coll. 1976 MA. B: 9/28/30. Add: Stearns Rd., Amherst 03031.

DIANNE L. HERCHEK (D)
    Doral Ave., Apt. 13E, Dover 03820.

JUDITH ANN HESS (R)
    1973-. Bds: V-Ch., Constitutional Revision Com.; Merrimack Cnty. Del. Prev: Del. N.H. Constitutional Conv. 1974-84. Org: Rep. Com. Educ: Simmons Coll. 1965 BS. Occ: Dir., Social Service. B: 12/16/43. Add: 9 Heather Dr., Hooksett 03106.

DONALDA K. HOWARD (R)
    Box 5, Glen 03838.

MILDRED S. INGRAM (R)
    Dreams Landing, Acworth 03601.

POLLY B. JOHNSON (R)
    35 Mountain Road, Concord 03301.

GRACE L. JONCAS (D)
    1969-. Dist: 5. Bds: Constitutional Revision Com.; Ch., Bd. of Selectmen; Budget. Party: Secretary-Treasurer, Dem. Town Com. 1968- . Prev: Supervisor of Checklist 1955-74. B: 12/22/23. Add: 15 Prospect St., Rollinsford, NH 03869.

JUANITA E. KASHULINES (R) **
    1973-. Rockingham 3. Party: Del., State Conv. Prev: Constitutional Conv. 1974. Org: OWL. Add: Rte. 1, Box 570, Windham 03087.

ALICE TIRRELL KNIGHT (R)
    1966-. Bds: Governor's Adv. Council on Alcoholism & Alcoholic Abuse; Statewide Health Coord. Council. Prev: Budget Com. 1965-71. Org: AWRT; BPW; Soroptimist; DAR. Educ: U. of N.H. 1925 BA. B: 7/14/03. Add: Addison Rd., Goffstown 03045.

ELAINE KRASKER (D) **
    1974-. Rockingham 22. Bds: Educ. Com.; Constitutional Revision Com.; Joint Bldg. Com. Party: Ward Selectwoman 1974- . Prev: Bd. of Educ. 1970-74; Library Trustee 1970-74. Org: LWV; WPC; Dem. Com. Educ: U. of NH 1949 BA. B: 4/18/27. Add: Little Harbor Rd., Portsmouth 03801.

ELIZABETH R. LADD (R) **
    1973-. Cheshire 3. Prev: Town Auditor. Org: Nursing Assoc.; Pres., Women's Club. Occ: Real Estate. B: 8/12/17. Add: Spring Hill Farm, Winchester 03470.

CATHERINE G. LAMY (D) **
    1971-. Hillsborough 35. Prev: Constitutional Conv. 1974. Org: OWL; Dem. Women's Club. Occ: Child Care Business. B: 2/15/40 Add: 607 Granite St., Manchester 03102.

BEATRICE M. LAYCOCK (D)
    8 Meisner Road, Salem 03079.

VIRGINIA K. LOVEJOY (R)
    12 South Main St., Derry 03038.

ELAINE T. LYONS (R) **
    1971-. Hillsborough 13. Bds: Legislative Administration; Resolution & Screening; Transportation; Assistant Majority Leader. Party: County Del.; Clerk, Exec. Com. 1971- . Educ: Boston U. Sargent Coll. 1949 BS. Add: Shore Dr., Merrimack 03054 (603)271-3661.

DONNA T. MAC IVOR (R)
    R.D. #5, Hardy Lane Boscawen, Penacook 03301.

HELEN MALOOMIAN (D) **
    1971-. Strafford 6. B: 7/24/18. Add: 8 Emory St., Somersworth 03878.

JOSEPHINE COSTER MARTIN (R) **
    1975-. Hillsborough 10. B: 9/26/55. Add: Farmlands Chestnut Hill Rd., Amherst 03031.

RITA C. MC AVOY (R)
    1977-. Bds: Statutory Revisions Com.; Exec. Bd., Grafton Cnty. Del. Party: State Del. 1976, '74; Women's Ch. Rep. Town Com. 1964-74; Rep. State Com. Adv. Bd. 1967-72; Rep. State Fund Raising Com. 1969- .; Rep. Exec. Com. 1974-75; Rep. State Policy Com. 1974- ; Grafton Cnty. Co-Ch. 1971-72. Prev: Assay Cmsn. of the US 1970- ; Dept. of Defense-Conservation Awards Com. 1974-76. Org: Fed. Rep. Women's Club; Citizens Scholarship Com.; Internat. Platform Assoc.; Historical Society; Bicentennial Com.; LWV; Citizens Educ. Com. B: 6/9/17. Add: Bethelehem Rd., Littleton 03561 (603)271-3310.

DONNA J. MC EACHERN (D)
    50 Meadow Road, Portsmouth 03801.

MARGARET L. MC GLYNN (D) **
    1973-. Hillsborough 21. Prev: Del., Constitutional Conv. 1974. Educ: Smith Coll. BA; Boston Coll. MA. Occ: Retired. B: 7/17/05. Add: 64 Kinsley St., Nashua 03060.

SUSAN NEIDLINGER MC LANE (R)
    1968-. Dist: 16. Party: State Del. 1977; Co-Ch., Ward 1958-60. Org: N.H. Council on World Affairs; LWV; N.H. Assoc. for Mental Health. B: 9/28/29. Add: 5 Auburn St., Concord 03301 (603)271-3663.

BERNADETTE MC NICHOL (R) **
1974-. Merrimack 5. Bds: Labor, Human
Resources & Rehabilitation. Prev: Clerk, School
Bd. 1972-74. Org: Legislative Ch., AAUW. Educ:
New England Coll. 1965 BS. B: 7/20/43. Add:
Allen Rd., Bow 03301 (603)271-3321.

GAIL C. MORRISON (R)
1976-. Bds: Constitutional Revision; Ch.,
Women's Equality Day Com. Party: State Del. 1974,
'76. Org: OWL; NOW. Educ: State Coll. of Salem,
Mass. BS. Occ: Potter. B: 5/27/43. Add: Cir.
Dr.,RFD #3, Hudson 03051 (603)889-4237.

THEODORA P. NARDI (D)
1971-. Dist: 27. Bds: State Fiscal Com.;
Govt. Adv. Budget Com.; V-Ch., Manchester Del.
Party: State Del. 1966-76; Nat. Alt. 1968; State
Dem. Com. 1970-78; Ch., Cnty. Dem. Com. 1968-78.
Org: Justice & Peace Com.; Dem. Party. Educ:
Manhattanville Coll. of the Sacred Heart 1944 BA.
Occ: Assistant Superintendent of Schools. B:
8/28/22. Add: 776 Chestnut St., Manchester
03104 (603)271-3165.

RUTH NEMZOFF-BERMAN (D)
1976-. Prev: Sub Com. on Educ. of NH 1972-73;
Status of Women Cmsn. 1972. Org: NH Personnel &
Guidance Assoc.; NOW; Women's Information Service;
Common Cause. Educ: Barnard Coll. 1962 BA;
Teachers' Coll., Columbia U. 1964 MA; Harvard U.
1976 CAS. Occ: School Consultant. B: 12/10/40.
Add: 57 Raymond St., Nashua 03060.

ESTHER R. NIGHSWANDER (R) **
1969-. Belknap 2. B: 5/19/12. Add: RFD #4,
Laconia 03246.

DOROTHEA O'NEIL (D)
1973-. Dist: 32. Bds: Ways & Means Com.
Party: State Del. 1976, '74, '71; Treasurer, Dem.
Ward Com. 1972-. Org: Common Cause; LWV. B:
12/16/19. Add: 24 Royson St., Manchester 03103.

JO ELLEN LINDA ORCUTT (D)
1973-. Bds: Dem. Policy Com.; Energy Com.;
Science & Technology Com. Party: State Del. 1972-
76; V-Ch. 1977-78. Educ: U. of Del. 1962 BA; U.
of NH 1973 MA. B: 7/22/40. Add: 7 Shirley Park,
Goffstown 03045.

EDNAPEARL FLORES PARR (R)
1970-. Bds: Ch., Conservation Cmsn.; Welfare
Fraud Cmsn.; Legal Aid Coop. Party: State Del.
1970-76; State Recording Secretary 1960-62; Cnty.
Co-Ch. 1972-76; Town Ch. 1974-76; Cnty. Co-Ch.
1976-78. Prev: Cnty. Bicentennial Cmsn. 1970-77;
Bicentennial Com. 1968-77; State Leg. Adminis-
tration 1975-77. Org: OWL; Nat. Assoc. of Par-
liamentarians; IWY; Women's Fed. Club; Rep. Club;
DAR. Educ: Sacramento Coll. 1943 AA; Strayer
Coll. 1954 BA. Occ: Broker. Add: 10 Emerald
Ave., Hampton 03842.

SUSAN W. PELTON (D)
New England College, Box 997, Henniker 03242.

MARJORIE Y. PETERS (R) **
1974-. Hillsborough 9. Bds: Constitutional
Revision; Bicentennial Cmsn. Org: OWL; Woman's
Rep. Club. B: 12/6/28. Add: 3 Church Rd.,
Bedford 03102.

CLAIRE PLOMARITIS (D)
Bridge St., Pelham 03076.

ELEANOR P. PODLES (R)
1976-. Dist: 25. Bds: Statuatory Com.
Party: State Del. 1977. Prev: Selectwoman 1975-
77. Org: Women's Rep. Club; City Rep. Club.
Occ: Librarian. B: 6/6/20. Add: 185 Walnut
Hill Ave., Manchester 03104.

NANCY J. PROCTOR (D) **
1974-. Cheshire 14. Bds: Exec. Depts. &
Administration. Party: Treasurer, County Com.
1974- . Org: Dem. Club. B: 4/24/36. Add:
187 North St., Keene 03431.

PHYLLIS JEANNE PUCCI (D)
1976-. Bds: Commerce & Consumers Affairs.
Party: State Del. 1966-76; Nat. Alt. 1976; State
Committeewoman 1974-76. Prev: Council on Aging
1974-81. Org: Salem Professional Women; Dem.
Club. B: 6/18/25. Add: 51 Lake Shore Rd.,
Salem 03079.

KATHERINE J. RALPH (D) **
1975-. Merrimack 13. Party: Ward Clerk.
Prev: City Treasurer; Postmaster. Occ: Retired.
B: 6/1/07. Add: 144 Woodbridge Rd., Franklin
03235.

MARGARET RUSSELL RAMSAY (D)
1976-. Dist: 5. Bds: Cnty.-City Ct. House
Bldg. Com. Party: State Del. 1972, '76. Prev:
OEO Adv. Com. 1969-72. Org: LWV. Educ: Keene
State Coll. 1956 BSEd; 1964 MEd. B: 1/4/35.
Add: Matthews Rd., Swanzey 03431 (603)271-3661.

MABEL LOWE RICHARDSON (R) **
1947-49; 1960-. Coos 4. Bds: Fish & Game;
Council of Towns; Municipal & County Government;
Veterans Affairs; County Finance Com.; State
Land Appraisal Bd. Party: Pres., State Party
1950- . Org: Grange; PTA; Women's Club. Add:
Box 14, Randolph 03593.

DORIS J. RILEY (D) **
1975-. Merrimack 6. Add: 1475 Hooksett
Rd., Hooksett 03106.

MYRTLE B. ROGERS (R) **
1972-. Rockingham 10. Bds: Environment &
Agriculture; Local Anniversary Bicentennial
Com.; Conservation Cmsn. Party: State Com.
1975- ; County Com. 1973- . Prev: Trustee of
Trust Funds 1970-73. Org: 4-H Leader; PTA. B:
3/24/25. Add: RFD 2, Box 435, Gale Vil. Rd.,
Newton 03858.

PATRICIA T. RUSSELL (D)
1975-. Bds: Dem. Policy Com.; Interstate Cooperation Com.; Bldg. Com. Party: State
Del. 1968-76; Nat. Alt. 1972; Nat. Committeewoman 1976-80; State Committeewoman 1962-77.
Prev: Ward Clerk 1962-70; Conservation Cmsn.
1974-76; Election Reform 1970-71. Org: Dem.
State Com.; NH Coalition of Retarded Citizens.
B: 3/8/31. Add: 74 Beech St., Keene 03431
(603)271-2136.

JANE F. SAUNDERS   (R)
    1976-. Dist: 4. Bds: Interstate Cooperation
Com.; State Song Selection Bd. Party: State Del.
1976; Cnty. Com. Org: Women's Rep. Club; Historical Society. Educ: Tufts U. 1970 BA. Occ:
Journalist. B: 7/26/48. Add: Box 97, Alton
03810.

JOAN M. SCHREIBER (D)
    Cherry Lane, RFD 2, Box 70A, Dover 03820.

ANNIE MAE SCHWANER   (R) **
    1962-. Rockingham 9. Bds: Resources, Recre-
ation & Dev. Com.; Draft Bd.; Legislative Del.
Party: State Platform Com. 1974-75. Org: OWL;
Women's Rep. Club. B: 4/24/12. Add: Elm St.,
Plaistow 03865.

ANDREA A. SCRANTON (R) **
    1973-. Cheshire 16. Bds: Architectural Bd.
Prev: County Exec. Com. Org: US Coast Guard
Women's Reserve; LWV. B: 11/7/19. Add: RFD #2,
Box 273, Hurricane Rd., Keene 03431.

IRENE JAMES SHEPARD (R)
    1974-. Dist: 4. Bds: Merrimack Cnty. Space
Com. Party: Asst. Ch. Rep. Town Com. 1972-78.
Org: Women's Rep. Club; Conservative Caucus; NOWL;
Women's Club. Educ: U. of MA 1944 BA. B:
5/14/22. Add: Gage Hl. Rd., Rt. 1, Concord 03301.

PATRICIA M. SKINNER (R)
    1973-. Bds: Ch., Labor, Human Resources &
Rehabilitation Com. Party: State Del. 1972-76;
V-Ch., Town Com. 1975-76. Org: Library Council;
NH Fed. of Rep. Women's Club. Occ: Newspaper
Correspondent. B: 12/3/32. Add: 68 Govenor
Dismore Rd., Windham 03087 (603)271-3661.

ALFREDA A. SMITH (D)
    35 Royal Circle, Salem 03079.

ROMA A. SPAULDING (R)
    1967-. Dist: 4. Bds: N.H. Foundation for
Medical Care; Health Systems Agency Mental Health
Adv. Council. B: 10/16/14. Add: 8 Maple Ave.,
Claremont 03743.

JUDITH M. STAHL (R)
    22 Cabot Drive, Nashua 03060.

JUDITH ST. GEORGE (D)
    1976-. Dist: 23. Party: State Del. 1974, '76.
B: 6/21/48. Add: 79 SW Highway S., Nashua 03860.

CAROL STOMBERG (D)
    Box 217, Canaan 03741.

BETTY JO TAFFE (R)
    1976-. Bds: House Educ. Com.; Supervisory
Union Bd.; Grafton Cnty. Exec. Com. Educ: Juniata
Coll. 1964 BA; U. of Chicago 1968 MAT. B:
11/19/42. Add: Quincy Rd., Rumney 03266 (603)
271-3333.

JOAN E. TERRY (D)
    19 Salisbury Rd., Keene 03431.

DORIS L. THOMPSON (R)
    95 Park Street, Northfield 03276.

GLYNETA B. THOMSON   (R)
    Mt. Cube Farm, Oxford 03777.

JANET B. TORREY (R) **
    1974-. Strafford 19. Bds: Educ. Com. Org:
BPW; OWL; NEA; OES; Women's Club. Educ: Flora
Stone Mather Coll. 1926 BA. Occ: Retired. B:
11/4/03. Add: 14 Elliot Park, Dover 03820
(603)271-1110.

MADELINE G. TOWNSEND (R)
    Storrs Hill, Lebanon 03766.

SARA M. TOWNSEND (R)
    1970-. Bds: NH State Council on Aging;
V-Ch., Exec. Dept. & Administration Com. Prev:
Finance Com. 1971-76; Cnty. Finance Com. 1971-
76; Conservation Cmsn. 1971-75; School Bd. 1959-
62. Educ: Middlebury Coll. 1941 BA. B:
12/30/19. Add: Box 65, Meriden 03770 (603)
271-3661.

IRIS VALLEY (R)
    129 Silver Street, Dover 03820.

ANNA S. VAN LOAN (R) **
    1963-66; 1969-. Hillsborough 9. Bds:
School Bd. Org: Rep. Women's Club; Women's
Club. Educ: Pembroke Coll. B: 8/12/20. Add:
62 Wallace Rd., Bedford 03102.

SARAH P. VOLL (D)
    1976-. Bds: Ch., Cnty. Criminal Justice
Com. Party: State Del. 1976; Co-Ch. Dist. Carter
Campaign 1975-76. Org: NOWL;DAR. Educ: Goucher
Coll. 1964 BA; Harvard U. 1966 MA; U. ot N.H.
1972 PhD. B: 11/13/42. Add: P.O. Box 511,
4 Croghan Ln., Durham 03824.

ZOE VRAKATITSIS (R)
    68 South St., P.O. Box 258, Keene 03060.

JEAN ROGERS WALLIN (D)
    1966-. Dist: 16. Bds: Ways & Means; Leg.
Administration; Hillsborough Cnty. Exec. Com.
Party: State Del. 1966-68; 1974-76; Nat. Del.
1968; Nat. Committeewoman 1968-73; V-Ch., Dem.
State Com. 1972-73. Prev: Bd. of Educ. 1968-
75; N.H. Constitutional Conv. 1974-84. Org: Bd.
of Realtors; BPW. Occ: Real Estate Sales Assoc.
B: 1/13/34. Add: 3 Durham St., Nashua 03060
(603)882-7230.

KATHLEEN W. WARD (R) **
    1974-. Grafton 1. Bds: Appropriations Com.
on Status of Women; Advisory Council. Party:
County Del. 1974- ; County Ch. 1972- ; State
Del. 1968-70; County V-Ch. 1968-70. Prev:
Budget Com. 1972-75; Distributor of Surplus
Food 1970-75. Org: Fed. Women's Club; Rep.
Women's Club. Occ: Office Manager. B: 8/9/28.
Add: 61 Pleasant St., Littleton 03561 (603)
271-3164.

GERALDINE G. WATSON (R)
    Amherst Road, Merrimack 03054.

EMMA B. WHEELER (R)
    1976-. Dist: 11. Bds: Environment & Agri-
culture Com. Educ: Plymouth Teachers Coll.
1963 BEd; Rivier Coll. 1959 MEd. Occ: Teacher.

B: 1/24/16. Add: 64 Amherst St., Milford 03055.

SHIRLEY J. WHITE (D)
 1975-. Bds: Ch., Human & Social Services.
Party: State Del. 1974-76; Cnty. V-Ch. 1976-78;
City V-Ch. 1976-78. Org: Dem. Party. Educ: U.
of NH 1975 AA. Occ: Realtor. B: 6/30/33. Add:
253 High St., Somersworth 03878.

HELEN FRANCIS WILSON (R) **
 1971-. Rockingham 2. Org: OWL; Women's Clubs.
Occ: Secretary. B: 1/23/21. Add: Rte. 1, Box
344, Manchester 03104.

CECELIA L. WINN (D) **
 1973-. Hillsborough. Party: Dem. City Com.;
Dem. State Com.; Del., Dem. Nat. Conv. 1972; Dem.
County V-Ch. Org: Pres., Dem. Women's Club.
Educ: Keene Teachers Coll. BS; U. of NH MA. Add:
12 Middle St., Nashua 03060.

MARGARET H. WISWALL (R) **
 1974-. Coos 1. Bds: Fish & Game Com. Prev:
Assistant Clerk for Com. on Fish & Game. Org:
OWL; Rep. Women's Club. B: 6/19/12. Add: Box
438, Edwards St., Colibrook 03576 (603)271-3323.

NEILA P. WOODWARD (D)
 9 First St., Groveton 03582.

JOYCE R. ZABARSKY (D)
 161 South Street, Portsmouth 03801.

County Commissions

Coos. MARIE C. HAWKINSON (D)
 1976-. Dist: 1. Bds: Cnty. Human Services
Coord. Council; Home Health Services; Berlin-
Gorham Outreach. Party: State Del. 1976; Local
V-Ch. 1950-52; Local Ch. 1976-77. Org: NH Assoc.
of Cnty's.; Human Services Coord. Council; Dem.
Club. B: 9/15/27. Add: 119 Sweden, Berlin
03570 (603)752-4100.

Grafton. BARBARA B. HILL (D)
 1972-. Dist: 1. Bds: Ch., Tri-Cnty. Council;
Ch., N.H. Assoc. of Cnty's.; Nat. Assoc. of
Cnty's. Criminal Justice. Party: State Del. 1972-
76; V-Ch., Cnty. Com. 1970-74. Org: N.H. Assoc.
of Cnty's.; Elected Women; Youth House; Human
Services Council; Women's Club. Educ: U. of
N.H. 1957 BA. B: 12/10/35. Add: 24 Messenger
St., Lebanon 03766 (603)787-6941.

Merrimack. EDNA C. MC KENNA (R)
 1973-. Bds: Citizens Adv. Com. Prev: City
Councilwoman 1960-72. Org: ANA; State Employees
Assoc.; Zonta; BPW; Women's Club; Women's Rep.
Club. B: 11/27/10. Add: 12 Kozy Trl., Concord
03301 (603)225-3065.

Rockingham. VESTA M. ROY
 County Courthouse, Exeter.

Mayors

Atkinson. HELEN V. WOODLOCK (D)
 1970-. Bds: Planning Bd.; Bd. of Health; Hwy.
Safety. Prev: Recreation Cmsn. Org: Welfare

Assoc. B: 5/24/24. Add: Summit Dr., Atkinson
03811.

Canterbury. MARY ELLEN FIFIELD
 Town Hall, Canterbury 03224.

Carroll. DOROTHY E. O'BRIEN **
 1976-. Bds: Planning Bd. Prev: School Bd.
1962-74; Council 1973-76. Occ: Self-employed
TV Sales. B: 1/13/31. Add: P.O. Box 97,
Airport Rd., Twin Mt. 03595 (603)846-5754.

Hill. JOYCE COLBY (I)
 1975-. Party: Nat. Alt. 1976. Prev: Clerk,
School Dist. Org: BPW. Occ: Para-Legal. B:
3/6/42. Add: Mountain View Dr., Hill 03243.

Hinsdale. MILDRED P. ZYWNA
 Town Hall, Hinsdale 03451.

Hudson. PHYLLIS M. KEENEY (R) **
 1976-. Bds: Budget Com.; Clerk, Police
Dept. Overseer; Welfare. Party: Secretary,
County Com. 1974- ; Town Exec. Com. 1963- ;
Del., State Conv. 1964-72. Prev: Council
1974-76. Org: AAUW; BPW; LWV; OWL; Zonta;
Women's Club. Educ: Penn. State 1946 BA;
Columbia U. 1952 MS. Occ: Librarian & Teacher.
B: 12/10/25. Add: Wason Rd., Hudson 03051
(603)889-1882.

Newfields. MARY HALLINAN
 P.O. Box 45, Newfields 03856.

Woodstock. BONNIE DAVIS HAM (R) **
 1976-. Bds: Budget Com.; Solid Waste
Disposal Study; Linwood Medical Center; Tri
County Council, Inc. Prev: Budget Com. 1971-
74; Town Clerk 1970-74; Council 1974-76. Educ:
Plymouth State Coll. 1969 BE. B: 10/5/47.
Add: Sargent St., North Woodstock 03262 (603)
745-8752.

Local Councils

Alstead. GLORIA SEDDON (I)
 1976-. Bds: Planning Bd. Prev: Planning
Bd. 1972-76; Regional Planning Cmsn. 1972-76;
Exec. Com. Regional Planning 1975-77. B:
4/14/31. Add: Main Rd., E. Alstead 03602
(603)835-2242.

Amherst. ANN SNOW
 Town Hall, Main St., Amherst 03031.

Andover. GRACIA HARRIS SNYDER (R)
 1976-. Bds: Planning Bd.; Health Officer;
Tax Assessor. Prev: Trustee of Trust Funds
1974-76; Conservation Cmsn. 1970-73. Occ:
Journalist. B: 7/25/28. Add: Main St., P.O.
Box 145, Andover 03216 (603)735-5332.

Bennington. GLADYS E. NEWHALL (I)
 1975-. Bds: Regional School Dist. Org:
Pres., Mass. School Nurse Org.; Amer. School
Health Assoc.; ANA; Reserve Officers Assoc.;
Retired Colonel-Army Nurse Corps.; Grange.
Educ: Nashua Memorial Hospital 1940 RN; Simmons
Coll. 1953 BS; Boston U. 1954 MEd. Occ: Health
Educator. B: 7/11/16. Add: Box 217, Bennington

Berlin. YVONNE COULOMBE (D) **
  1974-. Bds: Ch., Health, Educ., Welfare;
Environmental Control Com.; Finance Com.; Election
Com. Org: Hospital Bd.; Social Welfare. Educ:
NH Vocational Technical Coll. 1972 BA. B:
6/18/38. Add: 591 Third Ave., Berlin (603)
752-7532.

Claremont. MARY REESE (D) **
  1973-. Bds: Ch., Public Health Com.; Planning
& Dev. Com. Org: LWV; County Helping Service
Council. Educ: L.I.U. 1956 BS; Columbia U. 1959
BS. B: 10/16/35. Add: 13 Langseth Ave., Clare-
mont 03743.

Concord. BARBARA E. HENDERSON
  41 Green St., Concord 03301.

Concord. BARBARA UNDERWOOD (I)
  1974-. Bds: Ch., Recycling. Party: State
Del. 1970-74; State Ward Ch. 1974-77. Prev:
State Legislator 1971-76. Educ: Middlebury Coll.
1954 BA. B: 4/6/32. Add: 29 Rumford St., Concord
03301 (603)224-2391.

Derry. JANET M. CONROY (R)
  1976-. Bds: Overseer of Welfare; Alt., Southern N.H. Planning Cmsn. Org: LWV. B: 8/22/31.
Add: 16 High St., Derry 03038 (603)432-7724.

Dover. GERALDINE SYLVESTER
  Municipal Bldg., Dover 03820.

Dublin. LUCILLE MC DONALD
  Town Hall, Dublin 03444.

Epsom. NORMA J. DOWST
  Town Hall, Epsom 03234.

Exeter. ETHEL DOE (R)
  1975-. Bds: Planning Bd.; Town Hall Com.;
Safety Complex Com. Org: Child & Family Services;
Crisis Homes; NH Social Welfare Council; Rep.
Club; Area Resources Team. Educ: Wellesley Coll.
1938 BA; Brown U. 1943 MA. B: 6/25/16. Add:
92 High St., Exeter 03833 (603)778-0591.

Fremont. ROBERTA A. WADDELL
  Main St., Town Hall, Fremont 03044.

Hampton. HELEN W. HAYDEN
  136 Winnacunnet Rd., Hampton 03842.

Hanover. MARTHA S. SOLOW (D)
  1975-. Bds: Planning Bd., Health Council;
Library Trustee. Org: LWV; Common Cause. Educ:
Wellesley Coll. BA. Occ: Poll Interviewer. Add:
11 Rayton Rd., Hanover 03755 (603)643-4123.

Hebron. SUZANNE GASSETT SHEEHAN
  1976-. Bds: Planning Bd.; Common Historic
Dist. Cmsn. Educ: Plymouth State Col. 1971 BSEd.
B: 8/28/49. Add: Hobart Hill Rd., Hebron 03241
(603)744-2631.

Keene. PRISCILLA F. BATCHELDER (R)
  1974-. Bds: Parks, Recreation & Library Com.;
Leg. Review Com.; Air Service Com. Party: State
Del. 1977; Asst. Cnty. Ch. 1977-79. Org: Nat.
Fed. of Rep. Women; State Rep. Com.; Nat. Rep.
Party. Educ: U. of NH 1952 BA. B: 6/6/29.

Add: 6 Fairview St., Keene 03431 (603)
352-5211.

Keene. NANCY E. BAYBUTT
  3 Washington St., Keene 03431.

Keene. CECILE GOFF (D)
  1975-. Party: State Del. 1976. Prev:
Safety Bd. of Review 1973-75; Recreation Bd.
1970-73. Org: Amer. Personnel & Guidance Assoc.;
LWV; NH Social Welfare Council; Family Services;
PTA. Educ: Boston U. 1961 BS; Keene State Coll.
1977 MEd. Occ: Counselor. B: 7/9/39. Add:
37 Eastview Rd., Keene 03431 (603)352-5211.

Lebanon. PAMELA B. BEAN
  51 N. Park St., Lebanon 03766.

Lebanon. BARBARA H. JONES (I)
  1975-. Bds: City Charter Revision Cmsn.;
Health & Nursing Services Bd. Prev: Ward Clerk
1973-75. Org: LWV; Governor Cmsn. on Crime &
Delinquency. Educ: Denison U. 1963 BA; U. of
Mich. 1965 MA. Occ: Legal Secretary. B:
11/11/42. Add: 35 Seminary Hill Apt. 29, W.
Lebanon 03784 (603)448-4220.

Lee. SHIRLEY M. CLARK
  KAREN CURTIS
  RFD #1, Durham 03824.

Lyme Center. JEAN MARTZ
  Lyme Center 03769.

Nashua. ALICE L. DUBE
  City Hall, 229 Main St., Nashua 03060.

Nelson. TERRI UPTON
  Town Hall, Nelson 03457.

New Castle. MARGARET H. HARRINGTON (R)
  1974-. Bds: Historical Cmsn.; Mosquito
Control Cmsn.; Conservation Cmsn. B: 6/21/16.
Add: Box 216, New Castle 03854.

New Durham. ELOISE R. BICKFORD (D)
  1976-. Bds: Planning Bd.; Library Trustee;
Rural Dist. Health Council. Prev: Library
Trustee 1961-77. Org: Town Beautification Com.;
Rural Dist. Health Council; Local Archives &
Historical Collections Com. Educ: Symmes
Arlington Hospital School of Nursing 1948 RN.
Occ: RN. B: 12/25/25. Add: Old Bay Rd., New
Durham 03855 (603)859-2091.

Northfield. ROBIN D. STEADY
  P.O. Box 343, Tilton 03276.

Northumberland. NATALIE M. POTTER (R)
  1974-. Party: State Del. 1974-77. Prev:
State Repr. 1961-63; V-Ch., State Council on
Aging 1962-67. Org: BPW; OWL; OES. Occ: Secretary. B: 3/7/16. Add: RFD 1, Groveton
03582.

Pelham. MARIANNE H. THOMPSON (D)
  1976-. Bds: Budget Com.; Planning Bd.; Conservation Cmsn. Party: State Del. 1974-76;
State Com. 1976-78; Hills Cnty. Exec. Com. 1976-
78; Town Com. 1968-78. Prev: Budget Com. 1970-
76; Constitutional Conv. Del. 1974-84. Org: Adv.

Bd. Pelham Community; State Dem. Women. Educ:
Syracuse U. 1951 BA. Occ: Administrative Asst.
B: 3/30/30. Add: 298 Mammoth Rd., Pelham 03076
(603)635-7811.

Portsmouth. JOYCE YANCEY HANRAHAN (D)
1972-. Bds: Bd. of Dirs., Chamber of Commerce;
Special Citizens Com., Community Devt. Party:
Campaign Manager. Prev· Joint Bldg. Com. 1972-76;
Citizens Council-Community Improvement 1970-72;
City Council 1972-74. Org: Day Care Council of
Amer.; Nat. Assoc. for Educ. of Young Children;
NH Dems. Educ: U. of Ala. 1955 BA; U. of NH
1964 MEd. Occ: Exec. Dir. of Day Care Center.
B: 9/29/33. Add: 62 Marcy St., Portsmouth 03801
(603)436-4125.

Portsmouth. MARY M. KEENAN (D)
1975-. Bds: Joint Bldg. Com. Party: State
Del. 1970; Ward Selectwoman 1972-77. Prev:
Planning Bd. Org: Homemaker Home Aider; Family
Services; Dem. Club; Child Abuse Com. Occ:
Realtor. B: 9/8/36. Add: 85 Lawrence St., Ports-
mouth 03801.

Rochester. KATHERINE J. SHAFER
31 Wakefield St., Rochester 03867.

Rollinsford. GRACE L. JONCAS
Main St., Rollinsford 03869.

Salisbury. DOROTHEA LOVEJOY
Town Hall, Salisbury 03268.

Sanbornton. BARBARA PROKOSCH (D)
1976-. Bds: Hwy. Safety Com.; Historic Dist.
Cmsn.; Youth Assistance Program. Org: Historical
Society. Occ: Sales Manager. B: 5/6/42. Add:
RFD #1, Calef Hill Rd., Franklin 03235 (603)
286-4034.

Temple. JULIE HARLING
Town Hall, Temple 03084.

Winchester. HELEN G. MC FADDEN
Town Hall, Winchester 03470.

Windham. M. VIRGINIA BRADY (D)
1971-. Party: State Del. 1976; State Alt.
1974; Secretary, Dem. City Com. 1967-68; Ward
Committeewoman 1966-68. Prev: Planning Bd. 1972-
75. Org: NH Municipal Assoc.; Women's Club.
Educ: Lawrence General Hospital 1949 RN. Occ:
RN. B: 9/19/28. Add: 21 Birchwood Rd., Windham
03087 (603)432-7732.

Wolfeboro. LILLIAN O. BROOKES
Box 629, Wolfeboro 03894.

State Boards and Commissions

Office of the Governor, State Capitol Bldg.,
Concord 03301.

Accountancy, Board of
IRENE R. LEBEL
AIME PARADIS

Aging, Council on
CLARIA MONIER

Arts, Commission on the
CYNTHIA BEEBE
KAREN BROOK
JEANNE SACHS

Bank Advisory Board
SHIRLEY CLARK

Cancer Commission
MARY BOOTH LARNER

Cosmetology, Board of
ROBERTA SHEA

Education, Board of
CATHERINE R. CAOUETTE

High School Vocational-Technical Education
Consulting Committee
BARBARA ASH
HELEN COLL
VIRGINIA JANIK
ANN PLAYDON

Historical Commission
DOROTHY M. VAUGHAN

Human Rights, Commission for
IVOREY COBB
GAIL PAINE

Managers, Board of. New Hampshire Veteran's Home
SHIRLEY B. LUSCOMBE

Merrimack River Valley Flood Control Commission
CAROLYN JONES

Nursing Education and Nurse Registration, Board of
RITA BYRANT
DORIS GAGNON
MARGUERITE HASTINGS
JULIETTE PETILLO
MARILYN PROUTY
KATHLEEN J. YEAPLE

Parole, Board of
SHERRY KELLEY

Prison Trustees, Board of. State Prison
MARJORIE FIELD

Probation, Board of
RITA MC AVOY

Public Health Nursing
HOLLY BRICKER
ELIZABETH A. BURTT
MARY C. CAMINATI
JEAN DOOLEY
ELOISE DOUCET
MARIE ERICSON
JOAN GROSS
SANDRA HAIR
DOROTHY HOPKINS
SUSAN KARMERIS
BARBARA KRUGER
JUDITH LUCAS
PATRICIA NGAAM
CAROLE RYAN
ALISON SWEATT
DENCIE E. WARD

School Building Authority
    HELEN R. CROSSIN

State Library Commission
    ELIZABETH YATES MC GREAL

Sweepstakes Commission
    PHEBE L. PALAZZI

Technical Services in the Area of Health, Advisory
Board on
    JOANNE K. FARLEY
    PHYLLIS KEENEY
    ANNA PHILBROOK

Traffic Safety Commission
    MARY CARR

Trustees, Board of. New Hampshire Youth Development
Center
    M. MARY MORGAN

New Jersey

State Executive and Cabinet

JOANNE E. FINLEY (D)
    Commissioner of Health. 1974-. Bds: Ch.,
Health Care Facilities Financing Authority; State
Health Planning/Coord. Council; Health Care
Administration Bd. Prev: Dir., Public Health
1973-74; Dir., Health Planning Dept. 1968-72;
Comsr., Div. of Health 1966-68. Org: Amer. Public
Health Assoc. Educ: Antioch Coll. 1944 BA; Yale
1951 MPH; Case Western Reserve 1962 MD. Occ:
Physician. B: 12/28/22. Add: 57 Brookstone Dr.,
Princeton 08540 (609)292-7837.

ANN KLEIN (D)
    Commissioner, Department of Human Services.
1974-. Bds: State Bd. of Institutional Trustees;
State Law Enforcement Planning Agency; NJ Drug
Abuse Adv. Council. Party: State Del. 1972;
Secretary, 1972 Del. to Dem. Nat. Conv. Prev:
Assemblywoman 1972-74; State Tax Policy Cmsn.
1971-73; Governor's Council Against Crime 1968.
Org: LWV; NOW. Educ: Barnard Coll. 1943 BA;
Columbia U. 1945 MS. B: 7/23/23. Add: 9 Wood-
lawn Dr., Morristown 07960 (609)292-3717.

VIRGINIA LONG
    Commissioner of Banking. Add: 36 W. State St.,
Trenton 08625.

PATRICIA Q. SHEEHAN (D)
    Commissioner, Department of Community
Affairs. 1974-. Bds: Ch., NJ Housing Finance
Agency; Ch., NJ Urban Loan Authority; Ch.,
Hackensack Meadowland Devt. Cmsn. Party: State
Committeewoman; State Dem. Reform Cmsn.; Nat.
Dem. Adv. Council of Elected Officials. Prev:
Mayor, New Brunswick 1967-74; Governor's Tax
Cmsn. 1971-72. Educ: Trinity Coll. 1955 BA.
B: 2/22/34. Add: 5 Llewelyn Pl., New Brunswick
08903 (609)292-6420.

State Legislature

State Senate

ALENE S. AMMOND (D) *
    1973-. Dist: 6. B: 4/6/33. Add: 510 N.
Kings Highway, Cherry Hill 08034.

WYNONA M. LIPMAN (D)
    1972-. Bds: Senate Educ. Com.; Revenue,
Finance & Appropriations Com.; Institutions &
Agencies. Party: State Del. 1972; State Plat-
form Com. for Dem. Platform 1977; Cnty. Committee-
woman 1963-72; Town Ch., Municipal Com. 1969-
73. Prev: Cnty. Freeholder 1969-71; Dir., Cnty.
Freeholders 1971-72; Bd. of Trustees, NJ Bd.
of Public Welfare 1967-72. Org: NJEA; Cnty.
Faculty Assoc.; NJ Assoc. of Black Educators;
Nat. Council of Negro Women; NAACP; OWL; NJ
Fed. of Dem. Women; WPC. Educ: Talledega Coll.
BA; Columbia U. PhD. Occ: Assoc. Professor.
B: 11/17/29. Add: 555 Elizabeth Ave., Newark
0/112 (201)622-0007.

State House

JANE BURGIO (R)
    1973-. Bds: State Govt. & Interstate &
Federal Relations; Nursing Home Study Cmsn.
Party: State Del. 1975, '77; Nat. Alt. 1972;
Cnty. Com. 1965-72; V-Ch., Com. 1966-68; Local
Ch. 1969-72; Cnty. V-Ch. 1970-72. Prev: Cnty.
Bd. of Elections 1971-73. Org: BPW; LWV. B:
7/8/22. Add: 586 Mountain Ave., N. Caldwell
07006 (201)226-2747.

MARY KEATING CROCE (D) *
    1973-. Dist: 6. Party: V-Ch., State Plat-
form Com. 1975; Cnty. Committeewoman 1962- .
Org: PTA; Dem. Club; United Fund; NOW. B:
12/4/28. Add: 7520 Wyndam Rd., Pennsauken
08109.

BARBARA CURRAN (R) *
    1973-. Dist: 24. Party: Former Exec. Dir.
Rep. Party of NJ. Org: National Academy of
Television Arts & Science. Educ: St. Mary of
the Woods Coll. BA. B: 8/26/40. Add: Bassett
Bldg., 382 Springfield Ave., Summit 07901.

ALINA MISZKIEWICZ (D) **
    1975-. Dist: 32. Prev: Hudson Cnty. Free-
holder 1973-76. B: 1/10/40. Add: 821 Pavonia
Ave., Jersey City 07306.

MARIE A. MUHLER (R)
   1975-. Dist: 11. Bds: Assembly Educ. Com.;
Joint Com. on Public Schools. Party: State Del.
1975, '77; Nat. Alt. 1976; Cnty. Committeewoman
1970-72. Prev: Bd. of Educ. 1968-73, 1972-75;
Regional Bd. of Educ. 1975-77. B: 7/19/37. Add:
5 Oak Ln., Marlboro 07746 (201)462-9009.

HELEN CHIARELLO SZABO (D) *
   1976-. Dist: 13. Party: Cnty. Committeewoman
1956- ; V-Ch. 1961- ; Nat. Del. 1964. Org: Amer.
Cancer Soc.; Heart Fund. B: 4/17/23. Add: 276
Ashmore Ave., Trenton 08611.

County Commissions

Atlantic. LILLIAN E. BRYANT
   1917 Venice Ave., Atlantic City 08404.

Bergen. JOAN STARR LESEMANN (D)
   1975-. Bds: Liaison, Housing & Community Devt.
Com.; Ch., Youth Services Com. B: 1/17/34. Add:
66 Hamilton Ave., Englewood 07601 (201)646-2532.

Bergen. DORIS MAHALICK (D) **
   1966-69; 1975-. Party: County Com. 1960-65.
Prev: Mayor 1971-75; Councilwoman 1960-65. Org:
Citizen's Com. for Better Educ.; PTA. B:
10/23/24. Add: 41 Lexington Ave., Wallington
07057 (201)646-2502.

Bergen. JOAN E. STEINACKER
   36 Anne Ave., Ramsey 07446.

Burlington. CATHERINE AURORA COSTA (D) **
   1971-. Bds: Soil Conservation Dist.; Welfare
Bd.; Planning Bd. Party: County Com. 1960-75;
Party Ch. 1964-70; Party V-Ch. 1962-63; Del.,
Dem. Conf. 1968; Platform & Resolutions Com. 1968;
Secretary County Com. 1964-66. Prev: NJ State
Youth Commissioner 1964-68; Zoning Bd. Ch. 1968-
73. Org: V-Pres., State Nat. Resources Assoc.
B: 3/21/26. Add: 38 Rockland Dr., Willingboro
08046 (609)267-3300.

Essex. REITA GREENSTONE (D)
   1974-. Bds: Liaison, Cnty. Mental Health Bd.;
V-Ch., Cnty. Geriatrics Com.; Finance Com. B:
5/24/25. Add: 20 Ross Rd., Livingston 07039
(201)961-7084.

Hudson. ANNE O'MALLEY (D) **
   1972-. Party: V-Ch. City Com.; Ward Coordinator. Prev: Model Cities Citizens' Participation
Bd. Org: NAACP; Advisory Bd. Narcotics Educ.
Center; Advisory Bd. Urban Rodent Control Program.
B: 1912. Add: 123 Poplar St., Jersey City 07307
(201)795-0135.

Mercer. BARBARA BOGGS SIGMUND (D)
   1976-. Bds: Welfare Bd.; Park Cmsn.; Mental
Health Bd.; Planning Bd.; Cnty. & State Comsns.
on the Status of Women. Prev: Councilwoman 1973-
76; Ch., Public Works Dept. 1975. Org: Dem.
Women's Club; WEAL. Educ: Manhattanville Coll.
1961 BA. B: 5/27/39. Add: 8 Evelyn Place,
Princeton 08540 .

Middlesex. DOROTHY K. POWER
   1975-. Bds: Ch., Dept. of Educ. & Welfare;
Transportation Coord. Com.; Dept. of Corrections
& Institutions. Party: Cnty. Committeewoman;
Municipal V-Ch.; Cnty. V-Ch. 1970-74; State
Committeewoman 1974-77. Org: Dem. Social Club;
PTA; Family Service Assoc.; Human Services
Council; Nat. Secretaries Assoc. B: 7/14/32.
Add: 304 Patton Ave., Piscataway 08854
(201)463-3004.

Monmouth. JANE G. CLAYTON (R)
   1976-. Bds: Cnty. Planning Bd.; Council
Office on Aging; CETA Adv. Council. Party:
Nat. Alt. 1972; Cnty. Committeewoman 1951-77;
V-Ch., Rep. Exec. Com. 1969-77; Municipal Ch.
1965-77. Prev: Planning Bd. 1966-76; Cnty.
Election Cmsn. 1966-76. Org: Nat. Restaurant
Assoc.; Devt. Council; Fed. of Rep. Women;
Rep. Club. Occ: Buyer. B: 3/14/28. Add:
10 Woodmere Ave., Rumson 07760 (201)431-7416.

Morris. LEANNA BROWN (R)
   1972-. Bds: Ch., Planning & Devt. Com.; Ch.,
Bd. of Public Transportation. Party: Campaign
Coord. 1974, Pres., Rep. Club 1966. Prev:
Councilwoman 1969-72. Org: Zonta; LWV; AAUW;
Women's Club; Rep. Club; Cnty. Women's Club.
Educ: Smith Coll. 1956 BA. Add: 7 Dellwood
Ave., Chatham 07928 (201)285-6212.

Morris. EILEEN MC COY
   12 Colonial Dr., Convent Station 07961.

Ocean. HAZEL S. GLUCK (R)
   1976-. Bds: Ch., Parks & Environmental
Resources; Beach Erosion Liaison; Cultural &
Heritage Cmsn. Liaison. Party: Committeewoman
1977-78. Prev: Lakwood Mayor's Cmsn. on
Documentation of Poverty 1965; Bd. of Educ.
1965-68. Org: Soroptimist; Rep. Club; Cnty.
Finance Com.; Cnty. Council of Agencies; Cnty.
Municipal Consumer Agencies. Educ: U. of Mich.
1956 BA. B: 9/6/34. Add: 657 7th St., Lakewood 08753 (201)244-2121 x 222.

Passaic. LOUISE FRIEDMAN (R)
   1973-. Bds: Ch., Welfare Com.; Adminis-
tration; Law & Public Safety. Prev: Clifton
Bd. of Educ. 1963-65; Welfare Bd. 1970-73;
Mental Health 1968-70; Recreation Bd. 1973-74.
Org: Rep. Club; Cnty. Rep's.; Women's Club.
Educ: Flower 5th Ave. School of Nursing 1947 RN.
B: 4/18/24. Add: 1451 Van Houten Ave., Clifton
07013 (201)473-2600.

Somerset. DORIS W. DEALAMAN (R)
   1967-. Bds: Ch., Facilities & Services Com.;
Personnel Com.; Cnty. Welfare Bd. Party: Dist.
Committeewoman 1960-62; Municipal Ch. 1962-68;
Cnty. V-Ch. 1965- . Prev: Councilwoman 1965-67;
Ch., Cnty. Mental Health Bd. 1964-68. Org:
NASW; LWV; Rep. Club. Educ: Duke U. 1940 BA;
Columbia U. 1942 MS. B: 3/1/19. Add: Round
Top Rd., Bernardsville 07924 (201)725-4700.

Union. ROSE MARIE SINNOTT (R)
   1974-. Bds: Cnty. Economic Devt. Corp.;
Flood Control Cmsn.; Adv. Bd. on the Status of
Women. Party: Cnty. Committeewoman 1972. Prev:

V-Ch., Zoning Bd. of Adjustment 1967-72; Beautification Com. 1968-72; Ch., Adv. Bd. on the Status
of Women 1975. Org: BPW; LWV; Women's Rep. Club;
WPC. Educ: Marymount Coll. 1958 BA. Occ: Public
Relations Consultant. B: 10/4/36. Add: 2 Blackburn Pl., Summit 07901 (201)353-5000.

Mayors

Beechwood. CHRISTINA DE FOREST
    Municipal Bldg., 315 Atlantic City Blvd.,
Beechwood 08722.

Chester. JANET W. ABELES (D)
    1976-. Educ: Kean Coll. 1958 MA. Occ: Farmer.
B: 5/15/08. Add: 67 Budd Ave., Chester 07930
(201)879-7364.

Cranbury. PATRICIA H. SCOTT (R) **
    1976-. Bds: Planning Bd.; Shade Tree Com.;
Bd. of Health; Recreation Com.; Park Planning
Com. Party: County Com. 1968-74. Prev: Council-
woman 1974-76. Org: Treasurer, Woman's Club.
Educ: Trenton State Coll. 1953 BS. B: 3/17/32.
Add: 12 Ryan Rd., Cranbury 08512 (609)395-0544.

Cranford. BARBARA BRANDE
    8 Springfield Ave., Cranford 07016.

Delran. LORRAINE SCHMIERER (D) **
    1972-. Bds: Planning Bd. Party: County Com.
1965-70. Prev: Town Council 1969-72; Local
Assistance Bd. 1964-72. B: 9/25/34. Add: 500
Chestnut St., Delran 08075 (609)461-7734.

Englewood. SONDRA J. GREENBERG (D)
    1976-. Bds: Planning Bd.; Library Bd.;
Affirmative Action Com. Party: Cnty. Committee-
woman 1963-67; Registration Ch. 1963-65. Prev:
Ch., Downtown Beautification Com. 1967-68; Better
Englewood Com. 1972-73. Org: LWV; Dem. Club.
Educ: Cornell U. 1949 BA. B: 8/2/28. Add: 449
Liberty Rd., Englewood 07631 (201)567-1800
ext. 200.

Englishtown. EDNA L. HAMILTON (R) **
    1972-. Bds: Ch., Roads Com.; Deputy Police
Commissioner. Org: Senior Citizens. Occ: Deputy
Clerk, County Bd. B: 4/20/14. Add: 12 Main St.,
Englishtown 07726 (201)446-9235.

Hillsborough Twp. PATRICIA A. MC KIERNAN (R)
    1977-. Bds: Planning Bd.; Capital Planning
Com.; Police Com. Prev: Planning Bd. 1974-77;
Capital Planning Com. 1975-77; Ch., Finance 1975-
77; Deputy Mayor 1976-77. Org: Mobilization of
Resources; Rep. Club; Small Community Mayors
Assoc. B: 12/20/38. Add: Twp. Line Rd., Belle
Mead 08502 (201)369-4313.

Hopewell Township. CAROLINE E. WOODWARD
    RD #1, Box 332, Pennington 08534.

Maple Shade. JEANNINE A. GENDER (D)
    1975-. Bds: Ch., Local Planning Agency;
Planning Bd. Prev: Deputy Mayor 1975-77; Planning
Bd. 1975-76; Ch., Site Plan Review Bd. 1976-77;
Adv. Bd. of Commerce 1975- . Org: Helping Hand
Council; Dem. Club; PTA. B: 1/16/37. Add: 109
E. Roland Ave., Maple Shade 08052 (609)779-9610.

Millstone. MARY PATRICK (D)
    1977-. Party: State Del. 1973, '77; Nat.
Del. 1974; Nat. Alt. 1976; State Committee-
woman 1973-77; Precinct Leader 1961-71; Cnty.
Committeewoman 1953-70. Prev: Councilwoman
1971-77. Occ: Leg. Liaison for Dept. of Labor
& Industry. B: 5/3/26. Add: 11 Alley,
Somerville 08876.

Princeton Township. JOSEPHINE H. HALL
    State & Valley Rds., Princeton 08540.

Randolph. LEONORA P. WHILDIN (D)
    1974-. Bds: Planning Bd.; Landmarks Com.;
Library Bd. Prev: Bd. of Health 1973-74. Org:
ANA; LWV; WPC; Cnty. Fair Housing Council; Dem.
Club; Fed. of Dem. Women. Educ: Boston U.
School of Nursing 1954 BS; Columbia U. 1971 MS.
Occ: Nurse. B: 12/7/26. Add: 82 Radtke Rd.,
Randolph 07801 (201)361-8200.

Readington. VIRGINIA M. SWACKHAMER (D) **
    1976-. Bds: Bd. of Health; Planning Bd.;
Recreation & Park Cmsn. Prev: Councilwoman
1972-76; Org: County Visiting Homemakers. B:
5/10/25. Add: P.O. Box 462, Whitehouse Station
08889 (201)534-4051.

Rutherford. MARGARET K. SCHAK (D)
    1977-. Bds: Planning Bd. Prev: Council-
woman 1975-77; Finance Ch. 1976-77; Public
Works Ch. 1975-76; Liaison to Hackensack
Meadowland Devt. Com. 1975-77. Org: Bergen-
Passaic Health Systems Agency (HUD); Leg. Study
Cmsn. on Hackensack Meadowlands; Mayor's Munici-
pal Com. Meadowlands; Dem. Club. B: 6/5/21.
Add: 195 Wheaton Pl., Rutherford 07070
(201)939-0022.

Scotch Plains. ANNE B. WODJENSKI (D) **
    1976-. Bds: Recreation Com.; Bd. of Health.
Party: Com. 1973-74. Prev: Councilwoman 1974-
76. Org: Alert Parents for Good Schools; Dem.
Club; PTA. Educ: Coll. of New Rochelle 1953
BA. Occ: Medical Assistant. B: 10/1/31. Add:
2297 Elizabeth Ave., Scotch Plains 07076
(201)322-6700.

Springfield. JOANNE RAJOPPI (D)
    1975-. Bds: Ch., Union Cnty. Municipal Adv.
Council; Ch., Cnty. Consumer Affairs Adv. Com.;
Cnty. Revenue Sharing Com. Party: Ch., Voter
Registration 1975. Prev: Bd. of Educ. 1973-76.
Org: Nat. Assoc. of Press Women; LWV. Educ:
Case Western Reserve U. 1970 BA. Occ: Writer/
Editor. B: 12/25/47. Add: 66 Wabeno Ave.,
Springfield 07081 (201)376-5800.

Teaneck. ELEANOR MANNING KIELISZEK (D)
    1974-. Bds: Planning Bd.; Library Bd. Prev:
Councilwoman 1970-74; Planning Bd. 1966-70;
Community Relations Bd. 1963-66; Business Adv.
Bd. 1965-70. Org: LWV; Dem. Women of Bergen
Cnty. B: 9/25/25. Add: 184 Johnson Ave.,
Teaneck 07666 (201)837-1600.

Willingboro. BARBARA F. KALIK (D)
    1971-. Bds: Planning Bd. Party: V-Ch.,
Burlington Cnty. Com. 1970-77; Committeewoman
1964-77; Procedures & Compliance Officer 1975-76.
Prev: Adv. Shade Tree 1967-68; Adv. Youth Bd.

1974-75; Industrial Devt. 1972-73; Welfare Bd. 1973-74. Org: Dem. Club. Occ: Travel Agent. B: 11/8/36. Add: 48 Hillcrest Ln., Willingboro 08046 (609)877-2200.

Local Councils

Alpine. ZABELLE KEIL (I)
1976-. Bds: Ch., Bldg. Com.; Environmental Com.; Mental Health. Org: Rep. Club. Occ: Business Manager. Add: Bristol Ct., Alpine 07620 (201)768-6865.

Andover Borough. LOIS WILEY OKESON (R)
1976-. Bds: Ch., Celebration Public Events; Administrative & Exec.; Health & Welfare. Prev: Welfare Dir. 1950-51. Org: BPW; OES. Educ: Montclair State Coll. 1939 BA. Occ: Beauty Counselor. B: 1/5/19. Add: 33 Brighton Rd., Andover 07821.

Andover Township. DIANE C. BUCINO (D)
1977-. Bds: Recreation Cmsn. Party: Committee-woman 1974-75. Org: Dem. Club. B: 7/2/48. Add: RD 1, Box 815, Newton 07860 (201)383-6611.

Atlantic Highlands. HELEN M. MARCHETTI
99 Center Avenue, Atlantic Highlands 07716.

Barnegat Light. LUCILE B. PATRICK
1974-. Bds: Ch., Docks & Harbors; Ch., Health; Finances. Org: Conservation Society; Taxpayers Assoc.; Historical Society; Women's Club. B: 2/25/11. Add: 1503 Seaview Ave., Barnegat Light 08006 (609)494-2343.

Beachwood. EVELYN C. POTH (R)
1976-. Bds: Welfare & Recreation; Council Pres. Party: Cnty. Committeewoman 1957-77. B: 12/13/19. Add: 617 Compass Ave., Beachwood 08772 (201)349-8233.

Bedminster. ELIZABETH M. MERCK (R)
1974-. Bds: Ch., Police; Finance; Public Works. B: 1/23/20. Add: Cowperthwaite Rd., Bedminster 07921 (201)234-0333.

Bedminster. ANNE SHERMAN O'BRIEN (R)
1974-. Bds: Ch., Legal Com.; Public Works Com.; Zoning Com. Prev: Bd. of Adjustment 1974-75. Org: PTO. Educ: Duke U. 1951 BA. B: 7/16/30. Add: Ski Hill Dr., Bedminster 07921 (201)234-0333.

Belvidere. IRENE MACKEY SMITH (D)
1976-. Party: Nat. Del. 1968; Cnty. Committee 1946-70; Cnty. V-Ch. 1946-70; State Committee-woman 1971-81. Prev: Governor's Hwy. Safety Adv. Cmsn. 1973-75; Cnty. Coll. Study Com. 1975-76. Org: Soroptimist; DAR; Daughters of the Amer. Colonists; OES; Dem. Club. Occ: Congressional Aide. B: 4/9/10. Add: 628 3rd St., Belvidere 07823 (201)475-4672.

Berkeley Heights. MARIE ANNE KISSEBERTH (R)
1974-. Bds: Planning Bd.; Ch., Police; Leg. Repr. Party: State Alt. 1972; Cnty. Rep. Munici-pal Ch. 1970-75; V-Ch., Cnty. Rep. Party 1973-75; V-Ch., State Assoc. Rep. Party 1973-75; Leg. Aide to Assemblyman 1973-75. Prev: Mayor. Org: Women's

Club; BPW; Rep. Club. Occ: Travel Agent. B: 8/15/25. Add: 67 Webster Dr., Berkeley Hts. 07922 (201)464-2700.

Bernards. JOANNE L. HOWELL (R) **
1975-. Bds: Bicentennial Com. Org: AAUW; Rep. Club. Educ: U. of Md. 1952 BA. B: 10/10/29. Add: RD 1, 14 Hardscrabble Rd., Basking Ridge 07920 (201)766-2510.

Bernardsville. HOLLY M. LOCKHART (R)
1977-. Bds: Bd. of Health; Recreation; Library. Educ: Wellesley Coll. 1948 BA. B: 11/14/26. Add: 32 Mullens La., Bernardsville (201)766-2486.

Beverly. PHYLLIS HORTON
508 Jennings St., Beverly 08010.

Bloomsbury. FRANCES R. PETERMAN (R)
1976-. Bds: Ch., Health Bd.; Emergency Squad; Town Streets. Party: Cnty. Committee-woman 1930-52. Org: NEA; Local Election Bd.; Women's Club; Senior Citizens Council. Educ: Trenton State Coll. 1929 BSEd. B: 9/3/09. Add: 82 Main, Bloomsbury 08804.

Bloomsbury. JANET L. SULLIVAN (R)
1974-. Bds: Street Comsr.; Finance Com.; School Bd. Org: Women's Club. B: 5/21/26. Add: 46 Main St., Bloomsbury 08804 (201) 479-4412.

Bogota. ESTHER GARVEY (D) **
1973-. Bds: Planning Bd.; Library Bd.; Commissioner, Public Bldg. Party: County Com. 1969-74. Org: Pres., NJ Civil Defense; Dem. Club. B: 8/11/13. Add: 197 Beechwood Ave., Bogota 07603 (201)343-6241.

Boonton. LOUISE OAKLEY GREEN FRIEDMAN (D)
1976-. Bds: Housing Authority; Ch., Shelters for Battered Women; Ch., Health & Welfare. Party: Cnty. Committeewoman 1957-77; Election Bd. 1950-57. Prev: NJ Bd. of Examiners Cnty. Com. 1969-77. Educ: Cnty. Coll. of Morris 1974 AA; Montclair State Coll. 1977 BA. B: 5/18/26. Add: 145 Wootton St., Boonton 07005 (201) 335-2400.

Branchburg. LAURITA GABREE
27 Cedar Grove Road, Somerville 08876.

Bridgewater. CAROLANN AUGER (R) **
1974-. Bds: Planning Bd.; Environmental Com. Party: County Com. 1966-75. Org: State Nurses Assoc.; Pres., Mental Health Assoc. Educ: Adelphi U. 1960 BS. B: 10/31/38. Add: 239 Blossom Dr., RD 1, Basking Ridge 07920 (201)725-6300.

Brooklawn. MARION CONOVER
305 Town Center, Brooklawn 08030.

Butler. BARBARA J. RICKER (R)
1977-. Bds: Ch., Electric Dept.; Finance Com.; Water Com. Org: Butler Rep. Club. Educ: Gwenydd Mercy Coll. 1975 BA. Occ: Personnel Consultant. B: 5/31/44. Add: 93 Carey Ave., Butler 07405 (201)838-7200.

Byram. CAROL JEAN JACOBS (D) **
    1974-. Bds: Bd. of Health; Bd. of Public
Assistance. Party: State Com. 1973- ; County
Com. 1972-75. Org: Community Assoc.; Dem. Club;
PTA. B: 12/30/46. Add: Lake Dr., RD 2, Stanhope
07874 (201)347-2500.

Byram. CATHERINE VARIAN
    Cranberry Lake, RD #1, Andover 07821.

Califon. MARIE P. KOCH
    Railroad Ave., Califon 07830.

Califon. CYNTHIA E. WOERNER (R)
    1977-. Bds: Bd. of Recreation. Org: Women's
Club. Educ: Rutgers U. 1969 BA. B: 11/9/47.
Add: Hoffman Dr., Califon 07830.

Camden. HELEN MC HUGH
    City Hall, 6th & Market Sts., Camden 08101.

Chatham Borough. JANICE N. FENNER (R)
    1972-. Bds: Bd. of Health; Bd. of Adjustment;
Shade Tree Cmsn. Party: Cnty. Committeewoman
1963-67; Cnty. Finance Ch. 1966-67; Ch., Local
Com. 1965-67. Org: LWV; Rep. Club; PTA. Educ:
Middlebury Coll. 1955 BA. B: 9/2/34. Add: 96
Coleman Ave., Chatham 07938 (201)635-0674.

Chatham Borough. ARLINE PAILLER (R) **
    1972-. Bds: Mayor's Advisory Bd. to Dept. on
Aging. Prev: Bd. of Educ. 1960-65; Bd. of Health
1957-59. Org: Amer. Academy of Actuaries. Educ:
Case-Western Reserve U. 1937 BA; U. of Mich.
1938 MA. Occ: Consulting Actuary. B: 8/3/15.
Add: 80 Orchard Rd., Chatham 07928 (201)635-9012

Chatham Township. DOROTHY B. WILLIS (R)
    1976-. Bds: Bd. of Recreation; Bd. of Health;
Municipal Wildlife Refuge Cmsn. Prev: Bd. of
Recreation 1973-76. Org: Amer. Physical Therapy
Assoc.; PTA. Educ: Simmons Coll. 1956 BS. B:
12/12/34. Add: 30 Sunset Dr., Chatham Twp.
07928 (201)635-4600.

Cherry Hill. FRANCES BURNSTEIN
            ROSE MARIE HOSPODOR
    820 Mercer St., Cherry Hill 08002.

Chesilhurst. URSULA CHRISTINZIO (D) **
    1974-. Org: PTA; Dem. Club. Educ: U. of
Konigsberg, E. Prussia. Occ: Teacher. Add:
White Horse Pke., Chesilhurst 08089.

Chester. FRANCES BRANDER (D) **
    1974-. Bds: Water & Sewer Com.; Streets &
Roads; Finance. Org: NEA; NJEA; Dem. Club.
Educ: U. of RI 1951 BS. Occ: Nurse. B: 2/17/29.
Add: Grove St., Chester 07930 (201)879-5306.

Clifton. LOUISE FRIEDMAN (R)
    See Passaic County.

Clinton. ELLEN WILLIAMS (R)
    1976-. Bds: First Aid & Rescue Squad; Shade
Tree Cmsn.; Parks & Playgrounds. Org: LWV;
Women's Club; AAUW; Historical Society; Rep. Club.
Educ: Westminster Chair Coll. 1947 BA. B:
7/27/26. Add: 55 Center St., Clinton 08809
(201)735-8616.

Colts Neck. GLORIA L. PAMM
    22 Saratoga Dr., Colts Neck 07722.

Cresskill. MARGARET H. FOUDY (D) **
    1975-. Bds: Recreation; Senior Citizens;
Library Bd. Party: County Com. 1973-75. Org:
Dem. Club; PTA. B: 5/1/44. Add: 400 Grant
Ave., Cresskill 07626.

Delran. YVONNE J. DE WITT (D) **
    1974-. Bds: Multiple Dwelling Com.;
Bicentennial Com.; Assistance Bd.; Substandard
Housing Com. Party: Local Com. 1971-/5;
Secretary, Local Com. 1971-75; County Com.
1971-75. Org: PTA. B: 5/31/42. Add: 60C
Millside Manor, Delran 08075 (609)461-7734.

Demarest. JEANETTE M. FOLEY (D)
    1976-. Bds: Ch., Real Estate, Bldgs. &
Grounds; Recreation & Newsletter; Dept. of
Public Works. Party: Cnty. Committeewoman
1969-71. Prev: Planning Bd. 1971-75; N. Vly.
Planning Assoc. 1974-76. Org: LWV; Dem. Club.
Educ: St. John's 1952 BA. B: 6/27/30. Add:
30 Robin Rd., Demarest 07627 (201)768-0167.

Denville. ELIZABETH BELLOWS CANNARA (D)
    1971-. Bds: Sewer Ban Relief Com. Party:
Cnty. Committeewoman 1950-65. Prev: Environmental Cmsn. 1972-76. Org: LWV; Dem. Club.
B: 9/3/12. Add: Norris Rd., RFD, Denville
07834 (201)627-8900.

Deptford. SARA BAKER (D) **
    1968-. Bds: Auditing; Library. Party:
V-Ch., County Exec. Com. 1959-62; County Com.
1957-62. Prev: Bill Clerk, State Assembly
1959-63. Org: Dem. Club. B: 10/2/26. Add:
522 Hemlock Terrace, Woodbury 08096 (609)
845-5300.

Dover. JUDITH ANNE LOVAS (R)
    1977-. Org: Women's Rep. Club; Rep. Club.
Occ: Legal Secretary. B: 7/14/44. Add: 20
Sickle St., Dover 07801.

Dover. HELEN MC CAHILL
    3 E. Fairview Ave., Dover 07801.

Dumont. LOIS A. TULLY
    Municipal Bldg., 50 Washington Ave., Dumont
07628.

East Brunswick. NANCY E. BLETHEN (D)
    1974-. Bds: Ch., Recreation Adv. Bd.;
School Bd. Liaison. Prev: Bicentennial Com.
1975-76. Org: LWV; Dem. Club; Young Dem's.
Educ: Tufts U. 1962 BA; Rutgers 1972 MEd. Occ:
Leg. Aide. B: 11/11/40. Add: 4 Noel Ln.,
E. Brunswick 08816 (201)254-4600.

East Brunswick. GERALDINE M. WEBER (D)
    1976-. Bds: School Liaison Com.; Ad Hoc
School Site Com. Prev: Dir., Consumer Affairs
1974-76. Org: LWV; Dem. Club. Educ: Creighton
U. 1960 BA. B: 8/22/38. Add: 73 Stratford Rd.
E. Brunswick 08816 (201)254-4600.

East Orange. BERNICE J. DAVIS
    44 City Hall Place, East Orange 07019.

East Orange. NANCY JANE SCHRON (R)
1970-. Bds: Ch., Grants & Labor Negotiations; Finance Com.; Public Affairs Com. Party: Nat. Alt. 1972; Cnty. Committeewoman 1962-73; Ward Ch. 1972-73. Org: NEA; LWV; Rep. Women's Clubs; Fed. Rep. Clubs; PTA; Assoc. for Childhood Educ. Educ: Kean Coll. BS. Occ: Teacher. Add: 48 Fulton St., E. Orange 07017 (201)266-5120.

East Windsor. KATHRYN S. GOULD (D)
1975-. Bds: Planning Bd.; Economic Devt. Com.; Regional School Bd. Org: League of Municipalities, NJ; LWV; Dem. Club; Common Cause. Educ: U. of Wis. 1965 BA. B: 7/8/43. Add: 37 Hawthorne La., E. Windsor 08520 (609)443-4000.

East Windsor. SYLVIA DICHNER WEISS (D)
1975-. Bds: Welfare Bd, Recreation Cmsn. Prev: Senior Citizen Coord. 1974-75. Org: LWV; Dem. Club; Community Educ. Adv. Council. B: 10/27/14. Add: Wynbrook W. J-6, E. Windsor Twp. 08520 (609)443-4000.

Eatontown. JAMIE ONA MULLENAX
24 Barker Ave., Eatontown 07724.

Edgewater Park. NORMA J. WOOLMAN (R)
1976-. Bds: Planning Bd.; Riverfront Animal Control Cmsn.; Ch., Admin. Finance & Insurance. Party: Cnty. Committeewoman 1973-75; Municipal Ch. 1974-75. Prev: Industrial Adv. Cmsn. 1975-76. B: 5/31/26. Add: 134 W. Franklin Ave., Edgewater Park 08010 (609)877-2050.

Edison. DOROTHY K. DRWAL (I)
1975-. Bds: Bd. of Health. Party: Cnty. Committeewoman 1952-54. Org: NEA; Young Dem's.; United Dem's.; Edison Dem. Assoc.; PTA; PTSA. Educ: Rutgers U. 1952 BA. Occ: Teacher. B: 4/27/30. Add: 14 Overbrook Ave., Edison 08817 (201)225-3060.

Edison. MARGERY S. GOLIN (D)
1975-. Bds: Bd. of School Estimate. Prev: Planning Bd. 1973-75; Ch., Planning Bd. 1974-75. Org: LWV; WPC; Young Dem's. Educ: Columbia U. 1955 BS; Rutgers U. 1970 MEd. B: 6/6/33. Add: 74 Oliver Ave., Edison 08817 (201)287-0900.

Egg Harbor City. JEANNETTE T. GAUPP
424 Boston Ave., Egg Harbor 08215.

Egg Harbor City. HELEN M. HAUGAN (R)
1976-. Bds: Ch., Welfare Com.; Property Com.; Licensing Com. Org: Citizens in Action; Rep. Club. Occ: Real Estate Sales. B: 9/14/22. Add: 439 St. Louis Ave., Egg Harbor 08215 (609) 965-2189.

Egg Harbor City. FANNY D. RITTENBERG (R) **
1967-. Bds: Safety; Utility; Parks & Play-Ground; Trustee, Atlantic Community Coll. Org: NEA; NJEA; Chamber of Commerce; PTA; Rep. Club; Women's Civic Club. Educ: Syracuse U. BA, MS; U. of Pa. Occ: Principal, Elementary School. B: 2/25/05. Add: 29 Liverpool Ave., Egg Harbor City 08215 (609)965-0081.

Emerson. GRACE MAIER
CAROLINE OLSON
Municipal Place, Emerson 07630.

Englewood. SHIRLEY M. LACY
P.O. Box 228, Englewood 07631.

Englishtown. MARION A. PETER (R)
1976-. Bds: Ch., Finance & Administration; Co-Ch., Public Safety; Asst. Police Comsr. Org: NEA; Internat. Reading Assoc.; Rep. Club; PTA. Educ: Trenton State Coll. 1956 BS; 1972 MEd. Occ: Remedial Reading Specialist. B: 4/23/35. Add: 21 Wood Ave., Englishtown 07721 (201) 446-9235.

Fair Haven. NANCY ENGSTROM KERN (R)
1976-. Bds: Ch., Public Works; Finance & Administration; Fire, First Aid & Civil Defense. Org: NEA; Rep. Club. Educ: Allegheny Coll. 1956 BA; Colgate U. 1963 MA. Occ: Teacher. B: 8/18/34. Add: 79 Grange Ave., Fair Haven 07701 (201)747-0992.

Fair Haven. KATHERINE C. SHAFER (D)
1974-. Bds: Ch., Recreation, Environment & Health; Police Com.; Public Affairs & Planning. Party: Local-Cnty. Committeewoman 1972- Org: Children's Psychiatric Ctr.; Dem. Club; Young Dems. Educ: Wilson Coll. 1968 BA. Occ: Community Relations Asst. Planned Parenthood. B: 7/23/40. Add: 16 Gillespie Ave., Fair Haven 07701.

Fair Lawn. FLORENCE DOBROW (D)
1975-. Bds: Community Devt.; Mental Health; Senior Citizen Adv. Com. Party: Cnty. Committeewoman 1970- . Org: LWV; Independent Dems. Occ: Sales Exec. B: 3/18/18. Add: 14 Fulton Pl., Fair Lawn 07410 (201)796-1700.

Fairview. FLORENCE RYAN
Municipal Bldg., 58 Anderson Ave., Fairview 07024.

Fanwood. CAROL G. WHITTINGTON (D)
1974-. Bds: Ch., Health & Welfare Com.; Ch., Public Assistance Bd.; Bldg. & Zoning Com. Party: Cnty. Committeewoman 1972-75. Org: Right to Life; Dem. Club; PTA. B: 3/9/39. Add: 40 Forest Rd., Fanwood 07023.

Fieldsboro. ELEANORA CONWAY
20 Stewarts Lane, Fieldsboro 08505.

Fieldsboro. CATHERINE PROKOP (D) **
1974-. Bds: Finance; Property. Educ: West Jersey Hospital School of Nursing 1954 RN. B: 6/14/33. Add: 11 Adams La., Fieldsboro 08505.

Flemington. ELIZABETH YARD (D) **
Prev: Rent Leveling Bd. 1974-75; County Welfare Bd. 1971-74. Org: NJ Warehousemen's Assoc.; County Taxpayers Assoc.; Dem. Club. Occ: Self-employed. B: 8/29/16. Add: 24 Parker Ave., Flemington 08822 (201)782-2233.

Franklin. MILDRED H. HARDEN (D)
1974-. Bds: Public Assistance Bd.; Economic Cmsn.; Council Pres. Prev: Planning Bd. 1970-74; Cnty. Adv. Council for Title III 1977; Adv. Council Meals on Wheels & Outreach 1974- . Org: NEA; NJ Retired Teachers Assoc.; League of Municipalities. Educ: Cedar Crest Coll. 1931 BA; N.Y.U. 1944 MA. B: 10/17/08. Add: 7 Edsall Rd., Franklin 07416 (201)827-9280.

Franklin Lakes. ANITA ARDIA (R)
1975-. Bds: Bd. of Health; Hall of Honor Com. Party: Cnty. Committeewoman 1959-75. Org: Rep. Club. Occ: Writer. B: 2/12/17. Add: 358 Woodside Ave., Franklin Lakes 07419 (201)891-0048.

Franklin Township. PHYLLIS R. ELSTON (D)
1976-. Bds: Environmental Cmsn.; Bldg. Com. Prev: Bd. of Adjustment 1975-76; Secretary, Environmental Cmsn. 1975- . Educ: Rutgers U. 1973 BA. Occ: Saleswoman. B: 5/1/39. Add: RD, Annandale 08801 (201)735-4802.

Franklin Township. DOROTHY MARIE MAKLARY (R)
1975-. Bds: Real Estate Com. Org: Taxpayers Assoc.; Rep. Club. Occ: Bookkeeper. B: 4/22/41. Add: RD #1, 45 Crescent Dr., Princeton 08073 (201)873-2500.

Frenchtown. EVELYN F. EWALD
502 Harrison St., Frenchtown 08825.

Garfield. IRENE L. JAROSZ **
1972-. Bds: Housing Authority. Occ: Auditing Supervisor. B: 8/25/24. Add: 292 Outwater La., Garfield 07026.

Garwood. GEORGIANA GURREIRI (D)
1975-. Bds: Ch., Finance Com.; Laws & Licences; Ecology. Party: Dist. Committeewoman 1973-77; V-Ch., Dem. Com. 1973-77. Prev: Bd. of Adjustment 1974-75. Org: Historical Society; Dem. Club. Occ: Legal Secretary. B: 9/7/44. Add: 211 3rd Ave., Garwood 07027 (201)789-0710.

Garwood. DORIS COLWELL MANN (R)
1973-. Bds: Ch., Bldgs. & Grounds; Ch., Industrial; Ch., Ecology. Party: Cnty. Committeewoman 1977; Municipal Ch. 1973-77. Prev: Bd. of Health; Ch., Bicentennial 1973-76. Org: Rep. Club; PTA. Occ: Newspaper Correspondent. B: 8/5/26. Add: 252 Myrtle Ave., Garwood 07027.

Glen Ridge. HELENE E. KAPLAN (R)
1973-. Bds: Liaison to Cnty. Budget Hearings. Prev:Comsr., Essex Cnty. Charter Study 1973-74. Org: LWV; Rep. Club; Women's Rep. Club; NJ Fed. of Rep. Women. Educ: Queens Coll. 1956 BA. B: 11/12/35. Add: 76 Oxford St., Glen Ridge 07028 (201)748-8400.

Glen Rock. ELIZABETH H. ROUSSEAU (R)
1973-. Bds: Recreation Adv. Bd.; Youth Guidance Council. Org: LWV; PTA. B: 5/27/27. Add: 65 Concord Ave., Glen Rock 07452.

Gloucester. CONCETTA AUCELLO
Mun.Bldg., P.O. Box 8, Blackwood 08012.

Hackettstown. SUSAN J. WEST (D)
1976-. Bds: Planning Bd.; Ch., Ordinance & Municipal Affairs Com. Party: Cnty. Committeewoman 1976-77. Org: LWV; Dem. Club. Educ: Northern Ill. U. 1966 BS. B: 7/16/43. Add: 501 Plane St., Hackettstown 07840 (201)852-3130.

Hamburg. BEATRICE HESSLER (R) **
1972-. Bds: Bd. of Health; Bd. of Public Assistance; Finance. Org: NJEA. Occ: Cafeteria Manager. B: 6/5/28. Add: 198-200 Hamburg Turnpike, Hamburg 07419.

Hamilton Township. HELEN R. MC DONALD (R)
1975-. Bds: Local Bd. of Assistance; Environmental Adv. Cmsn.; Alcoholic Beverage Control Bd. Party: Cnty. Rep. Committeewoman 1969-77; Dem. Committeewoman 1950-68. Org: PTA. Occ: Beautician. B: 2/27/20. Add: 234 Sandalwood Ave., Hamilton Twp. 08619 (609)586-3500.

Hampton. HELEN S. BRIDGES (D)
1977-. Bds: Joint Municipal Ct., Joint Purchasing Com.; League of Municipalities. Prev: Zoning Bd. of Adjustment 1972-76. Org: NEA; PTA. Educ: Upsala Coll. 1956 BA; William Paterson Coll. 1972 MA. Occ: Teacher. B: 3/22/37. Add: RD 1, Box 105, Lafayette 07858.

Hampton. ARLENE GIBSON
Mun. Bldg., 67 Main St., Hampton 08827.

Hampton. ANNE VACCARO (R)
1975-. Bds: Planning Bd.; Tri-Regional Plan Bd.; Tri-Tregional Ct. Prev: Planning Bd. 1973-74; Ch., Plan Bd. 1974-75; Tri-Regional Plan 1975-77. Occ: Hairdresser. B: 3/22/30. Add: RD 4, Box 671, Newton 07860 (201)383-5570.

Harrington Park. MARION SUNDEN (R)
1976-. Bds: Bd. of Health; Bd. of Adjustment; Borough Newsletter. Prev: Recreation Cmsn. 1976-77; Fire Cmsn. 1976-77; Editor Borough Newsletter 1970-76. Org: Rep. Club; PTA. Occ: Tennis Instructor. B: 5/6/29. Add: 111 Old Hook Rd., Box 277, Harrington Park 07640 (201)768-1700.

Haworth. HARRIET E. MASON (R) **
1974-. Bds: Police Com.; Bd. of Health; Fire Com. Party: Com. 1968-71. Org: LWV; Rep. Club. Educ: Christ Hospital School of Nursing 1942 RN. B: 2/10/21. Add: 175 Pleasant St., Haworth 07641 (201)384-4785.

Haworth. BARBARA HANSON SHOTLIFF (R)
1972-. Bds: Library Bd.; Finance Com.; Editor, Newsletter. Party: Rep. Municipal Ch. 1968-72; Cnty. Com. 1966-72; Aide, State Assemblyman 1969-71. Prev: Ch., Parks & Playgrounds 1966-72; Planning Bd. 1972. Org: Rep. Club; Women's Club; AAUW. Educ: U. of Pa. 1940 BA. B: 9/28/18. Add: 209 Harrison St., Haworth 07641 (201)384-4785.

Hazlet. MARY JANE WILEY (R)
1976-. Bds: Bd. of Educ.; Welfare Bd.; Environmental. Party: Local Secretary 1971-72; Local Treasurer 1974-75; Cnty. Exec. Com. 1976-

77. Org: Rep. Club; PTO. B: 8/22/36. Add: 13 Monmouth St., Hazlet 07730 (201)264-1700.

Helmetta. ALICE FALKOWSKI
    31 Lake Ave., Helmetta 08828.

High Bridge. DOROTHY T. FARLEY (R)
    1974-. Bds: Ch., Water Com.; Finance Com.; Recreation; Public Bldgs. Party: Election Bd. 1966-73. Educ: Trenton State Coll. 1973 BS. Occ: Paralegal. B: 7/28/29. Add: 46 Tisco Ave., High Brg. 08829 (201)638-6455.

Highland Park. IRENE DWORECK (D)
    1974-. Bds: Community Affairs; Finance & Personnel; Ch., Dept. of Public Works. Party: Committeewoman 1966-74. Prev: Human Rights Com. 1974-75; Arts Com. 1974-75; Cmsn. on Aging 1974-75. Org: Dem. Club. B: 9/6/19. Add: 355 N 4th Ave., Highland Pk. 08904 (201)572-3400.

Hightstown. JOANNE O. FRAZER
    118 Harron Ave., Hightstown 08520.

Hightstown. WILMA C. SEHULSTER (R)
    1974-. Bds: Planning Bd. & Site Review Com.; Dept. of Welfare. Prev: Zoning Bd. of Adjustment 1973-74; Bd. of Health 1975-76. Org: BPW; Women's Club; Rep. Club. B: 4/26/16. Add: 116 Dutch Neck Rd., Hightstown 08520 (609)448-2188.

Hillsdale. CATHERINE CICORIA (R)
    1976-. Bds: Bd. of Health; Shade Tree; Environmental. Party: Cnty. Committeewoman 1968-77; Municipal Ch. 1973-77. Prev: Zoning Bd. of Adjustment 1971-75. Org: Women's Club; Rep. Club. Occ: Retail Sales Manager. B: 5/22/30. Add: 30 Bedford Rd., Hillsdale 07642 (201)666-4800.

Hi-Nella. SANDRA L. WILKIE (D)
    1976-. Bds: Planning Bd.; Police Com. Org: Dem. Club. Educ: Pierce Jr. Coll. 1965 AS. B: 5/25/45. Add: 9 Navajo Rd., Hi-Nella 08083 (609)784-6237.

Holmdel. ELAINE M. FREY (R)
    1976-. Bds: Bd. of Health; Welfare, Drug Abuse. Prev: Recreation Cmsn. 1967-76; Pool & Tennis Com. 1970-76; Bicentennial Com. 1974-76; Juvenile Conf. Bd. 1970-77. Org: Historical Society; Rep. Club. Occ: School Bus Driver. B: 8/1/25. Add: 4 Pky. Pl., Holmdel 07733 (201) 946-4330.

Hopatcong. CATHERINE REAM (R)
    1966-. Bds: Ch., License; Ch., Insurance; Real Estate. Org: Rep. Club. B: 8/28/18. Add: Hudson Guild Farm, Sparta-Stanhope Rd., Andover 07821 (201)398-5200.

Howell. ALICE ALATALO (R)
    1975-. Bds: Police Dept.; Recreation Dept.; Public Assistance Bd. Party: Cnty. Committeewoman 1972-75. Org: Rep. Club; Women's Dem. Club; Senior Citizens. B: 4/19/22. Add: 71 Darien Rd., Howell 07731 (201)938-4500.

Irvington. ESTHER D. SCHWARZ (D)
    1976-. Bds: Ch., Alcoholic Beverage Cmsn.; Property Maintenance Program. Prev: Citizens Mental Health Cmsn. 1971-77; Narcotics Cmsn.

1971-74; Fiscal Budget Com. 1975-76. Org: Dem. Club; PTA. Occ: Office Manager. B: 3/29/33. Add: 117 Webster St., Irvington 07111 (201)372-2100.

Island Heights. MARGARET W. KING (R) **
    1973-. Org: NEA; NJEA. Educ: SUNY at Albany 1936 BA. B: 5/31/14. Add: 29 Park Ave., Island Heights 08732.

Jackson. ARLEEN POLITO (D)
    1976-. Bds: Ch., Public Works, Health & Recreation; Welfare Bd. Prev: Jackson Bd. of Educ. 1971-76; Library Com. 1972-76; Bicentennial Com. 1976-77. Org: Dem. Club. Occ: Office Manager. B: 8/15/39. Add: 47 Goldweber Ave., Jackson 08527 (201)364-4909.

Jefferson Township. FRANCES SLAYTON (R)
    Cedar Terrace, Berkshire Vly. 07885.

Jefferson Township. GRACE R. TEESE (D)
    1975-. Bds: Environmental Protection Agency-Water Quality. Party: Municipal Ch. 1971-73; Cnty. Committeewoman 1970-73, '77. Prev: Pollution Abatement Com. 1965-67; Planning Bd. 1966-71. Org: Dem. Club; Grand Jurors Assoc. B: 6/25/25. Add: Clifton Rd., Oak Ridge 07438. (201)697-1500.

Jersey City. LOIS SHAW (D) **
    1973-. Party: Del. to Nat. Conv. 1972; Nat. Credentials Com. 1972; State Dem. Elector 1972. Org: LWV; Women's Political Caucus; Community Action Council. B: 5/4/42. Add: 244 Hancock Ave., Jersey City 07307 (201)434-3600.

Kenilworth. MARY KELLY (D)
    1968-. Bds: Bd. of Health; Welfare Bd.-Senior Citizens; Library Bd. Party: Cnty. Committeewoman 1958-63. Prev: Councilwoman 1968-71. Org: NEA; Dem. Club. Educ: Newark State Teachers Coll. 1941 BSEd. Occ: Teacher. B: 4/28/19. Add: 116 N. 14th St., Kenilworth 07033.

Knowlton. LYNNE J. STIRRAT
    Box 299, RD #1, Columbia 07832.

Lake Hopatcong. FRANCES SLAYTON
    Mun. Bldg., Weldon Rd., Lake Hopatcong 07849.

Lakehurst Borough. VIRGINIA KOCZYNSKI
    P.O. Box 54, Lakehurst Borough 08733.

Lambertville. BARBARA GILL
    RD #2, Lambertville 08530.

Lavallette. SUE C. JOHNSON
    5 1/2 White Ave., Lavallette 08735.

Lawnside. CORA N. FREEMAN (D)
    1975-. Bds: Ch., Finance; Ch., Personnel; Streets & Roads. Org: Dem. Club. Educ: Winston-Salem Teachers Coll. 1941 BS; Temple U. MS. Occ: Teacher. B: 9/15/20. Add: 116 E. Oak Ave. Lawnside 08045 (609)547-6133.

Lawnside. JOYCE GILCHRIST PIERCE (D) **
    1974-. Bds: Ch., Police & Fire Dept. Prev:
V-Ch., Bd. of Trustees, Children Shelter 1969-71.
Org: NEA; NJEA; Dem. Club. Educ: W. Va. State
1959 BA. Occ: Teacher. B: 6/18/38. Add: 12
Warwick Rd., Lawnside 08045 (609)547-6133.

Lawrence Township. MARY C.N. TANNER (R)
    1976-. Bds: Landscape Adv. Com.; Library;
Bd. of Condemnation. Org: LWV; Twp. Rep's.
Educ: U. of Vt. 1940 PHB; Mills Coll. 1942 MA;
Radcliffe Coll. 1955 PHD. B: 12/8/18. Add:
354 Cold Soil Rd., Princeton 08540 (609)
896-9400.

Leonia. MARGARET L. MUENSTERMANN
    511 Broad Avenue, Leonia 07605.

Leonia. ELLEN E. OPPENHEIMER (R)
    1976-. Bds: Police Comsr.; Ch., Recreation
Cmsn.; Fire Comsr. Prev: Law & Ordinance 1976;
Police Comsr. 1976-77; Fire Cmsn. 1976-77;
Ambulance Corps Dir. 1974-75; Ambulance Corps.
Personnel Dir. 1974-75. Org: "Project CARE";
Program for the Elderly; Rep. Assoc. Educ:
Hunter Coll. CPT. Occ: Real Estate & Construction
Co. B: 2/9/30. Add: 400 Greenway Dr., Leonia
07605 (201)944-6857.

Lincoln Park. CONSTANCE MIDKIFF
    4 Seneca Ave., Lincoln Pk. 07035.

Lincoln Park. JOYCE I. REINER (D)
    1976-. Bds: Environmental Com. Party: Cnty.
Committeewoman 1974-77. Prev: Citizens Adv. Com.
1975-76. Org: Dem. Club; PTA. Educ: Hunter Coll.
1959 BA. Occ: Substitute Teacher. B: 1/18/38.
Add: 29 Evergreen Dr., Lincoln Park 07035
(201)694-6100.

Lindenwold. KAY A. GARVEY
         ADRIAN NORWOOD
    Municipal Bldg., 1017 E. Linden Ave., Linden-
wold 08021.

Linwood. PEGGY OFF
    1450 Woodlynne Blvd., Linwood 08221.

Livingston. DORIS L. BECK (D)
    1974-. Bds: Senior Citizens Adv. Council;
Consumers Affairs Com.; Adv. Health Council.
Prev: Mayor 1975. Educ: Montclair State Coll.
1950 BA. Occ: Bank Dir. B: 3/15/29. Add: 70
Springbrook Rd., Livingston 07039 (201)992-5000.

Loch Arbour. MYRTLE P. ROBERTSON (R) **
    1973-. Bds: Bd. of Health. B: 8/1/26. Add:
421 Edgemont Dr., Loch Arbour 07711 (201)
531-4740.

Lumberton. MARGARET P. GEST
    6 Forrest Ct., Mt. Holly 08060.

Madison. ELIZABETH G. BAUMGARTNER (D) **
    1973-. Bds: Sanitation & Welfare; Bd. of
Health; Public Safety. Org: Amer. Nurses' Assoc.;
Zonta Club; NJ State Nurses' Assoc. Educ: Seton
Hall U. 1955 BSN; St. John's U. 1959 MS. Occ:
Professor of Nursing. B: 9/3/27. Add: 51 Fair-
wood Rd., Madison 07940 (201)377-0561.

Madison. FRANCES A. MANTONE (R)
    1976-. Party: Committeewoman 1975-77. Occ:
School Secretary. B: 10/12/37. Add: Hartley
Dodge Bldg., Kings Rd., Madison 07940.

Magnolia. CAROLYN JANE CARROLL (R) **
    1974-. Org: Rep. Club. B: 11/18/41. Add:
239 E. Washington Ave., Magnolia 08049.

Manahawkin. DOLORES M. BARNES (R)
    1976-. Org: Fed. Rep. Women; Cnty. Rep.
Org.; Rep. Club. B: 5/15/23. Add: 777
Delaware Ave., Manahawkin 08050.

Manchester Township. ADELAIDE PORTASH (R)
    1976-. Bds: Ch., Office on Aging; Police
Cmsnr.; Finance Officer. Org: Rep. Club; PTA.
B: 4/20/31. Add: 200 Wrangle Brook Rd.,
Manchester Twp. 08733 (201)657-8121.

Mannington. MARTYNA MC LEAN
    Old Kings Highway, Salem 08079.

Mansfield. GRETAL GOMETRO
    Karrville Rd., RD, Oxford 07863.

Manville. MARION B. DU DASH (D)
    1976-. Bds: Ch., Bldgs. & Grounds Com.;
Finance Com.; Fire & Water Com. Prev: Bd. of
Health 1973-76; Secretary, Bicentennial Com.
1976-77. Org: Dem. Club; Young Dems. Occ:
Patent Secretary. B: 10/3/45. Add: 706 Washing-
ton Ave., Manville 08835.

Matawan Borough. VIRGINIA CHRISTINAT (D)
    1975-. Bds: Recreation Cmsn.; Historic
Sites Cmsn.; Police Cmsn. Prev: Library Bd.
1972-75. Org: Women's Club; Dem. Club; Youth
Services. Add: 128 Ravine Dr., Matawan Borough
07747 (201)566-3898.

Matawan Borough. MARY ELLEN LUPI
    57 Sapphire Lane., Matawan 07747.

Maywood. JOYCE DEWLAND
    459 Maywood Ave., Maywood 07607.

Medford. JUDITH PALOMBI
    28 Main Trail, Medford 08055.

Medford. ELIZABETH WOODFORD
    Cedar Run Lake, Marlton 08053.

Mendham Borough. RUTH H. SMITH (R)
    1976-. Bds: Zoning & Subdiv. Cmsn.; Bd. of
Health; Planning Bd. Prev: Planning Bd. 1975-
76; Senior Citizen Housing Com. 1973-76. Org:
LWV; Educ: Hiram Coll. 1954 BA; Radcliffe
Coll. 1957 HRPBA. Occ: Leg. Consultant. B:
5/8/33. Add: 34 E. Main St., Mendham 07945
(201)543-7152.

Mendham Township. PATRICIA JOAN MAYNARD (R)
    1973-. Bds: Finance Com.; Ch., Recreation;
Ch., Bldgs. & Grounds. Party: Committeewoman
1974-77; Co-Ch., 1976 General Election.
Prev: Bd. of Recreation Cmsnrs. 1970-73. Org:
LWV; Women's Club; Rep. Club; Cnty. Women's
Rep. Club. Occ: Substitute Teacher. B:
5/24/34. Add: Old Mill Rd., Chester 07930
(201)543-4555.

Merchantville. GERTRUDE G. YATES (R)
1975-. Bds: Dir., Bd. of Health; Ch., Fees & Licenses; Water Cmsn. Prev: Planning Bd. 1960-65; Public Assistance 1965-68; Concerts in Park, Ch. 1962-77. Org: Rep. Club; Women's Club. Educ: Berwick Academy 1929 BA. B: 8/12/06. Add: 23 Clinton Ave., Merchantville 08109 (609)662-2474.

Metuchen. DIANE GABE FORNEY (D)
1976-. Bds: Liaison, Finance & Administration; Liaison,Borough Atty.; Borough Auditor. Party: Cnty. Committeewoman 1972-74. Prev: Local Assistance Bd. 1972-76. Org: LWV; Dem. Club. Educ: Syracuse U. 1965 BS; Rutgers U. 1976 MS. B: 5/24/43. Add: 54 Ross Ave., Metuchen 08842 (201)549-3600.

Millburn. ANN E. COOPER (D)
1974-. Bds: Planning Bd.; Ch., Cable Television Com.; Ch., Com. on Senior Citizen Needs. Party: Dem. Cnty. Com. 1970-74; V-Ch., Dem. Cnty. Com. 1973-76; Recording Secretary Dem. Cnty. Com. 1970-73. Org: Historical Society; LWV; Com. for a More Responsible Legislature; Dem. Club; Fed. of Dem. Women; PTA. Educ: Wellesley Coll. 1958 BA; Columbia U. 1962 MA. B: 12/12/36. Add: 9 Delbarton Dr.,Short Hills 07078 (201)376-2030.

Millburn. MAUREEN B. OGDEN (R)
1975-. Bds: Ch., Bldg. & Grounds Com.; Shade Tree & Recreation Cmsn. Party: Cnty. Committeewoman 1952-54. Prev: Ch., Environmental Com. 1973-75; Environmental Design Review Com. Org: LWV; Water Study; Jr. League; Women's Rep. Club; PTA. Educ: Smith Coll. 1950 BA; Columbia U. 1963 MA; Rutgers U. 1977 MCRP. B: 11/1/28. Add: 59 Lakeview Ave., Short Hills 07078 (201) 376-2030.

Millington. HELEN S. CLANCY
1434 Long Hill Rd., Millington 07946.

Montclair. BETTY EVANS (D)
1976-. Party: Cnty. Committeewoman 1948-51. Prev: Local Assistance Bd. 1953-57. Org: LWV; NJ Housing Coalition. Educ: Columbia U. 1970 BA. B: 9/17/10. Add: 14 Edgecliff Rd., Upr. Montclair 07043 (201)744-1400.

Montvale. SHARON K. MELENDES (R)
1975-. Bds: Recreation Com.; Youth Guidance Com.; Park & Playground Com. Org: Amer. Council to Improve our Neighborhoods; Rep. Club; PTA. Educ: Carroll Coll. 1961 BS. B: 1/24/39. Add: 31 Twin Oaks Dr., Montvale 07645 (201)391-5700.

Moonachie. MADELINE ORSINI
3 Jefferson Pl., Moonachie 07074.

Moorestown. MARY WELLS (D)
1974-. Prev: Health Adv. Council 1970-73. Org: NASW; Health Systems Agency, Burlington Cnty. Council; Health & Welfare Council of Burlington Cnty.; LWV; Dem. Club. Educ: Drew U. 1964 BA; Rutgers U. 1967 MSW. Occ: Co-Exec. Dir., Family Service of Burlington Cnty. B: 5/7/42. Add: 217 Paul Dr., Moorestown 08057 (609)235-0912.

Morris Plains. MARGUERITE ADAMS
Mun. Bldg., 531 Speedwell Ave., Morris Plains 07950.

Morristown. BEATRICE M. JENKINS (D)
1973-. Bds: Pres., Town Council; Bd.of Adjustment. Party: State Del. 1976. Org: Cnty. Urban League, NAACP; LWV; Nat. Fed. of Dem. Women; WPC. Occ: Note Clerk. B: 7/1/28. Add: 62 Wetmore Ave., Morristown 07960.

Mountain Lakes. CAROL RUFENER (R)
1977-. Bds: Citizens Advocate; Civil Defense Bldg. Com.; Sewer Com. Org: AAUW; LWV. Educ: Otterbein Coll. BS; N.Y.U. MBA. Occ: Writer. Add: 162 Lake Dr., Mtn. Lakes 07046 (201)334-3131.

Mount Holly. GRACE B. DONNELLEY
33 Bartram Ave., Mt. Holly 08060.

Mount Holly. ELIZABETH A. POTTER
Wilson Avenue, Mt. Holly 08060.

Mount Olive. SANDRA GEIGER (R)
1975-. Bds: Ch., Bd. of Health. Party: Cnty. Committeewoman 1973-75. Org: NJEA; School Nurse Assoc.; LWV; Rep. Club; Cnty. Women's Club. Educ: Albert Einstein Medical Ctr. 1960 RN; Jersey City State Coll. 1975 BA. Occ: Health Teacher/School Nurse. B: 8/21/38. Add: 5 Knollwood Rd., Flanders 07836 (201)691-0900.

Mount Olive. ELIZABETH KLEINBERG (D)
1977-. Bds: Bd. of Assistance; Water & Sewer Com. Prev: Environmental Cmsn. 1975-76. Org: LWV; Dem. Club; PTA. Educ: Brooklyn Coll. 1968 BS. B: 10/21/46. Add: 10 Edgewood Pl., Flanders 07836 (201)691-0900.

Neptune. MRS. ALMERTH BATTLE
Mun. Bldg., 25 Neptune Blvd., Neptune 07753.

Neshanic. THERESA SIEDLARCZYK
Mun. Bldg., Amwell Rd., Neshanic 08853.

Newark. MARIE L. VILLANI (D) **
1973-. Bds: Joint Meeting; Real Estate Cmsn.; Assistance Bd.; Commissioner Non-Emergency Transportation Systems. B: 7/4/21. Add: 586 Parker St., Newark 07104 (201)733-6572.

New Providence. MARY ELLEN IRWIN (R)
1971-. Bds: Ch., Community Dev. of Union Cnty.; Ch., Inter-governmental Com.; Ch., Legislative Com. Party: Nat. Alt. 1964; Cnty. Committeewoman 1958-71. Prev: Liaison, Cnty. Bd. of Freeholders 1970-71; Library Bd. 1969-71; Garden State Arts Center Council 1968-69. Org: United Way Bd.; LWV. Educ: Pomona Coll. 1954 BA; Occidental Coll. 1970 MUS. Occ: Eastern Repr.,Coro Foundation. B: 8/7/32. Add: 118 Possum Way, New Providence 07974 (201)665-1400.

Newton. NORMA IRENE CAPPOLA (R)
1976-. Bds: Bd. of Health. Org: NEA. Educ: Atlantic City School of Nursing 1949 RN; Jersey City State Coll. 1970 BA. Occ: Teacher. B: 5/5/27. Add: RD 2, Box 629, Newton 07860.

North Arlington. ROBERTA HAAG
Mun. Bldg., 214 Ridge Rd., N. Arlington 07032.

North Caldwell. BARBARA S. DOBBIN (R)
     1975-. Bds: Ch., Public Utilities Com.;
Public Safety Com.; Legal Ordinances Com. Party:
Ch., Rep. Party Charter Change 1975-76. Org:
Learning Consultants; Charter Change in Essex
Cnty.; NEA. Educ: Douglass Coll. 1953 BA;
Harvard 1954 EDM. Occ: Special Educ. Teacher.
B: 5/6/32. Add: 14 Highfield Ave., N. Caldwell
07006 (201)228-4400.

North Plainfield. ROSE C. MC CONNELL (R)
     1977-. Party: Cnty. Committeewoman 1965-77;
V-Ch., Cnty. Com. 1969-72. Prev: Green Acres
Com.; Recreation Cmsn. Org: NEA; Rep. Club.
Educ: Rider Coll. 1944 BS; Rutgers U. 1950 MEd.
B: 11/6/23. Add: 284 Leonard Pl., N. Plainfield
07060.

Oaklyn. JANE D. FITZPATRICK
     Munn, Bldg., 500 White Horse Pike, Oaklyn
08107.

Oceanport. MIRIAM S. BRYAN (R)
     1975-. Bds: Recreation Com.; Shade Tree Com.;
Bicentennial Com. Prev: Recreation Com. 1968-76.
Org: LWV; Oceanport Recreation Com.; Rep. Club.
Educ: Brookdale Coll. 1975 AA. Occ: Real Estate
Saleswoman. Add: 254 Arnold St., Oceanport
07757 (201)222-8221.

Ogdensburg. HELEN LUCAS
     29 Lincoln Ave., Ogdensburg 07439.

Old Bridge. SONJA K. FINEBERG
     307 Morgan Avenue, Old Bridge 08857.

Old Tappan. ISOBEL ELLIKER
     32 Irving Street, Old Tappan 07675.

Old Tappan. KELSEY LOBDELL SCHULZ (R)
     1974-. Bds: Ch., Police & Public Safety Com.;
Fire & First Aid Com.; Recreation & Golf Com.
Prev: Ch., Bldg. Com. 1975; Planning Bd. 1975;
Bd. of Adjustment 1975. Org: Org. Rep. Club;
PTA. B: 2/14/31. Add: 202 Orangeburg Rd., Old
Tappan 07675 (201)664-1849.

Oradell. ROSEMARY C. BERTRAM (R)
     1974-. Bds: Recreation Com. Party: Cnty.
Committeewoman 1970-77. Prev: Recreation Com.
1972-77. Org: AAUW; Rep. Club; State Fed. of
Rep. Women. Educ: Swarthmore Coll. 1960 BA. B:
4/24/38. Add: 202 Spring Vly. Rd., Oradell
07649.

Orange. PATRICIA JULIANO (D)
     1976-. Bds: Flood Control Com.; Ch., Study
Com.-Orange Animal Control; Ch., Council Special
Com. Party: Committeewoman 1975-76. Prev:
Trustee, Orange Opportunity Corp. 1967-68; Shade
Tree Cmsn. 1972-73. Org: Soroptimist; NJ League
of Municipalities; NJ Assoc. of Retarded Citizens;
Assoc. for the Deaf; LWV; Mental Health Assoc.
Educ: Essex Cnty. Coll. 1973 AS. B: 12/8/30.
Add: 390 Tremont Pl., Orange 07050 (201)266-4194.

Paramus. BLANCHE PATCHETT
     Mun. Bldg., Jockish Square, Paramus 07652.

Park Ridge. LUCY MESSICK HELLER (D)
     1975-. Bds: Ch., General Govt./Finance;
Police Com.; Liaison, Intergovt. Affairs.
Party: Del., Leg. Dist. 1977. Prev: Ch.,
Bergen Charter Study Com. 1973-74; Bd. of
Health 1973-75; Tri-boro Library Com. 1972.
Org: Internat. City Management Assoc.; LWV;
Health & Welfare Council; Historical Society;
Dem. Club. Educ: U. of Ala. 1955 BS. B:
3/6/34. Add: 80 S. 2nd St., Park Ridge 07656
(201)391-4626.

Parsippany-Troy Hills. MARIAN W. SMITH (D) **
     1973-. Bds: School Com.; Transportation
Com. Prev: Library Trustee, 1969-74; Tract
Com. 1970-71. Org: LWV; Dem. Club. Educ:
Jersey City State 1949 BS; Jersey City Medical
Center 1949 RN. B: 11/24/27. Add: 145
Marcella Rd., Parsippany-Troy Hills 07054
(201)334-3600.

Passaic. MARGIE SEMLER (D)
     1973-. Prev: Bd. of Educ. Org: Dem. Club.
Occ: Office Manager. B: 6/22/23. Add: 120
Van Houten Ave., Passaic 07055 (201)
GR1-3300.

Passaic Township. HELEN S. CLANCY (R)
     1434 Longhill Rd., Millington 07946.

Paterson. IRENE DI MARCANTONIO
     City Hall, Market St., Paterson 07505.

Paterson. MARIAN M. RAUSEHENBACH (R)
     1974-. Bds: CETA Adv. Com.; Task Force OEO;
Ch., Dept. of Human Resources. Prev: Mental
Retardation Adv. Council 1970-73; Devt.
Disability Council 1973-76; Pres., Bd. of Educ.
1969-73; City Councilwoman 1974-78. Org: Cnty.
Rep. Women. Educ: Skidmore Coll. 1932 BS. B:
8/2/18. Add: 612 E. 29th St., Paterson 07504
(201)684-5800.

Peapack. MARY E. HAMILTON (R)
     1975-. Bds: Ch., Police; Roads & Sewers;
Water. Prev: Bd. of Educ. 1957-67. B: 7/15/23.
Add: 164 Main St., Peapack 07977 (201)234-2250.

Pemberton Borough. JANE T. LORD (R)
     1976-. Bds: Com. to Develop a Master Plan;
Welfare Bd.; Ch., Finance. Org: Rep. Club;
AAUW. Educ: Gettysburg Coll. 1967 BA. B:
6/23/45. Add: 50 Budd Ave., Pemberton 08068
(609)894-8222.

Pemberton Township. JEAN DWANE (D)
     1976-. Party: Cnty. Committeewoman 1956-61,
1976- ; Ch., Cnty. Com. 1959-61. Prev: Planning
Bd. 1974-75; Cnty. Farmland Preservation 1976- ;
School Feasibility Study 1976- ; Welfare Bd.
1958-60; Ct. Clerk 1961-64; Road Dept. Head
1976; Ch., Bldgs., Grounds, Recreation 1977.
Org: Town Dem's.; Feasibility Study. Add:
RR 6, Box 6420, Browns Mls., 08015 (609)
894-8201.

Pennington. NANCY H. SCHLUTER (R)
     1975-. Bds: Recreation Com. Liaison; Park
Com. Liaison. Party: Cnty. Ch. 1975-77; State
Committeewoman 1965-75; Municipal Ch. 1963-75;

Cnty. Committeewoman 1961-75; State Rep. Platform Com. 1971. Prev: V-Ch., Mercer Cnty. Charter Study Cmsn. 1974-75. Org: Rep. Club; WPC. B: 1/1/29. Add: 205 S. Main St., Pennington 08534.

Pennington. BEVERLY P. THURMAN (R)
1972-. Bds: Bd. of Trustees, Free Public Library. Org: NJ Assoc. for Educ. of Young Children. Educ: Beaver Coll. 1949 BS. Occ: School Co-Dir./Teacher. B: 7/22/27. Add: 9 E. Curtis Ave., Pennington 08534 (609)737-0276.

Pennington. ROSEMARY H. WETHERILL (D)
1976-. Bds: Planning Bd.; Finance Com.; Public Safety Com. Occ: Store Manager. B: 8/15/27. Add: 23 W. Delaware Ave., Pennington 08534.

Pequannock. MARLOU BELYEA (R)
1976-. Bds: Rd. Alignment Com.; Planning Bd. Prev: Planning Bd. 1974-76. Org: AAUW; LWV; Rep. Club; Women's Club. Educ: Scripps Coll. 1947 BA. B: 9/11/26. Add: 134 Mountain Ave., Pompton Plains, 07444 (201)835-5700.

Perth Amboy. LORETTA LEWIS (I)
1974-. Prev: Planning Bd. 1970-72. Org: AFL-CIO; Federated Women's Club; LWV. Add: 213 High St., Perth Amboy 08861 (201)442-5098.

Pine Beach. NORMA BRUECKEER
709 Riverside Dr., Pine Beach 08741.

Piscataway. DOROTHY SONNENBERG (R)
1976-. Bds: Welfare Bd.; Ch., Public Safety. Party:Cnty. Committeewoman 1963-77; Rep. Registration Ch. 1967-69. Prev: Bicentennial Cmsn. 1975-76. Org: Municipal Welfare Assoc.; LWV; Piscataway Women's Reps.; NJ Fed. of Rep. Women. Educ: Kean Coll. 1963 BA. Occ: Teacher. B: 7/19/39. Add: 2 Dickerson Dr., Piscataway 08854 (201)981-0800.

Pitman. JUDITH L. LOHMANN (R)
1976-. Bds: Recreation Cmsn.; Bd. of Assistance; Public Property. Org: Helping Hands Com.; Rep. Club. Educ: Lebanon Vly. Coll. 1961 BS. Occ: Teacher. B: 1/13/40. Add: 330 Pitman Ave., Pitman 08071 (609)589-3522.

Plainfield. ANGELA SPINA PERUN (D)
1976-. Bds: Economic Devt. Com. Org: Union Cnty. Bar Assoc.; NOW; WPC; Dem. Club. Educ: Hunter Coll. 1944 BA. Occ: Lawyer. B: 3/14/21. Add: 632 Sheridan Ave., Plainfield 07060.

Plainfield. MARILYN A. SONNENSCHEIN (D)
1975-. Bds: Inter-Municipal Rail; Joint Sewer Cmsn.; Local Assistance Bd. Party: Nat. Del. 1976; Cnty. Committeewoman 1968-77; City Dem. Ch. 1972-75. Org: NJEA; Dem. Club. Educ: Queens Coll. 1956 BA. Occ: Teacher. B: 1/23/35. Add: 648 Sheridan Ave., Plainfield 07060 (201)753-3000.

Plainfield. NELLIE F. SURATT
306 Halsey St., Plainfield 07063.

Plainsboro. BARBARA W. WRIGHT (D)
1976-. Party: Municipal Committeewoman 1975-76. Prev: V-Pres., Regional School Bd. 1975-77. Org: ANA; Crisis Intervention Ctr.; Dem. Org. Educ:

Boston Coll. 1955 BS; Rutgers U. 1969 MEd; N.Y.U. 1976 MA. Occ: Nursing Professor. B: 8/3/33. Add: Davison Rd., Plainsboro 08536.

Point Pleasant. RUTH KANE (R)
1976-. Bds: Ch., Street Dept. & Drainage; Bd. of Health; Police Com. Party: Pres., Women's Rep. Club 1971-73. Prev: Pres., Bd. of Health 1967-75; NJ Rep. Fed. of Women 1972-74. Org: Rep. Party. B: 8/30/16. Add: 217 Ida Dr., Pt. Pleasant 08742 (201)892-3434.

Point Pleasant. JEANNE B. UHL (R)
1972-. Bds: Ch., Local Assistance Bd.; Bd. of Recreation; Ch., Finance Com.; Sewer; Water. Party: Cnty. Committeewoman 1973-75. Prev: Bd. of Public Transportation 1974-75; Shore Transportation Com. 1973-74; Local Assistance Bd. 1973-75. Educ: SUNY New Paltz 1951 BS. B: 6/30/31. Add: 1608 Calamus Place, Pt. Pleasant 08742 (201)892-3434.

Princeton Borough. LEONA MEDVIN (D)
1976-. Bds: Joint Cmsn. on Aging; Recreation Bd.; Housing Authority. Org: NJEA; NEA; Community Dem. Org. Educ: Hunter Coll. 1940 BA. Occ: Teacher. B: 6/13/19. Add: 27 Leavitt Ln., Princeton 08540 (609)924-3475.

Princeton Borough. NELSON VAN DEN BLINK (D) **
1974-. Bds: Intergovernmental Drug Com.; Alt. Sewer Operating Com.; Bd. of Health; Housing Authority; Local Assistance Bd. Party: County Com. 1972-74. Prev: Bd. of Health 1972-74. Org: Dem. Org. Educ: Smith Coll. 1956 BA. B: 10/26/34. Add: 82 Linden La., Princeton 08540 (609)924-3119.

Princeton Junction. CAROL L. BESKE (R)
Bds: Planning Bd.; Devt. Plan Review; Zoning Bd. of Adjustment. Party: State Del. 1971-73; State Alt. 1970, '74; Election Dist. Ch. 1969-74; Cnty. Committeewoman 1974-77. Prev: Zoning Bd. 1976-77. Org: Rep. Club. Educ: U. of Minn. BA. Occ: Tennis League Manager. B: 5/3/43. Add: 4 Berkshire Dr., Princeton Jct. 08550 (609)799-2400.

Princeton Township. MARGARET ROGERS BROADWATER (D)
1974-. Bds: Regional Health Cmsn.; Local Assistance Bd.; Intergovt. Coord. Com. on Drug Abuse Prevention; Joint Cmsn. on Aging; Bd. of Health. Party: Cnty. Committeewoman 1967-74. Prev: Zoning Bd. of Adjustment 1971-74. Org: APSA; Women's Caucus for Political Science; AAUP; Community Dem. Org. Educ: Georgetown U. 1954 BS; Rutgers U. 1976 MA, PhD. Occ: Asst. Professor. B: 7/2/32. Add: 54 Herrontown Cir., Princeton 08540 (609)924-5704.

Princeton Township. ELIZABETH HUTTER
Township Hall, State & Valley, Princeton 08540.

Ramsey. NANCY DURRETT HALL (R)
1977-. Bds: Bd. of Health; Swimming Pool; Youth Guidance. Educ: La. Tech. U. 1956 BA. B: 9/19/35. Add: 458 Elbert St., Ramsey 07446 (201)825-3400.

Ramsey. ELEANOR ROONEY (D)
    1975-. Bds: Ch., Community Devt. Com.; W.
Bergen Mental Health Ctr. Recreation Cmsn. Party:
Cnty. Committeewoman 1974-76. Prev: Environmental
Adv. Com. 1973-77. Org: LWV; Ramsey Residents for
Responsible Planning; Dem. Club. Educ: Skidmore
Coll. 1948 BS. B: 10/26/25. Add: 30 Timber Trl.,
Ramsey 07446 (201)825-3400.

Randolph. ELIZABETH L. JAEGER
    502 Millbrook Ave., Randolph 07801.

Randolph. LEONORA P. WHILDIN (D)
    82 Radtke Rd., RD 3, Randolph 07801.

Raritan Borough. MARIE PARIS (D)
    1972-. Bds: Ch., Finance; Bd. of Health;
Library Trustee. Party: Cnty. Steering Com.
1976-77. Prev: Recreation Com. 1970-71. Org:
League Municipal Leg. Com.; V-Pres. Somerset Cnty.
Govt. Officials; Fed. Women's Club; Dem. Club;
PTO. B:11/10/32. Add: 111 Avonridge Rd., Raritan
08869 (201)725-3951.

Raritan Township. HARRIET L. WOLFSON (R)
    1975-. Bds: Planning Bd.; Utilities Authority
Liaison; Industrial Com. Party: Cnty. Committee-
woman 1969-77. Prev: Mayor 1976-77. Org: NEA;
N.J. School Women; AAUW; Secretary, Hunterdon
Fund for Exceptional Children; Rep. Club. Educ:
N.Y.U. 1947 BSEd; Trenton State Coll. 1970 MA.
Occ: Guidance Counselor. B: 10/25/24. Add: RD 2,
Box 553, Flemington 08822 (201)782-2919.

Readington. TERESA H. MARTIN (R)
    1977-. Bds: Ch., Sts. & Rds.; Bd. of Health.
Org: Rep. Club. Educ: Mt. Holyoke Coll. 1959 BA.;
Mich. State U. 1965 MAT. Occ: Teacher. B:
3/19/39. Add: Potterstown Rd., RD 2 Lebanon
08833 (201)534-4031.

Ridgewood. HELEN H. MC ILWRAITH (R)
    1976-. Party: Cnty. Committeewoman 1959-65.
Prev: Ridgewood Planning Bd. 1973-74; Ch., Planning Bd. 1974-76. Org: LWV. Educ: Smith Coll.
1945 BA. Occ: Tax Consultant. B: 8/12/23. Add:
149 Brookside Ave., Ridgewood 07450 (201)444-
5500.

Riverton. ANNA LOUISE CANNON (R)
    1977-. Bds: Ch., Bd. of Health; Park & Rec-
reation; Ch., Planning & Evaluation. Party:
Election Judge 1975-76. Prev: Park & Recreation
1967-74; Bd. of Health 1974-76. Org: Triboro
Women's Club; LWV; Rep. Club. Occ: Bookkeeper.
B: 3/5/24. Add: 415 Elm Ave., Riverton 08077
(609)829-0120.

Rockaway. SUSAN R. SMALL (D)
    1974-. Bds: Planning Bd. Prev: Drug Abuse
Council 1972-73. Org: LWV; WPC; Dem. Club; Nat.
Fed. of Dem. Women. Educ: N.Y.U. 1963 BA. B:
2/21/42. Add: 21 Oneida Ave., Rockaway 07866
(201)627-7200.

Rockleigh. CATHLEEN JANE HESLIN (R)
    1973-. Dist: 9. Bds: Ch., Borough Historian;
Ch., Finance Com.; Ch., Historic Adv. Com.,
Planning Bd. Prev: Planning Bd. 1972-73. Org:
Society of Architectural Historians; Rep. Club;
Historical Society. Educ: Packer Collegiate

Institute 1950 AA. Occ: Textile Designer.
B: 2/24/29. Add: Piermont Rd., Rockleigh
07647 (201)768-4217.

Rocky Hill. VERONICA NAUGHTON (I)
    1975-. Prev: Bd. of Health 1963-74. Org:
ANA; ACLU; NJ Civil Service Assoc.; Rocky Hill
Comm. Group. Educ: Seton Hall U. 1954 BSN;
1958 MA; Mercer Cnty. Coll. 1974 AA. Add: 36
Crescent Ave., P.O. Box 136, Rocky Hill 08553
(609)921-7530.

Roosevelt. ESTHER POGREBIN
    Mun. Bldg., Boro Hall, Roosevelt 08555.

Roselle Park. VIRGINIA M. MC KENNEY (I)
    1974-. Org: Civic Assoc.; Historical Society;
Independent Voters of NJ. Occ: Office Worker.
B: 6/20/25. Add: 124 Filbert St., Roselle Pk.
07204 (201)245-6222.

Rutherford. BARBARA H. CHADWICK
    60 Raymond Ave., Rutherford 07070.

Saddle River. PEGGY S. PASSAGLIA (I)
    1976-. Bds: Ch., Public Information Person-
nel; Bldgs. & Grounds; Finance. Prev: Ch.,
Youth Guidance Council 1974-76; Juvenile Conf.
Com. 1975-76; Bd. of Health 1971-76. Org:
Historical Society; Rep. Org. Educ: Fairleigh
Dickenson U. 1961 BS. B: 4/21/32. Add: 15 E.
Saddle River Rd., Saddle Rvr. 07458 (201)
445-9466.

Salem. MARTYNA MC LEAN (R)
    1975-. Party: Municipal Leader 1976. Prev:
Ch., Public Health Adv. Bd. 1966- ; Addictive
Disease Adv. Council 1970-73. Org: Medical
Political Action of NJ; LWV; Historical Society;
Fed. of Rep. Women; Nat. Rep. Party. Educ:
Bittston Hospital School of Nursing 1946 RN.
B: 11/12/24. Add: 209 Old Kings Hwy., Salem
08079.

Sea Bright. TERRY ANNE MC GUIRE (D)
    1976-. Bds: Ch., Sewer & Sanitation; Admin-
istrative Public Bldgs.; Beach Com. Org: NOW;
ACLU; Right-to-Choose; Southern Pverty Law Ctr.;
Cnty. Women's Dem. Club. Occ: Hospital Admin-
istrator. B: 11/4/44. Add: 1201 Ocean Ave.,
Sea Bright 07701.

Seaside Heights. AGNES POLHEMUS
    261 Hancock Ave., Seaside Heights 08751.

Seaside Park. FLORENCE A. MITCHELL
    112 "M" Street, Seaside Park 08752.

Secaucus. PATRICIA DE FERRARI (D)
    1977-. Org: Dem. Regular Assoc.; PTSA; PTA.
B: 7/2/40. Add: 705 1st St., Secaucus 07094.

Shrewsbury. DOROTHY BLAIR MANSON (R)
    1973-. Bds: Finance & Insurance; Ch.,
Personnel & Welfare; Projects Funding; Council
Pres. Org: Cnty. Assoc. for Retarded Children;
Cnty. Assoc. for Social Service; Rep. Club; AAUW.
Educ: Wayne State U. 1938 BA. B: 9/29/15. Add:
15 Buttonwood Dr., Shrewsbury 07701 (201)
741-4200.

Somerdale. KATHLEEN DEMIANI
919 Pasadena Dr., Somerdale 08083.

Somers Point. KATHLEEN C. DEWEES
518 Pennsylvania Ave., Somers Point 08244.

Somerville. EDNA L. ALLENA
Mun. Bldg., 25 W. End Ave., Somerville 08876.

Somerville. DEE PAINTER (D)
1977-. Bds: Ch., Public Property, Bldgs. &
Grounds; Public Works; Citizen Adv. Liaison.
Party: Cnty. Committeewoman 1974-77; Municipal
V-Ch. 1975-77. Prev: Citizen Adv. 1975-76. Org:
Dem. Club. B: 8/26/32. Add: 23 Fieldstone Dr.,
Somerville 08876.

Somerville. MARILYN PEARLMAN
Mun. Bldg., 25 W. End Ave., Somerville 08876.

South Belmar. AMELIA REIFF
301 New Bedford Ave., South Belmar 07719.

South Bound Brook. DOROTHY G. WISBESKI
201 High Street, S. Bound Brook 08880.

South Brunswick. CAROLYN MC CALLUM
Mun. Bldg., Monmouth Junction 08852.

South Orange. VALERIE SHULMAN
Village Hall, Scotland Rd., South Orange 07079.

Spotswood. BARBARA J. KRAJCECK (I)
1976-. Bds: Council Pres. Prev: V-Ch.,
Charter Study Com. 1975; Ch., Rent Adv. Com.
1975; Bicentennial Com. 1975-76. B: 9/27/39.
Add: 19 Gaskin Ave., Spotswood 08884 (201)
251-3378.

Spring Lake. MARY F. GEIGER
15 St. Clair Ave., Spring Lake 07762.

Stanhope. HELEN ORROS
Mun. Bldg., 77 Main St., Stanhope 07874.

Stanhope. ELAINE M. STRUSS (D) **
1973-. Bds: Recreation Cmsn.; Finance Com.;
Public Safety Com.; Public Works Com. Occ:
Bookkeeper. B: 9/11/49. Add: 19 Hill Rd.,
Stanhope 07874 (201)347-0159.

Stockton. GIGI CELLI
Risler St., Stockton 08559.

Stratford. ANNE M. GRIFFIN (D)
1971-. Bds: Cnty. Transportation Adv. Council.
Org: Bicentennial Cmsn.; Dir. of Public Safety;
Women's Club. Add: 234 Winding Way Rd., Stratford 08084 (609)784-1588.

Summit. JANET L. WHITMAN (R)
1976-. Bds: Ch., Welfare Com.; Law Com.;
Youth Guidance Council. Org: Jr. League; Rep.
Women's Club; PTA. B: 9/10/37. Add: 16 Essex
Rd., Summit 07901.

Sussex. JULIA DEVINE (R)
1972-. Bds: Ch., Ct.; Ch., Industrial. Prev:
Welfare Dir. 1961-71. B: 7/6/20. Add: 4 Main St.
Sussex 07461 (201)875-4831.

Sussex. ELEANOR KING
RD #2, Sussex 07461.

Teaneck. DOROTHY SILVERSTEIN (D) **
1974-. Party: County Com. 1971-73. Org:
Dem. Club; PTA. B: 4/30/35. Add: 96 Herrick
Ave., Teaneck 07666 (201)837-1600.

Tenafly. EVELYN M. COMER (R)
1976-. Bds: Environmental Cmsn.; Senior
Citizens Adv. Com.; Fire Dept. Party: Cnty.
Committeewoman. Prev: Bd. of Adjustment; Bd.
of Health; Welfare Bd. Org: Women's Club.
Add: 7 Elm St., Tenafly 07670 (201)568-6100.

Tenafly. HARRIETT GREENWALD (D)
1974-. Bds: Ch., Dept. of Public Works; Bd.
of Health; Mayor's Com. Liaison, Community
Mental Health Ctr. Prev: Ch., Personnel &
Administration Bd. 1975-77; Bd. of Adjustment
1975-77; Youth Service Com.-Liaison 1975-77.
Org: LWV; Common Cause; Dem. Club; Citizen
Educ. Council; Women's Club. Educ: Smith Coll.
1952 BA; Yeshiva U. 1960 MA. Occ: Travel Agent.
B: 11/19/30. Add: 107 Oak St., Tenafly 07670
(201)568-6100.

Teterboro. JANE CAHILL
MARION J. GOLDING
Municipal Bldg., Teterboro 07608.

Tewksbury. LUCYANN PAMPALONE (R)
1977-. Prev: Twp. Planning Bd. 1975-77;
Environmental Cmsn. 1975-77. Org: AAUW;
Women's Club; Community Ctr.; Rep. Club; PTA.
Educ: Rosemont Coll. 1962 BA. B: 4/14/40.
Add: Scarlet Oak Rd., RD #1, Califon 07830
(201)439-2757.

Tinton Falls. ELIZABETH Q. BILLINGS
556 Tinton Ave., Tinton Falls 07724.

Tinton Falls. R. ELLEN BRANIN (R)
1975-. Bds: Ch., Finance Com.; Ch., Sewer
Com.; Public Safety. Party: Municipal Campaign
Coord. 1977. Prev: Bicentennial Com. 1975-77.
Org: Shore Professional Florist Assoc.; Rep.
Club; Fed. of Rep. Women; Historical Society.
Occ: Flower Shop Owner. B: 6/28/36. Add: 113
Water St., Tinton Fls. 07724.

Trenton. JENNYE W. STUBBLEFIELD (D)
1976-. Bds: Loans & Grants Com. Party:
Committeewoman 1969-71. Prev: Dir., Health,
Recreation & Welfare 1971-74. Org: Amer.
Dietetic Assoc.; LWV; NAACP; Black Caucus of
Health Workers; NJ Assoc. of Retarded Children;
Dem. Club. Educ: Tuskegee Institute 1946 BS;
Rutgers U. 1967 MS. Occ: Coord., Home Economic
Programs. B: 3/6/25. Add: 21 Alden Ave.,
Trenton 08618 (609)989-3185.

Verona. MAUREEN O'SULLIVAN LALLY (R)
1976-. Bds: Ch., Bldgs. & Grounds; Ch.,
Personnel; Water & Sewers. Org: Dem. Club.
Educ: Rosemont Coll. 1967 BA; Fordham U. 1966
MA. Occ: Asst. Professor of Psychology. B:
2/4/42. Add: 11 Winding Way, Verona 07044
(201)239-5508.

Wallington. MARY KONISZEWSKI
Maple Ave., Wallington 07057.

Wanaque. BESS DOTY
579 Ringwood Ave., Wanaque 07465.

Warren. SUSIE BLACKBURN BOYCE (R)
1974-. Bds: Planning Bd. Party: Cnty.
Committeewoman 1970-74. Prev: Bd. of Health
1973-74. Org: AAUW; LWV; Women's Club; Rep.
Club. Educ: Fla. State U. 1960 BA; Tulane U.
1962 MAT; Rutgers U. 1971 EdD. Occ: Coll.
Professor. B: 1/12/39. Add: 17 Rockage Rd.,
Warren 07060 (201)753-8000.

Washington Township. BONNIE KAY EBERHART
Mun. Bldg., Box 216, Long Valley 07853.

Washington Township. NANCY L. TINDALL (R) **
1973-. Bds: Bd. of Health; Bd. of Assistance.
Party: County Rep. Com. 1974. Org: V-Pres. Rep.
Club. Educ: Colby Coll. 1970 BA. Occ: Research
Analyst, NJ Nat. Bank. B: 6/12/48. Add: 123
Hillside, Robbinsville 08691 (609)259-7082.

Wayne. ESTELLE PERRY (D)
1971-. Bds: Ch., Vandalism Com.; Codes of
Ethics; Garage Site. Prev: Council Pres. 1976;
Planning Bd. Repr. 1972-75. Org: NJ League of
Municipalities; WPC; LWV; Cancer Care; League
for Conservative Legislators; Dem. Club. Educ:
Brooklyn Coll. 1953 BA. B: 3/11/32. Add: 8
Sequoia Pl., Wayne 07470 (201)694-1800.

Wenonah. LORETTA W. WARD (R)
1977-. Org: Cnty. Bd. of Realtors. Occ:
Real Estate Broker. B: 7/18/36. Add: 11 N.
Lincoln Ave., Wenonah 08090 (609)468-5228.

West Orange. GAYLE ROSEN (D)
1974-. Bds: Essex Cnty. Community Block Grant;
Cnty. Child Guidance Ctr. Party: Cnty. Committee-
woman 1968-73. Prev: Planning Bd. 1974-76; Reg.
Joint Meeting 1976-77; Rent Bd. 1973-74; NJ Ch.
UN Day 1975-76. Org: LWV; Mental Health; NJ Fed.
of Dem. Women. B: 6/6/34. Add: 9 Ridgeway Ct.,
W. Orange 07052 (201)736-2770.

West Paterson. KATHERINE CORNETTO
64 Jackson Avenue, W. Paterson 07424.

West Windsor. CAROL BASKE
Box 38, Princeton Junction 08550.

Wharton. DOROTHY V. HENNESSEY (D)
1972-. Bds: Planning Bd.; Environmental;
Council Pres. Party: Cnty. Committeewoman 1977-
78. Prev: Library Trustee 1968-72. Org: NJEA;
Dem. Club. Educ: Coll. of St. Elizabeth 1949 BA.
Occ: Librarian. B: 3/30/28. Add: 179 E. Central
Ave., Wharton 07885 (201)361-0481.

Woodbury. NANCY ELKIS (D)
1974-. Party: Committeewoman 1974-77. Org:
Common Cause; Dem. Club. B: 8/26/34. Add: 548
Hunter St., Woodbury 08096 (609)845-1300.

Woodcliff Lake. ELAINE ERCOLANO (D)
1974-. Bds: Bd. of Health; Ch., Youth
Guidance; Ch., Public Information. Party: State
Alt. 1974; Cnty. Committeewoman 1966-72. Org:
LWV; Common Cause; Dem. Club. B: 7/5/38. Add:
78 W. Hill Rd., Woodcliff Lake 07675 (201)
391-4977.

Woodcliff Lake. JOAN WRIGHT IRWIN
227 Pascack Road, Woodcliff Lake 07675.

Woodlynne. BRENDA C. BERICH (D)
1975-. Bds: Dir., Public Affairs; Ch.,
Bicentennial. Prev: School Bd. 1970-75. Org:
Dem. Club. Occ: Banking. B: 7/4/31. Add:
230 Powelton Ave., Woodlynne 08107 (609)
962-8300.

Wrightstown. EILEEN FOGA
9 McGuire St., Wrightstown 08562.

Judges

SONIA MORGAN
Superior Court Justice. Add: State House
Annex, Trenton 08608.

SYLVIA B. PRESSLER
Superior Court Justice. Add: State House
Annex, Trenton 08608.

State Boards and Commissions

Office of the Governor, State Capitol Bldg.,
Trenton 08625.

Adult Diagnostic and Treatment Center
LAURA HARDING
MARTHA Z. LEWIN

Aging, Commission on
CONSTANCE MIDKIFF

Agriculture, Board of
MELDA C. SNYDER

Alcoholism, Advisory Council on
NANCY BRACH

Architects, Board of
ELIZABETH MOYAHAN

Arts, Council on the
PEG M. BYRD
BARBARA FURST
RONI MONELL GOODMAN
MRS. WILLIAM MILLS
LUCILLE SWICK

Beauty Culture Control, Board of
JOAN DI FRANCESCO
RUTH N. LITTLE
ROSE ANN MORRIS
MARIE NOWIAK

Bicentennial Celebration Commission
    MRS. FREDERICK FRELINGHUYSEN
    MARY T. CAMPBELL

Blind and Visually Impaired, Commission for the
    NORMA KRAJCZAR
    MRS. AUGUSTUS C. STUDER, JR.

Bluestar Memorial Highway Council
    MRS. WILLIAM M. BOYD
    MRS. AUSTIN B. SAYRE
    MRS. ALBERT L. STILLMAN
    MRS. JAMES WOTHERSPOON

Carnival Amusement Ride Safety Advisory Board
    BLANCHE H. HOFFMAN
    EDNA ZDENEK

Cemetery Board
    PATRICIA S. BENNETT

Citizens Consumer Affairs Advisory Committee
    BARBARA P. BERMAN
    SUSAN T. BROOKS
    DENISE A. DEFAZIO
    JESTEEN GEBEL
    CAROLE JACOBSON
    SUSAN SIMON

Clean Air Control
    ROSLYN BARBASH
    MRS. EDGAR EISLER

Clean Water Council
    PATRICIA JACKSON

Community Mental Health Board
    MRS. DALE Y. CALDWELL
    MRS. WILLIAM N. GURTMAN
    GERTRUDE M. HARRIS
    MRS. JOHN F. HAYNIE
    VERONIQUE M. HENRIKSEN
    MRS. THOMAS J. MC COY
    SYLVAI S. RISKIN
    MRS. CURTIS L. SCHICK

Commuter Advisory Committee
    EILEEN HEARN

Correctional Institution for Women
    MRS. ARCHIBALD S. ALEXANDER
    MRS. BENJAMIN JONES
    MRS. WESLEY LANCE
    MRS. C. M. RUSSELL
    MRS. REEVE SCHLEY, JR.

County and Municipal Government Study Commission
    DORIS W. DEALAMAN

Dentistry, Board of
    GOLDANNA CRAMER
    ANNE M. SAGER

Developmental Disabilities Council
    BEATRICE ANTELL
    ELIZABETH M. BOGGS
    RUTH TOMLIN

Equine Advisory Board
    JOAN BROWN
    VIRGINIA BUCKLER
    ELAINE CHAPIN
    MRS. MERILLAT FROST
    NANCY HUTCHESON
    MARY KOSSATZ
    MAUREEN NIELSON
    MRS. MILTON QUIRK
    MRS. EUGENE VAN NESS
    MRS. LAWRENCE YETTER

Election Law Enforcement Commission
    JOSEPHINE S. MARGETTS

Election Law Revision Commission
    KATHERINE K. NEUBERGER

Energy Crisis Study Commission
    ELEANORE PETTERSEN

Ethical Standards, Executive Commission on
    ELAINE GOLDSMITH
    JUDY NALLIN

Governors, Board of. Rutgers-The State University
    LINDA STOMATO
    EMMA TWYMAN
    KATHERINE ELKUS WHITE

Health Care Administration Board
    BEVERLY N. DUNSTON

Health Coordinating Council
    BRENDA J. BACON
    NANCY DUNHAM
    MYRA R. ELLIOT
    DORIS G. HANSON
    VIVIAN HATCHER
    MARION E. PURBACK
    LOIS SHAW

Hearing Aid Dispensers Examining Committee
    LILA HERSH

Higher Education, Board of
    MARION EPSTEIN
    KATHERINE K. NEUBERGER

Highway Safety Policy Advisory Council
    IRENE SMITH

Historical Commission
    SANDRA ST. PHILLIP GARVEN

Historic Sites Council
    GRACE A. HAGEDORN
    MRS. JOHN KEAN

Housing Council
    GRETCHEN B. WAPLES

Institutional Trustees, Board of
    MRS. RAYMOND A. BROWN
    MRS. PHILIP H. ISELIN

"Jobs for Veterans" Task Force
    CATHERINE EASTBURN
    RICHA MIELE
    MRS. GEORGE F. WEINHEIMER, JR.

Juvenile Court Law Revision Commission
    MRS. MAXWELL BARUS

Juvenile Justice and Delinquency Prevention Advisory Committee
    SHARON H. GROSSMAN
    LILLIAN HALL
    ALCIIA NETTLES
    PAULA ROSENBLOOM
    PHYLLIS A. THOMAS

Law Enforcement Planning Agency
    ANN KLEIN
    ALICIA M. NETTLES
    MARGARET H. PERRYMAN
    PATRICIA Q. SHEEHAN

Local Finance Board
    BARBARA WERBER

Marriage Counselor Examiners, Board of
    VALERIE G. GLADFELTER

Master Plumbers, Board of Examiners
    LOUISE O. FRIEDMAN

Medical Assistance Advisory Council
    BETTY J. PHILLIPS

Medical Examiners, Board of
    MARY PAULA GAUTHIER

Mosquito Control Commission
    ELEANORE RENK

Motor Vehicle Study Commission
    MARSHA MORTKOWITZ

Natural Resources Council
    VIVIEN LI
    J. MARY NELSON
    ELEANOR ROONEY

New Jersey Legal Services Advisory Council
    BARBARA BROADWATER
    MARY E. JAMES

Noise Control Council
    HELEN B. LOEW

Nursing, Board of
    DOROTHY J. DE MAIO
    M. CATHERINE DULIO
    DOROTHY ANNE FARLEY
    SISTER TERESA LOUISE HARRIS
    LOUISE G. WALLHAUSER

Nursing Home Administrators' Licensing Board
    CONSULA CUCHURAL
    BEVERLY DUNSTON
    CLAIRE MANFREDI
    MILDRED OCHSE

Opthalmic Dispensers and Opthalmic Technicians, Board of Examiners
    ANN B. CRUMIDY
    MARIE D. MILLER

Optometrists, Board of
    FRANCES L. STARK

Pharmacy, Board of
    VIVIAN H. PETRO

Physical Therapy Advisory Committee
    VIRGINIA R. BERTHOLF
    RUTH DICKINSON
    ELIZABETH H. GEIGER

Psychological Examiners, Board of
    VIOLET FRANKS
    SYLVIA B. HERZ
    DORIS C. PERRY
    JOAN K. TAYLOR

Public Broadcasting Authority
    EDITH LURAY

Public Health Council
    ANITA OSPER LEONE
    MRS. J. DUNCAN PITNEY
    JANE B. ROBINSON

Public Welfare, Board of
    DORIS W. DEALAMAN
    MRS. ALFRED R. FELD
    ANNE S. HELZAPFEL
    MRS. RICHARD L. MARTIN
    MRS. AUGUSTUS C. STUDER, JR.
    MRS. BERNARD ZIMMER

Recreation Examiners, Board of
    ILENE ACKNER KASSON

Shorthand Reporting, Board of
    VALLERIE M. SAMUELS

Solid Waste Management, Advisory Council on
    HELEN MANOGUE

State Investment Council
    MARY G. ROEBLING

State Library Advisory Council
    DORIS L. BECK
    HELEN ELIZEY
    ESTHER W. FEATHERER
    RENEE SWARTZ

State Museum Advisory Council
    MARY G. ROEBLING
    BARBARA WESCOTT

State Scholarship Commission
    MARILYN BRODER BERGER
    SISTER ELIZABETH A. MALONEY

Status of Women, Advisory Commission on
    SUSAN REYNOLDS ARNDT
    SANDRA GRUNDFEST
    ELIZABETH M. HOGAN
    DORIS KULMAN
    ANNA LOPEZ
    JANE F. MEYER
    BARBARA B. SIGMUND
    ANITA E. VOORHEES
    CONSTANCE WOODRUFF

Trails Council
    MRS. WILLIAM GROAH
    CAROL MILLER
    EILEEN MOLLINEAUX
    MRS. ALBERT READING

Training School for Boys and Girls
    LUCIA BALLANTINE
    SALLY G. CARROLL
    MRS. WILLIAM L. HARRISON
    MRS. RICHARD R. STOUT
    MRS. EDWARD H. URION

Travel and Resort Industry Study Commission
    MILDRED FOX

Trustees, Board of. Division of Youth and Family
Services
    HATTIE E. TALLEY
    MRS. JOHN H. WRIGHT, JR.

Trustees, Board of. Educational Opportunity Fund
    JUDITH CAMBRIA
    VERONICA TAYLOR

Trustees, Board of. State Prisons
    EDYTHE M. HERSON

Uniform Construction Code Advisory Board
    CATHERINE A. COSTA
    ELEANORE PETTERSEN

Veterans' Facilities Council
    RUTH GROFT
    EMILY HERBERT
    HELEN YOUNG

Veterans' Services Council
    MARGARET M. MALONE

Veterinary Medical Examiners, Board of
    LUCILLE I. VAN SANT

Vocational Education Advisory Council
    DOROTHY COHEN
    ANITA GANS
    MARGE MORANO

Water Policy and Supply Council
    HERMIA LECHNER
    LILLIAN M. SCHWARTZ

X-Ray Technician Board of Examiners
    SISTER MARY ROSE

Youth Commission
    BESSIE H. MARSH

Youth Correctional Institution Complex
    BEATRIZ E. GOMEZ
    EMMA C. MC GALL
    HELEN VERHAGE
    MARGARET B. WALKER

New Mexico

State Executive and Cabinet

ERNESTINE D. EVANS (D) **
    Secretary of State 1967-. Bds: Public
Employees Retirement Bd.; State Canvassing
Bd.; State Com. of Public Records; Voting
Machine Com. Prev: State Representative
1940-41. B: 9/5/17. Add: 520 Acequia Madre,
Sante Fe 87501 (505)827-2717.

MAXINE GERHARDT
    Secretary, Department of Finance and
Administration. Add: State Capitol, Santa Fe
87503.

State Legislature

State Senate

GLADYS HANSEN (D) **
    1973-. Dist: 37. Bds: Finance Com.; Public
Affairs Comm. Interim Tax Study Com. Prev:
County Clerk 1969-72; City Clerk 1960-63. Org:
BPW; Dem. Women's Club; Real Estate Assoc. B:
1/29/20. Add: 1930 Gladys Dr., Las Cruces
88001.

State House

RUBY V. APPELMAN (R) **
    1975-. Dist: 20. Bds: Interior Election
Study Com.; Educ. Com.; Privileges & Elections.
Org: Chamber of Commerce; Pres., Fed. of Rep.
Women; PTA. Educ: W. Va. U. BA. Occ: Business
Manager. B: 4/17/30. Add: 1045 Santa Ana, SE,
Albuquerque 87123 (505)299-6084.

ADELE P. CINELLI (D) **
    1975-. Dist: 14. Bds: Taxation & Revenue;
Privileges & Elections. Org: OWL. Occ: Self-
employed, Investments. B: 8/6/33. Add: 901
Third St., SW, Albuquerque 87102 (505)
242-0535.

PAT I. HETH (R)
    1976-. Dist: 9. Bds: Western Conf. of State
Govt. Host Com.; Educ. Com.; Privileges &
Elections Com. Party: State Del. 1966-76;
Secretary, Rep. Central Com. 1966-70; V-Ch.,
GOP Central Com. 1970-72; State Central Com.
1968-74. Prev: Valencia Cnty. Clerk 1973-77.
Educ: Moorhead State Coll. 1952 AA; U. of NM
1967 BS. Occ: Cnty. Manager. B: 1/31/33.
Add: P.O. Box 43, Belen 87002 (505)865-9681.

SHARLYN M. LINARD (D)
Dist: 37. Bds: Labor Com.; Appropriations &
Finance Com.; Southwest Reg. Energy Council.
Party: Precinct Secretary; Precinct V-Ch. 1973- ;
Cnty. Secretary 1975- . Org: AAUW; OES. Educ:
NM State U. 1969 BA. B: 2/20/27. Add: 2013
Princess Jeanne, Las Croces 88061 (505)827-3131.

County Commissions

Catron. JUDY LAUGHTER NALDA (R) **
1974-. Party: County Com. 1970-74. B: 9/1/39.
Add: Diamond T. Ranch, Die Town 87827 (505)
533-6400.

Los Alamos. ALLENE H. LINDSTROM (R)
1976-. Party: State Del. 1976. Org: Nat.
Assoc. of Flight Instructors; LWV; Civil Air
Patrol. Educ: U. of Ore. 1954 BA. Occ: Data
Analyst. B: 4/8/33. Add: 327 Venado, Los Alamos
87544 (505)662-4122.

Los Alamos. SHERRY R. REISFELD (D)
1976-. Bds: Ch., Cnty. Atty. Search Com.
Org: ASPA; AAUW; Council on Alcoholism; Humanities
Council; Dem. Club. Educ: Pa. State U. 1956 BA;
U. of NM 1974 MA. Occ: Dir., Women's Center. B:
11/3/34. Add: 99 Osito, Los Alamos 87544

Rio Arriba. ELMA M. GARCIA (D)
1977-. Dist: 3. Bds: Cnty. Indigent Hospital
Bd.; Bd. of Finance. Party: State Del. 1976;
Precinct Member 1971-76. Occ: Reading Tutor. B:
11/11/38. Add: P.O. Box 98, Lumberton 87547
(505)759-3321.

Socorro. LEYLA A. TORRES (R)
1976-. Bds: Council of Govts.; SW Mental
Health Center Bd. Party: State Del. 1976, '66;
Precinct Secretary 1964-66. Educ: NM Institute
of Mining & Technology 1973 BS. Occ: Shoe Store
Owner. B: 6/30/44. Add: 1218 Hilton Dr.,
Socorro 87801 (505)835-0423.

Mayors

Bayard. LUCY M. ESCUDERO (D) **
1974-. Bds: Police Commissioner; Water Com.;
Landfill Com. Prev: Tax Assessor 1970-74; Tax
Assessor's Deputy 1964-70. Org: Municipal League;
Council of Governments; Internat. Assoc. of
Assessing Officers. B: 11/10/35. Add: P.O. Box
43, Bayard 88023 (505)537-3327.

Corrales. BARBARA ADELA CHRISTIANSON (D)
1971-. Party: State Del.; Cnty. Ch.; Cnty.
Central Exec.; State Exec. Org: LWV. B: 12/4/32.
Add: Star Rt., Box 492, Corrales 87048 (505)
898-7585.

Des Moines. ESTHER THOMPSON
City Hall, Des Moines 88418.

Folsom. FRAN EILAND
City Hall, Folsom 88419.

House. OPAL B. SNIPES (D)
1976-. Bds: Eastern Plains Council of
Govt.; Area on Aging. Party: State Del. 1942;
Precinct Ch. 1940-44. Prev: Community Devt.
Agency 1974-75. Org: NEA. Educ: U. of NM
1956 BA. B: 4/29/15. Add: Box 704, House
88121 (505)372-5252.

Jemez Springs. JOSEPHINE A. SHEPARD (R) **
1970-. Org: LWV; Municipal League Bd.;
County Planning & Dev. Assoc.; Dir., Medical
Clinic; Community Club. Educ: Coll. of
Albuquerque 1950 BS. B: 7/4/06. Add: 829-
3835, Jemez Springs 87025 (505)829-3540.

Lake Arthur. FLORENCE HART
City Hall, Lake Arthur 88253.

Loving. MIRANDA L. DARCY (D) **
1972-. Bds: Fed. Housing Bd.; Border Cmsn.;
Econ. Dev. Party: Ward V-Ch. 1971-72; Precinct
Secretary 1971-72; Party Secretary 1971-72.
Prev: Municipal Judge 1968-72. Org: PTA. Occ:
Office Manager Motor Vehicle Dept. B: 7/4/39.
Add: 113 1/2 N. 5th St., Loving 88256 (505)
745-3511.

Vaughn. CHRISTINE SIMPSON (D)
1968-. Bds: Eastern Plains Council of Govt.;
Municipal League on Nat. League of Cities;
Economical Devt. Assoc. Party: State Del. 1955-;
Precinct Ch. 1955-77; Cnty. Central Com. 1955-
77. Org: Cnty. Assoc.for Retarded Children;
Senior Citizens. Occ: Drycleaner. B: 4/14/14.
Add: P.O. Box 207, Vaughn 88353 (505)845-2301.

Local Councils

Albuquerque. SONDRA L. COHN WEST (R) **
1975-. Bds: Ch., Finance Com.; Health,
Welfare & Public Protection; Human Resources;
Environmental Quality Council; Human Rights
Advisory Bd. Org: LWV; Urban Coalition; Women's
Assoc. Educ: Millersville State Coll. 1954 BS;
U. NM 1969 MA. B: 6/15/34. Add: 1428 Columbia
NE, Albuquerque 87106 (505)766-7110.

Bloomfield. SHIRLEY ANN EVANS CURTIS (R) **
1974-. Org: Extension Club. Educ: NM State
U. 1966 BS. B: 2/16/44. Add: Box 662, Bloomfield 87413 (505)632-2997.

Bloomfield. MRS. ERVA LYNCH
City Hall, Bloomfield 87413.

Bosque Farms. THERESA J. BLAKE (R)
1976-. Bds: Ch., Animal Control Com.;
Community Devt. Com.; Co-Ch., Communications
Com. Party: Precinct Del. 1976-77. B: 4/28/35.
Add: Rt. 1, Box 1819, Albuquerque 87105 (505)
869-6611.

Cimarron. MARY LEAL COCA
City Hall, Cimarron 87714.

Columbus. MARY LEE GASKILL
City Hall, Columbus 88029.

Corona. PAMELA OWEN
     City Hall, Corona 88318.

Corrales. REBECCA B. CAPUTO (D)
     1976-. Org: Women's Dem. Club. B: 10/9/49.
Add: P.O. Box 38, Corrales 87048 (505)898-7585.

Corrales. DULCELENA CURTIS (D)
     1971-. Mayor Pro Tem. Bds: Historical
Society. Party: State Del. 1976, '77; Precinct
V-Ch. 1976-77. Prev: Cnty. Agricultural Stabil-
ization & Conservation Service 1966-69; Cnty.
Farms Home Administration 1977. Org: Farm Bureau;
Civic Assoc.; Dem. Women. B: 7/17/04. Add:
N. Star Rt., Box 264, Corrales 87048 (505)
898-7585.

Deming. JO HARELSON
     City Hall, Deming 88030.

Des Moines. ALMA ALLEN
     City Hall, Des Moines 88418.

Dexter. FAYRENE BUTLER POWERS (D)
     1974-. Org: NEA; NM Educ. Assoc.; NM Library
Assoc. Educ: E. NM U. 1950 BS; N. Texas State U.
1971 MLS. Occ: School Librarian. B: 10/12/28.
Add: 302 S. Elford, P.O. Box 271, Dexter 88230.

Eunice. BARBARA HAYES
     City Hall, Eunice 88231.

Folsom. SARAH CASTILLO
     City Hall, Folsom 88419.

Gallup. DANITSA HALL (D)
     1975-. Bds: McKinley Area Council of Govts.;
Ch., Historical Society Cmsn. Party: State Del.
1969- ; Precinct Leader; Cnty. Central Com.;
Dem. Cnty. Ch.; State Central Com. Org: Soroptimists; WPC. Educ: NM State U. 1958 BA. B:
1/23/37. Add: 1501 Red Rock Dr., Gallup 87301
(505)722-5055.

Grants. CHARLOTTE J. COTTON (D)
     1976-. Bds: Community Devt.; Midwest NM
Community Action Program. Prev: Cnty. Recreation
1974- . Occ: Clerk. B: 12/20/23. Add: 804
Jefferson, Grants 87020 (505)287-4444.

Grenville. RUTH WISEMAN (D)
     Party: Cnty. Alt. 1976. B: 7/8/32. Add: Box
213, Grenville 88424.

Hope. MRS. ROZELL DEAN
          MILDRED DONAGHE
          MARY EVELYN TEAGUE
     City Hall, Hope 88250.

Jal. BOBBIE MARTIN (D) **
     1974-. Bds: Streets & Zoning Com.; Water &
Sewer. Org: Dem. Women's Clubs. Occ: Teacher's
Aid. Add: 802 Iowa, Box 1176, Jal 88252 (505)
395-2222.

Jemez Springs. MAUDELL BERGLUND (R) **
     1970-. Party: Precinct Ch. & Registrar 1974-
75. Org: LWV; PTC. B: 12/31/23. Add: P.O. Box
65, Jemez Springs 87025 (505)829-3540.

Jemez Springs. ROSEMARY W. CART
     City Hall, Jemez Springs 87025.

Jemez Springs. GENEVIEVE A. SANDOVAL (D)
     1976-. Org: Wildlife Fed.
Occ: Dist. Office Clerk. B: 6/29/37. Add:
P.O. Box 61, Jemez Spgs. 87025 (505)829-3540.

Las Cruces. MARIANNE HOBBS THAELER (D)
     1974-. Bds: Del., Nat. League of Cities;
Environmental Policy Com.; Special Energy Task
Force. Party: State Del. 1976. Prev: NM
Municipal League Bd. of Dirs. 1974-76; NM-Mexico
Border Cmsn. 1974-75; Governor's Outdoor Recre-
ation Priorities Adv. Com. 1973-74. Org: ACLU;
Dem. Women's Club; Progress Club; Chamber of
Commerce. Educ: U. of Calif. 1957 BA. B:
3/2/36. Add: 2015 Huntington Dr., Las Cruces
88001 (505)526-0322.

Las Vegas. RACHEL WHORTON (D) **
     1974-. Bds: Ch., Park & Recreation Com.;
Police Com.; Sanitation Com.; Bicentennial
Com. Org: Las Vegas Women of Action; OES; PEO.
Occ: Account Exec. for Financial Corporation.
B: 5/6/17. Add: 1205 7th St., Las Vegas 87701
(505)425-9381.

Los Alamos. ALLENE L. LINDSTROM
     City Hall, Los Alamos 87544.

Los Alamos. SHERRY R. REISFELD (D)
     See Los Alamos County Commission

Los Ranchos de Albuquerque. VIRGINIA H. AHERN (R)
     1976-. Bds: Ch., Tax; Insurance Com.; Ch.,
Newsletter Com. Party: Cnty. Rep. Com. 1975-77.
Prev: V-Ch., Governor's Com. on the Status of
Women 1973-74; V-Ch., NM Com. on the Status of
Women 1974-75. Org: LWV; Nat. Council on Crime
& Delinquency; Jr. League; AAUW; Farm & Ranch
Bureau; Crisis Task Force; Library Assoc. Educ:
Wellesley Coll. 1942 BA. Occ: Land Manager.
B: 4/29/21. Add: 831 Chamisal Rd., NW,
Albuquerque 87107.

Mesilla ROSALIE ANN RADER (D)
     1974-. Occ: Music Teacher. B: 12/2/30.
Add: Box 418, Calle De Picacho, Mesilla
88046 (505)524-3262.

Pecos. MRS. BOB MARTIN
     City Hall, Pecos 87552.

Peralta. SHARON M. EASTMAN (R)
     1975-. Bds: Ch., Recreational Devt. Com.;
Postal Address Com. Party: Cnty. Precinct
Committeewoman 1975-77. Prev: Office Bldg.
Planning Com. 1975-77. B: 9/12/38. Add: Rt. 1,
Box 1676, Albuquerque 87105.

Questa. MRS. SELIMO RAEL
     City Hall, Questa 87556.

Roy. MRS. MONROE MACKEY
     City Hall, Roy 87743.

Santa Fe. DORA BATTLE (D)
    1976-. Bds: Community Action Program; Bd. of
Adjustment; Quadalupe Clinic Drug Rehabilitation.
Prev: City Action Com. 1972-74. Org: LWV; AAUW;
Dem. Women; WPC; PTA. B: 12/17/43. Add: 804
Los Arboles Ln., Santa Fe 87501 (505)982-4471.

Tatum. MELBA J. CARDWELL
    City Hall, Tatum 88267.

Texico. MARIE CHRISTIAN
    City Hall, Texico 88135.

Texico. RUBY MOORE GOFORTH (D) **
    1974-. Bds: Planning Council. Org: Chamber
of Commerce; Soroptomist. Occ: Administrative
Assistant. B: 10/6/30. Add: 409 Hutson, Texico
88135 (505)482-3314.

Tijeras. ELOISA BACA-GARCIA
          MARY HERRA
          THERESA JARAMILLO
          ETHEL SANDOVAL
    City Hall, Tijeras 87059.

Willard. JEANINE GARCIA
          LILA D. GONZALES
    City Hall, Willard 87063.

State Boards and Commissions

    Office of the Governor, State Capitol Bldg.,
    Santa Fe 87501.

Arts Commission
    KATY LOU ELY
    CONSUELO THOMPSON

Children and Youth, Committee on
    AMERITUS B. ANSLEY
    MARY MARTINEZ
    LOUISA ROMERO

Cosmetologists Board
    CANDY LOYD AMEZQUITA
    LESSIE J. BOYD
    EDITH F. HARDERN

Criminal Justice Planning, Council of
    MAUREEN A. LUNA

Developmental Disabilities Planning Council
    BEVERLY BABIK
    SHIRLEY BECHT
    CAROLYN BORLAND
    MARIANNE DIAZ
    NANCY JENNINGS
    CAROLYN LEVIN
    LILY MARTINEZ
    FAYE MILLER
    ANNA QUINTANA
    ALYCE RICHARDS
    RUTH SANDOVAL

Educational Finance, Board of
    PATRICIA Y. LAWRENCE
    THERESA MOULDS
    RUTH C. PADILLA

Employment of the Handicapped
    KATHY HARMON
    SADIE M. SCHREIBER

Food, Nutrition and Health Commission
    ELEANORA MAE SANDERS

Human Rights Commission
    VIOLA DOZIER
    DOLORES FRESQUEZ

International Space Hall of Fame
    VIRGINIA MARAGOS

Judicial Council
    RENA ROSEQUIST

Labor Commission - Apprenticeship Council
    SHARLENE MC MINN

Library Commission
    PAT HAMM

Mental Health - Drug Abuse - Alcoholism Advisory
Council
    AGNES BRANO
    MARIAN DAVIS
    KATIE EVILSIZER
    VIRGINIA KLAENHAMMER
    CIEL LONON
    JULIA LOPEZ

Nursing Home Administrators, Board of
    THELMA MC FEELEY

Physical Therapists Licensing Board
    BEVERLY ALARID
    ELIZABETH M. BARNETT

Public Broadcasting, Commission on
    ELIZABETH BAILEY
    GLADYS HANSEN
    RUTH PADILLA

Public Service Commission
    EILEEN GREVEY

Recreation Priorities Advisory Committee
    DEBBIE HAYS
    JENNIE MARIE HOLMES

Regents, Board of. Eastern New Mexico University
    JANIE MOBERLY

Regents, Board of. New Mexico Highlands University
    BEVERLY J. AGNEW

Regents, Board of. New Mexico School for the Deaf
    MARIAN V. KARLSON

Regents, Board of. New Mexico State University
    JULIE PAPEN

Regents, Board of. University of New Mexico
    COLLEEN MALOOF

Regents, Board of. Western New Mexico University
    MARY TUCKER

Search and Rescue
    LINDA ESTES
    GRACE OLIVAREZ

Status of Women, Commission on the
    KATHY DICKERSON
    GALE W. DOYEL
    MARGARITA MERCURE
    FRANCES WILLIAMS
    GRACE WILLIAMS

New York

State Executive and Cabinet

EILEEN D. DICKINSON *
    President, New York State Higher Education
Service Corp. 1975-. Prev: Village Educ. Adv.
Council; Ch., Cnty. Mental Health Bd.; State
Health Adv. Council 1975. Educ: Bryn Mawr Coll.
1941 BA; Columbia U. 1942 MA. Add: Empire State
Plaza, Tower Bldg., Albany 12250.

JOSEPHINE GAMBINO
    Civil Service Commissioner. Add: State Campus
Site, Civil Service Bldg., Albany 12239.

LOU GLASSE (D)
    Director, Office for Aging. 1976-. Bds:
Health Planning Cmsn.; Council on the Handicapped;
Crime Control Planning Bd. Party: Cnty. Issues
Com. 1966-73. Prev: Dir., Cnty. Office for Aging
1973-76; Cnty. Council of NY Cmsn. for Human
Rights 1962-68. Org: NASW; Nat. Council on
Aging; Nat. Council on Black Aging; NWPC; Women's
Dem. Club. Educ: U. of Okla. 1949 BA; U. of
Conn. 1952 MSW. B: 4/18/27. Add: Empire Plaza,
Agency Bldg. 2, Albany 12223.

MARY ANNE KRUPSAK (D) *
    Lieutenant Governor. 1974-. Prev: Assembly-
Woman 1968-72; State Senator 1972-74; Congress-
ional Administrative Asst. Educ: U. of Rochester
BA; Boston U. MS; U. of Chicago JD. B: 3/26/32.
Add: State Capitol, Albany 12224.

ROSEMARY S. POOLER (D)
    Director, Consumer Protection Council. 1975-.
Bds: Law Revision Cmsn.; Energy Cmsn. Party:
Nat. Del. 1974, '76; Cnty. Committeewoman 1972,
'75. Prev: Dir., City Consumer Affairs Unit
1972-74; City Councilwoman 1974-75. Org: Nat.
Assoc. of Consumer Affairs Administrators; Cancer
Society; NOW; WPC. Educ: Brooklyn Coll. 1959 BA;

U. of Conn. 1961 MA; U. of Mich. Law School
1965 JD. B: 6/21/38. Add: 1605 Euclid Ave.,
Syracuse 13224 (518)474-3514.

ERSA H. POSTON *
    Civil Service Commissioner. 1967-. Prev:
Pres., Civil Service Cmsn. 1967-75; U.S. Del.
to U.N. Gen. Assembly 1976; Dir., State Office
of Equal Opportunity; Youth Work Program
Coordinator, Division of Youth; Confidential
Assistant to the Governor. Org: Zonta; Urban
League; United Fund; Academy of Certified
Social Workers; BPW; NAACP; Nat. Assoc. of
Social Workers. Educ: Kentucky State U. BA;
Atlanta U. MSW; Union Coll. JD. Add: State
Office Bldg. Campus, 1220 Washington Ave.,
Albany 12239.

MURIEL F. SIEBERT
    Superintendent of Banking. Add: Empire State
Plaza, Bldg. 4, Albany 12223.

State Legislature

State Senate

CAROL BELLAMY (D)
    1972-. Dist: 25. Bds: Rules Com.; Ethics
Com.; Judiciary Com. Party: Cnty. Committeewoman 1972-76. Org: ABA; Assoc. of the Bar
of the City of N.Y. Educ: Gettysburg Coll.
1963 BA; N.Y.U. 1968 JD. Occ: Atty. B:
1/14/42. Add: 305 Henry St., Brooklyn 11201
(518)472-2157.

KAREN S. BURSTEIN (D)
    1972-. Dist: 9. Bds: Senate Health Com;
Senate Crime & Corrections Com.; Senate Judiciary
Com. Party: Nat. Del. 1976. Org: ACLU; NAACP;
WPC; Wilderness Society; Cnty. Bar Assoc. Educ:
Bryn Mawr Coll. 1964 BA; Fordham U. Law School
1970 JD. Occ: Professor of Law. Add: 1015
Cedar Ln., Woodmere 11598 (518)472-2127.

LINDA WINIKOW (D) **
    1974-. Dist: 38. Bds: Local Gov. Com.;
Finance Com.; Consumer Protection Com.; Corp-
orations, Authorities & Public Utilities Com.;
Agriculture Com. Party: Dem. Policy Com.
Prev: Town Zoning Bd. of Appeals 1968-71; Town
Councilwoman 1971-73; County Legislator 1973-
74; Ch., Public Service Cmsn.; Cmsnr., NY
Temporary Cmsn. on Living Costs & Economy.
Org: PTA; Dem. Women's Club; United Way; Histor-
ical Soc.; BPW; Cancer Care. Educ: Hofstra U.
1962 BA; Queens Coll. 1966 MA. Add: 62 Sutin
Place, Spring Valley 10977.

State House

JEAN AMATUCCI (D)
    1974-. Dist:98. Bds: Aging Com.; Agricul-
ture Com.; Child Care Com.; Health Com. Org:
Amer. Nurses Assoc.; NEA; NY Assoc. of Health,
Physical Educ. & Recreation; BPW; Assoc. of
Health Educators. B: 11/23/38. Add: RD 3, Box
92, Huguenot 12746.

ELIZABETH A. CONNELLY (D)
  1973-. Bds: Ch., Com. on Mental Health &
Retardation; Com. on Transportation; Com. on
Health. Party: Nat. Del. 1976; Cnty. Committee-
woman 1967- ; Zone Leader 1972-74. Org: BPW;
Westerleigh Improvement Society; N. Shore Dem.
Club. B: 6/19/28. Add: 94 Benedict Ave.,
Staten Is. 10314 (518)474-3100.

ESTELLA B. DIGGS (D) *
  1972-. Dist: 78. Bds: Social Services Com.;
Housing Com.; Child Care Com.; Mental Health
Com. Party: State Committeewoman. Org: NAACP;
BPW; Dem. Club. Add: 592 E. 167 St., Bronx
10456.

MARY B. GOODHUE (R) **
  1974-. Dist: 93. Party: V-Ch. Local Com.
1965-75. Educ: Vassar 1942 BA; U. of Mich. 1944
LLB. Occ: Attorney. B: 7/24/21. Add: McLain
St., Mt. Kisco 10549 (518)472-6230.

GERDI E. LIPSCHUTZ (D)
  1976-. Bds: Ch., Sub-Com. Senior Citizens
Safety & Security; Higher Educ. Com.; Housing
Com. Party: Dem. Com., NY 1969-71; Cnty. Dem.
Exec. Com. 1972- . Prev: Exec. Dir. of NYC
Mayor's Office of Voluntary Action. Org: Dem.
Party, Rockaway Health Council; Hadassah; Dem.
Club. B: 4/30/23. Add: 156 Beach 144 St.,
Rockaway Park, NY 11694 (212)634-4750.

MARY ROSE MC GEE (D) *
  1976-. Dist: 8. Party: Cnty. Committeewoman.
Prev: Dep. Town Clerk 1963; Town Clerk, 1967-76.
Org: LWV; BPW; Internat. Institute of Municipal
Clerks; Historical Soc.; Chamber of Commerce.
Add: 15 Brookside Dr., Huntington 11743.

County Commissions

Albany. VERONICA MEIER (D)
  1973-. Bds: Finance Com.; Social Services
Com.; Public Information Com. Org: Dem. Women's
Club. B: 12/30/36. Add: 157 Hudson Ave., Cohoes
12047 (518)445-7603.

Cattaraugus. ANNE MARIE COSTELLO
  MARIAN E. KRAMER
Courthouse, Court St., Little Valley 14755.

Chenago. JOYCE S. FLANAGAN
County Office Bldg., Norwich 13815.

Clinton. JANET L. DUPREY (R)
  1975-. Bds: Ch., Human Services Com.; Conservation & Cnty. Affairs; Educ. & Recreation.
Org: Council of Community Services; Peru Senior
Citizen Housing Com.; Social Services Adv. Council;
Cnty. Youth Bureau. Occ: Restaurant Owner. B:
11/27/45. Add: Telegraph St., Peru 12972
(518)561-8800.

Cortland. ELIZABETH I. BREVETT (R) **
  1974-. Bds: Home Care for Corland County;
Special Services Com.; Public Safety Com.; Consumer Protection Advisory Council. Org: LWV;
PTA; Women's Rep. Club. Educ: Smith Coll. 1946
BA; SUNY 1972 MS. B: 2/7/25. Add: 15 Morningside Dr., Cortland 13045.

Cortland. SHIRLEY A. FISH
  FLORENCE F. FITZGERALD
  ADELINE B. HIGGINS
  ELNA R. PHILLIPS
Courthouse, Corland 13045.

Cortland. ESTHER F. TWENTYMAN (R)
  1976-. Dist: 9. Bds: Transportation Com.;
Planning Com.; Water Quality Task Force. Party:
State Del. 1974; Nat. Alt. 1976; State Committee-
woman 1970. Prev: Town Planning Bd. 1973-77.
Org: Zonta Internat.; Farm Bureau; Cnty. Women's
Club. B: 5/16/24. Add: Rt. 2, Homer 13077
(607)756-2808.

Delaware. WANITA W. LEWIS (R)
  1973-. Bds: Ch., Health Com.; Ch., Election
Com.; Ch., Leg. Com. Party: Ch., Town Rep.
Com. 1962-65. Prev: Cnty. Treasurer 1971-77.
Org: Assoc. of Towns; Assoc. of Counties; Vlg.
Improvement Society; LWV; Women's Rep. Club.
Educ: State U. Coll.-Delhi 1971 AA. B: 8/27/14.
Add: 6 High, Delhi 13753 (607)746-2236.

Dutchess. JUDITH G. BLEAKLY
  MARGARET G. FETTES
  ROSALIE HODAS
County Office Bldg., Poughkeepsie 12601.

Dutchess. JEAN C. MURPHY (D)
  1967-. Bds: Ch., Human Services Com.;
Personnel Com.; Hudson Vly. Regional Council.
Party: Rep. Cnty. Committeewoman 1961-76. Org:
LWV; Women's Rep. Club. Educ: Parker Collegiate
Institute 1943 AA. B: 6/2/23. Add: 74 New
Hackensack Rd., Poughkeepsie 12603 (914)
485-9860.

Dutchess. LUCILLE P. PATTISON (D)
  1973-. Bds: Cnty. Supervisors Assoc. Org:
LWV; Mental Health Assoc.; Cnty. Dem. Women.
Educ: Syracuse U. 1957 BA. B: 10/31/35. Add:
97 Roosevelt Rd., Hyde Pk. 12538 (914)485-9860.

Erie. MARIE V. RICHARDSON (R)
  1975-. Dist: 19. Bds: Budget Com.; Social
Services Com.; Revenues & Assessments Com.
Org: BPW; Rep. Club. Educ:St. Lawrence U.
1955 BS. B: 7/21/33. Add: 75 Maple Ave.,
Hamburg 14075 (716)846-8653.

Fulton. EMMA KRAUSE
County Office Bldg., Johnstown 12095.

Monroe. PATRICIA BELL (D)
  1975-. Dist: 27. Bds: Asst. Dem. Minority
Leader; Health Systems Agency; Pure Waters
Administrative Bd. Party: Nat. Del. 1972;
Cnty. Committeewoman 1969-77; Cnty. Exec.
Committeewoman 1969-72; Secretary, Cnty. Com.
1970-71; V-Ch., Cnty. Com. 1971-72. Org:
Fed. of Women's Clubs; Neighborhood Assoc.;
Community Assoc.; Dem. Club. B: 5/10/42.
Add: 730 Seneca Pky., Rochester 14613 (716)
428-5352.

Monroe. NAN JOHNSON
39 Main St., W., Rochester 14614.

Monroe. LOUISE MC INTOSH SLAUGHTER (D)
1975-. Dist: 11. Bds: Pure Waters Bd. Party:
State Del. 1974; Nat. Del. 1972, '76; Cnty.
Committeewoman 1971- ; State Committeewoman 1974-.
Org: LWV; Common Cause; WPC. Educ: U. of Ky.
1951 BS; 1953 MS. B: 8/14/29. Add: 14 Manor
Hl. Dr., Fairport 14450 (716)454-3094.

Niagara. JEAN ANN BORGATTI (D)
1975-. Bds: Ch., Cnty. Mental Health Com.;
Co-Ch., Public Health Com.; Youth & Aging Com.
Org: Northwestern Zone School Nurse-Teachers;
ANA. Educ: Niagara U. 1963; U. of Buffalo 1971
EdM. Occ: Instructor of Nursing. B: 9/11/24.
Add: 2207 Woodlawn Ave., Niagara Falls 14301
(716)285-1212 x 337.

Oneida. MARY F. GRIFFITHS
800 Park Ave., Utica 13501.

Onodaga. DORIS CHERTOW (D)
1975-. Bds: Ch., Sub Com. on Children's
Services; V-Ch. Social Services Com.; Health Com.
Party: State Del. 1974, '70, '66; State Dem. Com.
1966-74; Cnty. Dem. Com. 1953- . Org: Cnty.
Legislators & Supervisors Assoc.; Assoc. for
Retarded Children; LWV; NOW; WPC; Cnty. Dems.
Educ: Hunter Coll. 1945 BA; Radcliffe Coll. 1948
MA; Syracuse U. 1968 PhD. Occ: Publication
Editor. B: 4/23/25. Add: 139 Sunnyside Park Rd.,
Syracuse 13214 (315)425-2170.

Onondaga. ELAINE LYTEL (D)
1974-. Dist: 9. Bds: V-Ch., Conservation &
Recreation; Educ. & Libraries; Social Services.
Party: Nat. Alt. 1974; Committeewoman 1964- .
Prev: Governor's Task Force on Public Adminis-
tration 1975- . Org: N.Y. State Supervisors &
Legislators Assoc.; LWV; NOWL; Women's Dem.
Club; WPC. Educ: Antioch Coll. 1945 BA; Syracuse
U. 1965 MPA. B: 9/10/23. Add: 222 Ambergate Rd.,
DeWitt 13214 (315)471-5043.

Oswego. NORMA BARTLE
County Bldg., Oswego 13126.

St. Lawrence. BETTY H. BRADLEY
Courthouse, Canton 13617.

Schenectady. ELIZABETH HARRIMAN BEAN (R)
1975-. Dist: 3. Bds: Citizens Adv. Com. to
the Capital Dist.; Reg. Planning Cmsn.; Ch.,
Physical & Environmental Planning Com. Prev:
Ch., State Citizens Information Service 1968-72;
Citizens Against Narcotics Com. 1970-71; Human
Services Planning Council 1974-76. Org: Assoc.
of Cnty's.; Supervisors & Cnty. Legislators
Assoc.; Bd. of Governors; Dir., Home Aide Service
of Eastern NY; Women's Rep. Club; Fed. of Women's
Club; AAUW; LWV; Planned Parenthood; Jr. League.
Educ: Smith Coll. 1945 BA. B: 9/23/23. Add:
2221 Stone Ridge Rd., Schenectady 12309 (518)
382-3282.

Schoharie. GAIL SHAFFER
County Bldg., Schoharie 12157.

Schuyler. MARIE EARL
County Bldg., Watkins Glen 14891.

Suffolk. ELAINE D. ADLER (D)
1975-. Dist: 16. Bds: Ch., Public Works/
Buildings & Grounds Com.; Leg. & Personnel
Com.; Public Safety & Judiciary Com. Party:
Cnty. Committeewoman 1967-77; State Committee-
woman 1971-73. Prev: Consumer Protection Bd.
1972-73; Zoning Bd. of Appeals 1973-75. Org:
NY Assoc. of Cnty Legislators & Supervisors;
Chamber of Commerce; Dem. Club. Educ: CUNY
1960 BA. B: 2/13/40. Add: 109 Dawson Dr.,
Greenlawn 11740 (516)427-9494.

Suffolk. JOYCE BURLAND
County Bldg., Riverhead 11901.

Suffolk. CLAIRE E. SAUER (D)
1975-. Bds: Salary & Classification Appeals
Bd.; Ch., Legislative & Personnel Com.; Edu-
cation & Youth. Party: Committeewoman 1974- .
Prev: Ch., Suffolk Cnty. Charter Revision Cmsn.
1967-70; Cnty. Youth Bureau 1972-74; Huntington
Youth Bd. Org: BPW; Chamber of Commerce; LWV;
ACTION for Preservation of N. Shore. Educ:
Cornell U. 1951 B-ILR. B: 3/12/29. Add: 1
Candlewood Ct., Huntington 11743 (516)673-9393.

Suffolk. MILDRED STEINBERG (D)
1974-. Bds: Ch., Environmental Control; Ch.,
Cultural Affairs; Human Services. Party: Nat.
Del. 1976; Committeewoman 1969-77; State
Committeewoman 1969-71. Org: LWV; Human Rela-
tions Council; NDC. Educ: Columbia U. 1938 BS;
MA. B: 5/8/12. Add: 4 Constance Ct., E.
Setauket 11733.

Sullivan. JEAN MC COACH
County Gov't. Center, Monticello 12701.

Tompkins. LE GRACE BENSON (D)
1972-. Bds: Cnty. Health Services Alliance;
Cnty. Alcoholism Council; Bd. of Dirs., Histor-
ical Society. Party: Cnty. Committeewoman 1968-
77. Prev: City Planning Bd. 1971-77. Org: Nat.
Assoc. of Women Deans & Counselors; Amer. Assoc.
for the Advancement of Science; ACLU; Cnty.
Co-op Extension. Educ: Meredith Coll. 1951 BA;
U. of Ga. 1956 MFA; Cornell U. 1975 PhD. Occ:
Assoc. Dean. B: 2/23/30. Add: 314 E. Buffalo
St., Ithaca 14850.

Ulster. BARBARA DE STEFANO (D)
1975-. Dist: 6. Bds: Public Health; Aging;
Tax Base Study. Party: Cnty. Committeewoman
1968-77; Ch., Town Committeewoman 1969-74.
Prev: Vlg. Trustee 1972-75. Org: Ulster Super-
visors & Legislators Assoc.; Dem. Club. Occ:
Medical Office Manager. B: 9/1/41. Add:S St.,
Box 278, Rosendale 12472 (914)331-9300.

Ulster. KATHLEEN QUICK
County Office Bldg., Kingston 12401.

Westchester. CAROLYN L. WHITTLE (D) **
1973-. Dist: 5. Bds: Community Affairs
Com. Org: LWV; Dem. Club; Women's Club. Educ:
Wellesley Northwestern U. 1967 BA; U. of Chicago
1968 MA. B: 2/22/45. Add: 25 Cushman Rd.,
White Plains 10606 (914)682-2325.

Yates. CATHERINE ELLIOTT
County Bldg., Penn Yan 14527.

Yates. CAROLYN M. SYMONDS (R) **
1973-. Dist: 4. Bds: Ch., Recreation Com.;
Ch., Planning Bd.; Public Health; Election;
Equalization; Workmen's Compensation. Party:
County Com. 1970-75. Org: BPW; OES; Women's
Rep. Club. Occ: Motor Vehicle Supervisor. B:
5/19/37. Add: Lincoln Ave. Ext., Penn Yan 14527
(315)536-4014.

Townships

Alexander. ELIZABETH WAGNER
Alexander 14005.

Almond. HELENE C. PHELAN (D)
1973-. Bds: Vlg. Bd. Repr. Prev: Vlg. Planning Bd. Org: Historical Society. Educ: UNC 1933
BA. B: 3/6/11. Add: 114 S. Main, Almond 14804.

Aurelius. DONNA K. REILLEY (D)
1973-. Bds: Cayuga Cnty. Supervisor Assoc.;
State Supervisor & Legislators Assoc. Party:
Cnty. Committeewoman. Prev: Town Clerk, Tax
Collector 1970-73. Org: Dem. Club. Occ: Account
Clerk. B: 3/10/30. Add: RD #3 W. Genesee Rd.,
Auburn 13021 (315)253-3578.

Aurora. JUNE M. GREENWOOD
1070 Falls Rd., W. Falls 14170.

Au Sable Forks. DOROTHY ELIZABETH MADDEN (I)
1976-. Bds: Water Cmsn.; Sanitary Landfill
Cmsn. Org: BPW; Chamber of Commerce; Mental
Health Assoc. Educ: Georgetown U. 1954 BSN.
Occ: RN. B: 8/16/32. Add: Main St., Jay 12941
(518)647-5595.

Babylon. SONDRA M. BACHETY (D)
1967-. Bds: Ch., Cultural Affairs; Ch., Park
& Recreation; Bldgs. & Grounds. Party: Nat. Del.
1974; Cnty. Committeewoman 1969-77. Prev:
Library Trustee 1965-75. Org: Women's Dem. Caucus;
LWV; NAACP; DAR; Dem. Club; PTA; Youth Center.
B: 3/28/32. Add: 259 W. 23rd St., Deer Park
11729 (516)957-3081.

Baldwin. ARLENE RAFFERTY (R)
1976-. Party: Cnty. Committeewoman 1968-76.
Org: PTA; OES. Educ: Tompkins-Cortland Community Coll. 1972 LPN. Occ: LPN. B: 5/10/33. Add:
RD #1, Federal Rd., Lowman 14861 (607)733-3984.

Bedford. PATRICIA V. HOTCHKISS (D)
1975-. Party: State Alt. Educ: Vassar Coll.
1950 BA. B: 7/31/29. Add: Box 67, RFD 1, Mt.
Kisco 10549 (614)666-5530.

Benson. WANDA MASON
Rte. 1, Northville 12134.

Bethel. JEAN BRUCHER (R)
1974-. Org: Amer. Institute of Banking; Rep.
Club; PTA. Occ: Bank Manager. B: 8/24/31. Add:
Dr. Duggan Rd., Bethel 12720 (914)583-4350.

Bethel. GRACE CAMPION
Kauneonga Lk. 12749.

Bethel. IRENE FOX
White Lake 12786.

Bethlehem. RUTH O. BICKEL
393 Delaware Ave., Delmar 12054.

Big Flats. BEVERLY F. MINIER (R)
1976-. Bds: Ch., Airport Land Use Study
for Chemung Cnty. Prev: Zoning Bd. of Appeals
1972-75. Educ: Skidmore Coll. 1952 BS; Ithaca
Coll. 1958 MS. Occ: Music Dir. B: 7/27/30.
Add: 754 Brookside Cir., Big Flats 14814
(607)562-8443.

Binghamton. LOIS D. MACKEY (R)
1961-. Org: Rep. Club. Educ: U. of N.H.
1941 BS. Occ: Coll. Instructor of Chemistry.
B: 12/12/20. Add: 2 Stone Rd., MR 98, Binghamton 13903.

Bleecker. GERTRUDE BULLERWELL
Bleecker Stage, Gloversville 12078.

Blooming Grove. HELEN B. DUELK
64 Duelk Ave., Monroe 10950.

Blooming Grove. SUZANNE V. WELLS
Dallas Rd., Monroe 10950.

Brant. BEVERLY A. WASMUND (R)
1973-. Bds: Hwy. Com.; Police Com. Org:
Rep. Club; OES; Chamber of Commerce. Occ:
Accountant. B: 9/21/2/. Add: 704 Commercial
St., Farnham 14061.

Brighton. JEANNE B. HUTCHINS (R)
1975-. Bds: Human Resources Council; Social
Security Task Force; Police & Public Works Com.
Prev: Ch., Citizens Adv. Com. 1972-77. Org:
Chamber of Commerce; Mental Health Coord. Group;
Rep. Club. Educ: Wells Coll. 1943 BA. B:
3/12/22. Add: 75 Indian Spring Ln., Rochester
14618 (716)244-5299.

Broome. BETTY M. CHICHESTER
RD #2, Middleburgh 12122.

Brunswick. JANE E. DOUGHNEY
RD #5, Box 257 1/2, Troy 12180.

Cameron. NELLIE P. BETTINGER
Box 16, Cameron 14819.

Canadaigua. FLORENCE NOTT
4112 W. Lake Rd., Canadaigua 14424.

Canton. ANNE PROUTY (R)
1973-. Bds: Youth Center Bd. Org: Agri-
Business Assoc.; Rep. Club. Occ: Cnty. Exec.
Dir. - USDA-ASCS. B: 11/23/34. Add: RR 4,
Canton 13617 (315)386-3735.

Carmel. LYNDA BERRIGAN (D)
1976-. Bds: Planning Bd. Liaison; Lighting
Dist.; Water Dist. Party: Cnty. Committeewoman
1972-77; Secretary, Town Com. 1974-77; Screening
Com. 1975-77. Org: Civic Assoc.; Dem. Club; PTA.

Educ: Hunter Coll. 1966 BA; Lehman Coll. MA. B: 6/26/44. Add: 24 Boniello Dr., Mahopar 10541 (914)628-1500.

Caroga. EMMA B. KRAUSE (R) **
    1965-. Party: Rep. Local Com.; Rep. Nat. Com. Org: Rep. Women's Club. Occ: Proprietor & Operator, Hotel & Restaurant. Add: Box 7, Caroga Lake 12032.

Caroline. SANDRA SARSFIELD
    2262 Slaterville Rd., Ithaca 14850.

Catskill. OLIVIA SCHMUCK
    RD #1, Box 129, Catskill 12414.

Centerville. FLORENCE PIXLEY
    RD #1, Farmersville Sta. 14060.

Chester. LORE M. HILDENBRAND (R)
    1974-. Bds: Dir., Loon Lake Park Dist.; Friends Lake Park Liaison; Town Planning Bd. Liaison. Prev: Secretary, Planning Bd. 1966-73. Org: Chamber of Commerce; Historical Society; Taxpayers Org.; Rep. Women; PTA. Occ: Resort Owner. B: 10/7/32. Add: RT #9, Chestertown 12817 (518)494-2711.

Clare. FLORENCE COLTON
    RFD #1, Russell 13684.

Clay. JUDITH V. FITZPATRICK (D)
    1976-. Bds: Ch., Dept. of Human Resources & Recreation; Ch. Zoning Bd. of Appeals. Party: Committeewoman 1974-78; Exec. Com., Onondaga Cnty. Dem. Com. 1975-77. Org: Nat. Assoc. Legal Asst's; Women's Dem. Club. Occ: Paralegal/Legal Secretary. B: 2/4/42. Add: 5085 Audrey Dr., N. Syracuse 13212 (315)474-7571.

Clinton. ANN D'ATTORE (R)
    1971-. Bds: Hwy. Com. Org: Rep. Club. Occ: Film Librarian. B: 8/26/36. Add: Shadblow La., Clinton Cors. 12514 (914)266-3748.

Cochecton. JEAN MC COACH
    RD, Cochecton 12726.

Colonie. MRS. MARIS C. HART
    16 Robert Dr., Albany 12205.

Conquest. MARGARET E. YOUNG (D)
    1974-. Party: Town Committeewoman 1968-77; V-Ch., Cnty. Com. 1977. Org: Cnty. Supervisor's Assoc.; Rural Letter Carriers Assoc.; Women's Club. B: 12/25/30. Add: RD #2, Prt. Byron 13140 (315)967-4555.

Corlandt. MURIEL H. MORABITO (I)
    1976-. Party: Dist. Leader 1943-45. Prev: Town Secretary-Clerk 1941-65; Town Clerk 1966-75. Org: Secretary Assoc. of Supervisors; V-Pres. Assoc. of Chief Elected Officials. B: 5/12/22. Add: 169 Seward St., Buchanan 10511 (914) 271-5196.

Cornwall. LORRAINE MEYERS BENNETT (R)
    1974-. Bds: Town Planning Bd.; Town Zoning Bd. of Appeals; Park Com. Party: Nat. Del. 1976; Ch., Rep. Com. 1971-77; V-Ch., Cnty. Rep. Com. 1975-77. Org: Women's Rep. Club; Rep. Club.

Educ: Empire State Coll. 1973 BS; N.Y.U. 1975 MA. Occ: School Nurse/Health Teacher. Add: Box 335, Vails Gate 12584 (914)534-3760.

Cuba. KIM B. CAMPBELL
    RFD 2, Friendship 14739.

Dayton. GALE A. INGERSOL
    P.O. Box 16, Dayton 14041.

Delaware. ANNE GORR
    Callicoon 12723.

Delhi. WANITA W. LEWIS (R) **
    1973-. Bds: Personnel Com.; Election Com.; Public Health Com.; Mental Health Bd.; Solid Waste Com. Prev: County Treasurer 1971. Org: BPW; OES; Village Improvement Society; Women's Rep. Club. B: 8/27/14. Add: 6 High St., Delhi 13753 (607)746-2237.

Dewitt. ELAYNE S. O'BRIEN
    103 Michaels Dr., Dewitt 13214.

Dryden. JANET GRAHAM
    12 Pleasant St., Dryden 13053.

Dunkirk. PATRICIA FORBES JOHNSON (D)
    1976-. Bds: Sewer Com.; Liaison, City of Dunkirk; Town Hall Renovation Com. Org: Bicentennial Com.; Dem. Club. Educ: SUNY at Fredonia 1950 BS. B: 7/3/29. Add: 5062 Shore-wood Dr., Dunkirk 14048 (716)366-4944.

Dunkirk. DOROTHEA M. KLAJBOR (D) *
    1973-. Bds: Inter-Municipal Planning Bd. Org: AAUW; Bar Assoc.; Nat. Lawyers Club; Senior Citizens Advisory Bd.; Volunteer Fire Dept.; Women's Dem. Clubs. Educ: Washington Coll. 1957 JD. B: 12/2/15. Add: 5081 W. Shorewood Dr., Dunkirk 14048 (716)366-2170.

East Hampton. MARY FALLON
    159 Pantigo Rd., E. Hampton 11937.

Elbridge. DORIS A. DAVIS
    Box 568, Jordan 13080.

Ellicott. FRANCES MORGAN
    19 N. Work St., Falconer 14733.

Ellicottville. LUCILLE J. POOLE
    1 Washington St., Ellicottville 14731.

Enfield. BETTY R. HOWARD (R)
    1976-. Party: Cnty. Committeewoman 1960-77. Org: Women's Rep. Club. Occ: Bookkeeper. B: 5/30/22. Add: 46 Podunk Rd., Trumansburg 14886.

Evans. DOROTHY H. ROSE (D)
    1971-. Bds: Ch., Recreation & Youth Com.; Police Com.; Water Com. Party: Town Committee-woman 1963- ; Cnty. Exec. Com. 1963-74. Prev: State Assemblywoman 1965-69. Org: Dem. Club; BPW. Educ: D'Youville Coll. 1941 BA; Geneseo State Coll. 1942 BS. Occ: Coll. Librarian. B: 9/21/20. Add: 974 Gold St., Angola 14006 (716)549-4038.

Farmersville. LESLIE D. BIGHAM
    R.D., Franklinville 14737.

Fleming. ELIZABETH ROSS
    W. Lake Rd., Auburn 13021.

Forestburgh. MARY GRUND (R)
    1974-. Org: Women's Club; Rep. Club. B:
6/7/09. Add: RD 1, Box 85, Monticello 12701.

Freedom. GLORIA M. KLEIN (R)
    1975-. Bds: Liaison, Recreation & Parks Com.
B: 1/7/35. Add: Maple Grove Rd., Freedom
14065 (716)492-1619.

Freetown. PATRICIA P. FOX
    R.D. #1, Cincinnatus 13040.

French Creek. ANNA LOU EMORY
    RFD #2, C/O French Cree, P.O. Clymer 14724.

Fulton. ALICE WASVARY
    RD #1, Box 56, Richmondville 12149.

Gates. BARBARA LETVIN (D)
    1975-. Bds: Conservation Adv. Bd. Party:
Cnty. Committeewoman 1976-77. Prev: Conservation
Bd. 1973-75. Org: LWV; Dem.Women's Club; PTA.
Educ: Ohio State U. 1964 BS; SUNY at Brockport
1969 MA. B: 6/19/42. Add: 42 Twin Circle Dr.,
Gates 14624 (716)247-6100.

Georgetown. LEONA GOODRICH
    R.D., Erieville 13061.

Goshen. DENISE A. LILLEY (D)
    1975-. Bds: Treas.-Orange Cnty. Assoc. of
Town Supervisors & City Mayors. Prev: Council-
woman 1974-75. Org: Assoc. of Town Supervisors;
Goshen Dem. Club; Homeowners Assoc. B: 2/19/44.
Add: 2 Fleetwood Dr., Goshen 10924 (914)
294-6996.

Granby. IRENE ARNOLD
    R.D. #7, Fulton 13069.

Greenburgh. LOIS TAPLIN BRONZ (D)
    1975-. Bds: Personnel; Recreation; Housing.
Org: Amer. Public Works Assoc.; Civic Assoc.;
Black Women's Political Caucus; Dem. Club; Black
Dem's. Educ: Xavier U. 1948 BA; Wayne State U.
1952 MEd. Occ: Educator. B: 8/20/27. Add:
282 Old Tarrytown Rd., White Plains 10603.

Greenburgh. BARBARA J. ROSEN (D)
    1973-. Bds: Ch., Police; Ch., Recreation; Ch.,
Consumer. Party: Committeewoman 1970-73. Org:
Assoc. of Towns; Amer. Public Works Assoc.;
Common Cause; LWV; Dem. Club; PTA. Educ: Vassar
Coll. 1956 BA. B: 5/19/34. Add: 32 Club Way,
Hartsdale 10530 (914)682-5272.

Greenville. BARBARA VALICENTI
    Norton Hill 12135.

Greig. HELEN E. PLATO
    Box 76, Greig 13345.

Guilderland. PAULINE PORTER
    Rte. 20, Guilderland 12084.

Halcott. WANNETA FINCH
    Halcott Ctr., 12437.

Hamburg. BARBARA C. WICKS (D)
    1973-. Bds: Ch., Town Recreation Com.;
Traffic Safety Bd.; Ch., Insurance Com. Party:
Cnty. Committeewoman 1968- . Prev: Town
Historian 1972-74. Org: BPW; LWV; Women's Dem.
Club; By-Laws Com., NY Assoc. of Towns. Educ:
SUNY 1964 BS; 1968 MS. B: 2/11/30. Add: 187
Charlotte Ave., Hamburg 14075 (716)649-6111.

Hannibal. DORIS Y. MC MILLEN (R)
    1974-. Educ: Oswego State Teachers Coll.
1946 BSEd. B: 7/12/24. Add: RD #1, Wall Rd.,
Hannibal 13074.

Harmony. GAIL A. JOHNSON
    R.D. Watts Flats, Ashville 14710.

Hinsdale. BETTY LINDERMAN (D)
    1975-. Party: Secretary, Cnty. Women Dem's.
1973-75. Prev: Election Bd. Inspector 1962-75.
Org: Cnty. Women Dem's. B: 7/28/36. Add:
RD #1, 3609 Rt. 16, Hinsdale 14743 (716)
557-2243.

Hopewell. CLARA STODDARD
    R.D. #2, Canandaigua 14420.

Hornby. ELEANOR Z. CONNELL (R) **
    1974-. B: 9/25/25. Add: Box 417, Hornby
Rd., RD 3, Corning 14830 (607)936-4805.

Ithaca. SHIRLEY A. RAFFENSPERGER (D)
    1976-. Bds: Ch., Park Com.; Cnty. Planning
Bd. Org: Civic Assoc.; PTA. Educ: Pa. State
U. 1953 BA. B: 9/5/32. Add: 139 Pine Tree
Rd., Ithaca 14850 (607)277-3909.

Ithaca. CATHERINE VALENTINO
    126 E. Seneca St., Ithaca 14850.

Kendall. ALICE WOLF
    1216 Norway Rd., Kendall 14476.

Kent. ETHEL M. FORKELL (I)
    1976-. Bds: Police Comsr.; Ch., Recreation;
Town Hall Bldg. Party: Committeewoman 1960-76.
Prev: Town Clerk 1955-75. B: 11/17/19. Add:
RD 7, Lk. Carmel 10512 (914)225-3954.

Kortright. IRIS HAGER
    1975-. B: 1/18/24. Add: RD 1, Box 52,
Bloomville 13739.

La Grange. MARJORIE BRONSON
    Stringham Rd., Pleasant Vly. 12569.

Lewisboro. JUNE CORY PATRICK
    Town House, Main St., S. Salem 10590.

Lewiston. JOAN E. GIPP (D)
    1975-. Party: Committeewoman 1972-75.
Educ: SUNY 1952 BS. Occ: Teacher. B: 6/24/29.
Add: 1468 Ridge Rd., Lewiston 14092 (716)
754-8214.

Lexington. EVELYN B. KELLY (D)
    1975-. Party: Cnty. Committeewoman 1975- .
B: 11/6/18. Add: Spruceton Rd., W. Kill 12492.

Litchfield. LEONA SLAUGHTER
RD #1, Ilion 13357.

Lumberland. ELIZABETH GEBA
Glen Spey 12737.

Lyndon. JOYCE SLOCUM (R)
1975-. Party: Local Committeewoman 1976-77.
Prev: Town Clerk 1969-71. Org: Women's Rep.
Club. B: 11/11/25. Add: RD #3, Cuba 14727
(716)676-9907.

Macomb. PHYLLIS TURNER (R) **
1973-. Bds: Environmental Conservation
Advisory Council. Prev: Town Clerk 1970-73.
Org: County Supervisor's Assoc. Occ: Milk Test-
ing Supervisor. B: 10/15/39. Add: RD 1, Rossie
13646.

Mendon. ROBERTA J. BARNES
9 N. Main St., Honeoye Falls 14472.

Milo. BARBARA S. PUTNAM (R)
1975-. Org: Nat. Retired Teachers Assoc.;
Rep. Club. Educ: Elmira Coll. 1929 BS; MA. B:
6/8/07. Add: 321 Main St., Penn Yan (315)
536-8911.

Montaque. NANCY GILLESPIE
R.D. #4, Lowville 13367.

Morehouse. DONNA E. UEBELE
Cold Brook 13324.

New Albion. MARILYN A. WASMUND (D)
1975-. Occ: Clerk. B: 7/6/33. Add: 78
Jefferson St., Cattaraugus 14719.

New Castle. NANCY FELCHER (D)
1973-. Bds: Hwy. Com.; Police Com.; Water
Com. Party: Committeewoman 1972- . Org: LWV.
Educ: Goucher Coll. 1964 BA. B: 12/12/42. Add:
54 Spring Ln., Chappaqua 10514 (914)238-4771.

New Haven. JUNE REED
R.D. #1, Oswego 13126.

Northeast. ELEANOR SINGLETON
Millerton 12546.

North Harmony. JUNE M. BUNGE (R)
1976-. Bds: Bldg. Com.; Parks Com.; Auditing
Com. Party: Cnty. Committeewoman 1975-77. Org:
Falconer Educ. Assoc.; NYS Teacher's Assoc.; PTA.
Educ: Fredonia State Teachers Coll. 1945 BS.
Occ: Teacher. B: 6/4/23. Add: R. 1, Quigley Pk.,
Ashville 14710.

North Hudson. EVELYN CLARK
N. Hudson 12855.

North Norwich. JUNE HORTON
No. Norwich 13814.

Ogden. GAIL SCHOTT
14 Sheldon Dr., Spencerport 14559.

Ontario. DOROTHY LEUZE
107 Ridge Road W., Ontario 14519.

Osciola. RUTH KEENEY
RFD, Redfield 13437.

Ossining. SUSAN D. FITZPATRICK
Municipal Bldg., Croton Ave., Ossining 10562.

Otego. VIRGINIA LIDDLE
R.D. #1, Otego 13825.

Owego. DIANE C. ALBRECHT (D)
1975-. Bds: Ch., Personnel Com.; Ch.,
Finance; Sewer & Water. Party: Cnty. Committee-
woman 1972- ; V-Ch., Town Dem. Com. 1975- .
Org: Health Systems Agency. Educ: SUNY 1973 BS.
B: 10/21/47. Add: RD #1, Box 296, Campville Rd.,
Endicott 13760 (607)754-2499.

Owego. DORIS B. SCOTT (R)
1974-. Bds: Ch., Playgrounds-Parks-Recre-
ation; Finance; Personnel. Party: Town Election Inspector 1969-73. Org: AAUW; Cnty. Rep.
Women; PTA. Educ: Keuka Coll. 1950 BA. B:
8/28/29. Add: Box 291, Apalachin Blvd.,
Apalachin 13732 (607)687-2194.

Pelham. MARCIA D. LIDSTONE (R)
1970-. Bds: Senior Citizens. Prev: Recreation Comsr. 1966-70; Ch., Recreation Cmsn.
1968-70. Org: Assoc. Visiting Nurse; Senior
Citizens Bd.; Women's Rep. Club; Jr. League.
Educ: Wellesley Coll. 1943 BA; Kutztown State
Coll. 1946 BS. B: 12/29/22. Add: 260 High-
brook Ave., Pelham 10803 (914)738-1021.

Penfield. ANNA R. BUNDSCHUH (R)
1975-. Bds: Ch., Parks, Recreation & Social
Services Com.; Parks & Recreation Adv. Bd.;
Narcotic Guidance & Youth Councils. Party:
Cnty. Committeewoman 1975-77. Org: LWV; Susan
B. Anthony Rep. Club; Women's Rep. Club; Real
Property Taxation Com. Educ: U. of Rochester
1948 BA. B: 12/5/27. Add: 40 Cobbles Dr.,
Penfield 14526.

Penfield. IRENE L. GOSSIN (D)
1972-. Party: Cnty. Committeewoman 1970-77.
Org: Monroe Cnty. Supervisor's Assoc.; Supervisors & Cnty. Legislators Assoc.; Heritage
Assoc.; Nature Conservancy. Educ: Eastman
School of Music, U. of Rochester 1941 BM. B:
2/1/19. Add:17 Parkview Dr., Rochester 14625
(716)377-5510.

Pinckney. IRENE A. WILLIAMS
Star Rte., Watertown 13601.

Pittsford. CAROL K. KAMAN (R)
1972-. Bds: Environmental Bd. Party: Rep.
Committeewoman 1962-77. Prev: Library Liaison
1974-76. Org: Rep. Club. Educ: U. of Pa.
1950 BA. Occ: Higher Educ. Assessment Specialist.
B: 2/23/29. Add: 65 Alpine Dr., Rochester
14618 (716)586-8649.

Pompey. GERALDINE GUYNUP
Watervale Rd., Manluis 13104.

Pompey. ELIZABETH A. SHEDLOCK (D)
1969-. Party: Committeewoman 1974-77. Prev:
Town Clerk 1964-69. Org: Dem. Club. B: 4/29/25.
Add: 7889 US Rt. 20, Manlius 13104 (315)682-9877.

Poughkeepsie. ANNA BUCHHOLZ (D)
    1975-. Bds: Joint Landfill Bd. of Governors;
Cnty. Solid Waste Agency; Ch., Bd. of Comsrs.
Special Benefit Dists. Party: Cnty. Committee-
woman 1967-75; State Committeewoman 1969-74.
Prev: Cnty. Reps. 1972-74. Org: AAUW; LWV; ADA;
ACLU; County Dem. Women. Educ: U. of Ky. 1940
BA; U. of Ill. 1941 MA; 1944 PhD. B: 12/29/20.
Add: 24 Edge Hill Rd., Wappingers Falls 12590
(914)471-8200.

Poughkeepsie. KATHRYN E. M. CARROLL (D)
    1975-. Bds: Ch., Labor Negotiating Com.;
Intergovt. Com.; Ch., Insurance Com. Party:
Secretary, Town Dem. Com. 1972-73; V-Ch., Town
Dem. Com. 1974-75; Public Relations Ch., Cnty.
Dem. Com. 1974-75; Cnty. Dem. Committeewoman
1972- . Org: Nat. Assoc. of Real Estate Brokers;
Common Cause; Cnty. Dem.; Women's Club. Occ:
Real Estate Broker/Real Property Appraiser. B:
2/17/37. Add: 11 Wildwood Dr., Poughkeepsie
12603 (914)471-8200.

Pound Ridge. PEARL L. GLASSMAN (D)
    1975-. Bds: Liaison, Conservation Adv. Bd.;
Liaison, Water Control Cmsn. Party: State Del.
1956. Prev: Zoning Bd. of Appeals 1968-75. Org:
LWV; Historical Society; Dem. Club. Educ: CCNY
1948 BBA; Fairfield U. 1970 MA. Occ: Guidance
Counselor. B: 6/5/27. Add: White Birch Rd.,
Pound Ridge 10576 (914)764-4633.

Prattsville. PHYLLIS RAEDER (D) **
    1974-. B: 1/19/37. Add: County Supervisor's
Office, Prattsville 12468 (518)299-3437.

Pulteney. ANNA HERMAN (R)
    1976-. Prev: Town Clerk 1950-62. B: 7/29/23.
Add: RD #2, Hammondsport 14840.

Putnam Valley. SALLIE S. SYPHER (D)
    1973-. Bds: Insurance Com.; Parks & Recreation;
Senior Citizens. Party: State Del. 1972-76; Nat.
Alt. 1974; State Committeewoman 1972-77; Cnty.
Committeewoman 1970-77; Town Ch. 1971-74. Org:
Dem. Club. Educ: Mt. Holyoke Coll. 1954 BA;
Cornell U. 1959 PhD. B: 2/1/33. Add: Roberts
Dr., RFD 3, Putnam Vly. 10579 (914)526-3280.

Red House. JOAN HOFFMAN
    R.D. #1, Salamanca 14779.

Rensselaerville. ZITA EASTMAN
    Rensselaerville 12147.

Rhinebeck. JANE GALLOW
    Rte. 308, Rhinebeck 12572.

Riga. PATRICIA WOITYRA
    8 S. Main St., Churchville 14428.

Rush. LUCY L. PARSONS (I)
    1974-. Bds: Conservation Bd.; Industry Con-
servation & Wildlife Management Adv. Com. Prev:
Trustee, Public Library 1960-73. Org: RUSH
Independents. B: 4/23/25. Add: 2782 Pinnacle
Rd., Rush 14543 (716)533-1312.

Salamanca. EILEEN GOODRICH
    R.D. #1, Box 206, Little Valley 14755.

Sandy Creek. FAY REID
    Lacona 13083.

Santa Clara. ERMA G. KIMPTON (D)
    1970-. Bds: Bd. of Dir's. Adirondack
Airport. Party: Local Committeewoman 1970-77.
Educ: Md. General Hospital School of Nursing
1933 RN. Occ: Asst. Caretaker. B: 6/26/12.
Add: Paul Smiths 12970 (518)327-3535.

Saugerties. JENNIFER PEETOOM
    Main St., Saugerties 12477.

Scarsdale. JEANNE A. RICHMAN
    Village Hall, Scarsdale 10583.

Scipio. CATHERINE LACEY
    R.D., Aurora 13026.

Shandaken. RUTH GALE
    Shandaken 12480.

Skaneateles. JANET ALLYN
    24 Jordan St., Skaneateles 13152.

Smithville. JOYCE FLANAGAN (R)
    1975-. Bds: Personnel Com.; Bills & Claims;
Youth Bd. Prev: Town Clerk 1959-71; School
Tax Collector 1973-75. Org: Women's Rep. Club.
B: 7/2/28. Add: Star Rt., Greene 13778
(607)656-8002.

Smithtown. JOAN FRANKE
    99 Main St., Smithtown 11787.

Southport. DIANE C. DICKERSON
    1139 Pennsylvania Ave., Elmira 14904.

Sparta. HELEN BABCOCK
    R.D. #1, Dansville 14437.

Springport. CORAL BENNETT
    R.D. 3, Auburn 13021.

Stephentown. PATRICIA MOHOS
    Stephentown 12168.

Sweden. JEAN W. MARTIN (R)
    1975-. Bds: Parks Cmsn. Party: Exec. V-Com-
mitteewoman 1973-75. Prev: Planning Bd. 1971-
75. Org: Right to Life; Women's Rep. Club.
Educ: Syracuse U. 1950 BM. Occ: Drive-In
Owner. B: 4/15/27. Add: 320 S. Main St.,
Brockport 14420 (716)637-2144.

Throop. ROBERTA SLAYTON
    RD #5, Turnpike Rd., Auburn 13021.

Throop. MARILYN SROLEA
    R.D. #5, Auburn 13021.

Tonowanda. GLORIA D. MC DONALD
    2919 Delaware Ave., Kenmore 14217.

Victory. FAY KASSON
    R.D. 2, Red Creek 13143.

Watertown. RUTH A. MISULIS
    Dry Hill Rd., Watertown 13601.

Webster. NANCY N. THOMAS   (R)
   1976-. Bds: Zoning Bd. of Appeals; Library
Bd.; Bd. of Health. Party: Committeewoman 1974-
77. Org: Women's Club; BPW; Chamber of Commerce;
LWV; Town & Cnty. Com.; Susan B. Anthony Club.
B: 8/18/28. Add: 402 Bittersweet Ln., Webster
14580 (716)872-1000.

West Bloomfield. CLAIRE F. ROBERTS   (R)
   1976-. Org: Women's Club. Occ: Medical Ward
Secretary. B: 6/11/24. Add: RD #2, 8338 Rt. 5
& 20, W. Bloomfield 14469.

West Bloomfield. GERALDINE E. SMITH   (D)
   1974-. Bds: Ch., Bicentennial Com.; Ambulance
Com. Prev: Zoning Bd. of Appeals 1970-73. Org:
Cen. School Non-Teaching Employees Org. Occ:
School Bus Driver. B: 5/29/29. Add: 2064
Factory Hollow Rd., RFD #1, Lima 14485.

West Seneca. JOAN F. LILLIS
   1250 Union Rd., W. Seneca 14224.

Wilmington. JEAN HUNTINGTON
   Wilmington 12997.

Wilna. BETTY MC LEAN
   Carthage 13619.

Windsor. JOAN H. EDWARDS
   Box 26, Windsor 13865.

Woodstock. VALERIE CADDEN   (R)
   1975-. Prev: Councilwoman 1974-75. Educ:
Georgian Ct. Coll. 1953 BS. B: 7/21/31. Add:
26 Van De Bogart Rd., Woodstock 12498 (914)
679-8597.

Woodstock. JANE VAN DE BOGART   (D)
   1974-. Bds: Woodstock Conservation Cmsn.,
Public Utilities; Sewage Study. Org: Concerned
Consumers of Ulster Cnty.; COPE; Woodstock
Nuclear Opponents; ACLU. Educ: Antioch Coll.
1964 BA; SUNY 1971 MA. Occ: Photographer. B:
8/24/41. Add: Wittenberg Rd., Mt. Tremper
12457 (914)679-2113.

Yorktown. NANCY R. ELLIOTT   (R)
   1976-. Bds: Sewer Com.; Recreation Cmsn.;
Expeditor Economic Devt. Com. Prev: Planning
Bd. 1973-76. Org: Assoc. of Towns; LWV; Community Help Com.; Rep. Club. Educ: Denison U. 1951
BA. B: 10/8/29. Add: Colonel Greene Rd., Yorktown Hts. 10598 (914)962-5722.

Yorktown. ANNE K. JANAK   (D)
   1973-. Bds: Recreation Cmsn.; Conservation
Bd.; Sewer Com. Party: Committeewoman 1973-77.
Prev: Citizen Adv. Com. on Housing 1972-73. Org:
LWV; Citizen Adv. Com. for Urban Devt.; Dem. Club.
Educ: Catherine Laboure School of Nursing 1960 RN;
Pace U. 1977 BA. B: 8/13/38. Add: 3548 Frost
Rd., Shrub Oak 10588 (914)962-5922 x 59.

Mayors

Albion. DONNA STRICKLAND RODDEN   (R)
   1973-. Bds: Exec. Com.-NW Frontier Assoc. of
Vlg. Officials. Prev: Planning Bd. 1971-73;
Orleans Cnty. Task Force on Alcoholism 1971-72.

Org: BPW; Internat. Platform Assoc.; Orleans
Cnty. Rep. Women; OES. Occ: Media Specialist.
B: 8/10/26. Add: 327 W. Bank St., Albion
14411 (716)589-9176.

Argyle. ELAINE MC INTYRE   (R)
   1974-. Bds: Vlg. Health Bd.; Police Chief,
Ch. Prev: Trustee 1961-74; Deputy Mayor 1973-
74. B: 5/11/21. Add: 2197 W. St., Argyle
12809.

Avon. MARY B. COLE   (D)
   1975-. Org: Delta Kappa Gamma; Cnty. Assoc.
of Vlg. Bds.; NY Conference of Mayors; LWV;
Common Cause; Cnty. Nutrition Program for Elderly; Dem. Club. Educ: U. of Rochester 1949
BA. Occ: Dir., Senior Community Service Employment Program. B: 7/14/27. Add: 350 N. Ave.,
Avon 14414 (716)226-8118.

Bloomingdale. HILDA HELMS
   Bloomingdale 12913.

Brushton. MARY KINGSLEY
   Brushton 12916.

Canajoharie. MARY K. PLANK   (R) **
   1975-. Bds: Bd. of Health; Bicentennial
Com. Party: Local Com. 1952-56. Org: Chamber
of Commerce; PTA; Rep. Club. B: 8/10/26.
Add: 34 Moyer St., Canajoharie 13317 (518)
673-5512.

Canton. RUTH C. BLANKMAN   (D)
   1974-. Bds: Planning Bd.; Council of Govt.
Prev: Vlg. Trustee 1974-75. Org: St. Louis
Cnty. Mayor's Assoc.; NY State Conf. of Mayor's
LWV; Women's Dem. Club. Occ: Buyer-Ladies
Apparel. B: 6/17/21. Add: 67 State St., Canton
13617 (315)386-2851.

Cherry Valley. LYNN J. THOMPSON
   Main St., Cherry Valley 13320.

Earlville. GRACE B. SUTTON   (R) **
   1974-. Bds: Opera House. Org: Co-Ch.,
County Rep. Club; Secretary Civic Club; Secre-
tary, Grange; Pres., Nurses Club. Educ: Nassau
Hospital School for Nurses 1930 RN. Occ:
Retired. B: 5/8/08. Add: 73 Main St., N.,
Earlville 13332 (315)691-2121.

East Setauket. HELEN M. JORDAN   (D)
   1973-. Prev: Bd. of Appeals 1964-68; Vlg.
Trustee 1968-73. Org: Civic Assoc. of Setauket.
B: 6/27/06. Add: 6 Maybeck Dr., E. Setauket
11733.

Geneva. HELEN P. MANEY   (D) **
   1974-. Prev: Councilwoman at Large 1963-74;
Pres., Common Council 1962-63; Councilwoman
1947-62. Org: LWV; School Administrators Assoc.;
Zonta; Free Library; Women's Dem. Club. Educ:
William Smith Coll. 1937 BA; Syracuse U. 1946
MA. Occ: V-Principal High School. B: 2/7/15.
Add: 197 Genesee St., Geneva 14456 (315)
789-5212.

Grand View on Hundson. LORRAINE MOSCOW
   87 River Rd., Grand View on Hudson 10960.

Hamburg. DOROTHY M. MELOY
    1975-. Prev: Planning Cmsn. 1964-69; Vlg.
Trustee 1969-75. B: 7/8/20. Add: 146 Main St.,
Hamburg 14075 (716)649-0200.

Hewlett Bay Park. ROSLYN T. LEA
    30 Piermont Ave., Hewlett 11557.

Madison. BRANDA TUBBS
    Madison 13402.

Marathon. EMOGENE B. PASSERY (R) **
    1972-. Party: Town Com. Org: County Recre-
ation Center; Women's Rep. Club. Occ: Accounting
Clerk. B: 9/9/27. Add: 12 Bradford St., Marathon
13803.

Mayfield. MRS. JACK WEMPLE
    Mayfield 12117.

Middleburg. THERESA YOUMANS
    367 Main St., Middleburg 12122.

Mohawk. DOROTHY A. MURPHY (R) **
    1973-. Bds: Landfill Corportation; Health
Bd. Org: PTA. Occ: Owner, Motor Repair Shop.
B: 11/22/37. Add: 10 N. Richfield St., Mohawk
13407 (315)866-4312.

Montour Falls. GWEN SNOW (D)
    1975-. Prev: Vlg. Trustee 1974-75. Org: OES.
B: 8/26/23. Add: 215 Henry St., Montour Fls.
14865 (607)535-7376.

Old Westbury. ELEANOR A. SIMPSON (R)
    1975-. Bds: Police Com.; Assessors; Water
Com. Prev: Vlg. Trustee 1972-75; Vlg. Planning
Bd. 1968-72. B: 1/27/31. Add: 35 Clork Tower
Ln., Old Westbury 11568 (516)626-0800.

Piermont. MARY C. BRYAN (D) **
    1974-. Prev: Village Trustee 1971-74. Org:
Civic Assoc.; Dem. Club; PTA. Educ: Rosemont
Coll. 1951 BA. B: 8/8/29. Add: 36 Bay St.,
Piermont 10968 (914)359-1258.

Port Jefferson. SANDRA SWENK (R) **
    1971-. Org: Beautification Com.; Historical
Society; PTA. B: 3/13/37. Add: 108 Prospect
St., Port Jefferson 11777 (516)473-4724.

Thomaston. CORINNE B. COE (I)
    1977-. Bds: Great Neck Vlg. Officials Assoc.
Prev: Deputy Mayor 1971-75; Trustee 1969-71;
Trustee Great Neck Library 1969-77. Org: LWV;
Great Neck Library Assoc. Educ: Madison Coll.
1945 BS. Occ: Home Economist/Teacher. B: 5/2/22.
Add: 1 Shadow Ln., Great Neck 11021 (516)
482-3110.

Warwick. MARY J. MURTIE (D) **
    1973-. Bds: Planning Bd.; Housing Authority;
Cable TV Cmsn.; Consolidation Study Cmsn. Org:
Conf. of Mayors. B: 8/11/28. Add: 23 Welling
Ave., Warwick 10990 (914)986-2031.

Wyoming. RHODA B. WARREN (I)
    1975-. Bds: Ch., Budget; Ch., Safety. Party:
V-Pres., Cnty. Women's Rep. Club. 1966-70. Org:
Rep. Town Com. Occ: Librarian. B: 6/22/22.

Add: 26 Sherman Ave., Wyoming 14591 (716)
495-6361.

Local Councils

Albany. GLORIA M. BALLIEN (D)
    1969-. Bds: Ch., Capital Hill Architect-
ural Cmsn.; Dept. of Commerce Acting Deputy
Cmsnr. & Counsel. Org: State Bar Assoc.;
Women's Bar Assoc.; Women Lawyers Assoc.;
Soroptimist; BPW. Educ: Columbia U. 1949 BS;
Albany Law School 1957 LLB/JD; NYU 1970 LLM.
Occ: Atty. Add: 32 Willett St., Albany 12210
(518)472-8140.

Baldwin. LEE G. MAC KEIL (R)
    1973-. Educ: NY State Agriculture & Tech-
nology 1960 AAS. Occ: Display Manager. B:
2/26/36. Add: Hoffman Holw. Rd., Lowman
14861.

Batavia. CATHERINE K. ROTH (R)
    1975-. Bds: Ch., Genesee Cnty. Sub-Area
Adv. Council; Ch., Traffic Com.; Mall Com.
Prev: Water & Sewer Adv. Bd. 1963-78. Org:
AAUW; Cnty. Women's Rep. Club; Assoc. for
Retarded Children; Preservation League of NY
State. Educ: William Smith Coll. 1942 BA. B:
8/23/20. Add: 255 East Ave., Batavia 14020
(716)343-8180.

Binghamton. MARY T. KEYES (D)
    1972-. Bds: State Assoc. of City Councils;
Council Pres. Org: BPW; State Assoc. of City
Councils; Health Access & Communications
Systems Ctr.; Cnty. Dem. Political Club; PTA.
Educ: Mercy Hospital School of Nursing 1947 RN.
B: 7/28/25. Add: 16 Dennison Ave., Binghamton
13901 (607)772-7236.

Brookhaven. REGINA SELTZER (D)
    1975-. Party: Town Committeewoman 1968-76.
Org: LWV. Educ: CCNY 1952 BBA; C.W. Post Coll.
1966 BLS. B: 9/4/29. Add: 30 S. Brewster Ln.,
Bellport 11713 (516)475-5500.

Carthage. BETTY MC LEAN
    439 N. Washington St., Carthage 13619.

Charlton. DAMASITA B. MINER
    RD #3, Vines Rd., Ballston Lk. 12019.

Cobleskill. PHYLLIS MERRILL
    31 Elm Street, Cobleskill 12043.

Cohoes. IRENE C. RIVET (R) **
    1967-. B: 11/25/01. Add: 77 Congress St.,
Cohoes 12047 (518)237-7811.

Conesus. MARTHA GANNON
    2075 E. Lake Rd., Conesus 14435.

Corning. ALEINE JANE MC KINNEY (R)
    1975-. Bds: Audit. Party: Committeewoman
1962-76. B: 7/21/02. Add: 178 W. 1st St.,
Corning 14830.

Cortland. MARY ELLEN OPERA (D)
   1975-. Party: Committeewoman 1972-77; City
Ch. 1976-77. B:11/4/31. Add: 161 Elm St.,
Cortland 13045.

Delhi. TRACY N. MATTHEWS
   23 Delview Ter., Delhi 13753.

Enfield. FERN SMITH
   R.D. #3, Newfield 14867.

Fenner. FRAN COSTELLO
   R.D. #1, Cazenovia 13035.

Glens Falls. LUCINDA HESS
   4 Horicorn Ave., Glens Falls 12801.

Grove. LYNN WEIDMAN
   Swain 14884.

Hartwick. JEANNETTE B. HANSEN
   R.D. #3, Cooperstown 13326.

Hector. DOROTHY W. MORRIS (R)
   1959-. Bds: Park. Prev: Grade School Trustee
1944-45. Org: Amer. Farm Bureau; NY State Grange.
B: 2/23/20. Add: RD #1, Montour Fls. 14865
(607)387-6300.

Highland. BARBARA MAAS
   Highland Lk. 12743.

Hoosick. JOAN H. ROGERS (D)
   1976-. Bds: Ch., Athletic Field. B: 12/24/30.
Add: 72 High St., Hoosick Fls. 12190.

Hudson. DOLORES EISNER (R) **
   1975-. Bds: Legal Com.; Street & Sewer Com.;
Youth Com. Party: Local Com. 1972-74. Org:
BPW; Rep. Club. Occ: Clerk. B: 6/6/32. Add:
358 Union St., Hudson 12534 (518)828-5205.

Hudson. GENEVIEVE A. KLUGO (D)
   1975-. Bds: Public Bldgs.; Cemetary; Public
Relations. Party: Secretary 1969- ; Election
Cmsnr. 1970-75; Committeewoman 1976. Org: Dem.
City Com.; Dem. Social Club. Occ: Management
Asst. B: 6/30/32. Add: 509 Union St., Hudson
12534.

Ithaca. NANCY R. MEYER (D) **
   1971-. Bds: Planning & Dev.; Human Services;
Transit; Environmental; Beautification; Mall
Steering Com.; Commons Advisory Bd.; Intergovern-
mental Com.; Revenue Sharing; Housing Bd.; Park;
Bicentennial; Ch., Revised Zoning Map & Ordinance.
Org: Art Teachers Assoc.; BPW; Downtown Business
Women. Educ: U. of Wisc. 1957 BS; U. of Wisc.
1967 MS. B: 4/4/34. Add: 214 Cascadilla Pk.,
Ithaca 14850 (607)272-1713.

Ithaca. ETHEL BARON NICHOLS (D)
   1969-. Bds: Ch., Charter & Ordinance Com.;
Human Services Com.; Bicentennial Cmsn. Party:
Cnty. Committeewoman 1966-. Prev: Youth Bd.
1973-74. Org: NEA; Economic Opportunity Bd.
Educ: U. of Minn. 1942 BA; Cornell U. 1951 PhD.
Occ: Teacher. B: 3/8/21. Add: 109 Lenroc Ct.,
Ithaca 14850 (607)272-1713.

Jamestown. JOYCE BATAITIS
   52 Arden Pkwy., Jamestown 14701.

Jamestown. ELIZABETH S. BLACK (D)
   1972-. Bds: Ch., Public Safety Com.; Ch.,
Ambulance Bd. Org: AAUP; AAUW; Bd. of Dir.,
Health System Agency. Educ: U. of Pittsburgh
1949 BS; St. Bonaventure U. 1972 MSEd.;
Deaconess Hospital 1946 RN. Occ: Nursing
Professor. B: 7/5/25. Add: 915 Newland Ave.,
Jamestown 14701.

Jamestown. VIVIAN A. TAYLOR
   31 W. 18th St., Jamestown 14701.

Junius. JANE L. DE WALL
   RD 2, Whiskey Hill Rd., Waterloo 13165.

Lincklaen. LYNN H. MOWERS
   Deruyter 13052.

Lockport. FRANCES A. RATH
   18 Harrison Ave., Lockport 14094.

Morehouse. JANE KELLEY
   Hoffmeister 13353.

Newburgh. REGINA MARY ANGELO (D) **
   1972-. Bds: Environmental Cmsn.; Ch.,
Beautification & Clean Up Com. Party: Local
Com. 1973-75; Co-Ch., County Com. 1973; City
Dem. Inspector 1964-70. Org: PTA; Women's
Dem. Club. Occ: Senior Library Clerk. B:
3/25/33. Add: 824 Broadway, Newburgh 12550
(914)565-3333.

New Castle. NELL TAYLOR
   200 South Greely Ave., Chappaqua 10514.

Newfane. JOSEPHINE N. BEILEIN (D)
   1976-. Bds: Deputy Supervisor. Party:
Committeewoman 1976-77. Org: Historical
Society; Right-to-Life; Newfane Dem. Club. B:
6/24/20. Add: 5448 W. Lake Rd., Bunt 14028.

Newfield. FERN B. SMITH (R)
   1975-. Bds: T.V. Cmsn. Occ: Office Clerk.
B: 8/10/26. Add: R.D. 3, Newfield 14867.

New York City. MARIAN FRIEDLANDER
   City Hall, New York 10007.

New York City. CAROL GREITZER (D)
   1969-. Bds: Ch., Consumer Affairs Com.;
Environmental Protection Com.; Finance Com.;
Ethics Com. Party: State Alt. 1962; Nat. Del.
1972; Dem. Dist. Leader 1961-69; Dem. Committee-
woman 1961- . Org: Abortion Rights Mobilization;
Vlg. Independent Dem's. Educ: Hunter Coll. BA;
NYU MA. Add: 59 W. 12th St., NYC 10011 (212)
D19-2466.

New York City. MARY PINKETT
   324 DeKalb Avenue, New York 11205.

New York City. LUCILLE ROSE
   Deputy Mayor of NYC, City Hall, New York
10007.

New York City.   AILEEN B. RYAN
    City Hall, New York   10007.

New York City.   ARLENE STRINGER
    2 Bennet Avenue, New York   10033.

Oneida.   MARJORIE I. O'BRIEN   (I)
    1976-.   Bds: Ch., Finance Com.; Senior
Citizens Com.; Senior Nutrition Com.   Prev:
Housing Authority 1974-76.   Org: Women of Rotary.
Educ: Green Mtn. Jr. Coll. 1938 AS; Syracuse U.
1942 BAEd.   B: 3/26/18.   Add: 420 Leonard St.,
Oneida 13421.

Oneonta.   JEAN M. SCORZAFAVA   (D)
    1975-.   Bds: Finance Com.; Bldg. Com.; Ch.,
Lighting Com.   B: 8/29/27.   Add: 37 1/2 Burnside
Ave., Oneonta 13820.

Poughkeepsie.   COLETTE LA FUENTE
    110 Hooker Ave., Poughkeepsie 12601.

Rochester.   BARBARA L. LETVIN
    235 Trabold Rd., Rochester 14624.

Rome.   PATSY SPADO
    126 McAvoy St., Rome 13440.

Rossie.   MAURINE EVANS
    Rossie 13646.

Rye.   PATRICIA T. LEVINE   (D) **
    1974-.   Bds: Youth Council; Bicentennial Cmsn;
Flood Control Com.   Org: Conservation Society;
LWV.   B: 1/12/34.   Add: 65 Drake-Smith La., Rye
10580   (914)967-5106.

Scarsdale.   MARCELLA S. KAHN
    1974-.   Prev: Safety Adv. Bd. 1969-72; Environ-
ment Adv. Council 1972-74; Environment Adv.
Council 1972-74.   Org: LWV; Vlg. Club.   Occ:
Credit Manager.   B: 10/24/27.   Add: 276 Mamaroneck
Rd., Scarsdale 10583   (914)723-3300.

Scarsdale.   JEANNE A. RICHMAN   (D) **
    1975-.   Bds: Environmental Com.; Planning;
Library Bd.   Party: State Platform Com. 1974-
75.   Prev: Local Governments Reappointment
Commissioner.   Org: LWV; Municipal League; Dem.
Club.   Educ: U. of Mich. 1944 BA; Columbia 1945
MS.   Occ: Project Director, Election Study.   B:
3/1/24.   Add: 110 Birchall Dr., Scarsdale 10583
(914)723-3300.

Schenectady.   KAREN BROWN JOHNSON   (D)
    1975-.   Bds: Ch., City Dev. & Planning Com.;
Health & Recreation Com.; Ch., Parking Com.
Party: Committee 1974- .   Org: LWV; Jr. League;
Human Service Planning Council.   Educ: Radcliffe
Coll. 1964 BA.   B: 5/12/42.   Add: 707 Union St.,
Schenectady 12305   (518)382-5089.

Syracuse.   JOYCE INGHAM ROSS   (D)
    1975-.   Dist: 5.   Bds: Ch., Metropolitan
Planning, Housing & Real Estate; Finance & Tax-
ation; Educ. & Human Resources.   Party: Cnty.
Committeewoman.   Prev: Administrative Asst. to
Mayor 1970-71; Personnel Dir. 1970.   Org: BPW;
ACLU; WPC; Dem. Women's Club; PTA.   Educ: Dickin-
son Coll. 1952 BA; Syracuse U. 1956 MSEd.   B:

7/24/30.   Add: 218 DeWitt Rd., Syracuse 13214
(315)473-2796.

Troy.   NORMA H. FATONE   (R)
    1976-.   Bds: V-Ch., Troy Urban Renewal
Agency; Ch., Public Safety Com.; Ch., Law Com.
Occ: Co-Owner.   B: 8/17/33.   Add:776 Rawling
Ave., Troy 12180.

Victor.   SUSAN E. MC NELLY
    1621 Victor Holcomb Rd., Victor 14564.

Webb.   DIANE BOWES
    Eagle Bay 13331.

West Seneca.   JOAN F. LILLIS
    1250 Union Rd., W. Seneca 14224.

White Plains.   JOYCE GORDON   (D)
    1975-.   Bds: Ch., Cnty. Criminal Justice
Coord. Com.   Prev: Special Asst. Westchester
Cnty. Exec. 1974-75.   Org: SAC; AFTRA; LWV.
Occ: Actress.   Add: 15 Hathaway La., White
Plains 10065   (212)252-7676.

White Plains.   MARY ANN KEENAM
    City Hall, Municipal Bldg., White Plains
10605.

Judges

BEATRICE S. BURSTEIN
    Supreme Court Justice.   Add: 10th Judicial
District, Supreme Court Building, Mineola
11051.

MAXINE K. DUBERSTEIN
    Supreme Court Justice.   Add: 2nd Judicial
District, 360 Adams Street, Brooklyn 11201.

ANN B. DUFFICY
    Supreme Court Justice.   Add: 11th Judicial
District, 88-11 Sutphin Blvd., Jamaica 11435.

JOAN M. DURANTE
    Supreme Court Justice.   Add: 11th Judicial
District, 88-11 Sutphin Blvd., Jamaica 11435.

MARGARET MARY J. MANGAN
    Supreme Court Justice.   Add: 1st Judicial
Distict, 60 Centre Street, New York 10007.

ANN T. MIKOLL
    Supreme Court Justice.   Add: 8th Judicial
District, Erie County Hall, Buffalo 14202.

HILDA G. SCHWARTZ
    Supreme Court Justice.   Add: 1st Judicial
District, 60 Centre Street, New York 10007.

State Boards and Commissions

Office of the Governor, State Capitol Bldg., Albany 12224.

Aging, Advisory Committee to the N.Y. State Office for the
RAMONA INTRIAGO
JEAN L. JANOVER
OLLIE RANDALL
ETHEL TORGESON

Agricultural Resources Commission
GRACE BAKER
ANITA MAXWELL
PAMELA ALISON MURTAUGH

Agriculture and Markets, Commission of
DORIS G. CADOUX

Alcoholism, Advisory Committee on
MRS. ALICE FORDYCE

Allegany State Park and Recreation Commission
JOAN A. MILLIGAN

American Revolution Bicentennial Commission
MARY BIONDI
JANE DES GRANGE
PATRICIA KENNEDY LAWFORD
MILDRED F. TAYLOR

Apprenticeship and Training Council
LOIS SPIER GRAY

Arts, Council of the
MIRIAM COLON EDGAR
GERALDINE FITZGERALD
SISTER M. IRENE FUGAZY
KITTY CARLISLE HART
VICTORIA E. LEVENE
BESS MEYERSON
MRS. RICHARD RODGERS
GERALDINE FITZGERALD SHEFTEL

Banking Board
ANNA ROSENBERG HOFFMAN

Capital Hill Architectural Review Commission
KATHERINE HARRINGTON

Central New York State Park and Recreation Commission
ESTHER M. ASWAD

Citizen's Policy and Complaint Review Council
SHANARA AYANA
LILLIAN MATEO
JANET S. WELCH

Community Affairs Advisory Board
ANNA BUCHHOLZ
MRS. HERBERT HOCKBERG
ANN M. HURLEY
OJETTA D. SMITH

Consumer Protection Board
ROSEMARY POOLER

Correction, State Commission of
DOROTHY B. WADSWORTH

Correction Medical Review Board
CATHERINE FINCH COLLINS
BETTY J. FRIEDLANDER
DR. PHYLLIS HARRISON-ROSS

Crime Control Planning Board
DR. JUNE JACKSON CHRISTMAS
DR. JUDIANNE DENSEN-GERBER
PAULINE FEINGOLD
EDITH MILLER
PEGGY WOOD

Dental Hygiene, Committee on
JUDITH H. SMITH
PATRICIA ZAHN

Dentistry, Board for
LILLIAN H. BACHMAN

Developmental Disabilities Act, Advisory Council to the
BARBARA FEINGOLD

Drug Abuse, Advisory Council on
JUANITA POITER

Economic Development Board
JUDITH PRICE

Education Commission of the States
SANDRA FELDMAN

Electric Generation Siting and the Environment, State Board on
MARLENE H. LINDQUIST
ELIZABETH MC LAFFERTY

Employment and Unemployment Insurance, Advisory Council on
MARY IDA GARDNER
ALICE B. GRANT

Engineering and Land Surveying
PHYLLIS B. BERGER
MARJORIE CARPENTER

Finger Lakes State Park and Recreation Commission
MARGARET L. CLYNES

Great Lakes Commission
CELESTINE J. MC GILL
LAURA R. PAUL

Guy Park House and Grounds
MRS. MICHAEL RAPHAEL

Health Advisory Council
EILEEN DICKINSON
MARGARET D. SOVIE

Health Coordinating Council, Statewide
BETTY H. BRADLEY
SHARON LEE DANIEL
SYLVIA F. HUNTER
REGINA M. KELLY
DR. ELEANOR LAMBERTSEN
PHYLLIS S. VINEYARD

Health Planning Commission
MRS. LOU GLASSE

Health Research Council
MRS. ALBERT D. LASKER
ALICE L. MILLER
MARIA I. NEW
DR. MARGARET D. SOVIE
MRS. LINDA TARR-WHELAN

Herkimer Home
MARY MARGARET MANLEY

Higher Education in the City of New York, Board of
EDITH B. EVERETT
PATRICIA CARRY STEWART

Higher Education Services Corporation
MRS. EDWARD T. DICKINSON
MRS. ROBERT A. LOW

Historic Preservation, Board of
DR. SHIRLEY GORENSTEIN
MRS. PATRICK HARRINGTON
MILDRED F. TAYLOR

Historical Records Advisory Board
MARCHARD M. FINNEGAN
DR. ELSIE M. LEWIS

Hospital Review and Planning Council
MARION ASCOLI
GLADYS BURROWS
PATRICIA M. COOK
SISTER ELLEN LAWLOR
ELIZABETH LAWRENCE
LILLIAN M. LEVEY
DR. ELENA PADILLA
NORA PIORE
MRS. GLENISS SCHONHOLZ

Housing Development Corporation, New York City
FRANCES LEVENSON

Hudson River Valley Commission
MRS. LEWIS GAGE
ROBIN MARTIN
MRS. GENE ROBB

Human Rights Appeal Board
IRMA VIDAL SANTAELLA

Insurance Fund
LOUISE COSTE

International Women's Year Committee
ANN T. MIKOLL

Job Development Authority
LOUISE M. SUNSHINE

Judicial Conduct, State Commission on
MRS. ALFRED DEL BELLO
MRS. LILLEMOR ROBB

Juvenile Justice Advisory Group
SHEILA ELAINE ANDERSON
NANCY ANN ASCH
MRS. ROBERT M. BLUM
MARIA RIVERA DE BUCHANAN
ADRIENNE L. FLIPSE

MARY E. GALBREATH
JUDGE FLORENCE M. KELLEY
THERESA M. MELCHIONNE
MRS. JOHN C. MITCHELL
SUZY L. NAGIN
CAROL J. PARRY
RENA K. UVILLER

Labor Relations Board
HELEN M. WOLFSOHN
MILDRED PAFUNDI ROSEN

Landscape Architecture, Board for
KATHARINE W. RAHN

Libraries, Governor's Conference on
DORIS FABER

Liquor Authority
DOROTHEA M. KLAJBOR

Long Island State Park and Recreation Commission
MS. JOYCE BURLAND

Manpower Planning Council
CORA CHANDLER
LOU GLASSE
SISTER ROSARIA HUGHES
KAREN TOBIN

Manpower Services Council
LOIS SPIER GRAY
CHARLOTTE SCHIFF JONES
AGNES LOUARD
ELSA LUKSICH
GERTRUDE G. MICHAELSON
JOYCE D. MILLER

Massage, Board for
ANN M. BURZYNSKI
EDITH L. KRISTELLER
ADELE MOLINSKI

Medical Advisory Committee
VIRGINIA WALTERS GALLAGHER
DR. PEGGY A. HANSON
BEVERLY JEAN HART
DR. BEATRICE KRESKY
MARGARET L. MC CLURE
GLENISS SCHONHOLZ

Medical Malpractice, Special Advisory Panel on
SISTER EVELYN M. SCHNEIDER

Medicine, Board for
EDITH C. REID

Mental Health Advisory Committee
ELEANOR MALLACH BROMBERG
DR. MARGARET M. LAWRENCE
ELIZABETH P. MAC LEOD

Mental Hygiene Council
KARIN A. BURGESS
ALICE FORDYCE

Mental Hygiene Planning, Council for
    KARIN A. BURGESS
    DR. JUNE JACKSON CHRISTMAS
    ALICE FORDYCE
    DR. MARGARET M. LAWRENCE
    JOAN R. SALTZMAN

Metropolitan Transportation Authority
    ROBERTA S. KARMEL

Mitchell-Lama Task Force
    FRANCES LEVENSON

New York State School for the Blind at Batavia
    SANDRA K. MALLORY

Niagara Falls Bridge Commission
    MRS. GEORGE HIGGS
    MRS. ROBERT W. RAMSEY

Nursing, Board for
    GRACE E. BROWN
    JULIA BROWN
    MARJORIE DOYLE
    SISTER RITA JEAN DUBREY
    LEOTA MC INTOSH
    HELEN MC NERNEY
    EVA M. NOLES
    MARY PILLEPICH
    MILDRED M. SCHMIDT
    EDITH SCHMITT
    JUNE SIMPSON
    BERNICE SMITH
    MARGARET SOVIE
    JENNIE D. WILBUR

Occupational Therapy, State Board for
    MILDRED C. EY
    ALICE FEINBERG
    MARIE L. FRANCISCUS
    BARBARA J. TEAL
    HARRIET J. TIEBEL

Olana Historic Site
    ELIZABETH J. KEELER
    ELAINE MORRISON
    NANCY TESTA

Ophthalmic Dispensing, Board for
    JOAN MACKOLIN

Optometry, Board for
    LIBBY SUKOFF

Palisades Interstate Park Commission
    DR. MAMIE PHIPPS CLARK
    MARY A. FISK

Parks and Recreation, State Council of
    MARIAN S. HEISKELL
    JEANNE F. LEWISOHN

Parole, Board of
    ADA F. JONES

Parole, State Board of
    WILHELMINA HOLLIDAY

Pharmacy, Board of
    DORIS H. CHAPIN
    PATRICIA KOPEC
    META SMITH

Physical Therapy Board
    JUDITH A. LURIE

Podiatry Board
    ELIZABETH ROBERTS

Postsecondary Education in New York State, T.S.C.
on the Future of
    LOIS DICKSON RICE

Project Finance Agency
    CAROL S. MORTON

Psychology, Board for
    RUTH LESSER
    VIRGINIA SEXTON

Public Accountancy
    M. JANE DICKMAN
    KATHARINE M. WEST

Public Disclosure, Board of
    RUTH ROBBINS

Public Employment Relations Board
    IDA KLAUS

Public Health Council
    JEANNE E. JONES

Public Service Commission
    MRS. CARMEL C. MARR
    ANNE F. MEAD

Public Work Advisory Board
    SUSAN COHEN

St. Lawrence-Eastern Ontario Commission
    MRS. H. FREDERICK BARTLE
    BETTY G. MC LEAN
    MRS. JAMES L. MASON

Saratoga-Capital District State Park and Recreation
Commission
    MRS. THOMAS CARLSEN
    ATHENA V. LORD

Security and Privacy Committee
    MARY JOHNSON LOWE

Senate House Association
    MRS. CYNTHIA BERARDI

Social Welfare, State Board of
    SANDRA RUIZ BUTTER
    TRUDY FESTINGER
    MARY ANN QUARANTA

Social Work, Board for
    AIDA BURNETT
    CATHARINE BUTLER
    BRAHANA D'ALOIS
    SISTER MARY GUNDELL

Speech Pathology and Audiology
    PATRICIA B. BEGNER
    ADELE MARKWITZ

Sports and Winter Olympics, N.Y. State Commission on
    MRS. CHARLES T. GROSSBERGER

State University Agricultural and Technical College at Canton
    MRS. BROOKE MC DOWELL

State University College at Buffalo, Council
    MRS. SYLVIA CALLISTEIN

State University College at Cortland, Council
    JERRENE M. WOODS

State University College at Oswego, Council
    PHYLLIS EASTMAN

State University College at Purchase, Council
    JOAN W. NIERENBERG

State University, Regents of
    LAURA B. CHODOS
    EMLYN I. GRIFFITH
    MARY ALICE KENDALL
    LOUISE P. MATTEONI

State University of New York, Board of Trustees of
    MRS. JAMES WM. JOHNSON
    MRS. MAURICE T. MOORE
    MRS. EDWARD SIEGEL
    MRS. WALTER N. THAYER

State University Trustees, Board of Trustees
    MRS. JAMES W. JOHNSON
    MRS. BILL MOYERS

Supreme Court Library at White Plains
    DORIS L. SASSOWER

Supreme Court Library at Troy
    JOYCE M. GALANTE

Taconic State Park and Recreation Commission
    JEANNE F. LEWISOHN

Thousand Island State Park and Recreation Commission
    NOREEN M. RYAN

Tourism, Board of
    HARRIET D. CORNELL
    KATHERYN V. FITZGERLAD
    RICELLE P. GROSSINGER
    ISABELLE LEEDS
    GAIL JONES LUMET
    JOYCE MILLER ROST
    LAURA VISCOME
    JOAN WOLF

Tri-State Regional Planning Commission, Citizens Advisory Panel
    ETHEL GEORGE BEDFORD
    ROSE MUSCIO

Upstate Medical Center
    MARGUERITE G. MC KENNAN

Visually Handicapped, Commission for the
    MARJORIE B. MC COY
    NANCY LONG STRURE

Washington's Headquarters, Board of Trustees
    MARJORIE K. INDZONKA

Westchester Community College
    MRS. RALYNN NEWMARK STADLER

Workmen's Compensation Board
    ILENE J. SLATER

Youth, Council on
    CHARLOTTE G. HOLSTEIN
    TERRY N. SAARIO

North Carolina

State Executive and Cabinet

SARA W. HODGKINS (D)
Secretary of Cultural Resources. 1977-.
Party: State Del.; State Alt.; Precinct Ch.,
1970-72; Precinct V-Ch. 1975-77; Cnty. V-Ch.
1968-69. Prev: Councilwoman 1976-77. Org:
State Employees Assoc.; Dem. Party. Educ:
Appalachian State U. 1952 BS. B: 11/25/30.
Add: 915 E. Indiana Ave., Southern Pines 28387
(919)733-4867.

DR. SARAH T. MORROW
Sec., Department of Human Resources. Add:
Albemarle Bldg., 325 North Salisbury Street,
Raleigh 27611.

State Legislature

State Senate

RACHEL G. GRAY (D)
1976-. Dist: 19. Bds: Transportation Com.;
Ways & Means Com.; Natural Economic Resources
Com. Party: State Del. 1976. Prev: Councilwoman 1973-76. Org: NC Women's Forum; Common
Cause. Occ: Gift Shop Buyer. B: 9/26/30. Add:
612 Gatewood Ave., High Point 27260 (919)
887-1054.

HELEN R. MARVIN (D)
119 Ridge Ln., Castonia 28052.

CAROLYN MATHIS (D)
1973-. Bds: Cmsn. on Children with Special
Needs; Council on Educ. Services for Exceptional
Children; V-Ch., Appropriations Com. on Educ.
Party: Nat. Committee-NC Fed. of Young Reps.
1971-72. Org: Young Dem's. Educ: UNC Greensboro
1963 BS; U. of NC 1970 MA. Occ: Teacher. B:
1/20/42. Add: 8045 Regent Park Ln., Charlotte
28210 (919)733-5658.

KATHERINE ANN HAGEN SEBO (D)
1974-. Dist: 19. Bds: Technical Adv. Com.
on Alternatives to Training School; N.C. Adv.
Com. on Non-Public Educ. Prev: Com. on the
Status of Women 1972-73. Org: AAUW; N.C. Political
Science Assoc.; ACLU; Altrusa; LWV; Women's Forum
of N.C.; Young Dem's.; North State Caucus. Educ:
Oberlin Coll. 1965 BA; American U. 1967 MA; PhD.
Occ: Coll. Professor. B: 7/9/44. Add: 907
McGee St., Greensboro 27403 (919)733-5706.

State House

MARILYN R. BISSELL (R) **
1972-. Dist: 36. Bds: Criminal Justice Train-
ing & Standards Council; Government Expenditure
Com. Party: Precinct V-Ch. 1968-70; V-Ch. 1970-72.
Org: AAUW; LWV; WPC; Charity League; PTA.
Educ: Grove City Coll. 1949 BS. B: 9/29/27.
Add: 2216 Providence Rd., Charlotte 28211
(919)829-5906.

LOUISE S. BRENNAN (D)
1969-. Dist: 36. Bds: Constitutional
Amendments Com.; Judiciary Com.; Appropriations.
Party: Nat. Del. 1972; Ch., Dist. Conv. 1970-
77; Ch., Mecklenburg Cnty. Dem. Party 1970-72;
State Exec. Com. 1968-77; Pres., Dem. Women's
Club 1967-68; Dist. Dir., N.C. Dem. Women 1968-
71; Precinct Ch. 1964-77. Prev: Charter Cmsn.
1969-71. Org: AAUW; N.C. Political Science
Assoc.; Women's Forum; WPC; Dem. Women's Club.
Educ: U. of N.C. 1970 BA. Occ: Coll. Professor.
B: 11/11/22. Add: 2101 Dilworth Rd. E.,
Charlotte 28203 (919)733-5889.

NANCY CHASE (D) **
1963-. Dist: 9. Bds: Com. to Study Emo-
tional Children; Governor's Study Com. on
Architectural Barriers; NC Land Planning; Com.
on Educ. & Employment of Women. Party: Del.,
Nat. Conv. 1968; Precinct Com. 1960-61. Prev:
School Bd. 1959-60. Org: State Farm Bureau;
Dem. Women's Clubs; Mental Health Assoc.; Women's
Clubs. Occ: Teacher. B: 10/12/03. Add: Box
226, Eureka 27830 (919)242-5633.

RUTH E. COOK (D) **
1974-. Dist: 15. Bds: Status of Women Cmsn.;
Consumers Council; Tax Reform Advisory Bd. Prev:
Exec. Dir., State Council for Social Legislation
1967-74. Org: Bd. Dir., ACLU; LWV; NC Educ.
Opportunities Center; Dem. Women's Clubs; PTA.
B: 11/11/29. Add: 3413 Churchill Rd., Raleigh
27607 (919)828-5863.

RUTH M. EASTERLING (D)
811 Bromley Rd., Apt. 1, Charlotte 28207.

JO GRAHAM FOSTER (D)
5600 Sea Croft Rd., Charlotte 28210.

PAT O. GRIFFIN (D)
2607 W. Cornwallis Rd., Durham 27705.

BERTHA MERRILL HOLT (D)
1975-. Dist: 22. Bds: V-Ch., Public
Libraries Com. Party: State Del. 1966-76;
Cnty. Pres., Dem. Women 1962-64; Ch., Head-
quarters Com. 1964, '68; State Dem. Exec. Com.
1964-76. Prev: Cnty. Social Services Bd. 1968-
72; Ch., Cnty. Social Services Bd. 1969-71;
Atty., Dept. of Interior 1942-43; U.S. Treasurer
for Funds Control 1941-42. Org: Grange; English
Speaking Union; Dem. Women; Women's Forum.
Educ: Agnes Scott Coll. 1938 BA; U. of Ala. 1941
LLR. B: 8/16/16. Add: 509 Country Club Dr.,
Burlington 27215 (919)733-5807.

PATRICIA STANFORD HUNT (D)
    1079 Burning Tree Dr., Chapel Hill 27514.

WILDA HURST (D)
    P.O. Box 309, Huburt 28539.

EDITH LEDFORD LUTZ (D)
    Route 3, Lawndale 28090.

MARY C. NESBITT (D)
    471 Fairview Rd., Asheville 28803.

JANET W. PICKLER (D)
    Route 1, New London 28127.

FRANCES E. SETZER (D) **
    1974-. Dist: 37. Educ: Bowling Green 1942 BA;
U. of NC 1957 MA. B: 11/27/22. Add: P.O. Box 265,
Newton 28658 (919)829-5773.

MARY P. SEYMOUR (D)
    1105 Pender Ln, Greensboro 27408.

LURA SELF TALLY (D) **
    1972-. Dist: 20. Bds: Appropriations;
Corrections; Educ.; Higher Educ.; Mental Health
& Social Services; Health. Org: AAUW; BPW; LWV;
Pres., Mental Health Assoc.; Women's Club. Educ:
Duke U. 1942 BA; NC State U. 1970 MA. Occ:
Teacher, Guidance Counselor. B: 12/9/21. Add:
3100 Tallywood Dr., Fayetteville 28303 (919)
484-4868.

MARGARET TENNILLE (D)
    1974-. Bds: NC Juvenile Code Revision Com.
Party: V-Ch., Precinct 1961-71. Prev: Bd. of
Educ. 1957-61. Org: NOWL; Women's Forum; Women's
Club; United Daughters of Confederacy; Dem. Women.
B: 3/25/17. Add: 2307 Greenwich Rd., Winston-
Salem 27104 (919)733-5900.

BETTY DORTON THOMAS (D)
    160 Glendale Ave., Concord 28025.

MYRTLE E. WISEMAN (D)
    Route 2, Mulleen Hill Rd., Spruce Pine 28777.

County Commissions

Beaufort. MRS. ARTHUR LEE MOORE (D)
    1974-. Bds: Mental Health Bd. Org: Dem.
Women's Club. Educ: E. Carolina U. 1950 BS; 1958
MA. B: 3/22/28. Add: Box 567, Washington 27889
(919)946-7721.

Buncombe. DORIS PATTON GIEZENTANNER (D)
    Bds: Health Systems Agency; Health Systems
Area Bd.; Mental Health Bd. Prev: Alderwoman
1971-76. Org: Dem. Women's Club; Dem. Club. B:
8/7/26. Add: P.O. Box 8462, Asheville 28807.

Buncombe. CARY C. OWEN (R)
    1972-. Bds: City-Cnty. Water-Sewer Com.;
Subdiv. Ordinance Com. Party: State Del. 1973.
Prev: Bd. of Educ. 1968-69. Org: Community Concert
Assoc.; Rep. Women's Club. Educ: U. of NC 1956
BA. B: 2/19/35. Add: 7 Greenwood Rd., Asheville
28803 (704)255-5533.

Caldwell. FAYE BEAL
    238 Tremont Park Dr. S.E., Lenoir 28645.

Carteret. MARY SUE NOE
    Morehead City 28557.

Cass. PATRICIA WOLD
    Fargo 58102.

Cass. JEANNETTE STANTON
    1522 N. 4th, Fargo 58102.

Catawba. BETTY PITTS COOKE (D)
    1977-. Bds: Co-Ch., Cnty. Water & Sewer;
Co-Ch., Cnty. Solid Waste; Ch., Cnty. Personnel.
Org: AAUW; Service League; Cnty. Dem. Club.
Educ: U. of N.C. 1948 BA. B: 8/23/28. Add:
Rt. 10, Box 551, Hickory 28601 (704)464-7880.

Durham. ELNA B. SPAULDING (D)
    Bds: Community Health Ctr.; Transportation
Adv. Com. Party: Cnty. Del. 1977. Org: Child
Advocacy Cmsn.; Founder of Women-In-Action for
Prevention of Violence, Inc.; Com. on Black
Affairs; Cnty. Dem. Club; Day Care Council. B:
1/23/09. Add: 1608 Lincoln St., Durham 27701
(919)688-3360.

Edgecombe. RUTH CHERRY
    Rt. 2, Rocky Mount 27801.

Forsyth. MRS. MAZIE S. WOODRUFF
    456 W. 24 1/2 St., Winston-Salem 27101.

Franklin. BETSY LEONARD PERNELL (D)
    1970-. Party: Precinct Leader 1952-64; Ch.,
Dem. Exec. Com. 1965-70. Org: Nat. Business
Educ. Assoc.; LWV. Educ: Atlantic Christian BA;
East Carolina U. MA. Occ: Professor. B:
6/26/31. Add: R-5 Box 100, Louisburg 27549
(919)496-5995.

Henderson. MILDRED BARRINGER
    3131 Wesley Way, Hendersonville 28739.

Madison. VIRGINIA ANDERSON
    Box 66, Marshall 28753.

McDowell. JANE G. GREENLEE (D)
    Party: State Del. 1968, '72, '76; Cnty.
Committeewoman. Prev: Bd. of Dir., N.C. Schools
for the Deaf 1968-73; Cnty. Planning Bd. Org:
State Dem. Women; Cnty. Dem. Women; United Way.
B: 4/2/20. Add: Marion 28752.

Mecklenburg. ELIZABETH G. HAIR (D)
    1972-. Bds: Library Bd.; Ch., Nat. Assoc.
of Cntys.; Tax & Finance. Party: State Del.
1964, '60. Prev: Ch., Cnty. Bd. of Elections
1960-72; Governor's Cmsn. of Educ. Beyond the
High School 1961-63; State Property Tax Study
Com. Org: BPW; United Community Service Bd.;
Dem. Women's Club; WPC. Educ: Wellesley Coll.
1941 BA. Occ: Advertising Sales. B: 1/2/20.
Add: 1522 Stanford Place, Charlotte 28207.

Moore. CAROLYN BLUE
    Eagle Springs 27242.

New Hanover. KAREN E. GOTTOVI (D)
    1976-. Bds: Bd. of Dir's. Social Services
Dept.; Airport Cmsn.; Downtown Area Revitalization
Effort. Party: V-Ch., Precinct 1975-77. Prev:
Citizens Planning Com. 1975-77. Org: NC Assoc.
of Cnty. Cmsnr's.; NC Library Assoc.; LWV; Jr.
League; Dem. Women; ACLU; Common Cause. Educ:
Wells Coll. 1962 BA; U. of NC 1971 MS. B: 2/2/41.
Add: Rt. 3, Box 344 F, Wilmington 28401 (919)
256-4849.

New Hanover. ELLEN WILLIAMS
    309 Northern Blvd., Wilmington 28401.

New Hanover. VIVIAN S. WRIGHT
    2809 Newkirk Ave., Wilmington 28401.

Pamlico. PATSY H. SADLER
    Hobucken 28537.

Randolph. MATILDA D. PHILLIPS (D)
    1976-. Bds: Piedmont Triad Council of Govts.
Party: State Del. 1970-76; State Alt. 1970-76;
Precinct V-Ch. 1970-72; Precinct Ch. 1972-76.
Prev: Cnty. Com. on the Status of Women 1975-76.
Org: Dem. Women. B: 6/15/41. Add: Box 966,
Liberty 27298 (919)629-2131.

Surry. ROXIE B. ROTH (D)
    1970-. Bds: V-Ch., Cnty. Mental Health; Land
Use, Housing Adv. Com.; NW Child Assoc. Party:
State Del. 1964; Cnty. Precinct Registrar 1964-
69. Org: Women's Club; Cnty. Dem. Club; Cnty.
Women's Club; PTA. B: 2/18/01. Add: 437 W.
Main, Elkin 28621.

Transylvania. JANICE L. BRYANT
    Box 386, Brevard 28712.

Wake. ELIZABETH BIAS COFIELD (D) **
    1972-. Bds: Social Services; School Com.;
Health Planning Council. Party: State Exec.
Com. 1973-75. Prev: School Bd. 1969-72. Educ:
Hampton Institute 1936 BS. Occ: Professor. B:
1/21/20. Add: 2322 Wade Ave., Raleigh 27607
(919)755-6160.

Wake. BETTY ANN KNUDSON (D)
    1976-. Bds: Cnty. Bd. of Health; Joint City-
Cnty. Tax Com.; Joint Land Use Code Com. Party:
Precinct V-Ch. 1975-76. Prev: Civic Ctr.
Authority 1974-77. Org: LWV; Goals for Raleigh/
Wake; Wake Environment; Conservation Council of
NC; Land Use Congress; WEAL; Dem. Women; WPC;
Assembly for Raleigh & Wake Educ.; Mental Health;
Women's Forum; Chamber of Commerce. Educ: U. of
Ga. 1948 BA. B: 10/10/26. Add: 617 Macon Pl.,
Raleigh 27609 (919)755-6160.

Washington. MAYME W. DAVENPORT
    Rt. 1, Creswell 27928.

Mayors

Aurora. GRACE H. BONNER (D) **
    1973-. Party: Precinct Ch. 1971-75. Org:
Bicentennial Cmsn.; Dem. Club; Mental Health. B:
12/27/30. Add: 101 Grace Dr., Aurora 27806
(919)322-4308.

Black Mountain. MARGARET G. SLAGLE
    225 W. State St., Black Mountain 28711.

Bolton. EDITH LUCILLE GREENE (D) **
    1973-. B: 10/29/19. Add: Box 129, Bolton
28423 (919)452-9945.

Carrboro. RUTH WEST
    P.O. Box 337, 509 W. Main St., Carrboro 27510

Elk Park. LUCILLE WINTERS
    P.O. Box 248, Elk Park 28622.

Fayetteville. BETH FINCH
    1975-. Bds: Governor's Crime Cmsn. Prev:
Fayetteville City Council 1971-75. Org: Cumberland Cnty. Govt. Assoc.; Dem. Women's Club; AAUW;
LWV; Women's Club. Educ: U. of NC 1942 BA. B:
11/13/21. Add: 2118 Winterlochen Rd., Fayetteville 28305.

Grimesland. MRS. RUBY HODGES
    P.O. Box 147, Pitt St., Grimesland 27837.

Harrisburg. MARTHA H. MARKS (R)
    1973-. Bds: Council of Govts. Org: NEA;
BPW. Educ: U. of NC 1943 BS; Georgia Coll.
1963 MEd. Occ: Teacher. B: 4/25/23. Add:
309 Hickory Ridge Rd., Harrisburg 28075
(704)455-2539.

Montreat. ELIZABETH H. MAXWELL
    P.O. Box 423, Montreat 28757.

Ocean Isle Beach. LA DANE WILLIAMSON
    P.O. Box 452, Ocean Isle Beach 28459.

Seven Springs. MRS. ORA G. SUTTON
    P.O. Box 198, 101 E. Spring St., Seven
Springs 28578.

Shady Forest. MRS. JOHN L. FOSTER
    P.O. Box 241, Rt. 1, Shallotte 28459.

Stem. MYRTIS H. GOOCH (D)
    1973-. Educ: U. of NC 1931 BA. B: 7/11/10.
Add: P.O. Box 97, Stem 27581 (919)528-2376.

Surf City. LUCILLE GORE
    P.O. Box 475, Surf City 28445.

Teachey. RUBY RAMSEY (D) **
    1965-. Prev: Town Cmsnr. 1962-65. Org:
Assoc. for Retarded Children; Exec. Bd. Mental
Health. Occ: Office Worker. B: 4/18/14. Add:
Box 115, Teachey 28464 (919)285-7564.

Yaupon Beach. LOUISE W. CORBETT (D)
    1975-. Prev: Town Cmsnr. 1975-79; Street
Cmsnr. 1975-76. Org: BPW. Occ: Activity Dir.,
Convalescent Ctr. B: 1/25/26. Add: 420 Trott
St., Star Rt. 2, Southport 28461 (919)278-5230.

Local Councils

Arapahoe. NEVA B. MC COTTER (D)
    1975-. Org: NEA; Retirement Club; Educ:
Atlantis Christian Coll. 1925 BA; E. Carolina U.
1960 MA. B: 9/2/08. Add: Arapahoe 28510
(919)249-3591.

Ashville. JO ANN M. SWILLING (D)
    1975-. Party: Precinct Committeewoman 1975-
76; Cnty. Precinct Del. 1976-77. Org: Council of
Fed. Women; Dem. Women; LWV. B: 5/15/40. Add:
91 Vermont Ave., Asheville 28806 (704)255-5476.

Atkinson. ANNIE MAE WALLACE
    P.O. Box 160, 1st Ave., Atkinson 28421.

Aulander. BETTY JO M. REDMOND (D)
    1975-. Org: PTA. Occ: Secretary. B: 12/2/46.
Add: 202 E. Canal St., Aulander 27805 (919)
345-3541.

Autryville. DONNA CASHWELL
    P.O. Box 10, Gray St., Autryville 28318.

Ayden. CAROL L. SPEIGHT
    P.O. Box 217, 221 W. Ave., Ayden 28513.

Bailey. HELEN BROOKS MURRAY (D) **
    1971-. Bds: Ch., Recreation Cmsn. B: 5/27/48.
Add: Box 14, Bailey 27807 (919)235-4265.

Belmont. JOHNNIE LOWRY FALLS (D)
    1975-. Org: Bank Admin. Institute; Council
on Status of Women. Occ: Banker. Add: 205 A
Glenway, Belmont 28012 (704)825-5331.

Black Mountain. RUTH DEAVER BRANDON (R)
    1975-. Bds: Nutrition Program Project Council;
Sourwood Tree Com.; Ch., Public Safety. Party:
V-Ch., Precinct 1974-75. Prev: Secretary, Black
Mtn. Planning & Zoning Bd. 1971-75. Org: Women's
Club; Cnty. Rep. Club; Citizens Com. for Better
Schools. Occ: Hardware Store Owner. B: 9/9/26.
Add: 722 Laurel Ave., Black Mtn. 28711 (704)
669-2255.

Blowing Rock. LINDA CRAIG (R)
    1975-. Bds: Recreation Cmsn.; Mayor's
Improvement Com. Party: State Del. 1974-77;
State Alt. 1972; Watauga Cnty. Rep. Exec. Com.
1974-76; V-Ch., Cnty. Rep. Exec. Com. 1977; NC
GOP State Exec. Com. 1977; Dist. Exec. Com. 1977;
V-Ch., Dist. Young Rep's. 1975-77. Org: Young
Rep's.; Rep. Women's Club. Educ: Appalachian
State U. 1973 BS; 1976 BA. Occ: Attendance
Counselor. B: 3/17/51. Add: P.O. Box 191,
Blowing Rock 28605 (704)295-3104.

Boiling Spring Lakes. JUDITH L. HOLOBAUGH COWAN (R)
    1975-. Bds: Firemans Relief Fund Bd.
Party: State Del. 1977; State Alt. 1972; Secretary, Cnty. Party 1976- . Prev: Cnty. Council
on the Status of Women 1975-76. Org: PTO. Occ:
Secretary/Bookkeeper. B: 8/18/43. Add: 55
Fairway Dr., Boiling Sprg Lks., Southport 28461
(919)253-4282.

Boiling Spring Lakes. LAVERNE D. MILLER
    City Hall, Southport 28461.

Bolton. REBECCA DANIELS
    P.O. Box 327, Bolton 28423.

Bostic. VICKI RICH
    P.O. Box 158, Bostic 28018.

Brevard. KATHERINE E. ANDERSON (R)
    1975-. Bds: Western Carolina Community
Action. Prev: Alcoholic Beverage Control Bd.
1974-76. Org: NC Assoc. Broadcasters; Chamber
of Commerce; W. Carolina Community Action.
Educ: U. of NC 1937 BS. Occ: Radio Station
Manager. B: 10/28/18. Add: 107 Park Ave.,
Brevard 28712 (704)883-9190.

Brunswick. LENA JARMAN
    P.O. Box 68, Brunswick 28424.

Bunn. BETTY BREWER
    P.O. Box 39, Bunn 27508.

Burlington. BARBARA T. MC CALL (D) **
    1973-. Bds: Transportation Planning
Advisory Council. Org: Common Cause; LWV.
Educ: Lake Forest Coll. 1967 BA; U. of Delaware
1969 MA. Occ: Elon Coll. Foundation Relations
Coordinator. B: 5/9/45. Add: 305 Laurel Hill
Dr., Burlington 27215 (919)227-3603.

Candor. STELLA REBECCA HARRIS WILLIAMS (D) **
    1971-. Party: Precinct Ch. 1964-65. Occ:
Secretary & Clerk. B: 5/18/40. Add: P.O. Box
575, Candor 27229 (919)974-4121.

Cape Carteret. PAXON MC LEAN HOLZ (D) **
    1974-. Educ: Queens Coll. 1969 BA. Occ:
Real Estate Broker. B: 9/12/47. Add: Rt. 1,
Box 480A1, Cape Carteret, Swansboro 28584
(919)326-8483.

Cape Carteret. CLAUDIA R. HULT (D)
    1975-. B: 7/18/40. Add: Rt. 1, Box 395,
Cape Carteret, Swansboro 28584.

Cape Carteret. BARBARA NEWMAN
    P.O. Box 1016, Swansboro 28584.

Carolina Beach. MRS. PAT EFIRD
    P.O. Drawer V, 118 Canal Dr., Carolina
Beach 28428.

Carrboro. NANCY WHITE
    P.O. Box 337, 509 Main St., Carrboro 27510.

Carthage. BILLIE MACKEY
    P.O. Box 842, Barrett St., Carthage 28327.

Centerville. MARIE G. DENTON
    Rte. 6, Louisburg 27549.

Cerro Gordo. SARAH N. BLACKWELL (D)
    1973-. Mayor Pro Tem. Bds: HUD Com.;
Bicentennial Com. Occ: Beautician. B: 1/8/40.
Add: Rt. 1, Box 354, Cerro Gordo 28430 (919)
654-5387.

Chapel Hill. SHIRLEY E. MARSHALL (D)
    1972-. Bds: Del., Council of Govts.; Cnty.
Council on Aging. Party: State Del. 1972;
Cnty. Dem. Judge 1969-72; Precinct Committee-
woman 1969- ; Pres., Cnty. Dem. Women 1977- .
Prev: Chapel Hill Appearance Cmsn. 1970-72.
Org: NC League of Municipalities; Nat. League
of Cities; Chamber of Commerce; Common Cause;
BPW; ACLU; LWV; NC Women's Forum; WPC. Educ:
Beaver Coll. 1947 BA. B: 4/27/25. Add: 707 E.
Franklin St., Chapel Hill 275514 (919)929-1111.

Charlotte. BETTY CHAFIN (D)
      1976-. Party: Precinct Chairwoman 1972; Nat.
Del. 1972. Prev: Munic. Information Review Bd.;
Cnty. Cmsn. on Status of Women. Org: LWV;
Voluntary Action Center; WPC; Women's Forum; Dem.
Women's Club; Young Dems.; ASPA; Nat. Assoc. of
Women Deans, Administrators & Counselors. Educ:
Greensboro Coll. 1964 BA; U. of NC 1972 MPA.
Occ: Associate Dean of Students, U. of NC. Add:
1912 Lombardy Circle, Charlotte 28203 (919)
377-4957.

Charlotte. PAT LOCKE (R)
      1973-. Bds: Ch., Public Works Com.; Health
Systems Agency; Human Resources Com. Party:
State Del. 1966-72; Rep. Women's Club Treasurer
1968-71; Rep. State Central Com. 1966-70; Pres.,
Rep. Women's Club 1968-70; Exec. Secretary, Rep.
Party 1966-70. Prev: Mayors Citizens Adv. Com.
1971-73. Org: LWV; WPC; Common Cause. Occ:
Insurance Agent. B: 6/28/30. Add: P.O. Box 4363,
Charlotte 28204 (704)374-2241.

China Grove. JAMIMA POWELL DE MARCUS (D)
      1975-. Mayor Pro Tem. Bds: Ch., Safety Com.;
Sanitation, Water, Sewage; Ch., Community Bldgs.
Party: State Del. 1960- ; Nat. Del. 1972; Cnty.
Precinct Ch. 1958-62; Dem. Women's Dist. 1970-72;
V-Pres. Dem. Women 1968-72; V-Ch., Cnty. Dem.
Party; Ch., Cnty. Dem Party 1977. Prev: Cnty.
Cmsn. on Historical Properties 1975- ; State
Cmsn. of State Goals & Policy Bd. 1977- . Org:
Chamber of Commerce; Women's Club; Cnty. Dem.
Party. Occ: Interior Designer. B: 12/12/24.
Add: 510 S. Main St., China Grove 28023.

Colerain. EVA J. WHITE (D)
      1974-. Party: Secretary, Cnty. Dem's. 1974- .
Prev: Cnty. Welfare Bd. 1950. Org: Women's Club.
Educ: Western Carolina U. BA. B: 3/12/06. Add:
P.O. Box 8, Colerain 27924 (919)356-2124.

Como. JOYCE B. SUMNER (D)
      1967-. Party: Precinct Treasurer-Secretary
1968-75. Org: Historic League. Educ: Radford
Coll. 1951 BS. B: 1/28/29. Add: P.O. Box 125,
Como 27818.

Conetoe. NAOMI BATCHELOR
      P.O. Box 63, Conetoe 27819.

Crossnore. EMMA S. FINK (D) **
      1969-. Party: County Com. 1968-72; Precinct
V-Ch. 1964-68. Org: AAUW; Med. Assoc. Educ:
Duke U. 1932 BA; Vanderbilt Medical School 1936
MD. Occ: M.D. B: 7/12/09. Add: Box 160,
Crossnore 28616 (704)733-9296.

Crossnore. ELIZABETH J. NELSON
      P.O. Box 129, Crossnore Dr., Crossnore 28616.

Danbury. CLARA B. NELSON
      Town Hall, Danbury 27016.

Davidson. NANCY H. MAC CORMAC (D)
      1973-. Bds: Town Park & Recreation Com.; Town
Planning Cmsn.; Bd. of Dir's., Community Services
Center. Party: State Alt.; Nat. Alt. Prev: Ch.,
Park & Recreation Com. 1970-73; Health Systems
Adv. Council 1976- ; Housing Adv. Council 1975-

Org: NC League of Municipalities; NC Parks &
Recreation Society; LWV; WPC. Educ: Conn.
Coll. 1957 BA. B: 10/28/35. Add: Box 561,
Davidson 28036 (704)892-7591.

Dillsboro. MARGARET C. MASON
      P.O. Box 157, Dillsboro 28725.

Durham. ISABELLE BUDD (D)
      1975-. Bds: Reg. Council of Govts.; Reg.
Com. on Criminal Justice; Reg. Com. on Water
Quality. Org: AAUW; Chamber of Commerce;
Historic Preservation Soc. Educ: U. of Mo.
1944 BS. B: 2/8/23. Add: 2753 McDowell St.,
Durham 27705 (919)683-4222.

Durham. MARGARET KELLER
      P.O. Box 2251, 120 Morris St., Durham
27702.

Earl. THELMA EARL
      Town Hall, Earl 28038.

East Arcadia. DELIAH BLANKS
      P.O. Box 273, Rte. 1, Riegelwood 28456.

East Bend. RINDA JESTER
                COLLIE TAYLOR
      P.O. Box 189, Main St., E. Bend 27018.

Elon College. SHERLEY MAE WHITE (D)
      1976-. Bds: Planning Bd. Party: State Alt.
1976; Precinct V-Ch. 1975-77. Org: Common
Cause. Educ: Mills Coll. 1951 BA. Occ: Art
Teacher. B: 5/18/23. Add: 216 Foster Dr.,
P.O. Box 872, Elon Coll. 27244 (919)584-0282.

Fairmont. MARGARET L. PERRY
      P.O.Box 248, Fairmont 28340.

Farmville. SARA HUMPHREY ALBRITTON (D)
      1973-. Bds: Ch., Recreation; Streets &
Sanitation; Fire & Safety. Party: State Del.
1966; Precinct Ch. 1977. Prev: School Bd. 1948-
56; Zoning Bd. 1956-60. Org: Cnty. Mental
Health; Cnty. Dem. Women. B: 2/18/12. Add:
204 S. George St., Farmville 27828 (919)
753-3059.

Fayetteville. MARIE W. BEARD
      234 Green St., Fayetteville 28301.

Forest City. MARION MICHALOVE
      12 Powell St., Forest City 28043.

Garland. MARY S. CARTER
      P.O. Box 207, Garland 28441.

Garner. KAY BEST DAUGHTRY (D)
      1957-. Party: State Del. 1973-76; Precinct
Ch. 1966-73; Pres., Cnty. Dem. Women 1971-73;
Secretary, State Exec. Com. 1973-74. Prev:
Governor's Study Cmsn. on Educ. 1971-72. Org:
Triangle J Council of Govts.; Women's Club; WPC;
Council on Aging; Dem. Women of N.C. Occ:
Hostess. B: 11/29/23. Add: 1107 Park Ave.,
Garner 27529 (919)733-5811.

Gatesville. MILDRED T. CARTER (D) **
     1969-. Org: NC Social Services Assoc.; Policy
Bd. of Law & Order Assoc.; Mental Health Interagency. B: 1/15/13. Add: High St., Gatesville
27938 (919)357-5411.

Gibson. VIRGINIA G. HARGRAVE
     P.O. Box 456, Main St., Gibson 28343.

Godwin. GEORGIA M. HONEYCUTT
     Town Hall, Godwin 28344.

Greensboro. LOIS M. MC MANUS (D)
     1975-. Bds: Cnty. Health Dept.; Planning &
Community Devt.; Senior Citizen Services. Org:
Nat. Meals Programs; Council on Aging; Retired
Senior Volunteer Program. B: 8/13/26. Add:
1506 Edgedale Rd., Greensboro 27408 (919)
373-2060.

Greenville. MILDRED T. MC GRATH (D)
     1971-. Mayor Pro Tem. Bds: Criminal Justice
Planning Bd.; Utilities Cmsn.; Planning & Zoning.
Org: WPC. Educ: E. Carolina U. 1960 BS; U. of
N. Colo. 1963 MA. Occ: Ch., Technical Institute.
B: 1/25/24. Add: 103 Deerwood Dr., Greenville
27834 (919)756-3130.

Grover. MARTHA BYERS
     Town Hall, Grover 28073.

Hamilton. ELIZABETH MATTHEWS CRAFT (D)
     1975-. Bds: Mid E. Regional Cmsn. Party:
State Del. 1976; Secretary, Cnty. Young Dem's.
1975-76; Precinct Ch. 1977. Org: Historic Cmsn.;
Cnty. Young Dem's. Educ: E. Carolina U. 1975 BA.
B: 4/5/52. Add: P.O. Box 153, Hamilton 27840
(919)798-2001.

Hamlet. MRS. RICHARD E. CARNES
     P.O. Box 1299, 201 Main St., Hamlet 28345.

Harrellsville. MAURA A. CALE (D)
     1976-. Org: PTA. Occ: Secretary-Treasurer.
B: 7/21/41. Add: P.O. Box 4, Harrellsville
27942.

Harrellsville. LINDA VAN LOTON
     P.O. Box 37, Harrellsville 27942.

Havelock. PATRICIA A. BAILEY (R)
     1973-. Bds: Library Bd.; Progression Cmsn.
Party: State Del. 1976. Org: Chamber of Commerce;
BPW; Rep. Club. Occ: Printer. B: 7/11/23. Add:
112 Miller Blvd., Havelock 28532 (919)447-1488/
3700.

Henderson. BARBARA PETROU
     P.O. Box 1434, 110 Young St., Henderson 27536.

Hertford. MATTIE R. BROUGHTON
     P.O. Box 32, 114 W. Grubb St., Hertford 27944.

Highlands. THELMA HOWELL
     P.O. Box 460, 4th St., Highlands 28741.

High Shoals. PHYLLIS CLINE
     P.O. Box 6, 101 N. Lincoln St., High Schoals
28077.

High Shoals. SHIRLEY RICE (D) **
     Org: Educ. Assoc. Educ: Guilford Coll. 1959
BA. Occ: Teacher. B: 9/18/36. Add: Box 261,
High Shoals 28077 (919)735-1621.

Hildebran. MILDRED C. MARTIN (D) **
     1971-. Bds: Finance. Org: PTA. Occ:
School Cafeteria Manager. B: 4/13/17. Add:
P.O. Box 66, 4th Ave., SE, Hildebran 28637
(919)397-3562.

Hildebran. BETTY SAIN
     P.O. Box 87, S. Center St., Hildebran 28637.

Hoffman. MAMIE G. CADDELL
     P.O. Box 165, Caddell St., Hoffman 28347.

Hoffman. JANICE GODWIN
     P.O. Box 165, Caddell St., Hoffman 28347.

Holden Beach. MRS. WYARIAN ATKINSON
     110 Rothschild St., Holden Beach 28462.

Holly Ridge. MARY E. PINER (D)
     1975-. Bds: Ch., Community Dev.; Recreation;
Ch., Beautification. Org: ANA; Assoc. of Oper-
ating Room Nurses; Lung Assoc. Educ: Roanoke
Rapids School of Nursing 1948 RN. B: 11/19/27.
Add: P.O. Box 203, Holly Ridge 28445.

Hookerton. LUVENIA SPEIGHT
     P.O. Box 296, Main St., Hookerton 28538.

Hope Mills. JUNE H. RITCHEY (D)
     1975-. Bds: Transportation Adv. Com. Educ:
Portland State U. 1965 BS. Occ: Ophthalmic Asst.
B: 7/25/37. Add: 5423 Thompson Cir., Hope Mills
28348 (919)425-7103.

Huntersville. MARION SPARROW
     P.O. Box 398, Old Statesville Ave., Hunters-
ville 28078.

Kenansville. BETTY C. LONG
     P.O. Box 420, Hill St., Kenansville 28349.

Kill Devil Hills. DIANE B. ST. CLAIR
     P.O. Box 719, Kill Devil Hills 27948.

Lake Waccamaw. NANCY M. SIGMON (D) **
     1973-. Org: Court Reporter's Assoc.; Women's
Club. Occ: Court Reporter. B: 2/9/35. Add:
P.O. Box 125, Lake Waccamaw 28450.

Lansing. IRENE CHASON
     Town Hall, Lansing 28643.

Lawndale. IRENE S. MAUNEY (D)
     1975-. Org: Fed. Women's Club; Cnty. Dem.
Women. Occ: Saleswoman. B: 3/28/11. Add:
208 Bridges St., Lawndale 28090 (704)538-7446.

Lenoir. ANNE BERNHARDT
     P.O. Box 958, 110 Main St., SW, Lenoir
28645.

Lillington. LYNN S. MANN
     P.O. Box 296, Main St., Lillington 27546.

Long Beach. PAULINE MORGAN
P.O. Box 217, Ocean Hwy., Long Beach 28461.

Louisburg. LOIS BROWN WHELESS (D) **
1969-. Bds: Council of Governments. Party:
Secretary, County Party 1970-75. Prev: Zoning
Bd. 1960-61. Org: LWV; NC Consumers Council;
Exec. Bd., Louisburg Coll. Trustee. Educ: U. of
NC 1944 BS. B: 2/28/22. Add: 106 John St.,
Louisburg 27549 (919)496-3566.

Love Valley. VELMA S. PONDER
DOROTHY S. WILLIAMS
P.O. Box 8, Love Valley 28677.

Lucama. ANN RENFROW
TERESA W. WOODWARD
P.O. Box 127, Main St., Lucama 27851.

Lumberton. JOAN BROWN BACOT (D)
1976-. Bds: Airport Cmsn. Org: Cnty. League
of Municipalities. Occ: Accountant. B: 10/13/45.
Add: 1001 Hardin Rd., Lumberton 28358 (919)
739-6031.

Madison. JEANNETTE GREEN RODENBOUGH (D)
1973-. Bds: Water Resources Com. Org: Dem.
Women. Educ: Randolph-Macon Women's Coll. 1955
BA; U. of NC 1973 MA. B: 9/18/33. Add: P.O. Box
46, Madison 27025.

Maiden. DOT LINEBERGER
P.O. Box 125, 113 W. Main St., Maiden 28650.

Matthews. EULA F. OUTEN
P.O. Box 398, 224 N. Trade St., Matthews
28105.

Maxton. THELMA GWINN
120 N. Florence St., Maxton 28364.

Maysville. CLAUDIA W. MATTOCKS (D) **
1974-. Bds: Industrial Dev. Com. Occ:
Retired. B: 10/23/12. Add: Box 6, Maysville
28555 (919)743-6551.

McAdenville. GAIL GUINN
Main Mill Office, McAdenville 28101.

Middleburg. DONNA NEATHREY
Town Hall, P.O. Box 59, Middleburg 27556.

Middlesex. ANN DANIEL LEWIS (D)
1973-. Bds: Public Library; School Beautification Com. Party: State Alt. 1976; Town V-Ch.
1975-77; Cnty. Leg. Dist. Exec. Com. 1977- . Org:
Industrial & Devt. Group. Occ: Insurance Agent
& Bookkeeper. B: 5/6/33. Add: P.O. Box 171,
Nash St., Middlesex 27557 (919)235-4077.

Mint Hill. AUDREY W. MAYHEW (D)
1973-. Bds: Council of Govts.; Southern
Piedmont Health Systems Agency Adv. Bd. Org:
BPW. Occ: Office Manager. B: 1/31/24. Add:
3339 Mintwood, Mint Hill, Charlotte 28212
(704)545-6881.

Mocksville. PATRICIA HAYES LATTA (D)
1975-. Bds: Planning Bd.; Fire Dept.; Bldg.
& Inspection. Party: Precinct Del. to Cnty.
Conf. 1976- ; Precinct Voter Registration
Worker 1977-78. Prev: Planning Bd. 1975. Org:
Women's Club; Cnty. Dem. Women; PTSA. Educ:
Catauba Coll. 1956 BA. B: 10/22/35. Add: P.O.
Box 251, Mocksville 27028 (704)634-2259.

Monroe. BILLIE GORDON KERR (D)
1975-. Bds: Housing Adv.-Centralina Council
of Govts. Party: State Del. 1976; State Alt.
1974; Secretary, Cnty. Party 1973-74. Org:
Nat. Assoc. of Realtors; BPW; Dem. Women. Occ:
Real Estate. B: 5/3/24. Add: 1111 Sunset Dr.,
Monroe 28110 (704)283-8165.

Morrisville. EMMA G. WALTON (D)
1975-. Bds: Del., Triangle J Council of
Govts.; Ch., Personnel Com. Occ: Bookkeeper.
B: 8/22/27. Add: P.O. Box 75, Morrisville
27560 (919)467-1876.

Morven. KAY PARKER
VIRGINIA WOODBURN
P.O. Box 219, Morven 28119.

Mount Holly. JOYCE CLARK
P.O. Box 406, 133 S. Main St., Mount Holly
28120.

Mount Holly. FAYE S. LITTLE (D) **
1973-. Bds: Council of Govt.; Liaison Com.;
Emergency Medical Service Council. Party:
County Party Exec. Com. 1962-70; Precinct Ch.
1966-70; V-Ch. 1962-66; Precinct Com. 1958-62.
Org: Nat. Assoc. of Regional Councils; Dem.
Women; PTA. B: 5/30/29. Add: 204 N. Hawthorne
St., Mt. Holly 28120 (704)827-3931.

Mount Pleasant. MAURA EVERHARDT
P.O. Box 98, Mount Pleasant 28124.

Mount Pleasant. MARGARET R. SCOTT (D)
1975-. Bds: Ch., Streets Cmsn.; Police Cmsn.
Org: PTA. Occ: Office Manager. B: 2/7/39.
Add: Pine St., P.O. Box 502, Mt. Pleasant 28124.

Murfreesboro. LESSIE V. DEANES
P.O. Box 6, 105 E. Broad St., Murfreesboro
27855.

Nashville. BECKY JONES BASS (D)
1975-. Bds: Ch., Library Cmsn.; Ch., Bldgs.
& Grounds Cmsn. Occ: Merchant. B: 1/19/39.
Add: 415 E. Green, Nashville 27856 (919)
459-2193.

New Bern. ELLA J. BENGEL
P.O. Box 1129, 300 Pollock St., New Bern
28560.

Newport. DORIS EDWARDS
P.O. Box 5, Howard Blvd., Newport 28570.

North Wilkesboro. PAT HADLEY DAVIS (D)
1975-. Bds: Bd. of Mental Health Dept. Party:
V-Ch., Cnty. Dem's., Exec. Com. 1973-77; V. Ch.,
Precinct 1971-73; State Del. 1975. Org: Dem. Club;
Dem. Women's Club. Educ: Wilkes Community Coll.
1969 AASS; Appalachian State U. 1976 BA. Occ:
Accountant. B: 8/16/26. Add: 1005 K St., N.
Wilkesboro 28659 (919)667-2151.

Ocean Isle Beach. RAE SLOANE
P.O. Box 452, Ocean Isle Beach 28459.

Old Fort. GLADYS B. GIBBS (D)
1973-. Bds: Isothermal Devt. Cmsn.; Emergency
Medical Service. Org: Southern Retail Florist;
Lighting Com. Occ: Florist. B: 10/27/17. Add:
Maple Ave., Old Fort 28762.

Oriental. INEZ S. HARGROVE
Town Hall, Oriental 28571.

Oriental. SUE S. RAGAN (D)
1975-. Prev: Bd. of Educ. B: 5/23/18. Add:
Ragan Rd., Oriental 28571 (919)249-9191.

Pine Knoll Shores. MARY CATHERINE BRADSHAW SMITH(D)
1975-. Bds: Finance Com. Party: Precinct Ch.
1935-45. Prev: City Clerk 1954-71. Org: Young
Dem's.; PTA. B:4/12/20. Add: 183 Oakleaf Dr.,
Rt. 1, Pine Knoll Shrs., Morehead City 28557
(919)726-8021.

Pollocksville. PENELOPE M. BENDER (D) **
1974-. Educ: U. of NC 1943 BS. B: 11/12/22.
Add: Green Hill St., Pollocksville 28573 (919)
224-6221.

Princeville. MARY E. BLACK
MARGARET HEATH
MAMIE S. PITTMAN
P.O. Box 485, Tarboro 27886.

Raleigh. MIRIAM BLOCK (D) **
Party: Precinct Ch. Org: Civic Assoc.; Dem.
Women; PTA. Educ: Eastern Ill. State U. Add:
Municipal Bldg., Raleigh 27600.

Randleman. ANN L. EARNHARDT (D)
1975-. Bds: Ch., Library Bd.; Recreation Bd.
Occ: Secretary. B: 3/1/25. Add: 516 Fox St.,
Randleman 27317 (919)498-2604.

Red Oak. ELIZABETH W. GRIFFIN (D)
1968-. Party: Precinct Secretary 1975-77.
B: 10/26/17. Add: Box 45, Red Oak 27868.

Red Oak. AGNES MOORE (D)
1970-. Bds: Treasurer. Party: Precinct Ch.
1975-77. Org: PTA; Women's Club. Educ: U. of NC
1947 BS. B: 10/29/26. Add: Box 8, Red Oak 27868

Roanoke Rapids. MARJORIE MIDGETTE
P.O. Box 38, Roanoke Ave., Roanoke Rapids
27870.

Rocky Mount. LYNDA H. HOMES (D)
1973-. Org: P.R. Society. Occ: Public Information Officer. B: 9/22/25. Add: 308 Villa St.,
Rocky Mount 27801 (919)977-2111.

Rolesville. LILLIAN W. EDDINS
P.O. Box 67, N. Main St., Rolesville 27571.

St.Pauls. SARAH GRANTHAM HAY (D) **
1973-. Bds: Recreation Com.; Legal Com.;
Publicity Com. Party: V-Ch., Precinct 1960-
70. Org: NEA; NC Educ. Assoc.; PTA. Educ:
Flora MacDonald Coll. 1939 BA. Occ: Teacher.
B: 9/4/18. Add: 500 W. Armfield St., St. Pauls
28384 (919)485-5126.

Sanford. JACKIE PEARCE
P.O. Box 338, 143 Charlotte, Sanford 27330.

Seagrove. LOUISE BELL
MARTHA COMER
Town Hall, Seagrove 27341.

Selma. MABEL S. LUCAS
P.O. Box 357, 100 N. Raeford St., Selma
27576.

Seven Springs. HILDA GIBBS
P.O. Box 198, 101 E. Spring St., Seven
Springs 28578.

Shelby. JUDY HOFFMAN BARRETT (D)
1976-. Add: 907 N. Lafayette St., #6,
Shelby 28150.

Southern Pine. SARA W. HODGKINS
P.O. Box 870, 145 SE Broad St., Southern
Pine 28387.

Southport. DOROTHY R. GILBERT
MARY MC HOSE
217 Dry St., Southport 28461.

Speed. FRANCES VIVIAN LUCAS (D) **
1972-. Bds: Elections. Org: Retired
Teachers. Educ: East Carolina U. 1940 BA.
Occ: Retired. B: 1/25/09. Add: Box 244,
Speed 27881 (919)823-8684.

Stallings. MARGARET E. MULLINA
Matthews 28105.

Stanley. GAIL R. BROTHERTON
P.O. Box 278, 230 S. Main St., Stanley 28164.

Star. NATALIE E. ALLEN (D)
Bds: Del., Council of Govts.; Library Com.
Org: Nat. Fed. of Postal Clerks; Dem. Women.
Occ: Postal Clerk. B: 9/11/23. Add: 705 S.
Main, Star 27356 (919)428-4623.

Statesville. MRS. J. C. FINK
P.O. Box 1111, S. Center St., Statesville
28677.

Stem. KATHERINE MANGUM
DOROTHY WATKINS
P.O. Box 95, Stem 27581.

Sunset Beach. TONYA GORDON EDWARDS (I) **
1973-. Bds: Finance Officer. Educ: East
Caolina U. 1969 BS. B: 10/19/47. Add: 11th
St. E., Sunset Beach 28459 (919)579-6297.

Topsail Beach. LETTIE LEE
    P.O. Box 89, 820 S. Anderson, Topsail Beach
28445.

Vanceboro. KATHLEEN CARAWON
    P.O. Box 306, Main St., Vanceboro 28586.

Vass. JO ANN HIPP
    P.O. Box H, Alma St., Vass 28394.

Waco. JUDY H. BARRETT
    P.O. Box 69, Waco

Wade. THELMA MC LAURIN
    P.O. Box 127, Wade 28395.

Wagram. BETTY J. GHOLSTON (D)
    1974-. Mayor Pro Tem. Bds: Ch., Cmsn. of
Library Services. Party: Cnty. Secretary/Treas-
urer 1975-77. Org: N.C. Assoc. of Educators;
NEA; Assoc. of Coll. Women; NAACP; Dem. Party;
Parent Involvement Org. Educ: N. Central U. 1963
BS. Occ: Teacher. B: 2/1/42. Add: Rt. 1, Box
283, Wagram 28396 (919)369-2964.

Wake Forest. DESSIE W. HARPER (R) **
    1961-. Bds: Ch., Finance. B: 4/4/07. Add:
312 N. Wingate St., Wake Forest 27587 (919)
556-3572.

Wake Forest. AILEY M. YOUNG (D) **
    1971-. Bds: Ch., Fire, Recreation & Cemetery;
Street & Sanitation; Finance. Party: Local Exec.
Com. 1974- ; Precinct V-Ch. 1970-72; Precinct
Secretary-Treasurer 1966-70. Org: Educ. Assoc.
Educ: Shaw U. 1943 BA. B: 4/11/03. Add: 337 E.
Spring Ave., P.O. Box 271, Wake Forest 27587
(919)556-2024.

Walnut Cove. MARY POWELL O'NEAL (D)
    1974-. Bds: Financial. Party: Cnty. Election.
B: 2/6/18. Add: Walnut Cove 27052.

Warrenton. ANNA GARDNER BUTLER (D)
    1972-. Bds: Ch., Planning; Ch., Zoning; Ch.,
Safety. Party: State Alt. 1968; Precinct
Committeewoman 1974-75; Alt., Cnty. Del. 1972-73.
Org: Daughters of Confederacy; Women's Club; Dem.
Women; Recreation Adv. Com.; Historical Assoc.
Occ: Bookkeeper/Secretary. B: 6/21/22. Add: 204
Cousin Lucy's Ln., Warrenton 27589 (919)257-3315.

Washington. CARLOTTA MORDECAI
    P.O. Box 850, Market St., Washington 27889.

Washington Park. ELIZABETH COWELL
    P.O. Box 298, Washington Park 27889.

Webster. LOUISE DAVIS
    Town Hall, Webster 28788.

Wendell. JUNE P. MANTYCH (D)
    1973-. Bds: Recreation Cmsn.; Wake Cnty.
Library Bd. Prev: Cnty. Opportunities Exec. Bd.
1974-75; Community Devt. Com. 1974-75. Org:
State Employees Assoc.; Women's Club; Cnty. Young
Dem's.; Debating Club; OES. Occ: Personnel Tech-
nician. B: 12/26/22. Add: 218 Cypress St.,
Wendell 27591 (919)365-4444.

Wendell. AILEEN PARISH
    P.O. Box 127, 4th & Pine Sts., Wendell
27591.

White Lake. ANNIE L. ATKINSON SMITH (D) **
    1973-. Bds: Clean Up Com. Party: County
Com. 1970-71. Prev: Registrar 1971-74; Judge
of Election 1964-71. Org: Amer. Business
Women's Assoc.; DAR. Occ: Legal Secretary.
B: 8/26/31. Add: P.O. Box 952, Elizabethtown
28337.

Whiteville. FLORA B. SINGLETARY
    P.O. Box 592, S. Madison St., Whiteville
28472.

Wilmington. MARGARET F. FONVIELLE (D) **
    1973-. Bds: Bicentennial; Regional Manpower.
Org: Bar Assoc.; Dem. Club; Women in Action for
Prevention of Violence. Educ: Greensboro Coll.
1938 BA; U. of NC 1943 LLB, JD. Occ: Attorney.
B: 1/19/18. Add: 529 Wayne Dr., Wilmington
28401.

Wilson. MARTHA K. WALSTON
    P.O. Box 10, Goldsboro St., Wilson 27893.

Winston-Salem. ERNESTINE WILSON
    P.O. Box 2511, 101 N. Main St., Winston-
Salem 27102.

Woodfin. DORIS P. GIERENTANNER (D) **
    1971-. Org: Dem. Women. Occ: Secretary. B:
8/7/27. Add: P.O. Box 8462, Ashville 28804
(704)253-4887.

Woodland. KATHRYN LEE
    P.O. Box 297, Spruce St., Woodland 27897.

Wrightsville Beach. FRANCES LOMAX RUSS (D)
    1974-. Bds: Council on Aging; Recreation
Adv. Com. Prev: Planning Bd. 1970-74. Org:
N.C. Bd. of Realtors; PTA. Educ: U. of N.C.
1951 BA. Occ: Realtor. B: 2/2/30. Add:
6 Pelican Dr., Wrightsville Bch. 28480 (919)
256-2245.

Zebulon. JO WARD
    111 E. Vance St., Zebulon 27597.

Judges

NAOMI MORRIS
    Court of Appeals Judge. Add: Box 888,
Raleigh 27603.

SUSIE MARSHALL SHARP (D)
    Chief Justice, Supreme Court. 1974-. Prev:
Special Judge, Superior Ct.; Assoc. Justice,
Supreme Ct. Org: ABA. Educ: U. of NC 1929 LLB.
B: 7/7/07. Add: Wade Ave., Raleigh 27605 (919)
733-3717.

State Boards and Commissions

    The membership of state boards and commissions
is available from:
        Governor's Appointments Office
        Administration Building
        Raleigh, North Carolina 27611

North Dakota

State Senate

STELLA H. FRITZELL (R)
1972-. Bds: Natural Resources; V-Ch., Business, Industry & Labor; Commercial Air Transportation Adv. Party: State Del. 1972, '74, '76. Prev: Park Cmsn. 1960-74; Planning & Zoning Cmsn. 1971-76. Org: BPW; Rep. Women. Educ: U. of Minn. 1931 BS. B: 10/3/09. Add: 1120 Cottonwood, Grand Forks 58201.

SHIRLEY W. LEE (R) **
1972-. Dist: 8. Bds: V-Ch., Resources Com.; Caucus Secretary; Finance & Taxation Com. Party: V-Ch., ND Org.; Ch., ND Org. 1964-66; County Organizer 1962-64; Secretary County Org. 1960-62. Org: Bd., Community Chest; Library Trustee; Bd., Rep. Women. B: 1/8/24. Add: Box J, Turtle Lake 58575.

BONNIE L. MILLER (D)
1976-. Bds: Ch., Interim Com. on Retirement; Interim Educ. Com. Party: State Del. 1976; Nat. Del. 1976; Dist Ch. 1976; State Policy Com. 1976. Org: NEA; LWV; Dem. Women. Educ: Valley City State Coll. 1959 BS. Occ: Teacher. B: 12/6/38. Add: 1028 Lake Ave., #3, Bismarck 58501.

State House

SISTER MARY BEAUCLAIR (D)
423 8th Ave. N., Carrington 58421.

PAULINE M. BENEDICT (D)
1976-. Bds: Agriculture Judiciary. Party: State Del. 1976, '74, '72. Prev: Postmaster 1935-44. Org: Dem. Ladies. B: 10/9/11. Add: Berthold 58718 (701)453-7825.

ROSIE BLACK (R)
1976-. Dist: 17. Bds: House Educ. Com.; House Political Subdiv. Com.; Interim Budget A Com. Party: State Del. 1976; Dist V-Ch. 1976-77. Org: Historical Society; Fed Rep. Women. B: 1/23/52. Add: 6104 - B Sunflake Cir., Emerado 58228.

ALOHA TAYOR EAGLES (R)
1966-. Bds: State Law Enforcement Council; Cmsn. on Status of Women; Com. on Criminology & Penology. Party: State Del. 1966-76; Dist. Exec. Com. 1970-72. Prev: Cmsn. on Youth 1967; Mayor's Youth Coord. Com.; Community Action Agency 1967; IWY, Sub. Com. on Reproductive Freedom 1976-77. Org: NOWL; LWV; Mental Health Assoc.; Rep. Women; Women's Coalition; NARAL. B: 11/8/16. Add: 1745 S. 8th St., Fargo 58102 (701)232-2193.

BRYNHILD HAUGLAND (R)
Box 1684, Minot 58701.

JEAN E. HERMAN (R)
3638 Fairway Rd., Fargo 58102.

TISH KELLY (D) **
1974-. Dist: 21. Bds: Industry, Business & Labor; Political Subdiv.; Public Service Cmsn. Study Com. Party: Del., Dist. & State Conv. 1962-72. Educ: U. of Md. 1954 BA. B: 8/2/32. Add: 404 South University, Fargo 58102.

MARJORIE L. KERMOTT (R) **
1972-. Dist: 5. Bds: Nat. Resources; State & Fed. Government Com.; Municipal Parking Authority; Library Bd. of Dir. Party: V-Ch., ND Rep. Party 1968-70. Org: OWL; Women's Fed. Rep. Club; Chamber of Commerce; Rep. Women. Educ: Presbyterian Hospital 1934 RN. B: 4/4/13. Add: 200 7th Ave., SE, Minot 58701.

FERN E. LEE (R)
1966-. Bds: State & Fed. Govt.; V-Ch., Political Sub-Div.; Transportation. Party: State Del. 1968-76; Precinct Committeewoman 1952-64. Org: Nat. Fed. Rep. Women; Chamber of Commerce; Rep. Women; Women's Club. Occ: Editorial Asst. B: 6/6/09. Add: 404 N. Main, Towner 58788.

JOANN WILKINSON MC CAFFREY (D)
1976-. Dist: 42. Bds: House Educ. Com.; Political Subdivisions Com. Party: State Del. 1976, '74, '72, '70; Precinct Committeewoman 1974- ; Party Exec. Bd. 1975- ; State Policy Com. 1975. Prev: ND Teachers Professional Practices Cmsn. 1974- . Org: NEA; ACLU; Dem. Women. Educ: Kan State U. 1957 BA; U. of ND 1974 MEd. Occ: Teacher. B: 2/23/29. Add: 403 N. 25th St., Grand Fork 58201.

RUTH MEIERS (D)
1974-. Party: State Del. 1974-76; Dist. Co-Ch., 1973-74. Prev: Bd., Dist. Health Unit 1968-77. Org: NOWL; Farmers Union; LWV; ND Conf. of Social Welfare; ND Public Health Conf. Educ: U. of ND 1946 BA. B: 11/6/25. Add: Box 56, Ross 58776 (701)755-3344.

CORLISS MUSHIK (D) **
1970-. Dist: 34. Bds: Budget Com.; Cmsn. on Status of Women; Bicentennial Cmsn.; Law Enforcement Com. Party: State Ch., Platform Com. 1974; Local Precinct Com. 1968-74; State Credentials Com. 1972; County V-Ch. 1968-70. Org: LWV; WPC; ND Women's Coalition; Dem. Club. B: 5/11/22. Add: 608 3rd St. NW, Mandan 58554 (701)663-3115.

ALICE OLSON (R)
1973-. Bds: Indian Cmsn. Party: State Del. 1971-77. State Alt. 1967-69; Pres., Rep. Women. Org: NOWL; Dist. 11 Rep. Women. B: 5/24/28.

Add: Cavalier 58220.

ANNA BERTHA JOSEPHINE POWERS (D) **
    1961; 1966-. Bds: Governor's Com. on Status
of Women; Citizen's Advisory Com. on Highway
Beautification; State Health Council; Provincial
Women's Bd. Party: State Central Com. 1961- ;
Precinct Com. 1950- ; Del., Nat. Conv. 1964.
Org: Dem. Women's League. B: 7/10/12. Add:
Leonard 58052.

BURNESS REED (R)
    211 Fenton Ave., Grand Forks 58201.

JANET MARIE NEFF WENTZ (R)
    1974-. Dist: 41. Bds: House Judiciary Com.;
House Political Subdivisions Com.; Interim Com.
Budget "A". Party: State Del. 1976. Org: LWV;
Quota Club; Rep. Party; Rep. Women. Occ:
Securities Salesperson. B: 7/21/37. Add: 505
8th Ave. SE, Minot 58701 (701)472-2109.

Mayors

Bantry. MARIE A. KUK (D) **
    1972-. Party: Precinct Com. 1974-. Prev:
Alderwoman 1971-72. B: 4/17/19. Add: P.O. Box
24, Bantry 58713 (701)768-2632.

Dazey. HELEN SHERLOCK
    P.O. Box 60, Dazey 58429.

Edmore. EVA SPARKS
    1966-. Bds: Area Low Income Council; N.
Central Planning Council; Water Bd. B: 3/24/18.
Add: City Hall, Edmore 58330 (701)644-2406.

Haynes. DOLORES EVANS (D)
    1976-. Prev: Alderwoman 1976. Org: Dem.
Women; BPW. Occ: Bar Owner. B: 3/16/23. Add:
Box 231, Haynes 58637 (701)567-9895.

Merricourt. ARLENE L. PAHL
    P.O. Box 2, Merricourt 58469.

Rawson. MARGARET LEER
    Alexander 58831.

Sentinel Butte. EINOR O. WALDAL
    P.O. Box 205, Sentinel Butte 58654.

Williston. DIANE L. BERVIG (I)
    1974-. Bds: Regional Council for Devt.;
Planning Bd.; ND Combined Law Enforcement Council.
B: 2/8/41. Add: 715 12th St. W, Williston
58801 (701)572-8161.

Local Councils

Alamo. BETTY E. OPPERUD (D)
    1976-. Occ: Cook. B: 10/24/35. Add: Box 33,
Alamo 58830.

Alice. SHARON KURTZ (I)
    1972-. B: 1/11/39. Add: Alice 58003.

Amenia. MYRTLE H. POYZER (R) **
    1974-. Prev: City Treasurer 1971-74. Org:
PTA. B: 10/18/11. Add: Amenia 58004.

Amidon. HILMA GRANGE
    Amidon 58620.

Arnegard. DONNA SCHULTZ
    Arnegard 58835.

Arnegard. KRIS STENSETH
    McKenzie County, Arnegard 58835.

Bantry. HELEN MYELLER
        DONNA SCHULTZ
    P.O. Box 41, Bantry.

Barney. NELLIE OLSON
    Barney 58008.

Bartlett. ELAINE HANSON
        DEBRA MARQUART
        CHERYL MILLER
    P.O. Box 2, Rt. 2, Lakota 58344.

Berthold. CONSTANCE E. JOHNSON (D) **
    1974-. Bds: Sewer Cmsnr.; City Anniversary
Com. Org: PTO. B: 1/15/27. Add: City Hall,
Berthold 58718.

Berwick. ALIDA FOSNESS
    Berwick 58788.

Bisbee. BARBRA OAKLAND
    Bisbee 58317.

Brinsmade. JANICE LUNDE
    Brinsmade 58320.

Burlington. VI WAHLER
    P.O. Box 159, Burlington 58722.

Cando. CAROL HAUGEN (R)
    1976-. Bds: Bd. of Health, Fire & Water,
Ch., Public Bldg. Org: Rep. Women's Club.
Educ: Sisters of St. Joseph School of Nursing
1954 RN. Occ: RN. B: 6/19/33. Add: 712 4th,
Cando 58324.

Casselton. PHYLLIS SPOONER
    P.O. Box 548, Casselton 58012.

Cathay. EDITH PETERSON
    P.O. Box 127, Cathay 58422.

Cathay. KAY RETZLAFF (R)
    1976-. Prev: City Treasurer 1968-74. Educ:
Vly. City State Coll. 1974 BS. Occ: Teacher.
B: 7/23/38. Add: Cathay 58422.

Churchs Ferry. INEZ CHRISTENSON (R) **
    1972-. Occ: Bar Maid. B: 9/19/19. Add:
Churchs Ferry 58325.

Cleveland. PHYLLIS LEYSRING **
    1970-. Bds: Park Bd. Org: PTO; Treasurer,
VFW. Occ: Post Office Clerk. Add: Cleveland
58424.

Conway. GRACE EISNER
    Forest River 58233.

Courtenay. DARLENE BURKHARDT
    1975-. Occ: Bookkeeper. Add: Courtenay
58426.

Courtenay. VIRGINIA C. TANATA
1973-. Bds: Ch., Keep ND Clean; Cnty. Library
Bd. B: 5/12/17. Add: Courtenay 58426 (701)
435-2269.

Deering. GLADYS L. HALL (D)
1975-. B: 4/10/11. Add: Deering 58731
(701)728-6474.

Dickey. ANN ARTHUR
P.O. Box 25, Dickey 58431.

Edinburg. MARIA PETERSON
P.O. Box 46, Edinburg 58227.

Epping. GERALDINE ENGET
Epping 58843.

Fargo. DONNA CHALIMONCZYK (R)
1976-. Bds: Lake Agassiz Regional Council;
Water Quality Bd. Party: State Del. 1976;
Precinct Committeewoman 1973- . Prev: Public
Service Com., Transmission Line Siting Adv. Com.
1975. Org: LWV; NOW; ND Women's Coalition; PTA;
WPC; IWY; GOP Women; Coord. Council for ERA.
Occ: Insurance Saleswoman. B: 1/4/33. Add: 1625
S. 14 1/2 St., Fargo 58102 (701)235-4269.

Gardena. MRS. HOWARD LENTZ
Gardena 58739.

Gardner. MARGARET BURIANEK
Gardner 58036.

Gilby. BONNIE J. MACHOVSKY (R)
1976-. Org: PTA. Occ: Secretary-Bookkeeper.
B: 2/21/40. Add: Gilby 58235.

Golva. MARILYN RISING
Golva 58632.

Hansboro. LOIS WOOD (D)
1976-. B: 7/8/47. Add: Box 214, Hansboro
58339.

Haynes. DELORES GALBREATH
1974-. Occ: Bookkeeper. B: 12/25/36. Add:
Box 191, Haynes 58637 (701)567-2509.

Haynes. ANITA JORGENSEN
1974-. Party: Precinct Committeewoman 1974-77.
Prev: School Bd. Org: Cnty. Dem. Women's Club.
Occ: Postal Clerk. B: 7/24/29. Add: Box 195,
Haynes 58637.

Haynes. L. SHIRLEY KAST (D)
B: 2/19/33. Add: Haynes 58637.

Hope. DOLORES PAUL (I)
1976-. Bds: Law Enforcement Council. Occ:
Saleswoman. B: 4/20/27. Add: Box 216, Hope
58046.

Horace. ROSEMARY LAMSETT
Horace 58047.

Hove Mobile Park. VICKIE BOLLIN
Hove Mobile Park 58229.

Lakota. AUGUSTA LARSON (R) **
1974-. B: 1/24/23. Add: 307 5th St., E.,
Lakota 58344 (701)247-2454.

Leonard. HELEN KISTLER
FLORENCE WEGGE
Leonard 58052.

Ludden. MARY ANN ANDERSON
ESTHER HAPALA
Ludden 58462.

Mandan. CAROLINE M. LUTKAT
110 Collins Ave., Mandan 58554.

Maxbass. ELAINE SCHILLING
MRS. VERYL THOMPSON
P.O. Box 14, Maxbass 58760.

McHenry. MARGARET D. SOMERVILLE
McHenry 58464.

Merricourt. BESSIE MALY
P.O. Box 2, Merricourt 58469.

Merricourt. RUTH C. TENNIS (R)
1976-. B: 8/18/42. Add: Box 6, Merricourt
58469.

Mohall. ORA FISHER (D) **
1972-. Bds: Water & Sewer Com.; Sanitation
& Equipment Com.; School Bd. Org: Bicentennial
Com.; Women's Club. Occ: Bookkeeper. B:
11/10/09. Add: Mohall 58761 (701)756-6452.

Perth MILDRED H. ARGABRIGHT (D) **
1972-. Org: Treasurer, Homemaker Club.
Occ: Postal Clerk. B: 3/27/29. Add: Perth
58363 (701)656-3651.

Pick City. CELIA FOWLER
CATHY J. RIME
Rt. #2, Hazen 58545.

Portland. HELEN KOEHNSTEDT
Portland 58274.

Rawson. IVY HEGGEN (I)
1975-. Party: Cnty. Secretary 1975-78.
Org: Cnty. Rep. Women's Org. B: 11/22/19.
Add: Rt. 2 - 339, Alexander 58831.

Ray. JULAINE A. CHRISTENSEN (D)
1974-. Bds: Park Bd. Occ: Restaurant
Manager. B: 7/8/41. Add: 24 W. St., Ray
58849 (701)568-2204.

Riverside. JO OLMSTED (I) **
1974-. Occ: Delicatessen Manager. B:
10/3/40. Add: 45 Center St., Riverside
58078 (701)282-6221.

Riverside. LUCY PAGE
108 W. Main Ave., West Fargo 58078.

Rolla. MAE C. NIEWOEHNER
1976-. Educ: Minot Coll. 1956 BS. B:
4/22/33. Add: 305 1/2 1st Ave., NE, Rolla
58367 (701)477-3180.

Ross. MARY JEAN HERMAN
     P.O. Box 8, Ross 58776.

Russell. FREDA DECKER
          ANN HAMEL
     Newburg 58762.

St. Thomas. PHYLLIS KENNELLY
     P.O. Box 177, St. Thomas 58276.

St. Thomas. JOSEPHINE G. MILLER (R) **
     1950-. B: 7/15/07. Add: St. Thomas 58276.

Sheldon. KATHRYN BUELING
     Sheldon 58068.

Sibley. MILDRED BUTTING
         EDYTHE HAGGLUND
     Sibley 58429.

Spiritwood Lake. JEAN BRADY
     P.O. Box 642, Spiritwood Lake 58401.

Spiritwood Lake. BARBARA C. LARAWAY (I)
     1974-. Org: Zonta. Occ: Store Owner. B:
     4/16/33. Add: 309 12th Ave NE, Jamestown 58401
     (701)252-8134.

Spring Brook. GUIDA PETERSON
     Spring Brook 58850.

Strasburg. RAMONA REIS
     1975-. Occ: Nurse. B: 9/13/49. Add:
     Strasburg 58573 (701)336-2645.

Warwick. KATHERINE SWENSON
     Warwick 58381.

Wheelock. LENORE G. BRADBURY
           GLADYS E. THUE
     P.O. Box 85, Wheelock 58855.

Wimbledon. EILEEN E. GRESHIK (D)
     1974-. Bds: Ch., Park Cmsnr. Org: Community
     Club; Election Inspector. B: 9/12/17. Add:
     Wimbledon 58492.

Wyndmere. ELEANORE SCHMIT
     P.O. Box 132, Wyndmere 58081.

State Boards and Commissions

     Office of the Governor, State Capitol Bldg.,
     Bismarck 58501.

Air Pollution Control Advisory Council
     VIVIEN RASK

Arts and Humanities, Council of
     KAY CANN
     RUTH EVERSON
     MRS. RUSSELL FREEMAN
     MRS. GORDON GRAY
     SYLVIA HAGEN
     MRS. A. J. PEDERSON
     ALMA STUDNESS
     MRS. WINIFRED STUMP
     MRS. LAWRENCE SUMMERS
     NANCY P. SWENSON

Business and Industrial Development Commission
     EDITH S. KJOS

Capitol Grounds Planning Commission
     GAIL HERNETT

Credit Union Board
     BETTY LEEHAN

Educational Broadcasting Council
     ELEANOR GOODALL
     BETTY MILLS

Employment of the Handicapped, Committee on
     EVELYN AMB
     GEORGENE EMARD
     RUTH ERICKSON
     NANCY HASS
     ELIZABETH MC COY

Examiners for Nursing Home Administrators, Board of
     DORIS M. STECKLER
     SISTER MADONNA WAGENDORF

Hairdressers and Cosmetologists, Board of
     GERALDINE ELKIN
     PALMA HATLESTAD
     ADELINE WOLFE

Health Council
     JOYCE CONRAD
     DAPHNA NYGAARD
     BERNICE PALMER
     MARALYN SALTING

Hearing Aid Dealers and Fitters
     LAURA M. SCHMALTZ

Higher Education, Board of
     GERALDINE CLAPP
     ELEANOR P. GRAHL

Higher Education Facilities Commission
     GERALDINE CLAPP
     ELEANOR P. GRAHL

Historical Society Board
     ROBERTA MC CREERY
     LOUISE STOCKMAN
     MARY YOUNG

Indian Affairs Commission
     ALBERTA WHITE CALFE
     ELIZABETH HALLMARK
     JUANITA J. HELPHREY
     ALICE OLSON

Laboratories Commission
     AILSA SIMONSON

Legislative Compensation Commission
     MRS. M. L. COUCHIGIAN
     FLORENCE OLSON

Massage, Board of
     GLADYS NEELS

Medical Center Advisory Council
     MRS. GILMAN PETERSON

Milk Stabilization Board
    MRS. SAM HILL

Nursing, Board of
    LEE ANN BARTHOLOMAY
    GERALDINE BAUMANN
    SUE EHLERS
    ADELE GORDER
    BETTY HALVORSON
    MRS. LA VONNE RUSSELL
    IRENE SAGE

Pardons, Board of
    BETTY LAVERDURE

Parole Board
    JO ANN YOCUM

Personnel Policy Committee
    JUANITA HELPHREY
    IRENE ROTH

Psychologist Examiners, Board of
    ALICE T. CLARK

Real Estate Commission
    MRS. NORMAN O'NEIL

Rehabilitation Services, Advisory Committee on
    ELVIRA W. JESTRAB
    JAN M. ROGNEBY

Social Service Board
    DARLENE LEINEN
    LAURA S. MAIXNER

State Personnel Board
    AILSA SIMONSON
    BEVERLY SOLBERG

Teachers Professional Practices Commission
    JUNE HOLTE
    JOANN MC CAFFREY
    MARLYS MARTWICK

Veterans Affairs, Administrative Committee on
    MRS. GAYLE DOHERTY

Water Conservation Commission
    ARLENE WILHELM

Wheat Commission
    JUDI ADAMS
    DEBBIE BROWN
    LINDA FASCHING
    MARY JANUSZ

Yellowstone-Missouri-Fort Union Commission
    LYLA HOFFINE

Ohio

State Executive and Cabinet

GERTRUDE W. DONAHEY (D)
    Treasurer. 1970-. Bds: Bd. of Deposit;
Sinking Fund Cmsnr.; Public Facilities Cmsn.
Party: State Del. 1964-76; Nat. Del. 1964, '68;
State Central Committeewoman 1966-71. Prev:
Senator's Administrative Asst. 1964-71. Org:
Oh. Assoc. of Mental Health; BPW; Municipal
Finance Officers Assoc.; Nat. Assoc. of Auditors,
Comptrollers & Treasurers. B: 8/4/08. Add:
2838 Sherwood Rd., Columbus 43209 (614)
466-2160.

HELEN W. EVANS (R) **
    State Dir., Industrial Relations 1975-.
Party: State Com. Prev: Dept. of Welfare
1939-51; Treasurer's Office 1951-57; State
Auditor 1958-63. Org: Rep. Club. B: 8/5/05.
Add: Rte. 5, Marysville 43040 (614)466-3271.

State Legislature

State Senate

MARIGENE VALIQUETTE (D)
    1969-. Bds: Ch., Judiciary Com.; Rules Com.;
Finance Com. Party: Nat. Del. 1974; Dem. Nat.
Com. 1976; V-Ch., Lucas Cnty. Exec. Com. 1970;
Oh. Dem., Exec. Com. 1974. Prev: State Repr.
1963-69. Org: LWV; BPW; Women's Club. Educ:
U. of Toledo BA; JD. Occ: Atty. Add: 3211
Parkwood, Toledo 43610 (614)466-5204.

State House

VIRGINIA AVENI (D) **
    Dist: 17. Bds: Energy & Environment; State
Government; Transportation & Urban Affairs.
Occ: Student. Add: 4911 Middledale Rd., Lynd-
hurst 44124 (216)291-2211.

HELEN H. FIX (R) **
    1974-. Dist: 26. Bds: Continuing Educ. Com.
Prev: Councilwoman 1967-74. Org: Newspaper
Women's Assoc.; Women in Communications; WPC;
County Rep. Club. Educ: Westhampton U. of
Richmond 1943 BA. B: 9/21/22. Add: 3141 Esther
Dr., Cincinnati 45213 (614)466-8247.

IRMA L. KARMOL (R) **
    1974-. Dist: 44. Bds: Human Resources;
Agriculture & Nat. Resources; Energy & Environment. Party: Com. 1964-74. Org: BPW; LWV;
OWL; Rep. Club. Educ: Miami U. 1945 BS. B:
4/13/23. Add: 3730 Chesterton, Toledo 43615
(614)466-8140.

FRANCINE M. PANEHAL (D)
1974-. Bds: V-Ch., Urban Cities Com. Party: Cnty. Exec. Com. 1971-77; Precinct Leader 1971-75. Prev: City Planning Cmsn. 1965-71; Councilwoman 1971-73. Org: AAUW; Women's Dem. Club; LWV; Dem. Club; Cnty. Dems.; WPC. Educ: Ursuline Coll. 1948 BA. B: 10/10/28. Add: 11502 Edgewater, Cleveland 44102 (614)466-8035.

DONNA POPE (R) **
1972-. Dist: 12. Bds: Nat. Conf. of Legislatures; Ohio Constitutional Review Cmsn. Party: County Exec. Com. 1966- ; Precinct Com. 1962- ; Ward Leader 1966-73; State Central Com. 1966-72. Org: Amer. Business Women's Assoc.; Internat. Platform Assoc.; OWL; Children Forever Haven Advisory Council; Citizens League; Women's Rep. Club. B: 10/15/31. Add: 3915 Longwood Ave., Parma 44134 (614)466-8120.

IRENE BALOGH SMART (D) **
1973-. Dist: 49. Bds: Agriculture; Commerce & Labor; Insurance; Utilities; Financial Institutions; Judiciary. Prev: Councilwoman 1960-72; State Bd. of Educ. 1945-46. Org: Bar Assoc.; Dem. Women's Clubs. Educ: Wittenberg U. 1942 BS; Harvard Med. 1943 MA; McKinley 1955 LLB. Occ: Physical Therapist. B: 3/24/21. Add: 3807 Third St., NW, Canton 44708.

MARIE TANSEY (I)
1977-. Dist: 72. Bds: House Energy & Environment Com.; House Govt. Affairs Com.; House Local Govt. Sub Com. Prev: City Council 1969-75; Pres. City Council 1973-75; Precinct Committeewoman 1965- . Org: Nat. Assoc. State Legislators; Amer. Leg. Exchange Council; Chamber of Commerce; Historical Society. B: 1/6/30. Add: 1201 State St., Vermillion 44089 (614)466-8100.

County Commissions

Athens. HELEN BAKER
County Court House, Athens 45701.

Athens. KAREN M. HARVEY (D)
1976-. Bds: Ch., Athens Cnty. Data Processing Bd.; Athens Cnty. Regional Planning Cmsn.; Bd. of Trustees - Tri-Cnty. Community Action Agency. Org: LWV; Ohio Citizens Council; Friends of Children's Services; Dem. Club; Dem. Women's Club. Educ: State U. of SD 1960 BA. B: 2/20/38. Add: 822 Ervin Rd., Athens 45701 (614)593-7988.

Highland. HARRIET STIVERS
Highland County Court House, Hillsboro 45133.

Monroe. MARGARET CLEGG
Monroe County Courthouse, Woodsfield 43793.

Montgomery. PAULA J. MAC ILWAINE (D)
1976-. Bds: Miami Vly. Regional Agency; Cnty. Planning Cmsn.; Miami Vly. Manpower Consortium. Org: Cnty. Assoc. of Ohio; Nat. Assoc. of Cntys.; LWV; Jr. League; Cnty. Dem. Club. Educ: Ohio Wesleyan U. 1962 BA. B: 2/11/41. Add: 200 Greenmount Blvd., Dayton 45419 (513)225-4015.

Ottawa. HELEN JEAN ROFKAR (D) **
1972-. Educ: Toledo Hospital School of Nursing 1968 LPN. B: 11/27/30. Add: 3495 NW Catawba Rd., Port Clinton 43452 (419)732-2523.

Tuscarawas. JOANNE LIMBACH (D)
1977-. Bds: Juvenile Multi-Cnty. Bd. Party: State Alt. 1975-76; Cnty. Committeewoman 1975-77. Prev: School Bd. 1972-77. Org: Ohio Educ. Assoc.; NEA; AAUW; Young Dem's.; WPC. Educ: Muskingum Coll. 1962 BA; Bowling Green 1968 MA. Occ: Teacher. B: 9/22/40. Add: 1383 Seven Mile Dr., New Philadelphia 44663 (216)364-8811.

Township Trustees

Allen. LYNNE W. HOADLEY
R.R.L., Van Buren 45889.

Archer. NANCY L. ALBAUGH
R.R. 5, Cadiz 43907.

Athens. KATHRYN WALBURN
R.R. 2, Athens 45701.

Bainbridge. ELEANORE L. MATTSON (R)
1975-. Bds: Cnty. Commissioners for Assoc. Township Trustees & Clerks. Org: Amer. Red Cross; Assoc. Township Trustees. Educ: Chatham Coll. 1949 BS; U. of Ill. 1950 MS. B: 2/21/28. Add: 7396 Ober Lane, Chagrin Falls 44022 (216)543-9872.

Bath. SARAH CHILDERS (D)
1971-. Bds: Cnty. Health Bd.; Cnty. Regional Planning Bd. Occ: Real Estate Agent. B: 8/20/23. Add: 936 Dayton Yell Spgs. Rd., Fairborn 45324 (513)767-9115.

Brown. LORAINE HORN
R.R. 1, Danville 43014.

Butler. JOAN M. HUBER
3900 Reinwood, Dayton 45414.

Catawba. NANCY ROBERTS
Cliff Dr., Port Clinton 43452.

Center. HELEN M. NOLD
9505 St. Rt. 45, Lisbon 44432.

Chatham. PATRICIA A. BROWN
8311 Chatham Rd., Medina 44256.

Chester. DOREEN KEARSCHNER
12059 Parker Dr., Chesterland 44026.

Colerain. HELEN B. AMBERCROMBIE
7845 Livingston Rd., Cincinnati 45239.

Delphi. VIRGINIA R. WITTE (I)
1975-. Bds: Cnty. Health Dept. Adv. Council; Reg. Council of Govts. Land Use Com.; Cnty. Economic Dev. Com. Prev: Zoning Cmsn. 1972-75. Org: Amer. Public Health Assoc.; Twp. Trustees & Clerks Assoc.; Women's Club; Bicentennial Com.; PTA. Educ: Mt. St. Joseph 1969 BS. Occ: Nurse. B: 5/5/47. Add: 4315 Copperfield 45238 (513)922-0145.

Enoch. ISADORE SNIDER
R.R. 4, Caldwell 43724.

Franklin. DORRIS HIGH
R.R. 3, Mt. Gilead 43338.

Franklin. VIRGINIA L. SPAHR (R)
1975-. Bds: Cnty. Health Dept.; Council on
Govts. Org: Cnty. Trustees & Clerks; Community
Council; Women's Club; PTA. B: 4/13/41. Add:
600 Yager Rd., Clinton 44216 (216)882-4324.

Greenville. JOYCE E. MICHAEL
290 Driftwood, Greenville 45331.

Hale. MABEL L. MC CALL
W. Taylor St., Mt. Victory 43340.

Jackson. DONNA L. FETTY
3026 W. Warren Rd., North Jackson 44451.

Jackson. BERNICE ROCKWELL
Town Hall, Patterson 45878.

Jackson. MARY G. TIBBE
R.R. 1, Winchester 45697.

Jefferson. LORAIN ALLEN
R.R. 1, Lore City 43755.

Jefferson. BINA TOLLE
R.R. 1, Box 13, Blue Creek 45616.

Latty. FAY P. SCARBROUGH
R.R. 1, Grover Hill 45849.

Laurel. RUBY FAST
R.R. 1, Rockbridge 43149.

Lee. MARTHA CLINE
R.R. 1, Albany 45710.

Lemon. DOROTHY L. INGRAM
2206 S. Dixie Hwy., Middletown 45042.

Logan. ANN JEFFRIES
RR #4, Harrison 45030.

Madison. LORAIN DENNEY
R.R. 2, Amanda 43102.

Madison. DORRIS DUFF
4003 Whiteston Ct., Dayton 45426.

Malta. SYLVA NORMAN
R.R. 2, Malta 43758.

Marion. MRS. CLEO H. BIERLY (D)
1968-. Org: Oh. State Assoc. of Twp. Trustees
& Clerks. B: 8/20/15. Add: 30360 Logan Horn's
Mill Rd., Logan 43138.

Miami. SHIRLEY ELAINE GRIESMEYER OMIETANSKI (R)
1976-. Bds: Community Devt. Adv. Block Funds
Com.; Solid Waste Adv. Com.; Miami Rvr. Corridor.
Org: Oh. Trustees & Clerks Assoc.; Civic Assoc.;
LWV; Nat. Audubon Society; Rep. Club; Women's
Club. Educ: Otterbein Coll. 1957 BSEd. Occ:
Teacher. B: 7/4/34. Add: 2418 Fox Run Rd.,
Dayton 45459 (513)433-9969.

Miami. BARBARA S. SMITH
5807 Mildren Ln., Milford 45150.

Milton. ALTA JENKINS
R.R. 4, Wellston 45692.

Nimishillen. DARLENE E. ODER (D)
1972-. Bds: Regional Planning Cmsn. Party:
State Del. 1972; Precinct Committeewoman 1974-
77. Org: LWV; Assoc. of Twp. Trustees & Clerks;
Dem. Women's Club. Educ: U. of Akron 1974 BA;
Allentown Hospital School of Nursing 1961 RN.
B: 12/18/40. Add: 6969 Pilot Knob N.E.,
Louisville 44641 (216)875-1963.

Northampton. HELEN R. BAUGHMAN
556 Portage Trail Ext., Cuyahoga Falls
44223.

Northampton. JOAN HENRICK
220 W. Steels Corners Rd., Cuyahoga Falls
44223.

Orange. CARRIE A. HUNT
8468 Azalea Rd.,SW, Dennison 44621.

Oxford. LORAINE MC CUNE
R.R. 3, Newcomerstown 43882.

Penn. DANA NEWTON
R.R. 1, Stockport 43787.

Pleasant. JANE KARN
6075 Lambert Rd., Orient 43146.

Pleasant. MARJORIE D. WOLLENHAUPT (D)
1971-. Org: Dem. Club. B: 2/8/05. Add:
RR #4, Van Wert 45891.

Richmond. CLARE N. CHAPMAN
R.R. 2, Andover 44003.

Roundhead. LACY SHIPP
Box 284, Roundhead 43346.

Russell. G. JEAN CROSS (R)
1976-. Bds: Steering Com.; Area Coord.
Agency. Prev: Cnty. Planning Bd. 1975-77; N.E.
Oh. Area Coord. Agency 1977. Org: LWV; Women's
Civic Club. B: 12/31/29. Add: 14905 Hillbrook
Cir., Russell 44072 (216)338-8912.

Short Creek. MARJORIE LANOY
Harrisville 43974.

Springfield. MARYLIN YODER (R)
1969-. Org: Twp. Rep. Club; Cnty. Assoc. of
Twp. Trustees & Clerks. Occ: Secretary. B:
1/15/33. Add: 6134 Estateland Ct., Maumee
43537.

Sylvania. LUCILLE IMOGENE LASKEY (R) **
1970-. Bds: Bikeway Com.; Solid Waste Coord.
Com.; Government Systems & Intergovernmental
Relations Com.; Regional Planning & Environ-
mental Resources Com.; County/Townships Drainage
Com.; Metropolitan Council of Governments;
Regional Area Plan for Action; County Health
Advisory Bd.; Safety Com. Party: Precinct Com.
1975. Prev: Zoning Appeals Bd. 1966-69. Org:

OES; Zonta; County Assoc. of Township Trustees & Clerks; Community Communications Council; Rep. Club. B: 1/9/18. Add: 4332 Dogwood La., Toledo 43623 (419)882-0031.

Union. CHRISTIE B. ROTH
R.R. 1, Bellefontaine 43311.

Vernon. HALLIE H. DRAS
6421 Bushnell-Campbell Rd., R.R. 1, Kinsman 44428.

Warren. F. IRENE FELGENHAUER
R.R. 1, New Philadelphia 44663.

Washington. SUE AUER (D)
1973-. Party: Cnty. Central Committeewoman 1952-77. Org: Fed. Dem. Women. B: 4/7/10. Add: 1598 Whitnauer Dr., Mansfield 44904 (419) 756-2574.

Washington. MARGARET V. RAPP
5246 Fortune Dr., Toledo 43611.

Wayne. PEARL REID
R.R. 2, Winchester 45697.

Mayors

Bedford Heights. LUCILLE J. REED
5661 Perkins Rd., Bedford Hts. 44146.

Bellevue. PHYLLIS A. ROBERTSON
City Hall, 108 W. Main St., Bellevue 44811.

Bergholz. VERDA STARN
Town Hall, 2nd St., Bergholz 43908.

Brunswick. HELEN L. WEST
4095 Center Rd., City Hall, Brunswick 44212.

Carrollton. LYNN R. FOX
Town Hall, 80 2nd St., SW, Carrollton 44615.

Cleveland Heights. MARJORIE B. WRIGHT
City Hall, 2953 Mayfield Rd., Cleveland Hts. 44118.

Coolville. MARIE DIXON (D)
1975-. Prev: Councilwoman 1974-75. Occ: Bookkeeper. B: 11/17/25. Add: 44 Campbell St., Coolville 45723 (614)667-3438.

Dalton. KATE SLUSSER (I)
1976- Bds: Ch., Planning Com. Party: Cnty. Rep. Exec. Com. 1976. Prev: Mayor 1960-68, Councilwoman 1968-72; Utilitiᵉ Bd. 1972-76. Occ: School Bus Driver. B: 1/29/09. Add: 7 West Main, Dalton 44618 (216)828-2221.

Deersville. DORIS J. MATTHEWS
Town Hall, Fire House, Deersville 44693.

Dexter City. MARY E. WARREN (R)
1972-. Bds: Regional Planning Com.; Cnty. Adv. Bd. Prev: Vlg. Clerk 1968-72. Org: BPW. B: 4/27/20. Add: Box 103, Dexter City 45727 (614) 783-2345.

Elyria. MARGUERITE E. BOWMAN (R)
1976-. Bds: Planning Cmsn.; Ch., City Health Bd.; Regional Council of Govts. Party: Precinct Leader 1961-77; Cnty. Exec. Com. 1961-77. Prev: Councilwoman 1964-65, 1968-75. Org: U.S. Conf. of Mayors; Oh. Mayor Assoc.; Rep. Women's Club. B: 5/9/18. Add: 1416 Ford Rd., Elyria 44035 (216)322-1829.

Kellys Island. HELEN A. MARCHKY (D)
1973-. Prev: Councilwoman 1972-73. Org: NEA; Altrusa. Educ: Bowling Green State U. 1933 BS; 1966 MS. B: 6/10/08. Add: Kelleys Is. 43438 (419)746-4101.

Loveland. VIOLA I. PHILLIPS
City Hall, 120 W. Loveland Ave., Loveland 45140.

Mantua. CAROLYN W. THOMPSON
1975-. Bds: Planning Com. Prev: Zoning Inspector 1959-66; Vlg. Councilwoman 1969-75. Org: Cemetery; Historical. Occ: Retail Business Owner. B: 11/27/22. Add: 4514 W. Prospect, Mantua 44255 (216)274-8776.

McComb. MARY E. STERRETT (R)
1976-. Occ: Assembler. B: 9/27/28. Add: 219 N. Todd St., McComb 45858 (419)293-3662.

Middle Point. BETTY J. RHODES
Town Hall, Main St., Middle Pt. 45863.

Mineral City. JUNE BRUNK
1976-. Bds: Police; Firemen. Prev: Councilwoman 1966-76. Occ: Packer. B: 1/24/32. Add: 1st St. Ext., Mineral City 44656 (216)859-2222.

Morral. SUEA M. FOSTER
Town Hall, Morral 43337.

Nelsonville. VIOLET HOLLENBAUGH
City Hall, 29 Fayette St., Nelsonville 45764.

New Knoxville. DELORIS R. FISCHBACH (R)
1971-. Bds: Pres., Mayors Assoc. of Oh.; Com. on Intergovt. Affairs; Auglaize Cnty. Regional Planning Cmsn. Party: State Del. 1976; Precinct Leader 1974; Cnty. Ch. 1974-76; Asst. Cnty. Ch. 1976. Org: Civic Assoc.; Cnty. Rep. Women; Soroptimist. Educ: Wright State U. 1973 BS. Occ: Grocery Store Owner. B: 3/29/23. Add: 511 S. Main St., New Knoxville 45871 (419) 753-2160.

Pitsburg. PATRICIA J. RICE (I)
1976-. Bds: Cnty. Health Com.; Rescue Squad. Org: PTA; OES. B: 8/2/36. Add: 322 N. Jefferson, Pitsburg 45358.

Powhatan Point. INEZ B. WRIGHT (D) **
1976-. Bds: Planning Com.; Police Com. Party: Dem. Exec. Com. 1952-75; Precinct Com. 1949-75. Prev: Notary Public 1954-75; Township Clerk 1948-65; Justice of Peace 1954-58. B: 4/1/11. Add: 112 Main St., Powhatan Point 43942 (614)795-4880.

Riverlea. CLARA G. GUTHERY
Town Hall, 302 Riverglen Dr., Riverlea 43085.

Rock Creek.   RUTH M. GYNN (R)
     1972-. Bds: Grand River Basin Planning; Cnty.
Council of Govts; Cnty. Planning. Prev: Councilwoman 1967-72. Occ: Antique Shop Owner. B:
11/12/18. Add: 2924 High St., Rock Crk. 44084
(216)563-3334.

Rushylvanica.   DOROTHY M. GILBERT
     Town Hall, Rushylvanica 43347.

St. Marys.   KAY E. ALBERT
     101 E. Spring St., St. Marys 45885.

Solon.   DOROTHY K. PORTZ (R)
     1975-. Bds: Planning Cmsn. Prev: Councilwoman
1972-75. Org: ABA; Ohio Bar Assoc.; Cnty. Bar
Assoc.; AAUW; Citizen's League. Educ: William &
Mary 1938 BA; Western Reserve U. 1948 JD. Occ:
Attorney. B: 1/23/16. Add: 5530 S.O.M. Center
Rd., Solon 44139 (216)248-1155.

Verona.   DOROTHY SEEKER (R)
     1977-. Prev: Councilwoman 1972-77. B:
10/25/20. Add: 111 W. Main St., Verona (513)
884-5155.

Local Councils

Adelphi.   PATRICIA POLING
     Town Hall, Adelphi 43101.

Akron.   KATHLEEN A. GREISSING
           ELSIE REAVEN
     City Hall, 166 S. High St., Akron 44308.

Alexandria.   PATRICIA ANN MC GLONE
     Town Hall, Liberty St., Alexandria 43001.

Amanda.   ELSIE DAVIS (D)
     1971-. Bds: Council Pres. B: 1/22/19. Add:
115 N. School St., Amanda 43102.

Amanda.   SARAH R. KENNEDY (R)
     1974-. Bds: Ch., Bicentennial. B: 12/14/31.
Add: Box 56, Amanda 43102.

Amberley Village.   GLORIA SCHOTTENSTEIN HAFFER
     1975-. Bds: Ch., House & Grounds Com.; Law
Com.; Police & Fire Com. Org: ABA Student Div.;
Jewish Community Relations Com. Educ: U. of
Cincinnati 1962 BA; Salmon P. Chase Coll. of Law
1977 JD. B: 1/28/41. Add: 8300 Arborcrest Dr.,
Cincinnati 45236.

Amberley Village.   BARBARA J. STEINBERG
     1975-. Bds: Ch., Health, Educ. & Welfare;
Recreation Com.; Roads, Public Utilities & Sewers.
Org: Women's City Club; Hamilton Cnty. Recreation.
Educ: U. of Cincinnati 1950 BS. B: 3/23/29. Add:
6602 E. Farm Acres Dr., Cincinnati 45237 (513)
531-8675.

Amsterdam.   VIRGINIA M. DAVIDSON
             HAZEL MASON
             LILLIAN WILLIGMAN
     Town Hall, Main St., Amsterdam 43903.

Aquilla Village.   CATHERINE C. BABBITT (D)
     1973-. Bds: Co-Ch., Safety. Org: VFW. B:
5/15/12. Add: 124 Cornelia Dr., Chardon
44024.

Arlington Heights.   ELLA MAE BUSTLE
     P.O. Box 15116, Cincinnati 45215.

Arlington Heights.   KAREN SUE FIELDS
     Town Hall, 601 Elliott Ave., Arlington
Hts. 45215.

Athalia.   PEGGY ULLAM
     Town Hall, Athalia 45669.

Aurora.   MARY L. DIMICK (R) **
     1972-. Bds: Ch., Parks & Recreation;
Service. Party: Com. 1968-72. Org: Women's
Rep. Club. B: 3/23/25. Add: 670 Eggleston
Rd., Aurora 44202 (614)562-8361.

Aurora.   JEANNE A. HARTMAN
     130 S. Chillicothe Rd., Aurora 44240.

Avon Lake.   JEANNE BAIR
              KATHRYN HARDMAN
     City Hall, 150 Avon Belden Rd., Avon Lake
44012.

Bairdstown.   DONNA M. KNAGGS (R)
     1975-. Occ: Secretary. B: 10/21/30. Add:
RR #1, N. Baltimore 45872 (419)454-2821.

Baltic.   BONNIE STEIN (R)
     1975-. Bds: Ch., Financial; Street & Sewer;
Utilities. Occ: Cosmetologist. B: 5/16/41.
Add: Main St., Baltic 43804.

Batesville.   MYRTLE BETTS (D)
     1966-. B: 12/21/28. Add: Rt. 2, Quaker City
43772.

Batesville.   MARY ANN CARPENTER (D)
     1974-. Bds: Pres., Town Council. B: 7/12/50.
Add: Rt. 2, Quaker City 43773 (614)679-2125.

Batesville.   DONNA EAGON
     Town Hall, Batesville 43715.

Beach City.   SHERRY MARIE
              SIDONIA RUTH VOGLEY
     Town Hall, 2nd NE, Beach City 44608.

Beaverdam.   RUTH FRITSCHI
             RENA HEYNEMAN
             JOYCE A. MC CLAIN
     Town Hall, Mill & Main Sts., Beaverdam 45801.

Bellaire.   CAROLINE COOPER
            MARIE SENATROE
     32nd & Belmont Sts., Bellaire 43906.

Belle Center.   MARY STIERHOFF
     Town Hall, Buckeye St., Belle Center 43310.

Belle Valley.   SANDRA SKLENAR (D)
     1976-. Bds: Ch., Street & House Numeration;
Ch., Sidewalk & Property; Ch., Funding Com.
B: 4/1/41. Add: 46 High, Belle Vly. 43717
(614)732-5394.

Bellville. MARGARET E. WALTER (R)
1975-. Bds: Ch., Ordinance Com.; Finance;
Zoning. Org: Historic Preservation; OES. B:
9/2/10. Add: 197 Dickerson Ave., Box 384,
Bellville 44813 (419)886-2245.

Belmont. LINDA BROWN
Town Hall, Market St., Belmont 43718.

Belmore. BETTY I. RAYLE
Town Hall, Belmore 45815.

Bentleyville. LUELLA KOERPER
Town Hall, 6253 Chagrin Rvr., Bentleyville
44022.

Berea. PATRICIA DORR
MARY J. PENROD
City Hall, 11 Berea Commons, Berea 44017.

Bethesda. JUDITH K. JENEWEIN
Town Hall, S. Main St., Bethesda 43719.

Beverly. MAXINE CLARK
Town Hall, 5th St., Beverly 45715.

Bexley. CAROLYN THOMAS WOOD **
1973-. Bds: Planning Cmsn.; Zoning Appeals
Bd. Educ: Conn. Coll. 1964 BA; Ohio State U.
1966 MA. B: 1/19/42. Add: 126 S. Parkview Ave.,
Bexley 43209 (614)252-3332.

Blanchester. MARGARET S. SCHNELL
Town Hall, Main & Broadway, Blanchester 45107.

Blue Ash. STEPHANIE STOLLER (R)
1973-. Bds: Ch., Safety Com.; Finance Com.
Org: Rep. Club. Educ: U. of Cincinnati 1957 BS.
Occ: Pharmacist. B: 4/24/35. Add: 5779 Bomark
Ct., Cincinnati 45242 (513)791-0330.

Bradford. LINDA S. MOORE
Town Hall, 115 N. Main St., Bradford 45308.

Bratenahl. JOHANNA A. IRISH
Town Hall, 411 E. 105th St., Bratenahl 44108.

Brecksville. KAY ELSAS BROUGHTON (R)
1975-. Bds: Ch., Utility Com.; Finance; Bldgs.
& Grounds. Prev: Recreation Cmsn. 1975-76. Org:
Society of Women Engineers; LWV; Citizens League;
Rep. Club. Educ: CCNY 1946 BChE; Columbia 1951
MSIE. Occ: Engineer. Add: 6703 Somerset Dr.,
Brecksville 44141.

Bridgeport. HAZEL MARIE ROTH (D)
1974-. Bds: Finance Com.; Garbage & Refuse;
Ch., Health. Party: Precinct Committeewoman 1972-
76. Org: Dem. Club. B: 1/23/20. Add: 710 High
St., Bridgeport 43912 (614)635-2424.

Brilliant. DELORIS A. QUINN
Town Hall, 409 Prospect St., Brilliant 43913.

Broadview Heights. EDNA M. DEFFLER
8938 Broadview Hts., Broadview Hts. 44147.

Brooklyn. PAULA ANN RITTER
7619 Memphis Ave., Brooklyn 44144.

Broughton. HELEN K. DOSTER
Town Hall, RR1, Paulding 45879.

Brunswick. JUDITH A. BEADELL
City Hall, 4095 Center Rd., Brunswick 44212.

Buckland. VIRGINIA V. FRY (D)
1975-. Bds: Street Com. B: 12/3/18. Add:
101 W. Water, Buckland 45819 (419)657-2252.

Buckland. JEANNETTE LAMBERT (D)
1974-. Party: Precinct Worker 1972-76. Occ:
Office Clerk. B: 1/12/36. Add: 308 S. Ridge
St., Buckland 45819 (419)657-2250.

Burbank. VIRGINIA H. LIVINGSTON (R)
1976-. Bds: Street; Park; Safety. Occ:
Restaurant Owner. B: 12/17/20. Add: 30 Front
St., Burbank 44214.

Burbank. MARGARET M. SMITH
DIANA WILES
Town Hall, 32 Front St., Burbank 44214.

Burton. GEORGIA A. HEDLUND
Town Hall, 14588 W. Park St., Burton 44021.

Burton. DOROTHY ADAMS WINTERMUTE (R)
1975-. Bds: Ch., Finance Com; Streets Com.
Org: Chamber of Commerce. Occ: Controller/
Office Manager. B: 7/9/26. Add: 14454 Hickox
St., Burton 44021.

Byesville. NANCY CONROY STERMER (R)
1969-. Bds: Legislative Com.; Utilities Com.;
Building Inspection. Org: Home & School Org.;
Bicentennial Com. Occ: Organist. B: 4/17/33.
Add: 204 High Ave., Byesville 43723 (614)
685-2702.

Cardington. BARBARA J. COWLES (R)
1973-. Bds: Ch., Fire & Safety; Equipment;
Service. Occ: Secretary-Bookkeeper. B: 9/15/35.
Add: 311 W. Main, Cardington 43315.

Carey. EDITH I. KITZLER
Town Hall, 127 N. Vance St., Carey.

Carroll. BESSIE BENSON (D)
Bds: Ch., Street Com.; Bldg. Com. B: 4/19/14.
Add: 66 Market St., P.O. Box 422, Carroll 43112
(614)756-4031.

Carroll. LINDA PIERCE
ELEANOR K. THOMPSON
Town Hall, 55 Park St., Carroll 43112.

Carrollton. ANN GREEN
Town Hall, 80 2nd St., SW, Carrollton 44615.

Carrollton. MARY ANN MILLER (R)
1975-. Bds: Bldg. & Zoning; Finance; Police
& Fire. Prev: Zoning Bd. of Appeals 1974-76.
Occ: Secretary. B: 1/1/37. Add: 80 2nd St. SW,
Carrollton 44615.

Casstown. DOROTHY ANN BUTLER (D)
1973-. Occ: Cashier. B: 12/13/27. Add:
12 N. Main, Casstown 45312 (513)339-1416.

Castalia. SYLVIA A. PUCHALSKI
    Town Hall, 106 S. Ave., Castalia 44824.

Castine. ALICE BAKER (D)
    1975-. Bds: Ordinances; Park Com. Occ:
School Cashier. B: 11/26/31. Add: 700 S. Oak,
Castine 45313.

Castine. MILDRED MC GRIFF
    Main St., Castine 45313.

Cecil. LOIS JACKSON
         THEDORA KEELER
    Town Hall, Cecil 45821.

Centerville. NAOMI BEMAN
              BEULAH MAE BOSTER
    Town Hall, Thurman, Centerville 43685.

Centerville. NORA E. LAKE (R)
    1974-. Bds: Miami Valley Reg. Planning Cmsn.;
Technical Adv. Program Steering Com.; Legal Com.
Party: State Alt. 1976; Precinct Leader 1970- ;
Ward Committeewoman 1972-78. Org: LWV; Rep.
Women's Club. Educ: U. of Dayton 1977 BA. Add:
1470 Black Oak Dr., Centerville 45459 (513)
433-7151.

Chagrin Falls. KATHRYN B. WATTERSON (R)
    1971-. Bds: Planning & Zoning Cmsn.; Bd. of
Zoning Appeals; Shade Tree Cmsn. Org: LWV;
Women's Club; Chamber of Commerce; Historical
Society. Educ: St. Lukes Hospital School of
Nursing 1954 RN. B: 10/23/33. Add: 544 North
St., Chagrin Falls 44022 (216)247-5050.

Chardon. BEVERLY J. CARVER
    Town Hall, 110 S. Hambden, Chardon 44024.

Chauncey. EDITH PIERRE COCHRAN (R)
    1968-. Bds: Ch., Finance; Ch., Parks; Ch.,
Beautification. Party: Clerk, Bd. of Elections
1971-77. B: 3/26/08. Add: 6 S. High St.,
Chauncey 45719.

Cheshire. ERNA CORNELUIS
    Town Hall, Cheshire 45620.

Cheviot. INEZ GINGERICH
          DOROTHY A. NEIHEISEL
    3814 Harrison Ave., Cheviot 45211.

Chillicothe. NANCY L. BELL (R)
    Bds: Ch., Health & Welfare Com.; Service &
Safety Com.; Parks & Recreation Com. Party:
Precinct Committeewoman 1973-79. Org: Nat. Assoc.
of Realtors; Community Improvement Assoc.; Rep.
Women; PTA. Occ: Realtor. B: 6/21/36. Add:
821 Woodhill Dr., Chillicothe 45601 (614)
773-3170.

Cincinnati. HELEN C. HINCKLEY
    Bds: Ch., Public Works & Traffic Safety Com.;
Urban Devt., Planning, Zoning & Housing Com.;
Finance Com. Org: Community Action Cmsn.; Com.
on Housing; Cincinnati Symphony Orchestra Policy
Bd. B: 8/24/22. Add: 17 Garden Pl., Cincinnati
45208.

Cincinnati. BOBBIE STERNE
    1971-. Bds: Retirement Bd., Criminal
Justice Regional Planning. Party: Charter
Committee, Field Division 1958-70. Org: Council
on Aging; Planned Parenthood. Educ: Akron U.
1942 RN. B: 11/27/19. Add: 4033 Rose Hill Ave.,
Cincinnati 45229 (513)352-3649.

Clarksburg. SHARON KAY COX (R)
    1976-. Bds: Street Cmsr.; Bd. of Adv.,
Community Action 1977- . Org: Community Action
Cmsn. B: 12/8/45. Add: 6th & High, Box 161,
Clarksburg 43115 (614)993-2501.

Clarksville. JUANITA LAVERNE HARVEY (R)
    1970-. Bds: Ch., Finance. Prev: Vlg. Clerk
1954-69. Org: OES. B: 6/24/19. Add: 42 Main
St., Clarksville 45113 (513)289-2652.

Clarksville. NEDA STANFIELD
    Town Hall, Main St., Clarksville 45113.

Clayton. VIRGINIA MALESKI (D)
    1975-. Org: Red Cross. Educ: Good Samaritan
Hospital School of Nursing 1957 RN. Occ: RN.
B: 10/5/36. Add: 55 W. Salem St., Clayton
45315.

Cleveland. MILDRED R. MADISON
    City Hall, 601 Lakeside Ave., Cleveland
44144.

Cleveland. MARY J. ZONE
    City Hall, 601 Lakeside Ave., Cleveland
44144.

Cleveland. MARY C. ZUNT (D)
    1973-. Bds: Ch., Leg.; Finance; Airport
Aviation. B: 8/16/39. Add: 17301 Elsienna
Ave., Cleveland 44135 (216)476-1777.

Cleveland Heights. LIBBY RESNICK
    City Hall, 2953 Mayfield Rd., Cleveland Hts.
44118.

College Corner. WILMA C. BLACK
    Town Hall, Eaton St., College Corner 45003.

Columbus. FRAN RYAN (D)
    1971-. Bds: Ch., Community Services; Safety;
Devt. & Planning. Party: State Del. 1972; Ward
Committeewoman 1968-71. Org: Young Dem's.
Educ: Ohio State U. 1956 BS. Occ: Dir., Senior
Companions Program. B: 1/4/34. Add: 1452
Fronwood Dr., Columbus 43229 (614)222-7380.

Conesville. CHRISTI DARR
    Town Hall, Conesville 43811.

Conesville. SHIRLEY IRENE DILE (R)
    1974-. Bds: Finance Com. Occ: Glove
Finisher. B: 8/13/35. Add: 405 Franklin Ave.,
Conesville 43811.

Conesville. WANDA JEAN HINDEL
    Town Hall, Conesville 43811.

Conneaut. JENNIE M. BROUGHTON
City Hall, 294 Main St., Conneaut 44030.

Corning. HOLLIE LOVE
Town Hall, Main St., Corning 43730.

Corwin. DIANE PURKERY
Town Hall, Corwin 45068.

Cuyahoga Falls. MILDRED A. MOLLI (D)
1975-. Bds: Ch., Public & Industrial Improve-
ments Com.; Public Affairs Com.; Housing Com.
Party: Precinct Committeewoman 1976-78. Org: ASPA;
Amer. Society of Planning Officials; Oh. Housing
Coalition; LWV; New Dem. Coalition; Dem. Women's
Study Club; Cnty. Fed. Dem. Women; Dem. Club;
PTA. Educ: Kent State U. 1975 BA; U. of Akron
1977 MA. B: 4/28/31. Add: 2751 Fairland St.,
Cuyahoga Fls. 44221 (216)923-9921.

Danville. MARTHA GRASSBAUGH
EDNA M. SHELDON
Town Hall, Danville 43014.

Darbyville Village. SARAH ANN BUCY (R)
1974-. Org: PTA. B: 2/26/46. Add: RR 1,
Williamsport 43164.

Darbyville Village. NOAMA GRIFFITH
TRUDY L. HUFFER
ROSEMARY LEACH
RUTH ANN MASSINGALE
ROSANETTE PERKINS
RR 1, Town Hall, Williamsport 43164.

Dayton. PATRICIA M. ROACH (D)
1976-. Bds: Ch., Data Control Bd.; Public
Access Facilitating Bd. Party: State Alt. 1974.
Prev: Housing Appeal Bd. 1972-75. Org: Economic
Resource Com.; Water Resources Com.; Battered
Women Com.; Oh. Public Interest Campaign; Dem.
Club; Nat. Assoc. of Regional Councils-Intergovt.
Affairs. Educ: Oh. State U. 1962 BSEd. Occ:
Professor. B: 3/2/40. Add: 1715 Shaftesbury Rd.,
Dayton 45406 (513)225-5148.

Defiance. RITA A. KISSNER
City Hall, 324 Perry St., Defiance 43512.

Delaware. JOAN CECILE DOCHINGER (D)
1973-. Bds: Planning Cmsn.; Ch., Cnty.
Council on Aging; Parks & Recreation Bd. Party:
State Alt. 1976; Precinct Leader 1976-78. Org:
AAUW; BPW; Common Cause; LWV; Oh. Citizens
Council; NOW; WPC; Oh. Cmsn. on Status of Women;
Dem. Women's Club; Arts Festival Bd.; Women's
City Club. Educ: Cornell U. 1953 BS. B: 5/11/31.
Add: 50 Pumphrey Ter., Delaware 43015 (614)
369-3183.

Delphos. EDNA JANE NOLTE (R)
1973-. Bds: Pres. City Council. Prev: Pres.,
Firemen's Pension Bd. 1958-66. Org: Rep. Club.
Occ: Insurance Repr. B: 6/28/20. Add: 990 N.
Jefferson St. #6, Delphos 45833 (419)692-3781.

Delta. NANCY K. WOODHOUSE
Town Hall, 401 Main St., Delta 43515.

Dipton. AUDRA ROBERTS
Town Hall, Court St., Dipton 44049.

Dover. JANET J. COMELLA (R)
1972-. Bds: Ch., Utility Com.; Finance;
Safety. Org: AAUW; Cnty. Medical Aux. B:
12/10/27. Add: 1203 N. Wooster Ave., Dover
44622.

Dublin. CATHERIN HEADLEE (D)
1972-. Bds: Park & Recreation Bd.; N. Area
Mental Health & Retardation Bd.; Bicycle Com.
Party: Precinct Judge 1966-77. Org: Farm Bureau;
Cnty. Dem's; Chamber of Commerce; Cnty. Mental
Health; PTO. Occ: Farmer. B: 2/5/29. Add:
7340 Brand Rd., Dublin 43017 (614)889-2175.

East Cleveland. MAE E. STEWART
City Hall, 14340 Euclid Ave., E. Cleveland
44112.

Eastlake. BARBARA BECKER
35150 Kake Shore Blvd., Eastlake 44094.

East Liverpool. BETSY F. MILLER
City Hall, 125 W. 6th St., E. Liverpool
43920.

Empire. HELEN SKINNER
Town Hall, Empire 43926.

Englewood. ALICE E. LEDFORD (R) **
1969-. Org: BPW; Women's Rep. Club. Occ:
Teacher's Aid. B: 3/27/38. Add: 307 Oldham
Way, Englewood 45322 (513)836-5106.

Evendale. EDNA RUTH CRESS
Town Hall, 10500 Reading Rd., Evendale
45241.

Fairlawn. MARILYN L. BALL
3487 S. Smith Rd., Fairlawn 44313.

Fairlawn. BETTY L. MC KINNEY (R) **
1974-. Bds: Park & Recreation Bd. Prev:
Planning Com. 1972-74. Org: Women's Club. B:
10/31/30. Add: 3133 Cot Dr., Fairlawn 44313
(216)666-8875.

Fairview. CLAUDETTE BENSON
Town Hall, Fairview 43736.

Fairview Park. MILDRED N. NYLAND
City Hall, 20777 Lorain Rd., Fairview Pk.
44126.

Farmersville. SHIRLEY BRADLEY
BEVERLY HAWES
Town Hall, 115 E. Walnut St., Farmersville
45325.

Forest Park. LORAINE E. BLACKBURN
City Hall, 1201 W. Kemper Rd., Forest Pk.
45240.

Fostoria. BARBARA LOUISE MARLEY (D)
1975-. Bds: Council Pres.; Seneca Cnty.
Reg. Planning Cmsn. Org: ABA; Altrusa; Bureau
of Concern; Red Cross; BPW; Dem. Club; Dem.
Women. Educ: St. Mary's Coll. 1969 BA; U. of

Toledo 1972 JD. Occ: Atty. B: 6/6/47. Add: 113 N. Union St., Fostoria 44830.

Fostoria. KAREN R. MILLER
City Hall, 213 S. Main St., Fostoria 44830.

Franklin. BARBARA L. THORNTON (R)
1974-. Bds: Oh.-Ind. Regional Council of Govts.; Cnty. Human Services Bd. Prev: Cnty. Bd. of Health 1973-74. Org: Chamber of Commerce; Women's Civic Org.; Women's Rep. Club. Educ: Centre Coll. 1962 BA. Occ: Retail Merchandiser. B: 3/2/40. Add: 313 Melanie Dr., Franklin 45005 (513)746-9921.

Frazeysburg. GERALDENE C. MORAN (R)
1971-. Bds: Ch., Safety; Finance. B: 6/28/22. Add: North State, Frazeysburg 43822.

Fredericksburg. ALICE MARCEILLE CRAMER (R)
1972-. Bds: Council Pres. Org: Rep. Women; OES. Occ: Accounting Clerk. B: 5/20/14. Add: 351 Diagonal, Fredericksburg 44627.

Fredericksburg. HARRIET ANN LEMON
Town Hall, N. Mill St., Fredericksburg 44627.

Gahanna. JUDY PETERSON
200 S. Hamilton Rd., Gahanna 43230.

Galena. HELEN G. CAMPBELL
Town Hall, Municipal Bldg., Galena 43021.

Galion. ELIZABETH A. MC HENRY (R)
1971-. Bds: Ch., Streets, Sewer & Alley Com.; Betterment Area; Police, Fire, Health Com. Party: State Del. 1970; Precinct Committeewoman 1966-77. Org: Rep. Women's Club. B: 12/21/27. Add: 1263 Hardingway E., Galion 44833 (419)468-1526.

Gambier. JOSEPHINE G. STROME (R) **
1974-. Occ: Secretary. B: 11/4/23. Add: 406 Wiggin St., Gambier 43022 (614)427-2671.

Garrettsville. MARY HELEN FOLGER
1970-. Bds: Ch., Parks & Recreation; Finance; Fire Dept. Dependency Bd. Prev: Cnty. Bd. of Health 1976-77. Org: Nat. Fed. of Press Women. Occ: Magazine Editor. B: 9/10/29. Add: 8215 Water, Garrettsville 44231 (216)527-2179.

Gates Mills. VIRGINIA BISHOP LANGMACK (R)
1972-. Bds: Ch., Public Relations; Safety Com.; Budget Com. Org: Community Club; Rep. Women's Club; WPC. Educ: Case Western U. 1951 BA. B: 1/24/20. Add: Gates Rd., Gates Mills 44040 (216)423-4405.

Geneva. CAROLINE C. HENN
81 E. Main St., Geneva 44041.

Geneva-on-the-Lake. MARTHA PERA WOODWARD (D)
1948-. Ch., Streets & Sidewalks; Police & Fire Safety; Sewers & Sanitation. Party: Cnty. Committeewoman 1940-60. Org: Dem. Club. Educ: Miami U. 1940 BA. Occ: Resort Owner/Operator. B: 4/8/17. Add: 5006 Mapleton Bch., Geneva-on-the-Lake 44043 (216)466-8650.

Georgetown. ELIZABETH ERNST
Town Hall, State St., Georgetown 45121.

Germantown. CATHERINE E. COGHILL
SUSANNE GREEN
Town Hall, Walnut & Center Sts., Germantown 45327.

Glenford. LORA M. RIDENOUR (R)
1974-. Bds: Ch., Bicentennial; Park Bd.; V-Pres., Firemen's Auxiliary. Party: Cnty. Committeewoman 1960. Org: Historical Society. B: 11/26/13. Add: S. Main St. #222, Glenford 43739.

Glenford. HELEN TAYLOR
Town Hall, Glenford 43739.

Glenmont. CAROLANN PURDY (D)
1976-. Bds: Council Pres. B: 12/5/41. Add: Box 97, Garland St., Glenmont 44628.

Glenmont. BIANCA M. WEAVER (D)
1975-. Add: Box 443, Glenmont 44628.

Glenwillow. NORMA L. HUMMER
Town Hall, 29500 Pettibone Rd., Glenwillow 44139.

Golf Manor. ROSEMARY HARDING
6540 Wiehe Rd., City Hall, Golf Manor 45237.

Golf Manor. ETHEL MITZMAN (D)
1975-. Bds: Ch., Transportation; Ch., Health; Finance. Party: Precinct Leader 1965-69; 1971-77. Prev: Dep. Registrar for License Plates 1971. Org: Women's Club. B: 2/4/31. Add: 6426 Wiehe Rd., Golf Manor 45237.

Gordon. MARTHA BERSTEIN
Town Hall, 300 Center St., Gordon 45329.

Grandview Heights. ANN LARRICK (I)
1974-. Bds: Bd. of Trustees, Health Planning Fed.; Areawide Bd. of Review; Ch., Human Resources Task Force. Org: Women's Org. Educ: La. State U. 1944 BS. B: 9/19/23. Add: 1082 Broadview Ave., Grandview Hts. 43212 (614) 486-6901.

Granville. JOAN BURROWS KENT (R)
1975-. Bds: Ch., Safety & Health; Finance. Org: United Way Bd. Educ: Denison U. 1957 BA. B: 8/20/35. Add: 555 Burg St., Granville 43023 (614)587-0707.

Greenfield. ROSE ANN BROWNELL (D)
1975-. Bds: Ch., Parks & Property Com.; Finance; Streets & Streetlighting. Org: BPW; AAUW; Dem. Club. Educ: Marshall U. 1960 BS; Toledo U. 1969 MA. Occ: Substitute Teacher. B: 9/9/38. Add: 728 Madison Pl., Greenfield 45123 (513)981-3048.

Green Springs. DAWN E. BLODGETT
Town Hall, 137 S. Broadway, Green Springs 44836.

Greenwich. HELEN M. WILSON
Town Hall, Main & Townsend, Greenwich 44837.

Grove City. ANN JENNETTE MYERS
City Hall, 42 E. Park St., Grove City 43123.

Hamilton. ANN ANTENEN (D)
1975-. Bds: German Vlg. Cmsn.; Ch., Budget Com.; Historic Preservation Survey Com. Prev: German Vlg. Cmsn. 1973-75. Org: Institute of Cultural Affairs. Educ: U. of Cincinnati 1946 BS. B: 5/19/25. Add: 30 Pinecrest Ln., Hamilton 45013 (513)868-5834.

Hammersville. MARY HANNAH
Town Hall, Hammersville 45130.

Hanoverton. PEGGY L. KNESTRICK (D)
1974-. Bds: Ch., Parks Com.; Ch., Bldg. Com.; Finance Com. Party: Precinct Committeewoman 1965-77. Org: Cnty. Exec. Com. B: 1/31/28. Add: 10138 Second St., Hanoverton 44423 (216)223-1081

Harbor View. MARY A. WEATHERWAX
Town Hall, 127 Lakeview Dr., Harbor View 43434

Harrison. ALICE A. MASON
Town Hall, 200 Harrison Ave., Harrison 45030.

Harveysburg. EVELYN BALL
Town Hall, Harveysburg 45032.

Heath. VIRA L. WISE (R) **
1971-. Party: Precinct Com. 1975- . Org: Amer. Business Women's Assoc.; Zonta; Women's Rep. Club. Occ: Accountant. B: 5/15/31. Add: 732 Radian Dr., Heath 43055 (614)522-4456.

Highland Heights. NANCY L. BIRD (R)
1975-. Bds: Safety & Service Com.; Park & Recreation Cmsn.; Area Recreation Council. Party: Precinct Leader Asst. Org: Women's Community Club; WPC; LWV; PTG. B: 1/7/41. Add: 722 Bishop Rd., Highland Hts. 44143 (216)461-2440.

Highland Heights. CAROL JEAN BROWNGARDT (D)
1975-. Bds: Ch., Leg. & Finance Com.; Drainage Com.; Mayfield Area Recreation Council. Org: LWV; WPC; Parent-Teacher Group. Educ: Oh. U. 1967 BSEd. B: 2/9/41. Add: 5917 Williamsburg Dr., Highland Hts. 44143 (216)461-2440.

Hoytville. CAROLYN F. KLINE
Town Hall, Hoytville 43529.

Hudson. ELAINE GRAHAM JOHNSTON (I)
1975-. Bds: Ch., Utilities Com.; Joint Govt. Facilities; Joint Cemetary Bd. Org: LWV. Educ: Baldwin-Wallace Coll. 1950 BA; Kent State U. 1972 BS. Occ: Librarian. Add: 35 Nantucket Dr., Hudson 44236 (216)653-6651.

Huron. VERA M. MC COMB
1973-. Bds: Com. on Age. Org: Ohio Retired Teachers Assoc. Educ: Oberlin Coll. 1932 BA; U. of Pa. 1936 MSW. B: 10/7/11. Add: 504 Cleveland Rd. W., Huron 44839 (419)433-5000.

Indian Hill. BETTY S. STEER
City Hall, 6525 Drake Rd., Indian Hill 45243.

Iron Dale. ETHEL M. NELSON
Town Hall, Iron Dale 43932.

Ironton. DOROTHY L. NENNI
City Hall, 4th & Railroad Sts., Ironton 45638.

Jacksonburg. BETH CROUT
BONNIE J. MARCUM
Town Hall, RR 1, Jacksonburg 45067.

Jackson Center. DORIS ANN WARE (D)
1974-. Bds: Ch., Public Property; Capital Improvement. Org: PTA; PTO; Girls Scouts. Occ: Truck Builder. B: 9/5/23. Add: 303 Davis St., Jackson Ctr. 45334.

Jamestown. PHYLLIS A. LANG (D)
1973-. Org: PTO. Occ: Accountant. B: 7/30/34. Add: 48 W. Xenia St., Jamestown 45335 (315)675-5311.

Jeromesville. CAROLINE C. ATTERHOLT (D)
Party: Dem. Central Committeewoman. Prev: Zoning Bd. 1976. B: 8/10/10. Add: 33 N. High St., Jeromesville 44840 (419)368-3086.

Kelleys Island. MARY SCHOCK (D)
1971-. Bds: Planning Cmsn. Occ: Post Office Clerk. B: 11/4/16. Add: Division St., Kelleys Island 43438.

Kent. BARBARA ROUSH WATSON (D)
1976-. Bds: Ch., Parks & Recreation, Finance, Personnel. Org: LWV; Dem. Women's Club; PTA; Ohio Federation Dem. Women. Educ: Ohio U. 1958 BA; Stephen Austin State U. 1963 MA. B: 11/13/36. Add: 1224 Fairview Dr., Kent 44240 (216)698-8100.

Kettering. NORMA H. KEISTER (I)
1975-. Dist: 3. Bds: Transportation Coord. Com.; Reg. Planning Com.; Open Space Com. Party: Precinct Captain 1973-75. Org: Municipal League; LWV; Planned Parenthood; Rep. Women's Club; PTA. B: 6/4/22. Add: 1100 Pepper Hill Dr., Kettering 45429 (513)296-2400.

Kingston. BEVERLY A. CONGROVE
Town Hall, Kingston 45644.

Kipton. JUDITH BRYDEN
Town Hall, Court St., Kipton 44049.

Kirtland. IRMA V. HAYDU (R) **
1973-. Bds: Planning-Zoning Cmsn. Org: ILGWU; Civic League. B: 4/24/09. Add: 8569 Euclid-Chardon Rd., Kirtland 44094 (216) 256-3332.

LaGrange. RUTH A. JOHNSON (R)
1963-. Bds: Finance Com.; Street Com.; Council Pres. Org: Civic Improvement League. Occ: Housekeeper. B: 8/31/13. Add: 310 W. Main, LaGrange 44050.

Lakeline. CARLA LOUISE CEFARATTI (D)
1975-. Bds: Asst. Finance Dir. Org: Ohio
Educ. Assoc.; Ohio Council for Soc. Studies.
Educ: Bowling Green State U. 1973 BS. Occ:
Teacher. B: 8/5/51. Add: 33811 Lake Shore Blvd.,
Lakeline 44094.

Lakeline. LOIS KAY
Town Hall, 33801 Lk. Shr. Blvd., Lakeline
44094.

Lancaster. URSULA LANNING (D)
1975-. Bds: Ch., Wage Negotiating Com.;
Finance Com.; Ch., Health Com. Party: Precinct
Committeewoman 1967-73. Prev: Library Bd. 1965-
69. Org: Dem. Club; Women's Dem. Club. Occ: Art
Teacher. B: 4/19/30. Add: 321 Brumfield Rd.,
Lancaster 43130 (614)654-1725.

Latty. DONNA GRAY
Town Hall, Alexander St., Latty 45855.

Lebanon. ELEANOR C. ULLUM (R) **
1973-. Bds: Street Com.; Park & Cemetery Com.;
Finance. Party: Precinct Poll Worker 1955-68.
Prev:Chief Deputy Probate Court Clerk 1948-61.
Org: BPW; Rep. Women's Club. B: 11/26/17. Add:
189 Summit St., Lebanon 45036 (513)932-2498.

Leesville. NANCY DEWALT
HAZEL GARTELL
Town Hall, Public Square, Leesville 44639.

Lewisburg. LINDA CREECH
BETTY H. GILMER
Town Hall, 112 S. Commerce, Lewisburg 45338.

Lewisville. DARLENE CARPENTER
NETTIE HILL
Town Hall, Railroad St., Lewisville 43754.

Lexington. RITA NEAL ERRE
Town Hall, 44 W. Main St., Lexington 44904.

Lima. DOROTHY J. RIKER (D)
1973-. Bds: Leg., Code & Judicial Com.; Land
Use, Building & Zoning; Planning & Devt. Party:
Precinct Committeewoman 1960-66; V-Ch., Cnty.
Com. 1960-64; State Del. 1960. Org: LWV; Dem.
Women's Club; YWCA; PTA. Occ: YWCA Administrative
Asst. B: 11/23/20. Add: 326 S. Collett St.,
Lima 45805.

Lincoln Heights. MARY L. EPPS (D)
1976-. Bds: Public Improvement; Law Com.
Party: Precinct 1973-75. Prev: Charter 1974-75.
Org: Day Care Pres. B: 10/28/33. Add: 1221
Congress Ct., Lincoln Hts. 45215 (513)733-5900.

Linndale. LORETTA BAISCH
RITA PAPCUM
Town Hall, 4016 W. 119th St., Linndale 44135.

Lockbourne. BETTY P. MC CUMBER
Town Hall, 85 Commerce St., Lockbourne 43126.

Lockington. CAROL SCHULZ
Town Hall, Lockington 45356.

Logan. SYLVIA LOUISE SMITH (R) **
1972-. Bds: Ch., Safety Com. Org: Senior
Citizens Council; County Rep. Women's Club.
Occ: Secretary. B: 6/28/20. Add: 388 N.
Mulberry St., Logan 43138 (614)385-3016.

Lyndhurst. DOROTHY ROBERTSON (R)
1976-. Bds: Service & Utilities Com.; Parks
& Buildings; Legislative. Org: LWV; Rep. Club.
B: 3/18/34. Add: 5268 Edenhurst, Lyndhurst
44124 (216)449-4159.

Macksburg. INA BATES
WILMA GILDOW
Town Hall, Macksburg 45746.

Madeira. MARY ANNE CHRISTIE (R)
1975-. Party: Precinct Exec. 1972-75. Org:
Historical Society; Cnty. Women's Rep. Club;
PTA. Occ: Realtor. B: 11/17/34. Add: 6225
Margo Ln., Cincinnati 45227 (513)561-7228.

Magnetic Springs. SHELIA KITCHEN
Town Hall, Magnetic Springs 43036.

Magnolia. THERESA L. RICH (D)
1974-. Bds: Planning Com. Party: Cnty.
Committeewoman 1971-78. Org: Dem. Club. Occ:
Office Clerk. B: 3/27/20. Add: 121 Brady St.,
Magnolia 44643.

Mansfield. VELITA W. KINNEY
City Hall, 27 W. 2nd St., Mansfield 44902.

Marietta. JANE CHOVAN (R)
1975-. Bds: Ch., Traffic & Transportation
Com.; Water & Sewer Com.; Streets, Sidewalks,
Bridges & Lights Com. Org: Rep. Exec. Com.;
Young Rep's. Occ: Dental Asst. B: 2/22/49.
Add: 401 Spring St., Marietta 45750.

Marietta. MARGARET A. YEAGER
City Hall, 301 Putman St., Marietta 45750.

Marion. RUTH I. KELLEY (D)
1971-. Bds: Ch., Utility Com.; Finance Com.;
Zoning Com. Party: Precinct Committeewoman
1974-75. Prev: Ward Councilwoman 1972-76. Org:
Industrial Club; Parents Without Partners; Cnty.
Dem. Club. Occ: Secretary. B: 10/23/28. Add:
889 Sheridan Rd., Marion 43302 (614)383-3123.

Marion. ELIZABETH ANNE MC KINLEY (R)
1975-. Bds: Ch., Codes & Regulations Com.;
Ch., Reg. Planning Cmsn.; Sewer Com.; Hospital
Com. Org: Rep. Club; Ohio School Counselors
Assoc. Educ: Ohio State U. 1949 BS; 1969 MEd.
Occ: School Counselor. B: 4/27/24. Add: 333
Reed Ave., Marion 43302 (614)383-3123.

Marysville. BARBARA J. TIMMONS
City Hall, 6th & Main Sts., Marysville
43040.

Mason. ELIZABETH PLANITX
City Hall, 202 W. Main St., Mason 45040.

Massillon. MARTHA A. HOWELL (D)
    1975-. Bds: Mayors Cmsn. on Aging; Bd. of
Health; Ch., Health & Welfare Com. Prev: Cnty.
Bd. of Mental Retardation 1976. Org: LWV;
Women's Dem. Club. Educ: Catholic U. 1947 BS.
B: 10/24/20. Add: 527 Grosvenor NW, Massillon
44646.

Massillon. HELEN E. MAIER
    City Hall, Municipal Gov't. Ctr., Massillon
44644.

Mayfield Heights. JOSEPHINE M. BRICE
    City Hall, 6154 Mayfield Rd., Mayfield Hts.
44124.

Mayfield Heights. MARGARET ANN RIEDEL
    1973-. Bds: Trustee, Cemetery; Ch., Leg. Com.;
Bldg. Com. Prev: Mayor's Adv.; Bd. of Zoning
Appeals 1968-71. Org: Citizens League; WPC; LWV;
PTA. Occ: Administrative Asst. B: 7/4/34. Add:
1681 Hawthorne Dr., Mayfield Hts. 44124 (216)
464-7816.

McComb. MARY E. STERRET
    Town Hall, McComb 45858.

Medina. SALLY A. GIOVINAZZO
    1973-. Bds: Recreation Cmsn.; Cnty. Manpower;
Cnty. Adv. Council. Prev: Citizens Adv. Com.
1970-73. Org: Chamber of Commerce; LWV; AAUW;
PTA. Educ: Oh. State U. 1959 BSEd. B: 9/9/38.
Add: 736 Weymouth Rd., Medina 44256 (216)
725-8861.

Medina. MARY LOUISE GREENWOOD (R)
    1976-. Bds: Planning & Zoning Cmsn.; Health,
Safety & Sanitation Com.; Public Properties Com.
Org: Hospital Women's Aux. B: 12/3/24. Add:
965 W. Liberty St., Medina 44256 (216)725-8861.

Mentor-on-the-Lake. VERNITA LOUISE SAVAGE (R)
    1975-. Bds: Ch., Ordinance Com.; Charter
Review Com.; Safety Com. Prev: Clerk of Council
1973-76; City Records Cmsn. 1975- ; Secretary,
Planning & Zoning Cmsn. 1972-74; Secretary,
Charter Review Cmsn. 1973-74; Income Tax Admin-
istrator 1968-72. Org: Right to Life Society;
Rep. Women; Nat. Org. of Rep. Women. B: 9/5/42.
Add: 7707 Fern Dr., Mentor-on-the-Lake 44060
(216)257-7216.

Middleburg Heights. DORIS LINGE
    City Hall, 15700 Bagley Rd., Middleburg Hts.
44130.

Middletown. MARY ALICE MACK (I)
    1971-. Bds: Park Bd. Occ: Accountant. B:
5/11/23. Add: 304 The Alameda, Middletown 45042
(513)425-7831.

Milan. EVELYN K. GILBERT
    Town Hall, 24 Public Sq., Milan 44846.

Miles. GEVENE C. SPREEANCENERE
    City Hall, 34 W. State St., Miles 44446.

Milledgeville. ANNA M. ANDERSON
    Town Hall, Main St., Milledgeville 43142.

Milledgeville. BARBARA A. GROOMS
    Box 31, Milledgeville 43142.

Milledgeville. WHANETTA HAFFNER
                PEGGY SLOAN
    Town Hall, Main St., Milledgeville 43142.

Millersburg. CYNTHIA BECK
                KAREN S. SNYDER
    Town Hall, W. Jackson St., Millersburg
44654.

Millersport. BETTY BUTATO
    Town Hall, Lancaster St., Millersport 43046.

Millersport. JUANITA B. CLARK (D)
    1974-. Bds: Drainage; Pres. Pro Tem. B:
5/21/28. Add: P.O. Box 5, Millersport 43046.

Mineral City. BETTY BELL
    Town Hall, N. High St., Mineral City 44656.

Minerva. LORRAINE R. SMITH
    Town Hall, 209 N. Market St., Minerva
44657.

Minerva Park. SHIRLEY MOURAS
    Town Hall, 2829 Minerva Pk. Rd., Minerva Pk.
43224.

Mogadore. PATRICIA A. MYERS (R)
    1974-. Bds: Ch., Safety Com.; Parks Com.;
Utilities. Org: PTA. B: 8/1/44. Add: 3421
Curtis St., Mogadore 44260 (216)628-9748.

Monroeville. KATHRYN R. MYERS (R)
    1971-. Bds: Planning Cmsn. Org: BPW;
Historical Soc. Occ: Journalist. B: 9/30/27.
Add: 3 Knob Hill, Rt. 1, Monroeville 44847
(419)465-2922.

Montgomery. ALMA M. BLAZIC (R)
    1973-. Bds: Ch., Finance Com.; Com. Con-
servation & Safety. Org: Women's Club; Rep.
Women; NE Women's Rep. Club. Educ: Cornell U.
1944 BA. B: 8/14/23. Add: 7465 Fourwinds Dr.,
Cincinnati 45242 (513)891-2424.

Montgomery. FLORENCE W. KENNEDY (R)
    1973-. Bds: Oh.-Ind.-Ky. Council of Govts.
Prev: Charter Cmsn. 1970- . Org: LWV; Rep.
Club. B: 10/10/20. Add: 7228 Pfeiffer Rd.,
Montgomery 45242 (513)891-2424.

Moraine. RUTH GERHARDT
                BEVE GILBERT
                INEZ LAWRENCE
    City Hall, 4200 Dryden Rd., Moraine 45439.

Moreland Hills. GERTRUDE E. CRUXTON (I)
    1976-. Party: Precinct Committeewoman 1974-
77. Org: Rep. Women's Club. B: 9/29/11. Add:
50 Hemlock La., Moreland Hills 44022 (216)
248-5906.

Moreland Hills. DOROTHY B. MAXWELL
    Town Hall, 4350 Som Center Rd., Moreland
Hills 44022.

Mount Blanchard. MARILYN ANN LEASE (R)
1976-. Bds: Cnty. Reg. Planning; Cnty. Park
Com. Prev: Vlg. Clerk 1972-76. Org: Cnty. Rep.
Women's Club. Occ: TV Sales Clerk. B: 5/7/36.
Add: 210 S. Main, Mt. Blanchard 45867.

Mount Healthy. MARIAN G. BLUM (D)
1973-. Bds: Ch., Public Relations; Safety;
Community Services. Org: Dem. Club; PTA. Educ:
U. of Cincinnati 1947 BS. Occ: Teacher. B:
12/9/25. Add: 7849 Elizabeth St., Mt. Healthy
45231.

Mount Healthy. ROSE MELVIN
Perry & McMakin Ave., Mt. Healthy 45231.

Mount Pleasant. JUDITH A ROBERTS (D)
1976-. Bds: Street Com.; Financial. B:
5/4/43. Add: Box 102, Mt. Pleasant 43939.

Mount Sterling. PATRICIA A. RILEY (D)
1976-. Bds: Ch., Finance Com.; Water & Sewer.
Org: FDIC Adv. Council; Historical Soc.; BPW.
Occ: Supervisor. B: 7/2/29. Add: 215 E. Main
St., Mt. Sterling 43143 (614)469-7301.

Mount Vernon. NANCY R. VAIL
40 Public Sq., Mt. Vernon 43050.

Mount Vernon. BETTY K. WINAND (D)
1976-. Bds: Civic Improvement Corp.; City
Planning Cmsn.; Ch., Senior Citizen Ctr. Prev:
Recreation Bd. 1969-76. Org: BPW; Soroptimist;
Chamber of Commerce. Occ: Accountant. B:3/7/29.
Add: 500 F. Gambler St., Mt. Vernon 43050
(614)392-8016.

Navarre. REBECCA S. SCHAUER (D)
1973-. Bds: Tree Cmsn. Prev: Bicentennial
Cmsn. 1975-77. Org: Nat. Assoc. Bank Women;
Amer. Institute of Banking; Historical Society.
Occ: Asst. V-Pres. & Manager, Bank. Add: 146
W. Wooster St., Navarre 44662 (216)879-5508.

Nelsonville. HOPE WOODSON
City Hall, 29 Fayette St., Nelsonville 45764.

New Athens. CAROL HUFFMAN
Town Hall, Fire House, New Athens 43981.

New Athens. MARY ALICE ROMSHAK
1968-. B: 4/2/22. Add: New Athens 43981
(614)968-3434.

New Boston. REBECCA FREMONT
Town Hall, 3940 Gallia St., New Boston 45662.

Newburgh Heights. ELEANOR F. SEJD (R)
Org: Rep. Club. B: 5/14/20. Add: 4421
Alpha Ave., Newburgh Hts. 44105 (216)641-4650.

New Knoxville. CAROL T. IRETON
Town Hall, Main & W. Bremen, New Knoxville
45871.

New Lebanon. BETTY JANE MITCHELL (D)
1969-. Bds: Safety Com. Org: Dem. Club.
B: 10/25/20. Add: 451 S. Clayton Rd., New
Lebanon 45345 (513)687-1341.

New Miami. GERALDINE RILEY (D)
1974-. Bds: Ch., Finance Com.; Water & Sewer
Com.; Streets & Lights. Org: Town Improvement
Assoc. B: 2/20/40. Add: 268 Whitaker Ave.,
New Miami 45011 (513)863-4227.

New Rome. BETTY J. FIFE
Town Hall, 30 Maple Dr., New Rome 43228.

New Straitsville. MARGARET BOYLE
BETTY ST. CLAIR
Town Hall, Clark St., New Straitsville
43766.

New Vienna. BONNIE WATTERS
Town Hall, Main St., New Vienna 45159.

New Weston. MARTHA S. GILLILAND
Town Hall, Main St., New Weston 45348.

North Baltimore. MURIEL A. HALDERMAN
GLORIA SPONSLER
Town Hall, 207 N. Main St., N. Baltimore
45872.

North Bend. MINNIE MAE FOSSITT
CORDA WALTERS
Town Hall, 25 Taylor Ave., N. Bend 45052.

North College Hill. MARGARET M. HILLER (D)
1973-. Bds: Ch., Streets & Hwys. Com.;
Public Utilities Com.; Laws & Rules Com. Org:
Dem. Club; PTA; Widow & Widowers & Singles.
Occ: Food Service Worker. B:4/4/27. Add:
1622 DeArmand Ave., N. College Hl. 45239
(513)521-7413.

North Fairfield. BONNIE R. D'ETTORRE
Town Hall, N. Main St., N. Fairfield 44855.

North Olmsted. JANET A. SARINGER (D) **
1971-. Bds: Ch., Environmental Com.; Ch.,
Long Range Planning; Bldg., Zoning & Dev.;
Recreation. Party: County Central Com. 1971- .
Org: WPC. B: 5/2/33. Add: 23336 Stoneybrook
Dr., North Olmsted 44070 (216)734-2419.

North Olmsted. DELORES D. SHARPE
5206 Dover Center Rd., N. Olmsted 44020.

North Ridgeville. LEOTA B. MITCHELL (D) **
1973-. Bds: Administrative Com. Prev:
County Recorder 1949-73; Bd. of Educ. 1934-36;
Supervisor, Dept. of Public Welfare. Org:
Assoc. of Trustees & Clerks; OES; Altrusa.
Occ: Retired. B: 2/6/01. Add: 33738 Bain-
bridge Rd., North Ridgeville 44039 (216)
327-5731.

North Ridgeville. SALLY L. RICHARDS
City Hall, 7307 Avon Beldon Rd., North
Ridgeville 44039.

North Robinson. MARTHA FROST (R)
B: 6/17/02. Add: Box 109, N. Robinson
44856 (419)562-6789.

North Robinson. REBA A. HUBER (D)
1970-. Bds: Council Pres. Occ: Nurse. B:
2/26/15. Add: Box 123, N. Robinson 44856.

North Robinson. MYRA WAGNER
    Town Hall, N. Robinson 44856.

Norton. SHIRLEY L. MC GUIRE
    City Hall, 3230 Greenwich Rd., Norton 44203.

Oberlin. GERALDINE CATHERINE DONALDSON (D) **
    1971-. Org: Black Political Assembly; Minor-
    ity Caucus; NAACP. B: 11/24/20. Add: 233 S.
    Pleasant St., Oberlin 44074 (216)774-1519;
    774-4357.

Octa. BEATRICE ROBERTS
    Town Hall, 8029 Allen St., NW, Octa 43160.

Ohio City. FLORENCE BRUBAKER (D)
    1970-. Bds: Council Pres. B: 10/23/08. Add:
    102 N. Main St., Ohio City 45874.

Olmsted Falls. BEVERLY B. SMITH (R) **
    1972-. Prev: Charter Cmsn. 1970-71. Org:
    Bicentennial Cmsn. Educ: Miami U. of Ohio 1959
    BA. Occ: Teacher. B: 9/9/37. Add: 8346 Lewis
    Rd., Olmsted Falls 44138 (216)235-3585.

Onatrio. BETTY J. MOHLER
    Town Hall, 377 Park Ave., Ontario 44862.

Oregon. MARY ANN CASHEN (D) **
    1974-. Bds: Ch., Public Utilities Com.; Drain-
    age & Roads Com.; Recreation & Parks. Party:
    Precinct Representative 1968-70. Org: BPW; Fed.
    of Teachers; Dem. Club. Educ: U. of Toledo 1952
    BA; U. of Toledo 1959 MA. Occ: Teacher. B:
    7/15/30. Add: 4134 Starr Ave., Oregon 43616
    (419)693-9371.

Orient. RUTH ALSPAUGH
        MARIE CRAWFORD
        BETTY SHERRICK
    Town Hall, 7869 Railroad St., Orient 43146.

Orrville. ELIZABETH K. HERBERT
    207 N. St., City Hall, Orrville 44667.

Orrville. ADA LOUISE PARKER XANDER
    1975-. Bds: Ch., Transportation Com.; Recre-
    ation & Parks; Health & Safety. Org: PTA; Rep.
    Club. Educ: State U. of Iowa 1950 BA. Occ:
    Tutor. B: 1/31/28. Add: 125 Wabash Ave.,
    Orrville 44667 (216)682-3931.

Otway. ETHEL HAMILTON
        VIRGINIA MILLER
        GLADYS RILEY
        MARY SANDERSON
    Town Hall, Otway 45657.

Oxford. CAROLINE H. HOLLIS
    City Hall, 101 E. High St., Oxford 45056.

Oxford. GEORGINA SILLIMAN (D)
    1973-. Bds: Planning Cmsn. Org: Urban
    League; Women's Club; OES. Educ: W. NM U. 1935
    BS; George Peabody Coll. 1939 MA. Occ: Insurance
    Sales. B: 5/27/06. Add: 6275 Timothy Lane,
    Oxford 45056 (513)523-4432.

Painsville. KATHLEEN M. COTTER
    City Hall, 7 Richmond St., Painsville 44077.

Parma. EVELYN M. KOPCHAK
        DORIS P. KRAWCZYK
    City Hall, 6611 Ridge Rd., Parma 44129.

Pataskala. BARBARA JORDON
           SUSAN WESTALL
    Town Hall, Main St., Pataskala 43062.

Pepper Pike. KATHRYN P. EAKEN (I)
    1969-. Bds: Com. on Road & Safety; Ch.,
    Com. on Public Relations. B: 11/30/08. Add:
    30699 Landerwood Dr., Pepper Pike 44124
    (216)831-8500.

Perrsburg. BETTY J. CALEVRO
           MARIE E. SNYDER
    City Hall, 201 W. Iniana Ave., Perrsburg
    43551.

Phillipsburg. MARY C. RAY HARTMEN
    Town Hall, 13 Eastman St., Phillipsburg
    45354.

Pioneer. EVELYN DEETZ
    Town Hall, Pioneer 43554.

Pitsburg. MARLENE BOOHER
          IVALOU CROSSLEY
    Town Hall, Lumber St., Pitsburg 45358.

Pleasantville. HAZEL ENGLE
    Town Hall, Columbus St., Pleasantville
    43148.

Poland. GRACE M.HEWIS
    Town Hall, Poland 44514.

Portage. KATHERINE LENHART
    Town Hall, Portage 43451.

Powell. DONNA M. LAWRENCE (I)
    1952-. Org: Retail Clerks Union; Civic Assoc.
    Occ: Cashier. B: 5/4/23. Add: 160 E. Olentangy
    St., Powell 43065.

Powell. MARY MATHENY
    Town Hall, Powell 43065.

Quincy. MARTHA STEWART (I)
    1976-. Bds: Regional Planning; Water &
    Agriculture Control. B: 6/12/21. Add: 303
    Carlisle St., Quincy 43343.

Racine. MAZINE S. WINGETT
    Town Hall, 3rd St., Racine 45771.

Rarden. BERTHA FOSTER
         LORETTA FOUCH
    Town Hall, Rarden 45671.

Rawson. CHARLOTTE ELLISON
         SHARON KELLY
    Town Hall, Main St., Rawson 45881.

Rawson. GLEANNA WARD (R)
    1977-. Bds: Park Bd.; Financial Com. B:
    6/3/20. Add: 150 Bolt St., Rawson 45881.

Rayland. VIRGINIA YOUNKINS
    Town Hall, 195 Main St., Rayland 43943.

Rendville. LUCY HARRIS
         DARLENE MAYLE
     Town Hall, Rendville 43775.

Revenna. IRENE A. ROTH
     City Hall, 210 Parkway, Revenna 44266.

Reynoldsburg. JO ANN DAVIDSON (R)
     1967-. Bds: Ch., Council Finance Com.;
Council Service Com.; Bd. of Trustees, Oh. Municipal League. Party: State Del. 1976; State Alt.
1974; Nat. Del. 1976; Cnty. Rep. Del. Ch. 1973-
77; Ward Committeewoman 1961-77. Org: Oh. Trade
Exec. Assoc.; WPC. Occ: Finance Specialist. B:
9/28/27. Add: 6571 Malone Dr., Reynoldsburg
43068 (614)866-6391.

Richfield. E. JUNE FEIBER (D)
     1967-. Bds: Pres., Vlg. Council. B: 6/25/22.
Add: 3761 Grant St., Richfield 44286 (216)
659-9700.

Richmond. CONNIE M. GEARY
     Town Hall, Richmond 43944.

Richmond. MABEL H. STEITZ (D)
     1962-. Org: Dem. Club. B: 1/9/11. Add:
Box 31, High St., Richmond 43944 (614)765-4329.

Richmond Heights. MARCIA J. STARKEY (D) **
     1973-. Bds: Recreation Bd. Party: Local
Precinct Com. 1963- . Org: Dem. Club; Women's
Traffic Club. Occ: Supervisor of Transportation.
B: 1/29/29. Add: 144 Brush Rd., Richmond Heights
44143. (216)486-2474.

Rittman. MURIEL JORDEN
         DELORIS WRIGHT
     City Hall, 30 N. Main St., Rittman 44270.

Rochester. BETTY WINFIELD
     Town Hall, State Rte. 511, Wellington 44090.

Rocky Ridge. DE ANNA M. BAUMERT
     Town Hall, 2nd St., Rocky Ridge 43458.

Rocky Ridge. BERNADINE L. LACER (D)
     Bds: Ch., Finance Com.; Ch., Fire Bd. Party:
Precinct Leader 1976-78. Org: Amer. Fed. of
Govt. Employees; Dem. Women's Club. Educ: Riverside Hospital School of Nursing 1932 RN. B:
2/28/09. Add: 1330 N. Main St., Rocky Ridge
43458.

Rocky River. BARBARA D. GIBBS (R)
     1975-. Bds: Ch., Planning & Zoning. Prev:
Charter Review Com. 1973. Org: LWV; Meals on
Wheels. Educ: Ia. State U. 1947 BS. B: 12/3/25.
Add: 3571 Dellbank Dr., Rocky Rvr. 44116 (216)
331-0600.

Roseville. DONNA BARKER
         HELEN KILDOW
     Town Hall, Main St., Roseville 43777.

Russells Point. LILLIAN J. BEATLEY
         GLADYS HASSAN
     Town Hall, Orchard Is. Rd., Russells Pt.
43348.

St. Bernard. CAROLYN E. UNGRUHE (D) **
     1973-. Org: Chamber of Commerce. Occ: Bank
Teller. B: 3/28/38. Add: 4342 Vine St., St.
Bernard 45217 (513)579-5525.

St. Marys. MARLENE E. SCHUMANN
     City Hall, 101 E. Spring St., St. Marys
45885.

Salem. SUSAN SCHMID
     230 W. 5th St., Salem 44460.

Salem. JOYCE S. WILSON
     City Hall, 231 S. Broadway, Salem 44460.

Salesville. MARTHA LONG
         SHIRLEY STILLION
     Town Hall, Salesville 43778.

Salineville. JOSEPHINE SHAFF (I)
     1975-. Bds: Ch., Safety Com. Org: NEA.
Educ: Penn State U. 1931 BA. B: 5/15/09. Add:
516 1/2 Jefferson St., Salineville 43945.

Shaker Heights. ELEANORE T. ADAMS (R)
     1966-. Bds: Ch., Communications; Ch.,
Community Housing; Commercial Areas Task Force.
Prev: V-Mayor 1971-76; Planning Cmsn. 1966-70.
B: 7/16/15. Add: 3031 Manchester Rd., Shaker
Hts. 44122 (216)752-5000.

Shaker Heights. KATHLEEN LUCAS BARBER (D)
     1973-. Bds: Ch., Bldg. & Housing Inspection;
Ch., Environment; Finance. Party: State Del.
1976; Nat. Del. 1976; Precinct Leader 1972-73.
Org: APSA; Oh. Assoc. of Economists & Political
Scientists; AAUP; Midwest Political Science
Assoc.; LWV; Citizens League; WPC; Dem. Club;
New Dem. Coalition; Historical Soc. Educ:
Wellesley Coll. 1944 BA; Case Western Reserve
U. 1965 MA; 1968 PhD. Occ: Coll. Professor.
B: 4/9/24. Add: 3005 Kingsley Rd., Shaker Hts.
44122 (216)752-5000.

Shaker Heights. LILLIAN JANIS (D)
     1975-. Bds: Council Com. on Aging; Bldg.
Dept. & Inspection Com.; Environment Com. Party:
Precinct Committeewoman 1970- ; Dem. Cnty. Exec.
Com. 1970- . Org: Dem. Club; ADA. B: 12/7/12.
Add: 18506 Lomond Blvd., Shaker Hts. 44122
(216)752-5000.

Sharonville. EILEEN B. HEYBRUCH (R)
     1969-72; 1975-. Bds: Reg. Planning. Party:
Ward Ch., 1970-72. Prev: Bd. of Health 1968-
69. Org: Rep. Club. Occ: Secretary. B:
6/27/37. Add: 3936 Sharonview Dr., Sharonville
45241 (513)563-1144.

Shawnee Hills. JANET B. BROWN
         JEANNIE BUTTS
         REGINA SWANSON
     Town Hall, R.R. 1, Powell 43065.

Sheffield. CATHERINE AGNES CSUBAK
     Town Hall, 4820 Detroit Rd., Sheffield
44035.

Sheffield. ROSEMARY REINHARDT
     City Hall, 609 Harris Rd., Sheffield 44054.

Sheffield. ROSEMARY K. SCHWARZ
1965-. Bds: Council of Govts.; Planning Cmsn.
Prev: Vlg. Treasurer 1963-65; Councilwoman 1965- .
B: 11/23/30. Add: 4520 Day St., Sheffield Vlg.,
44054 (216)934-6104.

Sheffield Lake. SUSAN ETTA FISHER (D)
1975-. Bds: Ch., Utilities & Insurance; Parks,
Recreation & Welfare; Ordinance. Org: Human
Resource Ctr.; PTO. B: 8/26/41. Add: 805 Roberts
St., Sheffield Lk. 44054 (216)949-7141.

Silver Lake. PATRICIA A. CREAMER
VIRGINIA M. KOEHLER
Town Hall, 2961 Kent Rd., Silver Lake 44244.

Silver Lake. MARGARET SITES VAN HORNE (R)
1973-. Bds: Community Liaison Com.; Park &
Recreation Bd. Org: Rep. Women's Club; Retired
Teachers Assoc.; Church Women United. Educ:
Ohio Wesleyan U. 1930 BA; Kent State U. 1966 ME.
B: 10/17/08. Add: 3112 Mayfield Rd., Cuyahoga
Falls 44224 (216)923-5233.

Silverton. HELEN C. CASSIDY (D) **
1973-. Bds: Park & Play Fields; Finance;
Public Bldgs. Org: PTA; Dem. Club. Occ: Secretary. B: 3/17/24. Add: 4225 South Ave.,
Cincinnati 45236 (513)891-1380.

Sinking Spring. LEONA M. WYLIE
Town Hall, Main St., Sinking Spring 45172.

Solon. JEAN ROWAN (R)
1975-. Bds: Ch., Public Properties Com.;
Safety Com.; Community Dev. Com. Party: Precinct
Committeewoman 1975-77. Org: Citizen League;
Rep. Club; PTA. B: 6/27/23. Add: 6651 Edgemoor
Ave., Solon 44139 (216)248-1155.

Somerville. IRMA E. BREITENBECHER
MARY WYATT
Town Hall, 146 S. Main St., Somerville 45064.

South Amherst. BEATRICE HOLM
Town Hall, 101 W. Main St., S. Amherst 44001.

South Vienna. HENRIETTA M. HOCTER (D)
1966-. Bds: Ch., Park Com.; Finance. Party:
Precinct Ch. 1976-78. B: 8/28/23. Add: 26 W.
North St., S. Vienna 45369 (513)568-4311.

South Zanesville. NANCY LEE ROBERTS
Town Hall, 7 Shawnee Ave., S. Zanesville
43701.

Springboro. NANCY ANNE HUFFMAN (R)
1973-. Bds: Ch., Finance Com.; Law Com.; HUD
Fund Application Com. Org: PTO; Smithsonian
Institute; Consumers' Union. Educ: Spring Hl.
Coll. 1965 BS. B: 12/26/42. Add: 165 Pinecone
Ln., Springboro 45066 (513)748-1048.

Springdale. MARGE BOICE (R)
1973-. Bds: Ch., Public Welfare, Safety &
Educ.; Planning Cmsn.; Tax Review Bd. Prev:
Planning Cmsn. 1971-73. Org: Women's Club. B:
12/31/32. Add: 236 Harter Ave., Springdale 45246.

Springfield. CAROL L. GOETTMAN (R)
1976-. Bds: Vice-Mayor; Park Bd., Recreation Bd.; Cnty. Art Program. Org: Ohio Munic.
League; LWV; Hospital Aux.; Rep. Women's Club.;
PTA. Educ: Washington U. 1956 BA. B: 10/12/34.
Add: 740 Westchester Pk., Springfield 45504
(513)325-0511.

Spring Valley. LANN PENCE
Town Hall, 7 W. Main St., Spring Vly. 45370.

Spring Valley. MELBA S. SACKETT
1974-. Bds: Adv. Bd., Cnty. Bd. of Health;
Alt. Del. Cnty. Planning Cmsn. Party: Precinct
Clerk 1963-65, '73. Occ: Clerk-Secretary. B:
2/16/37. Add: P.O. Box 54, Spring Vly. 45370.

Strasburd. EVELYN M. STRAUSS
Town Hall, 201 2nd St., Strasburd 44680.

Stratton. ANNE T. URICH (D)
1966-. Bds: Ch., Bldg. Com.; Ch., Park Com.;
Ch., Streets Com. Occ: Caterer & Grocery
Store Owner. B: 7/27/12. Add: Stratton 43961
(614)537-1911.

Streetsboro. SALLY S. HENZEL
City Hall, 2094 State Rte. 303, Streetsboro
44240.

Struthers. ELEANOR M. BURRIS (D)
Party: Precinct Committeewoman 1966-77.
Org: Dem. Fed. Women; PTA. B: 12/1/28. Add:
425 Creed St., Struthers 44471 (216)755-2181.

Sugar Grove. BETSY GROVES
CAROL RIGGS
Town Hall, Sugar Grove 43155.

Summerfield. BETTY I. KERNS (D)
1975-. Bds: Council Pres. Occ: Group
Leader. B: 1/17/26. Add: Box 65, Summerfield
43788.

Summitville. DONA A. BERGFIELD
SUE J. SABATINO
Town Hall, Summitville 43962.

Tarlton. JO ANN KARSHNER
NORTHA KARSHNER
Town Hall, Fire House, Tarlton 43156.

Tipp City. ABBY C. BOWLING
1975-. Bds: Community Services; Ch., Sub
Com., Recreation. Educ: Wittenberg U. 1970
BA. B: 12/27/47. Add: 861 Hawthorne Dr.,
Tipp City 45371 (513)667-8425.

Tipp City. CAROL V. TURNER
City Hall, 3 E. Main St., Tipp City 45371.

Toledo. JUNE ROSE GALVIN (R) **
1973-. Bds: Supervisory Council, Regional
Planning Unit; Ch., Standards & Goals Com.,
Regional Planning Unit; Task Force Women's
Occupational Dev. Center. Org: Area Government
Research Assoc.; Bar Assoc.; Pres., Legal Aid
Society; Council for Business; Counsel Neighbor-
hood Improvement Foundation. Educ: U. of Toledo
1960 BA; U. of Toledo 1964 JD. Occ: Attorney.

B: 6/25/38. Add: 3641 Christie Dr., Toledo
43606 (419)473-2675.

Trotwood. MARLENE JOYCE FLAGEL (D)
    1972-. Bds: Regional Planning Cmsn.; Housing
& Human Resources. Party: Precinct Committeewoman 1976. Prev: Human Relations Cmsn. 1968-71;
Charter Review Cmsn. 1971; Bd. of Zoning Appeals
1971-72. Org: LWV. Educ: Miami U. 1966 BSEd.
Occ: Real Estate Saleswoman. B: 7/8/45. Add:
728 Ellsworth Dr., Trotwood 45426 (513)837-7771.

Troy. MARY CATHERINE ROZELL
    City Hall, 100 S. Market St., Troy 45373.

Uhrichsville. CHARLOTTE BELL
                ETHEL M. GEPHART
    City Hall, 305 E. 2nd St., Uhrichsville
44683.

Uhrichsville. VERNA M. GREEN (D)
    1975-. Bds: Ch., Ambulance; Park; Public
Bldgs. Org: BPW; Nat. Sheriff's Assoc.; Cnty.
Right to Life; Dem. Club; Dem. Women's Club.
Occ: Deputy Sheriff. B: 10/26/14. Add: 218 E.
6th St., Urichsville 44683 (614)922-1243.

Uhrichsville. MARIE C. HILLYER
    City Hall, 305 E. 2nd St., Uhrichsville
44683.

Urbana. CAROLYN STRAPP
    City Hall, 205 S. Main, Urbana 43028.

Urbancrest. DELORES ZIGLAR
    Town Hall, 3492 1st Ave., Urbancrest 43123.

Utica. CYRENE EVANS
    Town Hall, Spring St., Utica 43080.

Valley Hi. LINDA L. PETERS
                CARRIE V. SHAFER
    Town Hall RFD, Zanesville 43360.

Valleyview. GERTRUDE NAVIN
    Town Hall, 436 N. Richardson, Valleyview 43204

Van Buren. CAROLE B. HUNTLEY
    Town Hall, N. Main St., Van Buren 45889.

Vandalia. JOY A. CLARK
    City Hall, 333 Bohanan Dr., Vandalia 45377.

Vermilion. MARGARET T. SHAFTS
    City Hall, 5335 Devon Dr., Vermilion 44089.

Verona. CAROL CLINARD
    Town Hall, 100 W. Main St., Verona 45378.

Vinton. EVELYN DAFT
    Town Hall, Vinton 45686.

Wadsworth. LOA M. GERBERICH (D)
    1976-. Bds: Ch., Public Ways; Safety; Finance.
Org: LWV; BPW; Dem. Club. Educ: Muskingum Coll.
1958 BA. Occ: Teacher. B: 9/12/36. Add: 144
West St., Wadsworth 44281 (216)336-7279.

Walbridge. IRIS CREMEAN
    Town Hall, N. Main St., Walbridge 43465.

Walbridge. LEILA MAE ROGERS (D)
    1974-. Bds: Ch., Safety Com.; Ch., Recre-
ation Com. Org: Women's Missionary; Dem. Club;
Bicentennial Com. Occ: Sales Coordinator. B:
4/28/35. Add: 613 S. Main, Walbridge 43465
(419)666-2782.

Warren. MARGARET R. O'BRIAN
    City Hall, 391 Mahoning, NW, Warren 44483.

Warrensville Heights. HATTIE JANE PRINCE
    4301 Warrensville Center Rd., Warrensville
Hts. 44128.

Washington Court House. BERTHA M. MC CULLOUGH (R)**
    1973-. Bds: Finance Com.; Personnel Com.;
Community Improvement Corporation. Org: BPW;
Rep. Women's Club. Occ: Telephone Company
Service Representative. B:11/14/19. Add:
431 W. Circle Ave., Washington Court House
43160 (614)335-5720.

Waterville. ELIZABETH W. MEMMER
                JOAN RIGEL
    Town Hall, 16 N. 2nd St., Waterville 43566.

Waynesburg. MARY L. CONNELLY (D)
    1973-. Bds: Ch., Insurance Bd.; Finance Com.;
Safety Com. B: 4/18/30. Add: 290 West Lisbon
St., Waynesburg 44688 (216)866-2644.

Waynesville. MARIAN SUE ANDERSON (I)
    1973-. Bds: Ch., Finance; Safety & Police.
Org: Chamber of Commerce; PTO. B: 6/4/39.
Add: 363 N. Main St., Waynesville 45068 (513)
897-5971.

West Carrollton. MAXINE GILMAN (R) **
    1971-. Bds: Bd. of Zoning Appeals. Org:
LWV; Rep. Club. Occ: Secretary. B: 9/18/32.
Add: 225 E. Main St., West Carrollton 45449
(513)859-5181.

Westerville. BARBARA LAIRD
    City Hall, 21 S. State St., Westerville
43081.

West Lafayette. M. LORENA SIMS (R)
    1974-. Bds: Finance Com. Org: Women's
Club; AAUW. Educ: Ohio State U. 1936 BS. Occ:
Cnty. Children's Services Bd. Exec. Dir. B:
10/13/14. Add: 428 E. Russell Ave., West
Lafayette 43845.

Westlake. MARGARITA PREMEN (R) **
    1973-. Bds: Ch., Public Bldgs. & Grounds;
Ch., Recreation; Ch., Public Transportation;
Ch., Civil Service. Party: Local Precinct
Com. 1956-65 & 1971-73. Org: LWV; Women's
Club. B: 5/11/25. Add: 2834 Clark Pkwy.,
Westlake 44145 (216)871-4186.

West Mansfield. JULIA ENGLISH
    Town Hall, W. Center St., W. Mansfield 43358.

West Millgrove. LEOTA MARY DIETERLE (R)
    1975-. B: 8/16/48. Add: W. Millgrove 43467.

West Milton. VIRGINIA A. HEMMERICH
                DOROTHY W. STOUT
    Town Hall, 701 S. Miami St., W. Milton 45383.

West Milton. F. CAROLYN WINEMILLER (D)
    1973-. Bds: Housing & Human Resources Com.;
Miami Valley Reg. Planning Cmsn.; Miami Metro-
politan Housing Authority Bd. Party: Precinct
Committeewoman 1968. Educ: Wright State U. 1972
BA. B: 9/16/39. Add: 222 Cedar Dr., W. Milton
45383.

Weston. DONNA SZORAD
    Town Hall, Weston 43569.

West Unity. MARY L. THOMAS
    Town Hall, W. Unity 43570.

Whitehouse. S. SUSAN MILLER (R)
    1974-. Bds: Finance Com.; Ch., Streets Com.
Party: Precinct Committeewoman 1975-76. Prev:
Master Plan Dev. 1973-74. Org: Chamber of Comm-
erce; Merchants Assoc. Occ: Art Gallery Owner.
B: 10/24/43. Add: 6027 Matthew Dr., Whitehouse
43571 (419)877-5383.

Willshire. PHYLLIS J. ACHESON (R)
    1974-. Bds: Bldg. Com.; Park Com.; Finance
Com. Party: Precinct Committeewoman 1970-77.
Org: Rep. Women. Educ: Vanwert Vocational 1968
LPN. Occ: LPN. B: 5/22/22. Add: 615 Ft.
Recovery Rd., Willshire 45898.

Woodstock. BERTHA L. FORSYTHE
    Town Hall, E. Bennett St., Woodstock 43084.

Wooster. MARGARET S. DEMOREST (R)
    1971-. Bds: Ch., Laws & Ordinances Com.;
Police & Fire; Water, Light & Sewers. Prev:
Cnty. Public Library Bd. of Trustees 1968-72.
Org: Quota Club. Educ: Ashland Coll. 1964 BSci.
Occ: Children's Librarian Asst. B: 3/30/22.
Add: 128 W. Henrietta, Wooster 44691 (216)
264-5326.

Xenia. ANN W. COATES
    City Hall, 101 N. Detroit St., Xenia 45385.

Yankee Lake. CLARE H. CLAFFEY
              ANGELA E. KRIVOSH
    Town Hall, Yankee Lk. Inn, Yankee Lk. 44403.

Yankee Lake. LILLIAN E. NUGENT (R)
    1965-. Occ: Nursing Home Owner. B: 8/5/22.
Add: Brockway Ave., RD #1, Brookfield 44403.

Yankee Lake. GRETCHEN SUTTON
    Town Hall, Yankee Lk. Inn, Yankee Lk. 44403.

Zaleski. SHARON BAY
          ELEANORE BOOTH
    Town Hall, Municipal Bldg., Zaleski 45698.

Judges

PATRICIA J. ANDERSON
    Judge, Court of Common Pleas. Add: Court
House, Carrollton 44615.

EVELYN W. COFFMAN (R)
    Judge, Court of Common Pleas. 1962-. Org:
ABA; Oh. Judicial Conf.; Rep. Women's Club. B:
6/12/18. Add: 700 Van Deman Ave., Washington C.H.
43160 (614)335-4750.

JUNE ROSE GALVIN (R)
    Judge, Court of Common Pleas. 1977-. Party:
Cnty. Exec. Com. 1973-76. Prev: City Councilwoman 1973-77. Org: Oh. Bar Assoc.; Oh. Assoc.
of Juvenile Ct. Judges; Oh. Cmsn. on the Status
of Women. Educ: U. of Toledo 1960 BA; 1964 JD.
B: 6/25/38. Add: 3641 Christie Dr., Toledo
43606 (419)259-8748.

CATHRYN L. HARRINGTON (R)
    Judge, Court of Common Pleas. 1958-. Org:
Probate Judges Assn., Juvenile Judges Assn.
Educ: Western of Miami 1938 BA; U. of Cincinnati
1941 JD. B: 5/1/17. Add: 239 N. Jefferson St.,
Van Wert 45891.

OLIVE L. HOLMES (R)
    Judge, Court of Common Pleas. 1968-. Prev:
Municipal Ct. Judge 1967-68. Educ: Ohio U.
1937 BA; U. of Cincinnati Law School 1943 LLD.
B: 10/4/16. Add: 7131 Fernbank Ave., Cincinnati
45233 (513)632-8022.

LILLIAN M. KERN
    Judge, Court of Common Pleas. 1976-. Prev:
Asst. Prosecuting Attorney, Montgomery Cnty.
1966-76. Org: Altrusa; ABA. Educ: U. of Miami
1951 BA; U. of Cincinnati 1964 JD. Add: Family
Court Center, 303 West Second St., Dayton 45402.

BLANCHE KRUPANSKY
    Judge, Court of Appeals. Add: Court House,
Cleveland 44113.

ANN MC MANAMON (D)
    Judge, Court of Common Pleas. 1976-. Prev:
Judge, Cleveland Municipal Ct. 1973-76. Org:
Cuyahoga Cnty. Bar Assoc.; Oh. State Bar Assoc.;
Women's Bar Assoc.; Fed. for Community Planning;
WPC. Educ: U. of Calif. 1945 BA; Cleveland
Marshall Law School 1950 JD. B: 11/27/24. Add:
3690 Melbourne, Cleveland 44111 (216)623-8706.

State Boards and Commissions

    Governor's Office, State Capitol Bldg.,
    Columbus 43204.

Adult Parole Authority
    LOUISE HARDY

Aging, Commission on
    MARJORIE J. ATER
    MURIEL M. ALLEN BERTSCH

Air Quality Development Authority
    PATRICIA ANN ALESSI
    GAYLE S. CHANNING

Akron University Board of Trustees
    FRANCES MC GOVERN

Alcoholism Advisory Council
    JUANITA DALTON
    DOROTHY MACK
    JEAN WICKUM

American Revolution Bicentennial Advisory Commission
    MAXINE CHARLTON
    MARIAN R. HEISER

Arts Council
        MARILYN F. ERICKSON
        RITA M. HOWLEY
        MAXINE LEVI
        MARION G. LIVINGSTON
        RACHEL REDINGER
        KATHERINE C. ROSE
        MARGARET V. SCHOTT

Ballot Board
        MARGARET COHN

Banking Board
        RUTH ANNA TOBEY

Bar Examiners, Board of
        ALICE MOORE BATCHELDER

Civil Rights Commission
        MARION R. SWEENEY

Constitutional Revision Commission
        LINDA ORFIRER
        KATIE SOWLE

Cosmetology, State Board of
        MARY R. BOYD
        JOAN FANNIN DOTSON
        VALERIA MC PHERSON

Criminal Justice Supervisory Commission
        LEONA M. BEVIS

Crippled Children's Services Medical Advisory
Committee, Bureau of
        NADENE COYNE, M.D.
        MARGARET G. ROBINSON, M.D.

Development Advisory Council
        ROSEMARY H. MARTIN

Developmental Disabilities State Planning Council
        ANTOINETTE PARISI EATON
        ELSIE D. HELSEL
        BEVERLY J. KANOVSKY
        MARIETTA S. KELLY
        MILDRED F. MADRY
        PATRICIA J. MOSS
        RUTH O'GRADY
        MARILYN PICKETT
        BETTY M. RAVENSCROFT
        NANCY J. WILLIS

Education, State Board of
        MARTHA BALTAN AGLER
        SUSAN DEAL GEORGE
        RUTH S. SCHILDHOUSE
        MARTHA W. WISE

Elections Commission
        PHYLLIS S. NEDELMAN

Employment Security, State Advisory Council for
        ANN B. WALKER

Engineers and Surveyors, State Board of Registration
for Professional
        MARION L. SMITH

Ethics Commission
        MARY K. LAZARUS
        BARBARA RAWSON

Expositions Commission
        CAROLINE P. SMITH

Historic Site Preservation Advisory Board
        LOUISE R. FARR
        HELEN JANES VAN METER

Historical Society
        VIRGINIA L. BAIRD
        HELDA BENTLEY
        VIRGINIA B. PLATT

Housing, State Board of
        MARY ANN CHRISTIE

Legal Services Corporation Advisory Council
        CATHERINE JACKSON
        SHIRLEY M. SMITH

Library Board
        JANE STERZER

Library Examiners, State Board of
        DORIS WOOD

Lottery Commission
        JEANNINE TAKACS

Maumee Watershed Conservancy District
        RUTH A. COONROD

Medical Board
        EVELYN L. COVER, D.O.

Mental Health and Mental Retardation Advisory and
Review Commission
        ELSIE D. HELSEL
        ELEANOR M. MERK
        CHRISTINE ROSENBAUM

Natural Areas Advisory Council
        JANE L. FORSYTH
        RUTH MELVIN

National Museum of Afro-American History and
Culture Planning Council
        KATHLEEN EVELYN DE LOACHE
        DAISY M. FLOWERS
        OLYMPIA A. HALL
        DORIS B. RANKIN

Nurse Education and Nurse Registration, Board of
        PATRICIA L. COLLINS
        PATRICIA JEAN DONLEY
        REBECCA P. EDEN
        SISTER MARY IMMACULATA KUSINA
        LEONA M. NEFF
        FRIEDA IMOGENE SHIRK
        MARIE A. TROUT
        HELEN M. YARMAN

Nursing Education and Nurse Registration, Advisory
Council to the State Board of
        MARY HAMMOND
        SISTER ALICE WARRICK

Nursing Home Administrators, Board of Examiners of
MARY ANTONITA METTERT

Ohioana Library Association Board of Trustees
MARTHA C. MOORE
FREDA MORIN
RUTH W. MOUNT
JEAN A. REILLY

Parks and Recreation Advisory Council
NORMA O. JACOB

Pharmacy, State Board of
BETTY J. NICHOL
PHYLLIS WILSON

Psychology, State Board of
BARBARA ANN GARWOOD
SANDRA B. MC PHERSON

Public Health Council
MARY A. AGNA, M.D.
T. JEAN OVERTON

Recreation and Resources Commission
NORMA O. JACOB
EDYTHE M. LEWIS

Regents, Board of
MARJORIE E. FAWCETT
MARY ELLEN LUDLUM

Rehabilitation Services Commission
JACQUELINE F. GILES

School Employees Retirement Board
BERTHE E. WEIST

Soil and Water Conservation Commission
BETTY L. SEKULA

Soldiers and Sailors Orphans Home, Board of Trustees
MARY E. LEE

Voting Machines, Board of Examiners for
DOROTHY F. HERBERT

War Orphans Scholarship Board
IRENE B. SMART

Youth Services Advisory Board
THERESA M. GABRIEL
DONNA M. HAMPARIAN
MARIE B. STINSON

Oklahoma

State Legislature

State Senate

MARY A. HELM (R)
1974-. Dist: 46. Bds: Public & Mental
Health; Revenue & Taxation; Business, Labor &
Labor Relations. Party: State Del. 1975-77;
State Exec. Com. 1975-77. Org: Rep. Women's
Club; Young Rep's.; Order of Women Legislators;
Bd. of Dir's. of Jr. Achievement of Oklahoma
City. Educ: U. of Ark. 1966 BS; U. of Ga. 1969
MS. B: 10/27/43. Add: 3201 NW 16th, Oklahoma
City 73107 (405)521-3421.

State House

HELEN T. ARNOLD (R)
1976-. Bds: Educ.; Environmental Quality;
Public Safety and Penal Affairs. Party: State
Del. 1962, '76, '77. Prev: Special Com. on
Constitutional Revision 1969- . Org: Nat. Conf.
of State Legislators; Common Cause; UN Assoc.;
AAUW. Educ: Kan. State U. 1949 BS. B: 6/17/27.
Add: 218 E. 29th St., Tulsa 74114 (405)
521-2711 x 226.

HANNAH D. ATKINS (D)
1968-. Bds: Ch., Mental Health & Retardation;
Appropriations & Budget; Public Health. Party:
State Del. 1972, '76; Nat. Del. 1972; Nat.
Committeewoman 1976-80. Org: ASPA; Nat. Assoc.
of Black Women Legislators; Nat. Conf. of State
Legislators; NAACP; Black Child Devt. Institute;
Nat. Urban League; NOW; WPC. Educ: St. Augustines
Coll. 1943 BS; U. of Chicago 1949 BLS. B:
11/1/23. Add: Rt. 4, Box 799, Oklahoma City
73111 (405)521-2711.

DOROTHY DELL CONAGHAN (R)
Bds: Common Educ.; Higher Educ.; Criminal
Jurisprudence. Party: State Del. 1961-77; Nat.
Del. 1968; Cnty. Exec. Com. 1961-75; City Ch.
1965-69; Cnty. V-Ch. 1961-65; Precinct Ch. 1961-
63. Org: OWL; Bicentennial Club; Chamber of
Commerce; Women's Club. B: 9/24/30. Add: P.O.
Box 402, Tonkawa 74653 (405)521-2711.

CLETA DEATHERAGE (D)
1976-. Bds: Com. on Appropriations & Budget;
Ch., Sub. Com. Higher Educ. Approprations;
Judiciary. Party: State Del. 1974, '72; Nat.
Del. 1972; Precinct Ch. 1972-76; State Party
Constitutional Com. 1974-77; State Exec. Com.
1976-77. Prev: Ch., Norman Reapportionment
Cmsn. 1974-76; Governor's Cmsn. on Status of
Women 1972-77. Org: Okla. Bar Assoc.; Cleveland
Cnty. Bar Assoc.; BPW; WPC; LWV; Coalition for
Equal Rights; Cnty. Dem. Women; Okla. Fed. of
Dem. Women. Educ: U. of Okla. 1973 BA; U. of
Okla Coll. of Law 1975 JD. Occ: Atty. B:9/16/50.
Add:816 S. Flood, Norman 73069 (405)521-2711x147.

JOAN KING HASTINGS (R) **
1974-. Dist: 67. Bds: Common Educ.; Oil &
Gas; Public Safety & Penal Reform; Wildlife.
Party: Nat. Com.; County V-Ch.; Precinct Official.
Org: Amer. Business Women's Assoc.; Chamber of
Commerce; Rep. Women's Club; Young Rep. Occ:
Owner, Private School. B: 10/7/32. Add: 10701
S. Sheridan, Tulsa 74135 (405)521-2711 X 208.

JUDY ANN SWINTON (D) **
1974-. Bds: Educ. Com.; Environmental Quality;
Governmental Reform; Tourism & Recreation. Party:
Precinct Secretary 1975- . B: 12/29/49. Add:
2712 N. Wheeler, Oklahoma City (405)521-2711.

County Commissions

Pottawatomie. JANICE GUDERIAN
Dist 1, Shawnee.

Sequoyah. HELEN WILLIAMS
Dist. 3, Sallisaw.

Washington. JOANNE RINEY BENNETT (R)
1972-. Bds: Ch., Cnty. Bd. of Health. Party:
State Del. 1964, '76; Precinct Leader 1954-56.
Org: Service League; Mental Health Bd. Educ: U.
of Kan. 1946 BA. B: 8/11/24. Add: Rt. 2, Box 20,
Bartlesville 74003 (918)336-0330.

Woods. MARIE LORD
Dist. 3, Waynoka.

Mayors

Calvin. GAIL DOCKREY
P.O. Box 134, Calvin 74531.

Canute. VIOLA D. PENICK (D)
1973-. Bds: Bicentennial Com.; Ch., Park Com.
Prev: City Cmsnr. 1965-73. Occ: Motel Owner. B:
5/2/21. Add: Box 146, Cotton Boll Motel, Canute
73626 (405)472-3205.

Cleveland. JEAN HANSON
100 S. Broadway, Cleveland 74020.

Fort Cobb. PAULA WIDENMAIER
202 Main, P.O. Box 34, Fort Cobb 73038.

Hardesty. ALICE EDWARDS (D) **
1974-. Prev: Councilwoman 1950-71. B:
10/17/02. Add: City Hall, Hardesty 73944 (405)
888-4508.

Harrah. ELSIE O. SUMMERS (R)
1975-. Bds: Bd. of Dir's., Assoc. Central
Okla. Govts. Educ: Okla City U. 1953 BS. Occ:
Bookkeeper. B: 7/5/24. Add: 2000 N. Dobbs Rd.,
Harrah 73045 (405)454-2951.

Kenefic. MRS. CHARLEY RACKLEY
P.O. Box 67, City Hall, Kenefic 74748.

Konawa. MARRENA SUE HART (D)
1976-. Occ: Store Owner. B: 10/11/40. Add:
421 W. 3rd St., Konawa 74849.

Leon. LEONA HYMAN
Main St., City Hall, Leon 73441.

McCurtain. VESTA SAWYER
Main & 1st Ave., P.O. Box 28, McCurtain
74944.

North Enid. JAUNITA PRITCHETT
230 Breckinridge Rd., N. Enid 73701.

Oakwood. MRS. DOVEY G. HEWITT
P.O. Box 237, City Hall, Oakwood 73658.

Oklahoma City. PATIENCE LATTING (D) **
Prev: City Council 1967; Governor's Advisory
Com. on Educ. 1964; Governor's Reapportionment
of Okla. Legislature Com. 1960. Org: AAUW; LWV;
PTA. Educ: Okla. U. BA; Columbia MA. B:
8/27/18. Add: 3600 Harvey Pkwy., Oklahoma City
73128.

Orlando. ALTA BRANEN
Community Hall, P.O. Box 27, Orlando 73073.

Pensacola. MRS. OPAL BLACK
Rte. 3, Vinita 74301.

Picher. NAOMI POOLE
213 E. Third, P.O. Box 247, Picher 74360.

Quapaw. ETHEL ALLISON
P.O. Box 647, Town Hall, Quapaw 74363.

Ramona. HOLLY C. WARD
4th St., P.O. Box 204, Ramona 74061.

Skedee. ATHLEEN BAILEY
R.R. 2, Pawnee 74058.

Valliant. MRS. GUSSIE THOMPSON
Municipal Bldg., P.O. Box 714, Valliant 74764.

Watts. MILDRED HERALD (D)
1974-. Prev: Trustee 1969-71. Occ: Rooming
House Owner. B: 10/21/05. Add: 1st St., P.O.
Box 67, Watts 74964 (918)254-3924.

Local Councils

Ada. LOUISE ROBBINS
City Hall, 13th & Townsend, Ada 74820.

Adair. PATSY RUDD
P.O. Box 198, Adair 74330.

Afton. JOYCE WILLIAMS
123 S. Main, P.O. Drawer 250, Afton 74331.

Aline. EVELYN DURHAM
GRACE C. MILLER
Town Hall, Main St., Aline 73716.

Allen. CHARLOTTE TATE
P.O. Box 402, Allen 74825.

Alva. N.J. STRASBAUGH (I)
1966-. Bds: Ch., Finance Com.; Police &
Safety Com. Party: Precinct Leader 1960-65.
Org: Okla. Municipal League; Dem. Women. B:
5/14/10. Add: 1232 Flynn, Alva 73717.

Anadarko. LORRAINE COX
115 W. Kentucky, P.O. Box 647, Anadarko 73005.

Ardmore. MAZOLA MC KERSON
23 South Washington, P.O. Box 249, Ardmore
73401.

Ashland. BEULAH JOHNSON
R.R. #1, Stuart 74570.

Avant. MRS. FOYE ALLEN
P.O. Box 147, Avant 74001.

Bennington. OLETA ROWAN
P.O. Box 476, Bennington 74723.

Bernice. VOLLIE E. CARTER
P.O. Box 564, Bernice 74331.

Bessie. VIRGINIA COTTEY
P.O. Box 38, Bessie 73622.

Big Cabin. LOIS FEARS
P.O. Box 102, Big Cabin 74332.

Bokoshe. LILLIAN SMITH
P.O. Box 278, Bokoshe 74930.

Boswell. ETHEL CAMPO
P.O. Box 378, Boswell 74727.

Bristow. BERNICE LOEFFLER (D)
1972-. Bds: War Memorials of VFW; Swimming
Pool. Prev: Councilwoman 1954-56. Org: BPW. B:
6/23/26. Add: 248 W. 6th Ave., Bristow 74010.

Bristow. CHRISTINE MATTOX
8th & Main, Bristow 74010.

Bristow. EVALYN E. PILANT
1976-. Bds: Service Com.; Trustee of Municipal
Authority; Budget Com. Org: BPW; Dir., of Recreation; Neighborhood Ch. B: 7/15/22. Add: Bristow
74010 (918)367-3730.

Bryant. MRS. SAM PROCTER
Rte. #1, Weleetka 74880.

Burbank. LOIS LEIBER
P.O. Box 59, Burbank 74633.

Butler. LOUISE FRAZIER
So. Main St., P.O. Box 84, Butler 73625.

Caddo. HELEN WHITTINGTON
124 Buffalo, Caddo 74729.

Calera. OLLIE MAE SULLIVAN (D) **
B: 7/23/18. Add: Calera 74730 (405)434-5424.

Canton. IONE M. WILLIE (R)
1975-. Prev: City Clerk 1944-47. Org: Okla.
Municipal League. Occ: Tax Practitioner. B:
6/7/22. Add: 705 N. Grant, Canton 73724.

Carnegie. BONNIE NETHERTON
P.O. Box 1, Carnegie 73015.

Carter. BERTIE LEE DENTON (D)
1972-. B: 8/18/01. Add: Carter 73627
(405)486-3248.

Checotah. KEITHA CHILDERS
201 N. Broadway, Checotah 74426.

Checotah. MRS. LEOLA THOMAS
201 N. Broadway, Checotah 74426.

Choctaw. SANDRA KINCANNON
2436 N. Main, P.O. Box 567, Choctaw 73020.

Claremore. ELIZABETH GORDON
104 S. Muskogee, P.O. Box 249, Claremore
74017.

Cleo Springs. MELBA SCHAPER
Town Square, Cleo Springs 73729.

Comanche. ANNA SCHAAK (D)
1976-. Party: State Del. 1976; Precinct Ch.
1960-75; Co-Ch., Dem. Party 1975-77; Ch., Cnty.
Dem. Party. Org: Communications Workers of
America AFL-CIO; Chamber of Commerce; BPW;
Women's Dem. Club. Occ: Telephone Operator.
B: 7/4/34. Add: Box 465, Comanche 73529
(405)439-8868.

Copan. MARION PURDUM
112 N. Caney, P.O. Box 218, Copan 74022.

Cyril. SHIRLEY PERRY
P.O. Box 448, Town Hall, Cyril 73029.

Davis. RUTH LOWRIMORE
300 E. Main St., Davis 73030.

Del City. KATHERINE KAY WILKINSON (D) **
1975-. Bds: Council of Governments; V-Pres.
Municipal Services; Health Planning Cmsn. Party:
State Del. 1970-75; Precinct Leader 1970-75.
Prev: Advisor to Governor on Real Estate Bd.
1974; Ch., City Planning Cmsn. Org: Amer.
Business Women's Assoc.; BPW; LWV; NOW; Advisory
Com. on Consumer Affairs; Bicentennial Cmsn.;
Parliamentarian, ERA Coalition of Okla.; Indust-
rial Trust Foundation & Okla. Planning Congress;
Bd. of Realtors; Chamber of Commerce; Dem. Women's
Club. Occ: Owner, The Home Finders, Inc. B:
10/6/30. Add: 4800 SE 19th St., Del City 73116
(405)677-8833.

Eufaula. BETTIE DOBBS
MARJORIE PYLE
64 Linden Ave., P.O. Box 684, Eufaula 74432.

Fairland. MRS. ILA BOYD
BEVERLY HILL
Conner & Main, P.O. Box 429, Fairland 74343.

Forgan. LUETTA BARNETT
Main St., P.O. Box 249, Forgan 73938.

Goltry. LENORE HODGES (D)
1975-. B: 9/15/27. Add: Box 23, Goltry
73939. (405)496-2441.

Goltry. RUBY M. RUST (D)
1974-. Occ: Babysitter. B: 1/20/17. Add:
P.O. Box 113, Goltry 73739 (405)496-2268.

Goltry. ROWENA J. SNIDER (R)
1973-. Occ: Beauty Operator. B: 7/12/44.
Add: Goltry 73739 (405)496-2441.

Goodwell. JOLENE STRONG
Main St., P.O. Box 759, Goodwell 73939.

Grainola. RUBY JACKSON
ALICE WEAVER
City Hall, Grainola 74639.

Grandfield. MARY FRANCES GEBHART
Grandfield 73546.

Granite. WANDA CHRISTIAN
418 N. Main St., P.O. Box 116, Granite 73547.

Grayson. KATHERINE BROOKS
Rte. 3, Box 355, Henryetta 74437.

Guthrie. ILLENE EDWARDS
300 W. Oklahoma Ave., P.O. Box 908, Guthrie
73044.

Guthrie. MADELINE GLOCK (D)
1975-. Bds: Alt., Okla. Assoc. Central Govt.;
Bd. Job Corp.; Bd., Civic Center. Org: BPW;
Chamber of Commerce. B: 12/17/15. Add: 220 N.
Capitol, Guthrie 73044.

Hastings. BOBBIE BOHOT
P.O. Box 67, Hastings 73548.

Healdton. GLORIA PICKELSIMER
312 Franklin, P.O. Box 926, Healdton 73438.

Hitchcock. JEAN DOBRINSKI (I)
1974-. Party: Precinct Leader 1973-76; Election Bd. Judge 1975-77. Org: Devt. Corp.; Cnty.
Rep. Women's Club. B: 6/14/45. Add: P.O. Box 134,
Hitchcock 73744.

Hitchcock. PAULINE OSBURN
BETTY SPAETH
City Hall, Hitchcock 73744.

Hobart. LUCILE P. DORSEY (D) **
1972-. B: 1/2/20. Add: 411 1/2 S. Tilden,
Box 48, Hobart 73651.

Hugo. ELLIS FORD
201 S. 2nd St., City Hall, Hugo 74743.

Idabel. ROSEMARY THOMAS (D)
1975-. B: 7/4/28. Add: 302 NW 15th, Idabel
74745 (405)286-7609.

Jay. MEDA UNDERWOOD
Whitehead Ave., P.O. Box 348, Jay 74346.

Jenks. MARION LIGHTFOOT
123 East Main St., Jenks 74037.

Lambert. EVA RUDY
Route 1, Cherokee 73728.

Lamont. EDNA BANNING
123 North Main, P.O. Box 222, Lamont 74643.

Lamont. BRETA MYERS (R)
1975-. B: 2/17/10. Add: 319 E. Madison,
Lamont 74643.

Langley. MINNIE MARIE MIDGETT (I)
1974-. Org: NEA; PTA. Educ: 1971 AA; Northeastern Okla. State U. 1974 BS. Occ: Teacher.
B: 5/15/42. Add: P.O. Box 96, Wildman Blvd.,
Langley 74350.

Langston. ANNA C. CORRADO (D) **
1973-. Bds: Council of Governments. Party:
Precinct Ch. 1973-75. Org: Educ. Assoc.;
Women's Dem. League. Educ: West Chester State
Coll. 1956 BS; Temple U. 1962 MA. Occ: Ch.,
Physical Educ. Dept. B: 8/28/33. Add: Box 297,
Langston 73050.

Lawton. BARBARA PIPES
JOYCE PURSELY
City Hall, 4th & "A" St., Lawton 73501.

Lenapah. KATHERINE LOWERY
Lenapah 74042.

Lexington. MARILYN NEWMAN
121 E. Broadway, P.O. Drawer D, Lexington
73051.

Loco. PAT MC CURRY
City Hall, Loco 73442.

Mannford. ROWENA C. LANGSTON (R)
1975-. Bds: Liaison, Senior Citizens Center;
Coord., 4th of July Celebration. Party: State
Del.; State Alt.; Ch., Precinct; Dir., Zone;
Dir., Cnty. Dist.; Cnty. Dist. Committeewoman
1969-70. Org: Cnty. Rep. Women. Occ: Company
Co-owner. B: 1/29/25. Add: 113 Gardenia Cir.,
Mannford 74044 (918)865-4314.

Marietta. LYNN PUCKETT
P.O. Box 160, Marietta 73448.

Maramec. MINNIE MARTIN
P.O. Box 40, Town Hall, Maramec. 74045.

Marble City. DOROTHY FULLER
MAYE TUNE
P.O. Box 326, Marble City 74945.

Marlow. MACKIE TERRY
318 W. Main, P.O. Box 113, Marlow 73055.

Maud. GEORGIA FORESEE
100 W. Main, P.O. Box 217, Maud 74854.

Meridian. MARY SMITH
P.O. Box 56, Meridian 73058.

Midwest City. DOROTHY JO ZACHRY (D)
1976-. Bds: License & Review Bd.; State
Health Com.; Insurance Com. Prev: Mid Del.
Youth & Family Ctr. 1970-75. Org: NEA. Occ:
Teacher. B: 1/22/36. Add: 3505 Rolling Ln.,
Midwest City 73110 (405)732-2281.

Millerton. BELLE ALLEN
P.O. Box 757, Millerton 74750.

Morris. BARBARA HOGUE
400 S. Hughes, P.O. Box 141, Morris 74445.

Mountain Park. EDNA HANKINS (D)
1975-. B: 5/28/16. Add: 702 S. Main, Mountain
Park 73559 (405)569-4234.

Mountain Park. VERA UPCHURCH
Spruce St., P.O. Box 126, Mountain Pk. 73559.

Mustang. LINDA JEAN HAGAN (R)
1975-. Bds: Alt., Assoc. of Central Okla.
Govts. Party: State Del. 1977; Precinct Secretary
1975-77. Org: Assoc. of Anti-Women's Groups.
Occ: Teletype Operator. B: 6/9/47. Add: P.O.
Box 117, Mustang 73064 (405)376-2475.

New Alluwe. ALICE MC KEE
JOANNA SHIPP
General Delivery, New Alluwe 74049.

Nicoma Park. REBA HECK
11600 N.E. 23rd, P.O. Box 545, Nicoma Pk.
73066.

Noble. ALMA BRADSHAW
106 S. Main, P.O. Box 557, Noble 73068.

Norman. LIBBA SMITH
111 North Peters, P.O. Box 370, Norman 73070.

Norman. LYNTHA NICKLAS WESNER (D)
1975-. Mayor Pro-Tem. Bds: Alt. Repr., Assoc.
Central Okla. Govt. Party: Precinct Co-Ch. 1973-
75; Precinct Ch. 1975. Prev: Budget Study Com.
1974-75. Org: LWV; Common Cause; PTA; Cnty. Dem.
Women. Educ: U. of Okla 1962 BA. B: 4/8/40.
Add: 616 Tulsa, Norman 73071 (405)321-1600.

Oakland. ELIZABETH NANCE
P.O. Box 344, Oakland 73452.

Oakwood. BETTY LANCE
CLEMMA ROBERTS
P.O. Box 237, City Hall, Oakwood 73658.

Oilton. MARY CAMPBELL
Main & "B" Street, P.O. Box 175, Oilton 74052.

Okarche. MARION PERDUE
116 W. Oklahoma Ave., P.O. Box 116, Okarche
73762.

Okemah. BONNIE MILLER
502 W. Broadway, Okemah 74859.

Oolagah. MRS. RUBY GARRISON
Alta & E. Boundary, Gen. Delivery, Oolagah
74053.

Osage. MARY M. CARGO
PHYLLIS TUCKER
Third & Main Sts., P.O. Box 43, Osage 74054.

Pawnee. WANDA BANTA (D)
1975-. Bds: Ch., Police, Fire, Ambulance Bd.;
Parks & Playgrounds. B: 3/6/36. Add: 609 Black-
bear, Pawnee 74058 (918)762-2658.

Pensacola. MARTHA ANDERSON
Rt. 3, Box 99, Vinita 74301.

Phillips. MAYBELLE FLAHAUT
Rte. 4, Box 31, Coalgate 74538.

Ponca City. BONNIE PHILLIPS
516 E. Grand Ave., P.O. Box 1450, Ponca City
74601.

Porum. CHARLOTTE SPAFFORD
2nd Street, P.O. Box 68, Porum 74455.

Ramona. IRENE STILLWELL
4th St., P.O. Box 204, Ramona 74061.

Ratliff. CAROLYN JAGGARS
Church St., P.O. Box 142, Ratliff City 73081.

Renfrow. EVA WHITE
Renfrow 73767.

Rentiesville. SUSIE MAGALINE NEARS (D) **
1972-. B: 9/30/16. Add: P.O. Box 55, Rentiesville 74459.

Rentiesville. JOSSIE REESE
P.O. Box 34, City Hall, Rentiesville 74459.

Ripley. MARIE SNAVELY
Main St., P.O. Box 66, Ripley 74062.

Rocky. MABEL ROBINSON
P.O. Box 287, Rocky 73661.

Roosevelt. ESTELLE L. PITTS (R)
1975-. B: 12/26/10. Add: P.O. Box 5,
Roosevelt 73564 (405)639-2414.

Ryan. PEARL LOMAN
7th & Washington Street, P.O. Box 489,
Ryan 73565.

Salina. CARRIE WARD
P.O. Box 276, Salina 74365.

Sand Springs. RUTH ELLEN HENRY (R)
1975-. Bds: Ch., Senior Citizens Adv.
Council. Org: Okla. Municipal League; Women's
Chamber of Commerce; Nat. League of Families of
Amer. POW/MIA's in S.E. Asia; Rep. Women; Child
Study Club. B: 4/26/44. Add: 1108 Pin Oak Ct.,
Sand Spgs. 74063 (918)245-8751.

Sasakwa. ALICE WILLIAM
P.O. Box 45, Town Hall, Sasakwa 74867.

Seminole. VIRGINIA STEWART
Evans at Main, P.O. Box 1218, Seminole
74868.

Shamrock. LILLIAN BEAVERS
GRACE GEMMELL
P.O. Box 351, Town Hall, Shamrock 74068.

Shattuck. EUNICE STARBUCK
405 S. Main, P.O. Box 285, Shattuck 73858.

Slick. PAULETTA HAYES
P.O. Box 111, Slick 74071.

Stidham. SIS ACORD
NADINE HALEY
Main St., Town Hall, Stidham 74471.

Stilwell. NANCY BURCHETT GARRETT (D)
1971-. Bds: Ch., Swimming Pool Com.; Council
Pres. Party: State Del. 1972; Precinct Co-Ch.
1968-70. Org: Library Bd.; Chamber of Commerce;
Cnty. Health Authority; Resource Conservation &
Devt. Com.; Vo-Tech. Adv. Council; Fed. Women's
Club. Occ: Firm Owner. B: 12/19/35. Add: 118
W. Olive St., Stilwell 74960 (918)774-2770.

Strang. MARY SHEARIN
Town Hall, Strang 74367.

Tecumseh. DOROTHY IVEY (D) **
1973-. Party: County Co-Ch. 1974-75; Precinct
Leader 1973-75. Org: Dem. Women's Club. Occ:
Saleswoman. B: 4/30/15. Add: 117 W. Jefferson,
Tecumseh 74873 (405)598-2161.

Tipton. MATTIE MAE HUFF
DIANA ROGERS
Town Hall, Tipton 73570.

Tulsa. NORMA EAGLETON (D)
1976-. Bds: Indian Nations Council of Govt.,
Bd. of Dir's.; Manpower Area Planning Council;
Ch., Insurance Com. Party: State Del. 1968;
Precinct Official 1966-76. Org: Community Service
Council; Dem. Club. Educ: Stephens Coll. 1954 AA;
U. of Okla. 1956 BA. B: 3/19/34. Add: 3210 E.
65th, Tulsa 74136 (918)581-5151.

Valley Brook. EDNA OSBAN
6201 Camille Ave., Valley Brook 73149.

Valliant. LILLIE CLINE
P.O. Box 714, Valliant 74764.

Vinita. SHARON MONTGOMERY
TONI MOORE
104 E. Illinois, Drawer "D", Vinita 74301.

Wakita. DONNA DANB
BUELAH TEMPLIN
117 Main, P.O. Box 53, Wakita 73771.

Watonga. BARBARA SMOLA
119 N. Wigel, P.O. Box 564, Watonga 73772.

Waynoka. MARGARET QUINLAN
CLARA MILLER
201 E. Cecil, Waynoka 73860.

Weatherford. LETHA SPANN
522 W. Rainey, P.O. Box 569, Weatherford
73096.

Webb City. ELSIE CAMPBELL
City Hall, Webb City 74654.

West Siloam Springs. NORMA WILLIAMS
ROSALINDA SMITH
Rt. 4, Siloam Springs, Ark. 72761.

Wetumka. BOOTS WHEAT (D)
1974-. Org: Okla. Municipal League. Occ:
Taxi Driver. B: 9/21/39. Add: 207 W. Grand,
Wetumka 74883 (405)452-3153.

Yale. KATHERINE LUKE
102 North Main, Yale 74085.

Yukon. BETTY THORNTON
Municipal Bldg., Drawer "A", Yukon 73099,

Judges

PATRICIA M. HOEBEL
Judge, District Court. Add: District Court
House, Tulsa.

MARGARET LAMM MC CALISTER
Judge, District Court. Add: District Court
House, Tulsa.

ALMA WILSON
Judge, District Court. 1975-. Bds: Ch.,
Library Bd.; Law & Citizenship Educ. Com. Prev:
Special Dist. Judge 1969-75. Org: AAUW; Assis-
tance League; Altrusa. Educ: U. of Okla. 1939
BA; 1942 LLB; 1970 JD. B: 5/25/17. Add: 300
S. Hal Muldrow Dr. #136, Norman 73069 (405)
329-5010.

State Boards and Commissions

Office of the Governor, State Capitol Bldg.,
Oklahoma City 73105.

Alcoholism Advisory Council
EULA DUNCAN
JEAN GUMERSON
JEANNE STEELF

Arts and Humanities Council
MRS. JACK CARTER
MRS. JOHN R. DANSTROM
MRS. ROBERT DOWNING
LUCY NAVE
MRS. CHARLES NESBITT
MRS. DENZIL POPE
MRS. BUCK SHUPERT
MRS. JOHN B. TOWNES

Capitol-Medical Center Improvement and Zoning
Commission Citizens Advisory Committee
MRS. RALPH BACHLE
MARGARET BEHRINGER
MRS. HOWARD MEREDITH
MAURINE MINK
THELMA MITCHELL
MARGARET RILEY
GWENDOLYN YOUNGER

Carl Albert Memorial Commission
MRS. ANTHONY D. ASHMORE
MRS. ROBERT POE

Claremore Junior College, Board of Regents
LAURA M. BUTNER
NADINE SMITH

Consumer Affairs, Commission on
SHIRLEY HARRIS
ANNA BELLE WIEDEMANN

Corrections, Board of
PATRICIA MONTGOMERY

Corrections Committee
ANN BYRD
PAULINE FAHLE
MAXINE LOOPER

Cosmetology, Board of
GLORIA BURSE MATTHEWS
ARDIS MILLER
MARCELLA THOMPSON
HELEN WALTER

Court System Committee
MARIAN OPALA

Crime Commission Executive Committee
ANN BYRD

Deaf and Hearing Impaired, Commission on the
JOAN FAUBION
MARGIE KERR
MARY WARNER
MRS. THOMAS A. WILKINS

Department of Libraries Board
CARLOTTA FRUIN
GEORGIA LA MAR
BESS MOORE
JANE PATTEN
FERN WARD
FLOSSIE WINESBERRY

Drug Treatment and Rehabilitation, Therapeutic
Advisory Council in
SISTER ANNE J. LAUF
ELLEN R. OAKES

Regents, Board of. Eastern Oklahoma State College,
Board of Regents
HAZEL PORTERFIELD

Education, Board of
ELNA JUERGENS

Education Council
MARY CHERRY
CLEO CROSS

Educational Television Authority
JUANITA KIDD
CARRIE MOTHERSHED
MARY SIMONDS
SUE LACKEY SMITH

Educational Television Authority Advisory Committee
VELMA FELKNER
MRS. M.E. KIBLER
JEAN SPRAGUE

Election Board
ELAINE ALLMAN

Electrology, Board of
DOROTHY LEA BURGTORF
CELIA P. MIDDLETON

Elmer Thomas Memorial Commission
RUTH HURT
MARTHA BEA JOHNSON
MARY SUE MASSAD

El Reno Junior College, Board of Regents
BETTY THORNTON

Employment of the Handicapped, Committee on
MARY CAROLINE COLE
MARY DEMKE
MILDRED BROOKS FITCH
FRANCES HOOPER
LOLA D. HUDSON
MRS. J. SAM JOHNSON
MARGIE KERR
KAY MUNDING
MRS. ROBERT L. PARKER
OLA MAE REETER
ESTHER ROBINSON
RUTH SUTTON

Employment Security Commission Advisory Council
MARY DEES

Environmental Protection, Board of Trustees
MARGARET SEAL

Health Facilities Advisory Council
ANDREA U. BIRCHER

Health Sciences Center Planning Committee
HANNAH D. ATKINS

Hearing Aid Dealers and Fitters, Board of
ELIZABETH BLOOMER
JEAN RUBY

Higher Education. Board of Regents
RUBYE M. HALL

Historical Preservation Board of Review
MARGARET RILEY

Historical Society Board
MRS. GEORGE L. BOWMAN
MRS. MARK R. EVERETT
MRS. CHARLES R. NESBITT
GENEVIEVE SEGER

Hospital Planning Advisory Council
BARBARA DILLON
JEARL SMART

Human Rights Commission
LEORA H. CHRISTIAN
CHRIS LEYJA
ANNABEL SAWYER
BARBARA WARE

Indian Affairs Commission
DANA KNIGHT
DORA SCHEXNIDER

Jim Thorpe Memorial - Athletic Hall of Fame
Commission
JONIECE FRANK
BERTHA FRANK TEAGUE

J. M. Davis Memorial Commission
LUCILLE SANDERS

Judicial Nominating Commission
HELEN PEARCE

Juvenile Delinquency Committee
LENA BENNETT
MARY LAYNE RALEY
NELLIE WELCH

Medical Care for Public Assistance Recipients,
Advisory Committee on
LOIS CHADRICK
JEARL SMART
FRANCES WADDLE

Mentally Retarded, Advisory Committee on
MRS. ROBERT I. HARTLEY
MRS. W. F. MATHEWS
MRS. CLYDE TAPP

Mental Health, Board of
KATHERINE SAPPINGTON
RUTH SUTHERLAND
MARIE WHITE RHODES

Murray State College, Board of Regents.
PAGE LAMBERT

Northern Oklahoma College, Board of Regents
ROWENA CORR
KAYE MC CARTY

Nurse Registration and Nursing Education, Board of
HELEN FRENCH
DORIS GOLAB
JUANITA MILLSAP
OLETA MITCHELL
LILLIE MURRAY
BERNICE J. REGALDO
BERNICE C. SLATER
JEARL SMART
DOROTHY THOMPSON
MARJORIE WILHELM

Nursing Homes, Board of
JUANITA HODGES
PEGGY MC MAKIN
JEARL SMART
SYBLE SCOTT

Oklahoma Colleges, Board of Regents
RUTH HOLMES

Pardon and Parole Board
DORIS MONTGOMERY

Physical Therapy Committee
ISOBELL KNOEPFLI
NANCY SNELL

Private Schools, Board of
ZULA BAY

Professional Practices Commission
BARBARA ANDERSON
BARBARA GRAYSON
HELEN MURRAY
DONNA TAYLOR
SHIRLEY WARD
ALICE WHITE

Professional Standards Board
RUTH A. ADAMS
MRS. CLETUS BOYER
JANE CLARK

DEVONNA MINNICH
MRS. FRANCES PERCIVAL
AVALON REECE
NADINE SMITH
MARY EVELYN SNIDER

Public Accountancy, Board of
SYLVIA DUNCAN

Public Employees Relations Board
MYRNA DUNN

Public Welfare Commission
MRS. ROBERT I. HARTLEY

Reorganization of State Government, Special
Commission on the
SHIRLEY WEEKS

Santa Claus Commission
MRS. JAMES P. GARRETT

Seminole Junior College, Board of Regents
PAULINE MARTIN

Shorthand Reporters, Board of Examiners of
HELEN M. SCARCE

Social Workers, Board of Registration for
PAULINE MAYER

South Oklahoma City Junior College, Board of Regents
JANE HARDIN

Speech Pathology and Audiology, Board of Examiners
for
RITA S. MC SHEA

State Personnel Board
JOYCE REICHELT

Student Loan Authority, Board of Trustees
BETTY SMITH

Tax Review, Court of
ALMA BELL WILSON

Teachers' Retirement System, Board of Trustees
JANIE BENNETT

Textbook Committee
NANCY BURKE
GWEN COX
EDDIE FAYE GATES
WANDA GREB
PAT HUNT
SHERRY MORGAN
EARLENE PARR
ELIZABETH PERRY
PAT ROSS
LUCILE WILCOXSEN

Transportation Commission
MRS. ROBERT L. PARKER

Tulsa Junior College, Board of Regents
ANNE MC WILLIAMS

University of Science and Arts of Oklahoma, Board of Regents
    KATHRYN EMPIE
    MARY ELLEN JENNINGS
    MARY E. RODDY

Vocational and Technical Education, Board of
    ELNA JUERGENS

Western Interstate Commission for Higher Education
    GLADYS MC COY
    BARBARA STALIONS

Western Oklahoma State College, Board of Regents
    MERNIECE UNDERWOOD

Oregon

State Executive and Cabinet

NORMA PAULUS (R)
    Secretary of State. 1976-. Bds: State Land Bd.; V-Ch., Public Contract Review Bd. Prev: State Repr. 1970-76; Marion-Polk Boundary Cmsn. 1969-71. Org: Ore. State Bar; BPW; Ore. Environmental Council; NAACP; WPC. Educ: Willamette Law School 1962 LLB. B: 3/13/33. Add: 3090 Pigeon Hollow Rd. S, Salem 97302 (503)378-4139.

State Legislature

State Senate

ELIZABETH W. BROWNE (D) **
    1969-. Dist: 22. Bds: State Civil Rights Com. Party: Precinct Ch. Prev: School Bd.; Org: ABA; Council of Governments; Dem. Party. Educ: U. of Chicago MA; U. of Ore. JD. Occ: Attorney. B: 4/4/26. Add: Box 737, Oakridge 97463 (503)378-8835.

BETTY R. ROBERTS (D)
    1964-. Dist: 10. Bds: V-Ch., Judiciary; Ways & Means; Aging & Minorities. Party: State Del. 1965- ; Nat. Del. 1968-76; Precinct Committeewoman 1960- . Prev: Ch., Solid Waste Disposal Adv. Com. 1972-74; Governor's Task Force Medical Malpractice 1975-77; Economic Devt. Cmsn. 1977- Org: Ore. Bar Assoc.; BPW; Soroptomist; ACLU; Urban League. Educ: Portland State U. 1958 BS;

U. of Ore. 1961 MS; Northwestern School of Law 1966 JD. Occ: Atty. B: 2/5/23. Add: 319 SE Gilham, Portland 97215 (503)378-8844.

MARY ROBERTS (D)
    1974-. Dist: 11. Bds: V-Ch., Human Resources Com.; Labor, Business & Consumer Affairs Com.; Local Govt. & Elections Com. Party: State Del. 1974; Nat. Del. 1974; Precinct Committeewoman 1970-72. Prev: State Repr. 1972-74. Org: WPC; Campaigners Club; Dem. Society. Educ: U. of Ore. BA; U. of Wisc. MA. Occ: Real Estate Salesperson/Curriculum Consultant. B: 12/19/44. Add: 105 SE 84th Ave., Portland 97216 (503) 378-8842.

State House

MARY MC CAULEY BURROWS (R) **
    1973-. Dist: 41. Bds: Local Government & Urban Affairs; Environment & Land Use Com. Party: Com. 1975- ; State Central Com. 1971-72; County Party Assembly 1962-65. Org: Young Rep. B: 8/27/32. Add: 3105 Firwood Way, Eugene 97401.

MARGARET ULRICKA DERELI (D) **
    Dist: 32. Bds: Educ.; Human Resources. Org: ACLU. B: 2/18/37. Add: 260 15th St., Salem 97301.

NANCIE PEACOCKE FADELEY (D)
    1970-. Bds: Ch., House Environment & Energy Com.; Energy Policy Review Com.; State Govt. Operations. Party: State Del.; Nat. Del. 1968; Precinct Leader. Org: Nat. Conf. of State Legislators; LWV; BPW. Educ: Central Methodist Coll. 1952 BA; U. of Ore. 1974 MA. B: 7/11/30. Add: 260 Sunset Dr., Eugene 97403 (503)378-8827.

GRETCHEN KAFOURY (D)
    1508 N.E. Stanton, Portland 97212.

VERA KATZ (D) **
    1972-. Dist: 8. Bds: Joint Com. on Alcohol & Drugs; Com. on Judiciary; Com. on Environment; Dist. Assoc. on Comprehensive Health Planning. Party: Precinct Com. 1969-74. Prev: State Nursing Cmsn. Org: Alcoholic Detoxification Center. Educ: Brooklyn Coll. 1954 BA; Brooklyn Coll. 1956 MA. B: 8/3/33. Add: 1214 NW 25th Ave., Portland 97210.

SANDRA L. RICHARDS (D)
    19103 N.E. Hassalo, Portland 97230.

MARY W. RIEKE (R) **
    1970-. Dist: 9. Prev: Ch., Nat. Educ. Dev. Advisory Council 1967-73; Bd. of Educ. 1958-70; Educ. Dist. Bd. 1964-68. Org: AAUW; LWV. Educ: Ore. State U. 1935 BS. B: 10/26/13. Add: 5519 SW Menefee Dr., Portland 97201 (503) 378-8179.

PAT WHITING (D)
    1972-. Dist: 7. Bds: Ch., Transportation Com. Party: State Del. 1972-76; Precinct Leader 1971-77. Org: Cnty. Community Action; Population Reference Bureau. Educ: San Jose State U. 1967 BA. Add: 8122 S.W. Spruce, Tigard (503)378-8794.

MAE YIH (D)
    1976-. Dist: 36. Bds: Educ. Com.; Social
Service Com.; School Bds. Party: State Del. 1976;
Precinct Committeewoman 1965-77. Org: Nat. School
Bd. Assoc.; AAUW; LWV; Mental Health Assoc.;
Retarded Citizens Assoc. Educ: Barnard Coll.
1951 BA. B: 5/24/28. Add: Box 274 - L, Rt. 2,
Albany 97321 (503)378-8858.

County Commissions

Benton. BARBARA ROSS
    County Bldg., Corvallis 97330.

Coos. IRENE L. JOHNSON
    County Bldg., Coquille 97423.

Crook. FRANCES L. BURGESS (D)
    1976-. Bds: Ch., Bd. of Equalization; Airport
Cmsn.; Manpower Council. Party: Secretary Central
Dem. Com. 1976- . Prev: Communities Service Bd.
1974-77. Org: Nat. Assoc. of Fed. Employees;
Central Dem. Com. B: 1/19/19. Add: Rt. 2, Box
606, Prineville 97754 (503)447-6555.

Jackson. CAROL N. DOTY (D)
    1976-. Bds: Bd. of Health; Economic Planning
& Devt. Com.; Human Resources Com. Prev: Gover-
nor's 4-C Council 1972-73; Cnty. Human Resource
Com. 1975-76; School Dist. Budget Com. 1975-77.
Org: Nat. Assoc. for Educ. of Young Children;
LWV; Historical Soc.; Eleanor Roosevelt League;
Common Cause. Educ: Berea Coll. 1960 BS; Kan.
State U. 1967 MS. B: 12/25/38. Add: 3655
Anderson Crk. Rd., Talent 97540 (503)776-7236.

Jackson. TAM MOORE
    County Bldg., Medford 97501.

Jefferson. MARY NORTON
    County Bldg., Madras 97741.

Linn. MARY T. KEENAN
    County Bldg., Albany 97321.

Multnomah. ALICE CORBETT (D)
    1974-. Bds: Administrative Services; Library
Bd.; Welfare Bd. Party: Nat. Del. 1960, '64, '68,
'72; Nat. Alt. 1956; V-Ch. Dem. Com. 1956-58;State
Dem. Party 1954-58; Nat. Com. of Dem. Women 1960-
78. Prev: State Senator 1959-67. Org: Dem. Club;
AAUW. Educ: U. of Ore. 1945 BS. B: 7/17/25.
Add: 2222 NE Schuyler, Portland 97212 (503)
248-5218.

Umatilla. BARBARA J. LYNCH (R)
    1975-. Bds: E. Central Ore. Assoc. of Cntys.;
Local Officials Adv. Com. to State; Human Services
Com. Prev: City Councilwoman 1969-75; Cnty.
Budget Com. 1973-75; Solid Waste Com. 1972-75.
B: 12/21/23. Add: 200 SW Butte Dr., Hermiston
97838 (503)276-7111 x 200.

Washington. VIRGINIA DAGG (D)
    1973-. Bds: Bd. of Dir's, Unified Sewerage
Agency; Health Systems Agency. Party: Precinct
Committeewoman Dem. Party 1965-67. Prev: Ch.,
Cnty. Traffic Safety Com. 1960-62. Org: Bd. of
Dir's, Child Care Coord. Council; Nat. Assoc. of
Women Hwy. Safety Leaders. B: 8/1/37. Add:
7075 SW 15th, Beaverton.

Mayors

Adair Village. CHARLINE R. CARR (R)
    1976-. Bds: Ch., Budget Com. Org: League of
Ore. Cities; Council of Govts. B: 8/5/38. Add:
162 Azalea Dr., - Adair Vlg., Corvallis 97330
(503)745-5274.

Chiloquin. BETH PAHLL
    P.O. Box 196, Chiloquin 97624.

Donald. RUTH J. BLAKE
    P.O. Box 388, Donald 97020.

Gates. PHILYIS SHELTON
    P.O. Box 577, Gates 97346.

Idanha. DALLES BENTON
    P.O. Box 396, Idanha 97350.

Jacksonville. CLARA L. WENDT
    P.O. Box 7, Jacksonville 97530.

Lyons. JUNE G. MC PHEETERS (R)
    1974-. Prev: Councilwoman 1970-74. B:
6/12/20. Add: 2112 E. Main St., Lyons 97358.

North Bend. BEVERLY L. HIGGINS
    P.O. Box B, N. Bend 97459.

Richland. FLORENCE NEDROW
    P.O. Box 236, Richland 97870.

Seaside. JOYCE C. WILLIAMS (R)
    1976-. Org: AAUW; Park & Recreational Bd.
Educ: Northern Ill. U. 1941 BSEd. Occ: Hostess/
Cashier in Restaurant. B: 2/23/19. Add: 2420
S. Edgewood, Seaside 97138 (503)738-5511.

Sumpter. LUCILLE MORIN (D)
    1977-. Bds: Blue Mtn. Intergovt. Council.
Prev: Planning Com. 1974-76. Org: Credit
Women's Internat.; OES. Occ: Loan Officer. B:
9/30/35. Add: P.O. Box 507, Sumpter 97877
(503)894-2314.

Local Councils

Amity. BONNIE JEAN JOHNSON (R) **
    1974-. Bds: Streets & Lights Com.; Park Com.;
Financial Com. Prev: Planning Bd. 1974-75.
Occ: Collection Agency Solicitor. B: 11/16/26.
Add: 300 Rosedell Ave., Amity 97101 (503)
835-3711.

Amity. LORIA M. MAC KABEN (D)
    1973-. Bds: Ch., Police Cmsn.; Ch., Council
Pres.; Budget Officer. Prev: City Councilwoman
1973-80; Council Pres. 1977-78. Occ: Teacher.
B: 7/4/24. Add: 107 6th St., P.O. Box 294,
Amity 97101 (503)835-3711.

Antelope. ANNE HICKS
    Town Hall, Antelope 97001.

Antelope. MARGARET WORKMAN HILL (R)
1974-. Educ: Emporia State U. 1943 BSEd. B: 1/26/21. Add: Box 45, Antelope 97001 (503) 489-3263.

Antelope. IDA ROSE KUHLMAN
P.O. Box 74-A, Antelope 97001.

Antelope. DORIS OLSON
IRENE WILSON
Town Hall, Antelope 97001.

Aumsville. DARLENE W. LOYD (D)
1976-. Bds: Ch., Parks & Recreation Cmsn.; Ch., Lights Cmsn.; Budget Com. Occ: Exec. Asst., Public Welfare Div. B: 9/28/44. Add: 620 Del Mar Dr., Aumsville 97325 (503)749-2030.

Bandon. MARINA STARFAS GARDINER (R)
1976-. Bds: City Charter Revision Com., Ch. Party: State Del. 1961, '76; Precinct Leader 1953-73; V-Ch., Jackson Cnty. Rep. Com. 1952-53. Prev: Budget Com. 1953-57. Org: Rep. Women; OES. B: 10/6/17. Add: 1220 Beach Loop Dr., Bandon 97411 (503)347-2851.

Bandon. ELEANOR C. LORENZ (R)
1974-. Bds: Council Pres.; Library Bd. Org: Ore. & Nat. Medical Record Assoc.; Day Care Center Adv. Bd. Occ: Hospital Administrator. B: 3/16/15. Add: 535 W. Harrison, Bandon 97411 (503)347-2426.

Banks. KAY WALFE
P.O. Box 428, Banks 97106.

Barlow. DORIS BOUTRIN
Rt. 3, Box 318, Barlow 97002.

Bay City. MARJORIE J. BIRK (D)
1976-. Bds: Streets & Roads; Parks; Fire & Police. Party: Precinct Woman 1975- . Org: BPW; Dem. Women. Occ: Dispatcher. B: 8/12/19. Add: P.O. Box 201, Bay City 97107.

Beaverton. RENEE CAROL FELLMAN (D)
1975-. Bds: Ch., Deferred Assessment;Water Supply; Audit Com. Prev: Mayor. Org: LWV; Common Cause; Women's Club. Educ: Northwestern U. 1964 BA. B: 12/24/43. Add: 5425 SW Chestnut Ave., Beaverton 97005. (503)644-2191.

Bend. RUTH R. BURLEIGH (D)
1974-. Mayor Pro Tem. Bds: Central Ore. Intergovt. Council. Org: Amer. Society of Medical Technologists. Occ: Medical Technologist. B: 3/25/26. Add: 127 N.W. Wilmington, Bend 97701.

Bonanza. LOUISE DYE
PATRICIA GIBNEY
JAUNITA SLOEHSLER
P.O. Box 247, Bonanza 97623.

Burns. JEAN RENWICK
90 W. Washington, Burns 97720.

Carlton. JANET DIXON
191 E. Main St., Carlton 97111.

Cascade Locks. MARY MC CULLEY
P.O. Box 308, Cascade Locks 97014.

Central Point. CANDACE L. JAZDZEWSKI (D) **
1974-. Bds: Streets & Recreation; Water & Sewer. Org: PTA. Occ: Secretary. B: 8/22/42. Add: 121 Bigham Dr., Central Point 97501 (503) 664-1201.

Chiloquin. RUBY HANAN
P.O. Box 196, Chiloquin 97624.

Clatskanie. BESSIE HAUSLER (D)
1975-. Bds: Pres., City Council. Org: Chamber of Commerce. Occ: Store Owner/Operator. B: 8/19/26. Add: 670 Conyers St., Clatskanie 97816.

Coburg. GERALDINE R. MYERS (R)
1977-. Org: PTA. Occ: Realtor. B: 7/26/37. Add: 440 E. McKenzie, Coburg 97401 (503)345-4946

Columbia City. VALERIE J. O'CONNOR (R)
1971-. Org: NEA; AAUW. Educ: Ore. Coll. of Educ. 1943 BSEd; U. of Ore. 1950 MEd. Occ: Librarian. B: 11/22/21. Add: 1925 The Strand, Columbia City 97018 (503)397-4010.

Columbia City. KAREN TWEED
1755 2nd Pl., Columbia City 97018.

Condon. JUANITA HARTLEY
P.O. Box 684, Condon 97823.

Condon. GAEL D. LIPTAK (D)
1977-. Bds: Parks & Golf Course Com. Occ: Dept. Store Clerk. B: 1/30/40. Add: P.O. Box 463, 333 N. Lincoln, Condon 97823.

Condon. COLLEEN SELBY
P.O. Box 684, Condon 97823.

Coos Bay. SHARON GOLBEK (D)
1976-. Bds: Bd. of Dir's., Bay Area Fun Festival; Swimming Pool Com.; Budget Com. Org: Amer. Business Women's Assoc.; Soroptimist; Citizen Involvement; PTA. Occ: Bookkeeper. B: 1/13/45. Add: 107 N. 12th, Coos Bay 97420 (503)267-7510.

Cornelius. KATHERINE REDWINE (D)
1976-. Bds: Civic Improvement Com. Prev: School Bd. 1971-76; Budget Com. 1972-76. B: 1/7/36. Add: 1599 S. Alpine, Cornelius 97113.

Corvallis. INGE CHRISTEL MC NEESE (D)
1976-. Bds: Public Works Com.; Public Services Com.; Housing Com. Org: LWV. Educ: Ore. State U. 1976 BA. B: 9/1/43. Add: 815 Seatwood Ave., Corvallis 97330 (503)757-6901.

Dayton. SHARON MAXWELL
416 Ferry St., Dayton 97114.

Dayville. CASSIE HOBBY
Town Hall, Dayville 97825.

Depoe Bay. NELLIE S. MUNSON
           MABEL I. REISINGER
           BEVERLY JEAN ROBINSON
    630 Highway 101 S.E., Depoe Bay 97341.

Detroit. GLADYS CHAMPION
    P.O. Box 589, Detroit 97342.

Drain. VESTA SARGENT BILLICK (D) **
    1972-. Org: Business Women's Club; Chamber
of Commerce. B: 7/14/26. Add: 232 W "C" St.,
Box 218, Drain 97435 (503)836-2251.

Dundee. MAXINE OLIVER
    P.O. Box 201, Dundee 97115.

Dunes City. SHIRLEY MERZ (R)
    1975-. Bds: Exec. Bd., Council of Govts.;
Pres., City Council. Party: State Del., 1964,
'66; State Alt., 1968; Cnty. Area Ch., 1960-68;
Cnty. V-Ch., 1964-66; Precinct Committeewoman
1960-75; Cnty. Leg. Alt. 1965-66. Prev: Zoning
Bd. 1974-75. Org: Rep. Club. Occ: Legal Secretary. B: 12/21/31. Add: N. Pioneer, Dunes City
97493 (503)997-8333.

Durham. MARY TAYLOR
    P.O. Box 23483, Tigard 97223.

Eagle Point. ROSE DRAPER (R) **
    1972-. Bds: Council of Governments. Occ:
Community Librarian; Student. B: 7/26/32. Add:
Box 33-221 Oretega, Eagle Point 97524 (503)
826-4212.

Echo. MARY ANN POWER
    P.O. Box 669, Echo 97826.

Elgin. BETTY J. KNAPP (D)
    1973-. Bds: Police Cmsn.; Community Ctr. Bd.;
Park Cmsn. Occ: School Secretary. B: 12/27/36.
Add: 1601 Division, Elgin 97827.

Elkton. MARY COLLY
    P.O. Box 508, Elkton 97436.

Elkton. LAWANDA SOLOMON (D)
    1972-. Occ: Grocery Clerk. B: 8/2/38. Add:
P.O. Box 536, Elkton 97436.

Eugene. BETTY L. SMITH (R)
    1977-. Bds: Budget Com.; V-Ch., Lane Cnty.
Social Services Adv. Com.; Metropolitan Wastewater Management Cmsn. Party: Precinct Committeewoman 1972-76. Prev: Nat. Cmsn. Observance of
IWY 1975-77; Community Goals Com. 1974. Org:
WPC; Jr. League. Educ: U. of Ore. 1957 BS. B:
5/19/35. Add: 2140 Agate St., Eugene 97403
(503)687-5010.

Fairview. SUSAN CLIFT
          GLADYS TREADWAY
    P.O. Box 395, Fairview 97024.

Florence. CAROLYNDA ERSKINE
    240 Hwy. 101, Florence 97439.

Forest Grove. LUCILLE F. HUNDLEY
    P.O. Box 326, Forest Grove 97116.

Gaston. EVA CULLERS
        GERALDINE THOMPSON
    P.O. Box 128, Gaston 97119.

Gearhart. NANCY BLACK
    Drawer "D", Gearhart 97138.

Gervais. NANCY HAVA SUTTON (D)
    1977-. Bds: Police Cmsnr. Occ: Cook. B:
11/1/33. Add: 1025 N. 3rd St., Box 127, Gervais
97026 (503)792-4222.

Gladstone. CONNIE WILLIAMS
    525 Portland Ave., Gladstone 97027.

Glendale. MINNIE A. KOBERNIK (R)
    1975-. Org: OES; Women's Assoc. B: 10/8/30.
Add: 1080 6th St., P.O. Box 331, Glendale
97442 (503)832-2106.

Glendale. FLORA C. SNYDER
    P.O. Box 361, Glendale 97442.

Gold Beach. ANN BROWNWELL
           LENA JAMES
           LORETTA MOCK
    540 S. Ellensburg Ave., Gold Beach 97444.

Gold Hill. FRANCES D. BROWN (R) **
    1969-. Bds: Budget Com.; Bicentennial Com.
Party: Precinct Com. 1972. Org: State Employees
Assoc. Occ: Librarian & Teacher's Aid. B:
8/2/25. Add: 1204 2nd Ave., Gold Hill 97525
(503)855-1031.

Grants Pass. BERNICE CARNES AYERS (D)
    1976-. Bds: V-Ch., City Budget Com.; City
Beautification Com. Party: State Del. 1976;
Precinct Committeewoman 1965-77. Prev: City
Budget Com. 1975-76. Educ: Rogue Community
Coll. 1975 AS; Southern Ore. Coll. 1977 BS.
Occ: Coll. Instructor. B: 10/25/25. Add:
1702 SW "K" St., Grants Pass 97526.

Greenhorn. LILLIAN POTTER
    775 S. Clematis Rd., W. Linn 97068.

Gresham. PAULA BENTLEY (D)
    1976-. Bds: Bd., Columbia Region Assoc. of
Govts. Party: Precinct Committeewoman 1974-76.
Prev: Planning Cmsn. 1975-76. Educ: U. of Okla.
1965 BA. Occ: Public Information Officer. B:
3/24/43. Add: 1787 SE Williams Ave., Gresham
97030 (503)666-3741.

Gresham. MARY C. OPRAY (R)
    1974-. Bds: Cnty. Economic Devt. Com.; Tri-
Cnty. Local Govt. Com. Org: Parents Assoc.
Occ: Budget Analyst. B: 11/27/23. Add: 1318
NE Hogan Dr., Gresham 97030.

Haines. RUTH BAHLER
        RUTH CLARK
    Box 14, Haines 97833.

Halfway. ETHEL M. DAVIS (D) **
    1973-. Prev: Postmaster 1963-65. Occ:
Library & Teacher Aid. B: 11/20/24. Add:
P.O. Box 424, Halfway 97834.

Halfway. EDWARDINE MALONE OLIVER (D)
    1976-. Org: ANA. Educ: Los Angeles Cnty.
General Hospital School of Nursing RN. Occ: RN.
B: 12/18/10. Add: P.O. Box 416, Halfway 97834.

Halfway. MRS. HERBIE SCOTT
    P.O. Box 738, Halfway 97834.

Halsey. LINDA COONROD
    P.O. Box 35, Halsey 97348.

Hammond. ELOUISE YORK (D)
    1975-. Bds: Ch., Water & Sewers Dept. Prev:
Adv. Council HUD 1975-76; Citizens Adv. Com. Hwy.
Dept. 1974-76. Org: NEA. Educ: Colo. U. 1951 BA.
Occ: Media Specialist. B: 6/16/29. Add: 535
Russell Dr., Hammond 97121 (503)861-1675.

Happy Valley. SANDRA H. COATS (D)
    1976-. Prev: Park Cmsn. 1972-76. Org: PTA.
Occ: Secretary. B: 5/12/38. Add: 10636 S.E.
Melita Dr., Portland 97236 (503)760-3325.

Harrisburg. MARTHA WOODS
    354 Smith St., Harrisburg 97446.

Hines. SOPHIE RODABAUGH
    P.O. Box 336, Hines 97738.

Hood River. DONNA J. DAVIS (R)
    1976-. Bds: Ch., Police Com.; Judiciary Com.;
Fire Com. Prev: St. Peter's Landmark Cmsn. 1967-
70; Economic Devt. Dist. 1969-70; Housing Com.
1975-77. Educ: Lewis & Clark Coll. 1956 BA. Occ:
Traffic Service Analyst. B: 10/19/34. Add: 825
Sherman St., Hood Rvr. 97031 (503)386-0392.

Hood River. MARY C. REED (R)
    1976-. Occ: Appliance & Television Store
Manager. B: 9/21/29. Add: 1304 Lincoln, Hood
Rvr. 97031 (503)386-2467.

Hubbard. BEVERLY KOUTNY
    BETTY ZACH
    P.O. Box 237, Hubbard 97032.

Huntington. BONITA GAY LE RANEY (D)
    1975-. Bds: Ch., Waste & Disposable. Occ:
Cook/Waitress. B: 7/7/33. Add: Box 82, Huntington 97907 (503)869-2424.

Idanha. ALICE STORMER
    P.O. Box 396, Idanha 97350.

Imbler. RUTH ANN ZEMKE (R)
    1976-. Occ: Secretary/Bookkeeper. B: 8/4/44.
Add: 5th & Esther, Imbler 97841.

Independence. NANCY GREER
    240 Monmouth St., Independence 97351.

Ione. LINDA LA RUE
    DOROTHY STEFANI
    Box 361, Ione 97843.

Irrigon. DOROTHY E. IRISH (R)
    1971-. Bds: School Long Range Planning Com.;
Senior Citizens Cnty. Adv. Council. B: 2/14/15.
Add: Rt. 2, Box 530, Irrigon 97844.

Jacksonville. CATHERINE KIMBALL
    P.O. Box 7, Jacksonville 97530.

Jefferson. DOREEN SALTER
    P.O. Box 83, Jefferson 97352.

John Day. DAISY KUIZENGA
    240 S. Canyon Blvd., John Day 97845.

Johnson City. DOROTHY FRANCIS
    CONNIE WEBB
    8021 S.E. Posey, Johnson City 97222.

King City. JEAN K. YOUNG (R) **
    1974-. Bds: Traffic Safety Commissioner.
Party: County Com. 1947- ; Precinct Com. 1936-;
Presidential Elector 1960-68; Secretary, State
Central Com. Prev: Ch., Ore. Wage & Hour Cmsn.
1948-58. Org: LWV; Altrusa; Fed. Women's Org.;
PTA; Rep. Women's Club. B: 5/1/04. Add: 12390
SW King Richard Dr., King City 97223 (503)
639-4082.

Klamath Falls. BERTHA LESTER HULTMAN (D)
    1977-. Bds: Parks & Recreation Bd. Party:
State Del. 1973-76; Ch., Dem. Cnty. Com. 1975-
77; State Exec. Bd. 1976-77. Prev: Teachers
Standards & Practices Cmsn. 1968-74. Educ:
U. of Wash. BS. B: 3/26/10. Add: 330 Pacific
Terrace, Klamath Falls 97601 (503)884-3161.

Lake Oswego. BEVERLY HENDERSON (R)
    1975-. Bds: Repr., Nat. Women in Municipal
Govt.; Water Study Com.; Heritage Assoc. Party:
State Del. 1972; Precinct Committeewoman 1970-
75; State Program Ch. 1968-70. Org: Fed. Women's
Club; Heritage Assoc.; Rep. Women's Club; Jr.
Historical Society. Occ: Administrative Asst.
Add: 2102 S.E. Country Club Rd., Lk. Oswego
97034 (503)636-3601.

Lake Oswego. CORKY KIRKPATRICK (D)
    1975-. Bds: Ch., Columbia Region Assoc. of
Govts. Org: Ore. Press Women. Educ: U. of Ia.
1961 BA; U. of Portland 1977 MA. Occ: Writer.
B: 7/4/38. Add: 2251 Fernwood Cir., Lk. Oswego
97034 (503)636-3601.

Lake Oswego. MARY H. NEELY (D)
    1976-. Org: LWV. Educ: U. of Ore. 1951 BA.
B: 8/24/30. Add: 3240 Upr. Dr., Lk. Oswego
97034 (503)636-3601.

Lebanon. BETTY MULKINS COLLINS (R)
    1974-. Bds: Ch., Finance Com.; Alt., Council
of Govts. Org: League of Ore. Cities; Chamber
of Commerce; LWV. B: 3/15/30. Add: 659 E.
Sherman St., Lebanon 97355 (503)258-3185.

Lexington. PATRICIA WRIGHT (D)
    1975-. Bds: Ch., Budget Com.; Ch., Curriculum
Com. Prev: Subdiv. Review Com. 1974-77; State
Grant Review Com. 1976-77; Cnty. Mental Health
Adv. Bd. 1974-77. Org: ANA; Grange. Educ: Good
Samaritan School of Nursing 1954 RN. Occ: RN.
B: 1/11/34. Add: Box 521, Lexington 97839
(503)989-8169.

Lonerock.   LOIS HOPKINS
        LORRAINE NICHOLS
    Town Hall, Lonerock   97823.

Long Creek.   BELLE DAVIS
    P.O. Box 148, Long Creek   97856.

Lostine.   ESTEL OLLIS
    P.O. Box 23, Lostine   97857.

Lowell.   MARLENE COWLISHAW   (D)
    1976-.   Bds: Citizens Adv. Com. on Economic
Devt.   Party: State Del. 1968; Precinct Committee-
woman 1964-68.   B: 7/21/35.   Add: 130 Hyland Ln.,
P.O. Box 164, Lowell   97452.

Lyons.   VIRGINIA GRIFFITH
        LOIS SLOVER
    541 5th St., Lyons   97358.

Madras.   REBA POWELL   (R) **
    1974-.   Bds: Finance Com.; Police Com.; Central
Ore. Intergovernmental Council.   Org: Ore. Assoc.
Community Educ.; County Literacy Council.   Educ:
Linfield Coll. 1960 BS.   Occ: Adult Learning
Center Instructor.   B: 9/6/38.   Add: 305 Hillcrest,
Madras   97741   (503)475-2344.

Malin.   MARTHA BROTHANEK (D)
    B: 5/4/09.   Add: Malin   97632.

Manzanita.   PAULA EDWARDS
    543 Laneda Ave., Manzanita   97130.

Medford.   VIRGINIA VOGEL
    Bds: Municipal Budget Com.; Administrative
Policy Com. of the Bear Creek Area Transportation
Study; Hospital Facilities Authority.   Org: Nat.
Secretaries Assoc.; BPW.   Educ: UCLA BA.   Occ:
Personal Service Repr. for Bank.   Add: 2252 Table
Rock Rd., #149, Medford   97501.

Maupin.   BETTY OLSON
        RITA ROLPH
    Maupin

Mill City.   ANN CAREY
    P.O. Box 256, Mill City   97360.

Milwaukie.   JOY B. BURGESS   (R)
    1972-.   Bds: Ch., Cnty. Growth Management Task
Force.   Prev: City Councilwoman 1972-76.   Org:
Parks & Beautification Com.; PTA.   B: 9/20/28.
Add: 12208 SE 22nd Ave., Milwaukie   97222   (503)
659-5171.

Molalla.   KIRBY KINDALL
    P.O. Box 248, Molalla   97038.

Monmouth.   PATRICIA JAFFER
    151 W. Main St., Monmouth   97361.

Monmouth.   JUDITH MILLER   (D)
    1974-.   Bds: Ch., Wage & Salary Com.; Ch.,
Rules Com.; Planning Cmsn.   Party: State Del.
1968-74; Nat. Del. 1972; Precinct Committeewoman
1968- ; V-Ch., Central Com. 1968-72; State Exec.
Bd. 1971-76; V-Ch., State Party 1975-76; Nat.
Campaign Com. 1976.   Prev: Cnty. Home Rule Charter

Com. 1972-75.   Org: Civic Club; WPC.   B:
10/14/42.   Add: 453 Scott St., Monmouth   97361
(503)838-0722.

Monroe.   DOROTHEA J. ANGEVINE   (D)
    1976-.   Bds: City Planning Cmsn.   Occ:
School Bus Driver.   B: 9/20/37.   Add: P.O. Box
171, 321 9th St., Monroe   97456   (503)847-5175.

Monroe.   CHARLETTE LINDSEY
    655 Commercial St., Monroe   97456.

Myrtle Creek.   JEAN NORTON
        KATHRYN PETERMAN
    P.O. Box 745, Myrtle Creek   97457.

Myrtle Point.   THELMA BUSHNELL
    424 5th St., Myrtle Point   97458.

Nehalem.   KAY ANDERSON
    8th & H Sts., Nehalem   97131.

Newberg.   JANE A. HARRIS   (D)
    1970-.   Bds: Cnty. Economic Devt. Com.; Bd.
of Dir's. Human Resources Center; Citizens
Involvement Adv. Com.   Party: Precinct Committee-
woman 1972-77.   Prev: Tri-Cnty. Council of Govts.,
Area Aging Agency 1973-76.   Org: BPW; Common
Cause; Public Citizen; Ore. Environmental Council.
B: 4/11/12.   Add: 212 W. 1st St., Newberg   97132.

Newport.   MONA OTTEM
    810 SW Alder St., Newport   97365.

North Bend.   SHIRLEY MORTENSEN
        NAN TEN EYCK
    P.O. Box B, North Bend   97459.

Ontario.   RAMONA SWAN
    241 SW 1st St., Ontario   97914.

Pendleton.   FHONA O'GARA
    P.O. Box 190, Pendleton   97801.

Philomath.   BONNIE CRAFT
    P.O. Box 549, Philomath   97370.

Philomath.   JANET TUNISON   (D)
    1976-.   Bds: Plan Cmsn.; Park & Recreation
Com.; Ch. Street Com.   Occ: Avon Repr.   B:
2/5/30.   Add: 2239 Applegate, Philomath   97370.

Phoenix.   JEANNE F. BARLOW   (R)
    1966-.   Bds: Ch., Park Cmsn.; Ch., Finance
Com.; Building Cmsn.   Org: Amer. Legion Aux.
Educ: La Salle U. 1977 CPA.   Occ: Accountant.
B: 11/6/25.   Add: Box 391, Phoenix   97535
(503)535-1955.

Phoenix.   ORLINZA A. BULLOCK
    P.O. Box 327, Phoenix   97535.

Pilot Rock.   KATHRYN MURRAY
    144 N. Alder, Pilot Rock   97868.

Portland.   CONNIE MC CREADY   (R)
    1970-.   Party: Nat. Alt. 1968; Precinct
Committeewoman 1950-70.   Prev: State Repr. 1967-
70.   Educ: U. of Ore. 1943 BA.   B: 8/20/21.
Add: 2407 NE 27th, Portland   97212   (503)248-4145.

Portland. MILDRED A. SCHWAB
1220 SW 5th Ave., Portland 97204.

Powers. JOAN ALTENBACH
P.O. Box 364, Powers 97466.

Powers. FRANCES ELLEN MC KENZIE (R)
1976-. Org: Chamber of Commerce. B: 6/7/21.
Add: 390 4th Ave., Powers 97466.

Powers. MABEL SHORB
P.O. Box 250, Powers 97466.

Prescott. NOMA CARTER
Rt. 2, Box 530, Ranier 97048.

Rainier. ELIZABETH VILHAUER (D) **
1974-. Bds: Ch., Finance & License. Occ:
Cashier & Customer Service. B: 10/8/30. Add:
520 E. 4th St., Rainier 97048 (503)556-4561.

Redmond. SHERI HAHN
MARY HODSON
455 S. 7th, Redmond 97756.

Reedsport. CONNIE GIBBONS
P.O. Box 358, Reedsport 97467.

Richland. E. LORRAINE SPECHT (I)
1976-. Org: Rural Mail Carriers Union; Grange.
Educ: St. Vincent Hospital Coll. of Nursing 1947
RN; Antelope Vly. Coll. 1956 AA. Occ: Rural Mail
Carrier. B: 10/6/26. Add: 3rd & Lake St.,
Richland 97870.

Riddle. PHYLLIS GARREN
NOVIDA SAMPLES
P.O. Box 143, Riddle 97269.

Rivergrove. JUDETTE C. HEMACHANDRA (D)
1976-. Educ: Portland State U. 1973 BS. Occ:
Marketing Staff Manager. B: 11/3/49. Add:
5650 SW Childs Rd., Rivergrove 97034 (503)
242-8132.

Rockaway. VIRGINIA CARRELL
P.O. Box 35, Rockaway 97136.

Rogue River. ANNA B. CLASSICK (D) **
1972-. Bds: Council of Governments; City
Planning Cmsn.; River Area Planning Cmsn. Org:
Civic Improvement Club; Dem. Club. B: 6/2/06.
Add: 419 Bergland, Rogue River 97537 (503)
582-3482.

Rufus. MRS. A. JORDAN
P.O. Box 27, Rufus 97050.

Salem. ELLEN C. LOWE
ELLEN A. SCHNEIDER
555 Liberty St. SE, Salem 97301.

Scio. JOYCE MORSE
ANN SAMPLE
P.O. Box 37, Scio 97374.

Scotts Mills. SHAREN JENSEN
Town Hall, Scotts Mills 97375.

Scotts Mills. JO ANN PINKHAM
Town Hall, Scotts Mills 97375.

Scotts Mills. CAROL ANN ROSENBLAD (R)
1972-. B: 4/10/32. Add: Box 85, Scotts
Mills 97375.

Shaniko. MARGARET JACOBS
JEANINE OAKES
MARSHA PALMER
P.O. Box 17, Shaniko 97057.

Sheridan. SHARON AGEE
DONNA JOHN
IRENE PANEK
139 NW Yamhill, Sheridan 97378.

Siletz. CAROLYN BROWN (D)
1974-. Bds: Ch., Fire Cmsnr.; Grant Writing;
Planning. Org: Ore. Personnel & Guidance Assoc.;
OES. Educ: Dan. State Teachers Coll. 1957 BSEd.;
Ore. Coll. of Educ. 1974 MSEd. Occ: School
Counselor. B: 8/24/29. Add: Box 87, Siletz
97380 (503)444-2521.

Sisters. PEGGY BARBEAU
P.O. Box 37, Sisters 97759.

Sodaville. LUCILLE JASMER
38087 Middle Ridge Dr., Lebanon 97355.

Springfield. SANDRA RENNIE
4th & North "A" Sts., Springfield 97477.

Sutherlin. NAOMI BENNETT
PATRICIA PUTMAN
Central Ave. & Umpqua, Sutherlin 97479.

Tillamook. ELIZABETH I. COULTER (D) **
1974-. Bds: Streets & Parks; City Planning
& Zoning; City Budget Com. Org: Advisory Bd.,
Family Planning; County Health Dept. Educ:
Mercy Hospital School of Nursing 1955 RN. Occ:
Supervisor, Obstetrics Dept. B: 5/12/34. Add:
3808 Alder La., Tillamook 97141 (503)842-4861.

Toledo. NANCY BOYER
P.O. Box 220, Toledo 97391.

Troutdale. HELEN F. ALTHAUS (R) **
1973-. Prev: Deputy City Attorney 1953.
Org: ACLU; Bar Assoc. Educ: U. of Ore. 1932
BA; Northwestern School of Law, Lewis & Clark
Coll. 1945 JD. Occ: Attorney. B: 3/26/10.
Add: Rt. 3, Box 1140, Troutdale 97060 (503)
665-5175; 297-1641.

Troutdale. BLANDINE EDWARDS
104 SE Kinbling St., Troutdale 97060.

Turner. WANDA WENDT (D) **
1974-. Bds: Park Commissioner; Street
Light Commissioner. Educ: Ore. Coll. of Educ.
1963 BS. B: 4/12/35. Add: Box 37, Turner
97392 (503)743-2155.

Umatilla. CORA JEAN CARTWRIGHT
911 6th St., Umatilla 97882.

Umatilla. SUE STAMATE (D) **
   1975-. Bds: Police Commissioner; Finance Com.
Org: Labor Union; PTA. Occ: Manager. B: 3/6/25.
Add: 1151 7th St., Umatilla 97882 (503)922-3761.

Umatilla. BETTY STEVENS
   911 6th St., Umatilla 97882.

Unity. PEGGA FISHBURN
   Town Hall, Unity 97884.

Veneta. PATRICIA TAYLOR
   24951 McCutcheon Ave. Veneta 97487.

Warrenton. DELLA WILSON
   147 SW Main, Warrenton 97146.

Waterloo. MARTHA CLARK
         DOROTHY WOODS
   30937 7th St., Lebanon 97355.

West Linn. DARLENE HOOLEY
   City Hall, W. Linn 97068.

Wheeler. MARGARET W. ADAMS
   775 Nehalem Bldv., Wheeler 97147.

Winston. VIVIAN A. BORGAES (D)
   1975-. Occ: Chamber of Commerce; Senior
Citizens. B: 9/25/20. Add: 270 S.E. Gregory,
Winston 97496.

Judges

MERCEDES F. DEIZ (D)
   Judge, Circuit Court. 1972-. Bds: Judicial
Conf., Public Information Com. Prev: Dist. Ct.
Judge 1970-72; Hearing Officer-Workmens Compen-
sation Bd. 1967-70. Org: ABA; Amer. Judicature
Society; Assoc. of Juvenile Ct. Judges; Profess-
ional Women's League; Queens Bench; Urban League;
NAACP. Educ: Hunter Coll. 1939 BS; Northwestern
Coll. of Law 1959 JD. B: 12/13/17. Add: 9144
N. Chautaugua, Portland 97217 (503)248-3229.

HELEN J. FRYE
   Judge, Circuit Court. 1971-. Party: Nat. Del.
1964; Precinct Committeewoman 1956-60. Educ: U.
of Ore. 1953 BA; 1955 MA; 1966 JD. B: 12/10/30.
Add: 39 Westbrook Way, Eugene 97405 (503)687-4258.

JEAN LEWIS
   Judge, Circuit Court. Add: Court Building,
Portland 97217.

JENA V. SCHLEGEL (R)
   Judge, Circuit Court. 1972-. Bds: Ch.,
Judicial Administration Com. of Judicial Conf.
Prev: Deputy Dist. Atty. 1958-64. Org: Zonta;
AAUW. Educ: U. of Okla. 1956 BS; Willamette U.
1958 JD. B: 5/5/34. Add: 1790 Corina Dr. SE,
Salem 97302 (503)588-5027.

State Boards and Commissions

   Office of the Governor, State Capitol Bldg.,
   Salem 97310.

Agriculture, Board of
   LEONA GILMOUR
   CLARA PEOPLES

Ambulances and Emergency Medical Technicians,
Advisory Council on
   CAROL FROST
   SHIRLEY TOBIASSON

American Revolution Bicentennial Commission
   JANET BAUMHOVER
   GERALDINE CHRISTIAN

Architectural Barriers, Advisory Committee on
   JOSEPHINE PEARSON

Arts Commission
   DORIS BOUNDS
   SHIRLEY GITTELSOHN
   MRS. E. CHARLES PRESSMAN
   ELAINE WITTEVEEN

Auctioneers, Board of
   HELEN MARIE WOOD

Bicycles, Advisory Committee on
   RUTH BASCOM
   IRVA D. DEURWAEDER
   LINNEA NELSON

Billing, Factoring and Collection Agencies Board
   FRANCES E. HUNTINGTON

Blind, Commission for the
   BARBARA KESLER

Builders Board
   LORA W. COX

Capitol Planning Commission
   SHARON FATLAND

Consumer Advisory Council
   JOYCE COX DIPPEL
   DORIS SALMON
   MARY JANE SORBER

Cosmetic Therapy, Board of
   GINGER HACKETT
   ISABELL HOYT
   JEAN L. HUNLEY
   MARJORIE I. LANGLEY
   ADRIENNE MILLER

Economic Development Commission
   HELEN JO WHITSELL

Education, Board of
   JOYCE BENJAMIN

Educational Coordinating Commission
   ELIZABETH JOHNSON
   EDITH MADDRON

Elevator Safety Board
KATHRYN L. BUSS

Emergency Medical Technicians II, III and IV,
Advisory Committee on
MARIETTA WALTER

Employment Relations Board
MARIAN CHURCHILL

Energy Facility Siting Council
MARIAN FRANK
M. DAWN DRESSLER

Energy Policy Review Committee
JOYCE COHEN
NANCIE FADELEY

Environmental Quality Commission
JACKLYN L. HALLOCK
GRACE S. PHINNEY

Ethics Commission
SHIRLEY F. CONKLIN

Fair Commission
DOROTHY HULT
MRS. JOSEPH W. SMITH

Fair Dismissal Appeals Board
IRENE CHELDELIN
BARBARA KLEIN
GRACE WILLIAMS
SHARI LEE WORTMAN
ALYCE YOSHIKAI

Field Sanitation Committee
JANET MC LENNAN

Filbert Commission
ELESA NEWELL

Fish and Wildlife Commission
MRS. ALLEN BATEMAN

Fryer Commission
MARGUERITE COXE
CHRISTINE TAYLOR

Furniture and Bedding Advisory Council
NANCY RAWLINSON

Geographic Names Board
PRISCILLA KNUTH
JOSEPHINE MOORE

Geology and Mineral Industries
LEEANNE G. MAC COLL

Health Commission
LORETTA DANIEL
SYLVIA NEMER DAVIDSON
BETTY HAUGEN
MARGUERITE REED

Higher Education, Board of
JANE H. CARPENTER
RUTH O. DANIELS
BETTY FEVES
VALERIE L. MC INTYRE

Housing Council
BETTY NIVEN

Instructional Television and Radio, Advisory
Committee on
ELLA FLOCCHINI
LOIS THOMAS

Intergroup Human Relations Commission
BRENDA GREEN
BERTHA HULTMAN
IRMA JANSEN

Land Conservation and Development Commission
DOROTHY ANDERSON
ANN SQUIER

Lane Transit District
ANNABEL KITZHABER

Law Enforcement Council
AMY BEDFORD
BETTY CROOKS
BRENDA GREEN
PEGGI TIMM

Liquor Control Commission
ELEANOR FORRESTER

Marine Board
ROBERTA SHOOK

Masseurs, Board of
MARIAN KOSZEGI-DABBOUS
DAWNIELLE LORREN

Minor Court Rules Committee
BEVERLY A. MC KELLER

Mobile Home Construction and Safety Standard
Advisory Board
ETHEL GALER

Natural Area Preserves Advisory Committee
PATRICIA HARRIS
MRS. A.E. SIDDALL

Nursery Advisory Committee
IRENE BURDEN

Nursing, Board of
HELEN CARTER
JOYCE COLLING
BETTY M. HAUGEN
ANNA M. HERBERT
LORENE L. PICKETT

Nursing Home Administrators, Board of Examiners
MARGARET DANNER
JOY O'BRIEN
MINNIE STRYFFELER

Parks and Recreation Advisory Committee
LUCILLE BECK

Parole, Board of
ISABEL HEMPE

Pharmacy, Board of
RUTH VANDEVER
BARBARA I. WATSON

Pennsylvania

State Executive and Cabinet

CARYL KLEIN
Secretary of Education. Add: State Capitol, Harrisburg 17120.

State Legislature

State Senate

JEANETTE F. REIBMAN (D)
1967-. Bds: Ch., Educ. Com.; Educ. Cmsn. of the States; Pa. Council on the Arts. Party: Exec. Com., Fed. of Dem. Women. Prev: State Repr. 1955-67. Org: AAUW; LWV. Educ: Hunter Coll. 1937 BA; Ind. U. 1940 JD. B: 8/18/15. Add: 711 Lehigh St., Easton 18042 (717)787-4236.

State House

MARGARET H. GEORGE (D)
1976-. Dist: 143. Bds: House Finance Com.; House Agriculture Com.; House Local Govt. Com. Party: Cnty. Committeewoman 1966-77. Org: AAUW; LWV; Common Cause. Educ: Ursinus Coll. 1949 BA. B: 4/5/28. Add: 79 Buttonwood Ln., Doylestown 18901 (717)783-8514.

HELEN D. GILLETTE (D)
1966-. Dist: 31. Bds: Appropriations; Insurance; Joint Air & Water Conservation Com. Prev: Justice of the Peace 1963-69. Org: NOWL; BPW; Community Service Club; Women's Club. Occ: Insurance Agency Owner. Add: 1917 Freeport Rd., Natrona Hts. 15065 (717)783-8808/8809.

RUTH HARPER (D)
1427 W. Erie Avenue, Philadelphia 19140.

JUNE N. HONAMAN (R)
1977-. Dist: 97. Bds: Ethics; Federal St. Relations; Joint Cmsn. on Election Reform. Party: Nat. Del. 1972, '68, '64; Precinct Committeewoman 1956-64; State Committeewoman 1958-64; V-Ch., Rep. Party 1964-76; Ch., Rules Com. Rep. Party 1973-75. Prev: Pa. Cmsn. on Status of Women 1964-70; Cmsn. on Election Reform 1972-73. Org: BPW; AAUW; Fed. of Women's Clubs; Pa. Council on Rep. Women. Educ: Beaver Coll. 1941 BFA. B: 5/24/20. Add: Landisville 17538 (717)787-5451.

ANITA PALERMO KELLY (D) **
1963-. Dist: 192. Bds: Bd. of Dir., Center for Child Guidance; Health & Welfare Com.; Issuance of Horse Racing Licenses; Professional Licensure; Ethics; Joint State Task Force on State Licensing of Professions & Occupations; Human Services. Party: Com.; Ward Exec. Com.

Org: Dem. Women's Club. Add: 61130 Master St., Philadelphia 19151.

PHYLLIS T. KERNICK (D) **
1974-. Dist: 32. Bds: State Government Com.; Fed. State Relations Com.; Professional Licensure; Ch., Citation Com. County Hospital Dev. Authority; Allegheny Regional Council; Governor's Justice Cmsn.; Cmsn. to Study Fiscal Needs of State Cultural Institutions. Prev: Township Treasurer 1970-76; Township Auditor 1966. Org: LWV; Nat. Fed. of Dem. Women; OWL; Chamber of Commerce; Mental Health; Mental Retardation; Western Pa. Conservancy; Zoological Society. B: 12/14/24. Add: 10753 Frankstown Rd., Pittsburgh 15235 (717) 783-1019.

AGNES M. SCANLON (D)
803 E. Allegheny Ave., Philadelphia 19134.

CARMEL A. SIRIANNI (R) **
Dist: 111. Party: Com. 1954; Del. Nat. Conv. 1964. Org: Rep. Women's Club; Counselors Assoc.; Women's Club. Educ: Bloomsburg State Coll. 1944 BS; Bucknell 1952 MSE; Marywood Coll. 1959 MSG. Occ: Teacher & Guidance Dir. B: 9/14/22. Add: Box 122, Hop Bottom 18824.

ELINOR Z. TAYLOR (R)
1977-. Dist: 156. Bds: Health & Welfare Com.; Educ. Com.; Higher Educ. Assoc. Agency. Prev: Councilwoman 1974-77; Recreation Cmsn. 1974-77. Org: Penna. Educ. Assoc.; Assoc. of Penna. State Coll. & U. Faculty; AAUW; United Fund; Penna. Assoc. of Health, Physical Educ. & Recreation. Educ: West Chester State Teachers Coll. 1943 BS; Temple U. 1958 MEd. B: 4/18/21. Add: 404 Price, West Chester 19380 (717) 787-4331.

DR. HELEN D. WISE (D)
1976-. Dist: 77. Bds: Ch., Sub-Com., Human Resources, Fed.-State Relations; Educ. Com.; Conservation. Org: NEA. Educ: Pa. State U. 1949 BS; Pa. State U. 1952 MEd; Pa. State U. 1969 DEd. B: 9/11/28. Add: 1127 S. Allen St., State Coll. 16801 (717)783-8515.

County Commissions

Columbia. CAROL T. HIDLAY (R)
1976-. Bds: Mental Health; Aging; Day Care. Org: AAUW. Educ: Bloomsburg State Coll. 1969 BS; Bucknell U. 1976 MS. B: 7/15/35. Add: 805 E. 4th St., Bloomsburg 17815 (717)784-1991.

Delaware. FAITH RYAN WHITTLESEY
773 Millbrook Lane, Haverford 19041.

Mc Kean County. LORETTA B. HARRINGTON (D) **
1967-. Bds: Conservation Dist.; Human Services.
B: 11/18/12. Add: R.D. 1, Smethport 16749 (814)
887-5571.

Monroe. NANCY SHUKAITIS (R)
1967-. Bds: Ch., Four Cnty. Task Force; Soil
Conservation Dist.; Economic Devt. Council.
Party: Twp. Committeewoman 1958-68; Secretary
Cnty. Com. 1962-66; V-Ch., Cnty. Com. 1966-68;
Ch., Cnty. Com. 1970- . Org: Del. Vly. Conser-
vation Assoc.; DAR; Save the Del. Coalition;
Soroptimists; Cnty. Council of Rep. Women; Rep.
Club. B: 3/3/25. Add: RD 5, E. Stroudsburg
18301 (717)424-5100.

Philadelphia. MARGARET M. TARTAGLIONE
City Hall, Rm. 136, Phila. 19107.

Potter. EMMALINE PERRY (D)
1974-. Bds: Ch., Bd. of Comsr's. Party: Cnty.
Committeewoman 1954-65; V-Ch., of Cnty. Dem.
Party 1956-61; Registration Ch. 1956-68; Cnty.
Treasurer 1968-70. Org: BPW. Occ: Bus Driver.
B: 11/15/25. Add: Box 147 A, RD #2, Genesee
16923.

Union. THELMA JOHNSON SHOWALTER (R)
1975-. Bds: Tax Reform. Party: State Del.
1974-77; Ch. Cnty. 1974; State V-Ch. 1936-38;
Nat. Committeewoman 1938-40; Nat. Co-Ch. 1940-42.
Prev: Cnty. Cmsnr. 1956-64. Org: State Assoc.
of Cnty. Cmsnr's.; Women's Club; Rep. Women; DAR.
Educ: Bucknell U. 1929 BA. B: 9/2/08. Add: 425
Market, Mifflinburg 17844 (717)524-4461.

Mayors

Boyertown. JANET E. SMITHSON (R)
1976-. Bds: Police Com.; V-Pres., Emergency
Bd. Prev: Councilwoman 1973-76; Planning Bd.
1973-76; Emergency Bd. 1973. Org: NEA; Civic
Ctr. Com.; Historical Society; Rep. Club. Educ:
Muhlenberg Coll. 1963 BS; Brown U. 1967 PhD.
Occ: Teacher. B: 1/24/42. Add: 108 Crest Dr.,
Boyertown 19512 (215)367-2688.

Brookhaven. VIRGINIA SIEDZIKOWSKI (D) **
1975-. Prev: Councilwoman 1973-75. Org: Dem.
Club. B: 1/1/28. Add: 3517 Victor Ave., Brookhaven 19015 (215)TR 4-2557.

Clarksville. ANN ROTA
Borough Bldg., Clarksville 15322.

Clintonville. EDNA ADKINS
Borough Bldg., Clintonville 16372.

Coatesville. FRANCES E. REGENER (D)
1972-. Party: Party Ch., 1960-62; Committeewoman 1956-60; Judge of Elections 1960-62. Prev:
Governor's Justice Com. 1974-77; Alderwoman 1966-
72. Org: Chamber of Commerce; Cnty. Women's Dem.
Club. B: 8/13/18. Add: 208 Charles St., Coatesville (215)384-0300/0301.

Corry. MARY ANN KIBLER **
Educ: Villa Maria Coll. 1958 BS; Nat. U. of
Mexico 1967 MD. Occ: M.D. Add: 303 N. Center
St., Corry 16407 (814)663-4162.

Glen Hope. VERNA L. BELL (R)
1963-. Occ: Baker. B: 2/3/09. Add: Glen
Hope 16645 (814)672-8148.

Harmony. MARY REMINGTON
Town Hall, W. Hickory 16370.

Hughesville. PAULINE R. MONTOGOMERY (D)
1974-. Party: Nat. Alt. 1972; Committeewoman
1974-78; Cnty. Exec. Com. 1974-78. Prev:
Councilwoman 1970-74. Org: Pa. Pharmacist Assoc.;
Women's Club. Educ: Temple U. 1950 BS. Occ:
Pharmacist. B: 6/20/29. Add: 165 N. Main St.,
Hughesville 17737 (717)584-2041.

Jermyn. ELEANOR CAWLEY
P.O. Box 40, Jermyn 18433.

Kennett Square. MARGARET WORRALL
Broad & Linden Sts., Kennett Square 19348.

Knox. JENNIFER WESNER
P.O. Box 366, Knox 16232.

Macungie. MILDRED D. ECK (D) **
1974-. Bds: State Police Dept.; Inter-
personnel Act Com.; Recreation Cmsn.; Mid-
Eastern Counties & Boroughs Assoc. Prev:
Councilwoman 1972-74. Org: BPW; Bicentennial;
PTA; Women's Club; Women's Dem. Club. Educ:
Allentown Hospital School of Nursing 1957 RN.
Occ: RN. B: 7/20/36. Add: 41 W. Chesnut St.,
Macungie 18062 (215)965-5400; 965-5755.

Mifflin. RUTH CRAMER WATERS (D)
1972-. Bds: Rcpr. Tri-Cnty. Boroughs; State
Resolutions Com. Prev: Library Bd. 1965-66,
1973- ; Councilwoman 1972-76. Org: NEA; BPW;
Bicentennial Com.; Dem. Women's Club. Educ:
Juniata Coll. 1939 BA; Pa. State U. 1957 MA.
Occ: Library Supervisor. B: 12/15/17. Add:
2 Main St., Mifflin 17058.

New Florence. MOLLIE SPORY
Borough Bldg., New Florence 15944.

Newry. MARY J. HITE (D)
1970-. Prev: Auditor. B: 8/30/15. Add:
200 Allegheny St., Newry 16665.

Richlandtown. MARY C. GRIDA (R)
1975-. Prev: Town Auditor 1973-75. Org:
Pa. Mayors Assoc. Occ: Restaurant/Grocery
Store Owner. B: 1/21/35. Add: 36 N. Main St.,
Richlandtown 18955 (215)536-2691.

Seven Springs. LOIS DUPRE (R) **
1967-. Prev: Councilwoman 1964-67. Educ:
Northwestern U. 1954 BS. B: 6/29/33. Add:
Seven Springs, Champion 15622 (814)926-2031.

Smithfield. MILLIE S. MOSER (D)
1976-. Prev: Bd. Member 1964-67. B:
11/17/05. Add: 16 Highhouse St., Smithfield
15478 (412)569-9567.

Sykesville. BARBARA HARVEY
Borough Bldg., Sykesville 15865.

Ulysses. MARY DOERING
Borough Bldg., Ulysses 16948.

Local Councils

Abbottstown. BETTY HOLLINGER
                DELORES SHAFFER
    Borough Bldg., Abbottstown 17301.

Addison. WILMA L. GEORGE
    Borough Bldg., Addison 15411.

Alba. EDNA MURRAY
    Borough Bldg., Alba 16910.

Allentown. THELMA BARNES
    City Hall, 435 Hamilton St., Allentown 18101.

Ambler. BONNIE M. KROLL (R)
    1976-. Bds: Chamber of Commerce. Party:
Committeewoman 1973- . Org: BPW; Mayor's Exec.
Com.; Rep. Club; PTA. Occ: Office Manager. B:
6/9/41. Add: 230 Belmont Ave., Ambler 19002
(215)646-1000.

Arendtsville. REBA ALBRIGHT
    P.O. Box 295, Arendtsville 17303.

Armagh. ANNA GRACE BIDLEMAN
                BESS RODGERS
    Borough Bldg., Armagh 15920.

Atglen. MARIE K. MALMBERG (D) **
    1974-. Org: Women's Club; Civic Assoc. Occ:
Secretary. B: 8/24/20. Add: 711 Valley Ave.,
Atglen 19310 (215)593-6692.

Atglen. EDYTHE A. WENTZ (D) **
    1973-. Bds: Finance; Streets. Party: Ch.,
Local Com. 1960-71. Prev: School Bd. 1961-67.
Educ: Knox Coll. 1930 BA. B: 1/25/10. Add:
235 High St., Atglen 19310 (215)593-6854.

Auburn. BEVERLY BAUER
    Borough Bldg., Auburn 17922.

Auburn. DOLORES J. BERGER (D)
    1976-. Bds: Ch., Zoning Com.; Ch., Lighting;
Finance Com. B: 10/19/31. Add: 235 Pine St.,
Auburn 17922.

Auburn. MYRTLE KOCH
    Borough Bldg., Auburn 17922.

Avalon. DOROTHY C. DOWNES (R) **
    1973-. Bds: Ch., Corporations, Utilities &
Planning; Health Com.; Interboro Relations. Org:
Civic Assoc.; Rep. Women. B: 9/4/13. Add: 717
Center Ave., Avalon 15202.

Avoca. IRENE TIMONEY MC DONALD (D)
    1969-. Bds: Council Pres.; Ch., Police Com.;
Ch., Road; Ch., Sanitation. Prev: Auditor 1964-
69. Org: Amer. Cancer Society; Amer. Heart Assoc.;
Women's Club. B: 7/12/11. Add: 741 Spring St.,
Avoca 18641 (717)457-4123.

Baldwin. MARY AGNES CONNORS
    3344 Churchview Ave., Baldwin 15227.

Baldwin. HELEN VENTRONE
    10 Community Park Dr., Pittsburgh 15234.

Barnesboro. EVELYN TRETINIK (D) **
    1973-. Bds: Recreation Com.; Civic Improve-
ments; Finance Com. Org: Dem. Club; Library
Assoc. B: 7/20/27. Add: 142, Park Ave.,
Barnesboro 15714 (814)948-8230.

Bath. ELIZABETH L. FIELDS (D)
    1974-. Bds: Mid-Boro Assoc. Org: Amer.
Medical Record Assoc.; Women's Dem. Club. Occ:
Professor. B: 9/2/41. Add: 119 N. Chestnut
St., Bath 18014 (215)837-6842.

Beech Creek. SARAH E. ELDER (R)
    1971-. Prev: Borough Auditor 1968-71. Org:
BPW; Friendship Community Services. Occ:
Secretary. B: 5/9/21. Add: Harrison St.,
Beech Creek 16822 (717)962-2291.

Bellevue. ROSEMARY HEFLIN (D)
    1976-. Bds: Ch., Parks & Recreation; Joint
Recreation; Works Dept. Party: Committeewoman
1970-77. Org: Dem. Women's Club; PTA. Occ:
Shoe Saleswoman. B: 12/8/32. Add: 545 Orchard
Ave., Bellevue 15202 (412)766-6164.

Ben Avon. MARIANNE WOLFE
    7101 Church Ave., Pittsburgh 15202.

Ben Avon Heights. NANCY K. HANSEN
    5 Biddeford Rd., Pittsburgh 15202.

Benezett. HELEN V. TUTTLE (R)
    1976-. Bds: Ch., Bd. of Supervisors. Prev:
Planning Cmsn. 1973-76. Org: NEA. Educ: Ind.
U. of Pa. 1954 BS. Occ: Art Instructor. B:
6/8/31. Add: Box #4 RD, Benezett 15821 (814)
787-4110.

Bernville. MARY ANN BROWN WATTS (D)
    1976-. Bds: Ch., Park & Recreation Com.;
Safety Com.; Finance Com. Prev: Com. on Aging
1964-65. Org: NEA; Women's Club; LWV; AAUW;
PTO. Educ: Cheyney State Coll. 1949 BS. Occ:
Teacher. B: 9/13/27. Add: Box 117, Bernville
19506 (215)488-1102.

Bethlehem. DOLORES W. CASKEY (D)
    Bds: Library Bd.; Redevt. Authority. Org:
LWV. Occ: Consumer Writer. B: 10/25/20. Add:
3112 Center St., Bethlehem 18017 (215)
865-7135.

Big Run. GLORIA BARBER
    Borough Bldg., Big Run 15715.

Birmingham. MAIDA HOOVER
                MARY PRYOR
                LUELLA SMITH
    Box 46-X, R.D. 1, Tyrone 16686.

Birmingham Township. HELEN A. BAUMAN
    Box 178, Chadds Ford 19317.

Blakeslee. CHARLOTTE J. DAVENPORT (R)
    1975-. Org: Women's Club; PTA; Community
Assoc. B: 5/12/33. Add: Fern Ridge, Blakeslee
18610 (717)646-2785.

Blooming Valley. HELEN DANGEL (D)
1975-. Party: Cnty. Committeewoman 1968-77.
Org: Labor Union. Occ: Cashier. Add: RD #2,
Saegertown 16433.

Brackenridge. ALYCE L. GILBOUX (D)
1973-. Bds: Ch., Finance Com.; Street Com.
Prev: Bd. of Educ. 1963-69; Bd. of Dir's., Senior
Citizens. Org: Dem. Guild. Add: 821 Cleveland
Ave., Brackenridge 15014 (412)224-0800.

Bradford Woods. JUDITH G. MC INTYRE (R)
1976-. Bds: N. Pittsburg Community Devt. Corp.;
Planning Liaison Com.; Planning Cmsn. Org:Parent
Faculty Group. Educ: Westminster Coll. 1959 BA;
U. of Pittsburgh 1961 MA. Occ: Educ. Consultant.
B: 2/4/38. Add: Box 153, Delmar Rd., Bradford
Woods 15015.

Bridgeport. ELEANORE M. WILKINSON (D)
1976-. Bds: Ch., Park & Recreation Com.;
Finance Com.; Health & Sanitation Com. Party:
Committeewoman 1965. Org: Bicentennial Com.;
Bridgeport Dem. Org. Occ: Scheduler. B: 10/21/20.
Add: 611 Green St., Bridgeport 19405 (215)
272-1811.

Bridgeville. DIANE L. EVANGELISTA (D)
1974-. Bds: Planning Cmsn.; Cnty. Boroughs
Assoc.; Ch., Administration. Prev: Govt. Study
Cmsn. 1973-74. Org: Dir., Public Library. Occ:
Cosmetologist. B: 2/24/24. Add: 514 Dewey Ave.,
Bridgeville 15017 (412)221-6012.

Bristol. L. MARIE MASCIA
Twp. Building, 2501 Oxford Valley Rd.,
Levittown 19057.

Brookhaven. JANICE M. SAWICKI (D)
1975-. Bds: Ch., Safety Com.; Public Works
Com.; Liaison, Fire. Party: Brookhaven Dem. Party
Ch. 1976-78. Org: Pa. Bar Assoc.; Cnty. Bar
Assoc. Educ: Pa. State U. 1972 BA; Widener Coll.
1975 JD. Occ: Atty. B: 10/4/51. Add: 4809
Shepherd St., Brookhaven 19015 (215)TR4-2557.

Brownsville. BERTHA HAWLL
Municipal Bldg., Brownsville 15417.

Burgettstown. JACQUELYN BIANCHI
115 Main St., Burgettstown 15021.

Burnside. JOAN BOUCH
Borough Bldg., Burnside 15721.

California. PATSY ALFANO
VIRGINIA PIPIK
Box 696, California 15419.

Callimon. SUSAN E. ALLMAN
R.D. #4, Meyersdale 15552.

Camp Hill. RUTH C. WYRE
2201 Market St., Camp Hill 17011.

Carbondale. BETTY ANN MORAN
City Hall, 1 N. Main St., Carbondale 18407.

Carmichaels. LUCILLE B. BUTLER
Box 318-E, Carmichaels 15320.

Carnegie. EILEEN PRESCOTT (D) **
1973-. Bds: Parks & Recreation; Finance
Com.; Bicentennial Com. Party: V-Ch. County
Com. 1960-75; County Com. 1956-75. Occ:
Department Head. B: 11/11/19. Add: 318 Dawson
Ave., Carnegie 15106 (412)355-4213.

Carroll Valley. SALLY B. CORTNER (D) **
1974-. Bds: Personnel, Finance; Municipal
Services Planning Cmsn.; Public Relations.
B: 5/28/08. Add: Box 266, Fairfield 17320
(717)642-8269.

Carroll Valley. BERENICE E. HESS (D)
1975-. Bds: Ch., Ordinance Screening; Parks
& Recreation; Planning Cmsn. Org: Common Cause;
Citizens Assoc. Educ: Milwaukee-Downer Coll.
1932 BA; Columbia U. 1947 MSW. B: 6/15/10.
Add: 23 Hilltop Trl., N.W., Fairfield 17320
(717)642-8269.

Cassandra. TERESA E. KULICK (D)
Prev: Judge of Election 1958-66. B: 9/13/16.
Add: P.O. Box 64, Cassandra 15925 (814)
736-4426.

Cassville. LUCILLE KUHNS
Borough Bldg., Cassville 16623.

Catasauqua. LOUISE M. PETERMAN (R)
1974-. Bds: Pres., Council. Prev: Recre-
ation Cmsn. 1972-74. Org: State Assoc. of
Boroughs; Mid.-E. Cnty's. Assoc. of Boroughs;
Fellowship in Serving Humanity. Educ: Seton
Hall Coll. 1959 BA. B: 10/30/37. Add: 306
Bridge St., Catasauqua 18032 (215)264-0571.

Center Valley. GLORIA B. WALSH
Box 278, Twp. Municipal Bldg., Center Valley
18034.

Centerville. DORIS O. FULLOM
Borough Bldg., Centerville 16404.

Central City. CATHERINE HILSHANSKY
124 Walnut St., Central City 15926.

Centralia. EVA MOREN
Borough Bldg., Centralia 17927.

Chalfant. DOLORES REPIC
218 North Ave., E. Pittsburgh 15112.

Chalfont. RITA BLANDIN
101 N. Main St., Chalfont 18914.

Cherry Tree. ROSE ANN FARABAUGH (D)
1974-. Org: Civic Club. B: 7/12/25. Add:
Box 106, Cherry Tree 15724 (814)743-6879.

Clarendon. GEORGIANNA SHEA
Borough Bldg., Clarendon 16313.

Clarion. RUTH HELEN SLOAN (D)
1969-. Bds: Ch., Adv. Com. Personnel; Property & Persons. Org: Dem. Assoc. Occ: Insurance
Agent. B: 6/24/10. Add: 23 E. 8th Ave.,
Clarion 16214 (814)226-8830.

Clarksville. MARGARET SHULSKY
Borough Bldg., Clarksville 15322.

Clearfield. CAROL BELIN
221 E. Market St., Clearfield 16830.

Cleona. LOTTIE E. PATTON (R) **
1973-. Bds: Shade Tree Cmsn.; Recreation Com.
Org: Women's Club. Occ: Secretary. B: 2/4/19.
Add: 556 E. Maple St., Cleona 17042 (717)
272-6151.

Clifton Heights. CLAUDIA FAGIOLI
EVELYN HESS
P.O. Box 151, Clifton Hts. 19018.

Clintonville. RAE SCHAEFFER
Borough Bldg., Clintonville 16372.

Clintonville. HARRIET TROJANOWSKI (D)
1975-. Bds: Ch., Sidewalk Com. Party: Local
Committeewoman. B: 2/27/27. Add: Box 75,
Emlenton St., Clintonville 16372.

Clymer. EVELYN DAVIS
Borough Bldg., Clymer 15728.

Coal Center. ISABELLE LORRAINE SETARO (D)
1976-. B: 12/13/17. Add: P.O. Box 227,
Federal St., Coal Ctr. 15423 (412)938-2626.

Coaldale. CAROL FORD
EMMA KERSSE
Borough Bldg., Six Mile Run 16679.

Coaldale. MARGARET SHARPE
Borough Bldg., Coaldale 18218.

Coalmont. BEVERLY BLACK
AUDREY MORNINGSTAR
R.D. 1, Saxton 16678.

Colebrook Township. PAULINE A. SIMCOX
Farrandsville 17734.

College Township. DOLORES A. TARICANI (R)
1975-. Bds: Ch., Regional Public Safety Com.
Party: Precinct V-Ch. 1965-69. Prev: Zoning Bd.
1965-75; Governor Study Cmsn. 1973-75. Org:
Rep. Women. Occ: Office Manager. B: 9/10/33.
Add: 224 Outer Dr., State Coll. 16801 (814)
238-3091.

Columbia. PHYLLIS GAMBER
3rd & Locust Sts., Columbia 17512.

Colwyn. MARGARET DRISCOLL
3rd & Spruce Sts., Colwyn 19023.

Confluence. ELOSIE HALVERSON
Box 85, Confluence 15424.

Conneaut Lake. LORETTA RHODES
P.O. Box 335, Conneaut Lake 16316.

Conneautville. AMELIA M. COLLINS (D)
1976-. Bds: Ch., Lights; Recreation; Planning
Cmsn. Org: Women's Club; Library Bd.; PTO. B:
8/13/36. Add: 504 Jefferson St., Conneautville
16406.

Connellsville. JOAN D. MILLER (D)
1976-. Bds: Ambulance Bd.; Health Bd.;
Firemans Pension Bd. Party: Committeewoman
1967-77. Org: AFL-CIO; BPW; Dem. Club. B:
12/26/32. Add: 1228 Chestnut, Connellsville
15425 (412)628-1127.

Connorvenessing. NORMA B. HARTER (R)
1970-. Bds: Council Pres. Org: BPW. Occ:
Saleswoman. B: 4/5/31. Add: Box 16,
Connorvenessing 16027.

Crafton. ELIZABETH CONLEY (R)
1974-. Bds: Ch., Leg.; Ch., Property & Wage
Tax; Ch., Parks. Party: Judge of Elections
1968-73; Committeewoman 1970-74. Org: Concerned
Tax Payers; Civic Club. B: 5/30/28. Add: 3 E.
Steuben Ave., Pittsburgh 15205 (412)921-0752.

Crafton. ELSIE A. MERRIMAN (R) **
1971-. Bds: Ch., Budget Com.; Ch., Finance;
Pool & Recreation Com. Party: Local Com. 1960-
75; Secretary to Com. 1960-75. Org: Amer.
Business Women's Assoc.; Civic Club; Rep.Council
of Women. Occ: Secretary. B: 2/28/22. Add:
21 Bell Ave., Pittsburgh 15205 (512)921-0752.

Cranberry Township. MARY LOU LASLAVIC (R)
1976-. Bds: Library Bd. Prev: Recording
Secretary, Municipal Sewer & Water Authority
1968-74; Twp. Planning Com. 1972-74. Org: Pa.
Assoc. of Twp. Supervisors; PTA; Civic Assoc.
B: 8/1/32. Add: 96 Sussex Dr., Zelienople
16063 (412)776-4806.

Darby. MARGARET GRIFFITH
EDYTHE MICHAEL
ISABELLE RAMSEUR
44 N. 9th St., Darby 19023.

Dauphin. ARLENE B. WISEMAN (D)
1974-. Bds: Parks. Occ: Beautician. B:
3/15/26. Add: 100 Schuylkill St., Dauphin
17018.

Dayton. JEAN ENTERLINE
JOANNE FOX
C/O Samuel P. Ettinger, Box 111, Dayton
16222.

Dayton. AGNES YOUMANS LEEK (R)
1967-. Org: Retired Teachers; Fed. of
Women's Club. Educ: Lake Erie Coll. 1919 BA.
B: 11/9/1897. Add: 213 Church St., Dayton
16222.

Delano Township. LOIS DATCHKO
Delano 18220.

Denver. DOLORES LEED
437 Main St., Denver 17517.

Derry. NANCY L. SHOMO
620 N. Chestnut St., Derry 15627.

Donora. AGNES GRIGER
Borough Bldg., Donora 15033.

Doylestown. LINDA FRANKLIN
    18 N. Main St., Doylestown 18901.

Doylestown. DIANE M. HERING (R)
    1976-. Bds: Del., Cnty. Assoc. of Twp.
Officials. Party: State Del. 1977; Dir., Rep.
Club 1974-75. Prev: Secretary, Planning Cmsn.
1973-75. Org: Pa. Assoc. of Twp. Officials. B:
10/8/42. Add: 2215 Turk Rd., Doylestown 18901
(215)348-9915.

Dravosburg. CAROLYN SAKAS (R) **
    1973-. Occ: Service Representative. B:
7/9/44. Add: 800 Valleyview Dr., Dravosburg
15034 (412)466-5200.

Driftwood. SALLY J. BAILEY (R)
    1973-. Prev: Tax Collector. Org: Recreation.
Occ: School Bus Driver. B: 5/31/38. Add: 3rd
St., Driftwood 15832 (814)546-2319.

DuBois. BARBARA DUGAN (R)
    1976-. Bds: Recreation Bd., Cnty. Youth Task
Force; Cnty. Planning Com. Party: Cnty. Rep.
Registration Com. 1976-77; Exec. Com., Cnty. Rep.
Com. 1976-77. B: 6/22/43. Add: 16 W. Scribner
Ave., DuBois 15801 (814)371-8826.

Dudley. THERESA R. REED
    Borough Bldg., Dudley 16634.

Dunbar. RUTH DE MICHELIS
    51 Connellsville St., Dunbar 15431.

Duncansville. MARY B. PATTON (R)
    1975-. Bds: Ch., Civic Com., Finance Com.,
Park & Recreation Cmsn. Occ: Retail Sales. B:
5/7/50. Add: 1504 3rd Ave., Duncansville 16635
(814)695-9548.

Duryea. LUCILLE A. MAZIARZ (D)
    1970-. Party: Nat. Del. 1972, '74; Nat. Alt.
1968, '76; Local V-Pres. 1976- . Org: Chamber
of Commerce; Dem. Club. Occ: Administrator.
Add: 626 Main St., Duryea 18642.

East Bangor. SHIRLEY ROWE
    Borough Bldg., E. Bangor 18013.

East Butler. PATRICIA THOMAS
                IRENE ZBUCKVICH
    Box 213, E. Butler 16029.

East Lansdowne. JOAN BINDER
    Lexington & Emerson Ave., E. Lansdowne 19050.

East McKeesport. MARY JANE SNEDDEN
    426 Miami St., E. McKeesport 15035.

Easton. CAMILLA H. COOMBS (R)
    1976-. Bds: Mid-Eastern Cnty's. Assoc. of
Boroughs; Del., Regional Adv. Com. of Joint
Planning Cmsn. Party: Nat. Alt. 1976; Dist.
Area Ch., 1974-76; Cnty. Exec. Com. 1974- ; Ward
Committeewoman 1972-77. Prev: Auditor 1973-76.
Org: LWV; Rep. Club; Young Rep. Club. Educ: U.
of Denver 1970 BA. Occ: Accountant. B: 9/8/44.
Add: 1726 Lehigh St., Easton 18042 (215)258-6142.

Easton. CAROL LEE HARMAN (D)
    1972-. Bds: Council Pres. Org: AFSCME.
Occ: Tax Appraiser. B: 7/10/45. Add: 169 E.
St. Joseph St., Easton 18042 (215)258-7518.

East Pennsboro Township. MARGARET M. FORAN
    243 Columbia Road, Enola 17025.

East Side Borough. ELIZABETH B. SIGLIN (I)
    Prev: Borough Secretary-Treasurer 1972-74.
Org: Common Cause. Educ: Rutgers U. 1935 BA;
BLS. B: 9/4/14. Add: RD #1, E. Side Borough,
White Haven 18661 (717)443-9429.

East Washington. MARY LOU DE HAAS
    Borough Bldg., E. Washington 15301.

Edgewood. RUTH H. LUTZ (R)
    1958-. Bds: Civil Service Cmsn.; Ordinance
& Information Com. Ch. Party: Committeewoman
1960-70. Org: Civic Club; Citizen's Adv. Com.;
Health System. Educ: U. of Louisville 1939
BA; 1940 MA. Occ: Teacher. B: 7/14/18. Add:
1207 Savannah Ave., Edgewood 15218 (412)
242-4824.

Edinboro. JEAN A. DAVIS (R) **
    1974-. Bds: Ch., Recreation Com.; Street
Com.; Personnel Com.; Transition Com. Org:
PTO; Women's Club. Educ: Edinboro State Coll.
BS. Occ: Graduate Assistant. B: 9/29/34.
Add: 305 Hillcrest Dr., Edinboro 16412
(814)734-1812.

Edinboro. CAROLINE ANNE RHODES (D)
    1975-. Bds: Co-Ch., Joint Recreation Com.;
Streets Com.; Personnel Com. Prev: Govt. Study
Cmsn. 1974-75. Org: NOW; AAUW; ACLU; Common
Cause; New Dem. Coalition; PTO. Educ: Syracuse
U. 1960 BA. B: 5/31/38. Add: 119 High St.,
Edinboro 16412 (814)734-1812.

Eldred. KATHALENE M. LONG (R) **
    1974-. Bds: Financial Com. Prev: Auditor
1962-74. Org: Bicentennial Com. B: 12/3/21.
Add: 1 Bennett St., Eldred 16731.

Elgin. GERTRUDE D. MC CRAY (R)
    1974-. B: 9/6/12. Add: R.D. 3, Corry
16407.

Elizabethville. JUNE CARVELL
    Borough Bldg., Elizabethville 17023.

Ellport. MARY C. SAVOR
             MARY ANN SHAFFER
    306 Jamison Ave., Ellport 16117.

Elverson. ANITA A. GEIGER (R)
    1976-. Bds: Boro Council Pres.; Ch., Recre-
ation. Org: NEA. Educ: Penn State U. 1949 BS;
Temple U. 1966 MEd. Occ: Teacher. B: 1/18/27.
Add: Box 222, Elverson 19520 (215)286-6420.

Emsworth. MARIE M. HAUGER
    Borough Bldg., Pittsburgh 15202.

Factoryville. CHRISTINE TYLER
    Borough Bldg., Factoryville 18419.

Fairfield. MARY S. MARTZ
Borough Bldg., Fairfield 17320.

Falls. DOROTHY S. VISLOSKY (D) **
1973-. Prev: School Dir. 1971-74. Org: Taxpayers Assoc. B: 1/9/30. Add: 725 Trenton Rd.,
Fairless Hills 19030 (215)295-4176.

Fayette City. ELIZABETH RUSSELL
Borough Bldg., Fayette City 15438.

Fountain Hill. ANN MARIE PEERSON
843 N. Clewell St., Fountain Hill 18015.

Foxburgh. ESTHER PAGE
Borough Bldg., Foxburgh 16036.

Fox Chapel. HELEN F. MATHIESON (R)
1975-. Bds: Environmental Adv. Council;
Sanitation; Community Relations. Party: Ward
Committeewoman 1959-61. Educ: Conn. Coll. 1952
BA. B: 12/7/29. Add: 10 Fairview Mnr.,
Pittsburgh 05238.

Frackville. HELEN APONICK
Borough Bldg., Frackville 17931.

Frankfort Springs. SUSAN BRODMERKEL
ANNA DEVITT
Borough Bldg., Hookstown 15050.

Franklin. NORMA BARTHEN
City Hall, 430 13th St., Franklin 16323.

Franklin. NORMA WEBB SHULTZ (D) **
1969-. Bds: Sewer Authority; Planning Com.;
Water Authority. Prev: Township Auditor 1959-63.
Occ: Secretary-Treasurer of Township. B: 4/22/24.
Add: Box 214, Waynesburg 15370 (412)627-5473.

Fredonia. JANET M. RUNKLE
Box 487, Fredonia 16124.

Freedom. NAOMI STRAYER
P.O. Box 67, Freedom 15042.

Freemansburg. AUDREY PHILLIP
600 Monroe St., Municipal Bldg., Freemansburg
18017.

Friendsville. BARBARA HENDRICKSON
MARJORIE WELCH
Borough Bldg., Friendsville. 18818.

Glasgow. SARAH MILLER
R.D. 1, Midland 15059.

Glen Campbell. EDNA ELLSMORE
BARBARA PEARCE
Borough Bldg., Glen Campbell 15742.

Glendon. ALICE DEROHN
Borough Bldg., Easton 18042.

Glendon. EMMA LOUISE EBNER (D)
1963-. Bds: Planning Cmsn.; Topics Com.;
Joint Planning Cmsn.; Cement Belt Assoc. Occ:
Soda Fountain Manager. B: 1/2/24. Add: 204 Lucy
Crossing, Easton 18042.

Glenfield. JOAN PICKENS
310 Kilbuck St., Glenfield 15143.

Gordon. LILLIAN RIEFF
114 Biddle St., Gordon 17936.

Great Bend. MADELINE COLLINS
Borough Bldg., Great Bend 18821.

Green Tree. MAUREEN E. GANNON
978 Greentree Rd., Pittsburgh 15220.

Hallam. MARIE HARMS
DORIS HEILAND
155 Broad St., Hallam 17406.

Hallstead. DOROTHY ELIZABETH BROWN FOOTE (R)
1976-. Bds: Cnty. Interborough Assoc. Org:
Civic Club; Rep. Women. Occ: Avon Dealer. B:
11/11/19. Add: 7 Jewett Ct., Hallstead 18822.

Hallstead. LINDA ROOD
Borough Bldg., Hallstead 18822.

Hanover. CHARLOTTE C. MILLER (R)
1976-. Bds: Zoning Bd.; Planning Cmsn.;
Public Service. Org: Retired Teachers; AARP;
Rep. Club. Educ: Hood Coll. 1936 BA. B:
2/25/14. Add: 201 High St., Hanover 17331.

Harmony Township. BARBARA D'ALESSANDRIS
Twp. Bldg., Woodland Road, Ambridge 15003.

Harris Township. ELLINOR GOODWIN GREEN
1974-. Bds: Finance Com.; Solid Waste Com.
Prev: Planning Cmsn. 1968-74. Educ: U. of Ia.
1943 BA. B: 2/1/22. Add: 115 Indian Hl. Rd.,
Boalsburg 16827 (814)466-6228.

Hartleton. MEDA STRUBLE
Box 43, Hartleton 17829.

Harveys Lake. MARGARET O.B. PURCELL (I)
1976-. Bds: Ch., Finance; Purchasing. B:
2/23/23. Add: Box 611-RD #1, Harveys Lk.
18618 (717)639-2113.

Hatboro. MARIE M. JOHN
120 E. Montgomery Ave., Hatboro 19040.

Haysville. ELLEN FLEIG
MARY GLEASON
12 River Rd., Sewickley 15143.

Heidelberg. ROSE MAHALCHAK
Borough Bldg., Heidelberg 15106.

Hempfield. ALICE VIRGINIA LOHR (D)
1976-. Bds: V-Ch., Bd. of Supervisors.
Party: Chairwoman Dem. Com. 1952-77; V-Ch.,
Cnty. Dem. Com. 1976-77. Org: State Twp. Supervisors Assoc.; Cnty. Supervisors Assoc., Civic
Assoc.; Health & Welfare; Cnty. Dem. Club; N.
Huntington Dem. Club. Occ: Roadmaster. B:
8/9/20. Add: RD 5, Box 80, Greensburg 15601
(412)834-7232.

Hermitage Township. SYLVIA A. STULL
Box 1046, Sharon 16146.

Herndon. LYNN K. GAW
        KATHRYN R. ZEIGLER
    Borough Bldg., Herndon 17830.

Highspire. MARGUERITE E. BLANCH (D)
    1976-. Bds: Ch., Safety; Leg.; Hwy. Org:
    AFSCME; Women's Club. Occ: Stenographer. B:
    4/28/17. Add: 496 Elizabeth, Highspire 17034.

Highspire. JOANNE KERA
    640 Eshelman St., Highspire 17034.

Honey Brook. THELMA UMBLE (D)
    1973-. Bds: Ch., Street Com.; Police Com.;
    Ch., Building Com. Prev: Inspector of Election.
    Org: Women's Club. B: 10/9/20. Add: Box 190
    RD #3, Honey Brook 19344 (215)273-3996.

Hookstown. GERTRUDE MOTT
    Borough Bldg., Hookstown 15050.

Hooversville. DOROTHY SNYDER
    Borough Bldg., Hooversville 15936.

Hopewell. IRENE LEIGHTY
    Borough Bldg., Hopewell 16650.

Horsham. PATRICIA E. JOHN
    1025 Horsham Rd., Horsham 19044.

Howard. MARY SCHENCK (R)
    1973-. Bds: Ch., Street Com.; Bldg. Com.
    Org: Women's Civic Club; Rep. Women. Occ:
    Machine Operator. B: 6/6/22. Add: Howard 16841.

Hunker. GLADYS GUIDAS
    Borough Bldg., Hunker 15639.

Huntingdon. LONA B. NORRIS (D) **
    1973-. Bds: Playground Com.; Government Trans-
    portation Com. Org: LWV. Educ: Juniata 1957 BA.
    Occ: Instructional Assistant. B: 7/27/35. Add:
    1529 Moore St., Huntingdon 16652 (814)643-3966.

Hyde Park. BETTY MARTIN
    Borough Bldg., Hyde Park 15641.

Indiana. MARGARET A. KONDRICK (D)
    1975-. Bds: Fox Chapel Area Coord. Com. Org:
    Pa. Assoc. of Notaries. Occ: Real Estate Agent.
    B: 1/22/35. Add: Lefever Hl. Rd. RD #1, Cheswick
    15024 (412)265-2048.

Indian Lake. DOROTHY PIELL
    RD #1, Central City 15926.

Irwin. VIRGINIA BETER DE PRIMIO (D)
    1976-. Party: Committeewoman 1972-78. Occ:
    Bookkeeper-Typist. B: 4/21/26. Add: 606 8th St.,
    Irwin 15642 (412)863-3515.

Ivyland. HELEN D. DUDBRIDGE (R) **
    1973-. B: 1/2/19. Add: 33 Wilson Ave., Ivy-
    land 18974.

Jackson Center. DOROTHY GATEWOOD
    R.D. 1, Box 86, Jackson Center 16133.

Jamestown. MARY ELLEN MORELAND (R)
    1976-. Bds: Ch., Water & Waste Water; Ch.,
    Street Lights; Police. Party: Committeewoman
    1966-70, 1974-78. Org: Planning Cmsn.; Fair
    Bd.; Council of Rep. Women. Educ: Youngstown
    State U. 1955 BME. B: 10/4/33. Add: 402 Main
    St., Jamestown 16134 (412)932-5211.

Jeannette. BETTY M. SANDELLA (R)
    1974-. Bds: Library Bd., Ch., Recreation
    Cmsn.; Police Pension Bd. Party: Cnty. Treasurer
    1975-76. Prev: Zoning Bd. 1972-73. Org:
    Chamber of Commerce; Historical Society; Greens-
    berg Council Rep. Women. B: 11/20/16. Add:
    72 Cayler Ave., Jeannette 15644 (412)834-8090.

Jefferson. ELEANOR J. BOWMAN (R) **
    1973-. Bds: Somerset Area Recreation Bd.;
    Planning Com.; Tax Bd. Org: Rep. Women. Occ:
    Antique Shop Owner. B: 11/24/25. Add: RD 6,
    Somerset 15501 (814)445-8357.

Jenkintown. MARY JANE REILLY (D)
    1975-. Bds: Public Works; Parking; Community
    Relations. Party: Committeewoman 1974-76; Leg.
    Dist. Finance Com. 1977. B: 8/11/48. Add:
    410 West Ave., Jenkintown 19046 (215)TU5-0700.

Jenkintown. GAIL WEST
    West Ave. & Leedom St., Jenkintown 19046.

Jersey Shore. GERTRUDE B. BITNER (R)
    1976-. Bds: Ch., Finance; Hwy. Com.; Recre-
    ation Com. Prev: Ch., Planning Cmsn. 1972-76;
    Dir., Library Bd. 1976-79. Org: NEA; Women's
    Club; Rep. Women's Club; Town Meeting; OES;
    Library Bd. Occ: Teacher. B: 3/8/14. Add:
    412 S. Main St., Jersey Shore 17740.

Johnstown. M. RITA CLARK (R) **
    1973-. Bds: Investigating Com.; Residency
    Com. Org: BPW; LWV; Chamber of Commerce. Educ:
    Lock Haven State 1937 BS. B: 9/12/15. Add:
    52 Rose St., Johnstown 15905 (814)539-8761.

Kane. RUTH J. MC CONNELL
    112 Bayard St., Kane 16735.

Kistler. MYRA ORDENOFF
    Borough Bldg., Mt. Union 17066.

Kittanning. JEAN NEIDIG
        KATHERINE STEIM
    P.O. Box 229, Kittanning 16201.

Knoxville. WANDA L. RODMAN
    Borough Bldg., Knoxville 16928.

Koppel. ALICE DOCCHIO
        HELEN TITA
    Arthur St., Koppel 16136.

Laflin. MARILYN SAIDMAN (R)
    1975-. Bds: Land Use Program Adv. Council;
    Borough Councilmen's Assoc. Nominating Com. Org:
    Wyoming Valley Flood Victims Action Council. B:
    12/31/30. Add: 2 Concord Dr., Laflin 18702
    (717)655-4107.

Lancaster. JULIA F. BRAZILL (R) **
    1969-. Bds: Ch., Intermunicipal Com.; Ch.,
Personnel Com.; Public Safety Com. Party: Ward
Ch., 1974-75; V-Ch., City GOP Com. 1972-74; Nom-
inating Com. 1968-72. Prev: Com. 1968-75. Org:
Amer. Assoc. for Advancement of Science; Amer.
Legion. Occ: Office Shipping & Finance. B:
4/6/22. Add: 728 S. Franklin St., Lancaster
17602 (707)397-3501 Ext. 37.

Langhorne. PATRICIA D. BAUDER (D) **
    1973-. Prev: Centennial Com. 1973-74; Plann-
ing Cmsn. 1972-74. Org: Historical Assoc.; PTO.
B: 9/11/42. Add: 151 N. Bellevue Ave., Langhorne
19047 (215)757-3768.

Langhorne Manor. MRS. JOHN OSBOURN
    Borough Bldg., Langhorne Manor 19047.

Lansford. EDITH MARKS
    P.O. Box 26, Lansford 18232.

Laurel Run. RENA THOMAS
    Borough Bldg., Wilkes-Barre 18702.

Leechburg. MARGARET P. WRAY (R)
    1973-. Bds: Ch., Finance Com.; Police Com.;
Ordinance Com. Org: Tourist Bureau; Council of
Rep. Women. B: 2/14/27. Add: 242 Main St.,
Leechburg 15656 (412)842-8511.

Leesport. ELVA V. HOTTENSTINE (D)
    1974-. Bds: Ch. Borough Authority; Recreation
Bd., School Bd. Prev: Auditor 1956-74; Judge of
Elections 1954-74. B: 3/6/1899. Add: 114 S.
Centre Ave., Leesport 19533 (215)926-2115.

Leetsdale. MADALINE S. BRETZ (R)
    1974-. Prev: Planning Cmsn. 1972-74. Org:
Nat. Retired Teachers Assoc.; Women's Club; BPW;
DAR. Add: 11 Valley Lane, Leetsdale 15056
(412)266-4820.

Leidy. GEORGIANNA M. SUMERSON (R) **
    1974-. B: 2/17/18. Add: Star Route, Renovo
17764 (717)923-0769.

Lemoyne. CONSTANCE MC ALLISTER
    665 Market St., Lemoyne 17043.

Lewisburg. JENNIE S. ERDLEY
    331 Market St., Lewisburg 17837.

Lewis Run. ANTIONETTE GILMORE
    P.O. Box 265, Lewis Run 16738.

Lewistown. HELEN I. PRICE (R) **
    1972-. Bds: Highway Com.; Law & Ordinance;
Flood Control. Org: Rep. Club. Educ: Penn. State
1943 BS. B: 3/4/04. Add: 117 Chestnut St.,
Lewistown 17044 (717)248-6715.

Library. MILDRED K. MONTUORO (D)
    1964-. Bds: Financial. Party: Local Ch.
1970-77; Cnty. Committeewoman 1962-77. Prev:
Planning Cmsn. 1964-70; Twp. Supervisor 1963.
Org: Chamber of Commerce; Women's Club; Twp. Dem.
Org. Occ: Chief Clerk, Cnty. Jury Cmsn. B:
5/31/23. Add: 3149 Ridgeway Dr., Library 15129
(412)831-7000.

Lilly. VICTORIA GUZIC
    Borough Bldg., Lilly 15938.

Lincoln. DOROTHY VAY
    R.D. 1, Box 224-B, Elizabeth 15037.

Little Meadows. LINDA PURCELL
    Borough Bldg., Little Meadows 18830.

Lock Haven. DIANN STUEMPFLE
    City Hall, 20 E. Church St., Lock Haven
17745.

Lower Allen Township. E. JEANNE EGGERT
    1993 Hummel Ave., P.O. Box 7, Camp Hill
17011.

Lower Providence Township. LOIS J. WOOD (D)
    1975-. Bds: Liaison, Administration. Party:
State Del. 1977; Cnty. Committeewoman 1968-77;
Lwr. Providence Twp. Ch. 1974-77. Org: LWV.
B: 1/12/35. Add: 3527 Ridge Pk., Collegeville
19426 (215)539-8020.

Lower Saucon Township. LOIS A. AUGUST
                          JACQUELINE PEEKE
    Box 464-A, R.D. 4, Easton 18042.

Lykens. JOYCE COOPER
        PHYLLIS MEEKER
    559 S. 2nd St., Lykens 17048.

Lyons. SUZANNE REED
    Lyon Station, Lyons 19536.

Macungie. LYNDA IPPOLITO
    P.O. Box 66, Macungie 18062.

Macungie. JEAN ANN NELSON (R)
    1973-. Bds: Regional Adv. Com. to Joint
Planning Cmsn.; Mideastern Cnty. Assoc. of
Boroughs; Ch., Finance & Personnel Com. Party:
Leg. Ch. 1975-77. Prev: Recreation Cmsn. 1954-
76; Bicentennial Com. 1973-76. Org: ANA; Fed.
Women's Club; World Hunger Appeal; Rep. Club;
Cnty. Rep's. Educ: U. of Rochester 1942 RN.
B: 7/15/21. Add: 61 Sycamore, Macungie 18062
(205)965-5400.

Madison. PATRICIA A. WALT (R)
    1973-. Org: OES; VFW. Educ: Westmoreland
Cnty. Community Coll. 1977 AA. B: 12/3/36.
Add: Main St., P.O. Box 7, Madison 15663.

Mahaffey. MYRTLE MAHAFFEY (D)
    Bds: Council Pres. Org: PTA. Occ: School
Bus Driver. B: 8/23/37. Add: Main St.,
Mahaffey 15757 (814)277-6317.

Manor. JUDY FINUCAN (D) **
    1973-. Bds: Recreation Bd.; Sewage Author-
ity. Org: Boroughs Assoc.; Dem. Club; PTA.
Occ: Statistician B: 1/25/45. Add: 32 Longview Dr., RD 6, Irwin 15642 (412)864-2422.

Manorville. NANCY GAUL
    Borough Bldg., Manorville 16238.

Manorville. HELEN J. HUFHAND (R)
1976-. Occ: Clerk. B: 7/7/23. Add: Box 227,
Manorville 16238 (412)763-1403.

Marianna. BETTY KIMINSKI
MAE ETTA MURPHY
LEONA THOMAS
Borough Bldg., Marianna 15345.

Marple Township. MARCIA W. TUCKER
29 Fairview Road, Marple.

Marshall Township. ROSE PARACCA
Box 94, Warrendale 15086.

Marysville. MARTHA W. DRUMHEISER
Borough Bldg., Marysville 17053.

Matamoras. NANCY B. VOCCI (D)
1973-. Bds: V-Pres. of Council. Party: Cnty.
Committeewoman 1971-75. Org: Recreation Adv. Bd.;
Cnty. Extension Bd.; Community Club. Occ: Com-
puter Operator. B: 1/25/37. Add: 805 Ave. N.,
Matamoras 18336.

Mayfield. MARY THERESA CARDAMONE (D)
1975-. Bds: Ch., Community Devt.; Ch., Recre-
ation Cmsn.; Planning Cmsn. Org: Pa. News Media
Assoc.; Consumer Protection Council Exec. Bd.
Occ: Photo Journalist & Tavern Owner. B: 5/9/33.
Add: 812 Penn Ave., Mayfield 18433 (717)876-9857.

McDonald. AGNES S. CLARK (R)
1976-. Bds: Ch., Ordinance Com.; Property
Com.; Ch., Printing & Public Relations. Org:
Women's Club; Chamber of Commerce. Educ:
Practical Nursing School 1962. Occ: Practical
Nurse. B: 5/1/16. Add: 222 4th St., McDonald
15057 (412)926-8711.

McKean. OLIVIA C. PURCHASE (R)
1976-. Bds: Ch., Road Com. Party: Committeewoman 1976-78. Org: PTA. B: 11/12/43. Add:
9058 Paula Way, McKean 16426.

McKeesport. FLORENCE SWANTACK (D)
1960-. Bds: Ch., Recreation Com.; Boro Devt.
Party: V-Ch. 1962-72. Prev: Secretary, State
Councilmen's Assoc. 1972-76. Org: Ladies
Political Club. Occ: Clerk Typist. B: 3/3/18.
Add: 3810 Liberty Way, McKeesport 15133.

McKeesport. CAROLYN O. YOUNG
201 Lysle Blvd., McKeesport 15132.

McKees Rocks. LORETTA MC CABE
Borough Bldg., McKees Rocks 15136.

Meadville. YOLANDA BARCO
984 Water St., Meadville 16335.

Mercer. THELMA STONE
Borough Bldg., Mercer 16137.

Middlesex Township. DARLENE WEINZETL
R.D. 2, Valencia 16059.

Mifflintown. CAROL MILLIKON
Courthouse, Mifflintown 17059.

Milesburg. KAY M. CRUST
Borough Bldg., Milesburg 16853.

Milford. SHIRLEY RIORDAN
Box 9, Milford 18337.

Millbourne. ELEANOR VANSICLEN
37 Inna St., Upper Darby 19082.

Millersville. DOROTHY R. BENDER (R)
1975-. Bds: Ch., Park Com.; Ch., Police
Com.; Finance Com. Party: Committeewoman 1974-
77. Prev: Planning Cmsn. 1969-75. Org: Women's
Rep. Club; Recreation Assoc. B: 10/13/20.
Add: 139 Landis Ave., Millersville 17551
(717)872-4645.

Millheim. PATRICIA WOLFE
142 E. Main St., Millheim 16854.

Mill Village. ISABEL M. BEAMAN (D)
1973-. Org: OES. Occ: Beautician. B:
10/14/22. Add: Box 61, Depot St., Mill Vlg.
16427.

Mill Village. MARY SZALL
Borough Bldg., Mill Village 16427.

Mont Alto. BARBARA SHANK
Borough Bldg., Mont Alto 17237.

Montgomery. ROBERTA MC CLINTOCK
Borough Bldg., Montgomery 17752.

Montgomery Township. BETTY BISS
R.D., Cherry Tree 15724.

Morton. NORMA MAC CLEASTER PICCONE (D)
1973-. Bds: Ch., Sewer Com.; Ch., Recreation;
Ch., Public Relations. Org: NEA. Educ: W.
Chester State Coll. 1953 BS; 1964 MS. Occ:
Teacher. B: 9/23/32. Add: 101 Locust Rd.,
Morton 19070 (215)KI3-4565.

Mount Carbon. MARTHA HAIN
DOLORES LAZERCHICK
Borough Bldg., Pottsville 17901.

Mount Pocono. MILDRED CRON (R)
1976-. Bds: Ch., Budget & Finance; Planning
Cmsn. B: 11/25/10. Add: 11 Rambling Way., Mt.
Pocono 18344.

Mount Union. MARGARET L. MAGLIERE
CATHERINE WEAR
P.O. Box 88, Mt. Union 17066.

Muncy. BETTY R. STUGART (D)
1972-. Bds: Council Pres. Party: Committeewoman 1968-72. Prev: Inspector of Elections
1956-68; Judge of Elections 1968-72. Occ:
Librarian. B: 8/30/26. Add: 28 N. Wash. St.,
Muncy 17756 (717)546-3952.

Nanty Glo. MARY ALICE MC DERMOTT
BETTY JEAN RAGLEY
Municipal Bldg., Nanty Glo 15943.

Nescapeck. EMMA JANE LYNN (R)
1976-. Bds: Ch., Community Welfare; Ch.,
Building. B: 7/3/25. Add: 328 Cooper St.,
Nescapeck 18635 (717)752-7224.

New Britain. EVELYN MOBERG
56 Keeley Ave., New Britain 18901.

New Britain. WILMA E. QUINLAN (R) **
1962-. Party: Local Com. 1958-60. Educ: U.
of Ill. 1925 BA. B: 4/3/03. Add: Box 52, New
Britain 18901.

Newburg. RAMONA E. CARTHEY (D)
1975-. Org: Pa. Educ. Assoc. Educ: U. of
Northern Ia. 1957 BA. Occ: Librarian. B: 4/1/25.
Add: Box 35, Newburg 17240.

New Buffalo. MARGARET V. BOSTDORF (D)
1974-. B: 9/5/08. Add: Creek Rd., New
Buffalo 17069.

New Columbus. NETTIE BOGERT
Borough Bldg., Stillwater 17878.

New Cumberland. ROSEMARIE C. PEIFFER
D. MARIE PHILLIPS
7th & Reno Sts., New Cumberland 17070.

Newell. MARY CORCIO
ESTHER SABOL
Box 27, Newell 15466.

Newell. VERONICA S. SOFRANKO (D) **
1966-. Bds: Parks, Arts & Recreation; Police
& Protection; Public Safety. Prev: Bd. of
Election 1950-66. Org: PTA. B: 7/25/26. Add:
Box 307, Newell 15466 (412)938-7430.

New Freedom. ALICE JEAN SHAFFER (R)
1975-. Bds: Ch., S. York Cnty. Water Control
Com.; Bd. of Governors- New Freedom Community
Center. Org: New Freedom Area Women's Club.
Educ: Peabody Coll. 1951 BS. Occ: Business Co-
owner. B: 1/4/30. Add: 124 Franklin St., New
Freedom 17349 (717)235-2337.

New Holland. JOAN L. DELP
12 N. Failroad Ave., New Holland 17557.

New Hope. JEAN K. NEY (D) **
1972-. Bds: Fire Com.; Light Com.; Zoning
Com. Occ: Assistant Librarian. B: 5/27/06.
Add: 40A Darien, Village II, New Hope 18938.

New Hope. NAOMI PFEIFFER (D)
1976-. Bds: Sewer Com.; Police Com.; Lights
Com. Party: Dem. Committeewoman; V-Ch. Cnty.
Dem. Committee. Prev: Planning Cmsn. 1974-76.
Org: LWV. B: 9/3/16. Add: 170 N. Main, Box 273,
New Hope 18938.

Newport. VIRGINIA MC GOWAN
231 Market St., Newport 17074.

Newry. MARJORIE E. HARKER (D)
1975-. Bds: Ch., Planning & Housing; Pres. of
Council. Party: Committeewoman 1975-78. Org:
State Council of Civil Defense; Cnty. Consumer

Action Com.; Dem. Women's Fed.; Dem. Club.
Occ: Office Manager/Secretary. B: 1/31/48.
Add: Box 31, Newry 16665.

Newry. LORRAINE KNISELY
MARTHA SHOEMAKER
Borough Bldg., Newry 16665.

Newton Hamilton. ERNA MC VEU
Borough Bldg., Newton Hamilton 17075.

Nicholson. RUTH HUNKLEY
Borough Bldg., Nicholson 18446.

Northampton. SANDRA OSWALD
1516 Main St., Northampton 18067.

North Apollo. FRANCES R. HARKCOM
Borough Bldg., N. Apollo 15673.

Northumberland. ELLEN JEAN NALLY (R)
Bds: Recreation Cmsn.; Library Bd.; Liberty
Pool Assoc. Bd.; V-Pres., Council. Party:
Precinct Leader 1974-77. Org: Civic Club; Rep.
Women's Club; PTA. Educ: St. Lukes Hospital
1954 RN. B: 11/12/33. Add: 912 Front St.,
Northumberland 17857 (717)473-3414.

North Wales. MARIE E. THOMPSON (D)
1975-. Bds: Public Works. Party: Committee-
woman 1976-78. Org: Cnty. Borough Assoc.;
Women's Dem. Club; LWV; OES. Occ: Real Estate
Sales. B: 6/29/21. Add: 814 E. Prospect Ave.,
N. Wales 19454 (215)699-4424.

North York. GRACE V. BENTZEL
Borough Bldg., N. York 19404.

Norwood. ELIZABETH CHRISTIANSEN (R)
1973-. Bds: Ch., Library Bd.; Ch., Insurance
& Pension Plans Com. Party: Committeewoman
1957-77; V-Pres., Exec. Com. 1976-77. Prev:
School Bd. 1969-72. Org: Women's Rep. Club;
Cnty. Rep. Women. Occ: Health Insurance
Service Repr. B: 1/15/24. Add: 305 Sylvan Ave.
Norwood 19074.

Norwood. JUNE A. RODGERS
P.O. Box 65, Norwood 19074.

Oakdale. RUTH A. SNATCHKO (D)
1974-. Bds: Ch., Finance Com.; Recreation.
Party: Town Secretary 1974- . Org: Women's
League. Occ: Data Entry Manager. B: 8/11/39.
Add: 577 Highland Ave., Oakdale 15071 (412)
693-9740.

Oakdale. SARAH YAMBER
Borough Bldg., Oakdale 15071.

Oakmont. DONNA E. DE TURCK
Municipal Bldg., 5th St. & Va. Ave., Oakmont
15139.

Ohiopyle. PAULINE BUNGARD
LAURA MARIETTA
Borough Bldg., Ohiopyle 15470.

Olyphant. MILDRED O'BOYLE
Borough Bldg., Olyphant 18447.

Orangeville. GRACE N. ALBERTSON (D)
    1973-. B: 3/21/25. Add: Main St., Orange-
ville 17859.

Osborne. MARYLOU SULLIVAN (D)
    1975-. Bds: Public Works; Public Safety. B:
12/15/42. Add: RD 2, 37 Sycamore Rd., Sewickley
15143 (412)741-4136.

Osceola Mills. MARGARET BURNS
                ELSIE PENNY
    Public Square, Osceola Mills 16666.

Palmyra. RUTH S. BALDWIN (R) **
    1973-. Bds: Chamber of Commerce. Party:
Local Com. 1950-62. Org: Women's Club. B:
7/22/10. Add: 24 N. Locust St., Palmyra 17078
(717)838-1720.

Pen Argyl. MARYELLA CORRELL
    Borough Bldg., Pen Argyl 18072.

Penn Lake Park. BETTY DINKELACKER
    Box 150-A, Star Rt., White Haven 18661.

Perkasie. THELMA A. BARINGER (D)
    1976-. Bds: Administration & Finance Com.
Party: Borough Auditor 1960. Prev: Borough
Auditor. Org: AFSCME; Dem. Club; Historical
Society; BPW; Women's Club. Occ: Graphic Artist.
B: 11/17/15. Add: 351 Market St., Perkasie
18944.

Perryopolis. HELEN DARKANGELO
    P.O. Box 304, Perryopolis 15473.

Petersburg. EDITH NALE
    Borough Bldg., Petersburg 16669.

Philadelphia. ETHEL D. ALLEN (R)
    1971-. Bds: Appropriation, Law & Govt. & Rec-
reation; Public Property & Works, Transportation
& Public Utilities, Commerce, Navigation & Air-
port Facilities. Party: Nat. Del. 1976; Nat.
Alt. 1972; Rep. Policy Com. 1971-77. Prev: Dist.
Councilwoman; Cmsn. on Gambling Policy 1972-77;
Cmsn. on IWY 1975-77. Org: Nat. Medical Assoc.;
Amer. Public Health Assoc.; Urban Coalition;
NAACP; Black WPC; WPC; Nat. Council of Negro
Women; Soroptimists. Educ: W. Va. State Coll.
1952 BS; Phila. Coll. of Osteopathic Med. 1963
DO. Occ: Physician & Surgeon. B: 5/8/29. Add:
2302 W. Nicholas St., Philadelphia 19121 (215)
686-3440/3441.

Philadelphia. BEATRICE K. CHERNOCK (R)
    1971-. Educ: Temple U. BS; MA. B: 5/30/09.
Add: 1820 Wynnewood Rd., Philadelphia 19151
(215)MU6-3452/3453.

Philadelphia. ANNA CIBOTTI VERNA
    Rm. 490, City Hall, Phila. 19107.

Pine Township. NANCY MANTIA (R)
    1976-. Bds: Parks & Recreation Bd.; Ch.,
Police Pension Fund Bd. Party: Committeewoman
1974-76; Secretary, Rep. Com. 1974-76. Org: LWV.
B: 5/15/31. Add: RD #4, Spruce Haven Dr., Wexford
15090 (412)625-1591.

Pitcairn. VERDA YAWORSKY
    320 Center Ave., Pitcairn 15140.

Pittsburgh. SOPHIE MASLOFF (D)
    Bds: Ch., Surveys & Service Com.; Ch., Cable
TV System. Party: Nat. Del. 1968; Dem. State
Com. 1971-75; Affirmative Action Com. 1971-75.
Prev: Administrative Div. of Ct. of Common Pleas
1946-75. Org: Fed. of Dem. Women's Guild of
Allegheny Cnty. Add: 3566 Beechwood Blvd.,
Pittsburgh 15217 (412)255-2137.

Pittsburgh. FRANCES R. VOEGE (R)
    1969-. Bds: Ch., Recreation; Planning; Ch.,
Public Facilities. Org: Amer. Academy of
Political & Social Science. Occ: Travel Agent.
B: 4/16/31. Add: 3907 Cloverlea St., Pittsburgh
15227 (412)884-1500.

Plumville. POLLY IRELAND
                JANET WEAVER
    Borough Bldg., Plumville 16246.

Pocopson Township. SALLY B. SUPLEE (R)
    1975-. Org: NEA. Educ: West Chester State
Coll. 1963 BSE; 1974 MA. Occ: Teacher. B:
4/24/30. Add: 550 W. Lafayette Dr., W. Chester
19380 (215)793-2151.

Polk. HARRIET KERR DAYE (R)
    1975-. Bds: Ch., Parks & Recreation. Org:
Zonta. Educ: Chatham Coll. 1949 BA; Clarion
State U. 1972 MS. Occ: Supervisor, Special
Educ. Program. B: 7/22/28. Add: Box 247
McClelland Ave., Polk 16342.

Portage. EVELYN G. COLEMAN (D)
    1971-. Bds: Police; Finance; Ch., Park.
Org: Home-School Assoc.; Ambulance Assoc. B:
12/9/36. Add: 622 Grant St., Portage 15946.

Portage. PHYLLIS MARIE KLEIN **
    1974-. Bds: Property Com.; Parks & Ordinance;
Electricity & Water. Org: Women's Club. B:
5/19/37. Add: 1025 Sonman Ave., Portage 15946
(814)736-9486.

Port Allegany. DOROTHY P. CARLSON (R) **
    1969-. Org: Library Bd.; Rep. Women's Club.
B: 8/3/18. Add: 314 Broad St., Port Allegany
16743 (814)642-2526.

Port Alleghany. DAWN JOHNSON
    Borough Bldg., Port Alleghany 16743.

Potter Township. EMILY J. DAVIS
    803 Pleasant Dr., Monaca 15061.

Pottstown. DORIS M. KOHLER
    241 King St., Pottstown 19464.

Punxsutawney. FLORINDA CRESSLEY
    Borough Bldg., Punxsutawney 15767.

Railroad. BRENDA L. STIFFLER (D)
    1974-. Bds: Ch., Recreation Assoc. Org:
Cnty's. Dem's. B: 2/5/50. Add: Main St.,
Railroad 17355.

Rainsburg. MARY ANDERSON
R.D. #4, Bedford 15522.

Reading. KAREN A. MILLER (D)
1975-. Bds: Ch-Dir., Accounting & Finance.
Party: Committeewoman 1974; Cnty. Exec. Com.
1974-75. Org: Municipal Finance Officers Assoc.;
Dem. Club. Educ: Indiana U. 1964 BA. B: 1/8/42.
Add: 120 N. 11th St., Reading 19601 (215)
373-5111.

Red Hill. CONSTACE TRUMBAUER
Borough Bldg., Red Hill 18076.

Richland. KATHRYN K. ROYER (R)
1975-. Bds: Ch., Historical Survey Cmsn.;
Ch., Finance Com.; Property Com. Party: Party
Worker at Election Polls 1960-64. Org: NEA.
Educ: Lebanon Vly. Coll. 1962 BS. Occ: Teacher.
B: 7/21/22. Add: 302 Chestnut St., Richland
17087 (717)866-5601.

Ridley Park. ALICE UTKUS
Borough Bldg., Ridley Park 19078.

Riegelsville. RUTH BANKO (D)
Bds: Ch., Public Relations; Recreation Bd.;
Property Com. Party: Committeewoman. Org: Pa.
Assoc. of Notaries; PTA; Adv. Com. for Educ. B:
3/28/31. Add: 449 Easton Rd., Riegelsville
18077.

Riegelsville. HELEN ENCELEWSKI
651 Easton Rd., Riegelsville 18077.

Riverside. PATRICIA J. HEATH (R)
1971-. Bds: Police; Personnel; Finance. Org:
LWV. B: 11/18/28. Add: RD 6, Danville 17821
(717)275-1751.

Rockwood. DOROTHY L. BURNWORTH
P.O. Box 58, Rockwood 15557.

Roseto. JO ANNE B. CASCIANO (R)
1975-. Bds: Ch., Finance; Safety; Law. Occ:
Business Owner. B: 7/27/31. Add: 405 Pa. Ave.,
Roseto 18013 (215)588-2237.

Rose Valley. MARY W. MC LAUGHLIN (D)
1949-. Bds: Pres. of Council. Educ: Bryn
Mawr Coll. 1938 BA. Occ: Bookkeeper. B:10/26/15.
Add: P.O. Box 196, Rose Valley 19065 (215)
LO6-2040.

Rosslyn Farms. ELIZABETH BELL MARTIN (D)
1973-. Bds: Cnty. Regional Planning Council;
Justice Cmsn. Org: Women's Club. Educ: Wellesley
Coll. 1947 BA; Carnegie Institute of Technology
1953 BArch. Occ: Real Estate Saleswoman. B:
10/2/25. Add: 31 Priscilla Ln., Rosslyn Farms
15106.

Royalton. ROSE BRETZ
SUSAN P. YOUNG
310 Wyoming St., Royalton 17057.

Rutledge. MARY M. JACKSON
200 Rutledge Ave., Rutledge 19070.

St. Clairsville. MARIE C. ICKES
Borough Bldg., St. Clairsville 16676.

St. Marys. ANNE M. GROSSER (R)
1973-. Bds: Codes & Ordinances Com.; V-Ch.,
Finance Com. Occ: Children's Retail Business
Owner. B: 5/6/23. Add: 540 Rock St., St.
Marys 15857.

St. Marys. CLARE G. SEMBERT (D) **
1971-. Bds: Public Safety; Finance Com.;
Municipal Services; Landfill Authority. B:
12/31/24. Add: 299 Maurus St., St. Marys
15857 (814)781-1718.

Saltsburg. ELAINE MC DIVITT
Point St., Saltsburg 15681.

Saxton. DORIS CAROTHERS
Borough Bldg., Saxton 16678.

Scalp Level. GWEN STRASHENSKY
508 1/2 Main St., Scalp Level 15963.

Schuylkill Haven. NANCY J. MONTZ (R)
1969-. Bds: Ch., Redevt. & Planning Com.;
Library Bd.; Electric Com. Org: BPW. Educ:
St. Luke's Hospital 1954 RN. Occ: R.N. B:
4/4/33. Add: 745 Garfield Ave., Schuylkill
Haven 17972.

Scottdale. MRS. DORCAS ECHARI
BETTY MARSH
P.O. Box 67, Scottdale 15683.

Scranton. GRACE O'MALLEY SCHIMELFENIG (D)
1973-. Bds: Ch., Community Devt. Com. Org:
AWRT; ABWA; BPW. Occ: Exec. Secretary. B:
2/9/31. Add: 216 Lk. Scranton Rd., Scranton
18505 (717)348-4154.

Selingrove. FRANCES A. NIMAROFF (D)
1974-. Educ: Eastman School of Music 1932
BM; Columbia U. 1951 MA. B: 5/15/09. Add:
10 1/2 N. High St., Selingrove 17870 (717)
374-2311.

Sellersville. NANCY COOMBS LYONS (R)
1976-. Bds: Public Works Com.; Historical
& Achievement Authority. Prev: Planning Cmsn.
1972-76. Org: Women's Guild. Educ: U. of Pa.
1946 BSEd. B: 3/19/25. Add: 36 Walnut St.,
Sellersville 18960 (215)257-5075.

Seven Springs. HELEN DUPRE
MARY DUPRE
LOUELLA G. MELLOTT
R.D. 1, Champion 15622.

Sewickley. MARY B. AZKUTNEY
4 Keystone Rd., Herminie 15637.

Sewickley Hills. FLORENCE OTT
MARGARET Y. SCHUETTE
R.D. 4, Henry Rd., Sewickley 15143.

Shade Gap. ELEANOR SNYDER
Borough Bldg., Shade Gap 17255.

Sharpsburg. LILLIAN RAJKOWSKI (D)
1976-. Bds: Civil Service Cmsn.; Police Com.;
Ch., Streets & Sewage Cmsn. Party: Cnty.
Committeewoman 1943-73; V-Ch. 1950-73; Ch., Cnty.
Committee 1973-77. Prev: School Dir. 1960-66.
B: 6/8/09. Add: 15 Fourth St., Pittsburgh
15215 (412)781-0546.

Sharpsville. ELIZABETH BOOKWALTER
Main & 3rd Sts., Sharpsville 16150.

Sheakleyville. NELLIE L. GRAVATT
Borough Bldg., Sheakleyville 16151.

Shippensburg. PATRICIA K. WELLER (D)
1975-. Bds: Ch., Finance Com.; Employee
Personnel Com.; Street Com. Prev: Sanitary
Authority 1974-75. Org: Amer. Assoc. of Women;
Dem. Club. Educ: U. of Colo. 1960 BS. Occ:
Medical Technologist. B: 2/25/38. Add: 117 S.
Prince St., Shippensburg 17257 (717)532-2147.

Shrewsbury. PATRICIA M. STEELE (D)
1976-. Bds: Home Health & Safety; Public
Buildings & Lands; Public Library. Org: Fed.
Women's Club. Occ: Pharmacy Clerk. B: 3/7/39.
Add: 7 Lexington Dr., Shrewsbury 17361.

Sinking Springs. EVELYN E. BUTKUS (R)
1976-. Bds: Ch., Property & Library Com.;
Law & Future Planning Com.; Streets & Refuse
Disposal Com. Org: Women's Club. Occ: Beautician
& Realtor. B: 7/10/21. Add: 918 Penn Ave.,
Sinking Spgs. 19608 (215)678-4903.

Smicksburg. DONNA FISHER
THELMA HYSKELL
ELLA STITELER
Smicksburg 16256.

Snow Shoe. ELEANOR M. KOSKI (R) **
1973-. Bds: Street Com. Org: NEA; Rep.
Women's Club. Occ: Teacher. B: 3/15/19. Add:
110 E. Olive St., Snow Shoe.

Snydertown. PATRICIA HEITZENDORF
Borough Bldg., Snydertown 17877.

South Heights. ANGIE MC COY
Borough Bldg., S. Heights 15081.

Southmont. CAROLYN R. SMITH
148 Wonder St., Johnstown 15905.

South Strabane. FRANCES R. HUDAK (D)
1976-. Party: Dem. Committeewoman 1954-56.
Prev: Sanitary 1975-76. B: 10/21/23. Add:
535 Manifold Rd., Washington 15301 (412)
225-9055.

Spangler. MARIE CANTELOPE
Spangler 15775.

Springboro. CLARINDA CARR
Box 25, Springboro 16435.

Springdale. JENNY A. ZALEPA (D)
1976-. Bds: Ch., Sewage Authority; Library
Bd. Org: PTA. B: 8/8/17. Add: 127 Center,
Springdale 15144.

Springfield Twp. (Montg. Co.) MRS. SAMUEL GARBER
Twp. Bldg., 1510 Paper Mill Road, Wyndmoor
19118.

State College. INGRID PEARSON HOLTZMAN
1973-. Bds: Ch., Finance Council; Senior
Citizens Adv. Cmsn.; Personnel Council. Prev:
Community Appearance & Design Review Bd. 1969-
73. Org: AAUW; LWV; Borough Councilmen's Assoc.;
Family Planning Council; Common Cause. Educ:
U. of Wash. 1939 BA. Add: 459 Martin Ter.,
State College 16801 (814)237-1411.

Stockertown. JEANNETTE ITTERLY
Borough Bldg., Stockertown 18083.

Stoneboro. JANA L. DEAN (D)
1976-. Bds: Sewer Com. Occ: Asst. Mgr.,
Hardware Store. B: 1/11/54. Add: Lake St.,
Stoneboro 16153.

Stoneboro. JANA MC CLEARN
Lake St., Stoneboro 16153.

Stoystown. TILLIE KIMMEL
Box 202, Stoystown 15563.

Sugar Grove. GAIL W. STEVENSON
R.D. 3, Greenville 16125.

Sugar Notch. HELEN GAVAZZI
MARY SHEA
Borough Bldg., Sugar Notch 18706.

Summit Hill. KATHLEEN LANZOS
18 E. Hazard St., Summit Hill 18250.

Suterville. H. ELIZABETH RUPERT (D)
1973-. Bds: Boro Law & Finance; Ch.,
Library. Occ: Newspaper Journalist. B:
3/28/19. Add: RR 1, Box 61, Suterville
15083 (412)751-3923.

Swarthmore. IRMA E. ZIMMER (R)
1972-. Bds: Ch., Recreation; Health &
Sanitation; Safety. Prev: Home Rule Study
Cmsn. 1972-73. Org: NEA; LWV; Recreation
Assoc.; Rep. Women. Educ: West Chester State
Coll. BSEd; U. of Pa. MA. B: 11/7/16. Add:
135 Ogden Ave., Swarthmore 19081 (215)
KI3-4599.

Tatamy. EDNA E. BARRALL
441 Broad Street, Tatamy 18085.

Telford. ALICE ANN STEPHENS (D)
1973-. Bds: Ch., Property Com.; Recreation
Com. Party: Committeewoman 1964-77. Org:
Dem. Com. Educ: Thomas M. Fitzgerald Mercy
Hospital of Nursing 1955 RN. B: 8/13/34.
Add: 26 Hamlin Ave., Telford 18969 (215)
723-5000.

Thornburg. MRS. JAMES MC CONOMY
501 Hamilton Rd., Pittsburgh 15205.

Tioga. JEAN WARD
P.O. Box 262, Tioga 16946.

Towanda. BILLIE CHILSON
    724 S. Main St., Towanda 18848.

Townville. EVA ELLIOTT
    Borough Bldg., Townville 16360.

Trafford. DOROTHY J. NOVAK (D)
    1973-. Bds: Ch., Streets & Hwys. Com.; Ch.,
Civil Defence Com. Org: Women's Club. B: 9/5/29.
Add: 9 Highland Ave., Trafford 15085.

Trafford. LUCY A. PETRINI (D)
    1976-. Org: Bicentennial Com. Occ: Secretary.
B: 3/27/33. Add: 109 1st St., Trafford 15085
(412)372-6559.

Troutville. MARY SHAFFER
    Borough Bldg., Troutville 15866.

Turtle Creek. IRENE SMITH
    125 Monroeville Ave., Turtle Creek 15145.

Tyrone. SUZANNE K. LINDER
    VIRGINIA G. WERNER
    1100 Logan Ave., Tyrone 16686.

Ulysses. CAROLYN WALIZER (R)
    1970-. Bds: Planning Cmsn.; Ch., Solid Waste
Com. Org: NEA; Women's Club. Educ: Indiana U.
of Pa. 1954 BS. Occ: Teacher. B: 12/16/31. Add:
P.O. Box 63, Ulysses 16948.

Upland. SELMA PARRIS
    Main & Castle Aves., Upland 19015.

Upper Darby. DOROTHY J. MAC NEIL (R) **
    1970-. Bds: Ch., Highway & Sidewalks; Water
& Light; Sanitation & Sewers. Party: County Com.
1971- . B: 7/4/28. Add: 44 Marian Court, Upper
Darby 19082 (215)FL2-1450.

Upper Frederick. ANNA M. GOTTSHALK (R)
    1976-. Bds: V-Ch., Bd. of Supervisors. Prev:
Secretary, Twp. Planning Cmsn. 1970- . Org:
Young Rep. Occ: Bookkeeper. B: 10/12/20. Add:
Box 406, Perkiomenville 18074 (215)234-8995.

Upper Makefield Township. MARGARET O. DISSINGER
    Taylorsville Rd., R.R. 1, Washington Crossing

Upper Makefield Township. CHARLOTTE L. DYER (R)
    1973-. Bds: Ch., Lethal Waste Com. Prev:
School Bd. Org: Cnty. Assoc. of Elected Officials.
Educ: Barnard Coll. 1931 BA; U. of Penna. 1948
MA; 1950 PhD. Occ: Farmer. B: 2/16/06. Add:
Diabase Farm, New Hope 18938 (215)968-3340.

Upper Merion. JOAN M. KELLETT (R) **
    1971-. Bds: Library; Park & Recreation;
Bicentennial. Org: Educ. Assoc.; Rep. Club.
Educ: Benedictine Coll. 1952 BS; Villanova 1966
MEd. Occ: Teacher. B: 3/16/31. Add: 532
General Learned Rd., King of Prussia 19406
(215)265-2600.

Upper Southampton Township. BETTY H. PARTRIDGE
    939 Street Rd., Southampton 18966.

Ursina. LOUISE KOONTZ
    JOANN ROMESBURG
    DORIS VAN SICKEL
    P.O. Box 26, Ursina 15484.

Valencia. LORRAINE HAY
    Box 185, Valencia 16059.

Vandergrift. IRENE R. BESAHA (D) **
    1972-. Bds: Recreation Com.; Library Com.;
Budget & Finance. Party: V-Ch., Local Com.
1974- . Org: Dem. Assoc.; PTA; Women's Club.
Occ: Exec. Dir. B: 12/20/18. Add: 122
Jefferson Ave., Vandergrift 15690 (412)
568-2311.

Venango. MARTHA BRADICK
    VIRGINIA CROWS
    Municipal Bldg., Venango 16440.

Verona. GRACE A. PYLE
    542 Ridge Ave., Verona 15147.

Warrior Run. CAROL A. LINKIEWICZ (R)
    1975-. Bds: Pres. of Council. Party:
Committeewoman 1976-77. Org: Warrior Run
Bicentennial. B: 9/10/44. Add: 417 Pine
St., Warrior Run 18706.

Waterford. JOAN C. BARTHOLME (R)
    1976-. Bds: Parks & Recreation; Buildings.
Org: Amer. Assoc. Respiratory Therapy. Educ:
Indiana U. of Pa. 1975 BS. Occ: Respiratory
Therapist. B: 4/30/53. Add: 137 E. 3rd St.,
Waterford 16441.

Waterford. ALETHA T. HOOD (R) **
    1971-. Bds: Parks-Trees-Recreation Com.;
Bldg. Com.; Special Bldg. Com. Party: Local
Com. 1969-70. Org: DAR; Historical Society.
B: 10/10/24. Add: 261 W. 3rd St., Waterford
16441 (814)796-4411.

Watsontown. DIANE W. DAWSON (D)
    1973-. Bds: Recreation Assoc.; Senior
Citizen Housing Corp.; Pres. Borough Council.
Party: Ward Committeewoman 1976. Prev:
Councilwoman 1973-75; V-Pres., Council 1976;
Pres., Council 1976- . Org: Jr. Women's Club;
Dem. Club; PTO. Educ: Bloomsburg State Coll.
1968 BS; Bucknell U. 1970 MS. B: 2/15/46.
Add: 303 Elm St., Watsontown 17777 (717)
538-1000.

Wattsburg. HARRIET WEAVER
    Borough Bldg., Wattsburg 16442.

Waymart. ELAINE L. FRIES (D)
    1974-. Bds: Road Com. Org: Civic Club.
Educ: Marywood Coll. 1958 BA. Occ: Substitute
Teacher. B: 1/23/37. Add: Sleepy Hollow Rd.,
Waymart 18472.

Waymart. JANE MARIE VARCOE (R)
    1973-. Bds: Road & Street Com. Org: NEA;
Historical Society; OES. Educ: E. Stroudsburg
State Coll. 1963 BSEd; U. of Scranton 1967 MSEd.
Occ: School Librarian. B: 1/27/41. Add: 211
South St., Waymart 18472.

West Carroll Township. ANNIE B. MYERS (D)
    1972-. Prev: Auditor 1972. B: 4/19/12. Add:
RD #1, Box 7, Carrolltown 15722 (814)344-8327.

West Elizabeth. NANCY LICHT
    Borough Bldg., W. Elizabeth 15088.

West Lawn. CAROL I. GARDECKI
    Borough Bldg., W. Lawn 19609.

Westover. PAULINE CAMPBELL
    Borough Bldg., Westover 16692.

West Sunbury. WILNIA YOUNG
    Borough Bldg., W. Sunbury 16061.

West View. MARY KAY BERNHARD (D) **
    1974-. Bds: Ch., Public Relations; Ch., Rec-
reation; Council of Governments; Bicentennial
Youth Com.; Bldg. Com.; Property & Purchasing.
B: 4/10/35. Add: 225 Martsolf Ave., Pittsburgh
15229 (412)931-2800.

West Whiteland Township. OLGA TAYLOR
    P.O. Box 210, Exton 19341.

Whitehall Township. CLAIRE A. LEVANDUSKI
    1265 Mickley Road, Whitehall 18052.

Wilkinsburg. MARY A. REICH (D) **
    1973-. Bds: Public Health & Sanitation Com.;
Public Property Com.; Finance Com.; Library Bd.
Org: VFW. B: 12/26/26. Add: 427 Center St.,
Wilkinsburg 15221.

Williamsport. SANDRA THORNTON
    City Hall, 454 Pine St., Williamsport 17701.

Wilson. CAMILLA M. HUMMEL
    20th & Hay Ter., Wilson 18042.

Wilson. JUDITH ANN LERCH (R)
    1972-. Bds: General Govt. Com.; Parks &
Recreation. Party: Committeewoman 1968-77. Org:
NEA; PTA; Wilson Boro Council of Rep. Women.
Educ: E. Stroudsburg State BS, MEd. Occ: Teacher.
B: 2/21/44. Add: 1917 Ferry St., Easton 18042
(215)258-6142.

Winterstown. ELLA JANE HESS (R)
    1974-. Educ: Ind. U. of Pa. 1962 BSEd. B:
8/12/40. Add: RD 1, Felton 17322.

Winterstown. YVONNE LAUER
    R.D. #1, Felton 17322.

Woodcock. SYLVIA CUMMINGS
    Borough Bldg., Saegertown 16433.

York. ELIZABETH N. MARSHALL (D)
    1971-. Bds: S. Central Pa. Adv. Council to
Governor's Justice Com.; Codorus Crk. Implement-
ation Com.; Transportation Club. Party: Exec.
Com., Cnty. Dem. Com. 1976-77. Prev: City Plann-
ing Com. 1973-74. B: 12/17/18. Add: 736 Florida
Ave., York 17404 (717)843-8735.

Judges

GENEVIEVE BLATT (D)
    Judge, Commonwealth Court. 1972-. Party:
State Del. 1936-68; Nat. Del. 1936-68; Dem.
State Com. 1949-59; Nat. Committeewoman 1970-
72. Prev: Asst. Solicitor, Pittsburgh 1942-45;
Dep. State Treasurer 1945-49; Sec. of Internal
Affairs 1955-67; Asst. Dir. Office of Economic
Opportunity 1967-69. Org: ABA; Nat. Assoc. of
Women Lawyers; LWV; AAUW; Nat. Council on Aging;
Soroptimist; Altrusa. Educ: U. of Pittsburgh
1933 BA; 1934 MA; 1937 JD. B: 6/19/13. Add:
Grayco Apts., Harrisburg 17101 (717)787-8816.

MARION K. FINKELHOR
    Judge, Court of Common Pleas. Add: Allegheny
Court House, Pittsburgh 15217.

LOIS G. FORER (D)
    Judge, District Court. 1971-. Prev: Atty.,
U.S. Senate Com. on Educ. & Labor 1938-40;
Atty., U.S. Rural Electrif. Administration 1940-
41; Atty., Office of Price Stabilization 1949;
Deputy Atty. General of Pa. 1955-63. B: 3/22/14.
Add: 2401 Pennsylvania Ave., Philadelphia 19130
(215)MU6-7328.

DORIS M. HARRIS
    Judge, Court of Common Pleas. Add:
Philadelphia Courthouse, Philadelphia 19130.

JUDITH J. JAMISON (D)
    Judge, District Court. 1973-. Bds: Contin-
uing Educ. Com.; Mental Health Com. Party:
Committeewoman 1953-73; Ward Secretary 1965-70;
Ward V-Ch. 1970-73. Prev: Asst. Atty. General
1957-62, 1970-73. Org: Amer. Judicature Society;
Nat. Coll. of Probate Judges; ABA; LWV; PTA.
Educ: Antioch Coll. 1946 BA; Temple U. 1949 JD.
B: 8/19/24. Add: 2119 Delancey Pl., Philadelphia
19103 (215)MU6-7032.

MERNA B. MARSHALL (D)
    Judge, Court of Common Pleas. 1971-. Prev:
Asst. U.S. Atty. 1961-71. B: 5/27/33. Add:
3900 Ford Rd., Philadelphia 19131 (215)
MU6-7358.

HARRIET MIMS
    Judge, Court of Common Pleas. Add: District
Courthouse, Doylestown 18901.

RITA E. PRESCOTT
    Judge, Court of Common Pleas. Add: District
Courthouse, Media 19063.

LISA AVERSA RICHETTE
    Judge, Court of Common Pleas. 1971-. Bds:
Calendar Judge, Felony Jury Program 1975-present.
Prev: Chief, Family Court Division, District
Attorney's Office 1956-64; Asst. District
Attorney, Philadelphia 1954-64. Org: Amer.
Judicature Soc.; ABA; Penna. Bar Assoc.; ACLU;
Justinian Society. Educ: U. of Penna. 1949 BA;
Yale 1952 LLB. Add: 1503 One East Penn Square,
Philadelphia 19107 (215)686-7354.

EUNICE ROSS (D)
Judge, Court of Common Pleas. 1972-. Party: Ward V-Ch., 1972; Cnty. Committeewoman 1972. Prev: Dir., Family Court 1970-72. Org: Penn. Bar Assoc.; Cnty. Bar Assoc.; Trial Judges Conference; Justice Cmsn.; BPW. Educ: U. of Pittsburgh 1945 BA; 1951 LLB. B: 10/13/23. Add: 1204 Denniston Ave., Pittsburgh 15217 (412) 355-5502.

JUANITA KIDD STOUT (D)
Judge, Court of Common Pleas. 1959-. Bds: Ch., Criminal Justice Com. of Bd. of Judges. Prev: Asst. Dist Atty. 1956-59. Org: ABA; Governor's Justice Cmsn. Educ: U. of Ia. 1939 BA; Ind. U. 1949 JD, LL.M. B: 3/7/19. Add: 1919 Chestnut St., Philadelphia 19103 (215) MU6-4221.

EVELYN M. TROMMER
Judge, Court of Common Pleas. Add: Philadelphia Courthouse, Philadelphia 15217.

State Boards and Commissions

A complete list of state boards and commissions, and of their membership, was not available for inclusion.

Rhode Island

State Executive and Cabinet

JEWEL DRICKAMER **
Dir., Dept. of State Library Services 1975-. Org: Common Cause; LWV; Library Assoc. Educ: Case Western Reserve U. 1940 BS; Western Coll. 1938 BA. Occ: Dir., Library Service Center. B: 10/10/17. Add: 10 Ormond Dr., East Providence 02915 (401)277-2726.

MARY C. HACKETT (D)
Director of Employment Security. 1969-. Bds: Governor's Adv. Com. on Women; State Planning Council; State Manpower Services Council. Org: AAUW; Save the Bay; Dem. Women. Educ: Seton Hill Coll. 1947 BA. B: 2/6/25. Add: 263 W. Main Rd., Middletown 02840 (401)277-3732.

ANNA M. TUCKER (R)
Director, Department of Elderly Affairs. Prev: RI Permanent Adv. Com. on Women 1971- ; Govt. Com. on Nursing 1977; Statewide Health Coord. Council 1977. Org: AAUW; NE Gerontology Institute; PTA. Educ: U. of RI 1941 BS. B: 3/17/19. Add: 3 School St., W. Warwick 02893 (401)277-2858.

State Legislature

State Senate

GLORIA KENNEDY FLECK (D)
1976-. Dist: 15. Bds: Judiciary Com.; Health Educ. & Welfare Com. Prev: Planning Bd. 1974-77. Org: WPC; Dem. Club. B: 10/16/49. Add: 13 Dryden Blvd., Warwick 02888.

RUTH GRIMES (D)**
1974-. Dist: 10. Bds: Finance Com.; Special Legislation. Party: Ward Com. 1964. Org: Women's Dem. Club. B: 7/26/26. Add: 663 Cranston St., Providence 02907 (401) 861-5030

LILA M. SAPINSLEY (R)
1972-. Dist: 2. Bds: Judiciary; Health, Educ. & Welfare; Finance. Party: Nat. Del. 1976; State Exec. Com. 1974. Org: LWV; Common Cause; Rep. Club. Educ: Wellesley Coll. 1944 BA. B: 9/9/22. Add: 25 Cooke St., Providence 02906 (401)277-2708.

IRENE P. SMITH (D)
1976-. Dist: 27. Bds: Senate Finance Com.; Senate Special Leg. Com.; Joint Com. on Water Resources. Prev: Town Moderator 1974-76; Ch., Town Govt. Study Com. 1975- ; Governor's Adv. Com. on Women 1971-76; Governor's Coord. Council

on Health Services 1977; Bd. of Administration
1971- . Org: Amer. Assoc. of Higher Educ.; Nat.
Business Educ. Assoc.; BPW; Heart Assoc.; Dem.
Women. Educ: Regis Coll. 1956 BA; Columbia U.
1964 MA. Occ: Educ. Consultant. Add: 61 Chapel
St., Harrisville 02830 (401)277-2292.

State House

DOROTHY BEATRICE EDWARDS (R) **
   Dist: 94. Party: State Central Com. 1966- ;
Town Com. 1962- . Org: Fed. Rep. Women's Clubs.
B: 3/22/24. Add: 25 Cove St., Portsmouth 02871.

THERESA M. HEALY (D)
   92 Chaplin St., Pawtucket 92861.

LORRAINE L. KANE (R)
   24 Nekick Rd., Warwick 02818.

MARY N. KILMARX (D)
   1974-. Dist: 88. Bds: Adv. Bd. of Library
Cmsnr's.; Joint Com. on the Environment; Com.
on Corporations. Party: Com. on Party Policy &
Org. 1973-75. Prev: Del., Constitutional Conv.
1973. Org: Common Cause; LWV; Dem. Women's
League. Educ: Mt. Holyoke Coll. 1949 BA. B:
12/12/27. Add: 56 Elm Ln., Barrington 02806
(401)277-2672.

VICTORIA LEDERBERG (D) **
   1974-. Dist: 4. Bds: Finance Com. Org:
Common Cause; LWV; Psychological Assoc.; Research
Org.; Women Educators. Educ: Pembroke Coll.
1959 BA; Brown U. 1961 MA; Brown U. 1966 PhD.
Occ: Associate Professor. B: 7/7/37. Add: 190
Slater Ave., Providence 02906 (401)277-2738.

MAUREEN E. MAIGRET (D) **
   1974-. Dist: 37. Bds: Governor's Advisory
Cmsn. on Women. Org: Nurses Assoc.; WPC. Educ:
RI Coll. 1974 BS; Memorial Hospital School of
Nursing 1964 RN. Occ: Nurse. B: 2/11/44. Add:
232 Vancouver Ave., Warwick 02886.

HELENA E. MC DERMOTT (D)
   293 Grove Ave., Warwick 02889.

Local Councils

Barrington. ANN H. HANSON (R)
   1975-. Bds: Sewer Com.; Youth Concerns; Cnty.
Solid Waste Com. Org: LWV; Rep. Town Com.; PTA.
Educ: U. of Vt. 1956 BS. B: 5/10/35. Add: 116
Nayatt Rd., Barrington 02806 (401)245-3103.

Charlestown. ELLEN F. ENNIS
   South County Trail, Box 372, Charlestown
02813.

Exeter. MURIEL ANN MYERS (R)
   1976-. Bds: Repr., Cnty. Council of Govts.
Party: Alt., Rep. State Central Com. 1977- ;
Rep. Town Com. 1976- . Org: R.I. Speech &
Hearing Assoc.; Civic Assoc.; Rep. Women; WPC;
Internat. Women's Assoc. Educ: Pa. State U.
1968 BA; U. of R.I. 1974 MS. Occ: Speech Path-
ologist. B: 9/20/47. Add: Glen Rock Rd., Exeter
02822 (401)295-7500.

Foster. MARGERY I. MATTHEWS (D)
   1976-. Bds: Pres. of Town Council. Party:
Dem. Com. 1970-74. Prev: Regional School Bldg.
Com. 1964-72. Org: RI Library Assoc.; Foster
Preservation Society; Historical Society.
Educ: U. of RI 1944 BS; 1968 MLS. B: 9/8/23.
Add: Box A30 RR2 Cucumber Hill, Foster 02825
(401)397-7771.

Hopkinton. OLIVE J. CHAMPLIN (R)
   1976-. Org: Rep. Club. Educ: Simmons Coll.
1932 BS; U. of RI 1967 MA. B: 5/23/09. Add:
P.O. Box 66, Bradford 02808 (401)377-8086.

Little Compton. JANE P. CABOT (R)
   1970-. Bds: Pension Com.; Council Pres.
Prev: Budget Com. 1965-70. Educ: U. of RI
1951 BS. B: 4/17/30. Add: W. Main Rd., Little
Compton 02837 (401)635-4400.

Middletown. KATHLEEN N. CONNELL
   233 Tuckerman Ave., Middletown 02840.

Middletown. JUNE GIBBS (R)
   1974-. Party: State Del. 1960-76; Nat. Del.
1968, '76; Rep. Nat. Com. Secretary 1977; Rep.
Nat. Committeewoman 1969- ; V-Ch., State Central
Com. 1960-69; Ch., Sub Com. on Housing 1975-76;
Rep. Nat. Conv. 1976. Prev: Charter Cmsn. 1967-
68; Beach Cmsn. 1954-67. Org: AAUW; WPC; Rep.
Women. Educ: Wellesley Coll. 1943 BA; Boston
U. 1947 MA. B: 6/13/22. Add: 163 Riverview
Ave., Middletown 02840 (401)847-0009.

Middletown. MARY M. NUNES
   127 West Main Road, Middletown 02840.

Newport. LILLIAN ROTHE GEE
   1975-. Bds: Tourist Promotion Cmsn.;
Mental Health Clinic; Ch., Gaslight Project
Liaison. Educ: U. of Lausanne 1967 BA. B:
1/2/45. Add: Endeavor, Narragansett Ave.,
Newport 02840 (401)846-7200.

Newport. ROSE E. MC GANN (D)
   1975-. Dist: 99. Bds: Bd. of Dir's., New
Visions; Bd. of Dir's., Potter League for
Animals; Adv. Bd., Liquor Licensing. Party:
State Dem. Com. 1972; City Dem. Com. Org: ANA;
Women's Dem. Club. Educ: St. Mary's School
of Nursing 1939 RN. Occ: RN. B: 11/25/16.
Add: 71 Merton Rd., Newport (401)846-7787.

North Kingstown. MARGUERITE NEUBERT
   20 Congdon Ave., North Kingstown 02852.

North Providence. ANN M. MC QUEENEY (D)
   1974-. Dist: 3. Bds: Council Claims Com.;
Public Welfare Com.; Finance Com. Prev: Del.,
State Constitutional Conv. 1973. Org: Teachers
Union; Dem. Women's Club; Women's Action Com.
Educ: R.I. Coll. 1970 BA; Providence Coll. 1974
MEd. Occ: Elementary School Teacher. B:
7/30/48. Add: 58 Capitol View Ave., N.
Providence 02911 (401)231-4711.

North Smithfield. ELIZABETH M. CESARIO (R) **
   1971-. Prev: Charter Cmsn. 1966-68;
Housing Authority 1970-71. Org: BPW; Bicentennial; Chamber of Commerce; Life Underwriters;

Women's Rep. Club. Occ: Owner of Business. B: 3/28/28. Add: Pond House Rd., Box 1348, North Smithfield 02895 (401)769-8151.

Portsmouth. DORIS M. PELTO
52 Brownell Lane, Portsmouth 02871.

Providence. CAROLYN F. BRASSIL
93 Governor Street, Providence 02906.

Scituate. ELEANOR M. CARPENTER
Chopmist Hill Road, No. Scituate 02857.

Tiverton. JEANNETTE N. TIDWELL (R)
1976-. Bds: Governor's Justice Cmsn.; Police-Fire-Hwy. Cmsnr. Org: Dem. Town Com.; WPC. Occ: Patient Account Repr. B: 8/20/26. Add: 191 Hayden Ave., Tiverton 02878 (401)624-4277.

Judges

CORRINNE P. GRANDE
Judge, Superior Court. Add: Providence County Courthouse, Providence 02903.

FLORENCE KERINS MURRAY
Judge, Superior Court. Prev: State Senator 1948-56; Governor's Judicial Council 1950-60; RI Com. on Youth & Children; RI Alcoholic Adv. Com. 1955-58; Governor's Adv. Com. on Mental Health 1954; Ch., RI Com. for the Humanities 1972; Governor's Adv. Com. on Revision of Election Laws; Governor's Adv. Com. on Social Welfare; 1950 White House Conf. on Youth & Children; 1952 Annual Assay Cmsn.; Nat. Defense Adv. Com. on Women in the Service 1952-58; Civil & Political Rights Com. of President's Cmsn. on Status of Women 1960-63. Org: Mass. Bar; RI Bar; US Dist. Ct.; US Supreme Ct.; US Tax Ct.; Internal Revenue Cmsn.; US Ct. of Military Appeals; Amer. Arbitration Assoc.; ABA; Ch., Nat. Endowment for the Humanities Com. Educ: Syracuse U. BA; Boston U. LLB. B: 10/21/16. Add: 2 Kay St., Newport 02840.

State Boards and Commissions

Office of the Governor, State Capitol Bldg., Providence 02908.

Abortions, Commission to Study Public Health Implications of
ROSALIE FALVEY

Aging, Advisory Committee on
ALIDA BOLAND
BETTY BRIGGS
JOSEPHINE FRATINI
ANN HILL
SUSAN MC GUIRL
ROSE SHOCKET

Alcoholics, Commission to Study Present Facilities and Treatment for
LOUISE BURNS
DOROTHY GADOURY
VIRGINIA LARKIN
CARLOTTA WHIRTY

Alcoholism, Advisory Council on
SISTER ARLENE VIOLET
PHILLIPPA ALMEIDA

Abulance Service Coordinating Board
CYNTHIA K. CLAY

American and Canadian French Cultural Exchange Commission
YVETTE D. BRUNI
RITA L. COUTURE
MRS. CHARLES A. POST

American and Irish Cultural Exchange Commission
FRANCES MAGUIRE

Apprenticeship Information Center, Advisory Committee of
PHILLIPPA ALMEIDA
JENNIE R. BROWN

Arts, State Council on the
ANNA R. BERNIER
CAROLE S. CASTELLUCCI
DOROTHY S. LICHT
FLORENCE N. WEINTRAUB

Auditorium Commission, State
MARIE C. SMITH

Automobile Wrecking and Salvage Yard Regulatory License Commission
SYBIL CHASET

Blind, Advisory Council for the
MARY J. CHERLIN
MARY V.B. STEPHENS

Building Code, State
MARIA LOPES

Children and Youth, Committee on
EMILY D. ALEXANDER
HELEN D. BENNETT
VIOLA M. BERARD
DOROTHY W. BURGESS
HELENE BURRELL
MARGARET A. CONNELLY
MABEL E. COONEY
VIRGINIA R. DAVIS
HELEN G. ENNIS
MARJORIE GILMORE
MARY HADE HICKEY
SARA L. KERR
LUCILLE P. LEONARD
GEORGIA C. LLOYD
HELEN C. MC LEISH
ANNA R. MULLANEY
RITA M. MURPHY
FLORENCE K. MURRAY
MARY W. L. MURRAY
BARBARA K. PAGANO
GLADYS P. SHEPLEY
RUTH T. SILVERMAN
DORIS S. VINER
SYLVIA P. WEISBERGER

Clinical Laboratories, Advisory Council for
RUTH F. THOMSON

Comprehensive Health Planning, Advisory Council to
RUTH GREENBERG
LUCILLE SULLIVAN
ADELINA WILLIAMS

Consumers' Council
ELEANOR MILLER

Correctional Services, Advisory Commission on
BEATRICE H. PIERCE
LUELLA RUSSELL
GLORIA SPEARS

Crime, Delinquency and Crime Administration,
Governor's Committee on
BEVERLY A. DWYER

Day Care Commission
CHRISTINE GAIL CHIACU
H. EILEEN COSTELLO
LYNDA J. DICKINSON
BARBARA MILDRAM
RAE KATHRYN O'NEILL
JOAN RETSINAS
TANYA ROMELLE SAUNDERS
BARBARA TUFTS

Developmental Disabilities, State Planning and
Advisory Council on
ALICE DONAHUE
NANCY D'WOLF
JUDY MYCROFT
CAROLE OLSHANSKY
BARBARA VAN WEST

Eastern States' Exposition Commission of Rhode
Island
MARION E. HOLLSTEIN

Economic Development Council
MILDRED T. NICHOLS

Education, Board of Regents for
MARY P. LYONS
DONNA MARIE PONTARELLI
NORMA B. WILLIS

Educational Television, Advisory Commission on
EILEEN D. DREW
MARY MC GOWAN

Education Commission of the States
SISTER ELIZABETH MORANCY
LILA M. SAPINSLEY

Electrolysis, Board of Examiners in
NINA FERRIE

Emergency Resources Planning Committee
MARY C. HACKETT
LORRAINE SILBERTHAU

Employment of the Handicapped, Governor's Committee
on
MILDRED A. BRADY
MEREDITH DONAHUE
HOPE FITTON
GAIL LEE GINALSKI
ELIZABETH KERSHAW
MARJORIE MC GARRY

Employment Security, Advisory Council on
MARGARET H. A. BURGESS

Environmental Quality, Council on
MARIE CAMPARONE
MILDRED CHASE
KATHLEEN MC DONALD
GRACE VALENTE

Firearms, Commission to Study the Safe Use and
Control of
LILLIAN POTTER

Foster Child Placement, Commission on
CATHERINE M. COONEY
JOYCE A. DESMARAIS
RUTH GRIMS
DR. JEAN M. MAYNARD
NAOMI OSTERMAN
LILA M. SAPINSLEY
LUCY RAWLINGS TOOTELL

Hairdressing, Board of
MARY CERRA
MARGO CHOBANIAN
ANGELA RINK

Handicapped, Governor's Commission on Recreation
for the
NANCY B. DE WOLF
EVA Y. RODIMON

Health Clubs, Commission to Study
GAIL CASTELLANO
VICKI WHITTIER

Health Facilities Construction, Advisory Council on
MARGARET VAN HOUTEN

Highway Safety, Council on
ETHEL T. GILDEA

Historical Preservation Commission
ELIZABETH G. ALLEN
ALFRED T. KLYBERG
NANCY HAY

Housing and Mortgage Finance Corporation
BARBARA A. SOKOLOFF

Housing and Mortgage Finance Corporation, Advisory
Committee to the
ADE BETHUNE
JOSEPHINE BYRD
BETTY JAE CLANTON
PHYLLIS MONROE

Human Rights, Commission for
RITA MICHAELSON

Judicial Tenure and Discipline, Commission on
ALICE D'ALESSIO

Justice Commission, Governor's
JOAN BUCHANAN
EUNICE SHATZ

Library Commissioners, Advisory Board of
VELMA M. BROWN
MARY V. MAGUIRE

Medical Education, Commission on
   LILA M. SAPINSLEY

Mental Health, Governor's Council on
   RITA M. ADAIR
   ELEANOR BRIGGS
   HARRIET BRUNELLE
   MAUREEN KEATES
   LILA M. SAPINSLEY
   L. ELLEN SCHROEDER

Mental Health Retardation and Hospitals, Advisory
Council on
   BARBARA J. GILROY
   RHODA MORRISON

Milk Sanitation Board
   CECILIA BLICKER

Motion Pictures, Board of the Classification of
   SANDRA CROLL
   CAROL C. CRONIN

Nurse Registration and Nursing Education, Board of
   HELEN E. JONES
   DORA FOWLER
   KATHLEEN LONERGAN
   CATHERINE I. MC GOLDRICK
   RITA SICARD
   CATHERINE STOCK
   HELEN STROK

Nurse Registration and Nursing Education, Committee
of Consultants to the Board of
   BEATRICE NELLE

Nursing Home Administrators, Board of Examiners for
   EVELYN HARRIS
   ELIZABETH MURPHY
   SISTER MARIETTA WALSH

Parole Board
   PAMELA C. MACKTAZ

Personal Data, Commission to Study Unfair Compiling
of
   LERA O'HARA

Personnel Appeal Board
   MARGARET H. LA ROSE

Pharmacy, Board of
   MARTHA M. GLASHEEN

Physical Therapy, Board of
   FLORENCE M. FILIPPO
   HAZEL E. GRIME

Physicians, Commission to Study the State's
Dependence on Foreign Trained
   ANN ROBINSON

Planning Council, State
   MARY C. HACKETT
   PAULINE LEVEN
   LUCY SCHMIDT
   MARION WOLK

Postsecondary Education Commission
   LUCILLE B. KEEGAN
   MARY P. LYONS
   DONNA MARIE PONTARELLI
   NORMA J. WILLIS

Present Facilities and Treatment for Epileptics,
and Local and State Laws Pertaining to Epilepsy,
Commission to Study in Depth the
   CAROLE OLSHANSKY

Psychology, Board of
   LENORA A. DE LUCIA

Public Building Authority
   EMILY GAGLIONE

Real Estate Commission
   ANN LAMB
   RITA STONE

Review, Board of
   ELIZABETH NORD

School for the Deaf, Advisory Council of the
   LUCILLE P. LEONARD
   SHIRLEY MC NELIS

Solid Waste Management Corporation
   ELEANOR F. SLATER

Solid Waste Management Corporation, Citizens
Advisory Board to the
   MARGARET K. KOSTER
   BETH PAUL MILHAM
   CHRISTINE A. MULLEN
   PEGGY GOYD SHARPE

Speech Pathology and Audiology, Board of Examiners
for
   RUTH FRITZ SIMONS
   JEAN MARIE HURT

Transportation Advisory Council
   PAMELA CRANDALL
   MARJORIE ZEUCH

Vocational Technical Education, State Advisory
Council on
   KAREN BOUCHARD
   MAUREEN E. MASSIWER
   MARIE RENZULLI
   ELEANOR F. SLATER

Women, Permanent Advisory Commission on
   LILLIAN T. CAPPUCCIO
   JOAN CORNELL
   BEVERLY A. DWYER
   FLORENCE GALLOGLY
   HARRIET HOLLAND
   GERTRUDE M. HOCHBERG
   LOUISE KING
   MAXINE V. S. NICHOLS
   MILDRED NICHOLS
   ROSE SACK
   IRENE SMITH
   SHEILA CABRAL SOUSA

South Carolina

JOSEPHINE CANNON
Executive Director, Children's Bureau. Add: Suite 400, Landmark E. Building, 3700 Forest Drive, Columbia 29211.

ESTELLENE P. WALKER
Librarian, State Library. 1970-. Party: State Alt. Prev: Adv. Com. on Library Services Program 1956-57; S.C. Com. for Humanities 1976. Org: Amer. Library Assoc.; S.C. Status of Women; S.C. Council for Common Good. Educ: U. of Tenn. 1933 BA; Emory U. 1935 BSLS. Add: 3208 Amherst Ave., Columbia 29205 (803)758-3181.

State Legislature

State House

SYLVIA K. DREYFUS (D)
10 Stone Lake Court, Greenville 29609.

LOIS EARGLE (D)
Conway 29526.

JUANITA W. GOGGINS (D) **
1974-. Dist: 49. Bds: Ways and Means Com.; Legislative Black Caucus. Party: Del., Nat. Dem. Conv. 1972-74. Org: Pres., Area Sickle Cell Anemia Foundation. Educ: SC State Coll. 1957 BS. Add: 1635 W. Main St., Rock Hill 29730 (803)758-8900.

JOYCE C. HEARN (R)
1975-. Dist: 76. Bds: Medical, Military & Municipal Affairs. Party: State Del. 1966, '68, '72, '74, '76; Precinct Leader 1974-77; Cnty. Ch. 1972-74; Dist. V-Ch. 1968-70; Cnty. V-Ch. 1968-70. Prev: Cmsnr., Cnty. Planning Cmsn. 1973-76; Bd., Cnty. Youth Center. Org: LWV; Urban League; Ct.-Up-Date; Rep. Women's Club; Women's Club. Educ: U. of Ga. 1949 BA; Ohio State U. 1957 BEd. B: 6/16/29. Add: 1316 Berkley Rd., Columbia 29206.

HARRIET KEYSERLING (D)
1976-. Dist: 124. Bds: Educ. Party: State Del. 1972, '74, '76. Prev: Cnty. Councilwoman 1974-76. Org: LWV; Dem. Party. Educ: Barnard Coll. 1943 BA. B: 4/4/22. Add: P.O. Box 1108, Beaufort 29902 (803)758-8825.

JEAN MYERS (D)
Dunes Club Sec., Myrtle Beach 29577.

IRENE K. RUDNICK (D) **
1972-. Dist: 85. Bds: House Ways and Means. Party: Ch., Treasurer, City Com.; State Exec. Com. 1974. Prev: Cnty. Superintendent of Educ. 1969-72. Org: Bar Assoc. Educ: U. SC 1949 BA; U. SC Law School 1952 JD. Occ: Attorney. B: 12/27/29. Add: 3425 Summit Dr., Aiken 29801.

NORMA RUSSELL (R) **
1973-. Dist: 90. Bds: V-Ch., Medical; Military; Public & Municipal Affairs. Party: Precinct V-Ch. 1970-72. Prev: Cnty. Rural Recreation Cmsn. 1968-69. Org: Citizens for the Advancement of the Physically Handicapped. Occ: Court Reporter. B: 8/23/37. Add: 92 Nob Hill Rd., Columbia 29210 (803)758-8541.

FERDINAN B. STEVENSON (D) **
1974-. Dist: 110. Org: OWL; Historical Society. Educ: Smith Coll. 1949 BA. B:6/8/28. Add: 14 Legare St., Charleston 29401 (803) 758-8825.

JEAN H. TOAL (D)
1974-. Dist: 75. Bds: House Judiciary Com.; State Workmen's Compensation Study; House Rules Com. Party: State Dem. Conv. 1972; Cnty. Dem. Conv. 1974; State Rules Com. 1974; Credentials Com., State Party 1972-74; State Del. 1972-76. Prev: State Human Affairs Cmsn. 1972-74. Org: ABA; Amer. Judicature Society; SC Bar Assoc.; BPW; Shandon Neighborhood Council, SC Defense Lawyers Assoc., Cnty. Young Lawyers. Educ: Agnes Scott Coll. 1965 BA; USC Law School 1968 JD. Occ: Lawyer. B: 8/11/43. Add: 2418 Wheat St., Columbia 29205 (803)799-9091.

County Commissions

Aiken. MIM WOODRING (R)
1976-. Dist: 4. Bds: Ch., Finance; Ch., Judiciary; Ch., Personnel. Org: Society of Professional Journalists; SC Press Assoc.; Chamber of Commerce; Bd. of Health; Rep. Women; Rep. Party. Educ: Juniata Coll. 1950 BS. Occ: Assoc. News Editor. B: 5/16/28. Add: P.O. Box 6095, N. Augusta 29841 (803)648-2996.

Berkeley. ALICE B. GEORGE
P.O. Box 454, Moncks Corner 29461.

Berkeley. BERNICE FRIENDLY
Box 817, Moncks Corner 29461.

Charleston. MAJORIE AMOS (D) **
1974-. Bds: Ch., Council Public Welfare & Educ. Com.; Council Finance Com.; Capital Improvements Com.; Industrial & Agricultural Dev. Com.; Legislative Com.; Bd. Dir., Amer. Dev. Corporation; Bd. Trustees Allen U.; Bd. Dir., Reid House Center. Party: V-Ch., City Party 1975- . Prev: Cnty. Tax Exempt Bd. 1973-74; Grand Jury 1972. Org: Dir., U.S. Dept. Housing & Urban Dev. Home Counseling Program. B: 1/13/26. Add: 361 Ashley Ave., Charleston 29403 (803)723-1626.

Hampton. MARCIA C. WOOD
    Box 508, Varnville 29944.

Lexington. ELSIE SUTHERLAND RAST (D)
    1973-. Bds: Ch., Transportation; Individual
Resource; Civil & Criminal Justice. Party: State
Del. 1972-76; Nat. Del. 1972; V-Ch., Cnty. Com.
1972-78. Prev: Cnty. Museum Cmsn. 1970-71. Org:
United Teaching Profession; SC Assoc. of Cntys.;
PTA; Grass roots Adv. Com. Educ: Wesleyan Coll.
1952 BA; Ariz. State U. 1959 MA; U. of SC 1971
MM. Occ: Teacher. B: 11/11/31. Add: Cedar
Pond Farm, P.O. Box 135, Pelion 29123 (803)
356-8103.

Marlboro. DOROTHY W. CROSLAND
    107 Townsend St., Bennettsville 29512.

Richland. SUSIE BUNCH NEWMAN (D)
    1976-. Bds: Judicial Ctr. Com.; Coats
Planning Com.; V-Ch. Justice & Public Safety.
Party: State Del. 1976; State Alt. 1974. Org:
Nat. Assoc. of Cnty's.; Mid-Carolina Council on
Alcoholism; Dem. Women's Club. B: 10/19/35.
Add: 192 Lions Gate Dr., Columbia 29204 (803)
254-7139.

Richland. CANDY YAGHJIAN WAITES (D)
    1976-. Bds: Ch., Administration & Finance
Com.; Planning & Devt. Com.; Liaison, Leg. Del.
Org: LWV; Central Midlands Regional Planning
Council; IWY Coord. Com.; Dem. Party; PTA. Educ:
Wheaton Coll. 1965 BA. B: 2/21/43. Add: 418
Edisto Ave., Columbia 29205 (803)254-7139.

Mayors

Clemson. CATHERINE J. SMITH (D)
    1975-. Bds: Bd. of Dir., SC Municipal Assoc.;
Recreation & Planning Cmsn.; Water & Sewer Com.
Prev: City Council 1967-75. Org: Municipal Assoc;
Women's Club. Educ: Furman U. 1938 BS. Occ:
Bookkeeper/Tax Preparer. B: 12/12/15. Add: 304
Wyatt Ave., Clemson 29631 (803)654-2636.

Eutawville. ROSEMARY MARTIN
    City Hall, Eutawville 29048.

Greeleyville. DORIS P. BROWDER (D)
    1976-. Bds: Cnty. Beautification Com. Party:
Cnty. Committeewoman 1976-77. Occ: Dry Cleaners
Owner. B: 9/9/18. Add: Main St., Greeleyville
29056 (803)426-2111/2426.

Hollywood. TERRI B. MAIN (R)
    1977-. Prev: Councilwoman 1975-77. Org: PTA.
Occ: Office Manager. B: 12/7/51. Add: P.O. Box
5183, Hollywood 29449 (803)889-2338.

Johnsonville. CONNIE S. DE CAMPS (I)
    1976-. Prev: Councilwoman 1974-76. Org:
Women's Club; Cnty. Beautification; SC Community
Devt. Assoc. B: 3/24/27. Add: Broadway St.,
Johnsonville 29555 (803)386-2069.

Manning. PANSY RIDGEWAY (D)
    1970-. Prev: Councilwoman 1962-70. Educ:
Furmon U. 1953 BA. Occ: Dress Shop Owner. B:
1/1/31. Add: 107 Sumter St., Manning 29102
(803)435-8477.

Ninety Six. MARY LANDER BELL (D) **
    1973-. Prev: Councilwoman 1972-73. Org:
Bd. of Dir., Chamber of Commerce; Amer. Red
Cross. Educ: Lander Coll. BA. B: 8/22/15.
Add: 400 N. Church St., Ninety Six 29666
(803)543-2200.

Local Councils

Anderson. BEATRICE THOMPSON
    City Hall, Anderson 29621.

Atlantic Beach. EARLENE EVANS
            MARY GLASS
    City Hall, Atlantic Beach 29016.

Blythewood. DOROTHY MILLER
    City Hall, Blythewood 29413.

Bonneau. NELL DENNIS
    City Hall, Bonneau 29413.

Carlisle. ANNE HAMILTON O'DANIEL DE HART (D) **
    1973-. Bds: Delinquent Tax Collector.
Occ: Teletype Operator. B: 10/3/51. Add:
Box 124, Carlisle 29031 (803)427-1505.

Chappells. IRENE D. PARNELL
    City Hall, Chappells 29037.

Charleston. MARY R. ADER (D)
    1975-. Bds: Ways & Means; Public Safety &
Traffic; Electric Wires & Lighting the City.
Org: Civic Club; Dem. Club; Women's Club. B:
1/20/28. Add: 1748 Somerset Cir., Charleston
29407 (803)571-2269.

Charleston. HILDA H. JEFFERSON
    City Hall, Charleston 29401.

Charleston. BRENDA C. SCOTT (D)
    1975-. Bds: Ways & Means Com.; Ch., Elect-
rical Wires & Lighting Com.; Public Safety &
Transportation Com. Party: V-Pres. Precinct
1976-78. Org: NEA; NAACP; Civic Club. Educ:
S.C. State Coll. 1971 BS. Occ: Teacher. B:
1/10/49. Add: 455-B Race St., Charleston
29403.

Clemson. MARY D. DUSENBERRY **
    1972-. Bds: Pres., Pickens County Munici-
pal Assoc. Org: AAUW; LWV; Pres., Community
Library; PTO. Educ: U. of SC 1962 BA. B:
9/26/40. Add: 111 Lakeview Cir., Clemson
29631 (803)654-2636.

Clemson. BETTY JANZEN
    City Hall, Clemson 29631.

Cope. LENA CROFT HAYDEN (R)
    1972-. B: 12/15/08. Add: P.O. Box 3, Cope
29038 (803)534-7703.

Darlington. BETTY BAKER (D) **
    1973-. Bds: Recreation Bd.; Park Com.
Party: Del., State Conv. 1974. Org: Dem.
Women. B: 4/13/37. Add: 706 James St.,
Darlington 29532.

Due West. RUTH COFFEY (D)
1976-. Org: AAUW. Educ: Maryville Coll.
1947 BA; Presbyterian School of Cristian Educ.
1949 MREd. B: 6/18/25. Add: Box 336, Due West
29639.

Eastover. EDNA SCOTT
City Hall, Eastover 29044.

Edisto Beach. MARGARET BOST
City Hall, Edisto Beach 29438.

Fairfax. OLIVIA COHEN
City Hall, Fairfax 29827.

Fountain Inn. BRENDA HALL
City Hall, Fountain Inn 29644.

Gifford. EARLENE DUNCAN
City Hall, Gifford 29923.

Goose Creek. MARGUERITE BROWN
SHIRLEY JOHNSON
NANCY LAWSON
City Hall, Goose Creek 29445.

Greenville. PATRICIA CORBIN HASKELL (R) **
1973-. Bds: Ch., Parks & Recreation Com.;
Public Service; Implementation Com. & Joint Law
Enforcement Center. Org: Urban League; Chamber
of Commerce; Mental Health Assoc.,; Rep. Club;
Rep. Women. Occ: V-Pres. & Manager of Business.
B: 1/29/31. Add: 285 Riverbend, Greenville
29601 (803)242-1250.

Greenwood. EMILY B. BOGGERO (D) **
1971-. Bds: Public Service. Org: Chamber
of Commerce; Literary Assoc. Occ: Secretary.
B: 4/19/25. Add: 205 Penn Ave., Greenwood 29646
(803)223-5463.

Greenwood. LERRYN U. CULBERTSON (D)
1976-. Bds: Com. on Human Resources; Municipal
Assoc. Org: ANA; Carolina Society for Health,
Educ. & Training; Rape Council. Educ: Lander
Coll. 1974 AA. Occ: R.N. B: 2/26/54. Add:
430 Grove St., Greenwood 29646 (803)229-3741.

Greer. SHIRLEE ROLLINS
City Hall, Greer 29651.

Hanahan. DOROTHY CEASE
MARY LOU STRICKLAND
City Hall, Hanahan 29410.

Hardeeville. DOROTHY MC GARVEY MARTIN (D)
Bds: Ch., Streets & Beautification. Org:
Chamber of Commerce. Occ: Motel Owner. B:
8/28/28. Add: 5 Carroll St., Hardeeville
29927 (803)784-2231.

Hartsville. PAM PARROTT FUNDER BURK (I) **
1975-. Org: BPW; PTA. Occ: Retail Buyer.
B: 3/5/48. Add: 1513 W. Carolina Ave., Hartsville 29550 (803)332-6463.

Hemingway. VIVIAN COLLINS
SARAH GALLOWAY
CAROL MORRIS
City Hall, Hemingway 29554.

Hollywood. JO ANN H. HARRISON (R)
1975-. Org: PTO. B: 8/29/33. Add: P.O.
Box 203, Hollywood 29449.

Kershaw. MRS. B.D. MC DONALD
City Hall, Kershaw 29067.

Lexington. SHARON R. RIGGS (D)
1975-. Org: NEA; Chamber of Commerce;
Bicentennial Cmsn. Educ: Newberry Coll. 1969
BA; U. of S.C. 1972 MAT. Occ: Teacher. B:
6/24/47. Add: 105 Blacksmith Rd., Lexington
29072 (804)359-4164.

Lexington. MARO K. ROGERS (D)
1975-. Bds: Ch., Finance Dept. Org:
Chamber of Commerce; Library Assoc. Educ:
Columbia Coll. 1956 BA. Occ: Teacher. B:
9/10/31. Add: Saxe Gotha Ln., Lexington
29072 (803)359-4164.

Loris. MAXINE T. DAWES
City Hall, Loris 29569.

Moncks Corner. IMOGENE T. RUSSELL (R)
1975-. Bds: Community Devt. Bd. Org: BPW;
Book Club. Occ: Merchant. B: 8/11/39. Add:
107 W. Main St., Moncks Corner 29461 (803)
899-6667.

Mount Croghan. CLARA R. HENDRICK (D)
1972-. Bds: City Treasurer; City Clerk.
Party: Precinct Secretary 1975-77; Del., Cnty.
Conv. Occ: Bank Teller. B: 11/3/32. Add:
P.O. Box 14, Mt. Croghan 29727 (803)634-6567.

Mount Croghan. VERA B. RIVERS
City Hall, Mt. Croghan 29727.

Mount Pleasant. DOROTHY B. KEARNS (R)
1976-. Bds: Ch., Budget & Finance; Ch.,
Parks & Public Buildings; Annexation. Party:
State Del. 1974, '72; State Alt. 1970; Precinct
Pres. 1974-76. Org: Women's Club. Occ: Account-
ant. B: 3/16/21. Add: 977 Tall Pine Rd., Mt.
Pleasant 29464 (803)884-8517.

Mullins. MRS. JESSIE D. LEWIS
City Hall, Mullins 29574.

Ninety Six. FRIEDA SCHUKOWSKY (D)
1975-. Bds: Chamber of Commerce; Municipal
Assoc. of SC. Org: BPW; Chamber of Commerce;
OES; Women's Club. Occ: Sales Coord./Corporate
Secretary. B: 11/8/45. Add: 115 Park St.,
Ninety Six 29666 (803)543-2711.

North Augusta. ELLEN S. SMITH (R) **
1971-. Org: Advisory Bd., Salvation Army;
Rep. Club; DAR. Educ: Kan. State U. 1940 BS.
B: 1/15/18. Add: 607 W. Woodlawn Ave., North
Augusta 29841 (803)279-0330.

North Charleston. PATSY W. HUGHES (D) **
1974-. Party: Precinct Com. 1968-74; Secre-
tary, Precinct 1967-68. Prev: Public Service
Commissioner 1969-72. Org: PTA. Occ: Monitor,
High School. B: 7/30/31. Add: 4924 France
Ave., North Charleston 29406 (803)554-5700.

North Myrtle Beach. MILDRED G. THOMAS (R) **
    1970-. B: 7/6/19. Add: 331 46th Ave., N,
North Myrtle Beach 29582 (803)272-5202.

North Myrtle Beach. JEAN N. WHITE (D)
    1976-. Prev: City Councilwoman 1964-67.
Occ: Account Exec. B: 6/2/36. Add: 709 14th
Ave. S, P.O. Box 1272,N. Myrtle Bch. 29582.

Orangeburg. SARA H. ALEXANDER (I)
    1975-. Org: Amer. Nurses Assoc.; Chamber of
Commerce; BPW. Educ: Orangeburg Reg. Hospital
School of Nursing 1952 RN. Occ: Nurse. B:
1/23/36. Add: 2025 Dogwood NE, Orangeburg
29115 (803)534-2525.

Pamplico. MARY K. MILLER
    City Hall, Pamplico 29583.

Paxville. AUDREY ARDIS
    City Hall, Paxville 29102.

Pine Ridge. SADIE LUCAS
    City Hall, Pine Ridge.

Quinby. MILDRED GALLUP (R)
    1976-. Bds: Ch., Recreational Facilities
Com. Occ: Teacher's Aide/Librarian. B: 3/28/27.
Add: 219 Creek Dr., Quinby 29501 (803)669-3031.

Ravenel. ETHEL W. COBB
          BETTYE GAINEY
    City Hall, Ravenel 29470.

Ravenel. ETHEL INABINETT (D)
    1976-. Org: PTA. Occ: Coord. B: 1/12/36.
Add: P.O. Box 104, Ravenel 29470 (803)889-2727.

Ruby. SYLVIA GULLEDGE BAILEY (D) **
    1971-. B: 7/22/39. Add: Box 133, Ruby 29741.

St. Shephen. BARBARA BARNETT
    City Hall, St. Shephen 29479.

Salley. DONNA C. BOYLSTON (D)
    1976-. Bds: Ch., Recreation; Ch., Streets.
Party: State Del. 1976; Exec. Committeewoman
1975-76; Local Ch. 1976. Org: Dem. Club. Educ:
Columbia Coll. 1969 BA; U. of SC 1976 MEd. Occ:
Teacher. B: 5/11/47. Add: Pine St., Salley
29137.

Sellers. GRACIE HORNER
    City Hall, Sellers 29592.

Springdale. ANN S. HINSON
    City Hall, Springdale 29169.

Springfield. REBECCA STEVERSON
    City Hall, Springfield 29146.

Stuckey. SYLVIA ARD
    City Hall, Stuckey 29554.

Summerton. ELLEN V. ARDIS
    City Hall, Summerton 29148.

Summerville. BETHEL WHITEHURST MC INTOSH (I)
    Bds: Regional Planning Council of Govts.; Ch.,
Lighting; Public Bldgs. & Grounds Com. Org:

Historical Society; Colonial Dames of Amer.;
Bicentennial Com.; Human Resources Com. Occ:
Medical Staff Asst. B: 4/10/20. Add: 603 W.
Richardson Ave., Summerville 29483 (803)
873-4310.

Sumter. COLLEEN H. YATES (D) **
    1970-. Bds: City, County Liaison; Regional
Planning Council; Cultural Com.; Municipal
Assoc. Party: Precinct Exec. Com. 1970- ;
Del., State Conv.; Congressional Representative;
Women's Dem. Council 1974-75. Prev: Election
Cmsn. 1960-70. Org: LWV; Chamber of Commerce;
Dem. Women's Council; Junior Welfare League.
Educ: Winthrop Coll. 1950 BS. B: 12/15/29.
Add: 437 W. Hampton Ave., Sumter 29150
(803)773-3371.

Tatum. EDNA B. GUILHERME
    1974-. Mayor Pro-Tem. Bds: Ch., Beautifi-
cation. Org: Nat. Assoc. of Post Masters;
Mental Health. Occ: Postmaster. B: 5/3/24.
Add: Stanton St., Tatum 29594.

Tatum. BETTY NEAL HINSON (D)
    1976-. Occ: Post Office Clerk. B: 1/24/39.
Add: P.O. Box 314, Tatum 29594 (803)523-5971.

Wellford. SALLIE A. PEAKE (D)
    1976-. Prev: Town Councilwoman 1976-77. B:
7/30/32. Add: P.O. Box 168, Wellford 29385
(803)439-4875.

Winnsboro. JEAN H. TRUSLOW (D)
    1975-. Educ: U. of Ill. 1939 BA. Occ:
Secretary. B: 11/10/17. Add: 311 Palmetto,
Winnsboro 29180 (803)635-4943.

State Boards and Commissions

    Office of the Governor, State Capitol Bldg.,
Columbia 29201.

Aging, Commission on
    MRS. BILLY L. ASHMORE
    ZENOBIA M. DIXON
    ANNA D. KELLY
    MRS. KENNETH G. MEDLIN
    MRS. GRANT RASH
    GLORIA TROWELL

American Revolution Bicentennial Commission
    MARTHA BEE ANDERSON
    MRS. JAMES F. DREHER

Arts Commission
    MRS. GORDON B. STINE

Bank Examiners
    JUNE B. MEICHEN

Blind, Commission for the
    MRS. T.E. BARHAM

Children's Bureau, Board of Directors of
    MRS. WILLIAM G. ALBERGOTTI
    AGNES DUNCAN
    MRS. O.H. GREEN

Chiropractic Examiners, Board of
    JUDITH R. EHLICH

Consumer Affairs, Commission on
    FRANCES MORRIS
    ELLEN HINES SMITH

Consumer Credit, Council of Advisors on
    BETH H. BROOME
    MRS. JOHN K. CAUTHEN
    MRS. JOE B. DAVENPORT
    MRS. M. MACEO NANCE, JR.

Corrections, Board of
    MRS. LOUIS E. CONDON

Cosmetic Art Examiners, Board of
    AURIE GOSNELL
    LAURA M. SIMS
    QUEEN ANN SIMS
    DELORES A. SINGLETARY

Dairy Commission
    MRS. J. ALLEN LAMBRIGHT
    JO ANN B. PRICE

Education, Board of
    SARAH D. BREWER
    LILLIE E. HERNDON

Education Council
    KAY PATTERSON

Educational System, Committee to Study State
    MRS. T. J. MIMS
    JEANETTE L. MULLEN

Educational Television Commission
    MRS. T. C. COXE, JR.

Election Commission
    SYLVIA A. MC CULLOUGH
    MARGARET TOWNSEND

Election Laws Study Committee
    ZILLA HINTON

Employment Agency Board
    VIRGINIA H. WEHUNT

Ethics Commission
    MINNIE W. JOHNSON

Governor's Mansion and Lace House Commission
    MRS. JAMES T. HARDY
    MRS. ROGER MILLIKEN
    MRS. JOSEPH YOUNG

Higher Education, Commission on
    WANDA L. FORBES

Highway Commission
    POSEY BELCHER

Hospital Advisory Council
    MRS. L.B. ADAMS
    LAURIE L. BROWN
    MRS. ALEX FANT
    MRS. WESSIE G. HICKS

    MRS. EDWARD SALEEBY
    MRS. G.J. SANDERS, JR.

Human Affairs Commission
    JEAN BOLUS
    ANGIE FRAZIER
    MARIAN G. HARTWELL
    JUDITH A. HELLER

Industrial Commission
    SARAH LEVERETTE

Juvenile Placement and Aftercare Board
    MRS. H.F. OWENS

Mental Retardation Commission
    BETTY P. STALL

Migrant Farm Workers Commission
    SUZETTE BAILEY

Museum Commission
    MRS. R. MAXWELL ANDERSON
    MRS. EDWARD P. GUERARD
    MRS. RIDGEWAY HALL
    MRS. JOHN F. RAINEY

Nursing, Board of
    BERTIE GIBSON
    HANNAH HOLMES
    LILLIAN LATHAM
    ROBERTA MANGIN
    LOIS WIDING

Nursing Home Administrators, Board of Examiners for
    CONSTANCE D. HARE
    LILLIE MAE TYLER

Old Exchange Building Commission
    LOUISE BURGDORF
    MRS. FRED W. ELLIS
    MRS. PHILIP PINCKNEY
    MRS. ARMINE RICHARDSON
    MRS. JAMES C. VAUGHN

Pharmaceutical Examiners, Board of
    MYRTLE E. MACKEY

Physical Therapists, Board of Examiners and Registration of
    VIRGINIA T. BESSINGER
    MARGUERITE HUTTO
    RAE M. LITAKER

Probation, Parole and Pardon Board
    MARION BEASLEY
    ELIZABETH M. MYERS

School for the Deaf and the Blind, Board of Commissioners of South Carolina
    MRS. L.M. DAVIS
    MRS. DANIEL R. MC LEOD
    MRS. WILLIAM BURKE WATSON

Social Services Advisory Committee
    DORIS JONES
    JUNE SVEDBERG
    SHIRLEY VAUGHN

Social Services, Board of
MRS. T.K. MC DONALD
LUCY THROWER
AGNES H. WILSON

Social Worker Registration, Board of
BARBARA L. HOLZMAN
JOSEPHINE R. TAGGART

State Employee Grievance Committee
MRS. WILLIE J. BROWN
ERLINE C. HOWELL
CHARLOTTE J. KOEHLER

State Library, Board of Directors.
THELMA BUSBEE
CARLANA HENDRICK

Tax Study Commission
JOSEPHINE ABNEY

Technical and Comprehensive Education, Board for
TRACY J. GAINES

Women, Commission on the Status of
BEVERLY T. CRAVEN
DOROTHY FILLIUS GREEN
DORIS WRIGHT JOHNSON
SARAH H. HAWKINS
BARBARA W. MOXON
IRENE L. NEUFFER
MARY G. PRUITT

Youth Services Board
LUCY T. DAVIS
LULA F. HARPER
BARBARA T. SYLVESTER

South Dakota

State Executive and Cabinet

JUDITH K. CALL (D)
Secretary of Health. 1975-. Org: Amer. Public Health Assoc.; Dem. Party. Educ: Bradley U. 1965 BS; U. of Id. 1970 MA. B: 3/30/43. Add: 1400 Edgewater, Pierre 57501 (605) 224-3361.

LORNA ROCHELLE DUCHENEAUX (I)
State Coordinator of Indian Affairs. 1976-. Bds: Governors Council on Aging; State Mental Health Adv. Bd.; Human Resources Sub. Com. Org: Nat. Congress of American Indians; Nat. Indian Educ. Assoc. B: 9/28/45. Add: 725 E. Wells, Apt. 28, Pierre 57501 (605) 224-3415.

LORNA B. HERSETH (D) **
Secretary of State 1972-. Bds: State Historical Dir.,; Cmsn. on Intergovernmental Relations; Labor Relations Bd. Prev: School Bd. 1944-58; County Superintendent of Schools 1937-39. Org: Century Club; Easter Seal Society; Historical Society; PEO. Educ: Northern State 1931 State Certificate. Add: 1100 E. Church, Pierre 57501 (605)224-3537.

ALICE KUNDERT (R)
State Auditor. 1968-. Bds: Bd. of Finance; Historical Society; Record Destruction Bd. Party: Pres. Elector 1968; State GOP Adv. Bd. 1965-67, 1973-77; State Teen-Age Rep. Adv. 1974-77. Prev: Cnty. Register of Deeds 1961-68; Clerk of Cts. 1955-60; City Treasurer 1965-68; State Local Study Cmsn. 1966-81. Org: Nat. State Auditor Assoc.; BPW; Rep. Women's Fed.; Rep. Women; Adv., Teenage Rep's. B: 7/23/20. Add: 407 N. Van Buren, Pierre 57501 (605)224-3341.

State Legislature

State Senate

FRANCES S. LAMONT (R) **
1974-. Dist: 2. Bds: Joint Appropriations Com.; Health & Welfare Com.; Interim Special Educ. Study Com.; Interim Joint Appropriations Com.; Council on Aging. Party: Local Precinct Com. 1960- . Prev: Governor's Com. on Elementary & Secondary Educ.; Governor's Com. on Status of Women 1964-73; Governor's Advisory Council, Women Civil Defense 1957-62; Cmsn. on Status of Women 1970-73; White House Conf. on Aging 1971. Org: AAUW; DAR; Interstate Assoc. of States; Nat. Council on Women; PEO; PTA; Rep. Club; Women in Communication; Zonta. Educ: U. of Wisc. 1935 BA; U. of Wisc. 1936 MA. B: 6/10/14.

MARY MC CLURE (R)
1974-. Bds: Ch., Senate Judiciary Com.; Interim Rules Com.; Exec. Bd., Leg. Research Council. Party: State Del. 1972; Nat. Del. 1976; Cnty. V-Ch. 1968-74. Prev: School Bd. 1970-74; Assoc. School Bds. 1972-74. Org: Rep. Party; PEO; Eastern Star. Educ: U. of S.D. 1961 BA. Occ: Substitute Teacher. B: 4/21/39. Add: 910 E. 2nd St., Redfield 57501.

State House

DEBRA RAE ANDERSON (R)
1976-. <u>Dist</u>: 11. <u>Bds</u>: Health & Welfare; Transportation. <u>Org</u>: LWV; WPC; Rep. Women's Club. <u>Educ</u>: Augustana Coll. 1971 BA. <u>Occ</u>: Waitress; Real Estate Sales. <u>B</u>: 6/13/49. <u>Add</u>: 1401 W. 6th St. #204, Sioux Fls. 57104 (605) 224-3851.

MARY B. EDELEN (R)
1972-. <u>Dist</u>: 13. <u>Bds</u>: House State Affairs; House Judiciary; Medical Adv. Com. <u>Educ</u>: U. of SD 1967 BA; Trinity U. 1968 MA. <u>B</u>: 12/9/44. <u>Add</u>: 301 Lewis, Vermillion 57069.

BEVERLY JANE HALLING (R)
1972-. <u>Bds</u>: Transportation Com.; State Affairs Com.; Billboard Study Com. <u>Prev</u>: State Indian Business Devt. Bd. 1974-76; Interim Rules Com. 1974-76. <u>Org</u>: BPW; Chamber of Commerce; City Rep. Women. <u>Occ</u>: Motel Owner. <u>B</u>: 9/16/31. <u>Add</u>: 346 W. Kansas, Spearfish 57783.

PATRICIA E. KENNER (D)
1974-. <u>Dist</u>: 27. <u>Bds</u>: State Mental Health Adv. Bd.; Judiciary Com.; Commerce Com. <u>Party</u>: State Del. 1976; Nat. Del. 1976; Nat. Committeewoman 1976-80. <u>Prev</u>: Planning Cmsn. 1972-76; Governor's Cmsn. on Exec. Reorg. 1971-73. <u>Org</u>: ANA; LWV; Common Cause; Dem. Forum; WPC. <u>Educ</u>: St. John's School of Nursing 1951 RN. <u>Occ</u>: RN. <u>B</u>: 7/9/29. <u>Add</u>: 109 San Marco, Rapid City 57701.

DORIS MINER (D)
Gregory 57533.

DOROTHY NEPSTAD (R) **
1969-. <u>Dist</u>: 17. <u>Bds</u>: Ch., Health & Welfare Com.; Local Government Com.; Local Government Study Cmsn. <u>Party</u>: Legislative Candidate Com. 1973-75; Office Manager Rep. Campaign Headquarters 1961-71; Precinct Com. 1960-69. <u>Prev</u>: Cnty. Auditor 1927-31. <u>Org</u>: BPW; PEO; Women's Rep. Club. <u>B</u>: 8/20/03. <u>Add</u>: 409 E. Fifth, Mitchell 57301.

County Commissions

Clark. RAMONA KIRKEBY
Vienna 57271.

Codington. MARLYS E. MULLER (D)
1972-. <u>Bds</u>: Ch., Planning & Devt.; Ch., Cnty. Park Bd. <u>B</u>: 11/6/22. <u>Add</u>: RR #1, Florence 57235.

Davison. MARY JO ARMSTRONG
1300 E. 4th, Mitchell 57301.

Kingsbury. JOYCE BARSTOW HODGES (R)
1977-. <u>Bds</u>: Extension Bd.; Cnty. Fair Bd.; Visiting Neighbor. <u>Party</u>: State Del. 1976. <u>Org</u>: Cnty. Rep. Women's Club. <u>B</u>: 5/20/30. <u>Add</u>: RR 1, Lk. Preston 57249 (605)854-3832.

Pennington. DELORES D. GHERE (R) **
1974-. <u>Bds</u>: Extension Bd.; Rural Dev.; Civil Defense; Weed Bd.; Weather Modification Bd.; State Bicentennial Com. <u>Prev</u>: Councilwoman 1969-74. <u>Org</u>: LWV; Zonta; Pres., PTA; Rep. Women. <u>Occ</u>: Bookkeeper. <u>B</u>: 11/14/38. <u>Add</u>: 1215 E. St. Francis St., Rapid City 57701 (605)343-1184.

Mayors

Cottonwood. MARJORIE HAZLETT
City Hall, Cottonwood 57728.

Eden. VIRGINIA GRUBY
City Hall, Eden 57232.

Garden City. WENDY HARTLEY (I)
1977-. <u>Prev</u>: Trustee 1975-77. <u>B</u>: 6/23/54. <u>Add</u>: Garden City 57236.

Gregory. CATHY J. WERNKE (R) **
1974-. <u>Bds</u>: Dist. Planning Com.; Combined Law Enforcement Com.; EPA Advisory Bd., Day Care Center Bd. <u>Party</u>: Precinct Com. 1964-68. <u>Org</u>: Fed. of Rep. Women. <u>B</u>: 10/27/33. <u>Add</u>: 1513 Logan St., Gregory 57533 (605) 835-5381.

Herrick. MARY LOUISE RUE (D) **
1968-. <u>Bds</u>: Parks Com.; Street Cmsn. <u>Org</u>: Pres., Cemetery Assoc.; PTA. <u>Occ</u>: Truck Driver. <u>B</u>: 11/27/34. <u>Add</u>: 906 Rorak, Herrick 57538 (605)775-2831.

Interior. LA VONNE O. GREEN (R) **
1972-. <u>Educ</u>: U. of Denver 1946 BA. <u>B</u>: 10/23/22. <u>Add</u>: Box 73, Interior 57750 (603) 433-5468.

Iroquois. ELLA SCHULZ
P.O. Box 111, Iroquois 57353.

Keystone. ELIZA PATTERSON
Box 326, Keystone 57751.

Watertown. MARY E. MOISAN (R) **
1974-. <u>Prev</u>: Councilwoman 1971-74. <u>Org</u>: BPW; Zonta. <u>Occ</u>: Lab Technician. <u>B</u>: 6/9/26. <u>Add</u>: 303 1st Ave., SW, Watertown 57201 (605) 886-4057.

Wilmont. BARBARA BERNSTEIN
City Hall, Wilmot 57279.

Local Councils

Alexandria. VESTA HILL (D)
1974-. <u>Bds</u>: Ch., Public Library Bd.; Bd. of Health; Ch., Beautification. <u>Party</u>: State Del. 1974; Cnty. V-Ch. 1970-77; State Central Committeewoman 1970-77. <u>B</u>: 6/6/07. <u>Add</u>: Alexandria 57311.

Bedfield. DOROTHY ALLEN
517 N. Main St., Bedfield 57469.

Bonesteel. IDA HALVERSON
Main Street, Bonesteel 57317.

Box Elder. ALICE DUSTER
DORIS RIEB
Box 27, Box Elder 57719.

Broadland. BONNIE HARTMAN
Rt. 2, Huron 57350.

Carter. MARJORIE JANSEN
City Hall, Carter 57526.

Carthage. ALBERTA STEVENS
P.O. Box 112, Carthage 57323.

Central City. PAT CHAMBERLAIN
Box 485 Deadwood, Central City 57754.

Chelsea. JULIANA MALLETT
City Hall, Chelsea 57431.

Custer. MARGARET BALLANTYNE
622 Crook St., Custer 57730.

Deadwood. PATRICIA ANN NOELLER (R)
1977-. Bds: Ch., Sanitation & Health; Ch.,
Library; Ch., Ways & Means. Org: Chamber of
Commerce; Rep. Women. Occ: Motel Owner. B:
12/4/33. Add: 137 Charles St., Deadwood 57732
(605)578-1611.

Dupree. ARLENE MARTIN
City Hall, Dupree 57623.

Eagle Butte. ELLEN A. MARSHALL (R)
1974-. Bds: Street Cmsnr. Org: OES. Occ:
Lodge Owner. B: 9/1/06. Add: Eagle Butte 59625.

Eagle Butte. GEORGE ANN SMITH
Main Street, Eagle Butte 57625.

Egan. MYRTLE KOTAN (R)
1976-. Occ: Cook. B: 7/13/15. Add: Box 157,
Egan 57024.

Elkton. LIL ANDERSON
LILLY CLAUSSEN
P.O. Box 158, Elkton 57026.

Erwin. PATRICIA PETERSON
City Hall, Erwin 57233.

Estelline. MARLENE M. SWENSON (D)
1976-. Bds: Ch., Law Enforcement; Ch., Park
& Airport; Streets & Dump. Org: Women's Study
Club. Educ: U. of ND 1967 BSEd. Occ: Substitute
Teacher. B: 6/3/45. Add: 208 N. 4th St.,
Estelline 57234 (605)873-2388.

Fairburn. CLOTILDA KRICK
City Hall, Fairburn 57738.

Flandreau. RITA BURNS
136 2nd Ave. East, Flandreau 57028.

Freeman. LOIS WILDE (R) **
1973-. Bds: Park & Pool Cmsn.; Bldg. Cmsn.;
Landfill Cmsn.; Library Cmsn. Occ: Grocery
Checker. B: 4/19/29. Add: 510 E. 2nd St.,
Freeman 57029 (605)925-7127.

Garretson. LOIS A. WIESE (R) **
1973-. Bds: Liquor Store Bd.; Dump Ground
Bd. Org: PTA. Educ; Mich. State U. 1953 BS.
Occ: Teacher. B: 7/23/31. Add: Box 223,
Garretson 57030 (605)594-3414.

Gregory. ALMA LARSON
120 W. 6th, Gregory 57533.

Hartford. GLENNA WARNE
City Hall, Hartford 57033.

Hecla. JANICE LANDRETH
P.O. Box 188, Hecla 57446.

Hetland. DORENE STRICKER
City Hall, Hetland 57224.

Hot Springs. GENEVA PARSONS (D) **
1974-. Bds: Bicentennial; Senior Citizens;
Arts Council; Housing Authority. Party:
Finance Ch. 1974; Cnty. Secretary 1972-73.
Org: BPW. B: 3/25/21. Add: 406 S. 6th St.,
Hot Springs 57747.

Interior. MARGARET SAUNDERS
City Hall, Interior 57750.

Lake Andes. HELEN RIECKMAN
City Hall, Lake Andes 57356.

Mellette. MARIE MURRAY (D) **
1969-. Bds: Cemetery Com.; Park Com.;
Water Com.; City Rezoning Com. Party: Precinct
Com. Prev: Cnty. Superintendent of Elections
1960-74; School Bd. 1955-58; City Assessor
1954-60. Org: Senior Citizens. B: 10/24/18.
Add: Town Hall, Mellette 57461 (605)887-3554.

Mellette. DORIS O'DONNELL
City Hall, Mellette 57461.

Mission Hill. KERRY KASULKA
KAY MAGORIEN
City Hall, Mission Hill 57046.

Oacoma. MARGARET PEDDYCOART
Box 23, Oacoma 57365.

Oldham. LILA I. LEE (R)
1975-. Org: Rep. Women. B: 2/25/16. Add:
Oldham 57051.

Pierre. GRACE PETERSEN (D) **
1972-. Bds: Dist. Planning; Bicentennial;
Municipal League; Liquor Control. Party:
Precinct Com. 1969-72. Org: PTA. Occ: Book-
keeper. B: 1/14/32. Add: 738 E. Dakota Ave.,
Pierre 57501 (605)224-5921.

Platte. ELIZABETH ALVIDA COOL (D)
1975-. Bds: Ch., Municipal Liquor; Parks &
Recreation. Org: Dem. Party; Municipal League.
Occ: Cosmetologist. B: 7/13/10. Add: 011
Ohio, Platte 57369.

Rapid City. DARLINE GERLACH
22 Main St., Rapid City 57701.

Rapid City. BERNITA G. LOUCKS (R)
    1972-. Bds: Ch., Public Safety Com.; Ch.,
Urban Renewal. Party: State Central Com., Women
from Pennington Cnty. 1964-68. Prev: SD Local
Govt. Cmsn. 1972-76. Org: Women's Org.; Fed.
Women's Club. Occ: Bank Teller. B: 2/23/24.
Add: 219 42nd St., Rapid City 57701 (601)
387-4110.

Rapid City. NORMA THOMSEN
    22 Main Street, Rapid City 57701.

Rosebud. PHYLLIS CORDIER (D)
    1976-. Party: State Del. 1973. Org: School
Bd. Occ: Project Director. B: 1/7/32. Add:
P.O. Box 143, St. Francis 57572 (605)747-2275.

St. Francis. ISABELL YOUNG
    City Hall, St. Francis 57572.

Salem. ALICE SCHALLENKAMP
    North Main St., Salem 57058.

Sturgis. RAMONA BRITTON (R)
    1974-. Bds: Library Bd.; Cemetery Bd.; Pres.
City Council. Org: NEA; AAUW; Cnty. Home Health
Agency; Teachers Adv. Educ: Black Hls. State
Coll. 1965 BSEd; 1969 MSEd. Occ: Teacher. B:
1/7/29. Add: 1439 Junction Ave., Sturgis 57785
(605)347-4422.

Timber Lake. CONNIE B. LABAHN (R)
    1975-. Bds: Dewey Cnty. Planning Cmsn. Org:
Senior Citizens-"Nutrition Site" Council. Occ:
Teacher. B: 3/11/45. Add: Timber Lk. 57656
(605)865-3659.

Trent. ADELE GULBRANSON (I)
    1977-. Org: Amer. Postal Workers Union; PTA.
Occ: Secretary. B: 10/22/26. Add: P.O. Box 846,
Trent 57065.

Volga. ILA KAYLEEN SWENNING (R)
    1977-. Bds: Police Cmsnr.; Ch., Civil Defense;
Fire Dept. Party: Committeewoman 1968-70. Occ:
Secretary & Clerk. B: 3/26/42. Add: 524 Marvin
Ave., Volga 57071 (605)627-9421.

Wessington Springs. SAUNDRA MEYER (D)
    1976-. Bds: Budget & Finance; Water & Sewer;
Ch., Personnel. Party: Cnty. Ch. 1973-75; Cnty.
Committeewoman 1975-77; Leg. Dist. Ch. 1975-77.
Org: Public Health Nursing Adv. Bd.; Professional
Practices & Standards Cmsn. Educ: Ball State U.
1966 BS. B: 11/12/42. Add: 312 S. Barrett Ave.,
Wessington Springs 57382.

Willow Lake. ELAINE HERKER
    City Hall, Willow Lake 57278

Judges

MILDRED RAMYNKE (D)
    Judge, Circuit Court. 1974-. Prev: State
Dist. Ct. Judge 1968-74; Cnty. Judge 1958-68.
Org: SD Bar Assoc.; SD Judges Assoc.; Criminal
Justice Dist. Com. Educ: SD State U. 1936 BA;
U. of SD 1939 LLB-JD. B: 2/6/17. Add: RR #1,
Peever 57257 (605)698-3395.

State Boards and Commissions

    Office of the Governor, State Capitol Bldg.,
Pierre 57501.

Abstracters' Board of Examiners
    BERGIT HINKLE
    BARBARA E. MANN
    ADELINE VAN GENDEREN

Administrative Internship Advisory Council
    MARGARET LEWIS
    JOANI NELSON

Aging, Advisory Commission on
    HAZEL BREKKE
    CAROL FLANAGAN
    PEG LAMONT
    FLORENCE OPBROEK
    BESSIE ST. PIERRE
    VADA THOMAS
    DOROTHY WILLIAMSON

Alcohol Abuse and Alcoholism Council
    LAURA LAMPHERE
    IRENE RICHARDSON

Banking Commission
    JO ANNE BARNETT
    ENID ROGERS

Capitol Grounds Enlargement and Beautification
Commission
    IRENE FENNELL

Charities and Corrections, Board of
    SYDNA CHEEVER

Children and Youth, Commission on
    JEAN ADLER
    KATHY AUGHENBAUGH
    JEAN BJERKE
    KAY BERYL FRASER
    NORENA HAROLD
    JULIE LAMBERT
    JANE NELSON
    CHARLENE RICHARDSON
    PHYLLIS WULF

Chiropractic Examiners, Board of
    ROSEANN MINOW

Cosmetology Board
    ELIZABETH ANTON
    PAT FOKKEN
    JANICE LIEBELT
    LOIS WISKUR

Criminal Justice Planning and Assistance,
Commission on
    ANN FLODEN
    BETTY HENDRICKSON

Cultural Preservation, Board of
    LOIS HABBE
    SHIRLEY LYONS

Dairy Products Marketing Commission
    GRACE BUBBERS
    DELORES BULLERT
    BONNIE PIERCE

Dentistry, Board of
MITZE JENSEN

Developmental Disabilities, Council on
DORIS BRUNS
MRS. GENE DEWES
NORMA HEESCH
LYNN KNUTSON
KATHY LE DUC
ARLEEN NELSON
NAOMI RENVILLE
MARILYN SHAW

Drug and Substances Control, Advisory Board on
DEBRA HOFER
MARY PATTERSON

Education, Board of
EVELYN BERGEN
JUDY OLSON

Educational Television, Board of Directors
HAZEL GERMAN

Education and Cultural Affairs Planning Commission
MARION HERSRUD
CELIA MINER
EVA NICHOLS
JUDITH OLSON

Education Commission of the States
SUE HEALEY

Emergency Medical Services, Advisory Committee on
WILMA MC KERCHER

Employment of the Handicapped, Advisory Committee on
RUTH AHL
ELEANOR CALDWELL
ZONA CHRISTIANSEN
EDITH DAILEY
MARILYN DUNKER
ARLIS FOUSEK
SYLVIA HENKIN
LILLIAN MYERS

Environmental Protection
GRACE PETERSON

Ethics Commission
LAURA M. ORVILLE

Fine Arts Council
FLORENCE BRUHN
LYNN FRIEFELD
CARROLL MC KENNA
DIANE PADRNOS
HARRIET PORTER
MARY WALLNER TURNER

Food Service Advisory Council
EUNICE FOSTER

Funeral Service, Board of
NOELLE C. BROWN

Health Coordinating Council
JUDITH CALL
MARGE HEGGE
JANE LAROUCHE

CATHY WERNKE
PHYLLIS WULF

Hearing Aid Dispensers, Board of
ELLEN LARSON

Hospital and Medical Facilities Advisory Council
MARION BERGAN
VERNICE JACKSON
DOROTHY MC DONALD

Human Rights, Commission on
DOROTHY BUTLER
KAY FOLKERTS
ESTER MUNDZ
BLANCHE ROBERTSON

Indian Affairs, Commission on
ROBBI FERON

Indian Business Development, Board of Directors
ELNITA RANK

Judicial Qualifications, Commission on
DONNA CHRISTEN

Juvenile Justice and Delinquence Prevention,
Advisory Council for
NADINE BAUER
PATTIE DVORAK
NANCY JORDAHL
JULIE KROGER
CHERYL LAPOINT

Legal Services, Advisory Council for
MARY DELL CODY
SHARON DENKE

Local Government Study Commission
ALICE KUNDERT

Manpower Planning and Service Council
ROCHELLE DUCHENEAUX
MARY LOUCKS

Massage, Board of
DELORES SALVIOLA
DELORES ZENS

Mental Retardation Facilities and Mental Health
Center Advisory Council
EVA ONE FEATHER
MRS. HAROLD STREET

Nursing, Board of
CAROLYN BELLMAN
MARALEE DENNIS
VIOLET EISENBRAUN
SISTER MARGARET MARY KEOGH
ANNA MC LEAN
SISTER EDNA NEMEC
PHYLLIS NEWSTROM
MYRTLE RASMUSSEN
JANICE JOFFER THOMPSON
KATHRYN VIGEN

Nursing Home Administrators, Board of Examiners for
ELLA BRADFIELD
DORIS ENQUIST
SARAH FLESNER

Outdoor Recreation, Advisory Council on
 SUE HANSON
 MAE VIK

Personnel Policy Board
 ELIZABETH SHREVES

Pharmacy, Board of
 SHIRLEY HEITLAND

Plumbing Board
 MARY SMITH

Professional Practices and Standards Commission
 CHERYL ENOS
 RUTH HANSEN
 LINDA JO JOY
 REGINA KATTKE
 SAUNDRA MEYER

Psychologists, Board of Examiners of
 ELEANOR SCHWAB

Public Health Advisory Committee
 EDITH MAGEDANZ

Real Estate Commission
 GEORGIA COOK

Regents, Board of
 BONNIE BUNCH
 CELIA MINER
 SUSAN NELSON
 BETTY REDFIELD

Renal Disease, Advisory Committee on
 MAXINE WHITE

Sanitarian Registration, Board of
 JANICE OVERBY

Social Services, Board of
 CAROL ANDERSON
 DOROTHY GILL
 GRACE HIGHLEY
 FRANCIE RUEBEL

Social Work Examiners, Board of
 NORMA CAMERON
 BONNIE MESSER

State Library Commission
 ARDETH KOCOUREK
 JANE KOLBE
 MRS. T.A. PETERSON

Tourism Development, Board of
 MARY ANN BURIAN
 JO ANN KELLY

Unemployment Insurance Advisory Council
 DOLORES BULLERT
 KAY COYLE
 WILDA DORSEY

Visually Handicapped, Advisory Committee on Service to
 HATTI GORSUCH
 REGINIA KATTKE

Vocational Education, Board of
 MARGARET MOORE

Vocational - Technical Education, Advisory Council on
 PHYLLIS DIXON
 EUNICE HOVLAND
 SUZANNE KNUDSON
 DONA WILLIAMS

Women, Commission on Status of
 RUTH ALEXANDER
 BARBARA BIEGLER
 ROSE BORDEAU
 LORRAINE COLLINS
 LONA CRANDAL
 ELAINE GUTHMILLER
 FRAN HOGARTH
 LOILA HUNKING
 EUNICE LARIBEE
 RUTH LINDEMANN
 SHARON SWANSON

Tennessee

State Executive and Cabinet

JEANNE M. BOWMAN
> Deputy Commissioner, Department of Human Services. Add: State Capitol, Nashville 37219.

JAYNE ANN WOODS (D)
> Commissioner, Department of Revenue. 1975-. Bds: Bd. of Equalization; Bd. of Claims; Oil & Gas Bd. Org: Federation of Tax Administrators; ABA; Federation of Dem. Women; WPC; NOW. Educ: Vanderbilt U. 1966 BA, 1968 JD. B: 2/26/44. Add: 3708 Abbott Martin, Nashville 37242 (615) 741-2461.

State Legislature

State Senate

ANNA BELLE CLEMENT O'BRIEN (D) **
> Dist: 36. Bds: Psychiatric Hospital Advisory Council; Bd. of Dir., Mental Health Center; Bd. of Dir., Nursing Home. Party: State Exec. Com. Prev: State Rep. Org: BPW; Beautification Assoc.; Chamber of Commerce; DAR; Dem. Women's Club. Add: Rte. 11, Lake Tansi Village, Crossville 38555.

State House

LOIS M. DE BERRY (D) **
> 1973-. Dist: 91. Bds: Education; General Welfare. Org: SCLC; Dem. Club; PTA. B: 5/5/44. Add: 1373 Valse, Memphis 38106 (901)774-6777.

PAM GAIA (D)
> Dist: 89. Bds: State & Local Govt. Com.; Commerce Com.; Subcom. on Small Business. Party: State Del. 1972, '74. Org: OWL; Cnty. Dem. Club; Tenn. Voters Council; BPW. Educ: Memphis State U. 1970 BA. B: 2/19/46. Add: Box 2341, Memphis 38101 (615)741-3875.

County Commissions

Anderson. CHARLOTTE J. HAYES
> 1966-. Bds: Ch., Cnty. HEW Com.; Ch., Cnty. Utility Bd.; Cnty. Planning Cmsn. Party: Cnty. Exec. Com. 1960- ; Pres., Cnty. Dem. Women's Club 1954-58. Org: Tenn. Magistrates Assoc.; Council on Aging; Cnty. Dem. Women's Club. Educ: Ohio Wesleyan U. 1944 BA. B: 11/17/23. Add: 120 Amherst Ln., Oak Ridge 37830.

Cheatham. HELEN HARPER
> DORIS SAWYER
> Ashland City 37015.

Cheatham. MARION I. WINTERS (R) **
> 1972-. Bds: Liquor Bd. B: 1/30/33. Add: 109 Gloria Cir., Ashland City 37015.

Chester. FAYE PATTERSON
> Rte. 1, Finger 38334.

Coffee. DORRIS DAVIS
> Rte. 1, Wartrace 37183.

Dickson. ANNA K. MILLER (D)
> 1970-. Bds: Budget Com.; Nursing Home Review Com.; Reapportionment Com. B: 4/17/18. Add: Celeste Hts., Charlotte 37036 (615) 789-5167.

Giles. WINFRED HELTON
> Rte. 1, Ethridge 38456.

Giles. VIVIAN R. LOCKETT (D)
> 1972-. Bds: Ch., Nursing Home Com.; Delinquent Tax Com.; Park & Recreation Com. Org: Dem. Women's Club; OES. B: 5/10/38. Add: 820 Ragsdale Ln., Pulaski 38478 (615)363-5300.

Greene. MARY JO SLAGLE (R) **
> 1972-. Bds: Airport Com.; Insurance Com.; Roby Center Advisory Bd. Party: Precinct Co-Ch. 1974- . Org: NEA; Rep. Fed. Women; TEA. Educ: Tusculum 1960 BS. Occ: Teacher. B: 6/14/30. Add: 1434 Tusculum Blvd., Greeneville 37743.

Hamblen. ANNE MITCHELL
> 400 E. 2nd North, Morristown 37814.

Hamilton. RACHEL ATCHLEY
> 1040 Floyd Dr., Chattanooga 37412.

Hamilton. MARY GARDENHIRE (R)
> 1972-. Judge Pro Tem. Dist: 3. Party: Nat. Del. 1976; Cnty. Rep. Steering Com. 1972- ; Cnty. Rep. Exec. Com. 1975-76. Org: Rep. Women. Educ: U. of Tenn. 1972 BA. B: 7/3/49. Add: 4610 Old Mission Rd., Chattanooga 37411.

Hamilton. JOAN LOCKABY
> 1436 Woodmore Ln., Chattanooga 37411.

Hamilton. ALMA E. SULLIVAN
> 128 Hood Circle, Daisy 37319.

Hancock. SARAH TRENT
> General Delivery, Sneedville 37869.

Hardeman. LOUISE DANIEL
> Rte. 2, Medon 38397.

Henry. LINDA J. PALMER (D) **
     1972-. Bds: Beer Bd.; Ambulance Bd.; Airport
Com.; Sanitary Land Fill; Hospital. Prev: Pres.,
Elective & Appointed Officials 1972. Org: Dem.
Club. Educ: Carver Institute 1950 BS. B:
2/20/23. Add: 403 Rison St., Paris 38242 (901)
642-1511.

Hickman. MILDRED C. COBLE (D)
     1975-. Occ: Hairdresser. B:4/23/20. Add:
Rt. 2, Lyles 37098.

Hickman. DORIS TURNER
     Rte. 2, Lyles 37098.

Jackson. ELLIE MC GUIRE
     Rte. 4, Gainesboro 38562.

Jackson. MRS. THEO SPIVEY (D)
     1972-. Bds: Ch. Nursing Home Com.; Budget
Com. Party: Cnty. Committeewoman 1973-74. B:
4/18/02. Add: Rt. 2, Gainesboro 38562 (615)
268-0966.

Jefferson. MARY CATE JONES
     Strawberry Plains 37871.

Knox. BEE DE SELM (R)
     1976-. Dist: 4. Bds: Metropolitan Planning
Cmsn.; Cnty. Ct., Finance Com.; Cnty. Ct.,
Ecology; Cnty. Ct. Party: Precinct 1976-77.
Prev: Cnty. Govt. Cmsn. 1975-76. Org: LWV; Cnty.
Rep. Women; Rep. Club. Educ: Ohio State U. 1946
BS; 1948 BS. B: 6/1/25. Add: 424 Hillvale Turn
W, Knoxville 37919.

Knox. MARY LOU HORNER (R)
     Bds: Ch., Welfare Com.; Educ. Com. Party:
V-Ch., Precinct 1976-78. Prev: Knoxville Transit
Authority 1973-78. Org: BPW; Rep. Women's Club.
Occ: Sales Manager. B: 11/21/24. Add: 3717
Thrall Dr., Knoxville 37918.

Madison. MRS. SWAN BURRUS, JR.
     7 Broadfield Dr., Jackson 38301.

Maury. DABNEY ANDERSON
     420 W. 7th St., Columbia 38401.

McNairy. MARTHA JO GLOVER
     Selmer 38375.

McNairy. EFFIE CARRIE WOODS (R)
     1972-. Bds: Budget Com.; Educ. Com. Party:
Cnty. Rep. Exec. Com. 1975-78. Org: Tenn.
Magistrates Assoc.; Rep. Women's Club. B:
10/24/24. Add: Rt. 1, Selmer 38375.

Monroe. FAYE C. TENNYSON (D)
     1976-. Bds: Hwy. Com.; Bldg. Com.; Purchasing
Com. Org: Cnty. Dem. Women's Club. Occ: Sub-
stitute School Teacher. B: 11/19/30. Add: 705
Broad, Sweetwater 37874 (615)442-3981.

Montgomery. LORENZA RIVES COLLIER (D)
     1972-. Bds: Bd. of Jail Inspectors & Penal
Farm Cmsnr's.; Cnty. Nursing Home for Indigents.
Party: State Del. 1970. Org: Community Service
Club; Cnty. Women's Dem. Club; Voc. Tech. Adv.

Com.; Practical Nursing Adv. Com. B: 3/13/20.
Add: 1150 College St., Clarksville 37046
(615)647-2613.

Montgomery. LETTIE M. PARKER KENDALL (D)
     1972-. Bds: Hwy. Liaison; Ch., Recreation
& Historical Bd.; Traffic Control. Org: NEA;
Magistrates Assoc. Educ: Ark. Baptist Coll.
1951 BA; Austin Peay State U. 1973 MA. Occ:
School Teacher. B: 5/2/30. Add: 388 "A" St.,
Clarksville 37040.

Montgomery. MABEL B. STEELEY
     1509 Golf Club Ln., Clarksville 37040.

Morgan. MELBA WILSON (I)
     1972-. Dist: 1. Org: Amer. Pharmaceutical
Assoc. Educ: U. of Tenn. 1970 BS. Occ: Pharm-
acist. B: 5/15/47. Add: Rt. 3, Box 498,
Harriman 37748.

Obion. MRS. GEORGE CLOYS
     Rte. 4, Union City 38261.

Rhea. JUNE FOURMAN (D) **
     1966-. Dist: 2. Bds: Law Enforcement;
Beer Bd. Prev: City Cmsnr. 1971-75; Cnty. &
Juvenile Judge 1969-71. Org: BPW; Health Care
Council; PTA. Occ: Self-employed. B: 3/22/32.
Add: Picadilly Ave., Spring City 37381 (615)
242-6673.

Rutherford. MARGARET M. HAYES
     739 N. Spring, Murfreesboro 37130.

Rutherford. CHRIS HUDDLESTON
     106 Eventide Dr., Murfreesboro 37130.

Rutherford. BETTYE JANE HUGGINS **
     1972-. Dist: 16. Bds: Welfare, Health,
Educ., Recreation; Investment Com.; Bldg. Com.;
School Bd. Party: Ch., Cnty. Com. Org: Tenn.
Magistrates Assoc. Educ: LSU BM; LSU 1954 MA.
B: 11/7/31. Add: 915 E. Main St., Murfreesboro
37130.

Rutherford. ISABELL K. ROBERTS
     301 S. Academy, Murfreesboro 37130.

Sequatchie. JOYCE DOTSON
            PATSY TATE
     Dunlap 37327.

Shelby. MINERVA JOHNICAN
     1265 Dunnavant, Memphis 38106.

Smith. MARY FLYE ALLEN
        EVELYN P. DILLEHAY
     Carthage 37030.

Smith. IRMA G. PASCHALL
     Gordonsville 38563.

Trousdale. MRS. RICHARD COX
            DOROTHY SMITH
     Rt. 2, Hartsville 37074.

Warren. MYRA ELIZABETH CHASTAIN (D)
    1968-. Bds: Educ. Com.; Health & Welfare
Com.; Hwy. & Bridge Com. Party: State Del. 1974,
'76; Precinct Del. 1973-77. Org: Tenn. Magisterial Assoc. Occ: Farmer. B: 11/26/19. Add:
Rt. 9, Box 141, McMinnville 37110 (615)668-8686.

Washington. ELLA VIRGINIA ROSS (R) **
    1970-. Bds: Budget Com.; Com. on Coms.; State
Bd. of Regents for Higher Educ. Party: Ch.,
Dist. Com. 1969-71. Prev: Constitutional Conv.
1953; Cmsn. on Status of Women 1972-73. Org:
Amer. Red Cross; BPW; DAR; Regional Bicentennial
Com.; Rep. Capital Club. Educ: East Tenn. State
U. 1928 BS; Duke U. 1932 MA; Harvard U. 1945 MEd.
B: 9/2/02. Add: 708 E. Unaka Ave., Johnson City
37601.

White. MARY N. KEISLING
    1974-. Bds: Mental Health Ctr.; Cnty. Health
Com.; Educ. Com. Party: Cnty. Committeewoman.
Prev: Secretary, State Arts Cmsn. 1971-76. Org:
Fed. Women's Club; Performing Arts Bd.; Fed. of
Women; DAR; State Alliance Arts Educ. Educ:
George Wash. U. 1938 BA. B: 1/3/16. Add: 507
Gaines, Sparta 38583 (615)836-3970.

White. NELL MARCHBANKS
    Bronson Bend, Sparta 38583.

Williamson. EMILY BROWN
    957 Glass St., Franklin 38064.

Williamson. ELIZABETH Z. FRYER (R)
    1966-. Bds: Ch., Recreation Com. Prev: State
Alcoholic Beverage Cmsn. 1970-74. Org: Tenn.
Cnty. Services Assoc.; Magistrates Assoc. of
Tenn.; WPC; Jr. League; Mental Health Assoc.;
Women's Rep. Club; Historic Assoc.; Historical
Society. Educ: U. of Cincinnati 1943 BA; Pea-
body Coll. 1951 MA. Occ: Librarian. B: 9/14/22.
Add: R. 8, Beech Crk. Rd., Brentwood 37027.

Williamson. JANE B. HARNESS
    River Oaks Rd., Brentwood 37027.

Wilson. DORIS BLAND
    Ligon Dr., Lebanon 37087.

Wilson. MILDRED HEARNE (D)
    1969-. Bds: Ch., Health & Welfare Com.;
Steering Com. Secretary. Party: Dem. Exec.
Com. 1967; Secretary-Treasurer 1977. Org: BPW;
Dem. Women's Club. B: 12/16/10. Add: 229 E.
Spring St., Lebanon 37087.

Mayors

Altamont. NINA BROWN
    City Hall, Altamont 37301.

Huntsville. NORMA JEAN POTTER
    P.O. Box 151, Huntsville 37756.

Iron City. SHERRY LUMPKINS (D) **
    1974-. Org: Dem. Women's Assoc.; PTA; Young
Dem. Occ: Hair Dresser. B: 1/13/43. Add: Box
142 W. 1st St., Iron City 38463 (615)845-4520.

Jonesboro. GRACE HAWS
    City Hall, Jonesboro 37659.

Lafayette. PAGE DURHAM
    P.O. Box 231, Lafayette 37083.

Maryville. JOANN WEBB
    Municipal Bldg., Maryville 37801.

Obion. EDDIE M. HUEY (D) **
    1973-. Bds: Finance Com.; Health Bd. Org:
PTA. Occ: Store Owner. B: 10/5/33. Add:
P.O. Box 528 Broadway St., Obion 38240.

Vonore. BLANCHE FARNSWORTH
    Rt. 1, Box 6, Vonore 37855.

Watauga. MARY PHIPPS
    P.O. Box 68, Watauga 37694.

Williston. JOETTA B. RAY (D)
    1974-. Bds: Ch., Utility Bd. Prev: State
Consumer's Panel 1976. Org: BPW. Occ: Secretary. B: 4/13/42. Add: Rt. 1, Box 2, Williston
38076.

Local Councils

Allardt. MARY JANE BROOKS
    City Hall, Allardt 38504.

Arlington. ELIZABETH C. OSBORNE (I)
    1975-. Bds: Ch., Finance & Records; Beer
Bd. B: 12/10/17. Add: 11912 Brown St.,
Arlington 38002 (901)867-2620.

Baxter. SHIRLEY HOLMES
    P.O. Box 335, Baxter 38544.

Bluff City. JEAN WYATT
    P.O. Drawer A, Bluff City 37618.

Columbia. NELL B. CRANFORD (R)
    1976-. Bds: Cnty. Library Bd.; Cnty.
Creative Arts Guild. Party: Rep. Exec. Com.
1972-77. Org: Rep. Women's Club; PTA; Assoc.
for Preservation of Tenn. Antiquities. Occ:
Bookkeeper. B: 3/16/20. Add: 208 Sewanee
Cir., Columbia 38401 (615)388-4400.

Cottage Grove. THELMA BELL
    City Hall, Cottage Grove 38401.

Cumberland Gap. HELEN RAMSEY (I)
    1974-. Bds: Finance Com.; Ch., Historical
Com.; Housing & Aging Com. Org: AAUW. Educ:
Lincoln Memorial U. 1926 BA. B: 3/31/05.
Add: Cumberland Gap 37724.

Cumberland Gap. DORIS SNYDER (D)
    1974-. Bds: Finance; Ch, Historical
Zoning. Prev: Cnty. Bicentennial 1975-76.
Org: BPW. Occ: Financial Secretary. B:
11/2/12. Add: Box 96, Cumberland Gap 37724
(615)869-2633.

Dover. BRENDA HARDIN
    P.O. Box 33, Dover 37058.

Dyer. GEORGIA M. ELLIS (D)
1973-. Bds: Street Com. Prev: Park Cmsn.
1972-74. Org: Business Women. B: 11/17/17.
Add: 979 S. Main, Dyer 38330 (901)692-3415.

Dyersburg. ANN LOWE BLURTON
1976-. Bds: Planning Cmsn. Prev: Bd.,
Selective Services 1971-76. Org: Women's Club.
Educ: Dyersburg State Com. Coll. 1976 AS. Occ:
Bookkeeper. B: 11/6/22. Add: 1911 Okeena Dr.,
Dyersburg 38024 (901)285-6321.

Erin. LORRAINE B. ROBIN (D)
1974-. Org: BPW; Dem. Women's Club. B:
12/24/01. Add: Rt. #1, Erin 37061 (615)
289-4403.

Greenbrier. LENA JUSTICE
Drawer G, Greenbrier 37073.

Henderson. JUANITA SIKES YOUNG (R)
1974-. Bds: Women in Govt. Org: BPW. Occ:
Social Services Coord. B: 2/20/36. Add: 316
White St., Henderson 38340 (901)989-4628.

Jonesboro. CHARLOTTE C. LAVENDER (R)
1976-. Bds: Ch., Traffic Control Com.;
Recreation Cmsn.; Beer Control. Educ: Tusculum
Coll. 1939 BA; E. Tenn. State U. 1975 MA. Occ:
Elementary School Teacher. B: 12/9/17. Add:
826 E. Main St., Jonesboro 37659 (615)753-3311.

Kingsport. MARY M. CUNNINGHAM (I)
1975-. Bds: Appalachian Regional Ctr. for
the Healing Arts Health Systems Agency; Kingsport Mental Health Ctr. Adv. Com. Prev: Citizens
Adv. Com. 1966-71 Org: LWV; Meals on Wheels.
Educ: Mt. Holyoke Coll. 1947 BA. B: 5/18/26.
Add: 300 High Ridge Rd., Kingsport 37660 (615)
245-5131.

Knoxville. BERNICE O'CONNOR
                 JEAN TEAGUE
P.O. Box 1631, Knoxville 37902.

Lafayette. EMMA JEAN HUNT (D)
1974-. Bds: Recreation Com. Prev: State
Revenue Dept. 1962; State Safety Dept. 1963-67;
City Police Dept. 1968-71; City Recorder 1971-
74. B: 1/6/39. Add: 506 1/2 Days Rd., Lafayette
37083 (615)666-4570.

Lafayette. MARY TOM LINK
P.O. Box 231, Lafayette 37083.

Lake City. NANCY H. TUCKER (R)
1976-. Org: BPW. Occ: Secretary & Bookkeeper.
B: 1/9/34. Add: Lindsay St., Lake City 37769.

Liberty. VIVA GAY VICKERS (D)
1975-. Org: OES. B: 3/8/37. Add: Rt. 1,
Main St., Liberty 37095.

Loudon. AILEEN K. RICHESIN
P.O. Box 189, Loudon 37774.

Lynnville. OLETA HEWITT
P.O. Box 116, Main Street, Lynnville 38472.

McKenzie. GINA H. MANNING (R)
1976-. Bds: Cmsnr., Fire & Ambulance
Dept.; Ch., Doctor's Clinic Com. Party: Cnty.
Secretary 1975-77. Org: Chamber of Commerce;
Young Rep's. B: 12/24/45. Add: 103 Stonewall
Cir., McKenzie 38201.

Medon. NANNY LEE SMITH
City Hall, Medon 38356.

Memphis. PATRICIA VANDER SCHAAF (R)
Bds: Ch., Public Utilities; Fire; Land
Planning-Zoning. Party: Rep. Party Steering
Com. 1972-76. Prev: Comprehensive Employment
Training Act Cmsn. 1974-76. Org: Community
Planning Council Bd.; Society for the Advance-
ment of Management; Women in Cable, Inc. Bd.;
Planned Parenthood Assoc.; Memphis Bank &
Trust Adv. Bd. Educ: Rider Coll. BS. B:
8/13/43. Add: 4019 S. Lakewood Dr., Memphis
38128 (901)528-2786.

Monteagle. BERNICE OLIVER
P.O. Box 785, Monteagle 37356.

Nashville. BETTY C. NIXON (D)
1975-. Bds: Schools Com.; Planning &
Zoning & Historical Com.; Public Safety Com.
Party: State Del. 1972. Org: Dem. Women; WPC.
Educ: Southern Methodist U. 1958 BA. Occ:
Asst. Press Secretary to Governor of Tenn.
B: 1/12/36. Add: 1607 18th Ave. S, Nashville
37212.

Niota. EVA BRAKEBILL
P.O. Box 191, Niota 37826.

North Huntington. VIRGINIA MURRAY
P.O. Box 666, 110 E. Third Ave., North
Huntington 38344.

Oak Ridge. JO H. ROE
P.O. Box 1, Oak Ridge 37830.

Obion. GRACIE M. ASHLEY (D)
1976-. Bds: Ch., Water Com.; Public Safety;
Police & Fire Protection. Prev: Councilwoman
1976-77. Org: Town Parade Ch.; PTA. Occ:
Bookkeeper. B: 1/13/38. Add: P.O. Box 384,
Obion 38240 (901)634-3466.

Oliver Springs. ROSE INGRAM
                       GLADYS VAN HOOK
P.O. Box 303, Oliver Springs 37840.

Philadelphia. EVELYN EVERETTE
City Hall, Philadelphia 37846.

Ramer. ELIZABETH HAMM (D)
1976-. Bds: Park Cmsn. Org: Community
Relations Team; AFL-CIO; PTA. Occ: Machine
Operator. B: 5/7/25. Add: Box 68, Ramer
38367.

Rossville. LILLIAN B. PULLIAM
P.O. Box 27, Third Street, Rossville
38066.

Savannah. NANCY KERR POLLARD
    1020 Main Street, Savannah 38372.

Scotts Hill. VERNICE BROADWAY
    P.O. Box 127, Scotts Hill 38374.

Selmer. DORTHENA ESTES
         JO MITCHELL
    144 N. Second St., Selmer 38375.

Signal Mountain. MARION PARKER SUMMERVILLE (R)
    1975-. Educ: U. of Ala. 1949 BS. B: 9/28/28.
    Add: 507 Barrington Rd., Signal Mountain 37377
    (615)886-2177.

Silerton. OPAL FITTS
           PHYLLIS NAYLOR
    City Hall, Silerton 38377.

Somerville. MAE BELLE SIMS (I) **
    1974-. Bds: Street; Finance; City Cemetery.
    Add: 504 S. Main St., Somerville 38068 (901)
    465-2704.

South Carthage. MABEL THOMPSON
    P.O. Box 28, South Carthage 37030.

Trenton. ESTHER NOWELL
    309 College Street, Trenton 38382.

Vonore. LOUISE STAMEY (D)
    1975-. Prev: Alderwoman 1975-77. B: 4/12/25.
    Add: Rt. 2, Box 4, Vonore 37885 (615)884-6321.

Walden. BILLIE BENNETT ANSELL (R)
    1975-. Org: Civic League; Rep. Women's Club;
    Women's Guild. Educ: U. of Chattanooga 1931 BA.
    B: 5/17/09. Add: 1524 E. Brow Rd., Walden 37377
    (615)886-2496.

Watauga. EDITH SMALLING
    P.O. Box 68, Watauga 37694.

Judges

MARTHA CRAIG DAUGHTREY
    Judge, Court of Criminal Appeals. 1975-.
    Org: ABA; Institute of Judicial Administration;
    NOW; WPC. Educ: Vanderbilt U. 1964 BA; 1968
    JD. Occ: Professor. B: 7/21/42. Add: 706
    Woodleigh Dr., Nashville 37215 (615)741-2119.

State Boards and Commissions

    A complete list of state boards and commissions,
and of their membership, was not available for
inclusion.

Texas

State Legislature

State Senate

BETTY ANDUJAR (R)
    1972-. Dist: 12. Party: State Del.; Nat.
    Del. 1968, '76; State Committeewoman 1964-76;
    Nat. Committeewoman 1976. Org: Tex. Medical
    Assoc.; BPW; Chamber of Commerce; Metropolitan
    Rep. Women's Club; Fed. of Rep. Women. Educ:
    Wilson Coll. 1934 BA. B: 11/6/12. Add: 2951
    Benbrook Blvd., Ft. Worth 76109 (512)
    475-2526.

State House

WILHELMINA R. DELCO (D) **
    1974-. Dist: 37-1. Bds: Public School
    Educ. Com.; Constitutional Revision Com.
    Party: Del., State Conv. 1974; V-Ch., State
    Conv. 1974. Prev: School Board Trustee 1968-
    72. Org: PTA. Educ: Fisk U. 1950 BA. B:
    7/16/29. Add: 1805 Astor Pl., Austin 78721
    (512)475-5973.

BETTY DENTON (D)
    P.O. Box 2910, Austin 78769.

ERNESTINE GLOSSBRENNER (D)
    P.O. Box 2910, Austin 78769.

EDDIE BERNICE JOHNSON (D)
    1972-. Dist: 33-0. Bds: Ch., Labor Com.;
    Constitutional Amendments Com. Party: State
    Del. 1972-76; Nat. Del. 1974, '76; State Dem.
    Party V-Ch. 1976-78; State Dem. Exec. Committee-
    woman 1972-76; Dem. Nat. Com. 1976-78. Org:
    Black Chamber of Commerce; NAACP; Nat. Council
    of Negro Women; Dem. Women; Urban League; Cnty.
    Dem. Progressive Voters League; LWV; NOWL.
    Educ: Tex. Christian U. 1967 BS; Southern
    Methodist U. 1976 MPA. Occ: Private Consultant.
    B: 12/3/34. Add: 2107 Lanark, Dallas 75203
    (512)475-5925.

SUSAN GURLEY MC BEE **
    Dist: 70. Occ: Teacher. B: 12/9/46. Add:
    P.O. Box 954, Del Rio 78840 (512)475-2763.

CHRIS MILLER (D)
    1972-. Dist: 32. Bds: Health & Welfare;
    Natural Resources; V-Ch., Rules. Prev: Human
    Relations Cmsn. 1969-72. Org: Women in Commun-
    ications; AWRT; NOWL; LWV; Common Cause; Child
    Care '76; Dem. Women's Club; WPC; House Study
    Group; BPW; Zonta. B: 6/15/26. Add: 1203 1/2
    Lake St., Fort Worth 78769 (512)475-5814.

IRMA RANGEL (D)
P.O. Box 2910, Austin 78769.

LOU NELL SUTTON (D)
P.O. Box 2910, Austin 78769.

SENFRONIA THOMPSON (D) **
1973-. Dist: 89. Org: LWV; NAACP; OES; WPC;
Dem. Club; Teachers Assoc. Educ: Tex. Southern
U. 1961 BS; Prairie View Agriculture & Mechanical
Coll. 1964 MEd. Occ: Teacher. B: 1/1/39. Add:
8611 Peachtree, Houston 77016 (512)475-3264.

SARAH RAGLE WEDDINGTON (D)
1972-. Dist: 37. Bds: Elections & State
Affairs Com.; Nat. Conf. of State Leg's. Party:
Del., Cnty. Conv. 1972; Ch., Dem. Cnty. Conv.
1976. Org: ABA; Educ. Cmsn. of the States;
IWY; WPC; WEAL; AAUW; BPW; NOW; NOWL; Historical
Cmsn. Nat. Reciprocal & Family Support Enforce-
ment Assoc. Educ: McMurny Coll. 1965 BS; U. of
Tex. 1967 JD. Occ: Atty. B: 2/5/45. Add: 709
W. 14th St., Austin 78701 (512)475-5975.

County Commissions

Bastrop. WILMA WILEY
County Courthouse, Bastrop.

Hamilton. WILLIE MAE ADAMS (D)
1976-. Bds: Central Tex. Manpower Planning
Council. B: 12/1/26. Add: Rte. 1, Hamilton
76531 (817)386-5823.

Jim Wells. LUCILLA DE LEON
County Courthouse, Alice 78332.

Kenedy. ELENA KENNEDY
County Courthouse, Sarita.

Kent. SARAH F. BYRD
County Courthouse, Jayton.

Lee. LENA GERMAN (D)
1971-. Bds: Manpower Adv. Planning Council;
Manpower Consortium Special Com.; Soil Conser-
vation Com. Org: Historical Cmsn.; PTA. Occ:
Farmer. B: 5/16/22. Add: Rt. 1, Box 180, Dime
Box 77853 (713)884-2284.

Loving. JERIANN BLAIR
County Courthouse, Mentone.

Lynn. JEWELL NELSON
County Courthouse, Tahako 79373.

Medina. TOBY TOMBLIN
County Courthouse, Hondo.

Moore. CAROLYN STALLWITZ (I)
1976-. Org: Tex. Fine Art Assoc.; Tex. Water-
color Soc.; Amarillo Art Ctr. Educ: W. Texas
State U. 1957 BS. Occ: Artist/Teacher. B:
4/27/36. Add: Box 1225, Dumas 79029 (806)
935-5588.

Nacogdoches. JOAN H. CASON (R) **
1972-. Bds: Exec. Com., Council of Governments; Workman's Compensation Insurance Fund.

Org: Rep. Women's Club. B: 6/2/29. Add:
1525 Redbud, Nacogdoches 75961 (713)564-8658.

Nolan. NOMA FRALEY
County Courthouse, Sweetwater.

Presidio. FRANCES E. HOWARD
County Courthouse, Marfa.

Somervell. ELIZABETH HAMMOND
County Courthouse, Glen Rose 76043.

Travis. ANN RICHARDS
1976-. Bds: Transportation Study; Social
Policy Adv. Com.; Metro-Austin Criminal
Justice Planning Unit Adv. Com. Party: State
Del. 1976. Prev: Westlake Hills Zoning &
Planning Cmsn. 1969-73. Org: Assoc. of Cnty.
Cmnsrs.; Parks & Recreation Society; LWV;
Common Cause; NWPC; PTA. Educ: Baylor U. 1954
BA. B: 9/1/33. Add: 810 Red Bud Trail, Austin
78746 (512)478-9606.

Upshur. BERNICE NOBLES
County Courthouse, Gilmer 75644.

Waller. JODY BOETTCHER
County Courthouse, Hempstead.

Ward. LENORA PRICE (D) **
1961-. Dist: 4. Org: Amer. Business
Women's Assoc.; UFW; Dem. Club. B: 10/25/24.
Add: Box 120, Pyote 29777 (915)943-3200.

Webb. ANGEL R. LAUREL
County Courthouse, Laredo.

Winkler. CHRISTINE MILLS
County Courthouse, Kermit.

Zavala. ELENA DIAZ
County Courthouse, Crystal City.

Mayors

Angleton. ELLEN LA VERNE WHITE SNOW (D) **
1975-. Bds: Cnty. Child Welfare Bd. Org:
Amer. Nurses Assoc.; LWV; Tex. Nurses Assoc.
Educ: Jefferson Davis School of Nursing, U.
of Houston 1945 RN. B: 5/6/25. Add: 202 E.
Cedar, Angleton 77513 (713)849-4361.

Balmorhea. HELEN K. HUMPHRIES
1976-. Org: Nat. League of Postmasters;
Chamber of Commerce. Educ: Simmons U. 1930
BA. B: 6/2/10. Add: Box 193, Balmorhea
79718 (915)375-2307.

Blue Mound. BETTY BEWLEY (D)
1976-. Bds: Civil Defense Dir.; Mayor's
Council. Occ: Operator & Receptionist. B:
1/12/31. Add: 1665 Tyson St., Blue Mound
76131 (817)232-0661.

Blum. MRS. RAY MC DEARMON
P.O. Box 613, Blum 76627.

Briar. DOROTHY JONES
Rte. 3, Box 150-B, Azle 76020.

Browndell. MRS. C.L. JACK WALKER
P.O. Box 518, Jasper 75951.

Clay. MARY F. MACK (D) **
1971-. <u>Party</u>: Cnty. Com. <u>Org</u>: Nat. Council
of Teachers. <u>Educ</u>: Prairieview A&M U. 1927 BS;
Tex. Southern 1958 MA. <u>Occ</u>: Teacher. <u>B</u>: 9/7/09.
<u>Add</u>: Box 75, Clay 77839 (713)272-8582.

Colorado City. MARION BASSHAM
1977-. <u>Prev</u>: City Councilwoman 1974-77.
<u>Educ</u>: Joseph Lawrence School of Nursing 1945 RN.
<u>Occ</u>: RN. <u>B</u>: 5/6/18. <u>Add</u>: 898 E. 8th St.,
Colorado City 79512 (915)728-3240.

Denton. ELINOR OTTS HUGHES (D) **
1975-. <u>Prev</u>: Council. <u>Org</u>: Citizens for
Modernized Corrections. <u>Occ</u>: Coordinator, Continuing Education & Community Services. <u>B</u>:
6/30/32. <u>Add</u>: 1821 Linden, Denton 76201 (817)
382-9601.

Dublin. JEWEL HUMPHREYS
213 E. Black Jack St., Dublin 76446.

Easton. ALMORA ELDER
Railroad Ave., P.O. Box 301, Easton 75641.

Fruitvale. HALLIE RANDALL
Rte. 1, Fruitvale 75127.

Gordon. CLEO PIERCE (D) **
1972-. <u>Bds</u>: Cnty. Cmsnr's. Court. <u>Party</u>:
Precinct Ch. 1970-75. <u>Org</u>: Fed. of Women's
Clubs. <u>B</u>: 9/12/13. <u>Add</u>: Box 336, Gordon 76453
(817)693-5676.

Gustine. MRS. CHESTER MARTIN
Town Hall, Gustine 76455.

Hilshire Village. RUTH TAPPAN KRENEK (R)
1972-. <u>Prev</u>: Bldg. Inspector 1963-65; Alderwoman 1965-72. <u>Org</u>: Civic Club. <u>Educ</u>: U. of
Okla. 1941 BS, B. of Arch. <u>B</u>: 1/21/21. <u>Add</u>:
1033 Wirt Rd., Houston 77055.

Josephine. INEZ HOWZE (D)
1974-. <u>Org</u>: Amer. Assoc. of Retired Persons.
<u>Educ</u>: St. Paul Hospital School of Nursing RN.
<u>B</u>: 1/13/13. <u>Add</u>: Box 1114, Josephine 75064
(214)694-3000.

Lyford. IRMA SALDANA
P.O. Drawer 310, Lyford 78569.

Menard. ESTELLE R. SMITH (I)
1974-. <u>Org</u>: State Bar of Tex.; Civic Beautification Council; OES. <u>Educ</u>: S. Tex. Coll. of
Law 1957 LLB. <u>Occ</u>: Atty. <u>Add</u>: P.O. Box 938,
Menard 76859 (915)396-4712.

Morgan's Point Resort. IVY BREAUX
P.O. Box 662, Belton 76513.

Oakwood. MAXINE E. MOORE
P.O. Box 96, Oakwood 75855.

Palmhurst. MRS. LAROY ROSSOW
Rte. 1, Mission 78572.

Rio Hondo. JUA NITA BRODECKY (I)
1973-. <u>Bds</u>: Pres., Lower Rio Grande Vly.
Official Assoc.; Greater S. Tex. Cultural
Basin. <u>Occ</u>: Bookkeeper. <u>B</u>: 11/27/26. <u>Add</u>:
P.O. Box 35, Rio Hondo 78583 (512)748-2102.

Roma. IRMA G. YNES
P.O. Box 947, Roma 78584.

Roman Forest. LORNA IMM (R)
1976-. <u>Prev</u>: Alderwoman 1975-76. <u>Org</u>:
Civic Assoc. <u>B</u>: 1/20/14. <u>Add</u>: 306 Canary,
New Caney 77357 (713)689-7419.

Sachse. MARY JO KILLINGSWORTH (D) **
1971-. <u>Bds</u>: Health, Welfare & Educ. <u>Prev</u>:
Council. <u>Org</u>: NEA; PTA. <u>Educ</u>: Tex. Women's
U. 1949 BS. <u>Occ</u>: Teacher. <u>Add</u>: Rt. 3, Box 57,
Wylie 75098 (214)495-1212.

San Antonio. LILA COCKRELL
1975-. <u>Bds</u>: Ch., Firemen's & Policemen's
Pension Fund; Public Service Bd.; Water Bd.
<u>Prev</u>: City Councilwoman 1963-75. <u>Org</u>: Zonta;
Military-Civilian Club. <u>Educ</u>: Southern Method-
ist U. 1942 BA. <u>B</u>: 1/19/22. <u>Add</u>: 3010 Charter
Crest, San Antonio 78230 (512)225-5661.

San Augustine. ALVIS HOWZE JUNIEL (I) **
1975-. <u>Org</u>: Mental Retardation Com.;
Women's Club. <u>B</u>: 6/24/19. <u>Add</u>: 310 E. Main
St., San Augustine 75972 (713)275-2121.

San Marcos. EMMIE CADDOCK
630 E. Hopkins, San Marcos 78666.

Seven Oaks. VIOLA JONES (D) **
1969-. <u>B</u>: 11/11/11. <u>Add</u>: Box 57, Leggett
77350 (713)398-2939.

Shady Shores. OLIVE STEPHENS **
1973-. <u>Add</u>: R. 4, Box 367, Denton 76201
(817)497-2202.

Waelder. TINA R. HOFFMAN
P.O. Box 427, Waelder 78959.

Local Councils

Allen. EILEEN RICE TOLLETT (D)
1976-. <u>Educ</u>: U. of Central Ark. 1969 BSE;
Southern Methodist U. 1972 MLA. <u>B</u>: 3/28/47.
<u>Add</u>: Box 235, Allen 75002 (214)727-3336.

Alvarado. GLENDA LASEMAN
P.O. Drawer L, 210 S. Frio, Alvarado 76009.

Alvarado. BETTY RAY (I)
1973-. Mayor Pro Tem. <u>Bds</u>: Ch., Citizens
Com. for Street Improvement. <u>Occ</u>: Secretary.
<u>B</u>: 6/26/21. <u>Add</u>: 106 E. Jessup Dr., Alvarado
76009 (817)783-3301.

Alvin. NANCY BENEFIELD (I)
1976-. Mayor Pro Tem. <u>Occ</u>: Office Manager.
<u>B</u>: 4/7/37. <u>Add</u>: 300 S. 2nd, Alvin 77511
(713)641-2074.

Amarillo. KATHRINE K. WILSON (D) **
   1975-. Org: Foundation for Health & Science
Educ. Educ: U. of Texas 1934 BA. B: 2/26/13.
Add: 600 Avondale St., Amarillo 79106 (806)
372-4211.

Angleton. MARY BATES
   121 S. Velasco, P.O. Box 726, Angleton 77515.

Angus. SHIRLEY HILL
   Rte. 3, Corsicana 75110.

Argyle. MYRTLE LYNCH
   P.O. Box 1035, Argyle 76226.

Argyle. VIRGIE NIMMS (D)
   1973-. B: 4/15/21. Add: RR 1, Argyle 76226.

Arlington. CAROLYN SNIDER
   200 W. Abram, P.O. Box 231, Arlington 76010.

Arlington. MARTHA WALKER (I)
   1972-. Bds: Ch., Greater Fort Worth Employment & Training Consortium; Regional Transportation Policy Adv. Com. Org: Tex. Municipal
League; Chamber of Commerce; Arlington Volunteer
Center; Together, Inc. Educ: U. of Okla. 1963
BA; U. of Tex. 1974 MA. Occ: Sales Repr. B:
11/14/33. Add: 1514 W. Lavender, Arlington
76013.

Aurora. HELEN DERTING
          RUTH MAYFIELD
   Rt. 1, Rhome 76078.

Austin. BETTY HIMMELBLAU (D)
   1975-. Bds: V-Ch., Exec. Bd., Capital Area
Planning Council; Secretary, Exec. Bd., Central
Tex. Health Systems Agency; Joint City-State
Leg. Com. Org: Women's Club; U. Ladies Club.
Educ: Stephens Coll. BS; U. of Wis. MA. B:
11/9/22. Add: 4609 Ridge Oak Dr., Austin 78731
(512)477-6511.

Austin. MARGRET HOFMANN (D) **
   1975-. Prev: Energy Conservation Com. &
Environmental Bd. 1973-75. Org: Dem. Club; PTA.
B: 7/3/25. Add: 610 Cardinal La., Austin 78704
(512)477-6511.

Austin. DR. EMMA LOU LINN
   124 W. 8th St., Box 1088, Austin 78767.

Bailey's Prairie. BARBARA JOURNEY
   Rte. 1, Angleton 77515.

Balch Springs. KAY OTTING
   1976-. Bds: Insurance Com.; Finance Com.;
Newsletter Com. Party: State Alt. 1975. Prev:
City Charter Cmsn. 1974-75; Planning & Zoning
Bd. 1975-76. Org: PTA. Occ: Secretary. B:
12/4/31. Add: 13001 Mitchell Dr., Balch Spgs.
75180 (214)286-4444.

Balcones Heights. LUCILLE WOHLFARTH
   123 Altgelt Ave., San Antonio 78201.

Barstow. MRS. JO ALLGOOD
   Community Center Bldg., Box 98, Barstow 79719.

Baytown. JODY LANDER
   2401 Market St., Box 424, Baytown 77520.

Baytown. MARY ELIZABETH WILBANKS (D)
   1972-. Dist: 6. Bds: Houston-Galveston
Area Council; Transportation Policy Com. Org:
Chamber of Commerce; Service League. Educ:
U. of Houston BA. Occ: Coll. Instructor. B:
1/17/41. Add: 610 Scenic Dr., Baytown 77520
(713)422-8281.

Beach City. OLGA MARIE BARROW (D)
   1977-. Mayor Pro Tem. Org: Historical &
Genealogical Society. Educ: U. of Houston 1959
BS. B: 9/23/17. Add: Rt. 2, Box 161, Baytown
77520.

Beach City. BETTI ENDERLI
   P.O. Box 455, Baytown 77520.

Beach City. GEORGIA MACKRELL **
   Bds: Bicentennial Com. Prev: City Treasurer.
B: 9/17/12. Add: Rt. 2, Box 126 B, Baytown
77520 (713)383-2235.

Beaumont. VI MC GINNIS
   700 Pearl St., Box 3827, Beaumont 77704.

Beckville. MRS. JOHNNIE HUGHES
   P.O. Box 97, Beckville 75631.

Bedford. ARNETTA LEDBETTER
   2000 Forest Ridge Dr., P.O. Box 157,
Bedford 76021.

Bellaire. LOUISE WARE
   7008 S. Rice Ave., Bellaire 77401.

Bellville. MARTHA B. HELLMUTH (R) **
   1975-. Bds: Library Bd.; Bicentennial.
Org: Teachers Assoc. Educ: Trinity U. 1956
BS; Trinity U. 1962 ME. B: 11/21/02. Add:
226 S. Live Oak, Bellville 77418 (713)
865-3136.

Benavides. MRS. PATRICIO GONZALES
   Drawer U, Benavides 78341.

Benbrook. LYDIA M. O'BRIEN
   101 B. Del Rio St., Fort Worth 75126.

Bertram. JOHNIE MAE WHEELER (D)
   1972-. Mayor Pro Tem. Party: State Del.
1975-76; State Alt. 1972, '74. Org: Chamber of
Commerce; OES; Ch., Mental Health & Retardation;
Cnty. Dem. Women; PTA. Educ: U. of Tex. 1941
BA; 1956 MEd. Occ: Elementary School Principal.
B: 11/2/20. Add: Rt. 2, Box 63, Bertram 78605
(512)355-2111.

Bickville. HAZEL AKINS
   Box 66, Bickville 75631.

Big Spring. MRS. FLOYD MAYS (R) **
   1973-. Bds: Tourism Com.; Parks & Recreation. Party: V-Ch. Local Com. 1964-66. Org:
Friends of the Library; Historical Survey Com;
Rep. Clubs. Educ: Kans. U. BS. Add: 602 Highland, Big Spring 79720.

Blooming Grove. GLADYS V. MAHONE (D) **
    1975-. Bds: Special Policeman; Beautification.
Org: Labor Union Member. Occ: Factory Worker.
B: 3/7/16. Add: Box 132, Blooming Grove 76626.
(214)695-2711.

Blossom. BILLIE JEAN HENRY (D)
    1976-. Occ: Filler Operator. B: 5/22/32.
Add: Hickory St., Box 253, Blossom 75416
(214)982-5939.

Blue Ridge. MRS. DANNIE CANTRELL
    P.O. Box 41, Blue Ridge 75004.

Boerne. CHRISTINE LA FON ELLIS (I)
    1974-. Bds: Health & Sanitation; Zoning &
Planning. Prev: Planning & Zoning 1972-74. Org:
Independent Teachers Assoc.; NEA; Chamber of
Commerce. Educ: Berea Coll. 1947 BA; U. of
Houston 1958 MEd. Occ: Teacher. B: 11/3/23.
Add: 108 Rock St., Boerne 78006 (512)249-2511.

Booker. MARION GUY (R)
    Occ: Insurance Agent. B: 3/11/42. Add: Rt.
2, Box 77, Booker 79005 (806)435-3626.

Boyd. ALICE SIMPSON
    P.O. Box 216, Boyd 76023.

Brackettville. CRIS GOMEZ
    P.O. Box 526, Brackettville 78832.

Branch. MRS. E. ANNE WEST
    Rt. 5, McKinney 75069.

Bremond. ELZIE GROHOLSKI
    Town Hall, Bremond 76629.

Briar. JOYLIN FONTES
        DOROTHY WALLING
    Rte. 3, Box 150B, Azle 76020.

Brownsboro. NETTIE JO MC LEAN
    P.O. Box 303, Brownsboro 75756.

Bryson. ALTA L. RUDOLPH
    P.O. Box 28, Bryson 76027.

Buckingham. PAULA HARKEY
    2022 1/2 Willingham, P.O. Box 75, Richardson
75080.

Buda. JUDY POWELL
    P.O. Box 1218, Buda 78610.

Buffalo. VIRGINIA LEE MARTIN
    P.O. Box 219, Buffalo 75831.

Buffalo Gap. PEGGY LOWE
    Vine & Lytle, P.O. Box 506, Buffalo Gap
79508.

Bunker Hill. SHIRLEY T. INMAN
    11977 Memorial Dr., Box 19404, Houston 77024.

Burkburnett. MRS. ROBERT NORRISS
    405 Ave. C, Burkburnett 76354.

Calvert. IOLA B. GRIFFIN (D) **
    1973-. Org: Mental Health Bd.; PTA. Occ:
Self-employed. B: 3/31/11. Add: 401 Texas
St., Calvert 77837 (713)364-2654.

Cameron. JANET WRIGHT LUECKE (D) **
    1975-. Bds: Street Improvement Com.;
Historical Survey Com.; Community Action Assoc.;
Outreach Clinic. Org: Friends of the Library.
B: 10/9/32. Add: 806 E. 7th St., Cameron
76520.

Canadian. PAT WATERS (D) **
    1973-. Bds: Bd. of Dir., Panhandle Regional
Planning Cmsn. & Manpower Com. Party: Precinct
Ch. 1968-70. Org: Bd. of Dir., Amer. Cancer
Society; Bicentennial Com.; PEO. Occ: Secre-
tary. B: 7/20/39. Add: 707 Kingman, Canadian
79014 (806)323-6473.

Castroville. VIRGINIA F. KEEFER
    1209 N. Florella St., P.O. Box 479,
Castroville 78009.

Cedar Park. BONNIE S. MERRILL
    P.O. Box 899, Cedar Pk. 78613.

Chandler. BETTY PHILLIPS
    P.O. Box 425, Chandler 75758.

Chillicothe. BOBBIE L. HORNER (D)
    1974-. Bds: Financial Cmsnr. Occ: Medical
Recorder. B: 3/14/31. Add: P.O. Box 533,
Chillicothe 79225 (817)852-5211.

China. GOLDEN HARDY
    P.O. Box 516, China 77613.

Christine. BETTYE HARRIS
        RUBY HOWARD
    P.O. Box 238, Christine 78012.

Cibolo. MARGE SMITH (D)
    1974-. Bds: Planning & Zoning Cmsn. Educ:
SW Texas State U. 1972 BSEd; MA. B: 10/10/33.
Add: 240 S., Cibolo 78108.

Cockrell Hill. MILDRED SUGGS
    4125 W. Clarendon, Dallas 75211.

Coleman. MATTIE B. ROGERS
    119 N. Concho, P.O. Box 592, Coleman 75834.

College Station. RUTH ANNE HAZEN
    1976-. Bds: Safety; School Bd.; Ch.,
Ambulance-Health. Prev: Safety Com. Sec. 1974-
76. Org: State Teachers Assoc.; School Health
Section for Nurses; LWV. Educ: U. of NH 1956
BA; Mass. General Hospital School of Nursing
1955 RN. Occ: Nurse. B: 9/10/31. Add: 1205-A
Munson Ave., College Station 77840.

Colorado City. JODY NEFF
    180 W. 3rd St., P.O. Box 912, Colorado
City 79512.

Columbus. LAURA ANN RAU
    605 Spring St., P.O. Box 87, Columbus 78934.

Commerce. SHARON L. FULKERSON (D)
1974-. Bds: Repr., N. Central Tex. Council
of Govt.; Regional Transportation Adv. Com. Org:
People & Services United Bd.; AAUW. Educ:
Southern Ill. U. 1963 BS, MS. B: 5/30/41. Add:
2905 Melmar Pk., Commerce 75428.

Coppell. HAZEL BEAL
P.O. Box 478, Coppell 75019.

Corpus Christi. RUTH B. GILL (D)
1975-. Bds: Coastal Bend Consortium; S. Tex.
Cultural Basin Cmsn.; Women In Municipal Govt.
Party: State Del.; Ch., Resolutions Com. 1976;
Election Judge 1962-75. Prev: Cnty. Community
Action Agency 1965-68, '75-77; Bldg. Standards
Bd. of Appeals; Library Bd.; City-Cnty. Health-
Welfare Adv. Bd.; Repr., Council of Govts. 1972-
75; Charter Revision Cmsn. 1973. Org: WPC; LWV;
Dem. Club. B: 12/31/23. Add: 1 Hewit Dr.,
Corpus Christi 78404 (512)884-3011.

Crawford. MARJORIE BURNS
P.O. Box 807, Crawford 76638.

Crawford. JOYCE HOLMES
P.O. Box 294, Crawford 76638.

Cross Roads. HELEN DIAMOND (R)
1974-. Educ: Lombard Coll. BS. B: 11/10/04.
Add: Rt. 1, Box 71, Aubrey 76227.

Cuero. SHARON D. STEEN
201 E. Main, P.O. Box 512, Cuero 77954.

Dallas. JUANITA CRAFT
Main & Harwood Sts., Dallas 75201.

Dallas. ADLENE HARRISON (I)
1973-. Bds: Ch., Council Community Devt. Com.;
Transportation; Arts Com. Prev: Cnty. Council
on Aging 1967-69; Planning Com. 1963-73. Org:
Save Open Space; Cnty. Heritage Society; Women
for Change; Dallas Alliance for Community Devt.
B: 11/19/23. Add: 5841 Burgundy, Dallas 75230
(214)748-9711 x 1481.

Dallas. LUCY P. PATTERSON (D)
1973-. Bds: Ch., Human Devt. Com.; Community
Devt. Com.; Intergovt. Affairs & Council Rela-
tions. Party: State Del. 1976. Prev: Pres.,
Municipal League 1975-77; V-Pres., Municipal
League 1974-75; Nat. League of Cities 1973-77.
Org: NASW; Nat. Assoc. of Black Social Workers;
Altrusa Internat.; Top Ladies Distinction;
United People for Action. Educ: Howard U. 1950
BA; U. of Denver 1963 MSW. Occ: Social Work
Educator. B: 6/21/31. Add: 2779 Almeda Dr.,
Dallas 75216 (214)748-9711.

Dallas. ROSE RENFROE
Main & Harwood Sts., Dallas 75201.

Dalworthington Gardens. AGATHA MARTIN
2600 Roosevelt Dr., Arlington 76016.

Dayton. LINDA RIGBY
111 N. Church St., Dayton 77535.

DeKalb. WANDA MC GILL
110 SE S. Front St., DeKalb 75559.

Del Rio. FRANCES F. PARET (R)
1968-. Bds: Middle Rio Grande Devt. Council;
Ch., Child Welfare Bd.; Mental Health-Mental
Retardation Adv. Bd. Prev: Mayor Pro Tem. 1974-
75. Org: Tex. Municipal League; Rep. Women;
PTA. Educ: Southern Methodist U. 1954 MAEd.
B: 4/27/33. Add: 105 Herrmann Dr., Del Rio
78840 (512)774-2781.

Deport. CHRISTINE SKAGGS (D)
1974-. Mayor Pro Tem. Occ: Farm Chemical
Store, Asst. Manager. B: 10/17/26. Add:
P.O. Box 181, Deport 75435 (214)652-3875.

De Soto. CANDACE S. HIGGINS (I) **
1965-. Bds: Council of Governments. Org:
Bicentennial. B: 9/14/46. Add: 1221 Hanna
Circle, De Soto 75115 (214)224-7344.

Dilley. HARRIET MANGUM
P.O. Box 230, Dilley 78017.

Douglassville. HELEN BAKER
MABEL MORRIS
MARY SWINT
Town Hall, Douglassville 75560.

Eastland. NANCY CHILDRESS
416 S. Seaman, P.O. Box 749, Eastland 76448.

Eastvale. NANCY DUGGER
Rte. 3, Box 358, Lewisville 75067.

Edcouch. OLGA BENAVIDEZ
206 Hill St., P.O. Box 86, Edcouch 78538.

Edgecliff. BETTY MARTIN
1605 Edgecliff Rd., Rte. 3, Box 69, Fort
Worth 76134.

Elgin. BETTY LYNN MEYER
114 Depot St., P.O. Box 591, Elgin 78621.

El Lago. PHYLLIS EGGLESTON
3802 Nasa Rd. 1, Apt. 27, Seabrook 77586.

El Lago. ELIZABETH F. LENOIR (D)
1977-. Bds: Park Cmsn.; Bd. of Equalization.
Org: PTA. Educ: Northeastern U. 1963 BA; U.
of Houston 1977 MA. Occ: Freelance Writer.
B: 5/21/42. Add: 431 Shadow Creek Dr., Seabrook
77586 (713)334-1951.

Elmendorf. ANITA PACHECO
P.O. Box 247, Elmendorf 78112.

El Paso. POLLY HARRIS (D)
1977-. Bds: Civic Ctr. Bd.; Conv. & Visitors
Bureau Bd.; Ampitheatre Bd. Prev: Bd. of Devt.
1972-74. Org: Advertising Fed.; Press Club;
Public Relations Society of Amer.; Assoc. of
Builders. Educ: Kan. City Jr. Coll. 1943 AA;
U. of Mo. 1945 BS. Occ: Pres., Public Relations.
Add: 6212 Papago Dr., El Paso 79903 (915)
543-6760.

El Paso. ARLENE S. QUENON (D) **
   1975-. Bds: Library Bd.; Museum Bd.; Parks
& Recreation Bd.; Zoo Bd.; Youth Services Bureau;
Bicentennial Cmsn.; Council of Governments.
Party: Local Precinct Del. 1972- ; County Del.
1972-74. Prev: City Housing Code Bd. 1972. Org:
LWV; Mental Health Assoc. Educ: U. of Tex. 1971
BA. B: 10/19/34. Add: 355 Pendale, El Paso
79907 (915)543-6052.

Emhouse. SHIRLEY RAY
   P.O. Box 205, Emhouse 75110.

Euless. WILLIE MAE MC CORMICK (D)
   1973-. Mayor Pro Tem. Bds: Waste Water Adv.
Bd. Party: State Alt. 1972. Org: Amer. Assoc.
of Women in Mathematics; AAUW; LWV; Ladies
Chamber of Commerce; Soroptimist; Women's Club;
PTA. Educ: Mary Hardin Baylor 1929 BA; Hardin
Simmons U. 1931 MA. B: 11/17/08. Add: Rt. 1,
Box 66, Euless 76039 (817)283-5381.

Eustace. ANN HUNT
   Town Hall, Eustace 75124.

Forest Hill. EARLENE GLASS
   6800 Forest Hill Dr., P.O. Box 15305, Fort
Worth 76119.

Forsan. SUSAN GASTON (D)
   1967-. Occ: Secretary/Bookkeeper. B: 10/28/
48. Add: Box 593, Forsan 79733 (915)457-2333.

Fort Stockton. LILA URIAS
   114 W. 2nd St., P.O. Box 1000, Fort Stockton
79735.

Frankston. JOSEPHINE A. LAKE (D)
   1973-. Occ: Grocery Store Owner. B: 3/29/18.
Add: Rt. 1, Box 140-1, Berryville 75763 (214)
876-3263.

Freer. IDA H. PEREZ
   HELEN SCHUENEMAN
   P.O. Drawer N, Freer 78357.

Fruitvale. EVELYN BURKHAM
   BEATRICE WHISENHUNT
   Rte. 1, Fruitvale 75127.

Galveston. EDNA LIVINGSTON FULLER (D)
   1977-. Mayor Pro Tem. Bds: Houston-Galveston
Area Council Projects Review; Parks & Recreation
Bd.; Galveston Marine Affairs Council. Party:
Nat. Del. 1976. Prev: City Councilwoman 1975-
77; Charter Review Cmsn. 1973-74. Org: LWV;
Sierra Club; Dem. Club; Historical Foundation.
Educ: Furman U. 1961 BS; Tulane U. 1963 MS. B:
11/24/39. Add: 7682 Chantilly, Galveston 77551
(713)766-2104.

Ganado. FRANCES STRAUSS
   204 W. Putnam St., Box 264, Ganado 77962.

Garland. DELORA LEWIS
   RUTH NICHOLSON
   200 N. 5th St., Box 189, Garland 75040.

Garland. GWEN SMALE (I)
   1976-. Bds: Downtown Devt. Com; Adult Educ.;
Data Services Review & Planning. Prev: Plann-
ing Cmsn. 1974-76. Org: AAUW. Educ: Southern
Methodist U. 1950 BA. B: 11/18/27. Add: 216
W. Rio Grande, Garland 75041.

Garrett. PEGGY STEWART
   BESSIE TUCKER
   Ferris St., Garrett 75119.

Giddings. BETTY GOODSON
   118 E. Richmond St., Giddings 78942.

Glen Heights. MRS. B.R. BARTON
   Rte. 1, Box 418A, De Soto 75115.

Graham. MARY MORRISON
   429 4th St., P.O. Box 690, Graham 76046.

Grandfalls. MAURINE GRIFFIN
   P.O. Box 375, Grandfalls 79742.

Grand Prairie. ANNE GRESHAM
   318 W. Main, P.O. Box 11, Grand Prairie
75050.

Granger. BRIDGET C. BOHAC
   P.O. Box 367, Granger 76530.

Greenville. MYRNA GILSTRAP
   2821 Washington St., PO. Box 1049, Greenville
75401.

Grey Forest. RUTH MORRIS
   VIRGINIA SPRINGER
   P.O. Box 258, Helotes 78023.

Groesbeck. ETHEL R. HANDER
   402 W. Navasota St., Box 277, Groesbeck
76642.

Harker Heights. MILDRED SHINE (D)
   1976-. Party: State Alt. 1970; Precinct Ch.
1964-77. Prev: Health & Sanitation Bd. 1968-
76. Org: Amer. Business Woman; State Election
Officials. Occ: Nurse. B: 10/20/21. Add:
1101 Mildred Lee, Harker Heights 76541 (817)
634-3115.

Harlingen. CONNIE DE LA GARZA
   118 E. Tyler, P.O. Box 2207, Harlingen
78550.

Haskell. LORAINE JOHNSON
   307 N. 1st St., Box 783, Haskell 79521.

Haslet. MRS. J.W. BRANAM
   Town Hall, Haslet 76052.

Hawley. CATHERINE PURCELL
   Town Hall, Hawley 79525.

Henderson. J. CAROLYN PARKER **
   1974-. Educ: Lamar Tech. U. 1965 BA;
Stephen F. Austin 1970 MA. Occ: Teacher. B:
8/25/38. Add: Rt. 6, Box 2, Henderson 75652
(214)657-6551.

Hewitt. MARIAN A. SKIVINGTON
    P.O. Box 610, Hewitt 76643.

Highland Village. COLLETTE JORDAN
    500 Highland Village Rd., Lewisville 75067.

Hill Country Village. DOROTHY COLEMERE
    114 Village Circle, San Antonio 78232.

Hitchcock. CAROLYN JEAN HOLT (D)
    1975-. Bds: Community Devt. Block Grant
Com.; Tax Break Com. Prev: City Cmsnr. 1975-77.
Org: Nat. Assoc. of Realtors; Political Coalition
League; Chamber of Commerce. Occ: Secretary.
B: 12/25/43. Add: 6720 W. Bayou Dr., Hitchcock
77563 (713)986-5591.

Holland. GEORGIA GROSSMAN
    P.O. Box 157, Holland 76534.

Hollywood Park. MRS. FRANCIS WEINHOLT
    #2 Mecca Dr., San Antonio 78232.

Howardwick. MARGARET BERRY
    P.O. Box 1143, Howardwick 79226.

Huntington. JANICE WILROY
    P.O. Drawer 349, Main St., Huntington 75949.

Huntsville. DELORA ROGERS KING (I)
    1974-. Bds: Tourist Council; Emergency
Medical Service. Org: BPW; Women's Forum; PTA.
Occ: Pharmacy Owner. B: 1/31/30. Add: 3407
Boettcher Dr., Huntsville 77340 (713)295-6471.

Hurst. MARGARET SLOAN
    1505 Precinct Line Rd., Hurst 76053.

Impact. NANCY PERKINS
    P.O. Box 3116, Abilene 79604.

Ingleside. RUTH INGRUM
    501 1/2 San Angelo St., P.O. Drawer 500,
Ingleside 78362.

Iowa Park. LITA HUGGINS WATSON (I)
    1976-. Mayor Pro Tem. Bds: Park & Recre-
ation Bd. Educ: Phillips U. 1951 BA. B:5/10/30.
Add: 520 Clara, Iowa Pk. 76367 (817)592-5454.

Iraan. JUNE E. HECK (D)
    1976-. Org: Soc. of X-Ray Technologists;
Chamber of Commerce; Nat. Taxpayers Union. Occ:
X-Ray Technician. B: 11/22/30. Add: Box 93,
Iraan 79744.

Irving. JOYCE J. PITTMAN (R) **
    1974-. Bds: Utilities Com.; Social Services
Com.; Civic Center Com.; Health Planning Council.
Party: Ch., County Precinct 1975-76. Org: Dir.,
Fed. of Rep. Women; Women's Chamber of Commerce;
Rep. Women's Club. Occ: Secretary. B: 8/31/40.
Add: 1401 Colony Dr., Irving 75061 (214)
254-6563.

Itasca. MRS. THOMASENE NORTON
    136 N. Hill, P.O. Box 99, Itasca 76055.

Jacksboro. MARTHA H. GREEN (I)
    1975-. Bds: Airport; Ch., Bd. for Employ-
ees for Salaries, Retirement. Org: BPW. Educ:
N. Tex. State U. 1930 BA; Colo. State Coll.
1936 MA. B: 10/9/09. Add: 1101 W. Archer,
Jacksboro 76056.

Jasper. MARCH COFFIELD
    272 E. Lamar, Jasper 75951.

Jewett. MRS. CARL PENCE
    P.O. Box 188, Jewett 75846.

Jones Creek. DONNA MC MINN
    Rte. 3, Freeport 77541.

Kemah. SYLVIA JACKSON
    6th & Bradford, Box 817, Kemah 77565.

Kemp. MARY DAILEY
    Main & 11th Sts., Box 276, Kemp 75143.

Kendleton. CAROLYN JONES
    P.O. Box 700, Kendleton 77451.

Kennedale. CLARA SANDERSON
            PAT TURNER
    201 New Hope Rd., P.O. Box 268, Kennedale
76060.

Kerens. FRANCES COLLINS
    115 W. 1st St., P.O. Box 160, Kerens 75144.

Kermit. BETTYE JONES
    114 S. Tornillo St., P.O. Drawer P, Kermit
79745.

Kirby. IRENE C. MILLER (D) **
    1973-. Org: Real Estate Bd.; Women's Club.
Occ: Real Estate Sales. B: 2/13/29. Add:
5239 Crown La., Kirby 78219 (512)661-3198.

Kirbyville. MRS. W.S. JINNETTE (D)
    1971-. Mayor Pro Tem. Bds: Deep E. Tex.
Council of Govts. Org: Amer. Dietetics Assoc.;
Women's Civic; Amer. Cancer Society. Educ:
Kan. State U. 1934 BS. Occ: Dietitian. B:
11/21/13. Add: 412 Trout St., Kirbyville
75956 (713)423-2451.

La Grange. ALMA PAINE
    155 E. Colorado St., Box 187, La Grange
78945.

Lake Tanglewood. THELMA LOFGREN
    Rt. 2, Box 44A40, Amarillo 79101.

Lakeview. NELLIE CAMPBELL (D)
    1976-. Occ: Bookkeeper. B: 10/19/26.
Add: Box 457, Lakeview 79239 (806)867-2111.

Lancaster. CAROLYN CORDILL FULTON (D) **
    1973-. Bds: Bicentennial Com.; Library
Bd. Org: Assoc. of School Librarians; Chamber
of Commerce; Municipal League; PTA. Educ:
Southern Methodist U. 1964 BA; Tex. Women's
U. 1970 MLS. Occ: Librarian. B: 3/8/30.
Add: 917 Sequoia Dr., Lancaster 75146 (214)
227-2111.

La Porte. VIRGINIA CLINE
    124 S. 2nd, P.O. Box 1115, La Porte 77571.

La Villa. ERNESTINA SAENZ
            HILDA WILT
    P.O. Box 101, La Villa 78562.

La Ward. THELMA DEYTON
           TILLIE TROJCAK
    P.O. Box 100, La Ward 77970.

Leonard. ELIZABETH NELL TREADWAY (D)
    1976-. Prev: City Secretary 1974-75. Org:
OES. B: 9/28/45. Add: Box 386, Leonard 75452
(214)587-2039.

Leon Valley. ANNA MARGARET REAVES (D) **
    1975-. Org: Fed. Employed Women. Org: Women
for Childrens Home. Occ: Inventory Management
Specialist. B: 4/19/24. Add: 6914 Forest Way,
San Antonio 78240 (512)925-6495.

Liberty. SANDRA PICKETT (I)
    1974-. Bds: Ch., Parks Com.; Light & Power;
Repr., Houston-Galveston Area Council. Party:
Secretary-Cnty. Convention 1974. Org: Historical
Cmsn.; Historical Society; Museum Bd. Educ: U.
of Tex. 1964 BS; U. of Houston 1969 MA. B:
12/29/42. Add: 5008 Lakeside Dr., Liberty
77515 (713)336-3684.

Lincoln Park. KAREN CANTRELL
               DENINSE GAMMAGE
    Rte. 1, Box 105, Aubrey 76227.

Live Oak. KAREN MC INTYRE
    8001 Shin Oak Dr., San Antonio 78233.

Lockhart. MARIE C. BURTON
    308 W. San Antonio, P.O. Box 239, Lockhart
78644.

Lometa. ANNYE B. WAGNER
    Town Hall, Lometa 76853.

Lone Star. MYRTLE DAVIS
    Jefferson & Center, P.O. Box 218, Lone Star
75668.

Loraine. LESLEY H. EASON
    204 Main St., P.O. Box 7, Loraine 79532.

Loraine. DORIS M. HENDERSON (D)
    1977-. Org: BPW. Occ: Bank Clerk. Add:
Box 473, Loraine 79532.

Lubbock. CAROLYN JORDAN (D)
    1972-. Bds: South Plains Assoc. of Govt.;
Health Systems Agency. Party: State Alt. 1974.
Org: AAUW; LWV; Friends of the Library. Educ:
Stanford U. 1957 BS, 1959 MA; Tex. Tech. U.
1977 JD. Occ: Law Clerk. B: 2/23/36. Add:
3249 62nd St., Lubbock 79413 (806)762-6411.

Lyford. IRENE JOHNSON
    P.O. Drawer 310, Lyford 78569.

Magnolia. JEAN VAJA
    510 Magnolia Blvd., P.O. Box 396, Magnolia
77355.

Marble Falls. NITA NUNNALLY (D)
    1976-. Occ: Real Estate. B: 12/29/24.
Add: P.O. Drawer 430, Marble Falls 78654
(512)693-4589.

Marietta. MRS. R.L. HARRIS
           MRS. HASKELL
    City Office, P.O. Box 247, Marietta 75566.

Marshall. MRS. JAMES K. ABNEY
    Houston St., P.O. Box 698, Marshall 75670.

Mason. MILDRED WALKER
    1976-. Org: PTA. B: 9/9/20. Add: 310 Fir,
Mason 76856.

Mathis. MARGARITA PAIZ RIVERA
    411 E. San Patricio, Mathis 78368.

Meridian. OLGA WORD
    111 N. Main, P.O. Box 205, Meridian 76665.

Mertzon. JANET B. EVANS (D)
    1976-. Org: State Teachers Assoc. Educ:
Sul Ross State U. 1954 BA. Occ: Teacher. B:
6/27/33. Add: Box 646, Mertzon 76941 (915)
835-4441.

Mesquite. BRUNHILDE WAGNER NYSTROM (R)
    1972-. Bds: Housing Com.; Housing Task
Force; Health Com. Org: BPW; Rep. Women's
Club. Educ: Chicago State U. 1949 BE. Occ:
Swimming Instructor. B: 1/14/26. Add: 1213
Majors Dr., Mesquite 75149 (214)288-7711.

Midlothian. PAT SIBLEY
    235 N. 8th St., P.O. Box 280, Midlothian
76065.

Mineral Wells. LOTTIE J. EUBANKS
    2803 North Murco Dr., Mineral Wells 76067.

Mingus. KATHI NOWAK
    P.O. Box 115, Mingus 76463.

Monahans. VIOLET NELMS POTTS (I)
    1975-. Bds: Regional Planning Com. Party:
State Del. 1972, '74; Precinct Secretary 1976-
77. B: 3/16/33. Add: 1307 S. James, Monahans
79756 (915)943-3335.

Monticello. EDITH CHILDERY
             MARY SMITH
    Rte. 3, P.O. Box 369, Mt. Pleasant 75455.

Morgan. FAY ALLEN
         MRS. JOHNNY L. SPEER
    Hutchison & Mary, Morgan 76671.

Morgan's Point Resort. PATRICIA F. PEEL (D)
    1975-. Bds: Bell Cnty. Health Dept. Org:
Disabled Amer. Veterans. Educ: Sacred Heart
Dom. Coll. 1953 BS. B: 8/10/31. Add: 2
Admiral Cir., Morgan's Pt. Resort 76513
(817)780-1384.

Moulton. ANN HINCIR
    City Hall, Moulton 77975.

Nacogdoches. JUDITH BARRETT MC DONALD (I)
    1977-. Org: Youth Enrichment Service. Occ:
Secretary. B: 2/10/38. Add: 1615 Redbud,
Nacogdoches 75961 (713)569-5304.

Nacogdoches. LA DONNA SIMPSON (I) **
    1973-. Bds: Council of Governments. Org:
Assoc. of Realtors. Occ: Realtor. B: 11/14/41.
Add: 2810 Colonial Dr., Nacogdoches 75961 (713)
564-6418.

Nassau Bay. SHIRLEY S. BOWCOCK (D)
    1976-. Bds: Galveston Area Council. Party:
State Alt. 1974. Org: Nassau Bay Civic Assoc.;
Nasa Area Dems. B: 3/17/32. Add: 1816 Saxony
Ln., Houston 77058 (713)333-2108.

Nassau Bay. MARY ANN HAGGENMAKER (R)
    1970-. Bds: Houston-Galveston Area Council.
Prev: Reg. Cmsnr. 1975-79. Org: ANA; Amer.
Public Health Assoc.; LWV; Cnty. Mayor's &
Councilmen's Assoc. Educ: Catholic U. of
America 1950 BSN; U. of Texas School of Public
Health 1974 MPH. Occ: Nursing School Asst.
Prof. B: 6/17/29. Add: 18322 Blanchmont La.,
Houston 77058 (713)333-2108.

New Braunfels. MARGARET NAEGELIN (D)
    1976-. Mayor Pro Tem. Bds: Community
Council; Finance; Master Plan Up-Date. Org:
Red Cross. Educ: N. Tex. State U. BS; S.W. Tex.
State U. MA. B: 7/29/14. Add: 681 Cross, New
Braunfels 78130 (512)625-3425.

Nolanville. BLANCHE KAISER
    100 Main St., Nolanville 76559.

Nolanville. JUANITA T. SIMS (D)
    1976-. Org: NEA. Occ: Teacher. B: 6/1/17.
Add: 300 N. Main, Nolanville 76559 (817)
698-6335.

Northlake. RUTH FAUGHT
    Rte. 2, Justin 76247.

North Richland Hills. JOAN GOODNIGHT
                       DOROTHY MC CLURE
    7301 N.E. Loop 820, P.O. Box 13305, N.
Richland Hls. 76118.

Oak Ridge. MRS. W.C. COFFMAN
    Rte. 2, Box 45A, Terrell 75160.

Oakwood. FRANCES C. HALE
    P.O. Box 96, Oakwood 75855.

Olmos Park. ELSIE S.MILLER
    119 W. El Prado Dr., San Antonio 78212.

Olton. BILLIE RICHARDS NORFLEET (R)
    1974-. Bds: Natural Resources Adv. Com.;
Dir., Municipal Recreation Ctr.; Criminal
Justice Adv. Com. Org: Recreation Ctr. B:
5/6/27. Add: 410 Ave. G, Olton 79064 (806)
285-2611.

Overton. MARY L. RHODES (D)
    Org: Nat. Assoc. of Realtors; Chamber of
Commerce. Educ: Tex. Real Estate Institute 1969
GRI Occ: Real Estate Broker. B: 2/7/24. Add:
P.O. Box 476 Hwy. 135 at City Limits, Overton

75684 (214)834-3481.

Ovilla. RACHEL HUBER
    Rte. 2, Box 275, Midlothian 76065.

Oyster Creek. SUE KALENDA
    Rt. 2, Box 415, Freeport 77541.

Paint Rock. PATRICIA SUE SIMS (I)
    1973-. B: 5/1/41. Add: Rt. 1, Paint Rock
76866.

Palmhurst. MRS. JOE GONZALEZ
    Rte. 1, Mission 78572.

Pantego. BETTY A. SHEAR (I)
    1974-. Bds: Police Cmsnr.; Ct. Supervisor;
Ch. Civil Defense. Org: Tex. Municipal League;
Dallas Securities Industries Assoc. B:4/27/42.
Add: 3301 Peachtree Ln., Pantego 76013 (817)
274-3585.

Pattison. ELEANOR BULLER (R)
    Bds: Houston & Galveston Area Council.
Party: State Del. 1968, '66; Cnty. Ch. 1967-76.
Org: Tex. State Teachers; Amer. Fed of Teachers.
Educ: U. of Houston 1965 BS; 1971 MA. Occ:
Instructor. B: 10/2/26. Add: Box 31, Brook-
shire 77423 (713)934-2595.

Pattison. MARIE D. PATTISON
    1973-. Mayor Pro Tem. Party: Cnty. Del.
1972. Educ: U. of St. Thomas 1969 BA; Prairie
View U. 1976 MEd. Occ: Teacher. B: 3/5/39.
Add: 1304 Ave. A, Pattison 77466 (713)
934-2585.

Payne Spring. MS. WILLIAMS
    Rt. 2, Mabank 75147.

Pilot Point. ESTELLE M. WHITLEY (D)
    1976-. Bds: Ch., Parks, Recreation, Lighting;
Water & Sewer; Sanitation & Streets. Org: Adv.
Council, Service Program for Aging Needs;
Historical Com.; Historical Society; AARP;
Nat. Retired Teachers Assoc. Educ: N. Tex.
State U. 1938 BA; 1939 MA. B: 10/25/14. Add:
Box 426, Pilot Pt. 76258.

Plainview. JEANE BROWNING
    901 Broadway, P.O. Box 1870, Plainview
79072.

Plano. LOUISE SHERRILL
    1117 15th St., P.O. Box 358, Plano 75074.

Pleasanton. ANTOINETTE G. WATERS (I)
    1973-. Mayor Pro Tem. Org: Chamber of
Commerce; NEA. Occ: Exec. Secretary. B:2/4/21.
Add: 215 Patrick Ave., Pleasanton 78064 (512)
569-3867.

Plum Grove. BRENDA MORROW
    Rte. 4, Box 322, Cleveland 77327.

Point Comfort. BETTY GRIFFITH
    108 Jones, P.O. Box 399, Pt. Comfort 77978.

Ponder. BETTY FOSTER
    Town Hall, Ponder 76259.

Portland. CHARLOTTE RUTH CAMPBELL GRIFFIN (I) **
1973-. Bds: Medical Planning Bd. Party: Del., County Conv.1974. Org: Concerned Citizens for Prevention of Drug Abuse; Legal Secretaries Assoc.; PTO. Occ: Self-employed, Advertising. B: 8/28/38. Add: 142 Catalina Circle, Portland 78374 (512)643-3757.

Poteet. HELEN OPPERMAN
530 Ave. H, P.O. Box 378, Poteet 78065.

Poyner. MRS. BENNIE R. PICKLE
Town Hall, Poyner 75782.

Prosper. VERA CLARY (D) **
1974-. Educ: Tex. Wesleyan Coll. 1936 BA; Tex. Christian U. 1944 MA. B: 1/5/1900. Add: Box 158, Prosper 75078 (214)347-2391.

Quinlan. LOIS CAGLE (D)
1976-. Occ: Garage Owner. B: 5/27/26. Add: P.O. Drawer 309, Quinlan 75474 (214)356-3533.

Refugio. DORIS MARIE MOORE
613 Commerce, Drawer Z, Refugio 78377.

Retreat. JUNE P. CLARK
Rte. 3, Corsicana 75110.

Richardson. MARTHA EVERLING RITTER (R)
1973-. Bds: Cnty. Health Council; General Studies Adv. Com.; Parks & Recreation Cmsn. Party: State Alt. 1974, '76; Precinct Ch. 1972-73. Org: Tex. Assoc. for Services to Children; Rep. Women. Educ: Drake U.1958 BSEd. Occ: Dir. Children's Emergency Shelter. B: 1/22/38. Add: 1505 Melrose Cir., Richardson 75080 (214) 235-8331.

Rio Honda. ERNESTINA SALDIVAR
130 Colorado, P.O. Box 396, Rio Hondo 78583.

Rio Vista. MRS. LONNIE GRAYSON
P.O. Box 347, Rio Vista 76093.

Rio Vista. GEORGIA L. JONES (D)
1975-. Org: OES; PTA. B: 4/7/43. Add: Rt. 1, Rio Vista 76093 (817)373-2588.

Roaring Springs. PEARL PALMER
209 Broadway, P.O. Box 27, Roaring Springs 79256.

Rockdale. MARGIE ABBOTT
140 W. Cameron, P.O. Box 58, Rockdale 76567.

Rollingwood. ERIN CARLSON
LINDA HYDE
403 Nixon Dr., Austin 78746.

Roman Forest. MARYSE IRIZARRY
CAROL WIANKOWSKI
1603 Roman Forest Blvd., P.O. Box 397, New Caney 77357.

Rosebud. PEGGY SMITH
117 N. 2nd St., Box 657, Rosebud 76570.

Rosenberg. LYNETTE SELF **
Prev: Chief Deputy. Org: PTA. Add: 1221 MacArthur St., Rosenberg 77471.

Sabinal. MARJORIE ANGERMILLER
501 N. Center St., Box 83, Sabinal 78881.

Sachse. MOZELLE HOOKER (D)
1976-. B: 8/13/24. Add: Rt. 2, Box 177M, Garland 75040.

Sadler. JANE CRANFORD (D)
1970-. Occ: Beauty Shop Owner. B: 1/11/30. Add: 101 E. Pecan, Sadler 76264.

Saginaw. MRS. DALE REED
404 S. Saginaw Blvd., Saginaw 76079.

St. Jo. HAZEL KAY BELLAL
220 E. Howell St., Box 186, St. Jo 76265.

San Antonio. MARGARET REAVES (D)
1975-. Occ: Real Estate Assoc. B: 4/19/24. Add: 6914 Forest Way, San Antonio 78240 (512)691-1300.

Sanger. MRS. T.W. MC DANIEL
201 Bolivar St., P.O. Box 57, Sanger 76266.

San Patricio. JOAN BLUNTZER
Rte. 2, Box 50, Mathis 78368.

Santa Anna. MRS. GALE A. BROCK
Ave. B & 2nd St., Box 188, Santa Anna 76878.

Schertz. GAIL HYATT (I) **
1975-. Prev: Citizens Advisory Com. 1974-75. Org: FHA. Occ: Secretary, Bookkeeper. B: 6/27/50. Add: 203 B Randolph Ave., Schertz 78154.

Seven Points. FRANCES COOK
Rte. 5, Kemp 75143.

Shenandoah. SHIRLEY CRONHARDT
29400 Driftwood, Conroe 77302.

Shepherd. KATHERINE HUNT CRUMLEY (D)
1972-. Mayor Pro Tem. Bds: Ch., Tax Bd. Prev: Cnty. Housing Coord. 1976-77. Org: Tex. Teachers Assoc.; NEA. Occ: Librarian. B: 4/22/19. Add: P.O. Box 41, Shepherd 77371 (713)628-3349.

Sherman. VIRGINIA E. MORRISS (D) **
1975-. Org: Altrusa; Licensed Child Care Assoc. Occ: Owner-Director Child Care Facilities. B: 12/28/25. Add: 2515 Monte Cristo Dr., Sherman 75090. (214)893-5514.

Shoreacres. MARY S. TAYLOR (D)
1964-. Prev: Zoning Cmsn. 1976; Planning Cmsn. 1960-64; Cnty. Transportation Study 1966-68. Org: Geological Aux.; Conservation & Preservation Assoc.; LWV; Friends of Library. B: 1/9/17. Add: 3546 Miramar Dr., P.O. Drawer A, La Porte, Shoreacres 77571 (713)471-2244.

Silsbee. MARJORIE B. ELDREDGE (D) **
1973-. Bds: Library Policy Com.; Regional Planning Cmsn. Org: Bd. of Realtors; Women's Club. Educ: La. State U. 1946 BS. Occ: Realtor. B: 9/8/25. Add: 1230 Maxwell Dr., Silsbee 77656 (713)385-2863.

Sinton. ROSALIE BROWN (D)
    1975-. Bds: Alt. Repr., Coastal Bend Council
of Govts. Party: Cnty. Del. 1973, '76. Prev:
V-Ch., Urban Renewal; Citizens Adv. Bd. 1967-
69; Bicentennial Cmsn. 1973-77. Org: Women in
Communication; Community Concerns; Chamber of
Commerce; Dem. Women; PTA. Occ: Office Manager.
B: 5/4/19. Add: 802 E. Main, Sinton 78387
(512)364-2381.

Somerset. GLADYS JAMES
    Town Hall, Somerset 78069.

Southmayd. LELA HIVELY
            ANNE TERRY
    P.O. Box 246, Southmayd 76268.

Splendora. HAZEL LUCILLE MC CRACKEN (D) **
    1968-. Org: Nat. Assoc. of Div. Order
Analysts. Educ: U. of Houston 1964 BA. Occ:
Supervisor, Div. Order Analysts. B: 11/15/13.
Add: Lucas Dr., Splendora 77372 (713)689-3197.

Spofford. MRS. FELIZ CASTILLO
           MRS. JOE J. CRUZ
           VIOLA JOHNSON
    P.O. Box 30, Spofford 78882.

Spring Valley. HARRIET LEISSNER
    1025 Campbell Rd., Houston 77055.

Stafford. REGINA AGNELLO
    2610 S. Main St., Stafford 77477.

Stafford. SANDRA B. GABLE (D)
    1975-. Bds: Emergency Com.; Repr., Houston/
Galveston Area Council. Org: Child Welfare Bd.
Occ: Realtor. B: 3/10/36. Add: 12938 Jebbia,
Stafford 77477 (713)499-4537.

Stephenville. BETTY HEATH
    354 N. Belknap St., Stephenville 76401.

Strawn. JENNIFER STEPHEN ELMORE (D) **
    1974-. Bds: Bicentennial Com.; Finance
Commissioner. Party: Local Precinct Secretary
1972-75; Cnty. Com. 1972. Org: Ladies Progressive Club; Teachers Assoc. Educ: Tarleton State
Coll. 1969 BA; Tarleton State Coll. 1973 MAT.
Occ: Teacher. B: 1/16/47. Add: Box 22, Strawn
76475 (817)672-5311.

Sunnyvale. HELEN BENNETT
    Long Crk. Rd., Rt. 2, Box 12, Sunnyvale
75182.

Sunset Valley. FRANCES BRADY UNDERWOOD (D)
    1975-. Bds: Ch., Public Safety; Ch., Budget
& Finance. Org: Women's Club. B: 12/11/23.
Add: 23 Pillow Rd., Sunset Vly., Austin 78745
(512)892-1384.

Sun Valley. JOSIE OSBORNE
    Rte. 2, Paris 75460.

Surfside Beach. CAROLYN CARLTON
                 PAULINE PERKINS
    Rte. 2, Box 485, Freeport 77541.

Sweeny. EDITH ROBERTSON
    111 W. 3rd St., Sweeny 77480.

Taft. MARY SYMA (D)
    1974-. Org: Nat. Real Estate Assoc.;
Chamber of Commerce; Nat. Dem. Party. Occ:
Real Estate Broker. B: 8/26/29. Add: 417
Victoria St., Taft 78390 (512)528-3050.

Tatum. AURELIA CLARK
    P.O. Box 868, Tatum 75691.

Taylor Lake Village. JANE WEIRICK
    1202 Kirby, Seabrook 77586.

Terrell Hills. AMANDA H. OCHSE (R) **
    1973-. Party: Alt., State Conv. 1972-73.
Prev: Historical Survey Com. 1973-75. Org:
Conservation Society. B: 4/28/21. Add:
116 Newbury Terrace, Terrell Hills 78209
(512)824-7401.

Three Rivers. LOUISE SHUMATE (I) **
    1972-. B: 10/12/22. Add: P.O. Box 220,
Three Rivers 78071 (512)786-2591.

Tom Bean. MARY CHUMBLEY
           ELIZABETH FEAGAN
    Britton St., P.O. Box 312, Tom Bean 75489.

Trent. ZULA DARBY
    P.O. Box 11, Trent 79561.

Trinidad. LAMESA LILLICK
    220 Park St., P.O. Box 345, Trinidad 75163.

Trinity. ELIZABETH CAUTHAN (D)
    1975-. Bds: Deep E. Tex. Council of Govts.
Org: Chamber of Commerce. B: 1/15/10. Add:
Trinity 75862 (713)594-2505.

Tuscola. MRS. E.G. HORTON
    Town Hall, Tuscola 79562.

Uncertain. MRS. DETTIE DANAHY
    Rte. 2, Karnack 75661.

Waelder. MARGRET KEMP
    P.O. Box 427, Waelder 78949.

Walnut Springs. MILDRED EHRHARDT
    P.O. Box 272, Walnut Springs

Weatherford. MRS. GERRI K. BURNS
    119 Palo Pinto St., P.O. Box 255, Weatherford
76086.

West Columbia. MRS. FRANK CROCKER
    300 E. Clay St., P.O. Drawer 487, W.
Columbia 77486.

West Columbia. DOROTHY P. MANSEL (I)
    1976-. Bds: Ch., Swimming Pool Com.; Parks
& Recreation Com. Org: Planning Cmsn.; PTA;
OES. Occ: Office Head Clerk. B: 2/24/22.
Add: 1000 S. Columbia Dr., W. Columbia 77486
(713)345-3123.

Westminster. THELMA JEAN HOOD
    E. Side Sq., P.O. Box 616, Westminster 75096.

Weston. VIRGINIA ATKINS
        MARIE PERRY
    P.O. Box 57, Weston 75097.

West Tawakoni. MRS. FERNEY SOUTHALL
    Rte. 1, Quinlan 75474.

West University Place. MARY ANN BINIG (R) **
    1972-. Bds: Council on Aging; Municipal
    League. B: 3/3/30. Add: 6634 Vanderbilt,
    Houston 77005 (713)668-4441.

Westworth Village. NANCY TSIVIS
    311 Burton Hill Rd., Fort Worth 76114.

White Settlement. SHIRLEY KEVIL
    214 Meadow Park Dr., White Settlement 76108.

Willis. FRANCES C. PURSLEY
    P.O. Box 436, Willis 77378.

Winfield. VERA MAE LINKER
    Town Hall, Winfield 75493.

Winnsboro. MADELINE MC CRARY
    201 Locust, P.O. Box 134, Winnsboro 75494.

Woodbranch. MRS. E. LAWSON
    P.O. Box 257, New Caney 77357.

Woodsboro. COLLEEN HENKHAUS
    121 Wood Ave., P.O. Box 63, Woodsboro 78393.

Woodway. CARLEEN BRIGHT
    P.O. Box 7485, Waco 76710.

Judges

RACHEL LITTLEJOHN (D)
    District Judge. 1974-. Bds: Juvenile Bd.
    Org: State Bar of Tex.; ABA; Local Bar Assoc.;
    BPW; AAUW; Family Counseling Assoc.; Dem. Party;
    OES. Educ: Baylor U. 1949 BA; Baylor U. Law
    School 1950 LLB; Texas Women's U. Denton MS.
    B: 6/14/22. Add: 812 E. Corpus Christi St.,
    Beeville 78102 (512)358-1839.

MARY LOU ROBINSON
    Associate Judge, Court of Civil Appeals. Add:
    7th District Courthouse, Amarillo 70186.

State Boards and Commissions

    Office of the Governor, State Capitol Bldg.,
    Austin 78767.

Aging, Committee on
    MRS. PRINTIS E. ELLIS
    LOUISE MASSEY

Arts and Humanities, Commission on the
    MRS. BROOKE BLAKE
    MARY LOU BRAYMER
    MRS. TRAMMELL CROW

    LAUREL DAMMIER
    VEDA W. HODGE
    MRS. W.C. HOLDEN
    MARY MOODY NORTHEN
    MRS. ROY RIDDEL, JR.
    MRS. JOHN M. WALLACE
    MRS. WESLEY WEST

Battleship Texas Commission
    MRS. MACK J. WEBB
    MRS. MURRAY EZZELL

Canvassers, Board of
    MRS. BLAKE SPARENBERG

Children and Youth, Commission on Services to
    VICKI LYNN BAKER
    TERESA DUNLAP
    PATSY DUNCAN
    LINDA ESCOBAR
    MRS. HENRY EWALD
    BRENDA JEFFERS
    MRS. JOHN T. MANRY III
    MRS. CHARLEY PRIDE
    CAROLYN V. WATKINS

College and University System Coordinating Board
    MRS. JESS HAY

Cosmetology Commission
    PEGGY GUTIERREZ

Criminal Justice Council
    CAROL S. VANCE

Cultural Basin Commission
    LILA COCKRELL

Deaf, Commission for the
    AUDREY W. KELTON
    SHIRLEY ANN PACETTI

Developmental Disabilities Planning and Advisory
Council
    CAROL CERVENKA
    MRS. FERRIS CLEMENTS
    MRS. WILLIAM H. WILLIAMS

Education, Board of
    MRS. RONALD SMITH
    JANE H. WELLS

Hearing Aids, Examiners in the Fitting and
Dispensing of
    MARGARETTE E. MAYHALL

Good Neighbor Commission
    MRS. JAMES DAY
    CONNA JEAN NYE

Health Resources, Board of
    MRS.JOHNNIE M. BENSON
    MARIA LA MANTIA

Historical Commission
    MRS. WESLEY B. BLANKENSHIP
    MRS. FRANK M. COVERT
    MRS. FRED M. LANGE
    MARY MOODY NORTHEN

MRS. DAN S. PETTY
MRS. ANICE READ
MRS. D.J. SIBLEY, JR.
MRS. CHARLES R. WOODBURN

Hospital Council Advisory
SISTER AUSTIN CUSIMANO

Intergovernmental Relations, Advisory Commission on
LILA COCKRELL

Kennedy Memorial Commission
JOHNNIE MAE RICE

Library and Historical Commission
MRS. WALTER S. MOORE

Library Examiners, Board of
KATHERINE SKINNER BROWN
HAZEL RICHARDSON

Mental Health and Mental Retardation Commission
MRS. HOWARD E. BUTT
MARGARET CIGARROA
LYNN DARDEN

Nimitz Memorial Naval Museum Commission
MRS. CARY ISENBERG

Nurse Examiners, Board of
EUNICE M. KING
SISTER REGIS MAILLIAN
SISTER MARY VINCENT O'DONNELL

Nursing Home Administrators, Board of Licensure for
MRS. JOHNNIE M. BENSON

Pardons and Paroles, Board of
SELMA WELLS

Physical Fitness, Commission on
MRS. ALAN L. BEAN
IRMA J. CATON
RHEA H. WILLIAMS

Physical Therapy Examiners, Board of
DORIS E. PORTER
HILDA F. MC KETHAN
RUTH WOOD

Private Employment Agency Regulatory Board
MILDRED J. BABICH
MARY E. EVINS
MRS. JESSIE BELLE NEWMAN

Public Accountancy, Board of
PAULINE THOMAS

Real Estate Research Advisory Committee
KATHERINE BOYD

Regents, Board of. A & M University System
MRS. WILMER SMITH

Regents, Board of. Midwestern University
MARY NELL GARRISON

Regents, Board of. Pan American University
MRS. MARIALICE S. SHIVERS

Regents, Board of. University of Texas System
MRS. LYNDON B. JOHNSON

Rehabilitation Commission
MARJORIE C. KASTMAN

San Jacinto Historical Advisory Board
LENNIE E. HUNT

Teacher Education, Board of Examiners for
VIRGINIA ALDERS
EVALYN AXELSON
DONNA BAKER
HENRIETTA BLEND
NORMA G. HERNANDEZ
FRANCES M. PHILLIPS
YOLAND M. REY
EDNA STEPHENSON

Teachers' Professional Practices Commission
VELMA R. BEDFORD
VIVIAN R. BOWSER
MARY LOU GARRISON
MARY E. HINDS
PATRICIA KELLY
NANCY H. RICHIE
EMMA J. TANNER

Technical-Vocational Education, Advisory Council for
GWENDOLYN M. FOSTER
DOROTHY ROBINSON

Teacher Retirement System, Board of Trustees to Administer
ANTOINETTE MILLER

Tuberculosis Advisory Committee
MRS. HERMAN JONES

Tuberculosis Nurse Examiners, Board of
MRS. TRAVIS MC NAIR

Vocational Nurse Examiners, Board of
BESS DAVENPORT
MINNIE B. OTTO
MRS. LOY PATTON
PATRICIA RACHEL
MRS. ARNICE F. SPENCE
MRS. BILLIE JO STEWART
WINNIE O. WARHOL

Youth Camp Safety, Advisory Council on
MRS. GARZA A. BOGGS
LOUISE FARGHER

Youth Council
MRS. ROBERT M. AYRES, JR.

Utah

BETH S. JARMAN (D)
Executive Director, Department of Community Affairs. 1977-. Bds: Ch., Ut. Housing Finance Agency. Party: State Del. 1972, '74, '76; Leg. V-Ch. 1972-74; Leg. Ch. 1974-76; Cnty. Central Com. 1974-76; Cnty. Exec. Com. 1974-76; State Central Com. 1974-76. Prev: State Repr. 1974-76; Administrative Asst. to Governor 1977. Org: NEA; Equal Rights Coalition; Dem. Women's Club; WPC. Educ: U. of Ut. 1964 BA; 1970 MA; 1977 PhD. B: 4/1/41. Add: 2529 E. 13th St. S., Salt Lk. City 84108 (801)533-5236.

State Legislature

State Senate

FRANCIS FARLEY (D)
1418 Federal Way, Salt Lake City 84102.

State House

GENEVIEVE ATWOOD (R)
1975-. Dist: 1. Bds: Ch., Social Services Com.; Ch., Earthquake Hazard Reduction Sub Com.; Natural Resources. Party: Cnty. Del. 1974- ; Prev: Blue Ribbon Energy Policy Task Force 1976; Intergovt. Panel on Science & Technology 1976-80. Org: Geological Society of Amer.; Jr. League; LWV; Common Cause; AAUW; Rep. Women. Educ: Bryn Mawr Coll. 1968 BA; Wesleyan U. 1973 MA. Occ: Geologist. B: 5/4/46. Add: 1216 1st Ave., Salt Lake City 84103.

VERVENE CARLISLE (D)
1971-. Dist: 4. Bds: Dem. Minority Leader of Devt. Services Appropriations Sub Com.; Business, Industrial Devt. & Consumer Concerns; Div. of State History. Party: Salt Lk. Cnty. V-Ch. Dem. 1970-75. Occ: Bank V-Pres. Add: 8 Hillside Ave., Salt Lake City 84103.

WYLLIS DORMAN-LEIGH (D)
634 E. 700 South, Salt Lake City 84102.

GEORGIA B. PETERSON (R)
6417 Highland Dr., Salt Lake City 84121.

BEVERLY WHITE (D)
1971-. Dist: 64. Bds: Ch., Social Services; Leg. Management; Asst. Minority Leader. Party: State Del. 1957-77; Nat. Del. 1968, 64; Nat. Alt. 1972; Dist. Ch.; Cnty. V-Ch. 1960-77; State Secretary 1970-77. Prev: State Bd. of Corrections 1964-70; Governor's Task Force for Disabled 1975-77; Mental Health Adv. Council 1970-77; Halfway House 1970-77; Juvenile Ct. 1971-77.

Org: Women's Club; Cnty. Dem. Women. Occ: Alcohol Program Developer. B: 9/28/28. Add: 122 Russell Ave., Tooele 84074 (801)533-5801.

Mayors

Cannonville. LAURIE DEA HOLLEY
1973-. Org: Nat. Assoc. of Postmasters. Educ: Brigham Young U. BS. Occ: Postmaster. B: 6/18/28. Add: Cannonville 84718 (801) 679-8743.

Cornish. KAY S. NEELEY
City Hall, Cornish 84308.

Francis. FAY MITCHELL
RFD Kamas, Francis 84036.

Virgin. BEULAH SEMMENS
City Hall, Virgin 84779.

Local Councils

Alta. BARBARA M. BANNON
City Hall, Alta 84070.

Altamont. DELAINE TIDWELL
City Hall, Altamont 84001.

Amalga. SHARAN BINGHAM
RFD #1, Smithfield, Amalga 84335.

Boulder. DONNA JEAN WILSON
City Hall, Boulder 84716.

Bountiful. PHYLLIS CLAYTON SOUTHWICK (R)
1974-. Bds: Planning; Power; Retirement. Org: NASW; Women's State Leg. Council; AAUW. Educ: U. of Ut. 1950 BS; 1967 MSW; 1976 DSW. Occ: Social Worker. B: 11/2/26. Add: 1314 E. Millbrook Way, Bountiful 84010 (801) 295-2301.

Cannonbille. ALMA D. FLETCHER
City Hall, Cannonbille 84718.

Centerfield. VAL JEAN HANSEN
City Hall, Centerfield 84622.

Clarkston. LA RAE L. GODFREY
1973-. Bds: Ch., Beautification; Ch., Planning & Zoning. Occ: Supervisor in Workshop for the Handicapped. B: 10/29/28. Add: Clarkston 84305.

Enterprise. JEANNINE H. HOLT (R) **
1973-. Bds: Community Dev.; Beautification; Planning; Zoning; Cnty. Fair Bd.; Ch., Cnty. Scholarship Pageant; Safety Council. Prev:

State PTA Bd. 1969-73. Org: PTA; Rep. Women's Club. Occ: Office Manager. B: 8/18/29. Add: P.O. Box 202, Enterprise 84725 (801)873-2325.

Ferron. JO ANN BEHLING
City Hall, Ferron 84523.

Garland. RUTH SHUMWAY
City Hall, Garland 84312.

Glendale. VIVIAN H. BRINKERHOFF (R)
1976-. B: 4/26/41. Add: Glendale 84729.

Gunnison. PHYLLIS GREENER
City Hall, Gunnison 84634.

Helper. MARY V. REBOL (D)
1974-. Bds: Ch., Bldg's. Com. Party: State Del. 1975. B: 5/23/14. Add: 164 Roosevelt, Helper 84526 (801)472-5391.

Kanosh. KAREN R. GEORGE (R)
1976-. Party: Precinct Leader 1969-70. B: 6/8/43. Add: Box 64, Kanosh 84637 (801) 759-2454.

Kaysville. ANN BUCHANAN
City Hall, Kaysville 84037.

Lehi. JO ANN K. BROWN
City Hall, Lehi 84043.

Lewiston. NORMA A. BODILY (I)
1976-. Org: NEA. Educ:1952 BS. Occ: Teacher. B: 9/11/28. Add: 1030 S. 800 W., Lewiston 84320.

Logan. CAROL WENNERGREN CLAY (R)
1976-. Bds: Recreation Bd. Party: State Del.; Rep. Precinct V-Ch. Prev: Task Force Ch., Forms of Govt. Cmsn. 1975. Org: Women's Leg. Council. Educ: Ut. State U. 1942 BS. B: 3/30/20. Add: 1219 E. 3rd N., Logan 84321 (801)752-3060.

Manila. JEAN G. WILSON
City Hall, Manila 84046.

Mantua. DIANE J. HALL (R)
1975-. Party: Conv. Del. 1975-76. Org: NEA; PTA. Educ: Utah State U. 1965 BFA. Occ: Teacher. B: 3/8/28. Add: Rt. 2, Brigham City 84302 (801)723-7679.

Marysvale. CLEORA PETERSON (D)
1973-. Occ: Agency Manager. B: 11/22/29. Add: Marysvale 84750.

Mendon. YVONNE EARL
City Hall, Mendon 84325.

Milford. LOU JEAN HANLEY (D)
1976-. Bds: Ch., TV Bd.; Volunteer Firemen's Com. Party: State Del. 1976-77, '73, '68; Cnty. Secretary 1972-73; Dist. Secretary 1969-77. B: 2/17/21. Add: Box 234, Milford 84751.

Moab. DIXIE L. BARKER (D)
1975-. Bds: Ch., Parks & Recreation; City-Cnty. Recreation Bd. Party: State Del. 1976, '74, '72; Ch., Dem. Cnty. Party 1969-70. Prev:

Bd., Cnty. Drug & Alcohol 1970-76; Cnty. Economic Devt. 1973-77; Cnty. Travel Council 1970-76. Org: Utah Broadcasters Assoc.; Utah Industrial Devt.; Exec. Assoc.; Chamber of Commerce. Occ: Radio Station Manager. B: 5/25/30. Add: 229 Walker, Moab 84532 (801) 259-5121.

Moab. MARJORIE R. TOMSIC
City Hall, Moab 84532.

Monroe. MURIEL C. MATHIS (R)
1975-. Bds: Ch., Beautification Com.; Planning & Zoning Cmsn.; Ch., Ordinance Book Com. Party: State Del. 1972-73, '75; V-Ch., Cnty. Rep. Party 1973-77; State Committeewoman 1973-74. Prev: School Dist. Adv. Bd. 1973-75; Cnty. Farm Bureau 1972-76. Org: Rep. Women's Club. B: 7/29/25. Add: 187 E. Center, Monroe 84754 (801)527-3511.

Monticello. MRS. PAT HOWELL
City Hall, Monticello 84535.

Moroni. ELSIE CHRISTENSEN
City Hall, Moroni 84646.

New Harmony. VIVIAN PRINCE
City Hall, New Harmony 84757.

North Logan. KAY D. BAKER
2053 No. 1200 East, North Logan 84321.

Ophir. GEORGIA R. RUSSELL
1974-. Occ: Secretary. B: 2/18/32. Add: RD #8, Ophir 84071 (801)882-9931.

Park City. ELEANOR BENNETT
City Hall, Park City 84060.

Parowan. GALE STOIK
City Hall, Parowan 84761.

Randolph. MRS. NATHELL HOFFMAN
City Hall, Randolph 84064.

Richfield. KAY KIMBALL
City Hall, Richfield 84701.

Richmond. FAVELL R. PLANT (R)
1975-. Bds: Ch., Public Bldgs.; Administration & Finance; Parks & Recreation. Party: State Del. 1976; Precinct Sec. 1967-76. Org: League of Cities; Nat. Fed. of Rep. Women. B: 2/21/13. Add: 170 W. Main St., Richmond 84333.

Riverdale. LOIS MANNING
City Hall, Riverdale 84403.

River Heights. JOYCE U. MILLER (R)
1972-. Bds: Utah League of Cities & Towns; Cnty. Com. for Change of Cnty. & Multi-Cnty. Govts. Party: State Alt. 1976; Precinct Ch. 1975-77; Cnty. Steering Com. 1976. Org: Nat. Assoc. of Realtors; Cnty. Women's Leg. Council; Ut. Women's Leg. Council. Occ: Realtor. B: 1/25/30. Add: 487 E. 6th S., Logan 84321 (801)753-5111.

Roosevelt. ELLEN RAWLINGS (D)
1976-. Bds: Planning Bd.; Ch., Beautification;
Ch., Cemetary. Prev: Ch. Bd. of Adjustment 1972-
76; Planning Bd. 1972-77; Cnty. Planning Bd.
1970-76. Org: BPW; Fed. Women's Club; PTA.
Educ: Brigham Young U. 1960 BS. B: 8/4/16. Add:
392 N. 5th St. E., Roosevelt 84066 (801)
722-5001.

Salina. LEAH J. CONOVER (R)
1976-. Bds: Ch., Civic Betterment;Ch., Library
Bd.; Zoning & Planning Com. Party: Cnty. Del.
1976-77. Occ: Bookkeeper/Secretary. B: 3/12/12.
Add: 135 Fast 1st N., Salina 84654 (801)
529-3311.

Scofield. BARBARA LEEK
JOY PODBEVSEK
City Hall, Scofield 84538.

Soldier Summit. NORA EBAUGH
City Hall, Soldier Summit 84658.

Springdale. BARBARA C. FELTON (I)
1976-. Educ: U. of Ariz. 1950 BA. Occ:
Farmer. B: 10/3/26. Add: P.O. Box 371, Springdale 84767.

Tremonton. MARJORIE Z. OYLER
City Hall, Tremonton 84337.

Virgin. MARILYN C. MATTHEWS (R)
1976-. Prev: Town Clerk 1974-76. Occ:
Teachers Aide. B: 7/15/52. Add: Kolob Rd.,
Virgin 84779 (801)635-4966.

Wendover. ELAINE W. DAHLSTROM (R) **
1973-. Org: Ladies Club; PTA. Occ: Administrative Assistant. B: 10/9/41. Add: P.O. Box
331, Wendover 84038 (801)665-2241.

West Bountiful. HARRIET STEPHENS
City Hall, West Bountiful 84087.

Willard. SUE MILLER (D)
1976-. Bds: Ch., Parks. B: 4/5/43. Add:
290 E. 1st S., Willard 84340.

State Boards and Commissions

Office of the Governor, State Capitol Bldg.,
Salt Lake City 84114.

Aging, Board of
STELLA OAKS

Aging Technical Review Committee
REES BENCH
FLORENCE LAWRENCE
RUTH E. PETERSON
CLARA RICHARDS

Agricultural Advisory Board
FLORA H. BARDWELL

Air Conservation Council
LOIS FREDERICK
VIRGINIA D. ROBERTS

Alcoholism and Drugs, Board of
ALICE JENSEN

American Revolution Bicentennial Commission
MARGUERITE COLTON
STEPHANIE CHURCHILL
MARION H. HAZLETON
SARA JENSE
DOROTHEA LIVINGSTON
ELEANOR S. OLSEN
JANET PRAZEN
ELIZABETH VANCE

Black Affairs, Advisory Council on
BERNEICE BINNS
ELSIE BROWN
ALBERTA HENRY
SUE MC INTOSH
RUBY PRICE
DOROTHY WATKINS

Capitol Hill Commission
MARY CHRISTENSEN

Cemetary Board
LYNN S. RICHARDS

Comprehensive Health Planning Advisory Council
MARION BENNION
MARGUERITE BROWN
ALICE CHASE
VIRGINIA COLE
IRENE CUTCH
OLIVE GALLEGOS
DONNA HARMER
MARION HAZLETON
CORALLENE MC KEAN
BERYLE MICHKELSON
MARILYN PARK
MARGERY PETERSON
JANET PRAZEN
IRENE SWEENEY

Consumer Credit, Council of Advisors on
FLORA BARDWELL
ELVA M. BARNES
IRENE JORGENSEN
MARGARET MERKLEY

Contractors Advisory Board
EDITH MELENDEZ

Corrections, Board of
EVELYN W. BROWN

Cosmetology, Board of
ALZINA H. BARTON
FERN H. EWER
BEATRICE G. LUND

Criminal Justice Administration, Council on
BARBARA BURNETT

Defense, Council of
BETH BROWN

Education and Vocational Education, Board of
LILA B. BJORKLUND
JOAN BURNSIDE

Visually Handicapped, Advisory Council for
    JOYCE BARNES
    ANNA S. TAYLOR

Vocational and Technical Education, Advisory Council for
    VERLA COLLINS
    ERNA ERICKSEN
    JOAN HADDEN
    LYNN J. MARSH
    DIANA MOORE
    DIXIE NELSON

Vocational Education, Board for
    LILA BJORKLUND
    JOAN BURNSIDE

Women, Commission on the Status of
    ZELMA B. BRUNDAGE
    BARBARA BURNETT
    IRENE CUCH
    JANET C. GORDON
    BETH GURRISTER
    CHIZUKO ISHIMATSU
    ELMA KLITGAARD
    ELEANOR S. LEWIS
    GAY MC DONOUGH
    ANITA MESTAS
    MARY L. OLSEN
    RUTH ROSS
    PHYLLIS SNOW
    BARBARA STUBBLEFIELD
    JAN L. TYLER

Vermont

State Executive and Cabinet

SISTER ELIZABETH CANDON
    Secretary of the Human Service Agency.
    Montpelier 05602.

State Legislature

State Senate

MADELINE B. HARWOOD (R)
    Bennington County, Manchester Center 05255.

ESTHER HARTIGAN SORRELL (D) **
    Dist: Chittenden, 4-9. Bds: Burlington
Housing Authority; Governor's Cmsn. on Employment
of Handicapped. Party: City & Cnty. Com. Org:
LWV; WPC; Dem. Women's Club. Educ: Trinity Coll.

BA. B: 4/24/20. Add: 23 Hickok Place,
Burlington 05401.

State House

CARMEL ANN BABCOCK (D)
    12 Sky Dr., Burlington 05401.

NANCY DEAN (R)
    Norwich 05055.

MARY EVELTI (D) **
    Dist: Chittenden, 4-8. Party: Clerk of
Ward 1971-74; Exec. Com.; City Com. Educ:
Burdett Coll. Occ: Real Estate Broker;
Medical Recorder. B: 5/16/20. Add: 4 Scarff
Ave., Burlington 05401 (802)864-5858.

THERESA G. FEELEY (D)
    Colchester 05446.

JANE KENDALL GARDNER (D) **
    Dist: Bennington, 2. Occ: Bd. of Dir. of
a Company. B: 12/9/26. Add: Arlington 05250
(802)375-2735.

LORRAINE H. GRAHAM (D) **
    1965-. Dist: Chittenden, 4-4. Bds: Food
Prices & Consumer Policy; Appropriation;
Library Bd.; Dev. Disabilities Legislative
Com. Party: City Membership Ch. 1965-69.
Prev: School Bd. 1970-73. Org: OWL; Dem. Club;
PTO. B: 7/20/25. Add: 280 N. Winooski Ave.,
Burlington 05401 (802)828-2228.

EVELYN L. JARRETT (D) **
    1967-. Dist: Chittenden, 409. Bds: City
Zoning Bd. Party: Platform Com. 1966, 1968;
County Dem. Com. Org: LWV; Vt. Children's
Aid Society; Bd. of Dir., Children's Center.
Occ: Realtor & Exec., Oil Co. B: 9/22/11.
Add: 101 Spruce St., Burlington 05401 (802)
846-5106.

ANNE JUST (D)
    RR 1, Box 141, Warren 05674.

ALTHEA P. KROGER (D)
    1976-. Bds: Govt. Operations Com. Party:
State Del. 1976. Prev: Planning Cmsn. 1974-
76. Org: APSA; Common Cause; Bread & Law Task
Force; Dem. Women's Club; LWV. Educ: St. Louis
U. 1969 BA; U. of Vermont 1974 MA. B: 10/9/46.
Add: 10 Church St., Essex Jct. 05452.

MADELEINE MAY KUNIN (D)
    1972-. Bds: Ch., Appropriations Com.; Emer-
gency Bd.; Joint Fiscal Com. Party: State Del.
1976, '72, '70; Nat. Del. 1976, '75; City Dem.
Com. 1972- ; Cnty. Dem. Com. 1972- . Prev:
Governor's Cmsn. on Status of Women 1964-67;
Governor's Cmsn. on Children & Youth 1972-77;
Governor's Cmsn. on Administration of Justice
1975-77. Org: LWV; ACLU; Common Cause; Dem.
Women. Educ: U. of Mass. 1956 BA; Columbia U.
1957 MS; U. of Vt. 1967 MA. Occ: Writer. B:
9/28/33. Add: 122 Dunber Rd., Burlington
05401 (802)828-2228.

MARY BARBARA MAHER (D) **
Dist: Chittenden, 5-2. Bds: City Planning
Cmsn.; State Election Law Reform Task Force;
Judicial Council; Capitol Complex Cmsn. Party:
City Com.; Cnty. Com. Org: LWV; Dem. Women's
Clubs. B: 4/30/33. Add: Box 2331, 660 Hinesburg
Rd., South Burlington 05401 (802)862-2840.

LUCILLE C. MOLINAROLI (R) **
1966-. Dist: Orange-Washington, 1-2. Org:
BPW; OWL; Altrusa; Women's Club. Occ: Businesswoman. B: 12/13/12. Add: 46 Webster St., Barre
05641 (802)476-3841.

GRETCHEN B. MORSE (R)
Lewis Creek Rd., Charlotte 05445.

EVA M. MORSE-SAYERS (R)
1970-. Dist: WA-2. Party: State Del. 1976,
'74, '72, '70; State Alt. 1968; Treasurer/Clerk
1968-76. Occ: Town Clerk/Treasurer. B:
10/28/38. Add: Calais 05688 (802)828-2228.

NOEL ANNE NEELY (R)
Woodstock 05091.

IRENE DURKEE SMITH (D)
10016 Bellevue Ave., Rutland 05701.

SALLIE SOULE (D)
Willowbank, Charlotte 05445.

MARION W. SPENCER (R) **
1974-. Dist: Addison, 1-2. Bds: Educ. Com.
Prev: School Bd. 1958-74. Org: Audubon Club;
Extension Homemakers; Rep. Women. Educ: Muhlenberg Hospital School of Nursing 1937 RN. B:
1/30/16. Add: RD 1, Box 72, Vergennes 05491.

THERESA D. STANION (D)
1974-. Dist: 2-1. Bds: Commerce Com. Party:
State Del. 1976, '72, '68; Cnty. Dem. Com. 1974-
78; V-Ch., Essex Town Dem. Com. 1974-76. Org:
LWV; AAUW; Cnty. Dem. Women. Educ: Notre Dame
Coll. 1960 BA; SUNY 1971 MA. B: 12/19/38. Add:
4 Wildwood Rd., Essex Junction 05452.

JUDITH B. STEPHANY (D)
1976-. Dist: Chittenden 4-6. Party: State
Alt. 1976; V-Ch., Ward Dem. Com. 1975-77. Org:
LWV; Dem. Women; PTA. Educ: LeMoyne Coll. 1965
BS. B: 6/1/44. Add: 108 Oakland Ter., Burling-
ton 05401.

LOUISE R. SWAINBANK (R) **
1970-. Dist: Caledonia, 1-3. Bds: Gover-
nor's Cmsn. on Status of Women; State Advisory
Com. on U.S. Civil Rights Cmsn.; Governor's
Cmsn. on Higher Educ. Planning. Party: Cnty.
Com. Educ: Smith Coll. 1939 BA. Occ: Teacher.
B: 11/3/17. Add: 49 Summer St., St. Johnsbury
05819 (802)748-3817.

RUTH H. TOWNE (R)
RD 2, Montpelier 05602.

HELEN W. WAKEFIELD (R) **
1973-. Dist: Orange-Windsor, 1. Bds: Vt.
Natural Resources Council; Planning Bd. Party:
State Com. Prev: Town Auditor. Org: Grange;

Historical Societies. B: 9/21/15. Add:
Rte. 2, Randolph 05060 (802)728-5288.

SUSAN HOWARD WEBB (R)
1973-. Bds: House Com. on Health & Welfare.
Prev: Planning Cmsn. 1973-78. B: 8/18/08.
Add: Brooksend, Plymouth 05056 (802)828-2228.

SADIE LUCY WHITE (D) *
1966-. Dist: Chittenden, 4-7. Org: Dem.
Women's Clubs. B: 12/9/01. Add: 89 Blodgett
St., Burlington 05401 (802)864-4679.

County Commissions

Chittenden. JANE L. WHEEL
County Court House, Burlington 05401.

Essex. VELMA C. AMES
County Court House, Guildhall

Washington. MARILYN M. DURANLEAU (R)
1975-. Party: State Del. 1968; Secretary,
Town Rep. Com. 1968-70; Repr., Cnty. Rep.
Com. 1974-75. Org: Vt. Asst. Judges Assoc.
Educ: U.C.L.A. 1960 AA. B: 8/12/24. Add:
Box 492, Barre 05641 (802)223-2091.

Townships

Athens. VERNA M. STEVENS (I)
1977-. Occ: Clerk. B: 5/3/17. Add:
Cemetery Rd., Athens 05141 (802)869-2394.

Bennington. LORRAINE N. EASTMAN (D)
1976-. Bds: Recreation Cmsn.; Opportunity
Council; Tax Stabilization Com.; Adv. Cmsn. on
Special Educ. 1977-79; Child Find Coord. of
S.W. Vt. 1977- . Prev: Governor's Wage Bd.
1958-59. Org: AAUW; Dem. Party; NEA; Amer.
Assoc. of Mental Deficiency. Educ: American
U. 1951 BA; Russell Sage Coll. 1971 MS. Occ:
Special Educ. Teacher. B: 11/4/28. Add:
169 North St., Bennington 05201 (802)
442-2626.

Brandon. DEBBIE KIRBY
Brandon 05733.

Brandon. MIM WELTON (D)
1977-. Party: Local V-Ch., Dem. Party 1976-.
Prev: Bd. of Zoning Adjustment 1975-77. Org:
Chamber of Commerce. Educ: Wagner Coll. 1951
BA. Occ: Newspaper Editor. B: 8/28/30. Add:
P.O. Box 207, Brandon 05733 (802)242-5721.

Brattleboro. HANNA K. COSMAN
City Hall, 3 Green Meadow, Brattleboro
05301.

Castleton. ELEANOR T. ANDERSON (R)
1975-. Party: State Alt. Prev: Justice
of the Peace 1973-75. Org: Women's Club.
Educ: Castleton State Coll. 1959 BSEd. Occ:
Teacher. B: 2/1/29. Add: E. Hubbardton Rd.,
Castleton 05735.

Dorset. KAREN BOVEY
        City Hall, Dorset 05251.

Dover. PHYLLIS C. SHIPPEE (R)
        1972-. Bds: Bicentennial Com.; Planning
Cmsnr. Prev: Bd. of Adjustment 1967-70; Finance
Com. 1973-76. Org: Parent-Teacher Club. B:
11/11/18. Add: Town Office, W. Dover 05356
(802)464-5100.

Dover. DIANA S. STUGGER (I)
        1975-. Prev: Planning Cmsn. 1972-75. Educ:
Mt. Holyoke Coll. 1965 BA. Occ: Asst. Manager
Ski Area. B: 11/30/43. Add: W. Dover 05356
(802)464-8000.

East Haven. CARRIE D. HAZARD
        East Haven 05837.

Elmore. MARY HOISINGTON
        City Hall, Lake Elmore 05657.

Essex. ANN P. HARROUN (D)
        1976-. Bds: Water Quality Management Com.
Party: State Del. 1960; State Alt. 1964; Precinct
Ch. 1960-64. Prev: Vlg. Clerk 1971-73; Planning
Cmsn. 1972-76; Recreation Com. 1973-74. Org:
LWV; Vt. Bikeways Coalition; Natural Resources
Council. B: 5/20/35. Add: 14 Wildwood Dr.,
Essex Jct. 05452 (802)879-0413.

Essex. BARBARA A. HIGGINS (R) **
        1974-. Prev: Clerk 1974-75; Tax Collector
1973-74. Org: LWV. Educ: U. of Vt. 1969 BA.
Occ: Assistant to Dir. B: 6/20/47. Add:
7 Cindy La., Essex Jct. 05452.

Essex Junction. MARY K. GAUTHIER (D)
        1975-. Bds: Water Bd.; Fire Warden. Party:
State Del. 1976; Town Committeewoman 1976-78.
Prev: Planning Cmsn. 1974-75. B: 4/23/40. Add:
50 West St., Essex Jct. 05452.

Grafton. MARGERY HAYES HEINDEL (I)
        1975-. Org: Amer. Occupational Therapy
Assoc.; Grafton Improvement Assoc.; Women's
Community Club. Educ: Tufts U. 1945 OTR. Occ:
Occupational Therapist. B: 9/3/23. Add:
Grafton 05146 (802)843-2419.

Greensboro. ELIZABETH E. WATSON
        1977-. Bds: Planning Cmsn. Prev: School
Dir. Occ: Real Estate Broker. B: 12/31/21.
Add: Box 158, Greensboro 05841 (802)533-2651.

Hartford. JUDITH BETTIS
        City Hall, W. Hartford Rd., White River Jct.
05001.

Hartland. DOROTHY H. CRANDALL (I)
        1976-. Bds: Town Planning Cmsn. Prev: Town
Planning Cmsn. 1974-76. Org: PTA; Smithsonian
Institute. Educ: Simmons Coll. 1932 BS. B:
11/20/11. Add: RD #1, Windsor 05089 (802)
436-2119.

Highgate. HYACINTHE BEAULIEU
        City Hall, RFD #1, Highgate Center 05459.

Johnson. FLORENCE C. LEVESQUE (R)
        1976-. Bds: Ch., Com. to Investigate Town
Manager Concept. Org: Cnty. Devt. Council.
Occ: Bookkeeper. B: 3/28/33. Add: Main St.,
P.O. Box 217, Johnson 05656 (802)635-2611.

Manchester Center. LOIS WILEY MATTISON (I)
        1973-. Bds: Civil Bd. of Authority. Prev:
Zoning Bd. of Adjustment 1972-73; Civil Bd. of
Authority 1973-77. B: 7/24/14. Add: Barnum-
ville Rd., Manchester 05255 (807)367-1313.

Marshfield. JEAN MATTHEW (D)
        1976-. Bds: Planning Cmsn.; Bd. of Civil
Authority. Party: Ch. Local 1975-77. B:
10/25/44. Add: Box 29, Marshfield 05658
(802)426-3305.

Middlebury. MARGARET F. MARTIN (I)
        1972-. Bds: Planning Cmsn.; Ch., Hwy. Study
Com.; School Bd. Prev: Planning Cmsn. 1971-72.
Org: LWV. Educ: Oberlin Coll. 1954 BA; Cornell
U. 1955 MEd. Occ: Mental Health Services Exec.
Dir. B: 11/30/31. Add: 33 Seminary St.,
Middlebury 05753.

Middlebury. ALICE WRIGHT
        City Hall, Middlebury 05753.

Montgomery Center. BEATRICE M. CHAFFEE (I)
        1972-. B: 12/9/16. Add: Main St.,
Montgomery Ctr. 05471 (802)326-4719.

Moretown. EUNICE FERRIS
        Moretown 05660.

Newark. CAROL J. KETCHAM (I)
        1973-. Bds: N.E. Vt. Devt. Assoc. Party:
Cnty. Secretary-Treasurer 1970-76. Org: Chamber
of Commerce. Occ: Office Manager. Add: RFD
Newark, W. Burke 05871.

Newfane. KATHLEEN B. SLATE (D)
        1975-. Bds: Ch., Bicentennial Com. Party:
Town Ch. 1960-68; Cnty. V-Ch. 1964-68. Occ:
Proofreader. B: 2/4/23. Add: RR #1, Box 171,
Newfane 05345 (802)365-7991.

New Haven. MARY PALMER MARSH (R)
        1976-. Bds: Cnty. Reg. Planning Com.
Party: State Alt. 1960; Secretary-Treasurer,
Rep. Com. 1952-75; Secretary, Rep. Com. 1975-77;
Del., Cnty. Rep. Com. 1962-64, 1975-77. Prev:
Town Clerk 1976-77; Civil Defense Dir. 1950-75;
Women's Civil Defense Adv. Bd. 1955-57. Org:
Women's Rep. Club; League of Vt. Writers.
Occ: Freelance Writer. B: 3/13/28. Add:
Beech Hill Rd., RD 1, New Haven 05472 (802)
453-3516.

Norwich. ALICE FLANNERY
        City Hall, Norwich 05055.

Pawlet. NATALE SMITH
        Pawlet 05761.

Pittsford. MARY C. CRAHAN
        City Hall, Pittsford 05763.

Pomfret. DOROTHY MOORE
    City Hall, North Pomfret 05053.

Roxbury. MARY JENNINGS
    City Hall, Roxbury 05669.

Stannard. MARGARET V. NICELY (D)
    1977-. Prev: Bicentennial Ch. 1976. Org:
Youth Service Group. Occ: Volunteers in Service
to Amer.-Dir., Hardwick Area Resource Group.
B: 9/29/40. Add: RFD Stannard 05842 (802)
533-2577.

Stannard. REGINA D. TROIANO (D)
    1975-. Bds: Bd. of Civil Authority. Prev:
Auditor 1974-75. Org: Women's Club. B: 3/29/47.
Add: RFD, E. Hardwick 05836 (802)533-2577.

Sunderland. MILDRED K. FERSH (D)
    1975-. Party: State Alt. 1976; Cnty. Dem.
Com. 1974-77; Secretary, Dem. Com. 1972-77.
Prev: Justice of the Peace 1974-76. Org:
Retired Teachers Assoc. Educ: NYU 1941 BS. B:
12/31/19. Add: Box 236, Earlington 05252.

Thetford. VIRGINIA S. BABCOCK
    Post Mills 05058.

Warren. LIZI FORTNA
    Warren 05674.

Waterbury. THERESA WOODWARD
    City Hall, Loomis Hill, Waterbury Center
05677.

West Haven. NANCY L. BURNS (R)
    1975-. Bds: Bd. of Civil Authority. Party:
State Alt. 1976. Educ: Prescott Coll. 1971 BA.
Occ: Farmer. B: 7/22/48. Add: RFD W. Haven
05743 (802)265-4291.

Westminster. BARBARA F. HURLEY
    RFD #3, Putney 05346.

Williston. JEANETTE J. ROUNDS
    1977-. B: 4/30/42. Add: RD 2, Box 288,
Williston 05495.

Wilmington. DENISE ALLEN
             JEAN CANEDY
    Wilmington 05363.

Worcester. MARY A. EVANS (R)
    1977-. Party: State Alt. 1976; Cnty. Committee-
woman 1975-77; Town Committeewoman 1975-77. Prev:
Town Service Officer 1975-77. Org: Bicentennial
Com.; Adv. Bd., Regional Medical Program. Educ:
U. of Wis. 1970 BA. Occ: Office Manager. B:
6/27/48. Add: Hampshire Hl., Worcester 05682
(802)223-2835.

Mayors

Brandon. PATRICIA SCOTT
    City Hall, Brandon 05733.

Panton. ELINOR SULLIVAN ADAMS (D)
    1974-. Bds: Bd. of Civil Authority. Prev:
School Dir. 1946-54. Occ: Teacher. B: 11/2/20.
Add: RD #3, Vergennes 05491 (802)475-2518.

Pittsfield. CHARLOTTE F. MILLS
    1975-. Bds: Planning Cmsn.; Fuel Coord.;
Ch., Bd. of Selectmen. Prev: Town Auditor
1973-75; Bicentennial Com. 1975- . Org:
Pittsfield Civic Club. Educ: Champlain Coll.
1963 ASS; Castleton State Coll. 1972 BS. Occ:
Elementary Teacher. B: 2/28/44. Add: Upr.
Mich. Rd., Pittsfield 05762 (802)746-8106.

Wilmington. SONIA DE LURY
    City Hall, Wilmington 05363.

Local Councils

Barre. FRANCES FLORUCCI
    Barre 05641.

Burlington. ELAINE M. CHARBONEAU
             BARBARA M. REUSCHEL
             JANET K. STACKPOLE
    City Hall, Burlington 05401.

Montpelier. JANICE ABAIR
             SARA RICE
    Montpelier 05602.

Rutland. ETHEL WING STEARNS (R)
    1960-. Party: State Del. 1970, '68, '67,
'65; City-Cnty. Treasurer 1965-76. Occ:
Court Officer Superior. B: 5/19/1900. Add:
57 Prospect, Rutland 05701 (802)775-5763.

St. Albans. ROSANNA F. GUYETTE (D)
    1976-. Bds: Ch., Liquor Bd.; Ch., Police
Cmsn.; Ch., Finance. Prev: Ch., Police 1976-
77; Public Works 1976-77; Finance. B: 9/24/32.
Add: 18 Russell, St. Albans 05478 (802)
534-4982.

St. Albans. JANET L. SMITH
    City Hall, St. Albans 05478.

South Burlington. CATHERINE M. NEUBERT
    City Hall, So. Burlington 05401.

Winooski. FLORENCE R. THABAULT (D)
    1976-. Prev: Ch., Library Bd. Org: Dem.
Women's Club. B: 12/26/13. Add: 36 Hood St.,
Winooski 05404 (802)655-0457.

State Boards and Commissions

    Office of the Governor, State Capitol Bldg.,
Montpelier 05602.

Administrative Coordination, Advisory Committee
on
    ESTHER H. SORRELL

Adult Education, Advisory Council on
    ESTHER H. COHEN
    MARIA A. KUCK
    ELLEN REID
    PEARL SOMAINI

Aging, Advisory Board to the Office on
    THERESA BRUNGARDT
    JOYCE CORNING
    HELEN CHAP

MRS. WALTER S. EDSALL
MRS. RAYMOND GRISWOLD
GENEVA HAYES
JUNE HOLMES
MARGUERITE LILLICRAP
MRS. ROYCE S. PITKIN
MARGARET WHITTLESEY

Air Quality Variance Board
HILDA WHITE

Alcohol Advisory Council
SUSAN HOPWOOD
JOAN KAYE
REGINA WALSH

Alcohol and Drug Abuse Education, Advisory Council on
MARIA ALBEE
ANNE A. BROSS
JEANNIE M. PILLSBURY

Arts and Crafts Advisory Council
HELEN S. BECKERHOFF
IRMA M. HEBARD
ANGELA HINCHEY

Arts, Board of Trustees of Council on the
MARILYNN ALEXANDER
MRS. FRANKLIN BILLINGS
JUDITH BROWN
MELISSA BROWN
KAREN MEYER

Bicentennial Commission
CATHERINE BEATTIE
GEORGIANA BRUSH
LILIAN CARLISLE
MADELINE B. HARWOOD
ELLEN MC CULLOUGH-LOVELL

Camel's Hump Forest Reserve Commission
ALICE DELONG
ERLENE BRAGG
MARY REAGAN

Certification Appeals Committee
LOUISE D. BARNES
LAURA K. HATHORN
MARGARET F. RAYMOND
BETTE STONE

Certification Review Board
SHIRLEY AITCHISON
ADELLE CLEWLEY
MARY C. CRAHAN
EVELYN DIKE
MARY D. GRAHAM
SHIRLEY HATHAWAY
AMY VANDERPOOL

Children and Youth, Committee on
ANNE BROSS
JOANNE E. CRISMAN
XAVIERIA EICHOLTZ
SUZANNE GIROUX
BARBARA GOLDMAN
EVELYN L. JARRETT
RUBY P. JENNESS
MADELEINE KUNIN

LISA MONAHAN
MARGARET F. MARTIN
ELEANOR C. PAINE
SARAH G. SMITH
JOAN SOLOMON
LINDA TOBORG
JANE WHEEL

Criminal Justice Training Council
GLORIA GIL

Comprehensive Employment and Training Council
ELSIE BERRY
SANDRA D. DRAGON
GLORIA GIL
EMMA HARWOOD
CONSTANCE L. KITE
AMY SYRI
VICTORIA TARDY

Cosmetology, Board of
BEVERLY DE MARINIS
PRISCILLA WIER

Dental Examiners, Board of
BARBARA HISELER
JEAN MEYER

Development and Community Affairs Advisory Board, Agency of
CAROL SIEGEL

Drug Rehabilitation Commission
MARGARET CHRISTOWE

Education, Board of
MARIE P. CONDON
JOAN HOFF
BARBARA W. SNELLING

Educational Advisory Council
MARILYNN ALEXANDER
ANNETTE BABCOCK
POLLY BISSON
MARIA BOVE
ALICE M. CHAPMAN
MONA MARY CSIZMESIA
JEAN S. DAVIES
JENNIFER HENDERSON
CHRISTINE HUTCHINS
SISTER CHRISTINE MORIARTY
MARY PIERCE
MARTHA PRINSEN

Educational Television Broadcasting Council
SISTER ELIZABETH CANDON
SISTER MARTHA O'BRIEN
RUTH W. PAGE
ANN REYNOLDS
JUDITH B.SAURMAN
ESTHER H. SORRELL

Elections, Board of
CATHERINE FRANK
FAITH PERRY

Employment Security Advisory Council
MADELYN S. DAVIDSON
PHYLLIS GRAHAM

Energy Policy Advisory Board
    FAITH PRIOR
    LOUISE SWAINBANK

Environmental Board
    MARGARET GARLAND

Forest Festival Week Committee
    CAROLYN ADLER
    SYLVIA FERRY
    DOROTHY P. SHEA

Handicapped, Committee on Employment of the
    EVELYN CANDON
    THEODORA CURTIS
    FAIRE EDWARDS
    EMMA HARWOOD
    CHRYSS A. JONES
    SALLY E. WILKINS

Health Board
    BARBARA GOLDMAN
    MRS. GEORGE B. MC KEON

Health Planning Advisory Council
    BETH ALLEN
    FLORA COUTTS
    JOYCE FELLOWS
    KATHLEEN HOUSE
    BARBARA LEAVENS
    MARY LEAVITT
    PATRICIA MULLEN
    BEVERLY O'NEILL
    LYDIA RATCLIFF
    CLARA THERRIEN
    ANN WALLEN

Higher Education Planning Commission
    SISTER ELIZABETH CANDON
    FLORENCE L. ROBILLARD
    LOUISE SWAINBANK

Hospital Advisory Council
    MARJORIE P. HOYT
    FRANCES S. MYERS
    BARBARA W. RICHARDS
    SISTER RITA VALLEE

Housing Authority
    LILIANE G. BROWN
    JUDITH O'BRIEN

Housing Finance Agency
    LYNN ALEXANDER

Human Rights, Commission on
    JENNIE C. HAYES
    MARGARET LUCENTI

Human Services Board
    MAUD E. DEVEREUX
    EMMA HARWOOD

Instructional Television Committee
    SHIRLEY BERESFORD
    SISTER CECILE BOUCHARD
    KARLENE V. RUSSELL

Interagency Craft Council
    SABRA JOHNSON
    LUELLA SCHROEDER
    LANDA WEISSMAN

Judicial Council
    BETTY A. KELLEY
    SUSAN RAVN

Judicial Selection Board
    RUTH P. BOGORAD

Justice, Commission on the Administration of
    DOROTHY B. ALLEN
    SUSAN K. BAKER
    GLORIA GIL
    MADELEINE KUNIN
    JUDY P. ROSENSTREICH

Libraries, Board of
    LORNA CROSS
    JEAN SWAIN
    MURIEL THOMAS
    JANICE WATERBURY

Library Services and Construction Act Advisory
Council
    ALICE BAYLES
    FRANCES G. CURTIS
    LORNA WHITEHORNE

Mental Health, Board of
    KAREN DRAPER
    HELEN DRELL
    SISTER JANICE RYAN

Mobile and Manufactured Housing, Advisory
Commission on
    LILIAN CARLISLE
    GRACE J. MC GUIRE

Municipal Bond Bank
    ANN H. SARGENT

Natural Gas and Oil Resources Board
    LUCILLE C. MOLINAROLI

Nursing, Board of
    MABEL M. BULEY
    MARY EDWARDS
    FAITH G. EMERSON
    ROSEMARY HITTLE
    HILDA PACKARD
    STELLA SKIBNIOWSKY

Nursing Home Administrators, Board of Examiners
for
    ELAINE ARMSTRONG
    LORRAINE DAY
    HAZEL PARRY

Opticians, Board of
    MARY MOORE

Optometry, Board of
    RENE LA PLANTE

Parole, Board of
FAITH OGDEN

Physical Therapy Registration
ELAINE M. ANDERSON
JUDITH COLBATH
INA KANE
DONNA KEEFE

Public Records Advisory Board
JEANNE L. ROUSSE

Radio and Television Technicians Licensing Board
JACQUELINE M. CORCORAN
JANET DIAZ

Real Estate Commission
MARY W. DAVIS LANDMAN

Recreation, Board of
DEBORAH BARLOW

Special Education, Advisory Council on
ARLENE ADAMS
ROBERTA COFFIN
JEAN GARVIN
SUSAN HASAZI
LOIS HOLBROOK
JANICE JOHNSON
JANE PAFFORD
DONNALEEN PARRISH
ELLEN REID
SISTER JANICE RYAN
KAY STAMBLER
GLORIA WASHBURNE
SUSAN WATSON
MARY WILSON
PATRICIA WRIGHT

State Colleges Board
JANET F. GILLETTE
MAUREEN MC NAMARA
RUTH W. PAGE
MARY F. TAYLOR

State Employees Compensation Review Board
JACQUEL-ANNE CHOUINARD

State Personnel Board
JACQUEL-ANNE CHOUINARD

State Planners
LUCINDA M. JONES

Student Assistance Corporation Board
MRS. DOMINIC FLORY

Student Interns in State Government, Council for
JEANNETTE FOLTA

Transportation Board
KATHLEEN D. WENDLING

Travel Information Council
EDNA M. COUTURE
HELEN L. MOORE

University of Vermont and State Agricultural
College, Board of Trustees of
MADELINE B. HARWOOD
CAREY H. HOWLETT
LOUISE R. SWAINBANK

Vocational-Technical Education, Advisory Council
for
CAROL CANTWELL
CELIA GEHLBACH
CONSTANCE L. KITE
SYLVIA MORSE
ELIZABETH RALPH
JANE STICKNEY

Women, Commission on the Status of
MARION ENGLISH
MARTHA FORSYTHE
GLORIA GIL
EMMA HARWOOD
KATHLEEN F. HOYT
IRIS LASH
JUDY G. MC ENTYRE
PHOEBE MORSE
MRS. THOMAS P. SALMON
LOUISE SWAINBANK
DOLORES STOCKER
JEANETTE SHERMAN
HELENA URE

Virginia

State Executive and Cabinet

PATRICIA R. PERKINSON (I)

Secretary of State. 1974-. Bds: Va. Interstate Cooperation Cmsn.; St.Leg. Conf.; Fiscal Affairs & Govt. Operations Com. Prev: Governor's Administrative Asst. 1966-70. Org: Richmond Public Relations Assoc. Educ: Richmond Professional Institute 1946 BS. B: 7/18/25. Add: 7702 Pinehill Dr., Richmond 23228 (804)786-2441.

State Legislature

State House

EVELYN HAILEY (D)

1973-. Dist: 39. Bds: Health, Welfare & Institutions; Conservation & Natural Resources; Agriculture. Party: State Del. 1976. Org: Winona Lafayette Civic Club; Tidewater Mental Health Assoc.; LWV. B: 4/12/21. Add: 1535 Versailles Ave., Norfolk 23509 (804)627-1546.

JOAN SHEPHERD JONES (D)

1973-. Dist: 11. Bds: House Educ. Com.; House Health Com.; Solid Waste Cmsn. Prev: School Bd. 1965-71. Org: LWV; WPC; Young Dem's. Educ: Wells Coll. 1948 BA; Lynchburg Coll. 1977 MEd. B:6/6/26. Add: 2209 Falcon Hl. Pl., Lynchburg 24503 (804)846-7295.

MARY A. MARSHALL (D)

1965-. Dist: 22. Bds: Ch., Leg. Cmsn. on the Needs of Elderly Virginians; Health, Welfare & Institutions Com.; Cities & Towns Com. Party: State Del. 1960, '64,'68; Nat. Del. 1964; Ch., Arlington Cnty. Dem. Com. 1961-63; Dem. State Central Com. 1977-79. Prev: State Library Bd. 1968-72, 1975-77; Joint Leg. Com. on Alcohol & Drug Abuse 1975-77. Org: BPW; Va. Assoc. on Aging; LWV; Nat. Assoc. for Mental Health; N. Va. Assoc. for Retarded Citizens; Va. Assoc. for Mental Health; Fed. of Dem. Women's Clubs; Young Dem. Club; AAUW. Educ: Swarthmore Coll. 1942 BA. B: 6/14/21. Add: 2256 N. Wakefield St., Arlington 22207 (703)786-8826.

DOROTHY S. MC DIARMID (D)

1959-. Dist: 18. Party: State Alt. 1976. Educ: Swarthmore Coll. 1929 BA. B: 10/22/06. Add: 9950 Meadowlark Rd., Vienna 22180.

BONNIE L. PAUL (R)

1975-. Bds: Agriculture Com.; General Laws Com.; Overall Adv. Council on Needs of Handicapped Children & Adults. Party: State Del. 1965-77; Nat. Del. 1976; Secretary, City Com. 1972-74. Prev: Dir., Shenadoah Vly. Soil &

Water Conservation Dist. 1973-75; Va. Public Telecommunication Council 1973-77. Org: Rep. Women's Club; PTA. Educ: Wilson Coll. 1962 BA. B: 6/6/40. Add: 504 S. Mason St., Harrisonburg 22801 (703)433-9166.

EVA MAE SCOTT (I) **

1972-. Dist: 31. Educ: Medical Coll. of Va., School of Pharmacy BS. Occ: Pharmacist. B: 5/6/26. Add: Rt. 1, Box 153B, Church Road 23833.

ELEANOR PARKER SHEPPARD (D) **

1968-. Dist: 33. Bds: Ch., House Educ. Com.; Finance Com.; Health, Welfare & Institutions; Cmsn. on the Status of Women; Educ. Cmsn. of the States; Services Bd. Prev: Councilwoman 1954-67; Mayor 1962-64; V-Mayor 1960-62. Org: BPW; PTA; Soroptimist. B: 7/24/07. Add: 1601 Princeton Rd., Richmond 23227 (804) 770-6700.

County Commissions

Albermarle. OPAL D. DAVID (D)

1975-. Bds: Planning Cmsn.; Urban Area Transporation Re-Study; NW Va. Health Systems Agency. Party: State Del. 1976; Cnty. Precinct Com. 1975-77. Educ: George Wash. U. 1940 BA. B: 9/9/06. Add: Rt. 5, Box 335-B, Charlottesville 22901.

Arlington. ELLEN M. BOZMAN (I)

1974-. Bds: Ch., N. Va. Planning Dist. Cmsn.; Ch., Health Center Cmsn.; Council of Govts. Party: Exec. Com. Arlingtonians for a Better Cnty. 1971-77. Prev: Planning Cmsn. 1971-73; Regional Park Authority 1963-67. Org: LWV. Educ: Northeastern U. 1946 BS. B: 4/21/25. Add: 4219 39th St. N, Arlington 22207 (703) 558-2261.

Arlington. DOROTHY TAPPE GROTOS (I)

1976-. Bds: N. Va. Planning Cmsn.; Regional Resources; Water Bd. Party: V-Ch., Cnty. Rep. Party 1972-74. Prev: N. Va. Park Authority Bd. 1967-71; Parks & Recreation Com. 1973-75; Nature Center Adv. Bd. 1972-74; Conservation Ch. 1966-69. Org: LWV; Women's Rep. Club; PTA. Educ: Southern State of Conn. 1952 BS; Cornell U. 1953 MS. B: 2/7/31. Add: 207 N. Irving St., Arlington 22201 (703)558-2261.

Botetourt. MARY D. PAULEY (D) **

1971-. Dist: Fincastle. Bds: Health Com.; River Com. Org: Dem. Women's Club; Improvement Assoc.; PTA. Educ: Chesapeake & Ohio School of Nursing 1951 RN. Occ: RN. B: 10/20/30. Add: Rt. 1, Eagle Rock 24085 (703)473-2816.

Buckingham. BETTIE D. MAXEY
Buckingham 23921.

Chesterfield. JOAN GIRONE (R)
1975-. Bds: Cmsnr., Regional Planning Dist.
Cmsn.; Agency on Aging; Personnel Com. Party:
State Del. 1972-76; Precinct Leader 1970-
Prev: Bd., Capitol Area Agency on Aging 1972-
Org: Rep. Women's Club; Cnty. Rep. Com. B:
8/30/27. Add: 2609 Dovershire Rd., Bon Air
23235 (800)748-1200.

Craig. MARY DOT CRUSH
1975-. Bds: Public Service Authority.
Party: State Del. 1976. Org: Improvement Assoc.;
PTA. B: 12/31/18. Add: Rt. 1, Box 56, 902
Meadow Ave., New Castle 24127 (703)864-6363.

Dickenson. BUELAH S. LAMBERT
County Bldg., Clinton 24228.

Fairfax. AUDREY C. MOORE (D) **
1972-. Dist: Annandale. Educ: U. of NH
1950 BA. B: 12/28/28. Add: 4104 Pineridge Dr.,
Annandale 22003 (703)256-4983.

Fairfax. MARTHA PENNINO (D) **
1967-. Dist: Centreville. Prev: Councilwoman 1962-67. Org: Common Cause; NOW; Civic
Assoc.; PTA. Educ: Emerson Coll. 1940 BA. B:
3/7/18. Add: 246 E. Maple Ave., Vienna 22180
(703)938-7993.

Fairfax. MARIE TRAVESKY
County Bldg., Fairfax 22030.

Hanover. NINA K. PEACE (D)
1975-. Bds: Recreation Cmsn.; Welfare Bd.;
Special Educ. Com. Party: State Del. 1976;
Local Committeewoman 1976. Org: Va. Bar Assoc.;
Young Dems. Educ: Goucher Coll. 1972 BA;
Georgetown U. 1973 JD. Occ: Atty. B: 8/1/50.
Add: Rt. 1, Box 25, Ashland 23005.

Prince William. ALICE E. HUMPHRIES (D)
1976-. Bds: Emergency Medical Services
Coord. Council; Disaster & Emergency Preparedness. Party: State Del. 1975-76; Ch., Cnty.
Dist. 1974-75. Org: Civic Assoc. Dem. Com.;
PTA. B: 9/13/37. Add: 13711 Joyce Rd., Woodbridge 22191 (703)368-9171.

Prince William. KATHLEEN SEEFELDT (D)
1976-. Bds: N. Va. Dist. Planning Cmsn.
Org: Lake Ridge Civic Assoc. Educ: Coll. of
St. Scholastica 1956 BA. B: 11/12/34. Add:
12991 Orleans St., Woodbridge 22192 (703)
368-0400.

Roanoke. MAY W. JOHNSON
County Bldg., Salem 24153.

Rockingham. WANDA DRIVER WILT (R)
1975-. Bds: Ch, Planning Com.; Buildings &
Grounds. Party: State Del. 1977. Org: Rep.
Women's Club. Occ: Television Advertising Sales.
B: 7/23/34. Add: 163 Third, Broadway 22815
(703)434-5941.

Smyth. MRS. CALLIE W. HOOVER
County Bldg., Marion 24354.

Warren. ELIZABETH W. MALTA
County Bldg., Front Royal 22630.

Wise. IRIS M. HENRY
County Bldg., Wise 24293.

York. SHIRLEY F. COOPER
County Bldg., Yorktown 23490.

Mayors

Accomac. MARY ALICE HEFFNER (D)
1974-. Org: NASW; Rural Health Initiative
Bd.; DAR. Educ: Goucher Coll. 1927 BA;
Catholic U. 1929 MA. B: 6/29/05. Add: Back
St., Accomac 23301.

Charlottesville. NANCY K. O'BRIEN (D)
1976-. Bds: Ch., Retirement Fund Cmsn.;
Ch., Urban Observatory. Prev: Planning Dist.
Cmsn. 1973-76; City Planning Cmsn. 1974-76.
Org: LWV; Dem. Women's Club. Educ: Mass.
Gen. Hospital School of Nursing 1957 RN. B:
11/16/36. Add: 1605 Concord Dr., Charlottes-
ville 22901 (804)296-6151.

Chesapeake. MARIAN P. WHITEHURST
City Hall, Chesapeake 23320.

Grundy. BARBARA BERRY
P.O. Box 711, Grundy 24614.

Hampton. ANN H. KILGORE
22 Lincoln Street, Hampton 23669.

Hopewell. HILDA M. TRAINA
300 Main Street, Hopewell 23860.

Leesburg. MARY ANNE NEWMAN
P.O. Box 88, 15 W. Market St., Leesburg
22075.

Petersburg. BARBARA P. SHELL (I)
1976-. Bds: Interstate Adv. Council;
Planning Dist's. Leg. Com; Community Devt.
Policy Com. Educ: Madison Coll. 1949 BS.
B: 9/3/28. Add: 1612 E. Tuckahoe St., Peters-
burg 23803 (804)733-1833.

Round Hill. VIRGINIA QUINN
P.O. Box 36, Round Hill 22141.

Troutville. SHIRLEY GRAYBILL
P.O. Box 176, Troutville 24175.

Local Councils

Alberta. BERNICE WALKER MARTINDALE (D)
1976-. Bds: Planning Cmsn. Prev: Planning
Cmsn. 1972-77. Org: NAACP. B: 11/4/20. Add:
P.O. Box 127, Alberta 23821 (804)949-7443.

Alexandria. BEVERLY BEIDLER (D) **
　　1973-. Bds: Alcohol & Drug Abuse; Land Use;
United Way Council. Org: ADA; AIP; LWV; Urban
League; PTSA. Educ: Albright Coll. 1950 BA. B:
1/23/29. Add: 403 Jackson Pl., Alexandria
22302 (703)750-6639.

Alexandria. NORA O. LAMBORNE
　　City Hall, 301 King Street, Alexandria
22313.

Alexandria. ELLEN PICKERING (I)
　　1976-. Bds: Energy Com.; Land Use Com.;
Human Resources Com. Prev: Ch., Beautification
Cmsn. 1969-76. Org: Civic Assoc.; PTA; Histor-
cial Society; LWV; AAUW; Common Cause. Educ:
Emerson Coll. 1951 BA. B: 7/6/29. Add: 123
W. Maple St., Alexandria 22301 (703)750-6531.

Bedford. MARJORIE RUCKER
　　P.O. Box 807, Bedford 24523.

Big Stone Gap. ANNE DYER SUTHERLAND (R) **
　　1974-. Bds: Finance Com. Org: Rep. Women's
Club. Educ: U. of NC 1968 BA. Occ: Owner Gift
Shop; Bookkeeper. B: 9/20/46. Add: 214 W. 3rd
St., Big Stone Gap 24219 (703)523-1115.

Blacksburg. RACHEL BROWN
　　Municipal Building, Blacksburg 24060.

Boones Mill. FRANCES B. MC NEIL (I)
　　1975-. Bds: Water Com. Org: PTA. Occ: Tax
Preparer. B: 10/8/36. Add: Rt. 2, Boones Ml.
24065.

Boones Mill. MARY W. RICHARDS (D)
　　1974-. Prev: Justice of the Peace 1972-74.
Educ: Mary Baldwin Coll. 1950 BA. Occ: Driver's
Educ. Teacher. B: 7/24/29. Add: Rt. 1, Box 11,
Boones Mill 24065.

Bowling Green. A. MAE BROOKS
　　P.O. Box 468, Bowling Green 22427.

Branchville. MARY F. VICK
　　1974-. Prev: Town Clerk 1966-77. Occ:
Fabric Store Employee. B: 4/8/21. Add: P.O.
Box 23, Branchville 23828.

Brookneal. MRS. AZILE B. ROARK
　　Municipal Building, Brookneal 24528.

Buchanan. LOIS R. ROBERT
　　Municipal Bldg., Main Street, Buchanan 24066.

Buena Vista. MARGARET UPDIKE
　　2039 Sycamore Ave., Buena Vista 24416.

Burkeville. THELMA J. CRADDOCK
　　Municipal Building, Burkeville 23922.

Cape Charles. MARY BRADFORD BOWEN (I)
　　1976-. Org: PTA. Occ: Salesclerk. B:
6/17/44. Add: 111 Monroe Ave., Cape Charles
23310.

Chatham. VIRGINIA L. SANDERS
　　P.O. Box 56, 24 Depot St., Chatham 24531.

Cheriton. PAGE OUTTEN
　　Municipal Building, Cheriton 23316.

Chincoteague. JOAN HILL
　　224 N. Main Street, Chincoteague 23336.

Claremont. BETTY COSTENBADER
　　　　　　　PATTI N. VANATTA
　　Municipal Building, Claremont 23899.

Cleveland. CARRIE JEAN BREEDING (D)
　　1976-. Bds: Ch., Christmas Parade Com.;
Town Hall Calendar. Org: Amer. Institute of
Banking; PTA. Occ: Bank Teller/Administrative
Asst. B: 12/28/46. Add: P.O. Box 244,
Cleveland 24225 (703)889-4365.

Clifton. SUZANNE WORSHAM
　　Municipal Building, Clifton 22024.

Clifton Forge. MARY W. MEADOWS
　　City Hall, Clifton Forge 24422.

Coeburn. MAUDE C. HAWKINS
　　P.O. Box 370, Coeburn 24230.

Colonial Beach. EDNA SYDNOR
　　P.O. Box 35, Colonial Beach 22443.

Colonial Heights. NANCY HALBERT
　　Municipal Bldg., James Ave., Colonial
Heights 23834.

Columbia. ALICE WALTON
　　　　　　CORA WALTON
　　Municipal Building, Columbia 23038.

Covington. BETTY R. CARPENTER (I)
　　1974-. Bds: V-Ch., Planning Cmsn.; Ch.,
Consolidation Study. Org: BPW; Mental Hygiene
Clinic; League of Older Amer. B: 10/23/17.
Add: P.O. Box 137, Covington 24426.

Culpeper. ALICE KAY POTTER
　　1974-. Bds: Ordinance Study Cmsn. Org:
Nat. Press Women; BPW; Women's Club; Adv. Com.
on Aging; Beautification Com.; Adv. Com. on
Special Educ.; Reading is Fundamental; Historical Society. Occ: Newspaper Writer & Photographer. B: 8/14/19. Add: 1067 Oaklawn Dr.,
Culpeper 22701 (703)825-6153.

Culpeper. HELEN DUNBAR SLAUGHTER
　　1976-. Bds: Ch., Bldg. Com.; Ordinance
Com.; Parks & Recreation Com. Org: Women's
Club; Historical Society; Amer. Assoc. of
Retired Persons. Educ: U. of Richmond 1965
BA. B: 9/16/14. Add: 2000 Cypress Dr.,
Culpeper 22701 (703)825-4700.

Damascus. LOUISE F. HALL (D)
　　1976-. Bds: Town Planning Cmsn.; Community
Action Agency. Prev: Councilwoman 1960-64.
Org: Cnty. Retired Teachers; Regional Mental
Health & Mental Retardation Bd. B: 12/2/11.
Add: 428 Laurel Ave., P.O. Box 130, Damascus
24236.

Dendron. LINDA COLLINS
　　P.O. Box 132, Dendron 23829.

Dendron. ALMA GERALDINE GIBBS (D)
1970-. Bds: Ch., Finance Com. Org: NEA; Va. Home Economics Assoc.; NAACP; PTA; Black Caucus; Youth Bd.; Planning Council. Educ: Va. State Coll. 1946 BS. Occ: Teacher. B: 7/24/14. Add: P.O. Box 227, Dendron 23839.

Dumfries. ELEANOR GUM
P.O. Box 56, 101 S. Main St., Dumfries 22026.

Dumfries. EILEEN STOUT (R)
1976-. Bds: Ch., Parks & Recreation Com. Party: Precinct Manager 1975-76. Org: NEA; Chamber of Commerce; Historic Dumfries; Rep. Party; Rep. Women's Club. Educ: Ladycliff Coll. 1966 BA; George Mason U. 1975 MA. Occ: Teacher. B: 1/23/45. Add: 2456 Kilpatrick Pl., Dumfries 22026 (703)221-5093.

Edinburg. VIRGINIA L. COFFMAN (R) **
1974-. Bds: Budget; Ordinance; Personnel. Org: Retired Teachers. Educ: Madison U. of Va. 1954 BS. Occ: Assistant Bookkeeper; Retired Teacher. B: 12/20/09. Add: Rt. 3, Box 275, Edinburg 22824 (703)984-4756.

Fairfax City. SUSANNE W. MAX (R)
1974-. Bds: Bd. of Dir., Council of Govts.; Community Appearance Com.; Water Resources Bd. Org: Rep. Women's Club; LWV. B: 5/14/32. Add: 10509 Center St., Fairfax City 22030.

Falls Church. CAROL W. DE LONG (I)
1976-. Bds: Ch., Appointments Com.; Ch., Tree Ordinance Com.; Water Com. Prev: Planning Cmsn. 1971-74. Org: Citizens for a Better City; Vlg. Preservation & Improvement Soc. Educ: Douglass Coll. 1952 BS; Wash. State U. 1954 MS. B: 6/25/30. Add: 213 W. Columbia St., Falls Church 22046 (703)532-0800.

Fincastle. IRIS HEDRICK
Municipal Bldg., Fincastle 24090.

Fincastle. BETTY ANN HICKENBOTHAM (D)
Occ: Restaurant Manager/Waitress. B: 8/7/43. Add: 307 Main St., Fincastle 24050.

Floyd. POSEY R. HARRIS
P.O. Box 286, Floyd 24091.

Floyd. HAZEL S. ROBERTSON
1974-. Occ: Florist. B: 12/2/11. Add: P.O. Box 56, Floyd 24091 (703)745-4165.

Fredericksburg. KATHRYN H. MASSEY
P.O. Box 239, Fredericksburg 22401.

Glasgow. ROBERTA B. BLACKE (D)
1974-. Bds: Streets & Lights. Org: NEA; NAACP; PTA; OES. Educ: Va. State Coll. 1958 BS; U. of Va. 1972 MEd. Occ: Teacher. B: 7/20/29. Add: Box 39, Glasgow 24555.

Glen Lyn. SHIRLEY SIMPSON
PAULINE THOMPSON
P.O. Box 88, Glen Lyn 24093.

Grundy. PAULINE RAINES TYLENDA (R) **
1974-. Occ: Office Manager, Auto Dealership. B: 3/8/24. Add: Watkins St., Grundy 24614.

Hampton. MARTHA AILOR
22 Lincoln St., Hampton 23669.

Haymarket. JANE M. BAKER
MURIEL GILBERTSON
Municipal Building, Haymarket 22069.

Herndon. E. CLARE OLSON (I)
1976-. Bds: Northern Va. Planning Dist. Cmsn.; Regional Resources Com. Org: Recreation. Educ: U. of ND 1965 BA. Occ: Clerk. B: 12/12/41. Add: 702 Ferndale Ave., Herndon 22070.

Herndon. ANNA LEE POWELL (I)
1976-. Bds: Planning Cmsn.; Ch.,Town Centennial Com. Org: BPW; Historical Society. Occ: Legal Secretary. B: 11/13/32. Add: 657 Stuart Ct., Herndon 22070 (703)437-1000.

Hillsboro. EVELYN TURBELVILLE
P.O. Box 24, Hillsboro 22132.

Hurt. MADELINE C. KEY (I)
1975-. Bds: Ch., Legal Com.; Sanitation Com.; Repr. to Planning Com. Prev: Town Councilwoman 1967-68; Planning Com. 1967-77. Educ: Alfred U. 1949 BS; Randolph Macon Women's Coll. 1973 MA. B: 11/22/27. Add: 102 Knollwood Dr., Hurt 24563 (804)324-4411.

Iron Gate. RITA MANN
JOY M. NICELY
P.O. Box 199, Iron Gate 24448.

Irvington. JAYNE VIEL JACKSON
1976-. Bds: Ch., Update Library. Educ: Shenandoah Coll. Conservatory 1954 BMEd. Occ: Teacher. B: 9/12/32. Add: Box 193, Irvington 22480.

Ivor. ELLEN H. STEPHENSON
1971-. Bds: Ch. Ordinance; Ch. Health. Educ: Longwood Coll. 1943 BS. B: 10/15/23. Add: Box 289, Ivor 23866.

Luray. CLARA M. BROYLES (I)
1973-. Bds: Ch., Budget & Finance Com.; Planning Comnsr.; Lord Fairfax Planning Cmsn. Org: NEA; Women's Club of Luray; NW Va. Systems Agency. Educ: Columbia Bible Coll. 1940 BA; Eastern Baptist Theological Seminary 1947 MRE; Madison Coll. 1967 MA. Occ: Teacher. B: 4/22/19. Add: 4 Terrace Ln., Luray 22835 (703)743-5511.

Manassas Park. MARY B. JAMES (D)
1976-. Bds: Ch., Emergency Operations Plan.; Asst. Editor of Newsletter; Bd. of Dir's Fire Dept. Party: State Del. 1976; City Committeewoman 1976- ; Parliamentarian 1976-
Org: Va. Municipal League; Women's Club. B: 4/6/50. Add: 183 Martin Dr., Manassas Pk. 22110 (703)369-1711.

Manassas Park. VIVIAN MARGARET PUGH (R) **
1974-. Bds: Health Planning Council; Recreation Com. Org: PTA. Occ: Florist. B: 5/31/41. Add: 122 Baker St., Manassas Park 22110 (703) 361-5186.

Marion. STELLA W. MALONEY
1974-. Bds: Ch., Ordinance; Ch., Building; Ch., Library. Occ: Radio Manager. Add: 214 Lee St., Marion 24350 (703)783-4113.

Melfa. KENNETHA A. MARTIN
P.O. Box B, Melfa 23410.

Middleburg. MILDRED CLARE GOUTHRO
10 West Marshall Street, Middleburg 22117.

Middletown. RACHEL L. MANUEL
P.O. Box 175, Middletown 22645.

Middletown. CATHERINE M. MONTE (Va. Amer. Pty.) **
1974-. Bds: Ch., Ordinance Com.; Street Com.; Water & Sewer Com. Org: VFW. B: 5/26/22. Add: Box 391-B, Church St., Middletown 22645 (703)869-2226.

Mineral. MRS. H.H. WALTON
P.O. Box 316, Mineral 23117.

New Castle. JANET HARDEN
WANDA LEE
GERTRUDE LOWERY
Municipal Building, New Castle 24127.

New Market. EMILY BRUCE
P.O. Box 58, New Market 22844.

Newport News. MARY SHERWOOD HOLT (D)
1972-. Bds: Peninsula Transportation Dist. Cmsn.; Oyster Pt. Devt. Authority; Peninsula Drug Abuse Council. Party: State Del. 1972, '76; Nat. Del. 1974; Nat. Alt. 1976; Dem. Com. 1970-77; Local Ch. 1970-72. Org: Jr. League; Human Services Coalition; Women's Dem. Club. Educ: Mt. Holyoke Coll. 1948 BA. B: 4/9/27. Add: 11 River Rd., Newport News 23601 (804) 247-8635.

Newport News. TONITA M. WARREN (D)
1976-. Bds: Peninsula Planning Dist. Cmsn. Party: State Del. 1976; Local Secretary 1976. Org: ABA; Va. State Bar; ACLU; WPC; Dem. Party. Educ: Westhampton Coll. 1966 BA; George Wash. U. 1969 JD. Occ: Atty. B: 7/27/44. Add: 632 Snug Harbor Ln., Newport News 23606 (804) 722-3947.

Newsoms. CARRIE COGSDALE
Municipal Bldg., Newsoms 23874.

Norfolk. ELIZABETH M. HOWELL
City Hall Building, Norfolk 23501.

Onancock. MRS. NORMAN HORSEY
Municipal Bldg., Onancock 23417.

Poquoson. FRANCES FREEMAN
Municipal Building, Poquoson 23662.

Purcellville. CLAIRE A. LARSON (R)
1974-. Bds: Ch., Personnel & Finance; Ch., Police & Ordinances; Va. Municipal League. Party: State Del. 1976-77; Ch., Magisterial Dist. 1974-78. Org: BPW; Women's Club; Rep. Cnty. Com. Educ: Boston U. 1948 AS. Occ: Real Estate. B: 7/6/28. Add: Box 787, Purcellville 22132 (703)338-7421.

Quantico. ROSALIE HELEN FRAZIER (D)
1976-. Party: Town Councilwoman. Occ: Asst. B: 7/30/38. Add: 211 Broadway, Quantico 22134 (703)640-7475.

Quantico. ANGELENA PANDAZIDES
405 Broadway, Quantico 22134.

Radford. MARGARET DUNCAN
619 Second Street, Radford 24141.

Radford. REESE EDMONDSON GOLDSMITH (I)
1972-. Bds: Planning Cmsn.; Regional Waste Water Authority. Prev: Recreation Cmsn. 1948-52. Org: Historical Society. Educ: Boston U. 1938 BS; Radford Coll. 1954 MEd. B: 9/18/10. Add: 316 Second St., Radford 24141 (703) 639-2681.

Richmond. WILLIE J. DELL (D)
1973-. Dist: 3. Bds: Ch., Housing Task Force; Transportation; Regional Planning Dist. Party: State Del. 1972. Prev: Human Relations Cmsn. 1972-73. Org: NASW; Urban League; NAACP; Crusade for Voters; Educ: St. Augustine's Coll. 1948 BA; Howard U. 1960 MSW. Occ: Senior Center Dir. B: 5/8/30. Add: 2923 Hawthorne Ave., Richmond 23222 (804)780-4288.

Roanoke. ELIZABETH T. BOWLES (I)
1976-. Mayor Pro Tem. Bds: Planning Dist. Cmsn.; Personnel Com.; Recodification Com. Prev: Library Bd. 1963-76. Org: Merchants Assoc.; Chamber of Commerce; Amer. Retail Bakers Assoc.; Va. Lung Assoc.; Parent Council; Roanoke Vly. Parliamentary Unit. Occ: Bake Shop Co-Owner. B: 4/26/21. Add: 3637 Grandview Ave. NW, Roanoke 24012 (703)981-2444.

Round Hill. ELIZABETH K. ENTWISLE (I) **
1974-. Bds: Public Relations; Bicentennial Com. Party: Cnty. Secretary-Treasurer 1968-74; Local Precinct Com. 1968-74; Del., State Conv. Prev: Mayor 1971-74. Org: Chamber of Commerce. Educ: Barnard Coll. 1943 BA. B: 4/27/22. Add: Rt. 1, Box 6B, Round Hill 22141 (703)338-2878.

Salem. JANE LITTS HOUGH (R) **
1972-. Bds: Planning Dist. Cmsn.; Human Resources Advisory Com.; Juvenile Detention Study Com. Org: Council of Community Services; Rep. Club. Educ: Randolph-Macon 1949 BA. B: 1/10/27. Add: P.O. Box 849, Salem 24153 (703)389-8601.

Saltville. SHIRLEY CARTER
DOROTHY GILLENWATER
P.O. Box 730, Saltville 24370.

Scottsville. SUSIE BLAIR
         MRS. CENNIE H. MOON
     P.O. Box 132, Scottsville 24590.

Shenandoah. EVELINE FISCHER
         MARGUERITE W. SULLIVAN
     416 First Street, Shenandoah 22849.

South Hill. BARBARA G. NANNEY (I) **
     1972-. Bds: Planning Com.; Manpower Cmsn.
Prev: Library Bd. 1967-75. Org: Municipal
League. Educ: Catawba Coll. 1960 BA. Occ:
Typesetter. B: 12/5/37. Add: 622 Windham Ave.
Drawer 37, South Hill 23970 (804)447-8050.

Staunton. KATHERYN B. HODGE
     1976-. Bds: Effective Govt. Com. & Reso-
lutions Com.; Joint Jail Com.; Crime Com.
Prev: Headwaters Soil & Conservation Dist.
1973-76. Org: Women's Club; Historical Society;
Teachers Assoc. Educ: James Madison U. 1972
BS. B: 11/19/19. Add: 101 Harper Ct.,
Staunton 24401 (703)885-5669.

Strasburg. EUNICE LAMBERT TAYLOR (I) **
     1974-. Bds: Water & Sewer Com.; Ch.,
Streets. Org: PTA. Occ: Secretary. B:
4/16/30. Add: 209 S. Holliday St., Strasburg
22657 (703)465-5230.

Strasburg. MARIE WILLIAMS
     P.O. Box 351, Strasburg 22657.

Stuart. BETTY SMITH CLARK (I)
     Org: OES; Homestead Learning Ctr. B:
10/6/35. Add: Blue Ridge St., Stuart 24171
(703)694-3811.

Stuart. ETHLYNE CREASEY
     P.O. Box 422, Stuart 24171.

Toms Brook. VIRGINIA REGER
         CHARLOTTE RINKER
     P.O. Box 107, Toms Brook 22660.

Troutville. SANDRA A. BARE (D)
     1976-. Bds: Water Com. Party: State Alt.
1976; Exec. Council 1975; Cnty. Org. Ch. 1976.
Org: Young Dems.; Cnty. Women Dem.; Va.
Municipal League. Occ: Student. B: 4/29/57.
Add: Rt. 2, Box 25, Troutville 24175.

Troutville. CAROL WADDELL
     P.O. Box 176, Troutville 24175.

Vienna. WANDA PELLICCIOTTO
     127 South Center Street, Vienna 22180.

Virginia Beach. MEYERA E. OBERNDORF (D)
     1976-. Bds: Cmsnr., Southeastern Regional
Planning Dist. Com.; Repr., Mayor's Youth
Council. Party: Dem. Committeewoman 1974-76.
Prev: Ch., Library Bd. 1967-76. Org: Va.
Municipal League; LWV; AAUW; Women's Club.
Educ: Old Dominion U. 1964 BS. B: 2/10/41.
Add: 5404 Challedon Dr., Va. Bch. 23462
(804)427-4111.

Wakefield. JESSICA C. MOORE (D)
     1976-. Bds: Ch., Beautification, Infor-
mation & Public Relations; Cemetary. Party:
State Alt. 1976. Org: Amer. Personnel &
Guidance Assoc.; Va. E.A.; Jr. Women's Club;
Young Dem's. Educ: Guilford Coll. 1968 BA;
E. Carolina U. 1970 MAEd. Occ: Guidance Dir.
Add: P.O. Box 92, Wakefield 23888.

White Stone. CATHERINE D. BELLOWS (D) **
     1960-. Bds: Christmas Decoration; Town
Planning. Org: Educ. Assoc.; PTA. Occ:
Teacher. B: 5/14/18. Add: White Stone
22578.

White Stone. PEGGY E. LAWSON (D)
     1970-. Bds: Budget Com.; Town Clerk. Org:
PTO. Occ: Secretary. B: 9/30/30. Add: P.O.
Box 274, White Stone 22578 (804)435-1622.

White Stone. ENID S. SOMERS (R)
     B: 9/6/13. Add: White Stone 22578.

Williamsburg. SHIRLEY PAYNE LOW (D)
     1974-. Bds: Peninsula Planning Dist. Cmsn.
Prev: Planning Cmsn. 1953-74. Org: Drug
Control Ctr. Educ: Kalamazoo Coll. 1926 BA;
U. of Mich. 1931 MA. B: 10/22/04. Add: 210
Nelson Ave., Williamsburg 23185 (804)
229-4821.

Winchester. MRS. EFFIE DAVIS
     Ronss City Hall, Winchester 22601.

Windsor. JEAN E. WOODWARD
     P.O. Box 307, Windsor 23487.

Woodstock. JOSEPHINE M. LYNN
     P.O. Box 169, Woodstock 22664.

State Boards and Commissions

     Office of the Governor, State Capitol Bldg.,
     Richmond 23219.

Aging, Advisory Board on the
     FANNIE B. JONES
     MARY ELLEN COX

Agricultural Foundation
     SHARON RAYMOND MILLER

Agriculture and Commerce, Board of
     MRS. M.B. PIERCE

Air Pollution Control Board
     ELIZABETH H. HASKELL

Airports Authority
     MRS. WILLIAM T. PEDIGO

Alcoholism Counselor Certification Committee
     BARBARA J. ANGLIN
     COLLEEN S. DILL
     FRANCES R. OLSON

Alexandria Historical Restoration and Preservation
Commission
   MRS. ELLIOTT T. DIMOND, JR.
   MRS. BERNHARD K. HAFFNER

Archaelogy, Advisory Committee on Virginia
Research Center for
   MILDRED F. COUNCILOR
   MRS. ROBERT B. EGGLESTON
   ELIZABETH GRAY
   MARY DOUTHAT HIGGINS
   VIRGINIA MABRY
   PAULINE MITCHELL
   D. EVE NEWMAN
   MRS. HAMPTON W. THOMAS

Art Commission
   MARIE PIETRI

Arts and Humanities, Commission on the
   MARY TENNANT BRYAN
   PHYLLIS GALANTI
   MARION P. LEWIS
   MRS. WILLIAM R. WILKINSON

Atlantic Rural Exposition, Inc., Committee on
   MRS. M. BLANTON PIERCE

Audiology and Speech Pathology, Board of
Examiners for
   CAROL J. COFEY
   MARGARET DUNKERLEY MC ELROY

Child Abuse and Neglect, Advisory Committee on
   MRS. CHARLES ELMORE
   MRS. E. DAVID FOREMAN
   SHIRLEY T. GREEN
   MRS. JAMES M. HALEY
   DR. CATHERINE SMITH

Children and Youth, Commission for
   MARY LOU ANTHONY
   O'LETA W. GOINS
   MARION EDWIN HARRISON
   KATHY L. MAYS
   MRS. GEORGE MC MATH
   MRS. WALTER RICE
   MRS. ROBERT S. SIMPERS
   MRS. RALPH STEINHARDT, JR.

Community College, State Board for
   MRS. HELMI E. CARR
   MRS. WALDO G. MILES

Corporation Commission
   JUNIE L. BRADSHAW

Corrections, State Board of
   MRS. JOHN J. DE HART

Criminal Justice, Council on
   CLAUDINE PENICK

Deaf, Council for the
   DOROTHY BLACK
   MRS. BERNARD W. MOORE
   MRS. MARVIN L. MYERS, JR.

Developmental Disabilities Planning and
Advisory Council
   MARY ELLEN CHEWING
   MRS. ARTHUR W. ORDEL, JR.
   MRS. W. CONRAD STONE
   CAROLYN M. STRICKLAND
   MRS. JAMES J. TRAINA
   ANNE VOGELWEDE
   RIZPAH WELCH

Drug Abuse Advisory Council
   MRS. ALTA NOBLES CURTIS
   PATTY W. FOWLER
   MRS. PHILIP LEE RUSSO
   JOAN A. VAN VLECK

Drug Counselor Certification Committee
   CAROL ELIZABETH JONES

Education Assistance Authority, Governing Board
   BARBARA J. HILDENBRAND
   JANE G. SWARTZ

Education Commission of the States
   ELEANOR P. SHEPPARD

Education for Health Professions and Occupations,
Committee on
   MRS. JESSE T. DAVIDSON, JR.
   ELEANOR J. SMITH

Education Loan Authority, Governing Board
   PRISCILLA M. LIGHT
   MRS. WILLIAM H. SARGENT

Education, State Board of
   ELIZABETH G. HELM
   ELIZABETH MORRIS ROGERS

Elections, State Board of
   JOAN STROUSE MAHAN

Emergency Medical Services, Advisory Committee
on
   ELIZABETH GRAY
   VIRGINIA MABRY
   PAULINE MITCHELL
   D. EVE NEWMAN

Energy Resource Advisory Commission
   MRS. CHARLES BRUCE MILLER

Equal Employment Opportunity Committee
   NINA ABADY
   MRS. JOHN N. DALTON
   MARY GUINES
   JUDITH S. JOHNSON
   MARGARET IVY LANE
   MRS. DAVID G. MELDRUM
   JOHNNIE MILES
   GAIL NOTTINGHAM

Executive Mansion, Citizen's Advisory Committee
on Furnishing and Interpreting the
   MRS. A. SMITH BOWMAN
   MRS. RICHARD E. BYRD
   MRS. GEORGE M. COCHRAN
   MRS. RICHARD CUTTS
   MRS. LEON DURE, JR.

MRS. GEORGE E. FLIPPIN, JR.
MRS. RICHMOND GRAY
MRS. J. HOWARD JOYNT
MRS. GEORGE M. KAUFMAN
MRS. B. B. LANE
MRS CHARLES BEATTY MOORE
MRS. W. TAYLOR MURPHY, JR.
MRS. BENJAMIN F. PARROTT
ANNE DOBIE PEEBLES
MRS. PAUL E. SACKETT

Hampton Roads Sanitation District, Governing Board
CAROLYN HOSKINS COFFMAN

Handicapped Children and Adults, The Overall Advisory Council on Needs of
DORIS D. FALCONER
EMMA MAE JONES
BONNIE L. PAUL
MRS. CHARLES H. PEERY
MARY L. WADE

Health, Board of
FOSTINE G. RIDDICK

Health Coordinating Council
ELIZABETH D. BUSBEE
VIRGINIA A. CROCKFORD
MILDRED D. GORDON
DOROTHY K. HEALY
ROSA HUDSON
MARGARET B. INMAN
PATRICIA ELLEN LUND
ANNE N. MASON
LAURA I. MC DOWALL
JANE C. PEERY
AMANDA G. VAUGHAN

Higher Education, State Council of
DR. DOROTHY N. COWLING
DOROTHY L. GIBBONEY
MRS. EARL R. STEGMAN

Highway Safety Commission
MRS.W. GOODE ROBINSON
RUTH O. WILLIAMS

Historic Landmarks Commission
NELLIE WHITE BUNDY
MARY DOUTHAT HIGGINS

Housing, State Board of
TIFFANY ARMSTRONG
BEVERLY R. MIDDLETON

Human Resources Priorities, Commission on
MRS. JOHN C. DOUD
PAULINE F. MALONEY

Independence Bicentennial Commission
CAROLYN MOSES LUSARDI
MRS. FAY S. MOORE, JR.

James Monroe Law Office Museum and Memorial Library, Board of Regents of the
MRS. JAMES W. RAWLES
MRS. ROBIN D.W. ROGER
HELEN MARIE TAYLOR
RUBY Y. WEINBRECHT
BARBARA WILLIS

Jamestown-Yorktown Foundation, Board of Trustees
MRS. GEORGE M. COCHRAN
SHIRLEY T. HOLLAND
MRS. VERN E. LENTZ

Library Board
MARJORIE L. DIETSCH
PATRICIA T. FRENCH
MARY A. MARSHALL
MRS. HARRY W. MEADOR, JR.

Mental Health and Mental Retardation Board
ELSIE R. CHITTUM
VIRGINIA H. LAMPE

Milk Commission
MRS. LE BRON J. HOLDEN

Museum of Fine Arts, Board of Trustees
MRS. HUNTER B. ANDREWS
MRS. RICHARD E. BYRD
MRS. JOHN M. CAMP, JR.
MRS. JOHN W. PEARSALL
MRS. FRED G. POLLARD
MRS. GEORGE A. REVERCOMB
MRS. WEBSTER S. RHOADS, JR.
MRS. CHARLES T. ROSE

National League Services Corporation, Advisory Council to the
ESTELLE GORE
LOIS MEAR

Nursing, State Board of
ANNE H. BISHOP
MARILYN A. BOYD
CORINNE FALCONER DORSEY
ALESE N. HAZELWOOD
ELEANOR J. SMITH
IONE H. STEPHENS
PATRICIA TEN HOEVE
HELEN W. WIESMANN

Nursing Home Administrators, Board of Examiners
AUDREY B. BUTLER
CAROL STICKNEY

Outdoors Foundation, Board of Trustees
MRS. BERTRAM FIRESTONE

Outdoor Recreation, Commission of
MARY STUART GILLIAM

Parole Board
MARGARET B. DAVIS

Physical Therapy, Advisory Committee on
MARIANNE MC DONALD

Plans and Specifications for School Building, Advisory Research Committee on
SUE B. MOSS

Professional and Occupational Regulation, Commission on
MRS. RUTH J. HERRINK
MRS. G. KENNETH MILLER

Professional Hairdressers, Board of Examiners of
    CORINNE B. BROOKS
    JEANNE M. BROWN
    POLLY A. FARMER
    MARY A. HUTCHINS
    COLLEEN SHUTTERS

Psychology, Board of
    LUCILE E. MICHIE

Public Highways, Advisory Committee on Outdoor Advertising in Sight of
    MRS. STEWART BELL

Public Telecommunications Council, Board of
    MRS. JOHN A. PAUL

Purchases and Supply, Board of
    RHEA BURTON LAWRENCE

Renal Advisory Committee
    MRS. H.R. BELL
    DIANA BERKSHIRE
    SUE FRANKE

Science Museum of Virginia, Board of Trustees
    MRS. T. FLEETWOOD GARNER
    DR. JANICE LEE HARRIS
    MRS. WILLIAM T. REED, JR.

Social Workers, Board of
    DIANA STRATTON COTHELL
    GRACE EDMONSON HARRIS
    MAUREEN J. HARRIS

Solid Waste Commission
    JOAN S. JONES

Substance Abuse Problems, Advisory Council on
    BETTY JO MARTIN

Transportation, Governor's Council on
    LOUISE BURKE
    MARY S. HOLT

Urban Assistance Incentive Fund Advisory Committee
    MARY SHERWOOD HOLT
    MARY WINN JOHNSON
    MRS. LOIS M. NELSON

Vocational Rehabilitation, Board of
    MRS. VAL LICHLENSTEIN, JR.

Voluntary Formulary Board
    NELL PUSEY

Welfare, Board of
    BARBARA K. WATKINS

Women, Commission on the Status of
    PEGGY P. ABEL
    MARTHA H. BOONE
    MRS. THEODORE J. BURR, JR.
    CLARICE CHRISTIAN
    MRS. LOU COOK
    MRS. JOHN N. DALTON
    MARTHA DANIELS
    JERILYN A. FARRAR

FRANCES V. GARLAND
DORIS E. KEAN
PHILLIS PENDERGRAFT
JADE CHRISTINE WEST
ROSALIE WHITEHEAD

Washington

State Executive and Cabinet

BETTY J. MC CLELLAND (D)
    Director, Department of Emergency Services. 1977-. Bds: Consultant, Internat. Assoc. of Fire Chiefs; Ad Hoc Inter-Agency Com. for Nuclear Response to Fixed Nuclear Facilities. Party: State Del. 1976; Cnty. Caucus Ch. 1975-76. Prev: Cnty. Dir., Emergency Services 1964-77; Cnty. Flood Control Bd. 1967-77; Cnty. Planning Cmsn. 1963-65. B: 4/25/29. Add: 408 3rd St., Hoquiam 98550 (206)753-5255.

DIXY LEE RAY (D)
    Governor. Prev: Ch., US Atomic Energy Cmsn. 1972-74; Asst. Sec. of State for Bureau of Oceans & International Environmental & Scientific Affairs 1975. Educ: Mills Coll. 1937 BA, 1938 MA; Stanford U. 1945 PHD. B: 9/3/14. Add: Governor, State Capitol, Olympia 98501.

R.Y. WOODHOUSE
    Director, Department of Licensing. Add: Hwys.-Licenses Bldg., Olympia.

State Legislature

State Senate

NANCY BUFFINGTON (R) **
    Dist: 34. Bds: Juvenile Court; Judiciary Com.; Social & Health Services; State Government. Org: Municipal League; Amer. Assoc. of Medical Technologists. Occ: Research Institute Program Coordinator. B: 1939. Add: 5919 47th St., SW, Seattle 98136.

SUE GOULD (R)
    1974-. Dist: 21. Bds: Governor's Com. on Law & Justice; Senate Educ. Com.; Senate Social & Health Services Com. Prev: School Bd. 1967-76. Org: AAUW; LWV; NOW; Chamber of Commerce; Rep. Club. Educ: U. of Wash. 1951 BS. B: 8/9/29. Add: 19225 92nd W, Edmonds 98020 (206)753-7640.

JEANNETTE C. HAYNER (R)
    1972-. Prev: Walla Walla School Bd. 1956-
63. Educ: U. of Ore. 1939 BA; U. of Ore.
School of Law 1942 JD. B: 1/22/19. Add: Box
454, Walla Walla 99362 (206)753-7630.

CAROL A. MONOHON (D)
    1977-. Dist: 19. Bds: Social & Health
Services; Parks & Recreation; Constitution &
Elections. Party: State Del. 1976, '74;
Precinct Committeewoman 1972-76; State
Committeewoman 1972-78. Prev: State Repr.
1976-77. Org: Women's Law Caucus; LWV; Dem.
Women's Fed. Educ: U. of Puget Sound 1975
BA. B: 7/15/45. Add: Rt. 1, Box 136, Raymond
98577 (206)753-7636.

LOIS NORTH (R)
    1974-. Dist: 44. Bds: Social Health
Services Com.; Local Govt. Com.; Ecology Com.
Party: State Del. 1976. Prev: State Repr.
1969-73; Cnty. Freeholder 1967-68; Cnty.
Boundary Review Bd. 1967-68. Org: Cnty.
Municipal League; LWV; Nat. Abortion Reform
League; Rep. Women; NOW; WPC; Community Club.
Educ: U. of Calif. 1943 BA. Occ: Local Govt.
Planner. B: 11/23/21. Add: 10126 Radford Ave.,
NW, Seattle 98177 (206)753-7686.

RUTHE B. RIDDER (D)
    1973-. Dist: 35. Bds: Ch., Senate Labor
Com.; Urban Devt. Com.; State Women's Council.
Party: State Del. 1968, '66; State Alt. 1970;
Precinct Committeewoman 1968-70, 1974-76.
Educ: U. of Wash. 1950 BS. B: 6/13/29. Add:
5809 S. Roxbury, Seattle 98118 (206)753-7668.

LORRAINE WOJAHN (D) **
    1969-. Dist: 27. Bds: State Women's
Council; Region V Advisory Council; State
Dept. of Social & Health Services; State
Judicial Council; Commerce; Higher Educ.;
Rules. Prev: State Repr. Occ: Public Relations
Add: 3592 E. Kay St., Tacoma 98404 (206)
753-7904.

State House

MARY KAY BECKER (D) **
    1975-. Dist: 42. Bds: V-Ch., Agricul-
ture; Ecology; Social & Health Services. Educ:
Western Wash. State Coll. BA. Occ: Writer.
B: 1946. Add: P.O. Box 81, S. Bellingham Sta.,
Bellingham 98225.

ELLEN CRASWELL (R)
    1976-. Dist: 23. Bds: Revenue Com.;
Education Com.; Parks & Rec. Com. Party:
State Del. 1976; State Alt. 1974. Org: Women's
Rep. Club. B: 5/25/32. Add: 11826 Kitsap
Way, Bremerton 88310 (206)753-7890.

PHYLLIS K. ERICKSON (D)
    1973-. Dist: 2. Party: State Del. 1976,
'74, '72; Precinct Committee 1949-51. Org:
LWV; Common Cause; Dem. Dist. Club. Educ:
U. of Utah 1946 BA; U. of Utah 1947 MSW. Occ:
Social Worker. B: 6/28/23. Add: P.O. Box
44488, Tacoma 98444 (206)753-7826.

HELEN FANCHER (R)
    Aeneas Route, Tonasket 98855.

ELEANOR A. FORTSON (D)
    1972-. Dist: 10. Bds: Ch., Constitution
Com.; Health & Social Services; V-Ch., Ocean-
ographic Cmsn. Party: State Del. 1954- ;
Nat. Del. 1968, '72, '76; Cnty. Precinct Com.
1954- ; State Committeewoman 1966-77. Org:
AAUW; Grange; Dem. Club. Educ: Western Wash.
Coll. BA, MA. B: 3/7/10. Add: 4008 SW Camano
Dr., Camano Is. 98292 (706)753-7838.

AUDREY LINDGREN GRUGER (D)
    1976-. Dist: 1. Bds: Sub. Com., Ch.,
Environmental Policy; V-Ch., Constitution
Com.; Sub. Com. Ch., Child Care. Party:
State Del. 1964; Precinct Chairperson 1961-
65, '1974-77. Prev: Firland Correction
Center Adv. Com. 1976-78. Org: Wash. Council
on Crime & Delinquency; LWV; AAUW; Common
Cause; Wash. Dem. Council; Metropolitan Dem.
Club; Cnty. Dem. Educ: U. of Wash. 1952 BA.
B: 5/17/30. Add: 3727 N.E. 193, Seattle
98155.

MARGARET HURLEY (D) **
    Dist: 3. Bds: Ch., Parks & Recreation;
State Government; Ways & Means, Revenue. Org:
OWL; Bar Assoc.; Citizens Against Residential
Freeways. Educ: Coll. of the Holy Names BA.
Occ: Teacher. Add: 730 E. Boone Ave., Spokane
99202 (206)753-7808.

ELEANOR LEE (R) **
    Dist: 33. Bds: County Policy Dev. Cmsn.;
Communities Plan Policy Advisory Bd.; Local
Govt.; Parks & Recreation; Transportation &
Utilities. Educ: Evergreen State Coll. BA.
Occ: Business Manager. Add: 1431 SW 152nd,
Seattle 98166.

PEGGY JOAN MAXIE (D) **
    1971-. Dist: 37. Bds: Ch., Higher Educ.;
Judiciary. Org: BPW; Nat. Assoc. Social
Workers. Educ: Seattle U. 1970 BA; U. of
Wash. 1972 MSW. Occ: Exec. Dir., Alcoholism
Council. B: 8/18/36. Add: 3302 E. Pine St.,
Seattle 98122 (206)753-7946.

GERALDINE MC CORMICK (D) **
    1969-. Dist: 5. Bds: Transportation &
Utilities; Financial Institutions; Local
Government. Org: Grange. Add: 1829 North-
ridge Court W, Spokane 99208 (206)753-7816.

FRANCES NORTH (D) **
    1972-. Dist: 47. Bds: Ways & Means;
Appropriations; Local Government; Parks &
Recreation; Governmental Conf. Prev:
Councilwoman 1968- . Org: BPW; Secretary's
Assoc.; Citizens for Transit. Add: Box 441,
North Bend 98045 (206)888-1211.

CATHY PEARSALL (D)
    1976-. Org: BPW; WPC. Educ: U. of Wash.
1954 BA. B: 4/18/32. Add: 2604 S. 76th,
Tacoma 98409 (206)753-7914.

MARION KYLE SHERMAN (D) **
1974-. Dist: 47. Party: Precinct Com. 1962-72; State Com. 1968-72; Exec. Bd. 1970-72. Org: Audubon Society; LWV; Chamber of Commerce; Citizens Com. on Highway Safety; Com. on Consumer Interests. Educ: U. of Wash. 1949 BA. B: 10/7/25. Add: 24629 SE 200, Maple Valley 98038 (206)753-7840.

HELEN SOMMERS (D)
1972-. Bds: Ch., Revenue Com.; State Govt.; Constitution. Party: State Del. 1974; Precinct Committeewoman 1973. Prev: V-Ch., Revenue Com.; Local Govt. Com.; Judiciary Com. 1973-74; Ch., Sub. Com. on Pensions 1976. Org: NOW; LWV; Common Cause; Public Pension Cmsn. Educ: U. of Wash. BA; MA. Occ: Research Analyst. B: 3/29/32. Add: 2516 14th W., Seattle 98119 (206)753-7940.

GEORGETTE W. VALLE (D) **
1965-. Dist: 31. Bds: Educ.; Ecology; Ways & Means; Appropriations. Party: Local Precinct Com. Org: Common Cause; LWV; Occupational Therapy Assoc.; Ralph Nader's Citizen; Dem. Women's Club. Educ: U. of Minn. BS. Add: 1434 SW 137th, Seattle 98166 (206) 753-7920.

SHIRLEY J. WINSLEY (R)
1974-. Dist: 28. Bds: Ch., Planning Com.; Ch., Chamber of Commerce Govt. Action. Party: State Del. 1964, '68, '72; State Alt. 1962; Precinct Committeewoman 1964-74; Dist. Ch. 1972-74. Org: LWV; Jr. League; Dem. Club; Rep. Club; Health Council; Community Club. Occ: Chamber of Commerce Manager. B: 6/9/34. Add: 539 Buena Vista Ave., Fircrest 98466 (206)753-7908.

County Commissions

Adams. DEANNA J. MC COY
210 W. Broadway, Ritzville 99169.

Benton. KATHY UTZ (D)
1976-. Bds: Public Transportation Benefit Area; Public Health Dept.; Council on Aging. Party: Precinct Committeewoman 1972-73. Org: LWV; AAUW; NOW; Dem. Central Com. Educ: U. of Pa. 1959 BS. B: 8/24/39. Add: 2320 Benson Ave., Richland 99352 (509)545-2496.

Clark. CONNIE KEARNEY (D)
1976-. Dist: 1. Bds: Mayors Com.; Ch., Energy Bd., Regional Planning Bd. Party: Precinct Committeewoman 1976-80. Org: Dem. Club. Educ: U. of Wash. 1967 BA. B: 2/25/43. Add: 2616 NE 116th St., Vancouver 98663 (206)699-2332.

Cowlitz. BERYL POWERS ROBISON (R)
1976-. Dist: 2. Bds: Social Services Coord. Bd.; Human Resources Cmsn.; Bldg. Com.; Hall of Justice. Org: NASW; Academy of Certified Social Workers; Jr. Service League; Chamber of Commerce; Cnty. Rep. Central Com.; Cnty. Rep. Women's Club; PTA. Educ: Hollins

Coll. 1961 BA; Portland State U. 1972 MSW. B: 3/9/39. Add: 1502 Kessler Blvd., Longview 98632 (206)577-3020.

King. RUBY CHOW (D)
1973-. Bds: V-Ch., Cnty. Council; Ch., Cnty. Health & Human Services Com. Org: Benevolent Assoc.; Chinese Community Service Org.; Adv., Chinese Parents Service Org. B: 6/6/20. Add: 6242 Chatham Dr. S., Seattle 98118 (206)344-4033.

King. BERNICE STERN (D)
1969-. Bds: Ch., Metropolitan Finance & Personnel; Puget Sound Conf. of Govts.; Metropolitan Council. Party: State Del. 1972; Nat. Del. 1972. Org: LWV; Urban League; Metropolitan Dem's. B: 7/25/16. Add: 2709 W. Galer, Seattle 98199 (206)344-3475.

Pacific. CLARA KOREVAAR
Memorial & Vine Sts., S. Bend 98586.

Thurston. MARJORIE YUNG (D)
1974-. Bds: Health Systems Agency; Community Health & Social Services Bd.; Regional Animal Control Bd. Party: Precinct Leader 1976-78. Prev: Olympia Com. of the Seventies 1974; Law & Justice Adv. Com. 1973-74; On Site Waste Com. 1973-74; Cnty. Planning Cmsn. 1972-73; Community Action Council 1975-76; Comprehensive Health Planning Council 1975. Org: LWV; NOW; Urban League; Thurston Action Com.; Cnty. Dem. Women. Educ: The Evergreen State Coll. 1975 BA; Good Samaritan Hospital School of Nursing 1957 RN. B: 5/1/35. Add: 3436 Sunset Beach Dr., NW, Olympia 98502 (206)753-8031.

Mayors

Aberdeen. FRANCES WHITE
200 E. Market St., Aberdeen 98520.

Airway Heights. LORRAINE D. HORTON
N. 206 Lundstrom, P.O. Box A, Airway Hts. 99001.

Chehalis. VIVIAN M. ROEWE (D)
1975-. Bds: Ch., Cnty. Public Transportation Benefit Area; Resolutions Com. Party: State Alt. 1965; Precinct Committeewoman 1963-70. Prev: Planning Cmsn. 1972-75. Org: Assoc. of Wash. Cities; Chamber of Commerce. Occ: Real Estate Saleswoman. B: 3/29/24. Add: 61 NE North St., Chehalis 98532 (206) 748-6664.

Darrington. GERALDINE INMAN
P.O. Box 418, Darrington 98241.

Des Moines. LORRAINE BODINE HINE (D)
1976-. Bds: Overall Economic Devt. Plan; Puget Sound Council of Govt.; Assoc. of Wash. Cities. Party: Precinct Committeewoman 1976. Prev: Councilwoman 1972-77. Org: Suburban Mayor's Assoc.; LWV. Educ: Wash. State U. 1952 BA. B: 5/1/30. Add: 1834 S. 229th, Des Moines 98188 (206)878-4595.

Entiat. MARIAN WOLF
   3rd & Kinzel, P.O. Box 228, Entiat 98822.

George. EDITH L. BROWN
   P.O. Box 5053, George 98824.

Hamilton. THELMA NELSON
   P.O. Box 444, Hamilton 98255.

Harrah. BARBARA HARRER (R)
   1977-. Bds: Cnty. Conf. of Govts. Prev:
Town Clerk-Treasurer 1966-70; Town Councilwoman 1972-77. Org: Pres., State 4-H Council;
Chamber of Commerce. Occ: Veterinary Asst.
B: 7/10/32. Add: Rt. 1, Box 14, Harrah 98933
(509)848-2432.

Kent. ISABEL K. HOGAN (R) **
   1969-. Bds: METRO Council; Puget Sound
Council of Governments. Prev: Park Bd. 1961-
69; School Bd. 1961-69. B: 2/3/21. Add: 616
Quiberson St., Kent 98031 (206)872-3355.

Lacey. KAREN R. FRASER (I)
   1973-. Bds: Ch., Regional Planning Council;
Bd. of Health; Intergovt. Human Resources Adv.
Council. Prev: City Council 1973- ; Lacey
Planning Cmsn. 1971-73; Citizens Adv. Com. on
Regional Transportation Planning 1971-73. Org:
WPC; IWY. Educ: U. of Wash. 1966 BA; 1969 MPA.
Occ: Policy Analyst. B: 9/12/44. Add: 821-C
Essex Place NE, Lacey 98506 (206)491-3210.

Mabton. THELMA SATTERFIELD
   P.O. Box 655, Mabton 98935.

Monroe. KATHARYN GRACE KIRWAN **
   1973-. Bds: Cnty. Law & Justice; Cmsnr.,
Hospital Dist.; Planning; Cnty. Community Dev.
Council. Prev: Councilwoman 1970-73. Org:
Amer. Cancer Society; Library Bd.; PTA. Educ:
Tex. Women's U. 1937 BA, BS; U.S. Naval War
Coll. 1970 Certificate. Occ: Owner, Manager
Ladies Ready-to-Wear. B: 12/1/13. Add: 538
S. Blakely St., Monroe 98272 (206)794-4880.

Pullman. KAREN KIESSLING
   SE 325 Paradise, P.O. Box 438, Pullman
99163.

Skykomish. JOYCE L. TIMPE
   P.O. Box 308, Skykomish 98288.

Snohomish. IONE GALE **
   1976-. Prev: Park Bd. 1970-72; Council.
Org: Music Teacher's Assoc.; Historical Society.
Occ: Piano Teacher. Add: 1230 Pine, Snohomish
98290.

Yakima. BETTY L. EDMONDSON (R)
   1976-. Bds: Ch., Cnty. Health Dist. Bd.;
Ch., City Police Relief & Pension Bd.; Cnty.
Emergency Service. Party: State Del. 1960-72,
1976; Nat. V-Ch. 1961-64; State Committeewoman
1964-68. Prev: City Councilwoman 1973-78;
Cnty. Alcohol Administrative Bd. 1973-80;
Govt. Com. Amer. Revolution Bicentennial 1970-
73; Govt. Com. Community Devt. 1976-77; Rape
Reduction Adv. Com. 1975-79. Org: BPW; Wa.
State Public Health Assoc.; Fed. Women's Club;
Rep. Women. B: 2/23/24. Add: 624 S. 34th
Ave., Yakima 98902 (509)575-6050.

Yelm. LORA B. COATES
   P.O. Box 479, Town Hall, Yelm 98597.

Local Councils

Airway Heights. MARYLYNN KRUMM
   N. 206 Sundstrom, P.O. Box A, Airway Hts.
99001.

Albion. VONNIE JENNINGS (R) **
   1973-. Bds: Planning Cmsn.; Street Com.;
Safety Com. Org: Women's Club. Occ: School
Cook. B: 9/16/36. Add: Box 1159, Albion
99102 (509)332-5095.

Algona. MARY NOEL
   402 Warde St., Algona 98002.

Algona. ALBERTA M. SUNDSTROM
   1971-. Bds: Ch., Utilities; Parks. Occ:
Bookkeeper. B: 1/17/15. Add: 633 Celery St.,
Algona 98002 (206)833-2741.

Anacortes. BETTYE D. BRYANT **
   1973-. Occ: Owner of Real Estate Business.
Add: 5314 Sterling Dr., Anacortes 98221
(206)293-3055.

Asotin. PATRICIA GUENTHER
   P.O. Box 25, Asotin 99402.

Auburn. LILLIAN KITCHELL
   20 "A" St., N.W., Auburn 98002.

Battle Ground. JANE S. JOHNSON (I)
   1975-. Bds: Ch., Street Com.; Finance Com.;
Bldg. Com. Educ: Portland State U. 1969 BS.
B: 6/2/38. Add: 509 N. Eaton Ave., Battle
Ground 98604 (206)687-2842.

Beaux Arts Village. HELEN L. LEWIS
   2804 107th SE, Beaux Arts Village 98004.

Bellevue. NANCY L. RISING (D)
   1969-. Bds: Ch., Public Safety; Metro
Council-Transit Com.; Puget Sound Council of
Govts. Party: State Del. 1964, '66, '68, '70;
Precinct Committeewoman 1964-70. Prev: Park
Bd. 1964-69. Org: Nat. League of Cities;
Urban League; NOW; WPC; LWV; Chamber of Commerce;
Dem. Club; Japanese Amer. Citizens League;
Municipal League. Educ: U. of Wash. 1953 BA.
B: 5/12/34. Add: 14438 NE 16th Pl., Bellevue
98007 (206)455-6800.

Bellingham. ROMA JEAN JONES (I)
   1976-. Bds: Library Bd.; Council Finance
Com.; Open Space Com. Prev: Mayors Adv. Com.
1974-75. Org: Bd. of Realtors; Soroptomist
Club. Educ: Realtor Institute 1974 GRI. Occ:
Real Estate Broker. B: 4/13/32. Add: 1425
N. State St., Bellingham 98225 (206)733-4350.

Benton City. KAY MYLER
     P.O. Box 218, Benton City 98320.

Blaine. JUDITH STEINBACH
     344 H St., P.O. Box 490, Blaine 98230.

Bonney Lake. KAREN S. MC BREER (R)
     1975-. Bds: Cnty. Law & Justice Planning
Com.; Water; Street. Org: U.S. Divorce Reform.
B: 12/11/43. Add: 19002 75th St. E., Bonney
Lk. 98390 (206)863-6319.

Brier. ELIZABETH HOWARD
     2901 228th S.W., Brier 98036.

Brier. KATHLEEN MAY PYNE (D) **
     1974-. Bds: Personnel Com. Educ: U. of
Southwestern La. 1960 BA. Occ: Secretary &
Bookkeeper. B: 5/15/30. Add: 23224 35th Pl.,
Brier 98036.

Buckley. MARTHA OLSEN
     Cedar & Pearl Sts., P.O. Box 344, Buckley
98321.

Bucoda. DOROTHY HURN
          DRUSILLA MORRIS
     7th & Nenant, P.O. Box 10, Bucoda 98530.

Burlington. SANDRA SCHEER
     500 Fairhaven Ave., Box 288, Burlington
98233.

Burlington. DOROTHY A. THOMPSON (I)
     1971-. Party: Precinct Committeewoman 1969-
71. Org: NEA; Friends of the Library; Educ.
Assoc. Educ: U. of Wash. 1951 BA. Occ:Teacher.
B: 7/1/28. Add: 500 S. Gardner Rd., Burlington
98233.

Camas. BERNICE HUGHES (I)
     1971-. Bds: Ch., Policy & Fire Com.;
Library Bd.; Southwest Wash. Health Dist. Org:
BPW. Occ: Music Teacher. B: 9/10/16. Add:
1201 NE 5th Ave., Camas 98607 (206)834-4626.

Camas. LILA W. TRAMMELL (D)
     1974-. Bds: Police & Fire Comsn.; Community
Educ. Bd. Party: State Del. 1976. Org: Amer.
Legion Auxilary. B: 7/12/16. Add: 655 NW
Trout, Camas 98607 (206)834-4262.

Carbonado. AUDREY BROWNING
              LOUISE CLAYTON
     Cor. of 5th & 8th, P.O. Box 2, Carbonado
98323.

Chehalis. FRANCES AUSTIN
            JOYCE VENEMON
     80 NE Cascade Ave., Box 871, Chehalis 98532.

Chelan. VIVIAN GAUKROGER
     143 Johnson Ave., P.O. Box 1669, Chelan
98816.

Chelan. MARTHA JANE MILLER (D)
     1973-. Mayor Pro Tem. Bds: Reg. Planning
Council; Health Cmsn.; Ch., Finance Com. Prev:
City-Cnty. Health Dist. Bd. 1974-76. Org:

Chamber of Commerce; Cnty. Dem. Club; OES.
Educ: Oregon State U. 1939 BA. B: 5/24/16.
Add: 225 E. Trow Ave., Chelan 98816 (509)
682-4037.

Cheney. VIRGINIA WHITE
     609 2nd St., Cheney 99004.

Chewelah. GLORIA DAVIDSON (R)
     1976-. Bds: Ch., Park & Airport Com.;
Finance Com.; Bldg. Com. Org: Master Florists;
Chamber of Commerce; Community Celebrations;
Women's Club. Educ: Kinman Business U. 1941
BEd. Occ: Florist. B: 3/15/24. Add: 709 W.
Clay, Chewelah 99109 (509)935-8555.

Cle Elum. IOLA BRAITHWAITE
            MARY J. GIAUDRONE
            DOROTHY NIXON
     301 Pennsylvania, Cle Elum 98922.

Colfax. BARBARA MC CRAY
     Mill & Island, P.O. Box 229, Colfax 99101.

College Place. HELEN ELIZABETH CROSS (I) **
     1971-. Bds: Finance Com. Org: Faculty
Women's Club. Educ: Hunter Coll. 1932 BA.
Occ: Book Editor & Proofreader. B: 4/23/11.
Add: 626 SE 4th St., College Place 99324.

Colton. JOANNE DAHMEN
          HELEN MOSER
     706 Broadway, Colton 99113.

Colville. GLORIA FUNK
     170 S. Oak, Colville 99114.

Colville. HELEN J. WHITE
     1975-. Bds: City Parking Cmsn.; Bd. of
Dirs. Tri-Cnty. Economic Devt. Org: Nat. Fed.
of Fed. Employees; Cnty. Bd.for 3rd Class
Dists.; OES. Occ: Resource Asst. B: 7/22/14.
Add: P.O. Box 215, Colville 99114 (509)
684-5221.

Concrete. BARBARA RIEHL (R) **
     1973-. Org: First Bank Independent Employ-
ers Assoc. Occ: Paying & Receiving Teller.
B: 10/27/32. Add: Box 273, Concrete 98237
(206)853-2141.

Connell. ALLEDA L. ARNOLD (D)
     1976-. Bds: Leg., Health & Sanitation;
Town Real Estate. Occ: Postal Clerk. B:
5/25/27. Add: 536 S. Almira, Box 328,
Connell 99326 (509)234-2701.

Creston. BETTY REED **
     1974-. Org: Labors Internat. Union. Occ:
School Bus Driver. B: 1/3/28. Add: Box 49,
Creston 99117.

Cusick. MARGARET OLSON
     Town Hall, Cusick 99119.

Darrington. CLARICE L. NESS **
     1973-. Org: Ch., Scholarship Fund. Educ:
Northwest Nazarene Coll. 1956 BA. Occ: Self-
employed. B: 11/21/34. Add: 815 Givens St.,
Darrington 98241.

Davenport. ELEANOR L. MAC DONALD **
    1974-. Org: Pres., Soroptimist. Occ: Cafe
& Lounge Owner. B: 6/27/25. Add: 1115 Marshall,
Davenport 99122 (509)725-2824.

Dupont. LORRAINE OVERMYER
    209 Barsdale Ave., P.O. Box 159, Dupont
98327.

Ellensburg. JANIECE L. COOK (I) **
    1974-. Bds: Law & Justice Com. B: 5/6/22.
Add: 103 S. Walnut, Ellensburg 98926 (509)
962-9863.

Ellensburg. IRENE MANN RINEHART (D)
    1967-. Bds: Cnty. Action Com.; Cnty. Conf.
of Govts.; Law & Justice Com. Educ: U. of Va.
1936 BA; 1938 MA; 1942 PhD. B: 5/27/16. Add:
1115 E 4th, Ellensburg 98926 (509)962-9863.

Everett. JOYCE EBERT
    3002 Wetmore, Everett 98201.

Fife. BARBARA BUTTON
    5209 Pacific Hwy. E., Fife 98424.

Fircrest. BEVERLY B. FOLEY
    115 Ramsdell St., Tacoma 98466.

Forks. MARJORIE HOWARD
    1st Ave. NE, P.O. Box 28, Forks 98331.

Garfield. ALICE J. ROCKHILL
    California & 5th, P.O. Box 218, Garfield
99130.

George. MARJORIE MERRIMAN
    P.O. Box 5053, George 98824.

Gig Harbor. RUTH M. BOGUE (I) **
    1969-. Bds: Park Bd.; Library Bd. Org:
Audubon Society; Alt., High School Advisory
Bd. B: 1/20/25. Add: Box 127, Gig Harbor
98335 (206)858-2116.

Gig Harbor. NANCY MELTON
    7716 Pioneer Way, P.O. Box 145, Gig Harbor
98335.

Gold Bar. BERTHA GILMORE
    501 Groft, P.O. Box 107, Gold Bar 98251.

Goldendale. MURIEL G. JACOBSEN **
    1973-. Bds: Ch., Water & Sewer; Ch.,
Financial & Judicial; Ch., Parks & Recreation;
Ch., Licenses; Bd. of Adjustment. Org: Exec.
Bd., Chamber of Commerce; Treasurer, PEO. B:
3/27/28. Add: Box 1, 405 E. Broadway, Golden-
dale 98620 (509)773-4288.

Grand Coulee Heights. IDA A. FLEISCHMANN (D)
    Bds: Ch., Audit; Ch., License; Ch., Library.
Party: State Del.; Precinct Committeewoman.
Prev: Mayor 1932-34. Org: Senior Citizens;
Dem. Women; Cnty. Central Com. Occ: Realtor.
B: 11/10/1900. Add: 530 Butler Sq., Grand
Coulee Hts. 99133.

Grand Coulee. RITA C. STOREY
    306 Midway, P.O. Box 180, Grand Coulee 99133.

Grandview. NANCY E. DAVIDSON (I)
    1975-. Bds: Ch., Parks & Recreation Com.;
City Property Com.; Planning Cmsn. Educ:
Big Bend Community Coll. 1967 AA; Central
Wash. State Coll. 1969 BA. Occ: Apartment
Manager. B: 12/5/46. Add: Rt. 3, Box 3508,
606 Cherry Ln., Grandview 98930 (509)
882-1237.

Granite Falls. BARBARA ALEXANDER
    206 S. Granite Ave., P.O. Box 64, Granite
Falls 98252.

Hamilton. JEWELL NATIONS
    P.O. Box 444, Hamilton 98255.

Harrah. SHARON SCHILPEROORT (R)
    1975-. Bds: Park Dir. Party: State Alt.
1976; Alt. Precinct Del. 1975-76. Educ:
Evangel Coll. 1969 BS. Occ: Pre-school
Teacher. B: 4/25/47. Add: Rt. 1, Box 12,
Harrah 98933 (509)848-2432.

Harrington. MARJORIE TANKE (D)
    1975-. Bds: Planning Cmsn. Party: State
Del. 1970, '72, '74, '76; Precinct Leader
1966-76; State Committeewoman 1970-76. Prev:
Ch., Civil Service, State Employee 1960-66.
Org: Wash. Assoc. of Wheat Growers; Chamber
of Commerce; Cnty. Dem. Women's Club. B:
8/6/17. Add: 507 S. 2nd, Harrington 99134.

Hartline. MEGAN HUNSAKER
    P.O. Box 34, Hartline 99135.

Hatton. IDA ERDMAN
    P.O. Box 148, Hatton 99332.

Hatton. VIVIAN LOUISE GOLDNER (D) **
    1972-. Occ: Floorlady, Potato Processing
Plant. B: 3/10/22. Add: Box 124, Hatton
99332.

Hatton. FRANCES JOHNSTON
        IRENE THOMPSON
    P.O. Box 148, Hatton 99332.

Hoquiam. GERTRUDE PEAK
        PHILLIS SHRAUGER
    609 8th St., Hoquiam 98550.

Hunts Point. DOROTHY J. KLINE (R) **
    1974-. Bds: Action Plan; Regional Shore-
line Technical Com. Party: Co-Precinct Ch.
1960-65. Prev: Water Cmsnr. 1973-74; Planning Cmsn. 1970-73. Org: Foundation for
Economic Educ.; Municipal League; World
Affairs Council; Fed. of Rep. Women; Rep.
Women. Occ: Secretary & Assistant Bookkeeper.
B: 11/29/23. Add: Box 1968, Bellevue 98009
(206)455-1834.

Index. JANE KELLY
    Town Hall, Index 98256.

Ione. ENID COOK **
    1971-. Bds: Park Cmsnr. B: 11/19/14.
Add: Houghton St., Ione 99139 (509)
442-3611.

Kalama. ELAINE E. BRADFORD (R) **
　　1973-. Bds: Planning Cmsn. Prev: Clerk-
Treasurer 1964-72. Org: Chamber of Commerce.
Occ: City Clerk; Treasurer; Secretary. B:
8/23/06. Add: 141 N. Second St., Kalama
98625 (206)673-4525.

Kennewick. SHELAH RENBERGER
　　210 W. 6th Ave., P.O. Box 6108, Kennewick
99336.

Kent. BILLIE RAE JOHNSON (D)
　　1973-. Bds: Finance Com.; Public Works
Com. Org: Women's Club. Occ: Company Coord.
B: 9/28/32. Add: 3901 Cambridge Ct., Kent
98031 (206)872-3357.

Kent. JEANNE MASTERS (R) **
　　1967-. Bds: Council of Governments. Party:
Precinct Com. 1969- . Org: PTA; Rep. Women's
Club. Occ: Secretary. B: 8/12/28. Add:
20038 68th Ave., S, Kent 98031 (206)872-3370.

Kettle Falls. ANN ANDERSON
　　　　　　HELEN HOUCK
　　P.O. Box 266, Kettle Falls 99141.

Kirkland. DORIS COOPER **
　　1971-. Bds: Central Business Dist.; Redev.
Advisory Com.; Council Finance Com. Party:
Del., Cnty. Conv. 1964. Prev: Regional Advisory
Com. 1973-74; Local Advisory Com.; Bd. of Adjust-
ment 1960-67. Org: PTA. Educ: U. of Wash.
1950 BA. B: 6/7/26. Add: 10640 NE 45th,
Kirkland 98033 (206)822-9271.

Krupp. EDNA LENZ
　　P.O. Box 227, Marlin 98832.

Lacey. JOSEPHINE GAUTHIER
　　5604 Pacific Ave. SE Drawer B, Lacey 98503.

La Conner. JUNE OVERSTREET
　　2nd & Douglas, P.O. Box 400, La Conner
98257.

Lyman. SUSAN RUSSELL
　　　　　SHIRLEY WIRTZ
　　104 W. 3rd St., P.O. Box 1248, Lyman 98263.

Lynnwood. TINA ROBERTS
　　19100 44th Ave. W, Lynnwood 98036.

Mabton. GRACE TODD
　　P.O. Box 655, Mabton 98935.

Marysville. RUTH ROUNDY (I)
　　1973-. Mayor Pro Tem. Bds: Cnty. Public
Transportation. Party: Precinct Committeewoman 1970-72. Org: Senior Club. B: 8/16/03.
Add: 1203 Cedar St., Marysville 98270.

Mc Cleary. SHIRLEY A. FINCH (D)
　　1973-. Occ: Clerk-Carrier. B: 12/9/38.
Add: 610 4th St., Box 542, Mc Cleary 98557
(206)495-3667.

Mc Cleary. KAREN ODLE
　　3rd & Simpson, P.O. Box 360, Mc Cleary
98557.

Medical Lake. FRAN LLEWELLYN
　　S. 124 Lefevre, P.O. Box 98, Medical
Lake 99022.

Medina. JULIE GERRARD
　　　　　MIRIAN LUCAS
　　501 Evergreen Pt. Rd., Box 144, Medina
98039.

Mercer Island. MARGUERITE M. SUTHERLAND
　　1971-. Bds: Planning Cmsn.; Puget Sound
Council of Govts.; Library Bd. Org: Environmental Council. Educ: U. of Mich. BS.
Add: 5425 96th SE, Mercer Is. 98040.

Mesa. MARY TSCHIRKY
　　3rd & Franklin, P.O. Box 146, Mesa 99343.

Monroe. DONETTA J. WALSER (D)
　　1975-. Bds: Ch., Audit & Finance;
Contracts & Insurance; Leases. Educ: U. of
Idaho 1966 BA. Occ: Realtor. B: 7/21/43.
Add: 682 Park La., P.O. Box 237, Monroe
98272 (206)794-7400.

Mossyrock. BETTY E. WORKMAN
　　P.O. Box 96, Mossyrock 98564.

Mountlake Terrace. LOIS ANDERSON
　　23204 58th Ave. W, Mountlake Terrace
98043.

Mount Vernon. RUTH E. GIDLUND
　　320 Broadway, P.O. Box 807, Mount Vernon
98273.

Mukilteo. VIRGINIA BERGSTROM (I)
　　1975-. Bds: Lower Snohomish Basin Facilities Planning Policy Com. Prev: Bd. of
Adjustment 1970-74. Occ: Bookkeeper. B:
9/10/15. Add: 1505 Mukilteo Ln., P.O. Box
291, Mukilteo 98275 (206)355-4141.

Mukilteo. ANNE JENKS
　　215 Park, P.O. Box 178, Mukilteo 98275.

Newport. KAREN ROTHSTROM
　　201 S. Washington, Box 546, Newport 99156.

North Bend. HELEN TROSTEL
　　201 Main St. N, P.O. Box 547, N. Bend
98045.

Northport. NORMA HAIGH
　　　　　ANN NEW
　　P.O. Box 177, Northport 99157.

Oak Harbor. PATRICIA COHEN
　　3075 300 Ave. W., Oak Harbor 98277.

Oakesdale. KAREN NEBEL
　　1st & Steptoe Ave., P.O. Box 105, Oakesdale
99158.

Oakville. GRACE MEILE
　　P.O. Box D, Oakville 98568.

Ocean Shores. MARGARET CARLSTON
　　Pt. Brown Ave., P.O. Box 317, Ocean Shores
98551.

Omak. DONNA SHORT
    1965-. Bds: Ch., Park Com.; Airport Com.;
Bd. of Adjustment. Org: Soroptimist; Ortho-
pedic Aux. Educ: Ullnatchie Valley Jr. Coll.
1977 AA. Occ: Employment Service Interviewer.
B: 6/27/26. Add: 628 Skyview Dr., Omak 98841
(509)826-0526.

Orting. LOUISE WISE
    100 N. Train, P.O. Box 665, Orting 98360.

Pacific. ROSALIE ANGEL
              AUDREY CRUICKSHANK
    100 3rd Ave. SE, P.O. Box 18, Pacific 98047

Palouse. CLARA A. MC DONALD
    P.O. Box 248, Palouse 99161.

Pateros. JANE HARVEY
    113 Lakeshore Dr., P.O. Box 8, Pateros
98846.

Pomeroy. WINNIFRED KUCKLICK (R) **
    1973-. Bds: Cemetery; Water, Sewer; Swim-
ing Pool; Fair Bd. Party: V-Ch., Precinct Com.
1975- . B: 3/26/29. Add: 234 Pataha, Pomeroy
99347 (509)843-1601.

Port Angeles. V. LORRAINE ROSS (R)
    1969-. Bds: Ch., Cnty. Govt. Conf.; Ch.,
Real Estate Com.; Olympic Health Dist. Party:
State Del. 1958-70; State Alt. 1976; State
Committeewoman 1960-64; Rep. State Elector
Coll. 1964; Asst. Cnty. Finance Ch. 1977-78.
Org: Nat. Assoc. of Realtors; Chamber of
Commerce; DAR; GOP Nat. Com.; Cnty. Rep.
Women. Occ: Real Estate Broker. B: 7/9/19.
Add: 413 E. Front, Port Angeles 98362 (206)
457-0411.

Port Orchard. MARY ROY WILSON (R)
    1976-. Bds: Ch., Fire & Light Com.;
Streets & Alleys Com.; Parks Com. Prev:
Planning Cmsn. 1975. Org: Amer. Fed.-State,
Cnty. & City Employees. Occ: Design Engineer.
B: 12/8/23. Add: 1306 West Ave., Port Orchard
98366.

Pullman. CRISTA EMERSON
    SE 325 Paradise, P.O. Box 438, Pullman
99163.

Pullman. BARBARA JEAN RAYBURN (I)
    1975-. Bds: Ch., Disability Bd. Org:
AAUW. Educ: Ind. U. 1965 BS. B: 3/7/43.
Add: NE 1830 Wheatland Dr., Pullman 99163
(509)332-2761.

Puyallup. PHYLLIS M. HALE (R)
    1971-. Bds: Parks & Recreation Bd. Party:
State Del. 1976; Club Pres. 1975-77. Org:
Teamsters Union; Rep. Club; OES. Occ: Epide-
miologic Investigator. B: 12/2/27. Add: 205
16th St. SW, Puyallup 98371 (206)845-1755.

Puyallup. MARY MEYER (D)
    1975-. Prev:Ch., Planning Cmsn. 1974-76.
Org: LWV; Dem. Club; PTA. Occ: Secretary. B:
1/30/39. Add: 2207 S. Meridan St., Puyallup
98371 (206)845-9158.

Quincy. MARILYN J. NEAVILL **
    1973-. Bds: Park Bd.; Alcoholism Bd.
Educ: Western Mich. U. BA. Occ: Teacher.
B: 6/26/37. Add: 409 I St., SE, Quincy
98848 (509)787-3523.

Reardan RUTH KELSO
    P.O. Box 228, Reardan 99029.

Redmond. DOREEN F. MARCHIONE (D)
    1975-. Bds: Ch., Public Administration
Com.; Planning Com.; Public Works. Party:
Precinct Committeewoman 1971- . Prev: V-Ch.,
Shorelines Adv. Com. 1973-74. Org: LWV.
Educ: Seattle U. 1961 BA. B: 11/6/38. Add:
7424 140th Pl. NE, Redmond 98052 (206)
885-2300.

Renton. PATRICIA SEYMOUR
    200 Mill Ave. S., Renton 98055.

Republic. GLADYSS APRILL
    P.O. Box 331, Republic 99166.

Ridgefield. BARBARA FAEH
    230 Pioneer Ave., P.O. Box 648, Ridgefield
98642.

Ridgefield. FRANCES QUIROGA **
    1972-. Bds: Finance Ch.; Park Com.;
Street Com. Prev: City Clerk 1970-72.
Org: Advisory Council, Community School;
Family Day Care Assoc.; Foresters; Foster
Parent Assoc.; Grange. Occ: Owner & Dir.,
Day Care Center. B: 8/1/40. Add: 113 S.
Main, Ridgefield 98642 (206)887-3557.

Ritzville. BERNICE ANN BASSO **
    1973-. Bds: Ch., Auditing Com.; Cemetery,
Park & Golf Course; Employee Relations. B:
3/11/36. Add: 403 E. 4th, Ritzville 99169
(509)659-0358.

Riverside. PATRICIA CHRISTOPH
                KATHRYN HUBBARD
                NORA MC KAY
    1st & State Sts., P.O. Box 188, Riverside
98849.

Rock Island. DIANA BAIRD
    P.O. Box 98, Rock Island 98850.

Rosalia. MARCIA NELSON
    1976-. Add: Box 201, Rosalia 99170
(509)523-2131.

Roslyn. DONNA M. GORDON (D)
    1973-. Bds: Cnty. Council of Govt.; Ch.,
Parks & Cemeterys Com.; Finance Com. Org:
Bd. of Realtors. Occ: Realtor. B: 8/8/32.
Add: 38 A St., Roslyn 98941 (509)649-3105.

Royal City. RUTH BROWN (D) **
    1969-. Bds: Park Cmsnr.; Bd. of Health.
B: 5/14/25. Add: Box 253, Royal City 99357
(509)346-2263.

Ruston. CORINNE D. JOHNSON
    B: 9/7/17. Add: 5227 N. Pearl, Tacoma
98407 (206)759-3544.

Ruston. MARY K. JOYCE
      DORIS L. SAGE
      5117 N. Winnifred, Tacoma 98407.

Seattle PHYLLIS LAMPHERE (I)
      1968-. Bds: Governor's Com. for Law &
Justice Planning Office; Puget Sound Council
of Govts.; Cnty. Sub-regional Council. Prev:
Ch., Intergovt. Relations Com.; V-Ch., Plann-
ing & Urban Devt.; Ch., Business & Occupation
Tax Force; Ch., Housing Policy Adv. Com.;
Puget Sound Health Planning Council, Exec.
Com.; Cnty. Air Pollution Control Adv. Bd.;
Governor's Adv. Com. on Community Devt. Org:
Nat. League of Cities; Neighborhood Housing
Services of Amer.; Nat. Ctr. for Productivity
& Quality of Working Life; U.S. Del., U.N.
Conf. on Human Settlements. Educ: Barnard
Coll. BA. Add: 1614 Edgewood SW, Seattle
98116 (206)583-2355.

Seattle. JEANETTE WILLIAMS (D) **
      1970-. Bds: Transit Com.; Finance Com.;
Council of Govts. Party: Local Precinct Com.
1939- ; Nat. Conv. Del. 1964, 1968, 1974;
Ch., Cnty. Central Com. 1963-68; Platform
Com. 1964, 1968; V-Ch., Cnty. Central Com.
1959-60; State Exec. Bd. Org: BPW; Common
Cause; LWV; NOW; Urban League; WPC; Musicians
Union. Educ: U. of Wash. 1937 BA; Amer. Conservatory of Music 1938 BM; Amer. Conservatory of Music 1939 MM. B: 6/11/17. Add:
7132 58th Ave., NE, Seattle 98115 (206)
583-2366.

Sequim. RENEE HANSEY
      JEANNE MOTAN
      152 W. Cedar, P.O. Box 295, Sequim 98382.

Snohomish. ANNA EASON
      EVELYN L. STROUT
      1009 1st St., Snohomish 98290.

Snoqualmie. MARY LOU STEVENS
      210 River St., P.O. Box 337, Snoqualmie

Soap Lake. MARINA ROMARY
      329 2nd Ave., SE, P.O. Box 187, Soap Lake
98823.

South Bend. HELEN MAE HILL (D)
      1973-. Bds: Ch., Parks, Docks, Bldgs.;
Ch., Planning Cmsn. Party: Precinct Committee-
woman 1958-62. Org: Literary Club. B:12/6/28.
Add: 1513 W. 1st St., S. Bend 98586.

Spokane. MARGARET JEAN LEONARD (R)
      1969-. Mayor Pro Tem. Bds: Ch., Fire
Pension Bd.; Ch., Police Pension Bd.; Employee
Retirement System. Party: State Del. 1968,
'70, '72; Precinct Committeewoman 1957-72.
Prev: City Councilwoman 1969-75; Mayor Pro
Tem 1975-77. Org: BPW; Grass Roots Citizens
Com.; Assoc. for Better Community; Rep. Party;
Dem. Party; Grange. Educ: Ellensburg Normal
School 1939 BA. B: 5/27/18. Add: 1117 E.
Mission Ave., Spokane 99202 (509)456-2643.

Spokane. MARILYN STANTON (D)
      1976-. Bds: Cnty. Air Pollution Bd.; Area
Agency on Aging. Party: Precinct Ch. 1972-77.
Org: Danforth Assoc.; Citizens Against Resi-
dential Freeways; AAUW; LWV; Dem's. for United
Action. Educ: Gonzaga U. BS; MA. Occ: Assoc.
Professor of Biology. B: 1/18/25. Add: E.
1540 S. Riverton, Spokane 99207 (509)
456-2678.

Springdale. HELEN HESKETT
      P.O. Box 157, Town Hall, Springdale 99173.

Stanwood. ROBERTA L. HANSON (D)
      1974-. Bds: Water Management Study; Ch.,
Finance Com.; Ch., Insurance Com. Org:
Historical Society; OES. B: 12/2/44. Add:
27011 - 81 Dr. N.W., Stanwood 98292 (206)
629-2181.

Starbuck. RUBY NORTON
      P.O. Box 296, Starbuck 99359.

Steilacoom. JOAN C. CURTIS
      1715 Lafayette St., P.O. Box M, Steilacoom
98388.

Stevenson. RUTH M. MEAGHERS (R) **
      1974-. Org: OES. Occ: Automotive Account-
ant. B: 8/12/20. Add: Box 306, Stevenson
98648.

Sultan. FLORENCE PREDHOMME
      P.O. Box 220, Town Hall, Sultan 98294.

Sumner. BARBARA SKINNER
      1976-. Bds: Cnty. Planning Cmsn. Citizen's
Adv. Com. Prev: Planning Com. 1975-76. B:
4/24/38. Add: 318 Valley Ave., Sumner 98390
(206)863-5263.

Sunnyside. IRENE BERK (D)
      1970-. Bds: Public Library; Airport Com.;
Fireman's Relief & Pension. Org: Retail
Store Employees Union; BPW. Occ: Bookkeeper.
Add: 115 Harrison Ave., Sunnyside 98944.

Sunnyside. MAXINE HOVORKA (D) **
      1973-. Bds: Cnty. Law & Justice Com.
Party: Del., Cnty. Conv. 1968. Prev: City
Library Bd. 1962-74. Org: Pres., Friends of
Library. Occ: Secretary. B: 12/31/24. Add:
1211 Cherry Ave., Sunnyside 98944 (509)
837-3782.

Tacoma. BARBARA J. BICHSEL (D)
      1975-. Bds: Human Relations Cmsn.; Puget
Sound Council of Govts. Party: State Del.
1976; State Alt. 1972; Precinct Committeewoman 1969-77. B: 9/24/25. Add: 3855 S.
Fawcett, Tacoma 98405 (206)593-4110.

Tekoa. HELEN JOHNSON
      P.O. Box 220, Tekoa 99033.

Tekoa. BILLIE MOORE (R)
      1969-. Bds: Ch. Tekoa Golf & Country Club;
Ch., Cemetary; Dump. Occ: Secretary & Accountant. B: 5/3/10. Add: Box 337, Tekoa 99033.

Tieton. BERNICE DILLEY
      P.O. Box 357, Tieton 98947.

Toledo. SHIRLEY ANN GRUBB (I)
      1974-. Bds: Utilities; Ch., Health &
Welfare, Finance Com. Educ: W.W.S.C. 1969 BA.
Occ: Teacher's Aide. B: 3/23/43. Add: 411
Hemlock, Toledo 98591 (206)864-4564.

Toppenish JUDITH BOEKHOLDER
      1976-. Bds: Cnty. Council of Govts. Org:
Women's Club. Educ: Ill. State U. 1964 BS;
1965 MS. Occ: Substitute Teacher. B: 8/9/42.
Add: 541 Lillie La., Toppenish 98948 (509)
865-2409.

Tukwila. CATHERINE HARRIS
      14475 59th Ave. S., Tukwila 98168.

Tukwila. PHYLLIS D. PESICKA (R)
      1975-. Bds: Public Works Com.; Community
Affairs Com. Party: State Del. 1974. Org:
Amer. Cancer Soc.; PTA. B: 6/29/34. Add:
14726 57th Ave. S., Tukwila 98168 (206)
242-7150.

Tumwater. CLORICE V. KENNEDY (I)
      Bds: Finance; Planning Com. Prev: City
Reasurer 1967-70. Occ: Clerical Supervisor.
B: 2/14/29. Add: 711 S. 4th, Tumwater 98502
(206)753-8750.

Twisp. MARIE RISLEY
      P.O. box 278, Twisp 98856.

Union Town. BETTY HEITSTUMAN (D) **
      1974-. Bds: Health & Welfare; Planning
Cmsn. Org: Credit Women of America. Occ:
Office Manager. B: 3/5/29. Add: P.O. Box 147,
Union Town 99179 (509)229-3581.

Vader. JEWEL HANCOCK
      P.O. Box 178, Vader 98593.

Vancouver. ROSE BESSERMAN
      210 E. 13th St., P.O. Box 1995, Vancouver
98663.

Vancouver. ETHEL K. LEHMAN (R)
      1973-. Bds: Ch., Project Central Park; Ch.,
Law & Justice Council. Party: State Del. 1976.
Prev: Planning Cmsn. 1971-73; Freeholder Cmsn.
1973- . Org: Grange; LWV. B: 6/1/20. Add:
602 Palo Alto Dr., Vancouver 98661 (206)
696-8211.

Walla Walla. ADELE BOWMAN ANDERSON (R)
      1973-. Party: State Del.; Area Ch. Prev:
Interagency Com. for Outdoor Recreation 1973-
76. Educ: Pomona Coll. 1956 BA; Claremont
Graduate School 1966 MA, PhD. Occ: Coll.
Professor. B: 6/20/34. Add: 221 Newell St.,
Walla Walla 99362 (509)525-1720.

Westport. JOY DAHLBERG
      N. Montesano St., P.O. Box 505, Westport
98595.

Winslow. ALICE B. TAWRESEY (R)
      1975-. Bds: Ch., Audit & Personnel;
Planning-Land Use. Party: State Del. 1974.
Org: Bainbridge Educ. Assoc.; Wash. Educ.
Assoc.; NEA. Educ: U. of Wash. 1975 BA. Occ:
Teacher. B: 6/14/47. Add: 136 Ferncliff Ave.
NE, Bainbridge Is. 98110 (206)842-4709.

Woodland. LEONA CARTY
      100 Davidson Ave., P.O. Box 9, Woodland
98674.

Yacolt. MARY ROSEANN DE SHAZER BECKER (I)
      1975-. Occ: Tupperware Dealer. B:
3/22/54. Add: 310 Railroad Ave., Yacolt
98675.

Yakima. NADINE WALKER (R)
      1976-. Bds: Cnty. Health Dist.; SE
Community Center; Retired Senior Volunteer
Program. Org: Wash. State Nurses Assoc.;
Amer. Business Women Assoc. Educ: Yakima
Vly. Coll. 1967 RN. Occ: RN. B: 4/16/18.
Add: 1005 S. 42nd Ave., #B, Yakima 98908.

Yarrow Point. JANNE WHITING
      4705 91st Ave. NE, Bellevue 98004.

Yelm. EVELYN SOUTHWORTH
      P.O. Box 479, Town Hall, Yelm 98597.

Judges

CAROLYN R. DIMMICK
      Judge, Superior Court. 1976-. Bds:
Judges Exec. Com.; Family Law Com. Prev:
Asst. Atty. General 1953-55; Deputy Prose-
cuting Atty. 1955-58, 1960-62; Dist. Ct.
Judge 1965-75. Org: ABA; Amer. Judges
Assoc.; World Assoc. of Judges; Altrusa.
Educ: U. of Wash. 1951 BA; 1953 JD. B:
10/24/29. Add: 15724 61st Ave. NE, Bothell
98011 (206)344-4058.

BARBARA DURHAM
      Judge, Superior Court. Add: King Cnty.
Courthouse, Seattle 98104.

NANCY ANN GATTUSO HOLMAN
      Judge, Superior Court. 1970-. Org: AAUW;
ABA; State Bar Assoc.; Bd., Assoc. of Family
Concillation Cts. Educ: Wheaton Coll. 1956
BA; Boston Coll. School of Law 1959 JD. B:
6/21/35. Add: 1608 Federal Ave. E., Seattle
98102 (206)344-4061.

JANICE NIEMI (D)
      Judge, Superior Court. 1972-. Bds:
Juvenile Ct. Com.; State Judges Criminal Law
Com. Prev: Dist. Ct. Judge 1971-72; Central
Area School Council 1969-70. Org: Wash.
State Bar Assoc.; ABA; Wash. Women Lawyers;
Child Abuse & Welfare Council; Urban League;
Jr. League. Educ: U. of Wash. 1950 BA; U. of
Wash. Law School 1967 JD. Occ: Superior Ct.
Judge. B: 9/18/28. Add: 1067 E. Blaine,
Seattle 98102 (206)344-4053.

State Boards and Commissions

Office of the Governor, State Capitol Bldg., Olympia 98504.

Accountancy, Board of
BETTY JEAN LUCAS

Affirmative Action, Governor's Review Committee
ALYCE ARGEL
JO GARCEAU
SALLY LEWIS
PAM LODEFINK
LOIS MEYER
MARY HELEN ROBERTS
EDITH SPANGLER
JANET WARD

Arts Commission
JACQUELINE F. DELAHUNT
MARGRET DICKINSON
MARY E. DUNTON
PEGGY GOLBERG
JOANNE B. PEEKEMA
JEAN SPRAGUE
JUDITH WHETZEL

Barber Examining Committee
PAULINE K. LANGNER

Beef Commission
TONI BENZEL

Building Code Advisory Council
BARBARA ALLEN
CHAO-LIANG CHOW
JOAN P. CLARK

Cemetery Board
MARY M. BOWLES

Chiropractic Examiners, State Board of
IRENE NAVRATIL, D.C.

Collection Agency Board
MRS. F. MARKS LANDLER

Columbia River Gorge Commission
NANCY BARNEY
ALICE P. BLAIR
MILDRED O'DONNELL

Community College Education Board
MRS. FRED RADKE

Community Development Advisory Commission
JEAN AMELUXEN
HAZEL BURNETT
NAOMI CUMMINGS
HELEN DYGERT
BETTY MAYOR EDMONDSON
DONNA HANSON
ELEANOR JOHNSON
ELAINE DAY LATOURELL
ELEANOR LEE
LOIS NORTH
VICTORIA PAVAL
CHRIS SMITH

Community Services and Continuing Education Advisory Council
FERN BRANDT
MARIE CAMERON
MARY LOU HARWOOD
ISABEL HOGAN
ANNE MARIE MC CARTAN
BARBARA WILLIAMS

Comprehensive Health Planning Advisory Council
ELISE CHADWICK
NANCY FALLER
JOYCE FIELDS
MAXINE HAYNES
MARY ELLEN HILLAIRE
LOIS MEYER
DOROTHY B. REID
KATHERINE RICKEY
SISTER CHARLOTTE VAN DYKE
RUTH WHITE

Conservation Commission
JEANNETTE C. HAYNER

Correctional Training Standards and Education, Board on
CHARLOTTE HACKMAN
JUDITH C. SMITH
VIRGINIA SWANSON

Cosmetology Examining Committee
OPAL E. LONON
MARIE H. MURPHY
BLANCHE MARIE SMITH
RUTH M. TAYLOR

Cosmetology Hearing Board
MINNIE DALGLEISH

Criminal Justice Training Commission
NANCY ANN HOLMAN

Deferred Compensation, Committee for
CHARLOTTE C. WHEAT

Developmental Disabilities Planning Council
KATHLEEN BARNETT
ELLA MAE CRAWFORD
DONNA DEVANEY
KATIE DOLAN
KATHERINE EPTON
CECILE LINDQUIST
HELEN A. PYM

Drug Abuse, Interagency Committee on
SALLY PERKINS

Drug Abuse Prevention
RITA FAY BURCHAM
MARILYN DECKER
JUNE LEONARD
ADELE PLOUFFE
MARITA STRENA
MARY ELLEN VAUGHAN

Ecological Commission
CAROLYN J. HAYEK
ANN WIDDITSCH

Economic Assistance Authority
    ELSE KORVELL

Education Commission of the States
    PHYLLIS ERICKSON
    CAROLE KUBOTA
    RUTHE RIDDER

Educational Television Commission
    GWEN R. CARLSON
    JUNE DILWORTH
    EVE JOHNSON
    SHARON MAEDA
    JUDITH MATSON
    SISTER MARIAN MC CARTHY
    NANCY WEBER

Electrical Contractors Examining Board
    SHARON Y. FUJITANI
    LAURIE FRANK MC CONNELL
    WINIFRED SAVERY

Emergency Medical and Ambulance Review Committee
    ANNA MAE ERICKSEN
    ZOE B. LUCKE

Employees' Insurance Board
    MARGARET OUCHI

Employee Suggestion Awards Board
    NANCY A. ALLEN
    DR. MARGARET P. FENN

Employment Agency Advisory Board
    SHIRLEY ADAMS
    SHIRLEY JONES MORGAN

Energy Facility Site Evaluation Council
    BETTY MC CLELLAND

Escrow Commission
    BEVERLY ERICKSON
    MARY E. KNUTSEN

Factory Built Housing, Advisory Board
    JUDITH FROLICH
    BEA HARDS

Family Practice Education Advisory Board
    BETTE EMERSON
    SISTER CHARLOTTE VAN DYKE

Forest Practices Advisory Committee
    MARJORIE SUTCH
    NANCY THOMAS

Forest Practices Board
    POLLY DYER

Gambling Commission
    MARY KNIBBS

Game Commission
    ELIZABETH MEADOWCROFT

Handicapped, Employment of the, Governor's
Committee on
    BARBARA ALLAN
    SUE AMMETER
    LUCILLE CHRISTIANSON

    KATIE DOLAN
    WINIFRED DUNCAN
    BARBARA DUNLAP
    JEAN FULTON
    POLLY GIBBS
    JULIA HALE
    JEANNE HUMMEL
    JOY ISHAM
    LETTIE JARRETT
    EMILIE JOHNSON
    MARGARET KENNEY
    JAN LA PRATH
    BONNIE LARSON
    PENNY LEWIS
    MARTY MARX
    DOROTHY MOORE
    SUE NEBEKER
    BEV PARKER
    LETHENE PARKS
    SALLY PUFF
    GLORIA SCHLEIFF
    ANNE SHUMWAY
    MURIEL TAYLOR
    JEAN TOEWS
    ANNE WALTZ
    MARILYN WARD
    PAT WILKINS

Health, State Board of
    JEANNE BENOLIEL
    BEVERLY FREEMAN

Hearing Aid Licensing Council
    MRS. WILLIAM L. BELL
    ROSE KALORIS SARIDAKIS

Highway Commission
    JULIA BUTLER HANSEN
    VIRGINIA GUNBY

Historical Records Advisory Board
    NANCY PRYOR

Historic Preservation, Advisory Council on
    PEGGY CORLEY
    CAROLYN FEASEY

Horse Heaven Hills Development (Select Committee on)
    DOROTHY PRIOR

Horse Racing Commission
    ANN MC LEAN

Hospital Commission
    SISTER CHARLOTTE VAN DYKE

Hospital Technical Committee
    KAREN CHAI
    IRMA GOERTZEN

Human Rights Commission
    WINIFRED DUNCAN
    LINDA S. HUME

Indian Advisory Council, Governor's
    RAMONA BENNETT
    VANETTA CHASE
    ANITA CHEER
    LORRAINE DOEBBLER
    MARILYN GEORGE

MARGARET GREENE
FLORENCE HARNDEN
ELOISE KING
MAYBELLE LITTLE
RAMONA MORRIS
PEARL PENN
ESTHER ROSS
FLORENCE SIGO
BEULAH WILSON

Indo-Chinese Advisory Committee
LUU TRANG KIM
DUONG-CHI NGUYEN

Institutional Industries Commission
MRS. JOSEPH ENTRIKIN

Intergovernmental Advisory Council
BETTY J. ANDERSON
DORIS COATES
DIANE WILLETT

Juvenile Justice Advisory Committee
DR. PATRICIA S. ANDERSON
MARY JO BUTTERFIELD
PATRICIA CLARK
ELEANOR F. CLIFTON
BRENDA M. GIVENS
EDNA L. GOODRICH
CAROLINA KOSLOSKY
MARY H. WAGONER
PEGGY G. WILLIAMS

Law and Justice, Governor's Committee on
PATRICIA S. ANDERSON
MONA BAILEY
SENATOR SUSAN GOULD
MURIEL HAGGLUND
HON. LENORE LAMBERT
HON. PHYLLIS LAMPHERE
BARBARA SCHLAG PETERSON
JOELENE UNSEOLD

Legal Service Advisory Council
ADDIE ROSE DUNLAP
RUTH NORDENBROOK

Lewis and Clark Trail Committee
HAZEL BAIN
DOROTHY ELLIOTT
WINIFRED FLIPPIN
VI FORREST
MARJORIE SUTCH

Librarians, State Board for the Certification of
DOREEN AMOROSO

Library Commission, State
BELINDA K. PEARSON
SHIRLEY TUCKER
VIVIAN WINSTON

Massage Examining Board
VIRGINIA E. PALMGREN

Medical Examiners, State Board of
NANCY S. NORDHOFF

Mexican-American Affairs Committee
MARGARET ZAMUDIO

Mobile Home and Recreational Vehicle Advisory Board
GLENNA TOLLETT

Nursing, State Board of
THELMA CLEVELAND
RUTH BARNEY FINE
BETTY J. HARRINGTON
LOUISE M. LEFEBVRE
BETTY JO NEILS
BEULAH M. SMITH
LYNNE BARBER VIGESAA

Nursing Home Administrators Board
SISTER M.L. FERSCHWEILER
DOROTHY KALLGREN
MERRIAM E. LATHROP
JEAN WALTERS OLDHAM
CAROLYN PAVLOFF
CAROLINE PRESTON

Oceanographic Commission
MARY KAY BECKER
ELLEN CRASWELL
ELEANOR FORTSON
RUTH WEINER

Outdoor Recreation, Interagency Committee for
HELEN ENGLE
MICAELA BROSTROM

Parks-Recreation Commission, State
KAY GREEN

Personnel Board, State
EDITH KOGENHOP

Pharmacy, State Board of
BARBARA NELSON
GERTRUDE H. REAVIS

Physical Therapists, State Examining Committee of
WILMA ZIEGLER

Pollution Control Hearing Board
CHRIS SMITH

Post Secondary Education, Council on
ALLISON COWLES
BETTY FLETCHER
RUTH SHEPHERD

Practical Nurse Examiners, State Board of
EVELYN M. BOYD, R.N.
MARGARET FROMHERZ
EVELYN KATZER
FRANCES H. GARVIE
CLARA SCHLOTFELDT

Prison Terms and Paroles, Board of
DIANNA F. OBERQUELL
HELEN RATCLIFF

Professional Development Fund Advisory Council
GENEVA DAVIDSON

Psychology, State Examining Board of
DR. MARIAN H. MOWATT
MARJORIE PANEK

Public Disclosure Commission
    JEAN DAVIS
    VIRGINIA GREGSON

Public Employment Relations Commission
    MARY ELLEN KRUG

Public Pension Commission
    DORIS J. JOHNSON
    FRANCES C. NORTH

Real Estate Commission
    EDRIS PHILLIPS

Securities Advisory Committee
    IRIS SPALDING

Social and Health Services
    RUTH COFFIN
    LILLIAN GIDEON
    SHERRIE M. MEYER
    JANET SKADAN
    KAY THODE
    DR. MARJORIE M. WILSON
    KATHY WOMER

Special Education Fiscal Task Force
    MARY PERKINS
    MARGO THORNLEY

Supply Management Advisory Board
    DOROTHY PLATH

Tax Board of Appeals
    JOAN THOMAS

Toll Bridge Authority
    VIRGINIA GUNBY
    JULIA BUTLER HANSEN

University of Washington, Board of Regents
    MARY GATES
    EDITH D. WILLIAMS

Vendor Rates, Advisory Committee on
    PRISCILLA V. BOWERMAN
    KRISTI WEIR

Veterans Affairs Advisory Committee
    DORIS MARTY MARX

Vocational Education Advisory Council on 687
    LOIS ANDRUS
    JOAN L. BERGY
    ANN DEWEY
    SUSAN C. EK
    ANNIE GALAROSA
    THELMA JACKSON
    JULIE SMILEY
    VENETTA STAPPLER
    MARGO THORNLEY

Women's Council, State
    JANET ALLISON
    JOAN BROWN
    MARY BURGESS
    DEBRA CLAUSEN
    ANN DEWEY

RITA DURAN
AUDREY GRUGER
CLAIRE HESS
MARILYN SCHELLER IRWIN
ELEANOR LEE
LOIS NORTH
CAROLYN PATTON
PEARL WARREN
LORRAINE WOJAHN

West Virginia

State Executive and Cabinet

MILDRED MITCHELL-BATEMAN **
    Director, Department of Mental Health 1962-.
Bds: South Regional Educ. Bd.; Cmsn. on Aging;
Cmsn. on Mental Retardation; Cmsn. on Status
of Women. Prev: Acting Dir., Dept. of Mental
Health 1962. Org: AMA; Amer. Psychiatric
Assoc.; Menninger Foundation; Bd. of Dir.,
Nat. Assoc. for Mental Health. Educ: Women's
Medical Coll. 1946 MD. Occ: Physician. B:
4/22/22. Add: State Office Bldg., Rm. 208,
Floor 2, Charleston 25305 (304)348-3211.

CAROLYN E. SMOOT (D)
    Director, Department of Employment Security.
1977-. Bds: Co-Ch., Governor's Com. on Employment of Handicapped; Co-Ch., Veterans Employment & Training Adv. Council; Cmsn, on Aging.
Org: NAACP. Educ: W. Va. State Coll. 1967 BS;
W. Va. Coll. of Graduate Studies 1975 MA. B:
9/24/45. Add: Box 222, Institute 25112
(304)348-2630.

VIRGINIA ROBERTS
    Director, Department of Motor Vehicles.
Add: State Capitol, Charleston 25305.

State Legislature

State House

THAIS BLATNIK (D)
    Party: State Del.; State Alt. Org: NOWL;
Cnty. Dem. Club. Occ: Journalist. B:
11/20/19. Add: RD 2, Triadelphia 26059
(304)348-3810.

MICHELE PRESTERA CRAIG (D)
    1972-. Dist: 11. Party: State Del. 1974.
Org: Jr. League; Community Mental Health Assoc.;
Dem. Women's Club. Educ: Queen Coll. 1967 BA.
Occ: Retail Merchant. B: 5/26/45. Add: 2030
Military Rd., Huntington 25701 (304)348-3810.

BETTY DORSEY CROOKSHANKS (D)
    1976-. Bds: Educ.; Labor & Industry;
Agriculture & Natural Resources. Party: State
Del. 1976. Org: OWL; Women's Club; BPW; Young
Dem's.; Dem. Women. Educ: W. Va. Institute of
Technology 1968 BA; W. Va. U. 1973 MA. Occ:
Teacher. B: 10/27/44. Add: Box 370, Rupert
25984.

PATRICIA OGDEN HARTMAN (D)
    1976-. Dist: 11. Bds: Educ. Com.; Leg.
Student Program Com.; State Federal Affairs
Com. Party: State Del. 1976; State Alt. 1972.
Prev: Cnty. Bd. of Educ. 1974-75; Bicentennial
Cmsn. 1975-76. Org: LWV; AAUW; Cnty. Dem.
Women's Club; Child Care Ctr., Bd. of Dir's.;
Women's Club. Educ: Marshall U. 1976 BA. B:
8/18/25. Add: 6224 Brenda Ct., Huntington
25705 (304)348-3810.

SARAH LEE NEAL (D)
    1972-. Dist: 20. Bds: V-Ch., Agriculture
& Natural Resources; State Police Reorgani-
zation; Finance Com. Party: State Del. 1976,
'72, '68, '64; State Exec. Com. 1964-72.
Prev: House Educ. Com. 1973-74; Health &
Welfare Com. 1973-74; Problems of Aged
Citizens 1973-76; Drug Abuse 1973-76. Org:
BPW; NOWL; Forest Fire Protection; Women's
Club; OES; Historical Society; Greenbrier
Dem. Women; WV Fed. of Women Voters; Dem.
Women; Young Dems.; Hwy. Safety; Pres.,
Library Bd.; Greenbrier Farm Bureau; Chamber
of Commerce. Occ: Realtor. B: 2/24/24.
Add: 310 11th, Rainell 25962 (304)348-2239.

JULIA LOCKRIDGE PITSENBERGER (D)
    1974-. Bds: Judiciary; Banking & Insurance.
Prev: Governor's Cmsn. on Alcoholism 1975-77;
Bd., Appalachian Mental Health Ctr. 1977-79.
Org: Nat. Vocational Guidance Assoc.; AAUW;
Women's Club; Young Dem's.; Cnty. Dem's.
Educ: W. Va. U. 1963 BS; 1964 MA. Occ:
Realtor. B: 5/2/41. Add: 110 Westview Dr.,
Elkins 26241 (304)348-3810.

HELAINE ROTGIN (D)
    1976-. Bds: Educ; Health & Welfare;
Agriculture & Natural Resources. Org: Central
Child Care Bd.; Citizens Recycling Council
Org.; Cnty. Dem. Women; Job Corps. Community
Relations Council. Educ: U. of Wis. 1936 BA.
Occ: Shop Owner/Manager. B: 12/26/15. Add:
4800 Virginia Ave. SE, Charleston 25304.

PAMELA SUE SHUMAN (D) **
    1974-. Dist: 2. Bds: Judiciary Com.;
Constitutional Revision; Ch., House Political
Subdiv.; Study of Volunteer Fire Depts.
Party: State Platform Com. 1972. Org: Dem.
Club; Women's Dem. Club. Educ: West Liberty
State Coll. 1973 BA. B: 6/11/51. Add: 170
Forest Dr., Wellsburg 26070 (304)348-3810.

CAROLYN M. SNYDER (D)
    Route 1, Summit Point 25446.

URSULA JAE SPEARS (D) **
    1974-. Bds: Health & Welfare; Educ.;
Constitutional Revision. Org: BPW; DAR; OWL;
Women's Club. Add: Box 181, Elkins 26241
(304)636-0350.

MARTHA WEHRLE (D) **
    1974-. Dist: 17. Bds: Com. on Health.
Party: Precinct Leader 1972-74. Org: Vocational Rehabilitation Foundation; Women
Builders Educ: Vassar 1948 BA; Harvard
1954 MA. B: 11/30/25. Add: 1440 Loudon
Heights Rd., Charleston 25314 (304)
348-3810.

W.W. JACKIE WITHROW (D)
    1960-. Dist: 18. Bds: Ch., Health &
Welfare; Cmsn. on Interstate Cooperation;
W.Va. State Plan for Comprehensive Mental
Health Services. Party: State Del. 1972-76,
'68, '64, '60; Nat. Alt. 1976. Prev: Cnty.
Park Bd. 1965-70; Cnty. Young Dem. Club
1955-66; Cnty. Library Cmsn. 1975-77. Org:
BPW; NOWL; Governor's Status of Women;
Women's Club; OES; Dem. Club; State Fed.
Dem. Women. B: 3/28/18. Add: 1301 Maxwell
Hill Rd., Beckley 25801 (304)348-0325/2239.

County Commissions

Gilmer. BILLIE JEAN SUMMERS (D) **
    1974-. Dist: Center. Org: PTA. Occ:
Secretary. B: 2/23/37. Add: Gilmer County
Courthouse, Glenville 26351.

Marion. BETTY E. GILL
    County Courthouse, Fairmont 26554.

Mason. AGNES A. ROUSH
    County Courthouse, Point Pleasant 25550.

Pleasants. JUANITA M. BAKER (D) **
    1971-. Party: Assoc. County Ch. B:
8/26/16. Add: W. Virginia State Rt. 2,
Belmont 26134 (304)665-2151.

Wetzel. SHIRLEY H. WAYNE (D)
    Cmsn. Pres. Bds: Reg. Council. Org: PTA.
Occ: Owner, Dairy-Confectionary. B: 10/23/28.
Add: Box 12, Hastings 26365 (304)455-3810.

Mayors

Beech Bottom. EVELYN PRUNTY
    City Hall, Beech Bottom 26030.

Durbin. KENNA REXRODE
    City Hall, Durbin 26264.

Huttonsville. WAUNITA TRICKETT (R)
    1973-. Bds: Planning & Devt. Council.
Educ: Nat. Coll. 1952 BA. Occ: Church &
Community Worker. B: 6/27/25. Add: P.O.
Box 147, Huttonsville 26273 (304)
335-2617.

Masontown. LYDIA D. MAIN (D)
1973-. Bds: Police Judge. Party: Committeewoman 1960-64. Org: W. Va. State Pharmaceutical
Assoc.; Health Council; Women's Fed. Club.
Educ: W. Va. U. BS. Occ: Pharmacist. B:
9/20/29. Add: Main St., Masontown 26542 (304)
864-5555.

Oakvale. O. BEE BOOTHE (D)
1973-. B: 10/18/18. Add: Rt. 4, Box 463,
Princeton 24740 (304)898-2641.

Paden City. EILEEN CALVERT SMITTLE (D)
1969-. Bds: Water Bd.; Finance; Park &
Pool. Prev: Councilwoman 1969-70, 1973-78;
Mayor 1970-71. Org: Cnty. Dem. Women's Club.
B: 10/2/19. Add: 115 Van Camp St., Paden
City 26159.

Pullman. LORENA SNODGRASS (D)
1969-. B: 4/12/09. Add: Box 666, Pullman
26421 (304)659-2113.

Ronceverte. VIRGINIA B. BLAKE (D)
1973-. Org: PTA; Women's Club. B: 12/15/21.
Add: 614 Monroe Ave., Ronceverte 24970 (304)
647-5455.

Local Councils

Bancroft. REBA HACKETT
City Hall, Bancroft 25011.

Beckley. LORRAINE K. SEAY (R) **
1971-. Bds: Recreation Bd.; Planning Cmsn.
Org: Educ. Assoc.; WSWP-TV Advisory Bd. Educ:
Bluefield State Coll. 1949 BS; W. Va. U. 1960
MA. B: 6/20/26. Add: 315 G. St., Beckley
25801 (304)252-8671.

Beckley. DOROTHY S. SMITH (D)
1970-. Bds: Co-Ch., Public Affairs Com.;
Finance Com. Org: Women's Club; Cnty. Dem.
Assoc. Educ: Morris Harvey Coll. 1973 BA.
Occ: Secretary. B: 7/3/19. Add: 905 Wood-
lawn Ave., Beckley 25801 (304)252-8671.

Beech Bottom. LUCILLE CAMPBELL
City Hall, Beech Bottom 26030

Beech Bottom. BESSIE JEAN GEISEL (R)
1976-. B: 6/22/23. Add: 18 2nd St.,
Beech Bottom 26030.

Beech Bottom. ANN LEWIS
City Hall, Beech Bottom 26030.

Bethany. MARIANNE DAVIS
HELEN FAIR
City Hall, Bethany 26032.

Bethlehem. DESSA MAY AUTEN (D)
1969-. Bds: Election Com.; Budget Com.;
Planning Com. Org: Cnty. News Media Org.;
PTA. B: 3/4/32. Add: 45 Wakut Ave., Bethlehem, Wheeling 26003 (304)242-4180.

Beverly. JOAN C. HART (D) **
Party: Cnty. Exec. Com. 1968-70. B:
4/6/31. Add: Box 344, Beverly 26253 (304)
636-5360.

Beverly. JOAN PLANT
City Hall, Beverly 26253.

Bramwell. KATHERINE BARRINGER
MRS. W.H. BOWEN
City Hall, Bramwell 24715.

Camden on Gauley. KAREN JOHNSON
City Hall, Camden on Gauley 26208.

Capon Bridge. BEULAH GILL
City Hall, Capon Bridge 26711.

Cass. ERNESTINE H. CLARKSON (D)
1975-. Party: State Del. 1976, '64; Cnty.
Precinct Leader 1964-76; Cnty. Committeewoman. Prev: Assoc. Cnty. Ch. Dem. Com.
1960-66. Occ: Secretary. B: 10/21/23.
Add: Cass 24927 (304)486-4865.

Charleston. EVELYN N. BALL
City Hall, Charleston 25301.

Charleston. JEAN S. HOLT (R)
Prev: State Repr. 1972-74. Org: Altrusa;
Rep. Women's Club. B: 11/15/13. Add: 1406
Quincy La., Charleston 25314.

Charleston. LINDA KESSEL MECKFESSEL (R)
1976-. Bds: Planning Com.; Recreation
Com.; Human Rights. Party: Precinct Captain
1972-75. Org: Jr. League; LWV; Community
Council; NOW. Educ: Stephens Coll. 1961 AA;
Washington U. 1964 BA; 1965 MA. Occ: Psychology Professor. B: 11/20/41. Add: 2113
Kanawha Ave. SE, Charleston 25304 (304)
348-6366.

Charleston. ANNEBELLE A. SHEETS
MARY JANE VANDERWILT
City Hall, Charleston 25301.

Charles Town. MARY ELIZABETH COYLE
ELIZABETH ANN WALL
City Hall, Charles Town 25414.

Clearview. MARY E. KING (D)
1976. Bds: Ch., Ordinance Com.; Sewage
Com.; Budget Com. Org: Civic League. Occ:
Bookkeeper. B: 10/1/32. Add: 28 Lyle Rd.,
Clearview, Wheeling 26003 (304)277-1177.

Davis. IDA A. COOPER (R)
1970-. Bds: Finance; Ordinance. Org:
Arts Council; OES. B: 9/15/19. Add: P.O.
Box 455, Davis 26260.

Dunbar. MARY HONAKER (D) **
Bds: Ch., Safety Com.; Financial Com.;
City Bldg. Com. Org: Dem. Club. B: 1/9/19.
Add: 407 19th St., Dunbar 25064.

Dunbar. CHARLOTTE LEGG
City Hall, Dunbar 25064.

Dunbar. AMIE MANETTA SMITH (D) **
     1972-. Bds: Ch., City Bldg.; Housing
Authority. Party: Local Com. 1968-72. Org:
Dem. Club. B: 3/9/27. Add: 103 Chestnut St..
Dunbar 25064 (304)768-2331.

Elk Garden. NEVA LYONS
     City Hall, Elk Garden 26717.

Ellenboro. FLORENCE HINTON (R)
     1972-. Educ: Salem Coll. 1941 BA; Marshall
U. 1948 MA. B: 12/3/05. Add: Box 104, Ellenboro 26346.

Ellenboro. MAXINE LEWIS (R)
     1975-. Org: PTA. B: 6/29/40. Add: Box
182, Ellenboro 26346.

Fairview. EDNA HAUGHT
     City Hall, Fairview 26570.

Falling Springs. FLORIDA BASSHAM
                 JOYCE CALLISON
     City Hall, Renick 24966.

Flatwoods. CAROLYN KNICELEY
            PEARL WOODALL
     City Hall, Flatwoods 26621.

Gassaway. JUDITH K. POTTS (D)
     1976-. Org: W. Va. Educ. Assoc.; NEA;
W. Va. Fed. of Women's Clubs. Educ: Glenville
State Coll. 1964 BA. Occ: Teacher. B:
9/12/42. Add: 714 Braxton St., Gassaway
26624.

Glendale. GENEVA JANE MOBLEY (R)
     1970-. Bds: Finance Com.; Ch., Fire &
Water; Park. Org: School Service Assoc.
Occ: Cook. B: 12/23/18. Add: 704 Orchard
Ave., Glendale 26038 (304)845-5511.

Grant Town. PATSY J. WEIR
     City Hall, Grant Town 26574.

Harpers Ferry. EDITH PERRY ALEXANDER (D)
     1973-. Bds: Treasurer, Library Cmsn. Org:
Women's Club; Environmental Council; Cnty.
Women's Dem. Club. Educ: Mt. Holyoke Coll.
1921 BA. B: 7/12/1900. Add: 800 Ridge St.,
Harpers Ferry 25425.

Harrisville. HELEN I. GARRETT (D)
     Party: State Del. 1976. Prev: Councilwoman
1975-77. Org: Dem. Com. B: 10/16/24. Add:
108 N. Penn Ave., Harrisville 26362 (304)
643-2498.

Hedgesville. KATHLEEN JOHNSON
     City Hall, Hedgesville 25427.

Hedgesville. ETHEL N. RUNKLES (D) **
     1973-. Occ: Seamstress. B: 6/20/18.
Add: 213 Mary St., Box 42, Hedgesville 25427.

Hillsboro. MARY ANN BEVERAGE (R)
     1973-. Occ: Store Manager. B: 1/11/31.
Add: Hillsboro 24946.

Huntington. PHYLLIS HART CYRUS (D) **
     1973-. Org: State Bar Assoc. Educ:
Marshall Coll. 1935 BA; W. Va. U. 1938 LLB.
Occ: Professor. B: 2/22/14. Add: 2940
Staunton Rd., Huntington 25702 (304)
523-5588.

Huntington. MRS. OWEN L. DUNCAN
     City Hall, Huntington 25701.

Hurricane. MARY HODGES
     City Hall, Hurricane 25526.

Kermit. GLARAY SUE ADKINS LACY (D)
     1971-. Org: NEA; Women's Club; DAR; OES.
Educ: Marshall U. BA; MA. Occ: Home Economics
Instructor. B: 12/20/37. Add: 20 Hill St.,
Kermit 25674 (304)393-3321.

Leon. RUTH DUNHAM
     City Hall, Leon 25123.

Lewisburg. ANN TATE BELL
     City Hall, Lewisburg 24901.

Lost Creek. LOUISE AZELVANDRE
     City Hall, Lost Creek 26385.

Lumberport. DOLLIE STIRE (D)
     1975-. Org: Retired Teachers. Educ:
Fairmont State Coll. 1957 BA. B: 12/15/08.
Add: 411 Chestnut, Lumberport 26386.

Madison. BETTY FOY
          JOY UNDERWOOD
     City Hall, Madison 25130.

Marlinton. ALICE WAUGH
     City Hall, Marlinton 24954.

Martinsburg. MARY BOYD KEARSE
     City Hall, Martinsburg 25401.

Mason. CHARLOTTE MAYE ROUSH JENKS (D)
     1975-. Bds: Recreation Cmsn. Prev:
Recorder-Clerk 1959-63; 1964-73; Mayor 1963-
64; 1969-71. Org: Historical Soc.; Dem.
Women's Org. B: 7/6/14. Add: 23 1st St.,
Mason 25260 (302)773-5201.

Mason. CATHERINE SMITH
     City Hall, Mason 25260.

Masontown. EDITH FORTNEY (D)
     1975-. Bds: Bldg. Permits; Ordinance.
B: 1/1/29. Add: Box 292, Masontown 26542.

Masontown. ELIZABETH PELL
     City Hall, Masontown 26542.

Matoaka. BRENDA THOMASON
     City Hall, Matoaka 24736.

Meadow Bridge. CELESTE B. ARRITT (D)
     Bds: Town Treasurer. Party: State Del.
1968; Cnty. Committeewoman 1966-70. Prev:
Human Rights Cmsn. 1966-70; Cnty. Mental
Health 1977. Org: AAUW; NEA. Educ: Marshall

U. 1932 BS; 1939 MA. Occ: Teacher. B:10/18/11.
Add: P.O. Box 218, Meadow Brg. 25976.

Meadow Bridge. EVA MC KEENY
        City Hall, Meadow Bridge 25976.

Mill Creek. FREDA KIESS
                EVELYN PARRACK
        City Hall, Mill Creek 26280.

Mitchell Heights. ANN HATCHER
        City Hall, Mitchell Heights 25601.

Montrose. BEULAH BARTLETT
        City Hall, Montrose 26283.

Montrose. JOYCE CANFIELD (D) **
        B: 7/16/38. Add: P.O. Box 24, Montrose
    26283 (304)636-2913.

Montrose. HELEN MURPHY (D)
        1971-. Org: NEA. Educ: W. Va. Wesleyan
    1965 BA. Occ: Teacher. B: 11/23/19. Add:
    P.O. Box 45, Montrose 26283.

Morgantown. DOROTHY COMUNTZIS
        City Hall, Morgantown 26505.

Nutter Fort. MARTHA F. DAVIS (D)
        1967-. Bds: Ch., Planning Cmsn.; Ch.,
    Beautification of the City. Org: Dem. Women.
    Occ: Deputy Assessor. B: 4/15/18. Add: 316
    Thomas Ave., Nutter Fort 26301 (304)622-7713.

Oakvale. ESTHER ROBERSON (R)
        1974-. Prev: Town Councilwoman 1974-77;
    Town Recorder 1977. B: 8/4/39. Add: P.O.
    Box 156, Oakvale 24739.

Oakvale. IMOGENE THOMAS
        City Hall, Oakvale 24739.

Osage. EARLINE TATE
        City Hall, Osage 26543.

Parkersburg. CHARLOTTE CORBITT
        City Hall, Parkersburg 26101.

Paw Paw. CARLA BOLYARD
        City Hall, Paw Paw 25434.

Peterstown. ELLEN HARLESS (D)
        1975-. B: 11/22/33. Add: 110 Thomas,
    Peterstown 24963 (304)753-9509.

Pine Grove. DOROTHY SPRINGER
        City Hall, Pine Grove 26419.

Pineville. EVELYN H. MARTIN
        1976-. Prev: Cnty. Welfare Bd. 1965-67;
    Airport Planning Cmsn. Org: PTA. Occ: Deputy
    Circuit Clerk. B: 4/12/31. Add: P.O. Box 612,
    Pineville 24874 (304)732-8000.

Pullman. CHARLENE CUNNINGHAM
            JEWEL CUNNINGHAM
            ANN HAYES
            EVA JETT
            VIOLET PRUNTY
        City Hall, Pullman 26421.

Ravenswood. NORMA JEAN COPE (R) **
        1973-. Bds: Ch., Bicentennial; Dev. Corp.
    Org: BPW. Occ: Co-owner Supermarket. B:
    3/31/33. Add: 501 Hillcrest Dr., Ravenswood
    26164 (304)273-2621.

Reedy. MAXINE GARRETT
            LUCILLE LAW
        City Hall, Reedy 25270.

Rhodell. RUBY AUGUSTINE
            ROSE MC KINNEY
            WILMA WIDDICK
        City Hall, Rhodell 25915.

Richwood. PATRICIA LOSCH
        City Hall, Richwood 26261.

St. Albans. MARTHA ELLEN SMITH (D) **
        1974-. Bds: Police Com.; Street Lighting;
    Bldg. & Grounds. B: 1/3/30. Add: 217 Carson
    St., St. Albans 25177 (304)722-3391.

St. Albans. PHYLLIS TROWBRIDGE
        City Hall, St. Albans 25177.

Sand Fork. LORRAINE FOSTER
            MRS. DAVID SHARPS
        City Hall, Sand Fork 26430.

Sophia. MARY MARTIN
        City Hall, Sophia 25921.

South Charleston. RUTH S. GOLDSMITH
        City Hall, Charleston 25303.

Star City. MARY PERVOLA
        City Hall, Star City 26505.

Stonewood. GRACE M. GABRIEL (D) **
        1973-. Prev: Recorder. Org: Dem. Women's
    Club; PTA. Occ: Secretary. B: 3/19/43.
    Add: 909 Cost Ave., Stonewood 26301 (304)
    623-2919.

Thomas. CAROLYN MONDAY
        City Hall, Thomas 26292.

Thurmond. MRS. W.E. PUGH
            ESTEL SMITH
        City Hall, Thurmond 25936.

Triadelphia. LORA JEAN MILLER
        City Hall, Triadelphia 26059.

Wayne. BETTY W. SMITH
        City Hall, Wayne 25570.

Weirton. MARY ELLEN BINKOSKI (D)
        1975-. Bds: Finance Com.; Planning Cmsn.
    Party: Cnty. Committeewoman 1970-78. Org:
    Dem. Women's Club; PTA; Ch., Cnty. Kidney
    Foundation. B: 1/22/35. Add: 133 Swartz
    St., Weirton 26062 (304)748-6831.

Wellsburg. PEARL CAMPAGNA
            VIRGINIA SEREVICZ
        City Hall, Wellsburg 26070.

West Milford. ALICE MARIE SOMERS (R)
     1975-. Party: State Alt. 1968; Cnty.
Committeewoman 1974-78. Org: Women's Club;
Cnty. Rep. Women. B: 3/27/23. Add: Box 24,
W. Milford 26451.

Weston. MARY GERTRUDE SLEIGH (D)
     1975-. Bds: Cemetery Authority. Occ:
Savings Teller. B: 12/26/21. Add: 570 Locust
Ave., Weston 26452 (304)269-3422.

Whitesville. MARY JANE HARLESS
     City Hall, Whitesville 25209.

Williamson. KAY WARD
     City Hall, Williamson 25661.

Womelsdorff. JOYCE JENNINGS
              MARY JONES
     City Hall, Womelsdorff 26257.

Worthington. HELENE Y. BROOKS
     City Hall, Worthington 26591.

State Boards and Commissions

     Office of the Governor, State Capitol Bldg.,
     Charleston 25305.

Aging, Commission on
     MRS. JOE L. MC QUADE

Arts and Humanities Council
     ELIZABETH A. ATWATER
     HELEN M. BIRKE
     CLAIRE FIORENTINO
     MRS. JAMES PAPPAS
     MRS. R.A. RAESE
     MRS. SCOTT H. SHOTT
     MRS. HARVEY M. SHREVE, JR.
     MRS. CHARLES JAY STEIN

Barbers and Beuticians, Committee of
     EVAUN FILES HARDMAN
     MARGARET M. NAFE

Carnifex Ferry Battle Ground Park Commission
     HELEN BOBBITT
     IDRA CARNIFEX CUTLIP

Citizens Legislative Compensation Commission
     MRS. WILLIAM R. ROSS

Consumer Affairs Advisory Council
     AUDREY GUTHRIE
     CHARLENE F. SIZEMORE
     JODY G. SMIRL
     JANE H. THEILING

Education Commission of the States
     CHRISTINE MC CUSKEY

Election Commission
     BARBARA M. RULEY

Emergency Services Advisory Council
     HELEN FAULKNER

Fire Commission
     GAIL C. ASH

Handicapped, Committee on Employment of the
     KATHERINE L. BROWN
     MRS. DELMAS MILLER
     EDITH SANDERSON

Health, Advisory Board to the Board of
     BETTY JANE VEACH

Historic Road Markers, Advisory Committee on
     MADGE MC DANIEL

Human Rights Commission
     ANCELLA BICKLEY
     IRIS BRESSLER
     ANNE MAXWELL

Interstate Cooperation, Commission on
     JUDITH A. HERNDON

Licensed Practical Nurses, Board of Examiners
for
     CINDA HOUS FOWLKES
     MARGARET M. HILL
     NANCY K. MARTIN
     MARY E. WALLS

Manpower Services Council
     MRS. WILLIAM CAMPBELL
     PHYLLIS GIVEN

Manpower, Technology and Training, Commission on
     LOIS KAUFELT

Mental Retardation, Advisory Committee to
Commission on
     RUTH E. ANDERSON
     MARY BOONE
     ROXANE BUTTS
     MRS. ARCH A. MOORE, JR.
     PATRICIA P. O'REILLY
     MRS. DONALD RHODES

Nursing Home Licensing Board
     MARIAN MC QUADE
     RENA PITOTTI

Nursing Home Administrators Advisory Council
     RENA PITOTTI

Physical Therapy, Board of
     MARCELLA CHANCEY

Real Estate Commission
     MRS. HENRY P. BUTTS

Registered Professional Nurses, Board of
Examiners for
     SANDRA S. BOWLES
     FRANCES L. JACKSON
     ELIZABETH O'CONNELL
     SISTER CHRISTINE RILEY
     GARNETTE THORNE

State Planning Council
 DIANE CRANE
 SALLY LOU DARST
 PEGGY MANGANO
 SADIE MC GHEE
 MRS. ARCH A. MOORE, JR.
 CORDELIA V. TOLES

Stonewall Jackson Memorial Fund
 VIRGINIA CORE

Teachers Retirement Board
 VELMA B. ALLEN

Welfare, Advisory Board to the Department of
 NETTIE DAVIS

Wisconsin

State Executive and Cabinet

SARAH DEAN (D)
 Secretary of Regulation and Licensing.
1975-. Party: State Del. 1976-77. Prev: Asst.
Dir. State Health Planning Agency 1972-75.
Educ: St. John's U. 1959 BS; Columbia U. 1971
MS. B: 11/22/32. Add: 2417 Joss Ct., Madison
53702 (608)266-8609.

VIRGINIA HART
 Ch. Industry, Labor & Human Relations
Commission. Add: State Capitol, Madison
53702.

BARBARA S. THOMPSON **
 State Superintendent of Public Instruction
1973-. Bds: U. of Wis. Bd. of Regents; State
Bd., Vocational, Technical, Adult Educ.;
Higher Educ. Aids Bd.; Educ. Cmsn. of States;
Educ. Communication Bd.; Agency for Instruc-
tional TV; Nat. Institute on Educ.; Research
& Dev. U. of Wis. Org: NAACP; Nat. Assoc. of
Childhood Educ.; Nat. Council of Administrative
Women in Educ.; Nat. Council of State Consult-
ants. in Elementary Educ.; NEA; Dept. of
Elementary School Principals; Wisc. Assoc. of
School Dist. Administrators; Assoc. for Supervi-
sion & Curriculum Dev.; Wis. Educational
Research Assoc.; PTA. Educ: U. of Wis. 1956
BS; U. of Wis. 1959 MS; U. of Wis. 1969 PhD.
B: 10/15/24. Add: 1 Springwood Circle,
Madison 53717 (608)266-1771.

State Legislature

 State Senate

KATHRYN MORRISON (D)
 1974-. Dist: 17. Bds: Joint Com. on
Finance; Senate Com. on Agriculture, Aging,
& Labor; Co-Ch. Joint Sub Com. on Juvenile
Alcohol & Drug Abuse. Party: State Del. 1973-
77; Exec. Bd., Cnty. Dem. Party 1974- . Prev:
Governor's Cmsn. on State-Local Relations
1975-77; Sewer & Water Cmsn. 1974-76. Org:
Amer. Economics Assoc.; Common Cause; WPC.
Educ: U. of Wis. 1964 BBA; 1965 MBA. B:
5/22/42. Add: 520 W. Main St., Platteville
53818 (608)266-1832.

MICHELE G. RADOSEVICH (D)
 1976-. Dist: 10. Bds: Minn.-Wis. Boundary
Area Cmsn.; Cmsn. on Interstate Cooperation;
Leg. Council. Party: State Del. 1976-77. Org:
Citizens for Clean Miss.; Dem. Party. Educ:
Marquette U. 1969 BA. B: 10/7/47. Add:
Riverside Dr. N., Hudson 54016 (608)266-5660.

 State House

MARCIA P. COGGS (D)
 2351 N. Richards Rd., Milwaukee 53212.

JULIA SHEEHAN DONOGHUE (R) **
 1973-. Dist: 35. Bds: Municipalities
Com.; State Affairs Com. Party: Del., Nat.
Conv. 1968. Prev: Assistant Coordinator,
White House Conf. on Food, Nutrition & Health
1969-70. Org: BPW. Educ: U. of Wis. 1967
BS. Occ: Assistant Management Analyst. B:
12/13/43. Add: 102 Cottage St., Merrill
54452 (608)266-7671.

JOANNE M. DUREN (D) **
 1970-. Dist: 50. Bds: Ch., Tourism Com.;
Educ. Com.; State Affairs Com. Party: Secretary, Congressional Dist. 1968-69. Prev:
School Bd. 1963-64. B: 10/11/31. Add: Box
234, Cazenovia 53924 (608)266-7694.

SUSAN SHANNON ENGELEITER (R)
 1974-. Bds: Commerce & Consumer Affairs
Com.; Assembly Local Affairs Com. Party:
State Del. 1975-77. Org: AAUW; New Rep.
Conf. Educ: U. of Wis. 1970 BS. Occ: Student.
B: 3/18/52. Add: 21725 Ann Rita Dr., Brook-
field 53005 (608)266-3756.

PATRICIA A. GOODRICH (R) **
 1975-. Dist: 72. Bds: Educ. Com.;
Enrolled Bills Com. B: 1/13/33. Add: 159
Oak St., Berlin 54923 (608)266-1526.

ESTHER DOUGHTY LUCKHARDT (R) **
 1962-. Dist: 54. Bds: Insurance & Bank-
ing; Agriculture; Com. on Equal Rights;
Governor's Com. on Status of Women. Org:
Mental Health Assoc.; Rep. Women's Club; VFW;
Women for Agriculture. Add: 211 Hubbard St.,
Horicon 53032 (608)266-1526.

SHARON METZ (D) **
    1975-. Dist: 90. Bds: Environmental
Quality Com.; Health & Social Services Com.;
Taxation Com. Occ: Tudent. B: 9/13/34. Add:
816 Shawano Ave., Green Bay 54303 (608)
266-7503.

MIDGE MILLER (D)
    1970-. Bds: Co-Ch., Commerce & Consumer
Affairs; Educ. Com.; Educ. Communications Bd.
Party: State Del. 1960-77; State Alt. 1958;
Nat. Del. 1968; Dem. Nat. Com. 1975-80. Org:
OWL; WPC. Educ: U. of Mich. 1944 BA; U. of
Wis. 1962 BS. B: 6/8/22. Add: 1937 Arlington
Pl., Madison 53705.

MARY LOU MUNTS (D)
    1972-. Dist: 76. Bds: Ch., Assembly
Environmental Protection Com.; Assembly
Judiciary Com.; Assembly Criminal Justice &
Public Safety. Org: Wis. Bar Assoc.; Assoc.
Retarded Children; LWV; Nature Conservancy;
Sierra Club; Audobon Society; Cnty. Dem. Party;
WPC. Educ: Swarthmore Coll. BA; U. of Chicago
MA; U. of Wis. JD. B: 8/21/24. Add: 6102
Hammersley Rd., Madison 53711 (608)266-3784.

LOUISE M. TESMER (D) **
    1972-. Dist: 19. Bds: Judiciary Com.;
Judicial Council; V-Ch., Commerce & Consumer
Affairs. Party: Del., State Conv. 1973- .
Prev: Municipal Justice 1966-67. Org: Amer.
Council of Young Political Leaders; OWL; State
Bar Assoc. Educ: U. of Wis. 1964 BA; U. of
Wis. 1967 JD. Occ: Attorney. B: 12/25/42.
Add: 4252 S. Nicholson Ave., St. Francis
53207 (608)266-8588.

County Commissions

Adams. MARCELLA HARDIN
    S. Grant, Adams 53910.

Adams. ELLEN MARTIN
    R.R., Adams 53910.

Bayfield. ILA BROMBERG
    1974-. Bds: Soil & Water Dist.; Cnty.
Foresters Assoc.; Ch., Unified Services Bd.
Occ: Free-lance Writer/Photographer. B:
5/3/24. Add: Rt. 1, Washburn 54891 (715)
373-5508.

Brown. EUNICE M. GARSOW (R)
    1974-. Dist: 37. Bds: Ch., Leg. Com.;
Steering & Advice Com.; Soil & Water Conser-
vation Dist. Party: State Del. 1975-77. Org:
Farm Bureau; Internat. Cultural Exchange.
Occ: Farmer. B: 9/28/31. Add: Rt. 3, DePere
54115.

Brown. ROSEMARY HINKFUSS (D)
    1974-. Bds: Ch., Protection & Welfare Com.;
City Plan Cmsn.; Mayor's Adv. Com. Org: LWV;
Astor Neighborhood Assoc.; Dem. Party. Educ:
Cardevial Stretch 1954 BS. B: 9/20/31. Add:
1002 S. Monroe, Green Bay 54301.

Brown. JEAN M. OLMSTEAD (R) **
    1972-. Bds: Ch., Agriculture & Extension
Educ.; Steering & Advice; Ad Hoc Study Com.
Org: LWV. Occ: Office Worker. B: 1/9/24.
Add: 480 W. Briar La., Green Bay 54301
(414)437-3211.

Brown. MARY ANN WALSH **
    1974-. Bds: Housing Authority; Arena;
Cmsn. on Aging; Museum; Public Works; Improvements. & Services. Prev: City Councilwoman
1974- . Educ: U. of Dayton 1951 BS. B:
2/25/29. Add: 2864 St. Ann Dr., Green Bay
54301 (414)468-0287.

Burnett. MARJORIE M. NYBERG
    1974-. Bds: Soil & Water Com.; Cnty. Aging
Com.; Social Service Com. B: 1/26/16. Add:
Rt. 2, Box 303A, Siren 54872.

Calumet. WILMA SPRINGER
    218 E. Hoover Ave., Appleton 54911.

Clark. ALICE SMITH (I)
    1976-. Dist: 12. Bds: Dept. of Social
Services; Educ., Technical & Vocational
Schools; Planning & Zoning. Org: BPW. B:
6/26/33. Add: Rt. 2, Box 320, Neillsville
54456.

Dane. ANNE R. DE WITT
    113 Longview Ave., Mt. Horeb 53572.

Dane. ELAINE GINNOLD (D)
    1976-. Dist: 20. Bds: Public Health Com.;
Hospital & Home Cmsn. Org: Wis.Public Health
Assoc.; Alliance for the Mentally Ill. Educ:
U. of N.C. 1962 BA; U. of Wis. 1973 MA. Occ:
Public Relations Dir. B: 1/18/41. Add:
1010 Mohican Pass, Madison 53711.

Dane. NAILA E. HARPER (D) **
    1974-. Bds: Affirmative Action Cmsn.;
Agriculture, Zoning, Planning; Water Re-
sources Com.; Soil & Water Conservation Dist.
Org: ACLU; LWV; Soil Conservation Society of
Amer.; Bd. of Dir., U. League; Consumer
Credit Counseling; Dem. Club. Educ: Higher
Teachers Coll. 1941 BA; U. of Conn. 1947 MA.
B: 11/25/23. Add: 3447 Edgehill Pkwy.,
Madison 53705.

Dane. BEATRICE A. KABLER (R)
    1976-. Dist: 19. Bds: Personnel Com.;
Mental Health Bd.; Hospital & Home Feasibility
Study. Party: State Del.; Cnty. Rep. Reso-
lutions Com. Prev: Div. of Health-Family
Planning "Hot Line" Com. 1975- . Org: Wis.
Citizen's for Family Planning; Nature Con-
servancy; Rep. Party; Common Cause; LWV; WPC;
Wis. New Rep. Conf. B: 2/9/28. Add: 5501
Varsity Hl., Madison 53705.

Dane. ROBERTA W. LEIDNER (D)
    1974-. Bds: Ch., Hwy. & Transportation
Com.; Regional Airport Cmsn.; Unified Assess-
ment Study Com. Party: State Del. 1956; Ward
Committeewoman 1963-69. Prev: Governor's
Mass Transit Com. 1968-71; Governor's Metro-
politan Problems Task Force 1970-72; State

Interim Leg. Hwy. Adv. Com. 1967-70; State All Mode Transportation Adv. Com. 1975- ; Mayor's Citizens Adv. Com. 1966-70; Mayor's Govt. Goals Com. 1971-72; Housing Design Selection Com. 1969. Org: Capital Community Citizens; Wis. Coalition for Balanced Transportation; Wis. Environmental Decade; Regent Neighborhood Assoc.; WPC; Dem. Party: PTA. B: 3/7/22. Add: 201 Lathrop St., Madison 53705 (608)266-4121.

Dane. JANICE REDFORD
2062 Hillside, R. 2, Cambridge 53523.

Dane. ELIZABETH SALMON (D)
1972-. Bds: Ch., Agricultural Extension Educ.; Zoning & Planning; Soil & Water Conservation Dist. Party: State Del. 1970-76; Precinct Leader 1970. Prev: Cnty. Parks Cmsn. 1972-76; V-Ch., Cnty. Bicentennial Com. 1974-76; Leg. Study Council Com. on Town Govt. Inc. 1975. Org: LWV; Community Citizens; Sierra Club; Cnty. Conservation League; Cnty. Dem's.; Nature Conservancy. Educ: U. of Mich. 1953 BSEd; U. of Wis. 1976 MS. Occ: Research Asst. B: 11/24/31. Add: 614 S. Segoe Rd., Madison 53711 (608)271-8820.

Dane. MARY LOUISE SYMON (D)
1970-. Bds: Ch., Public Protection Com.; Regional Planning Cmsn.; Solid Waste Com. Party: Precinct Committeewoman. Prev: Madison Equal Opportunity Cmsn. 1966-69. Org: Nat. Assoc. of Cnty's.; ACLU; LWV; NAACP; Urban League; Nature Conservancy. Educ: Wellesley Coll. 1943 BA. B: 4/7/22. Add: 1816 Vilas Ave., Madison 53711 (608)266-4360.

Dane. MARY D. WEISENSEL
R. 2, Sun Prairie 53590.

Dodge. LUCILLE E. BRAUNSCHWEIG (R)
1976-. Bds: Agriculture & Extension Com.; Cnty. Library Bd.; Cnty. Cmsn. on Aging. Party: State Del. 1977. Org: Wis. Women for Agriculture; Rep. Party. B: 6/20/41. Add: RR 1, Box 69, Rubicon 53078.

Door. GRACE MC CORMICK (D)
1976-. Bds: Property Com.; Solid Waste Com. Party: State Del. 1965; Cnty. Secretary 1963-65; City Repr. Bd. of Dirs. 1969-73. Prev: Cnty. Bd. 1964-68; Sturgeon Bay City Council 1964-68. Org: Dem. Party. Occ: Proofreader. B: 4/15/23. Add: 521 Nebraska, Sturgeon Bay 54235 (414)743-3321.

Door. DOROTHY MOSGALLER
438 S. Hudson, Sturgeon Bay 54235.

Douglas. REGINA B. HILL
1972-. Dist: 19. Prev: Alderwoman 1961-76. Org: Welfare Bd.; Housing Authority. Occ: Nutrition Dir. for Elderly. B: 4/28/18. Add: 1509 N. 4th St., Superior 54880 (715)394-0341.

Douglas. LORRAINE LEVALLE
2317½ Ogden Ave., Superior 54880.

Dunn. SUSAN HALL
1972-. Bds: Agriculture & Extension Educ.; Soil & Water; Law Enforcement. Educ: Earlham Coll. 1976 BA; U. of Chicago 1966 MA. B: 4/12/43. Add: 1103 Riverview Dr., Menomonie 54751.

Dunn. JOYCE L. QUILLING (R)
1967-. Bds: V-Ch., Recreation & Park Com.; General Claims & Cnty. Offices Com.; Cnty. Library Planning Com. Party: State Del. 1970; State Alt. 1969. Prev: City Councilwoman 1967-74. Org: LWV; Rep. Party. Occ: Clerk. B: 1/16/30. Add: 1109 4th St. E., Menomonis 54751.

Eau Claire. FRANCES R. DRESDEN
616 N. Dewey St., Eau Claire 54701.

Eau Claire. SISTER MARY FRANCES GEBHARD (D)
1972-. Bds: Ch., Personnel Com.; Social Services Com.; Unified Services Bd. Party: State Del. 1972-77; State Alt. 1971; Cnty. Secretary 1972-74; Cnty. V-Ch. 1975-76; Precinct Committeewoman 1972-76. Prev: Cnty. Bd. Supervisor 1972-76. Org: ANA; Wis. Assoc. of Social Services; NOW; Cnty. Dem. Party. Educ: U. of Wis. 1971 BS. Occ: Nurse. B: 6/1/32. Add: 1014 Oxford Ave., Eau Claire 54701.

Eau Claire. ESTHER E. KUHLMAN (D)
1976-. Bds: Personnel; Joint Liaison. Org: Peoples Rights Org.; Dem. Party. B: 2/9/26. Add: 820 Forest St., Eau Claire 54701 (715)839-4801.

Eau Claire. CORINNE B. UECKE
1011 State St., Eau Claire 54701.

Fond Du Lac. M. ANITA ANDEREGG
99 Meadowbrook Blvd., Fond Du Lac 54935.

Fond Du Lac. JANE BEHLEN (I)
1974-. Bds: Youth Service Bureau; Protection of Persons & Property Com. Org: LWV. Educ: St. Agnes School of Nursing 1948 RN. Occ: Nurse. B: 7/20/26. Add: 2912 Cnty. Trunk "K", Rt. 2, Fond Du Lac 54935.

Grant. MARILYN M. FITZGERALD
1976-. Dist: 12. Educ:Marquette U. 1962 BA. B: 7/16/37. Add: 1600 N. Elm, RR 3, Platteville 53818 (608)348-6301.

Grant. MARY LOU WIRTH (I)
1976-. Bds: Finance Com.; Law Enforcement & Civil Defense Com.; Ad Hoc Railroad Com. B: 11/11/27. Add: 1225 W. Hill, Platteville 53818.

Green. NAOMI B. BARNARD
1416 15th Ave., Monroe 53566.

Green. ELEANOR BRENNAN (D)
1973-. Bds: Ch., Cnty. Community Public Health Com.; Finance Com. Party: State Del. 1972; State Alt. 1974; Cnty. Ch. 1972-73. Org: Cnty. Day Care, Inc.; Cnty. Assoc.

Retarded Citizens; WPC; Cnty. Dem. Party. Occ: Farmer. B: 1/26/37. Add: Rt. 1, Browntown 53522.

Green. KATHRYN L. RUFENER (D)
1974-. Bds: Cmsn. on Aging; Publicity; Equalization of Assessments. Add: RR 3, Box 236A, Monroe 53566.

Green Lake. MARY J. WISE
113 W. Marquette St., Berlin 54923.

Iowa. CLAIRE GREENE
Avoca 53506.

Iowa. MARION PUSTINA
202 W. Clarence, Dodgeville 53533.

Jefferson. VIRGINIA W. FELLOWS (D)
1970-. Dist: 24. Bds: Special Educ.; Social Services Bd.; Ch., Coord. Council for Cnty. Bd. Party: State Del. 1971. Org: Project Review Com. of Health Planning Council. Educ: U. of Wis. 1969 BS. Occ: Music Teacher. B: 2/7/21. Add: 532 S. Fischer Ave., Jefferson 53549 (414)674-2500.

Kewaunee. ROSEMARY A. WEGNER (R)
1976-. Bds: Finance & Public Property. Party: State Alt. 1977. Org: Health Systems Agency; Cnty. Rep's. Occ: Dietary Supervisor. B: 7/21/29. Add: 324 Center St., Kewaunee 54216.

La Crosse. JOYCE M. ARTHUR (I)
1976-. Bds: Social Services; Landfill; Special Bldg. Com. Org: Wisc. Cnty. Assoc.; LWV; PTO. Educ: Brown U. 1961 BA; Yale U. 1962 MA; U. of Tenn.1969 PhD. B: 1/24/40. Add: 128 S. 26th St., La Crosse 54601.

La Crosse. ELIZABETH GUNDERSEN
R. 1, La Crosse 54601.

Marathon. MARY R. MC CLAIN (D)
1972-. Bds: Personnel & Labor Relations Com., Ch., Cmsn. on Status of Women, Human Rights Cmsn. Party: State Del. 1971, '72, '73; State Alt. 1969, '70. Org: Chamber of Commerce. B: 2/3/42. Add: 408 S. 9th Ave., Wausau 54401.

Marathon. JANE WILEY
2302 Park Rd., Wausau 54401.

Marinette. MRS. CLARYCE MAEDKE
R. 1, Box 37, Coleman 54112.

Marinette. JUDITH ANN WAGNER
1972-. Dist: 5. Bds: Forestry Outdoor Recreation Com. Org: Historical Society. Educ: U. of Wis. 1970 BS. Occ: Medical Secretary. B: 10/28/47. Add: RFD #1, Box 91A, Amberg 54102.

Milwaukee. BERNADETTE SKINBINX
1957 S. 12th St., Milwaukee 53204.

Monroe. JANICE M. WALL (R)
1974-. Bds: Health Cmsn.; Emergency Govt.; Ch., Bldg., Ground & Utilities. Org: Steering Com. for Status of Women; Rep. Women; Bicentennial Com.; PTA. B: 3/9/40. Add: 517 South St., Cashton 54619.

Outagamie. DIANE CUSATIS **
1974-. Bds: Cnty. Appointments; Agriculture, Extension Educ.; Social Services; Coordinating; Rules; Selection. Org: Human Rights Council; PTA. Occ: Professional Volunteer. Add: 1908 N. Racine, Appleton 54911 (414) 731-1883.

Outagamie. MARY D. GRUNDMAN
6 Meadowbrook Ln., Box 1, Appleton 54911.

Outagamie. ROSE SCHROEDER
222 E. Washington St., Appleton 54911.

Outagamie. BARBARA A. STEGER
744 W. Spencer St., Appleton 54911.

Ozaukee. ELLA B. OPITZ
2358 Shady Lane Rd., Saukville 53080.

Ozaukee. BERNADYNE M. PAPE
709 Heather Court, Grafton 53024.

Polk. ELSIE M. CHELL (I)
1974-. Bds: Ch., Cmsn. on Aging. B: 12/2/04. Add: 306 Pleasant Ave., Frederic 54857.

Polk. REGINA T. MILLER (D)
1976-. Bds: Social Services Com.; Public Health Com.; Nutrition Program Com. Party: State Del. 1970-72. Educ: U. of Wis. 1941 BS. B: 2/23/19. Add: 208 Madison St. N., St. Croix Falls 54024 (715)485-3161.

Portage. SHIRLEY JUANITA HANSEN GIBB (R)
1976-. Bds: Planning & Zoning Com.; Cmsn. on Aging; Ch., Judicial Com. Org: Natl. Assoc. for Educ. of Young Children; LWV; PEO. Educ: Monmouth Coll. 1959 BA; U. of Wis. 1973 MEd. Occ: School Program Coordinator. B: 12/20/36. Add: 1701 Clark St., Stevens Point 54481.

Portage. MARGARET M. SCHAD (I)
1975-. Bds: Ch., Human Services Bd.; Ch., Nursing Home Com.; Ch., Affirmative Action Com. Prev: Bd. of Park Cmsnr's. 1973- . Org: LWV; Common Cause. Educ: U. of Wis. 1951 BS. B: 11/14/30. Add: 623 Indiana Ave., Stevens Pt. 54481 (715)346-2113.

Racine. RUTH R. GEDWARDT (D)
1959-. Dist: 1. Bds: Law Enforcement & Legal Services. Party: State Del. 1958; Precinct Leader 1957-59. Prev: Cnty. Supervisor 1959-77. Occ: Counselor. B: 11/30/26. Add: 831 College Ave., Racine 53403 (414) 632-6141.

Racine. BETSY MARRON (I)
1975-. <u>Bds</u>: Human Services Bd.; Social Services Com.; Ch., Juvenile Services Com. <u>Prev</u>: Cmsn. on Human Rights 1971-73. <u>Org</u>: NOW; Southside Revitalization Corp. <u>Educ</u>: St. Joseph Coll. 1965 BA; U. of Wis. 1969 MA; 1976 MS. <u>Occ</u>: Program Dir., Girl Scouts. <u>B</u>: 10/15/43. <u>Add</u>: 1307 Main St., Racine 53403 (414)633-6332.

Richland. MILDRED M. ROTT (R) **
1974-. <u>Bds</u>: Social Services Bd.; Health Com.; Grievance Com.; Resolutions Com.; Criminal Justice Council. <u>Org</u>: Alcoholism Council; Educ. Assoc.; PTA. <u>Educ</u>: U. of Wis. 1974 BS. <u>Occ</u>: Dir., Day Care Center. <u>B</u>: 10/2/35. <u>Add</u>: RFD 1, Lone Rock 53556.

Rock. FRANCES KOCHICAS
440 Wisconsin Ave., Beloit 53511.

Rock. PATRICIA SEEFELDT (D) **
1970-. <u>Bds</u>: Ch., Handicapped Childrens Bd.; Staff Com. Member; Library Bd.; State Review Com. <u>Org</u>: Dem. Women's Club. <u>B</u>: 3/17/23. <u>Add</u>: 505 Walker St., Janesville 53545.

Rock. VIRGINIA SKELLY **
1971-. <u>Dist</u>: 13. <u>Bds</u>: Health Services. <u>Prev</u>: Town Clerk. <u>Org</u>: Altrusa. <u>B</u>: 8/19/22. <u>Add</u>: R 5, 2713 Hayner Rd., Janesville 53545 (608)752-3332.

St. Croix. MARY LOUISE HALLEN (I)
1975-. <u>Dist</u>: 12. <u>Bds</u>: Personnel Com.; Unified Bd. Health Ctr.; Unified Bd. Personnel Com. <u>Prev</u>: Alderwoman 1970-76. <u>Org</u>: NEA. <u>Educ</u>: U. of Wis. 1960 BS. <u>Occ</u>: Teacher. <u>B</u>: 11/12/36. <u>Add</u>: 614 Vine St., Hudson 54016 (715)386-5581.

Sauk. BETTY J. REPKA (D)
1975-. <u>Bds</u>: Law Enforcement; Personnel; Housing. <u>Party</u>: Precinct Committeewoman 1972-76. <u>Org</u>: Dem. Party; Community Club. <u>Occ</u>: Assessor. <u>B</u>: 7/24/21. <u>Add</u>: Rt. 1, Rock Springs 53961.

Shawano. SARAH HOLBROOK CARROLL
1975-. <u>Dist</u>: 7. <u>Bds</u>: Planning, Zoning, Solid Waste; Task Force. <u>Party</u>: State Del. 1973-74; State Alt. 1971-72; Precinct Leader 1965-69. <u>Org</u>: Cnty. Rep. Party; Cnty. Youth Adv. Bd.; PTA. <u>Occ</u>: Grocery Store Owner. <u>B</u>: 4/22/39. <u>Add</u>: 1124 Lake Dr., Shawano 54166 (715)526-6526.

Walworth. HARRIETTE S. KRUGER
56 Congress, Box 307, Williams Bay 53191.

Walworth. JOY M. SMAGE (R)
1976-. <u>Bds</u>: Data Com.; Judicial Com.; Bd. of Zoning Appeals. <u>Org</u>: Midwest Economics Assoc.; Rep. Women. <u>Educ</u>: U. of Wis. 1967 BEd. <u>Occ</u>: Economics Instructor. <u>B</u>: 6/14/29. <u>Add</u>: RR 3, Elkhorn 53121 (414)723-2597.

Walworth. KITTY D. STEWART (R)
1976-. <u>Bds</u>: Health Com.; Juvenile Affairs & Interagency. <u>Party</u>: State Del. 1964-67; State Alt. 1968-71. <u>Org</u>: Rep. Women. <u>Occ</u>: Travel Agent. <u>B</u>: 5/1/23. <u>Add</u>: 964 W. Charles St., Whitewater 53190.

Washington. MARCELLA JAEGER BERKHOLTZ
1214 Park Ave., West Bend 53095.

Washington. HELEN B. BUNKE (R) **
1960-. <u>Bds</u>: Public Property; Sheriff's Com. <u>B</u>: 5/14/08. <u>Add</u>: 528 Jackson St., West Bend 53095 (414)334-3491.

Washington. LORRAINE KRANIAK HARTMAN
1974-. <u>Dist</u>: 15. <u>B</u>: 8/31/18. <u>Add</u>: 741 Decorah Rd., Rt. 2, W. Bend 53095 (414) 334-3491.

Waukesha. MARY G. BIRDENER
4408 Deer Park Rd., Oconomowoc 53066.

Waukesha. BETTY J. COOPER (D)
1972-. <u>Dist</u>: 26. <u>Bds</u>: Admin.; Leg.; Negotiating. <u>Party</u>: State Del. 1974-77; Nat. Alt. 1976; Cnty. Dems. Admin. Bd. 1971-72. <u>Org</u>: Wis. Correctional Services; Dem. Party. <u>B</u>: 2/5/31. <u>Add</u>: 127 E. Newhall Ave., Waukesha 53186 (414)544-8160.

Waukesha. JO ELLEN MULDER
N84 W14981 James Ave., Menomonee 53051.

Waupaca. ROSELLA W. SPLITT
R. 1, Manawa 54949.

Winnebago. TERRI L. AARONS (D)
1974-. <u>Bds</u>: Cnty. Personnel & Finance Com.; Ch., Housing Adv. Com.; Exec. Com. <u>Party</u>: State Del. 1972-74; Precinct Captain 1972-73; Secretary 1974-76. <u>Prev</u>: Criminal Justice Standards & Goals Com. 1976. <u>Org</u>: Criminal Justice Planning Council; Home Opportunities Bd.; Dem. Party. <u>Occ</u>: Research Analyst. <u>B</u>: 4/16/47. <u>Add</u>: 2324 Island Beach Rd., Oshkosh 54901 (414)235-2500.

Winnebago. CAROLE BROAS
1647 S. Park Ave., Neenah 54956.

Winnebago. ALBERTA J. GOFF
1853 Fairview, Oshkosh 54901.

Winnebago. LILLIAN JERO
4266 Omro Rd., Oshkosh 54901.

Winnebago. ROSALINE PITZ
403 Merritt Ave., Oshkosh 54901.

Winnebago. MARILYN PROTHEROE
123 W. Peckham, Neenah 54956.

Winnebago. MARY ANN WARNING
1974-. <u>Bds</u>: Planning Zoning Com.; Bd. of Adjustment. <u>B</u>: 7/19/29. <u>Add</u>: 43 Zaling Ave., Oshkosh 54901.

Wood. PHYLLIS SULTZE
1976-. Bds: Health; Public Property Com.
Prev: Planning & Zoning Com. 1976-77. Org:
LWV. Educ: U. of Wis. 1939 BS. Occ: Teacher.
B: 2/4/18. Add: 731 Cook Ave., Wisconsin
Rapids 54494 (715)423-3000.

Mayors

Delafield. DOROTHY J. WHITE (I)
1974-. Bds: Ch., Plan Cmsn.; Ch., Budget
Com.; Water Pollution Control Cmsn. Org:
AAUW. Educ:Coe Coll. 1942 BA. B: 11/7/19.
Add: 2220 Key Pt. La., Hartland 53029 (414)
646-3761.

Delavan. ELIZABETH S. SUPERNAW (R)
1976-. Bds: Ch., Plan Cmsn.; Water &
Sewer Cmsn.; Ch., Dev. Corp. Party: State
Alt. 1952. Prev: Recreation Cmsn. 1965-70;
Alderwoman 1973-76. Org: BPW. Educ: U. of
Wis. 1952 BS. B: 11/5/30. Add: 518 Parish,
Delavan 53115 (414)738-5585.

Haugen. ANGELINE THOMPSON
Box 44, Haugen 54841.

Oconomowoc. FLORENCE G. WHALEN (D)
1976-. Bds: Ch., Planning Cmsn.; Utility
Cmsn. Prev: Wis. Task Force on Educ. Goals
1971-73; State Adv. Com. on Aging 1973-76;
Ch., Cable TV Com. 1974-76; Bd. of Appeals
1974-76. Org: LWV; Assoc. for Retarded
Citizens. B: 1/22/33. Add: 406 W. 3rd St.,
Oconomowoc 53066 (414)567-8143.

Rhinelander. CLARIBEL BEATRICE PROSSER (I) **
1972-. Bds: Electrical Bd.; Parking
Utility; Planning Cmsn.; Housing Com. Prev:
Councilwoman 1968-72; Supervisor 1968-72.
Org: Wis. Northwest Mayors; Bicentennial. B:
5/22/17. Add: 320 W. Kemp St., Rhinelander
54501 (715)369-2002.

Sheboygan Falls. GLADYS M. MORKEN
1976-. Bds: Ch, Plan Cmsn.; Ch., Bd. of
Review. Prev: Alderwoman 1964-67. Org:
Historical Soc. Occ: School Bus Driver. B:
3/22/26. Add: 65 Bryant Ct., Sheboygan Fls.
53085 (414)459-3191.

Spencer. LORAINE W. COOK
200 W. Buse Street, Spencer 54479.

Washburn. EDITH F. MERILA
City Hall, Washburn 54891.

Waunakee. ANN G. HELT
1975-. Bds: Ch., Fire Dist.; Ch., Planning
Cmsn.; Ch., Industrial Cmsn. Prev: Village
Trustee 1973-75. Org: PTA. Occ: Secretary.
B: 4/29/30. Add: 204 W. 3rd St., Waunakee
53597 (608)849-5626.

Local Councils

Wausau. MARY R. MC CLAIN (D)
See Cnty. Supervisor.

Judges

SHIRLEY SCHLANGER ABRAHAMSON
Judge, Supreme Court. Org: State Bar
Assoc.; LWV. Educ: NYU 1953 BA; Ind. U.
School of Law 1956 JD; U. of Wis. 1962 SJD.
Add: 2012 Waunona Way, Madison 53713 (608)
266-1885.

State Boards and Commissions

Office of the Governor, State Capitol Bldg.,
Madison 53702.

Accounting Examining Board
JUDITH S. METCALF
ELIZABETH S. PETERS

Aeronautics, Council on
MARIE GRIMM

Aging, Board on
ALICE GEORGE
MRS. ERNIE GOODWILL
MRS. FAY HILL

Agriculture, Board of
HELEN NELSON
JOCELYN RHEIN

Air Pollution Control Council
MRS. ROBERT JASKULSKI

Alcoholism, Citizens Advisory Council on
BESS HAYES
FERN SMITH

Arts Board
MARION BAUMANN
VELMA B. HAMILTON
RUTH DE YOUNG KOHLER
LYNN SAXER
SANDRA UTECH
MARY ALICE WIMMER

Barbers Examining Board
EVA ZIMMERMAN

Bingo Control Board
MARY BIRDENER
ELVERA TAYLOR

Boundary Area Commission
BARBARA A. FRANK
CATHERINE HEITING

Cosmetology Examining Board
LUVENIA VERLINE CHILDS
MARY E. KOLKA
VERNICE E. MAROUSEK
MARY CONNIE SCHMIEDER

Credit Union Review Board
  SUZANNE BARANOWSKI
  HELEN M. STORM

Developmental Disabilities, Council on
  ALETA BARMORE
  ADELE CARLEY
  JUNE DOBBS
  MARY MURPHY

Drug Quality Council
  KATHLEEN HICKSON
  DIANE O. JOHNSON

Dwelling Code Council
  DOROTHY COLLINS
  MARY PLATNER

Educational Approval Board
  GRACIE JEFFERSON
  WENDY MUSICH WITHERS

Educational Communications Board
  BARBARA M. HOLBROOK
  MARY E. KELLY
  MARILYN LANGDON
  DORIS ULLRICH

Elections Board
  ESTHER A. KAPLAN
  JOANNE WELLS

Environmental Council, Citizens
  ELIZABETH BARDWELL
  ELLEN FOLSUM
  SHARON IMES
  EILEEN MERSHART
  PEG WATROUS

Equal Rights Council
  HOPE CROSS
  MARIANNE EPSTEIN
  NESS FLORES
  CHARLOTTE FREEDMAN
  VELMA HERD
  LUCINDA MARTINEAU
  JULIA MINNICH
  SOPHIE LEE MROTEK
  TERESA E. OLIVARES
  CARRIE RANDLE
  BARBARA J. STENGER
  VEDA STONE
  ANNETTE WILLIAMS
  RUTH J. ZUBRENSKY

Ethics Board
  ANNRITA LARDY
  SISTER GRACE MC DONALD

Food Standards, Council on
  MARY A. BUSCAGLIA
  ERNA CARMICHAEL
  MRS. VINCENT ZEHREN

Health Facilities Authority
  JOY A. MOY

Health Policy Council
  EDITH BINGHAM
  DOLORES ECKER
  MARY HANRAHAN
  JENNIFER CLIFTON LEE
  ROSE M. NAMMACHER
  LORETTA NIKOLAI
  MARIAN PIPER
  FLORA SEEFELDT
  ELLEN SMITH
  PATRICIA STONE
  KIT SORENSON
  ALMA VAZQUEZ-BYRNE
  ANNELIESE WAGGONER
  SELMA WEISKOPF

Hearing Aid Dealers and Fitters Examining Board
  MARILYN MULLARKY

Higher Educational Aids Board
  MARIANNE H. EPSTEIN
  DEBORAH GARDNER
  ESTHER KAPLAN
  MARY BETH OLSON
  LOIS T. STAIR

Highway Safety, Council on
  LUCILLE FESSLER
  SHIRLEY SCHMERLING
  BARBARA THOMPSON

Housing Finance Authority
  JEAN C. BROEREN

Indian Education, Council on
  BARBARA BOWMAN
  JUNE COYHIS
  LORETTA ELLIS
  DOROTHY LE PAGE
  JANICE LINCOLN
  MARGE PASCLE
  ELAINE SHEPARD
  CHRISTINE WEBSTER

Industry, Labor and Human Relations Commission
  VIRGINIA B. HART

Interstate Indian Commission
  MARILYN C. SKENANDORE

Judicial Commission
  FRANCES W. HURST

Law Enforcement Standards Board
  JUDITH KAROFSKY
  MARY ANN SCHACHT

Library Development, Council on
  MARYON CIGLER
  SALLY A. DAVIS

Local Affairs, Council on
  ELEANOR M. FITCH
  SHARON K. IMES
  MARY LESCOHIER
  FLORA SEEFELDT
  ROSALIE TRYON

Medical Education Review Committee
  HELEN DORSCH

Medical Examining Board
  PATRICIA E. MC ILLECE

Mine Reclamation Council
  MEREDITH E. OSTROM
  ELIZABETH E. SALMON

Natural Resources Board
  VICTORIA MC CORMICK

Nursing, Board of
  HELEN GERMAN
  VALENCIA N. PROCK
  RUTH L. SMITH
  SISTER MARY A. TOUCHETT
  PAMELA J. WEGNER
  BARBARA JEAN WHITMORE

Nursing Home Administrators Examining Board
  ELLEN DEAN PATTERSON
  RUTH E. PAYNTER
  MARY SCHLIMGEN
  SISTER MARY CLAUDE SZYPERSKI

Nursing Home Reimbursement Appeals Board
  ELIZABETH REGAN

Optometry Examining Board
  ROSE MARIE BARON
  ANITA EBERL

Personnel Board
  LAURENE DE WITT

Pharmacy Examining Board
  JOSEPHINE MONTGOMERY
  THORA M. VERVOREN

Psychology Examining Board
  GEORGIA A. FELGER

Real Estate Examining Board
  MARCIA MILLS
  MARILYN SLAUTTERBACK

Retirement Fund Board
  FLORENCE BUREK
  NAILA HARPER

Snowmobile Recreational Council
  CAROL DIGGELMAN
  PHYLLIS PRESTON

State Employes Merit Award Board
  MARY M. GRAVE

Teachers Retirement Board
  MARCIA E. TOPEL

Tourism, Council on
  LOIS ALCORN
  VIRGINIA BURTNESS
  MILDRED PETERSON
  MAVIS PIGMAN
  JANE STAPLES
  EUNICE URBAN

University of Wisconsin Systems, Board of
Regents
  NANCY M. BARKLA
  JOYCE M. ERDMAN
  MRS. HOWARD V. SANDIN
  MARY M. WALTER

Vocational, Technical and Adult Education, Board
of
  ROSE DE RUYTER
  IRMA WEST

Watchmaking Examining Board
  KATHERINE CUMICEK

Wyoming

State Executive and Cabinet

THYRA G. THOMSON (R) **
Secretary of State 1962-. Bds: Land Bd.;
Reform Bd.; Capitol Bldg. Com.; Bd. of
Deposits; Collection Agency Bd. Org: Nat.
Assoc. of Secretaries of State; North Amer.
Secretaries Administration; Secretary, Wyo.
Fed. Women's Club 1946-47. Educ: U. of Wyo.
1939 BA. B: 7/30/16. Add: 204 E. 22nd,
Cheyenne 82001 (307)777-7378.

State Legislature

State Senate

JUNE BOYLE (D)
1962-. Party: State Del. 1960-76; Nat. Del.
1968, '72; Nat. Alt. 1964; Precinct Leader
1957-59; Cnty. Ch. 1959-61; Nat. Committeewoman 1964-76. Org: LWV; Fed. Women's Club;
Mental Health Assoc.; Dem. Women's Club. Educ:
U. of Colo. 1939 BFA. B: 9/30/17. Add: 706
S. 14th, Laramie 82070.

State House

ELLEN CROWLEY (R)
P.O. Box 287, Cheyenne.

ESTHER ESKENS (R)
1975-. Bds: Judiciary Com.; Labor; Health
& Social Services. Party: State Del. 1976,
'72. Org: ANA; BPW; NOWL. Educ: St. Mary
School of Nursing 1945 RN. Occ: RN. B:
11/30/24. Add: 15 E. 10th St., Lovell 82431.

MATILDA HANSEN (D)
1974-. Bds: Joint Judiciary Com.; Rules
& Regulations Sub-Com.; Liquor Recodification
Sub-Com. Party: State Del. 1974, '76; Precinct
Committeewoman 1972-74. Org: LWV; Common
Cause; ACLU; Dem. Women. Educ: U. of Colo.
1963 BA; U. of Wyo. 1970 MA. Occ: Dir., Adult
Educ. B: 9/4/29. Add: 1306 Kearney, Laramie
82070.

HELEN S. MELDRUM (R)
587 N. Main, Buffalo 82834.

CATHERINE M. PARKS (R) **
1972-. Dist: Campbell. Bds: Joint Interim
Labor Com.; Joint Interim Mines & Minerals Com.
Party: State Com. 1964-75; Del., Nat. Conv.
1972; Precinct Leader 1960-71. Org: Farm
Bureau; Rep. Women's Club; Dir., Fed. Land Bank;
Wyo. Stock Growers. Occ: Rancher. B: 4/27/20.
Add: Little Powder River Ranch, Weston 82731
(307)777-7702.

EDNESS KIMBALL WILKINS (D)
1955-. Bds: Interim Revenue Com.; Cmsn.
on Status of Women. Party: State Del. 1950-
76; Nat. Del. 1956, 1960; Precinct Ch. 1952- ;
Cnty. Ch. 1950-52. Prev: Asst. Dir. of U.S.
Mint 1933-47. Org: Stockgrowers Assoc.;
Farm Bureau; BPW; Zonta; Red Cross; Chamber
of Commerce; Dem. Women; WPC; AAUW. Occ:
Rancher. Add: 422 Milton Ave., Casper 82601.

County Commissions

Albany. MARGUERITE B. NELSON
1975-. Bds: Criminal Justice; Com. on
Aging; Com. on Alcoholism. Org: ANA; NEA;
Amer. School Health Assoc.; LWV; Common
Cause; Taxation with Representation. Educ:
N.Y.U. 1948 AN; U. of Wy. 1961 BS; 1962 MA.
Occ: School Nurse. B: 1/19/29. Add: P.O.
Box 489, Laramie 82070 (307)742-2149.

Laramie. WINIFRED HICKEY
County Courthouse, Cheyenne 82001.

Sheridan. RUTH GEIER RICE
County Courthouse, Sheridan 82801.

Sublette. LOIS E. COBB (R)
1977-. Bds: Resource Conservation & Devt.
Project. Org: Historical Society. Occ: Office
Manager. B: 11/16/28. Add: 454 S. Fremont
Ave., Pinedale 82941 (307)367-4321.

Teton. MARY FRENCH MOORE (D)
1976-. Bds: Water Quality Agency; Dept.
of Public Assistance & Social Services Bd.;
Planning Cmsn. Educ: U. of Colo. 1964 BA.
Occ: Potter. B: 2/25/38. Add: Box 161,
Wilson 83014 (307)733-4430.

Mayor

Hulett. JESSIE JOHNSON
P.O. Box 287, Hulett 82720.

Ranchester. MARION WONDRA
P.O. Box 236, Ranchester 82839.

Saratoga. KATHY GLODE (D)
1976-. Bds: Cnty. Joint Powers Bd.; Cnty.
Assoc. of Govts. Org: Historical & Cultural
Society; Dem. Women. Educ: Creighton U. 1971
BS. B: 7/1/49. Add: Box 605, Saratoga
82331 (307)326-5424.

Shoshoni. MRS. LEON MOREHOUSE
P.O. Box 267, 2nd & Wyoming, Shoshoni
82649.

Local Councils

Baggs. WILMA DIANE REED (I)
1974-. B: 3/23/45. Add: Box 148, Baggs
82321 (307)383-6245.

Basin. DORIS CROWELL
P.O. Box 599, Basin 82410.

Big Piney. MACILLE CARR
LUCY WILKERSON
P.O. Box 70, Big Piney 83113.

Casper. CLAUDETTE MC CRARY (I)
1977-. Bds: Health Bd.; Housing Community
Devt. Org: N. Casper Improvement Assoc.; Wyo.
Human Resources Council; LWV; AAUW. Educ: U.
of Wyo. BS. Occ: Home Economics Extension
Agent. B: 8/13/45. Add: 1240 S. Ill., Casper
82601 (307)265-8941.

Cheyenne. DARLENE K. BUNN
Rm. 208, City-County Bldg., Cheyenne 82001.

Cowley. LYNNE STROM
P.O. Box 215, Cowley 82420.

Dayton. LUCILLE ALLEY (R) **
1971-. Bds: Street Cmsn.; Cemetery Coordinator; OEO; Disaster & Civil Defense Agency.
Org: Bicentennial Com. Occ: Postal Clerk. B:
3/2/21. Add: Bridge St., Dayton 82836.

Diamondville. EDNA M. CRAWFORD (D)
1973-. B: 1/3/23. Add: P.O. Box 141,
Diamondville 83116 (307)877-3142.

Diamondville. THORMA HARRIS
P.O. Box 281, Diamondville 83116.

Dixon. JUANITA DANFORD
Town Hall, Dixon 82323.

Fort Laramie. KATHERINE ERSCHABEK (I)
Org: Cnty. Educ. Assoc. Educ: U. of Wyo.
1967 BS. Occ: Substitute Teacher. B: 12/31/10.
Add: Box 92, Ft. Laramie 82212 (307)837-2470.

Fort Laramie. CHRISTINE ARTHUR
P.O. Box 177, Fort Laramie 82212.

Glendo. FRANCES ELLER
P.O. Box 396, Glendo 82213.

Granger. MARIAM L. BANKS (I)
1976-. Occ: Sales Clerk/Asst. Manager.
B: 2/19/21. Add: 405 2nd St., Granger 82934.

Hartville. HARRIET B. RIZOR (D)
1976-. Occ: News Editor; Museum Curator &
Caretaker. B: 6/17/19. Add: Star Rt., Hartville 82215.

Hartville. EDNA VIOLA SPRAGUE (D)
1976-. Bds: Playground/Recreation Com.;
Christmas Decorating Com.; Environmental. Org:
AARP. Occ: Clerk. B: 1/6/14. Add: P.O. Box
71, Hartville 82215 (307)836-2580.

Kaycee. GLORIA STRATTON
P.O. Box 174, Kaycee 82639.

Kirby. VIRGINIA UITTO
P.O. Box 45, Kirby 82430.

Laramie. GERMAINE ST. JOHN
P.O. Box C, Laramie 82070.

Lingle. JANE SMITH
P.O. Box 448, Lingle 82223.

Marbleton. BETTY FINDLAY
STACEY GILLIAM
P.O. Box 611, Marbleton 83113.

Medicine Bow. POLLY DAVIS
JOYCE GRIFFITH
P.O. Box 156, Pine St., Medicine Bow 82329.

Mountain View. BETTIE B. BULLOCK
P.O. Box 249, Mountain View 82939.

Pavillion. ALICE WALKER
P.O. Box 15, Pavillion 82523.

Pinedale. DORIS BURZLANDER
P.O. Box 674, Pinedale 82941.

Ranchester. SONIA FISCHER
P.O. Box 236, Ranchester 82839.

Rawlins. JUNE R. AYLSWORTH (R)
1976-. Bds: Planning & Zoning Cmsn.; Cnty.
Council of Govt. Party: State Del. 1976;
State Alt. 1972, '74; Precinct Committeewoman
1964-66. Prev: Cnty. Museum Bd. 1975. Org:
Wyo. Assoc. of Municipalities; Red Cross; Rep.
Women's Club. B: 6/29/23. Add: Box 340,
1103 Mt. View, Rawlins 82301 (307)324-4425.

Rawlins. CAROL MOORE
P.O. Box 953, 5th & Buffalo, Rawlins
82301.

Riverside. OPAL INEZ MOORE (R)
Org: OES; PTA; Senior Citizens. Educ:
Chadron State Coll. BA. B: 3/28/03. Add:
Riverside 82325 (307)327-5255.

Riverton. LYNN M. COLEMAN (R)
1972-. Bds: Regional Airport Bd.; Wyo.
Assoc. of Municipalities Leg. Com.; Wyo.
Airport Operators Assoc. Party: Election
Judge 1959-61; Election Clerk 1958-59. Prev:
Water & Waste Water Quality Control Bd. 1974-
79; Certification Bd.; Control Bd. Org:
Soroptimist. Educ: Colo. Women's Coll. 1958
AA. Occ: Accountant. B: 10/29/38. Add:
114 S. 6th St. E., Riverton 82501 (307)
856-4816.

Rock River. ALICE EPPSE
P.O. Box 5, Rock River 82083.

Rock Springs. ROSE BELMAIN (R)
    1976-. Bds: Community Devt. Com.; Ch.,
Recreation Com. Prev: Urban Renewal Bd. 1974-
75; Planning & Zoning Cmsn. 1975-76. Org:
Chamber of Commerce. Educ: U. of Wy. 1967 BA.
Occ: Credit Bureau Manager. B: 2/6/44. Add:
406 Sapphire St., P.O. Box 459, Rock Springs
82901 (307)362-3911.

Sinclair. JUDITH A. FORSTER
    P.O. Box 247, Lincoln St., Sinclair 82334.

Sundance. RUTH FROLANDER (D)
    1976-. Party: State Del.; Cnty. Committee-
woman; Cnty. Precinct; Cnty. Treasurer 1976.
Prev: Cnty. Farmers Home Administration 1968-
71; 1976-79. Org: Life Insurance Underwriters;
Wyo. Farm Bureau; Wyo. Stock Growers. Occ:
Insurance Agent. B: 3/21/15. Add: 208 Park,
Sundance 82729 (307)283-3582.

Ten Sleep. VERNA B. DAVIS
    P.O. Box 5, Ten Sleep 82442.

Ten Sleep. FLORENCE SHRIVER
    P.O. Box 5, Ten Sleep 82442.

Upton. BARBARA SUHR
    P.O. Box 203, Upton 82730.

Van Tassell. MARCIA ZERBE
    Town Hall, Van Tassell 82242.

Wamsutter. EMMA GONZALES
    P.O. Box 6, Wamsutter 82336.

Worland. FAY ALEXANDER
    P.O. Box 226, 829 Big Horn, Worland 82401.

State Boards and Commissions

    Office of the Governor, State Capitol Bdg.,
Cheyenne 82002.

Aging, Advisory Committee on
    MRS. ARTHUR L. BUCK
    MRS. HUGH DUNCAN
    NELLIE E. FRIZZELL
    ALICE HAWKEN
    MARGARET KIRK
    MARY LEE
    MRS. JAMES PLATTS
    MRS. ALBERT TILLMAN
    HAZEL WILEY

Alcohol and Drug Abuse Advisory Council
    R. DEE COZZENS
    MARILYNN MITCHELL JUROVICH

Arts, Council on the
    CELIA DAVIS
    DONNA DICKSON
    RUTH LOOMIS
    SUZANNE TUMA

Beef Council
    VIRGINIA MC INTOSH

Bicentennial Commission
    MABEL E. BROWN
    PEGGY SIMSON CURRY
    MARY HELEN HENDRY
    RUTH LOOMIS
    CRONELIA P. METZ
    NORA REIMER
    HELEN L. REYNOLDS

Certified Public Accountants, Board of
    CYNTHIA M. BOYHAN

Child Care Facilities Certification Board
    RETA ONSTOTT

Child Care Facilities Certification Board
Advisory Committee
    ALICE COOK
    PAMELA RITTER
    SHIRLEY SMITH

Children and Youth, Council for
    LESLIE KOMINSKY
    LORRAINE KUHN
    EMILY ANN MACY
    SUSAN RUAN
    CAROL WEILANG

Children and Youth Council Advisory Committee
    CONSTANCE RICCI

Collection Agency Board
    LINDA RUSSELL
    THYRA THOMSON

Community College Commission
    MARGARET KAHIN
    NORA MIX
    MARIE STEWART

Cosmetology, Board of
    BARBARA M. CULLY
    LYNDA D. FREESE
    NELLIE MAE NELSON

Criminal Administration, Planning Committee on
    MAXINE PATTERSON

Developmental Disabilities, Planning and Advisory
Council for
    MARGARET ANDERSON
    SHARON BISHOP
    SUSAN BOEDEKER
    BEVERLY CREAGER
    WINIFRED HICKEY
    BETTY KLINE
    NANCY PETERNAL
    ANITA TUASON
    MARY KAY TURNER
    MARJ WOODS

Education, Board of
    KAREN HAND

Emergency Medical Services, Advisory Committee
on
    IMOGENE HANSON

Employment of the Handicapped, Committee for
JOAN L. ADRAGNA
MRS. DALE M. BARDO
SHARON FUNKHOUSER
GAYLE LACKEY
ANNETTA S. WALKER
RUTH CLARE YONKEE

Environmental Quality Council
LYNN DICKEY

Fair Employment Practices Commission
HAZEL SAGE

Hospital Advisory Council
ELIZABETH DAY
WILMA HUTCHINGS
JOYCE MAEDER

Jail Standards Advisory Committee
LINDA KIRKBRIDE
MAXINE PATTERSON

Land Use Advisory Committee
SHEILA ARNOLD

Land Use Commission
ELAINE BARTON

Library, Archives and Historical Board
JUNE CASEY
MARY EMERSON
SUZANNE KNEPPER

Manpower Affairs Council
BARBARA BANNISTER
MRS. BOBBY POTTER
JEAN SCHOECK

Medical Assistance and Services Act, Advisory
Committee for the
JOAN BEACHLER
JOYCE FITZHUGH
MRS. J.J. HICKEY

Nursing, Board of
A. PATRICIA DOCKINS
ROBERTA M. HARDING
JANICE K. POPE
DOROTHY M. RATZ
DOROTHY TUPPER

Nursing Home Administrators, Board of
R. DEE COZZENS
BARBARA GOETZ

Occupational Education, Advisory Council for
LA VERNE BOAL
ANITA LISEK
MARY K. SCHWOPE
MILDRED STROUD

Occupational Health and Safety Commission
JENNIE PARKER

Physical Therapy, Board of
MARY MC CULLEN

Public Assistance and Social Services
YOSHIYE TANAKA
GLENNA E. TIPPETS
VIRGINIA TOMINC

Recreation Commission
MRS. ROBERT FRISBY

Reorganization of State Government, Legislative-
Executive Commission on
MARGARET BROWN

Retirement System Board
RUTH F. ADAM
FERN A. BENDER
LYNN SIMONS
RITA WHITE

Speech Pathology and Audiology, Board of
Examiners for
RUTH BELL
JANIS A. JELINEK
DORIS M. LUCAS
KATHRYN H. SHEPHERD

Veterans Affairs Commission
BETTY HEMPHILL

Vocational Rehabilitation, Council on
MRS. DALE M. BARDO

Water Development, Council of
ADELLA LE BEAU

Water Quality Advisory Board
MAXINE PATTERSON

Women, Commission for
PATRICIA ALEXANDER
JANE BARDO
ELEANOR BECK
POLLY BOGGRESS
JUNE BOYLE
PATRICIA DUNCOMBE
RENEE FITZGERALD
MAXINE HAYWARD
FRANCES HOADLEY
LORA A. JOLLEY
OPLE JORGENSEN
JUDY KALLAL
DOROTHY KLEMENTS
KATHY LEBSACK
CLAUDIE M. MEYER
MEREDITH MORROW
ELEANORE O'NEILL
NANCY PETERNAL
CECILIA G. PICKETT
BETTY QUADE
PEGGY J. SANDERS
LOEVA SAWYER
MARTHA SCHROEDER
MARGARET TOBIN
CLARA LEE VORE
EDNESS KIMBALL WILKINS
EDNA L. WRIGHT

Women's Advisory Council, Commission for
    ELAINE AVERY
    VIOLET FLACK
    IRIS GUYNN
    VERDA JAMES
    IRENE KERR
    NETTA BELL LARSON
    ELSIE LOEHR
    MAE URBANEK

CATHERINE B. KELLY
    Judge, Superior Court. Washington DC

JULIA COOPER MACK
    Judge, Superior Court. Washington DC

Washington, D.C.

Local Councils

WILLIE J. HARDY (D)
    1974-. Bds: Ch., Special Com. on Adv.
Neighborhood Cmsn.; Com. on Educ., Recreation
& Youth Affairs; Com. on Public Safety & the
Judiciary. Party: Nat. Del.; Dem. State Com.
1960-64, 1968-70; JFK Inaugural Parade Coord.
1960-61. Prev: Deputy Dir., Dept. of Environ-
mental Services 1971-74; Deputy Dir., Mayor's
Office of Community Services 1970-71. Org:
Nat. Council of Negro Women. B: 7/18/22.
Add: 5046 Benning Rd. SE, Washington DC 20019
(202)724-8068.

HILDA MASON
WILHELMINA ROLARK
    City Hall, Washington DC

NADINE P. WINTER (D) **
    1974-. Bds: Council of Government; Ch.,
Housing & Urban Dev. Party: Del., Nat. Conv.
Dem. 1962, 1964, 1968, 1972; Ward Leader 1962-
70; Dem. Central Com. 1962-64. Prev: Model
Cities Cmsnr. 1970-75. Org: WPC; Dem. Women's
Club; Fed. of Civic Assoc.; Metropolitan
Assoc. of Settlement Houses; Political Educ.
Term of N.E.; V-Pres., Public Interest Civic
Assoc. Educ: Brooklyn Coll. BA; Federal City
Coll. 1972 MA. Occ: Exec. Dir., Hospitality
House. B: 3/3/24. Add: 1100 K St., NE,
Washington DC 20002 (202)638-2223 Ext. 64.

ADDENDUM

KENTUCKY

State Legislature

State Senate

Delete

DAISY THALER (D)
Dist: 34

State House

Delete

GLENNA A. BEVINS (D)
Dist: 77.

CHARLOTTE S. MC GILL (D)
Dist: 42.

Add:

CLAUDIA RINER
Dist: 36. Add: 1143 E. Broadway,
Louisville 40204.

NEW JERSEY

State Legislature

State Senate

Delete

ALENE S. AMMOND (D)
Dist: 6.

State House

Delete

ALINA MISZKIEWICZ (D)
Dist: 32.

Add

BARBARA BERMAN (D)
Dist: 6. Add: 12 Silvertop Ln., Cherry Hill

MILDRED BARRY GARVIN (D)
Dist: 26. Add: 15 Woodland Ave., East
Orange 07017.

BARBARA KALIK (D)
Dist: 7. Add: 48 Hillcrest Ln., Willingboro 07746.

GRETA KIERNAN (D)
Dist: 39. Add: 62 Spring St., Harrington
Pk. 07640.

BARBARA W. MC CONNELL (D)
Dist: 14. Add: R.D. 2, Box 505, Flemington 08822.

MARY M. SCANLON (D)
Dist: 28. Add: 145 Ivy St., Newark 07106.

ROSEMARIE TOTARO (D)
Dist: 23. Add: 69 E. Shore Rd., Denville
07834.

VIRGINIA

State Legislature

State House

Delete

ELEANOR P. SHEPPARD (D)
Dist: 33.

Add

ELISE B. HEINZ (D)
Dist: 23. Add: 2728 N. Fillmore St.,
Arlington 22207.

GLADYS B. KEATING (D)
Dist: 19. Add: 5911 Brookview Dr.,
Alexandria 22310.

MARY SUE TERRY (D)
Dist: 13. Add: P.O. Box 407, Stuart 24171.

APPENDIX: VARIATIONS IN TYPES OF OFFICES

In order to limit classification to a manageable number of categories, the editors have standardized designations for state and local offices and for governing bodies. In actual practice, nomenclature varies considerably from state to state, and within states at local levels. This appendix lists the most common variations of offices and provides citations to materials which give detailed explanations of variations in forms, functions, responsibilities and authority vested in the various governing bodies.

State Executive Offices and Cabinet Offices

The directory includes state executive offices which are filled by statewide election. Included in addition are those appointive offices designated as cabinet level by the executive office of the state. State boards of education and boards of university regents are not included in this section even if they are elected statewide. They can be found under the listings for boards and commissions.

The numbers and types of elective administrative offices vary from state to state. For a detailed listing of these offices, see The Book of the States, 1976-77 (Lexington, Kentucky: The Council of State Governments, 1976) pp. 121-123.

There is also great diversity in the offices which carry cabinet rank and in the way these offices are established and defined. In a few states the cabinet is authorized by the constitution or by statute. In most states the composition of the cabinet is determined by the Governor and can change with succeeding administrations. In some states cabinet status seems to be unofficial. For a partial listing of state cabinet and a list of the offices which compromise each state's cabinet, see Cabinets in State Government (Lexington, Kentucky: The Council of State Government, 1969).

State Legislature

Nebraska is the only state with a unicameral legislature.

Terms used to refer to both houses of the legislature:

> General Assembly Arkansas, Colorado, Connecticut, Delaware, Georgia, Illinois, Indiana, Iowa, Kentucky, Maryland, Missouri, North Carolina, Ohio, Pennsylvania,

Rhode Island, South Carolina, Tennessee, Vermont, Virginia

General Court Massachusetts, New Hampshire

Legislative Assembly North Dakota, Oregon

Legislature Alabama, Alaska, Arizona, California, Florida, Hawaii, Idaho, Kansas, Louisiana, Maine, Michigan, Minnesota, Mississippi, Montana, Nebraska, Nevada, New Jersey, New Mexico, New York, Oklahoma, South Dakota, Texas, Utah, Washington, West Virginia, Wisconsin, Wyoming

Terms used to refer to the separate legislative houses:

The upper house is uniformly referred to as the Senate

The lower house is most often called the House of Representatives, except in the following states:

> Assembly California, Nevada, New York, Wisconsin
>
> General Assembly New Jersey
>
> House of Delegates Maryland, Virginia, West Virginia

State Judges

The directory includes listings for judges in State Appellate Courts and in State Trial Courts of General Jurisdiction. State Appellate Courts commonly include the Appellate Court, the Court of Appeals and the Supreme Court. General Jurisdiction Courts usually include Circuit courts, District Courts and Superior Courts. The names of the courts in the fifty states are fairly standard. For a complete description of names and structures of all state courts, see State Court Systems, Revised (Lexington, Kentucky: The Council of State Governments, 1974).

State Boards and Commissions

States vary widely in the numbers and types of state boards and commissions they have established and there is no one source which lists or discusses them. Individual state manuals must be consulted for detailed information on the numbers, names, duties and powers of the boards and commissions.

County Governing Bodies

The 1972 Census of Governments counted 3044 organized and operating county governmental units. The following list summarizes the terms used to designate county bodies within the states. States in which practices vary are listed under each applicable category:

Board of Supervisors (often, Board of or Court of County Commission) Alabama, Alaska, Colorado, Florida, Georgia, Idaho, Illinois, Indiana, Kansas, Maine, Maryland, Massachusetts, Michigan, Minnesota, Montana, Nebraska, Nevada, New Hampshire, New Mexico, North Carolina, North Dakota, Ohio, Oklahoma, Oregon, Pennsylvania, South Carolina, South Dakota, Tennessee, Utah, Washington, Wyoming

Board of Chosen Freeholders New Jersey

Commissioners Court Texas

County Council Delaware, Illinois, West Virginia

County Court Vermont

Fiscal Court Kentucky

Police Jury, Parish Council Louisiana

Quarterly Court Tennessee

Quorum or Levying Court Arkansas, Delaware, South Carolina

For a more detailed state by state listing of the names of county governing bodies, see The U.S. Census of Governments, Vol. 1, Governmental Organization (Washington, D.C.; Government Printing Office, 1972). For an explanation of the variations in the duties and powers of county governments consult The U.S. Bureau of the Census Governing Bodies of County Governments (Washington, D.C.; Government Printing Office, 1973) and the National Association of Counties.

Townships

Twenty states have operating township governments in at least part of the state. Townships usually have limited functions such as the administration of public assistance programs, correctional systems, schools, the assessment of taxable property or the building and maintenance of roads. Township governments with jurisdiction exceeding the boundaries of the municipalities contained within them and which function as a separate form of government between the municipal and county level of government exist for all areas of Indiana and some areas in Connecticut, Kansas, Michigan, Missouri, Nebraska, New York, Ohio and Vermont. In Illinois townships function as county governments except in 17 counties and Cook county. These townships are, however, listed and counted as townships, not counties.

In the remaining 10 states (Massachusetts, New Hampshire, New Jersey, Pennsylvania, Rhode Island, Wisconsin, Maine, North Dakota, South Dakota and Minnesota) no geographic overlap exists between townships and municipalities. In this volume, these townships are classified and listed as the equivalent of municipalities.

For more information see The U.S. Census of Governments, Vol. 1, Governmental Organization (Washington, D.C.: U.S. Government Printing Office, 1972).

Local Governing Bodies

The terms used to designate chief officials and members of local governing bodies vary within each state as well as among states, usually according to the population or size of the localities and their subsequent classification (1st, 2nd, 3rd, class cities, towns, villages, boroughs, etc.), or according to the form of government chartered by law or optional plan (mayor-council, commission, trustee, alderman, etc.) In addition, most states have provisions for special charter or home rule cities, most of which take a mayor-council form of government. A few places have a combined city-county government. These include New York City, Denver, San Francisco, Juneau (Alaska), Jacksonville (Duval County, Florida), Columbus (Muscogee County, Georgia), Indianapolis (Marion County, Indiana), and Carson City (Ormsby County, Nevada). Generally, cities are governed by a mayor-council or commission form of government, while many towns and villages are governed by boards of supervisors, trustees or selectmen. The following list identifies various forms and names of local government operating within each state; a state may be classified in more than one category:

Mayor-Alderman (often President-Alderman) Alabama, Arkansas, Colorado, Florida, Louisiana, Michigan, Minnesota, Mississippi, New Hampshire, New Mexico, New York, North Carolina, North Dakota, Oklahoma, Tennessee, South Carolina, South Dakota, Texas and Wisconsin

Mayor-Council (often President-Council) Alaska, California, Idaho, Illinois, Indiana, Iowa, Kansas, Kentucky, Louisiana, Maryland, Massachusetts, Missouri, Montana, Nebraska, Nevada, New Jersey, New Mexico, New York, North Carolina, Ohio, Oregon, Rhode Island, South Carolina, South Dakota, Tennessee, Texas, Utah, Virginia, Washington, West Virginia, Wisconsin, Wyoming

Mayor-Board of Trustees Alaska, Arizona, Colorado, Illinois, Indiana, Kentucky, Michigan, Minnesota, Nebraska, New Jersey, New Mexico, New York, North Dakota, Oklahoma, South Dakota, Utah, Vermont, Wisconsin

City-Manager or Council-Manager Alabama,
Arkansas, Colorado, Idaho, Iowa, Kansas,
Louisiana, Massachusetts, Minnesota,
Mississippi, Missouri, Montana, Nebraska,
New Hampshire, New Jersey, North Carolina,
North Dakota, Ohio, Oklahoma, South
Carolina, South Dakota, Tennessee, West
Virginia

Commission Alabama, Arkansas, Iowa,
Kansas, Kentucky, Massachusetts, Minnesota,
Mississippi, Montana, Nebraska, New Jersey,
New Mexico, North Carolina, North Dakota,
Ohio, South Carolina, South Dakota, Texas,
Virginia, Wisconsin, Wyoming

Board of Selectmen Connecticut, Maine,
Massachusetts, New Hampshire, Vermont

Board of Supervisors California, North
Dakota, South Dakota, Washington, Wisconsin

Township Committee New Jersey

Home Rule, Individual or Special Charters
Connecticut, Delaware, Georgia, Maine,
Maryland, Michigan, Mississippi, Nebraska,
New Mexico, New York, Ohio, Oklahoma,
Pennsylvania, Rhode Island, Texas, Utah,
Vermont, Virginia, Washington, West Virginia

For detailed information, consult The U.S.
Census of Governments, Vol. 6, Popularly Elected
Officials of State and Local Governments (Washington, D.C.: U.S. Government Printing Office,
1967) and the Municipal League, the League of
Cities or the Legislative Reference Bureau
within each state.

PAGE COVERAGE OF INDIVIDUAL STATES

	Pages		Pages
Federal	1-6	Nebraska	249-256
		Nevada	256-259
Alabama	6-11	New Hampshire	260-268
Alaska	12-17	New Jersey	268-285
Arizona	17-22	New Mexico	285-289
Arkansas	22-29	New York	289-304
California	30-44	North Carolina	305-313
Colorado	45-53	North Dakota	314-318
Connecticut	53-64	Ohio	318-337
Delaware	65-68	Oklahoma	337-345
Florida	69-79	Oregon	345-354
Georgia	80-86	Pennsylvania	355-371
Hawaii	87-88	Rhode Island	371-375
Idaho	88-93	South Carolina	376-381
Illinois	93-97	South Dakota	381-386
Indiana	98-106	Tennessee	387-391
Iowa	107-124	Texas	391-404
Kansas	124-133	Utah	405-409
Kentucky	133-138	Vermont	409-415
Louisiana	138-141	Virginia	416-424
Maine	142-149	Washington	424-437
Maryland	150-158	West Virginia	437-443
Massachusetts	158-165	Wisconsin	443-450
Michigan	166-217	Wyoming	451-455
Minnesota	217-231		
Mississippi	231-233	Washington, D.C.	455
Missouri	234-245		
Montana	246-249		

NAME INDEX

In this index the surnames of all officeholders in the book are listed alphabetically, with page references to the full citation. To identify the state in which these officeholders serve, refer to page 460 where a list of states is given, with inclusive page numbers for each state.

Aalto, I. 181
Aalto, M. 178
Aarons, T. 447
Aase, H. 224
Abady, N. 422
Abair, J. 412
Abbott, B. 253
Abbott, C. 126
Abbott, M. 401
Abbott, P. 149
Abel, P. 424
Abeles, J. 270
Abell, E. 136
Abernethy, Mrs. D. 254
Abney, J. 381
Abney, Mrs. J. 399
Abraham, B. 224
Abraham, D. 92
Abrahamsen, L. 177
Abrahamson, S. 448
Abrams, R. 150, 156, 157
Abzug, B. 1
Acheson, P. 335
Achilles, H. 41
Achison, H. 129
Acker, J. 188
Acker, J. 231
Ackerley, M. 155
Ackerman, L. 24
Ackermann, B. 161
Acord, L. 231
Acord, S. 342
Adair, R. 375
Adair, V. 52
Adam, R. 454
Adams, A. 84
Adams, A. 415
Adams, B. 134
Adams, B. 192
Adams, B. 245
Adams, D. 86
Adams, D. 215
Adams, D.A. 216
Adams, E. 215
Adams, E. 332
Adams, E. 412
Adams, F. 82
Adams, F. 198
Adams, J. 74
Adams, J. 140
Adams, J. 318
Adams, K. 74
Adams, Mrs. L. 380
Adams, M. 62
Adams, M. 82
Adams, M. 104
Adams, M. 162
Adams, M. 277
Adams, M. 352
Adams, O. 66
Adams, R. 20
Adams, R. 104
Adams, R. 344
Adams, S. 435
Adams, V. 152
Adams, W. 392
Adamson, P. 195
Ader, M. 377

Adkins, E. 356
Adler, C. 414
Adler, E. 291
Adler, J. 384
Adragna, J. 454
Adrea, H. 244
Aeschilman, L. 260
Agee, S. 351
Agler, M. 336
Agna, M. 337
Agnello, R. 402
Agness, D. 106
Agnew, B. 288
Aguilar, R. 34
Ahearn, M. 20
Ahern, B. 68
Ahern, V. 287
Ahl, R. 385
Ahlering, B. 106
Ahmann, R. 218, 230
Ahrens, D. 218
Ahring, J. 129
Aiken, P. 150
Ailor, M. 419
Ainbiner, H. 68
Ainley, G. 260
Ainsworth, J. 240
Airriess, M. 205
Aitchison, S. 413
Aker, N. 194
Akers, E. 62
Akins, C. 106
Akins, H. 238
Akins, H. 394
Alarid, B. 288
Alatalo, A. 275
Albaugh, N. 319
Albaugh, R. 182
Albee, M. 413
Albergotti, Mrs. W. 379
Albers, B. 46
Albert, K. 322
Albert, P. 173
Albertson, G. 366
Albins, H. 240
Albrecht, D. 295
Albrecht, E. 174
Albright, A. 178
Albright, D. 227
Albright, R. 357
Albritton, S. 309
Albritton, V. 72
Alcorn, L. 450
Alcorn, M. 62
Alcott, K. 230
Alday, M. 71
Alders, V. 404
Alderton, B. 197
Alderton, E. 200
Aldrich, B. 146
Aldrich, V. 211
Alessi, P. 335
Alexander, A. 92
Alexander, Mrs. A. 283
Alexander, B. 186
Alexander, B. 429
Alexander, E. 373
Alexander, E. 440

Alexander, F. 161
Alexander, F. 453
Alexander, J. 11
Alexander, L. 414
Alexander, M. 139
Alexander, M. 413
Alexander, N. 119
Alexander, N. 136
Alexander, N. 232
Alexander, N. 254
Alexander, P. 233
Alexander, P. 237
Alexander, P. 454
Alexander, R. 79
Alexander, R. 386
Alexander, S. 379
Alfano, D. 358
Alfaro, A. 216
Alford, M. 28
All, P. 127
Allan, B. 435
Allard, M. 255
Allardice, M. 214
Allen, A. 111
Allen, A. 287
Allen, B. 341
Allen, B. 414
Allen, B. 434
Allen, C. 136
Allen, C. 230
Allen, C. 244
Allen, D. 24
Allen, D. 29
Allen, D. 240
Allen, D. 382
Allen, D. 412, 414
Allen, E. 366
Allen, E. 374
Allen, Mrs. F. 339
Allen, F. 399
Allen, J. 131
Allen, J. 229
Allen, J. 252, 258
Allen, L. 74
Allen, L. 77
Allen, L. 320
Allen, M. 6
Allen, M. 113
Allen, M. 120
Allen, M. 127
Allen, M. 241
Allen, M. 388
Allen, N. 312
Allen, N. 435
Allen, R. 244
Allen, V. 443
Allena, E. 281
Allensworth, A. 115
Alletson, F. 160
Alley, L. 198
Alley, L. 452
Allgood, J. 394
Allison, B. 48
Allison, E. 338
Allison, J. 437
Allison, O. 179
Allman, E. 343
Allman, S. 358

Allyn, J. 296
Alm, M. 111
Almada, A. 408
Almasi, M. 192
Almeida, P. 373
Almon, B. 22
Aloisio, M. 139
Aloupis, A. 142
Alspach, H. 90
Alspaugh, R. 331
Alston, L. 17
Alston, S. 123
Altenbach, J. 351
Althaus, H. 351
Altman, S. 85
Altvater, M. 147
Amaro, F. 18
Amatucci, J. 289
Amb, E. 317
Ambercrombie, H. 319
Ambler, M. 61
Ambrose, S. 84
Amdur, S. 57
Ameluxen, J. 434
Ames, M. 209
Ames, V. 410
Amezquita, C. 288
Amick, C. 158
Amidon, E. 177
Ammeter, S. 435
Ammond, A. 268
Ammons, N. 20
Amo, V. 171
Amore, A. 57
Amoroso, D. 436
Amos, M. 376
Amquist, Mrs. J. 20
Anastasia, Sister M. 148
Anderegg, M. 445
Andersen, B. 119
Andersen, C. 194
Andersen, M. 219
Andersen, M. 253
Anderson, A. 14
Anderson, A. 121
Anderson, A. 174
Anderson, A. 176
Anderson, A. 259
Anderson, A. 329
Anderson, A. 430
Anderson, A. 433
Anderson, B. 1
Anderson, B. 344
Anderson, B. 436
Anderson, C. 74
Anderson, C. 155
Anderson, Mrs. C. 156
Anderson, C. 212
Anderson, C. 386
Anderson, D. 83
Anderson, D. 90
Anderson, D. 223
Anderson, D. 353
Anderson, D. 382
Anderson, D. 388
Anderson, E. 15
Anderson, E. 50
Anderson, E. 66

Anderson, E. 87
Anderson, E. 213
Anderson, E. 410, 415
Anderson, G. 124
Anderson, G. 354
Anderson, J. 16
Anderson, J. 21
Anderson, J. 60
Anderson, J. 93
Anderson, J. 120
Anderson, J. 186
Anderson, J. 223
Anderson, K. 308
Anderson, K. 350
Anderson, L. 175
Anderson, L. 248
Anderson, L. 383
Anderson, L. 430
Anderson, M. 23
Anderson, M. 65
Anderson, M. 121
Anderson, M. 123
Anderson, M. 182
Anderson, M. 205
Anderson, M. 223
Anderson, M. 236
Anderson, M. 316
Anderson, M. 334
Anderson, M. 341
Anderson, M. 367
Anderson, M. 379
Anderson, M. 453
Anderson, N. 189
Anderson, P. 335
Anderson, Dr. P. 436
Anderson, R. 120
Anderson, R. 130
Anderson, R. 226
Anderson, Mrs. R. 380
Anderson, R. 442
Anderson, S. 302
Anderson, T. 254
Anderson, V. 194
Anderson, V. 306
Anderson, W. 184
Andolshek, E. 221
Andreas, D. 259
Andree, L. 15
Andresen, R.J. 216
Andrew, S. 15
Andrews, D. 255
Andrews, E. 14
Andrews, Mrs. H. 423
Andries, A. 122
Andrus, E. 184
Andrus, K. 148
Andrus, L. 437
Andujar, B. 391
Angel, R. 431
Angelo, R. 299
Angermiller, M. 401
Angevine, D. 350
Angle, C. 255
Anglin, B. 421
Angstead, S. 114
Anich, F. 49
Anschuetz, E. 183
Ansell, B. 391
Ansley, A. 288
Antell, B. 283
Antenen, A. 327
Anthony, M. 422
Anthony, S. 86
Anthony, S. 199
Anton, B. 228
Anton, E. 384
Antone, P. 20
Antonioli, G. 144
Antrim, I. 117
Apatiki, E. 15
Apley, D. 201
Aponick, H. 361
Apostle, M. 120
Appala, P. 254
Appel, M. 260

Appelman, R. 285
Applegate, S. 207
Aprill, G. 431
Arabian, M. 155
Arbuthnot, S. 21
Archambault, M. 239
Ard, S. 379
Ardia, A. 274
Ardis, A. 379
Ardis, E. 379
Arel, J. 225
Argabright, M. 316
Argel, A. 434
Argersinger, M. 126
Arm, Mrs. W. 139
Armantrout, M. 185
Armstrong, C. 85
Armstrong, D. 225
Armstrong, E. 173
Armstrong, E. 414
Armstrong, G. 52
Armstrong, J. 51
Armstrong, M. 382
Armstrong, N. 115
Armstrong, P. 168
Armstrong, Mrs. P. 253
Armstrong, R. 148
Armstrong, R. 258
Armstrong, S. 100
Armstrong, T. 423
Arnason, M. 225
Arndt, S. 284
Arndt, V. 191
Arnivik, S. 118
Arnold, A. 43
Arnold, A. 428
Arnold, D. 180
Arnold, H. 35
Arnold, H. 337
Arnold, I. 294
Arnold, J. 8
Arnold, L. 83
Arnold, M. 81, 86
Arnold, M. 180
Arnold, P. 233
Arnold, S. 11
Arnold, S. 454
Arntz, J. 183
Arritt, C. 440
Arsenault, N. 149
Arthur, A. 316
Arthur, C. 452
Arthur, J. 113
Arthur, J. 446
Ary, A. 32
Asbury, S. 8
Asch, N. 302
Ascoli, M. 302
Ash, B. 25
Ash, B. 267
Ash, G. 442
Ashbrook, P. 135
Ashburn, D. 127
Ashcraft, E. 29
Ashcraft, Mrs. R. 105
Ashe, L. 143
Ashford, C. 234
Ashler, E. 78
Ashley, G. 390
Ashlock, C. 51
Ashmore, Mrs. A. 342
Ashmore, Mrs. B. 379
Ashworth, E. 354
Ashworth, R. 131
Askenette, S. 259
Askin, B. 248
Aspel, M. 62
Aspell, M. 61
Aspy, J. 176
Asward, E. 301
Atchison, Sister J. 244
Atchley, Mrs. H. 233
Atchley, R. 387
Ater, M. 335
Atkins, H. 337

Atkins, H. 343
Atkins, P. 26
Atkins, S. 86
Atkins, V. 403
Atkinson, P. 216
Atkinson, Mrs. W. 310
Atpelesy, P. 241
Atterholt, C. 327
Atwater, E. 442
Atwood, G. 405
Atwood, P. 233
Aucello, C. 274
Audley, B. 38
Auer, S. 321
Aufdengarten, M. 253
Augenstein, E. 179
Auger, C. 271
Aughenbaugh, K. 384
August, L. 363
Augustine, C. 122
Augustine, R. 441
Augustus, G. 155
Ault, E. 147
Ault, M. 205
Ault, N. 240
Aust, J. 99
Austin, D. 209
Austin, D. 232
Austin, F. 428
Austin, J. 232
Auten, D. 439
Autumn, V. 42
Avalos, C. 20
Avellar, M. 160
Aveni, V. 318
Avery, E. 177
Avery, E. 455
Avery, M. 180
Awalt, M. 148
Awe, F. 21
Axel, J. 108
Axelson, E. 404
Ayana, S. 301
Ayers, A. 63
Ayers, B. 348
Ayres, I. 251
Ayers, V. 206
Aylsworth, J. 452
Ayotte, J. 56
Ayotte, M. 144
Ayres, Mrs. R. 404
Azelvandre, L. 440
Azkutney, M. 367

Babb, D. 195
Babbitt, C. 322
Babbitt, E. 189
Babcock, A. 413
Babcock, B. 1
Babcock, C. 409
Babcock, H. 296
Babcock, R. 100
Babcock, V. 412
Baber, M. 16
Babich, M. 404
Babik, B. 288
Baca-Barragan, P. 45
Baca-Garcia, E. 288
Bachar, H. 222
Bacher, C. 50
Bachety, S. 292
Bachle, Mrs. R. 342
Bachman, L. 301
Bachrach, A. 142
Bachtle, M. 224
Bachus, H. 141
Backer, B. 105
Backman, N. 408
Backstrom, R. 148
Bacon, B. 283
Bacot, J. 311
Badder, M. 172
Baedke, N. 118
Baehr, C. 241
Baehr, M. 122

Baetjer, Mrs. N. 156
Bagevaktuk, A. 14
Baggett, A. 6
Baggett, R. 233
Bagwell, C. 85
Bahler, R. 348
Bailey, A. 233
Bailey, A. 338
Bailey, B. 156
Bailey, C. 230
Bailey, Mrs. C. 245
Bailey, D. 168
Bailey, E. 1
Bailey, E. 288
Bailey, G. 27
Bailey, H. 24
Bailey, J. 21
Bailey, L. 354
Bailey, M. 18
Bailey, M. 436
Bailey, P. 76
Bailey, P. 175
Bailey, P. 310
Bailey, S. 251
Bailey, S. 360
Bailey, S. 379, 380
Bailey, T. 232
Baillargeon, J. 164
Bailor, J. 180
Bain, H. 436
Baines, B. 79
Bair, J. 322
Baird, A. 133
Baird, D. 431
Baird, M. 252
Baird, V. 336
Baisch, L. 328
Baize, S. 213
Bajoie, D. 138
Baker, A. 324
Baker, B. 51
Baker, B. 99
Baker, B. 115
Baker, B. 377
Baker, C. 155
Baker, D. 104
Baker, D. 404
Baker, E. 8
Baker, E. 103
Baker, E. 254
Baker, G. 301
Baker, H. 319
Baker, H. 396
Baker, J. 15
Baker, J. 42
Baker, J. 419
Baker, J. 438
Baker, K. 406
Baker, L. 10
Baker, L. 14
Baker, L. 192
Baker, L. 211
Baker, M. 137
Baker, R. 67
Baker, R. 99
Baker, S. 134
Baker, S. 236
Baker, S. 272
Baker, S. 414
Baker, V. 403
Bakewell, A. 221
Bakka, E. 181
Balanda, A. 61
Bald, M. 79
Baldridge, Y. 243
Baldus, W. 202
Baldwin, C. 148
Baldwin, C. 200
Baldwin, G. 116
Baldwin, J. 60
Baldwin, R. 366
Baldwin, W. 176
Balk, A. 111
Balkany, M. 72
Balkman, N. 29

Ball, B.   79
Ball, E.   163
Ball, E   327
Ball, E.   439
Ball, F.   232
Ball, G.   41
Ball, G.   116
Ball, M.   325
Ball, S.   8
Ballantine, L.   285
Ballantine, M.   167
Ballantyne, J.   120
Ballantyne, M.   383
Ballard, D.   132
Ballard, J.   23
Ballard, L.   136
Ballard, M.   10
Ballien, G.   298
Ballinger, M.   128
Ballock, R.   99
Balluta, E.   14
Balowski, D.   200
Balsiger, E.   223
Bamesberger, J.   254
Bamfield, C.   128
Banfield, M.   16
Bang, N.   47
Bangert, M.   254
Bangert, R.   237
Banko, R.   367
Banks, A.   244
Banks, B.   93
Banks, E.   66
Banks, I.   197
Banks, Mrs. J.   233
Banks, M.   452
Banning, E.   340
Bannister, B.   454
Bannon, B.   405
Bannon, F.   148
Banschback, T.   48
Banta, W.   341
Baraby, M.   148
Baralou, D.   91
Baranowski, S.   449
Baravetto, V.   202
Barbaret, A.   59
Barbash, R.   283
Barbeau, P.   351
Barbee, Mrs. W.   232
Barber, B.   27
Barber, G.   357
Barber, K.   332
Barbo, J.   224
Barbour, T.   21
Barboza, B.   38
Barco, Y.   364
Bardo, Mrs. D.   454
Bardo, J.   454
Bardwell, E.   449
Bardwell, F.   407
Bare, A.   244
Bare, C.   211
Bare, S.   421
Baresham, E.   169
Barfield, C.   84
Barham, Mrs. T.   379
Baringer, D.   121, 123
Baringer, T.   366
Barja, C.   77
Barker, B.   76
Barker, B.   199
Barker, D.   126
Barker, D.   332
Barker, D.   406
Barker, E.   164
Barkla, N.   450
Barkley, D.   233
Barlow, D.   415
Barlow, J.   19
Barlow, J.   350
Barmore, A.   449
Barmun, M.   240
Barnaby, L.   174
Barnard, J.   38

Barnard, M.   103
Barnard, N.   445
Barnes, Mrs. C.   93
Barnes, D.   54
Barnes, D.   276
Barnes, E.   407
Barnes, J.   94
Barnes, J.   409
Barnes, L.   413
Barnes, M.   7
Barnes, M.   176
Barnes, M.   192
Barnes, P.   7
Barnes, R.   82
Barnes, R.   295
Barnes, T.   357
Barnes-McConnell,P.   215
Barnett, B.   379
Barnett, E.   288
Barnett, H.   67
Barnett, J.   384
Barnett, K.   434
Barnett, L.   339
Barnett, M.   137
Barnett, M.   258
Barnett, P.   79
Barney, N.   434
Barnhart, D.   101
Barnhart, I.   39
Barnhart, T.   188
Barns, J.   213
Baron, R.   450
Barone, B.   21
Barr, D.   13
Barr, J.   155
Barr, J.   171
Barr, K.   36
Barrall, E.   368
Barrett, B.   179
Barrett, C.   132
Barrett, E.   100
Barrett, J.   312, 313
Barrett, L.   82
Barrett, M.   126
Barrett, Y.   59
Barrineau, M.   78
Barringer, K.   439
Barringer, M.   306
Barris, M.   205
Barron, H.   237
Barrow, O.   394
Barry, N.   102
Barsamian, Y.   215
Barteau, B.   104
Bartel, J.   354
Bartels, R.   193
Barter, J.   147
Barth, M.   215
Barthen, N.   361
Barthold, Mrs. C.   106
Bartholme, J.   369
Bartholomay, L.   318
Bartle, C.   190
Bartle, Mrs. H.   303
Bartle, N.   291
Bartlett, B.   441
Bartlett, E.   221
Bartlett, S.   258
Bartley, A.   22
Bartman, B.   14
Bartoletti, V.   197
Barton, A.   85
Barton, A.   407
Barton, Mrs. B.   397
Barton, C.   52
Barton, E.   454
Barton, J.   62
Barton, L.   93
Barton, M.   56
Barton, R.   10
Barus, Mrs. M.   284
Barysh, G.   57
Bascom, R.   352
Bashore, C.   194
Basile, K.   238

Baske, C.   282
Bass, B.   63
Bass, B.   311
Bass, C.   140
Bass, M.   21
Bass, M.   153
Bass, R.   160
Bass, W.   27
Bassham, F.   440
Bassham, M.   393
Basso, B.   431
Bataille, G.   121
Bataitis, J.   299
Batchelder, A.   336
Batchelder, D.   176
Batchelder, P.   266
Batchelor, N.   309
Bateman, A.   83
Bateman, A.   153
Bateman, Mrs. A.   353
Bater, B.   193
Bates, B.   48
Bates, I.   328
Bates, K.   112
Bates, K.   118
Bates, M.   394
Bates, S.   254
Bates, T.   241
Bates, W.   128
Batho, D.   175
Bathon, N.   155
Batson, J.   26
Batt, J.   56
Battenfeld, C.   226
Batterson, M.   213
Battin, M.   162
Battle, Mrs. A.   277
Battle, D.   288
Battle, M.   172
Bauder, M.   363
Bauer, B.   357
Bauer, L.   188
Bauer, M.   243
Bauer, N.   385
Bauger, M.   360
Baugher, N.   112
Baughman, D.   8
Baughman, D.   109
Baughman, H.   320
Baughman, M.   125
Baugous, T.   251
Baum, H.   120
Bauman, E.   126
Bauman, Mrs. G.   244
Bauman, H.   357
Bauman, M.   89, 93
Baumann, C.   257
Baumann, G.   318
Baumann, M.   448
Baumert, D.   332
Baumgartner, D.   209
Baumgartner, E.   276
Baumhover, J.   352
Baumhover, M.   123
Bavilla, S.   13
Baxter, A.   139
Baxter, E.   169
Baxter, L.   408
Bay, S.   335
Bay, Z.   344
Baybutt, N.   266
Bayer, J.   238
Bayles, A.   414
Beach, A.   202
Beach, E.   230
Beach, F.   237
Beach, G.   196
Beachler, M.   454
Beadling, E.   40
Beal, E.   144, 146
Beal, F.   306
Beal, H.   396
Beal, M.   233
Beal, S.   180
Beaman, I.   364

Beamer, B.   87
Beamon, M.   105
Bean, A.   148
Bean, Mrs. A.   404
Bean, E.   291
Bean, J.   24
Bean, N.   211
Bean, P.   266
Bean, W.   130
Beard, C.   129
Beard, J.   122
Beard, M.   309
Beard, V.   244
Bearden, F.   8
Beardslee, E.   199
Bearse, R.   174
Beary, S.   115
Beasley, M.   380
Beasley, R.   106
Beatie, A.   41
Beatley, L.   332
Beaton, J.   165
Beaton, R.   15
Beattie, C.   413
Beauclair, Sister M.   314
Beaudain, E.   185
Beaudett, F.   171
Beaulieu, H.   411
Beauregard, R.   189
Beaver, B.   49
Beavers, D.   254
Beaver, E.   19
Beaver, K.   408
Beavers, L.   341
Bechill, E.   191
Becht, S.   288
Bechtel, E.   84
Beck, A.   54
Beck, C.   329
Beck, D.   276
Beck, D.   284
Beck, E.   21
Beck, E.   454
Beck, L.   353
Beckenhauer, P.   256
Becker, B.   202
Becker, B.   325
Becker, K.   152
Becker, M.   425
Becker, M.   433, 436
Becker, P.   225
Becker, V.   101
Beckerhoff, H.   413
Beckner, J.   253
Beckwith, M.   202
Bedford, A.   353
Bedford, E.   304
Bedford, V.   404
Bedigan, M.   148
Bedsoe, N.   122
Bedtelyon, V.   177
Bee, B.   101
Beebe, C.   267
Beebe, E.   188
Beebe, N.   216
Beecher, E.   176
Beecher, M.   408
Beeding, E.   136
Beenken, A.   116
Beers, S.   194
Beggs, V.   183
Begner, P.   304
Behlen, J.   445
Behling, J.   406
Behling, T.   205
Behrens, V.   235
Behringer, M.   342
Behrle, E.   59
Beidler, B.   418
Beighle, L.   16
Beilein, J.   299
Beirne, H.   16, 17
Beitner, M.   217
Bekech, E.   63
Belaga, J.   54

Belcher, G. 58
Belcher, P. 380
Belden, P. 258
Belding, M. 194
Belen, L. 209, 214
Belin, C. 359
Bell, A. 440
Bell, B. 25
Bell, Mrs. B. 29
Bell, B. 329
Bell, C. 334
Bell, Mrs. H. 424
Bell, L. 244
Bell, L. 312
Bell, M. 128
Bell, M. 156
Bell, M. 377
Bell, N. 324
Bell, P. 290
Bell, R. 215
Bell, R. 216
Bell, R. 454
Bell, Mrs. S. 424
Bell, T. 389
Bell, V. 197
Bell, V. 356
Bell, Mrs. W. 435
Bellal, H. 401
Bellamy, C. 289
Bellamy, V. 86
Bellas, A. 257
Bellerue, S. 37
Bellman, C. 385
Bellows, C. 421
Belmain, R. 453
Beltrani, B. 23
Belusar, S. 187
Belyea, M. 279
Beman, N. 324
Bemis, J. 215
Benavidez, O. 396
Benaway, M. 193
Bench, R. 407
Benda, B. 252
Bender, C. 175
Bender, D. 364
Bender, F. 454
Bender, P. 312
Bender, R. 245
Bender, S. 59
Bender, V. 15
Bendl, G. 133
Benedict, P. 314
Benefield, N. 393
Beneke, L. 72
Beneke, M. 223
Benge, C. 204
Bengel, E. 311
Bengtson, E. 246
Benischek, G. 116
Benischek, L. 251
Benjamin, E. 203
Benjamin, J. 352
Benner, M. 228
Bennet, J. 338
Bennet, M. 153
Bennet, P. 62
Bennet, P. 283
Bennett, B. 95
Bennett, B. 132
Bennett, C. 66
Bennett, C. 296
Bennett, D. 216
Bennett, E. 250
Bennett, E. 406
Bennett, H. 373
Bennett, H. 402
Bennett, I. 50
Bennett, J. 344
Bennett, L. 201
Bennett, L. 293
Bennett, L. 344
Bennett, M. 26
Bennett, M. 62
Bennett, M. 99

Bennett, M. 126
Bennett, M. 143
Bennett, N. 351
Bennett, R. 435
Bennett, V. 14
Bennick, P. 202
Bennion, M. 407
Benoit, S. 142
Benoliel, J. 435
Benscoter, V. 115
Bensinger, D. 186
Benson, A. 177
Benson, B. 323
Benson, C. 325
Benson, E. 113
Benson, Mrs. J. 403, 404
Benson, K. 234
Benson, L. 1
Benson, L. 291
Benson, P. 255
Bent, L. 76
Bentley, H. 336
Bentley, P. 348
Bentley, R. 8
Benton, C. 38
Benton, D. 346
Benton, K. 235
Benton, Q. 244
Bentzel, G. 365
Benvenue, A. 200
Benzel, T. 434
Berard, V. 373
Berardi, C. 303
Berdell, M. 121
Beresford, S. 414
Berg, J. 146
Berg, P. 79
Bergan, M. 385
Bergen, E. 385
Berger, D. 357
Berger, L. 56
Berger, M. 284
Berger, P. 301
Bergfield, D. 333
Berghaus, N. 132
Bergin, K. 53
Bergin, K. 63
Berlin, L. 217
Berglund, E. 202
Berglund, M. 287
Bergman, B. 180
Bergman, C. 13
Bergman, I. 58
Bergman, L. 13
Bergmann, R. 177
Bergstrom, V. 430
Bergt, L. 15
Bergy, J. 437
Berich, B. 282
Berk, I. 432
Berk, Mrs. L. 156
Berkholtz, M. 447
Berkshire, D. 424
Berkson, P. 258
Berman, B. 283
Berman, B. 457
Berman, R. 54, 60
Bernard, M. 141
Bernard, M. 408
Bernard, Y 257
Bernert, R. 157
Bernhagen, B. 120
Bernhard, M. 370
Bernhardt, A. 310
Bernhardt, I. 238
Bernier, A. 373
Bernier, P. 165
Bernstein, B. 21
Bernstein, B. 382
Bernstein, D. 230
Beroza, M. 20
Berrigan, L. 292
Berry, B. 417
Berry, E. 29
Berry, E. 413

Berry, Mrs. G. 233
Berry, I. 81
Berry, M. 1
Berry, M. 27
Berry, M. 36
Berry, M. 398
Berry, T. 171
Berstein, M. 326
Bertholf, V. 284
Bertinuson, T. 54
Bertram, R. 278
Bertsch, M. 335
Berube, G. 142
Berviq, D. 315
Besaha, I. 369
Besbet, H. 33
Beske, C. 279
Besley, M. 116
Besserman, R. 433
Bessinger, V. 380
Bestful, P. 222
Bethel, H. 96
Bethke, J. 202
Bethune, A. 374
Betner, C. 28
Bettancourt, E. 32
Bettega, M. 162
Bettes, F. 131
Bettinger, N. 292
Bettinson, E. 89
Bettis, J. 411
Betts, L. 68
Betts, M. 322
Betway, L. 195
Beurmann, M. 175
Beusch, A. 157
Bevarley, M. 137
Beverage, M. 440
Beverly, V. 78
Bevins, G. 133
Bovis, Mrs. W. 79
Bewley, B. 392
Bhote, K. 95
Bianchi, J. 358
Bianchi, M. 205
Bichsel, B. 432
Bick, E. 248
Bickel, R. 292
Bickford, E. 266
Bickley, A. 442
Bickley, R. 81
Bickmore, M. 91
Bicknell, B. 99
Biddison, C. 46
Biddle, B. 66
Biddle, M. 186
Bideaux, J. 20
Bidleman, A. 357
Biegler, B. 386
Bienen, K. 156
Bienen, K. 157
Bienen, K. 150,156,157
Bierlein, M. 68
Bierly, Mrs. C. 320
Bifano, N. 20
Bifferato, M. 67
Bigelow, E. 223
Bigg, E. 188
Biggers, Mrs. J. 85
Biggins, C. 79
Bigham, L. 294
Billick, V. 348
Billings, E. 281
Billings, Mrs. F. 413
Billingsley, L. 85
Billsbrough, N. 211
Biloon, S. 53, 63
Binder, J. 360
Binger, P. 120
Bingham, E. 1
Bingham, E. 449
Bingham, S. 405
Bingley, M. 199
Binig, M. 403
Binkoski, M. 441

Binnie, N. 249
Binns, B. 407
Binsfeld, C. 166
Biondi, M. 301
Bira, V. 243
Bircher, A. 343
Bird, A. 104
Bird, N. 327
Bird, R. 44
Birdener, M. 447, 448
Birdsall, C. 113
Birk, M. 347
Birke, H. 442
Birney, J. 210
Bischoff, F. 202
Bishop, A. 74
Bishop, A. 423
Bishop, N. 146
Bishop, P. 239
Bishop, S. 453
Biss, B. 364
Bissell, M. 305
Bissinger, M. 188
Bisson, P. 413
Bissonette, M. 194
Bistline, B. 92
Bisulca, E. 147
Bitner, G. 362
Bittinger, J. 250
Bivens, B. 50
Bixby, G. 202
Bixel, E. 189
Bjerke, J. 384
Bjorklund, L. 407,408,409
Bjorndal, L. 247
Bjurman, L. 190
Black, B. 359
Black, D. 422
Black, E. 299
Black, J. 120
Black, K. 7
Black, M. 75
Black, M. 216
Black, M. 312
Black, N. 348
Black, Mrs. O. 338
Black, R. 314
Black, S. 78, 79
Black, W. 324
Blackburn, D. 91
Blackburn, D. 215
Blackburn, L. 325
Blacke, R. 419
Blackmore, L. 183
Blackstone, K. 253
Blackwell, C. 214
Blackwell, E. 242
Blackwell, G. 86
Blackwell, S. 308
Blaha, M. 114
Blahuta, R. 16
Blain, M. 182
Blaine, C. 232
Blair, A. 434
Blair, J. 392
Blair, S. 421
Blake, Mrs. B. 403
Blake, E. 115
Blake, R. 346
Blake, T. 286
Blake, V. 438
Blanch, M. 362
Blanchard, D. 147
Blanchard, K. 244
Blanchette, P. 260
Bland, D. 389
Blandin, R. 358
Blankenship, A. 10
Blankenship, A. 249
Blankenship, B. 134
Blankenship, J. 242
Blankenship, R. 252
Blankenship, Mrs. W. 403
Blankman, R. 297
Blanks, D. 309

Blanton, E. 83
Blatnik, T. 437
Blatt, G. 370
Blazic, A. 329
Bleakly, J. 290
Blees, F. 252
Bleesz, M. 49
Bleken, J. 248
Blend, H. 404
Blethen, N. 272
Blicker, C. 375
Blickman, M. 78
Bliesener, L. 214
Bliss, B. 408
Bliss, G. 78
Block, M. 312
Blodgett, D. 326
Blohm, M. 222
Blomdahl, E.K. 213
Bloom, B. 74
Bloom, E. 68
Bloom, E. 79
Bloomberg, H. 162
Bloomer, E. 343
Bloomquist, V. 227
Blonde, P. 189
Blood, D. 209
Blount, E. 156
Blue, C. 306
Blue, G. 18
Blue, K. 121
Blum, B. 1
Blum, B. 85
Blum, M. 330
Blum, P. 252
Blum, Mrs. R. 302
Blunck, H. 108
Bluntzer, J. 401
Blurton, A. 390
Blust, D. 31
Boal, L. 454
Board, Mrs. C. 78
Bobbitt, H. 442
Boccaccio, M. 156
Bock, M. 112
Boddie, R. 7
Boden, S. 74
Bodenhofer, G. 110
Bodily, N. 406
Bodine, J. 103
Bodlovick, A. 228
Boe, D. 89, 92
Boedecker, S. 453
Boeger, M. 244
Boekholder, J. 433
Boerhaue, L. 115
Boettcher, J. 392
Boeve, V. 182
Bogart, M. 125
Bogert, M. 189
Bogert, N. 365
Boggero, E. 378
Boggress, P. 454
Boggs, E. 283
Boggs, Mrs. G. 404
Boggs, L. 4
Bogorad, R. 414
Bogue, R. 429
Bohac, B. 397
Bohl, K. 119
Bohn, J. 89
Bohn, L. 198
Bohot, B. 340
Boice, M. 333
Boissoneau, M. 175
Boissy, D. 100
Boitscha, R. 114
Boland, A. 373
Boland, F. 119
Boles, C. 116
Bolles, D. 239
Bollhoefer, B. 109
Bollin, V. 316
Bolser, P. 175
Bolte, E. 118

Bolton, W. 244
Boltz, E. 154
Bolus, J. 380
Bolyard, C. 441
Boman, J. 198
Boman, P. 180
Bomar, B. 237
Bomer, I. 200
Bomer, L. 67
Bond, C. 210
Bonds, D. 25
Bonds, S. 184
Bone, C. 241
Boner, B. 248
Bonewitz, P. 113
Bong, C. 222
Bonge, L. 250
Bonilla, A. 63
Bonin, A. 173
Bonnell, N. 120
Bonner, G. 307
Bonnes, L. 113
Bonnichsen, L. 113
Boochever, C. 15
Booher, M. 331
Booi, C. 126
Bookwalter, E. 368
Boon, L. 207
Boone, F. 97
Boone, M. 424
Boone, M. 442
Boosalis, H. 249, 253
Booth, B. 150
Booth, E. 335
Booth, M. 231
Boothe, O. 439
Borboa, R. 36
Bordeau, R. 386
Bordeaux, P. 146
Borden, W. 257
Borders, D. 26
Borgaes, V. 352
Borgatti, J. 291
Borland, C. 288
Borman, S. 213
Born, D. 42
Bornhorst, M. 88
Borsheim, W. 231
Bortel, S. 189
Bosley, P. 172
Bosse, M. 134
Bossler, L. 119
Bost, L. 233
Bost, M. 378
Bostdorf, M. 365
Boster, B. 324
Boswell, J. 7
Bothman, E. 228
Bott, M. 190
Bottorff, P. 255
Bouch, J. 358
Bouchard, Sister C. 414
Bouchard, K. 375
Boucher, A. 241
Boughner, L. 180
Boulanger, M. 131
Bounds, D. 352
Bouquet, N. 156
Boushey, E. 33
Boutrin, D. 347
Bovard, E. 57
Bovat, C. 35
Bove, M. 413
Bovey, K. 411
Bowcock, S. 400
Bowden, S. 9
Bowen, M. 418
Bowen, N. 105
Bowen, P. 92
Bowen, Mrs. R. 86
Bowen, Mrs. W. 439
Bower, A. 19
Bowerman, P. 437
Bowers, A. 120
Bowers, M. 212

Bowers, V. 21
Bowers, D. 300
Bowler, B. 260
Bowles, E. 420
Bowles, M. 434
Bowles, S. 442
Bowley, A. 57
Bowley, D. 149
Bowley, J. 56
Bowling, A. 333
Bowling, E. 137
Bowman, Mrs. A. 422
Bowman, B. 449
Bowman, E. 362
Bowman, Mrs. G. 343
Bowman, J. 387
Bowman, K. 77
Bowman, M. 197
Bowman, M. 321
Bowns, B. 15
Bowns, G. 193
Bowser, V. 404
Box, M. 233
Boxer, B. 31
Boyce, L. 36
Boyce, S. 109
Boyce, S. 282
Boyd, A. 73
Boyd, E. 436
Boyd, I. 250
Boyd, Mrs. I. 339
Boyd, K. 404
Boyd, L. 61
Boyd, L. 288
Boyd, M. 336
Boyd, M. 423
Boyd, S. 48
Boyd, Mrs. W. 283
Boyer, Mrs. C. 344
Boyer, L. 65
Boyer, N. 351
Boyhan, C. 453
Boyle, C. 43
Boyle, J. 408
Boyle, J. 451, 454
Boyle, M. 330
Boyle, P. 213
Boylston, D. 379
Boyse, A. 206
Boyter, Mrs. I. 130
Bozich, M. 223
Bozman, E. 416
Bpada, N. 63
Brabon, L. 207
Bracco, G. 176
Brach, N. 282
Brack, R. 260
Brack, S. 190
Brackney, G. 27
Bradbury, L. 317
Braddock, E. 9
Braden, D. 113
Braden, J. 1
Bradfield, E. 385
Bradford, E. 430
Bradick, M. 369
Bradley, A. 176
Bradley, B. 125
Bradley, B. 291, 301
Bradley, D. 246
Bradley, Mrs. J. 63
Bradley, J. 145
Bradley, L. 21
Bradley, L. 82
Bradley, L. 210
Bradley, M. 241
Bradley, N. 76
Bradley, S. 325
Bradshaw, A. 341
Bradshaw, D. 232
Bradshaw, J. 422
Brady, J. 317
Brady, L. 120
Brady, M. 267
Brady, M. 374

Bragg, E. 215
Bragg, E. 413
Bragiel, K. 187
Braithwaite, I. 428
Brakebill, E. 390
Branam, Mrs. J. 397
Branchaud, S. 228
Brand, J. 182
Brand, J. 196
Brand, Sister M. 106
Brande, B. 270
Brandenburg, C. 181
Brander, F. 272
Brandl, F. 181
Brandon, L. 225
Brandon, R. 308
Brandt, D. 22
Brandt, D. 107
Brandt, F. 434
Brandt, J. 237
Branen, A. 338
Branin, R. 281
Brann, V. 147
Brannan, S. 82
Branning, H. 232
Brano, A. 288
Bransdorfer, P. 214
Branson, F. 122
Branson, M. 12
Brantley, S. 196
Brascugli, A. 219
Brasser, E. 111
Brassfield-Lee, Y. 74
Brassil, C. 373
Brataas, N. 217
Brattain, S. 100
Braumer, R. 242
Braun, T. 226
Braun, P. 230
Braunschweig, L. 445
Bray, D. 89, 91, 92
Bray, Mrs. W. 105
Braymer, M. 403
Brayson, A. 145
Brayton, S. 175
Brazil, Mrs. B. 28
Brazill, J. 363
Breaux, I. 393
Brechting, F. 171
Breckenridge, M. 182
Bredeweg, F. 180
Breeding, C. 418
Breeding, S. 74
Breeling, V. 115
Brehm, M. 194
Breitenbecher, I. 333
Brekke, H. 384
Bren, S. 227
Breneman, N. 135
Brennan, E. 248
Brennan, E. 408
Brennan, E. 445
Brennan, L. 305
Brennan, M. 187
Brennan, M. 321
Brennan, T. 149
Brenner, M. 247
Brenner, P. 122
Breslin, P. 94
Bressler, I. 442
Bretz, M. 363
Bretz, R. 367
Brevett, E. 290
Brewer, B. 308
Brewer, H. 48
Brewer, J. 82
Brewer, M. 145
Brewer, S. 380
Brewington, B. 247
Brice, J. 329
Brick, B. 137
Bricker, H. 267
Brickley, M. 216
Brickner, B. 241
Bridenstine, J. 108
Bridge, A. 100

Bridge, D. 253
Bridge, V. 32
Bridgers, J. 77
Bridges, H. 274
Bridges, S. 215
Bridgewaters, E. 106
Brietzke, B. 174
Brigger, Mrs. F. 109
Briggs, A. 154
Briggs, B. 373
Briggs, E. 375
Briggs, L. 188
Briggs, W. 131
Bright, B. 136
Bright, C. 403
Brighton, V. 186
Brink, M. 191
Brink, M. 196
Brinkerhoff, V. 406
Brinkley, M. 23
Brinkman, J. 102
Brinkman, M. 109
Brinkman, S. 236
Brinzo, R. 77
Bristol, B. 252
Bristow, C. 120
Britton, J. 180
Britton, R. 384
Broadwater, B. 284
Broadwater, M. 157
Broadwater, M. 279
Broadway, V. 391
Broas, C. 447
Brock, E. 195
Brock, Mrs. G. 401
Brockbank, C. 18
Brockman, A. 354
Brockman, J. 250
Brodecky, J. 393
Brodmerkel, S. 361
Brody, P. 61
Brody, S. 260
Broemmelsiek, B. 245
Broeren, J. 449
Brogg, L. 185
Brokas, M. 74
Bromberg, E. 302
Bromberg, I. 444
Bromley, E. 179
Bromley, L. 172
Broncho, N. 91
Bronner, Mrs. P. 238
Bronson, M. 294
Bronz, L. 294
Brook, K. 267
Brooke, M. 155
Brooker, R. 163
Brookes, L. 267
Brooking, D. 201
Brookman, E. 256
Brookman, E. 259
Brooks, A. 418
Brooks, B. 71
Brooks, C. 424
Brooks, D. 83
Brooks, E. 29
Brooks, G. 8
Brooks, H. 442
Brooks, J. 408
Brooks, K. 340
Brooks, Sister M. 105
Brooks, M. 389
Brooks, N. 208
Brooks, S. 257
Brooks, S. 283
Brooks, W. 137
Brooks, Y. 157
Broom, G. 253
Broome, B. 380
Bross, A. 413
Brostrom, M. 436
Brothanek, M. 350
Brotherton, C. 56
Brotherton, G. 312
Broughton, A. 137

Broughton, J. 325
Broughton, K. 323
Broughton, M. 310
Brouilette, C. 136
Browder, D. 377
Brower, L. 129
Brown, A. 78
Brown, A. 141
Brown, A. 213
Brown, A. 216
Brown, A. 225
Brown, B. 63
Brown, B. 147
Brown, B. 196
Brown, B. 407
Brown, C. 1
Brown, C. 63
Brown, C. 120
Brown, C. 148
Brown, C. 184
Brown, C. 351
Brown, D. 123
Brown, D. 212
Brown, D. 227
Brown, D. 318
Brown, E. 78
Brown, E. 251
Brown, E. 389
Brown, E. 407
Brown, E. 427
Brown, F. 348
Brown, G. 7
Brown, G. 13
Brown, G. 100
Brown, G. 303
Brown, I. 241
Brown, J. 83
Brown, J. 135
Brown, J. 283
Brown, J. 303
Brown, J. 332
Brown, J. 373
Brown, J. 405
Brown, J. 413
Brown, J. 424
Brown, J. 437
Brown, K. 113
Brown, K. 142
Brown, K. 259
Brown, K. 404
Brown, K. 442
Brown, L. 10
Brown, L. 89
Bown, L. 130
Brown, L. 188
Brown, L. 194
Brown, L. 269
Brown, L. 323
Brown, L. 380
Brown, L. 414
Brown, M. 63
Brown, M. 66
Brown, M. 90, 92
Brown, M. 91
Brown, M. 137
Brown, M. 149
Brown, M. 166
Brown, M. 378
Brown, M. 407
Brown, M. 413
Brown, M. 453, 454
Brown, N. 385, 389
Brown, P. 77
Brown, P. 131
Brown, P. 255
Brown, P. 319
Brown, R. 61
Brown, R. 86
Brown, R. 103
Brown, R. 120
Brown, Mrs. R. 283
Brown, R. 402
Brown, R. 418
Brown, R. 431
Brown, S. 26

Brown, S. 67
Brown, S. 110
Brown, V. 160
Brown, V. 242
Brown, V. 243
Brown, V. 374
Brown, W. 75
Brown, Mrs. W. 233
Brown, Mrs. W. 381
Browne, E. 345
Brownell, M. 255
Brownell, R. 326
Browngardt, C. 327
Browning, A. 428
Browning, J. 400
Brownwell, A. 348
Broyles, C. 419
Brubaker, F. 331
Bruce, E. 420
Bruce, H. 121
Brucher, J. 292
Bruck, M. 181
Brueckeer, N. 279
Bruhn, F. 385
Brumels, D. 196
Brumm, G. 176
Brundage, Z. 408
Brundage, Z. 409
Brunelle, H. 375
Brungardt, T. 412
Bruni, Y. 373
Bruning, V. 249
Brunk, J. 321
Brunner, C. 180
Bruns, D. 385
Bruns, L. 137
Brunt, D. 254
Brunton, C. 180
Brush, G. 413
Bruso, L. 181
Bryan, M. 64
Bryan, M. 278
Bryan, M. 298
Bryan, M. 422
Bryan, S. 105
Bryant, B. 427
Bryant, E. 109
Bryant, E. 162
Bryant, J. 239
Bryant, J. 307
Bryant, L. 144
Bryant, L. 269
Bryant, P. 25
Bryant, R. 267
Bryant, W. 7
Bryars, D. 7
Bryden, J. 327
Bubar, S. 147
Bubberd, G. 384
Bubnis, J. 257
Bucanan, G. 29
Buchanan, A. 406
Buchanan, C. 232
Buchanan, G. 126
Buchanan, J. 374
Buchanan, M. 45
Buchanan, M. 209
Buchanan, N. 92
Bucino, D. 271
Buck, Mrs. A. 453
Buck, C. 228
Buckholdt, T. 12
Buchholz, A. 296, 301
Buckingham, D. 121
Buckle, Mrs. K. 255
Buckler, V. 283
Buckley, A. 158
Buckley, L. 95
Buckman, Sister M. 245
Buckmater, E. 198
Bucknell, G. 110
Bucy, S. 325
Budd, I. 309
Budenholzer, L. 18, 21
Budnik, D. 190

Budreau, L. 208
Budzynski, H. 198
Buechler, M. 248
Bueling, K. 317
Buell, J. 62
Buell, M. 25
Buell, N. 215, 216
Buell, R. 179
Buergler, H. 29
Buersmeyer, J. 89
Buffington, F. 74
Buffington, N. 424
Buley, M. 414
Bull, J. 252
Bull, P. 149
Buller, E. 400
Bullert, D. 384, 386
Bullerwell, G. 292
Bullock, B. 452
Bullock, O. 350
Bulman, J. 35
Bunce, J. 192
Bunch, B. 386
Bunch, F. 235
Bundschuh, A. 295
Bundy, M. 145
Bundy, N. 423
Bundek, K. 66
Bungard, P. 365
Bunge, E. 295
Bungry, B. 68
Bunke, H. 447
Bunker, F. 35
Bunker, K. 145
Bunn, D. 452
Bunte, D. 158
Bunting, C. 186
Bunting, J. 64
Bunting, P. 88
Burch, D. 189
Burch, J. 171
Burch, M. 166
Burch, M. 183
Burch, S. 85
Burcham, B. 109
Burcham, R. 434
Burd, K. 52
Burden, H. 172
Burden, I. 353
Burdette, H. 135
Burek, F. 450
Bures, D. 76
Burford, B. 258
Burg, M. 250
Burgdorf, L. 380
Burgess, D. 373
Burgess, E. 354
Burgess, F. 346
Burgess, J. 123
Burgess, J. 350
Burgess, K. 302, 303
Burgess, M. 374
Burgess, M. 437
Burgess, Mrs. W. 23
Burgio, J. 268
Burgtorf, D. 343
Burgwald, B. 103
Buriaek, M. 316
Burian, M. 386
Burk, P. 37
Burk, P. 378
Burk, V. 245
Burke, C. 7
Burke, J. 93
Burke, L. 424
Burke, M. 125
Burke, N. 344
Burke, Y. 4
Burkemper, M. 241
Burket, E. 153
Burket, E. 223
Burkham, E. 397
Burkhardt, D. 315
Burkhart, A. 106
Burkhart, M. 19

Burkholder, V. 117
Burland, J. 291, 302
Burleigh, R. 347
Burlison, K. 169
Burman, K. 92
Burnam, B. 106
Burneister, L. 15
Burnett, A. 303
Burnett, B. 407, 409
Burnett, H. 434
Burnett, J. 172
Burnett, M. 257
Burnett, P. 216
Burnett, V. 226
Burnett, W. 176
Burney, Mrs. A. 254
Burnham, B. 27
Burns, C. 130
Burns, C. 162
Burns, E. 61
Burns, Mrs. G. 402
Burns, J. 25
Burns, L. 373
Burns, M. 83
Burns, M. 96
Burns, M. 366
Burns, M. 396
Burns,N. 115
Burns, N. 412
Burns, R. 383
Burns, S. 104
Burns, Y. 141
Burnsed, B. 69
Burnstein, F. 272
Burnside, J. 407, 408, 409
Burnworth, D. 367
Burr, E. 197
Burr, Mrs. T. 424
Burrell, H. 373
Burrill, S. 144
Burris, E. 333
Burris, I. 188
Burris, L. 67
Burritt, J. 57
Burrous, Mrs. K. 104
Burrow, C. 28
Burrows, D. 181
Burrows, E. 123
Burrows, G. 302
Burrows, M. 345
Burrows, P. 193
Burrus, Mrs. S. 388
Burstein, B. 300
Burstein, K. 289
Burtch, S. 177
Burtis, L. 254
Burtness, V. 450
Burton, A. 82
Burton, D. 236
Burton, E. 175
Burton, J. 187
Burton, M. 145
Burton, M. 243
Burton, M. 399
Burtraw, H. 199
Burtt, E. 267
Burwell, H. 157
Burzlander, D. 452
Burzynski, A. 302
Busbee, E. 423
Busbee, T. 381
Busby, C. 195
Busby, F. 231
Buscaglia, M. 449
Busch, M. 244
Bush, A. 31
Bush, A. 214
Bush, I. 128
Bushart, A. 152
Bushell, N. 146
Bushnell, H. 91
Bushnell, T. 350
Bushore, E. 101
Buskirk, V. 252
Buss, K. 353

Buss, S. 127
Bussa, M. 191
Bussanmas, F. 118
Bussanmas, P. 110
Bustin, R. 28
Bustle, E. 322
Butato, B. 329
Butcher, Mrs. L. 244
Butkus, E. 368
Butler, A. 313
Butler, A. 423
Butler, C. 303
Butler, D. 323
Butler, D. 385
Butler, E. 181
Butler, G. 73
Butler, H. 193
Butler, K. 110
Butler, L. 358
Butler, M. 226
Butler, N. 132
Butler, N. 149
Butler, P. 23
Butler, R. 43
Butler, R. 216
Butler, R. 227
Butler, V. 139
Butler, Z. 77
Butner, L. 342
Butt, D. 99
Butt, Mrs. H. 404
Butter, S. 303
Butterfield, A. 92
Butterfield, M. 436
Butterworth, M. 63
Butting, M. 317
Button, B. 429
Butts, G. 34
Butts, Mrs. H. 442
Butts, I. 176
Butts, J. 332
Butts, R. 442
Buxton, K. 174
Buyarski, D. 191
Buytaert, M. 201
Buzzi, W. 52
Buzzo, E. 194
Byars, J. 232
Bye, M. 222
Byers, M. 310
Bylington, B. 258
Bynum, W. 130
Byrd, A. 343
Byrd, J. 374
Byrd, P. 282
Byrd, Mrs. R. 422, 423
Byrd, S. 392
Byrn, K. 106
Byrne, M. 217
Byrnes, J. 62
Bysiewica, S. 64
Bystrom, L. 223

Cabe, Mrs. H. 28
Cable, M. 157
Cable, S. 402
Cabot,J. 372
Cabra, B. 140
Caddell, M. 310
Cadden, V. 297
Caddick, B. 181
Caddock, E. 393
Cade, J. 185
Cade, M. 185
Cadoux, D. 301
Cagle, L. 401
Cahill, J. 281
Cahill, M. 136
Cahlan, F. 259
Cain, R. 230
Cairns, A. 172
Cairns, M. 234
Cajero, C. 17, 21
Calahan, D. 254
Calas, K. 35

Caldwell, Mrs. D. 283
Caldwell, E. 385
Caldwell, G. 254
Caldwell, M. 48
Caldwell, P. 99
Caldwell, S. 122
Cale, M. 310
Calentine, B. 109
Calevro, B. 331
Calfe, A. 317
Calhoon, F. 123
Calhoun, B. 84
Calhoun, E. 67
Calhoun, M. 68
Calhoun, N. 13
Calhoun, T. 256, 257, 258
Calkins, D. 118
Calkins, R. 198
Call, J. 381, 385
Callison, J. 440
Callistein, S. 304
Calloway, D. 234
Calomino, P. 66
Calvert, L. 96
Calvey, R. 165
Calvi, A. 232
Calvrid, M. 238
Camara, K. 92
Camareno, A. 214
Cambria, J. 285
Cameron, J. 215
Cameron, M. 434
Cameron, N. 386
Camin, C. 20
Caminati, M. 267
Camp, H. 148
Camp, Mrs. J. 423
Camp, Mrs. R. 84
Campagna, P. 441
Camparone, M. 374
Campbell, A. 253,254,256,257
Campbell, B. 194
Campbell, E. 342
Campbell, Mrs. F. 139
Campbell, G. 19
Campbell, H. 326
Campbell, I. 137
Campbell, K. 293
Campbell, L. 250
Campbell, L. 439
Campbell, M. 134
Campbell, M. 139
Campbell, M. 240
Campbell, M. 249,253,260
Campbell, M. 283
Campbell, M. 341
Campbell, N. 398
Campbell, P. 173
Campbell, P. 235
Campbell, P. 370
Campbell, R. 193
Campbell, S. 8
Campbell, S. 114
Campbell, Mrs. W. 25
Campbell, Mrs. W. 442
Camping, G. 17
Campion, G. 292
Campo, E. 339
Campobasso, E. 158
Canady, E. 26
Candon, Sister E. 409,413,414
Candon, E. 414
Canedy, J. 412
Canfield, J. 441
Canfield, M. 189
Canja, E. 215
Cann, D. 68
Cann, K. 317
Cannara, E. 272
Canney, E. 260
Cannon, A. 280
Cannon, Mrs. D. 232
Cannon, J. 376
Cannon, M. 232
Cannon, W. 177

Canon, H. 258
Cantelope, M. 368
Canter, M. 21
Canto, M. 212
Cantrall, M. 186
Cantrell, Mrs. D. 395
Cantrell, K. 399
Cantrell, T. 135
Cantwell, C. 415
Canty, H. 80
Cantry, J. 52
Caouette, C. 267
Capecelatro, A. 63
Capin, E. 21
Caplan, C. 155
Capoccitti, V. 57
Capper, M. 109
Cappola, N. 277
Capps, E. 25
Cappuccio, L. 375
Caputo, R. 287
Carawon, K. 313
Card, B. 183
Card, M. 182
Cardamone, M. 364
Cardemas, B. 1
Cardin, S. 157
Cardwell, M. 288
Carey, A. 350
Carey, E. 67
Carey, Sister J. 64
Carey, M. 244
Carey, M. 254
Cargill, J. 148
Cargo, M. 341
Carleton, O. 147
Carleton, S. 143
Carley, A. 449
Carlile, M. 20
Carlin, G. 135
Carlin, M. 214
Carlisle, L. 413, 414
Carlisle, V. 405
Carlon, M. 207
Carlow, B. 71
Carls, V. 182
Carlsen, Mrs. T. 303
Carlson, B. 182
Carlson, C. 96
Carlson, C. 148
Carlson, D. 17
Carlson, D. 173
Carlson, D. 366
Carlson, E. 225
Carlson, E. 401
Carlson, G. 127
Carlson, G. 435
Carlson, J. 122
Carlson, J. 175
Carlson, M. 57
Carlson, S. 144
Carlson, V. 240
Carlson, V. 249
Carlston, M. 430
Carlton, C. 402
Carlton, F. 69, 79
Carlyle, M. 154
Carmack, R. 91
Carman, R. 205
Carmichael, E. 449
Carmichael, M. 10
Carmignani, K. 33
Carnes, Mrs. R. 310
Carney, C. 41
Carney, J. 117
Caron, E. 143
Caron, L. 148, 149
Caron, S. 79
Carothers, D. 367
Carpenter, B. 250
Carpenter, B. 418
Carpenter, D. 328
Carpenter, E. 373
Carpenter, J. 200
Carpenter, J. 353

Carpenter, L. 110
Carpenter, L. 131
Carpenter, M. 52
Carpenter, M. 175
Carpenter, M. 301
Carpenter, M. 322
Carr, C. 346
Carr, C. 368
Carr, F. 44
Carr, Mrs. H. 422
Carr, M. 268
Carr, M. 452
Carr, P. 92
Carr, S. 50
Carr, S. 254
Carrell, V. 351
Carrico, E. 151
Carrier, C. 144
Carrion, M. 214
Carrol, B. 240
Carrol, F. 15
Carrol, G. 20
Carroll, B. 198
Carroll, C. 276
Carroll, F. 16
Carroll, J. 228
Carroll, K. 296
Carroll, M. 260
Carroll, R. 157
Carroll, S. 285
Carson, D. 19
Carson, D. 79
Carson, E. 96
Carson, J. 98
Carson, J. 124
Carstenson, D. 254
Carswell, M. 260
Cart, R. 287
Carter, E. 35
Carter, G. 230
Carter, H. 81
Carter, H. 353
Carter, J. 19, 20
Carter, J. 191
Carter, J. 222
Carter, Mrs. J. 342
Carter, K. 157
Carter, K. 180
Carter, L. 79
Carter, M. 47
Carter, M. 62
Carter, M. 309
Carter, M. 310
Carter, N. 145
Carter, N. 351
Carter, P. 106
Carter, R. 185
Carter, S. 229
Carter, S. 248
Carter, S. 420
Carter, V. 29
Carter, V. 339
Carthey, R. 365
Cartwright, C. 351
Carty, L. 433
Carvell, J. 360
Carver, B. 104
Carver, B. 324
Cary, L. 117
Casareto, D. 224
Casciano, J. 367
Case, S. 186
Casey, J. 454
Cashen, M. 331
Cashwell, D. 308
Casiday, G. 200
Caskey, D. 357
Casler, M. 35
Cason, J. 392
Cason, M. 71
Cassey, S. 205
Cassiday, D. 64
Cassidy, H. 333
Cassidy, L. 68
Cassity, L. 238

Castallante, M. 203
Castellano, G. 374
Castelluci, C. 373
Castillo, Mrs. F. 402
Castillo, S. 287
Castle, M. 196
Casto, S. 48
Castor, E. 69
Caswell, B. 170
Caswell, C. 10
Catania, S. 94
Cates, B. 243
Cates, F. 149
Cathles, E. 62, 63
Cathroe, C. 252
Caton, Sister A. 245
Caton, I. 404
Caulbe, Z. 103
Cauthan, E. 402
Cauthen, Mrs. J. 380
Cavanaugh, F. 104
Cavarra, M. 52
Cave, C. 132
Cave, J. 59
Cavender, E. 110
Cavey, F. 156
Cawley, E. 356
Cayemberg, P. 208
Cease, D. 378
Cefaratti, C. 328
Ceigh, D. 253
Celli, G. 281
Cerenzia, M. 153
Cerra, M. 374
Cervenka, C. 403
Cesario, E. 372
Cetas, A. 182
Chace, L. 34
Chachere, D. 28
Chacon, V. 49
Chadrick, L. 344
Chadwick, B. 280
Chadwick, E. 434
Chadwick, L. 50
Chaffee, B. 411
Chaffee, Z. 195
Chafin, B. 309
Chai, K. 435
Chaich, J. 173
Chalimonczyk, D. 316
Chamberlain, J. 198
Chamberlain, Mrs. P. 245
Chamberlain, P. 383
Chambers, A. 1
Chambers, M. 260
Chambers, S. 236
Champion, G. 348
Champlin, O. 372
Chance, K. 233
Chancey, M. 442
Chandler, C. 302
Chaney, M. 100
Chaney, P. 9
Channing, G. 335
Chap, H. 412
Chapin, D. 303
Chapin, E. 283
Chapman, A. 26
Chapman, A. 413
Chapman, B. 59
Chapman, C. 320
Chapman, D. 121
Chapman, E. 94
Chappel, G. 27
Charboneau, E. 412
Charbonneau, R. 172
Charette, S. 146
Charlie, T. 14
Charlton, L. 121
Charlton, M. 335
Charpentier, S. 75
Charron, F. 148
Chase, A. 407
Chase, F. 62
Chase, Mrs. L. 17

Chase, L. 114
Chase, M. 374
Chase, N. 214
Chase, N. 305
Chase, R. 156
Chase, S. 147
Chase, V. 435
Chaset, S. 373
Chason, I. 310
Chastain, M. 389
Chatterton, C. 132
Chavaree, B. 146
Chaves, Y. 255
Chavez, L. 39
Chayes, A. 1
Cheatham, K. 8
Cheatham, R. 168
Chebuhar, E. 117
Cheer, A. 435
Cheeseman, J. 192
Cheever, S. 384
Cheldelin, I. 353
Chell, E. 446
Chelli, R. 145
Chenard, S. 183
Cheney, K. 61
Cherlin, M. 373
Chernik, E. 186
Chernock, B. 366
Cherry, G. 69
Cherry, H. 198
Cherry, M. 343
Cherry, R. 306
Cherry, S. 83
Chertow, D. 291
Chesley, A. 21
Chesley, B. 145
Chesnutt, Mrs. J. 28
Chevrie, D. 185
Chewing, M. 422
Chiacu, C. 374
Chiamp, C.L. 214
Chichester, B. 292
Childers, K. 339
Childers, S. 319
Childery, E. 399
Childress, Mrs. C. 140
Childress, L. 137
Childress, N. 396
Childress, V. 201
Childs, C. 63
Childs, L. 448
Childs, M. 211
Childs, P. 80
Chilson, B. 369
Chipps, L. 175
Chisholm, J. 21
Chisholm, S. 4
Chittum, E. 423
Choate, O. 141
Chobanian, M. 374
Chodos, L. 304
Chonko, L. 142
Chouinard, J. 415
Chovan, J. 328
Chow, C. 434
Chow, R. 426
Christen, D. 385
Christensen, A. 12
Christensen, E. 406
Christensen, J. 316
Christensen, M. 58
Christensen, M. 89
Christensen, M. 407
Christensen, Mrs. R. 254
Christenson, I. 315
Christenson, M. 117
Christian, C. 424
Christian, G. 352
Christian, H. 173
Christian, L. 232
Christian, L. 343
Christian, M. 288
Christian, W. 340
Christiansen, E. 365

Christiansen, M. 48
Christiansen, Z. 385
Christianson, B. 286
Christianson, L. 435
Christianson, P. 219
Christie, D. 104,106
Christie, M. 328,336
Christinat, V. 276
Christinzio, U. 272
Christmas, Dr. J. 301,303
Christoph, P. 431
Christopherson, R. 225
Christowe, M. 413
Christy, Sister M. 20
Chrystal, L. 12
Chumbley, M. 402
Church, L. 237
Church, R. 64
Churchill, M. 353
Churchill, R. 98
Churchill, S. 407
Cibulka, H. 258
Cicoria, C. 275
Cigarroa, M. 404
Ciglcr, M. 449
Cilek, L. 108
Cinelli, A. 285
Ciolfi, A. 79
Cirks, S. 144
Cisler, D. 119
Cisneros, C. 35
Cittadino, A. 191
Claffey, C. 334
Clagett, V. 151
Claiborne, R. 257
Clancy, H. 277,278
Clanton, B. 374
Clapp, G. 317
Clark, A. 153
Clark, A. 180
Clark, A. 318
Clark, A. 364
Clark, A. 402
Clark, B. 80
Clark, B. 107
Clark, B. 421
Clark, C. 75
Clark, C. 238
Clark, D. 199
Clark, D. 408
Clark, E. 114
Clark, E. 295
Clark, Mrs. H. 21
Clark, Mrs. J. 29
Clark, J. 148
Clark, J. 172
Clark, J. 217
Clark, J. 311
Clark, J. 329
Clark, J. 334
Clark, J. 344
Clark, J. 401
Clark, J. 434
Clark, L. 61
Clark, L. 96
Clark, L. 148
Clark, L. 230
Clark, M. 64
Clark, M. 184
Clark, Dr. M. 303
Clark, M. 323
Clark, M. 352
Clark, N. 142
Clark, N. 166
Clark, O. 164
Clark, P. 146
Clark, P. 436
Clark, R. 215
Clark, R. 348
Clark, R. 362
Clark, S. 266,267
Clark, W. 7
Clarke, C. 203
Clarke, D. 193
Clarke, E. 56,62

Clarke, J.   78
Clarke, J.   193
Clarke, M.   152
Clarke, R.   258
Clarkson, E.   439
Clary, V.   401
Classick, A.   351
Clausen, D.   437
Clauss, C.   1
Claussen, L.   383
Clavon, M.   215
Clay, B.   71
Clay, C.   373
Clay, C.   406
Clay, G.   18
Clay, M.   216
Claybrook, J.   1
Claypool, D.   119
Clayton, E.   29
Clayton, J.   269
Clayton, L.   428
Cleaver, E.   176
Clegg, M.   319
Clegg, R.   91
Cleghorn, G.   86
Cleland, V.S.   215
Clem, S.   48
Clemens, Y.   95
Clement, A.   189
Clements, Mrs. F.   403
Clemo, B.   209
Clemons, L.   126
Cleveland, S.   221
Cleveland, T.   436
Clever, J.   214
Clewley, A.   413
Click, E.   190
Clifford, M.   20
Clift, S.   348
Clifton, E.   436
Clifton, R.   29
Clinard, C.   334
Cline, L.   342
Cline, M.   320
Cline, P.   310
Cline, V.   399
Clinton, S.   156
Cloney, N.   71
Close, M.   96
Cloud, E.   68
Clough, E.   129
Clouser, M.   113
Cloys, Mrs. G.   388
Clum, P.   239
Clynes, M.   301
Coalson, D.   253
Coater, L.   72
Coates, A..   335
Coates, D.   436
Coates, L.   427
Coates, M.   128
Coates, D.   197
Coates,S.   349
Coatta, J.   192
Cobb, B.   105
Cobb, E.   267
Cobb, L.   451
Coble, M.   388
Coca, M.   286
Coceana, V.   75
Cochran, B.   62
Cochran, E.   324
Cochran, Mrs. G.   422,423
Cochran, Mrs. P.   135
Cochran, S.   245
Cockrane, V.   91
Cockrell, L.   393,403,404
Coder, C.   254
Coder, M.   253,255
Codley, M.   27
Cody, M.   385
Coe, B.   148
Coe, C.   298
Coens, M.   121
Cofey, C.   422

Coffey, B.   253
Coffey, R.   378
Coffey, V.   251,254,255
Coffield, M.   398
Coffin, R.   415
Coffin, R.   437
Coffman, C.   423
Coffman, E.   335
Coffman, J.   116
Coffman, V.   419
Coffman, Mrs. W.   400
Cofield, E.   307
Coggin, F.   11
Coggs, M.   443
Coghill, C.   326
Cogsdale, C.   420
Cohen, D.   76
Cohen, D.   285
Cohen, E.   35
Cohen, E.   148
Cohen, E.   412
Cohen, J.   353
Cohen, L.   134
Cohen, O.   378
Cohen, P.   430
Cohen, S.   303
Cohn, M.   336
Cohodas, L.   214
Cohrs, O.   209
Colbath, J.   415
Colberg, M.   191
Colby, J.   265
Cole, H.   51
Cole, J.   122
Cole, K.   203
Cole, M.   297
Cole, M.   343
Cole, S.   127
Cole, V.   407
Coleman, B.   154
Coleman, B.   230
Coleman, C.   166
Coleman, E.   366
Coleman, F.   156
Coleman, L.   452
Coleman, M.   213
Coleman, Mrs. M.   231
Coleman, M.   258
Colemere, D.   398
Colestock, D.   199
Coll, H.   267
Collet, B.   240
Colletta, P.   15
Collier, L.   388
Collier, P.   242
Colling, J.   353
Collins, A.   172
Collins, A.   359
Collins, B.   166
Collins, B.   349
Collins, C.   4
Collins, C.   301
Collins, D.   152
Collins, D.   170
Collins, D.   192
Collins, D.   247
Collins, D.   254
Collins, D.   449
Collins, E.   93
Collins, F.   398
Collins, J.   239
Collins, J.   245
Collins, L.   16
Collins, L.   386
Collins, L.   418
Collins, M.   52
Collins, M.   224
Collins, M.   361
Collins, P.   149
Collins, P.   336
Collins, R.   66
Collins, S.   15
Collins, S.   233
Collins, V.   378
Collins, V.   409

Collison, K.   121
Collison, M.   123
Collison, R.   151
Colly, M.   348
Colony, G.   189
Colson, D.   261
Colter, J.   82
Colton, F.   293
Colton, M.   407
Columbus, J.   248
Colvin, M.   18
Combs, G.   177
Comella, J.   325
Comer, E.   281
Comer, M.   312
Comfort, M.   196
Comly, M.   116
Comstock, S.   188
Comuntzis, D.   441
Conaghan, D.   337
Conaster, R.   9
Conaway, H.   259
Condon, M.   413
Conerly, J.   232
Coney, K.   141
Congrove, B.   327
Conkey, J.   67
Conklin, D.   133
Conklin, I.   200
Conklin, S.   353
Conley, A.   21
Conley, B.   248
Conley, E.   359
Conley, L.   178
Conley, S.   251
Conlin, J.   52
Conlin, R.   123
Conn, H.   105, 106
Conn, P.   259
Connaghan, R.   194
Connally, J.   81
Connell, E.   294
Connell, K.   372
Connell, P.   86
Connelly, B.   137
Connelly, E.   254
Connelly, E.   290
Connelly, M.   334
Connelly, M.   373
Conner, A.   121
Conner, F.   67
Conner, N.   96
Conner, T.   154
Conner, V.   18
Connerley, C.   252
Connolly, J.   67
Connolly, V.   54
Connon, S.   192
Connor, E.   61
Connor, R.   259
Connors, M.   357
Connors, S.   182
Conover, A.   63
Conover, E.   408
Conover, L.   407
Conover, M.   271
Conrad, D.   205
Conrad, J.   317
Conroy, J.   266
Conroy, T.   177
Constant, C.   238
Converse, V.   15
Conway, C.   62
Conway, E.   273
Coody, E.   85,86
Cook, A.   453
Cook, E.   429
Cook, F.   401
Cook, G.   386
Cook, H.   64
Cook, J.   35
Cook, J.   72
Cook, J.   429
Cook, L.   40
Cook, Mrs. L.   424

Cook, L.   448
Cook, M.   81
Cook, M.   147,149
Cook, N.   65
Cook, P.   302
Cook, R.   305
Cook, S.   126
Cooke, B.   254
Cooke, B.   306
Cooke, M.   216
Cooksey, P.   232
Cool, E.   383
Coombs, C.   360
Coon, L.   192
Coon, M.   257
Cooney, C.   374
Cooney, M.   373
Coonrod, L.   349
Coonrod, R.   336
Coons, B.   247
Cooper, A.   277
Cooper, B.   68
Cooper, B.   447
Cooper, C.   322
Cooper, D.   430
Cooper, E.   181
Cooper, G.   91
Cooper, I.   439
Cooper, J.   104
Cooper, J.   115
Cooper, J.   148
Cooper, J.   363
Cooper, K.   153
Cooper, M.   67
Cooper, P.   86
Cooper, S.   417
Cootware, D.   202
Coover, H.   214
Cope, N.   441
Copeland, R.   24
Copenhaver, M.   261
Copenhaver, W.   116
Coppolla, A.   20
Coppola, A.   216
Copes, J.   139
Corbett, A.   346
Corbett, L.   307
Corbin, G.   172
Corbitt, C.   441
Corcio, M.   365
Corcoran, J.   415
Corder, T.   116
Cordier, P.   384
Cording, D.   253
Cordova, C.   408
Cordsiemon, J.   238
Core, V.   443
Corey, A.   241
Corey, J.   171
Corey, L.   39
Corich, M.   52
Corkran, V.   75
Corlew, C.   192
Corlew, M.   173
Corley, P.   435
Cornell, E.   194
Cornell, G.   149
Cornell, H.   304
Cornell, J.   375
Corneluis, E.   324
Cornett, C.   148
Cornetto, K.   282
Cornick, P.   120
Cornile, Sister M.   85
Corning, J.   412
Cornwell, J.   62
Coro, M.   147
Corr, E.   179
Corr, M.   42
Corr, R.   344
Corrado, A.   340
Correll, M.   366
Correll, R.   47
Correll, R.   174
Cortner, S.   358

Cortser, L. 408
Corwin, J. 16
Cory, M. 75
Cos, L. 91
Cosand, V. 197
Cosentini, A. 61
Cosgriff, K. 62
Cosgrove, A. 157
Cosho, K. 91
Cosman, H. 410
Cossey, Mrs. O. 26
Costa, C. 269, 285
Costanza, M. 1
Coste, L. 302
Costello, A. 290
Costello, B. 73
Costello, E. 374
Costello, F. 299
Costello, M. 58
Costen, P. 86
Costenbader, B. 418
Costianes, F. 204
Cote, M. 261
Cothell, D. 424
Cotner, M. 103
Cotter, K. 331
Cotterman, M. 134
Cottey, V. 339
Cottman, R. 215
Cotton, B. 181
Cotton, C. 287
Cotton, M. 261
Cottrell, R. 103
Couch, L. 18
Couchigian, Mrs. M. 317
Couchman, L. 126
Coughenour, B. 103
Coughlon, M. 122
Coulombe, Y. 266
Coulson, C. 50
Coulson, D. 191
Coulson, R. 171
Coulter, E. 90
Coulter, E. 351
Council, R. 84
Councilor, M. 422
Counihan, G. 158
Counts, M. 10
Coup, J. 96
Courney, A. 175
Courtney, J. 235
Coutts, F. 414
Couture, A. 125
Couture, E. 415
Couture, R. 373
Couturier, F. 140
Cover, A. 89
Cover, E. 336
Covert, Mrs. F. 403
Cowan, J. 199
Cowan, J. 308
Cowan, K. 251
Cowart, J. 84
Cowart, S. 86
Cowell, B. 182
Cowell, E. 313
Cowles, A. 436
Cowles, B. 323
Cowley, Mrs. J. 233
Cowling, Dr. D. 423
Cowlishaw, M. 350
Cox, B. 128
Cox, C. 245
Cox, E. 235
Cox, E. 246
Cox, G. 344
Cox, J. 171
Cox, L. 69
Cox, L. 237
Cox, L. 339
Cox, L. 352
Cox, M. 116
Cox, M. 421
Cox, N. 6
Cox, P. 177

Cox, Mrs. R. 388
Cox, S. 324
Cox, V. 130
Coxe, M. 353
Coxe, Mrs. T. 380
Coyhis, J. 449
Coyle, B. 25
Coyle, K. 386
Coyle, M. 439
Coyne, N. 336
Coyner, A. 67
Cozzens, R. 453,454
Crabb, H. 121
Crabb, N. 70
Crabtree, C. 209
Cracken, S. 354
Craddock, A. 133
Craddock, T. 418
Craft, B. 350
Craft, E. 310
Craft, J. 396
Crahan, M. 411, 413
Craig, F. 108
Craig, G. 138
Craig, J. 408
Craig, L. 308
Craig, M. 438
Crain, J. 205
Craker, D. 188
Cramer, A. 326
Cramer, G. 283
Crandal, L. 386
Crandall, D. 411
Crandall, P. 375
Crane, A. 131
Crane, C. 248
Crane, D. 443
Crane, E. 191
Crane, F. 214
Cranford, J. 401
Cranford, N. 389
Crank, B. 354
Craswell, E. 425,436
Craven, B. 381
Craven, D. 200
Crawford, E. 167
Crawford, E. 434
Crawford, E. 452
Crawford, J. 244
Crawford, J. 256
Crawford, M. 154
Crawford, M. 331
Crawford, S. 173
Crawley, D. 241
Crawley, E. 220
Crawley, M. 24
Creager, B. 453
Creager, V. 177
Creamer, P. 333
Creasey, E. 421
Creech, L. 328
Creer, S. 408
Creigh, D. 253
Creiver, M. 197
Creque, B. 202
Cresmean, I. 334
Cress, E. 325
Cressley, F. 366
Crichton, A. 81, 86
Crilley, P. 195
Crim, B. 197
Crishal, M. 173
Crisman, J. 413
Crisp, I. 129
Crissman, J. 125
Crist, Mrs. H. 155
Cristofane, S. 152
Crocco, L. 60
Croce, M. 268
Crocker, D. 148
Crocker, D. 253
Crocker, Mrs. F. 402
Crocker, J. 204
Crockett, I. 259
Crockford, V. 423

Croft, G. 82
Croke, E. 48
Croll, S. 375
Cromer, J. 255
Cron, M. 364
Cronhardt, S. 401
Cronin, C. 375
Crooks, B. 353
Crookshanks, B. 438
Crory, E. 261
Crosbie, L. 62
Crosby, J. 99
Crosby, S. 254
Crosland, D. 377
Cross, B. 202
Cross, C. 19
Cross, C. 25
Cross, C. 343
Cross, G. 320
Cross, H. 428
Cross, H. 449
Cross, J. 68
Cross, L. 414
Crossin, H. 268
Crossland, L. 46
Crossley, I. 331
Crothers, D. 21
Crouch, E. 42
Crout, B. 327
Crow, B. 244
Crow, G. 238
Crow, L. 15
Crow, L. 222
Crow, R. 192
Crow, Mrs. T. 403
Crowe, B. 105
Crowe, Mrs. L. 243
Crowell, D. 452
Crowley, B. 31
Crowley, E. 451
Crowley, M. 160
Crowley, P. 64
Crows, V. 369
Crowson, R. 233
Crudginton, E. 60
Cruickshank, A. 431
Crumidy, A. 284
Crumley, K. 401
Crump, B. 232
Crump, L. 134
Crumrine, B. 127
Crush, M. 417
Crust, K. 364
Cruxton, G. 329
Cruz, Mrs. J. 402
Csizmesia, M. 413
Csubak, C. 332
Cuch, I. 409
Cuchural, C. 284
Cuddy, M. 245
Culbertson, L. 378
Cullen, F. 230
Cullens, J. 45
Cullers, E. 348
Cullin, P. 200
Cullinan, A. 21
Culliton, M. 77
Cullman, V. 127
Cully, B. 453
Culver, C. 178
Cumicek, K. 450
Cummings, B. 134
Cummings, M. 142,148
Cummings, M. 191
Cummings, N. 259
Cummings, N. 434
Cummings, S. 370
Cummings, W. 76
Cummins, J. 7
Cunningham, A. 232
Cunningham, C. 258,259
Cunningham, C. 441
Cunningham, J. 408
Cunningham, J. 441
Cunningham, M. 390

Curcio, E. 164
Curran, B. 105
Curran, B. 268
Curran, J. 238
Curran, T. 68
Currie, B. 86
Currie, Mrs. B. 354
Currie, J. 170
Currie, M. 98, 105
Curro, M. 231
Curry, M. 224
Curry, P. 453
Curt, D. 62
Curtain, M. 60
Curti, B. 258
Curtis, Mrs. A. 422
Curtis, D. 182
Curtis, D. 287
Curtis, F. 414
Curtis, H. 175
Curtis, J. 432
Curtis, K. 106
Curtis, K. 266
Curtis, M. 232
Curtis, P. 143
Curtis, P. 144
Curtis, R. 231
Curtis, S. 286
Curtis, T. 414
Curtis, V. 145
Curtiss, A. 246
Curtiss, F. 86
Curzan, A. 154
Cusatis, D. 446
Cushwa, P. 155
Cusimano, Sister A. 404
Custer, E. 225
Cutch, I. 407
Cutchall, L. 25
Cutler, J. 221
Cutler, L. 108
Cutlip, I. 442
Cutter, D. 180
Cutts, Mrs. R. 422
Cuyjet, M. 68
Cyrus, P. 440
Czinder, G. 178

Dack, D. 200
Dadd, V. 209
Daft, E. 334
Dagg, V. 346
Dagnon, E. 10
Dahl, N. 96
Dahl, P. 247
Dahl, R. 176
Dahlberg, J. 433
Dahlky, J. 90
Dahlquist, C. 254
Dahlstrom, E. 407
Dahmen, J. 428
Dahya, R. 216
Daigle, A. 147
Daigle, G. 147
Dailey, E. 385
Dailey, M. 398
Daily, Mrs. L. 255
Dale, J. 21
D'Alessio, A. 374
Dalgleish, M. 434
Dallafior, B. 185
Dallas, V. 59
Dallen, B. 125
D'Allessandris, B. 361
Dallman, B. 119
D'Alois, B. 303
Dalton, A. 193
Dalton, G. 255
Dalton, J. 192
Dalton, Mrs. J. 244
Dalton, J. 335
Dalton, Mrs. J. 422,424
Dalton, R. 259
Dalton, S. 216
Daly, C. 209

Daly, N. 48
Damen, K. 144
Damman, M. 116
Dammier, L. 403
Damon, M. 179
Damstrom, Mrs. J. 342
Dana, P. 147
Danahy, Mrs. D. 402
Danb, D. 342
Dancey, B. 156
Daner, M. 168
Danford, J. 29
Danford, J. 452
Danforth, B. 261
Dangel, H. 358
Daniel, L. 353
Daniel, L. 387
Daniel, S. 301
Daniels, C. 216
Daniels, E. 235
Daniels, H. 91
Daniels, J. 56
Daniels, M. 42
Daniels, M. 235
Daniels, M. 424
Daniels, N. 131
Daniels, R. 308
Daniels, R. 353
Danielson, A. 219
Danielson, J. 248
Dann, C. 258
Danneels, S. 174
Danner, M. 353
Danner, P. 2
Dapre, H. 367
Darby, A. 230
Darby, C. 132
Darby, Z. 402
Darcy, M. 286
Dardarson, D. 15
Dardeau, H. 141
Darden, L. 404
Dardis, M. 117
Dare, L. 27
Daresh, E. 195
Darga, E. 195
Darin, B. 216
Darkengelo, H. 366
Darr, C. 324
Darst, S. 443
Dast, C. 203
Dastrup, F. 39
Datchko, L. 359
D'Attore, A. 293
Daugherty, J. 135
Daugherty, O. 190
Daughtrey, M. 391
Daughtry, K. 309
Davenport, B. 404
Davenport, C. 357
Davenport, J. 2
Davenport, M. 307
Davey, A. 177
Davey, L. 215
Davick, D. 228
David, I. 141
David, O. 416
Davidson, G. 428,436
Davidson, J. 123
Davidson, J. 332
Davidson, Mrs. J. 422
Davidson, L. 106
Davidson, L. 118
Davidson, M. 413
Davidson, N. 429
Davidson, Mrs. R. 106
Davidson, R. 155
Davidson, S. 353
Davidson, V. 322
Davies, J. 413
Davilli, A. 161
Davin, F. 70
Davis, A. 113
Davis, A. 178
Davis, B. 163

Davis, B. 245
Davis, B. 272
Davis, B. 350
Davis, Mrs. C. 20
Davis, C. 29
Davis, C. 216
Davis, C. 453
Davis, D. 32
Davis, D. 188
Davis, D. 293
Davis, D. 349
Davis, D. 387
Davis, E. 99
Davis, E. 120,121,123
Davis, E. 154
Davis, E. 176
Davis, E. 190
Davis, E. 232
Davis, E. 248
Davis, E. 322
Davis, E. 348
Davis, E. 359
Davis, E. 366
Davis, Mrs. E. 421
Davis, F. 148
Davis, H. 69
Davis, H. 99
Davis, I. 26
Davis, J. 153
Davis, J. 168
Davis, J. 360
Davis, J. 437
Davis, L. 2
Davis, L. 39
Davis, L. 88, 92
Davis, L. 114
Davis, L. 146
Davis, L. 195
Davis, L. 313
Davis, Mrs. L. 380
Davis, L. 381
Davis, M. 125
Davis, M. 135
Davis, M. 160
Davis, M. 169
Davis, M. 202
Davis, M. 288
Davis, M. 399
Davis, M. 423
Davis, M. 439, 441
Davis, N. 443
Davis, P. 39
Davis, P. 312
Davis, P. 452
Davis, R. 158
Davis, S. 203
Davis, S. 258
Davis, S. 449
Davis, V. 118
Davis, V. 176
Davis, V. 182
Davis, V. 258
Davis, V. 373
Davis, V. 453
Davison, R. 187
Davitt, N. 67
Dawdy, J. 195
Dawes, M. 378
Dawson, A. 29
Dawson, B. 121
Dawson, D. 369
Day, A. 202
Day, C. 261
Day, D. 32
Day, E. 454
Day, J. 122
Day, Mrs. J. 403
Day, K. 250
Day, L. 73
Day, L. 414
Day, N. 157
Day, S. 183
Daye, H. 366
Dayhoff, N. 105
Days, R. 140

Days, V. 33
Deal, Mrs. R. 22
Dealaman, D. 269,283,284
DeAlmeida, M. 244
Dean, B. 247
Dean, E. 121
Dean, Mrs. J. 104
Dean, J. 368
Dean, M. 190
Dean, M. 239
Dean, N. 409
Dean, Mrs. R. 287
Dean, S. 34
Dean, S. 144
Dean, S. 443
Deanes, L. 311
Deardorff, V. 122
Deatherage, C. 337
DeAtley, C. 95
Deaton, I. 136
DeBerry, L. 387
Debes, I. 108
DeBlaker, K. 72
DeBlasis, J. 43
DeBoer, Y. 185
DeBoest, Mrs. H. 104
DeBuchanan, M. 302
DeCamps, C. 377
DeCaro, A. 75
DeCesare, G. 261
Decker, C. 58
Decker, F. 317
Decker, M. 434
Decker, P. 188
Decker, R. 133
Deddens, C. 233
Dedic, S. 251
Dedrick, C. 30
Deeds, T. 179
Deef, Mrs. R. 229
Deen, M. 71
Dees, M. 343
Deetz, E. 331
Defazio, D. 283
Deferrari, P. 280
Deffler, L. 323
Defoe, M. 215
DeForest, C. 270
DeFrank, M. 68
Degase, E. 184
DeGraff, A. 67
DeHart, A. 377
DeHart, Mrs. J. 422
DeHerrera, L. 45
Dehlinger, J. 96
Deike, D. 209
Deiz, M. 352
DeJong, A. 157
DeLaGarza, C. 397
Delage, J. 57
Delahunt, J. 434
DeLand, C. 231
Delauro, L. 60
DelBello, Mrs. A. 302
DelCarlo, L. 257
Delco, W. 391
DeLeon, L. 392
Dell, W. 420
Delley, N. 79
Dellinger, E. 126
DeLoache, K. 336
Delong, A. 413
DeLong, C. 419
DeLorenzo, M. 50
DeLouche, F. 259
DeLourdes, Mother M. 61
Delp, J. 365
DeLucia, L. 375
DeLury, S. 412
DeMaio, D. 284
DeMarcus, J. 309
Demarest, E. 200
DeMarinis, B. 413
Demiani, K. 281
Demientieff, J. 13

Demientieff, M. 13
Demke, M. 343
Demorest, M. 335
Demos, J. 219
Dempewolf, V. 126
Dempsey, D. 65
Demuth, P. 16
Deneen, M. 230
DeNise, J. 174
Denison, B. 205
Denison, M. 98
Denke, S. 385
Dennehy, M. 248
Denney, J. 111
Denney, L. 320
Denning, B. 216
Dennis, E. 13
Dennis, G. 173
Dennis, M. 201
Dennis, M. 255
Dennis, M. 385
Dennis, N. 377
Dennison, A. 145
Dennison, P. 255
Denniston, M. 116
Denny, M. 66
Denny, M. 131
Denny, N. 205
Densen-Gerber, Dr. J. 301
Denton, B. 128
Denton, B. 339
Denton, B. 391
Denton, F. 137
Denton, M. 308
Denzer, C. 220
DePalma, C. 42
DePearce, C. 92
Depew, C. 132
DePrimio, V. 362
DeProsse, C. 114
Dereli, M. 345
Dereniak, J. 179
Derenzy, H. 187
Derian, P. 2
Deriso, R. 86
Derohn, A. 361
DeRoso, D. 187
Derrickson, K. 67
Derry, P. 91
Derting, H. 394
Derusha, P. 186
DeRuyter, R. 450
DeSantis, V. 67
Desaulniers, R. 63
Descheeny, L. 18
DeSelm, B. 387
Desens, D. 227
DesGrange, J. 301
Desmarais, J. 374
Desmarteau, M. 129
DeSmedt, M. 195
DeSpain, P. 21
DeTar, P. 125
Detlefsen, B. 253
Dettmer, P. 130
D'Ettorre, B. 330
DeTurck, D. 365
Deurwaeder, I. 352
DeVall, J. 185
Devaney, D. 434
Devereux, M. 414
DeVille, P. 247
Devine, J. 248
Devine, J. 281
Devitt, A. 361
DeVoe, L. 106
DeVore,L. 111
DeWall, J. 299
Dewalt, N. 328
Dewees, K. 281
Dewes, Mrs. G. 385
Dewey, A. 437
Dewey, Mrs. G. 354
Dewey, P. 258
DeWitt, A. 444

DeWitt, L. 450
DeWitt, Y. 272
Dewland, J. 276
DeWolf, N. 374
Dexrode, K. 438
Dexter, D. 196
DeYoung, C. 15
Deyton, T. 399
DeZarn, I. 36
Diament, A. 34
Diamond, G. 171
Diamond, H. 396
Diaz, E. 392
Diaz, J. 415
Diaz, M. 288
Dick, N. 45
Dickason, B. 203
Dickerson, D. 296
Dickerson, K. 289
Dickey, B. 244
Dickey, C. 100
Dickey, L. 454
Dickey, M. 27
Dickinson, A. 149
Dickinson, A. 259
Dickinson, E. 289, 301
Dickinson, Mrs. E. 302
Dickinson, J. 199
Dickinson, L. 253
Dickinson, L. 374
Dickinson, M. 434
Dickinson, R. 284
Dickman, M. 247
Dickman, M. 303
Dickson, C. 245
Dickson, D. 453
Dickson, F. 9
Diebels, K. 17
Diedrich, F. 19
Diel, V. 129
Diemoz, F. 354
Diesburg, G. 114
Diesen, W. 209
Dieterle, L. 334
Dietsch, M. 117
Dietsch, M. 423
DiFrancesco, J. 282
Digel, L. 127
Digeronimo, E. 162
Diggelman, C. 450
Diggs, E. 290
Dike, E. 413
Dile, S. 324
Dilk, J. 53
Dill, C. 421
Dillard, J. 214
Dille, C. 89
Dillehay, E. 388
Dilley, B. 433
Dilley, J. 67
Dillin, K. 255
Dillon, B. 343
Dillon, E. 255
Dillon, J. 86
Dillon, L. 68
Dilworth, J. 435
DiMarcantonio, I. 278
Dimick, M. 322
Dimmick, C. 433
Dimond, Mrs. E. 422
Dinkelacker, B. 336
Dion, A. 261
Dion, L. 261
Dippel, J. 352
Dirks, E. 114
Dirks, L. 126
Dise, D. 216
Disher, B. 209
Dismukes, A. 81
Dissinger, M. 369
Ditmar, S. 254
Dittemore, B. 45
Diuble, G. 189
Dixon, A. 203
Dixon, A. 206

Dixon, B. 90
Dixon, J. 121
Dixon, J. 347
Dixon, M. 253
Dixon, M. 321
Dixon, P. 386
Dixon, R. 155
Dixon, S. 202
Dixon, Z. 379
Doane, M. 102
Dobberstein, L. 227
Dobbin, B. 278
Dobbs, B. 339
Dobbs, J. 449
Dobbs, P. 113
Dobbs, R. 184
Dobler, N. 87
Dobler, N. 91
Dobrinski, J. 340
Dobrow, F. 273
Dobson, P. 227
Docchio, A. 362
Docekal, A. 112
Dochinger, J. 325
Dochniak, I. 226
Dockery, G. 338
Dockins, A. 454
Doderer, M. 107,121,124
Dodge, D. 218,230
Dodson, R. 235
Dodson, Mrs. T. 28
Doe, E. 266
Doebbler, L. 435
Doebele, M. 129
Doele, C. 205
Doerer, A. 72
Doering, M. 356
Doggett, M. 242
Doherty, Mrs. G. 318
Dohse, B. 112
Dolan, A. 207
Dolan, K. 434,435
Dolan, R. 257
Doland, M. 18
Dolehanty, B. 183
Dolezal, L. 101
Dolezal, V. 178
Dolin, H. 85
D'Oliver, E. 9
Doll, D. 234
Dollahite, E. 233
Domonoske, Mrs. M. 258
Donahey, G. 318
Donahue, A. 374
Donahue, C. 178
Donahue, M.. 374
Donaldson, E. 32
Donaldson, G. 331
Donaldson, V. 28
Doncarlos, D. 120
Dondero, T. 257,258
Donley, P. 336
Donley, S. 202
Donnelley, G. 277
Donnelly, H. 261
Donnelly, Mrs. R. 156
Donoghue, J. 443
Donohue, C. 48
Donohue, M. 58,64
Donovan, E. 146
Donovan, K. 159
Dooley, J. 267
Dooley, R. 47
Dopkin, B. 155
Dorbecker, D. 98
Dorey, S. 161
Dorman, C. 192
Dorman-Leigh, W. 405
Dorr, P. 323
Dorsch, H. 450
Dorscher, M. 119
Dorsey, C. 423
Dorsey, L. 340
Dorsey, R. 156
Dorsey, W. 386

Dortch, Mrs. W. 29
Dorwart, L. 252
Dory, C. 21
Dose, B. 253
Doss, A. 202
Doster, H. 323
Doster, J. 187
Doten, K. 144
Dotson, J. 336
Dotson, J. 388
Doty, B. 282
Doty, C. 346
Dotzenrod, H. 221
Doucet, E. 267
Doud, Mrs. J. 423
Doud, M. 203
Dougan, Mrs. E. 25
Doughney, J. 292
Douglas, A. 185
Douglas, F. 33
Douglas, J. 12
Douglas, N. 185
Douglas, S. 146
Douglass, P. 178
Doversberger, A. 99
Dow, B. 186
Dow, B. 253
Dowd, L. 241
Dowell, B. 179
Dowling, B. 227
Downer, E. 9
Downes, D. 357
Downey, J. 182
Downham, C. 27
Downie, J. 103
Downing, J. 177
Downing, M. 67
Downring, Mrs. R. 342
Downs, R. 85
Downs, Z. 28
Dowst, N. 266
Doxey, S. 194
Doyel, G. 289
Doyle, B. 253
Doyle, C. 119
Doyle, E. 139
Doyle,M. 303
Doyle, S. 136
Dozier, S. 79
Dozier, V. 288
Dozzell, Mrs. C. 29
Dragon, S. 413
Drake, H. 354
Dranginis, A. 62
Draper, B. 175
Draper, K. 414
Draper, L. 256
Draper, M. 174
Draper, R. 348
Dras, H. 321
Draves, D. 212
Dreher, Mrs. J. 379
Drell, H. 414
Drennan, M. 123
Dresden, F. 445
Dressler, M. 353
Drevo, C. 256
Drew, E. 374
Drew, R. 225
Drewniak, D. 261
Dreyer, E. 106
Dreyfus, S. 376
Drickamer, J. 371
Drier, M. 200
Drill, V. 198
Drinkhouse, D. 243
Driscoll, M. 359
Drolet, E. 196
Dropiewski, A. 205
Drouse, J. 188
Drumheiser, M. 364
Drummer, L. 118
Drwal, D. 273
Dryden, A. 81
Dube, A. 266

Duberstein, M. 300
Dubey, C. 171
Dubey, E. 170
Dubois, D. 243
DuBois, I. 51
Dubrey, Sister R. 303
Ducheneaux, L. 381
Ducheneaux, R. 385
Duchin, M. 134
Ducker, L. 182
Duckworth, D. 126
Duclos, G. 148
Dudbridge, H. 362
DuDash, M. 276
Dudek, D. 252
Dudich, A. 47
Dudley, B. 91
Dudley, D. 260
Dudley, E. 19
Dudley, J. 207
Dudley, L. 250
Dudley, M. 155
Dudley, N. 27
Dudney, D. 79
Duelk, H. 292
Duewall, D. 22
Duff, D. 320
Dufficy, A. 300
Dugan, B. 360
Duggan, R. 238
Dugger, N. 396
Duke, B. 10
Dulio, M. 284
Dull, B. 114
Dull, K. 121
Dumas, M. 170
Dumas, M. 215
DuMont, M. 211
Dumsch, E. 170
Dunaway, P. 84
Duncan, A. 379
Duncan, E. 133
Duncan, E. 135
Duncan, E. 342
Duncan, E. 378
Duncan, Mrs. H. 453
Duncan, M. 420
Duncan, Mrs. O. 440
Duncan, P. 403
Duncan, R. 259
Duncan, S. 344
Duncan, V. 27
Duncan, W. 435
Duncombe, P. 454
Dunham, B. 16
Dunham, B. 193
Dunham, N. 283
Dunham, R. 440
Dunihue, A. 36
Dunkel, L. 174
Dunker, M. 385
Dunlap, A. 436
Dunlap, B. 435
Dunlap, T. 403
Dunn, B. 114,123
Dunn, C. 17
Dunn, J. 123
Dunn, J. 257
Dunn, M. 123
Dunn, M. 344
Dunning, Sister J. 255
Dunning, L. 148
Dunnington, S. 105
Dunson, C. 245
Dunson, F. 253
Dunston, B. 283,284
Dunton, M. 434
DuPont, Mrs. C. 156
DuPont, H. 201
Dupre, L. 356
Dupre, M. 367
Dupree, B. 202
Dupreee, G. 81
Dupree, J. 290
Dupuy, M. 112

Durak, A. 186
Duran, R. 437
Duran, S. 408
Duranleau, M. 410
Durante, J. 300
Durbin, B. 216
Durbin, P. 135
Durden, M. 83
Durdy, D. 47
Dure, Mrs. L. 422
Duren, J. 443
Durgin, L. 142
Durham, B. 433
Durham, E. 338
Durham, H. 67
Durham, I. 231
Durham, P. 389
Durocher, V. 174
Durrell, J. 54
Durrenburger, L. 73
Dusa, J. 199
Dusenberry, K. 18
Dusenberry, M. 377
Dusenbury, L. 81
Dussault, A. 246
Dusseau, M. 181
Duster, A. 383
Dustin, L. 149
Dutcher, N. 183
Dutson, N. 91
Duwe, B. 130
Duzenbury, D. 203
Dvorak, P. 385
Dwane, J. 278
D'Wolf, N. 374
Dworeck, I. 275
Dwyer, B. 374,375
Dye, L. 347
Dye, S. 17
Dyer, A. 144
Dyer, B. 84
Dyer, C. 369
Dyer, G. 94
Dyer, J. 240
Dyer, L. 247
Dyer, P. 435
Dygert, H. 434
Dykeman, R. 254
Dyrdahl, B. 248
Dyre, V. 113
Dysert, M. 96

Eads, M. 54, 62
Eagle, A. 198
Eagles, A. 314
Eagleton, N. 342
Eagon, D. 322
Eaken, K. 331
Eames, L. 191
Eargle, L. 376
Earl, M. 291
Earl, T. 309
Earl, Y. 406
Earnest, B. 252
Earnhardt, A. 312
Earwood, L. 121
Easley, B. 69
Eason, A. 432
Eason, L. 399
Eason, R. 408
Eason, S. 75
East, K. 92
Eastburn, C. 283
Easterling, R. 305
Eastman, J. 175
Eastman, L. 410
Eastman, P. 304
Eastman, S. 287
Eastman, Z. 296
Easton, T. 14
Eaton, A. 336
Eaton, B. 408
Eaton, G. 93
Eaton, J. 202
Ebaugh, N. 407

Ebberts, J. 74
Ebel, M. 117
Eberhardt, J. 213
Eberhart, B. 282
Eberl, A. 450
Ebersviller, B. 222
Ebert, B. 132
Ebert, J. 429
Ebner, E. 361
Ebona, N. 16
Eccker, K. 47
Echari, D. 367
Echeita, G. 89
Eck, M. 356
Ecker, D. 449
Eckert, J. 101
Eckhardt, L. 123
Eckl, E. 11
Ecklin, E. 182
Ecklund, D. 114
Eddington, M. 134
Eddins, L. 312
Eddy, H. 255
Eddy, N. 161
Edel, S. 229
Edelen, M. 382
Eden, R. 336
Edgar, M. 301
Edgerton, M. 194
Edgington, M. 236
Edmond, A. 239
Edmondson, B. 427
Edmondson, B. 434
Edmondson, S. 72
Edmunds, N. 213
Edo, M. 92
Edsall, Mrs. W. 413
Edson, B. 251
Edstrom, M. 188
Edward, M. 209
Edwards, A. 338
Edwards, B. 9
Edwards, B. 351
Edwards, D. 311
Edwards, D. 372
Edwards, F. 414
Edwards, G. 214
Edwards, I. 340
Edwards, J. 119
Edwards, J. 297
Edwards, M. 14
Edwards, M. 17
Edwards, M. 183
Edwards, M. 195
Edwards, M. 414
Edwards, P. 350
Edwards, S. 253
Edwards, T. 312
Efird, Mrs. P. 308
Egan, C. 222
Egeland, L. 30
Egenes, S. 107,121
Egert, S. 219
Eggert, E. 363
Eggle, D. 198
Eggleston, P. 396
Eggleston, Mrs. R. 422
Egrass, A. 14
Egress, A. 15
Ehlerding, A. 101
Ehlers, S. 318
Ehlert, L. 194
Ehlich, J. 380
Ehll, G. 243
Ehmke, S. 229
Ehrhardt, M. 402
Ehrlich, P. 93
Eichenberg, L. 188
Eichenberger, J. 252
Eichman, P. 52
Eicholtz, X. 413
Eichorn, J. 181
Eidson, Mrs. J. 233
Eiland, F. 286
Eilts, L. 115

Eisenberg, D. 258
Eisenbraun, V. 385
Eisenfeld, A. 210
Eisenhart, J. 16
Eisler, Mrs. E. 283
Eisner, D. 299
Eisner, G. 315
Ek, S. 437
Ekholt, E. 247
Ekstam, F. 106
Elam, W. 26
Elben, H. 119
Elder, A. 393
Elder, B. 181
Elder, E. 26
Elder, S. 357
Elders, J. 29
Eldredge, M. 401
Elenbaas, J. 195
Elias, M. 21
Elit, I. 222
Elizey, H. 284
Elkin, G. 317
Elkins, P. 148
Elkis, N. 282
Ellard, Mrs. J. 233
Ellenberger, V.M. 193
Eller, F. 452
Elliker, I. 278
Ellingson, I. 219
Ellington, A. 9
Ellington, J. 153
Elliot, M. 283
Elliott, A. 76
Elliott, C. 292
Elliott, D. 166
Elliott, D. 436
Elliott, E. 369
Elliott, H. 106
Elliott, N. 297
Ellis, C. 395
Ellis, D. 93
Ellis, D. 235
Ellis, F. 91
Ellis, Mrs. F. 380
Ellis, G. 72
Ellis, G. 145
Ellis, G. 390
Ellis, L. 449
Ellis, M. 100
Ellis, M. 156
Ellis, Mrs. P. 403
Ellis, S. 204
Ellison, B. 202
Ellison, C. 331
Ellison, I. 36
Ellison, P. 43
Ellison, S. 64
Elliston, L. 210
Ellman, D. 34
Ellsmore, E. 361
Ellwood, D. 121
Elmore, Mrs. C. 422
Elmore, J. 402
Elmore, M. 258
Elrod, I. 252
Elson, J. 12
Elston, P. 274
Elwood, R. 114
Ely, K. 288
Elzinga, J. 177
Emanuel, L. 123
Emard, G. 317
Embrey, E. 117
Embry, M. 136
Embry, M. 137
Emerick, P. 197
Emerson, B. 435
Emerson, C. 431
Emerson, F. 414
Emerson, M. 454
Emerton, S. 255
Emery, N. 211
Emmett, G. 21
Emmons, J. 174

Emmons, L. 54
Emory, A. 294
Emory, E. 66
Empie, K. 345
Encelewski, H. 367
Enderli, B. 394
Enemann, M. 208
Enersen, E. 253
Engdahl, M. 247
Engel, H. 129
Engel, M. 51
Engelbart, M. 110
Engelby, B. 229
Engeleiter, S. 443
Engels, B. 223
Engelsen, E. 225
Engesser, M. 219
Enget, G. 316
England, M. 91
Engle, H. 331
Engle, H. 436
Engle, L. 208
Englemann, T. 354
English, J. 334
English, M. 415
Ennis, E. 372
Ennis, H. 373
Eno, M. 157
Enos, C. 386
Enquist, D. 385
Enroth, J. 164
Enterline, J. 359
Entrikin, Mrs. J. 436
Entwisle, E. 420
Enyeart, V. 47
Epperly, J. 112
Epperson, J. 244
Epple, J. 179
Epps, M. 328
Eppse, A. 452
Epstein, M. 283
Epstein, M. 449
Epton, K. 434
Erb, D. 113
Erb, E. 57
Erb, M. 190
Erber, S. 205
Ercius, H. 77
Erckenbrack, E. 229
Ercolano, E. 282
Erdley, J. 363
Erdman, G. 161
Erdman, I. 429
Erdman, J. 450
Ericksen, A. 435
Ericksen, E. 408,409
Ericksen, R. 257
Erickson, B. 435
Erickson, E. 189
Erickson, E. 225
Erickson, F. 175
Ericson, M. 267
Erickson, M. 336
Erikson, N. 253,254
Erickson, P. 425,435
Erickson, R. 317
Erickson, S. 68
Ericson, G. 41
Eriquez, A. 60
Erlanger, M. 64
Erley, M. 57
Erlick, A. 106
Ernst, E. 326
Ernst, M. 76
Ernston, E. 223
Erre, R. 328
Erschabek, K. 452
Erskine, C. 348
Ervin, J. 73
Erwin, A. 148
Erwin, N. 156
Escobar, L. 403
Escudero, L. 286
Eskens, E. 451
Eskola, E. 170

Esmailka, M. 13
Espinola, M. 58
Essary, O. 206
Estell, B. 7
Estenson, J. 246
Estep, G. 23
Estep, M. 205
Esterly, A. 244
Estes, D. 391
Estes, L. 289
Esteves, C. 67
Ethen, G. 354
Etheridge, N. 10
Etie, E. 46
Eu, M. 30
Eubanks, E. 136
Eubanks, L. 399
Euse, M. 250
Evangelista, D. 358
Evans, A. 46
Evans, A. 158
Evans, A. 197
Evans, B. 29
Evans, B. 71
Evans, B. 122
Evans, B. 277
Evans, C. 214
Evans, C. 334
Evans, D. 315
Evans, E. 285
Evans, E. 377
Evans, F. 87
Evans, F. 253
Evans, H. 318
Evans, J. 399
Evans, M. 20
Evans, M. 67
Evans, M. 122
Evans, Mrs. M. 232
Evans, M. 300
Evans, M. 412
Evans, N. 19
Evans, P. 111
Evans, Mrs. W. 215
Evatt, P. 71
Evelti, M. 409
Evenson, L. 223
Everard, M. 181
Everett, B. 120,123
Everett, E. 302
Everett, Mrs. M. 343
Everette, E. 390
Everhardt, M. 311
Eversole, E. 100
Everson, R. 317
Everts, S. 91
Evilsizer, K. 288
Evins, M. 404
Ewald, E. 274
Ewald, Mrs. H. 403
Ewen, P. 60
Ewer, F. 407
Ewing, M. 88,92
Exber, D. 257
Ey, M. 303
Eye, W. 114
Eykamp, R. 104
Eyre, J. 258
Eyre, L. 178
Ezell, A. 257
Ezzell, Mrs. M. 403

Faber, D. 302
Fabiano, J. 58
Fadeley, N. 345,353
Faeh, B. 431
Fagioli, C. 359
Fahan, G. 109
Fahle, P. 343
Fahlen, D. 216
Fahrion, D. 51
Failor, B. 121
Fair, F. 240
Fair, H. 439
Fairbanks, L. 148

Fairchild, O. 25
Fairless, A. 32
Falco, K. 2
Falconer, D. 423
Fales, M. 191
Falkowski, A. 275
Faller, N. 434
Fallin, J. 141
Fallon, M. 293
Falls, J. 308
Falter, A. 93
Falvey, R. 373
Fancher, H. 425
Fannin, D. 21
Fant, Mrs. A. 380
Fantasia, M. 159
Farabaugh, R. 358
Farber, D. 117
Fargher, L. 404
Faris, J. 237
Farkas, K. 57
Farkas, L. 15
Farley, D. 275
Farley, D. 284
Farley, F. 405
Farley, J. 268
Farmer, P. 424
Farmer, V. 40
Farner, P. 77
Farnham, Mrs. C. 85
Farnsworth, B. 389
Farquhar, M. 157
Farr, L. 336
Farrand, J. 230
Farrar, J. 424
Farrell, C. 123
Farrell, J. 64
Farris, K. 255
Fasching, L. 318
Fashbaugh, M. 174
Fassina, H. 9
Fast, R. 320
Fateley, E. 132
Fatland, S. 352
Fatone, N. 300
Faubion, J. 343
Faught, R. 400
Faulis, D. 54
Faulkner, H. 442
Faulkner, J. 61
Faulkner, N. 82
Faust, M. 120
Faust, S. 11
Faux, A. 117
Fawcett, B. 183
Fawcett, M. 337
Feagan, E. 402
Fearnow, J. 126
Fears, L. 339
Feasey, C. 435
Featherer, E. 284
Fedon, B. 207
Feeley, T. 409
Feeney, D. 258
Feeney, G. 146
Feiber, E. 332
Feidelson, K. 63
Feigelson, M. 157
Feigenbaum, G. 21
Feigenbaum, R. 62
Feiger, A. 183
Feighner, J. 128
Feinberg, A. 303
Feingold, B. 301
Feingold, P. 301
Feinstein, D. 31
Feis, P. 255, 256
Feit, W. 253
Felcher, N. 295
Feld, Mrs. A. 284
Feldman, S. 301
Feldpausch, M. 206
Feldt, L. 215
Felgenhauer, F. 321
Felger, G. 450

Felker, E. 95
Felkner, V. 343
Feller, C. 199
Fellinger, Mrs. L. 108
Fellman, R. 347
Fellows, J. 414
Fellows, V. 446
Felt, B. 408
Felt, D. 408
Felt, J. 73
Felton, B. 407
Felton, D. 80
Fend, B. 183
Fender, H. 198
Fenical, J. 237
Fenn, M. 435
Fennel, I. 384
Fenner, J. 272
Fenner, N. 243
Fenske, J. 224
Fenstermacher, E. 249
Fenwick, M. 5
Ferguson, A. 196
Ferguson, B. 40
Ferguson, Mrs. B. 224
Ferguson, E. 29
Ferguson, F. 201
Ferguson, G. 172
Ferguson, Mrs. H. 29
Ferguson, Mrs. H. 244
Ferguson, J. 24
Ferguson, M. 153
Ferguson, M. 191
Ferguson, M. 15, 16
Ferguson, R. 166
Ferguson, S. 62
Ferguson, V. 57
Fernandez, P. 408
Feron, R. 385
Ferria, M. 116
Ferrie, N. 374
Ferris, E. 63
Ferris, E. 193
Ferris, E. 411
Ferry, S. 414
Ferschweiler, Sister M. 436
Fersh, M. 412
Fesnick, C. 173
Fessler, L. 449
Festinger, T. 303
Fetter, A. 58
Fetterman, E. 62
Fettes, M. 290
Fetty, D. 320
Fetzner, A. 97
Feves, B. 353
Fewins, V. 189
Fiala, K. 15
Fiedler, V. 113
Fiedler, V. 123
Fieghenne, R. 153
Fieker, L. 240
Field, M. 145
Field, M. 267
Fields, D. 157
Fields, E. 357
Fields, J. 434
Fields, K. 322
Fife, B. 330
Fifield, M. 265
Fike, C. 180
Fili, J. 232
Filiberti, M. 31
Filipowics, R. 79
Filippo, F. 375
Fillis, R. 202
Filter, C. 252
Finberg, S. 221
Finch, B. 307
Finch, R. 203
Finch, S. 430
Finch, W. 294
Findlay, B. 452
Fine, R. 436
Fineberg, S. 278

Finger, D. 189
Fink, D. 221
Fink, E. 309
Fink, F. 149
Fink, Mrs. J. 312
Fink, P. 244
Fink, R. 242
Finkbeiner, S. 167
Finkelhor, M. 370
Finkenbinder, C. 100
Finlan, P. 203
Finley, B. 77
Finley, B. 250
Finley, J. 268
Finn, J. 241
Finn, R. 20
Finnegan, K. 148
Finnegan, M. 302
Finnegan, Sister R. 79
Finneran, E. 243
Finnerty, M. 165
Finney, F. 252
Finney, J. 124
Finnigan, P. 144
Finnila, D. 180
Finnin, V. 129
Finseth, L. 223
Finucan, J. 363
Fiorentino, C. 442
Fiorot, L. 60
Firmage, M. 408
Firminhac, L. 220
Firovich, S. 226
First, L. 183
Fischbach, D. 321
Fischer, D. 452
Fischer, E. 186
Fischer, E. 421
Fischer, M. 223
Fischer, S. 253
Fiscus, C. 114
Fish, S. 290
Fishback, C. 100
Fishback, E. 51
Fishburn, P. 352
Fisher, A. 38
Fisher, D. 368
Fisher, L. 19
Fisher, L. 95
Fisher, M. 89
Fisher, M. 129
Fisher, O. 316
Fisher, S. 139
Fisher, S. 333
Fisher, V. 244
Fisher, Z. 111
Fishman, J. 56
Fisk, M. 303
Fitch, E. 449
Fitch, M. 343
Fitton, H. 374
Fitts, O. 391
Fitzgerald, Sister D. 62,63
Fitzgerald, F. 290
Fitzgerald, G. 253
Fitzgerald, G. 301
Fitzgerald, K. 304
Fitzgerald, M. 445
Fitzgerald, R. 454
Fitzhugh, C. 26
Fitzhugh, J. 454
Fitzloff, R. 219
Fitzpatrick, G. 188
Fitzpatrick, J. 278
Fitzpatrick, J. 293
Fitzpatrick, M. 236
Fitzpatrick, M. 295
Fitzsimmons, M. 220
Fix, H. 318
Fizer, B. 109
Flack, D. 408
Flack, V. 455
Flagel, M. 334
Flahaut, M. 341
Flahive, E. 165

Flanagan, C. 384
Flanagan, J. 290
Flanagan, J. 296
Flanagan, N. 261
Flanagin, M. 22
Flanery, P. 178
Flannery, A. 411
Fleck, B. 255
Fleck, G. 371
Fleck, J. 192
Fleig, E. 361
Fleihman, P. 243
Fleischmann, I. 429
Fleming, E. 134
Fleming, L. 67
Fleming, L. 130
Flemming, B. 115
Flemming, M. 232
Flesner, S. 385
Fletcher, A. 214
Fletcher, A. 405
Fletcher, B. 436
Fletcher, F. 174
Flickinger, F. 183
Flint, A. 115
Flippin, Mrs. G. 423
Flippin, W. 436
Flipse, A. 302
Flocchini, E. 353
Floden, A. 384
Flohr, J. 255
Flood, J. 112
Flores, C. 18
Flores, N. 449
Florucci, F. 412
Flory, Mrs. D. 415
Flowers, D. 336
Floyd, K. 233
Flynn, A. 25
Flythe, D. 81
Foerch, M. 215
Foga, E. 282
Fogarty, C. 227
Fogelberg, O. 219
Fojtik, K. 169
Fokken, P. 384
Folckemer, L. 25
Folds, J. 83
Foley, B. 429
Foley, E. 260
Foley, J. 272
Folger, M. 326
Folkers, M. 49
Folkerts, K. 385
Follett, B. 52
Follett, N. 95
Folsum, E. 449
Folta, J. 415
Foltz, A. 50
Foltz, A. 60
Folz, M. 134
Fong, L. ,259
Fonseca, M. 158
Fontaine, A. 149
Fontanini, T. 120
Fontenot, H. 139
Fontenot, M. 140
Fontenot, P. 141
Fontes, J. 395
Fonvielle, M. 313
Foote, D. 361
Foote, E. 208
Foote, H. 171
Foote, M. 256
Foote, V. 21
Footit, J. 160
Foran, M. 360
Forbes,M. 186
Forbes, P. 123
Forbes, V. 139
Forbes, W. 380
Force, P. 194
Ford, A. 80
Ford, C. 198
Ford, C. 359

Ford, E. 211
Ford, E. 340
Ford, F. 247
Ford, G. 214
Ford, J. 91
Ford, J. 255
Ford, N. 79
Ford, O. 86
Ford, V. 161
Fordham, P. 154
Fordyce, A. 301,302,303
Fordyce, M. 190
Forella, J. 62
Foreman, C. 2
Forer, L. 370
Foreman, Mrs. E. 422
Foresee, G. 340
Forest, J. 166
Forget, R. 194
Forkell, E. 294
Forner, L. 188
Forney, D. 277
Forrest, B. 176
Forrest, P. 19
Forrest, V. 436
Forrester, E. 353
Forsberg, C. 28
Forscha, P. 47
Forster, J. 453
Forston, A. 120
Forsyth, J. 336
Forsythe, B. 335
Forsythe, M. 217
Forsythe, M. 415
Fortier, R. 149
Fortino, B. 169
Fortna, L. 412
Fortney, E. 440
Fortson, E. 425,436
Forzano, M. 75
Foskey, H. 67
Fosness, A. 315
Fossitt, M. 330
Foster, Mrs. B. 28
Foster, B. 331
Foster, B. 400
Foster, C. 122
Foster, E. 385
Foster, G. 404
Foster, Mrs. J. 143
Foster, J. 305
Foster, Mrs. J. 307
Foster, L. 132
Foster, L. 250
Foster, L. 441
Foster, M. 15
Foster, M. 137
Foster, N. 96
Foster, R. 145
Foster, S. 321
Fouch, L. 331
Foudy, M. 272
Found, M. 261
Fountain, L. 220
Fountain, M. 354
Fountain, R. 47
Fourman, J. 388
Fournier, B. 172
Fousek, A. 385
Foutz, P. 257
Fowler, C. 316
Fowler, D. 375
Fowler, M. 253
Fowler, P. 422
Fowlkes, C. 442
Fox, A. 14
Fox, A. 184
Fox, A. 240
Fox, C. 201
Fox, C. 254
Fox, E. 28
Fox, E. 50
Fox, G. 120
Fox, G. 244
Fox, I. 292

Fox, J. 359
Fox, L. 321
Fox, M. 285
Fox, P. 201
Fox, P. 294
Fox, R. 69, 79
Fox, V. 212
Foxworthy, D. 252
Foy, B. 440
Frahm, R. 253
Fraley, N. 392
Frampton, A. 66
Frances, Sister H. 92
Francis, D. 349
Francis, E. 149
Francis, V. 147
Franciscus, M. 303
Frangiamore, Mrs. R. 85
Frank, B. 448
Frank, C. 413
Frank, Mrs. F. 254
Frank, J. 2
Frank, J. 343
Frank, M. 353
Frank, N. 16
Frank, P. 70
Frank, V. 120
Franke, J. 296
Franke, R. 239
Franke, S. 424
Frankenstein, M. 205
Frankin, V. 240
Franklin, L. 51
Franklin, L. 360
Franklin, M. 23
Franklin, R. 220
Franklin, S. 85
Frankmore, S. 51
Franks, V. 284
Franquet, R. 156
Franson, L. 91
Frantzen, J. 239
Franze, J. 103
Fraser, A. 2
Fraser, C. 247
Fraser, J. 109
Fraser, K. 384
Fraser, K. 427
Fraser, M. 71
Fratini, J. 373
Frazelle, D. 90
Frazer, Mrs. E. 85
Frazer, J. 275
Frazier, A. 380
Frazier, D. 23
Frazier, F. 42
Frazier, L. 339
Frazier, M. 26
Frazier, R. 420
Frederick, L. 407
Fredericks, M. 121
Frederickson, C. 196
Freedlander, L. 156
Freedman, C. 449
Freedman, S. 77
Freel, E. 176
Freel, M. 123
Freeland, V. 192
Freeman, B. 255
Freeman, C. 71
Freeman, C. 112
Freeman, C. 200
Freeman, C. 275
Freeman, F. 420
Freeman, I. 408
Freeman, L. 243
Freeman, M. 146
Freeman, M. 187
Freeman, M. 210
Freeman, M. 231
Freeman, Mrs. R. 317
Freese, L. 453
Freiman, S. 245
Frelinghuysen, Mrs. F. 283
Fremering, L. 13

Fremont, R. 330
French, H. 344
French, I. 130
French, J. 47
French, P. 423
French, V. 121
Frenzen, A. 123
Fresquez, D. 288
Frey, E. 275
Frey, H. 116
Frey, S. 196
Frick, C. 244
Fricke, M. 96
Fricke, M. 253
Friedlan, Mrs. L. 255
Friedlander, B. 301
Friedlander, M. 299
Friedman, K. 156
Friedman, L. 269,272,284
Friedman, L. 271
Friedman, Mrs. S. 85
Friefeld, L. 385
Friendly, B. 376
Fries, E. 369
Friesen, S. 251
Friess, S. 206
Friga, R. 241
Frink, B. 6
Frisbie, C. 178
Frisby, Mrs. R. 454
Frisch, S. 159
Fristoe, L. 78
Fritchie, U. 91
Fritchoff, S. 91
Fritschi, R. 322
Fritz, K. 187
Fritze, D. 176
Fritzell, S. 314
Frizzell, J. 157
Frizzell, M. 261
Frizzell, N. 453
Frizzell, P. 23
Froeb, A. 20
Froehler, F. 224
Frolander, R. 453
Frolich, J. 435
Fromherz, M. 436
Frost, C. 352
Frost, E. 215
Frost, Mrs. M. 283
Frost, M. 330
Frost, S. 95
Frost, S. 136
Frownfelter, K. 228
Frucci, P. 216
Frudden, S. 120
Fruechtenicht, S. 105
Fruin, C. 343
Fry, C. 255
Fry, D. 115
Fry, V. 323
Frye, E. 21
Frye, F. 205
Frye, H. 352
Fryer, E. 389
Fryett, J. 121
Fugazy, Sister M.I. 301
Fuhrhop, E. 197
Fuhrmann, D. 189
Fujitani, S. 435
Fulford, J. 33
Fulford, L. 8
Fulkerson, S. 396
Fullenwider, K. 210
Fuller, A. 51
Fuller, D. 233
Fuller, D. 340
Fuller, E. 203
Fuller, E. 397
Fuller, M. 37
Fuller, N. 137
Fullerton, E. 192
Fullom, D. 358
Fulstone, Mrs. R. 258
Fulton, C. 398

Fulton, J. 435
Fulton, M. 237
Fultz, E. 99
Funderburk, M. 83
Funk, G. 428
Funk, J. 117
Funk, V. 245
Funkhouser, S. 454
Furman, M. 223
Furr, L. 25
Furst, B. 282
Fuss, L. 189

Gabbert, S. 231
Gabriaudt, C. 38
Gabriel, D. 121
Gabriel, G. 441
Gabriel, T. 337
Gaby, R. 99
Gadoury, D. 373
Gaeden, L. 251
Gage, B. 261
Gage, H. 214
Gage, Mrs. L. 302
Gage, M. 112
Gaglione, E. 375
Gagne, E. 148
Gagnon, D. 267
Gagnon, G. 261
Gagnon, N. 261
Gaia, P. 387
Gaido, M. 37
Gaines, D. 203
Gaines, J. 46
Gaines, M. 230
Gaines, T. 381
Gainey, B. 379
Galante, J. 304
Galanti, P. 422
Galarosa, A. 437
Galbreath, D. 316
Galbreath, M. 302
Gale, I. 427
Gale, R. 296
Galer, E. 353
Galer, M. 80
Galila, P. 13
Gallagher, D. 225
Gallagher, J. 146
Gallagher, V. 302
Gallant, R. 147
Gallardo, P. 21
Gallegos, O. 407
Galleher, J. 17
Gallinger, M. 189
Gallo, G. 127
Gallogly, F. 375
Gallow, J. 296
Galloway, S. 378
Galloway, Mrs. V. 82
Gallup, M. 379
Galvanek, A. 185
Galvin, J. 333,335
Galvin, M. 91
Galyen, E. 25
Gamber, P. 359
Gambino, J. 289
Gamble, A. 11
Gamel, K. 242
Gammage, D. 399
Gandy, E. 231
Gandy, M. 24
Ganley, B. 261
Gann, B. 258
Gannett, A. 159
Gannon, M. 298
Gannon, M. 361
Ganoung, L. 20
Gans, A. 285
Gant, M. 234
Gantley, C. 137
Ganz, A. 225
Garbarino, J. 258
Garber, E. 106
Garber, Mrs. S. 368

Garceau, J. 434
Garcia, E. 286
Garcia, H. 52
Garcia, J. 288
Gard, B. 40
Gard, B. 102
Gardecki, C. 370
Gardenhire, M. 387
Gardiner, E. 184
Gardiner, M. 347
Gardner, D. 449
Gardner, E. 260
Gardner, G. 178
Gardner, G. 239
Gardner, Mrs. J. 29
Gardner, J. 161
Gardner, J. 409
Gardner, M. 181
Gardner, M. 242
Gardner, M. 301
Gardner, P. 173
Gardner, V. 155
Garey, J. 255
Garland, F. 424
Garland, M. 414
Garlock, J. 113
Garnder, S. 175
Garner, S. 241
Garner, Mrs. T. 424
Garofalo, I. 60
Garransson, M. 245
Garren, M. 10
Garren, P. 351
Garret, B. 245
Garrett, H. 440
Garrett, Mrs. J. 344
Garrett, M. 106
Garrett, M. 441
Garrett, N. 342
Garrison, M. 404
Garrison, Mrs. R. 341
Garsow, E. 444
Gartell, H. 328
Garten, L. 122
Garven, S. 283
Garvey, B. 164
Garvey, D. 185
Garvey, E. 271
Garvey, K. 276
Garvey, L. 156
Garvie, F. 436
Garvin, J. 415
Garvin, M. 457
Garwood, B. 337
Gasche, G. 125
Gasco, M. 179
Gashun, M. 73
Gaskill, M. 286
Gasper, M. 187
Gasperich, C. 130
Gass, A. 35
Gastl, D. 131
Gaston, S. 397
Gately, M. 47
Gates, B. 82
Gates, E. 344
Gates, M. 437
Gates, R. 67
Gatewood, D. 362
Gatrel, C. 241
Gaudette, M. 143
Gaukroger, V. 428
Gaul, N. 363
Gaupp, J. 273
Gauthier, G. 170
Gauthier, J. 430
Gauthier, M. 284
Gauthier, M. 411
Gauazzi, H. 368
Gaw, L. 362
Gay, H. 259
Gayle, M. 35
Geadelmann, P. 123
Gearhard, L. 202
Gearhart, R. 170

Geary, C. 332
Geasler, V. 190
Geba, E. 295
Gebel, J. 283
Gebhard, Sister M. 445
Gebhart, M. 340
Gedwardt, R. 446
Gee, L. 372
Gee, V. 408
Geen, P. 64
Gehlbach, C. 415
Geier, S. 225
Geiger, A. 360
Geiger, E. 284
Geiger, M. 281
Geiger, N. 197
Geiger, S. 277
Geilczuk, M. 187
Geisel, B. 439
Geisler, M. 206
Geissert, K. 43
Gelfman, M. 46
Gelman, E. 152
Gemmell, G. 341
Gender, J. 270
Genderen, A. 384
Geno, T. 231
Genry, K. 255
Genson, S. 171
Gentleman, J. 107
Gentley, B. 84
Gentry, B. 19
Gentry, J. 8
Gentz, H. 199
Geo-Karis, A. 94
George, A. 376
George, A. 448
George, D. 155
George, J. 17
George, J. 179
George, J. 239
George, K. 406
George, M. 87
George, M. 355
George, M. 435
George, P. 139
George, S. 14
George, S. 24
George,S. 336
George, T. 14
George, W. 357
Gephart, E. 334
Gerber, G. 119
Gerber, J. 238
Gerberich, L. 334
Gerencher, A. 222
Gerhardt, M. 285
Gerhardt, R. 329
Gerke, B. 194
Gerlach, C. 252
Gerlach, D. 383
Germain, A. 215
German, H. 385
German, H. 450
German, L. 392
Gerow, E. 259
Gerrard, J. 430
Gerrard, M. 232
Gerrish, J. 103
Gertz, R. 197
Gerweck, A. 182
Geske, S. 256
Gest, M. 276
Gestrin, D. 89
Getzwiller, P. 17
Geuder, P. 258
Geyer, J. 199
Geyer, M. 179
Gherardi, G. 42
Ghere, D. 382
Gholston, B. 313
Giacomelli, V. 206
Giannotti, A. 259
Giaquinta, J. 122
Giar, N. 176

Giardino, C. 71
Giaudrone, M. 428
Gibb, S. 446
Gibboney, D. 423
Gibbons, C. 74
Gibbons, C. 351
Gibbs, A. 419
Gibbs, B. 332
Gibbs, C. 140
Gibbs, E. 159,163
Gibbs, G. 312
Gibbs, H. 312
Gibbs, J. 372
Gibbs, N. 37
Gibbs, P. 435
Gibney, P. 347
Gibson, A. 189
Gibson, A. 274
Gibson, B. 380
Gibson, D. 112
Gibson, H. 116
Gibson, H. 220
Gibson, L. 249
Gibson, M. 110
Gibson, M. 216
Gibson, P. 214
Gideon, L. 437
Gidlund, R. 430
Gier, M. 187
Gierentanner, D. 313
Gierke, M. 182
Giese, C. 46
Giezentanner, D. 306
Gifford, I. 178
Gift, G. 153
Gignac, J. 18
Gigray, M. 91
Gil, G. 413,414,415
Gilbert, A. 49
Gilbert, A. 214
Gilbert, B. 329
Gilbert, D. 312
Gilbert, D. 322
Gilbert, E. 329
Gilbert, Mrs. J. 85
Gilbert, P. 130
Gilbertson,M. 419
Gilbo, D. 212
Gilboux, A. 358
Gilbreth, D. 26
Gilbride, H. 195
Gilchrist, I. 49
Gildea, E. 374
Gildow, W. 328
Giles, J. 337
Giles, K. 27
Gilette, G. 216
Gill, Mrs. A. 28
Gill, B. 142
Gill, B. 275
Gill, B. 438,439
Gill, D. 386
Gill, Mrs. L. 139
Gill, L. 177
Gill, M. 29
Gill, R. 396
Gillard, A. 57
Gile, I. 177
Gillenwater, D. 420
Gillespie, N. 295
Gillespie, V. 73
Gillett, L. 185
Gillette, H. 355
Gillette, J. 415
Gilliam, M. 423
Gilliam, S. 452
Gilliland, M. 330
Gillson, M. 223
Gilman, M. 67
Gilman, M. 334
Gilmer, B. 328
Gilmore, A. 363
Gilmore, B. 189
Gilmore, B. 429
Gilmore, J. 253

Gilmore, M.   373
Gilmore, S.   354
Gilmour, L.   352
Gilroy, B.   375
Gilstrap, M.   397
Ginalski, G.   374
Ginder, B.   109
Gingerich, I.   324
Gingrich, O.   198
Ginnold, E.   444
Ginop, L.   192
Giovinazzo, S.   329
Gipe, A.   128
Gipp, J.   294
Girbach, R.   182
Girolamo, S.   42
Girone,J.   417
Giroux, A.   148
Giroux, B.   413
Girven, J.   195
Gisel, E.   112
Giss, G.   19
Gittelsohn, S.   352
Gittler, J.   122
Given, P.   442
Given, Mrs. W.   10
Givens, B.   436
Gladfelter, V.   284
Glady, R.   172
Glasgow, J.   121
Glasheen, M.   375
Glasper, H.   408
Glass, E.   397
Glass, M.   377
Glasscock, J.   138
Glasse, L.   289, 302.
Glassman, C.   149
Glassman, P.   296
Gleason, M.   361
Gleason, S.   199
Gleeson, A.   200
Gleeson, H.   120
Gleeson, J.   258
Glendening, E.   103
Glenn, D.   134
Glenn, S.   71
Glenn, V.   66
Glennon, G.   164
Glick, B.   13
Glickert, E.   243
Glisson, D.   79
Glock, M.   340
Glode, K.   451
Glossbrenner, E.   391
Glover, H.   252
Glover, M.   78
Glover, M.   80
Glover, M.   388
Glover, P.   256, 259
Glowacki, T.   209
Glynn, L.   183
Glynn, M.   58
Godde, H.   204
Godejohn, D.   141
Godet, D.   139
Godfrey, L.   405
Godfrey, V.   139
Godwin, B.   85
Godwin, J.   310
Goebel, B.   215
Goehring, D.   229
Goertzen, I.   435
Goettman, C.   333
Goettsch, S.   21
Goetz, B.   454
Goetz, J.   180
Goetze, M.   155
Goetze, M.   179
Goff, A.   447
Goff, C.   266
Goff, E.   261
Goforth, R.   288
Goggins, J.   376
Gohlke, A.   211
Goike, G.   177

Goins, O.   422
Gojack, M.   256
Golab, D.   344
Golay, S.   90
Golbek, S.   347
Golberg, D.   434
Goldberg, E.   140
Goldberg, H.   62
Golden, L.   156
Goldenbogen, F.   188
Golder, J.   75
Golding, M.   281
Golding, V.   99
Goldman, B.   413
Goldman, B.   414
Goldman, C.   257
Goldman, J.   79
Goldman, J.   122
Goldman, L.   122
Goldner, V.   429
Goldrick, C.   375
Goldsmith, C.   176
Goldsmith, E.   283
Goldsmith, J.   156,157
Goldsmith, P.   20
Goldsmith, R.   420
Goldsmith, R.   441
Goldstein, S.   61
Goldwater, M.   150
Golin, M.   273
Gollinger, O.   183
Gomes, N.   256
Gometro, G.   276
Gomez, B.   285
Gomez, C.   395
Gomez, F.   255
Gonzales, E.   453
Gonzales, L.   255
Gonzales, L.   288
Gonzales, M.   62,63
Gonzales, P.   394
Gonzalez, Mrs. J.   400
Gonzales, R.   259
Gooch, M.   307
Good, P.   29
Goodall, E.   317
Goode, M.   159
Goode, S.   216
Goode, W.   50
Goodenberger, M.   254,256
Goodhue, M.   290
Gooding, D.   153
Goodman, J.   62
Goodman, M.   408
Goodman, R.   282
Goodnight, J.   400
Goodrich, A.   35
Goodrich, E.   296
Goodrich, E.   436
Goodrich, Mrs. G.   254
Goodrich, L.   294
Goodrich, P.   174
Goodrich, P.   443
Goodridge, R.   203
Goodroad, R.   255
Goodson, B.   397
Goodwill, Mrs. E.   448
Goodwin, C.   148
Goodwin, D.   55
Goodwin, K.   142
Goodwin, S.   27
Goolsby, M.   81
Gorden, D.   126
Gorden, J.   110
Gorder, A.   318
Gordon, A.   261
Gordon, C.   58
Gordon, D.   431
Gordon, E.   70
Gordon, E.   339
Gordon, J.   300
Gordon, J.   409
Gordon, M.   104
Gordon, M.   115
Gordon, M.   197

Gordon, M.   423
Gordon, R.   75, 78
Gordon, S.   230
Gore, E.   423
Gore, L.   307
Gorenstein, Dr. S.   302
Gorham, L.   156, 157
Gorr, A.   293
Gorsuch, A.   45
Gorsuch, H.   386
Gorum, N.   6
Gosnell, A.   380
Gossin, I.   295
Gottovi, K.   307
Gottschalk, E.   258
Gottschalk, G.   259
Gottshalk, A.   369
Goudreau, V.   180
Gough, E.   141
Goulais, E.   215
Gould, D.   92
Gould, J.   71
Gould, K.   273
Gould, R.   114
Gould, S.   424,436
Gourley, D.   126
Gourneau, J.   181
Gouthro, M.   420
Grabill, S.   183
Graboski, E.   58
Grace, B.   41
Grace, F.   164
Grady, T.   101
Grady, V.   244
Graf, K.   123
Graff, M.   134
Gragg, E.   99
Gragg, J.   132
Graham, A.   15
Graham, A.   148
Graham, B.   198
Graham, I.   232
Graham, J.   293
Graham, K.   110
Graham, L.   409
Graham, M.   413
Graham, P.   2
Graham, P.   146
Graham, P.   413
Graham, S.   28
Graham, S.   159,161
Grahl, E.   317
Grahn, E.   93
Gramkow, Mrs. E.   156
Gramlich, C.   253
Grande, C.   373
Grande, M.   62
Grange, H.   315
Granitz, W.   77
Granmo, L.   248
Grannes, J.   218,220
Grant, A.   301
Grant, D.   227
Grant, E.   123
Grant, G.   146
Grant, M.   90
Grant, M.   244
Grant, S.   109
Grantham, S.   233
Grapengeter, A.   117
Grassbaugh, M.   325
Grasso, C.   75
Grasso, E.   53
Gravatt, N.   368
Grave, M.   450
Graves, A.   86
Graves, D.   354
Graves, J.   102
Graves, M.   11
Graves, T.   256
Gravink, M.   53, 62
Gray, B.   137
Gray, B.   159
Gray, D.   170
Gray, D.   242

Gray, D.   328
Gray, E.   422
Gray, Mrs. G.   317
Gray, I.   52
Gray, I.   187
Gray, L.   115
Gray, L.   301, 302
Gray, L.   302
Gray, M.   164
Gray, N.   49
Gray, R.   305
Gray, Mrs. R.   423
Gray, S.   92, 93
Gray, S.   229
Gray, T.   98
Graybill, S.   417
Grayson, B.   344
Grayson, Mrs. L.   401
Greb, W.   344
Greeben, D.   76
Green, A.   10
Green, A.   73
Green, A.   323
Green, B.   353
Green, D.   201
Green, D.   381
Green, E.   55
Green, E.   57
Green, E.   361
Green, F.   41
Green, J.   6
Green, J.   31
Green, J.   137
Green, J.   162
Green, K.   123
Green, K.   436
Green, L.   26
Green, L.   232
Green, L.   382
Green, M.   178
Green, M.   185
Green, M.   398
Green, O.   25
Green, Mrs. O.   329
Green, S.   23
Green, S.   221
Green, S.   326
Green, S.   422
Green, V.   334
Greenbacker, E.   60
Greenberg, J.   157
Greenberg, R.   374
Greenberg, S.   270
Greene, C.   446
Greene, E.   262
Greene, E.   307
Greene, F.   43
Greene, M.   436
Greene, N.   145
Greener, P.   406
Greenfield, B.   67
Greenhouse, P.   28
Greenleaf, M.   121
Greenlee, J.   306
Greeno, A.   102
Greenspun, B.   259
Greenstone, R.   269
Greenwald, G.   121
Greenwald, H.   281
Greenwood, J.   292
Greenwood, M.   49
Greenwood, M.   329
Greenwood-Adams, L.   144
Greer, C.   78
Greer, E.   233
Greer, H.   204
Greer, H.   219
Greer, J.   125
Greer, M.   255
Greer, N.   349
Gregg, M.   120
Gregory, A.   60
Gregory, A.   242
Gregory, E.   129
Gregory, Mrs. H.   29

Gregson, V. 437
Greiffendorf, S. 177
Greiner, P. 179
Greissing, K. 322
Greitzer, C. 299
Gremillion, M. 141
Gresham, A. 397
Greshaw, B. 175
Greshik, E. 317
Greshman, R. 231
Grevey, E. 288
Grey, I. 193
Griak, R. 227
Gribben, R. 175
Grida, M.. 356
Griego, F. 56
Griep, P. 227
Grier, R. 176
Griffen, M. 223
Griffin, A. 281
Griffin, C. 401
Griffin, E. 312
Griffin, F. 81
Griffin, I. 395
Griffin, L. 75
Griffin, M. 38
Griffin, M. 397
Griffin, N. 201
Griffin, P. 305
Griffin, R. 262
Griffin, Mrs. W. 85
Griffith, A. 211
Griffith, B. 400
Griffith, E. 304
Griffith, J. 452
Griffith, M. 359
Griffith, N. 325
Griffith, V. 350
Griffiths, M. 216
Griffiths, M. 291
Griger, A. 359
Griggs, B. 132
Griggs, M. 135
Grigka, C. 172
Grime, H. 375
Grimes, A. 129
Grimes, R. 371
Grimm, M. 448
Grimme, L. 98
Grims, R. 374
Grinage, A. 199
Grindle, M. 143
Griswold, Mrs. R. /413
Grizzle, M. 70
Groah, W. 285
Grobmeyer, N. 134
Groen, N. 96
Groesbeck, D. 132
Groft, R. 285
Groholski, E. 395
Groner, B. 155, 156
Gronmark, J. 192
Grooms, B. 329
Grosch, V.L. 192
Gross, J. 267
Gross, L. 247
Gross, M. 255
Grossberger, Mrs. C. 304
Grosser, A. 367
Grossinger, R. 304
Grossman, E. 67
Grossman, G. 398
Grossman, L. 216
Grossman, R. 78
Grossman, S. 284
Grotos, D. 416
Grounds, B. 19
Grove, G. 40
Groves, B. 333
Growe, J. 217
Grubb, S. 433
Gruby, V. 382
Gruger, A. 425, 437
Grund, A. 220
Grund, M. 294

Grundfest, S. 284
Grundman, M. 446
Gruwell, L. 67
Gubbins, J. 98
Guber, S. 108
Guccione, I. 237
Guderian, J. 338
Guenther, P. 427
Guenthner, B. 136
Guerard, Mrs. E. 380
Guerrette, L. 144
Guerty, J. 76
Guess, C. 16
Guidas, G. 362
Guild, E. 91
Gilherme, E. 379
Guin, J. 7
Guines, M. 422
Guinn, G. 311
Guinn, N. 15
Guinn, N. 16
Guinn, S. 197
Guisc, B. 34
Gulbranson, A. 384
Gullette, E. 153
Gulley, K. 29
Gullingsrud, H. 218
Gum, E. 419
Gumerson, J. 342
Gunby, V. 435, 437
Gundacker, E. 116
Gundell, S. 303
Gunderson, E. 246
Gunderson, E. 446
Gunderson, M. 248
Gunn, Mrs. M. 245
Gunn, P. 232
Gunningham, B. 212
Gunter, A. 6
Gunter, N. 29
Guptill, C. 144
Gupton, N. 73
Gurnsey, K. 87
Gurreiri, G. 274
Gurrister, B. 409
Gurtham, Mrs. W. 283
Gustafson, M. 61
Guthery, C. 321
Guthmiller, E. 386
Guthrie, A. 442
Gutierrez, P. 403
Gutwillig, J. 21
Guy, F. 28
Guy, M. 395
Guyette, R. 412
Guynn, I. 455
Guynup, G. 295
Guzic, V. 363
Gwaydoskey, J. 149
Gwin, R. 119
Gwinn, T. 311
Gynn, R. 322

Haaf, M. 124
Haag, A. 200
Haag, R. 277
Haan, C. 194
Haapala, A. 44
Haapapuro, C. 195
Haart, L. 52
Haas, E. 9
Haas, M. 360
Habbe, L. 384
Haberer, Mrs. J. 255
Hackett, B. 136
Hackett, G. 352
Hackett, M. 371,374,375
Hackett, R. 439
Hackman, C. 434
Hadden, J. 409
Haddix, S. 137
Haden, W. 11
Hadley, D. 234
Hadley, H. 73
Haefele, B. 131

Haefner, J. 194
Haehl, J. 35
Haffer, G. 322
Haffner, Mrs. B. 422
Haffner, W. 329
Hagadon, B. 203
Hagadone, O. 246
Hagan, L. 341
Hagedorn, G. 283
Hagen, F. 110
Hagen, L. 192
Hagen, S. 317
Hager, D. 90
Hager, I. 294
Hagerty, B. 67
Haggenmaker, M. 400
Hagglund, E. 317
Hagglund, M. 436
Hagle, J. 191
Hagmeier, D. 116
Hahnel, J. 149
Haigh, N. 430
Haight, D. 165
Haight, G. 250
Haigler, N. 25
Haik, S. 227
Halley, E. 416
Hailey, S. 244
Hain, M. 364
Haines, H. 232
Hair, E. 306
Hair, G. 84
Hair, Mrs. R. 85
Hair, S. 267
Halbert, N. 418
Halderman, M. 330
Haldiman, B. 21
Hale, F. 400
Hale, G. 125
Hale, J. 233
Hale, J. 435
Hale, M. 24
Hale, P. 431
Haley, D. 110
Haley, Mrs. J. 422
Haley, M. 153
Haley, N. 342
Hall, A. 85
Hall, A. 163
Hall, B. 378
Hall, C. 96
Hall, D. 78
Hall, D. 252
Hall, D. 287
Hall, D. 406
Hall, E. 181
Hall, G. 316
Hall, J. 154
Hall, J. 222
Hall, J. 270
Hall, K. 98, 100
Hall, L. 284
Hall, L. 418
Hall, M. 16
Hall, M. 29
Hall, M. 176
Hall, M. 213
Hall, N. 22, 28, 29
Hall, N. 279
Hall, Mrs. O. 141
Hall, O. 336
Hall, P. 209
Hall, R. 343
Hall, Mrs. R. 380
Hall, S. 445
Hall, W. 20
Hallen, M. 447
Hallett, C. 30
Hallinan, M. 265
Halling, B. 382
Halling, Mrs. D. 227
Hallman, B. 211
Hallman, E. 186
Hallman, M. 117
Hallmark, E. 317

Hallock, J. 353
Hallows, J. 240
Halverson, E. 359
Halverson, I. 383
Halvorson, B. 318
Halvorson, O. 346
Ham, B. 265
Ham, C. 208
Ham, R. 147
Hamblet, F. 63
Hamburger, B. 155
Hamdorf, E. 124
Hamel, A. 317
Hamelin, G. 165
Hamer, M. 258
Hamilton, B. 127
Hamilton, E. 93
Hamilton, E. 143
Hamilton, E. 270
Hamilton, E. 331
Hamilton, G. 80
Hamilton, J. 41
Hamilton, M. 245
Hamilton, M. 258
Hamilton, M. 278
Hamilton, R. 62
Hamilton, S. 12
Hamilton, S. 84
Hamilton, V. 448
Hamline, M. 244
Hamm, B. 15
Hamm, Mrs. D. 255
Hamm, E. 390
Hamm, P. 288
Hammack, B. 76
Hammers, S. 251
Hammes, M. 228
Hammill, T. 193
Hammock, Mrs. Z. 83
Hammond, B. 196
Hammond, C. 68
Hammond, E. 392
Hammond, M. 184
Hammond, M. 336
Hammond, V. 9
Hammons, Mrs. O. 28
Hamon, E. 252
Hamparian, D. 337
Hampel, C. 110
Hampton, A. 66
Hamric, C. 73
Hamrick, J. 12, 14
Hanan, R. 347
Hance, M. 18
Hancock, I. 34
Hancock, J. 433
Hancock, M. 260
Hancock, Mrs. W. 95
Hand, K. 453
Hand, P. 93
Hander, E. 397
Handren, Sister M. 157
Hanie, B. 242
Hanieski, D. 215
Haniff, G. 230
Haniford, J. 103
Hanke, K. 113
Hankins, B. 160
Hankins, E. 341
Hanks, Mrs. J. 232
Hanks, L. 77
Hanks, L. 240
Hanks, M. 233
Hanley, L. 406
Hann, S. 351
Hanna, M. 254
Hanna, S. 16
Hannafious, W. 52
Hannagan, R. 122
Hannah, B. 20
Hannah, M. 372
Hannan, C. 123
Hannan, S. 15, 16
Hannasch, C. 228
Hannon, L. 24

Hanrahan, J. 267
Hanrahan, M. 449
Hansen, B. 149
Hansen, E. 92
Hansen, G. 75
Hansen, G. 285, 288
Hanse, J. 222
Hansen, J. 299
Hansen, J. 435, 437
Hansen, L. 112
Hansen, M. 171
Hansen, M. 247
Hansen, M. 451
Hansen, N. 357
Hansen, R. 251
Hansen, R. 386
Hansen, S. 21
Hansen, S. 252
Hansen, V. 180
Hansen, V. 405
Hansey, R. 432
Hanson, A. 372
Hanson, D. 283
Hanson, D. 434
Hanson, E. 111
Hanson, E. 315
Hanson, I. 225
Hanson, I. 453
Hanson, J. 258
Hanson, J. 338
Hanson, M. 223
Hanson, M. 227
Hanson, P. 224
Hanson, Dr. P. 302
Hanson, R. 432
Hanson, S. 220
Hanson, S. 386
Hanssen, L. 121
Hanzalek, A. 55
Hapala, E. 316
Happ, N. 247
Harbaugh, S. 203
Hardaway, A. 190
Harden, C. 105
Harden, J. 420
Harden, M. 274
Harden, T. 101
Harder, C. 120
Hardern, E. 288
Hardes, J. 21
Hardesty, A. 241
Hardie, O. 228
Hardin, B. 389
Hardin, J. 344
Hardin, M. 444
Harding, J. 147
Harding, L. 282
Harding, M. 243
Harding, P. 255
Harding, R. 326
Harding, R. 454
Hardman, E. 442
Hardman, K. 322
Hards, B. 435
Hardy, D. 186
Hardy, G. 395
Hardy, Mrs. J. 380
Hardy, L. 26
Hardy, L. 335
Hardy, S. 216
Hardy, W. 455
Hare, C. 380
Harelson, J. 17
Harelson, J. 287
Haremza, F. 128
Hargis, C. 130
Hargrave, D. 119
Hargrave, V. 310
Hargraves, S. 15
Hargrove, E. 214
Hargrove, I. 312
Hargrove, J. 116
Harju, D. 197
Harkcom, F. 365
Harker, B. 121

Harker, M. 365
Harkey, P. 395
Harknes, M. 153
Harlan, C. 48
Harlan, S. 239
Harland, M. 167
Harless, E. 441
Harless, M. 442
Harling, J. 267
Harman, C. 360
Harman, D. 177
Harmer, D. 407
Harmer, M. 182
Harmon, I. 43
Harmon, K. 288
Harms, B. 239
Harms, M. 361
Harnden, F. 436
Harness, J. 389
Harnois, P. 148
Haro, M. 21
Harold, N. 384
Harper, D. 193
Harper, D. 313
Harper, E. 8
Harper, E. 47
Harper, E. 257
Harper, H. 387
Harper, K. 206
Harper, L. 21
Harper, L. 381
Harper, M. 107
Harper, M. 215
Harper, N. 444
Harper, N. 450
Harper, R. 355
Harper, V. 123
Harrel, A. 22
Harrell, B. 105
Harrell, P. 20
Harrer, B. 427
Harrigan, A. 17
Harriman, T. 145
Harrington, B. 436
Harrington, C. 335
Harrington, E. 125
Harrington, K. 301
Harrington, L. 356
Harrington, M. 266
Harrington, Mrs. P. 302
Harrington, Z. 245
Harris, A. 76
Harris, B. 356
Harris, C. 105
Harris, C. 433
Harris, D. 370
Harris, E. 62
Harris, E. 101
Harris, E. 241
Harris, E. 375
Harris, G. 283
Harris, G. 424
Harris, H. 95
Harris, H. 215
Harris, J. 104
Harris, J. 235
Harris, J. 350
Harris, Dr. J. 424
Harris, L. 67
Harris, L. 332
Harris, M. 81
Harris, M. 200
Harris, M. 230
Harris, M. 424
Harris, P. 2
Harris, P. 353
Harris, P. 396
Harris, P. 419
Harris, R. 26
Harris, Mrs. R. 399
Harris, S. 155
Harris, S. 183
Harris, S. 342
Harris, Sister T. 284
Harris, T. 452

Harris, W. 86
Harrison, A. 396
Harrison, D. 244
Harrison, Mrs. G. 9
Harrison, H. 63
Harrison, H. 150,155,157
Harrison, J. 378
Harrison, M. 422
Harrison, S. 214
Harrison, Mrs. W. 285
Harrison-Ross, Dr. P. 301
Harroun, A. 411
Harshman, B. 127
Harson, G. 78
Hart, A. 73
Hart, B. 131
Hart, B. 302
Hart, C. 18
Hart, E. 83
Hart, E. 153
Hart, E. 187
Hart, F. 286
Hart, J. 439
Hart, K. 184
Hart, K. 212
Hart, K. 301
Hart, Mrs. M. 293
Hart, M. 338
Hart, P. 103
Hart, V. 443,449
Harter, N. 359
Hartford, M. 262
Hartgraves, A. 231
Hartley, J. 347
Hartley, Mrs. R. 344
Hartley, W. 382
Hartman, B. 383
Hartman, C. 37
Hartman, D. 92
Hartman, J. 322
Hartman, L. 447
Hartman, P. 438
Hartmen, M. 331
Hartnett, M. 255
Hartsema, A. 207
Hartung, A. 49
Hartwell, M. 380
Hartwick, L. 177
Hartwick, M. 318
Hartzell, V. 205
Harv, E. 149
Harvath, S. 197
Harvey, B. 356
Harvey, J. 324
Harvey, J. 431
Harvey, K. 319
Harwood, E. 413,414,415
Harwood, M. 132
Harwood, M. 189
Harwood, M. 205
Harwood, M. 409
Harwood, M. 413, 415
Harwood, M. 434
Hasazi, S. 415
Hasbrook, M. 118
Hascall, N. 172
Hasebroock, Mrs. W. 253
Hashim, E. 64
Haskell, E. 421
Haskell, P. 378
Haskell, Mrs. 399
Haslett, M. 127
Hass, N. 317
Hassan, G. 332
Hastings, J. 338
Hastings, M. 155
Hastings, M. 267
Hatch, D. 64
Hatcher, A. 441
Hatcher, S. 75
Hatcher, V. 283
Hatfield, A. 228
Hathaway, S. 413
Hathorn, M. 413
Hatlestad, P. 317

Haug, V. 125
Haugan, H. 273
Haugen, B. 353
Haugen, C. 315
Haugen, J. 228
Haugh, M. 224
Haught, E. 440
Haugland, B. 314
Hauser, M. 221
Hauserman, G. 125
Hauskins, D. 239
Hausler, B. 347
Hausler, I. 205
Havlik, B. 157
Hawe, M. 61
Hawes, B. 325
Hawken, A. 453
Hawkins, I. 92
Hawkins, K. 20
Hawkins, M. 70
Hawkins, M. 418
Hawkins, P. 69
Hawkins, S. 381
Hawkins, Mrs. V. 7
Hawkinson, M. 265
Hawley, E. 149
Hawll, B. 358
Haws, G. 389
Hawse, H. 18
Hay, J. 91
Hay, Mrs. J. 403
Hay, L. 369
Hay, N. 374
Hay, S. 312
Hayden, D. 136
Hayden, H. 266
Hayden, L. 377
Haydu, I. 327
Hayek, C. 434
Hayes, A. 215
Hayes, A. 441
Hayes, B. 29
Hayes, B. 77
Hayes, B. 136
Hayes, B. 246
Hayes, B. 287
Hayes, B. 448
Hayes, C. 387
Hayes, D. 288
Hayes, E. 244
Hayes, G. 413
Hayes, H. 84
Hayes, J. 33
Hayes, J. 414
Hayes, K. 256
Hayes, M. 388
Hayes, P. 341
Haymaker, J. 155
Haymaker, M. 99
Hayner, J. 425
Hayner, J. 434
Haynes, M. 434
Haynes, P. 154
Haynie, Mrs. J. 283
Hays, V. 105
Hayter, V. 97
Hayward, M. 454
Hayward, N. 354
Hayworth, A. 106
Hazard, C. 411
Hazard, Mrs. J. 78
Hazelbaker, J. 16
Hazeltine, B. 41
Hazelton, L. 196
Hazelwood, A. 423
Hazen, E. 256
Hazen, R. 395
Hazleton, M. 407
Hazlett, M. 382
Hazlewood-Brady, A. 148
Head, B. 100
Head, J. 262
Headlee, C. 325
Heald, D. 123
Healey, S. 385

Healt, T. 372
Healy, D. 423
Hearn, A. 24
Hearn, E. 283
Hearn, J. 376
Hearne, M. 389
Heath, B. 402
Heath, E. 217
Heath, H. 17
Heath, L. 191
Heath, M. 312
Heath, P. 367
Hebard, I. 413
Hebron, B. 195
Hecht, J. 214
Heck, J. 398
Heck, R. 341
Heck, V. 118
Heck, W. 105
Heckler, M. 5
Heckman, J. 40
Hedgecock, C. 119
Hedger, J. 135
Hedges, R. 131
Hedlund, G. 323
Hedrick, I. 419
Heeren, F. 95
Heesch, N. 385
Heffernen, L. 111
Heffner, M. 417
Heflin, R. 357
Heflin, T. 122
Hefner, M. 129
Heger, B. 239
Hegerhorst, V. 89
Hegge, M. 385
Heggen, I. 316
Heikkila, E. 182
Heikkinen, L. 229
Heil, I. 252
Heiland, D. 361
Heiller, F. 221
Heindel, M. 411
Heinen, M. 230
Heintz, N. 141
Heintzman, V. 195
Heinz, E. 457
Heinzman, J. 254
Heiser, M. 335
Heiskell, M. 303
Heiting, C. 448
Heitland, S. 386
Heitsman, T. 122
Heitstuman, B. 433
Heitzendorf, P. 368
Hejl, C. 172
Held, M. 48
Helgeson, K. 122
Helget, K. 221
Heller, E. 228
Heller, J. 380
Heller, L. 278
Heller, Mrs. M. 242
Hellmuth, M. 394
Helm, E. 422
Helm, L. 127
Helm, M. 337
Helmes, W. 157
Helms, H. 297
Helms, M. 236
Helphrey, J. 317, 318
Helsby, Z. 129
Helsel, E. 336
Helsel, J. 168
Helt, A. 448
Helton, W. 387
Helzapfel, A. 284
Hemachandra, J. 351
Hemenway, J. 165
Hemmerich, V. 334
Hempe, I. 353
Hemphill, B. 454
Hemstreet, M. 21
Hendel, P. 55
Hendershot, M. 171

Henderson, B. 9
Henderson, B. 29
Henderson, B. 266
Henderson, B. 349
Henderson, D. 147
Henderson, D. 399
Henderson, E. 206, 216
Henderson, G. 10
Henderson, H. 121, 122
Henderson, J. 137
Henderson, Mrs. J. 354
Henderson, J. 413
Henderson, K. 8
Henderson, L. 241
Henderson, M. 9, 10
Henderson, M. 73
Henderson, N. 197
Henderson, R. 229
Hendrick, C. 378
Hendrick, C. 381
Hendrick, M. 104
Hendrick, V. 245
Hendricks, O. 193
Hendricks, L. 28
Hendricks, P. 255
Hendricks, S. 240
Hendricksen, R. 252
Hendrickson, B. 361
Hendrickson, B. 384
Hendrickson, R. 28
Hendrickson, R. 187
Hendrix, J. 85
Hendry, H. 79
Hendry, M. 453
Heneage, J. 59
Henerson, H. 121
Henkhaus, C. 403
Henkin, S. 385
Henn, C. 326
Hennessey, D. 282
Hennessey, M. 63, 64
Henniges, M. 64
Henrichs, L. 248
Henrick, J. 320
Henricksen, I. 14
Henricksen, V. 283
Henry, A. 407
Henry, B. 259
Henry, B. 395
Henry, C. 23
Henry, Mrs. E. 240
Henry, I. 417
Henry, K. 16
Henry, Mrs. L. 29
Henry, L. 258
Henry, Mrs. M. 239
Henry, M. 254
Henry, R. 341
Henry, Mrs. T. 156
Hensel, C. 39
Henson, D. 111
Henzel, S. 333
Heppe, G. 193
Hepworth, C. 408
Herald, A. 216
Herald, E. 189
Herald, F. 180
Herald, M. 338
Herb, H. 100
Herbert, A. 353
Herbert, D. 337
Herbert, E. 285
Herbert, E. 331
Herbold, C. 123
Herbst, M. 58
Herchek, D. 262
Herd, V. 449
Hering, D. 360
Herker, E. 384
Herl, M. 196
Herman, A. 2
Herman, A. 296
Herman, J. 314
Herman, L. 17
Herman, L. 235

Herman, M. 317
Herman, R. 58
Hermon, B. 19
Hernandez, N. 404
Herndon, J. 442
Herndon, L. 380
Hernett, G. 317
Herr, H. 257
Herr, M. 106
Herra, M. 288
Herrink, Mrs. R. 423
Herrold, A. 117
Herron, G. 15
Herschleder, D. 20
Herseth, L. 381
Hersh, L. 283
Herson, E. 285
Hersrud, M. 385
Hertzog, N. 35
Herz, S. 284
Heskett, H. 432
Heslin, C. 280
Heslin, M. 53, 62, 63, 64
Hess, B. 358
Hess, C. 437
Hess, E. 359
Hess, E. 370
Hess, Mrs. J. 157
Hess, J. 262
Hess, L. 216
Hess, L. 299
Hess, M. 26
Hess, M. 212
Hess, R. 190
Hess, S. 124
Hesse, H. 125
Hessler, B. 274
Hester, E. 232
Hetchler, G. 229
Heth, P. 285
Hetherington, S. 106
Hetherington, T. 145
Hetrick, L. 118
Hetrick, M. 168
Heumpfner, C. 190
Hewis, G. 331
Hewitt, C. 203
Hewitt, Mrs. D. 338
Hewitt, L. 178
Hewitt, O. 390
Hewitt, P. 76
Hey, V. 179
Heybruch, E. 332
Heyneman, R. 322
Hiatt, P. 187
Hibbs, L. 162
Hibner, J. 98
Hickenbotham, B. 419
Hickey, A. 26
Hickey, Mrs. J. 454
Hickey, Mrs. M. 29
Hickey, M. 373
Hickey, N. 193
Hickey, V. 77
Hickey, V. 93
Hickey, W. 451, 453
Hicklin, C. 119
Hickling, B. 13
Hickman, N. 147
Hickok, R. 175
Hicks, A. 346
Hicks, D. 99
Hicks, D. 117
Hicks, H. 9
Hicks, H. 28
Hicks, L. 25
Hicks, L. 161
Hicks, M. 103
Hicks, V. 215
Hicks, Mrs. W. 380
Hickson, K. 449
Hide, M. 244
Hidlay, C. 355
Higbee, M. 206
Higby, J. 214

Higginbotham, J. 354
Higgins, A. 290
Higgins, B. 346
Higgins, B. 411
Higgins, C. 396
Higgins, M. 187
Higgins, M. 254
Higgins, M. 422, 423
Higgins, R. 129
Higgins, S. 68
Higgons, S. 127
Higgs, Mrs. G. 303
High, D. 320
Highley, G. 386
Hight, D. 128
Hightower, M. 68
Hildenbrand, B. 422
Hildenbrand, L. 293
Hilderbran, S. 74
Hilderbrant, L. 181
Hilger, M. 106
Hill, A. 373
Hill, B. 265
Hill, B. 339
Hill, C. 175
Hill, C. 238
Hill, D. 25
Hill, D. 117
Hill, D. 143
Hill, E. 157
Hill, F. 93
Hill, Mrs. F. 448
Hill, G. 131
Hill, Mrs. H. 104
Hill, H. 213
Hill, H. 432
Hill, J. 110
Hill, J. 418
Hill, L. 122
Hill, M. 56
Hill, M. 92
Hill, M. 103
Hill, M. 196
Hill, M. 203
Hill, M. 347
Hill, M. 442
Hill, N. 112
Hill, N. 328
Hill, O. 41
Hill, O. 125
Hill, R. 445
Hill, Mrs. S. 318
Hill, S. 394
Hill, V. 382
Hillaire, M. 434
Hillard, I. 92
Hilleary, J. 189
Hillebrandt, L. 22
Hiller, M. 330
Hillestad, L. 38
Hilliard, B. 207
Hilligan, J. 219
Hilligoss, M. 40
Hillstrom, L. 220
Hillyer, M. 334
Hilshansky, C. 358
Hilton, H. 176
Hilton, L. 148
Himm, A. 177
Himmelblau, B. 394
Himmelstein, F. 63
Hinchey, A. 413
Hincir, A. 399
Hinckley, H. 324
Hindel, W. 324
Hindenach, J. 190
Hinds, M. 404
Hinds, R. 96
Hine, L. 426
Hink, G. 108
Hinkfuss, R. 444
Hinkle, B. 384
Hinman, P. 93
Hinman, T. 255
Hinrichson, E. 119

Hinson, A. 379
Hinson, B. 379
Hinton, F. 440
Hinton, M. 101
Hinton, V. 236
Hinton, Z. 380
Hipp, J. 313
Hippman, L. 62
Hiseler, B. 413
Hisgen, M. 72
Hitchings, H. 72
Hite, C. 241
Hite, M. 356
Hittle, R. 414
Hitzler, J. 186
Hively, L. 402
Hixon, M. 7
Hixson, S. 150
Hjellen, E. 13
Hladky, I. 128
Hoadley, F. 454
Hoadley, L. 319
Hoagland, C. 214
Hoar, L.. 64
Hoare, R. 166
Hobart, I. 130
Hobbs, B. 19
Hobbs, C. 145
Hobbs, C. 241
Hobby, C. 347
Hochberg, G. 375
Hockberg, Mrs. H. 301
Hockstad, M. 207
Hocter, H. 333
Hodas, R. 290
Hodge, A. 77
Hodge, H. 253
Hodge, J. 34
Hodge, K. 421
Hodge, V. 403
Hodges, B. 51
Hodges, F. 82
Hodges, J. 344
Hodges, J. 382
Hodges, L. 339
Hodges, M. 193
Hodges, M. 440
Hodges, Mrs. R. 307
Hodgkins, S. 305
Hodgkins, S. 312
Hodo, B. 16
Hodson, M. 351
Hoebel, P. 342
Hoefler, B. 201
Hoefler, M. 254
Hoeve, P. 423
Hofer, D. 385
Hoff, B. 123
Hoff, J. 413
Hoffart, J. 253
Hoffine, L. 318
Hoffman, A. 301
Hoffman, B. 107
Hoffman, B. 283
Hoffman, E. 102
Hoffman, I. 226
Hoffman, J. 296
Hoffman, L. 155
Hoffman, L. 223
Hoffman, M. 174
Hoffman, Mrs. M. 406
Hoffman, T. 393
Hoffstetter, M. 240
Hofmann, M. 394
Hofschute, D. 16
Hogan, A. 63
Hogan, E. 284
Hogan, I. 427
Hogan, I. 434
Hogg, E. 84
Hoglund, C. 225
Hograth, F. 386
Hogue, B. 341
Hogue, C. 122
Hohman, J. 15

Hoisington, M. 172
Hoisington, M. 411
Hokanson, S. 217
Hoke, R. 76
Hokens, A. 190
Hokr, D. 226
Holbel, D. 215
Holbert, L. 257
Holbert, V. 230
Holbrook, A. 76
Holbrook, B. 449
Holbrook, L. 415
Holcomb, J. 199
Holcomb, M. 210
Holcombe, J. 25
Holden, D. 190
Holden, E. 252
Holden, H. 68
Holden, I. 91, 92
Holden, Mrs. L. 423
Holden, Mrs. W. 403
Holder, M. 75
Holdorf, L. 117
Holiday, B. 137
Holk, A. 226
Hollanel, E. 79
Holland, H. 375
Holland, I. 159
Holland, R. 241
Holland, S. 423
Holleger, H. 68
Hollenbaugh, J. 198
Hollenbaugh, V. 321
Hollenbeck, A. 207
Hollern, S. 227
Holley, L. 405
Holliday, W. 303
Hollinger, B. 357
Hollingsworth, K. 25
Hollingsworth, S. 140
Hollis, C. 331
Holm, B. 333
Holman, H. 237
Holman, N. 433,434
Holmbon, D. 146
Holme, B. 45
Holmes, H. 380
Holmes, J. 132
Holmes, J. 288
Holmes, J. 396
Holmes, M. 178
Holmes, M. 198
Holmes, O. 335
Holmes, P. 246
Holmes, R. 344
Holmes, S. 389
Holmes, W. 258
Holooman, N. 134
Holstad, M. 107, 121
Holstein, C. 304
Holstein, D. 253
Holstein, M. 374
Holt, B. 305
Holt, C. 86
Holt, C. 398
Holt, E. 173
Holt, J. 114
Holt, J. 405
Holt, J. 439
Holt, M. 5
Holt, M. 96
Holt, M. 420, 424
Holt, S. 15
Holte, J. 318
Holtzman, E. 5
Holtzman, I. 368
Holyoke, S. 253
Holysko, A. 182
Holz, P. 308
Holzman, B. 381
Homer, M. 92
Homes, L. 312
Honaker, M. 439
Honaman, D. 190
Honaman, J. 355

Hone, S. 34
Honeycutt, G. 310
Honig, Mrs. E. 155
Hood, A. 369
Hood, B. 185
Hood, T. 403
Hook, E. 91
Hook, J. 216
Hook, M. 153
Hooker, J. 23
Hooker, M. 401
Hooley, D. 352
Hoomes, E. 10
Hooper, F. 343
Hooper, S. 96
Hooton, M. 97
Hoover, Mrs. C. 417
Hoover, M. 357
Hoover, N. 32
Hoover, P. 233
Hope, E. 53
Hopkins, A. 157
Hopkins, B. 232
Hopkins, D. 267
Hopkins, L. 350
Hopkins, N. 239
Hoppe, A. 195
Hoppe, H. 184
Hoppe, S. 118
Hoppe, S. 155
Hopper, N. 13
Hopwood, G. 112
Hopwood, J. 171
Hopwood, S. 413
Horan, C. 135
Horan, M. 255
Horine, F. 96
Hork, J. 247
Horn, B. 15
Horn, B. 215
Horn, L. 319
Horner, A. 198
Horner, B. 395
Horner, G. 379
Horner, M. 387
Hornick, J. 222
Horphonois, E. 78
Horse, M. 250
Horsey, Mrs. N. 420
Hortenson, O. 171
Horton, B. 84
Horton,Mrs. E. 402
Horton, G. 24
Horton, J. 81, 83
Horton, J. 295
Horton, L. 426
Horton, P. 271
Horvath, M. 51
Hospodor, R. 272
Hossack, M. 216
Hotchkiss, J. 62
Hotchkiss, P. 292
Hottenstine, E. 363
Houck, H. 430
Hough, J. 420
Houk, C. 122
House, A. 102
House, B. 236
House, K. 414
Houser, E. 181
Houston, B. 86
Houston, M. 48
Hout, J. 15
Houvener, E. 195
Hovey, S. 92
Hovland, E. 386
Hovorka, M. 432
Howard, B. 140
Howard, B. 195
Howard, B. 293
Howard, C. 15
Howard, D. 182
Howard, D. 205
Howard, D. 255
Howard, D. 262

Howard, E. 92
Howard, E. 221
Howard, E. 428
Howard, F. 28
Howard, F. 392
Howard, H. 91
Howard, M. 66
Howard, M. 429
Howard, P. 75
Howard, R. 395
Howard, T. 83
Howard, Mrs. Z. 24
Howarth, P. 213
Howay, F. 201
Howe, A. 179
Howe, B. 68
Howe, G. 171
Howe, J. 191
Howe, M. 159
Howell, E. 381
Howell, E. 420
Howell, J. 271
Howell, M. 329
Howell, Mrs. P. 406
Howell, R. 123
Howell, S. 251
Howell, T. 310
Howie, J. 26
Howle, M. 133
Howlett, C. 415
Howlett, P. 123
Howley, R. 336
Howze, I. 393
Hoxsey, B. 94
Hoxey, J. 47
Hoyer, M. 210
Hoyt, I. 352
Hoyt, K. 415
Hoyt, M. 414
Hubbard, C. 78
Hubbard, C. 165
Hubbard, K. 431
Hubbard, V. 52
Hubbell, C. 122
Hubentahal, M. 92
Huber, I. 258
Huber, J. 319
Huber, M. 238
Huber, P. 23
Huber, R. 330
Huber, R. 400
Huber, S. 142
Huberty, S. 354
Hublar, V. 99
Hubler, S. 91
Huck, A. 235
Huck, V. 250
Hudak, F. 368
Hudak, L. 245
Huddleston, C. 388
Hudson, B. 54
Hudson, C. 72
Hudson, D. 243
Hudson, L. 250
Hudson, L. 343
Hudson, R. 423
Hudson, W. 16
Huefner, D. 408
Huelskamp. G. 72
Huey, E. 389
Huey, N. 72
Huff, B. 99
Huff, M. 202
Huff,M. 342
Huffer, T. 325
Huffman, C. 330
Huffman, N. 333
Huffman, P. 200
Hufhand, H. 364
Hufstedler, S. 6
Huggins, B. 388
Hughes, B. 428
Hughes, E. 393
Hughes, G. 73
Hughes, I. 200

Hughes, Mrs. J.   394
Hughes, L.   202
Hughes, M.   235
Hughes, N.   244
Hughes, P.   378
Hughes, R.   128
Hughes, Sister, R.   302
Hughes, S.   250
Hughes, T.   30
Hughs, F.   204
Huizenga, E.   214
Hulett, M.   184
Hull, A.   150
Hull, D.   92
Hull, D.   203
Hull, M.   174
Hull, M.   178
Hulsey, C.   85
Hult, C.   308
Hult, D.   353
Hultman, B.   349, 353
Hume, G.   45
Hume, L.   435
Humes, B.   128
Hummel, C.   370
Hummel, J.   206
Hummel, J.   435
Hummer, N.   326
Humphrey, D.   232
Humphreys, J.   393
Humphries, A.   417
Humphries, H.   392
Humphries, M.   224
Hund, Sister M.   252
Hundley, L.   348
Hunking, L.   386
Hunkley, R.   365
Hunley, J.   352
Hunnicutt, J.   21
Hunsaker, M.   429
Hunt, A.   354
Hunt, A.   397
Hunt, B.   182
Hunt, C.   68
Hunt, C.   320
Hunt, D.   157
Hunt, E.   390
Hunt, I.   14
Hunt, I.   96
Hunt, L.   404
Hunt, P.   306
Hunt, P.   344
Hunt, R.   227
Hunter, A.   109
Hunter, H.   153
Hunter, J.   21
Hunter, J.   149
Hunter, K.   104
Hunter, S.   301
Hunter, V.   96
Huntington, F.   352
Huntington, J.   297
Huntley, C.   119
Huntley, C.   334
Huntoon, C.   199
Hurchalla, M.   71
Hurd, I.   131
Hurley, A.   73
Hurley, A.   301
Hurley, B.   412
Hurley, K.   15, 16
Hurley, M.   149
Hurley, M.   425
Hurley, P.   236
Hurley, R.   190
Hurn, D.   428
Hurst, F.   449
Hurst, M.   120
Hurst, W.   306
Hurt, J.   375
Hurt, R.   343
Huschle, P.   222
Huse, M.   225
Huseman, C.   85
Hussong, D.   140

Hutcheson, N.   283
Hutchings, B.   85
Hutchings, M.   142
Hutchings, W.   454
Hutchins, B.   220
Hutchins, C.   413
Hutchins, J.   292
Hutchins, M.   424
Hutchinson, B.   66, 67
Hutchinson, G.   122
Hutchinson, N.   195
Hutchinson, S.   58
Hutson, E.   243
Hutler, E.   279
Hutto, M.   380
Hutton, M.   132
Hutton, P.   132
Hutton, R.   126
Huxtable, P.   216
Hyatt, G.   401
Hyde, C.   187
Hyde, J.   63
Hyde, L.   401
Hyde, S.   137
Hyder, M.   184
Hyman, L.   338
Hynes, C.   177
Hyskell, T.   368

Ibarra, J.   259
Ickes, M.   367
Ide, B.   244
Igoa, C.   257
Ikeda, D.   87
Iles, M.   73
Iliff, A.   230
Illes, L.   122
Imes, S.   449
Imm, L.   393
Inabinett, E.   379
Indzonka, M.   304
Ingalls, L.   15
Ingersol, F.   149
Ingersol, G.   293
Ingersoll, J.   199
Ingles, B.   119
Ingram, D.   320
Ingram, H.   21
Ingram, M.   262
Ingram, R.   390
Ingrum, R.   398
Injasoulian, M.   21
Inman, G.   426
Inman, M.   423
Inman, N.   182
Inojos, M.   243
Intriago, R.   301
Ippolito, L.   363
Ireland, P.   366
Ireton, C.   330
Irish, D.   349
Irish, J.   323
Irish, N.   171
Irizarry, M.   401
Irons, C.   122
Irrer, M.   173
Irvine, D.   148
Irvine, G.   48
Irwin, B.   237
Irwin, H.   95
Irwin, J.   282
Irwin, M.   277
Irwin, M.   437
Irwin, O.   201
Isaacson, D.   148
Isaacson, L.   227
Isabell, D.   15
Iselin, Mrs. P.   283
Isenberg, Mrs. C.   404
Isham, J.   435
Ishimatsu, C.   409
Israel, K.   244
Issac, I.   126
Itterly, J.   368
Ivary, M.   258

Iverson, A.   408
Ivey, A.   73
Ivey, D.   342
Ivkovich, P.   211
Izard, M.   86
Izzard, J.   177
Izzi, J.   186

Jack, F.   14
Jackinsky, H.   14
Jackinsky, Mrs. W.   16
Jacks, V.   23
Jackson, B.   79
Jackson, B.   137
Jackson, B.   238
Jackson, Mrs. B.   244
Jackson, C.   90
Jackson, C.   336
Jackson, D.   85
Jackson, E.   72
Jackson, F.   149
Jackson, F.   215
Jackson, F.   442
Jackson, G.   22
Jackson, J.   29
Jackson, J.   31
Jackson, J.   155
Jackson, J.   165
Jackson, J.   419
Jackson, L.   22
Jackson, L.   324
Jackson, M.   13
Jackson, M.   140
Jackson, M.   153
Jackson, M.   200
Jackson, M.   367
Jackson, P.   283
Jackson, R.   27
Jackson, R.   340
Jackson, S.   85
Jackson, S.   169
Jackson, S.   398
Jackson, T.   437
Jackson, V.   385
Jackston, P.   57
Jacob, J.   123
Jacob, N.   337
Jacobs, C.   272
Jacobs, E.   200
Jacobs, G.   112
Jacobs, M.   351
Jacobs, R.   184
Jacobs, V.   29
Jacobsen, E.   193
Jacobsen, M.   429
Jacobson, B.   255
Jacobson, C.   283
Jacques, A.   128
Jaegar, E.   280
Jaffee, L.   212
Jaffer, P.   350
Jaggers, C.   341
Jahn, M.   183
Jahnke, G.   129
Jakez, M.   31
James, B.   51
James, B.   233
James, G.   402
James, H.   96
James, J.   207
James, L.   348
James, M.   68
James, M.   284
James, M.   419
James, N.   231
James, O.   115
James, T.   214
James, V.   455
Jamieson, L.   168
Jamieson, L.   216
Jamison, A.   154
Jamison, J.   370
Janak, J.   297
Janda, L.   171
Janik, V.   267

Janis, K.   332
Jankowski, I.   224
Janover, J.   301
Jansen, I.   353
Jansen, J.   224
Jansen, M.   383
Jansseens, M.   196
Janssen, J.   222
Jansson, Mrs. H.   156
Janusz, M.   318
Janzen, B.   377
Jaramillo, T.   288
Jarboe, B.   102
Jarman, L.   308
Jarmon, B.   405
Jarosz, I.   274
Jarrard, M.   189
Jarrard, N.   171
Jarrell, J.   35
Jarrett, E.   409, 413
Jarrett, J.   241
Jarrett, L.   435
Jaskulski, Mrs. R.   448
Jasmer, L.   351
Jasper, B.   90
Jasper, J.   230
Jastak, S.   68
Jaworski, E.   208
Jazdzewski, C.   347
Jedele, L.   179
Jedlicka, S.   78
Jeffers, B.   403
Jeffers, D.   46
Jefferson, G.   449
Jefferson, H.   377
Jefferson, N.   173
Jeffreys, A.   8
Jeffries, A.   320
Jeffries, N.   132
Jefts, M.   178
Jeghelian, J.   165
Jelinek, J.   454
Jenewein, J.   323
Jenkins, A.   128
Jenkins, A.   320
Jenkins, B.   46
Jenkins, B.   277
Jenkins, C.   64
Jenkins, L.   83
Jenkins, S.   172
Jenks, A.   430
Jenks, C.   440
Jenner, J.   121
Jenness, R.   413
Jenniges, D.   51
Jennings, J.   100
Jennings, J.   442
Jennings, M.   345
Jennings, M.   412
Jennings, N.   288
Jennings, T.   70
Jennings, V.   427
Jense, S.   407
Jensen, A.   407, 408
Jensen, B.   186
Jensen, D.   226
Jensen, E.   42
Jensen, F.   126
Jensen, J.   110
Jensen, M.   226
Jensen, M.   385
Jensen, P.   111
Jensen, S.   117
Jensen, S.   351
Jerichow, A.   183
Jernigan, S.   79
Jero, L.   447
Jerome, M.   228
Jester, R.   309
Jestrab, E.   318
Jett, E.   441
Jewell, P.   206
Jinnette, Mrs. W.   398
Jobe, Mrs. R.   11
Johannsen, S.   108

Johansen, J. 254
John, D. 351
John, E. 131
John, J. 80
John, M. 361
John, P. 362
John, R. 403
Johnican, M. 388
Johns, M. 114
Johns, S. 191
Johns, W. 10
Johnson, A. 82
Johnson, B. 13
Johnson, B. 28
Johnson, B. 62
Johnson, B. 68
Johnson, B. 184
Johnson, B. 229
Johnson, B. 230
Johnson, B. 247
Johnson, B. 339
Johnson, B. 346
Johnson, B. 430
Johnson, C. 157
Johnson, C. 315
Johnson, C. 408
Johnson, C. 431
Johnson, D. 11
Johnson, D. 25
Johnson, D. 170
Johnson, D. 190
Johnson, D. 202
Johnson, D. 212
Johnson, D. 224
Johnson, D. 237
Johnson, D. 366
Johnson, D. 381
Johnson, D. 437
Johnson, D. 449
Johnson, E. 113
Johnson, E. 125
Johnson, E. 154
Johnson, E. 157
Johnson, E. 222
Johnson, E. 352
Johnson, E. 391
Johnson, E. 434
Johnson, E. 435
Johnson, F. 197
Johnson, F. 201
Johnson, G. 25
Johnson, G. 51
Johnson, G. 223
Johnson, G. 294
Johnson, H. 40
Johnson, H. 65
Johnson, H. 140
Johnson, H. 208
Johnson, H. 222
Johnson, H. 432
Johnson, I. 46
Johnson, I. 346
Johnson, I. 399
Johnson, J. 17
Johnson, J. 121, 123
Johnson, J. 155
Johnson, J. 225
Johnson, J. 228
Johnson, J. 243
Johnson, Mrs. J. 304
Johnson, Mrs. J. 343
Johnson, J. 415
Johnson, J. 422
Johnson, J. 427
Johnson, J. 451
Johnson, K. 110
Johnson, K. 300
Johnson, K. 439
Johnson, K. 440
Johnson, L. 7
Johnson, L. 14
Johnson, L. 117
Johnson, L. 186
Johnson, L. 218
Johnson, L. 397

Johnson, Mrs. L. 404
Johnson, M. 16
Johnson, M. 64
Johnson, M. 71
Johnson, M. 73
Johnson, M. 82
Johnson, M. 125
Johnson, M. 209
Johnson, M. 215
Johnson, M. 227
Johnson, M. 343
Johnson, M. 380
Johnson, M. 417, 424
Johnson, N. 54
Johnson, N. 251
Johnson, N. 290
Johnson, O. 156
Johnson, P. 187
Johnson, P. 209
Johnson, P. 262
Johnson, P. 293
Johnson, R. 115
Johnson, R. 229
Johnson, R. 327
Johnson, S. 171
Johnson, S. 232
Johnson, S. 275
Johnson, S. 378
Johnson, S. 414
Johnson, T. 121, 124
Johnson, V. 242
Johnson, V. 402
Johnson, Y. 73
Johnston, B. 20
Johnston, E. 327
Johnston, F. 47
Johnston, F. 429
Johnston, G. 176
Johnston, M. 224
Johnston, Mrs. S. 354
Jokela, N. 190
Jokinen, S. 218
Jolivet, A. 20
Jolley, L. 454
Joncas, G. 262, 267
Jondle, F. 111
Jones, A. 10
Jones, A. 303
Jones, B. 33
Jones, B. 232
Jones, B. 266
Jones, Mrs. B. 283
Jones, B. 398
Jones, C. 144
Jones, C. 204
Jones, C. 244
Jones, C. 267
Jones, C. 302
Jones, C. 398
Jones, C. 414
Jones, C. 422
Jones, D. 111
Jones, D. 182
Jones, D. 380
Jones, D. 392
Jones, E. 20
Jones, E. 423
Jones, F. 421
Jones, G. 124
Jones, G. 201
Jones, G. 401
Jones, Mrs. H. 8
Jones, H. 11
Hones, H. 71
Jones, H. 375
Jones, Mrs. H. 404
Jones, J. 15, 16
Jones, J. 112
Jones, Mrs. J. 235
Jones, J. 244
Jones, J. 303
Jones, J. 416
Jones, J. 424
Jones, K. 72
Jones, L. 45

Jones, L. 76
Jones, L. 92
Jones, L. 139
Jones, L. 415
Jones, M. 18
Jones, M. 26
Jones, M. 34
Jones, M. 82
Jones, M. 147
Jones, M. 153
Jones, M. 157
Jones, M. 179
Jones, M. 249
Jones, M. 251
Jones, M. 387
Jones, M. 408
Jones, M. 442
Jones, N. 93
Jones, N. 237
Jones, P. 12
Jones, P. 153
Jones, P. 247
Jones, R. 154
Jones, R. 199
Jones, R. 427
Jones, S. 16
Jones, S. 155
Jones, S. 408
Jones, V. 86
Jones, V. 393
Jones, W. 10
Jones, W. 238
Jordahl, N. 385
Jordan, Mrs. A. 351
Jordan, B. 5
Jordan, B. 57
Jordan, B. 82
Jordan, B. 166
Jordan, C. 398
Jordan, C. 399
Jordan, D. 14
Jordan, E. 144
Jordan, E. 149
Jordan, E. 245
Jordan, H. 125
Jordan, H. 297
Jordan, J. 78
Jordan, Mrs. J. 139
Jordan, L. 203
Jordan, O. 234
Jordan, R. 10
Jorden, M. 332
Jordon, B. 331
Jordon, L. 17
Jorgensen, A. 120
Jorgensen, I. 407
Jorgensen, M. 253
Jorgensen, O. 454
Jorgenson, A. 316
Jorgenson, Mrs. C. 254
Josephson, C. 214
Journey, B. 394
Journey, L. 103
Joy, L. 103
Joy, L. 386
Joyce, H. 242
Joyce, M. 432
Joyner, E. 64
Joyner, V. 219
Joynt, Mrs. J. 423
Jozwiak, J. 99
Jubelt, V. 168
Judd, D. 18
Judd, L. 90
Judson, S. 190
Juergens, E. 343, 345
Juidici, E. 204
Juliana, J. 191
Juliano, P. 278
Juniel, A. 393
Jurovich, M. 453
Jury, D. 184
Jury, J. 122
Just, A. 409
Justewicz, H. 208

Justice, E. 390
Justin, M. 186
Justus, A. 240
Justus, M. 131

Kaatz, L. 182
Kabler, B. 444
Kaczmarek, J. 202
Kadavy, P. 250
Kading, H. 92
Kaeckmeister, P. 203
Kafoury, G. 345
Kage, N. 173
Kagg, Mrs. H. 229
Kahin, M. 453
Kahn, M. 300
Kahn, P. 217
Kain, M. 95
Kaiser, B. 400
Kaiser, J. 181
Kaiser, M. 183
Kaiser, N. 238
Kaiser, S. 96
Kalbfleisch, J. 212
Kalemkiarian, R. 40
Kalenda, S. 400
Kalik, B. 270, 457
Kalkofen, M. 175
Kallal, J. 454
Kallgren, D. 436
Kallhoff, M. 250
Kallio, B. 222
Kalmes, H. 118
Kaltenbach, M. 238
Kaltenbrown, P. 241
Kamalii, K. 87
Kaman, C. 295
Kamenicky, B. 154
Kamm, L. 2
Kammer, L. 175
Kamp, L. 122
Kampa, N. 221
Kampen, J. 175
Kamper, C. 218
Kane, I. 415
Kane, K. 188
Kane, L. 372
Kane, M. 93
Kane, M. 142
Kane, R. 279
Kangas, H. 230
Kangas, J. 159
Kannegieser, S. 148
Kanovsky, B. 336
Kanoy, J. 66
Kantala, S. 83
Kany, J. 142
Kanzler, C. 62
Kapeller, E. 237
Kaplan, E. 449
Kaplan, H. 274
Kaplan, M. 179
Kaplan, N. 64
Kapusta, C. 172
Kardasen, I. 105
Karekel, B. 110
Karevich, P. 210
Karkiainen, B. 229
Karlson, M. 288
Karlstrom, F. 20
Karmel, R. 2
Karmel, R. 303
Karmeris, S. 267
Karmol, I. 318
Karn, J. 320
Karofsky, J. 449
Karp, N. 21
Karpiel, D. 95
Karpinen, G. 195
Karsen, E. 174
Karshner, J. 333
Karshner, N. 333
Karslake, R. 214
Karvonen, R. 168
Kasarskis, D. 180

Kashulines, J. 262
Kasson, F. 296
Kasson, I. 284
Kast, L. 316
Kasten, K. 226
Kasten, M. 245
Kastman, M. 404
Kastner, C. 223
Kasulka, K. 383
Kaszubowski, M. 191
Kattke, R. 386
Katz, E. 258
Katz, V. 345
Katzer, E. 436
Kaufelt, L. 442
Kauffman, E. 111
Kaufman, Mrs. G. 423
Kaufman, K. 255
Kaufman, L. 67
Kaufman, M. 78
Kaunisto, M. 167
Kaunitz, R. 63
Kavanaugh, S. 12
Kay, A. 111
Kay, L. 328
Kay, M. 215
Kaye, J. 413
Kaywood, M. 34
Kazanjian, N. 135
Kazmierzak, D. 105
Kean, D. 424
Kean, Mrs. J. 283
Kearnes, E. 87
Kearney, C. 426
Kearns, D. 378
Kearschner, D. 319
Kearse, M. 440
Keates, M. 375
Keating, G. 457
Keck, I. 204
Keddins, D. 82
Keefe, D. 415
Keefer, V. 395
Keegan, L. 375
Keehen, Sister C. 78
Keeler, E. 303
Keeler, M. 214
Keeler, T. 324
Keenam, M. 300
Keenan, M. 267
Keenan, M. 346
Keene, C. 68
Keene, S. 189
Keeney, P. 260,265,268
Keeney, R. 295
Keeslar, F. 175
Keetley, E. 154
Keeton, R. 151
Keever, M. 259
Keffaber, O. 104
Kegley, D. 133
Kehrer, B. 85
Keierleber, A. 255
Keil, Z. 271
Keisling, M. 389
Keister, N. 327
Keitges, B. 252
Keith, D. 247
Keker, L. 156
Keller, A. 230
Keller, C. 72
Keller, L. 207
Keller, M. 205
Keller, M. 309
Keller, P. 29
Kellermeyer, F. 195
Kellett, J. 369
Kelley, B. 414
Kelley, D. 144
Kelley, F. 302
Kelley, H. 215
Kelley, J. 173
Kelley, J. 259
Kelley, J. 299
Kelley, K. 194

Kelley, K. 257
Kelley, M. 197
Kelley, R. 301
Kelley, R. 328
Kelley, S. 267
Kelley, T. 38
Kellner, M. 181
Kellogg, H. 91
Kellogg, L. 16
Kellogg, M. 202
Kelly, A. 53
Kelly, A. 355
Kelly, A. 379
Kelly, C. 122, 124
Kelly, C. 455
Kelly, D. 122
Kelly, E. 218
Kelly, E. 294
Kelly, J. 165
Kelly, J. 386
Kelly, J. 429
Kelly, L. 159
Kelly, M. 164
Kelly, M. 275
Kelly, M. 336
Kelly, M. 449
Kelly, P. 51
Kelly, P. 169
Kelly, P. 404
Kelly, S. 62
Kelly, S. 252
Kelly, S. 331
Kelly, T. 314
Kelso, Mrs. J. 240
Kelso, R. 431
Kelso, V. 181
Kelton, A. 403
Kemler, J. 55
Kemp. A. 83
Kemp, M. 402
Kemp, Z. 181
Kemper, E. 67
Kempker, A. 168
Kendall, L. 95
Kendall, L. 388
Kendall, M. 169
Kendall, M. 304
Kende, A. 64
Kendle, P. 254
Kendrick, R. 52
Kenel, M. 174
Kennedy, C. 6
Kennedy, C. 64
Kennedy, C. 433
Kennedy, E. 392
Kennedy, F. 329
Kennedy, H. 41
Kennedy, J. 234
Kennedy, M. 121
Kennedy, N. 64
Kennedy, R. 102
Kennedy, S. 322
Kennedy, V. 215
Kennelly, B. 60
Kennelly, P. 317
Kenner, P. 382
Kenney, M. 435
Kenny, J. 258
Kent, J. 326
Kent, L. 82
Kent, L. 215
Kent, M. 94
Kent, M. 157
Kenwood, M. 28
Kenworthy, Mrs. D. 140
Kenyon, D. 200
Kenyon, K. 18
Keogh, Sister M. 385
Kephart, C. 118
Kepple, S. 110
Keppy, D. 121
Kera, J. 362
Kerchner, E. 96
Kermott, M. 314
Kern, C. 255

Kern, L. 335
Kern, N. 273
Kernan, L. 254
Kernick, P. 355
Kernohan, L. 76
Kerns, B. 333
Kerr, B. 311
Kerr, E. 124
Kerr, G. 131
Kerr, I. 455
Kerr, J. 106
Kerr, M. 122
Kerr, M. 343
Kerr, S. 373
Kershaw, E. 374
Kersse, E. 359
Keskine, L. 177
Kesler, B. 352
Kessel, E. 180
Kessel, M. 192
Kester, B. 16
Kester, V. 197
Kesterson, L. 257
Kesting, M. 89
Kestle, C. 98
Ketcham, C. 411
Ketcham, P. 34
Kettelkamp, M. 51
Kevel, S. 403
Kevis, M. 93
Kewatt, R. 224
Key, M. 419
Key, T. 248
Keyes, A. 257
Keyes, M. 15
Keyes, M. 298
Keyna, R. 93
Keys, M. 5
Keyserling, H. 376
Kibler, Mrs. M. 343
Kibler, M. 356
Kidd, H. 28
Kidd, J. 343
Kidd, M. 133
Kieliszek, E. 270
Kiernan, G. 457
Kiesler, M. 104
Kiess, F. 441
Kiessel, G. 207
Kiessling, K. 427
Kieswitter, Mrs. R. 104
Kildow, H. 332
Kilgore, A. 417
Kilgore, D. 90
Kilian, G. 132
Killebrew, G. 95
Killeen, M. 64
Killian, M. 173
Killingsworth, M. 393
Killoren, P. 237
Kills, D. 254
Killy, E. 61
Kilmarx, M. 372
Kilpatrick, C. 174
Kilpatrick, T. 163
Kilpatrick, V. 29
Kiltabidle, D. 115
Kim, L. 436
Kimak, J. 259
Kimball, C. 349
Kimball, D. 64
Kimball, K. 406
Kimball, M. 120
Kimball, R. 63
Kimber, L. 118
Kimbrell, V. 26
Kimbrough, B. 75
Kiminski, B. 364
Kimmel, T. 368
Kimpton, E. 296
Kimsel, C. 177
Kin, C. 184
Kincannon, S. 339
Kindall, K. 350
Kindel, S. 201

King, A. 67
King, B. 189
King, D. 398
King, E. 145
King, E. 161
King, E. 205
King, E. 404
King, E. 436
King, J. 21
King, J. 87
King, J. 97
King, J. 187
King, L. 187
King, L. 375
King, M. 2
King, M. 115
King, M. 215
King, M. 225
King, M. 275
King, M. 439
King, S. 104
King, Mrs. T. 28
King, V. 231
Kingore, W. 24
Kingsbury, J. 201
Kingsbury, L. 190
Kingsbury, M. 62
Kingsley, M. 297
Kinney, H. 97
Kinney, L. 250
Kinney, M. 92
Kinney, R. 191
Kinney, V. 328
Kinsellar, F. 62
Kinzel, D. 216
Kipp, P. 55
Kirbach, L. 207
Kirby, D. 410
Kirby, M. 255
Kirchhoff, H. 119
Kirchner, E. 113
Kirk, E. 43
Kirk, F. 27
Kirk, K. 173
Kirk, L. 177
Kirk, M. 453
Kirk, P. 195
Kirkbridge, L. 454
Kirkeby, R. 382
Kirker, M. 181
Kirkingburg, L. 196
Kirkman, V. 240
Kirkpatrick, C. 349
Kirwan, K. 427
Kirkwood, B. 123
Kirkwood, E. 162
Kirt, I. 176
Kisinger, E. 170
Kisor, V. 23
Kisseberth, M. 271
Kissner, R. 325
Kistler, H. 316
Kitchell, L. 427
Kitchen, S. 328
Kite, C. 413, 415
Kitsen, J. 63
Kittles, Dr. E. 79
Kitzhaber, A. 353
Kitzler, E. 323
Kivela, M. 200
Kizer, B. 28, 29
Kjar, Mrs. A. 253
Kjos, E. 317
Klaenhammer, V. 288
Klajbor, D. 293, 302
Klappmeir, M. 149
Klasen, D. 228
Klatskin, E. 63
Klaus, I. 303
Kleberger, L. 243
Klechner, B. 122
Kleiber, R. 72
Klein, A. 268
Klein, A. 284
Klein, B. 353

Klein, C. 355
Klein, E. 88, 92, 93
Klein, G. 294
Klein, J. 44
Klein, J. 212
Klein, Sister M. 132
Klein, M. 216
Klein, P. 366
Klein, S. 178
Klein, V. 76
Klein, V. 197
Kleinberg, E. 277
Kleinhardt, A. 185
Kleinke, A. 186
Klem, B. 163
Klement, C. 163
Klements, D. 454
Klenow, J. 172
Kline, B. 453
Kline, D. 429
Kline, K. 327
Kline, R. 108
Klingbeil, K. 198
Klinger, A. 31
Klingsmith, F. 243
Klinkers, J. 179
Klitgaard, E. 409
Klokkevold, D. 16
Kloser, D. 110
Klotz, S. 192
Kluck, J. 255
Klugo, G. 299
Klyberg, A. 374
Knaggs, D. 322
Knapp, B. 348
Knapp, C. 102
Knapp, G. 189
Knapp, L. 41
Knapp, M. 31
Knapp, M. 257
Kneeland, B. 145
Knepper, S. 454
Knestrick, P. 327
Knibbs, M. 435
Kniceley, C. 440
Knight, A. 262
Knight, C. 192
Knight, D. 343
Knight, F. 41
Knight, G. 86
Kniscly, L. 365
Knoepfli, I. 344
Knopf, V. 170
Knowles, A. 57
Knowles, L. 148
Knowles, S. 16
Knox, R. 157
Knudsen, M. 172
Knudson, B. 307
Knudson, S. 386
Knudtsen, M. 259
Knudtson, B. 50
Knuth, P. 353
Knutsen, M. 120
Knutsen, M. 435
Knutson, J. 223
Knutson, L. 385
Kobernik, M. 348
Kobs, D. 220
Koch, E. 251
Koch, L. 116
Koch, M. 272
Koch, M. 357
Kochalka, B. 200
Kochicas, F. 447
Kocina, J. 255
Kock, T. 118
Kocourek, A. 386
Koczynski, V. 275
Kodalen, L. 247
Koegh, E. 204
Koehler, C. 381
Koehler, R. 38
Koehler, V. 333
Koehnstedt, H. 316

Koelling, G. 96
Koelsch, D. 188
Koenig, J. 20
Koep, M. 221
Koerber, B. 110, 121
Koerper, L. 323
Koester, H. 117
Koester, Mrs. V. 106
Kogenhop, E. 436
Koger, M. 232
Kohl, Mrs. L. 221
Kohl, M. 203
Kohler, D. 366
Kohler, G. 194
Kohler, R. 448
Kohlman, M. 183
Kohn, E. 63
Kohtala, M. 143
Kohut, K. 165
Koivunen, A. 204
Kolb, A. 70
Kolb, L. 106
Kolbe, J. 386
Kolka, M. 448
Kollasch, M. 242
Komer, O. 215
Kominsky, L. 453
Komosa, M. 97
Kondrick, M. 362
Koniszewski, M. 282
Konald, S. 199
Konrad, M. 182
Konshuh, G. 198
Konya, E. 100
Koonce, S. 152
Koontz, L. 100
Koontz, L. 369
Kopchak, E. 331
Kopec, P. 303
Kopel, J. 115
Kopenski, H. 177
Kopietz, I. 174
Kopp, N. 150
Kordek, D. 20
Korevaar, C. 426
Koroch, B. 172
Koronka, L. 177
Korvell, E. 435
Kurt, R. 135
Korth, K. 250
Kosa, M. 215
Koschmeded, B. 117
Koscielniak, M. 177
Kosinski, J. 258
Koski, E. 199
Koski, E. 368
Koski, J. 186
Koskoff, G. 63
Koslosky, C. 436
Kosmo, H. 43
Koss, H. 151
Kossatz, M. 283
Koster, M. 375
Koszegi-Dabbous, M. 353
Kotan, M. 383
Kotch, K. 216
Kote, B. 117
Koutnik, R. 187
Koutny, B. 349
Kovac, K. 74
Kovalak, C. 172
Kovar, M. 43
Kowalczyk, S. 174
Kowalk, H. 188
Kowalski, B. 64
Kozkowski, M. 33
Kozlowski, I. 189
Kraft, P. 132
Krah, M. 62
Krajceck, B. 281
Krajczar, N. 283
Krall, M. 226
Kramer, A. 249
Kramer, M. 23
Kramer, M. 290

Kramer, P. 199
Krantz, B. 255
Kranz, M. 203
Krasker, E. 262
Kransnickas, A. 61
Krause, E. 290, 293
Krause, H. 254
Krause, N. 256
Krauskopf, J. 245
Krausz, F. 195
Kravitch, P. 85
Krawczyk, D. 331
Kraybill, M. 67
Kreft, M. 174
Kreifels, P. 253
Kreiger, M. 49
Kreiner, H. 179
Kreisle, M. 106
Kreiter, Sister C. 106
Krejmas, G. 162
Krell, E. 201
Kremers, M. 181
Krenek, R. 393
Kreps, J. 2
Kresky, Dr. B. 302
Kretzinger, J. 96
Kreutz, S. 253
Krevinghaus, L. 173
Krichmar, A. 196
Krick, C. 383
Krider, M. 255
Kriesch, C. 192
Krijci, L. 207
Krimm, E. 178
Kristeller, E. 302
Kristin, W. 121
Krivosh, A. 335
Kroetsch, V. 209
Kroger, A. 409
Kroger, J. 385
Krolak, E. 259
Kroll, B. 357
Kronholm, L. 63
Kronick, R. 58
Krotzer, E. 188
Krug, M. 437
Kruger, B. 267
Kruger, H. 447
Kruger, V. 188
Krull, M. 130
Krumm, M. 427
Krupa, M. 179
Krupansky, B. 335
Krupsak, M. 289
Kruse, R. 121
Kruse, R. 255
Kruse, S. 37
Krusen, M. 254
Kruzel, F. 196
Kubota, C. 435
Kuchynka, A. 220
Kuck, M. 412
Kucklick, W. 431
Kuebler, M. 170
Kuechler, R. 154
Kuehn, L. 39
Kugler, S. 93
Kuhlman, E. 445
Kuhlman, I. 347
Kuhn, L. 453
Kuhn, P. 21
Kuhn, S. 106
Kuhns, L. 358
Kuizenga, D. 349
Kuk, M. 315
Kukowski, C. 223
Kulander, N. 131
Kulick, T. 358
Kulman, D. 284
Kummer, E. 215
Kumpe, M. 79
Kundert, A. 381, 385
Kuney, R. 120
Kunin, M. 409,413, 414
Kunnen, E. 179

Kurek, M. 191
Kurtz, E. 104
Kurtz, F. 121
Kurtz, S. 315
Kusina, Sister M. 336
Kussmaul, F. 211
Kyer, M. 48
Kyle, M. 66

Labadie, J. 184
Labahn, C. 384
Labedz, B. 249
LaBrecque, M. 144
LaCase, N. 140
Lacer, B. 322
Lacey, C. 296
Lacey, R. 112
Lack, L. 26
Lackey, G. 454
Lackey, S. 39
Lackowsky, G. 29
Lacy, G. 440
Lacy, S. 273
Ladas, B. 72
Ladd, D. 96
Ladd, E. 262
Ladd, J. 172
LaFarge, F. 85
Lafferty, E. 301
LaFleur, M. 139
LaFluer, V. 161
LaFond, J. 161
LaForge, M. 143
LaFuente, C. 300
LaGrange, J. 119,123
Lahr, E. 227
Lai, M. 87
Laine, D. 33
Laing, J. 255
Laing, V. 188
Lainhart, C. 135
Lair, K. 133
Laird, B. 334
Laird, F. 100
Laise, C. 12
Lake, J. 48
Lake, J. 397
Lake, N. 324
Lalko, J. 208
Lally, M. 281
LaLonde, C. 191
LaMar, G. 343
Lamb, A. 71
Lamb, A. 375
Lamb, B. 66
Lamb, M. 13
Lamb, V. 12
Lamberson, L. 18
Lambert, A. 196
Lambert, B. 417
Lambert, D. 206
Lambert, I. 16
Lambert, J. 323
Lambert, J. 384
Lambert, L. 436
Lambert, N. 20
Lambert, P. 344
Lamberta, L. 68
Lambertsen, Dr. E. 301
Lamborne, N. 418
Lambright, Mrs. J. 380
Lamerand, G. 180
Lammert, E. 241
Lamont, F. 381
Lamont, L. 215
Lamont, P. 384
Lamoreaux, B. 44
Lamoreaux, D. 177
Lamp, L. 111
Lampe, V. 423
Lamphear, K. 130
Lamphere, L. 384
Lamphere, P. 432,436
Lamsett, R. 316
Lamy, C. 262

Lance, B. 341
Lance, Mrs. W. 283
Land, I. 74
Land, J. 84
Land, M. 113
Land, M. 200
Land, N. 131
Land, S. 62
Landauer, A. 127
Landberg, S. 188
Landenberger, J. 198
Lander, J. 394
Landheer, C. 168
Landingham, P. 43
Landis, E. 68
Landler, Mrs. F. 434
Landman, M. 415
Landon, M. 194
Landreth, J. 383
Landrum, R. 9
Landskov, C. 223
Lane, B. 52
Lane, Mrs. B. 423
Lane, C. 255
Lane, E. 113
Lane, H. 206
Lane, I. 81
Lane, M. 143
Lane, M. 144
Lane, M. 422
Lanegran, V. 228
Lang, P. 327
Lang, R. 89
Lang, T. 251, 254
Langdon, F. 123
Langdon, M. 449
Langdon, T. 15
Lange, E. 16
Lange, Mrs. F. 403
Lange, J. 115
Langenburg, J. 170
Langfeld, M. 221
Langford, E. 203
Langin, B. 116
Langley, M. 352
Langlois, B. 37
Langmack, V. 326
Langner, P. 434
Langston, R. 340
Langton, C. 62
Lanning, V. 328
Lanoy, M. 320
Lantz, B. 77
Lanzos, K. 368
Lapakko, T. 231
LaPlante, R. 414
LaPoint, C. 140
Lapoint, C. 385
LaPorte, J. 73
LaPrade, B. 18
LaPrath, J. 435
Laramore, B. 105
Laraway, B. 317
Lardenois, J. 129
Lardy, A. 449
Lare, C. 66
Largent, A. 130
Laribee, E. 386
Larkin, B. 170
Larkin, V. 373
Larner, M. 267
LaRose, M. 375
Larouche, J. 385
Larrick, A. 326
Larriva, Mrs. L. 20
Larsen, M. 13
Larson, A. 316
Larson, A. 383
Larson, B. 435
Larson, C. 420
Larson, E. 230
Larson, E. 385
Larson, F. 174
Larson, H. 180
Larson, J. 144

Larson, L. 92
Larson, M. 13
Larson, M. 16
Larson, M. 59
Larson, M. 125
Larson, N. 455
Larson, P. 16
Larson, V. 222
Larson, V. 252
LaRue, L. 349
Laseman, G. 393
Lash, D. 75
Lash, I. 415
Lasker, Mrs. A. 302
Laskey, L. 320
Laskey, N. 216
Laskos, N. 61
Laslavic, M. 359
Lasley, J. 196
Lassegne, C. 141
Lassek, H. 254,255
Lassila, D. 168
Latham, L. 380
Lathrop, C. 235
Lathrop, M. 436
Latourell, E. 434
Latta, P. 311
Latting, P. 338
Lauber, F. 31
Lauer, V. 202
Lauer, Y. 370
Lauf, Sister A. 343
Laughlin, E. 240
Laumner, D. 191
Laurel, A. 392
Laurent, N. 225
Lauria, L. 177
Lautner, A. 181
Lavelle, R. 60
Lavender, C. 390
Lavender, R. 193
Laverdure, B. 318
Lavoid, M. 247
Lavoil, D. 133
Law, L. 441
Law, V. 200
Lawford, P. 301
Lawler, L. 95
Lawlor, Sister E. 302
Lawniczak, C. 171
Lawrence, A. 28
Lawrence, B. 197
Lawrence, D. 331
Lawrence, E. 302
Lawrence, F. 407
Lawrence, I. 329
Lawrence, J. 24
Lawrence, Dr. M. 302,303
Lawrence, P. 288
Lawrence, R. 424
Lawrence, V. 123
Lawson, A. 84
Lawson, Mrs. E. 403
Lawson, M. 106
Lawson, N. 378
Lawson, P. 421
Lawson, V. 206
Laycock, B. 262
Layfield, F. 77
Layfield, V. 156
Layman, B. 203
Layman, J. 122
Layton, P. 135
Layton, R. 185
Lazarus, M. 336
Lazerchick, D. 364
Lea, R. 298
Lea, W. 7
Leach, D. 134
Leach, M. 240
Leach, M. 253
Leach, R. 325
Leach, S. 20
Lease, M. 330
Leavens, B. 414

Leavitt, J. 34
Leavitt, M. 414
Leavitt, R. 148
LeBeau, A. 454
Lebel, I. 267
Lebens, D. 228
LeBlanc, C. 139
Lebowitz, S. 62
LeBrun, J. 207
Lebsack, K. 454
LeCato, V. 156
Lechner, C. 14
Lechner, H. 285
Leckie, P. 211
LeClair, C. 51
LeClaire, J. 40
Lecours, R. 162
Ledbetter, A. 394
Ledbetter, Mrs. C. 29
Lederberg, V. 372
Ledesma, T. 216
Ledford, A. 325
LeDuc, K. 385
LeDudley, M. 21
Lee, B. 127
Lee, B. 147
Lee, D. 76
Lee, E. 122
Lee, E. 131
Lee, E. 425,434,437
Lee, F. 314
Lee, G. 95
Lee, G. 254
Lee, H. 191
Lee, J. 101
Lee, J. 132
Lee, J. 211
Lee, J. 449
Lee, K. 313
Lee, L. 151
Lee, L. 313
Lee, L. 383
Lee, M. 106
Lee, M. 209
Lee, M. 223
Lee, M. 337
Lee, M. 453
Lee, N. 148
Lee, P. 15
Lee, R. 9
Lee, S. 314
Lee, V. 178, 215
Lee, W. 420
Leed, D. 359
Leeds, I. 304
Leehan, B. 317
Leek, A. 359
Leek, B. 407
Leeka, E. 119
Leeks, M. 216
Leeper, D. 116
Leer, M. 315
Lefebvre, L. 436
Lefever, E. 82
Lefevre, M. 102
Lefkowitz, E. 38
LeGault, H. 63
Leger, J. 136
Legg, C. 439
Legg, G. 46
Legg, R. 175
Legg, S. 248
Legett, V. 231
Lehenbauer, M. 245
Lehman, E. 433
Lehman, H. 28
Lehmann, L. 122
Lehmbeck, N. 162
Lehner, C. 191
Lehrer, P. 67
Lehto, A. 217
Leibee, L. 254
Leiber, L. 339
Leick, J. 130
Leidner, R. 444

Leightver, D. 212
Leighty, I. 362
Leik, H. 112
Leikam, B. 221
Leinen, D. 318
Leininger, C. 171
Leipzig, M. 33
Leissner, H. 402
LeMaster, F. 9
LeMasters, D. 104
Lemcke, C. 230
Lemke, V. 167
Lemley, J. 29
Lemmer, J. 199
Lemon, E. 154
Lemon, H. 326
Lemon, R. 127
LeMoyne, S. 91
Lengel, J. 27
Lengemann, E. 249
Lenhart, K. 331
Lenhart, M. 118
Lenoir, E. 396
Lentz, Mrs. H. 316
Lentz, Mrs. V. 423
Lentz, W. 189
Lenz, Mrs. B. 259
Lenz, E. 430
Lenz, M. 189
Leod, Mrs. D. 380
Leonard, E. 55
Leonard, E. 136
Leonard, E. 140
Leonard, H. 102
Leonard, J. 434
Leonard, K. 179
Leonard, L. 373,375
Leonard, M. 167
Leonard, M. 432
Leone, A. 284
LePage, D. 449
Lepke, P. 120
Leppanen, J. 181
Lepper, S. 63
LeRaney, B. 349
LeRay, M. 138
Lerch, J. 370
Leschohier, M. 449
Lesemann, J. 269
Lesh, I. 204
Leslie, J. 82
Lesser, M. 92
Lesser, R. 303
Letendre, D. 170
Letson, B. 173
Lettick, A. 62
Letvin, B. 294,300
Leuthner, M. 220
Leuthold, C. 244
Leutz, P. 188
Leuze, D. 295
Levalle, L. 445
Levanduski, C. 370
Leven, P. 375
Levene, V. 301
Levenson, F. 302,303
LeVent, A. 212
Leverette, S. 380
Levesque, F. 411
Levesque, J. 160
Levetan, L. 80, 85
Levey, L. 302
Levi, M. 336
Levin, C. 288
Levine, A. 63
Levine, B. 86
Levine, P. 300
Levinson, V. 71
Levit, S. 32
Levitt, B. 20
Levy, J. 72
Levy, J. 91
Levy, R. 157
Levy, S. 30
Levzinger, U. 89

Lewandowski, M. 214
Lewies, L. 89
Lewin, M. 282
Lewis, A. 20
Lewis, A. 43
Lewis, A. 311
Lewis, A. 439
Lewis, C. 12
Lewis, C. 66
Lewis, C. 186
Lewis, D. 252
Lewis, D. 397
Lewis, E. 257
Lewis, Dr. E. 302
Lewis, E. 337
Lewis, E. 409
Lewis, G. 185
Lewis, H. 427
Lewis, J. 3
Lewis, J. 101
Lewis, J. 142
Lewis, J. 352
Lewis, Mrs. J. 378
Lewis, L. 85
Lewis, L. 279
Lewis, M. 34
Lewis, M. 126
Lewis, M. 174
Lewis, M. 205
Lewis, M. 384
Lewis, M. 422
Lewis, M. 440
Lewis, P. 157
Lewis, P. 169
Lewis, P. 257, 258
Lewis, P. 435
Lewis, R. 147
Lewis, S. 15
Lewis, S. 147
Lewis, S. 434
Lewis, W. 290, 293
Lewisohn, J. 303, 304
Lewton, L. 252
Lex, A. 153
Ley, D. 255, 256
Leyja, C. 343
Leysring, P. 315
Li, V. 284
Liabenow, N. 174
Libby, E. 56
Libhart, O. 149
Lichlenstein, Mrs. V. 424
Licht, D. 373
Licht, N. 370
Lichty, M. 119
Lickerman, C. 102
Liddicoat, M. 31
Liddle, V. 295
Lidstone, M. 295
Liebelt, J. 384
Lieber, A. 190
Lieber, D. 185
Liebhaber, H. 29
Lier, J. 76
Lifshitz, M. 58
Lifton, B. 64
Liggett, G. 50
Light, C. 48
Light, P. 422
Lightfoot, M. 64
Lightfoot, M. 340
Lightsey, Mrs. R. 11
Likar, M. 222
Likes, M. 255
Lilley, D. 294
Lillick, L. 402
Lillicrap, M. 413
Lillie, M. 44
Lilligren, P. 230
Lillis, J. 297, 300
Lilly, M. 19
Lilly, P. 62
Limbach, J. 319
Lin, P. 75
Linard, S. 286

Lincoln, G. 16
Lincoln, J. 449
Lindamon, D. 244
Lindberg, H. 121
Lindberg, J. 224
Lindbloom, F. 46
Lindell, J. 68
Lindeman, A. 17
Lindemann, R. 386
Linden, G. 64
Lindenau, J. 184
Linder, S. 369
Linderman, B. 294
Lindquist, C. 434
Lindquist, M. 301
Lindsay, I. 180
Lindsay, M. 125
Lindsay, S. 213
Lindsey, C. 350
Lindsey, Mrs. J. 23
Lindsey, M. 24
Lindsey, P. 91
Lindsey, R. 93
Lindstrom, A. 286
Lineberger, D. 311
Ling, K. 167
Linge, D. 329
Lingle, J. 126
Link, M. 199
Link, M. 390
Link, S. 132
Linker, K. 14
Linker, V. 403
Linkiewicz, C. 369
Linn, Dr. E. 394
Linna, A. 199
Linsenman, V. 193
Linstrom, A. 287
Linville, E. 238
Linville, P. 239
Lipman, T. 149
Lipman, W. 268
Lippincott, A. 61
Lipschutz, G. 290
Lipsky, J. 107
Liptak, G. 347
Lisek, A. 454
Lisle, R. 73
Lister, E. 194
Litaker, R. 380
Littich, C. 191
Little, A. 83
Little, D. 174
Little, D. 184
Little, F. 311
Little, M. 436
Little, R. 282
Littlefield, E. 149
Littlefield, K. 147
Littleton, R. 110
Litzenberger, L. 14
Litzner, S. 197
Liupakka, W. 176
Liuzzo, S. 49
Livengood, M. 130
Livesay, J. 137
Livingston, A. 23
Livingston, D. 407
Livingston, J. 132
Livingston, M. 336
Livingston, V. 323
Lianeza, V. 78
Llewellyn, F. 430
Llewellyn, Mrs. J. 28
Lloyd, A. 193
Lloyd, G. 373
Lloyd, I. 185
Lloyd, J. 247
Lloyd, K. 16
Lloyd, M. 5
Lobaugh, S. 16
Lobenherz, E. 183
Lock, N. 122
Lockaby, J. 387
Locke, L. 37

Locke, P. 309
Lockett, Mrs. T. 29
Lockett, V. 387
Lockhart, H. 271
Lockie, V. 115
Lockwood, L. 183
Lockwood, M. 253
Lockwood, V. 20
Lodefink, P. 434
Lodge, S. 42
Loeffler, B. 339
Loehr, E. 455
Loehr, R. 166
Loenning, D. 16
Loerwald, M. 114
Loew, H. 284
Loewen, B. 47
Lofgren, S. 20
Lofgren, T. 398
Logan, E. 43
Logan, F. 247
Logan, I. 25
Logan, J. 63
Logan, V. 178
Loggins, R. 83
Loh, Mrs. P. 27
Lohman, B. 216
Lohmann, J. 279
Lohr, A. 361
Loiederman, R. 157
Lolar, B. 147
Lomack, M. 13
Loman, P. 341
Lomen, M. 16
Lonardo, M. 59
Londry, M. 172
Lonergan, J. 107
Lonergan, K. 375
Long, B. 231, 233
Long, B. 310
Long, C. 27
Long, C. 74
Long, D. 27
Long, D. 36
Long, D. 239
Long, E. 229
Long, G. 26
Long, G. 176
Long, I. 175
Long, K. 50
Long, M. 85
Long, M. 99
Long, M. 127
Long, M. 332
Long, N. 153
Long, V. 268
Longfield, Y. 104
Lonnberg, A. 129
Lonon, C. 288
Lonon, O. 434
Look, S. 146
Loomis, R. 453
Looper, M. 343
Lopes, M. 373
Lopez, A. 284
Lopez, B. 20, 21
Lopez, B. 51
Lopez, E. 257
Lopez, J. 123
Lopez, J. 288
LoPiesti, A. 59
Lopiz, L. 408
Lord, A. 303
Lord, F. 64
Lord, J. 278
Lord, M. 14
Lord, M. 338
Lorenz, E. 347
Lormann, J. 75
Lorren, D. 353
Losch, P. 441
Losey, K. 84
Loss, F. 76
Lott, H. 259
Louard, A. 302

Loucks, B. 384
Loucks, J. 114
Loucks, M. 385
Loudermilk, E. 86
Loudon, J. 112
Loughlin, C. 259
Louis, E. 198
Lovas, J. 272
Love, A. 79
Love, H. 325
Love, L. 175
Love, R. 117
Lovegrove, M. 183
Lovejoy, D. 267
Lovejoy, V. 262
Lovette, N. 233
Lovette, S. 201
Lovvorn, E. 11
Low, Mrs. R. 302
Low, S. 421
Lowden, L. 61
Lowden, M. 143
Lowe, A. 75
Lowe, D. 122
Lowe, E. 351, 354
Lowe, M. 303
Lowe, P. 43
Lowe, P. 395
Lowenthalm, M. 138
Lowery, G. 420
Lowery, K. 340
Lowery, M. 255
Lowman, J. 82
Lowrimore, R. 339
Lowry, A. 136
Lowry, M. 73
Lowy, B. 13
Loy, A. 71
Loyd, D. 347
Loyd, H. 48
Lubay, K. 136
Lubberts, I. 223
Lubchansky, R. 62
Lubeck, M. 226
Lucas, B. 135
Lucas, B. 434
Lucas, D. 454
Lucas, F. 312
Lucas, H. 278
Lucas, J. 267
Lucas, M. 312
Lucas, M. 430
Lucas, R. 205
Lucas, S. 379
Luce, M. 52
Lucenti, M. 414
Lucius, R. 224
Lucke, Z. 435
Luckhardt, E. 443
Luckstead, N. 117
Ludlum, M. 337
Ludovissy, C. 116
Luecke, J. 395
Luff, E. 155
Luke, K. 342
Luksich, E. 302
Lumbard, C. 121
Lumet, G. 304
Lumpkins, M. 389
Luna, M. 288
Lund, B. 407
Lund, P. 190
Lund, P. 423
Lund, S. 148, 149
Lunde, J. 315
Lundgren, K. 255
Lunt-Aucoin, T. 148
Lupi, M. 276
Lupton, G. 129
Lupu, M. 20
Luray, E. 284
Lurie, J. 303
Lusardi, C. 423
Luscombe, S. 267
Luszczak, A. 63

Lutkat, C. 316
Lutterbie, P. 79
Lutz, E. 306
Lutz, R. 360
Lutz, S. 123
Lux, V. 205
Luxmoore, V. 212
Luyster, M. 43
Luzzati, R. 124
Lyall, K. 3
Lyke, J. 194
Lyke, M. 50
Lyman, Mrs. J. 245
Lynch, B. 346
Lynch, Mrs. E. 286
Lynch, M. 394
Lynn, E. 365
Lynn, J. 421
Lyon, E. 15
Lyon, E. 39
Lyon, E. 196
Lyon, J. 21
Lyon, J. 112
Lyon, L. 121
Lyon, W. 203
Lyons, C. 248
Lyons, D. 216
Lyons, E. 262
Lyons, L. 136
Lyons, M. 374,375
Lyons, N. 367
Lyons, N. 440
Lyons, P. 224
Lyons, S. 384
Lyte, Mrs. E. 157
Lytel, E. 291
Lytle, M. 183
Lytle, R. 169

Maag, J. 113
Maas, B. 299
Maas, E. 111
Mabbus, L. 232
Mabry, J. 9
Mabry, V. 422
Macaulay, S. 188
MacAvoy, C. 104
MacColl, L. 353
Macbeth, V. 64
MacCormac, N. 309
Mac Donald, B. 74
Mac Donald, E. 429
Mac Donald, V. 94
Mac Duff, B. 210
Mac Eachern, J. 258
Mac Farland, K. 132
Mac Gregor, E. 180
Mac Greger, N. 160
Machnicke, H. 237
Machovsky, B. 316
Maciag, K. 196
Maciasmedina, T. 255
MacIlwaine, P. 319
Macintosh, S. 162
Mac Issac, M. 149
Mac Ivor, D. 262
Mack, D. 335
Mack, J. 455
Mack, L. 36
Mack, M. 329
Mack, M. 393
Mack, S. 104
MacKaben, L. 346
MacKeil, L. 298
Mackenne, M. 162
Mackey, B. 308
Mackey, C. 9
Mackey, L. 292
Mackey, Mrs. M. 287
Mackey, M. 380
Mackie, B. 237
Mackin, J. 15
Mackin, R. 118
MacKinnon, N. 60
Mackolin, J. 303

Mackrell, G. 394
Macktaz, P. 375
MacLain, A. 36
MacLeod, E. 302
MacMarsh, S. 249
MacNab, B. 76
MacNeil, D. 369
MacPartin, A. 116
MacQueen, B.T. 216
MacVane, K. 84
Macy, B. 254
Macy, E. 453
Macy, F. 99
Madden, D. 292
Madden, L. 66
Madden, M. 15
Maddox, H. 197
Maddron, E. 352
Maddy, S. 235
Madison, M. 324
Madole, J. 51
Madry, M. 336
Maeda, S. 435
Maeder, J. 454
Maedke, Mrs. C. 446
Maffeo, M. 21
Magaro, J. 149
Magdalene, Sister M. 244
Magedanz, E. 386
Magee, L. 174
Magin, S. 302
Magliere, M. 364
Maglione, L. 161
Magnello, D. 62
Magnuson, J. 250
Magnusson, D. 255
Magorien, K. 383
Magowan, J. 258
Magruder, A. 236
Maguire, F. 373
Maguire, Mrs. J. 157
Maguire, M. 157
Maguire, M. 374
Mahaffey, M. 206, 216
Mahaffey, M. 363
Mahalchak, R. 361
Mahalick, D. 269
Mahan, E. 237
Mahan, J. 422
Mahannah, A. 57
Maher, J. 57
Maher, J. 259
Maher, M. 410
Maher, P. 201
Maher, W. 114
Mahlberg, D. 117
Mahnke, G. 250
Mahone, G. 395
Mahoney, J. 15
Mahoney, J. 32
Maier, G. 273
Maier, H. 329
Maier, T. 231
Maigret, M. 372
Maillian, Sister R. 404
Main, L. 439
Main, M. 200
Main, T. 377
Maisner, K. 217
Maixner, L. 318
Majeski, D. 229
Major, H. 253
Majors, M. 122
Majors, S. 255, 256
Maki, E. 170
Maki, G. 198
Maki, K. 196
Maki, M. 187
Makinen, A. 170
Maklary, D. 274
Makley, M. 213
Malavolti, M. 111
Malburg, G. 201
Malburg, L. 201
Malcho, B. 195

Malchon, J. 71
Maleski, V. 324
Malinowski, M. 193
Malkin, J. 201
Mallett, J. 383
Mallin, J. 283
Mallon, O. 202
Mallory, S. 303
Malmberg, M. 357
Malmsten, J. 230
Malnar, I. 190
Malone, H. 26
Malone, M. 285
Maloney, Sister E. 284
Maloney, M. 151
Maloney, Sister M. 253
Maloney, P. 423
Maloney, S. 420
Maloof, C. 288
Maloomian, H. 262
Maloy, G. 71
Malta, E. 417
Malutin, L. 15
Maly, B. 316
Malyjurek, M. 21
Mandes, R. 66
Mandl, N. 92, 93
Mandujano, M. 252
Maneke, G. 188
Maness, J. 16
Maness, J. 237
Maneval, O. 184
Maney, H. 297
Manfredi, C. 284
Mangan, N. 300
Mangano, P. 443
Mangin, R. 380
Mangione, M. 136
Mangrum, M. 23
Mangum, H. 396
Mangum, K. 312
Mangus, A. 242
Manifold, E. 7
Maniglia, D. 191
Manley, G. 85
Manley, M. 302
Manly, N. 232
Mann, B. 384
Mann, D. 274
Mann, F. 233
Mann, J. 11
Mann, L. 148
Mann, L. 310
Mann, R. 419
Mannering, A. 66
Manninen, M. 202
Manning, D. 181
Manning, G. 114
Manning, G. 390
Manning, H. 162
Manning, L. 406
Manning, M. 67
Manning, R. 236
Mannisto, E. 208
Manogue, H. 284
Manos, J.R. 214
Manry, Mrs. J. 403
Mans, R. 49
Mansel, D. 402
Mansfield, C. 121
Manson, D. 280
Mantia, M. 403
Mantia, N. 366
Mantone, F. 276
Mantych, J. 313
Manuel, R. 420
Maragos, V. 288
Maraman, B. 137
Marcantel, S. 140
March, M. 96
March, S. 86
Marchand, B. 31
Marchbanks, N. 389
Marchetti, H. 271
Marchione, D. 431

Marchky, H. 321
Marcott, M. 201
Marcotte, J. 20
Marcum, B. 327
Marcy, J. 153
Maresh, R. 255
Margetts, J. 283
Margolis, G. 70
Marie, Sister D. 63
Marie, Sister J. 28
Marie, S. 322
Marietta, L. 365
Marion, E. 155
Marix, Y. 76
Mark, M. 307
Markel, L. 177
Markey, M. 46
Marks, E. 363
Marks, J. 45
Marks, M. 245
Markwitz, A. 304
Marley, B. 325
Marousek, V. 448
Marquart, D. 315
Marr, Mrs. C. 303
Marriott, G. 234
Marrison, J. 236
Marron, B. 447
Marschall, C. 219
Marsh, B. 285
Marsh, B. 367
Marsh, L. 409
Marsh, M. 411
Marshall, A. 174
Marshall, E. 370
Marshall, E. 383
Marshall, G. 195
Marshall, G. 232
Marshall, M. 370
Marshall, M. 416, 423
Marshall, Mrs. O. 84
Marshall, P. 52
Marshall, S. 308
Marston, W. 16
Marsyla, E. 224
Martens, V. 120
Martin, A. 13
Martin, A. 143
Martin, A. 383
Martin, A. 396
Martin, B. 44
Martin, B. 158
Martin, B. 236
Martin, Mrs. B. 287
Martin, B. 287
Martin, B. 362
Martin, B. 396
Martin, B. 424
Martin, C. 12
Martin, C. 97
Martin, Mrs. C. 393
Martin, D. 378
Martin, E. 173
Martin, E. 367
Martin, E. 441
Martin, E. 444
Martin, F. 257
Martin, J. 28
Martin, Mrs. J. 138
Martin, J. 262
Martin, J. 296
Martin, K. 72
Martin, K. 186
Martin, K. 420
Martin, L. 94
Martin, M. 11
Martin, M. 42
Martin, M. 54
Martin, M. 85
Martin, M. 210
Martin, M. 237
Martin, M. 310
Martin, M. 340
Martin, M. 411, 413
Martin, M. 441

Martin, N. 155
Martin, N. 442
Martin, P. 94
Martin, P. 344
Martin, Mrs. R. 284
Martin, R. 302
Martin, R. 336
Martin, R. 377
Martin, T. 280
Martin, V. 395
Martindale, A. 90
Martindale, B. 417
Martindale, E. 177
Martindell, A. 3
Martineau, L. 449
Martinez, A. 3
Martinez, A. 354
Martinez, L. 52
Martinez, L. 288
Martinez, M. 288
Martinez, S. 408
Martini, E. 185
Martinko, Sister M. 86
Martinson, V. 182
Martz, J. 266
Martz, M. 361
Marvel, E. 67
Marvie, M. 145
Marvin, H. 305
Marx, D. 437
Marx, M. 435
Mascia, L. 358
Mascia, M. 61
Maser, C. 16
Masloff, S. 366
Mason, A. 327
Mason, A. 423
Mason, B. 259
Mason, H. 274
Mason, H. 322
Mason, H. 455
Mason, Mrs. J. 303
Mason, M. 309
Mason, Mrs. R. 78
Mason, W. 292
Massad, M. 343
Massaro, H. 77
Massey, B. 147
Massey, K. 419
Massey, L. 403
Massey, M. 48
Massingale, R. 325
Massiwer, M. 375
Mast, M. 148
Masters, J. 430
Masters, M. 196
Masterton, N. 143
Mateo, L. 301
Matheny, M. 139
Matheny, M. 331
Mathews, D. 113
Mathews, Mrs. W. 344
Mathias, Mrs. C. 157
Mathiesen, P. 50
Mathieson, H. 361
Mathis, C. 305
Mathis, F. 29
Mathis, M. 24
Mathis, M. 406
Mathis, S. 70
Matlack, A. 124
Matson, B. 197
Matson, J. 435
Matson, M. 223
Matteoni, L. 304
Matter, E. 171
Matters, W. 155
Mattes, D. 249
Matthew, J. 411
Matthews, A. 59
Matthews, C. 68
Matthews, D. 203
Matthews, D. 321
Matthews, E. 152
Matthews, G. 343

Matthews, H. 21
Matthews, L. 182
Matthews, M. 216
Matthews, M. 372
Matthews, M. 407
Matthews, R. 172
Matthews, T. 299
Mattie, P. 56
Mattison, L. 411
Mattocks, C. 311
Mattox, C. 339
Mattson, E. 319
Mattson, P. 191
Matuja, M. 211
Matushefske, L. 68
Matyas, D. 178
Matz, Mrs. R. 254,255
Matzke, L. 250
Matzke, Mrs. S. 253
Mauney, I. 310
Maupin, L. 50
Maurer, L. 151, 157
Maurer, L. 212
Mauro, M. 92
Maus, M. 104
Maus, Y. 127
Mause, W. 157
Mavis, J. 199
Max, S. 419
Maxey, B. 417
Maxey, C. 239
Maxey, J. 77
Maxheimer, B. 122
Maxie, P. 425
Maxson, D. 122
Maxwell, A. 301
Maxwell, A. 442
Maxwell, D. 329
Maxwell, E. 307
Maxwell, M. 233
Maxwell, S. 241
Maxwell, S. 347
May, A. 227
May, B. 255
May, M. 180
May, S. 168
May, S. 237
Mayer, B. 172
Mayer, L. 179
Mayer, O. 44
Mayer, P. 344
Mayfield, R. 394
Mayfield, S. 184
Mayhak, H. 185
Mayhall, M. 403
Mayhew, A. 311
Mayhew, J. 145
Mayle, D. 332
Maynard, B. 59
Maynard, D. 145
Maynard, J. 374
Maynard, P. 276
Mayne, J. 113
Mayne, M. 162
Mayo, E. 147
Mays, C. 82
Mays, Mrs. F. 394
Mays, K. 422
Maze, T. 101
Maziarz, L. 360
McAfee, E. 184
McAlear, M. 248
McAlister, K. 191
McAlister, T. 9
McAllister, C. 49
McAllister, C. 363
McAllister, F. 20
McAlpin, D. 62
McAlpine, J. 206
McAlpine, L. 198
McAnany, B. 237
McAnerney, L. 12
McAninch, B. 211
McAra, M. 179
McArdle, S. 56

McAvoy, R. 262,267
McBeath, S. 174
McBee, S. 391
McBirney, R. 92
McBreer, K. 428
McCabe, I. 190
McCabe, L. 364
McCabe, P. 16
McCaffery, D. 53
McCaffrey, J. 314, 318
McCahill, H. 272
McCain, P. 111
McCalister, M. 342
McCall, B. 308
McCall, F. 254
McCall, M. 320
McCallum, C. 281
McCally, G. 169
McCann, A. 108
McCann, C. 77
McCann, D. 88
McCann, S. 58
McCarran, Sister M. 257
McCartan, A. 434
McCarthy, B. 108
McCarthy, D. 17
McCarthy, J. 106
McCarthy, Sister M. 435
McCartie, N. 108
McCartney, R. 120
McCarty, K. 344
McCarty, R. 101
McCarty, V. 3
McCarver, C. 50
McCarville, M. 109
McCaslin, V. 137
McClain, D. 153
McClain, J. 322
McClain, M. 446, 448
McClary, C. 170
McClary, E. 181
McClearn, J. 368
McClellan, A. 180
McClellan, A. 232
McClellan, G. 43
McClellan, J. 408
McClelland, B. 183
McClelland, B. 424,435
McClelland, M. 174
McClendon, S. 156
McClintock, R. 364
McCloskey, A. 134
McClure, D. 85
McClure, D. 400
McClure, K. 34
McClure, R. 302
McCluskey, D. 55
McCoach, J. 291, 293
McColgan, M. 163
McCollough, L. 166
McComb, F. 180
McComb, R. 116
McComb, V. 327
McConnell, B. 457
McConnell, J. 113
McConnell, L. 435
McConnell, M. 98
McConnell, R. 278
McConnell, R. 362
McConomy, Mrs. J. 368
McCool, P. 28
McCord, W. 141
McCormack, D. 118
McCormack, M. 22
McCormick, G. 425
McCormick, G. 445
McCormick, V. 450
McCormick, W. 397
McCotter, N. 307
McCown, S. 251
McCoy, A. 368
McCoy, D. 426
McCoy, E. 132
McCoy, E. 269
McCoy, E. 317

McCoy, G. 345
McCoy, H. 179
McCoy, M. 304
McCoy, N. 106
McCoy, Mrs. T. 283
McCracken, A. 258
McCracken, H. 402
McCraner, O. 191
McCrary, B. 84
McCrary, C. 452
McCrary, F. 136
McCrary, M. 109
McCrary, M. 403
McCray, B. 428
McCray, G. 360
McCrea, L. 201
McCready, C. 350
McCreery, R. 317
McCreight, P. 130
McCue, S. 129
McCuin, A. 248
McCullen, M. 454
McCulley, M. 347
McCullough, B. 334
McCullough, S. 380
McCullough, V. 156
McCullough-Lovell, E. 413
McCumber, B. 222
McCumber, B. 328
McCune, L. 320
McCune, M. 9
McCurry, P. 340
McCuskey, C. 442
McCutcheon, F. 108
McDade, H. 231
McDaniel, E. 157
McDaniel, J. 6
McDaniel, J. 23
McDaniel, L. 22
McDaniel, M. 442
McDaniel, Mrs. T. 401
McDearmon, Mrs. R. 392
McDermott, E. 92
McDermott, M. 364
McDermott, P. 88
McDiarmid, D. 416
McDivitt, E. 367
McDonald, B. 15
McDonald, B. 50
McDonald, Mrs. B. 378
McDonald, C. 35
McDonald, C. 154
McDonald, C. 431
McDonald, D. 77
McDonald, D. 385
McDonald, G. 257
McDonald, G. 296
McDonald, Sister G. 449
McDonald, H. 120, 121
McDonald, H. 274
McDonald, I. 357
McDonald, J. 117
McDonald, J. 400
McDonald, K. 374
McDonald, L. 266
McDonald, M. 122
McDonald, Sister M. 258
McDonald, M. 423
McDonald, Mrs. T. 381
McDonnel, M. 214
McDonnell, J. 212
McDonough, G. 409
McDonough, M. 56
McDonough, M. 201
McDougal, M. 16
McDowall, L. 423
McDowell, Mrs. B. 304
McDowell, C. 239
McEachern, D. 262
McElrom, L. 121
McElroy, M. 422
McEntyre, J. 415
McEvoy, J. 59
McEvoy, M. 148
McFadden, H. 267

McFadden, J. 11
McFadden, M. 91
McFarland, Mrs. L. 242
McFarland, S. 239
McFarlin, Mrs. J. 29
McFeeley, T. 288
McFowland, D. 242
McGall, E. 285
McGann, R. 372
McGargill, B. 114
McGarry, M. 374
McGary, L. 144
McGee, E. 199
McGee, F. 152
McGee, J. 182
McGee, M. 290
McGee, P. 20
McGee, S. 93
McGehee, J. 28
McGehee, P. 140
McGhee, H. 127
McGhee, S. 443
McGhie, D. 257, 258
McGibbon, N. 146
McGill, C. 133
McGill, C. 301
McGill, S. 86
McGill, W. 396
McGillicuddy, H. 97
McGinnis, V. 394
McGlone, P. 322
McGlynn, M. 262
McGovern, B. 247
McGovern, F. 335
McGowan, B. 27
McGowan, R. 374
McGowan, V. 365
McGowen, D. 232
McGowen, R. 255
McGrath, A. 16
McGrath, C. 51
McGrath, M. 310
McGreal, E. 268
McGregor, C. 173
McGriff, M. 324
McGuckian, E. 156
McGuire, E. 387
McGuire, G. 414
McGuire, I. 203
McGuire, K. 64
McGuire, P. 153
McGuire, S. 331
McGuire, T. 280
McGuirl, S. 373
McHenry, E. 326
McHose, M. 312
McHugh, H. 272
McHugh, N. 120
McIllece, P. 450
McIllwain, B. 7
McIllwraith, H. 280
McInerney, B. 61
McInteer, M. 255, 256
McIntire, M. 255
McIntire, P. 163
McIntosh, B. 379
McIntosh, E. 216
McIntosh, L. 303
McIntosh, S. 407
McIntosh, V. 453
McIntyre, E. 297
McIntyre, H. 84
McIntyre, Mrs. H. 155
McIntyre, J. 358
McIntyre, K. 399
McIntyre, V. 353
McIver, I. 145
McIvor, N. 149
McKay, D. 198
McKay, L. 214
McKay, M. 34
McKay, N. 431
McKay, V. 51
McKean, C. 407
McKean, J. 123

McKee, A. 121, 122
McKee, A. 341
McKee, S. 241
McKeeny, E. 441
McKellar, D. 191
McKeller, B. 353
McKenna, C. 385
McKenna, E. 265
McKenna, M. 3
McKennan, M. 304
McKenney, V. 280
McKenzie, F. 351
McKenzie, J. 131
McKenzie, P. 7
McKeon, Mrs. G. 414
McKeon, J. 167
McKeown, Y. 193
McKercher, W. 385
McKernan, B. 144
McKerson, M. 339
McKethan, H. 404
McKiernan, P. 270
McKinley, E. 328
McKinley, L. 49
McKinney, A. 79
McKinney, A. 298
McKinney, B. 325
McKinney, E. 203
McKinney, H. 92, 93
McKinney, R. 220
McKinney, R. 441
McKnight, H. 213
McKnight, M. 10
McKown, J. 174
McLain, H. 115
McLane, E. 155
McLane, Mrs. G. 28
McLane, S. 262
McLane, V. 246
McLaughlin, A. 187
McLaughlin, F. 102
McLaughlin, M. 50
McLaughlin, V. 131
McLaurin, T. 313
McLean, A. 385
McLean, A. 435
McLean, B. 297, 298, 303
McLean, L. 201
McLean, M. 276, 280
McLean, N. 395
McLeish, H. 373
McLendon, I. 81
McLennan, J. 353
McLeod, C. 60
McLeon, C. 63
McLfan, M. 28
McLure, M. 381
McMacken, J. 179
McMahon, Mrs. C. 220
McMahon, M. 101
McMahon, S. 68
McMakin, P. 344
McManamon, A. 335
McManus, C. 214
McManus, L. 310
McMarth, J. 253
McMath, Mrs. G. 422
McMenimen, K. 165
McMillan, M. 198
McMillen, D. 294
McMinn, D. 398
McMinn, S. 288
McMurray, J. 122
McMurray, N. 102
McNabb, B. 78
McNabb, E. 140
McNair, Mrs. T. 404
McNally, B. 211
McNamara, A. 135
McNamara, M. 415
McNamara, S. 138
McNamee, C. 259
McNamee, R. 166
McNeeland, R. 145
McNeese, I. 347

McNeff, M. 230
McNeil, D. 196
McNeil, F. 418
McNeil, R. 192
McNeill, J. 43
McNeill, S. 157
McNelis, S. 375
McNelly, S. 300
McNerney, H. 303
McNichol, B. 263
McNulty, D. 64
McNulty, F. 164
McNulty, S. 33
McNutt, D. 133
McPheeters, J. 346
McPherson, Mrs. R. 220
McPherson, S. 337
McPherson, V. 336
McQuade, K. 34
McQuade, M. 442
McQueeney, A. 372
McRae, C. 128
McRae, W. 23
McShea, R. 344
McTigue, E. 122
McVea, E. 365
McWilliams, A. 344
McWilliams, C. 165
McWilliams, D. 138
Meacham, S. 22
Mead, A. 303
Mead, E. 201
Mead, M. 186
Mead, M. 212
Meador, Mrs. H. 423
Meadowcroft, E. 435
Meadows, M. 418
Meagher, Mrs. J. 136
Meaghers, R. 432
Mear, L. 423
Meckel, S. 255
Meckfessel, L. 439
Meckley, L. 198
Medeiros, C. 165
Medina, M. 154
Medina, S. 259
Medlen, G. 131
Medlin, Mrs. K. 379
Medori, Mrs. E. 85
Medvin, L. 279
Meehan, R. 103
Meeker, P. 363
Meents, Mrs. W. 255, 256
Mefferd, H. 121
Mehlberg, C. 199
Mehlhouse, M. 226
Mehney, V. 205
Meichen, J. 379
Meier, M. 254
Meier, P. 95
Meier, V. 290
Meierhenry, K. 252
Meiers, R. 314
Meikle, V. 189
Meile, G. 430
Meinecke, C. 144
Meininger, L. 251
Melby, D. 155
Melchionne, T. 302
Meldrum, Mrs. D. 422
Meldrum, Mrs. D. 422
Meldrum, O. 187
Melendes, S. 277
Melendez, E. 407
Melerine, C. 138
Melikian, E. 20
Mell, E. 90
Mellon, C. 30
Mellott, L. 367
Mellow, M. 33
Melloy, K. 137
Melovidov, A. 14
Meloy, D. 298
Melton, A. 78
Melton, N. 429

Melville, C. 42
Melvin, M. 183
Melvin, N. 21
Melvin, R. 330
Melvin, R. 336
Melvold, F. 124
Memmer, E. 334
Mendelson, M. 164
Menes, P. 151, 155
Mengebler, P. 167
Menke, Mrs. L. 106
Menke, M. 209
Mensinger, P. 38
Mercer, J. 79
Mercier, S. 140
Mercil, M. 226
Merck, E. 271
Mercure, M. 289
Meredith, Mrs. H. 342
Mergentime, M. 215, 217
Merila, E. 448
Merk, B. 238
Merk, E. 336
Merkel, L. 230
Merkel, R. 153
Merkey, H. 184
Merkley, M. 407
Merrell, B. 248
Merrell, M. 82
Merrill, B. 395
Merrill, J. 204
Merrill, K. 145
Merrill, M. 149
Merrill, P. 298
Merrill, R. 21
Merrill, U. 166
Merriman, E. 359
Merriman, M. 429
Merritt, L. 106
Mersch, E. 251
Mershart, E. 449
Merz, S. 348
Messer, B. 386
Messick, L. 104
Messina, F. 65
Mestas, A. 409
Metayer, E. 159
Metcalf, J. 448
Mettert, M. 337
Metts, J. 136
Metz, C. 453
Metz, S. 153
Metz, S. 444
Metzger, G. 192
Metzler, R. 103
Meyer, A. 55, 62
Meyer, A. 245
Meyer, B. 396
Meyer, C. 454
Meyer, E. 194
Meyer, H. 100
Meyer, I. 126
Meyer, J. 284
Meyer, J. 413
Meyer, K. 413
Meyer, L. 434
Meyer, M. 431
Meyer, N. 299
Meyer, S. 384, 386
Meyer, S. 437
Meyers, J. 124
Meyers, J. 222
Meyerson, B. 301
Meyner, H. 5
Mezler, P.A. 216
Michael, A. 76
Michael, D. 149
Michael, E. 359
Michael, J. 320
Michael, M. 135
Michael, M. 198
Michael, N. 24
Michael, R. 252
Michaelis, M. 221
Michaelson, G. 302

Michaelson, R. 374
Michalove, M. 309
Michaud, A. 148
Michaud, L. 149
Michelis, R. 360
Michie, L. 424
Michkelson, B. 407
Mickelson, H. 109
Mickevich, B. 198
Mickler, S. 8
Middlebrook, J. 188
Middlebrooks, M. 82
Middleton, B. 423
Middleton, C. 343
Middleton, M. 15, 16
Middleton, M. 16
Middleton, V. 182
Midgette, M. 312
Midkiff, C. 276, 282
Midkiff, Mrs. J. 25
Miele, R. 283
Miglionico, N. 7
Miilu, M. 184
Mikalevich, N. 235
Mikel, B. 133
Miklovich, C. 147
Mikoll, A. 300, 302
Mikulski, B. 5
Milam, M. 85
Milano, E. 19
Milberg, J. 228
Milbocker, R. 193
Mildram, B. 374
Miles, J. 422
Miles, Mrs. W. 422
Miley, M. 162
Milham, B. 375
Millard, M. 120
Miller, A. 32
Miller, A. 34
Miller, A. 302
Miller, A. 343
Miller, A. 352
Miller, A. 387
Miller, A. 404
Miller, B. 45
Miller, B. 127
Miller, B. 148
Miller, B. 314
Miller, B. 325
Miller, B. 341
Miller, C. 8
Miller, C. 177
Miller, C. 285
Miller, C. 315
Miller, C. 342
Miller, C. 361
Miller, C. 391
Miller, Mrs. C. 422
Miller, D. 55
Miller, D. 155
Miller, D. 202
Miller, D. 243
Miller, D. 377
Miller, Mrs. D. 442
Miller, E. 107
Miller, E. 154
Miller, E. 199
Miller, Sister E. 254
Miller, E. 301
Miller, E. 374
Miller, E. 400
Miller, F. 137
Miller, F. 288
Miller, G. 28
Miller, G. 125
Miller, G. 338
Miller, Mrs. G. 423
Miller, H. 92
Miller, H. 111
Miller, I. 398
Miller, Mrs. J. 105
Miller, J. 113
Miller, J. 116
Miller, J. 175

Miller, J. 302
Miller, J. 317
Miller, J. 350
Miller, J. 359
Miller, J. 406
Miller, K. 65
Miller, K. 208
Miller, K. 326
Miller, K. 367
Miller, L. 44
Miller, L. 178
Miller, L. 308
Miller, L. 441
Miller, M. 157
Miller, M. 168
Miller, M. 284
Miller, M. 323
Miller, M. 379
Miller, M. 428
Miller, M. 444
Miller, N. 240
Miller, O. 107
Miller, P. 93
Miller, P. 136
Miller, R. 59
Miller, R. 91
Miller, R. 446
Miller, S. 200
Miller, S. 335
Miller, S. 361
Miller, S. 407
Miller, S. 421
Miller, T. 229
Miller, V. 47
Miller, V. 194
Miller, V. 237
Miller, V. 331
Miller, W. 27
Miller, W. 52
Milligan, J. 301
Milliken, H. 214
Milliken, Mrs. R. 380
Millikin, V. 173
Millikon, C. 364
Millman, S. 60
Millner, L. 219
Mills, B. 245
Mills, B. 317
Mills, C. 96
Mills, C. 392
Mills, C. 412
Mills, D. 100
Mills, F. 133
Mills, L. 247
Mills, M. 450
Mills, Mrs. W. 282
Millsap, J. 344
Milton, D. 78
Mims, H. 370
Mims, Mrs. T. 380
Mindt, W. 254
Miner, C. 385, 386
Miner, D. 298
Miner, D. 382
Miner, E. 250
Miner, J. 186
Miner, P. 176
Minglin, M. 121
Mingus, M. 181
Minier, B. 292
Mink, M. 342
Mink, P. 3
Minkin, V. 173
Minnefield, H. 104
Minner, R. 65
Minnich, D. 344
Minnich, J. 449
Minor, A. 10
Minor, M. 162
Monow, R. 384
Minton, L. 208
Mirel, N. 41
Miriovsky, Mrs. F. 255,256
Mirt, G. 131
Mishoe, L. 68

Misulis, R. 296
Miszkiewicz, A. 268
Mitcham, J. 11
Mitchell, A. 387
Mitchell, B. 330
Mitchell, C. 27
Mitchell, D. 79
Mitchell, D. 116
Mitchell, D. 147
Mitchell, D. 158
Mitchell, D. 408
Mitchell, E. 83
Mitchell, E. 143, 148
Mitchell, F. 280
Mitchell, F. 405
Mitchell, I. 408
Mitchell, Mrs. J. 302
Mitchell, J. 391
Mitchell, L. 330
Mitchell, M. 3, 10
Mitchell, M. 114
Mitchell, M. 253
Mitchell, O. 9
Mitchell, O. 344
Mitchell, P. 191
Mitchell, P. 212
Mitchell, P. 422
Mitchell, T. 58
Mitchell, T. 342
Mitchell, V. 19
Mitchell, V. 77
Mitchell-Bateman, M. 437
Mitzman, E. 326
Mix, M. 172
Mix, N. 453
Mixon, E. 85
Mixon, Mrs. L. 29
Mixson, K. 85
Mleczewski, N. 194
Mobeland, M. 362
Moberg, E. 365
Moberly, J. 288
Mobley, G. 440
Mock, L. 348
Mockwitz, M. 90
Modders, J. 185
Modena, D. 211
Moe, R. 199
Moeller, D. 408
Moeller, J. 105
Moeller, J. 114
Moeller, V. 122
Moellman, C. 134
Moen, L. 160
Moershel, P. 124
Moezzi, P. 259
Moffat, M. 209
Moffatt, A. 100
Moffett, B. 93
Moffit, L. 215
Moffitt, L. 169
Mogg, E. 177
Mohler, B. 331
Mohony, Sister T. 408
Mohos, P. 296
Mohr, C. 177
Mohr, H. 104
Mohr, M. 113
Mohr, T. 115
Moisan,M. 382
Moises, J. 36
Mold, S. 218
Moldwin, S. 216
Molgaard, E. 221
Molinaro, G. 46
Molinaroli, L. 410,414
Moline, F. 170
Molinski, A. 302
Molli, M. 325
Mollineaux, E. 285
Mollon, M. 198
Molter, G. 187
Monahan, L. 413
Monday, C. 441
Monge, L. 224

Monier, C. 267
Monohon, C. 425
Monroe, E. 195
Monroe, P. 129
Monroe, P. 374
Monsey, J. 241
Monson, M. 252
Monson, S. 223
Montagna, M. 161
Montague, B. 74
Montague, E. 408
Montano, E. 16
Monte, C. 420
Monten, L. 187
Montgomery, D. 344
Montgomery, J. 255
Montgomery, J. 450
Montgomery, L. 22
Montgomery, M. 123
Montgomery, P. 9
Montgomery, P. 342
Montgomery, P. 356
Montgomery, S. 342
Montoya, V. 47
Montuoro, M. 363
Montz, N. 367
Monville, C. 193
Moody, J. 148
Moody, L. 148
Moon, C. 83
Moon, Mrs. C. 421
Moon, L. 123
Moon, M. 88, 93
Moon, S. 23
Moor, M. 233
Moore, A. 68
Moore, Mrs. A. 306
Moore, A. 312
Moore, A. 417
Moore, Mrs. A. 442,443
Moore, B. 29
Moore, B. 92
Moore, B. 135
Moore, B. 343
Moore, Mrs. B. 422
Moore, B. 432
Moore, Mrs. C. 17
Moore, C. 354
Moore, Mrs. C. 423
Moore, C. 452
Moore, D. 180
Moore, D. 239,244
Moore, D. 401
Moore, D. 409
Moord, D. 412
Moore, D. 435
Moore, E. 86
Moore, F. 166
Moore, Mrs. F. 423
Moore, G. 237
Moore, H. 109
Moore, H. 415
Moore, J. 135
Moore, J. 152
Moore, J. 163
Moore, J. 353
Moore, J. 421
Moore, L. 31
Moore, L. 36
Moore, L. 323
Moore, M. 233
Moore, Mrs. M. 304
Moore, M. 337
Moore, M. 386
Moore, M. 393
Moore, M. 414
Moore, M. 451
Moore, N. 51
Moore, O. 122
Moore, O. 148
Moore, O. 452
Moore, P. 17
Moore, P. 39
Moore, P. 71
Moore, P. 120

Moore, R. 89
Moore, R. 194
Moore, S. 111
Moore, T. 66
Moore, T. 342
Moore, T. 346
Moore, Mrs. W. 404
Moore, Z. 21
Moorhead, L. 58
Morabito, M. 293
Morales, B. 19
Moran, B. 358
Moran, G. 326
Moran, J. 215
Moran, M. 134
Morancy, Sister E. 374
Morano, M. 285
Mordecai, C. 313
Morehouse, K. 225
Morehouse, Mrs. L. 451
Moren, E. 358
Morfitte, L. 92
Morgan, B. 121
Morgan, B. 247
Morgan, E. 32
Morgan, F. 293
Morgan, J. 48
Morgan, J. 249
Morgan, K. 93
Morgan, Mrs. L. 255
Morgan, M. 239
Morgan, M. 268
Morgan, P. 311
Morgan, Mrs. R. 135
Morgan, S. 121
Morgan, S. 282
Morgan, S. 344
Morgan, S. 435
Morganti, M. 58
Moriarty, Sister C. 413
Morin, B. 149
Morin, L. 346
Morken, G. 448
Morley, Y. 203
Morneault, I. 64
Morningstar, A. 359
Morphis, E. 26
Moreell, S. 136
Morrey, L. 149
Morris, C. 378
Morris, D. 299
Morris, D. 428
Morris, F. 380
Morris, G. 64
Morris, J. 111
Morris, L. 255
Morris, M. 44
Morris, M. 160
Morris, M. 177
Morris, M. 396
Morris, N. 313
Morris, O. 65
Morris, R. 61
Morris, R. 282
Morris, R. 397
Morris, R. 436
Morris, Mrs. T. 140
Morris, T. 154
Morris, W. 96
Morrison, A. 84
Morrison, C. 221
Morrison, C. 230
Morrison, D. 108
Morrison, E. 95
Morrison, E. 333
Morrison, G. 263
Morrison, K. 443
Morrison, M. 254
Morrison, M. 397
Morrison, N. 23
Morrison, R. 375
Morriss, V. 401
Morrissey, M. 161
Morrissey, S. 254
Morron, M. 21

Morros, I. 258
Morrow, B. 400
Morrow, D. 136
Morrow, M. 215
Morrow, M. 454
Morrow, S. 305
Morse, G. 410
Morse, J. 351
Morse, N. 198
Morse, P. 415
Morse, S. 148
Morse, S. 415
Morse-Sayers, E. 410
Mortensen, S. 350
Mortkowitz, M. 284
Morton, A. 3
Morton, B. 27
Morton, C. 303
Morton, Mrs. E. 26
Morton, M. 55
Moscow, L. 297
Moseley, Sitter R. 258
Moser, D. 215
Moser, H. 428
Moser, M. 91, 93
Moser, M. 113
Moser, M. 356
Moses, W. 149
Mosgaller, D. 445
Mosley, B. 30
Moss, A. 58
Moss, B. 408
Moss, J. 39
Moss, M. 122
Moss, P. 336
Moss, S. 423
Mossey, D. 247
Mostad, K. 225
Mostoller, F. 224
Motan, J. 432
Mothershed, C. 343
Motley, B. 123
Motley, C. 6
Motley, C. 36
Motley, K. 238
Motley, N. 136
Mott, G. 362
Mott, H. 141
Mott, L. 178
Mottonen, E. 171
Moul, M. 255
Moulds, T. 288
Moulin, N. 86
Mount, R. 337
Mouras, S. 329
Movick, R. 119
Mowatt, Dr. M. 436
Mowers, L. 299
Moxon, B. 381
Moy, J. 449
Moyahan, E. 282
Moyer, L. 66
Moyer, M. 154
Moyers, Mrs. B. 304
Mraz, R. 149
Mrotek, S. 449
Muchelot, B. 62
Mudd, J. 243
Mueller, H. 95
Mueller, J. 241
Mueller, M. 255
Muellner, M. 223
Muenstermann, M. 276
Muenzenmay, M. 114
Muhler, M. 269
Muir, M. 171
Mulcahy, K. 232
Muldawer, C. 85
Mulder, J. 447
Mull, K. 86
Mullan, J. 208
Mullaney, A. 373
Mullarky, M. 449
Mullen, Sister A. 255
Mullen, C. 375

Mullen, J. 380
Mullen, P. 414
Mullenax, J. 273
Mullenix, P. 221
Muller, M. 110
Muller, M. 156
Muller, M. 382
Mullina, M. 312
Mullins, M. 231
Mullins, S. 123
Mulvena, J. 67
Mumah, J. 170
Mumford, R. 73
Munchrath, V. 112
Mundell, J. 114
Munding, K. 343
Mundy, D. 98
Mundy, G. 86
Mundz, E. 385
Mugner, P. 188
Munk, Mrs. D. 258
Munoz, I. 123
Munro, M. 193
Munsey, S. 163
Munson, E. 182
Munson, H. 197
Munson, N. 348
Munsterman, S. 242
Muntean, B. 85
Munts, M. 444
Murdock, B. 56
Murdock, D. 183
Murnan, V. 243
Murphey, D. 298
Murphey, J. 290
Murphy, B. 22
Murphy, B. 63
Murphy, B. 884
Murphy, D. 43
Murphy, E. 158
Murphy, E. 375
Murphy, H. 192
Murphy, H. 441
Murphy, Mrs. I. 232
Murphy, L. 149
Murphy, L. 186
Murphy, M. 67
Murphy, M. 122
Murphy, M. 217
Murphy, M. 230
Murphy, M. 364
Murphy, M. 434
Murphy, M. 449
Murphy, R. 232
Murphy, S. 17
Murphy, S. 246
Murphy, Sister W. 92
Murphy, Mrs. W. 423
Murray, E. 357
Murray, F. 373
Murray, G. 18
Murray, H. 308
Murray, H. 344
Murray, K. 350
Murray, L. 79
Murray, L. 199
Murray, L. 344
Murray, M. 58
Murray, M. 159, 162
Murray, M. 160
Murray, M. 170
Murray, M. 373
Murray, M. 383
Murray, S. 191
Murray, V. 390
Murtaugh, P. 311
Murtie, M. 298
Musch, D. 183
Muscio, R. 304
Musil, B. 178
Musselman, L. 195
Mustain, A. 51
Mustard, D. 40
Mustard, G. 113
Muter, L. 186

Muth, W. 30
Mutz, S. 197
Mycroft, J. 374
Myeller, H. 315
Myers, A. 327
Myers, A. 370
Myers, B. 340
Myers, E. 24
Myers, E. 180
Myers, E. 380
Myers, F. 414
Myers, G. 155
Myers, G. 347
Myers, Mrs. H. 106
Myers, J. 376
Myers, K. 329
Myers, L. 385
Myers, M. 372
Myers, Mrs. M. 422
Myers, P. 106
Myers, P. 329
Myers, R. 164
Myerson, E. 161
Myffler, Mrs. J. 255
Mykkanen, R. 196
Mylan, M. 216
Myler, K. 428
Myles, C. 137
Mynning, M. 202

Naddy, E. 230
Nadeau, R. 93
Nadeau, R. 145
Naegelin, M. 400
Nafe, M. 442
Nagata, F. 86
Nagel, R. 177
Nail, S. 121
Naito, L. 87
Najarian, M. 143
Najman, M. 251
Nalda, J. 286
Nale, E. 366
Nall, A. 9
Nall, L. 257
Nalls, J. 152
Nally, E. 365
Namie, N. 139
Nammacher, R. 449
Nance, E. 341
Nance, Mrs. M. 386
Nanney, B. 421
Nardi, T. 263
Nardini, H. 108
Narkawicz, M. 58
Nash, M. 28
Nash, V. 257
Nations, J. 429
Nations, W. 25
Naughton, V. 280
Nault, J. 148
Navajo, J. 408
Navarre, D. 168
Navarre, E. 198
Nave, L. 342
Navin, G. 334
Navratil, I. 434
Nawfel, L. 149
Naylor, P. 391
Nayokpuk, M. 14
Neakok, S. 15
Neal, H. 130
Neal, J. 153
Neal, L. 241
Neal, P. 85
Neal, S. 438
Neale, B. 45
Nears, S. 341
Neathrey, D. 311
Neavill, M. 431
Nebeker, S. 435
Nebel, K. 430
Nedelman, P. 336
Nedrow, F. 346

Neeley, K. 405
Neels, G. 317
Neely, M. 349
Neely, N. 410
Neenan, E. 108
Neeper, D. 183
Neering, E. 195
Neff, E. 178
Neff, J. 116
Neff, J. 395
Neff, L. 336
Neglaska, M. 13
Neher, R. 244
Neidig, J. 362
Neiditz, M. 64
Neifert, L. 49
Neiheisel, D. 324
Neil, K. 253
Neils, B. 436
Neilson, A. 173
Neisser, A. 21
Nejezchleb, M. 253
Neligh, R. 122
Nelle, B. 375
Nellis, K. 35
Nellis, W. 177
Nelms, E. 140
Nelson, A. 385
Nelson, B. 106
Nelson, B. 436
Nelson, C. 90
Nelson, C. 309
Nelson, D. 409
Nelson, E. 115
Nelson, E. 117
Nelson, E. 181
Nelson, E. 224
Nelson, E. 309
Nelson, E. 327
Nelson, F. 13
Nelson, F. 226
Nelson, H. 448
Nelson, I. 20
Nelson, J. 16
Nelson, J. 198
Nelson, J. 203
Nelson, J. 253
Nelson, Mrs. J. 258
Nelson, J. 284
Nelson, J. 384
Nleson, J. 384
Nelson, J. 392
Nelson, K. 175
Nelson, L. 352
Nelson, L. 424
Nelson, M. 14
Nelson, M. 39
Nelson, M. 143
Nelson, M. 225
Nelson, Mrs. M. 255
Nelson, M. 431
Nelson, M. 451
Nelson, N. 453
Nelson, P. 251
Nelson, S. 164
Nelson, S. 221
Nelson, S. 386
Nelson, T. 427
Nelson, V. 116
Nemick, M. 181
Nemec, Sister E. 385
Nemecek, S. 187
Nemo, C. 79
Nemzoff-Berman, R. 263
Nenni, D. 327
Nepstad, D. 382
Neptune, J. 147
Nesbit, O. 15
Nesbitt, Mrs. C. 342, 343
Nesbitt, M. 306
Nesmith, B. 8
Ness, B. 183
Ness, C. 428
Nessa, B. 118

Netherton, B. 339
Netsch, D. 94
Netteberg, R. 218
Nettles, A. 284
Neubauer, J. 200
Neuberger, K. 283
Neubert, C. 412
Neubert, M. 372
Neuffer, I. 381
Neugebauer, J. 43
Neuhauser, M. 109
Neumann, E. 101
Nevarez, L. 37
Neves, B. 86
Nevins, S. 129
New, A. 430
New, M. 302
New, V. 195
Newberry, P. 58
Newbold, M. 228
Newbrander, A. 40
Newcomb, B. 51
Newell, E. 353
Newell, M. 207
Newhall, G. 265
Newhouse, M. 187
Newhouse, S. 173
Newkirk, E. 64
Newman, B. 308
Newman, D. 26
Newman, D. 422
Newman, E. 157
Newman, E. 171
Newman, J. 138, 139
Newman, J. 194
Newman, J. 244
Newman, Mrs. J. 404
Newman, L. 192
Newman, M. 340
Newman, M. 417
Newman, S. 201
Newman, S. 377
Newsom, D. 175
Newstrom, P. 385
Newton, D. 320
Newton, N. 119
Newton, P. 172
Newton, S. 231
Ney, J. 365
Neyens, J. 43
Neylan, K. 122
Nez, D. 257
Ngaam, P. 267
Nguyen, D. 436
Nicely, J. 419
Nicely, M. 411
Niceum, Z. 130
Nicewander, N. 99
Nichol, B. 337
Nicholas, L. 254
Nicholls, D. 56
Nichols, B. 130
Nichols, C. 21
Nichols, C. 76
Nichols, E. 299
Nichols, E. 385
Nichols, G. 242
Nichols, J. 149
Nichols, L. 174
Nichols, L. 350
Nichols, M. 132
Nichols, M. 374, 375
Nichols, N. 168
Nichols, S. 48
Nicholson, D. 239
Nicholson, G. 236
Nicholson, J. 117
Nicholson, R. 397
Nick, B. 157
Nickerson, B. 67
Nickles, V. 110
Nicks, K. 37
Nicol, D. 99
Nicol, V. 184
Nicola, A. 148

Nicoli, D. 239
Niedens, M. 127
Niederman, M. 56
Niehues, A. 128
Niejadlik, B. 63,64
Nielsen, E. 200
Nielson, F. 47
Nielson, M. 178
Nielson, Mrs. M. 256
Nielson, M. 283
Niemela, T. 181
Niemi, E. 74
Niemi, J. 433
Nierenberg, J. 304
Nieschulz, H. 176
Nieto, D. 254
Niewoehner, M. 316
Nighswander, E. 263
Nikolai, L. 449
Niles, A. 124
Nimaroff, F. 367
Nimms, V. 394
Nitengale, C. 182
Niven, B. 353
Nix, P. 104
Nixon, B. 390
Nixon, D. 428
Nizolek, C. 61
Noack, W. 206
Noble, E. 158
Noble, H. 212
Noble, M. 121
Noble, M. 149
Noble, S. 213
Nobles, B. 392
Nock, M. 156
Noe, M. 306
Noekker, L. 113
Noel, M. 427
Noeller, P. 383
Nofzinger, E. 190
Nojima, Mrs. K. 258
Nolan, D. 29
Nolan, Mrs. W. 28
Nold, H. 319
Noles, E. 303
Nolin, V. 100
Noll, M. 29
Nolte, E. 325
Nopuolos, I. 112
Nord, E. 375
Nordenbrook, R. 436
Nordhoff, N. 436
Nordyke, K. 44
Nore, C. 255
Norfleet, B. 400
Norfleet, E. 137
Norgaard, T. 219
Norgard, B. 249
Norling, A. 149
Norman, G. 245
Norman, J. 76
Norman, S. 320
Norquist, J. 119
Norris, B. 250
Norris, L. 362
Norris, S. 200
Norriss, Mrs. R. 395
North, E. 425, 437
North, L. 425, 434, 437
Northen, M. 403
Northop, A. 123
Northup, K. 62
Norton, B. 13
Norton, E. 3
Norton, F. 192
Norton, J. 350
Norton, K. 118
Norton, L. 14
Norton, M. 346
Norton, R. 432
Norton, Mrs. T. 398
Nortwick, A. 196
Norwood, A. 276
Noteboom, S. 204

Noteware, B. 168
Nott, F. 292
Nottingham, G. 422
Nottingham, P. 202
Novak, D. 369
Novak, E. 180
Novotny, E. 253
Nowak, A. 185
Nowak, K. 399
Nowell, E. 391
Nowiak, M. 282
Nowlin, L. 247
Nowlin, Mrs. O. 106
Noyes, J. 149
Noyes, N. 144
Nugent, L. 335
Nunes, M. 372
Nunn, J. 219
Nunnally, N. 399
Nunnink, Mrs. J. 244
Nusbaum, V. 154
Nutting, E. 172, 216
Nyberg, M. 444
Nye, C. 403
Nye, M. 147
Nygaard, D. 317
Nyland, M. 325
Nystrom, B. 399

Oakar, M. 5
Oakes, E. 343
Oakes, J. 351
Oakes, V. 83
Oakland, B. 315
Oaks, S. 407
Oates, D. 8
Oatney, R. 90
Obenauf, M. 176
Obenreder, J. 76
Oberdorf, E. 201
Oberdorfer, S. 85
Oberndorf, M. 421
Oberquell, D. 436
Oberteuffer, M. 354
Oblinger, J. 93
O'Boyle, M. 365
O'Brein, J. 117
O'Brian, M. 204
O'Brian, M. 334
O'Brien, A. 271
O'Brien, A. 387
O'Brien, D. 265
O'Brien, E. 293
O'Brien, J. 162
O'Brien, J. 353
O'Brien, J. 414
O'Brien, L. 394
O'Brien, M. 300
O'Brien, Sister M. 413
O'Brien, N. 417
Ochse, A. 402
Ochse, M. 284
O'Connell, E. 442
O'Connell, H. 246
O'Conner, C. 196
O'Conner, M. 170
O'Conner, N. 113
O'Connor, B. 390
O'Connor, H. 354
O'Connor, J. 234
O'Connor, M. 41
O'Connor, S. 19
O'Connor, V. 347
Oczus, S. 217
O'Day, L. 68
Odegaard, S. 21
Odell, P. 122
Oder, D. 320
Oder, H. 76
Odle, K. 430
Odom, M. 83
O'Donnel, D. 383
O'Donnell, Sister M. 404
O'Donnell, M. 434

Oelsner, R. 132
Oesterle, C. 70
Oesterle, C. 202
Oetinger, C. 129
Off, P. 276
Offenbecker, M. 174
Ofstedahl, P. 21
O'Gara, F. 350
Ogden, F. 415
Ogden, S. 252
Ogden, W. 238
O'Gorman, M. 243
O'Grady, R. 336
O'Halloran, M. 108
Ohara, J. 114
O'Hara, L. 375
Oila, J. 171
Okeson, L. 271
Okesor, D. 132
Okie, L. 64
Olander, L. 230
O'Laughlin, C. 203
Oldaw, P. 14
Older, W. 62
Oldham, J. 436
Oldow, P. 12
Olean, E. 47
Oligney, M. 208
Olivares, T. 449
Olivarez, G. 3
Olivarez, G. 289
Oliven, M. 72
Oliver, B. 390
Oliver, E. 349
Oliver, H. 148
Oliver, Mrs. J. 28
Oliver, J. 203
Oliver, M. 178
Oliver, M. 348
Oliver, M. 408
Oliver, S. 143
Oliver, Mrs. W. 354
Olkon, N. 218
Ollila, E. 202
Ollila, S. 195
Ollis, E. 350
Olmstead, J. 444
Olmsted, J. 316
Olsen, E. 407
Olsen, H. 189
Olsen, J. 90
Olsen, L. 408
Olsen, M. 409
Olsen, M. 428
Olsen, P. 113
Olshansky, C. 374, 375
Olson, A. 90
Olson, A. 186
Olson, A. 314, 317
Olson, B. 350
Olson, C. 255
Olson, C. 258
Olson, C. 273
Olson, D. 347
Olson, E. 76
Olson, E. 111
Olson, E. 124
Olson, E. 419
Olson, F. 46
Olson, F. 317
Olson, F. 421
Olson, I. 193
Olson, J. 218
Olson, J. 225
Olson, J. 385
Olson, L. 257
Olson, M. 227
Olson, M. 428
Olson, M. 449
Olson, N. 315
Olstrom, A. 198
Olwin, J. 175
O'Malley, A. 269
Oman, P. 221
Omans, C. 113

Omer, S. 117
Omietanski, S. 320
O'Neal, H. 232
O'Neal, M. 313
One Feather, E. 385
O'Neil, D. 263
O'Neil, Mrs. N. 318
O'Neill, B. 414
O'Neill, E. 454
O'Neill, Mrs. H. 236
O'Neill, M. 162
O'Neill, R. 374
Ongley, B. 204
Ongtowasruk, A. 12
Onsgard, B. 223
Onstott, R. 453
Opala, M. 343
Opbroek, F. 384
Opera, M. 299
Opie, L. 83
Opitz, E. 446
Opperman, H. 401
Opperud, B. 315
Opray, M. 348
Orcuff, G. 55
Orcutt, J. 263
Ordel, Mrs. A. 422
Ordenoff, M. 362
Ordway, H. 178
O'Reilly, P. 442
O'Reilly, R. 171
O'Reilly, V. 149
Orfirer, L. 336
Orlinsky, J. 158
Orr, C. 244
Orr, J. 107
Orr, Mrs. R. 67
Orros, H. 281
Orsini, M. 271
Orten, B. 45
Orth, E. 176
Orthel, J. 109
Ortiz, M. 216
Orton, M. 23
Orville, L. 385
Orwig, V. 118
Osban, E. 342
Osborne, D. 57
Osborne, E. 389
Osborne, G. 242
Osborne, J. 61
Osborne, J. 402
Osbourn, J. 363
Osburn, P. 340
Osiecki, C. 55
Osier, E. 171
Osler, D. 55
Osman, P. 187
Ostby, R. 354
Osterhuis, E. 226
Osterlind, J. 354
Osterloh, J. 41
Osterlund, N. 123
Osterman, N. 172
Osterman, N. 374
Ostlund, Mrs. D. 115
Ostlund, E. 202
Ostrom, M. 450
Ostrow, B. 102
Ostrye, P. 39
Oswald, Mrs. L. 24
Oswald, S. 365
Otey, M. 29
Ott, B. 124
Ott, F. 367
Ott, S. 175
Ott, S. 222
Ottem, M. 350
Otting, K. 394
Otto, L. 217
Otto, M. 404
Ouchi, M. 435
Ouimette, L. 162
Outen, E. 311
Outten, P. 418

Overbey, J. 239
Overby, J. 386
Overfelt, J. 408
Overman, M. 239
Overmyer, L. 429
Overstreet, J. 430
Overton, T. 337
Owen, C. 306
Owen, F. 38
Owen, H. 134
Owen, J. 199
Owen, P. 287
Owen, V. 209
Owens, B. 74
Owens, C. 51
Owens, G. 9
Owens, Mrs. H. 380
Owens, R. 115
Owings, L. 134
Oxley, J. 108
Oyler, M. 407

Pace, G. 133
Pacetti, S. 403
Pacheco, A. 396
Pack, A. 211
Packard, D. 129
Packard, E. 20
Packard, H. 414
Packer, C. 195
Padgett, M. 24
Padie, M. 15
Padilla, R. 288
Padilla, Dr. E. 302
Padley, B. 110
Padrnos, D. 385
Paes, M. 165
Pafford, J. 415
Pagano, B. 373
Pagaran, B. 42
Page, A. 145
Page, D. 15
Page, E. 32
Page, E. 361
Page, L. 316
Page, R. 413, 415
Page, S. 225
Page, W. 208
Pahl, A. 315
Pahll, B. 346
Pailler, A. 272
Pails, V. 198
Paine, A. 398
Paine, E. 413
Paine, G. 267
Painter, A. 95
Painter, D. 281
Paiste, B. 241
Pajcic, A. 79
Pajnich, V. 181
Palazzi, P. 268
Palfini, D. 39
Palko, I. 59
Pallanck, A. 59
Pallister, E. 171
Pallotti, M. 62
Palmer, B. 317
Pamler, C. 146
Palmer, C. 191
Palmer, D 109
Palmer, G. 167
Palmer, G. 252
Palmer, K. 6, 8
Palmer, L. 388
Palmer, M. 184
Palmer, M. 351
Palmer, P. 401
Palmer, V. 145
Palmer, W. 146
Palmeri, G. 257
Palmgren, V. 436
Palombi, J. 276
Pamm, G. 272
Pampalone, L. 281

Pandázides, A. 420
Panehal, F. 319
Panek, I. 351
Panek, M. 436
Pangborn, M. 186
Panko, G. 147
Pankonin, S. 255
Papale, I. 58
Papanikolas, H. 408
Papcum, R. 328
Pape, B. 446
Papen, J. 288
Pappas, Mrs. J. 442
Pappert, R. 106
Paracca, R. 364
Paradis, A. 267
Paraschos, C. 106
Parent, L. 98
Parente, M. 163
Parenteau, C. 164
Paret, F. 396
Paris, M. 280
Parish, A. 313
Park, C. 234
Park, Mrs. M. 29
Park, M. 407
Parke, L. 65
Parker, A. 55
Parker, B. 435
Parker, C. 55
Parker, D. 105
Parker, G. 11
Parker, H. 100
Parker, H. 156
Parker, I. 186
Parker, J. 21
Parker, J. 121
Parker, J. 237
Parker, J. 397
Parker, J. 454
Parker, K. 311
Parker, L. 146
Parker, M. 138
Parker, M. 188
Parker, R. 102
Parker, Mrs. R. 343, 344
Parker, S. 50
Parker, S. 258
Parker, V. 11
Parker, V. 190
Parker, V. 195
Parkes, D. 199
Parks, C. 451
Parks, Mrs. J. 29
Parks, L. 255
Parks, L. 435
Parkton, D. 71
Parmelee, N. 42
Parnell, I. 377
Parr, E. 263
Parr, E. 344
Parr, K. 12
Parrack, E. 441
Parris, S. 369
Parrish, D. 415
Parrott, Mrs. B. 423
Parrott, G. 193
Parrott, M. 198
Parry, C. 302
Parry, H. 414
Parshall, J. 193
Parsons, B. 193
Parsons, B. 214
Parsons, D. 92
Parsons, E. 181
Parsons, G. 383
Parsons, H. 193
Parsons, L. 10
Parsons, L. 296
Parsons, M. 89
Parsons, S. 30
Parsons, S. 46
Parsons, S. 50
Partridge, B. 369

Paschall, I. 388
Pascle, M. 449
Pasco, C. 171
Passage, K. 245
Passaglia, P. 280
Passery, E. 298
Pastor, M.A. 214
Patchett, B. 278
Pate, B. 34
Pate, D. 79
Paterson, J. 46
Patovisti, E. 172
Patrick, D. 254
Patrick, J. 294
Patrick, L. 271
Patrick, M. 240
Patrick, M. 270
Patrick, S. 37
Patsy, M. 14
Patte, M. 93
Pattee, C. 113
Pattee, M. 203
Patten, E. 20
Patten, G. 35
Patten, J. 343
Patten, K. 243
Patten, S. 144
Patterson, C. 20
Patterson, E. 258
Patterson, E. 382
Patterson, E. 450
Patterson, F. 387
Patterson, J. 173
Patterson, J. 244
Patterson, K. 380
Patterson, K. 396
Patterson, M. 50
Patterson, M. 385
Patterson, M. 453, 454
Patterson, Z. 114
Pattison, L. 290
Pattison, M. 400
Patton, C. 437
Patton, L. 359
Patton, Mrs. L. 404
Patton, M. 360
Patton, V. 242
Paul, A. 13
Paul, B. 416, 423
Paul, D. 316
Paul, E. 50
Paul, Mrs. J. 424
Paul, L. 301
Paul, S. 131
Paulen, V. 194
Pauley, M. 416
Pauley, S. 222
Paulk, H. 70
Paulsen, G. 27
Pauly, H. 170
Paval, V. 434
Pavlak, B. 58
Pavloff, C. 436
Payne, B. 10
Payne, D. 209
Payne, E. 173
Payne, E. 240
Payne, V. 129
Paynter, R. 450
Payson, M. 145
Pazour, M. 115
Peace, N. 417
Peacock, M. 105
Peak, G. 429
Peake, S. 379
Pearce, B. 361
Pearce, H. 343
Pearce, J. 312
Pearce, L. 90
Pearl, H. 64
Pearl, P. 244
Pearlman, M. 281
Pearsall, C. 425
Pearsall, Mrs. J. 423
Pearson, B. 436

Pearson, C. 215
Pearson, J. 352
Pearson, L. 93
Pearson, Mrs. L. 222
Pearson, M. 122
Pearson, M. 143
Pearson, R. 251
Pecaut, D. 124
Peck, C. 132
Peck, L. 170
Peck, M. 123
Pecke, J. 363
Peddycoart, M. 383
Pederson, Mrs. A. 317
Pederson, D. 239
Pederson, J. 254
Pederson, M. 13
Pedigo, Mrs. W. 421
Peebles, A. 423
Peekema, J. 434
Peeks, S. 253
Peel, P. 399
Peer, P. 259
Peerson, A. 361
Peery, Mrs. C. 423
Peery, J. 423
Peetoom, J. 296
Peevy, G. 157
Peick, D. 122
Peiffer, R. 365
Peirce, G. 170
Pell, E. 440
Pellicciotto, W. 421
Pelloat, Mrs. P. 140
Pelto, D. 373
Pelton, S. 263
Pempek, L. 62
Pence, Mrs. C. 398
Pence, L. 333
Pencil, Mrs. L. 110
Pendell, L. 176
Pendergraft, P. 424
Pendergrass, P. 41
Penfold, P. 176
Penhune, N. 161
Penick, C. 422
Penick, J. 100
Penick, V. 338
Penn, P. 436
Pennell, R. 149
Penningroth, J. 108
Pennington, E. 137
Pennino, M. 417
Penny, E. 366
Penny, P. 25
Penrod, M. 323
Peoples, C. 352
Peratrovich, T. 13
Percival, Mrs. F. 344
Percival, N. 178
Perdue, M. 341
Perdue, N. 18
Perez, I. 397
Perez, M. 245
Perez, R. 255
Perillo, A. 67
Perillo, M. 61
Periou, V. 141
Perkins, E. 259
Perkins, J. 16
Perkins, M. 20
Perkins, M. 221
Perkins, M. 437
Perkins, N. 398
Perkins, P. 402
Perkins, R. 185
Perkins, R. 200
Perkins, R. 325
Perkins, S. 434
Perkinson, P. 416
Pernell, B. 306
Perotti, C. 21
Perreault, E. 200
Perrin, S. 156
Perrotti, C. 259

Perry, B. 9
Perry, C. 53
Perry, D. 61
Perry, D. 284
Perry, E. 282
Perry, E. 344
Perry, E. 356
Perry, F. 413
Perry, I. 221
Perry, L. 184
Perry, L. 233
Perry, M. 144
Perry, M. 309
Perry, M. 354
Perry, M. 403
Perry, P. 122
Perry, S. 339
Perryman, M. 284
Perschon, R. 184
Perttula, L. 186
Perun, A. 279
Pervola, M. 441
Peschon, I. 223
Pesicka, P. 433
Peter, M. 273
Peterman, F. 271
Peterman, K. 350
Peterman, L. 358
Peternal, N. 453, 454
Peters, B. 183
Peters, E. 448
Peters, L. 179
Peters, L. 334
Peters, M. 176
Peters, M. 192
Peters, M. 263
Peters, P. 96
Peters, P. 123
Petersen, G. 383
Petersen, M. 123
Petersen, M. 189
Petersen, V. 122
Peterson, A. 408
Peterson, B. 68
Peterson, B. 184
Peterson, B. 226
Peterson, B. 436
Peterson, C. 208
Peterson, C. 243
Peterson, C. 406
Peterson, E. 3
Peterson, E. 315
Peterson, Mrs. G. 317
Peterson, G. 317
Peterson, G. 385
Peterson, G. 405
Peterson, I. 229
Peterson, J. 179
Peterson, J. 249
Peterson, J. 253
Peterson, J. 326
Peterson, K. 223
Peterson, L. 67
Peterson, L. 106
Peterson, L. 122
Peterson, M. 46
Peterson, M. 112
Peterson, M. 126
Peterson, M. 153
Peterson, M. 200
Peterson, M. 209
Peterson, M. 221
Peterson, M. 255
Peterson, M. 316
Peterson, M. 407
Peterson, M. 450
Peterson, P. 383
Peterson, R. 407
Peterson, S. 250
Peterson, Mrs. T. 386
Peterson, W. 183
Petillo, J. 267
Petokas, I. 43
Petrini, L. 369
Petro, E. 181

Petro, V. 284
Petrou, B. 310
Petruny, A. 63
Pettersen, E. 283, 285
Pettersen, Mrs. P. 254
Pettis, S. 5
Pettit, G. 228
Petty, Mrs. D. 404
Pfaff, A. 178
Pfaffinger, A. 106
Pfannenstiel, C. 126
Pfeiffer, B. 118
Pfeiffer, N. 365
Pflaum, J. 15
Pflughoeft, A. 128
Phares, M. 132
Phelan, H. 292
Phelps, C. 193
Phelps, E. 8
Phelps, S. 85
Philbrook, A. 268
Phillip, A. 361
Phillip, J. 157
Phillipe, J. 156
Phillips, B. 70
Phillips, B. 93
Phillips, B. 147
Phillips, B. 284
Phillips, B. 341
Phillips, B. 395
Phillips, C. 17
Phillips, C. 56
Phillips, D. 24
Phillips, D. 182
Phillips, D. 365
Phillips, E. 184
Phillips, E. 217
Phillips, E. 290
Phillips, E. 437
Phillips, F. 404
Phillips, G. 11
Phillips, J. 21
Phillips, J. 244
Phillips, L. 50
Phillips, L. 233
Phillips, M. 121
Phillips, M. 201
Phillips, M. 307
Phillips, Mrs. P. 78
Phillips, R. 244
Phillips, S. 8
Phillips, V. 321
Phillips, Mrs. W. 233
Phillips, Mrs. W. 244
Philo, I. 178
Philon, L. 102
Phinney, G. 353
Phipps, M. 389
Phipps, V. 121
Phyfer, M. 232
Piana, G. 408
Picard, B. 140
Piccone, N. 364
Pickelsimer, G. 340
Pickens, J. 216
Pickering, C. 244
Pickering, E. 418
Pickering, P. 37
Pickett, B. 22
Pickett, C. 454
Pickett, L. 353
Pickett, M. 336
Pickett, P. 216
Pickett, R. 216
Pickett, S. 399
Pickle, Mrs. B. 401
Pickler, J. 306
Pickles, F. 238
Piddington, P. 210
Piell, D. 362
Pieper, A. 62
Pieper, Sister B. 123
Pierce, B. 374
Pierce, B. 384
Pierce, C. 393

Pierce, D. 101
Pierce, I. 200
Pierce, J. 276
Pierce, L. 323
Pierce, M. 413
Pierce, Mrs. M. 421
Pierre, B. 384
Pierson, J. 191
Pietri, M. 422
Pigman, M. 450
Pike, B. 158
Pike, M. 121
Pilant, E. 339
Pilchard, M. 61
Filippo, M. 196
Pilkington, G. 8
Pilkington, M. 25
Pilkington, P. 8
Pillepich, M. 303
Pillsbury, J. 413
Pinckney, Mrs. P. 380
Pine, S. 21
Piner, M. 310
Pines, L. 159
Pinkerton, M. 225
Pinkett, M. 299
Pinkham, J. 351
Pinner, E. 62
Pinney, B. 181
Pinson, B. 9
Piore, N. 302
Piotrowski, J. 79
Piotrowski, M. 182
Piper, M. 449
Piper, Sister T. 230
Pipes, B. 340
Pipik, V. 358
Pippert, D. 119
Pirsch, P. 253
Pisch, I. 57
Pisciotta, M. 242
Pitkin, Mrs. R. 413
Pitney, Mrs. J. 284
Pitoniak, J. 161
Pitotti, R. 442
Pitschmann, L. 63
Pitsenberger, J. 438
Pittman, E. 141
Pittman, J. 398
Pittman, M. 312
Pitts, C. 11
Pitts, E. 341
Pitts, F. 68
Pitz, R. 447
Pixley, F. 293
Plank, J. 152
Plank, M. 297
Plant, F. 406
Plant, J. 10
Plant, J. 439
Plantix, E. 328
Plas, J. 163
Plasencia, I. 122, 123
Plasters, Mrs. J. 255
Plath, D. 437
Platner, M. 449
Plato, D. 354
Plato, H. 294
Platt, J. 77
Platt, V. 336
Platte, Sister A. 212
Platts, Mrs. J. 453
Playdon, A. 267
Playford, J. 187
Plew, M. 185
Ploeg, M. 216
Plomaritis, C. 263
Plouffe, A. 434
Plummer, D. 255
Plummer, H. 154
Plummer, J. 198
Plunger, M. 191
Podbevsek, J. 407
Podles, E. 263
Poe, J. 123

Poe, Mrs. R. 342
Poe, S. 250
Poffenberger, V. 117
Pogrebin, E. 280
Pohjola, L. 181
Pohl, D. 190
Poindexter, M. 202
Poiter, J. 301
Poitevin, M. 90
Poitier, S. 72
Poland, K. 12, 16
Poldberg, J. 111
Polhemus, A. 280
Poling, P. 322
Polinsky, J. 55
Polito, A. 275
Polk, J. 128
Pollak, P. 67
Pollan, C. 22
Pollard, Mrs. F. 423
Pollard, J. 8
Pollard, N. 391
Pollard, S. 158
Pollick, J. 210
Pollina, L. 145
Pollock, M. 25
Polman, B. 229
Polman, C. 228
Polty, O. 14
Pomatto, M. 131
Pomeroy, S. 192
Pomroy, C. 149
Pomroy, N. 147
Ponce, V. 244
Pond, G. 63
Ponder, V. 311
Pontarell, D. 374, 375
Ponto, E. 230
Pool, M. 130
Poole, L. 293
Poole, N. 338
Pooler, R. 289, 301
Poore, S. 159
Pope, D. 225
Pope, D. 319
Pope, Mrs. D. 342
Pope, J. 454
Pope, Mrs. R. 156
Porlett, D. 95
Porreca, M. 163
Porritt, L. 193
Port, J. 245
Portash, A. 276
Porter, A. 96
Porter, A. 252
Porter, D. 99
Porter, D. 255
Porter, D. 404
Porter, E. 3
Porter, E. 75
Porter, E. 112
Porter, H. 385
Porter, L. 67
Porter, P. 294
Porter, R. 93
Porterfield, H. 343
Portman, M. 77
Portratz, A. 120
Portwood, L. 216
Portz, D. 322
Posey, J. 6
Post, B. 143
Post, C. Mrs. 373
Post, M. 105
Post, M. 408
Postlewait, R. 95
Poston, E. 49
Poston, E. 289
Poth, E. 271
Potter, A. 418
Potter, B. 190
Potter, Mrs. B. 454
Potter, E. 277
Potter, H. 258
Potter, L. 240

Potter, L. 348
Potter, L. 374
Potter, N. 266
Potter, N. 389
Potter, Mrs. R. 16
Potts, J. 440
Potts, M. 65
Potts, V. 399
Poulin, D. 145, 149
Poulin, Sister L. 149
Poulson, E. 187
Povondra, Mrs. J. 223
Powell, A. 216
Powell, A. 419
Powell, J. 395
Powell, K. 239
Powell, M. 9
Powell, M. 197
Powell, M. 209
Powell, R. 350
Powell, V. 140
Power, D. 269
Power, M. 348
Powers, A. 161
Powers, A. 208
Powers, A. 315
Powers, B. 210
Powers, D. 163
Powers, D. 252
Powers, F. 287
Powers, G. 133
Poyzer, M. 315
Pragman, J. 240
Prahl, M. 118
Praszker, F. 38
Prater, L. 252
Pratt, M. 197
Prazen, J. 407
Predhomme, F. 432
Premen, M. 334
Premer, M. 100
Prentice, P. 20
Prentice, P. 21
Prentice, R. 254
Prentiss, L. 148
Prescher, N. 222
Prescott, E. 358
Prescott, R. 370
Prescott, S. 145
Presnell, J. 245
Pressler, B. 200
Pressler, S. 282
Pressman, Mrs. E. 352
Preston, B. 228
Preston, C. 436
Preston, M. 84
Preston, M. 214
Preston, P. 450
Preuss, C. 196
Prevost, T. 16
Price, C. 121
Price, G. 245
Price, H. 363
Price, J. 301
Price, J. 380
Price, L. 19
Price, L. 392
Price, N. 91
Price, N. 198
Price, R. 407
Price, S. 192
Price, S. 214
Price, S. 259
Price, W. 74
Prickett, M. 101
Priddy, D. 133
Pride, Mrs. C. 403
Pridgeon, M. 176
Prielipp, A. 184
Prielipp, L. 203
Priest, W. 238
Primrose, S. 62
Prince, E. 198
Prince, F. 43
Prince, H. 334

Prince, V. 406
Princic, I. 49
Pringle, A. 129
Pringle, D. 109
Prinsen, M. 413
Prior, D. 435
Prior, F. 414
Pritchard, A. 130
Pritchett, J. 338
Pritchett, S. 213
Prochaska, M. 111
Prock, V. 450
Procter, Mrs. C. 339
Proctor, A. 7
Proctor, A. 164
Proctor, J. 26
Proctor, N. 263
Proctor, P. 174
Proctor, V. 28
Procunier, L. 184
Prokop, C. 273
Prokop, R. 3
Prokosch, B. 267
Prophater, I. 217
Prosser, C. 448
Prosterman, B. 155
Protheroe, M. 447
Prout, D. 187
Prouty, A. 292
Prouty, M. 155
Prouty, M. 267
Provitt, E. 214
Prown, S. 62
Pruente, B. 243
Pruitt, M. 238
Pruitt, M. 381
Prunty, E. 438
Prunty, V. 441
Pryor, G. 37
Pryor, M. 357
Pryor, N. 435
Pryor, Mrs. W. 231
Pucci, P. 263
Puchalski, S. 324
Puckett, L. 340
Puff, S. 435
Pugh, J. 11
Pugh, V. 420
Pugh, Mrs. W. 441
Pughe, A. 154
Pula, E. 171
Pulliam, L. 390
Pullin, P. 94
Pumphrey, H. 16
Pung, C. 189
Puorro, A. 206
Puotinen, K. 179
Purback, M. 283
Purce, I. 92
Purcell, C. 397
Purcell, L. 363
Purcell, M. 162
Purcell, M. 361
Purchase, O. 364
Purdum, M. 339
Purdy, C. 326
Purdy, J. 120
Purhonen, R. 259
Purinton, D. 254
Purkery, D. 325
Pursley, F. 403
Purves, I. 182
Purvis, B. 180
Purvis, E. 106
Purvis, H. 134
Purvis, J. 9
Pusey, N. 424
Pustina, M. 446
Putman, P. 351
Putnam, B. 295
Putnam, H. 33
Putnam, H. 191
Putnam, P. 181
Putney, C. 174
Putriment, P. 62

Putt, M. 202
Putzel, C. 156
Pyle, G. 369
Pyle, K. 49
Pyle, M. 339
Pym, H. 434
Pyne, K. 428

Quade, B. 454
Quain, G. 18
Qualls, J. 37
Quaranta, M. 303
Quarles, M. 6
Quarles, M. 153
Quee, R. 119
Quenon, A. 397
Quick, E. 200
Quick, K. 291
Quick, M. 205
Quigg, H. 249
Quillen, L. 66
Quilling, J. 445
Quimby, J. 49
Quinlan, M. 342
Quinlan, W. 365
Quinn, D. 323
Quinn, L. 75
Quinn, V. 417
Quintana, A. 288
Quintana, D. 50
Quirk, Mrs. M. 283
Quiroga, F. 431

Raasio, E. 196
Raatz, V. 228
Rabe, M. 244
Rachel, P. 404
Rackley, Mrs. C. 338
Radant, L. 250
Rader, M. 199
Rader, R. 287
Radford, N. 92
Radke, Mrs. F. 434
Radohl, M. 111
Radosa, B. 186
Radosevich, M. 443
Raeder, P. 296
Rael, Mrs. S. 287
Raese, Mrs. R. 442
Raffensperger, S. 294
Rafferty, A. 292
Ragan, S. 312
Raggio, D. 259
Ragley, B. 364
Raguckas, M. M. 214
Rahe, P. 104
Rahn, K. 302
Rainey, D. 102
Rainey, Mrs. J. 380
Rainey, L. 24
Rainville, A. 225
Rajala, G. 187
Rajkowski, L. 368
Rajoppi, J. 270
Raleigh, J. 210
Raley, M. 344
Ralph, E. 415
Ralph, K. 263
Ralph, R. 44
Ralston, E. 208
Rambosek, T. 15, 16
Ramey, H. 222
Ramey, K. 247
Ramhorst, B. 111
Ramig, T. 254
Ramirez, M. 216
Ramirez, D. 18
Ramsay, M. 263
Ramseur, I. 359
Ramsey, H. 389
Ramsey, M. 24
Ramsey, Mrs. R. 303
Ramsey, R. 307

Ramynke, M. 384
Randall, A. 156
Randall, H. 393
Randall, L. 184
Randall, O. 301
Randle, C. 449
Raney, M. 22
Rangel, I. 392
Rank, E. 385
Rankin, D. 336
Ranks, A. 254
Ransavage, J. 248
Ranse, E. 47
Ransohoff, Mrs. A. 64
Ransom, E. 197
Rapanos, J. 214
Raphael, Mrs. M. 301
Rapier, R. 47
Rappport, N. 55
Rapose, S. 59
Rapp, M. 321
Rappa, D. 216
Rash, Mrs. G. 379
Rask, M. 229
Rask, V. 317
Raskevitz, N. 162
Rasmussen, G. 123
Rasmussen, E. 16
Rasmussen, M. 385
Rassmussen, R. 214
Rass, N. 252
Rast, E. 377
Ratcliff, H. 436
Ratcliff, L. 414
Rath, F. 299
Rathbun, E. 180
Rathe, E. 120
Rathke, D. 113
Ratliff, P. 134
Rattazzi, A. 257, 258
Ratz, D. 454
Rau, L. 395
Raudenbush, J. 242
Raufaste, K. 153
Rausehenbach, M. 278
Ravencraft, J. 139
Ravenell, M. 78
Ravenscroft, B. 336
Ravenscroft, J. 104
Ravn, S. 414
Raw, B. 221
Rawhouser, F. 15
Rawles, E. 64
Rawles, Mrs. J. 423
Rawlings, D. 100
Rawlings, E. 407
Rawlinson, N. 353
Rawson, B. 336
Ray, B. 393
Ray, D. 15
Ray, D. 424
Ray, J. 389
Ray, S. 397
Rayburn, B. 431
Rayburn, D. 27
Rayburn, K. 230
Rayl, D. 169
Rayl, I. 118
Rayle, B. 323
Raymond, E. 63
Raymond, J. 118
Raymond, M. 30
Raymond, M. 413
Raymond, P. 197
Raymond, S. 51
Razzini, T. 104
Read, Mrs. A. 404
Reading, Mrs. A. 285
Reagan, L. 238
Reagan, M. 413
Ream, C. 275
Reames, D. 173
Reaven, E. 322
Reaves, A. 399
Reaves, M. 401

Reavey, D. 171
Reavis, G. 436
Reazin, V. 128
Rebol, M. 406
Rebrovich, E. 221
Reck, E. 188
Rector, M. 199
Rector, P. 51
Redd, E. 408
Reddy, R. 85
Redfield, B. 386
Redford, J. 445
Rediger, K. 116
Redinger, R. 336
Redmon, J. 189
Redmond, B. 308
Redmond, W. 196
Redner, C. 184
Redwine, K. 347
Reece, A. 49
Reece, A. 344
Reed, A. 179
Reed, B. 315
Reed, B. 428
Reed, C. 42
Reed, D. 89
Reed, D. 95
Reed, D. 207
Reed, Mrs. D. 401
Reed, E. 199
Reed, E. 219
Reed, J. 34
Reed, J. 67
Reed, J. 103
Reed, J. 295
Reed, L. 135
Reed, L. 321
Reed, M. 26
Reed, M. 93
Reed, M. 349
Reed, M. 353
Reed, P. 157
Reed, Mrs. R. 106
Reed, S. 68
Reed, S. 363
Reed, T. 360
Reed, Mrs. W. 424
Reed, W. 452
Reeder, Mrs. J. 103
Reeder, M. 408
Reeder, R. 15
Reese, B. 203
Reese, D. 157
Reese, D. 243
Reese, J. 341
Reese, M. 18
Reese, M. 266
Reese, S. 408
Reeter, O. 343
Reeves, M. 191
Regaldo, B. 344
Regan, E. 450
Regan, P. 246
Regener, F. 356
Reger, V. 421
Reginata, L. 259
Rehwalt, L. 92
Reibman, J. 355
Reich, M. 370
Reichart, H. 123
Reichelt, J. 344
Reichlin, Sister M. 92
Reid, A. 156
Reid, C. 59
Reid, D. 190
Reid, D. 434
Reid, E. 302
Reid, E. 412, 415
Reid, F. 296
Reid, M. 89
Reid, P. 321
Reid, R. 200
Reid, S. 228
Reid-Craigmont, L. 93
Reiff, A. 281

Reigan, M. 51
Reihman, V. 117
Reilley, D. 292
Reilly, J. 106
Reilly, J. 337
Reilly, M. 362
Reilly, N. 68
Reiman, J. 102
Reimann, S. 175
Reimer, D. 49
Reimer, N. 453
Reimers, B. 54
Reiner, J. 276
Reinhardt, R. 332
Reis, M. 163
Reis, R. 317
Reisfeld, S. 286, 287
Reisinger, M. 348
Reitz, L. 242
Remington, M. 356
Remmers, J. 127
Rempert, F. 172
Remsberg, J. 126
Renault, L. 73
Renberger, S. 430
Rendel, M. 195
Rendlen, S. 244
Renfro, S. 245
Renfroe, L. 232
Renfroe, R. 396
Renfrow, A. 311
Renk, E. 284
Rennie, S. 351
Reno, J. 79
Renville, N. 385
Renwick, J. 347
Renwick, M. 176
Renzulli, M. 375
Repic, D. 358
Repka, B. 447
Repo, M. 190
Repp, J. 122
Resnick, L. 324
Rethford, A. 193
Retsinas, J. 374
Retzlaff, K. 315
Reusch, T. 96
Reusch, V. 127
Reuschel, B. 412
Revercomb, Mrs. G. 423
Rey, Y. 404
Reynolds, A. 413
Reynolds, C. 14
Reynolds, C. 48
Reynolds, C. 58
Reynolds, D. 88, 92
Reynolds, H. 453
Reynolds, I. 173
Reynolds, I. 241
Reynolds, J. 21
Reynolds, K. 130
Reynolds, L. 160
Reynolds, M. 10
Reynolds, M. 97
Reynolds, M. 214
Rheault, M. 200
Rhein, J. 448
Rhinehalt, J. 147
Rhinesmith, D. 101
Rhoades, M. 255
Rhoads, Mrs. W. 423
Rhodes, B. 321
Rhodes, C. 360
Rhodes, Mrs. D. 442
Rhodes, J. 244
Rhodes, L. 359
Rhodes, M. 344
Rhodes, M. 400
Rhodes, S. 186
Ricard, M. 198
Ricci, C. 453
Riccio, Y. 59
Rice, Mrs. B. 134
Rice, G. 246
Rice, J. 404

Rice, L. 125
Rice, L. 192
Rice, L. 303
Rice, M. 81
Rice, P. 321
Rice, R. 451
Rice, S. 310
Rice, S. 412
Rice, Mrs. W. 422
Rich, E. 156
Rich, T. 328
Rich, V. 308
Richards, A. 61
Richards, A. 144
Richards, A. 288
Richards, A. 392
Richards, B. 414
Richards, C. 407
Richards, H. 52
Richards, L. 407
Richards, M. 202
Richards, M. 418
Richards, S. 64
Richards, S. 330
Richards, S. 345
Richards, V. 96
Richards, V. 192
Richardson, A. 10
Richardson, Mrs. A. 380
Richardson, C. 242
Richardson, C. 384
Richardson, D. 135
Richardson, E. 80
Richardson, E. 247
Richardson, H. 195
Richardson, H. 404
Richardson, I. 384
Richardson, L. 62
Richardson, M. 230
Richardson, M. 263
Richardson, M. 290
Richardson, R. 139
Richardson, S. 203
Richardson, V. 230
Richert, J. 134
Richesin, A. 390
Richette, L. 370
Richey, M. 6
Richey, M. 106
Richie, N. 404
Richman, J. 300
Richmond, L. 158
Richmond, M. 145
Richmond, R. 79
Richter, V. 253
Rick, L. 116
Ricker, B. 271
Ricketts, L. 96
Ricketts, V. 92
Rickey, K. 434
Rickey, M. 239
Ricklef, S. 111
Rickles, R. 36
Riddel, M. 19
Ridder, R. 425, 435
Riddick, F. 423
Riddle, Mrs. R. 403
Ridenour, L. 326
Rider, D. 27
Ridge, B. 52
Ridgeway, P. 377
Ridgeway, R. 3
Rieb, D. 383
Rieckman, H. 383
Riedel, M. 329
Rieff, L. 361
Riegle, P. 179
Riehl, B. 428
Rieke, M. 345
Rieke, R. 408
Riensche, E. 255
Ries, N. 182
Rigby, K. 88
Rigby, L. 396
Rigel, J. 334

Rigg, R. 172
Rigg, R. 214
Riggers, M. 92
Riggs, C. 333
Riggs, S. 378
Riha, A. 119
Riker, D. 328
Rilett, S. 185
Riley, Mrs. B. 86
Riley, C. 151, 156
Riley, Sister C. 442
Riley, D. 214
Riley, D. 263
Riley, F. 154
Riley, G. 25
Riley, G. 122
Riley, G. 330, 331
Riley, M. 342, 343
Riley, P. 26
Riley, P. 330
Riley, R. 229
Riley, S. 18
Rime, C. 316
Rimer, M. 62
Rindge, A. 202
Rinehart, I. 429
Riner, C. 457
Ring, M. 148
Ringeon, H. 118
Ringgenberg, L. 121
Rink, A. 374
Rinker, C. 421
Riordan, S. 364
Ripley, E. 253
Ripperdan, F. 101
Ripps, M. 259
Risch, D. 188
Rising, M. 316
Rising, N. 427
Riske, E. 182
Riskin, S. 283
Risley, M. 433
Risner, B. 175
Risner, B. 186
Ristline, Mrs. R. 105
Ritchey, J. 310
Ritchie, S. 61
Rittenberg, F. 273
Ritter, M. 401
Ritter, P. 323
Ritter, P. 453
Ritter, S. 201
Rivera, C. 255
Rivera, M. 62
Rivera, M. 399
Rivers, V. 378
Rivet, I. 298
Rizek, E. 251
Rizor, H. 452
Roach, A. 185
Roach, B. 149
Roach, P. 325
Roach, S. 81
Road, M. 110
Roane, I. 22
Roark, Mrs. A. 418
Roark, E. 47
Roback, S. 196
Robacker, K. 253
Robb, E. 237
Robb, Mrs. G. 302
Robb, Mrs. L. 302
Robbin, M. 93
Robbins, B. 76
Robbins, D. 220
Robbins, G. 238
Robbins, I. 9
Robbins, J. 123
Robbins, J. 161
Robbins, L. 338
Robbins, R. 303
Robbins, V. 112
Robel, R. 188
Roberson, A. 179
Roberson, E. 441

Roberson, K. 179
Robert, L. 418
Roberts, A. 77
Roberts, A. 115
Roberts, A. 245
Roberts, A. 325
Roberts, B. 116
Roberts, B. 331
Roberts, B. 345
Roberts, C. 77
Roberts, C. 297
Roberts, C. 341
Roberts, D. 130
Roberts, D. 147
Roberts, E. 303
Roberts, F. 96
Roberts, H. 259
Roberts, I. 26
Roberts, I. 238
Roberts, I. 388
Roberts, J. 47
Roberts, J. 53
Roberts, J. 330
Roberts, K. 196
Roberts, L. 86
Roberts, L. 187
Roberts, M. 210
Roberts, M. 345
Roberts, M. 434
Roberts, N. 319
Roberts, N. 333
Roberts, R. 120
Roberts, T. 430
Roberts, V. 407
Roberts, V. 437
Roberts, W. 138
Robertson, A. 117
Robertson, A. 162
Robertson, B. 385
Robertson, D. 328
Robertson, E. 402
Robertson, H. 419
Robertson, M. 9
Robertson, M. 276
Robertson, P. 321
Robertson, R. 239
Robertson, S. 83
Robertson, S. 179
Robertson, W. 20, 21
Robidue, A. 128
Robie, Mrs. W. 156
Robillard, F. 414
Robin, L. 390
Robins, S. 254
Robinson, A. 375
Robinson, B. 348
Robinson, C. 60
Robinson, D. 202
Robinson, D. 404
Robinson, E. 8
Robinson, E. 343
Robinson, I. 171
Robinson, U. 31
Robinson, J. 72
Robinson, J. 284
Robinson, M. 157
Robinson, M. 223
Robinson, M. 255
Robinson, M. 336
Robinson, M. 341
Robinson, M. 403
Robinson, R. 170
Robinson, S. 61
Robinson, Mrs. W. 423
Robison, B. 436
Robison, E. 43
Robson, M. 183
Rochefort, K. 186
Rocheleau, G. 173
Rocheleau, C. 67
Rochna, J. 164
Rocker, J. 79
Rockey, Z. 180
Rockhill, A. 429
Rocklage, Sister M. 244

Rockwell, B. 195
Rockwell, B. 320
Rockwell, E. 18
Rod, C. 180
Rodabaugh, S. 349
Rodden, D. 297
Rodden, M. 259
Roddy, M. 345
Rodenbough, J. 311
Roderick, B. 189
Roderick, M. 162
Rodgers, B. 357
Rodgers, J. 365
Rodgers, Mrs. R. 301
Rodgers, V. 207
Rodimon, E. 374
Rodman, W. 362
Rodrigues, C. 244
Rodriguez, S. 257
Rodriquez, A. 73
Roe, J. 390
Roebling, M. 284
Roedel, L. 68
Roehm, D. 213
Roethel, R. 210
Roethig, E. 180
Roewe, V. 426
Roewe, Mrs. W. 240
Rofkahr, J. 25
Rofkar, H. 319
Rogan, M. 44
Roger, Mrs. F. 79
Roger, Mrs. R. 423
Rogers, C. 236
Rogers, D. 342
Rogers, E. 176
Rogers, E. 384
Rogers, E. 422
Rogers, H. 108
Rogers, J. 106
Rogers, J. 299
Rogers, K. 354
Rogers, L. 334
Rogers, M. 233
Rogers, M. 263
Rogers, M. 378
Rogers, M. 395
Rogers, P. 153
Rogers, S. 149
Rogers, S. 239
Rogers, T. 39
Rogge, J. 131
Rogneby, J. 318
Rohret, B. 117
Rohlf, C. 14
Rolark, W. 455
Rollins, H. 3
Rollins, S. 378
Rolph, R. 350
Romanelli, D. 63
Romanko, P. 89
Romany, S. 63
Romary, M. 432
Romein, D. 101
Romer, D. 159
Romero, B. 51
Romero, J. 238
Romero, L. 288
Romesburg, J. 369
Rommell, E. 207
Romshak, M. 330
Roney, T. 11
Ronfeldt, S. 114
Rood, L. 361
Rooney, E. 280, 284
Roarda, J. 110
Roos, J. 74
Root, Mrs. C. 105
Root, E. 189
Root, G. 194
Root, Mrs. W. 156
Roppel, P. 16
Rosa, I. 26
Rosa, J. 186
Rosburg, N. 111

Roscoe, H. 170
Rose, A. 244
Rose, C. 173
Rose, Mrs. C. 423
Rose, D. 293
Rose, Mrs. F. 17
Rose, K. 336
Rose, L. 299
Rose, M. 155
Rose, Sister, M. 285
Rose, R. 68
Rose, R. 175
Rosell, L. 18
Rosen, B. 294
Rosen, G. 282
Rosen, J. 157
Rosen, M. 502
Rosenbaugh, W. 111
Rosenbaum, C. 336
Rosenvlad, C. 351
Rosenbloom, P. 284
Rosenkranz, V. 131
Rosenstangle, B. 113
Rosenstreich, J. 414
Rosequist, R. 288
Rosetti, B. 199
Ross, B. 112
Ross, B. 346
Ross, E. 294
Rosse, E. 371
Rosse, E. 389
Rosse, E. 436
Ross, H. 67
Ross, J. 123
Ross, J. 300
Ross, L. 128
Ross, M. 242
Ross, M. 255
Ross, N. 113
Ross, P. 344
Ross, R. 409
Ross, V. 431
Ross, Mrs. W. 442
Rosse, J. 149
Rosser, E. 105
Rossi, B. 57
Rossman, L. 203
Rossow, Mrs. L. 393
Rost, J. 304
Rota, A. 356
Rotgin, H. 438
Roth, A. 246
Roth, C. 298
Roth, C. 321
Roth, E. 27
Roth, G. 244
Roth, H. 323
Roth, I. 318
Roth, I. 332
Roth, R. 307
Rothell, S. 250
Rothstein, C. 210
Rothstrom, K. 430
Rott, M. 447
Rotter, H. 214
Rough, T. 173
Rounds, J. 412
Roundy, R. 430
Roush, A. 438
Roush, R. 127
Rousse, J. 415
Roussear, K. 10
Rousseau, E. 274
Routon, B. 11
Rovinson, B. 78
Rowan, J. 333
Rowan, O. 339
Rowden, C. 143
Rowe, I. 25
Rowe, M. 220
Rowe, M. 247
Rowe, N. 208
Rowe, P. 146
Rowe, S. 360

Rowland, G. 15, 16
Rowland, J. 179
Rowley, B. 183
Roy, E. 28
Roy, V. 265
Roybal, J. 47
Royer, K. 367
Roza, M. 192
Rozell, M. 334
Ruan, S. 453
Ruben, I. 151
Rubin, S. 155
Rubinson, M. 259
Ruby, J. 343
Rucinski, L. 215
Rucker, C. 125
Rucker, M. 418
Rudd, L. 12
Rudd, P. 338
Rudder, P. 137
Rudee, H. 31
Ruden, G. 123
Rudin, A. 41
Rudnick, I. 376
Rudnicki, K. 181
Rudolph, A. 395
Rudolph, E. 7
Rudolph, M. 236
Rudy, E. 340
Rue, M. 382
Ruebel, F. 386
Rufener, C. 277
Rufener, K. 446
Ruffin, R. 29
Rugg, M. 21
Ruggeberg, L. 115
Rule, Y. 48
Ruley, B. 442
Rumery, J. 204
Rummel, M. 211
Rundell, B. 36
Runkle, J. 361
Runkle, W. 114
Runkles, E. 440
Runyan, L. 23
Runyon, M. 211
Ruohonen, B. 199
Rupert, E. 368
Rupp, D. 212
Rupright, E.O. 216
Rusch, C.L. 192
Rush, K. 152
Rush, L. 146
Rushlo, M. 186
Russ, F. 313
Russ, J. 8
Russel, Mrs. C. 283
Russel, J. 167
Russell, A. 22
Russell, C. 66
Russell, E. 361
Russell, G. 132
Russell, G. 406
Russell, I. 378
Russell, K. 414
Russell, L. 168
Russell, Mrs. L. 318
Russell, L. 374
Russell, L. 453
Russell, M. 21
Russell, M. 134
Russell, N. 376
Russell, P. 38
Russell, P. 263
Russell, S. 430
Russo, Mrs. P. 422
Rust, C. 105
Rust, R. 340
Rust, S. 196
Rutherford, P. 57
Rutkowski, M. 151
Rutland, B. 139
Ryan, A. 300
Ryan, C. 239
Ryan, C. 267

Ryan, D. 1153
Ryan, D. 408
Ryan, E. 185
Ryan, F. 273
Ryan, F. 324
Ryan, Sister J. 414, 415
Ryan, L. 84
Ryan, M. 30
Ryan, M. 255
Ryan, N. 304
Ryan, P. 149
Ryan, R. 90
Ryan, S. 254
Rzepka, J. 173

Saari, F. 220
Saario, T. 304
Sabatino, S. 333
Sabaugh, C. 213
Saboe, R. 116
Sabol, E. 365
Saccamanno, P. 48
Sachs, C. 86
Sachs, D. 211
Sachs, J. 267
Sachs, M. 117
Sack, R. 375
Sacketti, E. 123
Sackett, M. 333
Sackett, Mrs. P. 423
Sackett, R. 120
Sadewasser, J. 169
Sadler, P. 307
Sadovich, M. 258
Saenz, E. 399
Sage, D. 432
Sage, H. 454
Sage, I. 318
Sager, A. 283
Sager, L. 95
Saidman, M. 362
Saiki, P. 87
Sain, B. 310
Sainio, D. 143
St. Clair, B. 330
St. Clair, D. 310
St. George, J. 264
St. John, G. 452
St. Onge, L. 149
Sakar, S. 13
Sakas, C. 360
Saklad, J. 163
Salame, G. 165
Salazar, G. 46
Saldana, I. 393
Saldivar, E. 401
Saleeby, Mrs. E. 380
Salek, H. 99
Salem, M. 221
Sallee, L. 27
Salletter, M. 79
Salmon, D. 352
Salmon, E. 445, 450
Salmon, Mrs. T. 415
Salo, A. 201
Salo, L. 220
Salter, D. 8
Salter, D. 349
Salting, M. 317
Saltzman, J. 303
Saltzman, V. 79
Salviola, D. 385
Sammons, E. 121
Sammons, F. 23
Sample, A. 351
Sample, D. 70
Samples, N. 351
Sampson, E. 97
Sampson, M. 256
Samson, P. 228
Samuels, D. 155
Samuels, V. 284
Sanchez, D. 216
Sandborn, M. 180

Sandella, B. 362
Sanders, B. 31
Sanders, B. 85
Sanders, B. 122
Sanders, E. 9
Sanders, E. 288
Sanders, G. 86
Sanders, G. 193
Sanders, Mrs. G. 380
Sanders, H. 93
Sanders, H. 237
Sanders, K. 127
Sanders, L. 343
Sanders, P. 454
Sanderson, C. 194
Sanderson, C. 398
Sanderson, E. 49
Sanderson, E. 442
Sanderson, H. 16
Sanderson, M. 331
Sandin, Mrs. H. 450
Sandomirsky, L. 58
Sandoval, E. 288
Sandoval, G. 287
Sandoval, R. 288
Sandusky, K. 120
Sandvik, G. 21
Sanford, E. 157
Sanger, S. 116
Sankey, J. 116
Sanofsky, R. 64
Santaella, I. 302
Santavenere, Mrs. O. 62
Santy, J. 61
Sapiel, E. 147
Sapinsley, L. 371, 374, 375
Sarabyn, R. 198
Sargeant, Mrs. W. 422
Sargent, A. 414
Saridakis, R. 435
Saringer, J. 330
Sarles, L. 354
Sarri, R. 214, 215
Sarsfield, S. 293
Sartor, P. 43
Sass, C. 193
Sassower, D. 304
Satteleberg, J. 181
Satterfield, J. 157
Satterfield, T. 427
Satterlee, J. 230
Satterlee, M. 104
Satterthwaite, Mrs. E. 156
Satterthwaite, M. 94
Sattler, V. 196
Sauer, J. 291
Sauls, P. 11
Saultz, C. 237
Saunders, C. 180
Saunders, J. 264
Saunders, M. 383
Saunders, T. 374
Saurman, J. 413
Savage, M. 67
Savage, V. 10
Savage, V. 329
Savanick, B. 220
Savery, W. 435
Savoie, W. 139
Savor, M. 360
Savoy, J. 208
Sawicki, J. 358
Sawyer, A. 343
Sawyer, D. 387
Sawyer, L. 188
Sawyer, S. 254
Sawyer, T. 85
Sawyer, V. 338
Saxer, L. 448
Saxman, G. 188
Saxman, P. 288

Saxton, B. 197
Saxton, K. 408
Say, M. 254
Sayers, G. 104
Sayers, L. 197
Sayes, G. 135
Sayre, Mrs. A. 283
Scanlan, A. 355
Scanlon, M. 457
Scarborough, M. 156
Scarbrough, F. 320
Scarce, H. 344
Schaaf, P. 390
Schaaf, T. 390
Schaak, A. 339
Schaake, E. 96
Schaber, P. 241
Schacht, M. 449
Schack, R. 70
Schad, M. 446
Schaeffer, R. 359
Schafer, A. 253
Schaferbein, M. 155
Schaffer, G. 53
Schak, M. 270
Schalk, I. 173
Schall, H. 99
Schallenkamp, A. 384
Schaller, M. 57
Schant, N. 93
Schaper, M. 339
Scharr, V. 129
Schatt, C. 21
Schaudigel, G. 194
Schauer, R. 330
Schectman, M. 120
Scheer, S. 428
Scheibeler, L. 130
Scheid, D. 248
Scheid, L. 218
Scheitlin, V. 248
Schemmel, M. 112
Schena, P. 60
Schenck, M. 362
Schenk, F. 125
Scherbring, J. 111
Scherer, C. 210
Scherrer, J. 241
Schexnider, D. 343
Schick, Mrs. C. 283
Schildhouse, R. 336
Schilling, A. 168
Schilling, B. 250
Schilling, E. 316
Schillo, Sister, G.
  253, 256
Schilperoort, S. 429
Schimelfenig, G. 367
Schimmelpenny, R. 175
Schinker, K. 255
Schissler, J. 156
Schlaack, H. 144
Schlabach, L. 20
Schlak, C. 86
Schleder, M. 181
Schlegel, J. 352
Schlegel, K. 193
Schleicher, J. 242
Schley, Mrs. R. 283
Schlicher, M. 201
Schlicting, M. 197
Schlieff, G. 435
Schlimgen, M. 450
Schloff, K. 215
Schlotfeldt, C. 436
Schlottman, L. 158
Schluter, N. 278
Schmaltz, L. 317
Schmerling, S. 449
Schmid, S. 332
Schmidbauer, J. 49
Schmidt, D. 224
Schmidt, E. 178
Schmidt, F. 120
Schmidt, J. 222

Schmidt, L. 230
Schmidt, L. 375
Schmidt, M. 123
Schmidt, M. 303
Schmidt, P. 206
Schmidt, Mrs. R. 132
Schmidt, V. 102
Schmieder, M. 448
Schmierer, L. 270
Schmit, E. 317
Schmitt, B. 113
Schmitt, E. 303
Schmitt, H. 190
Schmitt, M. 157
Schmitt, S. 77
Schmitz, V. 137
Schmuck, D. 213
Schmuck, O. 293
Schnebly, W. 121
Schneider, B. 210
Schneider, C. 174
Schneider, Sister E. 302
Schneider, E. 351
Schnell, M. 323
Schnoor, L. 124
Schnurer, H. 189
Schock, M. 327
Schoeck, J. 454
Schoenholtz, A. 211
Schoenrich, E. 156
Schondelmayer, S. 187
Schonholz, G. 302
Schoonover, F. 112
Schopieray, M. 176
Schopp, H. 179
Schott, G. 295
Schott, M. 182
Schott, M. 336
Schott, N. 185
Schotte, C. 194
Schragg, R. 212
Schram, V. 185
Schramm, D. 123
Schramm, P. 65
Schreffler, G. 121
Schreiber, J. 264
Schreiber, J. 354
Schreiber, S. 288
Schreier, S. 190
Schremp, J. 236
Schriner, R. 128
Schrock, K.M. 215
Schroeder, I. 255
Schroeder, L. 114
Schroeder, L. 375
Schroeder, L. 414
Schroeder, M. 19
Schroeder, M. 112
Schroeder, M. 454
Schroeder, P. 5
Schroeder, R. 127
Schroeder, R. 446
Schroer, C. 49
Schroer, I. 99
Schroll, M. 132
Schron, N. 273
Schuble, E. 100
Schueneman, H. 397
Schuessler, F. 293
Schuette, M. 367
Schuetter, D. 95
Schukowsky, F. 378
Schuldt, M. 119
Schuler, D. 181
Schulke, M. 113
Schulmeyer, M. 216
Schultz, D. 315
Schultz, M. 96
Schultz, M. 98
Schultz, M. 115
Schultz, M. 119
Schultz, P. 78
Schulz, C. 328
Schulz, E. 382
Schulz, K. 278

Schumacher, E. 128
Schuman, F. 220
Schumann, G. 254
Schumann, M. 332
Schumate, L. 402
Schunk, J. 177
Schuppel, C. 230
Schur, S. 163
Schuster, M. 155
Schuster, M. 208
Schutte, L. 108
Schutter, B. 123
Schutz, L. 183
Schwab, E. 386
Schwab, L. 253
Schwab, M. 351
Schwalm, R. 172
Schwaner, A. 264
Schwark, H. 213
Schwartz, H. 300
Schwartz, L. 285
Schwartz, M. 177
Schwartz, P. 196
Schwartz, R. 188
Schwartzkopf, B. 122
Schwarz, E. 275
Schwarz, R. 333
Schweinhaut, M. 150
Schwerdfeger, R. 128
Schwisow, M. 251
Schwope, M. 454
Scionequx, S. 140
Scorzafava, J. 300
Scott, A. 152
Scott, B. 81
Scott, B. 109
Scott, B. 178
Scott, B. 377
Scott, C. 179
Scott, C. 184
Scott, D. 157
Scott, D. 295
Scott, E. 378
Scott, E. 416
Scott, G. 154
Scott, Mrs. H. 349
Scott, M. 27
Scott, M. 75
Scott, M. 95
Scott, M. 206
Scott, M. 253
Scott, M. 311
Scott, N. 181
Scott, P. 270
Scott, P. 412
Scott, R. 41
Scott, R. 125
Scott, R. 189
Scott, S. 66
Scott, S. 85
Scott, S. 344
Scotti, N. 236
Scotto, H. 32
Scramlin, D. 188
Scranton, A. 264
Scriven, M. 127
Scrivens, M. 68
Scruggs, Mrs. E. 11
Scull, E. 152
Seagraves, B. 36
Seal, M. 343
Seaman, F. 148
Seaman, L. 189
Searcy, D. 39
Searles, D. 174
Sears, B. 71
Sears, C. 116
Sears, V. 45
Seaton, D. 82
Seaton, J. 86
Seaver, C. 184
Seay, L. 439
Sebastian, D. 52
Sebelius, K. 132
Sebo, K. 305

Sebree, I. 104
Secord, L. 190
Seddon, G. 265
Sederberg, M. 255
Sederlund, B. 180
Sedgeman, H. 221
Sedgwick, S. 230
Sedlacek, C. 254
Sedlacek, V. 194
See, E. 175
Seedall, E. 91
Seefeldt, F. 449
Seefeldt, K. 417
Seefeldt, P. 447
Seeker, D. 322
Seekins, D. 144
Seeley, M. 185
Seelye, L. 220
Seethaler, T. 205
Segal, C. 62
Seger, G. 343
Sehulster, W. 275
Seibert, C. 225
Seibert, M. 221
Seidel, D. 50
Seidel, J. 221
Seifert, M. 101
Seiler, C. 165
Seim, C. 215
Sejd, E. 330
Sekula, B. 337
Selby, C. 347
Seldmayr, L. 113
Self, L. 244
Self, L. 401
Selkregg, L. 13
Sellars, T. 92
Sellers, D. 89
Sellers, K. 100
Sellers, V. 44
Sellick, K. 196
Sellmeyer, Mrs. J. 24
Selner, B. 76
Seltzer, R. 298
Sembert, C. 367
Semler, M. 278
Semmens, B. 405
Senatroe, M. 322
Senegal, P. 104
Senior, A. 137
Sensabaugh, P. 185
Seppanen, A. 167
Serevicz, V. 441
Sergent, W. 191
Serke, E. 57
Seroczynski, M. 210
Sestak, J. 37
Setaro, I. 359
Settle, H. 121
Setzer, F. 306
Sevenski, C. 186
Sever, N. 77
Severance, B. 250
Sewall, C. 143
Seward, L. 129
Sewell, F. 71
Sewell, K. 180
Sexton, K. 172
Sexton, V. 303
Seymour, D. 126
Seymour, M. 306
Seymour, P. 431
Shaber, R. 92
Shackleford, Mrs. J. 28
Shackelford, L. 27
Shadduck, L. 92
Shafer, A. 181, 217
Shafer, C. 334
Shafer, K. 267
Shafer, K. 273
Shaff, J. 332
Shaffer, A. 365
Shaffer, D. 357
Shaffer, G. 291
Shaffer, J. 62

Shaffer, M. 219
Shaffer, M. 360, 369
Shalala, D. 3
Shanafelt, F. 185
Shanahan, E. 3
Shanahan, E. 124
Shank, B. 364
Shanks, J. 221
Shanks, M. 232
Shannon, I. 233
Shannon, R. 101
Shapard, V. 80, 85
Shapiro, C. 40
Shapiro, M. 64
Sharp, E. 408
Sharp, I. 140
Sharp, M. 122
Sharp, M. 206
Sharp, S. 255
Sharp, S. 313
Sharp, V. 79
Sharpe, D. 201
Sharpe, D. 330
Sharpe, H. 200
Sharpe, Mrs. J. 84
Sharpe, M. 359
Sharpe, P. 375
Sharps, Mrs. D. 441
Sharrett, D. 115
Sharron, J. 165
Shatz, E. 374
Shaw, Mrs. A. 7
Shaw, A. 40
Shaw, C. 120
Shaw, E. 107, 121
Shaw, E. 222
Shaw, G. 85
Shaw, J. 52
Shaw, L. 148
Shaw, L. 232
Shaw, L. 275, 283
Shaw, M. 385
Shaw, P. 185
Shaw, S. 172
Shaw, S. 216
Shay, L. 125
Shea, C. 163
Shea, D. 414
Shea, G. 358
Shea, H. 20
Shea, M. 368
Shea, R. 267
Shealy, M. 54
Shear, B. 400
Shear, S. 234
Shearer, C. 107
Shearer, C. 122
Shearer, R. 123
Shearin, M. 342
Sheats, L. 85
Shedlock, E. 295
Sheehan, E. 163
Sheehan, L. 151, 156
Sheehan, N. 192
Sheehan, O. 64
Sheehan, P. 268, 284
Sheehan, S. 266
Sheeley, B. 21
Sheets, A. 439
Sheffield, L. 202
Sheftel, G. 301
Shehee, V. 138
Sheid, V. 22, 28
Sheinberg, J. 157
Sheldon, B. 44
Sheldon, E. 325
Sheldon, G. 4
Sheldon, M. 14
Sheldon, M. 257
Sheldon, R. 256
Shelhart, K. 58
Shell, B. 417
Shelley, A. 180
Shelnutt, W. 85
Shelton, P. 346

Shepard, D. 212
Shepard, E. 449
Shepard, I. 264
Shepard, J. 286
Shepard, N. 224
Sheperd, K. 454
Sheperd, M. 127
Shepherd, R. 436
Shepley, G. 373
Sheppard, E. 416, 422
Sheppard, J. 130
Sheppard, L. 148
Sher, P. 155
Sherburne, D. 171
Sherlock, H. 315
Sherman, E. 131
Sherman, J. 415
Sherman, L. 123
Sherman, M. 426
Sherman, R. 228
Sherrerd, L. 255
Sherrick, B. 331
Sherrill, Mrs. C. 139
Sherrill, L. 400
Sherry, V. 185
Sherwin, E. 139
Sherwood, A. 96
Sherwood, D. 210
Sherwood, M. 169
Sherwood, M. 185
Shevin, Mrs. R. 78
Shiel, C. 172
Shields, V. 104
Shimanek, N. 108
Shine, Mrs. L. 106
Shipley, C. 27
Shipman, M. 239
Shipman, S. 57
Shipp, L. 320
Shippee, P. 411
Shippenburg, T. 62
Shirer, Mrs. A. 134
Shirk, F. 336
Shirley, E. 258
Shively, L. 125
Shivers, Mrs. M. 404
Shivlie, E. 182
Shoap, K. 157
Shocket, R. 373
Shockley, R. 67
Shockley, M. 244
Shoemaker, H. 105
Shoemaker, M. 365
Shoemaker, Mrs. R. 253
Sholtz, D. 177
Shomo, N. 359
Shook, R. 353
Shorb, M. 351
Shontz, P. 75
Shontz, P. 215
Shook, F. 115
Shooks, D. 176
Shooks, P. 192
Shores, J. 11
Short, D. 431
Short, N. 82
Shorliff, B. 274
Shott, Mrs. S. 442
Shotton, S. 131
Shove, R. 91
Showalter, S. 207
Showalter, T. 356
Shrauger, P. 419
Shrek, P. 354
Shreve, Mrs. H. 442
Shreves, E. 386
Shriver, F. 453
Shropshire, C. 254
Shrout, H. 137
Shroyer, B. 197
Shuck, D. 197
Shukaitis, N. 356
Shulsky, M. 359
Shultz, N. 361
Shumaker, S. 129

Shuman, P. 438
Shumway, A. 435
Shumway, R. 406
Shupert, Mrs. B. 342
Shutes, J. 174
Shutters, C. 424
Sibert, B. 176
Sibley, Mrs. D. 404
Sibley, P. 399
Sibson, S. 178
Sicard, R. 375
Sichts, J. 101
Sidars, V. 15
Siddall, Mrs. A.E. 353
Sides, S. 250
Sidles, S. 122
Sieben, V. 132
Sieberling, N. 122
Siebert, M. 289
Siebrecht, C. 113
Siedlarczyk, T. 277
Sidezikowski, V. 356
Siefkin, S. 38
Siegel, C. 413
Siegel, Mrs. E. 304
Sieger, L. 114
Siegers, C. 186
Siemer, D. 84
Sienknecht, K. 115
Sieting, L. 187
Sifriti, J. 79
Siggelkow, E. 92
Siglin, E. 360
Sigmon, N. 310
Sigmund, B. 269, 284
Sigo, F. 436
Silberthau, L. 374
Silliman, G. 331
Silvagni, O. 259
Silver, D. 113
Silver, M. 147
Silver, R. 157
Silverman, R. 373
Silverthorn, B. 191
Silvey, B. 236
Simcox, P. 359
Simeon, L. 13
Simila, C. 190
Simiraglia, C. 156
Simmons, J. 170, 215
Simmons, M. 237
Simms, H. 206
Simms, M. 68
Simon, R. 38
Simon, R. 216
Simon, S. 226
Simon, S. 283
Simon, V. 13
Simonds, B. 67
Simonds, M. 343
Simonetti, V. 22
Simons, C. 92
Simons, L. 454
Simons, R. 375
Simonson, A. 317, 318
Simonson, M. 21
Simpers, Mrs. R. 422
Simpson, A. 179
Simpson, A. 395
Simpson, C. 231
Simpson, C. 286
Simpson, D. 191
Simpson, E. 127
Simpson, E. 298
Simpson, J. 48
Simpson, J. 303
Simpson, L. 400
Simpson, M. 49
Simpson, R. 193
Simpson, S. 419
Simpson, V. 24
Sims, E. 92
Sims, E. 215
Sims, E. 216
Sims, Mrs. J. 8

Sims, J. 400
Sims, L. 238
Sims, L. 380
Sims, M. 391
Sims, M. 233
Sims, M. 334
Sims, N. 242
Sims, P. 400
Sims, Q. 380
Sims, R. 64
Simson, M. 169
Sinclair, B. 103
Singel, P. 154
Singer, A. 85
Singer, R. 164
Singletary, D. 380
Singletary, F. 313
Singleton, M. 77
Sinigaglio, M. 68
Sink, Mrs. J. 28
Sinklier, B. 238
Sinnott, R. 269
Siri, S. 258
Sirianni, C. 355
Sirk, C. 173
Sisk, S. 39
Sitarz, K. 63
Sittko, E. 220
Sitty, J. 57
Sitzema, M. 172
Sizemore, C. 442
Sizemore, E. 80
Sjaarda, B. 117
Skadan, J. 437
Skaggs, C. 396
Skanchy, E. 408
Skarritt, C. 191
Skelly, V. 447
Skenandore, M. 449
Skibniowsky, S. 414
Sinbinx, B. 446
Skinner, B. 176
Skinner, B. 432
Skinner, H. 325
Skinner, P. 264
Skivington, M. 398
Sklenar, S. 322
Skop, V. 185
Skupny, C. 168, 211
Skytta, M. 199
Slaglc, M. 307
Slagle, M. 387
Slate, K. 411
Slater, B. 344
Slater, E. 375
Slater, I. 304
Slaughter, H. 418
Slaughter, J. 197
Slaughter, L. 291
Slaughter, L. 295
Slautterback, M. 450
Slavin, P. 60
Slayton, F. 275
Slayton, R. 296
Sleigh, M. 442
Slekis, M. 61
Sliver, G. 58
Slights, J. 67
Sloan, J. 78
Sloan, M. 40
Sloan, M. 252
Sloan, M. 398
Sloan, P. 329
Sloan, R. 358
Sloane, R. 312
Sloat, H. 195
Slocum, G. 156
Slocum, J. 185
Slocum, J. 295
Sloehsler, J. 347
Slonaker, G. 198
Slooten, E. 195
Sloup, S. 253
Slover, L. 350
Slusser, K. 321

Slyvester, G. 266
Smack, S. 157
Smage, J. 447
Samle, S. 397
Small, E. 243
Small, S. 280
Smalley, E. 190
Smalling, E. 391
Smallwood, M. 35
Smart, I. 319, 337
Smart, J. 343, 344
Smeltzer, B. 123
Smendziuk, K. 175
Smiley, A. 99
Smiley, J. 437
Smirl, J. 442
Smith, A. 32
Smith, A. 49
Smith, A. 110
Smith, A. 111
Smith, A. 117
Smith, A. 167
Smith, A. 194
Smith, A. 197
Smith, A. 244
Smith, A. 258
Smith, A. 259
Smith, A. 264
Smith, A. 313
Smith, A. 440
Smith, A. 444
Smith, B. 102
Smith, B. 110
Smith, B. 114
Smith, B. 129
Smith, B. 132
Smith, B. 136
Smith, B. 138
Smith, B. 179
Smith, B. 189
Smith, B. 303
Smith, B. 320
Smith, B. 331
Smith, B. 344
Smith, B. 348
Smith, B. 434
Smith, B. 436
Smith, B. 441
Smith, C. 9
Smith, C. 16
Smith, C. 62
Smith, C. 196
Smith, C. 336
Smith, C. 368
Smith, C. 377
Smith, Dr. C. 422
Smith, C. 434, 436
Smith, C. 440
Smith, D. 21
Smith, D. 29
Smith, D. 207
Smith, D. 212
Smith, D. 388
Smith, D. 439
Smith, E. 34
Smith, E. 35
Smith, E. 149
Smith, E. 151
Smith, E. 173
Smith, E. 196
Smith, E. 206
Smith, E. 236, 244
Smith, Mrs. E. 253
Smith, E. 378
Smith, E. 380
Smith, E. 393
Smith, E. 422, 423
Smith, E. 441
Smith, E. 449
Smith, F. 299
Smith, F. 448
Smith, Mrs. G. 28
Smith, G. 50
Smith, G. 65, 67
Smith, G. 78

Smith, G. 92
Smith, G. 208
Smith, G. 297
Smith, G. 383
Smith, G. 408
Smith, H. 137
Smith, H. 215
Smith, I. 112
Smith, I. 176
Smith, I. 180
Smith, I. 198
Smith, I. 271, 283
Smith, I. 369
Smith, I. 371, 375
Smith, I. 410
Smith, J. 19
Smith, J. 25
Smith, J. 62
Smith, J. 130
Smith, J. 139
Smith, J. 172
Smith, J. 207
Smith, J. 236
Smith, J. 301
Smith, Mrs. J. 353
Smith, J. 354
Smith, J. 412
Smith, J. 434
Smith, J. 452
Smith, K. 72
Smith, K. 148
Smith, L. 125
Smith, L. 147
Smith, L. 181
Smith, L. 329
Smith, Mrs. L. 231
Smith, L. 339
Smith, L. 341
Smith, L. 354
Smith, L. 357
Smith, M. 17
Smith, M. 27
Smith, M. 49
Smith, M. 63
Smith, M. 84
Smith, M. 145
Smith, M. 153
Smith, M. 172
Smith, M. 175
Smith, M. 176
Smith, M. 178
Smith, M. 232
Smith, M. 235
Smith, M. 238
Smith, M. 278
Smith, M. 303
Smith, M. 312
Smith, M. 323
Smith, M. 336
Smith, M. 340
Smith, M. 373
Smith, M. 386
Smith, M. 395
Smith, M. 399
Smith, M. 441
Smith, N. 84
Smith, N. 255
Smith, N. 342, 344
Smith, N. 390
Smith, N. 411
Smith, O. 215
Smith, O. 301
Smith, P. 58
Smith, P. 62
Smith, P. 401
Smith, R. 11
Smith, R. 93
Smith, R. 134
Smith, R. 136
Smith, R. 144
Smith, R. 237
Smith, Mrs. R. 244
Smith, R. 276
Smith, R. 342
Smith, Mrs. R. 403

Smith, R. 450
Smith, S. 12
Smith, S. 24
Smith, S. 28
Smith, S. 91
Smith, S. 110
Smith, S. 115
Smith, S. 148
Smith, S. 188
Smith, S. 328
Smith, S. 336
Smith, S. 343
Smith, S. 413
Smith, S. 453
Smith, V. 5
Smith, V. 88
Smith, V. 121
Smith, V. 216
Smith, W. 237
Smith, Mrs. W. 404
Smithson, J. 356
Smittle, E. 439
Smola, B. 342
Smoley, S. 31
Smoot, C. 437
Smythe, M. 4
Snape, S. 164
Snatchko, R. 365
Snavely, M. 341
Snay, S. 195
Snedden, M. 360
Sneed, B. 156
Sneer, J. 229
Snell, N. 344
Sneller, F. 20
Snelling, B. 413
Snider, C. 394
Snider, I. 320
Snider, M. 344
Snider, R. 340
Snipes, O. 286
Snitchler, M. 172
Snodgrass, L. 439
Snodgrass, M. 9
Snodgrass, T. 208
Snow, A. 365
Snow, C. 194
Snow, E. 392
Snow, G. 255
Snow, G. 298
Snow, N. 149
Snow, P. 409
Snowden, D. 16
Snowden, J. 28
Snowe, O. 142, 148
Snyder, C. 438
Snyder, D. 362
Snyder, D. 389
Snyder, E. 367
Snyder, F. 348
Snyder, G. 265
Snyder, I. 176
Snyder, J. 16
Snyder, J. 257
Snyder, K. 329
Snyder, L. 251
Snyder, M. 104
Snyder, M. 282
Snyder, M. 331
Snyder, R. 179
Snyder, S. 72
Soderman, M. 95
Sofranko, E. 115
Sofranko, V. 365
Sohl, F. 252
Sokoloff, B. 374
Solberg, B. 318
Solberg, V. 293, 216
Solem, D. 226
Solheim, L. 120
Soloman, E. 141
Solomon, A. 12
Solomon, J. 413
Solomon, L. 348
Solow, M. 266

Solt, C. 219
Somaini, P. 412
Somers, A. 442
Somers, E. 421
Somerville, M. 316
Somerville, S. 185
Sommers, E. 173
Sommers, H. 426
Sonju, S. 36
Sonnenberg, D. 279
Sonnenschein, M. 279
Soper, Mrs. E. 166
Sorber, M. 352
Sorenson, K. 449
Sorey, M. 20
Sorrell, E. 409, 412, 413
Sorter, S. 9
Sosenko, E. 209
Soto, J. 20
Soule, S. 410
Soulliers, L. 177
Soumis, P. 177
Sousa, S. 375
South, J. 235
Southall, D. 15
Southall, Mrs. F. 403
Southard, A. 257
Southwell, M. 36
Southwick, P. 405, 408
Southworth, B. 64
Southworth, E. 433
Sovie, Dr. M. 301, 302, 303
Sowle, K. 336
Spado, P. 300
Spaeth, B. 340
Spaetzel, J. 191
Spafford, C. 341
Spafford, I. 178
Spagnotti, A. 204
Spahr, V. 320
Spalding, E. 64
Spalding, I. 437
Spalding, M. 259
Spangler, E. 434
Spangler, P. 227
Spanjers, Mrs. A. 79
Spann, L. 342
Sparenberg, Mrs. B. 403
Sparkman, E. 68
Sparks, E. 315
Sparks, H. 83
Sparks, L. 169
Sparks, M. 99
Sparks, Mrs. T. 28
Sparrks, S. 199
Sparrow, M. 310
Spaulding, E. 306
Spaulding, R. 264
Spear, J. 64
Spearks, J. 105
Spears, G. 374
Spears, U. 438
Specht, E. L. 351
Spector, R. 152
Speer, D. 123
Speer, Mrs. 28
Speer, R. 128
Speight, A. 232
Speight, C. 308
Speight, L. 310
Spellman, G. 6
Spence, Mrs. A. 404
Spence, W. 65
Spence, W. 127
Spencer, D. 156
Spencer, E. 192
Spencer, G. 354
Spencer, H. 189
Spencer, I. 46
Spencer, J. 158
Spencer, K. 49
Spencer, L. 213
Spencer, M. 172

Spencer, M. 410
Spencer, N. 197
Spencer, T. 101
Spencer, T. 172
Spengler, M. 161
Sperry, C. 169
Sperry, V. 177
Speth, J. 257
Spicer, Mrs. J. 136
Spiegel, F. 32
Spink, E. 235
Spivery, Mrs. T. 387
Splitt, R. 447
Spoden, E. 229
Spodis, J. 230
Spolar, E. 208
Spomer, D. 97
Sponsel, B. 110
Sponsler, G. 330
Spoon, M. 100
Spooner, A. 219
Spooner, P. 315
Spory, M. 356
Sprague, E. 452
Sprague, J. 165
Sprague, J. 343
Sprague, J. 434
Sprague, S. 14
Specker, J. 172
Spreeancenere, G. 329
Sprigg, J. 235
Spriggs, D. 134
Springer, D. 441
Springer, V. 397
Springer, W. 444
Sprinkle, G. 156
Spry, D. 206
Spurr, M. 136
Spybrook, M. 211
Squier, A. 353
Srolea, M. 296
Stabenow, D. 167
Stachnik, V. 187
Stakpole, J. 412
Stadler, Mrs. R. 304
Staender, Mrs. G. 354
Stafford, B. 23
Stafford, P. 149
Staggers, O. 76
Stahl, J. 97
Stahl, J. 264
Stahl, N. 187
Stair, L. 449
Stalions, B. 345
Stall, B. 380
Stallings, J. 85
Stallwitz, C. 392
Stalvey, K. 85
Stamate, S. 352
Stambler, K. 415
Stambough, L. 204
Stamey, J. 83
Stamey, L. 391
Stanard, M. 205
Stanek, L. 187
Stanely, F. 127
Stanfield, N. 324
Stanford, S. 33
Stanion, T. 410
Stanley, J. 137
Stanley, K. 87
Stanley, R. 146
Stansbury, D. 91
Stanton, A. 106
Stanton, J. 228
Stanton, J. 306
Stanton, M. 432
Stanton, V. 10
Staples, E. 217
Staples, J. 450
Stappler, V. 437
Starbuck, E. 341
Starcevich, R. 117
Starin, Mrs. A. 156
Stark, A. 117

Stark, B. 183
Stark, B. 235
Stark, F. 284
Stark, J. 213
Stark, Mrs. J. 255, 256
Stark, Mrs. L. 244
Stark, M. 177
Starkey, M. 332
Starks, B. 245
Starks, G. 21
Starkweather, J. 215
Starn, V. 321
Starner, M. 20
Starr, Mrs. J. 255
Starr, M. 233
Starr, R. 74
Starr, V. 21
Starrett, M. 20
Starring, J. 189
Statler, M. 121
Staton, B. 79
Staton, C. 106
Stauffer, D. 227
Stauffer, K. 240
Steady, R. 266
Stearns, E. 412
Stearns, P. 160
Stebbins, F. 83
Steckler, D. 317
Steckler, Mrs. W. 106
Steele, G. 37
Steele, J. 193
Steele, J. 342
Steele, P. 368
Steeley, M. 388
Steen, B. 123
Steen, S. 396
Steenbergen, Z. 136
Steer, B. 327
Steere, E. 62
Stefan, B. 212
Stefani, D. 349
Stefano, B. 291
Steffen, P. 51
Steffens, M. 215
Steffes, J. 132
Steffy, M. 105
Steger, B. 446
Stegman, Mrs. E. 423
Steiber, J. 63
Steiger, P. 122
Steim, K. 362
Stein, A. 408
Stein, B. 322
Stein, Mrs. C. 442
Stein, J. 132
Steinacker, J. 269
Steinbach, J. 428
Steinberg, B. 322
Steinberg, C. 80
Steinberg, G. 31
Steinberg, M. 291
Steiner, J. 18
Steinhardt, Mrs. R. 422
Steinmetz, K. 235
Steinnark, J. 46
Steitz, M. 332
Stellow, G. 187
Stenger, B. 449
Stenseth, K. 315
Stephany, J. 410
Stephen, C. 103
Stephens, A. 368
Stephens, B. 63
Stephens, H. 407
Stephens, I. 423
Stephens, J. 79
Stephens, M. 240
Stephens, M. 373
Stephens, O. 393
Stephenson, E. 404
Stephenson, E. 419
Stephenson, M. 244
Sterling, B. 92
Sterling, E. 85

Stermer, N. 323
Stern, B. 426
Stern, Mrs. H. 29
Sterne, B. 324
Sterner, M. 127
Sterner, M. 185
Sterret, M. 329
Sterrett, M. 321
Sterett, P. 197
Sterzer, J. 336
Sterzick, H. 173
Steuben, H. 49
Stevens, Mrs. A. 231
Stevens, A. 383
Stevens, B. 352
Stevens, C. 202
Stevens, C. 208
Stevens, J. 120
Stevens, J. 159
Stevens, L. 169
Stevens, L. 238
Stevens, M. 236
Stevens, M. 258
Stevens, M. 432
Stevens, R. 210
Stevens, S. 126
Stevens, V. 410
Stevenson, F. 376
Stevenson, G. 368
Stevenson, P. 38
Steverson, R. 379
Steward, Mrs. F. 244
Steward, H. 145
Stewart, Mrs. B. 404
Stewart, E. 139
Stewart, E. 408
Stewart, F. 85
Stewart, K. 447
Stewart, Mrs. M. 253
Stewart, M. 325
Stewart, M. 331
Stewart, M. 453
Stewart, N. 178
Stewart, Mrs. P. 137
Stewart, P. 302
Stewart, P. 397
Stewart, V. 341
Stickney, C. 423
Stickney, J. 415
Stiefel, R. 85
Stiefelmayer, K. 183
Stiehl, C. 94
Stierhoff, M. 322
Stiff, J. 44
Stiffler, B. 366
Stifler, J. 155, 157
Stiggers, I. 86
Stiglich, A. 186
Stiles, B. 111
Stiles, V. 141
Stillion, S. 332
Stillman, Mrs. A. 283
Stillwagon, D. 186
Stillwell, I. 341
Stimac, H. 198
Stimets, P. 148
Stine, Mrs. G. 379
Stine, J. 212
Stinebaker, S. 244
Stinson, M. 63
Stinson, M. 337
Stire, D. 440
Stirrat, L. 275
Stiteler, E. 368
Stivers, H. 319
Stock, C. 375
Stocker, Mrs. D. 106
Stocker, D. 415
Stockett, A. 151, 156
Stocking, P. 198
Stockley, C. 153
Stockman, L. 317
Stockman, S. 8
Stockton, R. 45
Stockwell, M. 163

Stoddard, C. 294
Stodolak, J. 199
Stoess, J. 258
Stogdill, E. 211
Stoik, G. 406
Stokes, F. 135
Stokesbary, S. 231
Stokus, V. 192
Stolar, M. 242
Stoller, S. 323
Stolt, L. 23
Stoltz, D. 167
Stomack, T. 194
Stomato, L. 283
Stone, B. 178
Stone, B. 413
Stone, Mrs. C. 422
Stone, J. 149
Stone, M. 27
Stone, N. 204
Stone, P. 449
Stone, R. 375
Stone, T. 364
Stone, V. 449
Stonebraker, L. 238
Stonebraker, S. 238
Stoner, J. 242
Stonorov, K. 16
Storch, D. 20
Storey, P. 145
Storey, R. 429
Storm, E. 192
Storm, H. 449
Stormer, A. 349
Storms, H. 252
Stormson, J. 258
Stotts, M. 253
Stouffer, C. 159
Stougard, V. 117
Stout, D. 334
Stout, E. 419
Stout, J. 371
Stout, Mrs. R. 285
Stovall, M. 9
Stovall, T. 133
Stover, E. 148
Strahl, C. 183
Strahl, D. 227
Strain, V. 238
Strandberg, L. 17
Strange, C. 93
Strange, M. 71
Strapp, C. 334
Strasbaugh, N. 338
Strashensky, G. 367
Strassburg, P. 15
Stratton, G. 452
Stratton, J. 119
Strauch, M. 179
Strauss, E. 333
Strauss, F. 397
Streaker, D. 157
Stream, E. 189
Strecker, S. 131
Street, D. 155
Street, Mrs. H. 385
Streeter, A. 59
Streeter, H. 164
Streit, S. 71
Strena, M. 434
Strew, Z. 195
Stricker, D. 383
Strickland, C. 422
Stricklan, H. 85
Strickland, M. 378
Strickland, V. 73
Stricklin, W. 21
Striebel, M. 160
Stringer, A. 300
Stringer, V. 85
Strohbehn, D. 112
Strohm, J. 229
Strok, H. 375
Strom, I. 224
Strom, L. 452

Strome, J. 326
Stromp, P. 175
Strong, J. 340
Strong, M. 174
Strotman, H. 98
Stroud, A. 85
Stroud, K. 123
Stroud, L. 90
Stroud, M. 454
Strout, E. 432
Struble, M. 361
Struckhoff, B. 126
Strunk, N. 255
Strure, N. 304
Struss, E. 281
Stryffeler, M. 353
Stuart, C. 16
Stuart, I. 237
Stubblefield, B. 409
Stubblefield, J. 281
Stubbs, S. 244
Stuckey, P. 253
Stuckum, C. 178
Studer, Mrs. A. 283, 284
Studness, A. 317
Stuempfle, D. 363
Stugart, B. 364
Stugger, D. 411
Stull, N. 255
Stull, S. 361
Stultz, L. 101
Stump, B. 19
Stump, Mrs. W. 317
Sturgill, L. 134
Sturgulewski, A. 13
Sturtevant, A. 147
Stuteman, E. 170
Stutheit, W. 255
Stutzman, C. 184
Stuwe, B. 49
Styron, M. 85
Styskal, H. 171
Sugar, P. 21
Suggs, M. 62
Suggs, M. 395
Sughrue, K. 124
Sugiyama, M. 93
Suhr, B. 454
Suhr, D. 256
Sukoff, L. 303
Sullenger, L. 190
Sullivan, A. 180
Sullivan, A. 387
Sullivan, C. 158
Sullivan, C. 196
Sullivan, J. 162
Sullivan, J. 271
Sullivan, K. 253
Sullivan, L. 92
Sullivan, L. 374
Sullivan, M. 62
Sullivan, M. 153
Sullivan, M. 173
Sullivan, M. 188
Sullivan, M. 254
Sullivan, M. 366
Sullivan, M. 421
Sullivan, O. 339
Sullivan, R. 196
Sultze, P. 448
Sumerson, G. 363
Summerlin, C. 86
Summers, B. 438
Summers, E. 338
Summers, J. 236
Summers, L. 114
Summers, Mrs. L. 317
Summers, M. 239
Summerville, M. 391
Sumner, J. 309
Sumner, M. 95
Sun, A. 255
Sunday, J. 180
Sundbeck, M.L. 215
Sundberg, R. 190

Sunden, M. 274
Sundstrom, A. 427
Sunshine, L. 302
Supernaw, E. 448
Suplee, S. 366
Suratt, N. 279
Sutch, M. 435, 436
Sutherland, A. 163
Sutherland, A. 418
Sutherland, M. 131
Sutherland, M. 253
Sutherland, M. 430
Sutherland, R. 344
Sutlief, E. 127
Sutton, G. 297
Sutton, G. 335
Sutton, L. 392
Sutton, M. 23
Sutton, N. 348
Sutton, Mrs. O. 307
Sutton, R. 343
Suttonm W. 245
Svedberg, J. 380
Svingen, I. 247
Svoboda, L. 108
Swackhamer, V. 270
Swain, J. 414
Swain, S. 171
Swainbank, L. 410, 414, 415
Swan, E. 129
Swan, M. 145
Swan, R. 350
Swank, G. 93
Swandon, B. 47
Swanson, B. 254
Swanson, E. 50
Swanson, G. 41
Swanson, K. 159
Swanson, K. 197
Swanson, K. 220
Swanson, L. 221
Swanson, R. 222
Swanson, R. 332
Swanson, S. 386
Swanson, V. 251
Swanson, V. 434
Swantack, F. 364
Swarts, B. 226
Swartz, B. 251
Swartz, J. 422
Swartz, M. 193
Swartz, R. 284
Swearengin, P. 236
Swearingen, V. 244
Swearingen, Y. 235
Sweatt, A. 267
Sweeney, I. 407
Sweeney, M. 336
Sweeney, P. 32
Sweeny, R. 42
Sweers, T. 176
Sweeter, B. 194
Swelander, G. 224
Swem, D. 194
Swenk, S. 298
Swenning, I. 384
Swenson, A. 50
Swenson, A. 219
Swenson, K. 317
Swenson, M. 383
Swenson, Mrs. N. 317
Swick, L. 282
Swift, L. 193
Swigert, R. 89
Swihart, K. 255
Swilley, H. 79
Swilling, J. 308
Swinehamer, D. 102
Swink, D. 42
Swint, M. 396
Swinton, J. 338
Swisher, J. 122
Switalski, N. 211
Switaski, A. 63

Switzer, A. 254
Switzer, D. 253
Swoboda, Mrs. F. 254
Sy, B. 173
Sydnor, E. 418
Syler, B. 209
Sylva, J. 37
Sylvester, B. 381
Syma, M. 402
Symanzik, C. 171
Symon, M. 445
Symonds, C. 292
Symons, A. 15
Symons, J. 166
Sypher, E. 51
Sypher, S. 296
Syri, A. 413
Sysak, P. 208
Syverson, D. 179
Szabo, H. 269
Szorad, D. 335
Szyperski, Sister M. 450

Taffe, B. 264
Taggart, J. 381
Tagliareni, D. 188
Tait, E. 79
Takacs, J. 336
Talarski, P. 241
Talaski, C. 204
Talbert, J. 408
Talbot, S. 47
Talley, H. 285
Talley, T. 140
Tallman, D. 171
Tallman, J. 36
Tally, L. 306
Talton, H. 354
Tamlyn, S. 204
Tanaka, Y. 454
Tanata, V. 316
Tanke, M. 429
Tanner, B. 105
Tanner, E. 404
Tanner, L. 233
Tansey, M. 319
Tapp, Mrs. C. 344
Tappe, M. 110
Tarciani, D. 359
Tardis, V. 143
Tardy, V. 413
Taritas, P. 215
Tarr, G. 143
Tarran, C. 217
Tarrant, S. 67
Tarr-Whelan, Mrs. L. 302
Tartaglione, M. 356
Tarutis, M. 157
Tarvin, M. 26
Tate, B. 147
Tate, C. 338
Tate, E. 441
Tate, N. 180
Tate, P. 388
Tate, R. 243
Tawes, J. 157
Tawresey, A. 433
Taylor, A. 14
Taylor, A. 45
Taylor, A. 409
Taylor, B. 11
Taylor, B. 71
Taylor, B. 242
Taylor, C. 92
Taylor, C. 309
Taylor, C. 353
Taylor, D. 95
Taylor, D. 344
Taylor, E. 158
Taylor, E. 355
Taylor, E. 421
Taylor, E. 448
Taylor, F. 132
Taylor, G. 78

Taylor, H. 141
Taylor, H. 326
Taylor, H. 423
Taylor, I. 29
Taylor, J. 189
Taylor, J. 284
Taylor, Mrs. L. 67
Taylor, L. 83
Taylor, M. 7
Taylor, M. 86
Taylor, M. 92
Taylor, M. 153
Taylor, M. 227
Taylor, M. 301, 302
Taylor, M. 348
Taylor, M. 401
Taylor, M. 415
Taylor, M. 435
Taylor, N. 299
Taylor, O. 370
Taylor, P. 27
Taylor, P. 352
Taylor, R. 72
Taylor, R. 179
Taylor, R. 354
Taylor, R. 434
Taylor, S. 14, 16
Taylor, S. 64
Taylor, S. 118
Taylor, S. 250
Taylor, T. 197
Taylor, V. 285
Taylor, V. 299
Taylor, Mrs. W. 253
Tea, E. 21
Teague, B. 148
Teague, B. 343
Teague, E. 99
Teague, J. 390
Teal, B. 303
Teare, J. 224
Teater, P. 112
Teddler, B. 25
Tedone, M. 60, 63
Teese, G. 275
Teeters, M. 200
Teich, V. 210
Teilbur, B. 112
Telson, R. 79
Tembruell, L. 188
Temple, B. 149
Templeton, J. 226
Templin, B. 342
Ten Eyck, N. 350
Tenhet, R. 233
Tennant, H. 200
Tenney, P. 215
Tennile, M. 306
Tennis, R. 316
Tenniswood, N. 171
Tennyson, F. 388
Tepper, M. 156
Terpening, L. 199
Terpstra, B. 176
Terrell, B. 47
Terrell, E. 208
Terrell, G. 134
Terrill, E. 62
Terry, J. 264
Terry, L. 49
Terry, M. 340
Terry, M. 457
Terwilliger, P. 216
Teryort, E. 38
Tesmer, L. 444
Testa, N. 303
Tester, J. 121
Thabault, F. 412
Thacker, I. 188
Thackery, H. 408
Thaeler, M. 287
Thaler, D. 133
Tharp, D. 240
Tharp, S. 106
Tharpe, M. 72

Thayer, B. 216
Thayer, N. 46
Thayer, V. 249
Thayer, Mrs. W. 304
Theeman, A. 146
Theiling, J. 442
Thein, L. 109
Thelander, L. 252
Therrien, C. 414
Thieln, D. 226
Thieme, P. 50
Thill, I. 182
Thill, S. 116
Thiman, T. 354
Thimmig, J. 52
Thode, E. 20
Thode, K. 437
Thoele, D. 223
Thoen, L. 221
Thomas, B. 84
Thomas, B. 90
Thomas, B. 306
Thomas, C. 99
Thomas, C. 198
Thomas, C. 242
Thomas, D. 85
Thomas, D. 187
Thomas, D. 188
Thomas, E. 244
Thomas, F. 39
Thomas, Mrs. H. 422
Thomas, I. 67
Thomas, I. 441
Thomas, J. 101
Thomas, J. 183
Thomas, J. 437
Thomas, L. 6
Thomas, L. 50
Thomas, L. 67
Thomas, L. 113
Thomas, L. 171
Thomas, L. 232
Thomas, L. 257
Thomas, Mrs. L. 336
Thomas, L. 353
Thomas, L. 364
Thomas, M. 110
Thomas, M. 244
Thomas, M. 335
Thomas, M. 379
Thomas, M. 414
Thomas, N. 297
Thomas, N. 435
Thomas, P. 284
Thomas, P. 360
Thomas, P. 404
Thomas, R. 340
Thomas, R. 363
Thomas, V. 384
Thomason, B. 440
Thompson, A. 448
Thompson, B. 377
Thompson, B. 443, 449
Thompson, C. 241
Thompson, C. 248
Thompson, C. 288
Thompson, C. 321
Thompson, D. 181
Thompson, D. 344
Thompson, D. 428
Thompson, E. 13
Thompson, E. 286
Thompson, E. 323
Thompson, G. 132
Thompson, Mrs. G. 338
Thompson, G. 348
Thompson, H. 103
Thompson, I. 429
Thompson, J. 26
Thompson, Mrs. J. 27
Thompson, J. 189
Thompson, J. 385
Thompson, K. 408
Thompson, L. 144
Thompson, L. 297

Thompson, M. 125
Thompson, M. 149
Thompson, M. 170
Thompson, M. 201
Thompson, Mrs. M. 245
Thompson, M. 247
Thompson, M. 266
Thompson, M. 343
Thompson, M. 365
Thompson, M. 391
Thompson, N. 10
Thompson, O. 60
Thompson, P. 108
Thompson, P. 419
Thompson, R. 173
Thompson, R. 255
Thompson, S. 123
Thompson, S. 138
Thompson, S. 145
Thompson, S. 248
Thompson, S. 392
Thompson, T. 31
Thompson, Mrs. V. 316
Thomsen, F. 19
Thomsen, N. 384
Thomson, G. 264
Thomson, M. 51
Thomson, R. 373
Thomson, T. 451, 453
Thorburn, G. 170
Thorne, G. 442
Thornley, M. 437
Thornton, B. 342, 343
Thornton, Mrs. R. 8
Thornton, S. 370
Thorpe, N. 259
Thorsby, M. 197
Thorsby, P. 192
Thorsen, R. 223
Thorton, B. 326
Thrasher, L. 154
Thrasher, M. 86
Thrasher, T. 16
Thrift, L. 73
Thrift, S. 81
Throckmorton, J. 105
Thrower, L. 381
Thrun, J. 201
Thudium, M. 122
Thue, G. 317
Thum, M. 127
Thurm, A. 72
Thurman, B. 279
Thurman, K. 72
Thurman, N. 244
Thurman, P. 117
Thurn, R. 129
Thurston, R. 128
Tibbe, M. 320
Tibbs, A. 253
Tice, E. 121
Tickner, E. 157
Tiderington, D. 171
Tidey, J. 178
Tidwell, D. 405
Tidwell, J. 373
Tiebel, H. 303
Tieman, N. 67
Tigges, L. 122
Tigges, W. 120
Tileston, P. 17
Tillapaugh, H. 63
Tille, A. 118
Tillion, D. 16
Tillman, Mrs. A. 453
Tilt, J. 188
Timm, P. 353
Timmer, E. 195
Timmons, B. 328
Timonen, N. 220
Timothy, R. 408
Timpe, J. 427
Tindall, N. 282
Tingle, F. 134
Tinker, I. 4

Tinsley, B. 135
Tinsley, Mrs. C. 106
Tinsley, R. 259
Tippets, G. 454
Tippin, Mrs. G. 29
Tirsell, H. 33
Tischler, L. 178
Tita, H. 362
Titus, G. 167
Titus, M. 93
Toal, J. 376
Tobar, L. 215
Tobey, R. 336
Tobias, R. 86
Tobiasson, S. 352
Tobin, K. 302
Tobin, M. 133
Tobin, M. 454
Tobin, Mrs. S. 23
Tobman, J. 257
Toborg, L. 413
Toby, A. 144
Todd, G. 240
Todd, G. 430
Todd, M. 235
Todd, N. 30
Todd, P. 114
Toepfer, M. 178
Toepke, M. 95
Toews, J. 435
Tolan, S. 176
Toland, C. 121
Tolbert, E. 152
Tolbert, V. 231
Tolentino, E. 104
Toles, C. 443
Toles, S. 137
Tolle, B. 320
Tollefson, M. 218
Tollett, E. 393
Tollett, G. 436
Tolmach, J. 39
Tolman, M. 185
Tolo, N. 244
Tomasek, A. 119
Tomber, I. 214, 215
Tomblin, T. 392
Tomek, N. 209
Tomer, E. 147
Tominc, V. 454
Tomlin, R. 283
Tomlinson, H. 181
Tomlinson, J. 255
Tomlinson, K. 171
Tompkins, R. 214
Tomsic, M. 406
Tondu, M. 174
Toney, J. 174
Tonkin, J. 73
Took, D. 211
Tootell, L. 374
Toothaker, G. 167
Topel, M. 450
Tordoff, F. 16
Torgeson, E. 301
Tornberg, J. 15
Toro, A. 62
Torp, R. 199
Torrence, J. 108
Torres, L. 286
Torrey, J. 264
Torrey, L. 145
Torrey, V. 145
Totaro, R. 457
Toth, J. 151
Totten, B. 231
Touchett, Sister,M. 450
Towne, R. 410
Towne, S. 14
Townes, Mrs. J. 342
Towns, B. 206
Townsend, J. 23
Townsend, M. 123
Townsend, M. 135
Townsend, M. 264

Townsend, M. 380
Townsend, P. 68
Townsend, S. 264
Track, J. 173
Tracy, C. 121
Tracy, F. 201
Trader, H. 157
Trafton, B. 143
Traina, H. 417
Traina, Mrs. J. 422
Trammell, L. 428
Trapp, H.Y. 215
Trask, E. 147
Traver, M. 190
Traver, N. 128
Travesky, M. 417
Traylor, V. 28
Treadway, E. 399
Tremaine, E. 91
Tremblay, Y. 15
Trembley, A. 192
Trenary, K. 213
Trendell, J. 131
Trent, S. 387
Trentham, V. 76
Treppler, I. 235
Tretheway, B. 189
Tretinik, E. 357
Trickett, W. 438
Tripp, C. 207
Triquet, D. 171
Troe, L. 222
Troiano, R. 411
Trojanowski, H. 359
Trojcak, T. 399
Trolz, B. 193
Trommer, E. 371
Trostel, H. 430
Trout, M. 337
Trover, H. 135
Trowbridge, P. 441
Trowell, G. 379
Troyer, H. 19
Truance, I. 205
Truckenbrod, M. 96
True, N. 10
Truex, Mrs. E. 64
Truex, R. 61, 64
Truitt, M. 66, 67
Trujillo, R. 33, 41
Trull, F. 91, 92
Trulock, C. 82
Truman, A. 19, 21
Trumbauer, C. 367
Trumps, F. 140
Trunick, M. 135
Truslow, J. 379
Tryon, R. 449
Tryon, S. 242
Tschirky, M. 430
Tsivis, N. 403
Tuason, A. 453
Tubbs, B. 298
Tuck, A. 75
Tuck, C. 164
Tuck, G. 79
Tucker, A. 371
Tucker, B. 397
Tucker, C. 106
Tucker, C. 191
Tucker, M. 288
Tucker, M. 364
Tucker, N. 390
Tucker, P. 341
Tucker, S. 436
Tuffelmire, E. 215
Tufts, B. 374
Tugend, E. 68
Tuggle, M. 86
Tully, D. 140
Tully, L. 272
Tulppo, E. 204
Tuma, S. 453
Tune, M. 340
Tunison, A. 214

Tunison, J. 350
Tuor, N. 354
Tupper, D. 454
Tupper, H. 146
Turbelville, E. 419
Turman, G. 408
Turnbull, C. 22
Turnbull, B. 242
Turner, A. 179
Turner, B. 85
Turner, B. 237
Turner, C. 333
Turner, D. 388
Turner, E. 120
Turner, F. 242
Turner, K. 49
Turner, L. 53
Turner, L. 106
Turner, M. 10
Turner, M. 209
Turner, M. 385
Turner, M. 453
Turner, P. 295
Turner, P. 398
Turnis, R. 123
Tutelain, N. 147
Tuttle, H. 357
Tutton, C. 112
Tuveson, J. 78
Tweed, K. 347
Twentyman, E. 290
Twilley, V. 66
Twyman, E. 283
Tyburski, J. 163
Tye, L. 83
Tyers, D. 192
Tylenda, P. 419
Tyler, B. 201
Tyler, C. 360
Tyler, J. 409
Tyler, U. 78
Tyler, L. 380
Tyndall, P. 254
Tyson, M. 37

Uda, B. 90
Uebele, D. 295
Uecke, C. 445
Uhl, J. 279
Uhlhorn, M. 229
Uitto, V. 452
Ullam, P. 322
Ulle, M. 155
Ullrich, D. 449
Ullum, E. 328
Ulman, M. 200
Ulrich, J. 190
Umble, T. 362
Umphress, J. 161
Underhill, L. 162
Underwood, B. 265
Underwood, F. 402
Underwood, J. 440
Underwood, K. 29
Underwood, M. 340
Underwood, M. 345
Ungricht, W. 88
Ungruhe, C. 332
Unrue, B. 205
Unruh, M. 96
Unseold, J. 436
Upchurch, V. 341
Updike, M. 418
Upjohn, Sister J. 408
Upshaw, D. 10
Upshaw, L. 244
Upton, A. 26
Upton, M.. 248
Upton, T. 266
Urban, B. 155
Urban, E. 450
Urbanek, M. 455
Urbany, K. 195
Ure, H. 415

Urias, L. 397
Urich, A. 333
Urion, Mrs. E. 285
Urton, E. 243
Urton, R. 199
Utech, S. 448
Utesch, E. 252
Utkus, A. 367
Utterback, H. 200
Utterback, L. 148
Utz, B. 53
Utz, K. 426
Uviller, R. 302

Vaccaro, A. 274
Vader, E. 167
Vail, C. 163
Vail, K. 244
Vail, N. 330
Vaja, J. 399
Valencia, V. 22
Valente, G. 374
Valente, J. 146
Valentine, B. 201
Valentino, C. 294
Valenzuela, E. 44
Valicenti, B. 294
Valiquette, M. 318
Valle, G. 426
Vallee, Sister R. 414
Valley, I. 264
Van, N. 233
Vanaken, F. 51
Vanatta, P. 418
Van Beek, Z. 93
Van Blarcom, E. 149
Van Buren, A. 171
Van Buskirk, G. 48
Vance, C. 96
Vance, C. 403
Vance, E. 407
Vance, M. 56, 58
Vance, M. 220
Vance, N. 11
Van Cleve, B. 106
VanCleve, V. 237
Vandagriff, M. 35
Van De Bogart, J. 297
Vandenbass, L. 175
Van Den Blink, N. 279
Van Den Heuvel, E. 122
Vendenhouten, L. 199
Vanderlaan, D. 192
Vander Laan, M. 220
Vanderpool, A. 413
Vanderpool, F. 48
Vanderwilt, M. 439
Van De Velde, M. 70
Vandever, R. 353
Van Doren, P. 56
Vandyk, M. 51
Van Dyke, Sister C. 434, 435
Van Hook, G. 390
Van Horn, D. 114
Van Horn, W. 66
Van Horne, M. 333
Van Houten, M. 374
Van Kleek, M. 227
Van Kooten, M. 16
Vanlandingham, B. 119
Van Loan, A. 264
Van Loo, C. 43
Van Loton, L. 310
Van Meter, H. 336
Van Meter, J. 255
Van Meter, V. 128
Vann, J. 28
Van Ness, Mrs. E. 283
Van Pelt, N. 136
Van Sant, L. 285
Van Sickel, D. 369
Vansiclen, E. 364
Van Sittert, B. 20

Vanstike, E. 18
Van Sumeren, M. 185
Van Tyle, J. 118
Van Vlack, E. 242
Van Vleck, J. 422
Van Wert, A. 123
Van West, B. 374
Van Winkle, B. 123
Van Winkle, L. 99
Van Zant, M. 134
Varble, A. 105
Varcoe, J. 369
Vargo, F. 174
Varian, C. 272
Varner, M. 242
Varney, H. 259
Varrati, J. 15
Vasko, E. 62
Vasold, P. 184
Vasquez, M. 48
Vassar, B. 27
Vaughan, A. 423
Vaughan, D. 267
Vaughan, M. 229
Vaughan, R. 215
Vaughn, C. 18
Vaughn, C. 79
Vaughn, F. 146
Vaughn, F. 240
Vaughn, Mrs. J. 380
Vaughn, M. 434
Vaughn, Mrs. P. 136
Vaughn, S. 380
Vaughn, V. 96
Vay, D. 363
Vazquez-Byrne, A. 449
Veach, B. 442
Vedoe, M. 165
Veihl, L. 182
Velez, J. 19
Venable, M. 104
Venell, R. 354
Venemon, J. 428
Vennert, B. 62
Vent, A. 12
Vent, M. 13
Ventrone, H. 357
Vercher, J. 74
Verhage, H. 285
Verna, A. 366
Verne, L. 58
Verner, E. 84
Vernon, J. 165
Verrilli, R. 59
Vertin, K. 218
Verville, D. 187
Vervoren, T. 450
Vest, D. 241
Viani, J. 257
Viau, R. 184
Vick, M. 418
Vickers, V. 390
Vickroy, P. 237
Vidmar, F. 221
Vieregg, V. 256
Viestenz, J. 242
Vigen, K. 385
Vigesaa, L. 436
Vigil, L. 52
Vik, M. 386
Vilhauer, E. 351
Villani, M. 277
Villines, E. 121, 122
Viner, D. 373
Vines, E. 158
Vineyard, P. 301
Violet, Sister A. 373
Virden, H. 122
Viscome, L. 304
Vislosky, D. 361
Visscher, V. 197
Vitale, C. 58
Vitale, C. 196
Vocci, N. 364
Voege, F. 366

Vogan, H. 177
Vogel, V. 350
Vogelaar, V. 197
Vogelwede, A. 422
Vogley, S. 322
Vogt, D. 224
Vogt, M. 255
Volkmer, H. 77
Voll, S. 264
Vollner, E. 174
Vollner, J. 4
Von Ammon, B. 18
Von Beroldingen, D. 31
Voorde, F. 4
Voorhees, A. 284
Vore, C. 454
Vorhaus, K. 123
Voth, E. 15
Vrakatitis, Z. 264
Vuich, R. 30
Vulk, F. 116
Vunovich, J. 204

Waddell, C. 421
Waddell, M. 19
Waddell, R. 266
Waddle, F. 344
Wade, B. 101
Wade, E. 81
Wade, M. 92
Wade, M. 423
Wade, P. 146
Wadley, E. 60
Wadsworth, D. 301
Wagendorf, Sister M. 317
Waggoner, A. 449
Wagley, A. 236
Wagner, A. 399
Wagner, B. 58
Wagner, B. 194
Wagner, E. 292
Wagner, G. 35
Wagner, J. 205
Wagner, J. 446
Wagner, L. 62
Wagner, M. 202
Wagner, M. 331
Wagner, S. 256
Wagoner, C. 132
Wagoner, L. 49
Wagoner, M. 436
Wahl, C. 201
Wahl, H. 130
Wahl, R. 230
Wahler, V. 315
Waite, Mrs. A. 85
Waite, B. 189
Waite, E. 214
Waites, C. 377
Waites, J. 8
Wakefield, A. 257
Wakefield, H. 410
Wakefield, K. 9
Wakeman, B. 56
Walburn, K. 319
Walch, V. 225
Walcott, S. 14
Wald, P. 4
Waldal, E. 315
Waldbaum, M. 253
Walden, O. 85
Waldo, K. 235
Waldron, C. 182
Waldstein, M. 109
Walfe, K. 347
Walizer, C. 369
Walker, A. 8
Walker, A. 24
Walker, A. 336
Walker, A. 452
Walker, A. 454
Walker, B. 83
Walker, C. 106

Walker, C. 251
Walker, Mrs. C. 393
Walker, E. 104
Walker, E. 376
Walker, G. 24
Walker, G. 71
Walker, G. 354
Walker, J. 79
Walker, L. 13
Walker, L. 48
Walker, L. 130
Walker, L. 186
Walker, M. 91
Walker, M. 248
Walker, M. 285
Walker, M. 394
Walker, M. 399
Walker, N. 433
Walker, Mrs. P. 244
Walker, S. 76
Walkmeyer, D.L. 214
Walkonen, S. 187
Wall, A. 90
Wall, E. 439
Wall, Mrs. J. 78
Wall, J. 446
Wallace, A. 113
Wallace, A. 308
Wallace, G. 12
Wallace, J. 205
Wallace, Mrs. J. 403
Wallace, L. 59
Wallace, S. 77
Wallen, A. 414
Waller, H. 224
Wallhauser, L. 284
Wallin, B. 12
Wallin, J. 264
Walling, D. 395
Wallinga, M. 122
Wallingford, M. 135
Walls, M. 442
Walser, D. 430
Walsh, B. 134
Walsh, G. 121
Walsh, G. 358
Walsh, Sister M. 375
Walsh, M. 444
Walsh, R. 413
Walstead, F. 170
Walston, M. 313
Walt, P. 363
Walter, A. 122
Walter, H. 343
Walter, M. 323
Walter, M. 353
Walter, M. 450
Walters, B. 14, 16
Walters, C. 330
Walters, J. 109
Walters, K. 15
Walters, L. 89
Walton, A. 418
Walton, B. 27
Walton, C. 418
Walton, D. 130
Walton, E. 184
Walton, E. 311
Walton, Mrs. H. 420
Walton, L. 86
Walton, W. 194
Waltz, A. 435
Wanatee, P. 122
Wander, A. 93
Wander, J. 110
Wanek, B. 250
Wangler, B. 202
Wanner, M. 90
Want, D. 255
Waples, G. 283
War, E. 258
Ward, B. 93
Ward, C. 341
Ward, D. 267
Ward, F. 343

Ward, G. 331
Ward, H. 152
Ward, H. 338
Ward, I. 232
Ward, J. 313
Ward, J. 368
Ward, J. 434
Ward, K. 34
Ward, K. 264
Ward, K. 442
Ward, L. 129
Ward, L. 282
Ward, M. 435
Ward, N. 56
Ward, P. 27
Ward, Mrs. S. 6
Ward, S. 183
Ward, S. 344
Warden, M. 246
Ware, B. 343
Ware, C. 180
Ware, D. 327
Ware, E. 254
Ware, L. 394
Ware, S. 105
Warhol, W. 404
Warling, M. 227
Warne, G. 383
Warner, C. 17
Warner, E. 40
Warner, L. 63
Warner, L. 202
Warner, M. 343
Warner, S. 106
Warner, T. 209
Warning, M. 447
Warnscholz, F. 253
Warr, M. 198
Warren, B. 15
Warren, B. 242
Warren, F. 85
Warren, J. 408
Warren, M. 83
Warren, M. 171
Warren, M. 321
Warren, N. 52
Warren, P. 437
Warren, R. 147
Warren, R. 298
Warren, T. 420
Warrick, Sister A. 336
Warsop, J. 182
Warwick, J. 15
Washburn, M. 212
Washburne, G. 415
Washington, C. 67
Washington, J. 85
Wasmund, B. 292
Wasmund, M. 295
Wassillie, E. 14
Wassillie, S. 14
Wassinger, A. 128
Wasson, E. 236
Wasuli, M. 14
Wasvary, A. 294
Wasylewski, J. 186
Waterbury, J. 414
Waters, A. 93
Waters, A. 122
Waters, A. 400
Waters, B. 204
Waters, M. 30
Waters, P. 395
Waters, R. 356
Watkins, B. 424
Watkins, C. 403
Watkins, D. 312
Watkins, D. 407
Watkins, E. 73
Watkins, I. 85
Watkins, I. 29
Watkins, M. 100
Watrous, P. 449
Watson, B. 4
Watson, B. 327

Watson, B. 353
Watson, E. 36
Watson, E. 76
Watson, E. 193
Watson, E. 411
Watson, G. 264
Watson, H. 62, 63
Watson, J. 8
Watson, L. 398
Watson, N. 44
Watson, S. 415
Watson, V. 7
Watson, Mrs. W. 380
Watt, B. 245
Watt, P. 205
Watters, B. 330
Watterson, K. 324
Watts, M. 357
Waugaman, N. 208
Waugh, A. 440
Waugh, C. 112
Waugh, H. 176
Waun, B. 190
Wax, E. 109
Wayne, J. 242
Wayne, S. 438
Wean, B. 106
Wear, C. 364
Weatherspoon, L. 233
Weatherwax, L. 205
Weatherwax, M. 327
Weaver, A. 340
Weaver, B. 183
Weaver, B. 241
Weaver, B. 326
Weaver, D. 158
Weaver, F. 211
Weaver, H. 369
Weaver, I. 118
Weaver, J. 239
Weaver, J. 366
Weaver, M. 238
Weaver, N. 33
Webb, C. 349
Webb, D. 186
Webb, D. 207
Webb, J. 389
Webb, K. 216
Webb, L. 81
Webb, Mrs. M. 403
Webb, Mrs. P. 78
Webb, P. 154
Webbs, S. 70
Webb, S. 112
Webb, S. 410
Webber, C. 181
Webber, P. 190
Webber, R. 73
Weber, B. 193
Weber, G. 272
Weber, H. 207
Weber, I. 185
Weber, M. 186
Weber, N. 122
Weber, N. 435
Weber, V. 181
Weber, W. 235
Webster, C. 449
Webster, F. 244
Webster, M. 237
Weddell, D. 118
Weddington, S. 4
Weddington, S. 392
Wedow, S. 258
Weed, D. 249
Weed, M. 8
Weeks, J. 152
Weeks, M. 17
Weeks, S. 44
Weeks, S. 344
Weers, L. 253
Wegge, F. 316
Wegner, P. 450
Wegner, R. 446
Wehrbein, J. 253

Wehrer, G. 53
Wehrle, M. 438
Wehrmeister, L. 191
Wehunt, V. 380
Weible, C. 72
Weidenfeld, M. 156
Weidman, L. 299
Weier, P. 244
Weiglein, R. 114
Weikel, E. 257
Weil, C. 73
Weiland, N. 121
Weilang, C. 453
Weimer, K. 18
Weinbach, V. 154
Weinberg, J. 157
Weinbrecht, R. 423
Weinel, L. 188
Weiner, R. 436
Weingart, Mrs. R. 246
Weinheimer, Mrs. G. 283
Weinholt, Mrs. F. 398
Weinreb, I. 32
Weinstein, E. 354
Weinstein, Mrs.H. 258
Weintraub, F. 373
Weinzetl, D. 364
Weir, E. 101
Weir, Mrs. G. 233
Weir, K. 437
Weir, P. 440
Weirick, J. 402
Weisbender, L. 132
Weisensel, M. 445
Weishaupt, M. 33
Weiskopf, S. 449
Weiss, B. 60
Weiss, S. 273
Weiss, V. 172
Weissman, L. 86
Weissman, L. 414
Weist, B. 337
Weitz, J. 52
Weitz, S. 48
Welch, B. 21
Welch, C. 189
Welch, E. 115
Welch, F. 23
Welch, J. 178
Welch, J. 301
Welch, M. 361
Welch, N. 230
Welch, N. 344
Welch, R. 422
Welcome, V. 150, 156, 158
Welford, N. 233
Well, R. 149
Weller, P. 368
Wellner, S. 173
Wells, B. 27
Wells, Mrs. D. 135
Wells, E. 232
Wells, I. 165
Wells, J. 403
Wells, J. 449
Wells, K. 239
Wells, M. 4
Wells, M. 205
Wells, M. 257
Wells, M. 277
Wells, S. 79
Wells, S. 292
Wells, S. 404
Welsh, C. 15
Welsh, Mrs. M. 105
Welter, J. 195
Welter, N. 121
Welton, M. 410
Welty, E. 195
Wemple, Mrs. J. 298
Wende, N. 67
Wendel, M. 160
Wendland, N. 195
Wendler, Mrs. W. 155

Wendling, K. 415
Wendt, C. 346
Wendt, W. 351
Wenger, M. 139
Wengert, S. 255
Wensel, R. 225
Wenta, M. 169
Wentworth, M. 184
Wentz, E. 357
Wentz, J. 315
Wenzel, M. 175
Werber, B. 284
Werkhoven, W. 63
Werner, D. 259
Werner, V. 369
Wernke, C. 382, 385
Wertheim, M. 4
Wertz, E. 113
Wescott, B. 284
Weseman, N. 219
Wesley, D. 191
Wesner, J. 356
Wesner, L. 341
Wesphal, P. 114
Wessberger, S. 373
Wessel, J. 216
Wesselman, M. 105
Wesselowski, J. 132
West, B. 95
West, C. 112
West, C. 210
West, E. 85
West, E. 232
West, Mrs. E. 395
West, G. 362
West, H. 321
West, I. 450
West, J. 424
West, K. 303
West, R. 29
West, R. 126
West, R. 307
West, S. 274
West, S. 286
West, W. 248
West, Mrs. W. 403
Westall, A. 79
Westall, P. 256
Westall, S. 331
Westbrook, E. 129
Westby, K. 229
Westenberg, M. 187
Westerhof, M. 121
Westgate, B. 157
Westphal, A. 25
Westrate, B. 208
Westrate, E. 178
Westrick, M. 178
Wetherall, C. 93
Wetherill, R. 279
Wetzel, B. 202
Wexler, A. 4
Weyant, G. 116
Weydert, D. 117
Weyhrich, D. 245
Weymann, B. 21
Whalen, F. 448
Whaley, A. 15
Whaley, B. 155
Whaley, E. 203
Whaley, M. 130
Wharton, A. 10
Wharton, D. 214
Whatley, C. 84
Wheat, B. 95
Wheat, B. 342
Wheat, C. 434
Wheatley, C. 155
Wheel, J. 410, 413
Wheeler, A. 92
Wheeler, B. 201
Wheeler, E. 264
Wheeler, F. 251
Wheeler, J. 394
Wheeler, M. 84

Wheeler, M. 148
Wheelock, Mrs. D. 185
Whelan, S. 180
Wheless, L. 311
Whetzel, J. 434
Whildin, L. 270, 280
While, V. 92
Whinery, F. 126
Whipple, L. 193
Whipple, L. 250
Whipple, M. 170
Whirty, C. 373
Whisehunt, B. 397
Whitcomb, E. 132
White, A. 114
White, A. 184
White, A. 344
White, B. 215
White, B. 405
White, C. 149
White, C. 197
White, D. 25, 26
White, D. 86
White, D. 99
White, D. 149
White, D. 152
White, D. 448
White, E. 179
White, E. 309
White, E. 341
White, Mrs. F. 106
White, F. 426
White, G. 62
White, H. 413
White, H. 428
White, Mrs. J. 25
White, Mrs. J. 106
White, J. 250
White, J. 379
White, K. 283
White, L. 7
White, L. 248
White, Sister M. 149
White, M. 149
White, M. 386
White, N. 86
White, N. 109
White, N. 308
White, P. 230
White, R. 354
White, R. 434
White, R. 454
White, S. 265
White, S. 309
White, S. 410
White, V. 14
White, V. 89
White, V. 191
White, V. 428
Whitecotton, M. 104
Whitehead, J. 58
Whitehead, R. 424
Whitehorne, L. 414
Whitehurst, F. 108
Whitehurst, M. 417
Whitesell, H. 102
Whiteside, J. 237
Whitford, M. 201
Whiting, J. 433
Whiting, M. 229
Whiting, P. 345
Whitley, E. 400
Whitlow, B. 95
Whitman, Mrs. E. 22
Whitman, J. 281
Whitman, D. 215
Whitmore, B. 450
Whitmore, D. 16
Whitmore, E. 49
Whitnel, E. 74
Whitney, G. 32
Whitsell, H. 352
Whitten, E. 215, 216
Whittier, V. 374
Whittington, C. 273

Whittington, H. 339
Whittle, C. 291
Whittle, N. 30
Whittlesey, F. 355
Whittlesey, M. 413
Whorton, R. 287
Wiankowski, C. 401
Wichert, M. 197
Wick, A. 227
Wick, S. 91
Wickersham, J. 105
Wickman, S. 184
Wicks, B. 294
Wicks, G. 93
Wickum, J. 335
Widdick, W. 441
Widditsch, A. 434
Widenmaier, P. 338
Widing, L. 380
Wiedemann, A. 342
Wieder, H. 32
Wiedmeyer, M. 121
Wiegmann, G. 123
Wiejaczka, M. 244
Wieland, E. 184
Wiemers, I. 123
Wienke, M. 20
Wiens, M. 129
Wier, P. 413
Wiescholek, R. 175
Wiese, L. 383
Wiesel, M. 68
Wiesmann, H. 423
Wignes, M. 219
Wike, M. 26
Wilbanks, M. 394
Wilber, E. 56
Wilbur, J. 303
Wilbur, K. 67
Wilcox, Mrs. D. 245
Wilcoxsen, L. 344
Wild, B. 140
Wild, M. 259
Wilde, L. 383
Wilder, F. 222
Wilder, M. 83
Wildt, J. 178
Wiles, D. 323
Wiles, L. 168
Wiley, C. 128
Wiley, H. 453
Wiley, J. 446
Wiley, M. 35
Wiley, M. 274
Wiley, W. 392
Wilhelm, A. 318
Wilhelm, C. 239
Wilhelm, G. 39
Wilhelm, M. 344
Wilhite, D. 242
Wilken, D. 72
Wilker, L. 226
Wilkerson, E. 232
Wilkerson, L. 452
Wilkerson, S. 128
Wilkes, H. 77
Wilkie, S. 275
Wilkin, R. 125
Wilkins, D. 191
Wilkins, D. 231
Wilkins, E. 451, 454
Wilkins, P. 435
Wilkins, R. 210
Wilkins, S. 414
Wilkins, Mrs. T. 343
Wilkinson, E. 358
Wilkinson, S. 67
Wilkinson, Mrs. W. 422
Wilkonson, D. 41
Wilkowski, J. 4
Wilks, L. 186
Willard, J. 194
Willer, A. 95
Willett, B. 26
Willett, D. 436

Willett, Sister E. 28
Willey, B. 75
Willey, L. 20
William, A. 341
Williams, A. 89
Williams, A. 186
Williams, A. 201
Williams, A. 374
Williams, A. 449
Williams, B. 17
Williams, B. 131
Williams, B. 434
Williams, C. 102
Williams, C. 122
Williams, C. 167
Williams, C. 210
Williams, C. 348
Williams, D. 67
Williams, D. 258
Williams, D. 311
Williams, D. 386
Williams, E. 21
Williams, E. 24
Williams, E. 272
Williams, E. 307
Williams, E. 437
Williams, F. 289
Williams, G. 7, 8
Williams, G. 389
Williams, G. 353
Williams, H. 338
Williams, H. 408
Williams, Mrs. I. 78
Williams, I. 295
Williams, J. 338
Williams, J. 346
Williams, L. 85
Williams, L. 110
Williams, L. 170
Williams, L. 214
Williams, M. 8
Williams, M. 28
Williams, M. 37
Williams, M. 90
Williams, M. 140
Williams, M. 215
Williams, M. 258
Williams, Ms. 400
Williams, M. 421
Williams, N. 78
Williams, N. 258
Williams, N. 259
Williams, N. 342
Williams, P. 20
Williams, P. 22
Williams, P. 76
Williams, P. 126
Williams, P. 436
Williams, R. 13
Williams, R. 24
Williams, R. 404
Williams, R. 423
Williams, S. 61, 63
Williams, S. 123
Williams, S. 232
Williams, S. 308
Williams, W. 134
Williams, Mrs. W. 403
Williamson, D. 384
Williamson, L. 307
Williamson, Y. 175
Willie, I. 339
Willigman, L. 322
Willingham, M. 11
Willis, A. 240
Willis, B. 423
Willis, D. 272
Willis, H. 216
Willis, K. 214
Willis, M. 140
Willis, N. 336
Willis, N. 374, 375
Willison, S. 214
Wilson, K. 180
Wilman, Mrs. R. 218

Wilroy, J. 398
Wilson, A. 91
Wilson, A. 342, 344
Wilson, A. 381
Wilson, B. 33
Wilson, B. 42
Wilson, B. 204
Wilson, B. 244
Wilson, B. 436
Wilson, C. 16
Wilson, C. 57
Wilson, C. 183
Wilson, D. 7
Wilson, D. 352
Wilson, D. 405
Wilson, E. 98
Wilson, E. 313
Wilson, G. 186
Wilson, Mrs. H. 67
Wilson, H. 154
Wilson, H. 265
Wilson, H. 327
Wilson, I. 48
Wilson, I. 210
Wilson, J. 24
Wilson, J. 92
Wilson, J. 199
Wilson, J. 236
Wilson, J. 332
Wilson, J. 354
Wilson, J. 406
Wilson, K. 394
Wilson, L. 69
Wilson, L. 116
Wilson, M. 62
Wilson, M. 182
Wilson, M. 388
Wilson, M. 415
Wilson, M. 431
Wilson, Dr. M. 437
Wilson, N. 176
Wilson, N. 245
Wilson, P. 131
Wilson, P. 175
Wilson, P. 337
Wilson, R. 74
Wilson, R. 201
Wilson, S. 41
Wilson, S. 78
Wilson, S. 123
Wilson, V. 214
Wilson, V. 244
Wilson, W. 100
Wilson, W. 237
Wilt, H. 399
Wilt, W. 417
Wiltjanen, M. 199
Wiltz, V. 140
Wimmer, C. 213
Wimmer, M. 448
Winand, B. 330
Winckler, B. 33
Windle, J. 244
Windschitl, V. 111
Winemiller, F. 335
Winesberry, F. 343
Winfield, B. 332
Winfree, F. 238
Wingate, A. 64
Wingett, M. 331
Winikow, L. 289
Winkleman, A. 223
Winn, C. 265
Winsley, S. 426
Winslow, J. 122
Winslow, P. 10
Winsor, K. 109
Winston, J. 242
Winston, J. 9
Winston, V. 436
Winter, M. 172
Wintermute, D. 323
Winters, F. 124
Winters, J. 209
Winters, L. 307

Winters, M. 387
Winton, J. 8
Wipfler, E. 97
Wirth, M. 445
Wirtz, S. 430
Wisbeski, D. 281
Wise, A. 162
Wise, E. 74
Wise, Dr. H. 355
Wise, J. 129
Wise, L. 431
Wise, M. 190
Wise, M. 336
Wise, M. 446
Wise, P. 251
Wise, V. 327
Wiseman, A. 359
Wiseman, L. 113
Wiseman, M. 306
Wiseman, R. 287
Wishman, T. 136
Wisienski, D. 175
Wiskur, L. 384
Wistedt, B. 76
Wiswall, M. 265
Witchell, D. 209
Witham, C. 99
Withchard, O. 11
Withers, W. 449
Witherspoon, A. 40
Withrow, W. 438
Witte, V. 319
Wittenberg, N. 79
Witteveen, E. 352
Wittie, G. 139
Wittman, M. 92
Wittmeyer, E. 52
Witulski, M. 255
Witzke, M. 175
Wixson, J. 173
Wodjenski, A. 270
Woehle, B. 74
Woerner, C. 272
Wohlfarth, L. 394
Woityra, P. 296
Wojahn, L. 425, 437
Wojda, D. 183
Wojtas, J. 56
Wojtowicz, J. 179
Wolak, V. 187
Wold, P. 306
Wolf, A. 63
Wolf, A. 294
Wolf, B. 122
Wolf, D. 129
Wolf, E. 63
Wolf, J. 304
Wolf, M. 62, 64
Wolf, M. 427
Wolfe, A. 317
Wolfe, D. 91
Wolfe, E. 91, 93
Wolfe, H. 25
Wolfe, J. 215
Wolfe, M. 357
Wolfe, P. 364
Wolfe, R. 254
Wolfsohn, H. 302
Wolfson, H. 67
Wolfson, H. 280
Wolgamott, M. 200
Wolk, M. 375
Wollenhaupt, M. 320
Wolman, J. 158
Wolner, A. 219
Wolstad, B. 15
Wolstrom, J. 255
Womack, D. 29
Womack, L. 24
Womack, V. 7
Womer, K. 437
Wondra, M. 451
Wood, C. 323
Wood, D. 336
Wood, E. 60

Wood, F. 36
Wood, F. 408
Wood, G. 247
Wood, H. 352
Wood, L. 316
Wood, L. 363
Wood, M. 377
Wood, P. 301
Wood, R. 404
Wood, V. 230
Woodall, P. 440
Woodard, L. 146
Woodbridge, T. 43
Woodburn, Mrs. C. 404
Woodburn, V. 311
Woodfin, Mrs. H. 29
Woodford, E. 276
Woodhouse, Mrs. C. 64
Woodhouse, N. 325
Woodhouse, R. 424
Woodke, E. 174
Woodley, G. 118
Woodlock, H. 265
Woodring, M. 376
Woods, J. 304
Woods, J. 387
Woods, K. 49
Woods, M. 83
Woods, M. 349
Woods, M. 453
Woods, P. 112
Woods, S. 132
Woodside, M. 254
Woodson, H. 330
Woodstra, B. 122
Woodward, A. 67
Woodward, A. 86
Woodward, C. 270
Woodward, J. 421
Woodward, M. 326
Woodward, N. 67
Woodward, N. 265
Woodward, T. 311
Woodward, T. 412
Woodward, Mrs. W. 28
Woodworth, P. 92
Wooer, J. 172
Wooldridge, Mrs. G. 156
Woolgar, R. 224
Woolman, N. 273
Woolridge, R. 243
Woolsey, S. 4
Wooten, J. 254
Wooten, L. 85
Word, O. 399
Worden, M. 194
Workman, B. 430
Workman, K. 16
Worman, M. 98
Worrall, M. 356
Worrey, M. 149
Worsham, S. 418
Worthen, A. 19, 20
Worthen, S. 65
Wotherspoon, Mrs. J. 283
Wortman, E. 124
Wortman, S. 353
Wothe, J. 222
Woyke, E. 67
Wracan, N. 177
Wray, M. 363
Wright, A. 63
Wright, A. 411
Wright, B. 160
Wright, B. 279
Wright, C. 67
Wright, D. 255, 256
Wright, D. 66
Wright, D. 332
Wright, E. 454
Wright, G. 85
Wright, G. 182
Wright, G. 354
Wright, I. 321
Wright, Mrs. J. 10

Wright, J. 67
Wright, J. 126
Wright, Mrs. J. 155
Wright, Mrs. J. 285
Wright, L. 60
Wright, L. 175
Wright, M. 95
Wright, M. 155
Wright, M. 321
Wright, N. 178
Wright, P. 17
Wright, P. 100
Wright, P. 349
Wright, P. 415
Wright, S. 157
Wright, U. 231
Wright, V. 307
Wrobel, L. 165
Wuertzer, H. 111
Wulf, P. 384, 385
Wunch, V. 189
Wunnicki, E. 4
Wurst, J. 195
Wyatt, J. 389
Wyatt, M. 104
Wyatt, M. 333
Wyckoff, M. 132
Wyeth, M. 217
Wylie, L. 333
Wylin, R. 173
Wyllie, J. 112
Wyman, L. 216
Wyman, N. 52
Wyman, P. 174
Wynia, A. 218
Wyre, R. 358
Wyrembelski, M. 195
Woodruff, C. 284
Woodruff, C. 284
Woodruff, Mrs. M. 306
Woodruff, W. 126
Woods, A. 44
Woods, D. 352
Woods, E. 4
Woods, E. 56
Woods, E. 388
Woods, H. 234

Yacavone, M. 56
Yakel, M. 226
Yamber, S. 365
Yancey, V. 236
Yantiss, Mrs. J. 130
Yard, E. 273
Yarman, H. 336
Yates, C. 379
Yates, G. 277
Yaworsky, V. 366
Yeager, M. 328
Yeaple, K. 267
Yearnd, P. 170
Yeary, B. 137
Yelverton, E. 10
Yetter, Mrs. L. 283
Yih, M. 346
Ynes, I. 393
Yocum, J. 318
Yoder, D. 178
Yoder, J. 91
Yoder, M. 115
Yoder, M. 320
Yankee, R. 454
Yori, D. 216
York, D. 200
York, E. 349
York, S. 184
York, V. 238
Yoshikai, A. 353
Yost, N. 253
Youmans, T. 298
Young, A. 313
Young, C. 164
Young, C. 252
Young, C. 364
Young, D. 171

Young, G. 28
Young, G. 67
Young, H. 164
Young H. 285
Young, I. 384
Young, J. 23
Young, J. 349
Young, Mrs. J. 380
Young, J. 390
Young, L 170
Young, M. 43
Young, M. 67
Young, M. 81
Young, M. 109
Young, M. 170
Young, M. 293
Young, M. 317
Young, P. 87
Young, P. 238
Young, R. 37
Young, S. 367
Young, V. 73
Young, V. 78
Young, W. 370
Youngblood, M. 215
Younge, W. 94
Younger, G. 342
Younger, R. 236
Youngs, E. 198
Younkin, J. 125
Younkins, V. 331
Yount, A. 71
Yukimura, J. 87
Yung, M. 426
Yurgaitis, P. 58

Zabarsky, J. 265
Zach, B. 349
Zachary, A. 29
Zackey, M. 19
Zachry, D. 340
Zahn, P. 301
Zahn, R. 226
Zajac, R. 257
Zalepa, J. 368
Zamudio, M. 436
Zanchetti, A. 164
Zanner, C. 198
Zavada, R. 189
Zbuckvich, I. 360
Zdenek, E. 283
Zecher, M. 44
Zeeb, V. 167
Zehnder, J. 58
Zehren, Mrs. V. 449
Zeigler, E. 44
Zeigler, K. 362
Zeimetz, E. 160
Zeldenrust, L. 184
Zelenka, J. 123
Zeller, M. 177
Zelt, E. 185
Zemke, R. 349
Zens, D. 385
Zepp, K. 233
Zerbe, M. 453
Zerlaut, J. 186
Zettel, V. 225
Zeuch, M. 375
Ziegelbein, J. 255
Ziegler, L. 137
Ziegler, W. 436
Zielinski, M. 205
Ziesing, L. 248
Ziglar, D. 334
Zimbicki, M. 177
Zimmer, Mrs. B. 284
Zimmer, I. 368
Zimmer, L. 125
Zimmerman, E. 448
Zimmerman, N. 156
Zimmerman, P. 259
Zimmerman, V. 185
Zink, M. 48

Zokosky, R. 37
Zone, M. 324
Zoob, R. 164
Zook, B. 22
Zopf, J. 154
Zornow, R. 21
Zothman, L. 227
Zozaya, J. 20
Zubeck, D. 128
Zubrensky, R. 449
Zumwalt, J. 28
Zunini, J. 259
Zunt, M. 324
Zupin, M. 175
Zuraitis, B. 58
Zurhorst, S. 147
Zuzich, A. 214
Zwonitzer, M. 239
Zychowski, B. 193
Zywna, M. 265